MW01011885

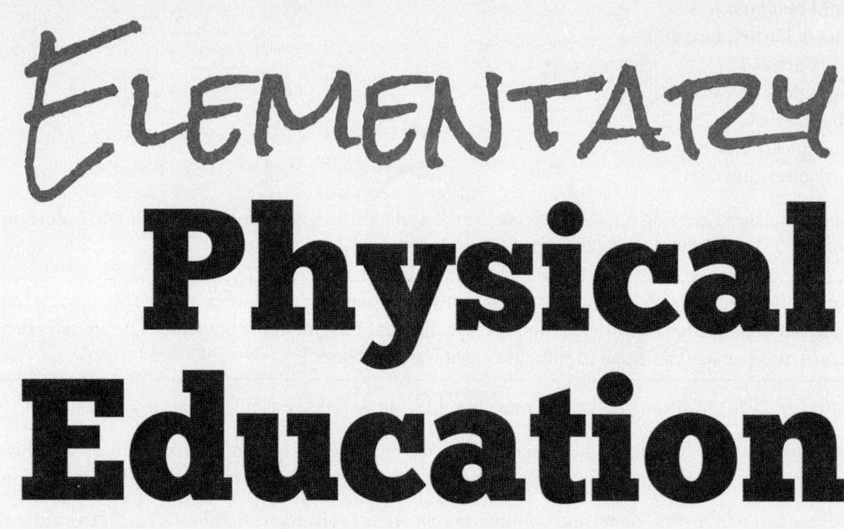

Elementary Physical Education

Curriculum and Instruction

Second Edition

Inez Rovegno
Professor Emeritus, University of Alabama

Dianna Bandhauer
Lecanto Primary School

JONES & BARTLETT
LEARNING

World Headquarters
Jones & Bartlett Learning
5 Wall Street
Burlington, MA 01803
978-443-5000
info@jblearning.com
www.jblearning.com

Jones & Bartlett Learning books and products are available through most bookstores and online booksellers. To contact Jones & Bartlett Learning directly, call 800-832-0034, fax 978-443-8000, or visit our website, www.jblearning.com.

Substantial discounts on bulk quantities of Jones & Bartlett Learning publications are available to corporations, professional associations, and other qualified organizations. For details and specific discount information, contact the special sales department at Jones & Bartlett Learning via the above contact information or send an email to specialsales@jblearning.com.

10376-2

Production Credits

VP, Executive Publisher: David D. Cella
Publisher: Cathy L. Esperti
Associate Acquisitions Editor: Kayla Dos Santos
Senior Developmental Editor: Nancy Hoffman
Associate Director of Production: Julie C. Bolduc
Director of Marketing: Andrea DeFronzo
VP, Manufacturing and Inventory Control: Therese Connell
Composition: Cenveo® Publisher Services
Cover Design: Kristin E. Parker
Rights & Media Specialist: Robert Boder
Cover Images: Illustration of park with school in background © leosapiens/iStock/Getty Images; boy passing basketball © R. Gino Santa Maria/Shutterstock; boy in yellow shirt jumping © michaeljung/Shutterstock; little boy with soccer leap © Zurijeta/Shutterstock; boy in red leaping © Jacek Chabraszewski/Shutterstock; girl jumping © MAHATHIR MOHD YASIN/Shutterstock; girl in striped top © Be Good/Shutterstock; girl playing soccer © Rob Marmion/Shutterstock
Printing and Binding: RR Donnelley
Cover Printing: RR Donnelley

Library of Congress Cataloging-in-Publication Data

Names: Rovegno, Inez. | Bandhauer, Dianna.
Title: Elementary physical education / Inez Rovegno and Dianna Bandhauer.
Description: Second Edition. | Burlington, MA : Jones & Bartlett Learning, [2017] | Includes bibliographical references and index.
Identifiers: LCCN 2015037236 | ISBN 9781284077988 (alk. paper)
Subjects: LCSH: Physical education and training—Study and teaching (Elementary)—United States. | Physical education and training—Curricula—United States.
Classification: LCC GV443 .R68 2017 | DDC 372.86—dc23 LC record available at http://lccn.loc.gov/2015037236

6048

Printed in the United States of America
20 19 18 17 16 10 9 8 7 6 5 4 3 2 1

We dedicate this textbook to Dr. Kate Ross Barrett, who committed her career to improving the quality of education for children, university students, and teachers. She has been, in our opinion, the leading and most influential scholar on children's physical education. We are grateful for what we learned from her.

Brief Contents

Contents

Foreword

Inez Rovegno and Dianna Bandhauer have put together one of the most comprehensive texts on teaching physical education to elementary students. The text takes a constructivist orientation to helping thinking and feeling children become skillful movers, recognizing the role that all subject areas in schools must play in the development of the cognitive, affective, and psychomotor domains. The approach to the content is a "movement education"/concept approach that facilitates children working at their own level and growing with the content as they are ready.

There is not another like it in terms of coverage. The theoretical underpinnings of teaching children in terms of motor development, motor learning, cognitive development, and the connections to research on best practice in teaching that form the basis for both curriculum and instruction are reviewed and applied in a language that teachers and teachers-to-be should find to be directly applicable.

Much of the theoretical material can probably be found elsewhere. What cannot be found elsewhere are the materials the authors have provided to help teachers understand how to plan for, teach, and assess educational games, educational gymnastics, and educational dance to develop skillful movers. The frameworks the authors have established to help teachers understand how to scaffold the material will be particularly helpful as teachers try to find their way to establish appropriate progressions for students at different levels. Knowing when to keep tasks open for exploration and when to teach and refine specific tasks more directly has always been the art of teaching in these content areas. The authors guide the teacher through this process with lots of very specific help in the form of sample lesson plans and learning experiences, assessment materials, and skill boxes that identify what good performance looks like.

Current issues related to the common core and health-related physical activity have impacted what physical education teachers are asked to do in schools. This new edition addresses the new physical education national standards, how to integrate the common core into lessons, and physical education's role in combating the obesity crisis in this country.

The material in this text cannot be learned in one course or in one reading. Pre-service teachers will want to keep this book and in-service teachers will want to purchase it and return to it often for help.

Judith Rink, PhD, MS, BS
Distinguished Professor Emeritus
University of South Carolina

Preface

Elementary Physical Education: Curriculum and Instruction, Second Edition, continues to present a relevant, up-to-date movement approach for the twenty-first century that is firmly rooted in both curriculum and instruction in historical movement approaches.

This text presents a comprehensive offering that can be used across several courses, including elementary physical education curriculum and instruction for physical education or classroom teachers, educational gymnastics, educational dance, educational games, and movement foundation courses. It also is a reference tool for field experience courses and student teaching.

What's New to this Edition?

National Standards for Physical Education and the Common Core and Other State Standards

First, we revised this edition to align with and strengthen the connections to the new National Standards for Physical Education (National Standards) and the Common Core and other State Standards (CCSS). The changes to this edition make it easier for students to recognize the importance and better understand the application of both the National Standards and the Common Core in physical education to guide teaching and planning.

We begin in Chapter 1 by describing the goal of physical education, the new National Standards, and sample grade level outcomes (Society of Health and Physical Educators [SHAPE], 2014). We describe why it is important for teachers to base their curriculum, program, and lessons on the National Standards. We emphasize physical education's focus on learning and how the National Standards are integrated and applied to the range of physical activities we teach. In addition, we begin each chapter by discussing the connection between the National Standards and the chapter content. We link all Sample Plans to the National Standards and highlight the connections between the National Standards and curriculum and instruction throughout the text.

In addition, we connect all chapters and all Sample Plans to the CCSS. We focus on CCSS for speaking, listening, collaboration, and communication. These sections of the CCSS work in tandem with National Standard 4 and are relevant during all group work in gymnastics, dance, games, and health-related physical activity (HRPA) lessons. Because most of our content and lessons for the upper elementary grades includes partner or group work, National Standard 4 and the CCSS are easily applied to lessons, and we demonstrate how to write objectives and design lessons that help students meet these standards. Sample tasks related to social responsibility and CCSS within Sample Plans are so labeled.

Dance and the Common Core Standards

In addition, to extend work on the Common Core, almost all creative dance lessons now integrate children's literature, informational texts, poetry, or vocabulary acquisition. We describe how to design dance lessons using reading content and have added several examples of lessons illustrating how to teach vocabulary.

Assessment

Second, we have greatly enhanced the information on assessment. We have combined what had been two chapters into one comprehensive chapter, adding more information about assessment and descriptions of how to design rubrics, rating scales, and checklists. We show students step-by-step how to link assessments to the National Standards.

Latest Research

One of the many strengths of this text is its support by research. We reviewed the research published since the first edition and integrated it into this second edition throughout the text.

Nowhere have recent research initiatives and reports had a more major impact on our field than the areas of health-related physical activity (HRPA), nutrition, and health-related physical fitness (HRF). For example, recently, the way we view the components of fitness (i.e., cardiorespiratory endurance, body composition, muscular strength, muscular endurance, and flexibility) has changed in two significant ways. It is now well established that "components of fitness change as a function of growth, maturation, development, and interactions among the three processes" (Malina, 2014, p. 165). Muscle power activities that contribute to bone strengthening are now recognized as important components of health-related fitness for children because these activities result in stronger bones, and there is evidence that this effect persists into adulthood (American College of Sports Medicine [ACSM], 2004). In turn, the components of fitness for children have changed, and muscle fitness is now viewed as multidimensional, including muscular strength, muscular endurance, muscular power, and flexibility (Corbin et al., 2014; Institute of Medicine [IOM], 2012; Plowman, 2014).

In regard to teaching nutrition concepts at the elementary level, the Academy of Nutrition and Dietetics' reviewed the research and stated that interventions combining nutrition education and increasing physical activity might be effective in improving body fat measures and behaviors associated with overweight (Hoelscher, Kirk, Ritchie, & Cunningham-Sabo, 2013). Research shows physical activity programs and teaching students about nutrition and HRPA along with parental involvement in these programs can be effective in improving health-related behaviors.

Comprehensive School Physical Activity Programs

Finally, the Centers for Disease Control and Prevention (2013), SHAPE America (NASPE, 2008), and the IOM (2013) have all issued reports and/or guidelines related to Comprehensive School Physical Activity Programs (CSPAPs).

All of the above research and information is discussed in the text and applied in sections on HRPA, HRF, and nutrition concepts. We have also added a section and lesson on how to design activity breaks.

Safety, Negligence, and Liability

Another major revision for the second edition was to significantly increase the amount of content on safety, negligence, and liability. In Chapter 1, we discuss the four elements of negligence that are required to prove liability. We discuss the major topics related to professional standards of practice, linking these to the National Standards. Further, in almost all chapters, we have added a feature box describing in detail the safety and liability directives linked to the chapter content. These directives inform physical education teachers about what they need to do to reduce the risk of liability, increase safety, and respond as a reasonably prudent teacher would in the same or a similar situation.

Modified Game Play and Tactics

Finally, we have combined the chapter on teaching students about game structures, designing games, and tag tactics (Chapter 19) with the chapter on level 3 invasion games tactics (Chapter 22) to create Chapter 20: Invasion Games: Designing and Modifying Games, Tactics for Tag, Passing, and Receiving with the Hands, Feet, and Hockey Sticks: Level 3. This change has put all the information on teaching modified invasion games when children are at developmental level 3 in one place. We then revised the Sample Learning Experiences to be easier to use to develop lesson plans.

Additional Resources

Accompanying this title is a suite of resources to aid in the instruction and learning of this content.

For the Instructor

- Answers to end-of-chapter Review Questions
- Sample Syllabi with additional activities and teaching tips
- Robust Test Bank with more than 1,800 assessments
- Slides with Lecture Outlines
- Key Image Review of more than 700 full-color photos and illustrations

For the Student

- Video clips featuring examples of in-class instruction of key concepts
- Additional Sample Lesson Plans and Learning Experiences
- Writeable Workbook Exercises
- Practice Activities

About the Authors

Inez Rovegno has taught elementary physical education methods in both small colleges and major research universities for 25 years. She continues to teach the approach used in this text in public schools to field test new lessons and demonstrate lessons for undergraduates and teachers. She has conducted research for 25 years on how undergraduates learn the approach, how expert teachers use the approach, and how children learn and respond to lessons based on the approach. She studied the approach in England at Chelsea College of Physical Education and at the Laban Art of Movement Studio under Lisa Ullmann, a student of Rudolf Laban. She has published more than 50 papers and chapters. She has given keynote addresses on the approach in Canada, France, Australia, Korea, Japan, and the U.S. and given more than 80 presentations at conferences. She was inducted into the National Academy of Kinesiology in 2007 and received the 2010 Honor Award from the Curriculum and Instruction Academy of the American Alliance for Health, Physical Education, Recreation and Dance (AAHPERD; now SHAPE America), the Senior Scholar Award, and the Exemplary Research Award from the Research on Learning and Instruction in Physical Education Special Interest Group of the American Educational Research Association, the Distinguished Alumni Award from the University of North Carolina at Greensboro, School of Health and Human Performance, and gave the twenty-third Distinguished Peter V. Karpovich Lecture at Springfield College in Springfield, Massachusetts.

Dianna Bandhauer has taught elementary physical education in Maryland, Connecticut, Hawaii, and Florida. She was on the standards writing committee for the National Board of Professional Teaching Standards for Physical Education. She has been on the editorial boards of *Teaching Elementary Physical Education* and the journal of the Florida Association of Health, Physical Education, Recreation, and Dance (FAHPERD; now SHAPE Florida). She has given more than 50 conference presentations about elementary school physical education. She has presented at AAHPERD National Conventions, as well as Southern District and state conventions in Hawaii, Florida, Georgia, Arkansas, North Carolina, North Dakota, South Carolina, Ohio, and New Hampshire. She was the FAHPERD Elementary Physical Education Teacher of the Year, the Lecanto Primary School Teacher of the Year, received the Physical Education Teacher of Excellence Award from Florida Governor Rick Scott's office, and was listed as the Most Admired Woman in Education by Altrusa. Her program was a Florida Department of Education (DOE) Demonstration School. She has also supervised student teachers, is a certified peer teacher in the Florida Performance Management System, and a Florida DOE Associate Master Teacher. She was on the Citrus County School District Curriculum Guide writing team and served on the Florida DOE Phase I, II, and III initial teacher certification and recertification examination test writing committee. She was on the Florida DOE validation committee for the state teacher exam in physical education and steering committee for physical education for handicapped students. She served on Citrus County's Gender Equity Committee and on the Lecanto Primary School and Lecanto High School Advisory Committee. She has been awarded numerous grants totaling more than $62,000, which includes a grant from the American Heart Association for her "Tar Wars: Teaching the Next Generation" after-school program to promote fitness with an anti-tobacco message, a National Diffusion Network Grant for her "Every Child a Winner" program to encourage daily physical education with the assistance of classroom teachers, a grant for developing aerobics videos for teachers to use when they must teach physical education in classroom spaces, and a grant to create a school garden with a micro-irrigation system.

Acknowledgments

As with the first edition, we are grateful for the team at Jones & Bartlett Learning for their guidance and assistance with the revisions, especially Kayla Dos Santos, Nancy Hoffmann, Julie Bolduc, and Robert Boder, and Kritika Kaushik and the folks at Cenveo Publisher Services. We are especially grateful for the many thoughtful reviewers of the second edition, including Kim Oliver, James Leech, and the faculty at the University of Northern Iowa, along with the reviewers of the first edition.

Reviewers of the *Second Edition*

Helena Baert
Physical Education Department
State University at Cortland

Janice Bibik
Behavorial Health & Nutrition
University of Delaware

Molly Hare
Kinesiology, Recreation, and Sport Department
Indiana State University

Christine J. Hopple
Department of Kinesiology
Penn State University

Anne Larson
Kinesiology Department
California State University at Los Angeles

Kevin Lorson
Kinesiology Department
Wright State University

Robert Martin
Education Department
Delaware State University

Reviewers of the *First Edition*

Robbi Beyer
Professor of Kinesiology
California State University, Los Angeles

Rebecca R. Bryan, PhD
Department of Kinesiology
Sonoma State University

Weiyun Chen, PhD
School of Kinesiology
University of Michigan

Connie Collier
Department of Physical Education
Kent State University

Sandi Cravens, PhD
Department of Kinesiology
Texas Woman's University/Irving ISD

Ari B. Fisher
Department of Kinesiology
Louisiana State University

Ritchie Gabbei
Department of Kinesiology
Western Illinois University

Grace Goc Karp
Department of Movement Sciences
University of Idaho

Gregory Green, PhD
Chair and Associate Professor
Fort Valley State University

Linda L. Griffin
School of Education
University of Massachusetts, Amherst

Tina J. Hall, PhD
Department of Physical Education
University of South Carolina

Peter Hastie
Department of Kinesiology
Auburn University

Jayne M. Jenkins
Associate Professor
Division of Kinesiology and Health
University of Wyoming

Pamela Hodges Kulinna
Division of Education Leadership and Innovative Policy
Arizona State University

Anne Larson, PhD
School of Kinesiology and Nutritional Science
California State University

Ann MacPhail, PhD
Department of Physical Education and Sport Sciences
University of Limerick

Sandra L. Nelson
Associate Professor of Physical Education
Coastal Carolina University

Lynda M. Nilges-Charles, PhD
Associate Professor of Physical Education Pedagogy
University of South Carolina

Deborah A. Sheehy, PhE
Associate Professor
Bridgewater State University

Margaret Stran
Department of Kinesiology
University of Alabama

Karen Weiller Abels, PhD
Kinesiology, Health Promotion and Recreation
University of North Texas

We thank Gopher Sport for providing us physical education equipment.

We also want to pay tribute to the many teachers who inspired us and taught us the movement approach, especially the faculty at Chelsea College of Physical Education, Martha Owens, Susan Rockett, Delores Curtis, Kate Barrett, and Jane Young, who also brought us together in 1989.

A final and most important thanks goes to the people who matter most to us in this world: our families, friends, and husbands, John Dolly and Bill Bandhauer.

How to Use this Book

Teaching elementary physical education instruction is a complex process that requires learners to build on the material they encounter, creating a layered approach to learning. To that end, we have developed a series of tables that provide readers with a guide to the content within this text and how that content builds, overlaps, and relates from chapter to chapter. These tables indicate where specific content can be found in the text and which lessons and activities support one another.

The first table is a content map for the entire text.

Content Map

Chapter	Content Mapping
Section I: Curriculum, Instruction, and Theoretical Support	

1: Physical Education Goals, Significance, and National Standards	• Introduces the goal and aims of physical education both historically and as discussed by SHAPE (2014).
	• Discusses the new National Standards and how the standards address the motor, cognitive, affective, and social domains and the integration of these domains into the physical activity content we teach.
	  • The integration of these standards is further explored in Chapters 9–12, Chapter 14 on planning, and Chapter15 on assessment and is illustrated in all Sample Plans.
	  • How the National Standards and CCSS can be applied is detailed in the text, Sample Learning Experiences, and Sample Plans in Chapters 17, 19–23, 26–29, and 31–33.
	• Introduces safety, liability, and negligence and the elements that define professional standards of practice:
	  • Supervision (specific guidelines discussed in Chapters 4, 8, 13, and 24).
	  • Instruction (specific guidelines discussed in Chapters 2, 4, 6, 7, 8, 9, 14, 16, 17, 18, 24, and 30 and all content chapters with lesson plans)
	  • Differentiated instruction and accommodating developmental levels (specific guidelines discussed in Chapters 4, 7, 9, 10, 11, and 12 and all content chapters with lesson plans)
	  • Physical environment (specific guidelines discussed in Chapters 4, 13, 18, 24, 29, 30, and 35 and all content chapters with lesson plans)
	  • Emotional environment (specific guidelines discussed in Chapters 11, 12, and 13)
	  • Professional development (specific guidelines discussed in Chapters 34 and 35)

2: An Overview of the Movement Approach and Philosophy	• The movement approach used in this text is introduced and contrasted to a recreational approach and a traditional sport approach.
	• Laban's framework is introduced and is further explored in Chapter 3.
	• The philosophy of the text is discussed in relation to the goal of physical education to develop physically literate individuals (SHAPE, 2014) and each of the five National Standards.
	• National Standards and the chapters in which they are applied include the following:
	  • Standard 1: Demonstrates competency in a variety of motor skills and movement patterns (Chapter 14 [planning], Chapter 15 [assessment], all content chapters ([18-33]).
	  • Standard 2: Applies knowledge of concepts, principles, strategies, tactics related to movement and performance (Chapters 3 [content overview]; Chapters 5, 6, and 10 [cognitive learning processes and higher-order thinking skills], and Chapters 18–33 [educational games, dance, and gymnastics content chapters]).
	  • Standard 3: Demonstrates knowledge and skills to achieve a health-enhancing level of fitness (Chapters 9 and 17).
	  • Standard 4: Exhibits responsible personal and social behavior (Chapters 11, 12, and 13 and Sample Plans in all content chapters).
	  • Standard 5: Recognizes the value of physical activity (Chapter 9 and 12 and Sample Plans in all content chapters).
	• Describes how to provide a program for diverse learners based on a developmental perspective and differentiate instruction to accommodate individual differences. Diversity, development, and individual differences are discussed in more detail in Chapters 4, 7, and 12 and are illustrated in Sample Learning Experiences and Sample Plans in Chapters 19–33.

3: Overview of the Content	• Describes the elements and movement concepts of the Laban framework adapted three ways to educational games, dance, and gymnastics. • How the movement concepts are applied and translated to content for teaching is shown across Chapters 18–33. • Strong illustrations of how movement concepts are applied to vary skills in game-like ways and their links to tactics can be found for catching, passing (Chapter 19), and dribbling (Chapter 21). Chapters 24–32 illustrate how to use movement concepts to extend children's range of responses in gymnastics and dance.
4: Motor Development and Learning	• Introduces how motor development theory and information guides teaching. This information is further discussed in the three-developmental-level progression for games and gymnastics and the two-developmental-level progression for dance presented in Chapters 18, 24, and 30 and illustrated in Chapters 19–23, 26–29, and 31–32.

Content Map (*continued*)

Chapter	Content Mapping
4: Motor Development and Learning (*continued*)	• Introduces the value of understanding and recognizing immature movement patterns and then aligning developmental feedback to children. Immature patterns and aligned feedback are discussed in detail in the Skills Boxes in Chapters 19–23, and throughout Chapters 26, 28, and 29. • Introduces constraints theory and how to design tasks and the environment to elicit appropriate movement responses. The impact of the environment is illustrated and expanded on in Chapter 19, (catching), Chapter 21 (dribbling), and Chapter 23 (forceful overhand throw). The role of the task and environment is further explored in Chapters 13 and 14. Constraints theory is applied across all content chapters and Sample Plans.
5: Cognitive Learning Theory	• Provides the theoretical basis for teaching cognitive concepts and performance techniques, described in greater detail in Chapters 6, 7, 8, and 13. • Introduces scaffolding, which is discussed in depth in Chapter 10.
6: Presenting Cognitive Content and Performance Techniques	• Builds on cognitive learning theory from Chapter 5, discussing how to teach cognitive concepts and performance techniques. • All Sample Plans illustrate how to teach cognitive concepts and performance techniques. Sample Learning Experiences include lists of potential questions for eliciting children's understanding of concepts. • The use of questions to facilitate learning and other inquiry-oriented strategies are discussed in detail in Chapter 10.
7: Task Design and Differentiating Instruction	• The focus of this chapter is on designing tasks to maximize practice time and ensure children are physically active 50% of their lesson time. • Multiple ways to differentiate instruction are discussed. Related challenges with large classes and limited equipment are discussed in Chapter 15.
8: Interactive and Reflective Teaching	• Continued discussion of teaching techniques introduced in Chapters 6 and 7, focusing on observing children's learning during tasks and then deciding on an appropriate teaching response, such as modifying the task or giving feedback. • Discusses the importance of reflecting on teaching in relation to children's learning outcomes, the National Standards, and a sound philosophy.
9: Motivation and Establishing a Learning Environment	• Discusses how to teach multiple motivation concepts, including a growth mindset and mastery orientation. • Provides sample ways to modify tasks to ensure students are challenged and successful, for example, teaching five levels of defensive intensity, which is covered in more detail in Chapters 19 and 20.
10: Higher-Order Thinking Skills and Inquiry-Oriented Teaching	• Builds on Chapters 5 and 6. Discusses five types of tasks that comprise inquiry-oriented teaching and develop higher-order thinking skills, including self-regulation, decision making, critical thinking, exploration, creative thinking, and problem solving. A brief overview of the process of designing dance and gymnastics sequences is provided; detailed discussion occurs in Chapter 25 and is illustrated in Chapters 26–28 and 31–33. • Teaching the problem-solving strategy for designing games and solving tactical problems is introduced here and covered in more detail in Chapter 20 and further illustrated in Chapters 21–23.
11: Social and Emotional Goals	• Discusses how to address National Standards 4 and 5, presented in Chapters 1 and 2. • Chapter 12 builds on the inclusion of diversity mentioned here. • Put-downs and harassing comments are covered in greater detail in Chapters 12 and 13. • Audience behavior is discussed in more depth in Chapter 25.
12: Diversity	• Describes multiple diversity issues. • Builds on ways to address National Standard 4, introduced in Chapter 11, and design programs that respect the needs of all children, introduced in Chapters 2 and 4.
13: Managing Behavior and Misbehavior	• Expands on teaching strategies introduced in Chapters 6–10 and on the importance of creating a safe, welcoming learning environment, introduced in Chapters 1, 4, 9, and 11. Discusses additional ways to address National Standard 4.
14: Planning	• Focuses on lesson, unit, and year-long plans based on the National Standards, introduced in Chapters 1 and 2. • Introduces progression of task difficulty and complexity, which is covered extensively in Chapters 18–23 and 26–33. • Draws on the principles for guiding task design found in Chapter 7.
15: Assessment in Educational Games, Gymnastics, and Dance	• Discusses assessment of learning outcomes based on the National Standards. • Discusses how to design assessments, including rubrics and rating scales. • Introduces how to assess using information on the development of immature patterns introduced in Chapter 4 and illustrated with specific information on hand dribbling. • Information on immature game skills is located in the Skills Boxes at the ends of Chapters 19–23. • Chapters 25, 26, and 29 provide information on immature patterns for gymnastics and dance skills. • Includes rubrics aligned with Sample Plans 26.5, 26.16, 26.17, 28.2, 28.3, 31.2, 31.5, 31.6, 32.3. • Levels of performance and sample rubrics for assessing elements of choreography and movement quality are discussed. These elements of sequence choreography and movement quality are discussed in detail in Chapter 25 and should be reviewed before creating an assessment.
16: Teaching Large Classes and Teaching in Small Spaces	• Discusses how to provide maximum practice time with large classes. Presents unit plans for teaching centers (stations) in gymnastics and game skills to classes of 70. Dance lessons that can be taught in large classes or in classrooms are drawn from Sample Plans 31.2, 31.4, 31.5, 31.6, 31.9, 31.15, 32.1, 32.2, 32.4, 32.9, 33.1, 33.9, and 34.10.

(*continues*)

Content Map (*continued*)

Chapter	Content Mapping
Section II: Health-Related Physical Activity	
17: Health-Related Physical Activity and Health-Related Fitness	• Discusses research on HRPA and HRF supporting physical education. Reviews issues specific to the elementary level and changes in the components of fitness for children. • Provides descriptions of HRPA, HRF, and nutrition concepts to teach. Integrating HRF concepts in dance, games, and gymnastics lessons is illustrated in Sample Plans in the text or on the text website. • The importance of teaching performance techniques is emphasized, and performance techniques for dance, gymnastics, and fitness movement are detailed in Chapter 25.
Section III: Educational Games	
18: Introduction to Educational Games	• Appropriate and inappropriate practices in teaching games are presented. • The three-level developmental progression for teaching games skills, tactics, and modified games used in all games chapters is discussed. • Chapters 18 and 20 further the discussion of competitive games from Chapters 9 and 11 and offer suggestions for discussion topics and actions to make a competitive environment a good, safe learning environment.
19: Invasion Games: Catching, Passing, Kicking, and Receiving with the Hands, Feet, and Hockey Sticks: Levels 1 and 2	• Applies the movement concepts from the Laban framework discussed in Chapter 3 to learning to vary skills in game-like ways. • Sample Plans illustrate setting task and environmental constraints to elicit more mature movements, first discussed in Chapter 4, teaching motivation and social concepts, presented in Chapters 9 and 11, and inquiry-oriented strategies, presented in Chapter 10. Refer back to Chapter 4 for a discussion of task and environmental constraints. • Chapter 23 continues the discussion on catching and throwing as they are performed in softball and baseball.
20: Invasion Games: Designing and Modifying Games and Tactics for Tag and Passing and Receiving with the Hands, Feet, and Hockey Sticks: Level 3	• Discusses how to teach children to design games and the impact of game structures (e.g., boundaries, rules, scoring goals) on tactics and game play, first for tag and then for invasion games. • Extends the discussion of the observation cycle begun in Chapter 8. • The teaching of motivation concepts, presented in Chapter 9, including a mastery orientation, and personal and social responsibility concepts, from Chapter 12, is discussed and then illustrated in Sample Learning Experiences and Sample Plans, as are inquiry-oriented tasks, discussed in Chapter 10. • Incorporates the five levels of defensive intensity, detailed in Chapter 19. • Teaching the anticipation of this is an example of learning the affordances of games, discussed in Chapter 4.
21: Invasion Games: Dribbling with the Hands, Feet, and Hockey Sticks: Levels 1, 2, and 3	• Applies movement concepts from Chapter 3 to varying dribbling in game-like ways. The development of hand dribbling movement patterns and in different task environments are presented in Chapter 4 • Chapter 14 includes a detailed lesson plan on dribbling with the hands while traveling at different speeds and stopping quickly. • You can combine the learning experiences from Chapter 19 with the learning experiences presented here to teach how to combine receiving with dribbling and dribbling with shooting or passing. • The section on modified dribbling games mirrors the tag unit described in more detail in Chapter 20. If you have not taught the tag unit, you will benefit from reading the more detailed version in Chapter 20. • Illustrates how to teach motivation and social concepts from Chapters 9 and 11 and inquiry-oriented teaching from Chapter 10.
22: Net/Wall Games: Skills, Tactics, and Modified Games: Levels 1, 2, and 3	• Applies the three-level developmental progression for content, described in Chapter 18, to net/wall skills, tactics, and modified gameplay. • Builds on the concept of "perfect" boundaries, as described in the tag units in Chapter 19. • Applies the idea of setting tasks and an environment that ensure challenge and success, discussed in Chapter 9, to getting children to successfully rally a ball using striking skills with body parts, paddles, or rackets.
23: Field Games: Overhand Throw, Batting, Catching with Gloves, and Modified Games: Levels 1, 2, and 3	• Applies the three-level developmental progression for content, described in Chapter 18, to field game skills, tactics, and modified gameplay. • Builds on the catching content covered in Chapter 19. • Discusses the impact of the environment on learning the overhand throw for force.
Section IV: Educational Gymnastics Content	
24: Introduction to Educational Gymnastics	• Introduces the content progression that is applicable to Chapters 25–29. • Expands on how to accommodate individual differences and differentiate instruction, introduced in Chapter 7. • Expands on and applies information on safety and liability, discussed in Chapter 1. • Expands on the three segments of a lesson and the use of centers (i.e., station), introduced in Chapters 14 and 15. • Discusses how educational gymnastics uses a range of teaching strategies from direct to inquiry oriented.
25: Sequence Choreography and Movement Quality in Gymnastics and Dance	• A progression for teaching elements of dance and gymnastics sequences introduced in this chapter is built on throughout Chapters 26–29. • Elements of sequence choreography, movement quality, and quality of sequence performances in dance and gymnastics are discussed on a continuum from immature through mature performance levels. Rubrics introduced in Chapter 15 are based on this information.
26: Foundational Gymnastics Skills and Combinations	• This chapter introduces the foundational skills for educational gymnastics, which are built on in Chapters 27 and 28. • Expands on the movement concepts introduced in Chapter 3. • Illustrates scaffolding, discussed in Chapter 10.
27: Using Movement Concepts as Themes	• Builds on content from Chapters 3 and 26 encompassing the foundational skills. • Presents lesson content focusing on movement concepts as themes.

Content Map (*continued*)

Chapter	Content Mapping
28: Partner and Group Work	• Builds on content from Chapter 26 working with partners and groups. • Discusses movement concepts that apply to partner and group work.
29: Technical Reference Information for Teachers About Gymnastics Skills	• Presents progressions for teaching specific skills and describes immature patterns. • Sample Plans in Chapter 26 illustrate how to include the progressions for mule kicks/handstands, cartwheels, and round-offs in lessons focused on the themes of balancing and step-like actions.
Section V: Educational Dance Content	
30: Introduction to Educational Dance	• Emphasizes the importance of teaching dance. • Describes dance instruction appropriate for school settings. • Discusses integrating dance and classroom content and illustrates how to design a lesson using children's literature, informational texts, or poetry. • Discusses the difference between movement and dance movement. • Chapters 31 and 32 provide sample dance lesson plans based on children's literature, informational texts, or poetry.
31: Creative Dance Level 1	• This chapter introduces movement concepts that are addressed at a more complex and difficult level in Chapter 32. • Movement concepts discussed in Chapter 3 are used as the basis for dance movement. • Topic themes are combined with movement themes to develop dance lessons. • Exploration, creative thinking, and critical thinking, discussed in Chapter 10, are applied in Sample Learning Experiences and Sample Plans. • Reviews the stop routine, described in Chapter 13.
32: Creative Dance Level 2	• Builds on the level 1 lessons introduced in Chapter 31 using movement concepts from Chapter 3 as lesson themes.
33: Folk, Square, and Line Dance	• Exploration, creative thinking, and critical thinking, discussed in Chapter 10, are applied in Sample Learning Experiences and Sample Plans. • Be sure to apply the lessons of respect for cultural diversity from Chapter 12.
Section VI: Working in Schools	
34: Continued Professional Development	• Promotes the importance of continued professional development. • Revisits the idea of reflecting on how and what your students are learning and feeling and how their learning is linked to your teaching, first raised in Chapter 8.
35: Managing the Politics of Schools	• Provides practical information to help new teachers understand and successfully deal with the politics of schools.

Common Core State Standards (CCSS)

The next table describes where the Common Core and other State Standards (CCSS) are discussed or used in the text. All Sample Plans illustrate how you can include at least one of the CCSS. In regard to the subsections of the CCSS, we believe physical education can make a strong contribution to address the standards related to speaking and listening because we use group work extensively in games, gymnastics, dance, and health-related physical activity lessons. We discuss how to meet the standards for speaking and listening in detail in Chapters 9–13 and give you ample examples of how to do this in practice. Physical education can also contribute to vocabulary acquisition and use across all content areas. We describe how to include vocabulary acquisition in Chapter 30. In addition, physical education can integrate literature and informational texts, in particular in dance lessons. We discuss how to use literature and informational texts along with how to design lessons based on these texts in Chapter 30. Almost all our dance lessons use either literature or informational texts as the basis for the lesson.

Selected CCSS Standards and Where They Are Addressed in the Text

CCSS Literacy Standards	Location in Text
Foundational Reading Skills: Fluency • Read with sufficient accuracy and fluency to support comprehension	Games Sample Plans 21.1 and 21.2

Speaking and Listening
• Comprehension and collaboration
  • Engage effectively in a range of collaborative discussions (one on one, in groups, and teacher led) with diverse partners on topics and texts, building on others' ideas and expressing their own clearly.
  • Recount or describe key ideas of details from a text read aloud or information presented orally or through other media.
• Presentation of knowledge of ideas
  • Report on a topic, tell a story, or recount an experience with appropriate facts and relevant descriptive details, speaking clearly at an understandable pace.
	How to teach standards for comprehension and collaboration is discussed in detail in Chapters 9–13 (see Table 9.1 for a summary).
	How to integrate these standards is illustrated in the following:
	Games Sample Plans 19.1, 19.2, 19.4, 19.7, 20.1, 20.2, 20.3, 21.2, 21.3, 22.2, 23.1, and 23.3
	Gymnastics Sample Plans 26.1, 26.2, 26.3, 26.6, 26.19, 27.6, 28.1, 28.2, 28.3, 28.4, 28.5, and 28.6
	Dance Sample Plans 31.1, 31.7, 32.3, 32.5, 32.7, 32.9, and 33.1

(*continues*)

Selected CCSS Standards and Where They Are Addressed in the Text *(continued)*

CCSS Literacy Standards	Location in Text
Vocabulary Acquisition and Use • Demonstrates understanding of word relationships and nuances in word meanings. • Identify real-life connections between words and their use. • Demonstrate an understanding of words by relating them to their opposites (antonyms) and to words with similar but not identical meanings (synonyms). • Acquire and use accurately grade-appropriate domain-specific words and phrases, including those that signal spatial and temporal relationships, precise actions, emotions, or states of being and that are basic to a particular topic.	How to teach vocabulary acquisition is discussed in Chapters 6 and 30. How to integrate these standards is illustrated in the following: Games Sample Plans 19.3, 19.6, 19.7, 20.2, 21.1, 22.1, 22.3, 23.2, and 23.3 Gymnastics Sample Plans 26.3, 26.4, 26.5, 26.6, 26.9, 26.12, 26.14, 26.18, 27.1, 27.2, 27.3, 27.5, 28.1, 28.2, 28.3, 28.4, and 28.8 Dance Sample Plans 31.2, 31.4, 31.5, 31.6, 31.8, 32.2, 32.5, 32.6, and 32.9 Health-Related Fitness Sample Plan 17.2

Literature and Informational Texts
• Key ideas and details
  • Ask and answer such questions as *who, what, where, when, why,* and *how* to demonstrate an understanding of key details in a text.
• Craft and structure
  • Determine the meaning of words and phrases in a text relevant to a topic or subject area.
• Integration of knowledge and ideas
  • Use the illustrations and details in a text to describe its key ideas.
	How to use literature and informational texts in your lessons and how to design lessons based on literature and informational texts are discussed in Chapter 30. The following Sample Plans in dance are based on children's literature, informational texts, or poetry:
	Literature: 31.1, 31.2, 31.3, 31.6, 31.7, and 31.8
	Informational texts: 31.2, 32.1, 32.2, 32.3, and 32.7
	Poetry: 31.5, 32.3, and 32.4
	How to integrate these standards is illustrated in the following:
	Gymnastics Sample Plans 26.7, 26.15, 26.16, and 26.17
	Dance Sample Plans 31.1, 31.3, 32.1, 32.2, 32.4, and 32.5

Modified by the authors from the Common Core State Standards Initiative. (2010). Common core state standards for English language arts and literacy in history/social studies, science, and technical subjects. Available: www.corestandards.org

Immature Movement Patterns and Performance Techniques

We describe immature movement patterns and list major performance techniques to teach at developmental levels in the Skills Boxes in the games chapters titled "Technical Reference Information for Teachers." The next table lists the manipulative skills and the chapter Skills Box that contains this information on immature patterns and performance techniques.

Where to Find Descriptions of Immature Patterns and Performance Techniques

Skill	Location Performance Techniques Discussed
Batting	Skills Box 23.1
Catching	Skills Box 19.1
Catching in field games	Skills Box 23.1
Catching with a glove	Skills Box 23.1
Cutting, catching, and receiving	Skills Box 19.1
Dribbling with the hands	Skills Box 21.2, Table 4.2
Dribbling with hockey sticks	Skills Box 21.2
Dribbling with the feet	Skills Box 21.2
Kicking with laces for power	Skills Box 19.1
Passing and receiving in games	Skills Boxes 20.1 and 21.1
Passing in football	Skills Box 19.1
Passing with the hands	Skills Box 19.1
Passing, lead	Skills Box 19.1
Push passes with hockey sticks	Skills Box 19.1
Passing, two-handed	Skills Box 19.1
Receiving balls with the feet or hockey sticks	Skills Box 19.1
Shooting at youth basketball hoops	Skills Box 19.1
Skills for children in wheelchairs	Skills Box 19.1
Striking with a racket	Skills Box 22.1
Striking with a racket for children in wheelchairs	Skills Box 22.1
Throw, overhand throw for force	Skills Box 23.1
Underhand rolling	Skills Box 19.1
Underhand serve	Skills Box 22.1
Underhand toss	Skills Box 19.1
Volleying with the hand or forearm	Skills Box 22.1
Volleying for children in wheelchairs	Skills Box 22.1

Dance lessons

The next table lists the dance lessons presented in the text and explains how they can be integrated with classroom subjects and texts.

Dance Lessons Integrating Classroom Content

Lesson Title	Science	Social Studies	Literature	Informational Texts	Vocabulary	Poetry
Down by the Cool of the Pool (Chapter 31)			X			
When Autumn Leaves Fall (Chapter 31)	X			X		
The Snowy Day (Chapter 31)			X			
If Not for the Cat (Chapter 31)	X					X
The Thunderstorm (Chapter 31)	X		X	X		
In the Small, Small Pond (Chapters 30, 31)	X		X			
Ashanti to Zulu (Chapter 32)		X	X			
Prey and Predators (Chapter 32)	X			X		
Invasive Species (Chapter 32)	X			X		
The Sea and the Shore (Chapter 32)						X
Journey Through the Solar System (Chapter 32)	X			X		
The Dimensional Cross (Chapter 32)					X	
Shelter in a Storm (Chapter 32)	X			X		
Row, Row, Row Your Boat (Chapter 32)						
Sport Tableaux (Chapter 32)						
Song Within My Heart (Chapter 33)			X			
Where the Wild Things Are (Chapter 17)			X			
All Folk Dance Lessons in Chapter 33: Native American Tribal, Hawaiian, Irish, Italian, Greek, Serbian, Japanese, Mexican		X				

Additional Features

Elementary Physical Education: Curriculum and Instruction, Second Edition, incorporates a number of engaging pedagogical features to aid in the student's understanding and retention of the material.

Each chapter starts with **Pre-reading Reflection** questions, which ask students to consider their prior experiences, opinions, and questions about the chapter content.

Chapters also begin with **Objectives** students will learn, which highlight the critical points of each chapter, and **Connection to Standards**, which indicates how the chapter content links to the new National Standards for Physical Education and the Common Core and other State Standards.

Further, a list of **key terms and concepts** is included, bolded where defined in the chapter, and all key terms and concepts are provided in a new end-of-text glossary.

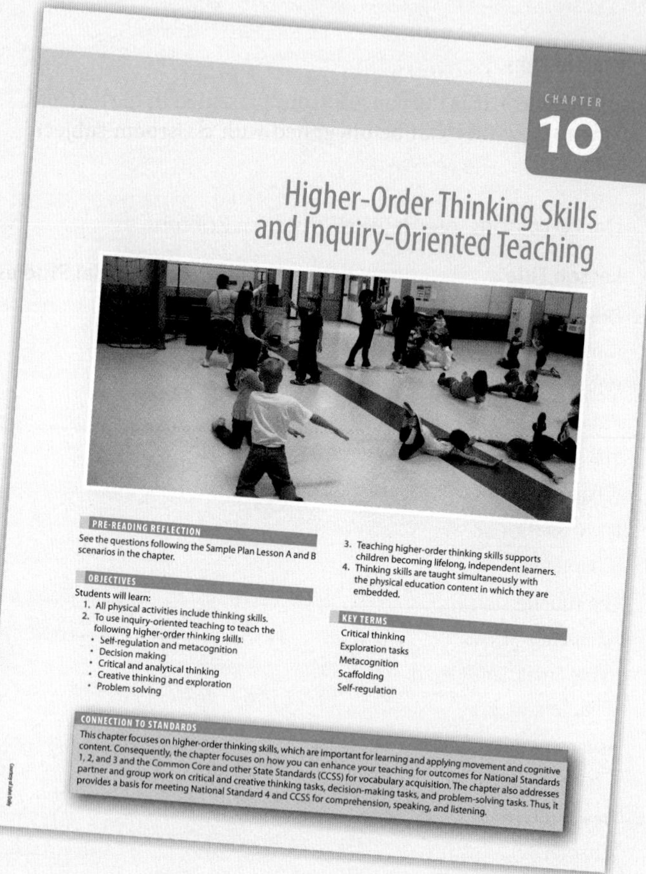

CHAPTER 10

Higher-Order Thinking Skills and Inquiry-Oriented Teaching

PRE-READING REFLECTION

See the questions following the Sample Plan Lesson A and B scenarios in the chapter.

OBJECTIVES

Students will learn:

1. All physical activities include thinking skills.
2. To use inquiry-oriented teaching to teach the following higher-order thinking skills:
   - Self-regulation and metacognition
   - Decision making
   - Critical and analytical thinking
   - Creative thinking and exploration
   - Problem solving
3. Teaching higher-order thinking skills supports children becoming lifelong, independent learners.
4. Thinking skills are taught simultaneously with the physical education content in which they are embedded.

KEY TERMS

Critical thinking
Exploration tasks
Metacognition
Scaffolding
Self-regulation

CONNECTION TO STANDARDS

This chapter focuses on higher-order thinking skills, which are important for learning and applying movement and cognitive content. Consequently, the chapter focuses on how you can enhance your teaching for outcomes for National Standards 1, 2, and 3 and the Common Core and other State Standards (CCSS) for vocabulary acquisition. The chapter also addresses partner and group work on critical and creative thinking tasks, decision-making tasks, and problem-solving tasks. Thus, it provides a basis for meeting National Standard 4 and CCSS for comprehension, speaking, and listening.

Summary

Motor development and motor learning provide important tools that can help you teach physical education based on how children learn. Developmental sequences describe in detail qualitative markers of change from less to more mature patterns through which children will progress as they learn motor skills. Knowing the developmental steps in the sequence helps teachers observe and assess children's skills, anticipate children's responses during planning, select relevant performance techniques, and design tasks to facilitate children's learning.

The precepts of Newell's constraints theory, along with concepts from ecological psychology and dynamical systems theory, help teachers understand the role of individual, task, and environmental constraints on performance and learning.

Motor learning is a form of discovery learning in which the learner explores the relations among individual, task, and environmental constraints in performing motor skills. These theories guide teachers in designing tasks that elicit the movement patterns they want children to practice.

Understanding development helps you, as a teacher, see children from a developmental perspective, and teach developmentally appropriate content. Using a developmental perspective, you can better recognize children's progress along developmental continua, recognize individual differences, and match your content to children's capabilities, helping them improve.

Review Questions

1. Compare and contrast a developmental perspective with an error model. Which do you hold now, and why?
2. What does the phrase "Development is age related, not age determined" mean? What are some implications for teachers?
3. Select any skill you know well from any sport, such as the front crawl in swimming, blocking in football, or spiking in volleyball. Based on your experience in teaching, coaching, or learning the skill, hypothesize an intratask developmental sequence for it, and list, in order, developmental patterns for components and/or phases of the movement.
4. Briefly describe Newell's constraints theory.
5. Give two specific examples of how task or environmental constraints can have a negative effect on children's movement patterns.
6. Give one specific example of a task that can elicit the movement response you want children to practice.
7. Define open and closed skills, giving examples of skills from each end of the open–closed continuum.
8. Where on the continuum from open to closed skills would you classify the following skills and why? (Describe which aspects of the skills you used as a basis for your decision.)
   - Shooting in basketball
   - Dribbling in soccer
   - Breaststroke in swimming
   - Football pass
   - Batting off a tee
9. Briefly describe the three stages of motor learning and their implications for teaching physical education.

References

Allison, P. C., & Barrett, K. R. (2000). *Constructing children's physical education experiences: Understanding the content for teaching.* Boston: Allyn & Bacon.

Barrett, D. D., & Burton, A. W. (2002). Throwing patterns used by collegiate baseball players in actual games. *Research Quarterly for Exercise and Sport, 73*, 19–27.

Boyce, B. A., Coker, C. A., & Bunker, L. K. (2006). Implications for variability of practice from pedagogy and motor learning perspectives: Finding a common ground. *Quest, 58*, 330–343.

Chen, D. (2011). Creative paradoxical thinking and its implications for teaching and learning motor skills. *Journal of Physical Education, Recreation, and Dance, 82*(9), 19–23, 49.

At the end of each chapter, a **Summary** reviews key ideas and helps students remember the different concepts discussed in the chapter and how the concepts interact.

Review Questions are designed to help students assess what they have learned and to further enhance their understanding of the content in the chapter. **References** allow students the opportunity for further research on their own.

Throughout the text, there are hundreds of boxed features to aid in the learning and retention of the material. These supplemental features complement the text with the voices of students, teachers, parents, and researchers.

What the Research Says boxes provide brief summaries of research that supports the curriculum and instruction discussed in the text to further demonstrate how the material is evidence based.

What the Research Says

Do Young Children Benefit from Fundamental Skill Instruction or Should We Simply Provide Recess with Plenty of Equipment?

Some people question why we need to provide instruction in fundamental skills to preschoolers and young children, claiming that children simply need opportunities to play and that skills will develop naturally through maturation. The research, however, suggests that a sound physical education program that teaches children fundamental skills has a significant impact on children's skill levels. By comparison, control groups who played in well-equipped play environments but received no instruction showed no significant improvements in skills (Goodway & Branta, 2003; Robinson, 2011; Robinson & Goodway, 2009).

Experienced Teachers Talk features include engaging commentary from teachers in the field that cover an array of issues that future teachers are likely to encounter in the real world.

Experienced Teachers Talk

Teaching Children to Ignore Distractions

Here is a story I tell my children when we have distractions that cannot be avoided:

How many of you have ever been watching cartoons when your mother says, "Why don't you come when I call you?" Of course, you're thinking to yourself, "I never heard her." That happened because you were concentrating so hard on the cartoon that you blocked out any distractions. The kind of concentration that kept you from hearing any other noise is what you need to do today while I am talking.

TEACHING TIP

Eliciting Exploration Quickly

When you give an exploration task and a child responds quickly, say, "I see someone balancing on two hands and one foot; I see someone balancing on their hips." Other children will start exploring by trying to find different body parts because they want you to call out their ideas, too. This positive approach works better than saying, "Get busy and do what I told you to do."

Teaching Tip boxes describe how concepts and teaching techniques from theory and research on motor learning, cognitive learning, motivation, higher-order thinking skills, cooperative learning, social responsibility, and multicultural diversity work in practice.

Student Tales

One of our colleagues told us this story:

My nephew came home with his PE report card in kindergarten and the teacher stated that he needed to work on skipping. I said, "John, I know you can skip. What happened?" He said, "My teacher taught me to skip a different way than you did. Watch." In slow motion he tried, unsuccessfully, to step and hop first on one foot and then on the other. The teacher had broken down skipping into parts, and the fragmentation totally messed up his performance of the skill as a whole.

Student Tales boxes reflect real-life reactions to students' physical education experiences. This allows readers to see the effect of teaching methods, curriculum, and attitudes toward practice.

SAFETY AND LIABILITY 4.1

Increasing Safety and Decreasing Risk of Liability: Guidelines Relevant to Content in this Chapter

In this box, we discuss specific guidelines built on information discussed earlier in this text on professional standards of practice, negligence, and liability. The goals of these guidelines are to increase children's safety and decrease teachers' risk of negligence and liability.

- Ensure all tasks are developmentally appropriate for every child in relation to skill level, size, age, strength, and other physical capabilities. Differentiating instruction to accommodate these developmental differences is important for decreasing your risk of liability.
- In partner and group activities in which there is the potential for contact or harm due to unequal size, weight, or other physical characteristics and capabilities (e.g., pairs balancing in gymnastics), pair and group children with others of similar physical attributes and developmental levels.
- The younger the children, the more closely they need to be supervised.

Sources: (Hart & Ritson, 2002; Halsey, 2005)

Safety and Liability boxes provide critical guidelines to support a safe, effective, and supportive learning environment for children.

Safety tips include governing laws and regulations, suggestions for supervision and safe equipment use, and differentiated instruction for smaller or larger groups and differently abled learners.

Sample Learning Experiences and Sample Plans

A strength of this text is the detailed descriptions of content and how children learn that content along with ample specific examples of how to translate content into learning experiences and lesson plans that illustrate how to teach the content to children. These descriptions are found in the content chapters and in the Skills Boxes, Sample Learning Experiences, and Sample Plans throughout the text.

SAMPLE LEARNING EXPERIENCES 19.6

Level 2A: Passing and Receiving with the Feet or Hockey Stick

1. Moving to Receive a Ball/Puck with the Feet or Hockey Stick

With a peer coach, explore moving to receive a ball with the feet or hockey stick. Learn to move to the left and to the right so that you line up behind the ball to receive it with the feet or hockey stick, control it, reposition to pass, and pass it back to your peer coach. The peer coach remains stationary. Decide a fair way to switch roles.

2. Passing Balls/Pucks Over Different Distances Using the Right Amount of Force

- With a teammate, explore passing over different distances.
- Compare and contrast the different movement patterns you need to kick or push pass for short, medium, and long distances.
- Experiment to discover the longest distance over which you can pass accurately.

3. Receiving Balls with Different Amounts of Force

- Explore receiving and passing balls with different amounts of force.
- Experiment to learn how to adjust your body actions when you receive a ball/puck with different amounts of force, such as how quickly you need to travel to get in line with the ball/puck and how to adapt the speed and distance you need to absorb the force of the ball/puck.

SAMPLE PLAN 14.2

Plan for a Dribbling Center

Objectives

As a result of this center, the children will improve

Motor

1. Dribbling on different pathways looking up.

Social

2. Their sensitivity to the need of their partner to have a fair amount of space by looking up and not infringing on their partner's space.

Task

Working with your partner, put the cones anywhere you want in your area. Dribble on different pathways all around the cones any way you want. Be sure to look up to see whether you are letting your partner have a fair amount of space.

ME You can choose to practice dribbling while traveling slowly and focus on pushing with your finger pads rather than slapping the ball.

In the content chapters, games and gymnastics content is organized into a three-level developmental progression and dance into a two-level progression. Starting each games, dance, and gymnastics chapter is a list of the relevant content (i.e., skills, movement concepts, movement themes, and/or tactics) in a progression. Sample Learning Experiences for each developmental level expand on the content progression list and describe a progression of tasks and/or learning experiences that prospective teachers can develop into lesson plans. Sample Plans then illustrate how a set of learning experiences can be developed into lesson plans. These plans include objectives; links to the National Standards; potential refinements and performance technique to teach based on the likely developmental levels of children; ways to integrate relevant motivation, social responsibility, and/or affective concepts into lesson plans; and safety issues that can arise. Sample Plans bring alive the content and help prospective teachers imagine how teaching the content might look in actual learning environments. The Sample Plans have a clear focus on learning and improving motor skills and show teachers how to shift among a range of teaching strategies, from direct to inquiry-oriented, reflecting how instruction of a movement approach occurs in real-world settings.

For every major motor skill and tactic, the **Skills Box** feature includes the typical immature movement patterns students can expect to see, descriptions of the mature performance techniques, and potential performance cues to teach, arranged from the most basic to the more advanced techniques children can develop through practice.

SKILLS BOX 4.1

Using Descriptions of Developmental Movement Patterns to Guide Teaching: An Example with Dribbling

Teaching the Hand/Wrist/Arm Component

Hand/Wrist/Arm Movements Observed

Immature: Palm slaps ball. The child slaps or hits the ball with the palm of the hand (see Figure 4.2).

Performance Techniques to Teach to Help Children Progress to the Mature Pattern

- Push the ball with the finger pads or fingerprints; don't slap the ball.
- Your hand is like a spider spread over the ball.

Potential Tasks (Level 1 Content)

- Remaining in your personal space, try bouncing the ball as many times in a row as you can.
  - Give both hands practice.
  - Try to increase the number of times you can bounce the ball without missing it or having it bounce out of your personal space.
- Try bouncing the ball as many times in a row as you can while walking and then jogging easily.
  - Give both hands practice.
  - Try to increase the number of times you can bounce the ball and keep it with you without losing control of it. If you have problems keeping the ball with you, practice dribbling in your personal space.

Teaching the Body/Head Component

Body/Head Movements Observed

Intermediate: Glances up. Knees are slightly bent, and the child is mostly upright. The child glances up to see where he or she is going but tends to look primarily at the ball.

Based on the concept of observation as a critical teaching skill, **Sample Observation Plans** are tied to the interactive teaching observation–interpretation–decision-making cycle. Observation allows students to understand the process of teaching and it is the basis for later reflecting on practice. We describe the observation cycle and the reflecting on practice cycle in detail in Chapter 8 and then, throughout the remainder of the book, we use the **observation cycle icon** to indicate where you'll find important observation points.

SAMPLE OBSERVATION PLAN 8.1

Second-Grade Games Task

Task: Self-toss and -catch a foam ball, working on reaching to catch.

1. Check whether children are far enough apart so no one will bump into another child.
2. See if any child appears to be afraid to catch the ball.
3. Determine whether children are tossing accurately enough to practice catching.
4. Watch their arms and hands, and assess if they are reaching.

Notes: For this task, we plan to observe whether the tosses are accurate enough before checking whether the children are reaching to catch. This sequence is appropriate because the environmental constraints (an accurate toss) must be right to enable the children to practice catching. Then, we will focus on reaching for the ball, which is the lesson objective.

© Jones & Bartlett Learning. Photographed by Sarah Cebulski.

Which children are tossing accurately enough to practice catching? Which are not?

ASSESSMENT 15.5

Sample Checklist with Descriptions of Immature and Mature Performance Techniques

Dribbling with Hands in Place

Name	Immature Performance Level: Slaps ball, no pushing action, makes contact with ball using palm	Mature Performance Level: Pushes with finger pads
Mia	X	
Jill	X	
Bill		X

Assessment boxes provide readers with solid tools to assess a range of outcomes, such as throwing (physical), describing feelings (affective), task engagement (motivation), and self-regulation (cognitive).

References

American College of Sports Medicine (ACSM). (2004). Physical activity and bone health. *Medicine and Science in Sports and Exercise, 36*(11), 1985–1996.

Centers for Disease Control and Prevention (CDC). (2013). *Comprehensive School Physical Activity Programs: A Guide for Schools.* Atlanta, GA: U.S. Department of Health and Human Services.

Common Core State Standards Initiative. (2010). *Common core state standards for English language arts and literacy in history /social studies, science, and technical subjects.* Available: www .corestandards.org

Corbin, C. B., Welk, G. J., Richardson, C., Vowell, C., Lambdin, D., & Wikgren, S. (2014). Youth fitness: Ten key concepts. *Journal of Physical Education, Recreation, and Dance, 85*(2), 24–31.

Hoelscher, D. M., Kirk, S., Ritchie, L., Cunningham-Sabo, L. (2013). Position of the Academy of Nutrition and Dietetics: Interventions for the prevention and treatment of pediatric overweight and obesity. *Journal of the Academy of Nutrition and Dietetics, 113*, 1375–1394.

Institute of Medicine (IOM). (2012). *Fitness measures and health outcomes in youth.* Washington, DC: National Academy of Sciences.

Institute of Medicine (IOM). (2013). *Educating the student body: Taking physical activity and physical education to school.* Washington, DC: National Academy of Sciences.

Malina, R. M. (2014). Top 10 research questions related to growth and maturation of relevance to physical activity, performance, and fitness. *Research Quarterly for Exercise and Sport, 85*, 157–173.

National Association for Sport and Physical Education (NASPE). (2008). *Comprehensive school physical activity programs.* Reston, VA: Author.

Plowman, S. A. (2014). Top 10 research questions related to musculoskeletal physical fitness testing in children and adolescents. *Research Quarterly for Exercise and Sport, 85*, 174–187.

Society of Health and Physical Educators (SHAPE). (2014). *National standards and grade-level outcomes for K–12 physical education.* Champaign, IL: Human Kinetics.

SECTION I

Curriculum, Instruction, and Theoretical Support

In this section, we begin in Chapters 1 through 3 by describing the goals, national standards, and significance of physical education, including a brief history of this field, and then provide an overview of the movement approach that constitutes the curricular and instructional model presented in this text. In Chapters 4, 5, and 9, we describe the development, learning, and motivation theories that support our approach. We describe instruction in Chapters 6, 7, 8, 10, and 13, thereby linking instruction to how children learn and develop. Chapters 11 and 12 discuss teaching social responsibility, emotional goals, and respecting and valuing diversity. Planning, assessment, and their links to national standards are discussed in Chapters 14 and 15. Section I is followed by descriptions of the content of the curricular and instructional model, including the sample lesson plans presented in Sections II, III, and IV. As part of these discussions, we link the content to the theoretical support, national standards, and instructional methods discussed in Section I.

CHAPTER

1

Physical Education Goals, Significance, and National Standards

PRE-READING REFLECTION

1. Did you enjoy physical education at each level: elementary, middle, and high school?
2. Was the program at each level an instructional program in which the teacher taught you skills, or did you just play games and sports?
3. Did you have any health-related physical fitness lessons? If so, did you enjoy them?

OBJECTIVES

Students will learn:

1. Until the early twentieth century, physical fitness was the goal of physical education.
2. In the twentieth century, games, sports, dance, and outdoor recreational activities became prominent goals.
3. In the 1960s, motor, cognitive, social, and emotional goals to help the child develop into a fully functioning person became important.
4. All three types of goals—(a) health-related physical activity; (b) sports, dance, and recreational activities; and (c) cognitive, social, and emotional goals—are important today.
5. "The goal of physical education is to develop physically literate individuals who have the knowledge, skills, and confidence to enjoy a lifetime of healthful physical activity" (Society of Health and Physical Educators [SHAPE], 2014, p. 11).
6. To achieve this goal, SHAPE has set five national standards.
7. Teachers have differing value orientations. Their unique orientations affect the extent to which they emphasize different goals.
8. Physical education is significant because it teaches about and provides health-related physical activity and fitness, which benefit health, and because it teaches sports, dance, outdoor, and recreational activities, which are significant cultural activities.

KEY TERMS

Breach of duty
Damage
Disciplinary mastery value orientation
Duty
Ecological integration value orientation
Friedrich Ludwig Jahn
Gymnastics wars
Johann Christoph Friedrich Guts Muths
Learning process value orientation
mens sana en corpore sano
Negligence
Per Henrik Ling
Proximate cause
Self-actualization value orientation
Social responsibility value orientation

CONNECTIONS TO STANDARDS

In this chapter we introduce the National Standards for Physical Education and the Common Core State Standards, explain their importance, and describe the connections between the National Standards for Physical Education and the motor, cognitive, social, and affective domains.

A Brief History of Physical Education

History can help you understand which curriculum goals have guided and continue to guide our field, why educators considered these goals beneficial, and why new perspectives emerged. Studying history also can help you appreciate the long, proud heritage of physical education. Finally, knowing your history can help you prepare for teacher certification tests, which often include historical questions.

Early Greek and Roman Influences

Until the 1900s, many physical educators were physicians, and all physical education was called gymnastics. The aim of this field was to improve health and correct physical ailments. Greek and Roman physicians were the first to develop these physical education programs, which still influence our field today—although we no longer exercise naked, as was the practice then. These historical figures used the term *gymnastics* to describe their activities because they conducted their programs in a gymnasium (Freeman, 2012).

The physician Galen (who lived from circa 130 to 200 A.D.) was the first writer to develop a medical gymnastics program to improve health, although the belief that exercise is connected to health dates back in written records at least to Hippocrates (for whom the physicians' Hippocratic Oath is named) in the fifth century B.C. (Gerber, 1971). Galen's gymnastics program included exercise, wrestling, throwing the discus, climbing ropes, carrying heavy loads, running, shadow boxing, and exercising with a small ball. In some European countries today, people exercise with small balls in ways similar to Galen's program, even though this program originated 1,800 years ago (Gerber, 1971). Likewise, today we continue to promote the ancient Greek and then Roman ideal of ***mens sana en corpore sano*** (a strong mind in a healthy body) (Patterson, 1998).

German Gymnastics

Guts Muths: The Grandfather of Physical Education

The modern era of physical education began in Germany in the late 1700s, as part of a movement led by **Johann Christoph Friedrich Guts Muths** (1759–1839) (Gerber, 1971). Guts Muths was a physical education teacher who taught and wrote about his work for more than 50 years (Freeman, 2012). Historians call him the grandfather of physical education. Guts Muths provided individualized gymnastics programs for students, focusing on wrestling, running, leaping, throwing, balancing, climbing, lifting, skipping rope, swimming, dancing, hiking, and military exercises (see **Figure 1.1**). He also included games that contributed to building strength, speed, and flexibility.

Jahn: The Father of Physical Education

Born in Prussia, **Friedrich Ludwig Jahn** (1778–1852) is considered the father of physical education and modern gymnastics. Influenced by the ideas of Guts Muths, he was a leader in developing "German gymnastics" and *Turnverein* (gymnastics

Figure 1.1 Early German gymnastics

Reproduced from G. Muths, J.C. Friedrich. Gymnastics for youth: or A practical guide to healthful and amusing exercises for the use of schools. Printed for P. Byrne, 1803. Courtesy of the Harvard Medical Library in the Francis A. Countway Library of Medicine [HOLLIS number 003017820].

societies). So-called Turners (i.e., gymnasts) exercised on the horizontal and parallel bars, vaulting horse, balance beam, climbing ropes, and ladders; they also participated in wrestling, hoop and rope jumping, throwing, running, broad jumping, pole vaulting, and lifting weights (Gerber, 1971; Lumpkin, 1986). Gymnastics was seen primarily as a means of developing fitness (Patterson, 1998). The military, for example, used gymnastics for training troops—the horse apparatus was modeled after live horses used in the cavalry. Even by the early 1900s, some horse apparatus still had the front end pointed up and the tail end pointed down.

Jahn's Arrest for Teaching Physical Education

At one point, the German government arrested Jahn because it perceived him to be a political threat. Jahn and his followers conducted German gymnastics outdoors in large groups (of approximately 400 people). The Turnverein societies promoted German nationalism, and the Turner motto translated into "Gymnasts are vigorous, happy, strong, and free" (Gerber, 1971, p. 131). Because these organizations promoted nationalism and freedom, the government attempted to stop Turnverein activity. Nevertheless, Turnverein societies continued to operate "underground" in some German states, and German immigrants brought the system to the United States, where it soon spread. At the Chicago World's Fair in 1893, for example, 4,000 Turners demonstrated large group gymnastics activities (Gerber, 1971).

Swedish Gymnastics

The second major influence on the modern era of physical education was the Swedish system of gymnastics developed by **Per Henrik Ling** (1776–1839). Like the German system, the Swedish system promoted nationalism, was used as part of military training, and focused on large groups of people performing mass drills. The Swedish system emphasized exercises and body positions performed in highly precise ways, much like many aerobic and fitness classes today (see **Figure 1.2**). Swedish exercising concentrated on posture development rather than the stunts employed in German gymnastics. Ling invented a variety of apparatus for his system, including the stall bars and the Swedish box used for vaulting. We still use these and similar apparatus today (see **Figure 1.3**).

The Gymnastics Wars

Much as in the "reading wars" and the "math wars" of recent times, educators in the late 1800s debated whether the German or Swedish system was best. Educators sometimes called these debates the **gymnastics wars** or the "battle of the systems" (Freeman, 2012).

New Goals: Teaching Games, Sports, Dance, and Recreational Activities

In the twentieth century, educators began to promote a second set of subject matter goals for physical education—namely, that students learn games, sports, dance, and recreational activities. After World War I, the Roaring Twenties were in full swing. The United States entered a new era after the war with "unprecedented confidence," a "quest for the 'good life,'" and a feeling that "anything was possible" (Swanson, 1985, p. 18). John Dewey, whose work is still influential today, and other educators proposed a new view of schooling called progressive education that focused on developing the whole child. This spirit of progressive education soon captured the field of education.

In 1927, Thomas Wood and Rosaline Cassidy wrote a book titled *The New Physical Education*, which advocated a shift from the regulated fitness regimes of German and Swedish gymnastics to teaching movement skills and physical activities, such as games, sports, and dance. It makes sense that physical educators moved away from the German and Swedish systems when addressing the general public because these systems were developed, in part, for military training. By the 1920s, World War I was over, Europe was "over there," and people were optimistic. Educators of this era viewed fitness exercises as inadequate for a total program of physical education; instead, they

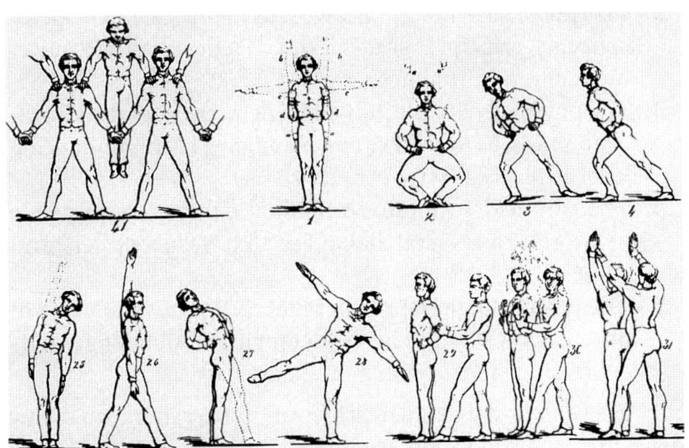

Figure 1.2 Swedish gymnastics

Reproduced from P.H. Ling. The gymnastic free exercises of P.H. Ling, arranged by H. Rothstein. Groombridge & Sons, 1853. Courtesy of the Boston Medical Library in the Francis A. Countway Library of Medicine [HOLLIS number 005693194].

Figure 1.3 Child today vaulting over a Swedish box

claimed that health would be an outcome of children learning skills and activities that they could enjoy in their everyday lives (Swanson, 1985).

At the same time, educators called for the development of children's mental capabilities and moral character so they could become productive citizens of a democratic society. They believed that these goals could be met through games and sports (Freeman, 2012).

The dual goals of engaging in health-related activities and teaching games, sports, dance, and recreational activities have coexisted since the 1920s, and they continue to influence physical education today. In some years, health-related goals predominated; in other years, the teaching of sports, dance, and recreational activities assumed primary importance. Two additional events had a major influence on elementary physical education; one occurred in England and the other in the broader field of education.

Historical Influences on Elementary Physical Education

The English Movement Approach

In the late 1940s and 1950s, there was growing interest in England among physical education teachers to apply Rudolf Laban's work in modern educational dance (what we would label creative or educational dance today) to games and gymnastics (Riley, 1981). In addition, teachers found that children enjoyed exploring apparatus such as cargo nets and parallel ropes, which were originally used to train the armed forces for World War II.

During the same era, *Moving and Growing* (1952) and *Planning the Programme* (1953) were published by the Department of Education in England as replacements for the national syllabus that had been maintained since 1933. These texts promoted a curriculum and instructional model called a movement education or a movement approach, which included exploration, repetition, discovery learning, and versatility and quality in movement. The new syllabus led to changes in elementary physical education curricula and instruction across England. In the late 1950s and 1960s, adoption and development of the English movement approach by North American physical educators increased dramatically.

ASCD Promotion of Individual Development as a Goal of Education

In 1962, the Association for Supervision and Curriculum Development (ASCD) published a yearbook that brought individual development goals to prominence. Many physical educators embraced the goals outlined in the ASCD yearbook; as a consequence, the yearbook had a lasting impact on American elementary schools.

The major aim articulated in the yearbook was to help the child develop into a "fully functioning" person with the capabilities needed to live a "good life." A good life, according to this source, is a life that is satisfying, meaningful, and productive. A fully functioning person has a sense of confidence, is open to new challenges, and accepts change with optimism and hope that the change will be enriching and enhancing.

Another key aim was for children to develop autonomy and the ability to make wise decisions about what is meaningful and important to them. The yearbook also proposed that programs focus on helping children develop social responsibility, form cooperative relationships with others, and care about the well-being of people in their communities.

In the 1960s, the goals articulated in the ASCD yearbook contributed to the interest of North American physical educators in adopting the movement approach. The movement approach was based on comparable goals and introduced new teaching techniques and a new view of content that allowed teachers to design programs to meet the goals promoted in the yearbook. Teachers and university faculty brought the movement approach to North America, and its use in elementary physical education has grown ever since.

We turn now to a discussion of the goals of physical education and national standards.

The Goals of Physical Education and the National Standards

According to the Society of Health and Physical Educators (SHAPE), the national organizational for physical education, "The goal of physical education is to develop physically literate individuals who have the knowledge, skills, and confidence to enjoy a lifetime of healthful physical activity" (SHAPE, 2014, p. 11). The term *literate* in this sense means educated, and it is currently used across many subject areas to describe their goals (e.g., to be mathematically literate). The reference to preparing students to enjoy a lifetime of healthful physical activity indicates that our goals are not simply to keep children physically active and having fun, but, more importantly, to lay an educational foundation in physical literacy that will support them throughout adulthood. It is a goal worthy of our best efforts as teachers and has broad, nationwide support.

To provide a framework to guide physical education programs, this broad goal has been broken down into the following five national standards (SHAPE, 2014, p.12):

1. The physically literate individual demonstrates competence in a variety of motor skills and movement patterns (see **Figure 1.4**).
2. The physically literate individual applies knowledge of concepts, principles, strategies, and tactics related to movement and performance.
3. The physically literate individual demonstrates the knowledge and skills to achieve and maintain a health-enhancing level of physical activity and fitness.
4. The physically literate individual exhibits responsible personal and social behavior that respects self and others.
5. The physically literate individual recognizes the value of physical activity for health, enjoyment, challenge, self-expression, and/or social interaction.

These national standards identify for teachers what students are expected to achieve in physical education from kindergarten through grade 12 (K–12).

As you can see, the historical motor goals for learning both physical activities and health-enhancing physical activity remain prominent today, as do broader goals for individual development, such as developing social responsibility

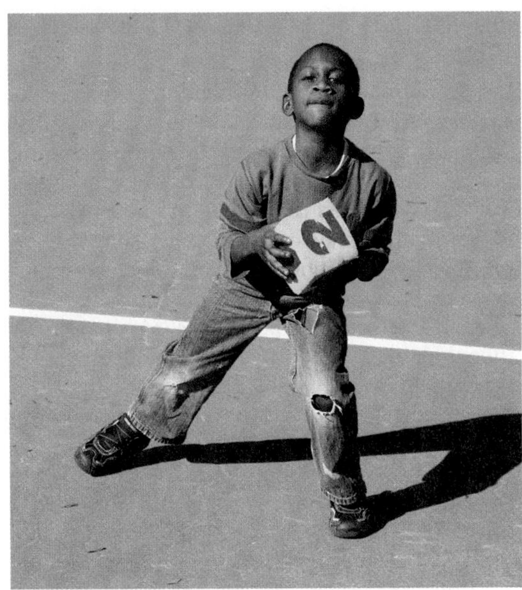

Figure 1.4 Engaged in developing competence in motor skills

and learning to value the enjoyment and challenge of physical activities.

Accompanying the national standards are grade-level outcomes that describe more specific content that students are expected to learn and master in each grade level. For example, outcomes third-graders are expected to master for National Standards 1, 2, and 3 are as follows (SHAPE, 2014):

- "Dribbles with the feet in general space at slow to moderate jogging speed with control of ball and body" (p. 29)
- "Applies simple strategies and tactics in chasing [i.e., tag] activities" (p. 33)
- "Demonstrates, with teacher direction, the health-related fitness [HRF] components" (p. 35)

Thus, grade-level outcomes give teachers guidance that is more specific for planning their grade-level curriculum.

Based on national standards, each state developed a set of state standards or a state course of study that is more specific than the national standards and thus offers teachers more precise guidance in planning what skills, knowledge, and attitudes they will teach in their program.

State standards are especially important because many states are now using those standards to hold teachers and schools accountable for student learning outcomes (Rink, 2013; Ward, 2013). Students are tested as to whether they have met the standards, and the extent to which they have met the standards is used, at least in part, as a basis for evaluating teacher effectiveness. Traditionally, teachers were evaluated by principals and sometimes peers who observed their teaching using an assessment tool that described qualities of effective teaching, along with a rating scale to assess whether the teacher was effective. Now, however, at least 30 states also require teachers to provide evidence of effectiveness using measures of student learning outcomes linked to state standards (Rink, 2013; Ward, 2013).

National standards and outcomes represent the collective professional judgment of teachers, administrators, and researchers about what students need to learn in schools. If students meet these standards and outcomes, they are considered to be physically literate and well on their way to a lifetime of physical activity. In addition, these standards, along with curriculum guidelines and policies published by SHAPE America (e.g., *Opportunity to Learn,* NASPE, 2010; *The Essential Components of Physical Education,* SHAPE America, 2015; *Appropriate Instructional Practice Guidelines for Elementary School Physical Education,* NASPE, 2009), define elements of professional standards of practice. Professional standards of practice are used by courts in lawsuits to determine if a teacher's actions or lack of action is negligent in relation to harm or injury to a student. Although we discuss specific safety and liability issues in relevant chapters throughout the text, we introduce negligence here to help you understand the importance of adhering to the national standards and generally accepted characteristics of professional practice.

Negligence, Liability, and the National Standards

As undergraduates, we both memorized the definition of **negligence**, that is, a failure to do what a reasonably prudent person would do in the same or similar circumstances. We recommend you do the same. Following the standard of professional practice to do as a reasonably prudent person would do will decrease your chances of being held liable for a student's injury, and failing to do so will increase your chances of liability (Eickhoff-Shemek, Herbert, & Connaughton, 2009). It is critical to remember that in a negligence lawsuit, you will be judged not on what a reasonably prudent person in the general population would do, but what another, well-trained, knowledgeable, reasonably prudent *physical educator* would do (Eickhoff-Shemek et al., 2009; Hart & Ritson, 2002). For example, if you teach a lesson and don't follow a developmentally appropriate progression for teaching a skill based on the national standards and learning outcomes for physical education, and a student is injured and claims your instruction was inadequate to prevent injury, you could be held liable in a negligence lawsuit for failing to follow the professional standards of practice described in the National Standards for Physical Education, written by other physical education professionals and published by our professional association, SHAPE America.

To understand negligence, we direct your attention to the Safety and Liability box. In this box we explain the elements of negligence. Throughout the text, we discuss specifically what you must do to meet professional standards of practice related to the content of each chapter. For example, the following are the major topics covered by professional standards of practice:

- *Supervision*: Students in the physical education space must be supervised at all times by a qualified supervisor (i.e., a certified teacher). The younger the children, the more closely they must be supervised.
- *Instruction*: Students must receive instruction on how to perform skills and movement patterns following a developmentally appropriate progression that ensures students' safe participation. Teachers must prepare written lesson plans that include teaching of safety in relation to lesson

content. Students must be instructed about the potential danger of various physical activities.

- *Developmental level*: Physical activities must be matched to each student's developmental level, and students must participate with other students at comparable developmental levels in regard to safety variables. Instruction must be differentiated for students of different developmental levels, abilities, and characteristics.
- *Environment*: Teachers and administrators must maintain a physically safe environment, including facilities, grounds, apparatus, and equipment. Teachers must also ensure the class organization provides adequate space for the movements of children, balls, and equipment such as bats and racquets.
- *Emotional environment*: Teachers and administrators must maintain an emotionally safe environment, including management of bullying and harassment.
- *Training*: Administrators must provide teachers opportunities for training in current professional practice and safety procedures, such as cardiopulmonary resuscitation (CPR) and first aid.
- *Accident reports*: Administrators and teachers must maintain records of accidents and injuries.

The national standards are important for many reasons, not least of which is giving you guidance on how to maintain professional standards. These standards will serve you well in decreasing your risk of liability.

The Focus on Learning in the National Standards for Physical Education

As you reflect on the goals of physical education and the five national standards, you can see that the focus is on student learning (SHAPE, 2014). For example, developing competence in motor skills and acquiring knowledge of concepts related to movement and performance, health-related physical activity, and fitness directly focus on learning. This focus reflects physical education's location in schools, which have a mission to educate children and young people across subject areas. Children and adults can also participate in sports, fitness, and recreational physical activities in a range of community settings. These settings sometimes provide educational lessons; however, more often the focus is on providing opportunities for recreation and participation in physical activities. To support and align with the educational mission of schools, physical education focuses on learning (Ennis, 2014). In other words, physical education is not recess or simply an opportunity to work out; physical education is an opportunity for students to learn the skills, knowledge, and dispositions that will support participation in physical activities throughout adulthood.

National Standards and the Physical, Cognitive, Social, and Affective Domains

At first glance, it may appear that the five national standards are separate and address four different domains: physical (Standard 1), cognitive (Standards 2 and 3), social (Standard 4), and

SAFETY AND LIABILITY 1.1

Negligence

Negligence is the "failure to exercise reasonable care that a reasonably prudent person would have exercised in the same or similar circumstances" (Nohr, 2009, p. 17). In a lawsuit, the injured student must prove all four of the following elements of negligence.

Duty

Duty means there is some relationship between individuals, such as employer and employee, teacher and student, or coach and players, and that the potential for harm by an action or lack of action was foreseeable (Eickhoff-Shemek et al., 2009; Nohr, 2009). Some events and accidents are not foreseeable, such as a meteorite landing on a child. For those events that are predictable, teachers have a duty to anticipate dangers and exercise reasonable, professional care to prevent harm.

Breach

Breach of duty means the teacher failed to meet the standard of professional care of the child that a reasonably prudent teacher would have met in the same or a similar situation. A breach of duty can be an action or a failure to act.

Proximate Cause

Proximate cause means the teacher's actions or failure to act caused the injury or harm to the child. For example, if the child asked to try a back handspring (a difficult gymnastics skill) and the teacher said yes but failed to spot the child and the child was injured, the failure to provide spotting is a proximate cause of the injury. To help you understand proximate cause, you can apply the "but for" test. *But for* the teacher's negligence in not providing spotting, the child would not have been injured.

Damage

The final element of negligence that must be proven is that the child suffered actual **damage** or that an actual injury occurred. Thus, if the child tried the back handspring and fell, but was not injured, claiming he or she could have been seriously injured is not sufficient to prove negligence.

affective (Standard 5). The physical domain refers to movement and motor skills; the cognitive domain reflects knowledge and thinking skills; the social domain focuses on social interactions; and the affective domain focuses on emotional feelings. Many physical educators define the affective domain as including both social interactions and emotional feelings, and others use the terms *affective* and *social* interchangeably. For clarity, in this text, we maintain a distinction between social and affective aspects.

Although we may discuss these four domains separately, in fact, these domains are fully integrated within physical activities. All physical activities have physical, cognitive, social, and affective aspects. For example, a class of third-graders given the task of dribbling a soccer ball (all at the same time), each traveling on different pathways (straight, curved, and zig zag) about the gymnasium, is practicing a motor skill, acquiring cognitive knowledge about different pathways and using thinking skills to decide when to change pathways to avoid bumping into a classmate, learning why changing pathways is important for working safely in a social environment, and feeling the excitement of dribbling successfully through a crowd. All four domains are part of the task.

The fact that all movement tasks you assign children include aspects of all four domains is critical because it allows you to focus on one (or more) of the national standards while also having students work on the primary aim to become competent in skills supporting a lifetime of physical activity. For example, in the soccer dribbling task, you might focus on improving the children's performance techniques (Standard 1). Or, you might instead focus on helping the children apply their knowledge of straight, curved, and zigzag pathways to avoid classmates or as a tactic to avoid defenders in game-like situations (Standard 2). You might also use the task to teach the children about the cardiorespiratory endurance needed in game-like situations (Standard 3), or you could emphasize the importance of exhibiting personal and social responsibility by not bumping into classmates (Standard 4). Finally, you might focus on helping the children recognize how the task is valuable because it is enjoyable and challenging (Standard 5). You can't focus on all five national standards at the same time, but movement tasks allow you to focus on whichever standard is most relevant at a given time and place.

The Common Core and Other State Standards

In addition to the national and state physical education standards, most states have also adopted a set of standards for literacy that apply to all subject areas. Many states use what are called the Common Core State Standards (Common Core State Standards Initiative, 2010), whereas other states have modified and adapted the Common Core to better meet specific needs. In this text, we call these standards the Common Core and other State Standards and use the label CCSS to identify these standards and note when they are included in the physical education lessons. We use the language of the Common Core because these standards are currently the most widely adopted.

The CCSS were developed by the states due to widespread concern about the English language literacy skills of American students and widespread agreement that teachers in all subject areas must contribute to students' abilities to read, write, speak, listen, and use higher-order thinking skills, as well as to collaborate with partners and small groups in discussions, projects, and problem-solving tasks. Although our goal and primary responsibility in physical education is to develop physically literate individuals, we can address CCSS without compromising our primary focus. We will show you how to do so throughout this text.

Teachers' Values and Goals

With all of the national and state standards that exist, you might be wondering if there is any room for teachers' personal values and goals. In fact, there is. In a large number of studies, Dr. Catherine Ennis found that teachers have both motor goals and broader goals for children's development. However, the extent to which they value and emphasize different goals varies. Ennis studied five value orientations that physical education teachers hold: disciplinary mastery, self-actualization, learning process, social responsibility, and ecological integration (Ennis, 1992; Ennis & Chen, 1993; Jewett, Bain, & Ennis, 1995). We summarize these orientations in the remainder of this section.

On the text website, you will find a Value Orientation Inventory that you can take to see which orientations you currently value most and least. Recognizing your own value orientations can stimulate you to think about goals you might not have considered in the past. As you read the description of each orientation, think about the extent to which you want your physical education program to reflect the goals described. You might want to rank the five orientations and compare your ranking to your scores on the Value Orientation Inventory.

Disciplinary Mastery

Teachers with a **disciplinary mastery** value orientation focus on subject-matter mastery as the primary goal of instruction. Thus, the first priority for these teachers is that children develop skillful movement in games, dance, and gymnastics; acquire knowledge of health-related physical activities; and learn about the disciplinary concepts of biomechanics, exercise physiology, the sociology and psychology of physical activity, and the history of sports and fitness.

Self-Actualization

Teachers who value **self-actualization** as their primary orientation focus on individual development and help children develop autonomy, self-confidence, self-management skills, self-understanding, and the ability to identify and work toward their own goals. Teachers select physical activities that children find meaningful and relevant and aim to develop children's individual capabilities.

Learning Process

Teachers with a **learning process** orientation help children learn how to learn. They not only teach physical activities, but also teach the process of learning these activities, such as how to improve performance, how to make decisions, and how to solve problems. They want children to be lifelong participants in physical activities and consequently focus on helping children learn how to engage in physical activities throughout their lives.

Social Responsibility

Teachers who prioritize **social responsibility** goals focus on developing responsible citizenship. This perspective includes teaching children how to cooperate and work responsibly and positively with others, why respecting the rights of others is important, and how to exert positive leadership, avoid conflict, and negotiate conflict resolutions (Ennis, 1994; Ennis & Chen, 1995).

Ecological Integration

Ecological integration emphasizes the integration of the individual within the total physical, social, and cultural environment. The teacher's primary objective is to prepare children for living in a global, interdependent society in which neither individual nor social needs predominate. Ecological integration has a future orientation, and teachers balance subject matter with individual and societal goals.

Research on Teachers' Value Orientations

Ennis and her colleagues have studied the value orientations of physical education teachers in elementary, middle, and high school settings. According to these researchers, most teachers have a disciplinary mastery orientation. Nevertheless, only 7.6% of the teachers in urban schools in their study reported valuing disciplinary mastery (Ennis, Chen, & Ross, 1992); instead, these urban teachers tended to emphasize social responsibility (Ennis, 1994).

Ennis and her colleagues also found that teachers have different value profiles. A profile indicates the extent to which you believe in each of the five value orientations. For example, some teachers believe strongly in one or two orientations and are only minimally concerned about the others. Other teachers will be concerned equally with most value orientations. Still other teachers will score high on one orientation, low on another, and be neutral on the other three.

You can discover your own profile by completing the Value Orientation Inventory on the text website and then scoring your answers using the scoring method provided. Keep in mind that your profile is not set in stone. Research shows that undergraduates' orientations change as they progress through teacher education (Solmon & Ashy, 1995).

What is critical is for you to reflect on your values and implement a program that reflects what you believe. The National Standards for Physical Education include goals that reflect different orientations. In this text, we present curriculum and instructional practices that you can use to implement a program in keeping with any of the five value orientations. We hope to challenge you to become the kind of teacher you want to be.

The Significance of Physical Education

The significance of physical education relates directly to its goals. We begin by considering the significance of health-related physical activity (HRPA).

The Significance of Health-Related Physical Activity

There is considerable support for the importance of HRPA and the role of physical education in its promotion from government agencies, such as the Centers for Disease Control and Prevention (CDC), the Surgeon General of the United States, the American Heart Association (AHA), and SHAPE, as well as researchers and physical education teachers. Specifically, a substantial body of research shows that HRPA produces the following benefits:

- Lower risk of early death
- Lower risk of coronary heart disease
- Lower risk of stroke
- Lower risk of high blood pressure
- Lower risk of adverse blood lipid profile
- Lower risk of type 2 diabetes
- Lower risk of metabolic syndrome
- Lower risk of colon cancer
- Lower risk of breast cancer
- Prevention of weight gain
- Weight loss, particularly when combined with reduced calorie intake
- Improved cardiorespiratory and muscular fitness
- Prevention of falls
- Reduced depression
- Better cognitive function (for older adults) (U.S. Department of Health and Human Services [USDHHS], 2008, p. 9)

In addition, the CDC (2010) has confirmed a link between physical activity and academic achievement:

- There is substantial evidence that physical activity can help improve academic achievement, including grades and standardized test scores.
- The articles in this review suggest that physical activity can have an impact on cognitive skills and attitudes and academic behavior, all of which are important components of improved academic performance. These include enhanced concentration and attention, as well as improved classroom behavior.
- Increasing or maintaining time dedicated to physical education may help, and does not appear to adversely impact, academic performance (p. 6).

Thus, physical activity is not only beneficial to health, but increasing time in physical education does not correspond to decreased test scores, even if less time is spent in subjects such as reading and mathematics.

In response to this research, the Surgeon General (USDHHS, 2010) made the following recommendations.

To promote physical activity, school systems should

- Require daily physical education for students in pre-kindergarten through grade 12, allowing 150 minutes per week for elementary schools and 225 minutes per week for secondary schools.
- Require and implement a planned and sequential physical education curriculum for pre-kindergarten through grade 12 that is based on national standards.
- Require at least 20 minutes of daily recess for all students in elementary schools.

- Offer students opportunities to participate in intramural physical activity programs during after-school hours.
- Implement and promote walk- and bike-to-school programs.
- Establish joint-use agreements with local government agencies to allow use of school facilities for physical activity programs offered by the school or community-based organizations outside of school hours (p. 9).

There is little doubt that physical activity can make a significant contribution to good health. In turn, physical education is significant because it offers the following benefits:

- Provides opportunities for children to engage in physical activity
- Develops a foundation of motor skills that enable children to enjoy participation in a range of physical activities as children and into adulthood
- Teaches children information about HRPA and HRF, including their benefits and ways to improve fitness levels
- Teaches children the motivational attitudes that contribute to increased participation, such as the belief in their abilities to be physically active
- Promotes the joy of movement, which contributes to increased participation

We once thought that fitness lessons for children meant having them engage in adult forms of fitness activities, such as calisthenics and running laps. "No pain, no gain" was the prevalent ideology, and the model for the teacher was the drill sergeant. This perception changed with the landmark report in 1996 from the Surgeon General (CDC, 1996). Based on research findings, the report recommended that adults engage in moderate physical activity for approximately 30 minutes most days of the week and included a broad range of physical activities considered effective in enhancing health. The current guidelines for children call for 60 minutes or more of moderate to vigorous physical activity every day, including activities such as skateboarding, hiking, games involving running, walking to school, bike riding, and jumping rope (USDHHS, 2008). Therefore, the emphasis in physical education today is on a variety of enjoyable health-related physical activities that can lead to lifelong participation.

The Significance of Learning Sports, Dance, Outdoor Activities, and Physically Active Play

The many forms of physical activity are significant parts of human life. Physical education is the only subject area in school devoted to teaching children the skills they need for meaningful participation. Siedentop (2002) argues, "The cultures of physically active play [are] fundamentally important to collective social life, and that bringing children and youth into contact with those cultures through educationally sound practices [is] sufficient to justify physical education as a school subject" (p. 411).

Physically active play—including sports, dance, outdoor activities, children's games, and recreational sports—is undeniably an important activity in society today. One of the key roles of schools is to educate students about ideas and events and to prepare students to participate in activities that are important

What the Research Says

Support for the Significance of Physical Education's Contribution to Children's Education

Learning movement skills is both an outcome in itself, as well as a means for physical education to contribute to the general goal of education to develop the whole child in all domains: physical, cognitive, social, and emotional. Educational researchers support the importance of physical education's contribution to the whole child.

Howard Gardner's Research

There is no doubt that one goal of education is to develop children's intelligence. But what is intelligence? Does it consist of a score on an I.Q. test? Howard Gardner, a Harvard University psychologist, says no. In his influential books, *Frames of Mind: The Theory of Multiple Intelligences* (1983) and *Intelligence Reframed: Multiple Intelligences for the 21st Century* (2000), Gardner argues that the old view of intelligence based on verbal and mathematical abilities is far too narrow to define intelligence.

In his research, Gardner has identified eight different intelligences: linguistic, logical-mathematical, spatial, musical, bodily-kinesthetic, interpersonal, intrapersonal, and naturalist. Individuals have different strengths among these eight intelligences, but all of these capabilities are important, valuable intelligences that help humans to function in society.

One implication of Gardner's work is that schools should develop all of the intelligences that will help students function well and contribute to their communities. We live and work in a complex world where we rarely acquire and use isolated pieces of information. Instead, the challenges we face, the problems we must solve, daily living, and work tasks require us to use multiple intelligences.

A second implication of Gardner's work is that children acquire knowledge and skills using multiple intelligences. Some children will learn more easily through one mode of learning; others will benefit from another approach. Relying on only one mode of learning does a disservice to children who might better understand a given topic if the teacher used multiple sources and modes of learning. Providing more than one source of information and multiple modes of learning can help all children develop a deeper understanding of subject matter.

Teachers and schools across North America have embraced Gardner's work because it has given them a broader, more comprehensive framework for understanding intelligence. Schools applying such a framework have succeeded in improving student achievement (Campbell & Campbell, 1999).

Courtesy of John Dolly

© muzsy/ShutterStock, Inc.

© Rubberball Productions

© Stockbyte/Thinkstock

Figure 1.5 Physical activity contributes to health and the quality of life

in their society. Literature, poetry, biology, earth science, geography, art, music, and history are all justified as subject areas, in part because they include ideas, events, and activities that were significant throughout history and remain important to today's society.

From the sports pages of most every newspaper to the Friday night lights of high school football, sports are part of the fabric of our communities. Across the country, parks and recreation departments provide swimming pools; access to lakes for fishing; trails for hiking, biking, and walking; tennis courts; golf courses; recreation centers offering a variety of leisure activity classes; and playgrounds for children. Sport agencies offer youth programs in soccer, basketball, softball, baseball, swimming, volleyball, cheerleading, gymnastics, dance, ice hockey, and other sports and activities. Television offers sports and sport-related shows 24 hours a day.

Clearly, learning sports, dance, and other physical activities is a critical part of children's education, enabling them to know about and participate in culturally significant activities. These activities contribute to the quality of their lives and support a lifetime of participation in health-enhancing, recreational physical activity in their communities (see **Figure 1.5**).

Summary

Until the twentieth century, many physical educators were physicians whose primary aim was to improve the health of their "patients." In the nineteenth century, German and Swedish systems of exercise predominated, and traces of these systems persist within modern-day approaches to physical education. In the twentieth century, educators promoted the goals of having students learn games, sports, dance, and outdoor recreational activities. In the 1960s, emphasis was placed on motor, cognitive, social, and emotional goals to help children develop into fully functioning people. All of these goals are valued today and are evident in the National Standards for Physical Education.

There is wide consensus that the "goal of physical education is to develop physically literate individuals who have the knowledge, skills, and confidence to enjoy a lifetime of healthful physical activity" (SHAPE, 2014, p. 11). To provide a framework to guide physical education programs, this goal has been broken down into five national standards. Teachers plan their curriculum and lessons in order to ensure their students meet the National Standards for Physical Education and their state's standards for physical education. In addition, education in all subject areas is expected to contribute to students' meeting the Common Core or other State Standards for English language literacy.

Teachers differ in the extent to which they value different goals. Researchers have identified five value orientations: disciplinary mastery, self-actualization, learning process, social responsibility, and ecological integration.

The significance of physical education relates directly to its goals. A substantial body of research shows that HRPA leads to health benefits. In addition, physical activity and academic achievement are linked. Increasing time for physical education does not detract from academic performance. Sports, dance, outdoor activities, children's games, and recreational sports are undeniably significant cultural activities. Physical education is the only subject area in school devoted to teaching children the skills they need for meaningful participation.

Review Questions

1. Describe the goal of physical education prior to the 1900s.
2. What were the gymnastics wars?
3. In the early 1900s, what became the second subject-matter goal of physical education, and why did teachers shift to this goal?
4. In your own words, describe the goal of physical education as defined by SHAPE (2014).
5. Link the four domains discussed in this chapter to the five National Standards for Physical Education.
6. Describe a task to practice a motor skill in an elementary school grade and identify the physical, cognitive, social, and emotional aspects of that task.
7. Pretend you are back in elementary school physical education. Rank the five value orientations that you would want your teacher to emphasize. Now assume that you are a parent, and rank the five value orientations that you would want your child's physical education teacher to emphasize. Discuss the reasoning underlying your rankings.
8. Reflect on the following situation. You are a high school physical education teacher in a rural community, and a senior girl who often confides in you asks your opinion about what she should do. All her life, she has wanted to be a fashion designer; now, because of her talent, she has the opportunity to attend a famous fashion institute in New York. Her family runs the only grocery store in their small town. Her parents are getting old and rely on her to run the store. If she leaves for New York, the store will likely have to close, which will affect both her family and the community. What do you say to her? What do you think she should do? Identify which value orientations reflect what you think she should do.
9. Pretend you are meeting with a principal. Explain the significance of physical education as a school subject.

References

Association for Supervision and Curriculum Development (ASCD). (1962). *Perceiving, behaving, becoming: A new focus for education.* Washington, DC: Author.

Campbell, L., & Campbell, B. (1999). *Multiple intelligences and student achievement: Success stories from six schools.* Alexandria, VA: Association for Supervision and Curriculum Development.

Centers for Disease Control and Prevention (CDC). (1996). *Physical activity and health: A report of the Surgeon General.* Atlanta, GA: Author.

Centers for Disease Control and Prevention (CDC). (2010). *The association between school-based physical activity, including physical education, and academic performance.* Atlanta, GA: U.S. Department of Health and Human Services.

Common Core State Standards Initiative. (2010). *Common core state standards for English language arts and literacy in history/social studies, science, and technical subjects.* Available at http://www.corestandards.org

Department of Education and Science & Central Office of Information. (1952). *Moving and growing.* London: Her Majesty's Stationery Office.

Department of Education and Science & Central Office of Information. (1953). *Planning the programme.* London: Her Majesty's Stationery Office.

Eickhoff-Shemek, J. M., Herbert, D. L., & Connaughton, D. P. (2009). *Risk management for health/fitness professionals: Legal issues and strategies.* Philadelphia: Wolters Kluwer/Lippincott Williams & Wilkins.

Ennis, C. D. (1992). The influence of value orientations in curriculum decision making. *Quest, 44,* 317–329.

Ennis, C. D. (1994). Urban secondary teachers' value orientations: Social goals for teaching. *Teaching and Teacher Education, 10*(1), 109–120.

Ennis, C. D. (2014). The role of students and content in teacher effectiveness. *Research Quarterly for Exercise and Sport, 85,* 6–13.

Ennis, C. D., & Chen, A. (1993). Domain specifications and content representativeness of the revised Value Orientation Inventory. *Research Quarterly for Exercise and Sport, 64*, 436–446.

Ennis, C. D., & Chen, A. (1995). Teachers' value orientations in urban and rural school settings. *Research Quarterly for Exercise and Sport, 66*(1), 41–50.

Ennis, C. D., Chen, A., & Ross, J. (1992). Educational value orientations as a theoretical framework for experienced urban teachers' curricular decision making. *Journal of Research and Development in Education, 25*, 156–163.

Freeman, W. H. (2012). *Physical education, exercise, and sport science in a changing society* (7th ed.). Burlington, MA: Jones & Bartlett Learning.

Gardner, H. (1983). *Frames of mind: The theory of multiple intelligences.* New York: Basic Books.

Gardner, H. (2000). *Intelligence reframed: Multiple intelligences for the 21st century.* New York: Basic Books.

Gerber, E. W. (1971). *Innovators and institutions in physical education.* Philadelphia: Lea & Febiger.

Hart, J. E., & Ritson, R. J. (2002). *Liability and Safety in Physical Education and Sport.* Reston, VA: National Association for Sport and Physical Education.

Jewett, A. E., Bain, L. L., & Ennis, C. D. (1995). *The curriculum process in physical education* (2nd ed.). Madison, WI: WCB Brown & Benchmark.

Lumpkin, A. (1986). *Physical education: A contemporary approach.* St. Louis, MO: Times Mirror/Mosby.

National Association for Sport and Physical Education (NASPE). (2009). *Appropriate instructional practice guidelines for elementary school physical education* (3rd ed.). Reston, VA: Author.

National Association for Sport and Physical Education (NASPE). (2010). *Opportunity to learn guidelines for elementary, middle and high school physical education.* Reston, VA: Author.

Nohr, K. M. (2009). *Managing risk in sport and recreation: The essential guide for loss prevention.* Champaign, IL: Human Kinetics.

Patterson, J. (1998). Historical perspectives. In B. S. Mohnsen (Ed.), *Concepts of physical education: What every student needs to know* (pp. 137–158). Reston, VA: National Association for Sport and Physical Education.

Riley, M. (1981). *A history of the influence of English movement education on physical education in American elementary schools: The fifties.* Working draft available from Kate Barrett.

Rink, J. E. (2013). Measuring teacher effectiveness in physical education. *Research Quarterly for Exercise and Sport, 84*, 407–418.

SHAPE America. (2015). *The essential components of physical education.* Reston, VA: Author.

Siedentop, D. (2002). Sport education: A retrospective. *Journal of Teaching in Physical Education, 21*, 409–418.

Society of Health and Physical Educators. (2014). *National standards and grade-level outcomes for K-12 physical education.* Champaign, IL: Human Kinetics.

Solmon, M. A., & Ashy, M. H. (1995). Value orientations of preservice teachers. *Research Quarterly for Exercise and Sport, 66*, 219–230.

Swanson, R. A. (1985). History of elementary school physical education 1920–1950. In National Association for Sport and Physical Education (NASPE) (Ed.), *The history of elementary school physical education, 1885–1985* (pp. 18–24). Reston, VA: NASPE.

U.S. Department of Health and Human Services (USDHHS). (2008). *2008 physical activity guidelines for Americans.* Washington, DC: Author. Retrieved September 19, 2011, from http://www.health.gov/paguidelines

U.S. Department of Health and Human Services (USDHHS). (2010, January). *The Surgeon General's vision for a healthy and fit nation.* Rockville, MD: Office of the Surgeon General.

Ward, P. (2013). The role of content knowledge in conceptions of teaching effectiveness in physical education. *Research Quarterly for Exercise and Sport, 84*, 431–440.

Wood, T. D., & Cassidy, R. F. (1927). *The new physical education.* New York: MacMillan.

CHAPTER

2

An Overview of the Movement Approach and Philosophy

PRE-READING REFLECTION

1. What do you value about physical education?
2. What do you think elementary physical education can do for children?

OBJECTIVES

Students will learn:

1. The movement approach uses the Laban framework to analyze and describe movement.
2. The movement approach focuses on children learning skills and movements that are the foundation for lifelong participation in healthy physical activities.
3. The movement approach builds a strong foundation based on conceptual knowledge, motivation and thinking, emotional, and social skills that support children's learning.
4. The movement approach uses numerous teaching methods, including explicit instruction, problem solving, decision making, exploration, giving specific feedback, and asking questions.
5. The movement approach is committed to developmentally appropriate physical education for *all* children, regardless of their gender, race, ethnicity, sexual orientation, religion, physical ability, or physical characteristics.
6. The movement approach is a focused curriculum designed for children.

KEY TERMS

Beehive soccer
Developmentally appropriate
Differentiated instruction
Laban's framework
Middle childhood
Movement approach
Traditional sport approach

CONNECTIONS TO STANDARDS

The goal of the movement approach described in this text is the same as the goal of the National Standards for Physical Education: to develop "physically literate individuals who have the knowledge, skills, and confidence to enjoy a lifetime of healthful physical activity" (Society of Health and Physical Educators [SHAPE], 2014, p. 11). This chapter describes how the movement approach is designed to meet all five national standards.

Introduction

In this chapter, we provide an overview of the movement approach described in this text. We also link the movement approach to the National Standards for Physical Education.

Overview of the Movement Approach

The physical education program described in this text is based on the **movement approach**: a curricular and instructional model that has a long, proud history dating back to Laban's original work in educational dance (Laban, 1948). Many variations of the movement approach have been developed. The version described in this text traces its roots back to influential texts published in England in the 1960s, including the Inner London Education Authority's *Movement Education for Infants* (1969), Mauldon and Redfern's *Games Teaching: A New Approach for the Primary School* (1969), Morison's *A Movement Approach to Educational Gymnastics* (1969), Mauldon and Layson's *Teaching Gymnastics* (1965), and Preston-Dunlop's *A Handbook for Modern Educational Dance* (1980; originally published in 1963).

The movement approach described in these early texts was further developed, first in Canada by Shelia Stanley in *Physical Education: A Movement Orientation* (1969), and then in the United States in *Physical Education for Children: A Focus on the Teaching Process* (Logsdon et al., 1984; originally published in 1977) and *Constructing Children's Physical Education Experiences: Understanding the Content for Teaching* (Allison & Barrett, 2000).

Movement approaches have evolved over the years as our research on teaching, learning, and curriculum development has helped refine them. Critical to this text's approach is its foundation in current research, particularly research on learning, development, and motivation. Over the past 20 years, researchers have made incredible gains in understanding the learning process. This information is a powerful tool for teachers.

Teachers are more effective if their teaching accommodates how children learn, develop, and are motivated. For example, when you understand learning and development, you know how to design tasks better. You know more about how to establish a learning environment that will lead to success and achievement. You understand the best ways to introduce information to children and to make this information meaningful to them. You know the attitudes and dispositions to teach to children that will contribute to their having a positive perception of themselves as learners.

Although many variations of the movement approach exist, all movement approaches have four characteristics. We discuss these next.

Use of a Movement Framework

First, movement approaches use a conceptual movement framework. This text uses **Laban's framework**, which is a conceptual framework to analyze movement and describe its content.

Provision of a Foundation for Enjoying Lifelong Participation in Physical Activities

Second, the goal of movement approaches is to develop "physically literate individuals who have the knowledge, skills, and confidence to enjoy a lifetime of healthful physical activity" (SHAPE, 2014, p. 11), which is also the goal of the National Standards for Physical Education. Thus, movement approaches provide the movement, cognitive, affective, and social foundations for lifelong participation in a range of healthy physical activities. For example, we teach fundamental game skills, such as throwing, catching, kicking, dribbling, and striking, that serve as the foundation for children's later participation in sports such as basketball, softball, baseball, volleyball, soccer, hockey, tennis, badminton, and racquetball. We teach other fundamental skills, such as jumping, sliding, skipping, climbing, and balancing, that are foundational to all sorts of activities, including all forms of dance, gymnastics, track and field, fitness, and outdoor pursuits. Based on the goal, movement approaches, in turn, are committed to children meeting the five national standards, the connections to which we discuss in the next major section.

Teaching of a Variety of Movement Patterns of Skills

Third, in addition to a focus on fundamental skills, movement approaches teach children how to vary skills in different situations. This strategy is appropriate because people use skills in physical activities with a variety of movement patterns (see **Figure 2.1**). For example, ways of throwing a ball in baseball range from a short underhand toss from shortstop to second base to a long, overhand throw from the outfield. Ways of throwing a ball in basketball range from a soft, high, two-handed toss to a fast, low, bounce pass around a defender and a host of other passes done from a variety of body positions to a variety of levels. Children need to be able to perform skills in many different ways in different situations if they are to enjoy and become competent participants in physical activities throughout their lives (see **Figure 2.2**).

Use of a Range of Teaching Methods

Fourth, movement approaches advocate using a range of teaching methods. Often, teachers will design tasks that have children making decisions, solving problems, and exploring a variety of ways to perform skills. At other times, when appropriate, teachers will explain how to perform a skill, demonstrate

Figure 2.1 Catching balls in game situations

the point they are making, or give specific feedback on children's performance. Three rationales support teachers' use of a wide range of teaching methods—all of which are closely linked to current research and reflect our own experience.

One reason for using a range of teaching methods is that research on learning has shown the importance of having children learn to solve problems, make decisions, and think critically and creatively. These thinking skills require teaching methods in which the teacher sets tasks such as having children identify and solve tactical problems, think critically about their performance and select an appropriate performance technique to practice, and think creatively about what movements to include in a dance. In addition, to accomplish these tasks, children must have accurate information available to them about tactics, performance techniques, and aesthetic criteria for selecting dance movements. Providing that information requires more explicit instruction by the teacher. Thus, to best facilitate learning, teachers must use a range of methods.

A second reason for using a range of teaching methods is to address children's individual differences. Children have many developmental differences, and teachers will need to use a range of instructional methods to meet the needs of all children.

Finally, different methodologies are necessary because of the vast range of content we teach—from a creative dance sequence, to batting a ball off a tee, to sending passes to open receivers. For example, creating a dance sequence representing prey and predators requires teachers to use exploration and problem-solving tasks because there is no predetermined end product. In contrast, learning to bat a ball requires explicit instruction because children have to know certain performance techniques to be successful. Meanwhile, learning to see and select the appropriate open receiver requires teachers to provide explicit instruction about some aspects of sending lead passes while also setting up decision-making tasks in which children practice making tactical decisions.

Contrasting the Movement Approach with Other Physical Education Approaches

Before the movement approach came along, elementary physical education consisted of countless activities organized in categories, such as low organized games, relay races, lead-up games, stunts, and self-testing activities (Barrett, 1997). As equipment companies developed many types of elementary equipment, teachers added activity categories based on this equipment, such as beanbag activities, wand activities, and parachute activities.

Activity categories proliferated without teachers evaluating whether those categories were substantive or worthwhile (Langton, 2007). Teachers thought of the activities or the equipment used as the content of lessons (e.g., a beanbag lesson). They explained the activity or taught the rules of the game and then had children do the activity or play the game. Little attention was paid to analyzing the content within the activity category or teaching children the skills, tactics, and concepts they needed to play the game or perform the activity skillfully. Consequently, lessons were more recreational than instructional.

(A) (B)

Figure 2.2 (A) Jumping in a variety of ways in games (B) Jumping in a variety of ways in dance

Another older approach is the **traditional sport approach**. In this approach, teachers focused on traditional sports, often using regulation equipment and the rules of adult versions of the games. Although a few highly skilled children could play the regulation sport, the vast majority of children did not have the skills or tactical knowledge to do so successfully. SHAPE (2014) said the traditional sport approach was "a concern for the profession. The evidence clearly indicates

Experienced Teachers Talk

The Positive Impact of the Movement Approach

The research on teachers who transition from a recreational approach to a movement approach suggests that this change benefits not only the children, but also the teachers' status within their schools. The following are quotes from a teacher in one study (Pissanos & Allison, 1996, p. 12):

> I truly feel that it [physical education] was thought of as recreational, that it was simply time for them [classroom teachers] to have their planning period, that what the children were doing during that time was not important. I don't believe that they felt that there was any true learning going on. I'm not sure that there was at that time either...we played a lot of games, kiddie games.
>
> I felt the reaction to my program from all of the classroom teachers changed after that year [I changed my program]. I felt that they looked upon me as part of the curriculum and that what I was doing had direct relationship to what they were doing.... They were seeing that there was more than just games [to physical education]. It was the concepts of right and left, relationship of body parts, and the sequencing of movement to make a throw [that made the difference]. I think they were very impressed that they could see that there was a science involved in it. And that it was not just all fun and games. I think there was a very definite change in their approach to what was going on in the gym.

that this type of competitive sport curriculum alienates many students, particularly girls and less-skilled students" (p. 10).

Movement approaches bring a different perspective to the content and teaching of elementary physical education. With movement approaches, lessons are not merely a series of activities, but rather comprise a progression of tasks focused on developing children's skills aiming to meet National Standards 1 and 2. For example, a lesson might include a series of tasks teaching children how to dribble at different speeds while changing directions, thereby improving children's dribbling skill and *the movement variety needed to be successful* in game-like situations. Although movement approaches use equipment such as beanbags, the intent of the task is to teach children a skill. For example, we use beanbags to teach children how to catch because beanbags are more developmentally appropriate than hard balls and because beanbags elicit the grasping action of a catch.

Teachers value this approach because the content is substantive and worthwhile. In other words, the content will develop skillful movement that supports children's lifelong participation in significant, healthful physical activities. **Table 2.1** summarizes how the content of the movement approach differs from a recreational activities approach. **Table 2.2** summarizes how the movement approach differs from a traditional sport approach.

Philosophy of the Movement Approach and the Connections to National Standards

We next describe the philosophy of the movement approach of this text. By *philosophy*, we mean a core set of beliefs and goals that teachers hold in regard to children's physical education. It is important to understand the basis of a physical education program. We explain ours so that you can reflect on it and understand how a philosophy supports the decisions teachers make about curriculum and instruction. If you examine this set of beliefs and goals carefully, you may find it helpful. In job interviews, principals will often ask you about your beliefs and the kind of program you plan to implement. It is important that you are able to articulate a set of goals for and beliefs about physical education and that you feel confident that they

Table 2.1 Comparison of the Movement Approach to a Recreational Activities Approach

Movement Approach	Recreational Activities Approach
Teachers teach the skills, movement concepts, tactics, health-related physical activity concepts, and choreographic concepts within games, dance, and gymnastics tasks. The focus is clearly on developing skill and movement variety.	Teachers select activities based on the equipment. Categories of activities and equipment are used to organize the curriculum (e.g., beanbag activities, jump rope activities, parachute activities, ball activities).
Progression: Teachers plan tasks within the lesson and across the unit in a small-stepped progression so that children develop skills and knowledge to successfully perform the culminating activity at the end of the unit, such as a dance or gymnastics sequence. Teachers break down and teach the skills and tactics of games (even games such as tag); they use small-sided games.	Progression: Teachers teach the rules of low-organized games and then have children play the game. Teachers divide the lesson into unrelated segments that do not build in a progression, such as an introductory activity, a fitness activity, and games.
Teachers select content and design tasks to meet the lesson objectives and desired learning outcomes. All tasks have a specific goal for improving some aspect of children's movement and knowledge within the games, gymnastics, dance, and health-related physical activity content areas.	Teachers select activities because they work to keep children "busy, happy, and good."

Table 2.2 Comparison of the Movement Approach to the Traditional Sport Approach

Movement Approach	Traditional Sport Approach
Teachers select skills and tactics related to invasion games (e.g., basketball, soccer), net/wall games (e.g., volleyball, racquetball), field games (e.g., softball), and target games (e.g., golf, bowling) as learning objectives. Teachers provide appropriate situations for practicing the skill or tactic and modify all games to be small-sided.	Teachers teach adult versions of traditional sports, often with regulation-sided games (e.g., 5v5 basketball).
Teachers teach skills, such as passing, emphasizing the variety of ways individuals use passing in games. The teachers' goal is to develop versatile games-players who can think and act quickly and make tactical adjustments during game play.	Teachers teach traditional skills related to a specific sport, such as a chest pass, bounce pass, or overhand pass in basketball.
Teachers and children modify the rules to match the children's developmental levels. Teachers focus on teaching children the meaning of rules. Children learn how to design their own games that work as learning experiences for all children.	Teachers emphasize memorizing and playing within the regulation rules of the sport.

are educationally sound. Understanding our philosophy is a place to start.

A teacher's philosophy is like a compass: it guides you in the direction you want to go. It also helps you figure out where you don't want to go. This may surprise you, but we have found that it is often just as helpful to know where you don't want to go as where you do want to go. As a physical education teacher, you will be inundated with catalogs from equipment companies showing a ton of physical education equipment that they claim will enhance your program. You will receive advertisements for books listing literally hundreds of activities the authors claim will work with your students. Some will be trash; some will be treasure. In any event, the number of choices can be overwhelming. Having a sound philosophy can help you make your way through the jungle to implement a program that matches your beliefs and emphasizes what you value.

The philosophy of the movement approach described in this text is based on the National Standards for Physical Education, as well as current research, theory, and scholarly thinking within the field of education. The curriculum of the movement approach represents an excellent physical education program. It is educationally sound and worthwhile—worth the children's time and worth the time, energy, and resources required to teach it. The following beliefs guide this approach.

What the Research Says

The Value of a Sound Philosophy

The research on accomplished teachers suggests that having a sound philosophy is critical and can sustain you when you are faced with the problems that you, like all teachers, will inevitably face. The following quote is taken from a study in which an accomplished teacher discusses this point:

> A lot of people see what you do and like it, but go and say, "It won't work in my school," or "My kids will never do that," because they never were instilled in the deeper meaning. I mean, really, that is a real crucial thing—the deeper meaning of what all this is going to do for kids....
>
> Every workshop that I went to, the books that I would read, I always kept reinforcing [the philosophy]. So, I had something ingrained in me and I didn't want to let that go. Those things were right for children, and no matter what anybody else says, I wasn't going to get off that path, no matter how hard it was. I was going to stay on that path. Maybe that's what allowed me to keep going ahead. Maybe it's the pedigree that kept me going" (Rovegno & Bandhauer, 1997, p. 145).

The Movement Approach Provides the Movement Foundation for a Lifetime of Physical Activity (National Standards 1 and 2)

As argued by SHAPE (2014), physical education ought to focus on learning. The goal of the movement approach is to provide the movement foundation for a lifetime of healthful physical activity, which matches the goal defined by the national standards. Meeting this goal means teaching children fundamental skills, such as throwing, catching, skipping, hopping, rolling, and balancing, as required by National Standard 1 (see **Figure 2.3**). Next, children learn how to use these fundamental skills in games, dance, gymnastics, and health-related physical activity contexts that are more complex. For example, once children learn the fundamental skill of dribbling, they learn to dribble on different pathways, at different speeds, and in different directions, as required by National Standard 2. This enables them to learn children's games, such as dribble tag, and small-sided, modified basketball-type games. Similarly, once children learn the fundamental skills and movements of dance, they can design their own dances expressing their ideas and learn social, cultural, and aerobic dances.

When children leave elementary school, they ought to be competent and confident movers. They ought to be well prepared to continue to develop their motor abilities in any sport

Figure 2.3 Focusing on learning a fundamental skill

or physical activity they choose, from basketball to ballroom dance.

In addition, the research shows that competence in fundamental skills is linked to increased levels of physical fitness as adults and increased levels of physical activity in children and adolescents (Barnett, van Beurden, Morgan, Brooks, & Beard, 2008, 2009; Castelli & Valley, 2007; Okley, Booth, & Patterson, 2001; Stodden, Langendorfer, & Roberton, 2009). Thus, skillfulness is critical to setting the stage for lifelong participation (Ennis, 2010).

Physical education differs from recreation and recess, which offer children opportunities to play and socialize. Recess and physically active recreation after school are critical for children's health, development, and quality of life. Research shows that play is an important part of childhood that contributes significantly to youths' development (Pronin, Fromberg, & Bergen, 2006). Whereas children accrue many benefits from unstructured play, physical education is the only time in the school day devoted to teaching children significant motor skills and concepts that will enable their lifelong participation in healthy physical activities.

You might wonder why we even need to discuss the importance of learning in schools, because this point seems obvious. After all, what else would we do in schools? Unfortunately, many physical education programs are recreational in nature. A recreational program focuses on children participating in activities with no clear intent by the teacher to focus on learning. Students may be exposed to a variety of activities, but they are not given the instruction and time to practice skills needed to develop the competence necessary for lifelong participation in physical activity (Ennis, 2010).

One reason why it is imperative that physical education be instructional is the fact that, for many children, school-based activities represent the only opportunity for quality instruction in physical activities. Children who live in poverty or who come from working-class families rarely have the money to participate in community sports or take private lessons. Physical education is their only opportunity to get instruction in skills and physical activities that are important for them. Many middle- and upper-class families provide opportunities for their children to receive instruction in dance, sports, martial arts, swimming, gymnastics, tennis, and a multitude of other physical activities. Other parents do not have the time or resources available to offer their children such opportunities. Finally, some of the instruction in community sports does not match the caliber of instruction that a certified teacher can offer.

As teachers, we need to step up to the challenge of providing the best education we can for our children. We live in an age of accountability and standards—all of which aim to hold teachers accountable for ensuring that all children learn. The National Standards for Physical Education focus on learning. Likewise, state departments of education set courses of study requiring teachers to focus on children's learning. In addition, for many years, the federal government has had an agenda to improve the quality of education and hold teachers and schools accountable for ensuring that their students learn. Physical educators, like all teachers, are paid to provide the best education possible for children.

The Movement Approach Provides the Cognitive and Social Foundations for a Lifetime of Physical Activity (National Standards 2, 3, and 4)

In addition to building a foundation of skills and movement patterns, the movement approach lays a groundwork of conceptual knowledge; motivation; thinking, emotional, and social skills; and dispositions to support children's learning of skills and physical activities. Moreover, this cognitive and social foundation facilitates children's participation in healthful physical activities outside of school at all ages and throughout their lives.

Conceptual Knowledge

The movement approach focuses on four categories of conceptual knowledge. First, children are taught movement principles and concepts related to performing efficient and effective movement (National Standard 2). These include biomechanical principles and the movement concepts of the Laban framework.

Second, children learn concepts and principles related to maintaining a health-enhancing level of physical activity and fitness (National Standard 3). This information includes the benefits of physical activity, the components of fitness, and ways to improve fitness.

Third, children need to understand tactical concepts and game structures (National Standard 2). In the same way that certain skills, such as catching, are basic to many physical activities, so tactical concepts and game structures cross over and are basic to many games. For example, the tactic in which players on offense run into open space to receive a pass is basic to games such as basketball, football, and lacrosse, to name a few.

Fourth, children need to understand basic choreography and movement quality concepts (National Standard 2). Many of these concepts are used not only in physical arts such as dance, gymnastics, circus arts, and mime, but also drama, music, art, and beyond, in areas such as website design, automotive design, and architectural design. For example, contrast, line, and dynamics are relevant to several art forms and contribute to what makes a gymnastics sequence memorable, a dance

What the Research Says

Teachers Who Transition from Recreational Approaches to Movement Approaches

Research on teachers who have changed their method of instruction from recreational approaches that kept children busy playing games to a movement approach focused on learning suggests that these educators viewed the transition as important for the children and satisfying for them as teachers (Pissanos & Allison, 1996, p. 6; Rovegno & Bandhauer, 1997, p. 142). The following are quotes from teachers who participated in some of these research studies.

> [Before I changed approaches,] I felt that my content was marginal....I couldn't see that my kids had changed any before or after the instruction....You know when I started to see them increase in their skillfulness in games, dance, and gymnastics...it changed my opinion of what I was doing....What I could see was the end product, not just that they were skillful, but I could see their pleasure in being able to do it [the skill]....That fostered a lot of my pleasure in being a physical educator and my feelings that my content was important, that it did have an impact on the lives of the children.
>
> I was considered one of the best teachers. People came and watched, observed me, and watched my lessons because I was real energetic, the kids liked PE, and I did a lot of after-school activities. But it was terrible PE! I just picked the books that said "Elementary School PE" and that said "These games are second grade." I played those games in second grade. That's scary that a person could be that crummy, have no content knowledge from undergraduate work, be crummy, and have the reputation of being good just because everybody was busy doing something....But then I started reading the literature and going to conferences, and they were talking about making PE educational—[what I was doing,] it really wasn't educational. They were having fun, but that wasn't enough. And so over time I became interested in the movement approach and focused on learning.

sequence an aesthetic experience, and an architectural design work well within a given space (see **Figure 2.4**).

Figure 2.4 Children showing the concept of line in gymnastics also shown in the mural on the gymnasium wall

Courtesy of John Dolly

Motivation and Thinking Skills

In the same way that movements and cognitive concepts cross many physical activities, so motivation concepts and thinking skills cross physical activities and support children's learning. For example, all gameplay involves making tactical decisions. Creating a dance, jump rope, or gymnastics sequence involves thinking creatively and critically. This is why the grade-level outcomes for National Standard 2 include both motor and cognitive aspects.

National Standard 2 asks children to *apply* (emphasis added) "knowledge of concepts, principles, strategies and tactics related to movement and performance" (SHAPE, 2014, p. 12). Applying knowledge during movement tasks is complex and requires children to comprehend and synthesize information, analyze a situation and think critically about when and how a particular principle is relevant, make decisions about strategies, and solve tactical problems. In the movement approach described in this text, children learn the basic thinking skills that are part of physical activities and relevant to National Standard 2 (see **Figure 2.5**).

In addition, the Common Core and other State Standards (CCSS) include similar thinking skills. For example, students must "integrate and evaluate information presented in diverse media and formats...evaluate a speaker's point of view, reasoning, and use of evidence and rhetoric...and make comparisons and contrasts and analyze and synthesize a multitude of ideas in various domains" (CCSS, 2010, p. 22).

Motivational dispositions are also important in learning skills, as these dispositions lead to student confidence and

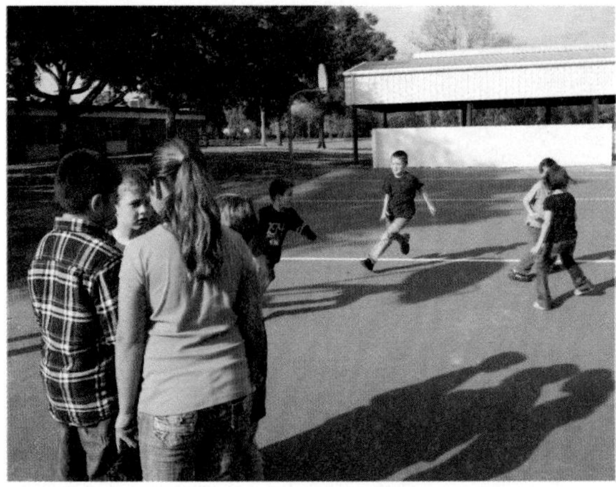

Figure 2.5 Thinking critically about their game tactics

success. A large body of research shows that learning and the likelihood of continued participation are greater in a success-oriented climate when children view achievement as based on effort, not ability; perceive themselves to be competent and able to learn new skills; and are motivated by self-improvement rather than by comparing themselves to others (Ennis, 2010; Solmon, 2006).

Social and Emotional Skills (National Standard 4)

The movement approach has long focused on the social and emotional domains. It aims to build a community of learners, to teach children to care about the experiences of all children in their class, and to discuss concepts and make decisions within a group based on a sense of fairness, caring, and reason. The goal is to teach children to treat their classmates with respect and empathy, value diversity, and work willingly with children of different races, genders, ethnicities, and abilities. These social and emotional goals are the focus of National Standard 4.

Quality group discussions, respecting peers, and problem solving are also central to many CCSS standards, in particular within the standards for speaking and listening. For example, second-grade students are expected to learn to

a. Participate in collaborative conversations with…peers and adults in small and larger groups
b. Follow agreed-upon rules for discussions (e.g., gaining the floor in respectful ways, listening to others with care, speaking one at a time about the topics and texts under discussion).
c. Build on others' talk in conversations by linking their comments to the remarks of others.
d. Ask for clarification and further explanation as needed (CCSS, 2010, p. 23).

It is important to integrate these goals and standards in partner and small-group tasks, which are used often in movement approach lessons (see **Figure 2.6**).

Affective Content (National Standard 5)

Finally, and most significantly, a goal of the movement approach from its inception has been for children to experience the joy of movement and, in turn, to appreciate how physical activities can be enjoyable, challenging, and meaningful. National Standard 5 and the affective domain can contribute to the learners' disposition to value physical activity throughout their lives.

Thinking, motivation, social, and emotional skills and dispositions not only enhance learning in physical education, but also contribute to the educational goal of developing the whole child—that is, the physical, cognitive, social, and affective domains. We know developing the whole child is a tall order, but we think it is worthy of our best efforts.

The Movement Approach Curriculum Is for All Children

Physical education programs are for *all* children, regardless of their gender, race, ethnicity, sexual orientation, economic status, religion, physical ability, or physical characteristics. This is a powerful statement. When you believe physical education is for all children, you care about the learning experiences of children who are low skilled, those who are average, those who are frail, those who are obese, those with disabilities, those who love physical education, and those who don't. We think being a teacher means being committed to all children and making a difference in their lives.

To reach this goal, you need to ask yourself some difficult questions: Are you offering a curriculum that appeals primarily to the high-skilled boys and girls who enjoy sports? Are you focusing on only those activities that you enjoy teaching? Are you hearing only the high-skilled, verbal children who pester you daily to play a game, and not listening with your heart to the shy, quiet children who find such games to be arenas of intimidation? Are you giving children with disabilities just as good of an experience as children without disabilities, or are they sitting on the sidelines because you cannot figure out how to involve them or you fear the teams will not be fair? Are you serving well the children who love gymnastics and dance (see **Figure 2.7**, **Figure 2.8**, and **Figure 2.9**)?

Figure 2.6 Practicing a child-designed partner sequence based on Tinikling, a Philippine folk dance

Figure 2.7 Enjoying dance

Courtesy of John Dolly

Figure 2.8 Enjoying gymnastics, self-taught
Courtesy of John Dolly

To offer a curriculum for all children, you must teach a range of activities across the school year and be sure you are teaching the basic skills and movements that will support children's participation in whatever physical activity *they* may choose as adolescents and adults. Children have the right to expect that, at some point during the school year, we will teach them their favorite activities and that we will do our best to make all lessons positive learning experiences. We have found that once children have quality instruction, they enjoy most, if not all, physical activities we teach in physical education.

The Movement Approach Is Designed for Children, Not Adolescents or Adults

In elementary schools, teachers ought to provide a curriculum designed for children, rather than provide a watered-down high school curriculum. The movement approach is designed for children much in the same way that we give children tricycles and bicycles designed just for them, enabling them to travel like the wind and explore their world on wheels.

To meet this goal, teachers need to base curriculum decisions on children's motor, cognitive, and social development. The elementary school years, called **middle childhood**, constitute a phase of life that is qualitatively different from adolescence and adulthood. During this phase, children are full of energy, curiosity, and playfulness. They are inventive and creative and like to build things, try new activities, play with friends, and develop competency (Berk, 2010). The kinds of physical activities meaningful to children are the antithesis of the regimented exercise workouts that adolescents and adults enjoy in health clubs across America.

Figure 2.9 Enjoying gymnastics
Courtesy of John Dolly

Many physical educators enjoyed high school sports and want to share their enjoyment with children by providing the same kinds of experiences they had in high school. A secondary school curriculum does not work with children, however: Their skills are not mature enough to support regulation gameplay. For example, you cannot get children to play a successful game of 6v6 volleyball. You can't get a good game going; there are no rallies. Children argue. Some children never touch the ball, whereas others are ball hogs. Walk around any city park in which young children are playing youth soccer games and you will see **beehive soccer** in which crowds of children chase after one ball like a mass of bees swarming about a hive. There is no passing, no attempts to get into an open space, and no defense other than intimidation and trying to run and kick the ball somewhere—anywhere.

When the adult versions of sports don't work, the physical education teacher waters the sport down to a version that won't create disastrous behavior problems and has all the children playing one game that the teacher can control—for example, playing volleyball and putting half of the children on each side of the net or playing softball and putting six kids in the outfield. Sometimes the teacher is the one getting the most practice by acting as the pitcher. The problem with watered-down sports is that few children get opportunities to touch the ball, and consequently, few get to practice and learn.

There are many other reasons why adult versions of sports don't work with children. The good news is that you don't need to water down the adult version of sports to do a good job preparing children to play sports when they get older. You can teach skills and tactics and have children invent and play in small-sided, modified games designed to teach different aspects of gameplay (see **Figure 2.10**). A movement approach is an excellent way to prepare children to play a sport, if they so choose, and to encourage them to participate in a range of lifetime physical activities as they get older.

Figure 2.10 Skillfully playing a children's game called Hit-the-Pin

The Movement Approach Provides Developmentally Appropriate Physical Education

The movement approach is, by its very nature, "developmentally appropriate," as it is committed to reaching *all* children. Teachers using this approach respect the individual nature of children and are able to use their rich knowledge base of how movement changes over time to design and implement an effective curriculum. This point of view is often termed *holding a developmental perspective*. Both phrases are used in many curriculum documents, teacher certification exams, state standards, and teacher evaluation instruments. Being **developmentally appropriate** means that your curriculum and instructional approach (1) take into account children's developmental capabilities in the motor, cognitive, social, and affective domains; and (2) differentiate instructional tasks to accommodate individual differences among children.

Accounting for Children's Developmental Capabilities

First, teachers using the movement approach select content and design tasks that match the developmental level of the children they're teaching. Notice in **Figure 2.11** the children are practicing throwing overhand forcefully at a wall using soft balls that roll gently back to them, a task matched to their developmental level and one that will develop their overhand throwing skill. Children are both challenged and successful at their specific level of development—that is, physically, cognitively, socially, and emotionally—while learning the content. In another example, beehive soccer behavior results from asking children to participate in a game context that is developmentally *inappropriate* for them. Because young children view gameplay from an egocentric position, socially they are not ready to engage in the complex game of soccer. Game tactics require that children understand multiple roles and appreciate the perspectives of both the defense and offense simultaneously. You can have young children play eleven-a-side soccer, but the game has a very different meaning to them than it has for older players—it means kicking and chasing a ball all at the same time! At younger ages, it is a better use of children's time to focus on developing fundamental skills and learning how to use those skills in a variety of small-sided game-like situations; such content would be considered more developmentally appropriate

Using Differentiated Instruction to Accommodate Individual Differences

Teachers who teach from a developmental perspective are able to modify and adapt content and feedback, design tasks, select

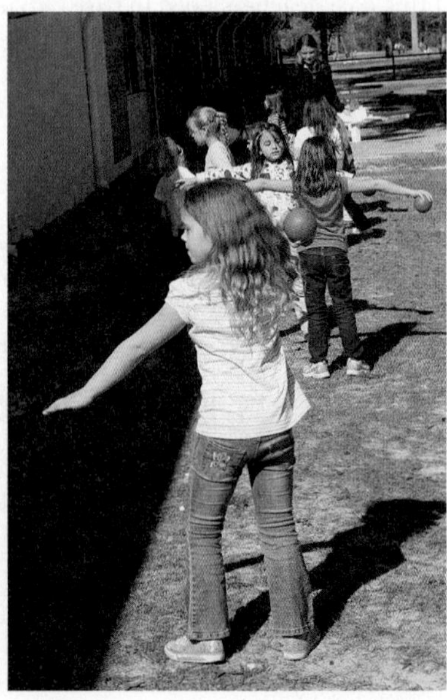

Figure 2.11 Kindergartners practicing throwing

What the Research Says

Teachers Who Recognized Gender Bias in the Curriculum

Research on teachers who recognized gender bias in the curricula at their schools and then made changes suggests that the process of change begins with a critique of the effect of team sport programs on girls. The following are quotes from a teacher who participated in the study (McCaughtry, 2004, p. 406).

> When I ask many of my female friends why they don't work out, they often say, "When I was in PE, all we ever did was play sports. I hated sports. I was no good and always got picked on....I guess I grew up hating to be active because all there ever was to do was play sports." I think a lot of girls had the same feelings here. They hated this because all we did was sports.
>
> I guess forcing girls into this rigid team sport box only said that it didn't matter what they wanted. Yeah, some girls really got into it, but a lot didn't. To keep on doing the same thing when so many girls weren't following says, "We don't care."

Experienced Teachers Talk

Learning About a Developmental Perspective

In my early years when I was teaching high school, one student, Maryrose, was not skilled in volleyball. When we played games, she was so unhappy, she just hated it, and it broke my heart. She could not get the ball over the net when she served. I helped her learn as best I could, and she developed a serve that was almost a throw rather than a strike. It was technically an illegal serve because it did not quite match the mature movement pattern required by the rules. I didn't recognize it as an immature pattern or as a problem with the rules that I set.

But she never missed, even using the immature pattern. I looked at her face when she served, and she smiled as the ball sailed over the net into play. She stood up to serve and she was confident. Her classmates were confident in her and knew she would never miss (some of them missed). Never in a million years could I ever have blown the whistle and called her serve illegal.

This was when I first learned that the rules and boundary lines of the adult versions of sport can be developmentally inappropriate for some students, even in high school, and that my job as a teacher was to find ways to put the needs of students first. I learned more from Maryrose than she learned from me.

equipment, change group sizes, and make other adjustments to match the developmental levels of different children within one class. This method of teaching is called **differentiated instruction**. For example, within one class some children will be ready to practice volleying with a trainer volleyball, whereas others will need to use beach balls. In another example, when teaching children rolling in gymnastics you will find that some children do not have the arm strength or skill to safely roll backward or forward because these skills require children to support the entire weight of their body on their hands while their head and neck are underneath. If their arms and body collapse on their head and neck, this can cause injury. Consequently, you must differentiate instruction and teach children who are not ready to learn forward or backward rolling safely to learn rolling sideways and diagonally in different shapes, which are developmentally appropriate rolls for them. At the same time, you need to teach children who are capable of learning rolling forward and backward how to do so safely.

Differentiated instruction and teaching from a developmental perspective are challenging but rewarding tasks. In this text, we teach you how to be consistent with this perspective when you plan and implement your programs.

The Movement Approach Is a Focused Curriculum

Physical educators need to provide a focused curriculum for children. By *focused*, we mean that the teacher focuses on important skills and concepts and does not try to teach everything and anything. Some teachers believe that they should expose children to as wide a range of activities as possible. Then, when children get older, they can choose which activity they want to learn in depth. This strategy is sometimes labeled the exposure curriculum. The problem with the exposure curriculum is that children never learn any skills or activities to a level of competence that will allow them to participate successfully in the activity (Ennis, 2010).

Recent research comparing U.S. students' achievement in classroom subjects with the achievement of students worldwide has shown that the curriculum in top-scoring international countries focuses on a more limited set of important concepts and topics studied in depth, whereas the U.S. curriculum is "a mile wide and an inch deep"—meaning students study a lot of concepts but never anything in depth. When students learn a powerful set of concepts and skills in depth, their knowledge is robust; it sticks with them and serves to support future learning. With this perspective, students recognize how parts connect to the whole and understand how they can apply skills and concepts in different situations and to solve new problems.

The idea that in-depth learning of a limited number of important skills, concepts, and activities leads to robust knowledge and higher levels of achievement is summarized in what seems a paradoxical phrase: "Less is more." When faced with an endless array of equipment in catalogs and limitless choices of activities, it helps to remember that if you value children's learning, less is more. The movement approach focuses on major skills, tactics, and concepts in games, gymnastics, dance, and health-related physical activity and does not overwhelm you with hundreds of activities to choose from.

Having a Sound Philosophy

There are many good physical education teachers. Unfortunately, there are also some teachers whom Herman Weinberg labeled the "three-Rs PE teachers": They call *roll*, *roll* out the ball, and *rest* in the shade, leaving the students to play on their own. You must decide which kind of physical education teacher you will be. A good start to being a great physical education teacher is to develop an educationally sound philosophy on which you can build your program.

We have discussed goals and beliefs on which you can build your own philosophy and program. Some of these ideas might appeal to you immediately, whereas others might sound unrealistic because they do not resemble the physical education programs you have experienced or because you have yet to develop the teaching skills needed to apply the ideas easily.

Your prior experiences in physical education and sports will inevitably influence your beliefs as an undergraduate. We hope that your coursework in your college or university will also influence your beliefs. Texts such as this one, as well as documents promoted by SHAPE, are based on research and ideas that have the support of teachers. The programs presented work for teachers and children in a wide variety of school settings—and they can work for you.

Research shows that in learning to teach, prospective educators benefit if they can suspend their judgment of new ideas. Be willing to experiment with content and instructional techniques that are new to you, even if you do not understand them fully or you are not sure how they will work in your school. It helps to think of your program as a work in progress. In other

What the Research Says

Teachers Being Continual Learners

Research shows that accomplished teachers are continual learners who are always looking for ways to improve their programs. They recognize, however, that learning new approaches and trying new teaching techniques takes time. The following quote discussing this point is from an experienced teacher who participated in a research study conducted by Cothran (2001, p. 76):

> You're always looking for that instant fix or something that is so wonderful that everybody will just say, "Yes, this is it!" But it just doesn't work that way. You know you have to adapt so many things to your situation or your personal strength. It's an evolving process to see how this works. It's a work in progress as to how it will end up. Next year maybe I'll try something different and look for the next natural step to take.

words, you should always be trying to improve on what you do. Good teachers are continual learners; they are always working to find better ways to do their jobs.

The research on accomplished teachers shows it takes many years for teachers to develop expertise. Rome was not built in a day—so take your time. As you gain experience and reflect on the children's learning experiences in your lessons, your philosophy will evolve.

Learning to teach physical education is an exciting challenge, and you will need to persist and work hard to learn how to be a good teacher. There's an old saying: "What looks easy from the classroom seats looks very different from behind the teacher's desk." Don't be discouraged if your first attempts at teaching do not go as smoothly as you would like—there is nothing wrong with you; it is simply that teaching is more difficult than it appears.

We hope that as you gain knowledge about elementary physical education that you develop a philosophy of which you are proud. Teaching is a very satisfying career when you take pride in what you do and know that you make a difference in the lives of your students.

Summary

Your philosophy is a core set of beliefs and goals that you hold related to children's physical education. In this chapter, we described the movement approach, its philosophy, and connections to the national standards. The movement approach differs from the recreational activity approach and recess in that the movement approach focuses on learning. It lays the groundwork for children's participation in a range of physical activities throughout their lives. In addition, the movement approach builds a foundation of conceptual knowledge; motivation; and thinking, emotional, and social skills that support children's learning of and desire to participate in physical activities.

The movement approach reflects what we know about learning and development. It is committed to providing developmentally appropriate physical education for *all* children, regardless of their gender, race, ethnicity, religion, sexual orientation, physical ability, or physical characteristics.

The movement approach is designed for children and is not a watered-down high school curriculum. It focuses on in-depth learning of a limited number of important skills, concepts, and activities, which leads to more robust knowledge and higher levels of achievement than are possible with an exposure curriculum. Teaching is a very satisfying career when you take pride in your philosophy and know it makes a difference in the lives of your students.

Review Questions

1. Pretend you are about to go to a job interview. One of your friends teaches first grade at that school and tells you the physical education teacher, who recently quit, taught using a recreational approach. She says the principal wants to hire a physical education teacher who will "teach" content just like classroom teachers teach content. Describe the movement approach in ways the principal can understand. Explain how the movement approach differs from a recreational, activity-based approach.
2. Which ideas in this chapter did you find most appealing, and why? Put them somewhere safe—this is the start of your philosophy.
3. Which ideas in this chapter did you find least appealing or most dubious, and why?
4. Discuss why physical education should focus on learning.
5. Identify three thinking skills. Give an example not cited in this chapter of how each can be used in a physical education practice task.
6. Why are emotional and social skills important to teach in physical education? Give examples to support your argument.
7. Critique the claim that elementary physical education should focus solely on preparing children to play the major team sports (e.g., basketball, football, softball/baseball). Then outline an argument that elementary physical education should focus on a curriculum that includes dance and gymnastics and a wider range of lifetime skills.
8. Discuss why elementary physical education should be designed for children rather than consisting of a watered-down high school curriculum.

9. Define the two major criteria for developmentally appropriate physical education, and describe the implications of each for teaching.

10. What are the problems with an exposure curriculum? What are the benefits of studying fewer concepts in depth?

References

Allison, P. C., & Barrett, K. R. (2000). *Constructing children's physical education experiences: Understanding the content for teaching.* Boston: Allyn & Bacon.

Barnett, L. M., van Beurden, E., Morgan, P. J., Brooks, L. O., & Beard, J. R. (2008). Childhood motor skill proficiency as a predictor of adolescent physical activity. *Journal of Adolescent Health, 44,* 252–259.

Barnett, L. M., van Beurden, E., Morgan, P. J., Brooks, L. O., & Beard, J. R. (2009). Does childhood motor skill proficiency predict adolescent fitness? *Medicine and Science in Sports and Exercise, 40,* 2137–2144.

Barrett, K. R. (1997). Movement education in children's physical education, 1958–1990. In M. A. Roberton (Ed.), *Motor development: Research and reviews,* volume *1* (pp. 200–229). Reston, VA: National Association for Sport and Physical Education.

Berk, L. E. (2010). *Development through the lifespan* (5th ed.). Boston: Pearson Education.

Castelli, D. M., & Valley, J. A. (2007). The relationship of physical fitness and motor competence to physical activity. *Journal of Teaching in Physical Education, 26,* 358–374.

Common Core State Standards Initiative. (2010). *Common core state standards for English language arts and literacy in history/social studies, science, and technical subjects.* Available at http://www.corestandards.org

Cothran, D. J. (2001). Curricular change in physical education: Success stories from the front line. *Sport, Education and Society, 6,* 67–79.

Ennis, C. D. (2010). On their own: Preparing students for a lifetime. *Journal of Physical Education, Recreation and Dance, 81*(5), 17–22.

Inner London Education Authority. (1969). *Movement education for infants.* London: Author.

Laban, R. (1948). *Modern educational dance.* London: MacDonald & Evans.

Langton, T. (2007). Applying Laban's movement framework in elementary physical education. *Journal of Physical Education, Recreation and Dance, 78*(1), 17–24, 39, 53.

Logsdon, B. J., Barrett, K. R., Ammons, M., Broer, M. R., Halverson, L. E., McGee, R., & Roberton, M. A. (1984). *Physical education for children: A focus on the teaching process* (2nd ed.). Philadelphia: Lea & Febiger.

Mauldon, E., & Layson, J. (1965). *Teaching gymnastics.* London: MacDonald & Evans.

Mauldon, E., & Redfern, H. B. (1969). *Games teaching: A new approach for the primary school.* London: MacDonald & Evans.

McCaughtry, N. (2004). Learning to read gender relations in schooling: Implications of personal history and teaching context on identifying disempowerment for girls. *Research Quarterly for Exercise and Sport, 75,* 400–412.

Morison, R. (1969). *A movement approach to educational gymnastics.* London: J. M. Dent & Sons.

Okley, A. D., Booth, M. L., & Patterson, J. W. (2001). Relationship of physical activity to fundamental movement skills among adolescents. *Medicine & Science in Sports & Exercise, 33,* 1899–1904.

Pissanos, B. W., & Allison, P. C. (1996). Continued professional learning: A topical life history. *Journal of Teaching in Physical Education, 16,* 2–19.

Preston-Dunlop, V. (1980). *A handbook for modern educational dance* (rev. ed.). Boston: Plays.

Pronin Fromberg, D., & Bergen, D. (Eds.). (2006). *Play from birth to twelve: Contexts, perspectives, and meanings* (2nd ed.). New York: Routledge.

Rovegno, I., & Bandhauer, D. (1997). Psychological dispositions that facilitated and sustained the development of knowledge of a constructivist approach to physical education. *Journal of Teaching in Physical Education, 16,* 136–154.

Society of Health and Physical Educators (SHAPE). (2014). *National standards and grade-level outcomes for K–12 physical education.* Champaign, IL: Human Kinetics.

Solmon, M. (2006). Learner cognition. In D. Kirk, D. MacDonald, & M. O'Sullivan (Eds.), *The handbook of physical education* (pp. 226–241). London: Sage.

Stanley, S. (1969). *Physical education: A movement orientation.* Toronto: McGraw-Hill of Canada.

Stodden, D., Langendorfer, S., & Roberton, M. A. (2009). The association between motor skill competence and physical fitness in young adults. *Research Quarterly for Exercise and Sport, 80,* 223–229.

CHAPTER

3

Overview of the Content

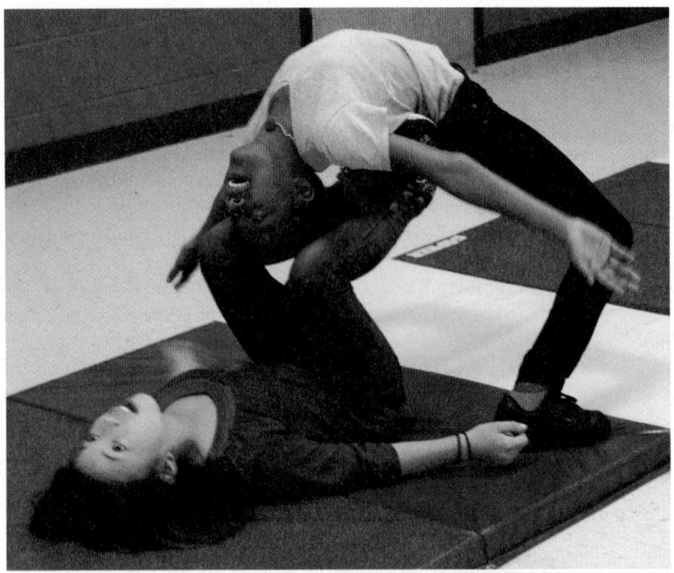

PRE-READING REFLECTION

1. If you had a magic wand and could make one wish with it, what would you do to make physical education better for children?

OBJECTIVES

Students will learn:

1. Games, dance, and gymnastics are three forms of movement.
2. The form of movement determines the goal of the movement, performance techniques to emphasize, and movement variety.
3. Movement approaches use the Laban framework to analyze and describe movement. The Laban framework provides a consistent movement vocabulary across games, gymnastics, and dance.
4. The Laban framework includes four aspects: body, space, effort, and relationship. Each aspect includes many movement concepts.
5. Movement concepts describe where and how a skill or body action is performed.
6. Movement concepts help teachers identify and teach movement variety.

KEY TERMS

Body aspect of the Laban framework
Dance forms of movement
Effort aspect of the Laban framework
Effort movement concepts
Game forms of movement
Gymnastics forms of movement
Locomotor skills
Manipulative skills
Movement concepts
Nonlocomotor skills
Relationship aspect of the Laban framework
Relationship movement concepts
Shape movement concepts
Space aspect of the Laban framework
Space movement concepts
Weight transfer skills

CONNECTIONS TO STANDARDS

This chapter describes and helps you to analyze the content you teach to ensure students meet National Standards 1 and 2.

Introduction

In this chapter, we provide an overview of the content of physical education. We then discuss this content in more detail in sections on educational games, educational gymnastics, educational dance, and health-related physical activity and fitness. This chapter also introduces the Laban framework, a theoretical framework for describing and analyzing movement.

Games, Dance, and Gymnastics as Forms of Movement

We divide the content of physical education into three forms of movement: games, dance, and gymnastics.

- **Game forms of movement** include functional movements, skills, and tactics related to games and sports.
- **Dance forms of movement** include movements that are expressive and rhythmical and occur within creative, folk, square, line, and social dances.
- **Gymnastics forms of movement** are broadly defined and include functional (i.e., not expressive) movements used to demonstrate bodily skill, strength, flexibility, power, precision, and prowess. You might find the term *gymnastics* confusing because of its association with the Olympic sport of gymnastics. Educational gymnastics is much broader; it includes movements from the sport of gymnastics such as balancing and rolling, skills such as jumping for height and distance (associated with track and field), and swinging and climbing (associated with outdoor pursuits and adventure activities). Gymnastics forms of movement also include most of the exercises associated with fitness, which are functional movements. (Health-related physical activity and fitness are a cognitive content area—not a form of movement.)

Why Include Only Games, Dance, and Gymnastics? Where Are Swimming and Other Sports?

We will answer the second question first. We do not include swimming because few elementary schools have access to swimming pools and because teachers need special certification to teach swimming. Swimming is certainly an essential physical activity for all children to learn. It is not only a lifetime physical activity but is also necessary for safety whenever children or adults are near water. Fishing, boating, canoeing, and sailing are just some of the many recreational sports for which the ability to swim is important for safety reasons.

The quick answer to why physical education content includes only games, dance, and gymnastics is that if you define gymnastics broadly to include the wide range of functional movements discussed here, there are only three forms of movement. We use this classification scheme only at the elementary school level, where we focus on fundamental skills and movements that will support participation in a range of physical activities.

The longer answer is that our definition of gymnastics is historically based. As you will recall, prior to the 1900s all physical education was labeled "gymnastics." Gymnastics aimed to improve strength, endurance, agility, balance, speed, flexibility, and skillfulness in activities such as climbing, jumping, vaulting, and throwing the discus. It was geared toward improving health and fitness and for military training. From their inception in the 1940s, educational gymnastics movements have been broadly defined and performed on a wide range of apparatus (see **Figure 3.1**).

Why the Form of Movement Is Important

The three forms of movement (game, dance, and gymnastics) are important because they determine the goal of the movement. For example, jumping is a skill that is important in all three forms of movement (see **Figure 3.2**). The goal of jumping, however, changes with each form. The goal of the movement tells you which kind of feedback is important, which performance techniques should be emphasized, and which kinds of movement variety you should teach the children.

In games, the goal is functional. You jump to get height because the situation requires it, such as jumping to catch a ball or shoot a ball into a basket. In dance, the goal of jumping is expressive. Children might jump to create a weird, twisted shape representing some prehistoric creature, or they might jump and skip about the space lightly, representing happiness. In gymnastics, the goal is both functional and to demonstrate precision, bodily skill, and prowess. Children might

Figure 3.1 A school that is well equipped with educational gymnastics apparatus

(A)

(B)

(C)

Figure 3.2 (A) Jumping in a game (B) Jumping in gymnastics (C) Jumping in dance

Courtesy of John Dolly

do a split jump and attempt to jump as high as possible with their toes pointed and legs in a perfectly straight line. In gymnastics and dance, it matters a great deal if you point your toes. In games, you score points if you jump, shoot, and the ball swishes through the hoop. It does not matter if you point your toes during this action; what matters is that you are ready to respond to the demands of the game situations. To help children improve each of these jumps, your feedback differs based on the unique goal of each movement.

The Laban Framework

This text uses the Laban framework as a conceptual framework to analyze movement and describe content. You can apply it to any movement, not just the movements we teach in physical education. In fact, Laban used the effort aspect of the framework to teach drama and to improve the efficiency of workers in industry. Some drama teachers still use Laban's model today. This framework to analyze movement can be a powerful tool that children can apply throughout their lives.

The Laban framework provides a consistent movement vocabulary across games, gymnastics, and dance. It helps you as a teacher because it means that you can use the same vocabulary across lessons; children, in turn, will understand and be able to apply the vocabulary in new situations. For example, you might teach children how to travel quickly on a zigzag pathway to represent lightning in a dance lesson. Later, when you teach them how to dribble on a zigzag pathway to get by a defender, they will already understand the term "zigzag pathway" and will understand how to travel on a zigzag pathway without a ball.

In this section, we describe the four aspects of the Laban framework and then define the major movement concepts within each aspect. These four aspects are as follows:

1. **Body aspect**: What the body is doing and the shape of the body.
2. **Space aspect**: Where in space the body moves.
3. **Effort aspect**: How the body moves.
4. **Relationship aspect**: The relationships between the body or body parts and the equipment or apparatus, between individuals, and among individuals in groups.

All movements include all four of these aspects all of the time. For example, when a child leaps over an obstacle, he or she (1) is performing a skill—that is, a leap from the body aspect; (2) is at a high level moving in a forward direction from the space aspect; (3) is using strong force from the effort aspect; and (4) has a relationship to the obstacle—that is, leaping over it.

Movement Concepts

Movement concepts are elements of the four aspects of the Laban framework and describe where and how a skill or body action is performed. In the lists below, movement concepts are italicized.

Shape movement concepts (within the body aspect) describe the shape of the body—for example,

- Jumping to make *wide, round, angular, and straight shapes*
- Rolling in a *round shape*

Space movement concepts describe where the body is moving in space—for example,

- Running in a *forward direction*
- Rolling in a *sideward direction*
- Dribbling on a *zigzag pathway*
- Catching balls at *high, medium, and low levels*

Table 3.1 Using Movement Concepts to Describe a Skill

Content Area	Body Skills, Shape Movement Concepts: What the Body Is Doing	Space Movement Concepts: Where the Body Is Moving	Effort Movement Concepts: How the Body Is Moving	Relationship Movement Concepts: The Relationships that Occur During Movement
Game skills	Running	In a forward direction	At a fast speed	Ahead of the tagger (in a game of tag)
	Dribbling a ball with the feet	On angular pathways	Tapping the ball lightly	Keeping the ball close to you while going around a defender
Dance skills	Stretching and curling	At different levels	Using light force	Matching a partner
	Making angular shapes	Facing different directions	With strong force	In a group of three, representing anger
Gymnastics skills	Jumping	To a high level	Using strong force	Over an obstacle
	Rolling in a round shape	At a low level	At a slow speed	On a mat

Effort movement concepts describe how the body is moving—for example,

- Throwing a ball using *strong force*
- Making a *soft* gesture in dance using *light force*
- Running *fast*
- Walking *slowly*

Relationship movement concepts describe the relationship between the body and the equipment, between one individual and other individuals, or between body parts and other body parts—for example,

- Striking a ball upward by getting your hands *under* the ball
- Leaping *over* an obstacle
- *Copying* a partner's dance movement

Table 3.1 provides some specific examples of how movement concepts describe a skill or body action.

Next we describe the movements and movement concepts of each of the four aspects of the Laban framework.

Body Aspect: Skills and Shape Movement Concepts

Skills

- **Locomotor skills** are skills used to travel on your feet, such as skipping, walking, running, hopping, galloping, sliding, jumping, and leaping. Locomotor skills are used in games, dance, and gymnastics. We typically first teach locomotor skills to young children in dance and gymnastics lessons because they can focus on learning the locomotor skill without having to control a ball as they would in a games lesson. In this text, we illustrate how to teach skipping, galloping, and sliding in the dance chapters and hopping, jumping, and leaping in the gymnastics chapters.
- **Manipulative skills** include skills such as throwing and striking, in which the body manipulates equipment such as balls and bats.
- **Weight transfer skills** include skills such as rolling and step-like actions (e.g., cartwheels) in which the body travels and is supported by a sequence of different body parts.
- **Nonlocomotor skills** are skills in which the body remains in one place, such as balancing, turning, twisting, stretching, and curling. Nonlocomotor skills can also be elements of other skills, such as stretching to catch a ball and twisting the belly button to the target during a forceful overhand throw.

Shape Movement Concepts

It includes the following shapes (see **Figure 3.3**):

1. Straight shapes, which are typically narrow or pin-like
2. Round, curled, tucked, or ball-like shapes
3. Angular or pointed shapes
4. Twisted shapes
5. Wide, wall-like, or flat shapes
6. Symmetrical shapes, in which the shapes of both sides of the body are the same
7. Asymmetrical shapes, in which the shapes of the two sides of the body differ

Space Movement Concepts

Areas: General and Personal Space

General space is all of the space in the room, gymnasium, or playground in which children can move during physical education. *Personal space* is the space surrounding the child that the child can reach with her or his arms and legs.

We teach the concepts of general and personal space at the beginning of the school year as part of management routines. When learning these routines, children become aware of the boundaries of their own and others' personal space and learn to travel about general space without bumping into anyone or invading others' personal space. Knowing how to move appropriately in personal and general space allows them to work productively and safely all at the same time. We then apply general and personal space concepts to the content areas of games, dance, and gymnastics (see **Figure 3.4**).

Figure 3.3 Straight, round, angular, twisted, and wide shapes

Figure 3.4 Catching in different areas of personal space

Figure 3.5 Dribbling on curved, zigzag, and straight pathways

Levels

Three levels are distinguished in physical education. High is above the shoulders or while jumping in the air. Medium is between the shoulders and the knees. Low is below the knees and traveling low on the floor. Sample content in games includes learning to catch balls at different levels. In dance, sample content includes making shapes at different levels.

Pathways

Three pathways are used in physical education: straight, curved, and zigzag (see **Figure 3.5**). Sample content in games includes dribbling on straight pathways when there is no defender and dribbling on curved and zigzag pathways around defenders.

Directions

Five main directions are identified in physical education: forward, backward, sideways (left and right), upward, and downward. Traveling on a diagonal combines two or more of the five main directions. Sample content includes rolling in different directions in gymnastics and traveling forward, backward, and sideways with a partner in folk dance.

Effort Movement Concepts

Each of the movement concepts of effort exists on a continuum, meaning you can analyze the movement from one extreme to the other and anywhere in between.

Time includes the *speed* and *duration* of movement. Speed is a continuum from slow to fast and includes acceleration and deceleration. Duration is a continuum from short to long.

Force is a continuum from light to strong (see **Figure 3.6**). An example of light force is a dance movement in which you pretend to catch a bubble in the palm of your hand. An example of strong force is an overhand throw from the outfield.

Use of space is a continuum from direct to indirect. Direct use of space means moving on a direct pathway using a minimal amount of space to achieve your goal. A sprinter running

Figure 3.6 Sinking with light force in dance

100 meters uses space directly. Indirect use of space means moving in a meandering, flexible way using a lot of space—in fact, indulging in space. Many hip-hop dance movements use space flexibly.

Flow is a continuum from bound to free; it is concerned with the control of the flow of the movement. Bound flow means being able to stop the movement instantly, which usually entails moving hesitantly and with restraint. Free flow means unstoppable, as when sledding down a snowy hill or running very fast. Most of the time, children work in between bound and free flow when controlling their movements. Another element of flow is its continuity—that is, whether the movement stops or flows continuously. Cooperatively hitting a tennis ball back and forth with a friend is an example of continuity of game flow.

Relationship Movement Concepts

Relationships differ greatly among game, dance, and gymnastics content areas. Relationships include the following arrangements.

Relationship of Body or Body Parts to Equipment, Apparatus, and Other Body Parts

Focusing on the relationship of body parts to balls and the relationship of equipment such as bats and rackets to balls is important content in games—for example, getting the forearms under the ball to strike the ball and move it upward. The relationship of body parts to other body parts is important in dance such as when we position both arms and one leg pointing to the same place in space to direct the observer's eye to that place. Traveling on, off, over, under, and through different apparatus and equipment is a major relationship theme we teach in gymnastics.

Partners and Groups

In gymnastics and dance, relationships between partners include, for example, matching and contrasting. Group relationships include formations such as circles and actions such as moving in unison. In games, relationships are tactical, such as those among teammates on offense and defense and those between offensive players and defenders. Game relationships also include the tactical relationships between players and the boundaries and scoring goals.

The Laban Framework Adapted for Educational Games, Gymnastics, and Dance

The Laban framework was first used in physical education in the realm of dance (Laban, 1948; Preston-Dunlap, 1980). Over time, the use of Laban's work expanded. Some texts, including this one, use three adaptations of the Laban framework to identify movement concepts specific to each content area: educational games, educational dance, and educational gymnastics. These variations are discussed in **Table 3.2**, **Table 3.3**, and **Table 3.4**, respectively.

As you compare these tables, you will see that the body, space, effort, and relationship aspects and many movement concepts are the same. In each case, however, we use vocabulary appropriate for games, dance, and gymnastics, and we include movement concepts specific to one content area but not the other two areas. For example, we list game tactics only within the games framework and gestures only within the dance framework.

Movement Concepts and National Standards 1 and 2

The Laban frameworks analyze and provide a consistent vocabulary for describing content we teach at the elementary school level to meet National Standards 1 and 2. National Standard 1 requires students to demonstrate competency in performing motor skills, whereas National Standard 2 requires students to apply their knowledge of movement concepts in a variety of game, dance, and gymnastics contexts. For example, one grade-level outcome for grade 4 is for students to apply "the concepts of direction and force when striking an object with a short-handled implement [such as a racquetball racket], sending it toward a designated target" (Society of Health and Physical Educators [SHAPE], 2014, p. 32). A grade-level outcome for grade 2 is for students to combine "shapes, levels and pathways into simple travel, dance and gymnastics sequences" (SHAPE, 2014, p. 32).

Movement Concepts and Movement Variety

The movement concepts are excellent tools for helping you identify the movement variety content within game, dance, and gymnastics content that children need to develop to meet National Standards 1 and 2. To become skillful, children need to practice and perform skills in a variety of ways. The movement concepts will help them achieve this goal. The following lists provide several examples of how the movement concepts are used to identify movement variety content.

Table 3.2 The Laban Framework Adapted for Educational Games

Body	Space Movement Concepts
Locomotor skills used in games: running, sliding, jumping, galloping, skipping Manipulative skills: • Throwing overhand and underhand • Passing • Catching • Striking • Volleying • Kicking • Dribbling • Receiving (gaining possession of a ball with hockey stick or feet) • Carrying (carrying a football or a lacrosse cradle) Nonlocomotor skills: pivoting, alert ready position, stretching, curling, twisting, turning	Areas: personal, general Levels: high, medium, low Pathways on the ground: straight, curved, zigzag Pathways of balls in the air: straight, curved Directions: forward, backward, sideways, upward, downward, diagonal Extensions: near, far
Effort Movement Concepts	**Relationship Movement Concepts**
Speed: • Slow—fast • Accelerate—decelerate Force: • Light—strong • Producing—receiving Use of space: direct—indirect Flow: • Bound—free • Continuity of flow In relation to performance techniques: • Using appropriate amounts of force and muscle tension • Using appropriate amounts of space • Using appropriate amounts of speed • Controlling the flow of movement	Body or body parts to equipment (e.g., rackets, balls, bats): • In front of, behind • To the side of • Over, under Individuals and groups within game situations: Defensive tactics (examples): • Denying space • Covering space • Gaining possession and intercepting • Knowing when to commit • Marking: ball side/goal side • Backing others up • Closing the passing lane • Shifting quickly to attack Offensive tactics (examples): • Cutting into appropriate open space • Sending lead passes • Passer/receiver relationships • Creating space for self or others • Supporting the person with the ball • Making the defense commit • Hitting to open space • Making the defense shift or move from coverage • Shifting quickly to defense Game structures: rules, boundaries, consequences, scoring goals, scoring systems

Source: Data from Barrett, K. R. (1984). Educational games. In B. J. Logsdon, K. R. Barrett, M. Ammons, M. R. Broer, L. E. Halverson, R. McGee, & M. A. Roberton (Eds.), *Physical education for children: A focus on the teaching process* (2nd ed.) (pp. 193–240). Philadelphia: Lea & Febiger.

Dribbling (with the Hands, Feet, or a Hockey Stick): Game Content

1. Dribbling on different pathways (straight, curved, and zigzag)
2. Accelerating dribbling, stopping dribbling, decelerating quickly, and changing directions
3. Dribbling at different speeds
4. Dribbling while changing speeds, directions, and pathways
5. Dribbling while protecting the ball or puck against defenders
6. Hand dribbling at low and medium levels
7. Hand dribbling in different body positions and under and around body parts

Table 3.3 The Laban Framework Adapted for Educational Dance

Body	Space Movement Concepts
Locomotor skills: walking, running, hopping, jumping, leaping, galloping, skipping, sliding, marching, stomping, prancing, darting, slithering, skittering; *assemblé, sissone, schottische*, step-hop, step-together-step/*chasse*; polka, waltz, grapevine Nonlocomotor skills: • Stillness and motion • Turning, spinning, swirling • Stretching, curling, twisting • Rising, falling • Opening, closing • Gathering, scattering • Shaking, wiggling, bouncing, shivering, quivering • Pushing, pulling • Swinging, swaying, swooping • Use of body parts (emphasizing, leading with, gesturing) • Body positions (standing, sitting, kneeling, lying) Shape movement concepts: wide, round, straight, twisted, angular, symmetrical, asymmetrical Manipulative skills: use of props such as scarves, canes, and ribbons	Areas: personal, general Levels: high, medium, low Pathways: straight, curved, zigzag Directions: forward, backward, sideways, upward, downward, diagonal Dimensional cross and related body actions: • Up/down (rise/fall) • Left/right (close/open) • Forward/back (advance/retreat)
Effort Movement Concepts	**Relationship Movement Concepts**

Time:
• Speed: slow—fast, accelerate—decelerate
• Duration: short—long
• Accent, rhythm (even, uneven) and meter (e.g., 3/4, 4/4)
Force, static and kinetic:
• Fine/light—firm/strong
• Anti-gravity—heavy
Use of space: direct—indirect
Flow:
• Bound—free
• Continuity of flow
Eight basic effort actions: wring, press, slash, jab, flick, dab, float, glide
In relation to movement quality:
• Using appropriate amounts of force
• Maintaining appropriate amounts of muscle tension
• Using appropriate amounts of space
• Using appropriate amounts of speed
• Controlling the flow of movement
	Body or body parts to other body parts and partners:
	• In front of, behind
	• To the side of
	• Over, under
	In relation to movement quality:
	• Maintaining appropriate body part alignments
	Partners:
	• Copying
	• Matching, mirroring, contrasting, complementing
	• Responding to, acting, reacting
	• Meeting, parting, passing by
	Groups:
	• Group formations (lines, double lines, circles, squares, triangles, V shape, leader and group)
	• Group shapes
	• Group actions:
	  • Canon, unison
	  • Action, reaction
	  • Assembling, dispersing
	Choreography elements:
	• Sequences have a beginning, middle, and end.
	• All parts fit together logically with fluid transitions.
	• Originality
	• Expressing an idea
	• Contrasts and aesthetic highlights
	• Relationships of body parts: line, focus, and clarity
	Choreography topics
	• Theme and variations
	• Stories and narratives
	• From science, social studies, poetry, children's literature, and art
	• Music

Table 3.4 The Laban Framework Adapted for Educational Gymnastics

Body	Space Movement Concepts
Locomotor skills: jumping for height and distance, hopping for distance, leaping, galloping, sliding, skipping, running, *assemblé, sissone* Skills: • Balancing, weight bearing • Rolling, rocking • Transferring weight (step-like actions) • Sliding • Stretching, curling • Twisting, turning • Vaulting-type flight • Hanging, gripping, swinging, climbing Shape movement concepts: wide, round, straight, twisted, angular, symmetrical, asymmetrical	Areas: personal, general Levels: high, medium, low Pathways: straight, curved, zigzag Directions: forward, backward, sideways, upward, downward, diagonal
Effort Movement Concepts	**Relationship Movement Concepts**
Speed: • Slow—fast • Accelerate—decelerate Force: light—strong Use of space: direct—indirect Flow: • Bound—free • Continuity of flow In relation to movement quality: • Using appropriate amounts of force • Maintaining appropriate amounts of muscle tension • Using appropriate amounts of space • Using appropriate amounts of speed • Controlling the flow of movement in skills and landings	Body or body parts to apparatus: arrive on, dismount off of, over, under, through In relation to movement quality: • Maintaining appropriate body part alignments Partners: • Copying • Matching, mirroring, contrasting, complementing • Counterbalancing • Engaging in countertension • Supporting, being supported, performing pairs balances Groups: • Group shape • Canon and unison Choreography elements: • Sequences have a beginning, middle, and end. • All parts fit together logically with fluid transitions. • Originality • Expressing an idea • Contrasts and aesthetic highlights • Relationships of body parts: line, focus, and clarity

8. Dribbling on straight pathways when there is no defender between the player and the goal
9. Dribbling on curved and zigzag pathways to avoid defenders

Catching: Game Content

1. Catching a variety of balls
2. Catching at high, medium, and low levels
3. Catching in all areas of personal space
4. Moving to the left, to the right, and forward to catch
5. Catching balls thrown with different amounts of force
6. Catching balls thrown near to and extending far from you

Balancing: Gymnastics Content

1. Balancing on different body parts
2. Balancing on large and small body parts
3. Balancing in different ways on your hands and feet
4. Balancing in different shapes (straight, wide, curled, twisted, angular)
5. Balancing at different levels
6. Balancing on different pieces of apparatus
7. Balancing on like and unlike body parts
8. Balancing on upper body parts
9. Connecting balances to rolls
10. Connecting balances to step-like actions

Figure 3.7 Mirroring shapes at different levels
Courtesy of John Dolly

11. Connecting balances to other balances
12. Matching, mirroring, contrasting, and complementing a partner's balance (see **Figure 3.7**)
13. Counterbalancing with a partner
14. Engaging in countertension with a partner

Rising and Sinking: Dance Content

1. At different speeds
2. Using strong and light force
3. Leading with different body parts
4. To and from different levels
5. For different durations
6. Making different gestures
7. To and from different body positions (standing, sitting, kneeling, lying)
8. Adding a turn
9. Ending in different shapes
10. To different rhythmic beats
11. Using continuous and discontinuous flow
12. Matching, mirroring, contrasting, and complementing a partner

Frequently Asked Questions

Does the Movement Approach Teach Skills?

Yes. Skills are movements. The movement approach is a skill approach, but it approaches skills broadly. For example, instead of teaching a chest pass and a bounce pass performed in one way to a person standing about 10 feet away, we focus on teaching passing using a wide variety of passing movement patterns.

Does the Movement Approach Ever Teach Games Like Real Kickball?

As Barrett (1984) said, "No, we do not teach real kickball or real volleyball. If we taught them, we would teach a modified version" (p. 195). The problems with "real" kickball are that few children are active at any one time (many never touch the ball at all), and the rules do not accommodate individual differences.

We teach skills that can be performed in a variety of ways and the basic tactics of games. We do so in ways that are developmentally appropriate, and we give children maximum opportunities to practice. We will tell you one true story that happened to one of the authors (Dianna) to illustrate how the movement approach teaches the skills and tactics used within games but does not teach real kickball:

> It was my first year teaching at Lecanto Primary School. The state was evaluating our district. The state inspector came in, interviewed me, and asked me, "Do you teach kickball?" I was really worried because I didn't know what the right answer would be for *him*, and I didn't have tenure (and I certainly never had children play kickball and don't believe in it). So, I said, "Well, I teach children how to run and kick a ball. I teach them how to catch balls coming in the air and on the ground. I teach them how to throw accurately to different distances. I teach them how to throw the ball to the base ahead of the runner. I teach them how to cover space on defense. I teach them how to send the ball to the open space on offense. Yes, I teach the skills and tactics associated with kickball, if that's what you mean." A few days later, a man walked into my office and introduced himself as the superintendent. He said, "The state inspector said I either had a great PE teacher or a crazy one. So I came over here to see for myself."

Summary

The approach used in this text is a movement approach. Movement approaches use the Laban framework to describe and analyze movement. Games, dance, and gymnastics are three forms of movement. The form of movement determines the goal of the movement, performance techniques to emphasize, and movement variety. The Laban framework includes four aspects: body, space, effort, and relationship. Each aspect consists of many movement concepts. Movement concepts describe where and how a skill or body action is performed. In this text, we present three adaptations of the Laban framework: one adaptation each for game, dance, and gymnastics content. Within the three adaptations, we focus on vocabulary and content relevant to the three content areas.

Helping children develop the ability to perform skills in the variety of ways in which those skills are used in games, dance, and gymnastics is central to this text. The movement concepts from the Laban framework help teachers identify and teach this movement variety.

Review Questions

1. Describe the three forms of movement.
2. Within which form of movement would we categorize the following activities: rock climbing, jumping rope, lifting weights, and swinging from a rope tied to a tree limb, letting go, and landing in a lake?
3. Select a familiar skill and describe in detail all four aspects (body, space, effort, and relationship) of the skill using as many movement concepts as you can.

References

Barrett, K. R. (1984). Educational games. In B. J. Logsdon, K. R. Barrett, M. Ammons, M. R. Broer, L. E. Halverson, R. McGee, & M. A. Roberton (Eds.), *Physical education for children: A focus on the teaching process* (2nd ed.) (pp. 193–240). Philadelphia: Lea & Febiger.

Laban, R. (1948). *Modern educational dance*. London: MacDonald & Evans.

Preston-Dunlop, V. (1980). *A handbook for modern educational dance* (rev. ed.). Boston: Plays.

Society of Health and Physical Educators (SHAPE). (2014). *National standards and grade-level outcomes for K–12 physical education.* Champaign, IL: Human Kinetics.

CHAPTER

4

Motor Development and Learning

PRE-READING REFLECTION

1. Go where you can observe people of different ages walking (e.g., a park or mall). Watch the walking movement patterns (leg actions and positions, feet actions and positions, arm actions, speed, and consistency) of a child between 1 and 1.5 years of age, a child between 2 and 3 years old, an adult, and a person who is very old. Take notes on how the movement patterns differ by age.

OBJECTIVES

Students will learn:

1. Development is age related, not age determined.
2. Motor skill development is highly related to opportunities to practice.
3. Development in all domains occurs in a relatively predictable pattern.
4. Researchers have documented sequences describing the changes from immature to mature movement patterns of fundamental skills.
5. Understanding developmental changes guides teachers in observing children's developmental levels and then providing developmentally aligned feedback and tasks.
6. The movement pattern of skills results from the interaction of individual constraints, task constraints, and environmental constraints.
7. Skills can be classified on a continuum from open to closed based on the extent to which the environment changes.
8. Learning occurs in three stages:
   - Stage 1: The child acquires the basic movement pattern of the skill.
   - Stage 2: The child learns to vary the movement pattern.
   - Stage 3: Skill performance is automatic, and the child can focus attention on gameplay and tactics.

KEY TERMS

Adult error detection model
Affordances
Closed skills
Developmental perspective
Developmental sequence
Discovery learning
Environmental constraints
Individual constraints
Intertask developmental sequence
Intratask developmental sequence
Motor development
Newell's constraints theory
Open skills
Proficiency barrier
Stages of motor learning
Task constraints
Variable practice

CONNECTIONS TO STANDARDS

Motor development and learning provide the theoretical basis for the progression of motor and cognitive content used in this text to meet National Standards 1 and 2.

Introduction

An understanding of motor development and learning has long been considered essential for teachers. To be an effective teacher, you need to know how children learn and develop. This knowledge allows you to design effective, developmentally appropriate content, instruction, and assessments that best match the ways children learn and their developmental characteristics.

Key Ideas about Motor Development

Development Is Sequential

Motor development is defined as "changes over time in motor behavior that reflect the interaction of the human organism with its environment" (Wickstrom, 1983, p. 3). Because of the interactions of humans with their environment, development is a sequential process—that is, it proceeds in a relatively predictable pattern (Haywood & Getchell, 2005). For example, the sequence of major milestones in the development of human locomotion (called an intertask sequence) is for children to creep, then stand alone, and finally to walk before they can run. This sequence is predictable.

Not only is the sequence predictable, but changes in the movement of body components within skills also are relatively predictable (called an intratask sequence). For example, as children develop the ability to walk, their walking movement patterns change from the wide, short, flat-footed steps and wobbly, side-to-side movements of a toddler to the long strides with the heel landing first and the arms swinging in opposition of a six-year-old striding to be first in line at the drinking fountain.

Multiple Domains of Development Are Important to Teachers

Motor development is only one domain of development; development occurs in the cognitive, emotional, and social domains as well. As physical education teachers, we are responsible for the motor domain, but we are concerned about children's development in all domains, too—not only because physical activities draw on all domains but also because, like all good teachers, we are concerned about the whole child.

Development Is Age Related, Not Age Determined

Development in all domains is age related but not age *determined*. In other words, different domains develop at different rates, and the rate of development for each domain differs among different children. This is a critical concept for teachers to understand. Some children will develop earlier and more rapidly in the language domain; others will develop earlier and more rapidly in the social or motor domain. Within any one class, children will be at different developmental levels in different domains. Any one child might be more developed in some domains and less developed in others. Because development is age related, you can anticipate certain behaviors across children at different ages, but it would be a mistake to draw conclusions about a particular child's potential. You cannot assume a child is more "talented," "smarter," "uncoordinated," or "inept" in comparison to her or his classmates in any domain because development is only *related* to age, not *determined* by age. The "slower" child might simply need more time and will eventually catch up to or even surpass her or his classmates.

A classic example of this phenomenon is seen with middle school basketball players who begin their growth spurt early and reach their adult height earlier than other adolescents. Simply because of the greater height, basketball coaches have such students play and develop the skills required of centers. But by the end of high school and college, however, classmates who experienced their growth spurts later are likely to have caught up to and possibly to have surpassed the early bloomers' height. Because early developers are more likely to have played center throughout middle school and early high school, they may have not developed the skills they need to play guard, which may be the position best matched to their adult height. As a consequence, their abilities to continue in basketball are limited. This is one reason why good teachers and coaches insist that all children learn the skills required to play all positions.

What the Research Says

Do Young Children Benefit from Fundamental Skill Instruction or Should We Simply Provide Recess with Plenty of Equipment?

Some people question why we need to provide instruction in fundamental skills to preschoolers and young children, claiming that children simply need opportunities to play and that skills will develop naturally through maturation. The research, however, suggests that a sound physical education program that teaches children fundamental skills has a significant impact on children's skill levels. By comparison, control groups who played in well-equipped play environments but received no instruction showed no significant improvements in skills (Goodway & Branta, 2003; Robinson, 2011; Robinson & Goodway, 2009).

Development Results from the Interaction Between the Individual and the Environment

Most significantly, development results from the interaction between the child and the many environments in which he or she develops. These environments include peers, family, school, community, and broader (sometimes multiple) cultures. For example, children who have enriched verbal and language environments will likely be further along the developmental sequence in reading and vocabulary compared to children who lack access to similar environments. Likewise, preschool children with older siblings or parents who teach them motor skills, take them to the playground, and join with them in a variety of physical activities often enter elementary school with far more developed motor skills than children who have not enjoyed an enriched motor environment. Teachers regularly see a few kindergarten children with highly developed throwing skills—acquired by time spent throwing and catching with their siblings or parents during their preschool years. This ability does not mean they will always be more skilled than their classmates. Once other children have the opportunities to develop in an enriched motor environment, such as the environment provided by a good physical education program, they will gain experience and instruction, and their motor skills can become highly developed as well.

Development of Fundamental Motor Skills Takes Time and Practice

Although to adults, fundamental motor skills seem simple, they are actually complex movement patterns that take children considerable time and practice to develop. Development will not occur automatically—in fact, many adolescents and adults never develop the mature form of many basic skills (Williams, 2004). Moreover, teachers can expect to see wide variations in the rate at which children learn skills because of individual differences (Davids, Button, & Bennett, 2008). Children differ in their level of neural, cognitive, physical, emotional, and social development. They also have different capabilities, such as different physical fitness levels. Because learners do not begin with the same set of characteristics, they will learn skills at different rates.

The Proficiency Barrier

Seefeldt (1980) argued that there is a **proficiency barrier**, which is a minimal level of proficiency in fundamental motor skills that children must acquire to allow for enjoyable participation in physical activity and active recreation throughout their lifespan. If children do not develop fundamental motor skills beyond this barrier, their options for adult engagement in physical activities will be limited. Recent research supports Seefeldt's argument (Stodden, True, Langendorfer, & Gao, 2013). Consequently, the first three years of the elementary curriculum focus primarily on developing skills that will provide the foundation for later participation in games, sports, dance, and other physical activities.

Developmental Changes from Immature to Mature in the Movement Patterns of Skills

Understanding the predictable changes from immature to mature movement patterns of skills is essential for improving your ability to observe children's skill levels and then designing developmentally appropriate tasks and giving appropriate feedback to help each child improve (see **Figure 4.1**). Immature patterns arranged in a **developmental sequence** describe the qualitative changes that occur in children's movement patterns of skills as they develop from less mature to more mature levels of performance. Developmental sequences are not judgmental; they are simply descriptive. Two types of sequences can be distinguished: intertask and intratask.

An **intertask developmental sequence** is a sequence of different skills that develop or emerge across time. For example, walking emerges before running, which emerges before hopping, which emerges before skipping. An **intratask developmental sequence** describes the most common changes that occur in the movement patterns of one skill over time as children learn the skill. For example, when very young children first throw, they do not step with either foot as they throw; this

Figure 4.1 Giving developmentally aligned feedback

What the Research Says

Beginning Teachers Who "Blame the Students"

If you remember that fundamental skill development takes considerable practice, this can help you better interpret the responses you see. For example, suppose you are teaching dribbling with the hand to kindergarteners and your lesson focuses on the performance technique of pushing the ball with the finger pads rather than slapping the ball. You also provide corrective feedback to children who continue to slap the ball. Yet, after two lessons, you see some children continuing to slap the ball. What does this mean?

Research on beginning teachers found that when this type of situation occurred, some undergraduates assumed that such children were "not listening," "not trying," or "did not understand the instructions." In fact, these children were listening and trying hard—they just had not yet developed that component of the skill.

Listen to the words of Robin:

I seem to have found that you can tell them, "Throw it in front of the person," or tell them to do something, and they might really be trying to do that. They just can't.... They're just not to that [developmental] level.... And before, I thought it was like [a] "Don't you understand what I'm saying?" type thing. But it's actually just a developmental thing (Rovegno, 1991, p. 210).

Often children will perform the "new" movement pattern sometimes but not on all occasions. This inconsistency typically means they are in the process of developing and consolidating the new movement pattern. When you see this happening, remember that skill development takes many practice opportunities. Don't blame the children or yourself; be patient, and provide more time for them to practice.

is labeled an immature pattern. As they develop, an intermediate pattern is to take a step as they throw, but they will step with the foot on the same side of their body as their throwing arm. A second intermediate pattern is to take a step with the opposite foot. With practice (and instruction), they will learn the mature pattern to take a long step with the opposite foot (Roberton & Halverson, 1984).

Beginning Teachers Talk

Being a Student Versus Being a Teacher

Before I took methods class, I was very worried about what I was going to teach in elementary PE. I figured I would teach throwing one day, catching the next, kicking the next, and then I had no idea what you were supposed to do the rest of the year. Now I understand how much time it takes kids to learn skills and how many different tasks you can use to do it.
—Undergraduate student

It has been my experience in high school PE that getting into games is most important. In my school, they had a departmental-type philosophy where they would teach skills, run through drills, and then begin games. This held true for all activities and all the teachers. It ran like clockwork. This used to be my philosophy until I learned that all children develop differently at different rates. Because I was skilled, I didn't realize that not everyone was skilled. When the time came to play games, this didn't affect me, but it affected those who were not ready to play games. Because the teachers did not allow each individual to progress at their own rate, many students did not accomplish anything or improve their skills. Now I realize that the content I teach has to allow for this because if it doesn't, these students are just wasting time.
—Undergraduate student

Developmental sequences describe observable markers of qualitative changes in the components of motor skills (e.g., leg action, arm action, preparation phase). Once you know what to look for, the elements of developmental sequences are easy to see. Thus, these patterns can help you recognize developmental progress even though children may not yet have mastered the mature pattern.

Dr. Lolas Halverson and Dr. Mary Ann Roberton are the leaders of this line of research. We based our descriptions of immature patterns on their work and researchers who followed in their footsteps. Where no research exists for a particular skill, we describe immature patterns we have observed across our years as teachers. Researchers have studied and proposed developmental sequences or characteristics for the following motor skills: running, skipping, hopping, jumping, catching, overhand throwing for force, punting, overhand striking (e.g., a tennis serve), forward rolling, hand dribbling, lacrosse cradling, cutting into a space to receive a pass, and sending lead passes.

Table 4.1 presents examples of descriptions of immature, intermediate, and mature patterns for dribbling with the hand within different task constraints. This table is based on the work of Wickstrom (1983); Chen, Rovegno, Todorovich, and Babiarz (2003); and our experiences teaching dribbling. Notice that the developmental sequence breaks dribbling down into six components: (1) hand, wrist, and arm actions (with two levels of performance); (2) body and head actions (with three levels of performance); (3) ball control (with two levels of performance); (4) traveling on different pathways (with four levels performance); (5) dribbling at different speeds (with four levels of performance); and (6) dribbling against a defender (with four levels of performance). Different skills have different numbers of components, and some developmental sequences break the skill down into phases, such as the take-off phase and landing phase of jumping.

Table 4.1 Descriptions of Developmental Movement Patterns for Dribbling with the Hand in Different Task Conditions

Hand/Wrist/Arm Component	
Immature: Palm slaps ball	The child slaps or hits the ball with the palm of the hand (see **Figure 4.2**).
Mature: Finger pads (or prints) ride and push ball	The child uses the finger pads; the hand rides the ball up to the top of the bounce and then pushes the ball down to bounce again (see **Figure 4.3**).
Body/Head Component	
Immature: Head down, knees almost straight	The child looks at the ball and keeps the head almost over the ball and the knees almost straight (see Figure 4.2).
Intermediate: Glances up	Knees are slightly bent, and the child is mostly upright. The child glances up to see where he or she is going but tends to look primarily at the ball.
Mature: Looks up, keeps head in line	Knees are bent, the child is upright, the head is in line with body, and the eyes are looking around (see Figure 4.3).
Ball Control Component	
Immature: Ball controls child	The ball seems to control the child; the child chases the ball, and bouncing is inconsistent. Sometimes the ball bounces and the child does not make contact with the ball; sometimes the ball is too far in front and sometimes too close to the child's feet. The ball is directly in front of the body. Sometimes the child dribbles with two hands. The child never uses the nondominant hand except immediately following the teacher's instruction to dribble with the nondominant hand.
Mature: Controls ball, lower than chest height	The child controls the ball; that is, the child maintains contact on consecutive bounces and applies appropriate force and speed so the ball remains under control. Ball height is at the chest or lower, and while moving forward, the ball is to the front and side of the body.
Dribbling While Traveling on Different Pathways	
Immature: Ball controls child	The child follows the pathway of the ball and does not control ball placement.
Intermediate: Controls ball on straight pathways	The child can control the ball while dribbling on straight pathways but cannot direct the ball on curved or angular pathways.
Intermediate: Controls ball on curved pathways	The child can dribble around obstacles (cones or defenders) and on curved pathways. Angular pathways are rounded, not sharp.
Mature: Controls ball on sharp, angular pathways	The child can dribble around obstacles on sharp, angular pathways by planting a foot, bending a knee, and pushing off forcefully. The child uses a crossover dribble when appropriate.
Dribbling at Different Speeds and Stopping	
Immature: Standing in place	The child dribbles standing in place or chases the ball. When traveling, the child needs to take several steps before being able to stop.
Intermediate: Slow, walking speed	The child can control the ball while walking and can stop traveling forward and dribble in place without losing the ball.
Intermediate: Medium, jogging speed	The child can control the ball while jogging or walking and can stop suddenly without losing ball control.
Mature: Fast, running speed	The child can control the ball while running fast, jogging, or walking and can quickly change speeds or stop.
Dribbling Against a Defender	
Immature: No response to defender	The child seems unaware of or unable to respond to the defender.
Intermediate: Turns back	The child keeps his or her back toward the defender, seems to hover over the ball, and protects the ball by turning. The child dribbles the ball directly in front of the body.
Intermediate: Watches defender, uses only dominant hand	The child turns his or her head toward the defender, watching and responding to the defender while dribbling the ball, dribbles with the dominant hand only, and keeps his or her body between the ball and the defender.
Mature: Faces action, can use nondominant hand	The child watches the defender or game action while dribbling the ball on the side away from the defender, keeping his or her body between the defender and the ball. The child dribbles with whichever hand is away from the defender.

Figure 4.2 Immature dribbling

Using Knowledge of Changes from Immature to Mature Movement Patterns in Teaching

Once you know the immature, intermediate, and mature movement patterns of motor skills, you can use this knowledge as a "model in your head" as you observe children (Allison & Barrett, 2000). This model provides the details of how children's body components move and change in predictable ways as they learn motor skills. This knowledge will help you with the following tasks:

- Observe and assess children's skills
- Recognize progress in the development of skills even when children appear not to have mastered the mature pattern
- Anticipate children's responses
- Based on children's capabilities, select content, design tasks, and determine assessment tools to facilitate learning
- Provide feedback and select developmentally aligned performance techniques to teach

Research shows when teachers know the immature and intermediate movement patterns of skills and give children feedback that is developmentally aligned, children improve to a greater extent than children who received feedback that is not aligned developmentally (Cohen, Goodway, & Lidor, 2012). **Skills Box 4.1** illustrates how you can use the descriptions of changes from immature to mature dribbling described in **Table 4.1** in teaching.

Having a Developmental Perspective

Learning about the developmental changes of motor skills from immature to mature will help you understand the developmental perspective supported and promoted by the Society of Health and Physical Educators (SHAPE) (2014), which is also part of certification exams. Teaching based on a developmental perspective will also help you increase safety and decrease your risk of liability as described by scholars who study court cases on negligence (see the Safety and Liability box).

When you have a **developmental perspective**, you recognize individual differences and what each child can do along the developmental continuum, and you design developmentally appropriate lessons by matching tasks and feedback to the capabilities of individual children to help them progress (Allison & Barrett, 2000; Cohen, et al., 2012). When children's movement patterns are positioned toward the less mature end of the continuum, they are not considered wrong or incorrect. If you see these immature patterns as wrong, you are most likely using what we refer to as the **adult error detection model**—that is, you are comparing what you see to the adult or expert model and perceiving any deviation from adult performance

Figure 4.3 Mature dribbling

SKILLS BOX 4.1

Using Descriptions of Developmental Movement Patterns to Guide Teaching: An Example with Dribbling

Teaching the Hand/Wrist/Arm Component

Hand/Wrist/Arm Movements Observed

Immature: Palm slaps ball. The child slaps or hits the ball with the palm of the hand (see Figure 4.2).

Performance Techniques to Teach to Help Children Progress to the Mature Pattern

- Push the ball with the finger pads or fingerprints; don't slap the ball.
- Your hand is like a spider spread over the ball.

Potential Tasks (Level 1 Content)

- Remaining in your personal space, try bouncing the ball as many times in a row as you can.
  - Give both hands practice.
  - Try to increase the number of times you can bounce the ball without missing it or having it bounce out of your personal space.
- Try bouncing the ball as many times in a row as you can while walking and then jogging easily.
  - Give both hands practice.
  - Try to increase the number of times you can bounce the ball and keep it with you without losing control of it. If you have problems keeping the ball with you, practice dribbling in your personal space.

Teaching the Body/Head Component

Body/Head Movements Observed

Intermediate: Glances up. Knees are slightly bent, and the child is mostly upright. The child glances up to see where he or she is going but tends to look primarily at the ball.

Performance Techniques to Teach to Help Children Progress to the Mature Pattern

- Look up to see your classmates.
- Look up to see what your partner is doing.

Potential Tasks (Level 2 Content)

- Everyone has a ball. The whole class dribbles in a scattered formation, looking up to avoid bumping into classmates.
- Decrease the size of the space and continue to dribble in a crowd in a scattered formation, looking up to avoid bumping into classmates.
- With an assigned partner, play follow-the-leader with the leader dribbling, moving the body and body parts in different positions, bouncing the ball under and around the body and different body parts, and changing hands. The follower must look up to follow the leader.

Teaching Dribbling While Traveling on Different Pathways

Movements Observed

Intermediate: Controls ball on curved pathways. The child can dribble around obstacles (cones or defenders) and on curved pathways. Angular pathways are rounded, not sharp.

Performance Techniques to Teach to Help Children Progress to the Mature Pattern

- When you dribble on an angular pathway, make quick, sharp changes in direction.
- Plant the outside foot, bend the knee, lean in the opposite direction, push off forcefully, and do a crossover dribble, changing the ball to the other hand.

Potential Tasks

- Cones are scattered about the physical education space. Everyone has a ball. The whole class dribbles in a scattered formation using zigzag pathways to dodge classmates and the cones, which are pretend defenders.

SAFETY AND LIABILITY 4.1

Increasing Safety and Decreasing Risk of Liability: Guidelines Relevant to Content in this Chapter

In this box, we discuss specific guidelines built on information discussed earlier in this text on professional standards of practice, negligence, and liability. The goals of these guidelines are to increase children's safety and decrease teachers' risk of negligence and liability.

- Ensure all tasks are developmentally appropriate for every child in relation to skill level, size, age, strength, and other physical capabilities. Differentiating instruction to accommodate these developmental differences is important for decreasing your risk of liability.
- In partner and group activities in which there is the potential for contact or harm due to unequal size, weight, or other physical characteristics and capabilities (e.g., pairs balancing in gymnastics), pair and group children with others of similar physical attributes and developmental levels.
- The younger the children, the more closely they need to be supervised.

Sources: (Hart & Ritson, 2002; Halsey, 2005)

as an error. Your teaching would focus on teaching adult performance techniques without concern for developmental alignment. A developmental perspective stands in contrast to this adult error model.

Here's an example to help you see the difference between a developmental perspective and an adult error model more clearly. Suppose you are observing a group of children forcefully throwing a yarn ball against a wall when you notice that with many of them, their trunk faces forward throughout the throw. If you hold a developmental perspective, you know that this movement pattern represents the most immature movement pattern for the trunk action in (forceful) throwing and is a movement pattern all children use early in the development of throwing. Your job is to align your feedback to the child's developmental level and design tasks to help children move along the continuum by progressing toward more mature patterns (trunk rotation) and finally the most mature pattern (differentiated rotation in which the hips rotate forward before the shoulders). Thus, your feedback would be aimed at teaching children to start with their side pointing to the target to help them begin to learn trunk rotation (see **Figure 4.4**). You would not spend time discussing that the hips rotate forward before the shoulders rotate forward, because this information is more information than the children need at their level of development. Their current pattern would not be seen as "wrong" or an "error," but rather as merely being at the less mature end of the continuum. In contrast, if you use the adult or expert model or hold an "error attitude," you would assume the current pattern to be an error and thus would design tasks to "correct" it, not taking into consideration the concept of development and how components of the forceful throwing pattern develop with practice over a considerable amount of time.

You teach differentiated rotation when children need to know it and are able to use the information to improve their throwing. If there are some children in the class ready to learn differentiated rotation, you would teach it to those children, thus accommodating individual differences by differentiating instruction.

Assessing the Developmental Level of Skills Rather than the Product

When teachers assess children's skills, it is critical to assess the developmental level of the performance techniques (i.e., the movement patterns) as opposed to the product, such as the distance jumped. The reason for qualitatively assessing movement patterns is that quantitative products in many skills, such as the number of inches jumped, is highly related to the size of the children. For example, a tall child with a qualitatively less

Figure 4.4 Starting side to target, pointing to target

mature pattern might jump farther than a short child with a more mature pattern. In other words, rather than assessing learning, with a taller and shorter child in the same grade, you are assessing growth. Growth is a factor neither the teacher nor the child can control. Taking a developmental perspective allows you to recognize that the tall child is less skilled and needs instruction and practice to progress to a more mature pattern.

Newell's Constraints Theory

Karl Newell (1986) proposed a constraints theory of motor performance that has proved to be a helpful tool for both motor development researchers and teachers alike. **Newell's constraints theory** states that the movement patterns of skills exhibited by an individual result from interactions among three sets of constraints: (1) individual constraints; (2) environmental constraints; and (3) task constraints. **Figure 4.5** illustrates this interaction.

Individual Constraints

Individual constraints include factors such as the child's height, strength, and fitness level; physical, cognitive, and social development; and current ability level. Individual constraints also include anxiety, motivation, attention, knowledge, and memory (Haywood & Getchell, 2005).

Individual constraints should not be perceived as negative, as they simply describe the child's capabilities and development at a particular point in time. Moreover, many individual constraints, such as knowledge, motivation, and anxiety, can be changed by teachers through instruction of performance techniques and establishment of a classroom climate that enhances motivation and decreases anxiety.

Environmental Constraints

Environmental constraints include physical constraints such as gravity, the weather, and the type of surface (e.g., a slippery gymnasium floor, an uneven field, a hard-surfaced playground). Physical constraints also include the amount of space, light, and noise in the environment.

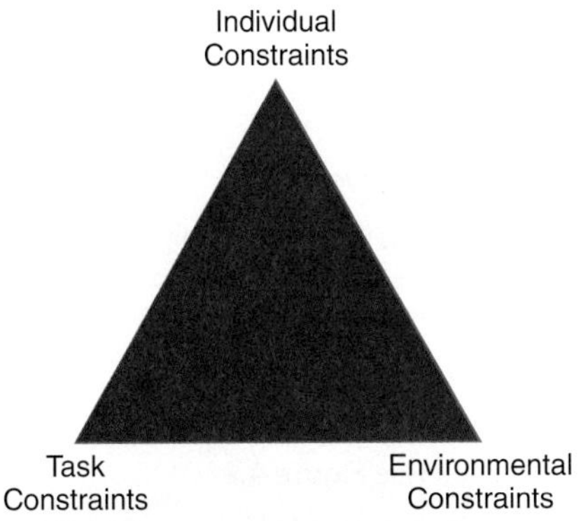

Figure 4.5 Newell's constraints model

Source: Data from Newell, K. M. (1986). Constraints on the development of coordination. In M. G. Wade & H. T. A. Whiting (Eds.), Motor development in children: Aspects of coordination and control (pp. 341–360). Amsterdam, Netherlands: Martinus Nijhoff.

Other environmental constraints that play a critical role in motor development and learning are social and cultural constraints, which include the influence of classmates, teachers, peer groups, parents, siblings, societal expectations, and cultural expectations and support. For example, in some cultures, physical activity is viewed as a male domain, and girls are not encouraged to participate. Sometimes classmates support and other times hinder an individual child's performance. Societal expectations for achievement in physical activities, which often differ by gender, race, and culture, play a major role in students' motivation to learn, practice, and achieve.

Another major cultural constraint you will need to manage when teaching is the culture fostered by professional, collegiate, and elite sport, in which winning is portrayed as the most important outcome of a contest. This cultural conception can have a negative effect on children because it can shift their focus away from learning and toward simply winning.

Task Constraints

Task constraints include the goals of the activity, movements specified, rules, equipment, and number of players. As a teacher, you have control over the task constraints. When you design tasks, you will manipulate task constraints in relation to the individual and environmental constraints so that children practice the skill movement patterns you want them to practice.

Movement Patterns: The Result of the Interactions Among Individual, Task, and Environmental Constraints

Newell's constraints theory has profound implications for teachers. The movement pattern you observe a child performing does not necessarily represent that child's developmental level for the skill. Instead, it results from the interactions among individual, task, and environmental constraints (see **Figure 4.6**). For example, if two highly skilled children play catch standing 15 feet apart indoors, they will typically not turn their side to the target or step on the opposite foot. In this setting, their throwing resembles the immature pattern, even though they can throw at a mature level. These children are limiting their range of motion to adapt to the indoor environment and their distance apart. In a throw from the outfield, they would exhibit the mature overhand throwing pattern. In the indoor setting, however, the task and environmental constraints influence their throwing movement patterns.

A study of elite baseball players counted the number of throws by all players in actual games and coded the developmental levels of the backswing, forearm, and step (Barrett & Burton, 2002). The researchers found players used a less mature pattern in more than half the throws due to the tactics (i.e., the task constraints) of the game situation. The pitchers and outfielders studied used the mature pattern 95.7% and 86.4% of the time, respectively. By comparison, catchers and infielders used less mature patterns 95.9% and 85.8%, respectively. Thus, the task (such as the catcher's throws back to the pitcher and a shortstop's quick throws to second base without taking a time-consuming full backswing) determined the movement pattern performed.

Of course, the throwing patterns of the collegiate athletes in this study were simple to interpret because the researchers knew that the athletes could all throw at a mature level. Thus,

Figure 4.6 Task constraints eliciting less mature arm action

we can easily recognize the roles of the task and the environment in this scenario. In contrast, children may or may not be able to perform a given skill at a mature level. This is why in teaching, and especially in assessing the overhand throw, you should always design the task and environment so that children can throw as forcefully as possible. As with the catchers and infielders in the research study, once accuracy or other factors, such as the distance of a partner catching the ball, become part of the task, throwers will adapt their movement pattern because maximal force production is not the overriding goal.

Assessment of children's developmental levels can be even more complicated. For example, in one study of third-grade children dribbling, task constraints elicited less mature patterns in some components and more mature patterns in others (Chen et al., 2003). **Table 4.2** summarizes the findings.

The results from this study demonstrated that simply observing the child in one task does not reveal the child's potential developmental level on all components of dribbling. We expect mature dribbling performance techniques that children can do but have not mastered to the point of automaticity (e.g., pushing with finger pads) will become less mature (e.g., slapping the ball) when the task is more difficult, because children must manage a more complex environment in more difficult tasks. However, more difficult task constraints in this study also elicited the more mature pattern of looking up, which is in contrast to what we typically see. The need to see where they were going so they would not bump into anyone in the more difficult tasks brought out more mature movement patterns of looking up among study participants. This finding implies that you need to use a variety of tasks with different constraints for both teaching and assessment of dribbling.

Dynamical Systems and Ecological Psychology

Over time, motor control and learning researchers expanded on Newell's work and described what they called a "constraints-led approach," integrating principles from ecological psychology, which addresses perception, and dynamical systems theory, which addresses motor control (Davids et al., 2008). This section summarizes five key principles from these theories.

Links Between Perception and Action

Learners actively seek and perceive information directly from the environment in relation to their current capabilities and intended action (Gibson & Pick, 2000; Gibson, 1979/1986). Thus, perception and action are linked. For example, in catching, children attend to the flight of the ball. The flight path gives them information about where to move to catch the ball, and the height of the ball tells them whether to put their thumbs together with hands up for a high fly ball or their pinkies together with hands down for a grounder. Through practice, learners become more attuned to the information in the environment and can perceive information more precisely.

Affordances

J. J. Gibson (1979/1986) called what learners perceive within the environment as "affordances." **Affordances** are possible actions that the environment allows (i.e., affords) in relation to the individual's capabilities and goals. A chair to an adult affords sitting, while a chair to a baby just learning to stand affords something to hold onto while trying to stand.

Table 4.2 Research Findings on Dribbling Under Different Task Constraints

Task Constraints	Movement Patterns Observed
More difficult task constraints: • Dribble at a fast speed • Dribble traveling on zigzag or curved pathways in a crowded space • Dribble following a partner leader • Dribble against a defender	*Resulted in the following less mature movement patterns* (see **Figure 4.7**): • Slapped the ball more • Ball chest high or higher • Lost control of the ball more often *Resulted in the following more mature movement patterns:* • Head up, looking up (see **Figure 4.8**)
Less difficult task constraints: • Dribble at a moderate or slow speed • Dribble on a straight pathway	*Resulted in the following more mature movement patterns:* • Slapped the ball less • Maintained control of the ball *Resulted in the following less mature movement patterns:* • Head down, looking down

Source: Data from Chen, W., Rovegno, I., Todorovich, J., & Babiarz, M. (2003). Third grade children's movement responses to dribbling tasks presented by accomplished teachers. *Journal of Teaching in Physical Education*, 22(4), 450–466.

Figure 4.7 Dribbling fast, which elicits a less mature pattern of ball rebounding (face high)

Figure 4.8 Task constraints that elicit looking up and slapping the ball more

What the environment affords for the capabilities of one individual will be different from what the same environment affords for the capabilities of another individual. For example, a fifth-grader who is skilled in dribbling will perceive a defender as a challenge who can be successfully (and enjoyably) dodged by going either left or right and choosing among several dodging options. In contrast, a first-grader who has problems controlling the ball while dribbling will perceive the defender as a stressful barrier and as someone who will likely steal the ball (and the fun). With only limited capabilities to control the ball, the first-grader will likely not attempt to dodge, but rather will turn her or his back to the defender and hover over the ball.

Inseparability of the Learner and the Environment

Because learners always perceive the environment in relation to their capabilities and intended actions, the learner and the environment are inseparable (Gibson & Pick, 2000). In turn, ecological psychology and dynamical systems theory support the idea that teachers should not break skills down into small steps or decontextualize skills—that is, teach skills in isolation from key environmental and task constraints within which the skill will eventually be performed (Davids et al., 2008; Renshaw, Chow, Davids, & Hammond, 2010).

Of course, teachers must simplify the environment and tasks to teach skills to children. For example, kindergarteners cannot learn to dribble by playing 5v5 basketball. The goal is for teachers to simplify tasks enough so that children can be successful, while maintaining key components relevant to how they will perform the skill in more complex environments.

Variable Practice

Motor learning research has shown that once learners develop the basic movement pattern of skills, they benefit from practicing a skill under a variety of task and environmental constraints (Boyce, Coker, & Bunker, 2006; Davids et al., 2008). Through **variable practice**, children learn to adapt to variations in environmental and task constraints, which occur not only in skills, such as a soccer dribble when performers adjust to changing game situations, but also in skills with less variability, such as batting a ball. In fact, from a dynamical systems perspective, learning is described as an "adaptive change or behavior change in relation to a specific task goal" (Wee Keat Tan, Chow, & Davids, 2012, p. 336). Although repetitive practice of the same movement pattern has some short-term benefits for older students, practicing with a variety of task constraints (e.g., different balls, boundaries, or distances) is better for long-term learning (Chen, 2011).

Discovery Learning

According to dynamical systems and ecological psychology, perception and action are processes in which the performer actively seeks information from the environment and discovers which movement to produce by exploring the relations among individual capabilities and the current task and environmental constraints. Whether the exploration occurs at a conscious or subconscious level, the performer is always exploring these relationships. A constraints-led approach aims to help performers learn how to search and discover the relationships among constraints (Davids et al., 2008). From this perspective, learning is viewed as a discovery process.

Discovery learning is one way teachers can encourage students to become independent, autonomous learners. Autonomy is a strong motivator for student engagement and learning in physical education. In addition, there is some evidence in motor learning research that discovery learning is either equivalent or superior to explicit instruction (Chen, 2011). Effective teaching means knowing when you need to provide explicit instruction and when you need to just let children practice without any interventions within the assigned tasks but with appropriate task and environmental constraints.

Implications for Teaching

Researchers point out that (1) individual, task, and environmental constraints; (2) the inseparability of the individual from the environment; and (3) affordances have important implications for teachers (Chen et al., 2003; Chow, Davids, Button, Shuttleworth, Renshaw, & Araujo, 2007; Davids et al., 2008; Mally, 2006; Renshaw et al., 2010; Rovegno, Nevett, Brock, & Babiarz, 2001). These implications are described in the remainder of this section.

Design Task Constraints to Elicit the Performance Techniques that Children Should Practice

Design task constraints to elicit the most mature movement patterns the children can perform and to foster their development toward the most mature pattern. For example, if your objective is for children to practice stepping on the opposite foot to improve their ability to generate force when throwing, you must create practice conditions that allow them to throw as forcefully as they can (e.g., throwing yarn balls against a wall, throwing across a field with no accuracy constraints). If the children are too close together, they might step with the opposite foot, but they will not use the step in a coordinated way to generate force, which was the goal of the lesson. They will step with the opposite foot to please the teacher, but will not learn to step with the opposite foot as part of the coordination for throwing because they do not need to step to generate force when they are too close together.

Other examples include the following:

- Research on teaching young children jumping showed that if they are told to jump from two feet to as far as they can over a pretend swamp filled with alligators (drawn on paper), they will improve their leg actions (Sweeting & Rink, 1999). If children jump around a cone, they will not use their arms to generate force, as in the mature pattern, because they don't need much force to jump a short distance. To elicit the most mature pattern children are capable of, they must jump forward as far as they can, which requires a task and an environment designed to encourage them to do so.
- Research on dribbling showed that if you want children to practice looking up while dribbling, you need to use tasks that require children to look up, such as dribbling fast, dribbling on different pathways in a crowded space, or dribbling in different ways following a leader (Chen et al., 2003). Otherwise, children tend to look up only immediately after the teacher says, "Look up," and not on their own.
- Setting a task constraint in 3v3 basketball in which players can mark or guard only one player and can steal the ball from only that player helps defenders learn to stay close to their assigned player (Harvey, 2007).

Determine Whether the Task and Environmental Constraints Are Having a Negative Effect

The second implication is a correlate to the first. During teaching, observe the children's movements and decide whether the task or the environment is having a negative effect on performance or learning. For example, is a child trying to shoot a ball into a basket using a sidearm slinging action or an underhand throw because the ball is too heavy and the basket too high? Is the tagger in a tag game never able to tag any runner because the three other children in the group are all faster runners? Is a child unable to do a circular swing with a racket because the racket is too heavy?

When task and environmental constraints are having a negative effect and bringing out a less mature pattern, you can modify the task, equipment, or environment to eliminate the problem. Returning to the earlier examples, you might give the child shooting at the basket a smaller, lighter ball and lower the basket height, group children with similar running speeds when teaching tag-type games, and give the child practicing a circular swing a lighter racket.

If you can keep Newell's model in your head as you observe your classes, you will be better able to decide if the movements the children are doing represent their true developmental level or are a result of task or environmental constraints. You will also be better prepared to design and modify tasks during the lesson to create better practice conditions for the children. As Mally (2006) suggests, teachers need to stop assuming that the children's failure to perform a skill technique is due to individual constraints, such as the child being too slow or too weak or lacking skill, and instead examine the effects of task and environmental constraints.

Design Tasks that Include Key Elements of the Skill as It Is Performed in Games

As much as possible, have children practice skills within an environment that reflects key aspects of the environment in which the skills will be used eventually, while at the same time matching the difficulty of the task and environment to the motor, cognitive, perceptual, and social capabilities of the children (Davids et al., 2008).

Deciding how to break down games into tasks that retain key elements of games that make the games meaningful yet are simple enough for children to manage successfully is one of the most difficult decisions you will make as a teacher (Rink, 2001). A child who cannot control the ball while dribbling will not benefit from dribbling against an opponent. A child who cannot rally back and forth with a partner will not benefit from playing a competitive game of tennis. In addition, most young children have not reached a level of cognitive, social, and emotional development to play games in ways that enhance their learning of motor skills.

Nevertheless, there are many tasks you can use that both capture key elements of the game environment and are developmentally appropriate.

Teach Children to Attend to Affordances

Teach children to attend to key affordances of the task and environment, such as perceptual and tactical aspects. For example, teaching children how to see the apex in the arch of a ball in flight will help them learn where to move to catch the ball. Teaching children how to anticipate the moment a teammate cutting to receive a pass will be free from a defender will help them learn when to send a lead pass.

Provide a Variety of Tasks that Allow Children to Explore Different Task and Environmental Constraints

Being able to vary and adapt skills as required in different game, dance, and gymnastics situations is critical for children to become skillful movers. Motor development theory supports the importance of providing varied task constraints for learning (Boyce et al., 2006; Chow et al., 2007). Moreover, game, dance, and gymnastics content is, by its very nature, varied. For children to participate successfully in games, dance, and gymnastics, they must have multiple opportunities to explore the effects of different task and environmental constraints on skill performance. To encourage such exploration, you can provide a wide variety of tasks to practice each skill. In the content chapters, we show you how to design a variety of tasks and give you many examples for each skill.

Classification of Skills: The Open–Closed Continuum

Motor learning researchers classify motor skills on a continuum from closed to open—a schema that is helpful for teachers seeking to understand how to design practice conditions. "**Closed skills** are performed in stable, unchanging environments. The goal for the learner in these types of movement situations is the development of a consistent movement pattern that can be performed in exactly the same way from trial to trial" (Rose & Christina, 2006, p. 217). Examples include cartwheels and basketball free throws. **Open skills** are "skills that are performed in variable environments and therefore must be repeatedly adapted to the changing demands of the environment" (p. 217). Examples include soccer dribbling, catching, and volleyball striking.

We classify some skills in between the open and closed ends of the continuum. For example, a fairway golf swing with irons is performed in an environment that is relatively stable (no defender is trying to steal the golf ball, and the target is not moving). The performer decides when to swing. Nevertheless, wind direction, the condition of the ground, and the distance to the hole provide considerable variability. The movement pattern of batting a ball is somewhat consistent but will change depending on where the ball is pitched, what the ball speed is traveling at, and where the batter plans to hit the ball. The batter does not determine when to start the swing, as the timing depends on the pitcher.

The open–closed continuum can help teachers in planning tasks and practice conditions. Think about the way skills are used in games, dance, and gymnastics, and then plan tasks that reflect the variability of the movement patterns of the skill and teach learners how to adapt the movement pattern to the task and environmental constraints. With this kind of program, your students will develop both movement variety and adaptability.

Stages of Motor Learning

Motor learning researchers have proposed that learning occurs in broad stages. The **stages of motor learning** guide teachers regarding what to expect as children learn motor skills and which tasks are appropriate at each stage. Rose and Christina (2006) suggest that three researchers have developed especially helpful stage models: Fitts (1964), Gentile (1972), and Vereijken (1991). Table 4.3 summarizes and compares the three models.

For teachers, the three stages of learning have clear curriculum implications. These stages serve as the basis for the games chapters in this text:

Stage 1: In the first stage, teachers focus on teaching children the basic movement patterns of skills. Children will not be

Table 4.3 Summary of Stages of Learning Models

Fitts (1964)	Gentile (1972)	Vereijken (1991)
Cognitive stage 1: • Learners try to understand and then perform the basic components of the skill. • Learners are cognitively engaged, watching demonstrations and listening to cues and feedback. • Inconsistent performance and immature movement patterns are noted.	*Getting the idea of the movement:* • Learners try to understand and perform the basic components of the skill. • Learners can be distracted by irrelevant aspects of the environment and try to learn which elements are important.	*Novice stage:* • Learners tend to freeze out some of the joint actions of the skill to make the skill easier to control; for example, a child may throw without trunk rotation (freezing the trunk action) or without stepping on the opposite foot (freezing opposition and leg actions).
Associative stage 2: • Learners begin to coordinate components of the skill (e.g., legs and arms in jumping). • Learners begin to adapt the skill to different movement contexts (e.g., catching a ball coming from different levels).	*Fixation/diversification stage:* • For closed skills performed in a stable environment, learners work to develop a consistent outcome (e.g., performing a cartwheel on a line). • For open skills in an environment that changes, learners work to develop versatility (e.g., dribbling a ball in a game-like environment).	*Advanced stage:* • Learners use and coordinate more joint actions and body components (e.g., coordinating stepping with the opposite foot with the arm action of the overhand throw).
Autonomous stage 3: • The skill can be performed without cognitive attention to the movement so that learners can attend to the context (e.g., the game tactics). • Skill performance is consistent, with few immature movements.		*Expert stage:* • All joint actions and body components work together and work with external forces, such as friction, in an efficient and coordinated way to achieve the optimal technique.

Sources: Data from Magill, R. A. (2011). *Motor learning and control: Concepts and applications* (9th ed.). New York: McGraw-Hill; and Rose, D. J., & Christina, R. W. (2006). *A multilevel approach to the study of motor control and learning* (2nd ed.). San Francisco: Benjamin Cummings.

able to perform all the techniques of the adult pattern, nor will they be able to coordinate all body components. Consequently, teachers must select the most relevant performance techniques for the children's developmental level. Children's initial attempts will be inconsistent. Tactics and gameplay will not be meaningful and will be a waste of time because beginners need to concentrate their attention on performing the skills.

Stage 2: Once children can perform the basic movement pattern, teachers can focus on helping children develop versatility and adapting the movement to different environmental conditions. For example, once children have mastered the basic movement pattern of dribbling—that is, they can successfully make contact with the ball on consecutive bounces—children can learn to vary that pattern by dribbling on different pathways and at different speeds in game-like tasks.

Stage 3: In the third stage, as children become proficient, they do not need to think consciously about their movements and can then attend to complex game situations.

Summary

Motor development and motor learning provide important tools that can help you teach physical education based on how children learn. Developmental sequences describe in detail qualitative markers of change from less to more mature patterns through which children will progress as they learn motor skills. Knowing the developmental steps in the sequence helps teachers observe and assess children's skills, anticipate children's responses during planning, select relevant performance techniques, and design tasks to facilitate children's learning.

The precepts of Newell's constraints theory, along with concepts from ecological psychology and dynamical systems theory, help teachers understand the role of individual, task, and environmental constraints on performance and learning. Motor learning is a form of discovery learning in which the learner explores the relations among individual, task, and environmental constraints in performing motor skills. These theories guide teachers in designing tasks that elicit the movement patterns they want children to practice.

Understanding development helps you, as a teacher, see children from a developmental perspective, and teach developmentally appropriate content. Using a developmental perspective, you can better recognize children's progress along developmental continua, recognize individual differences, and match your content to children's capabilities, helping them improve.

Review Questions

1. Compare and contrast a developmental perspective with an error model. Which do you hold now, and why?
2. What does the phrase "Development is age related, not age determined" mean? What are some implications for teachers?
3. Select any skill you know well from any sport, such as the front crawl in swimming, blocking in football, or spiking in volleyball. Based on your experience in teaching, coaching, or learning the skill, hypothesize an intratask developmental sequence for it, and list, in order, developmental patterns for components and/or phases of the movement.
4. Briefly describe Newell's constraints theory.
5. Give two specific examples of how task or environmental constraints can have a negative effect on children's movement patterns.
6. Give one specific example of a task that can elicit the movement response you want children to practice.
7. Define open and closed skills, giving examples of skills from each end of the open–closed continuum.
8. Where on the continuum from open to closed skills would you classify the following skills and why? (Describe which aspects of the skills you used as a basis for your decision.)
   - Shooting in basketball
   - Dribbling in soccer
   - Breaststroke in swimming
   - Football pass
   - Batting off a tee
9. Briefly describe the three stages of motor learning and their implications for teaching physical education.

References

Allison, P. C., & Barrett, K. R. (2000). *Constructing children's physical education experiences: Understanding the content for teaching.* Boston: Allyn & Bacon.

Barrett, D. D., & Burton, A. W. (2002). Throwing patterns used by collegiate baseball players in actual games. *Research Quarterly for Exercise and Sport, 73*, 19–27.

Boyce, B. A., Coker, C. A., & Bunker, L. K. (2006). Implications for variability of practice from pedagogy and motor learning perspectives: Finding a common ground. *Quest, 58*, 330–343.

Chen, D. (2011). Creative paradoxical thinking and its implications for teaching and learning motor skills. *Journal of Physical Education, Recreation, and Dance, 82*(9), 19–23, 49.

Chen, W., Rovegno, I., Todorovich, J., & Babiarz, M. (2003). Third grade children's movement responses to dribbling tasks presented by accomplished teachers. *Journal of Teaching in Physical Education, 22*(4), 450–466.

Chow, J. Y., Davids, K., Button, C., Shuttleworth, R., Renshaw, I., & Araujo, D. (2007). The role of nonlinear pedagogy in physical education. *Review of Educational Research, 77*, 251–287.

Cohen, R., Goodway, J. D., & Lidor, R. (2012). The effectiveness of aligned developmental feedback on the overhand throw in third-grade students. *Physical Education and Sport Pedagogy, 17*, 525–541.

Davids, K., Button, C., & Bennett, S. (2008). *Dynamics of skill acquisition: A constraints-led approach.* Champaign, IL: Human Kinetics.

Eickhoff-Shemek, J. M., Herbert, D. L., & Connaughton, D. P. (2009). *Risk Management for Health/Fitness Professionals: Legal Issues and Strategies.* Philadelphia: Wolters Kluwer/Lippincott Williams & Wilkins.

Fitts, P. M. (1964). Perceptual-motor skills learning. In A. W. Melton (Ed.), *Categories of human learning* (pp. 243–285). New York: Academic Press.

Gentile, A. M. (1972). A working model of skill acquisition with application to teaching. *Quest*, Monograph XVII, 3–23.

Gibson, E. J., & Pick, A. D. (2000). *An ecological approach to perceptual learning and development.* Oxford, England: Oxford University Press.

Gibson, J. J. (1979/1986). *The ecological approach to visual perception.* Boston: Houghton Mifflin.

Goodway, J. D., & Branta, C. F. (2003). Influence of a motor skill intervention on fundamental motor skill development of disadvantaged preschool children. *Research Quarterly for Exercise and Sport, 74*, 36–46.

Hart, J. E., & Ritson, R. J. (2002). *Liability and Safety in Physical Education and Sport.* Reston, VA: National Association for Sport and Physical Education.

Halsey, J. J. (2005). Risk Management for Physical Educators. In H. Appenzeller, (Ed.). *Risk Management in Sport: Issues and Strategies*, (2nd ed.), (pp. 151–163). Durham, NC: Carolina Academic Press.

Harvey, S. (2007). Using a generic invasion game for assessment. *Journal of Physical Education, Recreation and Dance, 78*(4), 19–25, 48–50.

Haywood, K. M., & Getchell, N. (2005). *Life span motor development* (4th ed.). Champaign, IL: Human Kinetics.

Magill, R. A. (2011). *Motor learning and control: Concepts and applications* (9th ed.). New York: McGraw-Hill.

Mally, K. K. (2006). Creating positive task constraints. *Teaching Elementary Physical Education, 17*(3), 28–30.

Newell, K. M. (1986). Constraints on the development of coordination. In M. G. Wade & H. T. A. Whiting (Eds.), *Motor development in children: Aspects of coordination and control* (pp. 341–360). Amsterdam, Netherlands: Martinus Nijhoff.

Nohr, K. M. (2009). *Managing Risk in Sport and Recreation: The Essential Guide for Loss Prevention.* Champaign, IL: Human Kinetics.

Renshaw, I., Chow, J. Y., Davids, K., & Hammond, J. (2010). A constraints-led perspective to understanding skill acquisition and game play: A basis for integration of motor learning theory and physical education praxis. *Physical Education and Sport Pedagogy, 15*, 117–137.

Rink, J. E. (2001). Investigating the assumptions of pedagogy. *Journal of Teaching in Physical Education, 20*, 112–128.

Roberton, M. A., & Halverson, L. E. (1984). *Developing children: Their changing movement.* Philadelphia: Lea & Febiger.

Robinson, L. E. (2011). Effect of a mastery climate motor program on object control skills and perceived physical competence in preschoolers. *Research Quarterly for Exercise and Sport, 82*, 355–359.

Robinson, L. E., & Goodway, J. D. (2009). Instructional climates in preschool children who are at risk. Part I: Object control skill development. *Research Quarterly for Exercise and Sport, 80*, 533–542.

Rovegno, I. (1991). A participant-observation study of knowledge restructuring in a field-based elementary physical education methods course. *Research Quarterly for Exercise and Sport, 62*, 205–212.

Rovegno, I., Nevett, M., Brock, S., & Babiarz, M. (2001). Teaching and learning basic invasion game tactics in fourth grade: A descriptive study from situated and constraints theoretical perspectives. *Journal of Teaching in Physical Education, 20*, 370–388.

Rose, D. J., & Christina, R. W. (2006). *A multilevel approach to the study of motor control and learning* (2nd ed.). San Francisco: Benjamin Cummings.

Seefeldt, V. (1980). Developmental motor patterns: Implications for elementary school physical education. In C. H. Nadeau, W. R. Halliwell, K. M. Newell, & G. C. Roberts (Eds.), *Psychology of motor behavior and sport—1979* (pp. 314–323). Champaign, IL: Human Kinetics.

Society of Health and Physical Educators. (2014). *National standards and grade-level outcomes for K-12 physical education.* Champaign, IL: Human Kinetics.

Stodden, D. F., True, L. K., Langendorfer, S. J., & Gao, Z. (2013). Associations among selected motor skills and health-related fitness: Indirect evidence for Seefeldt's proficiency barrier in young adults. *Research Quarterly for Exercise and Sport, 84*, 397–403.

Sweeting, T., & Rink, J. E. (1999). Effects of direct instruction and environmentally designed instruction on the process and product characteristics of a fundamental skill. *Journal of Teaching in Physical Education, 18*, 216–233.

Vereijken, B. (1991). *The dynamics of skill acquisition.* Unpublished dissertation. Free University, Netherlands.

Wee Keat Tan, C., Chow, J. Y., & Davids, K. (2012). How does TGfU work?: Examining the relationships between learning design in TGfU and a nonlinear pedagogy. *Physical Education and Sport Pedagogy, 17*, 331–348.

Wickstrom, R. L. (1983). *Fundamental motor patterns* (3rd ed.). Philadelphia: Lea & Febiger.

Williams, K. (2004). What's motor development got to do with physical education? *Journal of Physical Education, Recreation, and Dance, 75*(6), 35–39.

CHAPTER

5

Cognitive Learning Theory

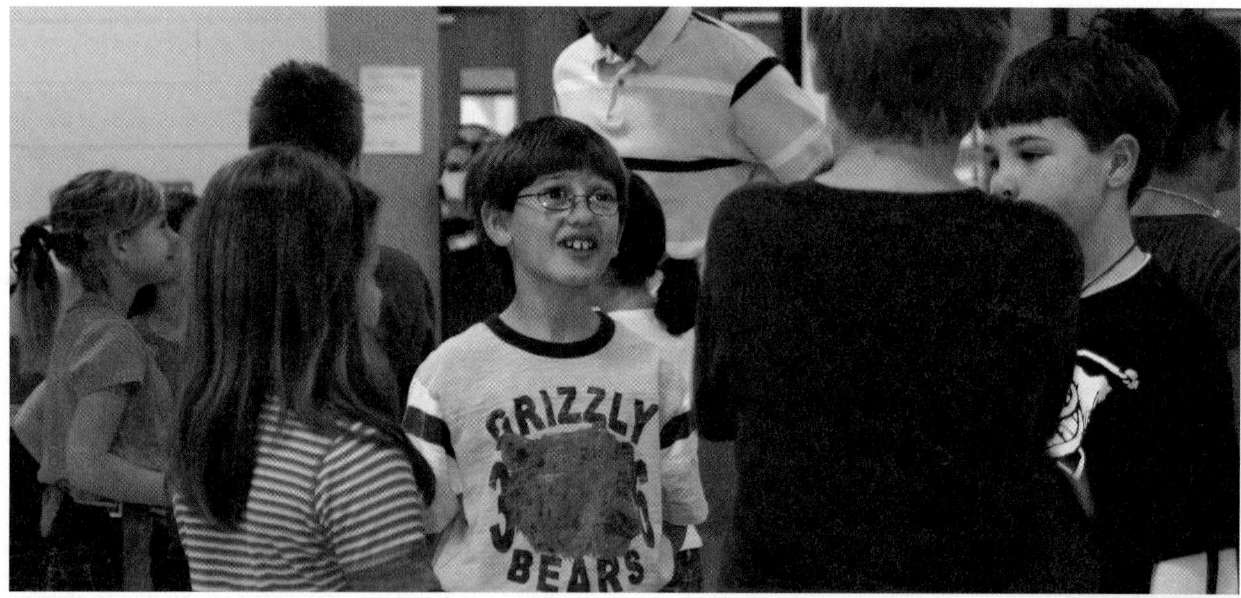

PRE-READING REFLECTION

1. Rank the following items in terms of how you believe K–5 students prefer to learn. Then, rank the following items in terms of how you preferred to learn when you were in elementary school (feel free to have ties). How do you prefer to learn as a college student?
   - Listening to a lecture and taking notes
   - Doing hands-on activities or lab experiments
   - Experimenting on your own
   - Watching a demonstration
   - Listening to a short explanation and then trying the ideas on your own
   - Reading on your own
   - Discussing ideas with classmates
   - Interacting with others via the Internet
   - Searching the Internet and then reading information
   - Searching in the library and then reading information
   - Other learning situations not listed here (as many as you want)

OBJECTIVES

Students will learn:

1. Successful learning results in broad and deep knowledge structures in which chunks of information are well connected and can be flexibly transferred to other contexts.
2. Learning is an active process of constructing knowledge structures.
3. Children construct new knowledge based on their prior knowledge. They always have some prior knowledge or experience related to what we teach.
4. During learning, knowledge, thinking skills, and motivation are intertwined.
5. Being "child centered" means the teacher focuses on what children are experiencing and learning, how they are thinking and feeling, and what they can do.
6. Through social interactions, students construct knowledge together and can gain deep and accurate understandings of subject matter.

7. The cultural environment plays a critical role in learning.
8. Understanding and applying principles of constructivism is challenging. Research shows that undergraduates and teachers can easily develop misunderstandings.

KEY TERMS

Child-centered teaching
Constructivism
Inert knowledge
Pop culture
Situated cognition
Social constructivism

CONNECTIONS TO STANDARDS

This chapter describes how children acquire cognitive knowledge, which is the focus of National Standards 2 and 3 and the Common Core and other State Standards (CCSS) for vocabulary acquisition. We describe the role of social interactions in the construction of knowledge, which is part of National Standard 4 and CCSS on collaboration, speaking, and listening.

Behaviorism

Behaviorism was the first psychological theory in the United States applied widely to teaching physical education. Behaviorism focuses on the impact of environmental conditions on students such as how teachers' reinforcement of desired student behaviors, an environmental condition, contributes to student's learning and success. Behavioral techniques are used by all teachers. For example, positive reinforcement of the desired motor response and appropriate behaviors, cues, prompts, and feedback are common, proven teaching techniques. In addition, helping students generalize the common elements of different environmental situations to facilitate the transfer of learning is a widely used instructional technique derived from behavioral psychology (Ward, 2006). Most significantly, behavioral theories focus on the role of the environment in facilitating learning. Having teachers emphasize the effects of the conditions of the environment, including the physical, social, and emotional environments created by the teacher, peers, and tasks, is critical for effective teaching and is a concept supported by Newell's constraints theory.

In fact, instructional techniques derived from behavioral theory are so commonplace that we often think of them as simply "good teaching," without contemplating their underlying theoretical base. Many teaching techniques have their theoretical roots and research support in behavioral theory.

In this chapter, we focus on information for teachers based on cognitive theories of learning and motivation. In the same way that motor development theory informs teachers about how children learn motor skills, so cognitive learning theories inform teachers about how children process information and construct knowledge.

This chapter concentrates on one broad cognitive learning theory called **constructivism**. Constructivism has many implications for teaching. Even so, it is not a theory of instruction, nor does it tell teachers how to teach. In the constructivist approach, teaching and learning are considered to be two sides of the same coin: they are connected, but one side does not dictate what the other side must look like. To use this theory effectively, you must apply the principles of constructivism with intelligence and sensitivity to the children you teach and the subject matter you are teaching.

Key Ideas of Constructivist Theory

Researchers developed constructivist theory over many years based on the results of thousands of studies. The key ideas highlighted in this section summarize how children learn based on constructivist theory; in addition, examples are provided for how you can apply these ideas in teaching. The more you understand how children learn, the better you will be able to teach. In addition, you will be able to base your teaching on current, research-based principles that have been shown to produce achievement in school settings.

Knowledge Is Like a Web with Multiple Connections

Research on experts' knowledge shows that successful learning results in two outcomes:

- Broad and deep knowledge structures in which chunks of information are well connected and organized around broad, meaningful concepts and principles
- Knowledge that can be flexibly transferred to other contexts (Chi, Feltovich, & Glaser, 1981; deGroot, 1965; Glaser, 1987)

Thus, knowledge is like a web, with multiple connections centered on big ideas. Many research studies in physical education have replicated these findings. The application of knowledge to different contexts is the primary task for meeting National Standard 2. The development of deep, well-connected knowledge structures is a focus of National Standards 2 and 3 and many CCSS.

Figure 5.1 illustrates the well-connected knowledge of a fifth-grader about hand dribbling. You can see how components of knowledge connect to other components and how components of this knowledge can be transferred to dribbling with the feet.

When asked by the U.S. government to summarize what we know about learning and the implications of this understanding for teachers, the National Research Council (1999)

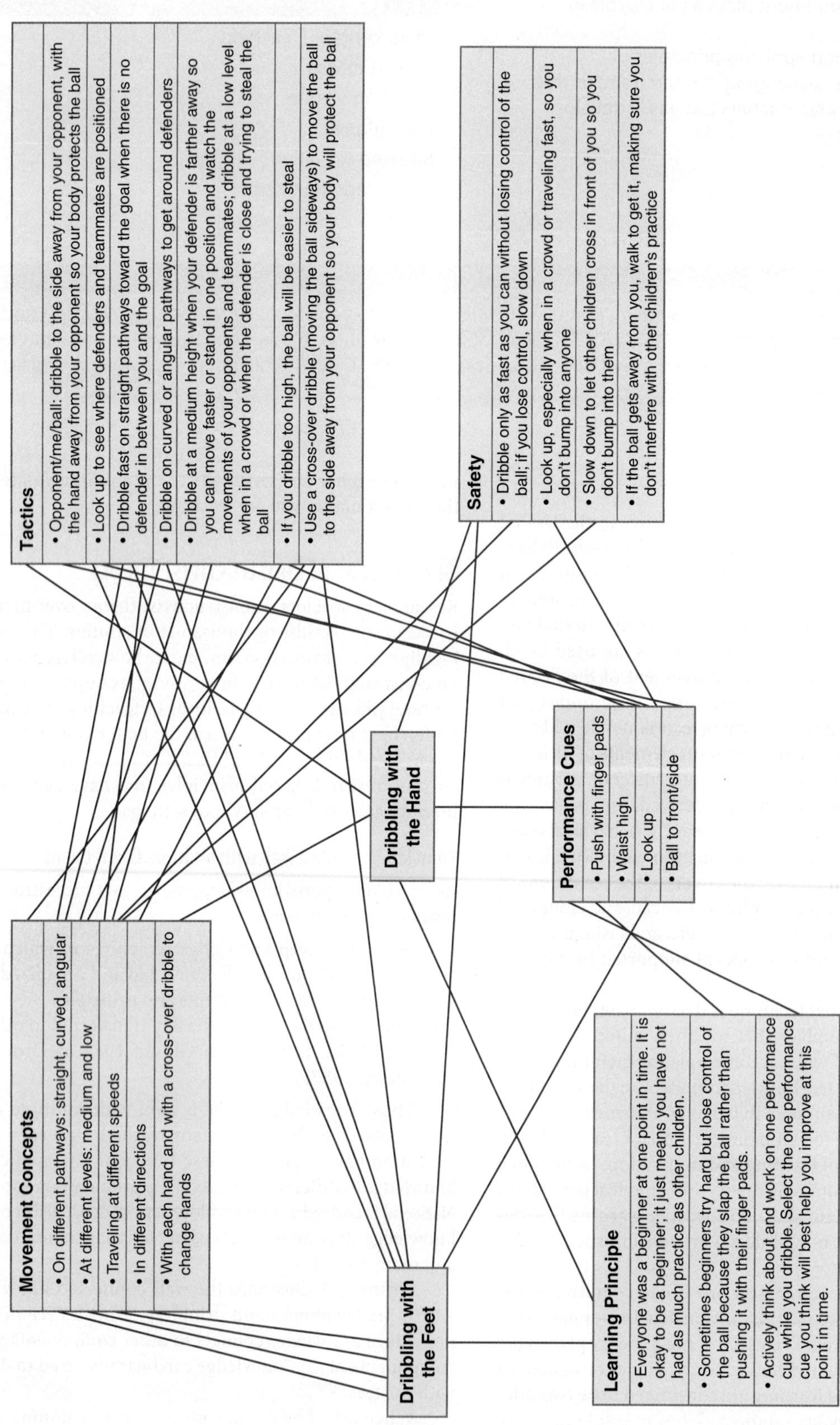

Figure 5.1 A fifth-grade child's well-connected knowledge of hand dribbling

Source: Data from Rovegno, I., Chen, W., & Todorovich, J. (2003). Accomplished teachers' pedagogical content knowledge of teaching dribbling to third grade. *Journal of Teaching in Physical Education*, 22, 426–449.

recommended that teachers ensure students acquire more than surface-level information through rote memory. Its report suggested that teachers should focus on helping students develop a deep, well-connected understanding of subject matter so that knowledge can be applied or transferred to new problems and new situations.

Why is this deep, well-connected knowledge important? Knowledge that is not well connected is called **inert knowledge**—a label indicating that it is not used and often forgotten. Inert knowledge isn't very meaningful to children. In contrast, when students have deep and well-connected knowledge, they can apply concepts and principles in a range of situations, including new situations. Imagine how beneficial it can be for students to understand a game tactic and then be able to apply and adapt that tactic in a range of situations and even in other sports. Compare the well-connected knowledge of the child in Figure 5.1 to the knowledge of child who has not been taught connections, but instead has simply listened to a teacher present a few performance techniques of dribbling. Which child has knowledge that is more useful when playing dribbling games?

In addition, the research implies that teachers should focus on the big ideas (i.e., key concepts) within the subject matter they are teaching and help children understand how lesson content connects to these big ideas. For example, big ideas for tactics in the upper elementary grades include cutting into an open passing lane, sending lead passes to teammates who are open, and receiving the ball and quickly passing before defenders can reposition themselves. Teaching these big ideas about tactics helps children understand how to use skills in game-like situations and how these skills and tactics can be transferred to other situations.

Learning Is an Active Process of Constructing Knowledge

Children are active learners—that is, they learn by constructing their own understanding and building knowledge structures. We assume that you have studied educational psychology and learned how the active construction of knowledge is an important part of the theories of Lev Vygotsky, Jean Piaget, Jerome Bruner, and John Dewey.

Broadly speaking, cognitive science confirms Piaget's claim that people must *construct* their understanding; they do not simply register what the world shows or tells them, as a camera or a tape recorder does. To "know" something, indeed, even simply to memorize effectively, people build a mental representation that imposes order and coherence on experience and information (Resnick & Williams-Hall, 1998, p. 100).

The goal of teaching is to actively engage children in learning movement and thinking about and feeling that movement during the learning process. Active engagement is the opposite of "going through the motions"; it includes emotional engagement in learning.

Physical, cognitive, and emotional engagement leads to a deeper understanding than does rote memorization. For example, memorizing rules of sports, such as the three-second rule in basketball, has little or no meaning to children *until* they (1) experience (in a small-sided game) the frustration that comes when the offense is allowed to stand forever in front of the goal; (2) discuss this problem with classmates; and (3) design their own type of three-second rule that prevents the problem from occurring. This process leads to a deeper understanding of the three-second rule than if students were just to memorize the rule and then regurgitate it on a quiz. Many teachers will tell you that when students simply memorize the three-second rule, many think the rule applies to the defense!

The implications of active learning for teaching include providing opportunities for children as individuals and within groups to construct, analyze, discover, create, explore, and experiment with movement content. For example, you can have children engage in the following tasks:

- Explore different movements within gymnastics and dance themes (see **Figure 5.2**).
- Experiment with different tactical solutions in game situations and different choreographic solutions in dance situations.
- Design different health-related physical activity workouts to address different goals.
- Answer questions and explain the reasoning of the answers.
- Make connections between the content of the day's lesson and other physical education content, classroom content, and aspects of their everyday lives.
- Select the equipment, performance cue, or task to practice based on what is best for their learning.
- Assess a peer and offer appropriate feedback.
- Design obstacle courses, gymnastics routines, dance sequences, or games.

Giving children such opportunities encourages them to apply and discuss their knowledge; "muck about" with ideas; and explore possible options with peers. These processes increase children's active engagement in learning and give them ownership of their learning. Although it might appear as if constructivist-oriented teaching will decrease physical activity time, research shows there is little risk of this outcome (Chen, Martin, Sun, & Ennis, 2007).

Cautions

It is tempting to try to understand the implications of constructivism by saying a teaching practice either is constructivist and facilitates active learning or is traditional and does not. An

Figure 5.2 Children exploring different themes in dance

Courtesy of John Dolly

example of such either/or thinking is the following statement: "Lecturing is traditional; problem solving is constructivist." However, either/or thinking can lead you astray. Listening to a lecture can also involve actively constructing knowledge. A better way to think about teaching practices that facilitate the construction of knowledge is to view those practices as existing on a continuum from less active to more active:

Less Active	More Active
Lecturing about the rules of a sport requires less active engagement as learners construct knowledge.	Having children design and modify their own game rules requires more active engagement as learners construct knowledge.

Learners Construct Knowledge Based on Their Prior Knowledge, Feelings, and Experiences

The National Research Council (1999) reports that substantial research evidence indicates that children enter classrooms "with a range of prior knowledge, skills, beliefs, and concepts that significantly influence what they notice about the environment and how they organize and interpret it. This, in turn, affects their abilities to remember, reason, solve problems, and acquire new knowledge" (p. 10).

As Alexander (2006) explains, children construct new knowledge based on their prior knowledge: They always have some prior knowledge, feelings, or experiences related to what we teach. In addition, prior knowledge and experiences affect students' goals and their beliefs about whether they will fail or succeed in a task, and whether they think something is interesting, relevant, or important (Shen & Chen, 2006). According to the National Research Council (1999), "There is a good deal of evidence that learning is enhanced when teachers pay attention to the knowledge and beliefs that learners bring to a learning task, use this knowledge as a starting point for new instruction, and monitor students' changing conceptions as instruction proceeds" (p. 11).

Taken collectively, these findings suggest that you need to find out what children already know about the content you are planning to teach. You also need to attend to whether children's prior knowledge, feelings, and experiences are having positive or negative effects on their learning. For example, if children have played soccer at a young age and been intimidated by other, more aggressive children who simply chased and attempted to kick the ball (often missing and kicking other children), this prior experience will likely affect their later experiences in learning to dribble and pass a soccer ball in your class.

Thinking Skills and Motivation Are Critical Aspects of Learning

Constructivist theory considers thinking skills and motivation to be critical aspects of acquiring knowledge (Resnick & Williams-Hall, 1989; Sun & Chen, 2010). For example, decision making is an essential aspect of all game tactics. Creative dance includes exploration and problem solving. Designing health-related physical activity workouts includes analysis, goal setting, and attention to motivation.

When teachers teach thinking skills and motivational attitudes, student achievement increases. For example, physical education research indicates that when coaches and teachers do not teach decision making in tactics, this omission impairs the development of students' gameplay; in contrast, when tactical decision making is taught, gameplay improves (French, Nevett, Spurgeon, Graham, Rink, & McPherson, 1996; French, Spurgeon, & Nevett, 1995; Nevett & French, 1997; Oslin & Mitchell, 2006). In addition, research shows that expert teachers recognize the importance of teaching thinking skills and motivational attitudes relevant to the movement content of the lesson and address these issues when they teach (Chen, 2001; Chen & Rovegno, 2000; Ennis, 1991; Rovegno, Chen, & Todorovich, 2003).

Being Child Centered

Teachers often refer to constructivism as a "child-centered" approach. A teacher using this approach focuses on what children are learning and experiencing, how they are thinking and feeling, and what they can do. Child-centered teaching means teachers look at the children and see what they need—teachers don't simply teach a curriculum script that doesn't respond to children's learning or lack of learning.

To be child centered, ask yourself questions such as the following:

- What does this child understand about what I am saying?
- What is this child's level of development, and how will that affect her or his response to this task?
- What will help this child learn at this moment?
- What did Kawanda learn today? What did Emilio experience?

Being child centered means constantly and consistently assessing children's learning both formally, by using assessment tools, and informally, by asking children what they know and how they feel, and then adjusting what or how you are teaching based on the outcome of the assessment. When you focus on children's learning, thinking, and feelings, you are better able to respond when problems arise or when learning progresses faster than you anticipated (see **Figure 5.3**).

Figure 5.3 Focusing on children's responses

Courtesy of John Dolly

The bottom line on being child centered is that what matters is not what you *teach*, but what the children *learn*. This constructivist point of view helps to ensure instruction results in children's learning.

The Role of Social Environments

While some branches of constructivist theory are individually oriented, others, based on the work of Vygotsky, focus on learning in social settings (Alexander, 2006). **Social constructivism** emphasizes the primary role of social interactions with parents, peers, teachers, and other individuals in children's learning. In school settings, research gives considerable support to group work as an effective tool for learning across a variety of subject areas (National Research Council, 1999; Slavin, 1996). During group work, for example, students explain their ideas, justify their opinions, generate possible solutions to problems, offer different perspectives, and negotiate differences. Through social interactions, students construct knowledge together and can gain deep and accurate understandings of subject matter.

Being able to work productively in groups is viewed as a necessary skill for twenty-first–century jobs. Accordingly, the CCSS include many standards related to collaboration with partners and within small groups, and Physical Education National Standard 4 focuses on social responsibility and working well with peers.

The use of group work has increased not just in physical education, but across the field of education as a whole. Physical education research on curriculum models such as Sport Education, Teaching Games for Understanding, Project Adventure, and the Movement Approaches has demonstrated that both teachers and students find group work beneficial and effective (Dyson, 2006; Kinchin, 2006; Oslin & Mitchell, 2006).

The Role of Cultural Environments and Situated Cognition

The cultural environment also plays a critical role in learning. Similar to research related to the constraints theory and ecological psychology, research on what is referred to as **situated cognition** has shown how the individual, the activity in which he or she is engaged, and the social–cultural environment are inseparable parts of what is learned and how learning occurs (Lave & Wenger, 1991; Rogoff, 1990). In turn, situated cognition argues against teaching decontextualized skills and knowledge, in favor of authentic activities that are meaningful to learners. It implies that teachers must be familiar with the multiple cultural environments of their students and the effects of popular (pop) culture.

Cultural Constructions of Knowledge

Constructivism also addresses the way knowledge is constructed within our culture. Knowledge changes over time, of course: Sports change, rules change, and new sports are invented. As a consequence, what was a "fact" 50 years ago might not be a fact today. For example, the physical education profession's knowledge about and recommendations for health-related physical activity have changed dramatically since the 1950s. In 1996, the landmark U.S. Surgeon General's report summarized current research on physical activity and health and proposed new guidelines regarding the frequency, duration, and intensity of health-related physical activity, which we still use today.

Because knowledge changes over time, we need to prepare students to have the skills and attitudes necessary to seek and adapt to new information. They need to understand that knowledge changes and that the amount of information humans know is growing at exponential rates. Most of today's students are preparing for jobs that don't even exist right now. And their leisure-time activities are evolving as well; for example, recreational activities such as snowboarding, racquetball, and beach volleyball didn't exist 50 years ago.

Cultural constructions of knowledge also include **pop culture**—that is, how sports, fitness, dance, and the body are represented by television, magazines, Internet sites,

SAFETY AND LIABILITY 5.1

Increasing Safety and Decreasing Risk of Liability: Guidelines Relevant to Content in this Chapter

In this box, we discuss specific guidelines built on information discussed earlier in this text on professional standards of practice, negligence, and liability. The goals of these guidelines are to increase children's safety and decrease teachers' risk of negligence and liability.

- Instructions about how to perform skills appropriately and safely and instructions about safety procedures and the dangers inherent in specific physical activities need to be age appropriate and based on students' prior knowledge, skills, and beliefs so children clearly understand the information.
- Assessing informally and formally what students actually learned about what you taught about how to perform skills appropriately and safely is important for decreasing your risk of liability.
- Unsafe behaviors children see in professional and collegiate sport (e.g., sliding into second base trying to tackle the defensive player making the tag in baseball, contact in basketball) will affect children's understanding of your instructions about safety and rules. You must counteract the inappropriate models from professional and collegiate sport to ensure children accept and follow your instructions and rules.
- Cultural values placed on thinness can contribute to children's understanding of your instructions about unsafe health behaviors. You must counteract children's misconceptions about health and fitness to ensure they understand, accept, and follow your instructions and rules.

advertisements, radio, peers, and adults in children's daily lives. Pop culture contributes a significant part of the knowledge and experiences children bring to physical education classes. Peers and what is currently popular exert powerful pressure on older children and adolescents, in particular.

One of the implications of social and cultural constructivism is that teachers need to help children think critically about how pop culture may affect—either positively or negatively—their experiences in physical education. For example, the cultural value placed on thinness pressures individuals to be excessively thin and can lead to unsafe health behaviors and decreased self-esteem. The negative behaviors of professional athletes that children see on television can lead to problems during gameplay in physical education.

Common Fallacies About Constructivism

It is challenging to understand and apply the principles of constructivism because many undergraduates have not experienced much, if any, physical education teaching based on this approach. Research shows that undergraduates and teachers can easily develop misunderstandings or incomplete and, in turn, inaccurate conceptions. For example, such misinterpretation may arise when a comparison is made between traditional teaching and teaching based on constructivist principles, and then particular teaching techniques are classified as either traditional or constructivist. This either/or thinking can lead to misconceptions. To help you avoid misunderstandings about constructivism, we briefly summarize suggestions from the research in the remainder of this section (Rovegno & Dolly, 2006).

Fallacy: Constructivism Means Not Telling Children What to Do

Constructivism implies that teachers do not simply lecture and dictate every movement that they expect children to do. Instead, they use techniques such as asking questions and setting problem-solving and exploration tasks during which children actively construct their understanding of the content. Children also make decisions about skills, select equipment and performance techniques to practice, and design games, dances, and gymnastics sequences.

Although this description may sound as if teachers don't tell children what to do, this perception is inaccurate. Constructivist-oriented teachers often tell children what to do and provide explicit information. For example, a teacher might tell children to design a gymnastics sequence with one balance, one roll, and one jump. The teacher may not specify the exact balance, roll, and jump, but the children have clear constraints on what they can do. Moreover, a teacher also may explicitly give children criteria for performance techniques, such as staying tight and pointing their toes.

Fallacy: If You Set an Exploration or Problem-Solving Task, Children Will Figure Everything Out on Their Own

Considerable evidence indicates that "hands-on" learning in which children explore ideas, conduct experiments, or solve problems is effective in engaging children and helping them develop a conceptual understanding of principles. This statement, however, is overly simplistic. For exploration and problem-solving tasks to work correctly, the teacher must carefully structure the experience, attend to children's misconceptions both prior to and during the task, and ensure that children acquire accurate knowledge. Then, the teacher needs to help children make the connections between the concrete, hands-on learning task and the abstract concept or principle. Finally, the teacher needs to help children learn to transfer and apply their knowledge in other settings. None of these steps will happen automatically, and children won't figure everything out on their own, without the guiding hand of the teacher (see **Figure 5.4**).

Fallacy: Being Child Centered Means There Are No Standards

This fallacy comes from the (misguided) idea that being child centered means you allow children to select the content they will learn based on only their interests. If the content includes a creative product, then anything the child produces is acceptable, according to this perception. Both of these statements reflect misunderstandings.

Constructivist-oriented teachers do care about what interests children and what they find relevant and meaningful, but that does not mean that they don't ensure children acquire the skills and knowledge specified in national and state standards. There is room in a standards-based curriculum for children to make choices and to modify activities in ways that are meaningful to them. For example, you might have a class work in small groups on a tactical concept, such as how to maintain possession of the ball by passing quickly, and tell them to design a game to practice that concept. Some groups might design a highly competitive game and keep score, some groups might design a competitive game and not keep score, and other groups might design a game that is more cooperative than competitive. All of these groups will learn the tactical content to the appropriate standard, yet will be able to practice that content in ways of interest to them.

In relation to creative products, clear standards of quality exist for what constitutes an aesthetic and well-designed product in all of the arts and, specifically, in dance and gymnastics in physical education. Teachers sometimes hesitate to apply standards to a child's creative product, believing that

Figure 5.4 Helping children design gymnastics sequences

Courtesy of John Dolly

they will stifle creativity and violate the aim of constructivism to allow children to express their own ideas. In reality, teaching children about standards of quality will help them clarify their ideas and express them in more effective and powerful ways. If taught well, information about standards of quality will enhance, rather than stifle, creativity.

Fallacy: Teachers Stand Back and Do Not Intervene in Group or Individual Work in Constructivist-Oriented Classrooms

Nothing could be further from the truth. Constructivist-oriented teaching means the teacher is highly active monitoring and guiding children's learning. Because children are typically not all doing the same thing at the same time, the teacher must be especially active in responding to the range of activities and scaffolding learning in different ways for different groups and individuals. Scaffolding entails providing enough support and guidance to learners to enable them to successfully perform the activity or learn the concept. Teachers create scaffolding in many ways, including prompting, demonstrating, asking questions, clarifying, giving feedback, redefining tasks, modifying tasks to make them simpler or more difficult, and breaking down the content into more manageable chunks. While the hallmark of constructivist-oriented teaching is active children, this approach requires an equally active teacher to be effective.

Summary

Constructivist learning theory describes how children learn. It provides guidelines for instruction but does not dictate or limit instructional techniques. According to this theory, learning is an active process of constructing knowledge structures that include chunks of information that are well connected to big ideas and transferable to other contexts. Children construct new knowledge based on their prior knowledge, feelings, and experiences. They always have some prior knowledge, feelings, or experience related to what we teach.

When you are child centered, your teaching is based on ongoing assessments of what children are experiencing, feeling, learning, and can do. This approach stands in contrast to a teaching strategy based on a planned progression of tasks that disregards what children's prior knowledge is and what they are successfully or not successfully learning during the lesson. The social interactions of group work can facilitate learning. Both the social and cultural environments are part of what and how children learn.

Review Questions

1. Take a skill you know well (not the example in the chapter), and, using the web in Figure 5.1 as a model, draw a detailed web illustrating your knowledge of the skill and the connections among the chunks of information related to that skill.
2. What does it mean to say, "Learning is an active process of constructing knowledge"?
3. Why is active learning important? What are some teaching techniques that facilitate active learning?
4. What role do prior knowledge, feelings, and experience play in learning? Give an example (not one used in the chapter) of when you experienced the negative or positive effect of your own or someone else's prior knowledge, feelings, or experiences on learning something new.
5. Why is it important to teach relevant thinking skills and knowledge of tactics at the same time?
6. What does it mean to be child centered?
7. Why is group work important in physical education?
8. Describe something negative children will see in the mass media from pop culture (not one of the examples in the chapter), and explain how you can help children recognize why is it inappropriate or harmful to them.
9. Describe two common fallacies about constructivism, and explain why you think these fallacies developed.

References

Alexander, P. A. (2006). *Psychology in learning and instruction.* Upper Saddle River, NJ: Pearson.

Chen, A., Martin, R., Sun, H., & Ennis, C. D. (2007). Is in-class physical activity at risk in constructivist physical education? *Research Quarterly for Exercise and Sport, 78,* 500–509.

Chen, W. (2001). Description of an expert teacher's constructivist-oriented teaching: Engaging students' critical thinking in learning creative dance. *Research Quarterly for Exercise and Sport, 72,* 366–375.

Chen, W., & Rovegno, I. (2000). Examination of expert and novice teachers' constructivist-oriented teaching practices using a movement approach to elementary physical education. *Research Quarterly for Exercise and Sport, 71,* 357–372.

Chi, M., Feltovich, P., & Glaser, R. (1981). Categorization and representation of physical problems by experts and novices. *Cognitive Science, 5,* 121–152.

deGroot, A. D. (1965). *Thought and choice in chess.* The Hague, Netherlands: Mouton.

Dyson, B. (2006). Students' perspectives of physical education. In D. Kirk, D. MacDonald, & M. O'Sullivan (Eds.), *The handbook of physical education* (pp. 326–346). London: Sage.

Eickhoff-Shemek, J. M., Herbert, D. L., & Connaughton, D. P. (2009). *Risk Management for Health/Fitness Professionals: Legal Issues and Strategies.* Philadelphia: Wolters Kluwer/Lippincott Williams & Wilkins.

Ennis, C. D. (1991). Discrete thinking skills in two teachers' physical education classes. *Elementary School Journal, 91*, 473–487.

French, K. E., Nevett, M. E., Spurgeon, J. H., Graham, K. C., Rink, J. E., & McPherson, S. L. (1996). Knowledge and problem solution in youth baseball. *Research Quarterly for Exercise and Sport, 67*, 386–395.

French, K. E., Spurgeon, J. H., & Nevett, M. E. (1995). Expert–novice differences in cognitive and skill execution components of youth baseball performance. *Research Quarterly for Exercise and Sport, 66*, 194–201.

Glaser, R. (1987). Thoughts on expertise. In C. Schooler & W. Schaie (Eds.), *Cognitive functioning and social structure over the life course* (pp. 81–94). Norwood, NJ: Ablex.

Hart, J. E., & Ritson, R. J. (2002). *Liability and Safety in Physical Education and Sport.* Reston, VA: National Association for Sport and Physical Education.

Halsey, J. J. (2005). Risk Management for Physical Educators. In H. Appenzeller, (Ed.). *Risk Management in Sport: Issues and Strategies*, (2nd ed.), (pp. 151–163). Durham, NC: Carolina Academic Press.

Kinchin, G. D. (2006). Sport education: A view of the research. In D. Kirk, D. MacDonald, & M. O'Sullivan (Eds.), *The handbook of physical education* (pp. 596–609). London: Sage.

Lave, J., & Wenger, E. (1991). *Situated learning: Legitimate peripheral participation.* Cambridge, UK: Cambridge University Press.

National Research Council. (1999). *How people learn: Brain, mind, experience, and school.* Washington, DC: National Academies Press.

Nevett, M. E., & French, K. E. (1997). The development of sport-specific planning, rehearsal and updating of plans during defensive youth baseball game performance. *Research Quarterly for Exercise and Sport, 68*, 203–214.

Nohr, K. M. (2009). *Managing Risk in Sport and Recreation: The Essential Guide for Loss Prevention.* Champaign, IL: Human Kinetics.

Oslin, J., & Mitchell, S. (2006). Game-centered approaches to teaching physical education. In D. Kirk, D. MacDonald, & M. O'Sullivan (Eds.), *The handbook of physical education* (pp. 627–651). London: Sage.

Resnick, L. B., & Williams-Hall, M. (1998). Learning organizations for sustainable education reform. *Daedalus, 127*(4), 89–118.

Rogoff, B. (1990). *Apprenticeship in thinking: Cognitive development in social contexts.* New York: Oxford University Press.

Rovegno, I., Chen, W., & Todorovich, J. (2003). Accomplished teachers' pedagogical content knowledge of teaching dribbling to third grade. *Journal of Teaching in Physical Education, 22*, 426–449.

Rovegno, I., & Dolly, J. P. (2006). Constructivist perspectives on learning. In D. Kirk, D. MacDonald, & M. O'Sullivan (Eds.), *The handbook of physical education* (pp. 242–261). London: Sage.

Shen, B., & Chen, A. (2006). Examining the interrelations among knowledge, interests, and learning strategies. *Journal of Teaching in Physical Education, 25*, 182–199.

Slavin, R. E. (1996). Research on cooperative learning and achievement: What we know, what we need to know. *Contemporary Educational Psychology, 21*, 43–69.

Sun, H., & Chen, A. (2010). A pedagogical understanding of the self-determination theory in physical education. *Quest, 62*, 364–384.

Ward, P. (2006). The philosophy, science, and application of behavior analysis in physical education. In D. Kirk, D. MacDonald, & M. O'Sullivan (Eds.), *The handbook of physical education* (pp. 3–20). London: Sage.

CHAPTER

6

Presenting Cognitive Content and Performance Techniques

PRE-READING REFLECTION

1. Reflect on your knowledge of constructivist theories of learning. Predict three teaching techniques that might help children construct knowledge.
2. A child of a friend of yours plays volleyball on a year-round basis. Her high school coach yells out what the team members should do on every hit. Her club coach teaches team members to think about the game situation and decide what to do based on both the immediate game situation (e.g., whether they have a sure scoring opportunity) and the game situation that will occur if the ball is returned. Which coach do you think is more successful? Which coach would you want to have coaching you and your child, and why?

OBJECTIVES

Students will learn:

1. When teaching new content, it is best to start by activating children's prior knowledge and experiences.
2. Children will practice more persistently if they understand the value of what they are learning.
3. Asking questions is a primary teaching technique for eliciting prior knowledge and helping children make connections and construct knowledge.
4. Making connections and teaching for transfer help children construct robust knowledge.
5. When presenting new information, it is best to be brief and clear, focus on a few performance techniques, and use stories, metaphors, and images to help children understand and remember information.
6. Demonstrations are critical for helping children learn.

KEY TERMS

Bloom's taxonomy
Cold calling
Critical performance techniques
Eliciting tasks
Inquiry-oriented teaching
Peer assessment
Personal interest
Situational interest
Teaching for transfer

CONNECTIONS TO STANDARDS

This chapter focuses on teaching the cognitive content from National Standards 2 and 3. In addition, we discuss how you can meet the Common Core and other State Standards (CCSS) for vocabulary acquisition that address making connections between words and concepts and their use in real-life situations and understanding the meaning of metaphors.

Introduction

In this chapter, we discuss facilitating children's construction of knowledge. Acquiring knowledge about skills and concepts is a critical part of physical education and is the focus of National Standards 2 and 3 (SHAPE, 2014). From principles of health-related physical activity to tactical concepts, principles of choreography, movement concepts, and the performance techniques of skills, teachers help children construct knowledge in every lesson and apply that knowledge while performing skills and physical activities.

You may recall that children learn by constructing knowledge. In turn, a critical role of the teacher is to encourage children's active thinking and engagement during the learning process. One primary way teachers do this is through **inquiry-oriented teaching**—that is, by setting exploration, creative and critical thinking, problem-solving, and decision-making tasks and asking questions. These teaching strategies require children to think and engage actively in constructing knowledge.

Asking Questions

A primary teaching technique for helping children construct knowledge is asking questions (see **Figure 6.1**). Questions differ in terms of the amount and complexity of cognitive processing required for the child to answer them. Teachers often use **Bloom's taxonomy** (which you probably studied in your educational psychology course) to determine the level of cognitive processing required for questions, tasks, and lesson objectives (Bloom, Engelhart, Furst, Hill, & Krathwohl, 1956). Bloom's taxonomy describes six levels of cognitive processing (see **Table 6.1**). We typically think of Levels 1 to 3 as requiring lower-order thinking and Levels 4 to 6 as requiring higher-order thinking. Although most of the time teachers ask lower-order questions, it is important to also plan higher-order questions for each lesson.

Even beginning teachers should get in the habit of asking questions whenever possible. Start your lessons with questions that will stimulate interest, review information pertinent to the new lesson, or get children engaged in the topic. Put feedback in the form of a question. During the lesson, ask questions that check whether children understand what you are teaching. Close the lesson with questions asking children what they learned. Plan ahead of time to ask questions that require children to think about and discuss the ideas you are teaching. Ask open-ended questions that may have multiple answers. Ask questions that require children to make connections. Write questions on a whiteboard that students can refer to during the lesson. The more you learn to ask questions, the more your children will construct knowledge that they remember and is meaningful to them.

Wait Time

Research has shown that increasing teachers' wait time is effective in improving children's learning. Wait time is the amount of time a teacher waits after asking a question before calling on

Figure 6.1 Asking questions

Courtesy of John Dolly

Table 6.1 Bloom's Taxonomy of Educational Objectives

Level 1: Knowledge

Recalling information; vocabulary terms; methods for performing; and principles already taught. Sample questions:

- What are the performance techniques for catching a ball that you learned in the last lesson?
- What does "accelerate" mean?

Level 2: Comprehension

Understanding and being able to use the information; explaining; summarizing; predicting; extending an idea; and reordering or rearranging parts. Sample questions:

- What are two ways to use the boundaries on defense to deny offensive players space?
- Predict how this game will change if we add another player.
- What is another example of a movement that works on arm strength?

Level 3: Application

Applying abstract ideas, principles, and concepts to different situations. Sample questions:

- In dance yesterday, you learned to add a contrast in speed and levels to make your dance sequence more interesting. How can you apply the idea of contrast to improve your gymnastics sequence today?
- How can you set up your defense in this net game to deny space for the offense to score?

Level 4: Analysis

Categorizing, classifying, breaking down a whole into parts; identifying relationships among elements; identifying a hierarchy of principles or ideas. Sample questions and tasks:

- As a team, analyze how and why you were successful on offense. Then tell your opponents what they did that allowed you to score easily.
- Compare and contrast Louisa's and Shakita's dance sequences.
- Compare and contrast the four balls we used for striking.

Level 5: Synthesis

Creating something new by combining ideas or elements; designing or composing a new whole from multiple parts; developing abstract principles from a set of concrete experiences or basic information. Sample questions and tasks:

- With a partner, discuss what you learned about matching, contrasting, and complementing shapes, and create a partner gymnastics sequence that has variety and originality of shapes.
- Working in groups of four, design a game that will allow you to practice getting free from a defender and cutting into open spaces to receive passes.
- Ask yourselves, "Which tactics did your opponents use that were successful?" Then devise a way to counteract them.

Level 6: Evaluation

Critiquing something based on a set of criteria; making judgments based on evidence and standards; and making recommendations based on criteria. Sample questions and tasks:

- What is your opinion of the aesthetic qualities of your partner's dance sequence?
- Based on the criteria for designing a good health-related physical activity plan, assess your own plan and justify your choices.
- As a team, evaluate the tactics you used in the game and find at least two ways to improve them.

Source: Data from Bloom, B. S., Engelhart, M. D., Furst, E. J., Hill, W. H., & Krathwohl, D. R. (1956). *Taxonomy of educational objectives—Handbook 1: The cognitive domain*. New York: McKay.

a child. It is also the amount of time a teacher waits after the child answers for that child to expand on his or her answer or for other children to offer additional information. Long wait times—12 seconds or longer—will encourage more students to respond and lead to more complex answers, better discussions, more confidence, less confusion, and improved quality of answers to higher-order questions (Orlich, Harder, Callahan, & Gibson, 2001). Silence can be worrisome to a new teacher, but if you remember the benefits of wait time for children's learning you will soon become comfortable asking questions, pausing, and watching the nonverbal reactions of the children before calling on a child to answer. If the silence bothers you, say, "Take your time and think."

What If I Ask a Question but the Children Don't Know the Answer or Answer Incorrectly?

Your response depends on why you asked the question. If you asked a question to find out what children learned previously or outside of your class and no one knows the answer, then provide the answer yourself.

If you asked an application, analysis, synthesis, or evaluation question to generate information based on children's experiences during the lesson, give them time to discuss the question with a partner or in groups. Prompt them with additional questions that will help elicit ideas. Most higher-order questions have multiple correct and viable answers, and children will readily offer at least some answers.

Sometimes, however, children may answer with inaccurate information that, if uncorrected, will hinder their further learning. If this occurs, you must make sure that you get a correct and complete answer.

There are several ways to achieve this goal. If a student gives an incorrect answer, ask another student for the answer, and then ask the original student the question again. This practice sends the message that although you got the wrong answer, you can still learn the right answer. Calling on the original child again prevents children from saying, "I don't know," simply to avoid participating in class (Lemov, 2010).

Other techniques to correct erroneous answers are to clarify the part of the question the child did not understand and then ask the child the question again. Sometimes if you simply ask a child, "What was your thinking on that?" the child will self-correct as he or she explains the answer. You can also reiterate the part of the answer the child gave correctly and then ask for more information about other parts (Orlich et al., 2001). For example, if you ask, "What is an open passing lane?" and a child answers, "Where you pass the ball," you can say, "Great start; that's where you pass the ball. Now tell us more about an open passing lane." As Lemov (2010) suggests, don't accept an answer that is partially correct, and don't be tempted to simply repeat the part of the answer the child got right and then add the rest of the answer yourself. Let the children know what was right, and ask questions to get the rest of the answer.

When children give an incorrect or incomplete answer, it is important to avoid being negative because such a response may cause not only that child, but also other children, to avoid participating in class discussions. Of course, it is equally important for that child and the rest of the class to learn the correct and complete answer. Let children know that if they give an incorrect or incomplete answer, someone—either you or a classmate—will help them get it right.

Challenges Teachers Face in Asking Questions

Research has shown that teachers face six challenges when asking questions (Orlich et al., 2001). First, teachers tend to repeat questions and explanations, often three times. This repetition wastes time. Even worse, if children know you will repeat a question or an explanation, they will not listen to you until the third time, if they listen at all. Train yourself to ask questions or give instructions only one time. Speak slowly and clearly, and then wait for the children to respond. Even if children's classroom teachers have trained them not to listen the first time a teacher says something, they will quickly learn that in your class they must listen the first time.

Second, teachers tend to repeat students' responses. This habit also wastes time, and it does not reinforce the idea that children are viable sources of information. Children won't bother listening to other children if they know you will repeat the answer.

Third, teachers tend to ask and then answer their own questions. Again, this practice lets children know that they don't really need to think about an answer because the teacher is the source of information.

Fourth, some teachers ask a question but then do not watch the children or appear to be interested in hearing them respond.

Fifth, some teachers interrupt when children are answering and don't let them finish talking. Both of these behaviors cause children to stop participating and stop trying to think on their own.

Sixth, teachers sometimes select the same children to answer questions, which suggests to their classmates that those children are "special" in the teacher's eye. Children are very quick to notice who teachers appear to like best. Playing favorites will cause a decrease in other children's attempts to contribute to class discussions. It is all too easy to fall into the trap of calling on the same children because you know they will give a correct answer and you want to move on. Try to remember that your responsibility is to teach all children; answering questions allows quiet children to participate and enables you to know what all children know. Good teachers make it a habit to call on every student at some point. This practice lets students know you expect everyone to be thinking about the answer and to participate (Lemov, 2010).

Cold Call

Increasingly, teachers and researchers are recommending teachers to not have children raise their hands to indicate that they want to answer a question (McTighe & Wiggins, 2013). Instead, they suggest you rely on the "cold call" strategy (Lemov, 2010, p. 111). **Cold call** means you always select who will answer the question. Students soon learn that they can't avoid participating in class because you will call on them at some point in time. Nor can they sit and not listen, knowing that if they don't raise their hands they can avoid engaging in the lesson.

Reinforcing that Children Are Viable Sources of Information

When children answer questions or work on exploration, problem-solving, or decision-making tasks, it is critical that they look to themselves and to other students as possible sources of information. In summarizing the research, Alexander (2006) reports that teachers must emphasize that knowledge can come from many sources, including the children themselves. If children look to the teacher as the only source of information, then they will simply try to figure out and then tell the teacher what he or she wants to hear and will be unwilling to take risks to think on their own. To avoid this problem, Alexander (2006) suggests that teachers create a risk-free environment that is open to new ideas from multiple sources.

For example, in games lessons, it is critical that children learn to think of and devise tactics. If they move only when and where the teacher tells them to move, they will never develop into skilled games players—which requires quick thinking and tactical decision making on the field. Likewise, if the teacher does not allow students to explore and make decisions in dance

Figure 6.2 Children solving problems with the dance sequences they are designing

and gymnastics, they will not develop their creative and critical thinking abilities, nor will they learn to trust their own judgments. For children to move beyond basic skills in games, dance, and gymnastics, teachers must provide opportunities for them to make decisions, think critically and creatively, solve problems, explore, and answer questions (see **Figure 6.2**).

Eliciting Children's Prior Knowledge

Research shows that children's prior knowledge has a strong influence on their learning of new information. When teachers attend to children's prior knowledge, their reactivation of this memory facilitates learning. There is no true "first" day. As one expert teacher said, "Students always bring something to the table."

Figure Out What Children Already Know

The first guideline implied by the research findings is to start by figuring out what children already know (see **Figure 6.3**). If you are about to teach a skill you have never taught students before, ask them what they know about that skill. If you are starting a unit by reviewing a skill you taught the previous year, ask questions and elicit a review of the skill from the children. With this approach, you can determine what they remember and what they don't.

Don't Reteach What Students Already Know—Build on It

More significantly, if children already know something, you don't need to teach it again. Students can get very bored at the beginning of a unit if teachers repeat explanations about performance techniques and then have children repeat the same drills year after year. Children may not throw at a mature level,

Figure 6.3 Eliciting children's prior knowledge

but if they are cognitively aware of the performance techniques, you can elicit this information from them and begin with tasks designed to build on their existing levels of knowledge and skill development.

Listen for Possible Misconceptions

Sometimes children's prior knowledge includes misconceptions, especially in the area of health-related physical activity and fitness. For example, research shows that students often believe that if they do sit-ups, they will lose their abdominal fat (Placek, Griffin, Dodds, Raymond, Tremino, & James, 2001). They also believe that fitness equals being thin and that you can sweat off fat in saunas. In games, children believe that the goalie cannot come out and steal the ball until the opponent shoots. If you assess students' prior knowledge, you can then address their misconceptions directly through planned activities that can help them refine their understanding.

Making Connections

Making Connections to Understand the Value of New Content

Many state and national guidelines for effective teaching suggest that teachers tell children what they will be learning, what the goals of the lesson are, and why the content is valuable to learn. Research on motivation and constructivism clearly shows that children will learn more and practice more persistently if they understand the value of what they are learning and if the content has meaning for them (Alexander, 2006; Solmon, 2006). Thus, teachers need to find ways to make content relevant to, and valued by, children.

One way to help children understand the value of content is to explain how the new content connects to skills, concepts, tactics, and activities students will learn later on. For example, you might explain how being skilled at catching in all areas of their personal space will help them be good at softball, football, and basketball in middle school or how a good dancer is admired within adolescent cultures.

What the Research Says

Situational and Personal Interest

Dr. Ang Chen and his colleagues have studied **situational interest**, which is interest in an activity created by a teacher in a school situation. **Personal interest** is interest that students already possess based on their own experiences or opinions of activities. What is important is that teachers can create situational interest even in activities children might not find personally interesting (A. Chen, 2001; Chen, Ennis, Martin, & Sun, 2006). At the elementary school level, teachers can get children interested in learning new content by designing tasks that meet one of the following criteria: The tasks (1) are novel; (2) are challenging; (3) demand the children's attention; (4) give them opportunities to explore; or (5) are instantly enjoyable (A. Chen, 2001; Sun, Chen, Ennis, Martin, & Shen, 2008).

A second way to help children find content meaningful is to help them understand connections to their prior knowledge and experiences, other classroom subjects, and their lives outside of school, thereby making the new information personally meaningful. For example, in gymnastics, learning to jump, land, and roll—a maneuver called "safety rolling"—is relevant because it can keep children safe from injury when they fall, whether at school or outside of school. It can be meaningful to them when they recognize the use of safety rolling by actors on television during chase scenes or by paratroopers. Safety rolls are also relevant to other sports—for example, in diving to catch a football and diving to do a forearm pass in volleyball, followed by rolls to safely control momentum and recover to the feet.

Content doesn't have to be relevant or interesting to children before you teach it. Research in physical education shows that teachers can create interest in activities, even in activities students have not found personally interesting prior to the lesson (Chen & Darst, 2001; Chen & Ennis, 2004). During lessons, teachers can help children understand the value and significance of new content, leading them to become excited about learning new activities. For example, just because children don't think dance is relevant before they have learned any dance, it does not mean they won't find it relevant once they are engaged in a dance unit (Shen, Chen, Tolley, & Scrabis, 2003).

Making Connections to Build Robust Knowledge and meet CCSS

In addition to helping students understand the relevance and value of new content, making connections helps children build robust knowledge structures. The goal of building robust knowledge structures—which have multiple connections to other concepts—is one reason the CCSS require students to identify real-life connections between words and their use (Common Core State Standards Initiative, 2010a). For example, the movement concept of pressing in dance is defined as slow movements using strong force and firm tension in the muscles. Pressing can be connected to the following real-life situations:

- Pulling something heavy
- A weight lifter lifting a heavy weight
- A boa constrictor squeezing a victim
- A tug-of-war
- Bracing yourself against a strong wind
- The pressure of the earth forming diamonds

Consequently, to help children meet CCSS whenever possible, help children make connections between the content you are teaching real-life situations. For example, you might start a lesson by saying, "Last week we worked on different pathways in dance. What were three different pathways? [Straight, curved, and angular.] Right. Now think about what you did playing outdoors yesterday. Did you travel on straight, curved, or angular pathways? What were you doing? Let's think about the letters that you are learning to write. Which letters have straight pathways? Curved pathways? Angular pathways? Great answers. Today we will be traveling on different pathways while dribbling."

Following this line of inquiry, when children learn to dribble on different pathways, they will be applying the movement concept of pathways in a new context making a new connection. Such integration of concepts in different contexts will contribute to a more robust, well-connected knowledge structure.

Literacy researchers suggest several strategies for teaching concepts and vocabulary words (Ruddell, 2009). Vocabulary words are learned most effectively in context, whether that context is an informational text or a movement task, because the context gives children information about the meaning of the word. Either before or during the lesson when, in the context, *children need to know* what a word means, you can ask the children if anyone knows or has some clues about what the word might mean. Next, clarify the meaning of the word, or, if you had no answers from the children, directly define the word briefly. Then, return to your lesson using the word or concept in the movement context.

Then, discuss the meaning of the word or concept during lesson closure. By waiting until the end of the lesson, children will have experienced using the word in context during the lesson, giving them some understanding upon which you can build more robust knowledge. Suggestions for closure are listed next:

- On a whiteboard, draw a web with the movement concept (or the new word) in the center. Then have the class generate words or describe real-life situations related to the central movement concept and write the students responses as the ends of the spokes of the web. Having children read the words is critical because the goal is to extend their use of the new word in reading, writing, and speaking. It is important for children to understand that words can be spelled differently from the way they sound.
- Have students in pairs discuss and then share with the class real-life connections between the movement concept and events, images, objects, emotions, or other contexts. They can also discuss antonyms for one of more of the vocabulary words.

In addition to making connections to real-life situations, whenever possible, try to help children make connections to classroom content. For example, the following is a list of gymnastics concepts that connect with classroom content:

- Symmetrical, asymmetrical, and congruent shapes are taught in mathematics and are required concepts in the CCSS (Common Core State Standards Initiative, 2010b).
- Sequencing is taught in literacy.
- Balance and force are taught in science.
- Choreographic principles of line, unity, contrast, originality, and aesthetic highlights are taught in art.
- Transitions are taught in story writing.

Talking to children's classroom teachers about what you are teaching and what the children are learning in the classroom is a good way to identify possible connections. Moreover, it is good politics to let classroom teachers know that you think their content is important enough for you to reinforce it in physical education. If you don't talk to the classroom teachers, they will not have a clue about what you are doing.

Finally, research suggests that when children understand how parts connect to big ideas, and how big ideas connect to other big ideas, they are more likely to transfer their knowledge to new situations. In summarizing the research, Alexander (2006) concluded,

> There seems to be no question that transfer is an essential dimension of competent performance in any complex domain: Students cannot achieve competence in history, mathematics, reading, or any other field without applying knowledge across tasks and across contexts (p. 140).

Making Connections to Teach for Transfer

Teaching for transfer means that you want children to be able to use and apply the skills, movement concepts, and tactics you teach in one context within other contexts. For example, we teach children in the lower elementary grades skills such as throwing and catching so that they will be able to use these skills effectively in different games in the upper elementary grades. We teach basic tactics such as receiving and passing quickly before the defense can reposition its members so that children can transfer this knowledge to basketball-type, soccer-type, and hockey-type games. The content of games, dance, and gymnastics in this text is organized around big ideas (using the Laban framework to label concepts whenever relevant) in an effort to facilitate the transfer of learning from one context to another.

Transfer, however, does not happen automatically—you have to explicitly teach for transfer by helping children make connections between previously learned content and new content and by helping them understand similarities and differences in performance when the context changes. For example, the movement patterns of an overhand throw and an overhead striking action share certain similarities. Motor learning research suggests that the more similar the movement patterns of skills, the more likely there will be positive transfer. Pointing out the similarities (and differences) to throwing (a skill they typically learn much earlier) can be helpful for giving children a general idea about how to perform the movement pattern of an overhead strike in volleyball (Magill, 2011).

What the Research Says

Comparing and Contrasting

The research suggests that comparing and contrasting help children construct robust knowledge structures. For the teacher, it is critical to help students identify similarities and differences between concepts, skills, tactics, and contexts in which skills and tactics are used, or whatever content you are teaching. This effort leads to better transfer (Alexander, 2006).

More significantly, research suggests that for transfer to occur, children must understand the concept deeply. In particular, they must spend time using these concepts in a variety of contexts (Alexander, 2006). For example, teaching children that defenders stand on the goal side of the offensive players (which is not a simple concept for children to learn) takes practice in many different situations before children will easily transfer that tactical concept to new contexts.

Presenting New Information: Brevity and Clarity

Although assigning problem-solving, creative thinking, and exploration tasks is central to helping children construct knowledge, as a teacher you will often present new information explicitly. Regardless of the age of students, it is critical when you teach students how to perform a new skill or tactic to limit the amount of information you introduce at one time. A problem that is not uncommon, especially for beginning teachers, is to teach a skill by describing thoroughly how to perform the skill. For example, teachers may describe the starting position, actions of each major body component, and ending position. No learner can remember all that information. As one report on motor learning research states, "Short-term memory (STM) for once-presented materials is limited in capacity to just a few items [and] forgetting is rapid (occurring in about 30 seconds)....Therefore, practitioners should remember that if their instructions contain more than one or two key points, learners are likely to forget them before they get around to attempting the skill" (Schmidt & Wrisberg, 2004, p. 222).

The issue of brevity is even more critical at the elementary level because young children often have very short attention spans. The KISS principle—Keep It Short and Simple—is an essential guideline for elementary-age children. Try lecturing to a class of children about how to perform a skill and you will soon see them fidget—impatient to be moving—or become bored (see **Figure 6.4**). Even if they appear to be listening, it is likely that they are thinking about something other than your lecture.

Children may also get confused when presented with overly technical information. As a teacher, you need to plan how to parse complex information into clear, brief statements. You might wonder how children will know what to do if you don't explain how to perform the skill. In fact, children need

Figure 6.4 Children listening to a teacher who is lecturing too long

Keeper of the Word

When introducing children to new vocabulary words and performance cues, it helps to assign one child to be the "keeper of the word." (Write the assigned word next to the child's name on the class list so you can keep track of who has which word and who doesn't have a word yet.) That child is responsible for remembering the word and its meaning. All performance techniques, movement concepts, and any new terms will have a keeper of the word. It won't take long before everyone in the class is the keeper of at least one word. When a child asks you a question about a word, you tell him or her to ask the keeper of that word. This method contributes to creating a community of learners who rely on one another, not just on the teacher, for knowledge.

only a demonstration and one simple, brief cue to start learning a skill. Moreover, they cannot think about more than one performance technique at a time (even adults have problems thinking of more than one at a time).

Focus on a Few Critical Performance Techniques

Research on expert elementary physical educators has shown that across a unit, expert teachers teach children only two to four performance cues for each skill (Rovegno, Chen, & Todorovich, 2003). As a teacher, you want to select the most **critical performance techniques**—the key elements of the skill that will help children make the most improvement.

For example, expert teachers tend to teach the same performance techniques for dribbling with the hand, although each teacher introduces only about three of the following cues:

- Push with your finger pads; don't slap the ball.
- Dribble at a waist-high level.
- Keep the ball to the front and side.
- Keep your eyes and head up.

These performance techniques are critical, not trivial. The first three are critical for ball control and the last three are critical dribbling tactics—that is, dribbling waist high or lower and to the front and side, with your body protecting the ball, makes it more difficult for defenders to steal the ball, and keeping your eyes up enables you to see defenders and teammates. Presenting other information about dribbling, such as the angle of the bend at the knees and hips and the action of the shoulder and elbow, would likely prove overwhelming to children, for whom such technical information is not critical to learning the skill or using it later in game situations.

We also recommend that you teach only one performance technique at a time. Across several days in a unit, you can teach two or three performance techniques by having children focus on one technique each day. If you focus on one at a time, you can ensure children understand the technique and know how to concentrate on it during practice. As they become more knowledgeable, they can think critically about their skill performance and select the performance technique on which they will focus.

How Do You Know Which Performance Techniques Are Best to Teach?

Studying the content is critical for learning which performance techniques are most important to teach. Although you might be an expert baseball player, your status as an athlete does not mean you are an expert at teaching throwing to young children. The research on expertise reveals that experts often cannot describe what they know, especially to a beginner. A study of four teachers teaching jumping noted that the teacher who produced the greatest improvements in children's jumping had studied jumping just prior to the start of the study (Werner & Rink, 1989). We know that the best teachers continuously study their content to improve their teaching.

Many professional resources are available to help you get started. Physical education methods texts, such as this one, include many suggestions. The *Journal of Physical Education, Recreation, and Dance* and *Strategies* regularly include articles on teaching skills. *Teaching Cues for Basic Sport Skills* by Fronske and Wilson (2002) also is an excellent source. Finally, the Internet provides a wealth of information from teachers, coaches, sport organizations, and participants about teaching skills. As you study and gain experience with teaching skills and carefully observing children's responses, you will figure out which performance techniques are most effective for helping children learn in your school.

Select the Performance Technique Based on Children's Developmental Levels

The art of selecting performance techniques is in choosing those that are most critical in relation to children's developmental levels. For example, pushing the ball, rather than slapping it, is the most basic technique to teach for dribbling, while keeping your head up is more appropriate for children who have already acquired basic ball control.

Some skills, such as throwing and batting, take many years of practice before children develop the mature form. With these skills, you might focus on one to three performance techniques per year. As children's skills develop, you progress to more difficult performance techniques.

Is Teaching Performance Techniques Always Helpful?

The research literature, in general, supports the importance of students learning critical performance techniques related to skills and tactics but suggests that the information presented during such lessons needs to be brief and clear (Rink, 2001). *In general* means that for some skills, teaching performance techniques will not impact all components of the skill (Weimar, Martin, & Wall, 2011). In addition, research also indicates that students can learn skills through **eliciting tasks**—tasks designed to elicit a particular movement pattern or performance technique through task and/or environmental constraints designed by the teacher—without having to hear explicit information.

A few studies, however, have found that providing some kinds of information about how to perform certain skills could be detrimental to learning. In their study, Wulf and Weigelt (1997) taught two groups of students how to perform a slalom ski action on a ski simulator, which is a small platform that slides on two arched rails. One group was given no information on how to perform the skill, whereas the second group was given the correct biomechanical information to operate the simulator—namely, to push down on the platform by extending the knees after the platform reached the top of the arch. Those participants who were not given any biomechanical information learned the skill faster and maintained a higher level of performance when tested for retention.

What is important to remember about the Wulf and Weigelt study, and about all research in this area, is that researchers typically study *only* one movement with one age group. Based on one or even several studies, you cannot generalize the findings to all age groups and all skills. What works for one skill may not work for another; there are always exceptions to the rules.

How do you know whether teaching performance techniques are a help or a hindrance? In general, such instruction is helpful, but you must be open-minded and willing to question whether the performance technique you selected is effective in a particular situation. Beginning teachers want to know the right way to teach and exactly what they need to do, but you cannot avoid the fact that teaching isn't a simple process—it is an art as well as a science. When you teach a performance technique, carefully observe your children, and note how your instruction influences their skill development. A performance technique that is helpful to one child might not be helpful to another. If you are an observant, reflective teacher, you will be able to make these judgments, and with experience you will acquire a teaching repertoire that supports student learning.

The Value of Guided Peer Assessments for Learning

Peer assessments can make a significant contribution to what and the extent to which students learn. When teachers prepare a checklist or other assessment tool that describes specifically what peer assessors need to look for and assess in their partners, this is called peer assessment. Research has shown that students learn and retain more than students doing the same lesson without the peer assessment tool (Iserbyt, Elen, & Behets, 2010; Vande Broek, Boen, Claessens, Feys, & Ceux, 2011). The reason peer assessment works is because the specific performance techniques or actions the students are supposed to learn that lesson is described in detail, focusing students' attention on the learning objective and reinforcing knowledge acquisition. More significantly, however, the peer assessors are actively using that knowledge to make judgments about peers' performances. Using knowledge repeatedly in a meaningful context contributes to robust knowledge.

Using Metaphors, Stories, and Images to Teach Performance Techniques

The CCSS require students to explain the meaning of metaphors and similes in context. In physical education, we frequently use metaphors to describe performance techniques of

SAFETY AND LIABILITY 6.1

Increasing Safety and Decreasing Risk of Liability: Guidelines Relevant to Content in this Chapter

In this box, we discuss specific guidelines built on information discussed earlier in this text on professional standards of practice, negligence, and liability. The goals of these guidelines are to increase children's safety and decrease teachers' risk of negligence and liability.

- To decrease risk of liability for negligence, provide instruction about appropriate and safe performance of all skills and physical activities and about safety procedures for all tasks and activities. In addition, warn students of inherent dangers within these skills and physical activities, as well as behaviors that can lead to injury (Hart & Ritson, 2002; Halsey, 2005).
- Select performance techniques for instruction that match the children's developmental levels.
- Elicit children's prior knowledge of and misconceptions about safety and safe and appropriate ways to perform skills in order to understand what you need to teach to ensure the children understand safety procedures and performance.
- Teach children the connections between following rules and personal and peers' safety and the connections between disregarding safety procedures and getting injured as a result.
- Teach children to think critically about skills, tasks, and physical activities and to self-identify potential dangers and behaviors that can lead to injuries. Then discuss as a class what they identified.
- Teach children why rules and safety procedures are important so these rules and procedures become personally meaningful to them and not simply rules they must follow to please the teacher.

skills and movement quality in dance and gymnastics. Metaphors help students better understand how they need to move, and, in turn, they learn the meaning of the metaphor.

Expert teachers have been noted to tell stories and use images and metaphors to teach performance techniques (W. Chen, 2001). In teaching the hand position of dribbling, for example, experts might say, "Your hand is like a spider," (fingers curved and spread on top of the ball) or, "The ball is like an egg" (that you push rather than slap). In teaching throwing, one expert described the immature arm position with the elbow bent and palm facing up near the shoulders looking like a server carrying a pizza to a restaurant table. She'd joke, "No pizza for lunch," to remind children to lift their elbow to shoulder height. The following are some of the many metaphors you can use when teaching skills:

- Give; be like a sponge to absorb the force of the ball when catching.
- No loose, floppy fish ankles when kicking a ball.
- Don't grip the hockey stick like a broom.
- When shooting a ball in a basket, follow through like a duck's head.
- The ball should make a McDonald's arch when you shoot.
- Cut on a straight pathway to receive a pass, not on a banana pathway.
- When setting a volleyball, follow through with Superman arms.

Here is a longer example of using a metaphor to help children remember performance cues—in this case, "pencil legs" (see **Figure 6.5**):

Pencil Legs

Keeping legs straight with feet and toes pointed is a critical performance technique for almost all gymnastics skills. Your legs and feet should be straight and end in a point just like a pencil. Therefore, when I mention the performance technique "pencil legs" or "sharpen your pencils," you know that I am reminding you to point your feet and toes and keep your legs straight.

Children love to laugh, and they love hearing stories. If you joke and tell stories about performance techniques, your teaching will both capture their attention and help them remember what you're teaching them. For example, in teaching children to shoot a basketball, teachers in one school tell the children to make a duck's head when they follow through. To help the children aim their fingers at the hoop rather than follow through too low, they say, "But don't drown the duck by sticking its bill in the water."

Figure 6.5 Pencil legs
Courtesy of John Dolly

Sample *Question Me* Assignment

An excellent idea for helping children remember big ideas, major concepts, or simply vocabulary terms is to send home a sheet with three to five questions that parents can ask children about content taught in PE that week. Briefly explain what you taught, put the questions in italics, and include the answers. Here is a sample.

Question Me!

There are several concepts students need to understand so they can become skillful game players. This week we have focused on the offense and defense. Ask your child to answer the following questions (in italics) about their PE lessons. The answers are provided.

1. *In a game, who is on offense?* The team with the ball that is trying to score.
2. *In a game, who is on defense?* The team without the ball that is trying to steal it and/or keep the other team from scoring.
3. *What is a passing lane?* It is the space between the player with the ball and a teammate with no defenders in the lane.
4. *Why is it important for the offense to keep the passing lane open?* Open passing lanes allow the offense to pass the ball toward the goal to score. If a defender blocks the passing lane, the possibility of interception (loss of possession) is high.
5. *What helps you to decide when to pass?* The location of the defender and how close I am to the goal.

Most of the time, however, children practice skills without a teacher standing next to them, reminding them to think about a particular performance technique; they need to have knowledge that supports practicing independently. Here is a story to capture children's attention and help them remember a performance technique essential for safety. You can modify the story to be about Nearly Headless Suzanne, a cousin of Nearly Headless Nick from the Harry Potter stories, or use it as a Halloween story about the Headless Roller for classes that learned about Ichabod Crane and the *Legend of Sleepy Hollow*.

Use Strong Arms When You Roll to Protect Your Head

This is the story of the headless roller. It is like the story of the headless horseman who rode through Sleepy Hollow, scaring people on Halloween. The headless roller is a ghost named Todd who lived a long time ago. Todd loved gymnastics, and he loved the thrill of doing dangerous things. His teacher told him to always use strong arms to protect his head, but Todd thought it would be much more fun to throw his body in the air like a ghost and then not worry about the landing—ghosts don't have a solid body, so landings are not a problem for them. So Todd ignored his teacher and thought he could fly like a ghost. And one day that is just what happened: Todd became a ghost and no one ever saw him again because he became the headless roller.

Demonstrations

In addition to presenting content verbally, physical education teachers use demonstrations as a highly effective way to show children what to do. The adage "A picture is worth a thousand words" certainly applies to teaching physical education. One reason demonstrations are essential is that some children learn more easily visually, by seeing what they need to do, whereas others benefit more orally, from hearing instructions. Consequently, teachers need to both show and tell children what they want them to learn and how the task is organized.

Setting Up the Demonstration

Before you demonstrate or have a child demonstrate, you need to organize your class so that children will be able to see the demonstration. This means every child must have an unobstructed view of your presentation.

In addition, be aware that it is difficult to see with sun glare. If you are outside, position children so you face the sun and the children have their backs to the sun. If you are in a location with distractions, such as multiple classes being taught simultaneously, recess, traffic, or construction, demonstrate the task in a corner, along a wall, or with the children's backs to the distraction.

Finally, make sure the children will see the action from the most appropriate angle. For example, if you want to demonstrate the body positions in the flight phase of a jump, the children need to see the body from the side. From this angle, they can see the extension of the legs and the reach of the arms in flight.

Cuing Children on What to Look For

When watching a demonstration, children will not know which components are important to watch and which are not. They may focus on the color of the demonstrator's shirt or the ball and not even look at your movements. Before demonstrating, tell them what to look at and what is important.

One way to help children construct knowledge about skills through demonstrations is to have them watch a particular child who is successful and then see if they can figure out why. For example, you might say, "Juan and Jill have been very successful at holding their balance. Watch as they demonstrate how they do this, and tell me what you see."

Demonstrating Fully

A common problem with beginning teachers is the tendency to do partial demonstrations—what dancers call marking or walking through a dance. You need to demonstrate the task fully, doing the full skill or action at the appropriate energy level and speed. If you look lackadaisical or lethargic, the children will copy your movements and energy level. In addition, if the practice situation involves four children, then demonstrate it with four children—not you and one other student.

You can effectively demonstrate the task in slow motion to emphasize critical body positions. You can also demonstrate one portion of a skill, such as the arm action of the jump. Even with these demonstrations, however, you need to pay attention to your energy level and the position of your whole body so children will understand how the part works in relation to an accurate whole.

Some research suggests children learn better from a peer demonstrating at a comparable developmental level. If you have a child demonstrate, ask the child in advance if he or she is willing, and be sure you have observed them perform the technique you want to show the class. Be conscious of equity and diversity in who you ask to demonstrate (e.g., equal numbers of boys and girls, children of different ethnicities and races, and both high- and low-skilled children demonstrating something they do well).

There are Always Exceptions

Although demonstrations are valuable, there are always exceptions to any rule about teaching. One study examined the effects of a teacher demonstrating and describing the mature arm and leg actions of the hop to kindergartners. The researchers found that following this lesson, the hopping patterns of 78% of the children were disrupted (Roberton, Halverson, & Harper, 1997). In other words, demonstrating and describing the mature pattern did more harm than good! The demonstration was not developmentally aligned with the children's capabilities. For teaching hopping, the most important thing to do is to give children lots of practice. When they can do several hops in a row without losing control or their balance, have them hop for longer distances. As they continue to improve, have them attempt to travel a longer distance with each hop. The task of hopping for distance will bring out more mature arm and leg patterns.

Assessing Your Teaching

On the text website, we provide a rubric based on the work of Weiyun Chen (1997) that will help you self-assess your teaching in terms of the information presented in this chapter.

Experienced Teachers Talk

Teaching Children to Ignore Distractions

Here is a story I tell my children when we have distractions that cannot be avoided:

How many of you have ever been watching cartoons when your mother says, "Why don't you come when I call you?" Of course, you're thinking to yourself, "I never heard her." That happened because you were concentrating so hard on the cartoon that you blocked out any distractions. The kind of concentration that kept you from hearing any other noise is what you need to do today while I am talking.

Summary

To help children construct new knowledge, start by activating their prior knowledge and experiences. Teach them the value of what they are learning. Asking questions is a primary teaching technique for eliciting prior knowledge and helping children make connections and construct knowledge. When you ask questions about the content you taught, be sure the child gives a correct and complete answer before continuing with the lesson; don't settle for partially correct answers. Give children plenty of time to think about the answers to your questions.

Making connections and teaching for transfer help children construct robust knowledge that they can then transfer to new situations. Make these connections explicit.

When presenting new information about skills, be brief and clear, focus on a few critical performance techniques, select performance techniques related to children's developmental levels, and use stories, metaphors, and images to help children understand and remember information.

Demonstrations are critical for helping children learn. Be sure every child can see the demonstration. Tell children exactly what you want them to notice in the demonstration. Demonstrate fully, showing the movement using an appropriate energy level. If you demonstrate only part of the movement, show children how the part fits into the whole.

Review Questions

1. Why do teachers elicit children's prior knowledge of new content?
2. Describe what you can say to help children understand the value of two skills or tactics (not an example from the chapter).
3. Write an example of a question related to physical education content for each of the six levels in Bloom's taxonomy.
4. Why does wait time enhance the quality of children's answers to questions?
5. Which broader goals of education are you supporting when you teach children that they are viable sources of information?
6. Give an example of how you can teach for transfer using skills or tactics not discussed in this chapter.
7. Explain why is it critical to be brief and limit the amount of new information you teach at one time.
8. Make up a story, image, or metaphor for three different performance cues for teaching one skill or several skills.
9. What are guidelines for good demonstrations?

References

Alexander, P. A. (2006). *Psychology in learning and instruction.* Upper Saddle River, NJ: Pearson.

Bloom, B. S., Engelhart, M. D., Furst, E. J., Hill, W. H., & Krathwohl, D. R. (1956). *Taxonomy of educational objectives—Handbook 1: The cognitive domain.* New York: McKay.

Chen, A. (2001). A theoretical conceptualization for motivation research in physical education: An integrated perspective. *Quest, 53,* 59–76.

Chen, A., & Darst, P. W. (2001). Situational interest in physical education: A function of learning task design. *Research Quarterly for Exercise and Sport, 72,* 150–164.

Chen, A., & Ennis, C. D. (2004). Goals, interests, and learning in physical education. *Journal of Educational Research, 97,* 329–338.

Chen, A., Ennis, C. D., Martin, R., & Sun, H. (2006). Situational interest: A curriculum component enhancing motivation to learn. In S. N. Hogan (Ed.), *New developments in learning research* (pp. 235–261). Hauppauge, NY: Nova Science Publishers.

Chen, W. (1997). *Differences between constructivist-oriented teaching practices of expert and novice teachers in elementary physical education.* Unpublished doctoral dissertation, University of Alabama, Tuscaloosa.

Chen, W. (2001). Description of an expert teacher's constructivist-oriented teaching: Engaging students' critical thinking in learning creative dance. *Research Quarterly for Exercise and Sport, 72,* 366–375.

Common Core State Standards Initiative. (2010a). *Common core state standards for English language arts and literacy in history/social studies, science, and technical subjects.* Retrieved from http://www.corestandards.org.

Common Core State Standards Initiative. (2010b). *Common core state standards for mathematics.* Retrieved from http://www.corestandards.org

Fronske, H., & Wilson, R. (2002). *Teaching cues for basic sport skills for elementary and middle school students.* Boston: Benjamin Cummings.

Halsey, J. J. (2005). Risk Management for Physical Educators. In H. Appenzeller, (Ed.). *Risk Management in Sport: Issues and Strategies,* (2nd ed.), (pp. 151–163). Durham, NC: Carolina Academic Press.

Hart, J. E., & Ritson, R. J. (2002). *Liability and Safety in Physical Education and Sport.* Reston, VA: National Association for Sport and Physical Education.

Iserbyt, P., Elen, J., & Behets, D. (2010). Instructional guidance in reciprocal peer tutoring with task cards. *Journal of Teaching in Physical Education, 29,* 38–53.

Lemov, D. (2010). *Teach like a champion: 49 techniques that put students on the path to college.* San Francisco: Jossey-Bass.

Magill, R. A. (2011). *Motor learning and control: Concepts and applications* (9th ed.). New York: McGraw-Hill.

McTighe, J., & Wiggins, G. (2013). *Essential questions: Opening doors to student understanding.* Alexandria, VA: ASCD.

Orlich, D. C., Harder, R. J., Callahan, R. C., & Gibson, H. W. (2001). *Teaching strategies: A guide to better instruction* (6th ed.). Boston: Houghton Mifflin.

Placek, J. H., Griffin, L. L., Dodds, P., Raymond, C., Tremino, F., & James, A. (2001). Middle school students' conceptions of fitness: The long road to a healthy life study. *Journal of Teaching in Physical Education, 20*, 314–323.

Rink, J. E. (2001). Investigating the assumptions of pedagogy. *Journal of Teaching in Physical Education, 20*, 112–128.

Roberton, M. A., Halverson, L. E., & Harper, C. J. (1997). Visual/verbal modeling as a function of children's developmental levels in hopping. In J. E. Clark & J. H. Humphrey (Eds.), *Motor development research and reviews* (*vol. 1*) (pp. 122–147). Reston, VA: National Association for Sport and Physical Education.

Rovegno, I., Chen, W., & Todorovich, J. (2003). Accomplished teachers' pedagogical content knowledge of teaching dribbling to third grade. *Journal of Teaching in Physical Education, 22*, 426–449.

Ruddell, R. B. (2009). *How to teach reading to elementary and middle school students: Practical ideas from highly effective teachers.* Boston: Pearson

Schmidt, R. A., & Wrisberg, C. A. (2004). *Motor learning and performance* (3rd ed.). Champaign, IL: Human Kinetics.

Shen, B., Chen, A., Tolley, H., & Scrabis, K. A. (2003). Gender and interest-based motivation in learning dance. *Journal of Teaching in Physical Education, 22*, 386–409.

Society of Health and Physical Educators (SHAPE). (2014). *National standards and grade-level outcomes for K–12 physical education.* Champaign, IL: Human Kinetics.

Solmon, M. (2006). Learner cognition. In D. Kirk, D. MacDonald, & M. O'Sullivan (Eds.), *The handbook of physical education* (pp. 226–241). London: Sage.

Sun, H., Chen, A., Ennis, C., Martin, R., & Shen, B. (2008). An examination of the multidimensionality of situational interest in elementary school physical education. *Research Quarterly for Exercise and Sport, 79*, 62–70.

Vande Broek, G., Boen, F., Claessens, M., Feys, J., & Ceux, T. (2011). Comparison of three instructional approaches to enhance tactical knowledge in volleyball among university students. *Journal of Teaching in Physical Education, 30*, 375–392.

Weimar, W. H., Martin, E. H., & Wall, S. J. (2011). Kindergarten students' qualitative responses to different instructional strategies during the horizontal jump. *Physical Education and Sport Pedagogy, 16*, 213–222.

Werner, P., & Rink, J. (1989). Case studies of teacher effectiveness in second grade physical education. *Journal of Teaching in Physical Education, 8*, 280–297.

Wulf, G., & Weigelt, C. (1997). Instructions about physical principles in learning a complex motor skill: To tell or not to tell. *Research Quarterly for Exercise and Sport, 68*, 362–367.

CHAPTER

7

Task Design and Differentiated Instruction

PRE-READING REFLECTION

1. Think back to your experiences in physical education, youth sports, and interscholastic sports. Do you remember standing in line waiting for your turn to practice a skill? Think back to reading in elementary school. Did you ever have to stand in line waiting to read a book?
2. Did you ever participate in a sport, dance, or other physical activity class in which you were one of the lowest skilled and the lesson tasks were too difficult for you? If so, how did you feel, and what was the result of this experience? If this never happened to you, ask a friend, parent, child, or sibling if that happened to them, how they felt, and what was the result of the experience.

OBJECTIVES

Students will learn:

1. Designing tasks that provide maximum practice opportunities for every child is one of the most critical aspects of good teaching.
2. The importance of designing tasks that reflect whether the skill is open or closed.
3. The importance of designing tasks that match the stage of learning and the developmental capabilities of the children.
4. To teach most skills as a whole and use part–whole teaching only when the skills are complex and parts interact only to a small extent.
5. To use eliciting tasks whenever possible—that is, to set task and environmental constraints to elicit the movement patterns and performance techniques you want children to practice.

6. All tasks have motor, cognitive, and affective aspects.
7. There are many ways to design tasks to accommodate individual differences.

KEY TERMS

Inclusion tasks
Large-group, one-ball games
Mastery progressions
Wave organization

CONNECTIONS TO STANDARDS

In this chapter, we describe how to design tasks to meet all five national standards, although we focus primarily on tasks for learning skills addressing National Standard 1 and the application of movement concepts, principles, and tactics in movement tasks from National Standard 2.

Introduction

In this chapter, we describe how to apply development and learning theories to task design. We begin with the single most important topic: practice time.

The Importance of Practice

It seems so obvious that you might wonder why we even need to write this, but the only way to learn motor skills is by doing them. We could explain in detail how to perform a back handspring, and we could have a gymnast demonstrate the skill for you, but the only way you could perform a back handspring is to spend a considerable amount of time mastering the skills that are foundational to a back handspring and then even more time practicing a back handspring with considerable assistance from an instructor.

The same is true for children. To learn the fundamental skills of games, gymnastics, or dance, they must spend a considerable amount of time practicing those skills. As motor development research shows, mastery of mature patterns takes many years of practice (Haywood & Getchell, 2005). Research on developing expertise also reveals the importance of deliberate practice—that is, practice designed to improve performance over many years (Ericsson, Krampe, & Tesch-Romer, 1993). Finally, research on teaching physical education indicates that the amount of appropriate practice is the key variable leading to student learning (Silverman, Tyson, & Morford, 1988; Solmon & Lee, 1996; van der Mars, 2006).

The implication for teaching is that you must provide considerable time for practice. Although this sounds easy, the research on the amount of physical activity during physical education classes shows that, on average, students spend only 31% to 36% of class time being physically active (Trost, 2006). The Institute of Medicine (2013), in their efforts to improve children's health and skill development, presented guidelines for quality physical education and stated children must be moderately to vigorously active for greater than 50% of lesson time, and they proposed assessing physical education to see if the 50% target is met.

Good teachers know how to provide practice for 50% or more of lesson time. Some of the ways they ensure children have plenty of time to practice skills are to provide brief presentations, use effective organization, and minimize the amount of time children spend in transition from one task to the next. Here we focus on designing tasks to maximize practice time.

Design Tasks that Provide Maximum Practice Time for Every Child

To maximize practice opportunities, the goal is to design tasks in which all children are actively practicing most of the time. The three rules of thumb highlighted in this section will help you achieve this goal.

Provide Every Child (or Pair) with a Ball or Equipment

The first rule of thumb at the elementary level is that every child or pair of children should have a ball or whatever piece of equipment you are using. If you are teaching tactics and gameplay that requires more than two children, such as two offensive players versus one defender (2v1) on a fast break, then use the smallest group possible. Children should not have to wait for their turn to practice. Can you imagine a reading class in which there was only one book and the children had to wait for their turn to practice reading? Can you imagine waiting for each of the students sitting in the row of desks in front of you to finish using a pencil, and then pass it back to the next person in the row to use, until it finally reaches you? Students never wait for essential supplies in the classroom, and they should not wait in a physical education setting, either.

Eliminate Lines

Second, eliminate time spent standing in line. This means eliminating squad lines in which children wait for their turn to dribble down the field or shoot a ball into a goal. It also means eliminating lines for waiting to use gymnastics equipment. Most importantly, eliminate having all of the children in the class wait in line for the teacher to toss one ball to a student one at a time. The only person getting any practice with this organization is the teacher!

Eliminate Large-Group, One-Ball Games

Finally, eliminate **large-group, one ball games**. In these games, typically only one or two children are active and practicing at a time. The classic examples of games that lack maximum opportunities for practice are kickball and softball. Typically, only the pitcher and catcher get many opportunities to practice, with some children in the outfield never having the opportunity to catch or throw the ball during the entire lesson. The same problem occurs in volleyball when the teacher divides the class into two teams playing one game over one net.

Even large-group games in which every child has a ball can result in some children getting lots of practice while others just stand around. For example, in whole-class dribble tag, some children will not be chased at all. Even when half of the class tries to steal the ball from the other half, some children will not be chased and, consequently, will not practice dribbling against a defender, which is the object of dribble tag. To provide more practice opportunities for children in tag games, use groups no larger than 3v3.

In summary, to provide maximum practice opportunities:

- Have children all practice at the same time, typically in a scattered formation throughout general space (see **Figure 7.1**).
- Set up enough centers (also called stations) so that there is no waiting, with two or three children working at each center and enough equipment at each center for all children to practice at the same time.
- Use small-sided games with a maximum of two, or rarely three, children on a team.
- For group work (to design dances, games, jump rope routines, etc.) have a maximum of four children per group.

Exceptions to the Rule

Of course, as with all rules of thumb, there are exceptions to the rules presented here. For example, sometimes equipment such as a ball machine, springboard, or vaulting box might require a short wait. In these cases, limit groups at that center to two or three children.

Another exception occurs when children must practice a skill, such as dribbling or galloping, at a fast speed and you teach in a small space. The **wave organization** is designed to accommodate these constraints. With this approach, you have as many short lines as you can while still ensuring enough room between the lines. Assign a maximum of two to four children to each line. The first children in line are wave 1, the second are wave 2, and so on. Tell the first wave to start. When they are roughly one-third of the way down the gym, tell wave 2 to start. When wave 2 is one-third of the way down the gym, start wave 3. In the meantime, wave 1 stops at cones set up approximately 8 feet from the wall and forms a line facing the direction from which they started. As each wave finishes, its members get in line and you repeat the task moving in the other direction. With this strategy, most children are active most of the time, and each child has enough space to travel safely at a fast speed without worrying about another child crossing his or her path.

What Can I Do If I Don't Have Enough Equipment?

Sometimes teachers new to a school will not have enough equipment for all children to perform the same skill at the same time. In these situations, we suggest you use centers (stations) and have children work on different tasks at different centers (see **Figure 7.2**). For example, you might have one-third of the space set up for practicing dribbling, one-third for practicing throwing, and one-third for practicing catching.

If you don't have enough equipment to divide the class into thirds, then take out all of your equipment and set up as many centers as you need. We have seen classes of more than 100 children effectively practicing motor skills because the teacher and aides set up 60 different centers.

Assess Your Teaching: Practice Time

We believe that maximizing practice time is so important that it is worth assessing your teaching to see if you are providing as much practice time as possible. On the text website, we include

Figure 7.1 Practicing in scattered formation

Figure 7.2 Using centers to maximize participation

Experienced Teachers Talk

The Quest to Acquire Adequate Amounts of Equipment

There is no doubt that many beginning teachers who get jobs in schools find that the physical education teachers who preceded them were not committed to providing excellent physical education, and, consequently, they have little equipment. In addition, many inner-city schools or rural schools in low-income areas have little, if any, equipment budget. We sympathize with teachers in these situations, and we encourage you to be creative and persistent in your quest to get adequate amounts of equipment to provide maximum practice opportunities for every child.

When Dianna Bandhauer first arrived at Lecanto Primary School, she had little equipment at her disposal. The challenge inspired her to use creative problem solving. Bandhauer taught punting using plastic gallon milk jugs. She found a foam mattress and cut it up into squares to teach kicking. She started fundraising and built up her stock of equipment little by little. Twenty-five years later, she has seven pitching machines, gymnastics mats for each child in a class, a variety of wall-mounted gymnastics equipment, portable climbing and balancing equipment, and enough balls, bats, rackets, and other small equipment for all her children to learn any skill she selects. She even organized a donation campaign so every child in her school who wanted a bicycle could have one.

Homemade equipment works very well and is something to be proud of because it shows how much you care about your children's learning. Plastic cups left over in the football stadium make excellent cones. Two sheets of newspaper tightly rolled (starting from one corner and rolling diagonally to the other, then secured with a piece of tape) make perfect canes that you can use as obstacles for teaching jumping. You can form these same canes into 8-inch rings and have children throw them like Frisbees for learning net game tactics. Surprisingly, you can make excellent trainer volleyballs with donated broken beach balls and Styrofoam peanuts (cut an 8-inch slit in the ball, stuff it tightly full of peanuts, and use duct tape to close the opening). Water bottles with pea gravel make dance shakers. Asking parents for donations of old sports equipment or to assist in making gymnastics equipment such as 2 × 4 balance beams or balance beams made with 6- to 12-inch-diameter PVC pipe has worked for many teachers. Home improvement stores sometimes donate wood and PVC pipe to schools, and scraps can be found for free.

An inspiration to us is a colleague, Dr. John Todorovich, who taught eight years in an elementary school with many portable classrooms and no indoor space for physical education. Through fundraising and donations of supplies and labor, he built a gym! It is a simple metal frame building with a concrete floor, but it is an excellent instructional setting, especially when it rains or is cold or hot.

It takes persistence and dedication to acquire the equipment you need. However, providing maximum practice opportunities for children to learn skills and be physically active is probably the single most important task of teaching physical education.

three assessments that can help you determine the amount of practice you are providing students.

Design Tasks that Reflect Whether the Skill Is Closed or Open

"*Closed skills* are performed in stable, unchanging environments" (Rose & Christina, 2006, p. 217). *Open skills* are "skills that are performed in variable environments and therefore must be repeatedly adapted to the changing demands of the environment" (p. 217). In designing tasks, you need to ask yourself, "Is the skill closed or open, and in which ways does that skill vary in games, gymnastics, or dance?" Then, you need to design tasks that reflect the variability of movement patterns for that skill.

For a closed skill, design tasks in which the children practice the skill in a stable environment to develop consistent performance. Such a task requires children to repeat the same movement pattern. In contrast, open skills require children to learn how to adapt the skill to different environmental demands. Consequently, across lessons and units you want children to practice the skills in a variety of ways.

To design tasks that match the variability of open skills, we apply the movement concepts from the Laban framework and consider all the ways performers use those skills in games. For example, balls are thrown with different amounts of force and speed, ranging from a short gentle toss to a forceful overhand throw that travels a great distance, and at every force and distance in between. Balls are thrown to still targets in baseball and softball and to moving targets in basketball and football. They are thrown while the player is standing still and on the run. They are thrown from different levels to avoid defenders and in different directions. They are thrown from one hand, from two hands, and from equipment such as lacrosse sticks.

After analyzing an open skill, we plan tasks that teach children how to perform that skill in multiple ways under different environmental conditions (e.g., different speeds, levels, directions, to moving teammates, while avoiding defenders). This builds a strong foundation for children to be able to play games skillfully and to perform gymnastics and dance with versatility.

A far less effective way to teach open skills that is not supported by research or theory (but is all too common) is to teach open skills as if they were closed skills. For example, the only task and environment used to teach a chest pass and bounce pass is to make these passes to a partner standing about 10 feet away. This task limits children's abilities to use those skills in game situations; in turn, gameplay suffers because the children have practiced passing only in limited environmental conditions. In the content chapters, we show you how to apply movement concepts to skills and plan lessons that develop versatility and adaptability to different environmental conditions.

Match the Task to the Stage of Learning

In designing tasks, you also need to take into account the developmental level of the children and their stage of learning. Recall that children in the first stage of learning are working to acquire basic movement patterns. Thus, they should not have to worry about adapting movement patterns to meet changing environmental conditions. Once children have control over their body (and the ball), practice tasks can then focus on practicing the skill in a variety of ways.

For Most Skills, Design Tasks to Practice the Whole Skill

When designing tasks, you have to decide whether to have children practice the skill as a whole or in parts. Most skills at the elementary level should be taught as a whole. For example, most teachers have children practice the whole skills of throwing, catching, dribbling, kicking, and striking. They have children work on particular performance techniques by focusing on one part of the skill, such as pushing with the finger pads while dribbling with the hand, but the children perform the skill as a whole.

Motor learning researchers have developed principles that can guide you in deciding whether whole or part–whole teaching is more appropriate. The first principle is specificity of learning—that is, "the notion that the best learning experiences are those that most closely approximate the movement components and environmental conditions of the target skill and target context" (Schmidt & Wrisberg, 2004, p. 234). This means that you should, if possible, teach the skill as a whole. If you have students practice parts of skills, have them practice the whole as soon as possible.

Other tasks are so complex that simplifying the task is necessary for learners to acquire the basic pattern of the movement. For example, having children practice batting off a tee, which eliminates the movement of a pitched ball, is beneficial when they are first tackling the task of batting.

A second principle based on motor learning research is that if the parts of a skill interact with each other to only a small extent, then practicing parts is effective; in contrast, if the parts interact to a large extent, then practicing parts is ineffective (Schmidt & Wrisberg, 2004). For example, practicing batting without running to first base is effective because running does not interact very much with batting. Practicing segments of a dance is effective because the parts don't interact as long as students also practice the dance as a whole. In general, you should plan for children to practice the whole skill unless the skill is complex with a number of parts and high environmental demands; even while performing the whole skill, however, children can focus on its various parts (Magill, 2011).

What the Research Says

Support for Variable Practice

Although the very nature of open skills suggests that it is essential to provide practice of skills in a variety of ways, research on motor learning theory also supports variable practice. Schmidt's theory of motor learning proposes that a generalized motor program is used to produce the action of skills; for example, children develop a generalized motor program for throwing and a different generalized motor program for kicking (Schmidt & Wrisberg, 2004). Once children have acquired the generalized motor program of a skill, motor learning research reports that it is beneficial to practice that skill in a variety of ways, such as by throwing different balls for different distances (Boyce, Coker, & Bunker, 2006; Schmidt & Wrisberg, 2004).

Student Tales

One of our colleagues told us this story:

My nephew came home with his PE report card in kindergarten and the teacher stated that he needed to work on skipping. I said, "John, I know you can skip. What happened?" He said, "My teacher taught me to skip a different way than you did. Watch." In slow motion he tried, unsuccessfully, to step and hop first on one foot and then on the other. The teacher had broken down skipping into parts, and the fragmentation totally messed up his performance of the skill as a whole.

Consider the Motor, Cognitive, and Affective Aspects of Tasks

All tasks have motor, cognitive, and affective aspects (Barrett, 1972). For example, the motor aspects of striking a ball cooperatively with a partner and trying to hit as many consecutive shots as possible include swinging and aiming with the racket so that the ball goes over the net. The affective aspects include the feeling of the continuity of flow and the feeling of cooperation. The cognitive aspects include deciding whether to hit a forehand or backhand shot and then deciding where to send the ball so that your partner can return the shot to keep the rally going.

Although the motor aspects of tasks are usually the most obvious, the cognitive, affective, and also social, aspects are also critical to consider because they can affect students' responses. For example, without understanding the affective dimensions of the task, some students just hit the ball with the racket as hard as they can, so that their partners then must spend their time fetching the ball. If a child is nervous about or lacks confidence in performing a task, these emotions can negatively affect that child's experience. If a tactical task requires a child to make a quick decision and that proves difficult, the child can get frustrated, especially if the gameplay continues and the child is left behind or is overcome by the defense.

When you design tasks, pay careful attention to all three domains. To make a task work, you need to discuss and teach children about the cognitive and affective aspects in addition to the motor aspects. The integration of the motor, cognitive, affective, and social domains in physical activities is why National Standards 2, 4 and 5 are so critical to the success of your program.

Whenever Possible, Design Eliciting Tasks

Eliciting tasks are tasks that elicit a particular movement pattern or performance technique through task and/or environmental constraints designed by the teacher. First promoted by Lolas Halverson (1966), a motor development researcher, eliciting tasks ensure that children perform a skill using the most mature pattern they are capable of performing. For example, telling children to throw a yarn ball as hard as they can—a task constraint—will elicit their most mature throwing pattern. Rink (2001) calls this approach "environmental design."

Think about the research and theory that describe the important roles of individual, task, and environmental constraints on learning. When you design tasks, you need to think about whether there is a task constraint or a way to design the environment that will elicit the movement pattern you want the children to practice. For example, having children jump and try to touch a balloon hanging out of reach over their heads is likely to elicit a reach with their arms, which is a mature performance technique of jumping that we want children to master.

Research has shown that eliciting tasks can be effective in helping children improve performance techniques. Sweeting and Rink (1999) found that having young children jump over a pretend swamp elicited more mature leg actions. Chen et al. (2003) discovered that the following tasks encouraged children to lift their heads to look up while dribbling: dribbling fast, dribbling in a crowded space, dribbling following a leader, and dribbling against a defender. In addition, having children change dribbling speeds when the teacher held up a green (fast), yellow (slow), or red (in place) card also elicited a greater frequency of children looking up.

Several factors explain why eliciting tasks are effective. In particular, the task and environment bring out the performance technique without the teacher constantly needing to remind children to concentrate on a performance cue. Thus, children can practice independently of the teacher's verbal commands. In addition, eliciting tasks motivate children. Finally, because eliciting tasks bring out the performance technique you want children to practice, these tasks provide productive practice time.

Student Tales

I took ballet lessons as a little girl. When I became too advanced for our neighborhood teacher, my mother switched me to a ballet school in the middle of the year. The lessons were too difficult for me. I did okay as long as I stood in the back of the class where I could copy the girls in front of me. But, every third week, my row was in the front of the class and I was lost and embarrassed. The teacher did nothing to differentiate instruction. All he had to do was let me remain in the back row until I caught up with the new steps and terminology of the new school. I was too young to know I could speak up and ask my mom to get me reassigned to an easier class. Even though I loved to dance, I quit ballet after one semester.

Differentiate Instruction by Designing Tasks to Accommodate Individual Differences

Differentiated instruction means using different instructional tasks emphasizing different performance techniques for different children based on their developmental levels. Differentiated instruction accommodates individual differences by providing optimal challenges for all students.

In physical education, it is critical that all tasks account for the individual differences of children's capabilities to perform skills and allow you to differentiate instruction. Accommodating individual differences is obviously essential when teaching children with disabilities. Differentiated instruction is included in many documents published by professional organizations as an element of professional practice and is necessary for increasing safety and decreasing risk of liability (see the Safety and Liability box).

Designing tasks matched to the students' individual capabilities will enhance appropriate practice, student learning, persistence, motivation, autonomy, engagement, and enjoyment. In contrast, tasks that are too easy or too difficult can lead to boredom, off-task behavior, lack of motivation, disengagement, frustration, embarrassment, and little learning. In this section, we describe seven ways to differentiate instruction through task design.

Same Task, But Children Select Different Performance Techniques on Which to Focus

Many tasks naturally accommodate differences in individual capabilities. As the teacher, you can readily differentiate your instruction by having children work on different performance techniques selected to match the developmental level of your students. For example, having children throw a yarn ball against a wall is appropriate for children at all developmental levels. Some children might work on starting with their side to the target and rotating the trunk while throwing, whereas others might work on the more mature movement of rotating the hips before the shoulders.

Inclusion Tasks: Same Task, But Children Select the Level of Difficulty of the Movement

You can also present tasks that have built-in choices for the level of difficulty, such as modifications in speed, force, height, or distance. The most famous of these tasks was designed by Muska Mosston. Called the "slanty rope," it served as the basis for Mosston's inclusion style of teaching (Mosston & Ashworth, 2002). In this task, children jump over a rope with one end anchored low to the ground and the other end attached to a support at a higher level. The child jumps over the rope at the height appropriate for her or his ability. You can also use a slanty rope on the ground for practicing standing long jumps, with children choosing which distance to jump. We have labeled

SAFETY AND LIABILITY 7.1

Increasing Safety and Decreasing Risk of Liability: Guidelines Relevant to Content in this Chapter

In this box, we discuss specific guidelines built on information discussed earlier in this text on professional standards of practice, negligence, and liability. The goals of these guidelines are to increase children's safety and decrease teachers' risk of negligence and liability.

- Instruction must be in keeping with professional standards recognized in the field. This includes providing enough details about safe, appropriate performance techniques of skills to support safe participation, feedback on performance techniques, and sufficient practice (Hart & Ritson, 2002).
- "The curriculum includes strategies for differentiation of instruction and modification for students of all ability levels. Every physical education class presents a multitude of student needs, and plans for differentiation of instruction are essential for ensuring effective teaching....A physical educator is responsible for providing a customized education experience that meets the needs of each student" (Society of Health and Physical Educators [SHAPE], 2015, p. 6).
- "The reasonably prudent physical educator...avoids teaching to the masses and individualizes instruction wherever appropriate" (Hart & Ritson, 2002, pp. 52–53) and "keeps activities within the ability level of individual students" (p. 115).
- Differentiate instruction for students with special needs and those returning to school from illness or injury.
- Do not coerce students to perform a skill which they perceive is difficult for them or for which they have expressed fear in performing. Coercion includes grading based on the difficulty of the skills as one criterion.
- Teach skills using a safe progression that allows an individual student to progress at his or her rate of learning.
- Sequence the physical activities in the curriculum matching state and national recommendations for sequencing by grade, age, and ability level.
- Modify equipment based on individuals' capabilities. Do not require all children to use the same equipment or perform the exact same skills unless the equipment and skills are developmentally appropriate for every child.

all such tasks **inclusion tasks** based on Mosston's work (see **Figure 7.3**).

You can apply the same principle to tasks requiring speed. For example, you can have children to dribble about general space, going as fast as they can without losing control of the ball. Those who are more skilled will travel faster, working at a higher difficulty level, and those with less skill will travel at a slower speed, making the task easier and more appropriate for their developmental level. Allowing children to match the speed of their movement to their ability is critical for safety. One of the many reasons why relay races are inappropriate is that it is dangerous if children are pressured to perform skills at speeds faster than they can control safely.

Figure 7.3 An inclusion task

You can also design inclusion tasks for skills requiring force. For example, when practicing catching, you can tell the children to throw a ball to their partner at a speed that matches their partner's developmental level in catching. If the children are self-tossing, tell them to toss only to a height from which they can successfully catch the ball.

Exploration, Movement Variety, and Child-Designed Tasks: Children Select the Level of Difficulty of the Movements

Exploration tasks, tasks for practicing skill variability, and child-designed tasks are hallmarks of the movement approach and naturally accommodate individual differences (see **Figure 7.4**). In these tasks, children choose the movement, movement variety, or activity they will practice. An example in gymnastics would be a task to practice balancing on different body parts. Children with experience in gymnastics can practice balancing on two hands or even one hand, whereas beginners can practice balancing on their hips or feet.

In educational dance and gymnastics, we rely on children to design their own sequences by selecting movements that are appropriate for them. In educational games, children are encouraged to design their own games by deciding whether

Figure 7.4 The task to combine a balance, roll, and balance accommodates individual capabilities

the game will be competitive, competitive but with the score not kept, or cooperative. Another example is giving children a range of small equipment and having them design an obstacle course for practicing dribbling or different targets for practicing throwing. These tasks all allow children to select the movements they will practice and, therefore, accommodate individual differences.

Provide Multiple Tasks and Have Children Select Which Task to Practice

A fourth way to accommodate individual differences is to provide multiple tasks and have children select the task they want to practice. For example, you might design the following tasks to practice dribbling and have children choose their task:

1. Design an obstacle course to practice dribbling.
2. With a partner, play follow-the-leader while dribbling in different ways.
3. With a partner, play a 1v1 dribbling game.

Another way to provide multiple tasks is to establish a range of centers and let students select the centers at which they will practice. You can also let children decide how long to practice at a center (as long as they share the center fairly). This approach allows children who need more practice at a center with easier task and environmental constraints to progress at their own rate, rather than requiring them to work at a center that is too difficult.

Provide Task Modifications that Are Easier and More Difficult and Let Children Select Which Modification to Practice

After you present a task, give children easier and more difficult options. For example, you might say, "I want you to practice dribbling on straight, curved, and angular pathways. For those of you who are ready for more of a challenge, dribble quickly on sharp angular pathways and do a crossover dribble while working with your nondominant hand as if you were going around a defender." An example in gymnastics would be this: "I want you to practice combining jumping from the stacked mat, landing, and rolling. Which modifications would make this task more difficult? [Answers: Making different shapes in the air when you jump and rolling in different directions.] Those are great answers. What would make this task easier? [Answers: Starting from the floor mat, do a low jump, and then do a sideways safety roll.] You decide which modifications are best for you."

Throughout the lesson plans presented in this text, we describe and label modifications to make the task more difficult (MD tasks) and modifications to make the task easier (ME tasks). Beginning teachers, in particular, need to plan MD and ME tasks because it is difficult to anticipate the appropriate level of difficulty for children whom you do not know well. When you present a task and see that the level of difficulty is inappropriate, it helps enormously if you have planned MD and ME tasks. Then you can proceed like an expert and modify your lesson plan on your feet easily, without getting flustered.

We also recommend teaching children how to modify tasks to be easier and more difficult. When children work in centers or when teachers have large classes, children will need to know how to modify tasks so they can practice at an appropriate level of difficulty. You need first to teach them the criteria for making these modifications—that is, how to practice at a level that allows them to be both challenged and successful.

You also will need to teach children that it is okay to modify tasks to improve practice conditions to facilitate learning, but it is not okay to change the task and do anything they want. In other words, children must stay on task and meet the content objectives you established. Children readily understand the difference between being on task and fooling around.

Use Mastery Progressions

A tried-and-true teaching technique for accommodating individual differences is to teach skills using **mastery progressions**. This approach can be especially useful in gymnastics. With a mastery progression, you break the skill down into a series of subskills that increase in difficulty. You teach the series of subskills and tell the children to work on the subskill that is developmentally appropriate for them. They should move on to the next subskill only if they feel confident, competent, and sure they can safely progress.

What the Research Says

Student Autonomy

You have probably noticed that our suggestions for accommodating individual differences include providing options and respecting students' abilities to make decisions about their learning. In motivation research, this strategy is called "teacher support for student autonomy." Considerable evidence across fields and growing evidence in physical education indicate that (1) offering choices in task difficulty and activities; (2) accommodating individual differences; and (3) respecting and supporting students' capabilities to make autonomous decisions can enhance learning and motivation (Bryan & Solmon, 2007; Koka & Hagger, 2010; Prusak, Treasure, Darst, & Pangrazi, 2004; Shen, McCaughtry, Martin, & Fahlman, 2009). Motor learning research also supports the benefits of enhancing student autonomy. As shown in multiple studies, when students control their practice conditions and when they receive feedback, they learn more (Chiviacowsky & Wulf, 2005; Wulf & Toole, 1999).

Children deciding which ball to use

What Children Think

The following quote from a 10-year-old girl with low skill ability is from a research study on children's perspectives (Rovegno, 2010):

> Emily: They have softballs and you can use the tennis balls if you don't want to use the softballs and stuff like that.
>
> Researcher: Why do they give you choices like that?
>
> Emily: 'Cause some people feel more comfortable with the tennis ball than the softball, and some people don't like to use softballs 'cause it's a little more harder than the tennis ball and it could hurt.
>
> Researcher: So, do you like having choices or do you not like having choices?
>
> Emily: I like having choices.

The following is a list of the subskills for teaching a mule kick and a handstand:

- *Subskill 1:* Starting position: Knees are bent and body is tucked in a ball with most of the weight on the feet and some weight on the hands, which are flat on the mat. Lean forward so more of your weight is on your hands.
- *Subskill 2:* Same starting position; put weight on hands and straight arms; push off with both feet (jumping) about 1 inch from the floor, with the body remaining in tucked position.
- *Subskill 3:* Weight on hands; one foot in front of the other; lift back foot; push off with front foot about 2 inches from the floor; switch feet in the air; land on the original back foot, which is now the front foot.
- *Subskill 3:* Lift your feet a little higher each time.
- *Subskill 4:* Mini–mule kick. Start in a lunge with all weight on feet with the front knee bent, back leg straight, and body upright; put weight on hands, lift the back leg parallel to the ground, push off with front leg, switch legs in the air, and land on original back foot.
- *Subskill 5:* Full mule kick.
- *Subskill 6:* Cartwheeling out of a handstand.
- *Terminal skill:* Full handstand.

Modify the Equipment to Match Individual Capabilities

A final way to accommodate individual differences through task design is to have children select the equipment that best matches their developmental level. For example, children can all work on dribbling, with some using basketballs (the most difficult to dribble), others using nylon-bound playground balls, and still others using large playground balls that are not nylon bound (the easiest to dribble). When playing a 3v3 game of modified basketball with no dribbling, the more skilled children can use basketballs while the less skilled can use foam balls, which are easier to catch and elicit more confidence in children who are afraid to catch passes thrown with force.

The goal when modifying equipment is to find equipment that allows the children to best approximate the skill technique or tactics that are the objective of your lesson. For example, if you want children to work in pairs and strike a ball continuously over a low net with a racket, the following is a progressive list of ME tasks (modifications to make the task easier) and MD tasks (modifications to make the task more difficult), with task 5 being the task you planned based on your objective. Task 5 is your best guess at the appropriate equipment that will work for this objective, matched to the skill level of your class. You know, however, that you will likely need to modify the equipment for some children to make the task easier or more difficult. Equipment changes include changes in the ball, racket, and net height, as well as the addition of boundaries. Tactics are added in task 7, which increase in complexity and skill demands. Changes are highlighted in **bold**.

ME: Modifications to Make Task 5 Easier

1. Strike a large, light, bouncy vinyl ball back and forth with a partner, using your hands and letting the ball bounce once before you hit it.
2. Strike a large, light, bouncy vinyl ball back and forth **over a net or rope set at about 3 feet**, using your hands and letting the ball bounce once before you hit it.

3. Strike a large, light, bouncy vinyl ball back and forth over a net, using **a short-handled, light racket** and letting the ball bounce once before you hit it.
4. Strike a **large indoor foam bouncy ball** back and forth over a net, using a short-handled, light racket and letting the ball bounce once before you hit it.

Planned Task

5. Strike a **small, low-compression, slow, tennis ball** back and forth over a net using a short-handled, light racket and letting the ball bounce once before you hit it.

MD: Modifications to Make Task 5 More Difficult

6. Strike a small, low-compression, slow, tennis ball back and forth over a net, using a short-handled, light racket and letting the ball bounce once before you hit it, while **keeping the ball within marked boundaries**.
7. Strike a small, low-compression, slow, tennis ball back and forth over a net using a short-handled, light racket and letting the ball bounce once before you hit it, while keeping the ball within marked boundaries and **trying to hit the ball into an open space (not hitting it directly to your partner)**.
8. Strike a small, low-compression, slow, tennis ball back and forth over a net, using a short-handled, light racket and letting the ball bounce once, while keeping the ball within marked boundaries, **trying to hit the ball into an open space, and trying to make your partner have to shift from side to side on every hit**.
9. Strike a small, low-compression, slow, tennis ball back and forth over a net using a short-handled, light racket and letting the ball bounce once, while keeping the ball within marked boundaries, trying to hit the ball into an open space, and trying to make your partner have to shift from side to side **and/or front to back on every hit**.
10. Strike a small, low-compression, slow, tennis ball back and forth **using a tennis racket** over a net while keeping the ball within marked boundaries, trying to hit the ball into an open space, trying to make your partner have to shift from side to side and/or front to back on every hit.

It is highly unlikely you will ever have a class with children whose developmental levels vary to the extent that you would need to use all 10 of these tasks. However, it is helpful as a teacher to have a mental model for how you might modify the equipment and task to meet the needs of the most and least skilled children in a class. This mental model will enable you to modify the task on your feet and to be prepared to make changes on the fly using a range of equipment options.

Rink's Criteria for Appropriate Learning Experiences

Rink (2014) provides a set of criteria that summarize well how you can judge whether the learning experiences and tasks you design are appropriate:

- Does the learning experience have the potential to improve motor skill performance? In other words, is the learning experience likely to lead to movement learning, or is it primarily focused on providing physical activity, recreation, or social experiences?
- Does the learning experience provide maximum practice time?
- Is the learning experience developmentally appropriate for all children's capabilities?
- Does the learning experience have the potential to integrate motor, cognitive, and affective goals?

Using these criteria, you can design effective lessons that will enhance your students' learning and positive experiences.

Summary

Providing maximum practice opportunities is one of the most critical characteristics of good tasks. In addition, you need to design tasks that reflect whether the skill is a closed skill with little variability or an open skill requiring considerable variability of practice. Tasks also must match the developmental capabilities of all children in the class, thereby allowing children with different abilities to learn successfully. To achieve this goal, you will need to differentiate instruction by designing multiple tasks, providing modifications to make tasks either easier or more difficult, and having students choose the movement, task, level of task difficulty, and/or performance technique to practice. Whenever possible, set task and environmental constraints to elicit the movement patterns and performance techniques that you want children to practice. Because physical activities have motor, cognitive, and affective aspects, ideally you will design tasks that allow you to work on all three domains simultaneously.

Review Questions

1. What are the current guidelines for the amount of time children should engage in moderate to vigorous physical activity during a physical education lesson? Why do you think teachers in some research studies had children active only 31% to 36% of class time?
2. Describe the wave organization for practice tasks.
3. Based on the practice conditions important for open skills, select three open skills and design an appropriate practice task for each (do not use examples from the chapter).

4. Which guidelines does motor learning research suggest for whole and part–whole practice?
5. What are the motor, cognitive, and affective aspects of the task of practicing catching balls tossed (between partners) to all areas of each child's personal space?
6. Why are eliciting tasks effective? Select one skill and design a task to elicit a performance technique important for that skill.
7. Discuss how to accommodate individual differences with tasks.

References

Barrett, K. R. (1972). I wish I could fly: A philosophy in motion. In R. Cobb & P. Lepley (Eds.), *Contemporary philosophies of physical education and athletics* (pp. 3–18). Columbus, OH: Charles E. Merrill.

Boyce, B. A., Coker, C. A., & Bunker, L. K. (2006). Implications for variability of practice from pedagogy and motor learning perspectives: Finding a common ground. *Quest, 58*, 330–343.

Bryan, C. L., & Solmon, M. A. (2007). Self-determination in physical education: Designing class environments to promote active lifestyles. *Journal of Teaching in Physical Education, 26*, 260–278.

Chen, W., Rovegno, I., Todorovich, J., & Babiarz, M. (2003). Third grade children's movement responses to dribbling tasks presented by accomplished teachers. *Journal of Teaching in Physical Education, 22*(4), 450–466.

Chiviacowsky, S., & Wulf, G. (2005). Self-controlled feedback is effective if it is based on the learner's performance. *Research Quarterly for Exercise and Sport, 76*, 42–48.

Ericsson, K. A., Krampe, R. T., & Tesch-Romer, C. (1993). The role of deliberate practice in the acquisition of expert performance. *Psychological Review, 100*, 363–407.

Halverson, L. E. (1966, Spring). Development of motor patterns in young children [Monograph]. *Quest, VI*, 44–53.

Hart, J. E., & Ritson, R. J. (2002). *Liability and Safety in Physical Education and Sport.* Reston, VA: National Association for Sport and Physical Education.

Haywood, K. M., & Getchell, N. (2005). *Life span motor development* (4th ed.). Champaign, IL: Human Kinetics.

Institute of Medicine. (2013). *Educating the Student Body: Taking Physical Activity and Physical Education to School.* Washington, DC: National Academy of Sciences.

Koka, A., & Hagger, M. S. (2010). Perceived teaching behaviors and self-determined motivation in physical education: A test of self-determination theory. *Research Quarterly for Exercise and Sport, 81*, 74–86.

Magill, R. A. (2011). *Motor learning and control: Concepts and applications* (9th ed.). New York: McGraw-Hill.

Mosston, M., & Ashworth, S. (2002). *Teaching physical education* (5th ed.). San Francisco: Benjamin Cummings.

Prusak, K. A., Treasure, D. C., Darst, P. W., & Pangrazi, R. P. (2004). The effects of choice on the motivation of adolescent girls in physical education. *Journal of Teaching in Physical Education, 23*, 19–29.

Rink, J. E. (2001). Investigating the assumptions of pedagogy. *Journal of Teaching in Physical Education, 20*, 112–128.

Rink, J. E. (2014). *Teaching physical education for learning* (7th ed.). New York: McGraw-Hill.

Rose, D. J., & Christina, R. W. (2006). *A multilevel approach to the study of motor control and learning* (2nd ed.). San Francisco: Benjamin Cummings.

Rovegno, I. (2010). *Children's perspectives on physical education.* Unpublished manuscript, University of Alabama, Tuscaloosa.

Schmidt, R. A., & Wrisberg, C. A. (2004). *Motor learning and performance* (3rd ed.). Champaign, IL: Human Kinetics.

Shen, B., McCaughtry, N., Martin, J., & Fahlman, M. (2009). Effects of teacher autonomy support and students' autonomous motivation on learning in physical education. *Research Quarterly for Exercise and Sport, 80*, 44–53.

Silverman, S., Tyson, L. A., & Morford, L. M. (1988). Relationships of organization, time, and student achievement in physical education. *Teaching and Teacher Education, 4*, 247–257.

Society of Health and Physical Educators (SHAPE). (2015). *The essential components of physical education.* Reston, VA: Author.

Solmon, M., & Lee, A. M. (1996). Entry characteristics, practice variables, and cognition: Student mediation of instruction. *Journal of Teaching in Physical Education, 15*,136–150.

Sweeting, T., & Rink, J. E. (1999). Effects of direct instruction and environmentally designed instruction on the process and product characteristics of a fundamental skill. *Journal of Teaching in Physical Education, 18*, 216–233.

Trost, S. G. (2006). Public health and physical education. In D. Kirk, D. MacDonald, & M. O'Sullivan (Eds.), *The handbook of physical education* (pp. 163–187). London: Sage.

van der Mars, H. (2006). Time and learning in physical education. In D. Kirk, D. MacDonald, & M. O'Sullivan (Eds.), *The handbook of physical education* (pp. 191–213). London: Sage.

Wulf, G., & Toole, T. (1999). Physical assistance devices in complex motor skill learning: Benefits of a self-controlled practice schedule. *Research Quarterly for Exercise and Sport, 70*, 265–272.

CHAPTER

8

Interactive and Reflective Teaching

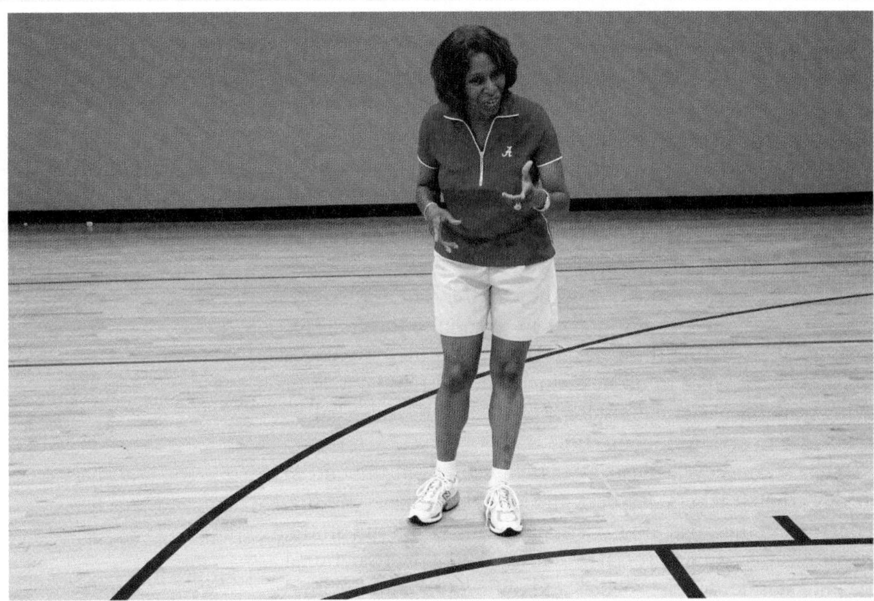

PRE-READING REFLECTION

1. List three of your strongest beliefs about teaching.
2. Describe how you will know if you are teaching in keeping with these beliefs.

OBJECTIVES

Students will learn

1. Observation is a critical teaching skill that informs you about children's safety and learning.
2. Checking for understanding helps you know what children are thinking during the lesson.
3. Interactive teaching is a cycle of observing, interpreting, and making decisions about what to do in relation to what you have observed.
4. Accomplished teachers assume problems they observe are due to some aspect of teaching that they can change. Some beginning teachers may fall into the trap of blaming the children for problems.
5. Beginning teachers should plan alternative strategies and tasks to use when what they planned is not working.
6. There are different kinds of feedback that enhance learning.
7. When you reflect on your teaching, you consider carefully your teaching, curriculum, and children's responses in relation to long-term goals, professional standards, your beliefs, and your philosophy.

KEY TERMS

Alternative strategies
Checking for understanding
Congruent feedback
External feedback
Feedback
Feedback in the form of a question

Focused observations
Interactive teaching
Intrinsic feedback
Observation plan
Praise (general, positive feedback)
Reflective teaching
Scanning
Think–pair–share

CONNECTION TO STANDARDS

In this chapter, we discuss reflective teaching. **Reflective teaching** occurs when teachers reflect on long-term goals, such as the goal of physical education defined in our national standards, and the extent to which their teaching, curriculum, and the responses of children in the motor, cognitive, affective, and social domains indicate children are likely to meet these goals. We also discuss the cycle of observation, interpretation, and decision making used during lessons to ensure lessons focused on learning, which is the purpose of physical education as defined by our national standards.

Introduction

In this chapter, we continue our discussion of teaching techniques. Here, we focus on interactive teaching—that is, what teachers do and how they respond "on their feet" during lessons—and we discuss reflective teaching. We describe interactive and reflective teaching as two cycles. First, we discuss teaching as a cycle of observing the children's motor, cognitive, affective, and social responses in relation to the goals for learning, interpreting these observations, and then making a decision about what to do next, such as modifying a task or giving students individual feedback. This cycle has been called "reflection in action" (Schön, 1983, 1987).

The second cycle starts after the lesson or at the end of the day, when teachers step back and look at the bigger picture, reflecting on their teaching, curriculum, and children's motor, cognitive, affective, and social responses in light of our national goal and standards, their beliefs and philosophy, and the kind of teacher they want to be. Next, teachers decide what changes they might make in their curriculum and instruction to better match their intentions and goals. This cycle has been called "reflection on action" (Schön, 1983, 1987). Careful attention to both cycles is indicative of a reflective teacher.

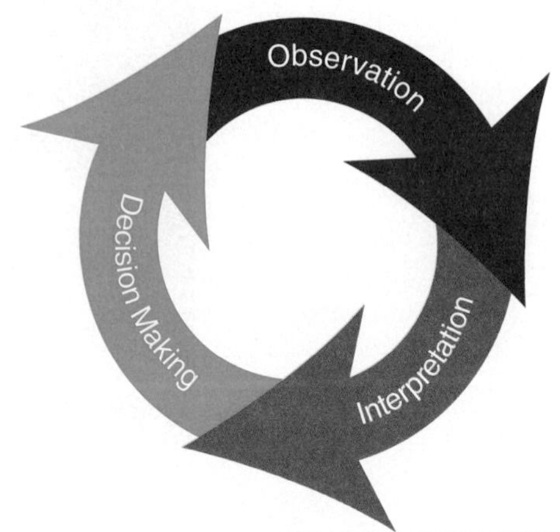

Figure 8.1 Teaching as observing, interpreting, and decision making

Observation as a Critical Teaching Skill

Dr. Kate Barrett, who studied observation as a teaching skill for many years, described **interactive teaching** as a cycle of observing the children, interpreting those observations, and then making a decision about what to do (Barrett, 2009). **Figure 8.1** depicts this cycle graphically. The cycle begins with observation.

Research on expert teachers reveals that one reason such teachers are considered experts is their ability to observe and focus on critical details relevant to student learning (Schempp & Woorons-Johnson, 2006). Research on novices has shown that beginning teachers have difficulty seeing the details of the movements that they need to see in order to make judgments about children's learning (Barrett, 2009).

Teachers' abilities to observe critical details rely on their knowledge of the specific content they are teaching and their knowledge of the movement patterns they need to look for to tell them the extent to which students are learning that content and responding productively. For example, if you know that a critical detail of performing an overhand throw for force is a straight line, rather than an acute angle, between the shoulders and humerus, you will know what to look for to determine the developmental level of the arm action of the throw.

The good news is that you can improve your knowledge of the skills, movement concepts, principles, and tactics you teach, and you can develop your observation skills—even as a beginner. One effective way to improve your observation skills is to write a plan for what to observe (Barrett, 1984). You will need to plan to observe for safety and learning.

Planning to Observe for Safety

Observation plans involve two key elements: planning for safety and planning for learning. Start with safety. In writing your observation plan, think about which safety problems could arise in your tasks and what you need to look for to be sure the children are safe. (See the Safety and Liability box for other important safety issues.) For example, when children throw a yarn (or any) ball forcefully at a wall, you need to observe to be sure that no child throws when another child is in front of the

SAFETY AND LIABILITY 8.1

Increasing Safety and Decreasing Risk of Liability: Guidelines Relevant to Content in this Chapter

In this box, we discuss specific guidelines built on information discussed throughout this text on professional standards of practice, negligence, and liability. The goals of these guidelines are to increase children's safety and decrease teachers' risk of negligence and liability.

- All students are always supervised and observed while they are in the physical education space and during transit to this space. Teachers cannot leave the children alone to step into the hallway for any reason, even to deal with an emergency situation, without another qualified supervisor in the physical education space. Classroom and physical education teachers must communicate when they transfer supervisory duties from one to the other.
- Supervision must be done by a qualified person, which typically means a certified teacher. Student teachers and custodians are not considered qualified (Halsey, 2005).
- "Safety issues are identified in all lessons and are monitored continually during each lesson/activity" (National Association of Sport and Physical Education [NASPE], 2010, p. 9). Potential safety issues and dangers should be written into lesson plans.
- Teachers must actively scan the class, traveling around the perimeter of the space to make sure all children are within their view at all times.

wall retrieving a ball. When children are striking with rackets, you need to look to be sure children are far enough apart so there is no chance they will hit another child with their racket.

Planning to Observe for Learning

Next, focus on learning. Ask yourself, "What is my lesson objective for this task, and what will I need to observe and assess to determine whether the children are meeting this objective?" To answer this question, you need to think about the details: the performance techniques or the movement variations you want children to learn. Which body parts do you need to observe? What are the critical components of the movement? Which specific actions should you assess? Once you plan what to look for, it will be easier to see.

Following are sample lesson tasks, along with observation plans. We also explain our reasons for what we chose to observe about the children's movements. Note that we always start by observing for safety related directly to the task being performed.

How to Observe: Scan and Focus

The first way to observe is to scan the class. **Scanning** involves starting at one side and systematically scanning the class so that you observe every child. When you scan, you sweep your eyes across the class back and forth, without stopping to watch a particular child. After you give a task, we suggest that you scan the class first for safety, second to see whether the children are doing the task you assigned, and third for positive emotional reactions (e.g., interested, engaged, not frustrated, not angry, not confused).

What the Research Says

Beginning Teachers' Observations

One study asked undergraduates to describe in writing what they saw in a field experience early in their coursework. Only 10% of the statements focused on the movement responses of the children, and none focused on the impact of the learning environment. The authors of this study suggest that "If improving student movement skills is a primary objective of physical education teachers, this relatively small number of statements suggests that, in early field experiences, student movement responses do not capture the preservice teachers' attention" (Bell, Barrett, & Allison, 1985, p. 88).

Dr. Sandy Stroot and Dr. Judy Oslin (1993) videotaped undergraduates teaching children how to throw. They found the undergraduates watched the children and taught performance techniques that the children were already performing well but neglected to teach performance techniques that children needed to improve. It appears that the novices were unable to observe the details of children's movements and respond in ways that matched the children's actual performance.

The following quotes are from a research study on junior undergraduates teaching and trying to observe children's movements accurately in field experiences:

> What my mind was thinking about was just organization, making sure everybody was doing it. And I was just trying to see and it was really difficult....All I could see were people and balls going....It was the first time I've ever had that many people, so I was overwhelmed by that....And I guess if I were to really set out to look for skill I might have been able to see it, but honestly....as far as skill, I saw nothing. I saw nothing. I couldn't even tell you if anybody caught a ball (Rovegno, 1991, p. 208).

> I guess I've had a big "eureka" since then, and it's like I figured out part of how to teach....The key, to me, is to know exactly what the focus is at that moment in your teaching. And before...I was getting all jumbled up with everything....So that's what I'm working on now. It's like before the lesson begins, I kind of have my focus for each task and I know what I'm looking for (Rovegno, 1992, pp. 73, 76).

SAMPLE OBSERVATION PLAN 8.1

Second-Grade Games Task

Task: Self-toss and -catch a foam ball, working on reaching to catch.

1. Check whether children are far enough apart so no one will bump into another child.
2. See if any child appears to be afraid to catch the ball.
3. Determine whether children are tossing accurately enough to practice catching.
4. Watch their arms and hands, and assess if they are reaching.

Notes: For this task, we plan to observe whether the tosses are accurate enough before checking whether the children are reaching to catch. This sequence is appropriate because the environmental constraints (an accurate toss) must be right to enable the children to practice catching. Then, we will focus on reaching for the ball, which is the lesson objective.

Which children are tossing accurately enough to practice catching? Which are not?

SAMPLE OBSERVATION PLAN 8.2

Third-Grade Games Task

Task: Practice batting off the tee, working on keeping the front foot closed and the back foot pivoting. (As you hit the ball, your front foot remains parallel to the "pitcher" and the back foot pivots with the heel up.)

1. Observe whether children wait to hit when another child is retrieving a ball.
2. Look at the position of the feet after the hit.

Note: In this task, we plan to observe the specific performance techniques that were taught in the lesson and were in our lesson objectives.

Which children have back foot pivot and front foot closed?

In addition to scanning, you need to engage in **focused observations**, in which you pause and observe one child or one group of children long enough to see how they are learning. When you do so, you must frequently look up and scan the entire class, only then returning to focusing on the smaller group or individual. At the elementary level, you must scan frequently, as children can get off task and into unsafe situations very quickly.

Teacher Location While Observing

We use the slogan "Put your back against the wall and keep moving" to describe where you should position yourself as you teach, especially as a beginning teacher (Barrett, 1984). When you are teaching outdoors, stay at the perimeter of the space (see **Figure 8.2**). You don't want to let children get behind you or out of your vision, because they can and will quickly do things you don't want them to do. We have watched too many videos of lessons that show children watching the teacher and then, the instant the teacher cannot see them, doing things like back handsprings, handstands, kicking the ball instead of throwing it as the task required, tearing equipment, or poking a classmate. If you need to talk to a particular child or group, call that child over to you and talk to him or her as you continue to scan the rest of the class periodically.

The reason you keep moving is to enable you to be close to all children in the class at least some of the time and to be in a position to observe their movements. This kind of monitoring lets all children know you care about them and their learning. If you stay in one place, children who want to go off task will drift as far away from you as possible. Simply positioning yourself near a child who is off task can prompt that child to get back on track quickly. In addition, children cannot hide in the back if you are in the back as much as the front of the space.

Experienced teachers who know their children will be able to move from the perimeter to the middle and then back out (they develop "eyes in the back of their heads"), as can middle and high school teachers. Of course, even the best teacher will find that children sometimes go off task when the teacher is not looking. At the elementary level where children do not always exercise the best judgment as to what is safe and what is not safe, we recommend all beginning teachers put their backs against the wall and keep moving.

Figure 8.2 Strategy for beginning teachers: Put your back against the wall and keep moving

Checking for Understanding and Informally Assessing Knowledge Acquisition

While observing can give you information on children's movements, and to some extent on their understanding of the task, sometimes you need to know what children understand about cognitive content. A teaching strategy you can use to gather information is **checking for understanding**. With this strategy, once you teach a concept or give instructions about a task, you check whether the children understand what you have just said.

Ask Questions

The easiest way to check for understanding is to ask questions about what you have said. Initially call on at least five children.

SAMPLE OBSERVATION PLAN 8.3

First-Grade Gymnastics Task

Task: Jump while making wide, curled, and straight shapes in the air with toes and ankles pointed and legs straight when they are supposed to be straight.

1. Watch whether children are landing on their feet safely and returning to the starting position without crossing another child's pathway.
2. Watch whether children are keeping their legs straight and toes and ankles pointed when they are supposed to be (i.e., extended in a straight line).

Note: For this gymnastics task, we plan to observe one performance technique common to all jumps in gymnastics—that is, pointing toes and ankles—and one performance technique that varies depending on the jump. When the children do a curled or tucked jump, they should tuck the legs in tightly. When they make a shape intending for one or both legs to be straight, they should extend the leg straight at the knees. Pointing toes and ankles and keeping legs straight is a common problem (even with elite gymnasts) and a cue that teachers must consistently emphasize.

(*continues*)

SAMPLE OBSERVATION PLAN 8.3

First-Grade Gymnastics Task (*continued*)

Which children have toes/ankles pointed? Which children have legs straight when they are supposed to be straight?

Courtesy of John Dolly

SAMPLE OBSERVATION PLAN 8.4

Fourth-Grade Games Task

Task: The cones scattered about the space are pretend defenders. Dribble on straight, curved, and angular pathways—on straight pathways when you have space to travel fast and no defenders are near, and on curved and angular pathways to get around defenders.

1. Watch whether children are maintaining a safe amount of space between themselves and others.
2. Observe whether a change of direction on an angular pathway is a sharp angle.

Note: In this task, we focus on looking for a movement we know is an immature pattern that we are likely to see—that is, rounding the angle rather than making a sharp, angular change in direction.

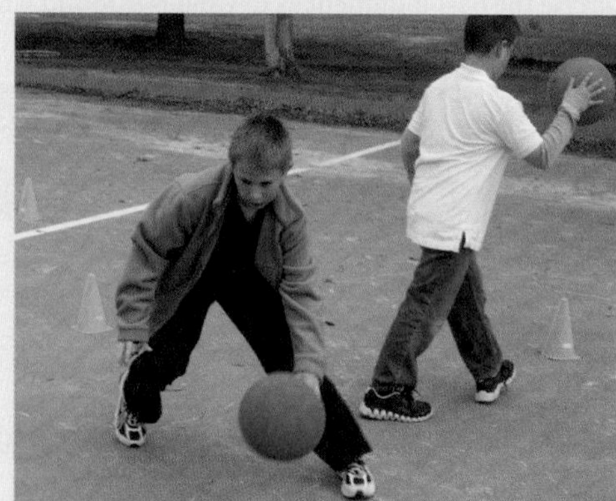

Which child is making a sharp, angular change in direction and which is not?

If you do this several times, the children will develop the expectation that they will have to repeat your instructions and will begin to listen more carefully. Call on children without having them raise their hands. This technique tells children that they each need to be ready to answer questions and not let those who raise their hands do all of the thinking and paying attention for the class. You can then cut down on the number of children you call on to respond. Teachers typically check for understanding after each major task, after teaching new information, and as a review at the end of a lesson.

Partners Describing Each Other's Knowledge

Another strategy for informally assessing children's understanding of cognitive content during the lesson is to put children in pairs and provide a direction, such as "Partner A, tell your partner what you know about throwing a lead pass. Partner B, tell your partner what you know about defending a lead pass." Walk around and listen to the conversations. After a minute or so, randomly select one student to tell the class what his or her partner said. Repeat this step two or three times and write the answers on a whiteboard. Then ask, "Would anyone like to add something we missed on either list?" This technique keeps all the children actively listening and talking, rather than the entire group sitting and listening (or not) to one child answering the question.

Think–Pair–Share

A third way to check for understanding is called **think–pair–share**. In this technique, you ask the class a question and have children think on their own for approximately 30 seconds about the answer. Next, put the children in pairs and have them share their answers and discuss any differences. Finally, you have pairs share their answers with the entire class.

Interpreting Your Observations

When you observe a class, you must interpret what you have seen. For example, if children look bored, do they have that attitude because the task is too easy, or because the task is too hard and they try to look bored so they don't appear incompetent? Suppose you see children who don't generate much force in their kicking: Is it because their performance technique is immature, or are they too close together?

One of the best suggestions we can give you in interpreting observations is to avoid the temptation to blame the children. It is not uncommon for beginning teachers to say, for example, "But I told them to bend their knees in the volleyball forearm pass, but they didn't do it; they must not be trying." This statement indicates the teacher saw an immature developmental pattern and assumed the problem lay with the students' attitudes. In fact, it takes a lot of practice before students develop the mature pattern of using the legs to help generate force.

Good teachers take responsibility for their students' learning. They don't simply present a lesson and assume that it is the children's responsibility to learn the material. When veteran teachers see problems, they first consider their own tasks and actions. They look at the impact of environmental constraints and ask questions such as the following:

- Does the space allow for the speed and force of the skills being practiced?
- Is the space constraining the children's responses?
- Is the ground slippery?
- Is the sun shining in the children's eyes?

They also assess the task constraints and the movement patterns that resulted:

- Did the task elicit the most mature movement patterns the children are capable of performing?
- Did the task accommodate individual differences?
- Is the equipment too heavy, too light, too long, or developmentally inappropriate?
- Are the balls bouncing too high, too low, or too fast?
- Are the balls too big or too small, too hard or too soft?

What the Research Says

Blaming the Students

Several studies have shown it is easy for undergraduates to initially blame the students for problems, claiming the students don't listen, don't try, or don't understand. After teaching and reflecting on their lessons, they learn that their initial impressions were inaccurate and that the problems arose either because of the tasks or because of their interpretations of the students' actions (McCaughtry & Rovegno, 2003, pp. 360–361; Rovegno, 1991, p. 210).

Initial Impressions Early in the Unit

- "I tell them not to hit it so hard, but they do it anyway. That tells me they aren't listening. Whenever I tell them to aim it, it goes all over the place. I don't understand why they can't pay attention when I show them."
- "They don't care what they are doing wrong because they don't want to be there and try. All they had to do was try."
- "It is their problem and effort more than our teaching. I know if they tried, they could do it."

What the Undergraduates Learned During the Unit

- "I really got it wrong. I figured they would be skilled like I had been. I had no idea. I just didn't do a good job anticipating what we would have to deal with. I feel bad because I feel like I really took the lead, so it was my fault."
- "They got a bad first impression because we didn't make the drills at their level. But the biggest problem was that we didn't see it; we thought it was all them and not us."
- "They really don't do things on purpose that you think are bad and you want to choke them. [Laughs.] They're not doing it on purpose. It might just be a matter of development....And, it's not being bad like I always thought it was."

Finally, they consider their task presentation:

- Did they give clear instructions?
- Did they ensure all children could see their demonstration and hear their cues?
- Were their cues clear?

Of course, sometimes children don't try, and sometimes they don't listen. When you see a child performing an immature movement pattern and you have thoroughly taught a more mature performance technique, a guideline we find helpful is to ask the child if he or she remembers the performance technique to practice. If the child knows the performance technique and is not fooling around, then you can assume that the child is at a stage in developing that skill when he or she simply needs more practice. This is the time to encourage children's efforts. Tell them that learning takes time and that they will learn the skill because they are working hard. Remind them that everyone was a beginner at one point in time and that you know they are trying to improve.

In addition, it helps to remember that children often don't tell you about their problems. Perhaps they are having problems at home or in the classroom that are affecting their work in physical education. Try to give children the benefit of the doubt, and focus on what you can do to change the situation in the class.

Experienced Teachers Talk

Inaccurate Interpretations

This did not happen to me—it happened to a friend, but I won't ever forget the story. She was a student teacher at the time, was working on her management skills, and wanted to be sure that all children did exactly what she told them to do. She was teaching first grade and had all the children stand in a circle holding hands. One little girl refused to hold hands, keeping her arms tight to her sides. My friend kept insisting the girl hold hands until finally she did. To my friend's horror, the little girl's underpants fell down to her ankles because the elastic had worn thin. She had been holding up her underpants. All her classmates saw this happen. My friend learned the hard way that you could never know if there are serious personal reasons why children might not want to do what you are asking them to do and that it can be very difficult for young children to explain their predicaments to adults.

The 20 mats were set up under the trees in a long line so the children could practice gymnastics in the shade. I was down at one end helping a child and scanned to make sure everyone was working. I noticed at the far end two boys looked like they were trying to make their mat slide in the leaves. So I walked down there and in a gruff voice said, "What are you doing?" They looked up and said, "We are trying to do a cartwheel, and it is the hardest thing in the world." I often wonder if they would have ever attempted to do a cartwheel again if I had accused them of fooling around. I felt bad about my gruff voice, but luckily they ignored it.

Decision Making Based on Observations and Interpretations

Once you have observed and interpreted your observations, you then must decide what to do. You might react in any of the following ways:

- Revise your instructions to make them clearer.
- Modify the task.
- Modify the equipment being used.
- Modify the environment.
- Give group feedback.
- Give individual feedback.
- Move on to the next task in the lesson.

In making your decisions, try to keep in mind what excellent teachers do. They go after learning aggressively, focusing on what they can control as teachers; they pursue children's success relentlessly. If children are not progressing, good teachers differentiate their instruction accordingly and change what they are doing until they find tasks, equipment, and an environment that work for each individual. No decision is final. If one ball doesn't work, try another. If a task works for some children but not others, change it so all children are working productively at a task that works for everyone.

Regardless of what you decide, the cycle begins again. You observe and assess the impact of your decision, interpret what you have seen, and then make another decision about what to do next. The cycle of observing, interpreting, and decision making continues throughout the lesson.

Planning What to Do If Your Tasks Don't Work

Even the best lesson plans will require some modifications. What works with one group of children, for example, might not work with another group. Consequently, you need to be prepared to modify tasks on the fly. This type of adjustment is much easier for an experienced teacher who has taught tons of tasks and has a large repertoire from which to draw. For beginning teachers, we recommend planning ways to modify tasks if what you're doing isn't working—in other words, having **alternative strategies** at the ready to use on your feet. The easiest alternative strategies to plan are modifications to make tasks easier (ME tasks) and modifications to make tasks more difficult (MD tasks).

Information Feedback

One primary response after observing and interpreting children's movement is to give feedback on what you observed. **Feedback** is information you (or a peer) give to a child about his or her responses in relation to the learning goal of the task. Feedback gives students specific information about their responses that tells them if, how, and the extent to which they are learning the objective of the lesson or task. Good feedback is descriptive, not evaluative. For example, let's say the objective of the lesson is dribbling by pushing with the fingerprints. Feedback is more likely to lead to learning when you say, "I see that most of the time you are successfully pushing the ball with your fingerprints when you dribble, but a few times you slapped the ball with your palm and you lost control of the ball," as opposed to saying, "Good job," or "Don't slap the ball." When you say "good job," which is evaluative and not descriptive, the child doesn't know what "job" he or she is doing well or the extent to which he or she is learning the objectives of the lesson. When you say, "Don't slap the ball," the child might be unaware that he or she ever slapped the ball and consequently might think, "What is he talking about? I *am* pushing with my fingerprints." Then, the child might ignore your feedback, as it is only a partial description of the child's performance and thus appears to be inaccurate. Children need to know their teacher's feedback is trustworthy and accurate (Wiggins, 2012) so that they will use this feedback to self-correct skill performance when the teacher is not there.

The same applies to cognitive or social goals, such as how to use a game tactic, apply a principle of choreography, or follow rules for productive social interactions in a small group discussion. With these cognitive and social objectives, the nature of good feedback remains the same. Describe in a nonevaluative manner what you saw or heard in relation to the objective you set for the task.

Use of Smartphones and Tablets for Information Feedback

This may be hard to believe, but in the not so distant past, only coaches regularly used films and videotapes to provide feedback. With the rapid growth of technology, the capability to use videos to provide informational feedback instantly is in the hands of most teachers today.

As a teacher, you likely have access to a smartphone or tablet. You can use these devices to record the students and have them see their performance during the lesson. You can both show and explain what you observed. Then remove the recording from the device. This feedback strategy is particularly helpful when you want students to see what the audience sees in a dance or gymnastics sequence. It is also helpful to show them what the passer sees when looking for an open receiver. Children sometimes think they are open when they're not, and a video from the passer's perspective can help them reinterpret their actions as receivers. There are also apps for drawing lines over a video performance or adding audio commentary to teach students exactly how the body should be positioned. Before recording students' performances, check your school policies on videotaping students.

Congruent Feedback

The use of **congruent feedback** is a strategy to help you and the children focus on the learning goal of the task, that is, ensuring your feedback matches the performance technique you gave as the focus of the task (Rink, 2014). It can be very frustrating for children when you ask them to focus on one performance technique and then give them feedback on something completely different. What typically happens is that the child has successfully performed the technique you taught but has difficulty with a different performance technique. When you notice this issue, instead of giving the child positive, specific feedback on the original performance technique assigned, you move on to the next performance technique you think the child needs to learn. Although this response is understandable, it is better to take the time to give feedback on the performance technique you discussed first. This action rewards the child for paying attention and learning what you asked; then you can move on to the next performance technique.

Figure 8.3 Giving positive feedback

Courtesy of John Dolly

Positive and Negative Feedback

There is consensus in the research that positive specific feedback (see **Figure 8.3**) on children's performance is more effective and important to both learning and motivation (Bryan & Solmon, 2007; Chiviacowsky & Wulf, 2002, 2007; Koka & Hagger, 2010; Silverman, Tyson, & Krampitz, 1992; Sun & Chen, 2010). In contrast, negative nonverbal feedback has a negative effect on motivation (Koka & Hagger, 2010), and feedback after unsuccessful trials is less successful in enhancing learning than feedback after successful trials (Chiviacowsky & Wulf, 2002, 2007; Silverman et al., 1992).

Feedback on How to Improve

Once children understand the relevant details of their performance, provide them with one specific way they can improve their performance. Address either the process (the child's movement pattern) or the outcome, and you should focus on improvement, rather than comparing that child to others (Bryan & Solmon, 2007; Koka & Hagger, 2010; Sun & Chen, 2010).

Don't overload them with information. For example, you can say, "I saw your knees bend during your cartwheel. Next time, try to extend your legs so straight they reach the sky." This feedback gives the child one image on which to focus, as opposed to saying, "Keep your knees straight, toes pointed, and legs tight," which will also result in straight legs, but requires the child to think of three performance techniques at once.

Don't be tempted to skip the description of what you saw, and, instead, immediately give them advice on how to improve. The child needs to understand why you are making your suggestion in the first place and trust that you saw their performance and recognized their attempts to meet the lesson goals (Wiggins, 2012).

Feedback in the Form of a Question

Putting **feedback in the form of a question** asks children to reflect back on their performance and tell you what they did well in relation to the goal and what they might try to do next to improve. This kind of feedback contributes to children becoming independent learners and learning how to think critically and analyze their skills. With only one teacher and many children, it is critical that children become independent learners capable of generating their own feedback. When you make a habit of giving feedback in the form of a question, the children soon learn that they will be accountable for paying attention to what you teach, knowing the performance techniques on which you expect them to focus, and then focusing on these techniques during practice.

It's easier than you might think to put feedback in the form of a question. A helpful guideline is to think about what feedback you want to give and then put it in the form of a question.

Praise or General, Positive Feedback

Praise such as "Good job," or a big smile and a thumbs-up are welcomed by children. They need to know you are happy with them and their efforts. **Praise (general, positive feedback)** is general, nonspecific feedback that makes a positive statement about student performance. General, positive feedback contributes to a positive classroom climate, enhances student motivation, and lets children know you are pleased with their efforts (Koka & Hagger, 2010). Thus, general, positive feedback serves a different purpose than specific feedback on how to improve performance. The problem with praise occurs, however, when you follow praise with other feedback. In these instances, students focus on the praise and don't pay attention to the other information provided by the teacher (Hattie, 2012). Praise is important, but children must perceive praise as sincere and linked to their immediate actions, rather than as habitual comments made by the teacher at the end of every task. **Table 8.1** describes different types of feedback that can be given to students.

Group and Individual Feedback

Feedback can be given to the whole group, a small group, or individual children. To give feedback to the entire class (i.e., whole group), scan and see what feedback would help most children. Then say something appropriate: "Many of you are doing a great job pushing with your finger pads," or "I can see that many of you have really improved your dribbling today because you are keeping the ball waist high or lower. Think to yourself what you did to improve, remember what you did, and give yourself a pat on the back." You can also use whole-group feedback to address the most pressing problems you see. For example, you might say, "Some of you are losing control of the ball, and it is interfering with other children's practicing. What do you need to do to keep better control of the ball? [Answers: Dribble more slowly; don't push the ball too far ahead.] Those are great answers. Let's try the task again and see if you can control the ball the entire time."

Whole-group feedback is beneficial for the following reasons:

- It tells the children you are observing all of them in relation to the goal of the task.
- It reminds children to focus on one component of the skill.
- It helps refocus children's attention if they are drifting off task.
- It functions as a management technique by reminding the children to focus on learning.

Individual feedback is given to an individual child. If you teach small classes, this kind of feedback is both possible and desirable. If you teach large classes, you will not be able to give individual feedback to every child on every task. In addition, it

Table 8.1 Types of Feedback

Type of Feedback	Description	Examples
Specific and informational	Provides specific information about the student's performance in relation to the objective of the task or learning goal of the lesson	You did a great job bending your knees when you landed. Excellent tension in your body as you held your final position. You worked very hard on your transitions in your gymnastics sequence, and consequently the sequence was very smooth. I can hear this group is all listening to each other, and everyone is making a contribution to the discussion.
Congruent	Addresses the exact performance technique the teacher told the children to work on during the task	I saw you dribble waist high.
In the form of a question	Requires the child to self-evaluate and tell the teacher something he or she did well and how he or she might improve	You improved that time; what, specifically, did you do better? What are you working on? Where did the ball go when you tossed it? What do you think you need to do to toss the ball straight up?
Praise (general, positive feedback)	Nonspecific, positive statements about student performance	Good job! You got it! Excellent.

What the Research Says

Feedback

Research on the impact of feedback has yielded inconsistent results. One study showed it had little effect; rather, the amount of practice was what accounted for learning (Silverman, Tyson, & Morford, 1988). Another investigation found that giving both specific feedback on how to perform a complex skill and motivational feedback was more effective than simply giving motivational feedback or no feedback (Fredenburg, Lee, & Solmon, 2001). Research also suggests that the most effective form of feedback probably depends on the skill.

Feedback focused on the outcome rather than performance techniques was found to be more effective in a forearm pass and volleyball serve (Silverman et al., 1992). Focusing on techniques proved more effective than focusing on ball flight in a study of a golf shot (Wulf, McNevin, Fuchs, Ritter, & Toole, 2000). In a balancing skill, research indicated that learners benefited more from focusing on an external point in space as opposed to the body (Wulf, Shea, & Park, 2001).

In regard to positive and negative feedback, research reveals that when learners control when they receive feedback, they prefer to get feedback after they have performed the skill successfully and that feedback after successful attempts enhances learning more than feedback after unsuccessful attempts (Chiviacowsky & Wulf, 2002, 2007). Another study also found positive feedback related to achievement (Silverman et al., 1992). These authors note that traditional views of feedback assume that feedback is most helpful after a poor performance; their results, however, contradicted this contention. In addition, research on motivation clearly supports that positive feedback should be given related to how a child improved, rather than comparing that child to other children (Bryan & Solmon, 2007; Koka & Hagger, 2010; Sun & Chen, 2010).

is difficult to give large amounts of individual feedback when you also must scan frequently to ensure safety (Morgan & Kingston, 2008). Group feedback when you teach large classes is a viable alternative.

Give Feedback Often but Briefly

Typically, beginning teachers do not give enough feedback, especially group feedback. A good guideline is to talk often, but briefly. If you stand quietly watching the class, the children will more quickly go off task. Interactive teaching requires an active teacher who is moving and responding to the class in a positive manner, thereby encouraging the children to learn.

One way to help you improve on the amount, accuracy, and specificity of your feedback and the positive climate of the class is to videorecord your lesson and then code which type of feedback was provided, to whom the feedback was given, whether the feedback was congruent with the assigned task, and whether it reflected an accurate assessment of the children's movements. Again, check your school's policies on video recording lessons before doing so. On the text website we provide a tool for assessing your feedback.

Other Forms of Feedback

Teachers who teach large classes know they cannot give each child a lot of individual feedback. It helps to remember that children are getting other forms of feedback on every trial. **Intrinsic feedback** is feedback children get through their own senses, such as the feeling of hitting a ball. In addition, children often get **external feedback** about the results of their movement. We call this "knowledge of results," and it includes things like seeing whether the ball hit the target and seeing whether a kicked ball went into the air or traveled along the ground. These are powerful forms of feedback that clearly contribute to learning (Schmidt & Wrisberg, 2004).

We do not yet have strong support from research conducted in school settings indicating that teacher feedback to individual students is *directly* linked to student learning; in other words, we cannot claim that the more students receive individual feedback, the more they will learn (Rink, 2003). Some studies have shown that less frequent feedback is more beneficial than high rates of feedback, such as after every trial (Rose & Christina, 2006). This does not mean that teacher feedback isn't important, but rather that its importance will depend on which skill is being attempted, the ability level of the students, whether the learner is just beginning to learn the skill or is refining performance, and whether other forms of intrinsic and extrinsic feedback are available.

Because skills and learners vary so greatly, research cannot conclusively tell teachers how much feedback is best. However, it is certainly important for children to know that their teacher is watching them, encouraging them to learn and work hard, and noticing improvements and giving positive, specific feedback on these improvements.

Reflecting on Teaching

The observation, interpretation, and decision-making cycle occurs during a lesson, and the teacher is reflecting in action. A second cycle, similar in form, occurs when you reflect carefully on your teaching, content, and children's responses and then evaluate your program in relation to long-term goals, professional standards, your beliefs, and your philosophy.

Being a reflective teacher both during and after lessons is a characteristic of excellent teachers. Research shows that teachers who effectively reflected on their teaching improved their teaching and how they accommodated individual differences (Jung, 2012). Moreover, reflecting regularly and deeply allowed them to understand and critique their beliefs and then change their beliefs in ways they viewed to be positive.

Reflecting on your teaching means thinking about the big picture and asking some difficult questions, such as the following:

- Do the motor, cognitive, affective, and social responses of each child you teach indicate the likelihood that they are developing the "knowledge, skills and confidence to enjoy a lifetime of healthful physical activity" (Society of Health and Physical Educators [SHAPE], 2014, p. 11)?
  - Are all your children learning, or are you being successful with only those athletic children who are just like you?
  - Are you paying attention to the emotional responses of all children?
  - Are the overweight and obese children happy, successful, and part of the class community, or are they alienated and teased?
- Can you justify your curriculum in relation to the National Standards for Physical education?
- Are you teaching based on a consistent philosophy of which you are proud?
- Are you having the kind of impact you want?
- Are you the kind of teacher you want to be?

Reflecting on teaching in relation to your beliefs can help you clarify these beliefs and better understand the connections between what you do daily and your overarching philosophy. Reflecting on teaching can also help you notice issues or problems you don't notice in the hectic pace of a school day. It can start you on the road to addressing these issues and solving these problems. Reflecting on teaching can help you grow as a teacher.

Summary

Interactive teaching is a cycle of observation, interpretation, and decision making. This cycle can be referred to as reflecting in action. A characteristic of expert teachers is their ability to observe critical details that are important for learning (Schempp & Woorons-Johnson, 2006); in contrast, novices tend to have difficulty seeing details (Bell et al., 1985). You can learn to be an excellent observer of children's movement by learning about the details of the content you are teaching and through practice, assisted by the development of a plan of what to observe.

To interpret children's responses, consider the role of the task and the environment, children's developmental levels, and other factors that can affect children's responses. Based on your interpretations, you then make decisions about how to respond.

When and which kind of feedback to give to children are decisions you will frequently make. Feedback is information that you (or a peer) give to children about their motor, cognitive, social, and motivational responses in relation to the learning goals of the lesson.

Reflecting on teaching occurs after the lesson or at the end of the day. When you reflect on teaching, you look at your curriculum, instruction, and children's motor, cognitive, affective, and social responses in relation to long-term goals, professional standards, your beliefs, and your philosophy. You then decide if you need to make changes to what and how you teach. Being a reflective teacher is a sign of excellence and is beneficial for beginners as well as veterans.

Review Questions

1. Write a task, and then describe what you will need to observe to ensure children's safety while they are completing the task.
2. Write two different lesson tasks for any elementary grade, and then write an observation plan for each task.
3. As a novice teacher, where should you locate yourself during lessons and why?
4. What is checking for understanding? Describe three ways to check for understanding.
5. What is congruent feedback, and why is it important?
6. What is whole-group feedback, and why is it beneficial?
7. What are intrinsic feedback and knowledge of results?
8. What is reflecting on teaching, and why is it important?

References

Barrett, K. R. (1984). The teacher as observer, interpreter, and decision maker. In B. J. Logsdon, K. R. Barrett, M. Ammons, M. R. Broer, L. E. Halverson, R. McGee, & M. A. Roberton (Eds.), *Physical education for children: A focus on the teaching process* (2nd ed.). (pp. 295–355). Philadelphia: Lea & Febiger.

Barrett, K. R. (2009). *From carbon (paper) to computer chips: A personal retrospective on the art of informing research through teaching.* In L. D. Housner, M. W. Metzler, P. G. Schempp, & T. J. Templin (Eds.), *Historic traditions and future directions of research on teaching and teacher education in physical education* (pp. 15–21). Morganton, WV: West Virginia University, Fitness Information Technology.

Bell, R., Barrett, K. R., & Allison, P. C. (1985). What preservice physical education teachers see in an unguided, early field experience. *Journal of Teaching in Physical Education, 4*, 81–90.

Bryan, C. L., & Solmon, M. A. (2007). Self-determination in physical education: Designing class environments to promote active lifestyles. *Journal of Teaching in Physical Education, 26*, 260–278.

Chiviacowsky, S., & Wulf, G. (2002). Self-controlled feedback: Does it enhance learning because performers get feedback when they need it? *Research Quarterly for Exercise and Sport, 73*, 408–415.

Chiviacowsky, S., & Wulf, G. (2007). Feedback after good trials enhances learning. *Research Quarterly for Exercise and Sport, 78*, 40–47.

Eickhoff-Shemek, J. M., Herbert, D. L., & Connaughton, D. P. (2009). *Risk Management for Health/Fitness Professionals: Legal Issues and Strategies.* Philadelphia: Wolters Kluwer/Lippincott Williams & Wilkins.

Fredenburg, K. B., Lee, A. M., & Solmon, M. (2001). The effects of augmented feedback on students' perceptions and performance. *Research Quarterly for Exercise and Sport, 72*, 232–242.

Halsey, J. J. (2005). Risk Management for Physical Educators. In H. Appenzeller (Ed.), *Risk management in sport: Issues and strategies*, (2nd ed.). (pp. 151–163). Durham, NC: Carolina Academic Press.

Hart, J. E., & Ritson, R. J. (2002). *Liability and Safety in Physical Education and Sport.* Reston, VA: National Association for Sport and Physical Education.

Hattie, J. (2012). Know thy impact. *Educational Leadership, 70*(1), 18–23.

Jung, J. (2012). The focus, role, and meaning of experienced teachers' reflection in physical education. *Physical Education and Sport Pedagogy, 17*, 157–175.

Koka, A., & Hagger, M. S. (2010). Perceived teaching behaviors and self-determined motivation in physical education: A test of self-determination theory. *Research Quarterly for Exercise and Sport, 81*, 74–86.

McCaughtry, N., & Rovegno, I. (2003). The development of pedagogical content knowledge: Moving from blaming students to predicting skillfulness, recognizing motor development, and understanding emotion. *Journal of Teaching in Physical Education, 22*, 355–368.

Morgan, K., & Kingston, K. (2008). Development of a self-observation mastery intervention program for teacher education. *Physical Education and Sport Pedagogy, 13*, 109–129.

National Association of Sport and Physical Education (NASPE). (2010). *Opportunity to learn: Guidelines for elementary, middle, and high school physical education: A side-by-side comparison.* Reston, VA: Author.

Nohr, K. M. (2009). *Managing Risk in Sport and Recreation: The Essential Guide for Loss Prevention.* Champaign, IL: Human Kinetics.

Rink, J. (2003). Motor learning. In B. Mohnsen (Ed.), *Concepts of physical education: What every student needs to know.* Reston, VA: National Association of Sport and Physical Education.

Rink, J. E. (2014). *Teaching physical education for learning* (7th ed.). New York: McGraw-Hill.

Rose, D. J., & Christina, R. W. (2006). *A multilevel approach to the study of motor control and learning* (2nd ed.). San Francisco: Benjamin Cummings.

Rovegno, I. (1991). A participant-observation study of knowledge restructuring in a field-based elementary physical education methods course. *Research Quarterly for Exercise and Sport, 62*, 205–212.

Rovegno, I. C. (1992). Learning to teach in a field-based methods course: The development of pedagogical content knowledge. *Teaching and Teacher Education, 8*, 69–82.

Schempp, P. G., & Woorons-Johnson, S. (2006). Learning to see: Developing the perception of an expert teacher. *Journal of Physical Education, Recreation, and Dance, 77*(6), 29–33.

Schmidt, R. A., & Wrisberg, C. A. (2004). *Motor learning and performance* (3rd ed.). Champaign, IL: Human Kinetics.

Schön, D. A. (1983). *The reflective practitioner.* New York: Basic Books.

Schön, D. A. (1987). *Educating the reflective practitioner: Toward a new design for teaching and learning in the profession.* San Francisco: Jossey-Bass.

Silverman, S., Tyson, L., & Krampitz, J. (1992). Teacher feedback and achievement in physical education: Interaction with student practice. *Teaching and Teacher Education, 8*, 333–344.

Silverman, S., Tyson, L. A., & Morford, L. M. (1988). Relationships of organization, time, and student achievement in physical education. *Teaching and Teacher Education, 4*, 247–257.

Society of Health and Physical Educators (SHAPE). (2014). *National standards and grade-level outcomes for K–12 physical education.* Champaign, IL: Human Kinetics.

Stroot, S. A., & Oslin, J. L. (1993). The use of instructional statements by preservice teachers for overhand throwing performance of children. *Journal of Teaching in Physical Education, 13*, 24–45.

Sun, H., & Chen, A. (2010). A pedagogical understanding of the self-determination theory in physical education. *Quest, 62*, 364–384.

Wiggins, G. (2012). Seven keys to effective feedback. *Educational Leadership, 70*(1), 11–16.

Wulf, G., McNevin, N. H., Fuchs, T., Ritter, F., & Toole, T. (2000). Attentional focus in complex skill learning. *Research Quarterly for Exercise and Sport, 71*, 229–239.

Wulf, G., Shea, C., & Park, J. H. (2001). Attention and motor performance: Preferences for and advantages of an external focus. *Research Quarterly for Exercise and Sport, 72*, 335–344.

CHAPTER

9

Motivation and Establishing a Learning Environment

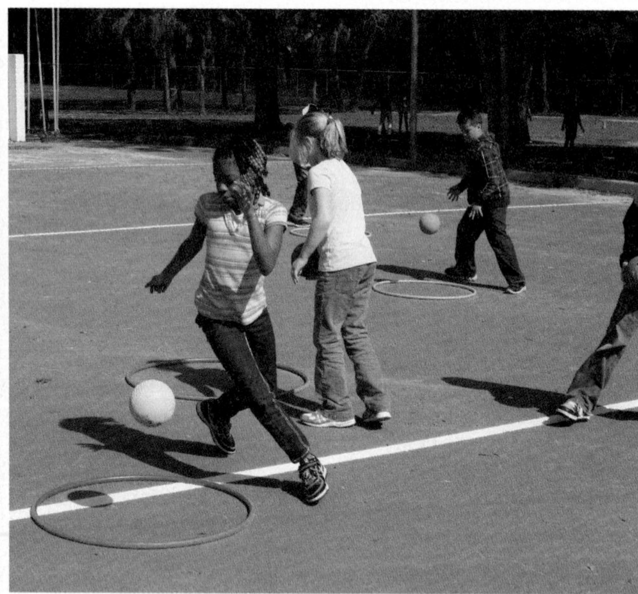

PRE-READING REFLECTION

1. Have you ever played a game (such as racquetball, tennis, or 1v1 basketball) against an opponent who was so much better or so much worse than you that it wasn't a good game? Did you or your opponent simply run up the score and go home early, or did you or your opponent modify your game (such as by serving only returnable serves, eliminating kill shots, or winning points only by using drops, drives, or passing shots)? What is your opinion about what players should do in these situations?
2. When you play softball at a family picnic or other mixed-age social gathering and a small child comes up to bat, do you pitch the ball fast or slow so the little kid can get a hit? Why?

OBJECTIVES

Students will learn:

1. Research has shown that some students find physical education alienating and humiliating.
2. Two "Hall of Shame" practices that lead to a negative environment are putting children on display and having captains publicly pick their teams.
3. Helping children develop a mastery orientation and growth mindset, believe they can be successful, and develop perceptions of competence and autonomy contributes to a positive learning environment.
4. Students with a mastery orientation are most concerned about mastering the content and self-improvement. They embrace challenging tasks and persist when faced with difficult problems.
5. Students with an ego orientation focus most on how their performance compares to others and seek to have others perceive that they are smart and have high abilities.

6. Students with a growth mindset believe that they can improve their abilities and intellect through hard work. For these students, success is due to effort.
7. Students with a fixed mindset believe that success is due to ability, rather than to working hard or making a good effort.
8. Teachers can teach a mastery orientation and a growth mindset and increase student achievement, satisfaction, and enjoyment in physical education.
9. Teachers contribute to a positive learning environment when they create opportunities for student autonomy and ensure students are challenged but can be successful.

KEY TERMS

Autonomy
Ego orientation
Fixed mindset
Growth mindset
Hall of Shame practices
Mastery orientation
Perceived competence

CONNECTION TO STANDARDS

Broadly speaking, this chapter discusses motivation for learning. Consequently, it addresses all National Standards for Physical Education (National Standards) and Common Core and other State Standards (CCSS). In particular, we describe principles of learning motor skills that are included under National Standard 2 and the value of challenge included under National Standard 5. Research on motivation for learning motor skills mirrors research on learning cognitive knowledge, and both fields address related social and affective dimensions of learning. The principles and suggestions for teaching derived from research on motivation provide powerful teaching strategies for meeting the National Standards and CCSS.

Introduction

Our goal in this chapter is to describe how to create a positive learning environment. A positive learning environment is one in which students are motivated to learn, think positively about their abilities to learn and succeed, work hard and persistently, and embrace challenging tasks. We will start with what research has shown to be negative aspects of some physical education environments and discuss two teaching practices to avoid. Just like the Hippocratic Oath taken by physicians, we start with this imperative for teachers: "First, do no harm."

Next, we briefly summarize the large body of research on motivation that shows how teachers can create a positive learning environment. We end with examples demonstrating how you can easily apply these research findings in your classes.

Alienation in Physical Education

Physical education can be frightening for children in relation to both their emotional safety and their physical safety. Recall that children enter physical education with prior knowledge and experiences. Unfortunately, for some children these experiences may have been negative—even humiliating and embarrassing—and physical education can sometimes be an alienating place, especially for low-skilled children (Carlson, 1995; Dyson, 2006; Portman, 1995; Spencer-Cavaliere & Rintoul, 2012).

In one study, low-skilled, alienated students reported feeling powerless, frustrated, uninterested, and embarrassed. They did not enjoy physical education and withdrew from participation (Spencer-Cavaliere & Rintoul, 2012). In another study, boys who had masculinities that were not the dominant masculinity and were taunted and mocked by students and teachers resisted physical education by finding clever ways to appear as if they were participating without actually doing so. The boys enjoyed physical activities outside of school where the purpose was play oriented and not winning in a highly competitive environment. In physical education programs, however, their body language (e.g., guarded, making their bodies small, curling into a ball with head down, avoiding eye contact, not smiling at teachers' jokes) expressed their anxiety and fear. The researchers asked, "Why do certain students wear so much anguish in physical education?" (Tischler & McCaughtry, 2011, p. 47).

Although, in general, young children like physical education, believe that they are competent, and are motivated to learn (Lee, Carter, & Xiang, 1995; Xiang, Lee, & Williamson, 2001; Xiang, McBride, & Guan, 2004; Xiang, McBride, Guan, & Solmon, 2003), by the end of elementary school, more and more have become alienated. As physical education teachers, it is our job to turn this attitude around.

Hall of Shame Practices that Alienate Students and Harm the Learning Environment

One reason that the physical education environment can be embarrassing and alienating to children is that everyone can see their bodies and performance. Consequently, everyone knows who is highly skilled and who is not. You might do poorly on a math test, but only the teacher will know. By comparison, the whole class can see if you miss the ball in physical education.

Hall of Shame practices are inappropriate teaching behaviors that do not meet professional standards of practice because they alienate students and harm the learning environment. Neil Williams (1992, 1994, 1996) nominated a number of common teaching practices and games for the "The Physical Education Hall of Shame." Here we highlight two common teaching practices that he included in the "Hall of Shame" because of their negative impact on the learning environment. The National Association of Sport and Physical Education (NASPE), which is now called the Society of Health and Physical Educators (SHAPE), has also identified these practices as inappropriate (NASPE, 2009).

Putting Children on Display

As Williams (1996) states, having one child perform while all the other children watch can be a devastating experience for low-skilled and average-skilled children. This situation may arise in elimination games such as dodgeball in which the less skilled children are singled out and eliminated first, relay races in which the entire class watches to see who caused a team to finish last or lose the race, whole-class games like kickball in which only one child is performing at a time, and gymnastics or other classes when children stand on line waiting their turn.

Try to put yourself in the children's shoes: Would you want to have your high school and college grades posted on the classroom wall? One way to eliminate these situations is simply to have all children work individually or in small groups at the same time. If everyone is concentrating on their own work, no one will be put on display.

Having Captains Publicly Pick Their Teams

Most physical education majors were among the highly skilled students in their elementary schools and consequently did not experience the humiliation of being among the last children picked to be on a team. As we all know, captains pick friends and the best players first, while the less skilled children stand uncomfortably on display, feeling not only incompetent but also disliked.

You might think picking teams is simply part of childhood rituals with no impact later in life; however, the evidence suggests the contrary. In one study, 31% of participants reported they had been picked last for a team, and these participants were significantly less physically active as adults than adults who had not experiences being picked last (Cardinal, Yan, & Cardinal, 2013). In another study, 93.4% of teachers surveyed knew that having captains pick teams was an inappropriate professional practice, but only 71.4% never used this team selection practice (Strand & Bender, 2011). Researchers Cardinal, Yan, and Cardinal have this to say about the practice:

> The practice of choosing sides or teams using a pecking-order approach must be stopped. It has the exact opposite effect of what is ultimately desired in physical education. It causes real and long-lasting harm to people's psyches and their physical activity participation levels. It is a humiliating experience that only serves to marginalize and disadvantage those left standing on the line waiting and wondering when their name will be called, hoping they will not be called last (2013, p. 53).

Some teachers think having captains pick teams is the only way to ensure fair teams. In reality, students are rarely accurate judges of their peers' abilities. There are many ways to select fair teams. We suggest you do it yourself and focus on assigning children to groups in ways that facilitate learning.

Remember that the goal of physical education is learning and establishing lifelong motivation to participate in physical activity, not in setting up "fair" competitions where the emphasis is on winning.

You might also consider that the national organization that represents physical education in the United States, SHAPE America, states that the practice of having captains publicly pick their teams is inappropriate. Highly competitive environments that publicly privilege those who are highly skilled are

SAFETY AND LIABILITY 9.1

Increasing Safety and Decreasing Risk of Liability: Guidelines Relevant to Content in this Chapter

In this box, we discuss specific guidelines built on information discussed throughout this text on professional standards of practice, negligence, and liability. The goals of these guidelines are to increase children's safety and decrease teachers' risk of negligence and liability.

- To decrease risk of liability, teachers follow professional standards of practice that are published by professional organizations.
- Developing autonomy by giving children choices about task difficulty is one way to differentiate instruction, which is a characteristic of professional practice promoted by SHAPE.
- For safety reasons, it is important in educational gymnastics to teach a mastery orientation, not a competitive ego orientation. You will always have some children who take gymnastics lessons. The skills they can perform are fun, and other children want to learn them. If the learning environment is ego oriented, some children might attempt to perform skills they are not ready to learn or perform safely and become seriously injured.

damaging. If a child gets hurt or parents complain and you are using practices that the national organization representing physical education educators states are inappropriate, you are vulnerable to charges that your actions were unprofessional, negligent, and caused emotional harm.

Motivation and a Positive Learning Environment

To create a positive learning environment, you must do more than simply eliminate harmful practices. In this section, we discuss research on ways to improve student motivation and create positive learning environments.

A large body of compelling research on motivation in education, physical education, and sport settings emphasizes the importance of children having

- A mastery orientation
- A growth mindset
- Perceived competence and autonomy
- Positive perceptions of and intrinsic interest in lesson content

Mastery Orientation Versus Ego Orientation

Students who have a **mastery orientation** are most concerned about learning the content, mastering the task or skill, and accomplishing their own self-improvement (Ames, 1992; Solmon, 1996; Treasure & Roberts, 2001). Children with mastery orientations embrace challenging tasks, don't give up when the going gets tough, and persist in working hard even when they encounter difficulties in learning the content. The priority for students with a mastery orientation is what they learn, rather than which grades they receive or how they compare to others. They enjoy mastering new skills (see **Figure 9.1**).

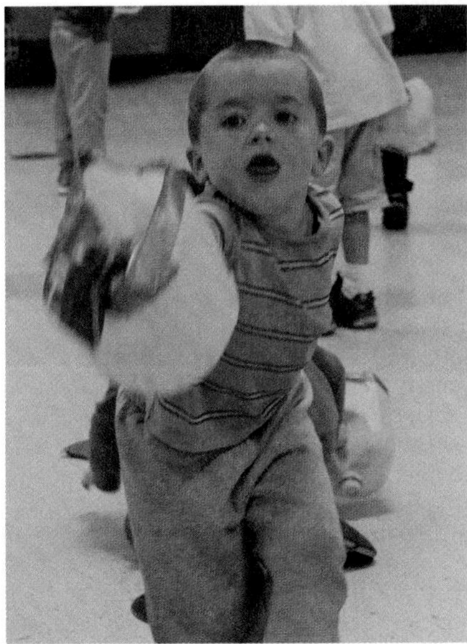

Figure 9.1 Focusing on mastery

Courtesy of John Dolly

> **Experienced Teachers Talk**
>
> Picking Teams
>
> In one school we know, the teachers successfully eliminated the practice of having captains publicly pick their teams whenever children were on school property, including at recess, before and after school, and on weekends. The teachers simply banded together, taught the children why this practice was harmful, and gave them alternative ways to select teams. When children would say, "We played this really cool game," the teachers would ask, "How did you pick teams?" Most children admitted the truth, and eventually the culture of the playground changed.

In contrast, students who have what researchers call an **ego orientation** (or performance orientation) focus most on how their performance compares to the performance of others (Ames, 1992; Solmon, 1996; Treasure & Roberts, 2001). Their goals are high grades and high rankings compared to peers. They are very concerned with looking good and having others perceive that they are smart and highly skilled. They don't like challenging tasks because they are afraid they will fail and

> **What the Research Says**
>
> Mastery Orientation
>
> In physical education, when students have mastery orientations, their skill development, engagement, and expectations of success are greater, and they perceive physical education as interesting, important, and useful (Treasure & Roberts, 1995; Xiang et al., 2003; Xiang et al., 2004).
>
> In addition, teachers can create a mastery-oriented climate, thereby having a positive impact on students' motivation. Teachers who structure mastery-oriented climates have been found to significantly increase student achievement, satisfaction, beliefs that success is based on effort, the number of times students practiced a skill, students' persistence, and the difficulty level of the tasks they chose to practice (Ames, 1992; Parish & Treasure, 2003; Solmon, 1996; Treasure & Roberts, 1995). By comparison, in an ego-oriented climate, students did not prefer challenging tasks or taking risks and were less motivated or lacked motivation to engage in physical activity (Parish & Treasure, 2003; Treasure & Roberts, 2001).
>
> When physical educators provide tasks at an appropriate developmental level and allow children to choose the difficulty level (see **Figure 9.2**), they are more likely to develop a mastery orientation, which involves practicing more, exerting more effort, and trying more challenging tasks (Byra & Jenkins, 1998; Solmon, 1996, 2006; Solmon & Boone, 1993). When children are engaged in lesson activities and motivated, they have more positive attitudes (Subramaniam & Silverman, 2000, 2002)—a goal worthy of all physical education teachers.

Figure 9.2 Children choosing the difficulty level

Courtesy of John Dolly

appear inept. This attitude, in turn, has a negative impact on learning, because such individuals will be reluctant to attempt skills they have not already mastered. An example in physical education is students who focus only on winning games and don't mind playing games where there is no challenge because they are much better than their opponents. They don't want to risk losing. They like having all the good players on their team.

Attributing Success to Effort Versus Ability: Growth and Fixed Mindsets

Another component of motivation is students' theories about whether intelligence and abilities can grow or are fixed. Dweck (2007) labels these attitudes a **growth mindset** and a **fixed mindset**, respectively. (The technical terms, which you might have learned in educational or sport psychology courses, are an entity implicit theory of ability for a fixed mindset and an incremental implicit theory for a growth mindset.)

Students with a growth mindset believe that they can develop their abilities (Dweck, 2007). They attribute success to effort and hard work, rather than to innate abilities. They believe that if they work hard they will become more skilled and more intelligent, and consequently will perform better. If they make mistakes or fail at a task, they view the setback as simply a sign that they need to work harder or find a different way to tackle the task. No better example of this attitude can be cited than the Olympic athletes who, when asked about their success, discuss how pleased they are that all of their hard work paid off.

Students with a fixed mindset believe that either you are athletic or not, intelligent or not, good at mathematics or not, good at reading and writing or not—and there is nothing you can do to change your abilities, because they are fixed traits. Students with fixed mindsets attribute success to ability, rather than to effort and hard work (Dweck, 2007). When they make mistakes or fail at a task, they believe this result shows that they lack ability, are not smart, and that working harder will not make any difference. Because they attribute success to ability, such individuals believe that smart, talented, and athletic students don't have to work hard; they equate working hard to what students who are not smart, talented, or athletic must do.

When students attribute their success to their abilities, they can be devastated when, as inevitably occurs, they are assigned more difficult tasks in which they are less successful, because they assume this outcome means they are no longer smart, talented, or athletic. When faced with challenging tasks, they can become anxious and afraid to take risks. These students think they have no control over their success or failure because the outcome is due to their ability; in turn, when tasks are difficult, they demonstrate an attitude of helplessness.

Benefits of a Mastery Orientation and a Growth Mindset

The benefits of having a mastery orientation and a growth mindset are many, including increased achievement, higher levels of effort, more persistence, greater skill development, and higher levels of engagement in learning tasks. When students believe that through hard work, effort, and persistence they can become smarter and more skilled, they actually do so, and they deal better with any difficulties or obstacles they face during the learning process.

The best athletes are excellent examples of the benefits of having a mastery orientation and a growth mindset. Although they are performance oriented during games or meets (because of the nature of competition), they look for and expect critiques of their performance so that they can improve through hard work and effort. They don't assume they will get better simply because of their ability; they know the necessity of engaging in hard work and facing challenges.

Students' Beliefs About Their Potential for Success, Perceived Competence, and Autonomy

When children enter a classroom believing that they can be successful and competent in the content being taught, then they are, in fact, more successful (Solmon, 2006). In addition, if children believe they will be competent, they are more willing to engage in practice, concentrate, pay attention, and work hard (Solmon & Lee, 1996). The reverse also has been shown. When low-ability students don't believe they can be successful, they become less successful and have difficulty figuring out how to improve (Solmon & Lee, 1996).

What the Research Says

Growth and Fixed Mindsets

Research in physical education has shown that a growth mindset leads to more skill development, greater enjoyment of physical activities, and increased satisfaction in physical education, whereas a fixed mindset leads to increased anxiety, lack of motivation, lack of interest, less enjoyment, less effort, and less skill development (Biddle, Wang, Chatzisarantis, & Spray, 2003; Li, Lee, & Solmon, 2005; Ommundsen, 2001, 2003). In addition, when students have a growth mindset, they demonstrate increased intrinsic motivation (i.e., motivation to engage in an activity for its own sake, personal enjoyment, and meaning), persistence, and improved performance (Li et al., 2005). Research has also shown that an ego-oriented class climate can contribute to a fixed mindset, whereas a mastery-oriented climate can contribute to a growth mindset (Xiang & Lee, 1998; Xiang et al., 2001).

Figure 9.3 "You've worked hard! Now you've got it."
Courtesy of John Dolly

Competence and autonomy are basic human needs (Deci & Ryan, 2002). Research in physical education has shown that higher levels of perceived competence have many benefits, including increased intrinsic motivation, engagement, and physical activity levels (Bryan & Solmon, 2007). **Perceived competence** occurs when children enter a classroom believing that they can be successful and competent in the content being taught.

Autonomy is the extent to which you have choices and control your behaviors. Student autonomy leads to increased engagement, self-sufficiency, and enjoyment (Standage, Duda, & Ntoumanis, 2003; Treasure & Roberts, 1995). When students perceive that they are competent and have autonomy in physical education, they increase effort, concentration, and persistence (Zhang, Solmon, & Gu, 2012) (see **Figure 9.3**).

Teachers can enhance motivation and learning when they support student autonomy in the following ways:

- Respecting and supporting students' capabilities to make decisions
- Respecting and accommodating individual differences among students
- Offering choices among activities
- Offering choices in skill test item difficulty
- Offering choices in task difficulty (Bryan & Solmon, 2007; Johnson, Prusak, Pennington, & Wilkinson, 2011; Koka & Hagger, 2010; Prusak, Treasure, Darst, & Pangrazi, 2004; Shen, McCaughtry, Martin, & Fahlman, 2009)

Students' Perceptions of the Value of Physical Activities

Research in physical education has shown that the extent to which students appreciate the value (i.e., usefulness, importance, and intrinsic interest) of physical activities can contribute to their motivation to learn and participate in physical activities (Chen, Martin, Ennis, & Sun, 2008; Xiang et al., 2003; Xiang et al., 2004). For children, interest appears to be the most significant influence on student motivation (Xiang, Chen, & Bruene, 2005), whereas the value of the task appears to motivate cognitive learning (Ding, Sun, & Chen, 2013). Thus, teachers should teach children the usefulness and importance of what they are learning so as to pique their interest and increase their motivation (Chen et al., 2008).

Strategies to Establish a Mastery-Oriented Climate, Teach a Growth Mindset, and Promote Autonomy

It might seem that having a mastery orientation, attributing success to effort, and maintaining perceptions of competence would simply be part of students' personalities or result from their past experiences with a particular content area, such that teachers can do little to change students' basic mindsets. The good news is that this isn't so. Research conducted on students ranging from elementary through college age clearly shows that teachers can teach students a growth mindset, which in turn will result in increased achievement, effort, persistence in the face of difficulties, and choice of challenging tasks (Dweck, 1999; Dweck & Molden, 2005). More importantly, teachers can

Sport Slogans Emphasizing a Mastery Orientation and Attributing Success to Effort

Many coaches and athletes have promoted a mastery orientation through a focus on effort and hard work. Common locker room slogans and clichés reflect this orientation:

- The only place where success comes before work is in the dictionary.
- When the going gets tough, the tough get going.
- Winners never quit, and quitters never win.
- If you think you are green, you'll ripen. If you think you're good, you'll rot.
- When you're through improving, you're through.
- If you have done your best, you have won.
- The person who wants to do something finds a way; the other kind finds an excuse.
- Often the roughest road may be the best way to where you want to go.
- "A lifetime of training for just 10 seconds!" (Jesse Owens, Olympic gold medalist sprinter)
- "Every single day I wake up and commit to myself to becoming a better player." (Mia Hamm, professional soccer player)
- The glory is not in never failing, but in rising every time you fall.
- "It does not matter how many times you get knocked down; it matters how many times you get up." (Vince Lombardi, NFL football coach)

What the Research Says

Is Providing Tasks that Ensure Success Enough?

Carol Dweck (1999) and her graduate students and colleagues have conducted many studies on having a growth mindset versus a fixed mindset. In one set of studies, they tested whether having a history of success (such as bright girls with excellent grades in math in elementary school) would contribute to confidence and ensure continued success as tasks became more difficult in middle school. This is a commonly held belief among teachers—that success breeds success and that self-confidence supports students' willingness to attempt more challenging work.

What the researchers found was surprising. Students who had fixed mindsets (that is, they believed they succeeded because of their abilities and that their abilities were a fixed trait) did not fare well when they faced difficult and challenging tasks. This was especially true for bright girls. Instead, their performance decreased. When students with a fixed mindset were given the choice of tasks, they chose tasks that were easy so that they would not make mistakes. They were afraid of failure, because to them failure meant they were not smart. In contrast, students with growth mindsets (who believed intelligence could be developed through effort and hard work) were resilient when they faced difficult work and continued to improve.

The researchers then focused on the students with fixed mindsets who blamed their failures on their ability and responded to challenging tasks with helplessness. Half of these students were given training that included only tasks in which they succeeded. The other half was trained to reinterpret their failures. Instead of blaming mistakes on their ability, they were taught that when they made mistakes, it meant they needed to try harder. In other words, these fixed-mindset students were taught to have growth mindsets.

After the training sessions, the students who experienced success the entire time showed no difference in their performance when faced with challenging tasks; the performance of some even decreased. The students who were taught to take a growth mindset and view mistakes as meaning they had to try harder performed much better on difficult tasks. In addition, they began to show greater persistence by working longer on difficult tasks rather than giving up.

The researchers concluded that when students have a fixed mindset, ensuring success and confidence is not enough to encourage them to tackle difficult tasks or to respond to failure with resilience. However, you can teach such students to have a growth mindset and change a helpless attitude into one that encourages children to persist and work harder when they face difficult and challenging tasks.

establish a mastery-oriented climate that promotes a growth mindset, effort, competence, and embracing challenges, and supports student autonomy.

In the remainder of this chapter, we describe instructional strategies for applying motivation concepts in your lessons. We summarize this information in **Table 9.1** and align each instructional strategy with the three levels of games and gymnastics content and the two levels of dance content. Table 9.1 and our descriptions and illustrations will help you select skills and concepts that you can include in lessons to meet both the National Standards and CCSS.

Teacher Beliefs and Reflection

A. Have a Growth Mindset and Believe Physical Education Is About Mastering Skills

The very first step is to start with your mindset. You need to believe that your students are capable of increasing their motor, cognitive, affective, and social capabilities. Studies have found that teachers who demonstrated fixed mindsets did not produce as much achievement as those who had growth mindsets (Dweck & Molden, 2005). One reason for this difference was that teachers with fixed mindsets made quick judgments about what students could achieve. Teachers with growth mindsets, in contrast, viewed students as capable of changing; they both recognized growth and viewed students' current abilities as simply an assessment of where they were at that moment in time. A growth mindset is the same as taking a developmental perspective. You also need to believe that physical education is about learning, not about playing games to determine a winner.

B. Reflect on Your Teaching in Relation to Motivation Principles

The most important way to maintain a mastery orientation and a growth mindset is to hold these attitudes and then act accordingly. Many times an ego orientation arises because children and teachers simply accept the attitudes and behaviors that seem appropriate and predominant in professional, collegiate, and interscholastic high school sports. You need to step back from the games and reflect on what you observe. Ask yourself the following questions:

- Do you emphasize the information that children have learned, the enjoyment of the game, and the value of effort?
- Do you or the children accept negative, hurtful behaviors as simply "part of the game"?
- Does any child feel incapable? Alienated? Humiliated?
- Do the children feel good about their performance and effort in a well-played game regardless of the score?
- Do the children value the challenge of working hard against a good opponent?
- If the children won but played poorly, didn't improve, and didn't try hard, did they gloat and claim they were successful?
- Have you taught children the tactics and tactical skills needed for the game (e.g., how to throw a lead pass, defend a receiver, and develop game tactics)?

Table 9.1 Motivation, Higher-Order Thinking Skills, and Social Responsibility Concepts

Game Content		
Level 1: Developing fundamental game skills	***Level 2:*** Developing fundamental skills into tactical game skills	***Level 3:*** Learning to use tactical game skills in modified gameplay
Gymnastics Content		
Level 1: Developing foundational skills	***Level 2:*** Combining skills, using movement concepts from the Laban framework to extend movement variety, partner work	***Level 3:*** Group work and more difficult themes
Dance Content		
Level 1: Body, effort, space, relationships	***Level 2:*** More complex body, more complex effort, more complex space, more complex relationships	
Motivation: Meets National Standards 1 and 2 for concepts and principles related to learning. Meets National Standard 5 for concepts related to challenge.		
Teacher Beliefs and Reflection		
A. Have a growth mindset about your students and believe that physical education is about mastery and learning, not competing in games to determine a winner. *Example:* View students as capable of changing, and view students' current abilities as simply an assessment of where they are at this moment in time.		**B.** Reflect on your teaching in relation to motivation principles. *Example:* Are you emphasizing what children have learned, the enjoyment of the game, and the value of effort? Do the children feel good about their performance and effort in a well-played game regardless of the score?
Challenge and Success		
A. Ensure tasks are developmentally appropriate and children are challenged and can experience success. *Example:* Set developmentally appropriate tasks with the appropriate balance between challenge and success. **B.** Differentiate instruction. *Example:* Dribble while traveling as fast as you can without losing control of the ball. This will be a different speed for everyone in the class.	**C.** Teach children to make decisions about the level of task difficulty so they are challenged and successful. *Example:* Practice jump, land, and roll. You can choose to jump from the single-level trapezoid or the double-level. You can make a shape in the air. You can roll in any way you choose. The key is to make choices so you are challenged but also successful. **D.** In partner work, teach children how to modify tasks to ensure challenge and success for both children. *Example:* Were you both successful with the skills you put in your jump rope routine?	**E.** Teach children to modify game-like experiences and games to ensure challenge and success for teammates and opponents during modified gameplay. *Sample Feedback* "Is your game allowing for the success of both teams, or is one team always on defense and never getting the opportunity to score?"

(*continues*)

Table 9.1 Motivation, Higher-Order Thinking Skills, and Social Responsibility Concepts (*continued*)

Autonomy		
A. Begin to develop autonomy: Have children choose equipment to practice game skills and skills for sequences of locomotion and body actions in gymnastics and dance.	**B.** Continue to develop student autonomy by having them make decisions alone and with a partner about equipment and tasks based on the criteria of what will help them improve. *Example:* Select the ball that will help you to improve the most. *Example:* Select movements for your partner sequence that you both will enjoy and can learn successfully.	**C.** Continue to develop autonomy by having students design their own games, dances, and gymnastics sequences in small groups.
Growth Mindset		
A. Directly teach a growth mindset. *Example:* The single most important thing I can teach you is that you do not have to be "athletic" to learn motor skills. All you have to do is practice and work hard. **B.** Praise students for their effort, not their abilities. *Example:* You tried so hard to stay tight when you held that balance. Good for you! *Example:* We did challenging activities today, and I am so proud of how hard you worked.	**C.** Teach children that making mistakes is part of learning motor skills and that it doesn't mean they're not good at sports or dance. Help them develop the grit not to give up when tasks are difficult and they make mistakes. Tell them that mistakes simply mean they need to try harder and practice more. *Example:* How long will it take before you master dribbling? [Years of practice.] **D.** Explicitly teach children about the importance of persistence and effort, and encourage resilience on challenging tasks. *Example:* Skills are hard to learn; you just have to keep trying. *Example:* Challenging tasks are fun to practice and will help you improve.	**E.** Set challenging tasks and have children practice until perfected. *Example:* With a partner or small group, design a game, dance, or gymnastics sequence that is challenging and practice it until you have it perfected and are proud of your work.
Mastery Orientation		
A. Teach children the gym is a learning place—a place to master skills, not a stage for performing. *Example:* You're working hard to improve your throwing and catching. This lets me know you appreciate the gym as a learning place for all students.	**B.** Teach children to value self-improvement, not how they compare to other children: De-emphasize an ego orientation. *Example:* I thought you really improved today. Give yourself a pat on the back. **C.** Base assessments on self-improvement rather than on a comparison with classmates' performances. *Example:* Did your score improve from the start of the unit to now?	**D.** Teach children game play is not about winning or showing you are better than your opponent; it is about everyone improving. **E.** Teach children how to design, critique, and modify small-sided games to create a positive learning environment for all group members. *Sample Task* "Within your teams, discuss which tactics you used to score successfully. Then have a whole-group discussion and tell the other team which tactics they need to use to stop you from scoring. Play again. Notice if the other team has improved, and compliment them if they have."

If you don't observe mastery orientations and growth mindsets in your students, then change the task, have a class discussion, or give children individual feedback on their perspectives. If you are persistent, you can change the motivation climate of the class, even during competitive games.

Challenge and Success

A. Ensure Tasks are Developmentally Appropriate and Children Are Challenged and Can Experience Success

For children to develop mastery orientations and growth mindsets, teachers must design tasks that are developmentally appropriate and thus balance challenge and success (Treasure & Roberts, 1995). Children need to be challenged to learn more difficult skills and understand increasingly complex concepts. However, putting children in situations that are too challenging can result in children withdrawing effort because they don't believe they have any chance of succeeding (Solmon, 2006). Tasks are developmentally appropriate when children both are challenged and can succeed (see **Figure 9.4**).

B. Differentiate Instruction

Because students enter class with a wide range of skill levels, it is important to differentiate instruction so that all students can work at an appropriate developmental level. Research conducted on motivation supports the importance of differentiating instruction (Treasure & Roberts, 1995). In studies in which low-skilled students were given a progression of tasks that began with and built on their ability level, they had more success and greater perceptions of competence (Hebert, Landin, & Solmon, 2000; Solmon, 2006). If you differentiate your instruction and plan developmentally appropriate tasks, you can convince students that they can succeed and become competent.

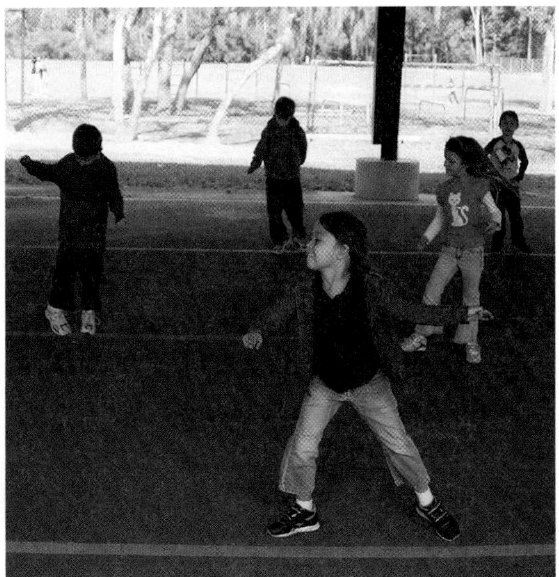

Figure 9.4 Learning to slide is challenging for kindergarteners, but they can succeed.

C. Teach Children to Make Decisions About the Level of Task Difficulty So They Are Challenged and Successful

You can help children develop a mastery orientation and a growth mindset by teaching them how to modify a task to make it harder or easier so they are challenged but also can succeed. Recall that you can modify tasks to make them either more difficult (MD) or easier (ME). When you present a task, you can explain how the children can modify it or ask them for suggestions for making the task easier or more difficult. What is critical is to teach children that the criterion for the task is to work at a level that is challenging enough to help them improve but not so difficult that they feel frustrated, helpless, or unable to succeed.

Sample Feedback

- "Is this center too easy?"
- "Is this station challenging you?"
- "After working at your center, if your center is boring and too easy, change the arrangement of the equipment and apparatus to make it more challenging. If your center is frustrating and too difficult, change the equipment and apparatus to allow you to succeed."

Sample Messages to Teach

- "You won't improve without trying difficult tasks."
- "Challenging yourself with difficult tasks is very important to learning."
- "Isn't it fun to try challenging tasks?"

Sample Objective

- By the end of the lesson, children will know how to modify the centers to make them easier or more difficult and appropriately choose the level of difficulty that is best for their self-improvement."

D. In Partner Work, Teach Children to Modify Tasks to Ensure Challenge and Success for Both Children

In level 2 content, children often work with a partner, and they must make decisions to ensure challenge and success for both partners. For example, when they design a challenge course for practicing a skill, a jump rope routine, or dance and gymnastics sequences, or play follow-the-leader, they must respond to the developmental level of their partner so both children are challenged to improve, but also both capable of success.

Example

- "Were you both successful with the skills you put in your jump rope routine?"

E. Teach Children to Modify Game-Like Experiences and Games to Ensure Challenge and Success for Teammates and Opponents During Modified Gameplay

In level 2 game-like experiences and level 3 game play, children will need to design and modify games to be learning environments so that children of all abilities can be successful and challenged within the game. This means partners and children within groups might practice using different equipment, rules, or boundaries. In addition, in invasion games, children will need to modify the intensity level of the defense.

Figure 9.5 "Set boundaries, and select the net and balls that are right for you."

Sample Modifications

- In striking games, have a smaller boundary on the side of the less skilled child, thereby creating more of a challenge for the more highly skilled child (see **Figure 9.5**).
- In striking games, have each child use a racket that is developmentally appropriate for her or him.
- In striking games, have each child hit the ball directly to the opponent if the opponent has problems keeping a rally going or hit the ball to the open space if the partner is more skilled.
- In batting games, pitch more slowly to less skilled batters and faster to more highly skilled batters.
- Have uneven numbers of players on teams—for example, 2v1 in a racket striking game or 4v2 in a volleyball-type striking game.
- Modify the level of defense for each individual player if necessary. We teach five levels of defense for invasion games, including dribbling games, keep-away games, and passing games:
  1. Feet still, arms still
  2. Feet still, arms wave and move
  3. Feet move, can't touch the ball
  4. Soft guarding (feet and arms can move, but defenders put gentle pressure on the offense)
  5. Full guarding

Sample Objective

- By the end of the lesson, students will understand that helping their partner requires them to find a level of defense that matches their opponent's abilities.
- By the end of the lesson, students will have created a 2v2 dribbling game with rules ensuring everyone can be successful when they play.

Sample Feedback

- "How did you challenge your partner but also help your partner succeed?"
- "This game seems to be one-sided. Dave has not scored at all, while Juanita scores every time. What changes can you make in this game to make it fair and fun for both of you?"
- "I noticed that Shelia and Shakita are not receiving their fair share of passes. Figure out why. Is there something Shelia and Shakita are doing or not doing that makes you not pass them the ball? Can you modify your game so everyone gets the same opportunities to improve?"
- "Is your game allowing for success for both teams, or is one team always on defense and never getting the opportunity to score?"

Autonomy

A. Begin to Develop Autonomy in Level 1 Content

You can begin to develop autonomy even in the youngest grades by offering children choices. When children are working on fundamental skills, offer them choices of balls to catch and have them explore the differences. Have them choose their shapes, locomotor skills, and body actions in dance and gymnastics. For example, "Design a dance that starts in a shape you find interesting, do one locomotor skill you enjoy performing, and end in another shape you like."

B. Continue to Develop Autonomy in Level 2 Content

In level 2 content, continue to develop autonomy by giving children choices about equipment and tasks. Teach them to choose equipment based on the criteria of what is best for their learning. For example, you can provide several different appropriate balls (e.g., playground balls and basketballs or playground balls and foam balls). Then explain that they need to select the ball that will most help them improve at this point in time (see **Figure 9.6**). Provide a variety of tasks in centers or in different sections of the physical education space. Then teach children to select the task that will best help them improve.

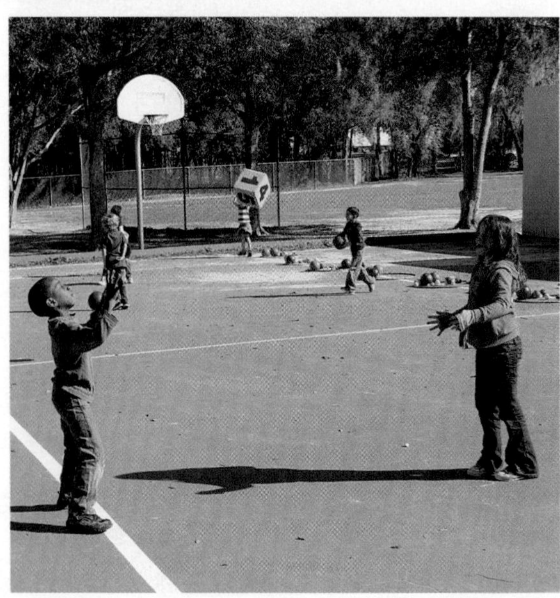

Figure 9.6 "Select the ball that's best for you."

Sample Discussion

- "Today you get to choose which ball you will use to dribble. How do the balls differ?" [Answers: The yellow balls are larger, the red balls are smaller, and the basketballs are in between.] "You have used these balls in the past; what other differences do you remember?" [The yellow balls bounce higher and are easier to make contact with. The small, red balls are harder to bounce, but you can get your hand around them and direct them more easily. The basketballs are harder to bounce and harder to control.] "On what criteria do you base your choice of ball?" [The ball that will most help me improve.]
- "Today your team gets to choose which ball to use in your passing game. Those who love action might prefer the ball that travels the fastest. Those who like to plan their tactics as the ball moves might prefer the ball that travels more slowly. Some people like the smaller ball because of how it feels in their hand. Some like the big ball because of how they can make it move where they want it to go. As a group, select the ball that is best for all of you to improve your passing and tactics."

Sample Experiment

- "Today you will get to select your practice ball. When I say 'Go,' you will have one minute to experiment with each ball. Then we will compare and contrast the value of using each ball, and you can select the ball that will best help you improve. This section of the class is group A, and they will start with the yellow balls. This section is group B, and they will start with the red balls. This section is group C, and they will start with the basketballs. I will tell you when to switch balls. Go."

C. Continue to Develop Autonomy in Level 3 Content

In level 3 when children work in small groups, continue to develop autonomy by having them design their own games, dances, and gymnastics sequences.

A Growth Mindset

Some of the most interesting experiments are those in which researchers have instilled a fixed or growth mindset in comparable groups of students. The fixed-mindset group was told that success in learning the skill would be related to their innate ability; the growth-mindset group was told that success in learning the skill would be related to how hard they worked and how much effort they demonstrated. The growth-mindset groups outperformed the fixed-mindset groups—a result indicating that teachers can instill a growth mindset and increase achievement. Moreover, many studies have tested the impact of workshops designed to teach a growth mindset to low-achieving students. Studies consistently report that students can change their mindset, with their effort and achievement in school subsequently improving (Dweck, 2007).

A. Directly Teach a Growth Mindset

Sample Messages to Teach

- "Everyone can learn skills if they work hard."
- "The single most important thing I can teach you is that you do not have to be 'athletic' to learn motor skills. All you have to do is practice and work hard."
- "Being highly skilled results from practice and hard work, not natural ability."
- "Learning motor skills takes lots of time and practice."
- "When you see an athlete on television, do you think he or she practiced hard for many, many years? Yes. To become an elite athlete takes years of practice."
- "Did you know that Michael Jordan, who many people think is the greatest basketball player ever, did not make his varsity high school basketball team as a sophomore because he was not good enough? What he did was work hard and improve until he was the best in the world."

B. Praise Students for Their Effort, Not Their Abilities

As Dweck (2007) explains, praising ability can backfire. In the short term, the child feels good. In the long term, however, such feedback leads to students avoiding effort and being afraid to work on challenging tasks for fear it will prove they are inept. Praising effort and attributing successes to their hard work will develop a growth mindset (see **Figure 9.7**).

Sample Feedback

- "You tried so hard to stay tight when you held that balance. Good for you!"
- "You all worked so hard today on swinging your arms when you jumped."
- "I am so proud of how much work you put into creating your dance sequence."
- "You selected the most difficult task to practice, and you practiced hard. That's great!"
- "Did you work hard today? [Yes.] I noticed."

C. Teach Children that Mistakes Are Part of Learning Motor Skills and to Develop the Grit Not to Give Up When Tasks Are Difficult and They Make Mistakes

Mistakes are part of learning motor skills and do not mean that a child is not good at sports or dance. Emphasize that mistakes

Figure 9.7 "You've worked so hard! Give yourselves a cheer."

Courtesy of John Dolly

simply mean you need to try harder and practice more. Encourage students to approach difficult tasks with a positive spirit and the grit to not give up if they make a mistake (Goodwin & Miller, 2013). Help them assume the attitude that mistakes are simply opportunities to learn.

Sample Stories to Tell and Messages to Teach

- "Suppose I brought 10 cars to your repair shop, and you could fix only four. A few days later, I brought you 10 more cars, and you could still fix only four. Do you think you would be in business very long if you could fix only a few cars out of the total number brought in for repair? But if you were a baseball player and you had hits four out of every 10 times you came to bat, you would be a millionaire and in the Hall of Fame. Sport is a place you will often fail more than you will succeed, and that's okay. Rickey Henderson used to hold the record for the most stolen bases. He also held the record for the most put-outs trying to steal a base. He was the best and the worst at the same time. Could someone be the best overall math student in your class and be the worst at the same time? No. Sports are different from other subjects."
- "Sometimes you will be trying very hard to catch a fly ball and you will miss it. That does *not* mean you are not good at catching. It simply means you need more appropriate practice. Think about your performance technique: reach and give and try, try again."
- "Don't let mistakes get you discouraged. All beginners make mistakes when they are learning new skills."
- "It's okay to be a beginner" (Rink, 2004).

Sample Objective

- At the end of this lesson, children will understand that mastering motor skills takes years and years of practice.

Sample Questions

- "How long will it take before you master dribbling?" [Lots of practice in a variety of situations; years of practice.]
- "What do you need to do to improve your dribbling?" [Practice a lot.]

D. Explicitly Teach Children About the Importance of Persistence and Effort, and Encourage Resilience on Challenging Tasks

As with other aspects of a growth mindset and mastery orientation, you can directly teach children to value persistence, effort, and hard work, especially when tasks are challenging. Reinforce the idea that to learn, you must challenge yourself with difficult tasks, and highlight the importance of being resilient and not giving up when you have difficulties when initially performing a task. Encourage risk taking. Explain to the children that they need to take risks and work at the edge of their developmental level. Teach them that challenging themselves is fun and that they should approach challenging tasks with a willing, positive spirit. Provide, as options, tasks that are challenging, fun, and captivating.

It can help if you teach children what effort feels like. One suggestion is to have children rate their effort on a scale from 1 to 10 (Jacobson, 2013). When children complain that they can't do something and it is too hard, ask them to rate their effort. Most children will respond with an honest self-evaluation, and you can reinforce the message that motor skills are difficult to learn and take lots of practice to master.

Experienced Teachers Talk

Keeping Score

I always offer children the choice of whether to keep score or not or to play a cooperative game. My kids are used to these choices. I chuckled one day as I listened to a group [of two teams] design their game and one team announced, "We don't want to keep score. You can keep score if you want, but don't tell us."

Sample Feedback and Messages

- "Don't give up. It's hard to get free from the defender."
- "Skills are hard to learn, but you've got to keep trying."
- "Those of you who were successful, please share some tips."
- "You can't improve if you play it safe and only do what you already know how to do."

E. Set Challenging Tasks and Have Children Practice Until Perfected

Succeeding at a challenging task and knowing this was due to your hard work can reinforce a growth mindset. Set a challenging task. Tell children the task is challenging and if they persist, work hard, and support each other, they can succeed. Give them the time to practice, structure their practice to help them stay focused, insist they aim to do the best job they can do, and help them critique their work so they know what they need to do to improve.

Sample Task

- With a partner or small group, design a game, dance, or gymnastics sequence that is challenging, and practice it until you have it perfected and are proud of your work.

Mastery Orientation

A. Teach the Children that the Gym Is a Learning Place—A Place to Work on Mastering Skills, Not a Stage for Performing

Teach children the important message that the gym is a learning place, that is, a place to work on mastering skills, not a stage for performing or showing off. You need to reinforce frequently that the physical education lessons are for all children to improve their skills. For young children, you also need to teach that physical education is not recess. Remember, for most kids, doing physical activities means play time. At recess, they play games for fun. Because our subject matter is fun for children, you will need to teach children that physical education class is about learning movement and that learning is fun. With

Parents and Youth Sports Leagues

What is the first question parents typically ask their children when they come home from a youth sports league game? The answer: "Did you win?" We hear this question even from parents and other adults who really don't care whether the child won, but rather whether the child is having fun, being physically active, and learning skills. The first questions parents should ask are these: "Did you have fun? Did you try your best? How did you play today?"

young children, in particular, you need to reinforce frequently that physical education is their chance to practice and improve and have fun while doing so.

Sample Feedback

- "You're working hard to improve your throwing and catching. This lets me know you appreciate the gym as a learning place."
- "You did a great job today improving your striking skills. Isn't it fun to learn new skills?"
- "Did you improve from the start of the lesson to the end?"
- "You did some very interesting and unusual balances today. You're getting better and better at making your balances creative."
- "Remember, the gym is a learning place and what matters is that you improve your skills."

B. Teach Children to Value Self-Improvement, Not Comparisons to Other Children: De-Emphasize an Ego Orientation

You can teach children directly that what really matters is how much they improve, not whether they are better than their classmates. Explain that some children have older brothers or sisters and parents who teach them skills after school or during holidays. Other children might take private lessons or be members of a youth sports team and have had many more opportunities to practice. The amount of practice and effort determines your skill level.

If you value and reinforce self-improvement, the children will hear your message. In games lessons, avoid making comparisons, focusing on winning and losing, constructing class rankings, and posting scores. Instead, focus on how hard the children tried and how their effort led to improved play and skills (see **Figure 9.8**).

For safety reasons, it is equally important in educational gymnastics to teach and emphasize explicitly and repeatedly a mastery orientation, not a competitive ego orientation. Many classes will include some children who have learned gymnastics skills outside of school and are more skilled than their classmates. If the learning environment in gymnastics becomes competitive and children take on ego orientations, some might attempt to perform skills they are not ready to learn or perform safely. This behavior could lead to serious injury. Others will give up and never try at all.

Figure 9.8 "I'm so proud of how hard you're working!"
Courtesy of John Dolly

Sample Feedback and Messages

- "Today your goal is to improve your own performance. If you caught five balls in a row yesterday, try to improve on your record today."
- "Remember, there are always some people who are more and less skilled than you are. What really matters is whether you improve your own performance."
- "I thought you really improved today. Give yourself a pat on the back."

Sample Teacher Behaviors and Attitudes

- In gymnastics, emphasize the quality of sequences rather than the difficulty of the skills.
- In gymnastics, be just as enthusiastic about the quality of the less difficult sequence as you are about the spectacular, difficult performance.
- In dance and gymnastics, recognize and celebrate children for the variety of ways they perform movements in a theme and for their ability to find inventive, creative movement solutions to exploration tasks.

Sample Objective

- By the end of the lesson, students will have learned to select skills and movements for their gymnastics sequences that they can perform safely, confidently, and successfully.

C. Base Assessments on Self-Improvement Rather than a Comparison with Classmates' Performances

To set a mastery-oriented climate, base assessments on improvement (Treasure & Roberts, 1995). In addition to teacher assessments, you can have children and peers assess their own and each other's improvement.

Sample Objective

- By the end of the lesson, students will know how to assess their improvement without comparing their performance to their partner's.

Sample Feedback

- "Did you do better the second time?"
- "Did your score improve from the start of the unit to now?"

D. Teach Children Game Play Is Not About Winning or Showing You Are Better than Your Opponent—It Is About Everyone Improving

Games and game-like situations must be opportunities for all children to improve their skills and tactics. Competition, by definition, is a social comparison. Although we can easily eliminate or de-emphasize competition in dance, gymnastics, motor skills learning, and cooperative games, we cannot and should not eliminate or even avoid competition in physical education. Competition is the structure of gameplay and one of our most important content areas.

Nevertheless, teachers can do much to encourage a mastery orientation rather than an ego orientation during competitive tasks and games. First, we can offer children choices as to whether to play a competitive game, a cooperative game, or a competitive game without keeping score. Second, we can teach children that the purpose of competitive games within physical education is for all children to improve their tactics and skills—that is, to develop a mastery orientation. Third, we can explicitly highlight the link between working hard, learning, and winning games—reminding students that learning is permanent, but winning a game is only a temporary occurrence.

It is not difficult to convince children that school and physical education are places where all children should get equal opportunities to learn and to improve. Unfortunately, it can be difficult to teach them how to maintain a mastery orientation during competitive games because the sports models they see on television all appear to be about winning, not learning. There is a difference between the ethic of competition in high school interscholastic, intercollegiate, and professional sports (which are focused on winning) and the ethic of competition in an educational setting or in sports for children younger than 13 years old (which is focused on learning and development for all children).

The problem isn't competition per se (it can be either beneficial or harmful), but rather the way in which children interpret competition and the learning environment established by the teacher. If the teacher doesn't talk about the winner, children don't focus on winning. If the teacher focuses on learning, so will the children.

Throughout games units, you need to teach and reinforce the message that although children compete against one another, the primary goal is not winning, but rather helping yourself and your classmates improve. In your feedback and conclusion to each lesson, you can emphasize the points the children have learned, the enjoyment of the game, and the value of effort. If children have acquired a mastery orientation over several units or years, they will be able to maintain a mastery orientation even during the most competitive games.

Sample Messages to Teach

- "In sports, you can play well and win. You can also play well and lose. You can play poorly and still win, and you can play poorly and lose. What matters is doing your best and improving every day." (If students look at "losses" and "wins" in this way, they are more likely to focus on learning rather than the score.)
- "What is the purpose of physical education?" [To learn and improve.]
- "What did you learn today in your game?"
- "Compare and contrast the play of the different partners you played with today. What did each one do to be successful?"
- "You are screaming every time you score. What's going on? What's important in PE? Right, whether you and your classmates learn and improve."
- "What did you learn about tactics in the past three minutes?"

E. Teach Children How to Design, Critique, and Modify Small-Sided Games to Ensure a Learning Environment for All Group Members

In level 3 games content, children learn to design games. They need to learn to recognize when the game is not a learning environment for all children and to modify it to solve the problem. A game is not an equitable learning environment when

- Children are eliminated from the game
- Some children never get the ball
- Some children or one team is always on defense
- Some children or one team never gets the chance to score
- The score is lopsided

For a game to be a learning environment for all children,

- No child can be excluded from play by teammates refusing to pass that child the ball
- Children experience playing all positions for equal amounts of time (no one is stuck far away behind everyone in "out" outfield)
- Everyone has opportunities to score
- Time spent on offense and defense is roughly equal
- Neither the offense nor the defense overpowers the other
- Neither team overpowers the other

To make games equitable learning experiences, you will need to teach children to design rules and consequences for breaking rules that do not exclude children from practice or send children out of bounds to do exercise as punishment, as these practices will not contribute to learning.

Children also need to be sensitive to children who never get the ball or the chance to score and insist teammates treat each other fairly, or, if the problem is that the child does not know how to get into an open position to receive a pass, then teammates or their opponents need to help them learn how to do so. To solve the problem of one team overpowering the other, children can design an uneven scoring rule. For example, you could say, "When one team is six points ahead, two players must switch teams, and the entire group must discuss how to improve play to make the game more challenging." The change-of-possession rule is often the problem when time spent on offense and defense is not equal. This rule can be modified to rectify the situation, such as by having the ball change possession if the offense drops the ball or if the defense touches the ball. Issues such as the lack of opportunity to play offense or the defense overpowering the offense can occur because at the elementary level, children's defensive abilities tend to be stronger than their offensive abilities, as they do not have to control the ball on defense. You can solve this problem by playing with fewer defenders, such as 3v2 or 3v1, and you can teach children how to limit their defensive intensity based on the capabilities of their opponents. We show you how to teach children to limit the defense in the games chapters.

Sample Feedback

- "Is everyone getting a fair chance to score? If not, find a way to solve this problem."
- "Is everyone receiving passes? If not, what can you do to solve this problem?"
- "What is your change-of-possession rule? Is it working to give both teams equal time on offense and defense?"
- "Within your teams, discuss which tactics you used to score successfully. Then have a whole-group discussion, and tell the other team which tactics they need to use to stop you from scoring. Play again. Notice if the other team has improved, and compliment them if they have."

Summary

Although we want physical education to be a positive learning environment for all students, some children may find physical education alienating and humiliating due to teachers' and peers' behaviors and attitudes. For example, putting children on display and having captains publicly pick their teams are harmful practices.

A large body of research in education and physical education indicates that teachers can create a mastery-oriented learning environment and teach children to have a mastery orientation and growth mindset, believe they can be successful, and have perceptions of competence and autonomy. This process contributes to student achievement, satisfaction, and enjoyment in physical education.

Review Questions

1. What are two "Hall of Shame" (Williams, 1996) practices that contribute to a negative learning environment?
2. Why do you think some teachers continue to use "Hall of Shame" practices?
3. Describe a mastery orientation and its effects on students' actions and attitudes.
4. Describe an ego orientation and its effects on students' actions and attitudes.
5. Describe a growth mindset and its effects on students' actions and attitudes.
6. Describe a fixed mindset and its effects on students' actions and attitudes.
7. Why do you, as a teacher, need to have a growth mindset about your students?
8. Why is it important for students to have perceptions of competence and autonomy?
9. Describe how to teach children to modify tasks to ensure challenge and success for all children during gameplay.
10. Describe how you can develop (a) a growth mindset and (b) a mastery orientation in your students. Give examples of feedback or messages to teach for each.

References

Ames, C. (1992). Classrooms: Goals, structures, and student motivation. *Journal of Educational Psychology, 84,* 261–271.

Biddle, S. J. H., Wang, C. K. J., Chatzisarantis, N. L. D., & Spray, C. M. (2003). Motivation for physical activity in young people: Entity and incremental beliefs about athletic ability. *Journal of Sport Sciences, 21,* 937–989.

Bryan, C. L., & Solmon, M. A. (2007). Self-determination in physical education: Designing class environments to promote active lifestyles. *Journal of Teaching in Physical Education, 26,* 260–278.

Byra, M., & Jenkins, J. (1998). The thoughts and behaviors of learners in the inclusion style of teaching. *Journal of Teaching in Physical Education, 18,* 26–42.

Cardinal, B. J., Yan, Z., & Cardinal, M. K. (2013). Negative experiences in physical education and sport: How much do they affect physical activity participation later in life. *Journal of Physical Education, Recreation and Dance, 84*(3), 49–53.

Carlson, T. B. (1995). We hate gym: Student alienation from physical education. *Journal of Teaching in Physical Education, 14,* 467–477.

Chen, A., Martin, R., Ennis, C. D., & Sun, H. (2008). Content specificity of expectance beliefs and task values in elementary physical education. *Research Quarterly for Exercise and Sport, 79,* 195–208.

Deci, E. L., & Ryan, R. M. (2002). Overview of self-determination theory: An organismic dialectical perspective. In E. L. Deci & R. M. Ryan (Eds.), *Handbook of self-determination research* (pp. 3–36). Rochester, NY: University of Rochester Press.

Ding, H., Sun, H., & Chen, A. (2013). Impact of expectancy-value and situational interest motivation specificity. *Journal of Teaching in Physical Education, 32,* 253–269.

Dweck, C. S. (1999). *Self-theories: Their role in motivation, personality, and development.* Philadelphia: Taylor and Francis/Psychology Press.

Dweck, C. S. (2007). The perils and promises of praise. *Educational Leadership, 65*(2), 34–38.

Dweck, C. S., & Molden, D. C. (2005). Self-theories: Their impact on competence, motivation, and acquisition. In A. J. Elliot & C. S. Dweck (Eds.), *Handbook of competence and motivation* (pp. 122–140). New York: Guilford Press.

Dyson, B. (2006). Students' perspectives of physical education. In D. Kirk, D. MacDonald, & M. O'Sullivan (Eds.), *The handbook of physical education* (pp. 326–346). London: Sage.

Eickhoff-Shemek, J. M., Herbert, D. L., & Connaughton, D. P. (2009). *Risk Management for Health/Fitness Professionals: Legal Issues and Strategies.* Philadelphia: Wolters Kluwer/Lippincott Williams & Wilkins.

Goodwin, B., & Miller, K. (2013). Grit + Talent = Student Success. *Educational Leadership, 70*(1), 74–76.

Halsey, J. J. (2005). Risk Management for Physical Educators. In H. Appenzeller, (Ed.). *Risk Management in Sport: Issues and Strategies,* (2nd ed.), (pp. 151–163). Durham, NC: Carolina Academic Press.

Hart, J. E., & Ritson, R. J. (2002). *Liability and Safety in Physical Education and Sport.* Reston, VA: National Association for Sport and Physical Education.

Hebert, E., Landin, D., & Solmon, M. A. (2000). The impact of task progressions on students' practice quality and thought processes. *Journal of Teaching in Physical Education, 15,* 338–354.

Jacobson, M. D. (2013). Afraid of looking dumb. *Educational Leadership, 71*(1), 40–43.

Johnson, T. G., Prusak, K., A., Pennington, T., & Wilkinson, C. (2011). The effects of the type of skill test, choice, and gender on the situational motivation of physical education students. *Journal of Teaching in Physical Education, 30,* 281–295.

Koka, A., & Hagger, M. S. (2010). Perceived teaching behaviors and self-determined motivation in physical education: A test of self-determination theory. *Research Quarterly for Exercise and Sport, 81,* 74–86.

Lee, A. M., Carter, J. A., & Xiang, P. (1995). Children's conceptions of ability in physical education. *Journal of Teaching in Physical Education, 14*, 384–393.

Li, W., Lee, A. M., & Solmon, M. A. (2005). Relationships among dispositional ability conceptions, intrinsic motivation, perceived competence, experience, persistence, and performance. *Journal of Teaching in Physical Education, 24*, 51–65.

National Association for Sport and Physical Education (NASPE). (2009). *Appropriate instructional practice guidelines for elementary school physical education* (3rd ed.). Reston, VA: Author.

Nohr, K. M. (2009). *Managing Risk in Sport and Recreation: The Essential Guide for Loss Prevention*. Champaign, IL: Human Kinetics.

Ommundsen, Y. (2001). Pupils' affective responses in physical education classes: The association of implicit theories of the nature of ability and achievement. *European Physical Education Review, 7*, 219–242.

Ommundsen, Y. (2003). Implicit theories of ability and self-regulation strategies in physical education classes. *Educational Psychology, 23*, 141–157.

Parish, L. E., & Treasure, D. C. (2003). Physical activity and situational motivation in physical education: Influence of the motivational climate and perceived ability. *Research Quarterly for Exercise and Sport, 74*, 173–182.

Portman, P. A. (1995). Who is having fun in physical education classes? Experiences of sixth-grade students in elementary and middle schools. *Journal of Teaching in Physical Education, 14*, 445–453.

Prusak, K. A., Treasure, D. C., Darst, P. W., & Pangrazi, R. P. (2004). The effects of choice on the motivation of adolescent girls in physical education. *Journal of Teaching in Physical Education, 23*, 19–29.

Rink, J. E. (2004). It's okay to be a beginner. *Journal of Physical Education, Recreation, and Dance, 75*(6), 31–34.

Shen, B., McCaughtry, N., Martin, J., & Fahlman, M. (2009). Effects of teacher autonomy support and students' autonomous motivation on learning in physical education. *Research Quarterly for Exercise and Sport, 80*, 44–53.

Solmon, M. A. (1996). Impact of motivational climate on students' behaviors and perceptions in a physical education setting. *Journal of Educational Psychology, 88*, 731–738.

Solmon, M. A. (2006). Learner cognition. In D. Kirk, D. MacDonald, & M. O'Sullivan (Eds.), *The handbook of physical education* (pp. 226–241). London: Sage.

Solmon, M. A., & Boone, J. (1993). The impact of student goal orientation in physical education classes. *Research Quarterly for Exercise and Sport, 64*, 418–424.

Solmon, M., & Lee, A. M. (1996). Entry characteristics, practice variables, and cognition: Student mediation of instruction. *Journal of Teaching in Physical Education, 15*, 136–150.

Spencer-Cavaliere, N., & Rintoul, M. A. (2012). Alienation in physical education from the perspectives of children. *Journal of Teaching in Physical Education, 31*, 344–361.

Standage, M., Duda, J. L., & Ntoumanis, N. (2003). A model of contextual motivation in physical education: Using constructs from self-determination and achievement goal theories to predict physical activity intentions. *Journal of Educational Psychology, 95*, 97–110.

Strand, B., & Bender, V. (2011). Knowledge and use of appropriate instructional strategies by physical education teachers. *The Physical Educator, 86*, 2–17.

Subramaniam, P. R., & Silverman, S. (2000). Validation of scores from an instrument assessing student attitude toward physical education. *Measurement in Physical Education and Exercise Science, 4*, 29–43.

Subramaniam, P. R., & Silverman, S. (2002). Using complementary data: An investigation of student attitude in physical education. *Journal of Sport Pedagogy, 8*, 74–91.

Tischler, A., & McCaughtry, N. (2011). PE is not for me: When boys' masculinities are threatened. *Research Quarterly for Exercise and Sport, 82*, 37–48.

Treasure, D. C., & Roberts, G. C. (1995). Applications of achievement goal theory to physical education: Implications for enhancing motivation. *Quest, 47*, 475–489.

Treasure, D. C., & Roberts, G. C. (2001). Students' perceptions of the motivational climate, achievement beliefs, and satisfaction in physical education. *Research Quarterly for Exercise and Sport, 72*, 165–175.

Williams, N. F. (1992). The Physical Education Hall of Shame. *Journal of Physical Education, Recreation and Dance, 63*(6), 57–60.

Williams, N. F. (1994). The Physical Education Hall of Shame, part II. *Journal of Physical Education, Recreation and Dance, 65*(2), 17–20.

Williams, N. F. (1996). The Physical Education Hall of Shame, part III: Inappropriate teaching practices. *Journal of Physical Education, Recreation and Dance, 67*(8), 45–48.

Xiang, P., Chen, A., & Bruene, A. (2005). Interactive impact of intrinsic motivators and extrinsic rewards on behavior and motivation outcomes. *Journal of Teaching in Physical Education, 24*, 179–197.

Xiang, P., & Lee, A. (1998). The development of self-perceptions of ability and achievement goals and their relations in physical education. *Research Quarterly for Exercise and Sport, 69*, 231–241.

Xiang, P., Lee, A., & Williamson, L. (2001). Conceptions of ability in physical education: Children and adolescents. *Journal of Teaching in Physical Education, 20*, 282–294.

Xiang, P., McBride, R., & Guan, J. (2004). Children's motivation in elementary physical education: A longitudinal study. *Research Quarterly for Exercise and Sport, 75*, 71–80.

Xiang, P., McBride, R., Guan, J., & Solmon, M. (2003). Children's motivation in elementary physical education: An expectancy-value model of achievement choice. *Research Quarterly for Exercise and Sport, 74*, 25–35.

Zhang, T., Solmon, M. A., & Gu, X. (2012). The role of teachers' support in predicting students' motivation and achievement outcomes in physical education. *Journal of Teaching in Physical Education, 31*, 329–343.

CHAPTER

10

Higher-Order Thinking Skills and Inquiry-Oriented Teaching

PRE-READING REFLECTION

See the questions following the Sample Plan Lesson A and B scenarios in the chapter.

OBJECTIVES

Students will learn:

1. All physical activities include thinking skills.
2. To use inquiry-oriented teaching to teach the following higher-order thinking skills:
   - Self-regulation and metacognition
   - Decision making
   - Critical and analytical thinking
   - Creative thinking and exploration
   - Problem solving
3. Teaching higher-order thinking skills supports children becoming lifelong, independent learners.
4. Thinking skills are taught simultaneously with the physical education content in which they are embedded.

KEY TERMS

Critical thinking
Exploration tasks
Metacognition
Scaffolding
Self-regulation

CONNECTION TO STANDARDS

This chapter focuses on higher-order thinking skills, which are important for learning and applying movement and cognitive content. Consequently, the chapter focuses on how you can enhance your teaching for outcomes for National Standards 1, 2, and 3 and the Common Core and other State Standards (CCSS) for vocabulary acquisition. The chapter also addresses partner and group work on critical and creative thinking tasks, decision-making tasks, and problem-solving tasks. Thus, it provides a basis for meeting National Standard 4 and CCSS for comprehension, speaking, and listening.

Introduction

The following are common elementary school experiences:

- Memorizing state capitals
- Memorizing dates in history
- Using mathematics formulas by rote without understanding why
- Looking up vocabulary words in the dictionary and then memorizing definitions
- Memorizing the rules of sports
- Repeating the same decontextualized skill drills every year in physical education

Not only are these activities boring, but they are also ineffective learning experiences because there is little transfer of knowledge to the more complex contexts in which these skills and concepts are intended for use.

Contrast Lesson A, an all-too-common basketball lesson for grade 4, with Lesson B (see **Sample Plan 10.1**). Would Lesson A or B be more likely to engage children's thinking skills in game-like situations and in making tactical decisions?

Higher-Order Thinking Skills and Inquiry-Oriented Teaching

A large body of research across all fields in education during the past 20 years has shown that there are better ways to teach than relying on memorization of facts and practicing decontextualized skills. When teachers assign problems and activities that engage children in thinking critically about the subject matter, discussing their ideas, experimenting, and evaluating solutions, children not only learn more, but are also more engaged and interested in what they are learning (Costa, 2008; Swartz, 2008). We call these forms of teaching "inquiry-oriented teaching."

Terms that are commonly used to describe inquiry-oriented teaching in physical education include "problem-solving approaches," "guided discovery," and "exploration." The terms we use in this text are more specific:

- Decision-making tasks
- Critical thinking tasks
- Creative thinking and exploration tasks
- Problem-solving tasks

These types of tasks, along with asking questions, are the major forms of inquiry-oriented teaching in elementary physical education.

There is widespread consensus that teachers need to connect content to a meaningful or authentic context and simultaneously teach the thinking skills used in that context (Costa, 2008; Resnick, 2010). We show you simple and effective ways to achieve this goal in this chapter.

The Importance of Higher-Order Thinking Skills and National Standards

Thinking skills are important for meeting the National Standards for Physical Education because they are critical parts of all physical activities and are essential to the learning process. For example, using tactics in games requires making decisions about what to do, which skills to use, where to move, and when to act. Self-regulation is used to enhance skill performance and to monitor one's own thinking during motor skill learning to ensure effective practice. Thus, teaching the thinking skills that are part of physical activities and support learning motor skills will improve students' motor competency, which is the key requirement of National Standard 1.

National Standard 2 directly addresses the fact that all physical activities have motor and cognitive aspects because it requires students to *apply* knowledge. Applying knowledge is complex and requires students to think critically and creatively, make decisions, and solve problems. Thus, National Standard 2 addresses the integration of movement, cognitive knowledge, and thinking skills to develop students' competencies in physical activities. For example, solving choreographic problems is central to designing dance and gymnastics sequences—the culminating activity for lessons and units. To do so, students need to acquire knowledge of principles and elements of choreography and then apply that knowledge, along with creative and critical thinking, to the problem-solving task of designing a sequence. Students need to acquire knowledge of the principles and concepts of health-related physical activity (HRPA) and fitness (HRF) and then apply that knowledge using critical and creative thinking to generate and evaluate solutions to problems related to their health and well-being. In addition, students need to learn to use thinking skills during physical activities. Telling students about an offensive game tactic is not enough to teach them how to apply that tactic in a small-sided game practice. Students need to learn to solve offensive tactical problems and make tactical decisions in game-like situations. Movement and thinking skills are not separate.

A third reason thinking skills are important to achieving National Standards is that assigning problem-solving, critical thinking, creative thinking, and decision-making tasks, along with fostering a mastery orientation and growth mindset, supports the development of autonomy, enabling children to become independent, successful learners. The goal of developing autonomy is to enhance the likelihood that after graduation, students will be physically literate, with the motor, cognitive, affective, and social skills and dispositions to learn new skills and participate in the physical activities of their choice across their lifetime.

A final reason to have children work on problem-solving, critical thinking, creative thinking, and decision-making

SAMPLE PLAN 10.1

Lessons A and B

Lesson A

Warm-up

1. The teacher says, "Run a lap for warm-up."
2. "Get in your squad lines and let's do 40 jumping jacks together. I will count for you. 1, 2...40. Now do 10 sit-ups."

Skill Practice (in Squads)

3. "Time to practice your chest passes. Squads 1 and 2, pass the ball back and forth. Squad 3, work with squad 4, and squad 5, work with squad 6."
4. Repeat the drill, but with bounce passes.
5. "Squads, move down behind the end line. Squad leader, set up eight cones in a line from the end line to the center line, starting in front of your squad. Each squad member should dribble in a figure eight pattern around the line of cones. When you get to the center line, dribble back and hand the ball to the next child in line."
6. "I will assign each squad a basket. Practice your shooting."

Game

7. "Now we will play a game of sideline basketball. Squad 1 will play 5v5 against squad 2. Squads 3, 4, 5, and 6, line up on the two sidelines. Squads 1 and 2 can pass the ball to anyone on squads 3, 4, 5, and 6, who will then pass to someone on the squad who passed them the ball. After 5 minutes, we will rotate in squads 3 and 4. They will get 5 minutes to play, and then we will rotate in squads 5 and 6."

Compare this lesson to the following scenario.

Lesson B

The teacher says, "In today's lesson, we will continue working on how the offense can create space by passing quickly, but today we will use a different game. When I say 'go':

1. Get in the same groups of five children with whom you worked in the past three lessons.
2. Design a 3v2 game in which the goal is to throw a ball to knock down a cone in the center of your space (see **Figure 10.1**).
3. Use your critical thinking and decision-making skills to decide
   - Which ball to use (e.g., small foam, medium foam, playground)
   - Which kinds of boundaries you will need (use jump ropes and saucer cones in the baskets)
   - What the rules are and what the consequences for breaking those rules are
4. Experiment playing your game until you have a good game working. What are the criteria for a good game? [Answers from the children: It is fair for both offense and defense; there is balance so that neither the offense nor the defense dominates play; the game doesn't stop all the time, but continues; we don't argue over the rules because we figured out fair rules, and everyone knows the rules we agreed on.] Great answers.
5. Raise your hands to let me know when you get a good game going. You have designed your own games many times before, so this should not take longer than 5 minutes. Then we will start working on our major objective for today—that is, to explore different ways the offense can create space to score. Go.
6. Now explore different ways the offense can create space to shoot at the cone. Discuss and experiment with different tactics.
7. Share your results with the class. [Quick passes that force the defense to shift positions can result in an open shot; when you send a high loopy pass over the defenders, it gives the defenders time to reposition themselves.]
8. Practice again, trying to improve on your passing skills and tactics.
9. Discuss the tactical principle you learned. [The offense must pass quickly—time is the enemy of the offense and a friend of the defense.]"

Reflection

Would Lesson A or B be more likely to engage children's thinking skills? Which would more likely improve children's tactical knowledge and decision making in games?

Figure 10.1 Creating space for the offense to shoot in "Hit the Pin"

tasks is to contribute to your school's efforts to meet CCSS. Assigning these tasks and teaching thinking skills necessary for task completion contribute directly the CCSS categories of comprehension, collaboration, and presenting knowledge and ideas under the listening and speaking sections.

Regardless of the standards your state sets, a key goal of education across states is to help children develop their abilities to think. Physical education can contribute to this goal just like any other subject area (Noddings, 2008).

Overlap Among Thinking Skills and Inquiry-Oriented Tasks

In the next section, we discuss the five major high-order thinking skills, including ways to teach each one. **Table 10.1** summarizes these instructional strategies, organizes them into a three-level progression, and aligns this progression with the three levels of games and gymnastics content and the two levels of dance.

Research shows that thinking skills overlap to some extent. For example, all creative thinking involves a degree of critical thinking (e.g., when you evaluate the creativity of an idea). Self-regulation, critical thinking, and creative thinking include decision making. Problem solving includes all other thinking skills.

Don't worry about deciding whether a task demonstrates one thinking skill or another. Trying to draw clear distinctions between inquiry-oriented tasks and different thinking skills is a mistake; it will distract you and limit your ability to plan inquiry-oriented tasks that work for the subject matter in your lessons. You need to think about inquiry-oriented teaching in fluid ways, focusing on how best to help children learn the content you are teaching. In the following sections, focus on the main ideas and not on rigid categories.

Teaching Self-Regulation and Metacognition

Metacognition means "reflecting on and evaluating one's own thoughts and learning" (Alexander, 2006, p. 157). **Self-regulation** is defined somewhat more broadly and is the term we will use in this chapter. It means reflecting on and evaluating your motor, cognitive, and emotional responses and the environment during learning (Alexander, 2006). Self-regulation includes the following components:

- Self-talk about a performance technique as you practice (e.g., "I need to reach and give to catch the ball.")
- Thinking about your own thinking (e.g., "I need to think about a performance technique each time I throw.")
- Motivational self-talk (e.g., "I can do this.")
- Knowing the most effective way to practice and learn (e.g., "I need to challenge myself," "I can learn if I work hard.")
- Knowing the most effective way to think (e.g., "When we first start designing our dance, we need to brainstorm as we try different movements and not be critical of our ideas; critique comes later.")
- Knowing how to control emotions (e.g., "Katie and I are about to argue. I need to step back, take a deep breath, and calm down before I say anything.")

Experienced Teachers Talk

Learning to Teach Self-Regulation

I remember the day I learned that quite a few children did not understand self-regulation. This was a second-grade class. I told the students to dribble waist high or lower, and most did. But a good number of them did not, and it appeared to me that they should have been able to change what they were doing and dribble only waist high. After repeating my demonstration and describing the performance technique "waist high" several times, nothing changed. I finally realized that they didn't know I meant *they* had to think about the performance technique and *they* had to make a change in their dribbling. They politely listened to me, but did not self-regulate. They thought simply dribbling was being on task and doing what I told them to do. They had yet to understand there was such a thing as self-regulation. So, I taught them about thinking about one performance technique while they were dribbling and focusing on making a change in their dribbling pattern.

What the Research Says

Self-Regulation

There has been considerable research into the role of self-regulation in education (Costa, 1991) and in sport (Zourbanos, 2013). Some studies in physical education have demonstrated the benefits of self-regulation and self-talk in learning (e.g., Anderson, Vogel, & Albrecht, 1999; Kolovelonis, Goudas, & Dermitzaki, 2011; Lidor, 2004; Luke & Hardy, 1999; Singer, 2000; Zourbanos, Hatzigeorgiadis, Bardas, & Theodorakis, 2013). Research also shows that expert teachers explicitly teach children self-regulation strategies, which suggests they learned that these strategies were critical to children's learning (Rovegno, Chen, & Todorovich, 2003).

Table 10.1 Teaching Higher-Order Thinking Skills

Game Content		
Level 1: Developing fundamental game skills	***Level 2:*** Developing fundamental skills into tactical game skills	***Level 3:*** Learning to use tactical game skills in modified gameplay
Gymnastics Content		
Level 1: Foundational skills	***Level 2:*** Combining skills, using movement concepts from the Laban framework to extend movement variety, partner work	***Level 3:*** Group work and more difficult themes
Dance Content		
Level 1: Body, effort, space, relationships	***Level 2:*** More complex body, more complex effort, more complex space, more complex relationships.	
Higher-Order Thinking Skills: Meets National Standards 1, 2, 3, and 4 for applying concepts and principles related to learning motor skills and developing social responsibility during partner and group work. Meets multiple CCSS standards for speaking and listening.		
Self-Regulation and Metacognition		
A. Explicitly teach children to think about and concentrate on one performance technique while practicing. *Sample Content to Teach* Think about pushing with your finger pads while you are dribbling. **B.** Explicitly teach children the importance of self-regulation so they can become independent learners. *Sample Content to Teach* Remember, I can't be in your backpack in middle school. You need to be in charge of your learning. It has to come from you. I can't learn this for you.	**C.** Teach children to think about their thinking (metacognition) *Sample Feedback* Check up on how you've been thinking during practice. Have you been thinking about one part of the skill so you can improve? **D.** Teach children to engage in positive motivational self-talk *Sample Feedback* "Have you been saying positive things to yourself?"	**E.** Teach self-regulation in group thinking strategies. *Sample Content to Teach* Ask yourselves as a group, "Are we experimenting and trying out our ideas? Or are we being judgmental too early?"

(*continues*)

Table 10.1 Teaching Higher-Order Thinking Skills (*continued*)

Decision Making		
A. Have children make decisions about equipment and tasks. *Sample Content to Teach* You select the ball. You can experiment with different balls. **B.** Clarify choices and demonstrate possible decisions. *Sample Content to Teach* You can choose to jump over several pieces of equipment or no equipment. You can choose to jump from a box or from the mat. **C.** Teach the criteria for making decisions. *Sample Content to Teach* You may increase your speed as long as you can so do safely.	**D.** Give feedback on children's decisions. *Sample Content to Teach* You made a good decision when you put the goal where you did, because it won't interfere with other children's practicing. **E.** Have children make decisions with a partner. *Sample Content to Teach* You and your partner decide which equipment you want to include in your dribbling obstacle course. **F.** Teach children to critique their decisions. *Sample Feedback* Stop and decide whether you are making a good decision or a poor decision about your running speed.	**G.** Have children make decisions in small groups. *Sample Content to Teach* For your dance sequence, decide as a group which formations will look the best **H.** Teach affective dispositions and attitudes that support decision making. *Sample Content to Teach* The willingness to • Consider their own and others' feelings • Take responsibility for their decisions • Have, express, and justify their opinion
Critical Thinking		
A. Teach children to think critically about their performance and select a performance technique on which to focus. *Sample Feedback* Think critically about your dribbling, and select one performance cue that will most help you improve on that. **B.** Elicit critical thinking by putting feedback in the form of a question. *Sample Feedback* You really improved this time; what did you do better? **C.** Have children compare and contrast. *Sample Discussion Topic* Compare and contrast how Madison's sequence and Marquis's sequence used changes of level to add interest.	**D.** Include peer teaching and peer assessment. *Sample Task* Use the checklist with two performance cues to assess if your partner is using the performance techniques. Then help her or him improve. **E.** Partner work: Explicitly teach the affective dispositions that contribute positively to critical thinking. *Sample Content to Teach* Be open-minded to new ideas. Carefully listen to the ideas of others. Resist impulsivity. Give logical reasons for opinions.	**F.** Group work: Teach more sophisticated dispositions and attitudes supporting critical thinking in relation to multiple criteria. *Sample Content to Teach* Give reasons for opinions. Suspend judgment when the group doesn't have adequate evidence. Keep asking questions until children understand the ideas of their classmates. Make defensible arguments.

Creative Thinking and Exploration

A. Explore individually using the creative thinking strategy.

Generate many ideas.

Generate varied ideas.

Find some unusual ideas.

Add to your ideas to make them better.

B. Scaffold exploration.

C. Teach children to move while they think and to think while they move.

D. Establish a positive, emotionally safe classroom climate.

Sample Content to Teach

Do not to be critical of ideas as you are brainstorming. You may have an idea that seems silly at first but ends up being great.

E. Explore with a partner to generate many, varied, and some unusual ideas; then elaborating on your ideas.

F. Teach affective dispositions and attitudes that support creativity.

Sample Content to Teach

Be broad and adventurous.

Defer criticisms.

G. Explore with small groups trying to generate many, varied, and some unusual ideas; then elaborating on your ideas.

H. Teach affective dispositions and attitudes that support exploration and contribute to CCSS.

Sample Task

As a group, explore different ball-like, wall-like, and pin-like group shapes.

Sample Content to Teach

Suspend judgments.

Be open-minded.

Have a few wild and crazy ideas.

Build on classmates' ideas.

No negative body language.

Comment on what you like about other's ideas.

Problem Solving

A. Set problem-solving tasks that call for working individually on simple problems.

Sample Task

Design a dance sequence with a starting shape, a traveling movement, and an ending shape.

B. Scaffold the problem-solving process.

Example

Teach children how to explore options. Give them examples of potential options. Explain possible ways to select their ideas.

C. Set problem-solving tasks for partners: Teach problem-solving strategies for gymnastics and dance sequences, jump rope and dribbling routines, and challenge courses using game skills.

Sample Task

Design a partner gymnastics sequence based on matching and contrasting shapes and body actions.

Sample Task

Design a hand dribbling routine with your partner dribbling in different ways, in different body positions, and in different relationships to your partner. You may include passing or exchanging the balls.

Example of Strategy

1. Explore options
2. Select and arrange ideas
3. Refine and practice

D. Set problem-solving tasks for small groups: Teach problem-solving strategies for designing games and solving tactical problems.

Sample Task

Design a 1v1 dribbling game with boundaries, rules, and consequences for breaking rules.

Sample Strategy

Play–discuss–play cycle:

1. Play
2. Discuss problems, identify options, and make a decision.
3. Play and try out your ideas.

E. Teach the affective dispositions and attitudes that support problem solving and contribute to CCSS.

Examples

- Anchor your ideas to what you experienced.
- Have the courage to express your ideas.
- Provide reasons to support your solutions.
- Have humility and suspend judgment.

Self-regulation enables children to learn more effectively and independently without the teacher controlling their every thought and movement—a goal of physical education and education overall.

We begin teaching self-regulation during the learning of motor skills. We have children work individually and learn to self-regulate their own thinking about their skill performance. Research shows that self-talk about elements of a skill is particularly helpful for beginners (Zourbanos, 2013). We then extend this to the regulation of group work.

A. Explicitly Teach Children to Think and Concentrate on One Performance Technique While Practicing

The first step is to teach self-regulation explicitly. Although adults know to think about a performance technique to learn a skill, young children do not. To children, simply doing the skill is the same as intentionally practicing that skill to make improvements in particular performance techniques. You need to teach children that to learn a skill they need to think about and concentrate on one performance technique during practice (see **Figure 10.2**).

Typically, children need to think about the technique *just before* practicing discrete skills, such as batting and throwing, which happen quickly. They need to think about one performance technique *during* continuous skills, such as hand dribbling, when they need to think about pushing the ball with their finger pads (not slapping the ball) *while they are dribbling.*

B. Explicitly Teach Children About the Importance of Self-Regulation So They Can Become Independent Learners

Expert elementary physical educators know that they cannot control what every child is thinking in the class. If we want children to be able to learn skills independently from teachers in physical education, after school, and in adult life, we need to teach them the importance of self-regulating their learning. As one expert said to her classes, "I can't be in your backpack in middle school," and as another teacher told students, "If you want to improve, it has to come from you. I can't do it for you. You need to think about your performance techniques" (Rovegno et al., 2003).

Figure 10.2 Thinking about a performance technique while practicing

Sample Objective

- At the end of this lesson, children will understand and improve their ability to think about one learning cue—pushing the ball while dribbling.

Sample Feedback

- "What should you think about while you dribble? [Pushing the ball.] Yes, go!"
- "What were you thinking about just before you hit the ball with the bat? [Front foot closed, back foot pivot.] That's great—you were thinking about a performance technique."
- "While you were dribbling, were you actively thinking about your finger pads pushing?"

C. Teach Children to Think About Their Thinking (Metacognition)

Once children understand the importance of thinking about their movement patterns, the next step is to teach them to think about their thinking. In other words, they need to learn to monitor their thinking during learning and ask, "Was I thinking about one performance technique?"

Sample Feedback

- "Were you the boss of your thinking?"
- "Check up on how you've been thinking during practice. Have you been thinking about one part of the skill so you can improve?"
- "Check up on your thinking. Were you thinking about staying tight while balancing?"

D. Teach Children to Engage in Positive Motivational Self-Talk

When children talk positively to themselves during learning, they will improve more (Alexander, 2006). Some children engage in negative self-talk, such as "I'm not very good at rolling," or "I won't be able to catch that ball." The emotional dimensions of self-regulation need to be positive and self-affirming, such as "I *can* reach way up high with my arms to jump high," or "I *can* keep control of this ball while I dribble."

Sample Feedback

- "Have you been saying positive things to yourself?"

E. Teach Self-Regulation in Group Thinking Strategies

After children learn how to think about performance techniques while performing skills and use motivational self-talk, we take them a step further—that is, we teach them to assess not only their own thinking, but also the thinking of their group. In the upper elementary grades, children will be working in groups doing such tasks as solving tactical problems, making decisions about game rules, thinking creatively about elements of their dance, and thinking critically about their partner or group gymnastics sequences. All of these inquiry-oriented tasks require the use of several higher-order thinking skills (e.g., decision making, critical thinking, problem solving), and children will need to monitor how they are using those thinking skills in their group.

Teachers can use two strategies to help children self-regulate during partner and group work. First, they can remind children to think about their thinking as a group. Second, they can appoint one child to be in charge of assessing the group's work and reminding the group to follow the guidelines for effective decision making, critical thinking, exploration, and/or problem solving.

Sample Explanations

- "Today, as you and your partner try to think of creative shapes, be sure to remember to think about your thinking. Remember what we said about how to be a good creative thinker? [Think of many, varied, and unusual shapes.] Right. Today, pay attention to whether you are being good creative thinkers."
- "In your group discussions to solve your tactical problems, I want one person to be in charge of monitoring your group discussions to be sure you are using the problem-solving strategies we discussed in the last lesson. If not, remind your classmates what they need to do."

Sample Feedback

- "Don't forget that an important part of critical thinking is to give your partner reasons for your opinions. Remember to think about your critical thinking as you and your partner talk."
- "As you are exploring different ideas for your gymnastics sequence, monitor your group's explorations. Ask, 'Are we experimenting and trying out our ideas? Or are we being judgmental too early?'"

Teaching Decision Making

Decision making is an important thinking skill across physical education content areas. All game tactics require students to make decisions. In HRPA and HRF, students make decisions while designing their own programs of activities; in dance and gymnastics, they make decisions about which movements to perform and what to include in their sequences.

More significantly, to develop autonomy and become independent, lifelong learners, children need to learn how to make decisions about learning and practicing skills. When you give students opportunities to make decisions, you enhance learning, enjoyment, and motivation.

A. Have Children Make Decisions About Equipment and Tasks

To help children learn to be effective decision makers requires that teachers begin at the youngest grades by having children make simple decisions about which equipment to use or which task to practice (see **Figure 10.3**). Start by giving them only two choices, such as making a decision between two different balls for practicing a skill. Then expand the range of choices, so that children make a decision by selecting from three different options, for example.

> **What the Research Says**
>
> **Student Decision Making**
>
> Considerable evidence supports the idea that teachers should give students opportunities to make decisions about task difficulty, feedback, activities, and assessments (Bryan & Solmon, 2007; Chiviacowsky & Wulf, 2002; Johnson, Prusak, Pennington, & Wilkinson, 2011; Koka & Hagger, 2010; Prusak, Treasure, Darst, & Pangrazi, 2004; Shen, McCaughtry, Martin, & Fahlman, 2009; Standage, Duda, & Ntoumanis, 2003; Treasure & Roberts, 2001; Wulf & Toole, 1999). Such an approach leads to increases in the following areas:
>
> - Engagement
> - Learning
> - Self-sufficiency
> - Motivation
> - Enjoyment

B. Clarify Choices and Demonstrate Possible Decisions

Expert teachers explicitly teach and scaffold the decision-making process (Chen, Rovegno, Cone, & Cone, 2012; Rovegno et al., 2003). To do so, experts first clarify which decisions children will be making. Then, they discuss possible choices the children can make, as options that may seem obvious to teachers are not always obvious to children.

Sample Explanation

Suppose the task is to set up an obstacle course to practice galloping and leaping with each child having two poly spots as the starting and ending place and two hurdles (foam rods set on high cones). To help the children understand their choices, the teacher makes the following statement:

> You might start on one poly spot and then arrange the two hurdles far apart so you can gallop a short distance and

Figure 10.3 Children having a choice of rackets, nets, and balls

What the Research Says

Teaching Tactical Decision Making

Research on children playing shortstop showed that baseball coaches who had shortstops practice throwing to first and throwing to second *without runners to add authenticity*, and who then simply yelled to the shortstop, "Play is at second," were teaching children to listen to the coach and then throw to where the coach said. The researchers found that the children could perform the tactic, but they did not understand the tactic themselves. The children did not learn how to look at the game situation (e.g., number of outs, the location of runners), recognize that the play was at second base, and then make a decision to throw to second. The studies showed that even 12-year-olds with years of baseball practice had not learned how to recognize game situations and make appropriate tactical decisions due to inadequate coaching and practice of tactical decision making (French, Nevett, Spurgeon, Graham, Rink, & McPherson, 1996; French, Spurgeon, & Nevett, 1995; Nevett & French, 1997). The implications of this research are that children need to practice not only the skills but also the tactical decision making that occurs in authentic situations (e.g., a baseball scenario with runners).

leap, then gallop a long distance and leap. Or, you might put the hurdles close together so you can gallop a long distance, gaining speed and then do two leaps in a row. You might put the hurdles close to the poly spots so you can take one step and leap, gallop a long distance, leap, and stop quickly. You decide where you place the hurdles.

C. Teach the Criteria for Making Decisions

Expert teachers also provide criteria for making decisions, thereby teaching children that there are good decisions and bad decisions. Teachers may use many criteria, most of which will be focused on ensuring student learning. The following three criteria are always important. After you teach these three points, children should know you expect them to meet these criteria, whether you remind them explicitly or not.

- *Be safe.* Safety is the most critical criterion. Although children are allowed to make decisions, they are not allowed to make choices that might potentially harm either themselves or their classmates.
- *Don't hurt others' feelings.* Other poor choices include those that can make partners feel bad, such as making an obstacle course that is too difficult for the partner to navigate but allows the course creator to show off.
- *Be fair.* Another category of poor decisions includes those in which one child infringes on other children's opportunities to learn. For example, if children are allowed to make decisions about the centers at which they will practice and one child remains at a center for the entire class, thereby preventing other children from practicing at that center, it is a poor decision because it is not fair to all children.

Sample Tasks

- "For your gymnastic sequence today, select three different balances and put them together in a smooth sequence. Select balances that you can do safely and hold for a count of 3 [*criterion*]."
- "Set up eight cones any place you want in the space for your center. Dribble all around the cones on different pathways. Make sure your partner has as much space to dribble around the cones as you do. Don't hog the space [*criterion*]."
- "Today you get to select which ball to use to practice your tossing and catching skills. In your baskets are plenty of small foam balls, large foam balls, yarn balls, rubber band balls, and nubby balls. Practice with three, four, or five different balls, and then select a ball you can catch successfully but also challenges you to improve [*clarifying options, criteria*]."

D. Give Feedback on Children's Decisions

In the same way that teachers provide feedback on motor skill performance, so they should also provide feedback on thinking skill performance. With decision making, this means acknowledging the good decisions children have made, describing the positive aspects of those decisions, or, if necessary, explaining how their decisions were inappropriate (e.g., not safe).

Sample Objective

- At the end of this lesson, children will learn to make decisions about which rolls to practice (side, diagonal, forward, backward) based on the criterion of safety.

Sample Feedback

- "I can see each of you is working on rolls that are safe for you. You made good decisions because you remembered and followed the rule for safety."

Sample Objective

- At the end of this lesson, the children will learn to make decisions about what to include in their dance sequence based on the criterion of which movements are original and interesting.

Sample Feedback

- "Which part of your sequence do you think is most original and interesting? [The middle.] Yes, I thought you made excellent decisions about the middle. It is quite creative. Think back to some of your earlier ideas, and decide if you can make your beginning and ending shapes as original and interesting as the middle."

Sample Feedback

- [You observe that children have set up the apparatus and they are jumping, but not in task conditions that challenge them enough so they will improve their arm or leg actions.] "I don't see that your apparatus arrangement is helping you improve your arm actions. How can you modify it so you work on swinging your arms over your head?" [We can set the lines farther apart; we could hang the balloon higher so we would have to reach to touch it, rather than hitting it like we are doing now.]

E. Have Children Make Decisions with a Partner

Once children can make appropriate decisions alone, you can teach them to make decisions with a partner. Working with partners and small groups requires social skills. Start by having partners make simple decisions about setting up equipment, selecting movements for sequences, and meeting criteria for only one element of choreography, such as that sequences must have a beginning, middle, and end. Then progress to more complex decisions about designing games and longer, multipart dance and gymnastics sequences.

F. Teach Children to Critique Their Decisions

Next, teach children to critique their own decisions in relation to the criteria established by the teacher.

Sample Feedback

- "Your partner and you need to discuss the decisions you made about your dribbling obstacle course. First, ask yourselves, 'Is it safe?' Then, ask yourselves, 'Is it challenging both of you to improve your dribbling skills? Is there anything you can do to improve your course?'"
- "Now that you have your gymnastics sequence planned, think critically about it, and decide whether you need to improve the transitions."
- "Do you think you chose the ball that is working well for everyone in your group?"

G. Have Children Make Decisions in Small Groups

After children can make decisions with a partner, they can work on making group decisions. Typically, group tasks require more difficult and complex decisions about what to include in dance and gymnastics sequences and physical activity workouts based on multiple criteria. Tactical decisions also are more complex because the children must consider multiple defenders and teammates.

Sample Tasks

- Play 2v1, and practice anticipating when the receiver will get free and sending the ball into the space ahead of the receiver.
- Play the 2v2 modified hand-passing game we played in the last lesson, and work on tactical decisions about cutting into open passing lanes.
- Play the 3v3 passing (with the feet) game, and work on tactical decisions about not bunching up in front of the goal.
- Play 1v1, striking a ball with your hand over a low net, and practice the tactical decision of striking the ball into the space where your opponent is not standing.

H. Teach Affective Dispositions and Attitudes that Support Decision Making

Expert teachers explicitly teach dispositions and attitudes that will support better decision making. These dispositions include the following characteristics (adapted from Perkins, Jay, & Tishman, 1993):

- The willingness to consider one's own and others' feelings in making decisions
- The willingness to take responsibility for one's decisions
- The willingness to think independently and make decisions
- The drive to get it right and make good decisions
- The willingness to have, express, and justify an opinion
- The desire to clarify factors affecting decisions

The first two dispositions address behaving in a socially responsible way and thus allow you to work on National Standard 4. The last two dispositions relate to standards from the speaking and listening section of the CCSS, such as asking questions to clarify information and presenting an opinion using appropriate facts and relevant, descriptive details about a topic.

Sample Explanations

- "Now that you are a big kid and no longer in kindergarten, you will be making more of your own decisions in PE. This means you are more independent and must decide whether the decision you are about to make is a good decision or a poor decision."
- "When you are in charge of making your own decisions, you get to select what you want, but you must also take responsibility for your decisions. Maybe you want to use the playground ball instead of the foam ball for passing and catching, but then you will be responsible for throwing passes that are soft enough for your teammate to catch."

Sample Feedback

- "Which criteria did I discuss for making decisions about the gymnastics movements to include in your sequence? [Must have one balance with an interesting shape, one roll, and a smooth transition.] Are you working hard to make good decisions to get the sequence just right?
- "What a great decision you made to travel at a speed you can control safely. You made a responsible decision because you considered your and your classmates' safety."

Sample Tasks

- With a partner, set up an obstacle course for practicing dribbling at different speeds. You have three jump ropes, four cones, and three hoops available to you. Make all decisions together, and discuss your reasons for suggesting a particular equipment arrangement. Try to design an obstacle course that is challenging.
- With a partner, design a dance sequence with matching and mirroring shapes and movements (see **Figure 10.4**). If you have problems matching exactly, make a different decision about the shape or movement so that both of you feel the sequence works. Try to get it right. To get it right, you will need to not only practice, but also make good decisions about your shapes and movements and find ones that work for both of you.
- Play 1v1, striking a ball with your hand over a low net, and practice the defensive tactical decision to be in the ready position on the court so you cover as much space as possible.

Teaching Critical Thinking

Dr. Ron McBride (1991), a leader in promoting critical thinking, proposed that **critical thinking** in physical education be defined as reflective thinking that is used to make reasonable

Figure 10.4 Designing a dance with matching and mirroring shapes and movements

Figure 10.5 Thinking critically about skill performance

Courtesy of John Dolly

and defensible decisions about movement tasks or challenges. *Reflective* refers to the ability to draw upon information from one's general and domain-specific knowledge areas. *Reasonable* implies a logical thought process, and *defensible* refers to being held accountable for the decisions made from the critical-thinking process (p. 115).

Examples of critical thinking tasks in physical education include the following:

- Thinking critically about whether a dance sequence has good transitions and originality—two criteria of good choreography that children learned in the lesson
- Thinking critically about which tactics would be most appropriate in a modified game

To begin to teach children about critical thinking, we start with thinking critically about the children's own motor skill performance. We progress to working with a partner and critiquing skills, tactics, and short dance and gymnastics sequences. Then we progress to small groups and thinking critically about more complex tactics, modifying game rules and consequences for breaking rules, and elements of choreography in dance and gymnastics.

A. Teach Children to Think Critically About Their Performance and Select a Performance Technique on Which to Focus

After children have learned two or three performance cues for a skill, teach them to think critically about how they are performing that skill and then select the one performance technique that they think will most help them improve (see **Figure 10.5**). Then, have them focus on that technique during practice.

B. Elicit Critical Thinking by Putting Feedback in the Form of a Question

Put feedback in the form of a question so that children must analyze and critique their movement to answer your question. Recall that teachers should think about the kind of feedback they need to give to a child and then put that feedback in the form of a question.

Sample Feedback

- "You really improved this time. What did you do better?"
- "You really improved this time. What were you thinking about during or before the movement?"
- "Why do you think your roll was so smooth and quiet?" [I used strong arms and tucked tightly.]
- "Think critically and tell me what you can do to hold your balance. [Be tighter.] Sounds like a good idea. Try it and see if that helps."
- "Which performance technique do you think you need to work on to improve your kicking? [Turn my knee and foot out in the squash-the-bug position.] Yes. You did a great job thinking critically about your kicking."
- "Which performance techniques might you think about while balancing? [Answers: Staying tight, stretching through the spinal column, pointing feet and toes.] Select one and keep working hard the way you have been doing."

C. Have Children Compare and Contrast

To extend children's abilities to analyze and critique movements, teachers may have them compare and contrast two different performances. *Comparing* means to identify what is similar, whereas *contrasting* means to identify what is different. For example, children can compare and contrast the gymnastics sequences of two volunteers in terms of how each child successfully completed the assignment. We cannot emphasize enough that these whole-class discussions must be limited to positive comments and compliments only. Children can also compare and contrast the impact of different game rules, such as what happens when you put the scoring goal in the corner of the boundaries or in the middle of the end lines.

What the Research Says

Critical Thinking

There has been considerable interest in critical thinking in physical education, with researchers studying how expert teachers teach critical thinking to children (Chen, 2001; Chen & Cone, 2003; Cleland & Pearse, 1995). It appears that teachers teach critical thinking explicitly and scaffold critical thinking skills. In scaffolding, teachers provide temporary guidance and prompts. Research shows that when teachers teach critical thinking and use tasks that promote this thinking skill, children learn more and improve their critical thinking skills.

Comparing and contrasting are thinking skills used extensively in meeting many CCSS. Understanding vocabulary words and how concepts and objects fit into similar or different categories requires children to compare and contrast, which are central to elementary school CCSS for comprehension and vocabulary acquisition.

D. Include Peer Teaching and Peer Assessment

As students become adept at critiquing their own skill performances, they can help a partner learn as well. In peer teaching, students observe one another and, with very specific guidance from the teacher about what to look for, give their peer feedback. Peers can also effectively assess one another's skills using checklists provided by the teacher. Research has shown peer teaching and assessment to be very effective in enhancing learning in physical education (Byra, 2006; Iserbyt, Elen, & Behets, 2010; Vande Broek, Boen, Claessens, Feys, & Ceux, 2011).

E. Partner Work: Explicitly Teach the Affective Dispositions that Contribute Positively to Critical Thinking

Teachers also need to integrate into their lessons guidelines related to the affective aspects of critical thinking (Perkins et al., 1993; Tishman & Perkins, 1995). These guidelines include teaching children to do the following:

- Be open-minded to new ideas
- Carefully and respectfully listen to and consider the ideas of other students
- Resist impulsivity and evaluate the pros and cons of many options
- Give logical reasons for their opinion

Teaching the affective aspects of critical thinking is important because partner discussions will be ineffective if children become egocentric and refuse to listen to the opinions of others. Being open-minded is essential for a full analysis of the activity and to judge which responses are important. Giving reasons for their opinions helps children begin to learn to make defensible decisions, which are part of the CCSS standards under speaking and listening. Little critical thinking will happen if children act impulsively and simply accept the first idea a child mentions, as opposed to being reflective about the task and evaluating multiple options. These aspects of critical thinking also allow you to address socially responsible behaviors from National Standard 4 related to listening carefully and respectfully and being open to and caring about the ideas of other students.

Sample Tasks

- *Peer teaching:* Today, we will be doing peer teaching. Here is a check sheet listing the performance techniques we have learned for jumping. Watch your partner, and put a check under the column "Mastered" for each performance technique he or she has mastered. Put a check under the column "Not yet" for each technique he or she has not mastered yet. Use your critical thinking skills.
- *Partner work:* After you and your partner have designed your gymnastics sequence showing matching and contrasting shapes, use the self-assessment rubric I gave you to think critically about your sequence and decide if your originality is at level 1 (plain shapes), level 2 (varied shapes), or level 3 (original shapes). Then revise your sequence to see if you can improve it.
- *Partner work:* You have done a nice job designing 1v1 dribbling games. Now play your games, and think critically about your tactics. Stop and discuss with your partner which offensive tactics worked to score and which did not work, and why. Then play again, with both of you trying to improve your use of offensive tactics.

Sample Feedback

- "In your partner discussion, have you tried to be open-minded about new ideas?"
- "This pair did such a great job in analyzing which tactics worked and why. Their presentation was detailed, and each point was justified."
- "What I was most pleased about today was that I heard many children tell their partner the reasons why they liked the partner's dance sequence. That's great critical thinking."
- "Let's compare and contrast how our volunteers, Jose and Dontea, added exciting interest to their gymnastics sequences. [Yes. Both of them used a dramatic change of speed.] What was different? [Right, Jose did a very original balance, whereas Dontea did several rolls using interesting shapes]."

F. Group Work: Teach More Sophisticated Dispositions and Attitudes Supporting Critical Thinking in Relation to Multiple Criteria

In level 3 content, children often work in small groups and think critically about more complex games, dance, gymnastics, and HRPA and HRF content. They can now use multiple criteria to analyze and critique their work. The affective components of group work become more difficult in older grades. These elements include the following (adapted from Perkins et al., 1993):

- Giving reasons for opinions and weighing the strength of each reason to decide which ones are more pertinent
- Suspending judgment when the group doesn't have adequate evidence—for example, not judging the use of a tactic until the group has tried the tactic several times

- Having the desire for clarity and persisting in asking questions until children understand the ideas of their classmates in detail
- Making sound, reasonable, and defensible arguments for their point of view by using logic, citing evidence to support their views, and referring to the criteria set for the task

All these elements support meeting CCSS within the speaking and listening section. Standards include asking and answering questions to clarify comprehension, providing reasons and evidence to support a claim, and determining the main idea and supporting details about the topic under discussion.

Sample Tasks

- *Group work in games:* You have been playing 3v3 modified soccer. Within your team, think critically about your offensive tactics. Decide which tactics worked, which didn't, and why.
- *Designing sequences in dance:* As a group, critique your sequence based on your knowledge of what makes a sequence original and interesting. Make sure to give reasons for your opinions.
- *Designing sequences in gymnastics:* As a group, critique the transitions in, and the originality of, your group routine. Figure out how to improve. Be open-minded and listen carefully to the opinions of others.

Sample Feedback

- "The members of this group were awesome in clearly explaining their ideas and discussing in detail how to solve the tactical problem."
- "Are your tactics working? [No.] Everyone, tell me why you think they are not working."

Teaching Creative Thinking and Exploration

Although all content areas can include creative thinking, dance and gymnastics, in particular, offer teachers excellent opportunities to help children develop their creative thinking skills. As is true with the other higher-order thinking skills, to develop creative thinking teachers need to

- Set tasks and establish a learning environment that support children's creative thinking.
- Explicitly teach creative thinking strategies and dispositions.

Torrance (1962), the first psychologist to study creativity in depth, defined four aspects of creative thinking: fluency, flexibility, originality, and elaboration. Schlicter (1986) translated Torrance's ideas into what she labeled "kid talk." We find her model helpful and adapt it here.

Creative Thinking Strategy

When using creative thinking, children can use the following strategy:

- Generate "many ideas" (fluency).
- Generate "varied ideas" (flexibility).
- Find some "unusual ideas" (originality).
- "Add to your ideas to make them better" (elaboration) (Schlicter, 1986, p. 26).

The Role of Knowledge in Developing Creative Thinking

Knowledge plays a critical role in developing creative thinking. When children are asked to use their creative thinking skills in any content area, they must have knowledge to use as a springboard for their creative thoughts. For example, in dance, to think creatively about the theme of rising and sinking, children need to know they can rise and sink by making different shapes, leading with different body parts, moving at different speeds, and using different amounts of force. They also need to know elements of choreography that contribute to a quality product. For students to think creatively about different ways to work on cardiorespiratory endurance, they need to have knowledge about what that is and how to achieve it.

Exploration Tasks

In physical education, we call creative thinking tasks **exploration tasks**. When teachers give exploration tasks, they ask children to discover, invent, find different solutions to a problem, and generate multiple responses. For example, a teacher might ask children to find different ways to balance on different body parts. Of course, many of these balances will have been discovered or invented by many other children. The main goal is neither to invent a balance that has never been performed before, nor to discover the right way to balance (e.g., headstands, handstands). Rather, the goal is to extend each child's movement vocabulary—that is, the variety of ways he or she can perform games, gymnastics, and dance skills and tactics (see **Figure 10.6**).

A. Explore Individually Using the Creative Thinking Strategy

The first step in teaching children how to explore is simply to teach them the creative thinking strategy discussed earlier—that is, to think of many, varied, and unusual ideas, and then to add to those ideas. Focus on one key word at a time. The following is an example that demonstrates how to define what you mean by "explore" and how to teach the meaning of the

Figure 10.6 Exploring wide shapes in dance

Courtesy of John Dolly

key words in the creative thinking strategy. The example uses curled shapes in dance.

Example of How to Teach the Creative Thinking Strategy

1. When I say "Explore," I want you to experiment freely and try to find as *many* different ideas as you can. For example, when I say, "explore many different curled shapes," this means you want to find as many different ways to make curled shapes as you can. Let's try some.
   - Do a curled shape, now another, now another.
   - Do a different curled shape, and another. Great! You have started to find many curled shapes.
2. The word "varied" means that you have discovered as many different curled shapes as you can. Explore and try to find varied curled shapes—that is, a wide range of curled shapes (see **Figure 10.7**). Let's do this together.
   - Make a curled shape at a medium level.
   - Now curl your spine a different way. Some of you are curling forward, some to the side, and some backward. You have curled in a variety of directions.
   - Now let's change the level. Find a variety of different curled shapes at a low level.
   - Now try to find at least three different symmetrical curled shapes. Now try to find six different asymmetrical curled shapes.
   - Now curl and move your arms to a different position each time.
3. We have now explored a wide variety of curled shapes. "Unusual" means very different, very original, and very creative. These shapes can even be weird!
   - Create an unusual curled shape by moving your arms and legs into very different positions (see **Figure 10.8**).
4. When I say, "Add on to your ideas to make them better," I want you to take several of your ideas and see if you can make them more interesting. So, when I say "Explore," I want you to experiment freely and try to generate many, varied, and unusual ideas. Then add to your ideas to make them better. I have written the creative thinking strategy on the whiteboard so if you forget what to do, you can just look at the board to help you remember.

Figure 10.7 Varied curled shapes
Courtesy of John Dolly

Figure 10.8 An unusual curled shape
Courtesy of John Dolly

Sample Tasks

- Find as many different ways as you can to catch balls in all areas of your personal space (e.g., left and right sides, above your head, near your feet). (*Fluency/many*)
- Strike a ball up with your forearms as many times as you can, exploring different amounts of force. (*Fluency/many*)
- Explore a variety of ways to rise and sink, ending in a different shape each time. (*Flexibility/varied*)
- Jump in the air and try to make a very unusual shape with your legs that you have never made before. (*Originality*)
- Make a balance, do a movement, and then make another balance. Repeat these skills a second time, and try to make the shape of your legs different. Repeat the skills a third time, and change the speed of the connecting movement. (*Elaboration*)

Sample Feedback

- "That is a very unusual shape. Excellent creative thinking."
- "I saw you do at least five different rolls with different shapes. Wonderful exploring to come up with many rolls."

B. Scaffold Exploration

Another important teaching technique is to scaffold exploration. Research shows that expert teachers teach children how to explore in dance and in designing games by scaffolding the exploration process (Chen & Cone, 2003; Chen et al., 2012).

The term *scaffolding* is used because the process resembles the creation of scaffolds used in constructing buildings. In the building trades, a scaffold is a temporary structure that you build to help with the construction process. Similarly, in teaching thinking skills, a scaffold is a temporary structure that teachers remove when children no longer need its support.

Scaffolding in physical education includes temporary sets of procedures, prompts, assistance, and equipment modifications to help children learn a motor, cognitive, or social skill. Examples of common equipment scaffolds in physical education include low-level beams in gymnastics, swim aids,

TEACHING TIP

Eliciting Exploration Quickly

When you give an exploration task and a child responds quickly, say, "I see someone balancing on two hands and one foot; I see someone balancing on their hips." Other children will start exploring by trying to find different body parts because they want you to call out their ideas, too. This positive approach works better than saying, "Get busy and do what I told you to do."

modified equipment such as foam balls and trainer volleyballs, hitting fairway irons off a golf tee, and batting tees.

In educational games, gymnastics, and dance, teachers almost always need to scaffold the exploration process with beginners—of any age. To scaffold exploration, take the students through the exploration process step-by step using a set of tasks that have children explore only one or two choices or movement concepts while you make specific suggestions.

The following examples of scaffolding come from a lesson on balancing on different body parts and illustrate three levels of scaffolding: massive, moderate, and light.

Task: Explore balancing on different body parts.

Massive Scaffolding of Exploration

1. Today we're going to explore balancing on different body parts. I want you to get into the same position as me. [Demonstrate a balance on hips with legs tucked in curled position and arms out.]
2. Which body part am I balancing on? [Answer: Hips.] Yes. Follow me. I want you to try to balance on another body part. [Demonstrate.] Now we are balancing on our sides, now our hands and shins, now our bellies.
3. Which body parts can you balance on? [Answers: Hips, belly, back, shoulders, shins, forearms, hands, feet] [If anyone answers "head," tell the child that "head" is an accurate answer, but state that children are not to balance on their heads today because there are special rules for balancing on your head, which you will work on at a later time.] When I say, "Go," I want you to select a body part on which you can balance. Go.
4. Now balance on another body part: Go. Now another: Go. Another: Go. [Repeat several more times.]
5. I have not seen any balances on your side. Let's all try that.

Moderate Scaffolding

1. Today we're going to explore balancing on different body parts. Let's start with hands and feet. Explore different ways to balance on your hands and feet.
2. Change to another balance on your hands and feet. Change again to a different balance on your hands and feet. Change. Change. Change again. [Repeat several times.]
3. Now explore balancing on your hands and feet with three parts touching the mat. You can balance on two feet and one hand, or on two hands and one foot. Be sure the foot in the air is pointed. Go. Change. Change. [Repeat several times.]
4. Now using just your hands and feet, try to find different ways to balance on two body parts.
5. Sometimes when balancing on your hands and feet, you have your belly facing the mat and sometimes your back. Try balancing on your hands and feet sometimes with your belly facing the mat and sometimes with your back facing the mat. You decide. Go. [Repeat several times.]
6. You can balance on many different body parts. Let's generate a list of possible body parts. [Call on children until you have a relatively complete list.] Now explore balancing on different body parts.

Light Scaffolding

1. When I say "Start," I want you to explore balancing on different body parts. Start.
2. Which body part did you use? Great; now try some others.
3. Which body parts are not good supports for balancing? Great answers. Try to find body parts that are good supports.
4. Now that you have explored several different body parts for supporting your weight in a balance, try to ensure you have many, varied, and a few unusual balances. Go.

Using Logic to Identify Movement Concepts for Breaking Down the Exploration Process

One problem teachers often have when scaffolding exploration is identifying the more detailed content (i.e., movement concepts) relevant to each skill. To do this, we use the Laban framework.

While looking at the Laban framework, think about the skill, try to apply each of the movement concepts, and evaluate whether a logical connection exists. For example, it is logical to vary jumping using the movement concepts of making different shapes in the air and taking off and landing on one or two feet. Varying the speed of jumps isn't logical, however, because you can't jump in slow motion—it takes a certain speed to generate enough force to leave the ground.

Next, evaluate whether the variations represent worthwhile content for children to learn and practice. For example, in gymnastics, it is important for children to learn to jump from apparatus at low, medium, and high levels and to jump onto apparatus at low, medium, and high levels. Combining jumping and changes in levels in these ways constitutes substantive gymnastics content that progresses in difficulty. It is probably not worth the effort for children to devote much time to exploring jumping at low levels or different speeds (because the speed of a jump for height and distance is linked directly to generating force). In contrast, having children practice generating as much force with their arm and leg actions to achieve as much height as they can during a jump is valuable content to learn. Jumping at different speeds and low levels is relevant in jumping rope and would be important in lessons covering that content.

5. Which body parts are the easiest to balance on? Which balances are hard to hold? Why? Work on balances that are more difficult for you to hold—challenge yourself.

As a teacher, your goal is to use the least amount of scaffolding necessary and to remove scaffolding when the children no longer need it. In several lessons in the content chapters, we illustrate three levels of scaffolding: massive, moderate, and light. These three levels do not represent a progression; in other words, you don't start with massive and progress to light scaffolding. Instead, you use the amount of scaffolding the children need to meet your lesson objectives.

Research shows that expert teachers change the amount of scaffolding throughout a unit, increasing and decreasing it based on task difficulty, children's responses, and lesson objectives (Chen et al., 2012). They have strong, extensive knowledge of the movement concepts from the Laban framework that will help scaffold exploration, and they can shift on their feet from light to moderate scaffolding when they observe children having problems exploring.

When children are beginners at exploration tasks, you need to be prepared with a backup plan to use massive amounts of scaffolding, increasing and decreasing the amount of scaffolding based on the children's actual responses. In addition, as a beginning teacher, planning massive scaffolding even if you won't need it will help you think about the movement concepts from the Laban framework that children can use in exploring a theme. Your thinking during planning will help build your content knowledge so that it becomes more like the knowledge of experts.

C. Teach Children to Move While They Think and to Think While They Move

A common response when children first learn to explore is to sit and think rather than to explore by trying out different movements. You explore through movement, not by thinking about which movements you could do. If you simply remind children to move while they are thinking and, of course, to think while they are moving, their responses will quickly improve.

Sample Feedback

- "Remember to explore by moving and trying ideas. Don't sit and think—just try it."
- "Move while you think, and think while you move."

> **TEACHING TIP**
>
> **Older Children**
>
> With older children who have not had dance or gymnastics classes before, you must insist they don't laugh at one another. Many older children (and undergraduates) laugh at others because they feel uncomfortable doing something different themselves and they are afraid they will appear incompetent to their classmates. We find it necessary to approach this problem directly by discussing it before we have children explore.

D. Establish a Positive, Emotionally Safe Classroom Climate

When teaching exploration, it is important to establish a positive classroom climate (Chen et al., 2012). Children need to be encouraged to experiment freely. Avoid criticism of ideas during the exploration phase. Don't allow children to laugh at or make fun of one another. Recognize and reward new and original ideas. Children need to feel emotionally safe to take risks and try new ideas.

E. Explore with a Partner to Generate Many, Varied, and Some Unusual Ideas, and Then Elaborate on Your Ideas

In level 2 content, children often work with a partner. Review the creative thinking strategy but with a partner.

F. Teach Affective Dispositions that Support Creativity

Psychologists have identified affective dispositions and attitudes that support creative thinking (Perkins et al., 1993). We begin our discussion of these dispositions here.

Be Broad and Adventurous

Teach the dispositions to be broad and adventurous. Emphasize that being adventurous is fun; it is fun to "play" with a movement concept or skill to see if you can uncover some new ways to perform.

Defer Criticism

It is also important to teach children the disposition to defer criticism about the ideas they generate. If they become critical of their ideas too early in the process, they might limit the number and quality of the ideas they generate. Tell them that sometimes a movement that feels silly, boring, dull, trivial, or weird will lead to a different idea that is very good.

Be Safe and Remain on Task

The only restrictions we suggest are to limit children's movements to those that are safe and related to the task. For example, in gymnastics, balancing on either elbows or kneecaps is an accurate response to a task calling for balancing on body parts, but these balances can hurt and be unsafe and, therefore, are not appropriate. Crawling on hands and knees can be accurately called weight transfer or a step-like action, but it is not an appropriate gymnastics movement and isn't a worthwhile skill for children to practice; crawling is a skill they learned as babies. Nevertheless, children might do crawling-like movements that they can develop into interesting, valuable gymnastics movements. Part of the art of teaching is to recognize accurate but inappropriate responses and help children to modify their ideas.

Sample Feedback

- "What an adventurous class you are. I saw so many different ways to dodge and dribble around defenders. Your efforts will pay off when you play soccer."
- "Don't forget that some ideas seem boring, but you may be able to expand on an idea and make it exciting."

Sample Tasks

- Set up two cones as pretend defenders and two more cones along the fence as a soccer goal. Find as many ways

Typical Immature Patterns

Children will not automatically know how to explore a theme, nor will they be instantly proficient with creative processes and design interesting and original movements. They will be beginners at creative thinking in the same way that they will be beginners at performing motor skills. Teachers can expect to see several typical beginner responses.

They All Copy One Another: What Does This Mean?

Research in other subject areas suggests that when children repeat what they hear another child say, this response is simply how they begin to discuss their own ideas with one another and explore their understanding of a topic. We suspect a similar process occurs in physical education. Copying what another child does is one way children begin to explore their own ideas, better understand themes, and elaborate on the range of appropriate responses. We don't worry about copying; instead, we view it as part of the developmental process. Children will, if given the time, develop their own ideas. The one time you must prevent copying is when children in gymnastics see other children demonstrating a skill that is beyond their ability. Tell them they can copy ideas they like, but only skills they can perform safely and skillfully.

They Are Doing the Same Thing Over and Over; They Are Not Creative: Is This a Problem?

Repetitive behavior may or may not be a problem. Repetition may indicate that the children do not know the movement concepts that they can apply to vary the skill they're working on. For example, if you ask children to balance in different ways, they might know that they can vary the supporting body parts but not think about varying the shape and level of their balances. Thus, they might repeat the same balance over and over.

Repetition also may indicate that the children do not know enough about each of the movement concepts that are relevant to a skill. For example, if they aren't familiar with the five kinds of shapes—wide, straight, round, angular, and twisted—they won't be able to explore different shapes by intentionally varying their shapes in these ways.

Another problem might be that only a few options are available to children that are safe. Rolling in different directions is a perfect example. Low-skilled children might have only one direction—sideways—in which they can roll safely and confidently.

Another reason why children might repeat the same movement over and over is because they like the movement they have discovered. They want to practice it over and over for the sheer joy of doing it.

Finally, children might do the same thing over and over because they are off task or not listening to the teacher—a judgment about the children's responses we suggest teachers try to defer. Blaming the children is easy to do, but it doesn't solve the problem.

We offer two suggestions for remedying the problem in this scenario. First, assume that the children do not understand the options available, and explicitly teach them the relevant options. Second, try scaffolding the exploration process, thereby helping children learn how to explore. You can say, "If you understand, you may begin; if not, stay here and I will explain some more."

The Children Don't Want to Explore; All They Do Is Stand Around and Watch

There are many good reasons why children might stand and watch rather than join in. It takes a while for children to adapt to learning in a new way and working in a new learning environment. Children who have never been given choices in physical education or in their classroom will not know how to respond when a teacher gives an exploration or problem-solving task. They might be waiting for the teacher to tell them what to do and assume that if they watch other children, they will figure out what the teacher wants. If they are used to traditional games, gymnastics, and dance classes, they also might be afraid that other children will watch them; it will take a while before they understand that other children are doing their own work. Finally, they might think there is only one right answer and fear that their ideas will be unacceptable to the teacher. It takes time for children to understand that there are multiple right answers to exploration tasks posed by the teacher.

as you can to dribble with your feet around the defenders, faking them out and protecting the ball. Then, shoot to score.

- Play a 1v1 hand dribbling game in which both of you dribble while trying to touch your partner's ball. Try to use a different tactic each time.
- With a partner, design a dance sequence representing the theme of prey and predator. Begin by exploring different actions the predator might use to move stealthily close to the prey without the prey seeing or hearing the predator. Don't criticize your ideas—remember, this is the exploration phase of creating your dance.
- With a partner, find as many ways as you can to make contrasting shapes with one partner jumping and making a shape high in the air and the other balancing or rolling and making a contrasting shape at a low or medium level. We are just experimenting right now, so use your creative thinking strategy. I have written it on the whiteboard in case you need a reminder of this strategy.

G. Explore Tasks with Small Groups, Trying to Generate Many, Varied, and Some Unusual Ideas

The progression for teaching exploration follows the progression for teaching other thinking skills first for individuals, then partners, and finally small groups. This progression aligns with levels' 1, 2, and 3 content. Although the process gets more complex because of increased social demands in level 3 content, the creative thinking strategy remains the same.

H. Teach Affective Dispositions and Attitudes that Support Exploration and Contribute to CCSS

Having explored in younger grades, by the older grades children should be comfortable with the process of exploring and ready to engage in partner and group work. The social aspects of group work, however, add emotional complexity to the exploration process, causing some children to be reticent to speak as they lack confidence in their ideas. Others are afraid of looking foolish or incompetent, while still others fear their classmate will laugh at or make fun of their ideas. Thus, it is critical to maintain an emotionally safe class climate that supports children brainstorming, exploring ideas, and working on creative thinking with peers.

In addition, within the CCSS speaking and listening section are standards related to partner and group discussions. Included are standards for listening carefully, building and elaborating on classmates' ideas, being supportive and respectful, and expressing thoughts, feelings, and ideas clearly. Children can work on all of these standards when they explore tasks with partners and small groups.

Psychologists have identified a set of affective disposition and attitudes that characterize good thinking (Perkins et al., 1993) and support group discussions that meet CCSS standards. These affective dispositions and attitudes include the following:

- Be broad and adventurous
- Play with new ideas
- Generate many options
- Defer criticism
- Suspend judgments
- Be open-minded
- Have a few wild and crazy ideas
- Build on classmates' ideas
- Watch out for negative body language; it will halt good brainstorming
- Comment on what you like about other group members' ideas

You can teach these dispositions one at a time or keep a list on a whiteboard to remind the groups about the importance of maintaining these attitudes. You can assign individuals roles for monitoring the group's exploration process. One role can be the equity officer in charge of making sure everyone listens, everyone speaks and makes a contribution, and everyone is accepted, supported, and treated respectfully. Another role can be the strategy monitor, who reminds the group to remember the creative thinking strategy to think of many, varied, and unusual ideas and to build on their and their classmates' ideas. A final role might be the encourager, who encourages everyone to have a few wild and crazy ideas.

> **TEACHING TIP**
>
> **Stories**
>
> One story you can tell to help children not be critical too early is about computers. The first computer was about the size of a building. Where would we be now if someone said, "Oh, let's try to make the computer the size of a briefcase," or "Let's try to connect all of the computers together in a worldwide web," or "Let's try to make a wireless connection from computer to computer," and everyone else responded, "That's not a good idea," or "That won't work," or "Why would you want to do that?"

Teaching Problem Solving

Problem-solving tasks include all four of the thinking skills we have discussed so far. Thus, they are typically bigger and broader tasks and build on what children have learned about other thinking skills. Problem-solving tasks are used extensively in games, gymnastics, dance, and HRPA lessons (see **Figure 10.9**). In fact, such tasks are often the culminating activity of lessons and units. They are the backbone of the curriculum for grades 3 through 5.

Problem-solving tasks are used to

1. Design a practice task to practice a skill or tactic
2. Design (or modify) the rules of a game
3. Design game tactics to solve tactical problems
4. Design gymnastics or dance sequences to solve a choreographic problem
5. Design an HRPA or HRF workout or program to meet a fitness objective

If you have studied secondary physical education curriculum models such as Sport Education, Teaching Games for Understanding, and Project Adventure, you will notice that the problem-solving tasks in this text form a progression that leads up to these secondary models. For example, teaching children to design tasks for practicing tactics and to work as a group to solve tactical problems are progressions for the tasks students do in a Sport Education unit.

At the elementary level, problem-solving tasks present authentic problems about some aspect of content. Recall, for example, the scenario at the beginning of this chapter in which children were asked to design a game and then explore and critique offensive tactics for creating space to score. Because

Figure 10.9 Brainstorming ideas for a dance with positive attitudes

Courtesy of John Dolly

of their inherently challenging nature, problem-solving tasks are engaging and relevant to children.

In almost all problem-solving tasks, there is no single right answer. That is, we don't use problem solving narrowly to figure out the one answer the teacher wants all the children to provide. Rather, because tasks are authentic, there is typically a range of appropriate options children can explore. For example, a problem-solving task to design a dance sequence showing movements at different levels will lead to as many different dance sequences as there are children in the class. Similarly, a tactical problem will have multiple solutions. Although some tactics will be better than others, there is typically more than one viable solution.

A. Set Problem-Solving Tasks that Call for Working Individually on Simple Problems

In the same way that we start teaching other thinking skills, in the youngest grades we teach children how to solve simple problems and continue to build their efforts toward solving more complex problems throughout all elementary grades. For example, a simple problem-solving task in dance would be to create a sequence with a starting shape, one traveling movement, and an ending shape. We also start by having children work alone to solve problems.

B. Scaffold the Problem-Solving Process

In the same way that you can scaffold the exploration process, so you can scaffold the problem-solving process by talking the class through the process while offering prompts and suggestions on how to make the problem-solving strategy work better for them. For example, during the first part of a gymnastics or dance lesson, you would guide the class through the process of exploring each part of the final sequence. Then, in the culminating activity, you would guide the children in selecting and arranging their best ideas from the exploration phase. You would end the lesson by guiding the refinement and practice of the children's sequence or practice task.

Think-Aloud Scaffold Using the Example of a Challenge Course

Another way to scaffold the problem-solving strategy is to use a think-aloud teaching technique. In this technique, the teacher demonstrates how to solve a problem by working through it while talking aloud about what he or she is thinking. In this way, you make the thinking process, which usually happens quietly in your head, visible to the students.

The following example demonstrates how to use this technique while designing a skill practice task. The teacher says aloud:

> I'm supposed to design a challenge course to practice dribbling at different speeds. That means I need to have some places where I travel fast and some places where I go slowly. To go fast, I need lots of room, so I better set up two cones far apart from each other. If I put some cones close together in zigzags, I'll have to travel more slowly. It would be really challenging if I make the zigzags have sharp angles. I can pretend these are defenders, and when I finally break free, it will be fun to sprint and dribble fast, as if I'm a superstar. So, I'll do the zigzag first and then put the last cone far away. [Teacher puts out the zigzag cones.] Oh, no, if I put the last cone here, then I might run into Clarisa because her cones will cross mine. Where can I put mine? Oh. I see a safe space. [Teacher puts the last cone down.] There, it's done. Now let me test it out.

What the Research Says

Problem-Solving Strategies

Cognitive psychologists have studied problem solving extensively; through their research, they have developed general problem-solving strategies that can transfer from one subject area to another and positively affect student achievement (Woolfolk, 1993). Other researchers have studied subject-specific problem solving and have shown that the use of these strategies can enhance student learning. Thus, in physics lessons, students learn scientific methods for solving physics problems; in mathematics, they learn specific methods for solving quadratic equations and geometry proofs. All the research in this area reinforces the importance of teaching students both the content and the strategies to solve problems within that content area.

C. Set Problem-Solving Tasks for Partners: Teach the Problem-Solving Strategy for Designing Gymnastics and Dance Sequences

As children's social skills develop, we assign problem-solving tasks to children in pairs working on longer gymnastics and dance sequences applying elements of choreography. We teach the problem-solving strategy for designing gymnastics and dance sequences, jump rope and dribbling routines, and challenge (obstacle) courses using game skills. The problem-solving process not only can be taught, but also needs to be nurtured in children (Swartz, 2008). In other words, many children will not spontaneously figure out and use a thoughtful process for solving problems without the teacher's help.

The Problem-Solving Strategy for Designing Gymnastics and Dance Sequences (also used for jump rope, dribbling, and fitness routines)

The process of designing dance and gymnastics sequences in detail requires further discussion. Here, we provide a brief

TEACHING TIP

Watch Me! Watch Me!

Sometimes children get very excited about their solutions to problems and want you to watch them. They call out your name or run over to you and say, "Come see this! I've got to show this to you." Before you know it, many children are yelling, "Watch me," or "Come see me." Teachers can establish a protocol ahead of time to prevent this. Tell them you will walk around the room to see everyone. They do not need to call out your name to show you their work; you will watch everyone. If they have a question or need help, they can raise their hands and you will respond.

overview to describe the similarities to the problem-solving strategies used in skills and games. The process is the same for a child working alone as it is for working with partners and in small groups. You will see that other thinking skills are embedded in the problem-solving process.

Sample Tasks

- Design a dance based on the themes of rising and sinking, opening and closing.
- Design a partner gymnastics sequence based on the themes of matching, contrasting, and complementing.
  1. *Explore movement options.* In phase 1, children explore, invent, discover, and experiment with movements associated with the theme of the sequence assigned by the teacher. Children use creative thinking to generate many, varied, and some unusual ideas without critiquing these ideas. They physically try out their ideas as they are exploring.
  2. *Select and arrange ideas.* When children begin phase 2, they use critical thinking and decision-making skills to evaluate the quality of their ideas, select the best ideas, and arrange the movements in a sequence. During this process, they try out their ideas as they are making decisions about what to include.
  3. *Refine and practice.* In phase 3, the children try out their ideas as a whole sequence and then evaluate their sequence. They may explore and test new options to refine parts that are not working. Then they practice the sequence until they can repeat it accurately and the quality of their movements is the best they are capable of.

D. Set Problem-Solving Tasks for Small Groups: Teach the Problem-Solving Strategy for Designing Games and Solving Tactical Problems

When children are working in small groups, the social, motor, and cognitive content becomes more complex. Dance and gymnastics sequences are based on more sophisticated themes and more difficult choreographic elements. They also design or modify small-sided game rules, boundaries, and consequences for breaking rules, and they solve and practice more complex tactical problems. In HRPA and HRF, they deal with group routines, personal issues, and ways that fitness sources and the media portray the body.

Starting in grade 3, we teach the problem-solving strategy for designing games and solving tactical problems. Because it shares characteristics with the problem-solving strategies we have taught and used in skill practices, dance, and gymnastics, the children can learn this new strategy quickly.

The Problem-Solving Strategy for Designing Games and Solving Tactical Problems

- *Task:* Design a game.
  1. *Use a play–discuss–play cycle.* When designing games and solving tactical problems, the children play the game, stop and discuss the game, and then play again. This cycle of play–discuss–play continues throughout the lesson. Sometimes you begin with the discussion phase of the cycle and sometimes with the play phase. Regardless of where you begin, the goal is for children to remain physically active throughout the problem-solving tasks, thereby testing their ideas in game situations. Discussions are typically brief. Thus, the children begin to play with a basic set of rules or a basic tactical plan and then revise their ideas throughout the lesson based on trying their ideas in game situations.
  2. *Discuss.* In the discussion phase, the children use the following thinking skills:
     a. Think critically about the game, identifying what worked and did not work (see **Figure 10.10**).
     b. Identify options (*creative thinking*). If the children are designing a game, have them identify possible rules and consequences for breaking those rules. If the children are planning tactics, have them discuss possible tactics. Ask them to anticipate what might happen when they play the game again, and critique each tactical or rule option (*critical thinking*).
     c. Make a decision as group. Try to reach a consensus, but if that is not likely, then vote on the decision. Before playing, check for understanding with everyone in the group. The most common problem with group work is that some children understand the discussion and make decisions while others don't. When play resumes, those who didn't hear or didn't know the rules or tactics the group decided upon either inadvertently violate the rules or use different tactics, and gameplay falls apart.
  3. *Play the game and try out the tactics or rules.*
  4. *Discuss.* When problems develop or on a signal from the teacher, stop play and discuss the game again. Evaluate how the rules or tactics worked using steps A, B, and C. Repeat the play–discuss–play cycle.

When children are first learning the problem-solving process, as the teacher you need to anticipate problems they will encounter in each phase. For example, children will not check for the understanding of each group member before starting to play their game unless you remind them frequently about how important this step is for successful gameplay.

Figure 10.10 Children solving a problem with their game

E. Teach the Affective Dispositions and Attitudes that Support Problem Solving and Contribute to CCSS

As a teacher, you need to teach the affective attitudes and dispositions that are components of good thinking (Perkins et al., 1993) and support success in partner and group problem solving. According to the literature, people who approach tasks in reasoned, thoughtful, planned, and strategic ways—as opposed to hastily trying to solve the problem—do better both in school and in adult life (Alexander, 2006).

In addition, as part of the CCSS speaking and listening section, standards require children to express their ideas clearly and discuss reasons and evidence for their claims or proposed solutions. They must be able to elaborate on classmates' ideas and draw conclusions based on information presented in their group discussions. They must ask and answer questions and recount experiences, providing relevant, detailed information about the topic. In physical education, the problem-solving processes of designing games, coming up with tactical solutions, and designing gymnastics and dance sequences have children working on each of the components of the speaking and listening CCSS standards. Thus, we suggest teachers teach and reinforce the following attitudes and affective aspects of thinking (adapted from Perkins et al., 1993):

- Observe closely to find problems or instances of confusion or lack of clarity.
- Anchor your ideas to what you experienced.
- Have the courage to express your ideas.
- Provide reasons to support your solutions.
- Have humility and suspend judgment.
- Persevere when the going gets tough.
- Guard against being impulsive. Plan! Think and talk before you act.

Summary

All physical activities include thinking skills. Thinking skills are taught simultaneously with the movement and cognitive knowledge content in which they are embedded. A large body of research has shown that when teachers assign problems, projects, and activities that engage children in thinking critically about the subject matter, discussing their ideas, exploring and experimenting with different options, and discovering and evaluating possible solutions to problems, children not only learn more, but also are more engaged and interested in what they are learning. This kind of inquiry-oriented teaching includes decision-making, critical thinking, creative thinking and exploration, and problem-solving tasks in addition to asking questions.

Review Questions

1. List three reasons thinking skills are important in physical education.
2. Select a skill you know well and describe what you would say to a class to explain what self-regulation means in relation to that skill.
3. Write a task for designing a game, dance sequence, or gymnastics sequence. Then describe how you would teach children the decision-making aspects of your task.
4. Describe how you would explain or teach two dispositions that support decision making. Do not use the examples provided in the text.
5. How does putting feedback in the form of a question elicit critical thinking?
6. What are the four components of creative thinking? What is the creative thinking strategy?
7. Read the examples in the text and describe the specific differences that distinguish massive, moderate, and light scaffolding.
8. Describe the problem-solving strategy for designing games and solving tactical problems.

References

Alexander, P. A. (2006). *Psychology in learning and instruction*. Upper Saddle River, NJ: Pearson.

Anderson, A., Vogel, P., & Albrecht, R. (1999). The effect of instructional self-talk on the overhand throw. *The Physical Educator*, *56*, 215–221.

Bryan, C. L., & Solmon, M. A. (2007). Self-determination in physical education: Designing class environments to promote active lifestyles. *Journal of Teaching in Physical Education*, *26*, 260–278.

Byra, M. (2006). Teaching styles and inclusive pedagogies. In D. Kirk, D. MacDonald, & M. O'Sullivan (Eds.), *The handbook of physical education* (pp. 449–466). London: Sage.

Chen, W. (2001). Description of an expert teacher's constructivist-oriented teaching: Engaging students' critical thinking in learning creative dance. *Research Quarterly for Exercise and Sport*, *72*, 366–375.

Chen, W., & Cone, T. P. (2003). Links between children's use of critical thinking and expert teacher's teaching in creative dance. *Journal of Teaching in Physical Education*, *22*, 169–185.

Chen, W., Rovegno, I., Cone, S. L., & Cone, T. P. (2012). An accomplished teacher's use of scaffolding during a second grade unit on designing games. *Research Quarterly for Exercise and Sport*, *83*, 221–234.

Chiviacowsky, S., & Wulf, G. (2002). Self-controlled feedback: Does it enhance learning because performers get feedback when they need it? *Research Quarterly for Exercise and Sport, 73,* 408–415.

Cleland, F., & Pearse, C. (1995). Critical thinking in elementary physical education: Reflections on a yearlong study. *Journal of Physical Education, Recreation, and Dance, 66*(6), 31–38.

Costa, A. L. (Ed.). (1991). *Developing minds: A resource book for teaching thinking.* Alexandria, VA: Association for Supervision and Curriculum Development.

Costa, A. L. (2008). The thought-filled curriculum. *Educational Leadership, 65*(5), 20–24.

French, K. E., Nevett, M. E., Spurgeon, J. H., Graham, K. C., Rink, J. E., & McPherson, S. L. (1996). Knowledge and problem solution in youth baseball. *Research Quarterly for Exercise and Sport, 67,* 386–395.

French, K. E., Spurgeon, J. H., & Nevett, M. E. (1995). Expert–novice differences in cognitive and skill execution components of youth baseball performance. *Research Quarterly for Exercise and Sport, 66,* 194–201.

Iserbyt, P., Elen, J., & Behets, D. (2010). Instructional guidance in reciprocal peer tutoring with task cards. *Journal of Teaching in Physical Education, 29,* 38–53.

Johnson, T. G., Prusak, K., A., Pennington, T., & Wilkinson, C. (2011). The effects of the type of skill test, choice, and gender on the situational motivation of physical education students. *Journal of Teaching in Physical Education, 30,* 281–295.

Koka, A., & Hagger, M. S. (2010). Perceived teaching behaviors and self-determined motivation in physical education: A test of self-determination theory. *Research Quarterly for Exercise and Sport, 81,* 74–86.

Kolovelonis, A., Goudas, M., & Dermitzaki, I. (2011). The effects of instructional and motivational self-talk on students' motor task performance in physical education. *Psychology of Sport and Exercise, 12,* 153–158.

Lidor, R. (2004). Developing metacognitive behavior in physical education classes: The use of task-pertinent learning strategies. *Physical Education and Sport Pedagogy, 9,* 55–71.

Luke, I., & Hardy, C. A. (1999). Appreciating the complexity of learning in physical education: The utilization of a metacognitive ability conceptual framework. *Sport, Education and Society, 4,* 175–191

McBride, R. E. (1991). Critical thinking: An overview with implications for physical education. *Journal of Teaching in Physical Education, 11,* 112–125.

Nevett, M. E., & French, K. E. (1997). The development of sport-specific planning, rehearsal and updating of plans during defensive youth baseball game performance. *Research Quarterly for Exercise and Sport, 68,* 203–214.

Noddings, N. (2008). All our students thinking. *Educational Leadership, 65*(5), 8–13.

Perkins, D. N., Jay, E., & Tishman, S. (1993). Beyond abilities: A dispositional theory of thinking. *Merrill-Palmer Quarterly, 39,* 1-21.

Prusak, K. A., Treasure, D. C., Darst, P. W., & Pangrazi, R. P. (2004). The effects of choice on the motivation of adolescent girls in physical education. *Journal of Teaching in Physical Education, 23,* 19–29.

Resnick, L. B. (2010). Nested learning systems for the thinking curriculum. *Educational Researcher, 39,* 183–197.

Rovegno, I., Chen, W., & Todorovich, J. (2003). Accomplished teachers' pedagogical content knowledge of teaching dribbling to third grade. *Journal of Teaching in Physical Education, 22,* 426–449.

Schlicter, C. L. (1986). Talents unlimited: Applying the multiple talent approach in mainstream and gifted programs. In J. Renzulli (Ed.), *Systems and models for developing programs for the gifted and talented* (pp. 21–44). Mansfield Center, CT: Creative Learning Press.

Shen, B., McCaughtry, N., Martin, J., & Fahlman, M. (2009). Effects of teacher autonomy support and students' autonomous motivation on learning in physical education. *Research Quarterly for Exercise and Sport, 80,* 44–53.

Singer, R. N. (2000). Performance and human factors: Considerations about cognition and attention for self-paced and externally-paced events. *Ergonomics, 43*(10), 1661–1680.

Standage, M., Duda, J. L., & Ntoumanis, N. (2003). A model of contextual motivation in physical education: Using constructs from self-determination and achievement goal theories to predict physical activity intentions. *Journal of Educational Psychology, 95,* 97–110.

Swartz, R. J. (2008). Energizing learning. *Educational Leadership, 65*(5), 26–31.

Tishman, S. & Perkins, D. (1995). Critical thinking and physical education. *Journal of Physical Education and Recreational Dance.* 66 (6), 24–30.

Torrance, E. P. (1962). *Guiding creative talent.* Englewood Cliffs, NJ: Prentice-Hall.

Treasure, D. C., & Roberts, G. C. (2001). Students' perceptions of the motivational climate, achievement beliefs, and satisfaction in physical education. *Research Quarterly for Exercise and Sport, 72,* 165–175.

Vande Broek, G., Boen, F., Claessens, M., Feys, J., & Ceux, T. (2011). Comparison of three instructional approaches to enhance tactical knowledge in volleyball among university students. *Journal of Teaching in Physical Education, 30,* 375–392.

Woolfolk, A. E. (1993). *Educational psychology* (5th ed.). Needham Heights, MA: Allyn and Bacon.

Wulf, G., & Toole, T. (1999). Physical assistance devices in complex motor skill learning: Benefits of a self-controlled practice schedule. *Research Quarterly for Exercise and Sport, 70,* 265–272.

Zourbanos, N. (2013). The use of instructional and motivational self-talk in setting up a physical education lesson. *Journal of Physical Education, Recreation and Dance, 84*(8), 54–58.

Zourbanos, N., Hatzigeorgiadis, A., Bardas, D., & Theodorakis, Y. (2013). The effects of self-talk on dominant and non-dominant arm performance on a handball task in primary physical education students. *The Sport Psychologist, 27,* 171–176.

CHAPTER

11

Social and Emotional Goals

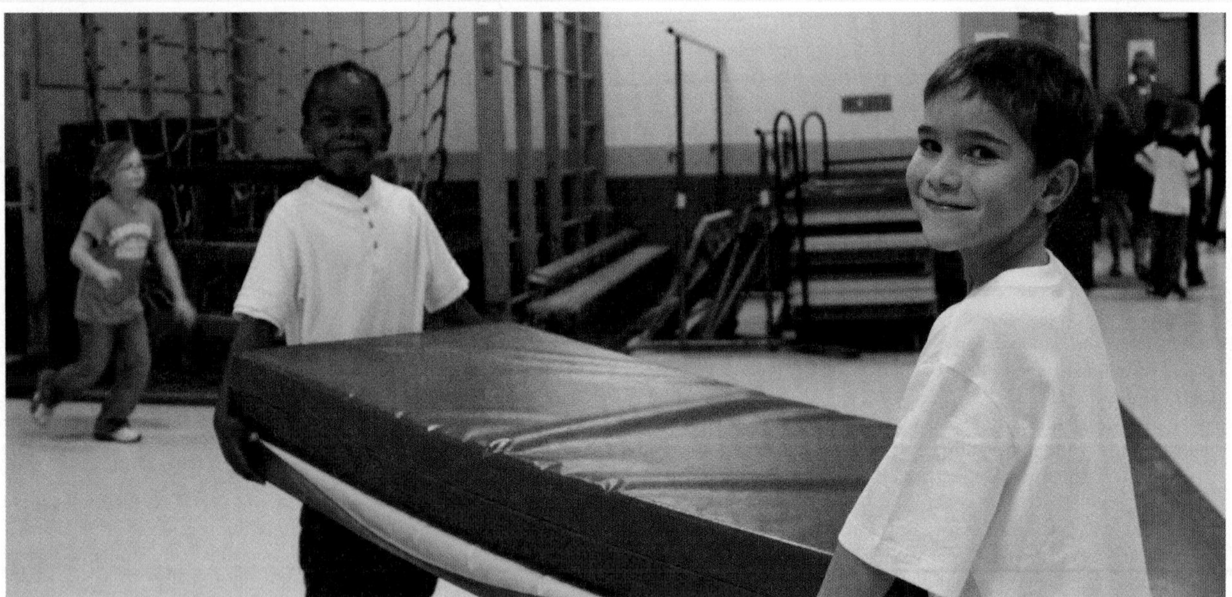

PRE-READING REFLECTION

1. Identify your favorite teacher or other adult in a teaching-related profession, such as an age-group coach (not a relative), who has had an impact on your life. Describe that person and explain why he or she was your favorite teacher.
2. Why do you want to be a teacher?

OBJECTIVES

Students will learn:

1. Within the social and emotional domains, there are four overlapping categories of goals for elementary physical education: (a) developing caring and respect for others; (b) developing collaboration skills; (c) developing personal and social responsibility; and (d) valuing the affective aspects of physical activities.
2. Each category can be broken down into specific behaviors and content.
3. Teachers need to describe explicitly the social and emotional behaviors and content they want children to learn.
4. Decision-making and cooperative learning tasks are used to work on social and emotional goals.

KEY TERMS

Cooperative learning
Egocentrism
Individual accountability
Positive interdependence

CONNECTION TO STANDARDS

The focus of this chapter is to describe how you can teach behaviors and attitudes that meet National Standards 4 and 5 (Society of Health and Physical Educators [SHAPE], 2014). In addition, we describe in detail how you can teach the skills required for students to meet the standards for speaking, listening, collaboration, and comprehension in the Common Core (Common Core State Standards Initiative [CCSS], 2010).

Introduction

In this chapter, we discuss goals for facilitating children's social and emotional development in physical education. These goals have a long history in our field. From the 1800s through the present day, physical educators, coaches, and even the general public have believed that sports can develop positive social and moral qualities in children and youth (Theodoulides & Armour, 2001). Historically, many of the leaders in our field have argued that our two primary goals are education *of* the physical (i.e., teaching physical activities) and *through* the physical (i.e., promoting character development) (Freeman, 2012; Hellison & Martinek, 2006). National Standards for Physical Education (National Standards) 4 and 5 focus on teaching social and emotional goals.

Teachers well recognize the importance of social and emotional goals in their classrooms. In a series of studies, Dr. Catherine Ennis found that urban teachers, in particular, place a high value on teaching social responsibility (Ennis, 1994a, 1994b; Ennis & Chen, 1995). Dr. Nate McCaughtry and his colleagues found that teachers attend carefully to students' emotional states, which then guide teachers' decisions about lesson activities, the curriculum, and teaching techniques (McCaughtry, 2004; McCaughtry, Barnard, Martin, Shen, & Hodges Kulinna, 2006).

In addition, research shows that teachers can help children develop socially and emotionally. Moreover, school-based programs designed to achieve this aim have proved successful in reducing antisocial, disruptive, and aggressive behaviors (Osher, Bear, Sprague, & Doyle, 2010).

Finally, a goal of many physical education teachers is to make a difference in the lives of their students. It is not simply that we want to share the joys and benefits we experienced in sports, fitness, gymnastics, and dance settings; we also want to help students grow socially and emotionally so they can lead happy, productive lives.

What the Research Says

Facilitating Social and Emotional Development

Several studies have examined the effectiveness of school programs designed to improve children's moral judgments, social and personal responsibility, and sense of fair play. These studies reveal that teachers can make a difference and help children improve in terms of their attitudes and behaviors, such as self-control and self-responsibility, respect for rules and opponents, positive attitudes toward equitable participation for all, and moral reasoning (DeBusk & Hellison, 1989; Gibbons, Ebbeck, & Weiss, 1995; Romance, Weiss, & Bockoven, 1986; Wandzilak, Carroll, & Ansorge, 1988). However, simply participating in physical education or sports does not appear to contribute to changes in children's behaviors and attitudes. The implications are clear: If you want children to develop a sense of fairness, responsibility, justice, and caring, you need to teach for these goals.

Do Sports Build Character?

Although teachers strongly support the idea of using sport and physical activities to facilitate students' social and emotional development, some evidence suggests that character development does not happen automatically through sport participation (Theodoulides & Armour, 2001). If you want to develop children's social and emotional skills, you need to teach them explicitly. The good news is that research shows planned programs for developing children's social and emotional abilities are effective.

Organization of the Chapter, National Standards 4 and 5, and the Common Core and other State Standards (CCSS)

We begin by discussing children's social and emotional development, teaching strategies for content from the social and emotional domains, and Hellison's "Taking Personal and Social Responsibility" approach. We then discuss the social and emotional behaviors and content you can teach, organized in four sections:

- *Caring and respect for others:* This section aims to develop the ethics of caring and respect and addresses the National Standard 4 sections on working with others and personal responsibility.
- *Collaboration:* This section aims to develop an ethic of cooperation and the critical skills needed for cooperative learning with partners and small groups. We address behaviors and content from the standards for comprehension and collaboration within the speaking and listening section of the CCSS. We also address the section on accepting feedback within National Standard 4.
- *Personal and social responsibility:* This section aims to develop an ethic of social responsibility and fairness and addresses the National Standard 4 sections on personal responsibility, rules and etiquette, and safety. An ethic of social responsibility and fairness also includes issues related to diversity, including the equitable and just treatment of individuals regardless of race, gender, ethnicity, sexual orientation, religion, body shape, disability, or ability. Diversity is so important that it is worthy of its own chapter.
- *Valuing the affective aspects of physical activities*: This section addresses National Standard 5.

Social and Emotional Development

Industry and Competence

As you may recall from your coursework in educational psychology, Erikson's theory (1950) states that the primary task for middle childhood (ages 6–11) is to develop industry and a sense of competence versus inferiority. When development progresses in positive directions, children learn they are competent and can master skills (Berk, 2010). They develop a sense of responsibility and the ability to cooperate with peers. When development does not progress in a positive direction, however, children feel inferior and experience a sense of helplessness when asked to demonstrate competence.

The implications of this theory for teachers include the importance of teaching a mastery orientation and a growth mindset. In addition, the importance placed on developing industry supports the goal of elementary physical education to focus on children learning skills.

Self-Regulation of Emotions

During middle childhood, children also increase their ability to self-regulate their emotions (Berk, 2010). This capacity gives them a sense of control, a positive self-image, and optimism, and it contributes to the development and maintenance of successful peer relationships. When children don't learn to self-regulate their emotions, this failure can leave them overwhelmed by negative feelings and unaccepted by peers. The implication is that teachers need to help children learn to self-regulate; in particular, we need to help those children whose emotional reactions jeopardize their ability to maintain friendships.

Understanding the Perspective of Others

Middle childhood is the stage of life when children develop from a standpoint of **egocentrism** (in which they believe their perspective is the only perspective) to being able to recognize the existence of multiple perspectives on the same situation (Berk, 2010). The ability to see an issue or situation from the perspective of another child is critical in the development of empathy and a sense of fairness. It is also important for forging friendships and for being able to work successfully in cooperative groups. Thus, understanding others' perspectives is an important ability for teachers to help children develop.

Peer Groups and Friendships

Although peers do not play as central a role in children's development in elementary school as they will in middle and high school, younger children do learn to develop friendships based on trust. They learn to rely on friends for support, build emotional commitments, and resolve conflicts while maintaining the friendships. These are the years in which children form clubs with special handshakes, secret languages, clubhouses, and rules (Berk, 2010).

While peer groups can be positive—enabling children to learn how to get along with others, be trustworthy members of a team, and develop leadership skills, for example—these groups can also be exclusive cliques and harmful to children outside of the clique. Starting in about third grade, aggression against outsiders begins, with girls typically using gossip and exclusion as their favored weapons and boys being more overt with insults and taunts (see **Figure 11.1**) (Berk, 2010).

It is essential for teachers to recognize and respond to the negative effect of cliques. Children who are the victims of such aggression can be devastated, become isolated, and fail to develop the important social skills and self-esteem necessary for their well-being. Children who are rejected by their peers are isolated and unhappy and begin to have academic, social, and emotional problems. Rejected children who are passive are more at risk for becoming victims of bullying. Rejected children who are aggressive may become hostile, impulsive, angry, and unable to self-regulate their negative behavior (Berk, 2010).

Figure 11.1 Peer groups can be either positive or exclusive and harmful to other children.

Physical education teachers must become part of the team that seeks to help rejected children develop self-esteem and learn positive social skills. Because our subject matter includes games and play situations, physical education teachers might be the first adults to recognize a child's social and emotional problems. There is much we can do to improve matters on this front. As discussed later in this chapter, we can teach children social skills and help them develop emotional self-regulation and a positive affect. We can also refer children to the guidance counselor and talk to parents and classroom teachers.

Teaching Strategies

Define the Goal, Behaviors, and Attitudes

Researchers and practitioners alike suggest that you need to begin teaching social and emotional goals by defining for children the behavior or attitude you want the children to learn.

> **Experienced Teachers Talk**
>
> **The Story of the Farm Boy**
>
> I noticed that none of the children wanted to be a partner with this one boy. He seemed to be a nice boy, so I asked one of the children why, and she said, "Because he smells." And I discovered that he did. Every morning he had farm chores and his shoes smelled from manure. It is a terrible experience for a child to be isolated and have no one want to be with him. I called his mother and told her to have him change his shoes just before he got on the bus, and the problem was solved.

Experienced Teachers Talk

The Story of the Girls' Club

I saw a mother of a girl in my classes (I'll call her Lela) at a high school sport event. She said to me that her daughter hated PE. I said to Lela's mom, "That surprises me so much. She acts happy in class. She never causes any problems, and I never have to reprimand her for anything." So I knew there was a serious problem, and I referred Lela to the guidance counselor. The guidance counselor found out that a group of girls had formed a club, and one of the rules was that you could not talk to or play with Lela. So, in PE, she was always left out, and no one would talk to her. The guidance counselor called a meeting of all of the parents of the girls in the club and told them what was going on. The parents put an end to the club.

We deal with this issue every year. Sometimes the organizer of the club says, "You can't talk to her or him, or you can't be her or his friend." There are other clubs in which no one in the club can talk to anyone else, and they use membership in the club to bully other children. So we have learned as a school to watch for signs of this behavior, because we know it happens, and it happens in places where teachers can't hear it or see it.

The definition must be presented in language the children will understand and at a conceptual level matched to their developmental level. Kindergarteners need concrete explanations linked simply to what is good versus bad behavior. Older children can understand more complex definitions and can recognize how context might influence behavior.

In addition, your definition must be linked to behaviors and attitudes related to the content you are teaching. For example, if you want to teach children cooperation with a partner (see **Figure 11.2**), and the task is to practice catching a ball tossed to the side so the child must move to catch it, you need to explain what cooperation means:

- Making each toss catchable
- While making each toss catchable, also toss far enough to the side to challenge your partner to improve
- Complimenting your partner when he or she works really hard to catch the ball
- Not making your partner spend time retrieving balls you tossed too far to the side
- Standing as close to or as far apart as you need to toss accurately

Use Decision-Making and Cooperative Learning Tasks

Practitioners and researchers agree on the kinds of tasks that are necessary for developing caring, respect, collaboration, and social responsibility. First, tasks must have a decision-making component. Recall that decision-making, critical thinking, exploration, and problem-solving tasks all include some element of decision making. These tasks give children opportunities to learn to care for others, to take responsibility for their own and others' learning, to be fair to others, and to have autonomy over what they practice and how their learning process evolves.

Figure 11.2 Selecting an appropriate distance apart for your partner's needs

Second, tasks must have a cooperation component. Children need to learn how to work cooperatively with others, first alone while sharing space and equipment with classmates, and then with partners and in small groups.

Cooperative learning is the term for group work in which students work together cooperatively to complete a project. Cooperative learning has been extensively researched across all age groups and subject areas within education (Dean, Hubbell, Pitler, & Stone, 2012; Dyson & Grineski, 2001). Research consistently shows that cooperative learning leads to deeper learning, increased motivation due to feeling a part of and a sense of responsibility toward their group, and improved attitudes toward school (Dean et al., 2012). Improved social interactions and relationships, however, do not happen automatically (Brock, Rovegno, & Oliver, 2009; Byra, 2006). Cooperation must be taught.

The Impact of Student Status on Group Work

Research has shown that student status often determines who has a voice in group discussions, who is heard, and who gets to make the group's decisions (Cohen, 1994). Unfortunately, students with high status often dominate discussions and decision-making processes. In turn, they learn more than students with low status do. In both classroom subjects and physical education, students assign high status to group members who have athletic ability, academic ability, popularity, high socioeconomic status, and attractiveness (Brock et al., 2009; Cohen, 1994). Race and gender also can affect status.

The implications of this practice are that teachers must attend to issues of student status and ensure that all children have equitable opportunities to contribute to the group's work. Cohen (1994) presents a number of techniques to help teachers improve the quality of group work. First, she suggests that teachers teach norms for how to behave in groups (p. 46). These norms include the following behaviors:

- Listening to other children
- Asking for others' opinions
- Ensuring everyone contributes
- Giving reasons for your opinion
- Reflecting on what others have suggested

- Showing and explaining how to do things
- Helping others

Second, she recommends teaching group processes related to the content and task assigned. For example, one possible group process for designing a game based on Cohen's work is as follows (see **Figure 11.3**):

Group Process for Designing a Game

1. Design boundaries, rules, and consequences for breaking rules.
2. Everyone talks; everyone listens. (Each person gives his or her opinion, and everyone must listen to it. Don't be bossy.)
3. Encourage quiet classmates to contribute. You can say, "What do you think, Jesse?"
4. Before you play, make sure that everyone understands the rules of the game.
5. Play the game, and then stop and critique the boundaries, rules, and consequences. Make revisions to solve problems.
6. If you feel angry in the game, it usually means someone is not following what *you think* is a rule. Take a deep breath, stop the game, and calmly discuss the problem. First, check whether you made a rule that covered the situation. For example, if you did not make a rule that there is no running with the ball, then you can't penalize a person for doing that. Second, make the rule (if necessary), and define the consequences for breaking the rule. Then continue playing. No retroactive rules are permitted. If everyone agreed there was a rule, then apply the consequences.

Third, Cohen suggests assigning roles to students to ensure that the group works in fair and productive ways. Student roles teach children to be responsible for their group work. In addition, one teacher cannot hear the discussions of multiple groups at the same time and will not be able to guide each group individually to follow appropriate norms. The following are student roles that can be helpful in physical education:

- *Facilitator:* The facilitator keeps the group working on the task assigned, ensures that each group member participates, and monitors whether the group is following the group processes. Cohen emphasizes that the facilitator does not control the group's decisions.
- *Harmonizer:* The harmonizer attends to the emotional feelings of group members and reminds classmates, when necessary, to be kind and positive.
- *Checker:* When designing games, the checker makes sure that every group member understands the rules before the group plays the game. When designing skill tasks or dance and gymnastics sequences, the checker makes sure that every group member understands what to do.
- *Equity officer:* The equity officer is in charge of making sure every group member gets a fair chance to participate, suggest ideas, voice opinions, and be heard.

Research on cooperative learning provides many of the same suggestions. The two most consistently emphasized are "positive interdependence" and "individual accountability" (Dean et al., 2012). **Positive interdependence** means that group members must work together to complete the project, help each other, depend on each other, and care about the success of the group and that everyone must contribute to the project and the learning of other group members (Dean et al., 2012; Slavin, 2014). **Individual accountability** means that everyone is responsible and held accountable through assessments for learning and skill development. Slavin (2014) explains that without individual accountability, a class will typically have some "free riders," who don't contribute any work to the group assignment, and "know-it-alls," who dominate group decisions.

Suggestions for ways to encourage equitable contributions and individual accountability are to assign different parts of the project, such as different parts of a dance sequence or challenge (obstacle) course, to different group members and then assess each part as well as the whole and then use techniques along the line of the "Random Reporter" (Slavin, 2014). In "Random Reporter," each group member has a number from 1 to 4 or 5, depending on the size of the group. The teacher asks a question and then randomly selects an index card with a number. The child with that number must answer for the entire group. The group can be awarded points or extra privileges for correct answers. Because the group knows the teacher will select the reporter randomly, they make sure each group member knows the answer or can present the group's solution to the problem assigned.

The widespread promotion of cooperative learning is evident in the CCSS section on speaking and listening and the subsections of comprehension and collaboration, and presentation of knowledge and ideas. The CCSS aim to prepare students for college and careers. Twenty-first-century jobs require successful collaboration with diverse groups of individuals. To be ready for the world of work, students must learn how to be effective group members, carry their fair share of the load, cooperate with and support the success of diverse partners. Collaborative behaviors and cooperative attitudes can be learned though teaching and practice in appropriate group tasks.

Figure 11.3 Designing a challenge course

Role-Play Demonstrations

Another teaching strategy for helping students learn social behaviors and attitudes is role-play demonstrations. For example, teachers can use role-play to demonstrate how to design a challenge course for practicing jumping with a partner. Using a think-aloud technique, the teacher demonstrates how to listen carefully, resolve conflicts, and cooperate to design a course that both partners like.

Role-Playing the Design of a Challenge Course

Teacher (to aide or child demonstrator): Okay, we have to select six pieces of equipment. What do you want to use?

Aide: I want to use hoops and low hurdles.

Teacher: Me, too. I also want to use cones. Is that okay with you?

Aide: Yes. I will get two hoops and two low hurdles and meet you back here. You get the cones.

Teacher: What if we start with the low hurdles?

Aide: Okay.

Teacher: You decide what goes next.

Aide: Actually, now that I think about it, I'd rather start with the hoops and then the hurdles and then the cones because our challenge course will get harder at the end.

Teacher: I like that idea. I'll set up the first part of the course and you do the end.

One colleague of ours, Robin Litaker, is adept at using role-play to teach her children social skills. For example, she has the children, while working with the same partner, rotate through a large number of centers for two weeks. Inevitably, several children will be absent at times and their partners will need to work with different partners or in groups of three. When the original partner returns to school, Ms. Litaker knows that there will be the potential for hurt feelings. So she and an aide act out what children need to do in this situation and what could happen if they forget to be attentive to everyone's feelings.

Ms. Litaker (pretending to be a child while speaking her thoughts aloud): Oh, look, my original partner is back at school. I've been having a great time with my temporary partners, but Ms. Litaker's rule is to go back with my original partner. I need to say something to my temporary partners so their feelings won't be hurt. [Waves to original partner.] I'll be right there. [Walks over to an aide pretending to be the temporary partner, who looks very sad.] I've had such a great time playing with you, but the rule is I need to go back with my original partner. Thanks for being so helpful when my partner was home sick. I'll miss you. [Ms. Litaker looks sadly at the aide. The aide smiles brightly. Ms. Litaker walks to the original partner and smiles.] I'm so glad you're back at school and we can be partners again.

Ms. Litaker (to class): Would you prefer to be treated that way, or this way? [Ms. Litaker walks to the temporary partner but then sees the original partner. She frowns, sighs, and turns her back on the temporary partner and with a slouching posture walks over to the original partner.]

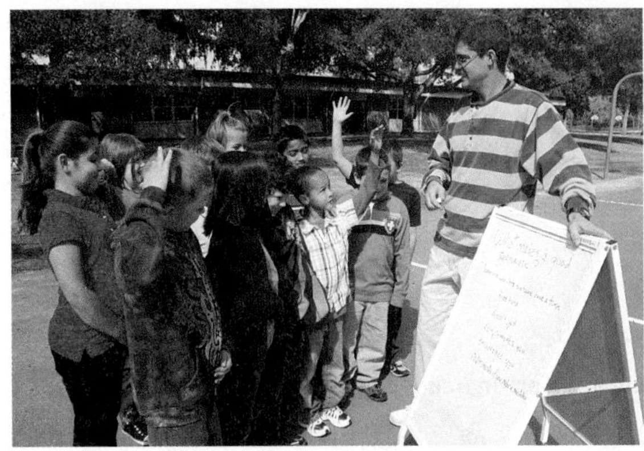

Figure 11.4 What makes a good teammate?

Ms. Litaker (to class): Put your hands up if you would prefer the first example. Tell me why that example was better. How do you think the original partner and the temporary partner felt in the second example?

Class Discussions and Self-Assessments

Holding class discussions is another important teaching technique for developing children's social and emotional skills. Typically, the teacher selects a discussion topic related directly to the lesson tasks. For example, you might ask the class to generate a list of characteristics of what makes a good partner versus a poor partner (see **Figure 11.4**). **Table 11.1** illustrates a list of such characteristics generated by a class of children.

Class discussions are also valuable at the end of a lesson to assess how the children met the social or emotional objective. You can ask the children to discuss what happened during the lesson and what they learned about the objective. Alternatively, you can hand out brief written self-assessment forms for children to complete. The self-assessment instrument might consist of a simple checklist of behaviors or a rating scale, for example. **Table 11.2** shows two different self-assessment tools.

Table 11.1 Children's Descriptions of Good and Poor Partners

What Makes a Good Partner?	What Makes a Poor Partner?
Does not fight; works together with the other partner	Goofs around
Cooperates	Pitches an attitude
Shares stuff	Argues
If you want to do different things, takes turns doing your ideas	Talks too long and wastes playing time
Plans together, and doesn't just use their ideas	Talks back
Listens	Doesn't do what the partners agreed to do

Table 11.2 Sample Self-Assessment Tools for Social Interactions

How helpful were you in your peer teaching today? Rate yourself on a scale of 0–5, where 5 is the absolute greatest and 0 is the weakest.					
I gave my peer tons of feedback.					I didn't say very much to my peer.
5	4	3	2	1	0
I complimented my peer.					Everything I said was negative.
5	4	3	2	1	0
I watched my peer closely.					I was distracted and didn't watch.

Rate yourself on being a group member by putting a check in the appropriate column.			
	Did This All of the Time	**Did This Sometimes**	**Did Not Do This**
Listened to everyone			
Contributed ideas			
Encouraged quiet peers to contribute			
Gave reasons for my opinions			
Checked to be sure everyone understood the rules			

Hellison's "Taking Personal and Social Responsibility" Approach

Hellison (2003) has spent more than 30 years working with underserved children and youth, teachers, and recreation specialists to help children become more personally and socially responsible. He developed the "Taking Personal and Social Responsibility" (TPSR) approach for this purpose and has tirelessly tested his ideas in schools and after-school programs in some of the United States' most underserved urban environments. He has been the physical education profession's strongest proponent for helping children and youth take more personal responsibility for their well-being and contributing to the well-being of others.

TPSR is what Hellison calls a "loose" teaching and learning progression. In other words, you do not need to teach the progression in a rigid order, but rather can adapt the ideas to your teaching situation and beliefs. In fact, throughout the text *Teaching Responsibility Through Physical Activity* (now in its second edition), he provides many examples of ways teachers have flexibly adapted his ideas.

Hellison (2003, p. 26) favors presenting his progression of levels of responsibility in the following three categories:

Beginning	Level I: Respect
	Level II: Participation
Advanced	Level III: Self-direction
	Level IV: Caring
Most Advanced	Level V: Outside the gym

- *Level I: Respect.* Hellison describes Level I goals as teaching children to have self-control and respect the rights of other children. This includes the right of other children to play in an emotionally safe environment without being subjected to abuse or bullying.
- *Level II: Participation.* Level II relates to personal responsibility and development. The goal is for children to participate with effort in class activities without the teacher having to prompt them. The children are self-motivated at least at a basic level of engagement.
- *Level III: Self-direction.* Level III extends children's level of participation to self-directed participation in which children can work independently of the teacher.
- *Level IV: Caring.* Level IV is related to social responsibility and includes caring about and being willing to help others, as well as making a positive contribution to the group.
- *Level V: Outside the gym.* Level V entails taking what children have learned in physical education and applying it to other life contexts, such as the classroom, home, playground, and after-school activities.

We recommend that anyone interested in using Hellison's approach to physical education purchase his highly readable book. It provides detailed descriptions of how his ideas work in practice.

Teaching Social and Emotional Behaviors and Attitudes

In this section, we describe teaching strategies for social and affective content related to National Standards 4 and 5. We begin with **Table 11.3**, which summarizes these strategies and organizes them into the three levels of games and gymnastics content and the two levels of dance content. Thus, when you plan lessons and units you can refer to this table to assist you in selecting social and affective goals that match the developmental level of the tasks of your lessons.

Table 11.3 Teaching Social and Emotional Behaviors and Attitudes

Game Content		
***Level 1*:** Developing fundamental game skills	***Level 2*:** Developing fundamental skills into tactical game skills	***Level 3*:** Learning to use tactical game skills in modified gameplay
Gymnastics Content		
***Level 1*:** Foundational skills	***Level 2*:** Combining skills, using movement concepts from the Laban framework to extend movement variety, partner work	***Level 3*:** Group work and more difficult themes
Dance Content		
***Level 1*:** Body, effort, space, relationships	***Level 2*:** More complex body, more complex effort, more complex space, more complex relationships	
Social and Emotional Goals: This entire chapter addresses National Standards 4 and 5. The chapter also addresses multiple standards within the speaking and listening section of the CCSS and meets the National Standard 4 sections on working with others and personal responsibility.		
Caring and Respect for Others		
A. Teach children to see the class as a community, to care about others' feelings, and to support others. *Sample Discussion* What can you do to make people feel included in this class community? Which comments and behaviors keep the class from being a community? *Sample Content to Teach* Listen to and look at their classmates, and then respond to their classmates' feelings by saying something nice or encouraging. **B.** Teach children to avoid put-downs, negative comments, and negative body language, and to make amends. *Sample Discussion* How do you know when you hurt someone's feelings? Which body language is hurtful? **C.** Teach children that they are responsible for telling you if someone is hurting them, hurting someone else, or damaging equipment. *Sample Content to Teach* • If someone is hurting you or someone else, it is important that you tell me. • If you see someone damaging equipment, you need to tell me.	**E.** Use peer tutoring: Teach children to help their partners learn in a supportive way. *Sample Discussion* How can you evaluate your partner without being mean or bossy? **F.** Teach children impulse control and ways to react when they get angry. *Sample Procedure* 1. Calm down (take deep breaths; talk to yourself). 2. Think aloud how to solve the issue. 3. Think about it later. (Why was I angry? Why did I do that?) **G.** Teach children to be a respectful audience. *Sample Rules* 1. Watch quietly. 2. Don't laugh. 3. Think of compliments. 4. Clap at the end.	**H.** Teach children to coach and compliment opponents and other groups. *Sample Content to Teach* • Give your opponents a thumbs-up when they make a nice play. • Tell the group what you liked about their dance. **I.** Teach children criteria for caring and respect within the tasks of the lesson. *Sample Criteria* In passing and catching tasks, be sure you send passes that are catchable. In designing gymnastics sequences, be sure you select only those movements both of you can do safely and confidently.

(*continues*)

Table 11.3 Teaching Social and Emotional Behaviors and Attitudes (*continued*)

Caring and Respect for Others		
D. Teach children to treat others the way they want to be treated. *Sample Content to Teach* • Be willing to work and cooperate with anyone in the class. • Don't exclude others; be inclusive and nice to everyone.		
Collaboration		
A. Teach children to listen to the teacher and respond appropriately. *Sample Content to Teach* Listen to the teacher's directions, and do what the teacher said. Listen and respond positively to the teacher's cues and feedback. **B.** Teach children to ask and answer questions about the teacher's instructions. *Sample Task* Turn to your assigned partner. One of you asks the other a question about the cue I just taught you about throwing overhand. The other person answers the question. **C.** Teach children to speak audibly and explain their ideas clearly. *Sample Question* Which ball did you like the best for catching: the large foam, small foam, string, or yarn ball? Then explain why you liked it best.	**D.** Teach children how to listen carefully to a partner's ideas, care about a partner's opinions and feelings, and share a decision. *Sample Content to Teach* • Listen attentively. • Ask for your partner's opinion. • Find ways to incorporate your partner's ideas. **E.** Teach children it is important for both partners to contribute ideas and work on the project. *Sample Content to Teach* The discussion must be an exchange of ideas with each of you discussing your ideas and the ideas of your partner.	**F.** Teach children how to be good group members and use cooperative group processes so their group work is caring. *Sample Discussion* • What can you do when one person in your group won't talk? • Which actions or attitudes can stop a group from coming up with lots of ideas? • How can you get every student to contribute ideas? **G.** Teach children to improve the quality of their discussions. *Sample Content to Teach* • Build on what other children say; elaborate on their ideas. • Connect your ideas to other children's ideas. **H.** Teach children to persist when the going gets tough. **I.** Teach children about individual differences in ways people share ideas and how to respond appropriately. *Sample Content to Teach* Some people will think of and publicly share lots of ideas; if you criticize an idea, they will tell you another one. Other people think of lots of ideas privately but will share only ideas they really like. These people will care very much if their idea is criticized.

Personal and Social Responsibility

A. Teach children that being fair and responsible means not infringing on classmates' time, personal space, or opportunities to learn.

Sample Discussion

- What should you remember when you share a center with a partner?
- If you lost your ball, how can you get it without disrupting your partner?

B. Teach children how to practice skills and use equipment safely.

Sample Question

When you dribble fast, what do you need to do to be able to stop safely without falling down?

C. Teach children how to carry, set up, and put equipment and apparatus away safely.

Sample Rules

- Always use two children to carry a mat; the mat must be carried (not dragged on the floor) at about waist height (not over your head).
- Balls need to be placed (not thrown) in the ball container.

D. Teach children to take responsibility for their actions.

Sample Content to Teach

Avoid blaming others and using "they made me" or "they told me to" statements.

E. Teach children to take turns fairly.

Sample Content to Teach

- Turns need to be equal in number or length of time.
- Don't hog the ball.

F. Teach children to challenge themselves safely without disrupting others.

Sample Task

Dribble as fast as you can *without* losing control.

G. Teach children to take responsibility for their school's property after school.

Sample Content to Teach

- After school, don't hang on the basketball hoops. If big kids do, remind them that this is our community and our school.
- After school, don't smash bottles on the playground.

H. Teach children what contributes to being a good teammate and a good opponent.

Sample Discussion

What makes a poor teammate?

- Someone who always wants it their way.
- Someone who only wants the best players on their team.
- Someone who always wants the ball.

I. Help children learn how to interpret other children's actions more accurately and then resolve the problem when they think someone "cheated," played unfairly, or intentionally broke a rule.

Sample Content to Teach

Don't take it for granted that everyone knows the rules. If you don't make it a rule, then it isn't a rule. Make sure everyone hears and understands every rule you design.

J. Teach children to self-referee.

Sample Content to Teach

- Admit and call a violation on yourself.
- Don't use negative body language to intimidate a child who calls a foul.
- Don't pretend you are fouled.

K. Teach conflict resolution strategies.

Sample Strategy

1. Stop, calm down, and think before you speak.
2. State the problem and describe how you feel.
3. Try to look at the problem from the other person's perspective.
4. Set a positive goal.
5. Try to think of many possible solutions.
6. Decide on a solution and try it out.

L. Teach children to critique the etiquette and ethics they see in different sport settings.

M. Identify and critique media images.

Valuing Affective Aspects

Sample Objectives

Appreciate the emotional and kinesthetic feeling within your body.

Recognize the feeling of excitement when doing movements such as leaping, running fast, chasing, jumping high, and swinging on gymnastics apparatus.

Enjoy challenging yourself.

Appreciate the joy of effort.

Value the satisfaction of knowing you tried your hardest.

Sample Objectives

Value the feeling of total involvement in a game-like task or dance or gymnastics performance.

Value the feeling of skillfulness, power, control, and/or precision while performing skills.

Enjoy working with your partner to express your ideas about the topic you selected for your dance.

Sample Objectives

Feel the joy in playing the game all out and challenging yourself to do your very best.

Appreciate the uplifting feeling of teamwork in a game or in a well-executed dance or gymnastics group performance.

Appreciate the excitement of playing in a game between equal opponents.

Value the feeling of satisfaction for persisting to the end of a physically demanding lesson.

Caring and Respect for Others

A. Teach Children to Recognize That the Class Is a Community, to Care About Others' Feelings, and to Support Others

Repeatedly explain to children that the class is a community, and explain that being part of a community means we care about one another and help one another. When a group is a community, its members are kind to everyone and make everyone feel included and important. "Everyone" in this context means everyone, regardless of race, ethnicity, gender, ability, disability, body shape, sexual orientation, or economic status.

In addition, teach children how important it is to care about their classmates and to support them (see **Figure 11.5** and **Figure 11.6**). Teaching children to care contributes to developing empathy—a critical part of social development. Learning to support other children helps children grow from being egocentric to caring about the feelings of others.

Sample Discussion

- Which comments and behaviors make you feel good about being in the class community?
- Which comments and behaviors keep the class from being a community?
- What can you do to make people feel included in this class community?

Sample Content to Teach

- Listen to and look at classmates, and then respond to your classmates' feelings by saying something supportive or encouraging.
- Do a favor for someone, such as helping another child set up a boundary or retrieve a ball.
- When your classmates do a good job or show they care about others, compliment them.

Figure 11.5 Supporting a classmate

Figure 11.6 Caring about others

B. Teach Children to Avoid Put-Downs, Negative Comments, and Negative Body Language and to Make Amends

Children need to learn to realize when they've hurt someone's feelings and to make amends. This teaching point includes discussing comments and behaviors that can be hurtful (such as laughing at someone when he or she makes a mistake or turning your back on someone who wants to play with you), as well as put-downs such as "You're a loser," and "You're no good."

You can teach children to ask their partners if they've hurt their feelings; to say, "I'm sorry," when they've been hurtful; to not laugh at others; and to encourage their partners. When doing so, you have to guard against the "fake sorry," when children say they're sorry simply to get out of trouble. Watch the children involved to see if the apology stops the inappropriate behavior. If it doesn't, you need to take further action (e.g., calling parents, timeout).

You also will need to teach children that negative body language is hurtful and, therefore, unacceptable. To address this issue, you might start with a class discussion identifying negative body language, such as turning your back on someone to let that person know you don't want to be with her or him, pouting, rolling your eyes, making faces, dramatic sighs, and stomping when the partner misses the catch. One effective approach is for the teacher to demonstrate negative body language through role-play, and then to lead a group discussion about how children would feel if someone did that to them.

One simple way to reduce negative body language and exclusionary behaviors, while at the same time teaching children they must learn to work with diverse partners, is for the teacher to *always* assign partners and groups. Both authors agree strongly with Dr. Dolly Lambdin's comments in the nearby "Experienced Teachers Talk" box. If teachers never have children select their own partners, they won't jockey to be near their friends when the teacher is presenting a task,

Experienced Teachers Talk

Selecting Partners

Over the years, I have developed a strong opinion about the consequences of allowing students to choose partners or members of a team. Although students do often report that they like choosing their own partners, it has been my observation that this rarely works without producing some intensely negative fallout. Almost invariably, at least one or two children are left out or are confronted by obvious rejection—no matter how momentary it is or how it is resolved. Because our teaching action sets that rejection up to happen, we are responsible, which is absolutely unacceptable.

No matter how enjoyable and natural children may find the process of choosing their own partners, a process that does harm to any child disqualifies the process as a management tactic. Forcing children to confront rejection, just as with forcing them to engage in a public activity in which they only experience failure, is not justified by the argument that most kids enjoy what is happening.

Source: Dolly Lambdin, in Locke, L. F., & Lambdin, D. (2003). *Putting research to work in elementary physical education: Conversations in the gym* (p. 81). Champaign, IL: Human Kinetics.

negative body language against children unwanted as partners will decrease, and they will learn to work with diverse partners. When children never have the opportunity to choose a partner, they will not expect to have the choice. When the first author taught seven days in the second author's school, in which the teachers always assign partners and groups, she never once saw a child take part in any form of negative body language when assigned a partner in a group—*not once in seven days*. The children simply went to work on the assigned task.

Sample Discussion

- How do you know when you hurt someone's feelings?
- What things hurt your feelings or someone else's feelings?
- When you work with a partner, what kinds of comments can be hurtful?
- Which body language is hurtful?

Sample Content to Teach

- If you hurt someone's feelings, say you're sorry and stop doing whatever you were doing.

Sample Objective

- The children will understand that negative body language, such as sighing, rolling their eyes, and stomping when their partner misses the catch, is hurtful.

C. Teach Children that They Are Responsible for Telling You if Someone Is Hurting Them (Physically or Emotionally), Hurting Someone Else (Physically or Emotionally), or Damaging Equipment

Teaching children to make amends when they hurt someone's feelings is a good place to start on developing the social skill and disposition to right wrongs. Learning to take action to right wrongs is critical in helping children refrain from being bystanders when they witness hurtful behaviors, such as harassment and bullying. Learning to right wrongs is a long-term goal that crosses the K–12 curriculum, but you must begin teaching this at the elementary level.

For children to learn how to right wrongs, you can start by teaching them to tell you (or another adult) when they see hurtful or potentially unsafe behavior. An experienced teacher put it this way:

> You need to teach children that they are responsible for telling you if someone is being hurt. Over the years, I have learned to say it simply in kid terms and give them plenty of examples in multiple contexts. I tell them to tell me if someone is
> - Hurting you [physically or emotionally]
> - Hurting someone else [physically or emotionally]
> - Tearing something up [damaging equipment]

The child does not need to make a public statement. Children can speak to you privately or they can give you a note saying, "See me," which you have discussed in advance is a code for a child witnessing hurtful behavior. Children need to understand there is a difference between tattling and reporting. Children are not tattling when they report someone being hurt; they are being socially responsible.

Sample Discussion

- Why do you think it's important to tell an adult when you see hurtful or unsafe behavior?

Sample Content to Teach

- If someone is hurting you or someone else, it is important that you tell me.
- If you see someone damaging equipment, you need to tell me.
- If you see someone doing something that isn't safe, tell me as soon as possible.
- If you see someone doing something hurtful, say something like "That wasn't nice," "That was mean," or "Let's try to be nice."
- If you see someone feeling excluded, do something to help include that person.

D. Teach Children to Treat Others the Way They Want to Be Treated

Teaching children the criteria for treating others the way they want to be treated is a topic many teachers discuss. It gives children a universal moral principle on which they can base their understanding of appropriate social behavior. You can apply this principle to a wide range of situations. Thus, you can refer back to it frequently, helping children understand its broader meaning and applications. For example, you can connect each of the following specific attitudes and behaviors to the criteria for treating others the way they want to be treated.

Sample Content to Teach

- Be willing to work and cooperate with anyone in the class.
- Don't exclude others; be inclusive and nice to everyone.
- Listen to what your peers are saying.

- Be kind to others; think of others first.
- Treat everyone fairly, regardless of whether they are highly skilled or less skilled, boy or girl, fat or thin.
- Keep your hands and feet to yourself.
- Don't hit anyone, even if you are REALLY mad.

Sample Discussion

- Let's make a list of how you want to be treated when you share a center with a partner.

Related to these ideas, but more specific, is the importance of teaching children that they must treat everyone with respect, even peers they don't like.

Sample Discussion

- When you're an adult at work, what do you think will happen if you don't treat your coworkers with respect?
- Describe a time when you were excluded, and how you felt as a result. I am going to list everyone's experiences on this side of this poster board. Now describe a time you were included, and describe how you felt. I'm going to list these experiences on the other side of the poster board. Read both lists and see if you can identify critical places and times when children feel excluded and included.

E. Use Peer Tutoring: Teach Children to Help Their Partners Learn in a Supportive Way

Research shows peer tutoring is effective in helping students learn (Ward & Lee, 2005). You can teach children how to observe carefully and evaluate the movements or body positions of a classmate's skill using simple peer assessment tools. Research has found that when teachers provide an assessment tool that describes specifically what movements or body positions the peer tutor should look for and assess in their partners, students learn more than students not using the assessment tool (Iserbyt, Elen, & Behets, 2010; Vande Broek, Boen, Claessens, Feys, & Ceux, 2011).

In addition, you need to teach children how to give their peer feedback in a positive, supportive way and to encourage their partner's efforts and persistence. Research on third- through fifth-grade students' descriptions of the social skills of partners who were good collaborators found that good partners provided valued support (Ladd, Kochenderfer-Ladd, Visconti, Ettekal, Sechler, & Cortes, 2014). For example, students valued partners who

- Made encouraging comments, like "Nice job," or "Good try."
- Responded to their partners' feelings, such as being positive when the partner felt bad or angry.

Sample Content to Teach

- Pay attention to your partner's feelings, and respond by being positive and supportive.
- Compliment your partner's effort.
- Compliment your partner after they successfully perform the skill technique.

Sample Discussion

- What were different ways you helped your partner at the centers today?
- How can you evaluate your partner or group sequence without being mean or bossy?
- How can you tell your partner how to improve in a caring, respectful way?

F. Teach Children Impulse Control and Ways to React When They Get Angry

One cause of problems when children treat others with a lack of respect and caring is a lack of impulse control. Developing impulse control is critical for children's emotional development. Children without impulse control have problems making friends and maintaining positive social relationships.

You can teach strategies to help children manage their emotions when problems occur (see **Figure 11.7**). The following approach was described on a poster in an article by Phillips (1997, p. 43):

What to Do When You Are Angry

1. Calm down:
   - Take three breaths.
   - Count backward slowly.
   - Think calming thoughts.
   - Talk to yourself.
2. Think out loud to solve the issue.
3. Think about the incident later:
   - Why was I angry?
   - Why did I do that?
   - What worked? What didn't work?

G. Teach Children to Be a Respectful Audience

Performing in front of an audience happens in dance and gymnastics lessons, when children show their sequences, and in games, when they are demonstrating the obstacle challenge course or game they designed. Audience behavior is an important topic, although the discussion here is abbreviated. In brief, you can have a class discussion about respectful and disrespectful behavior. Respectful behavior includes watching quietly, not laughing, sitting still, thinking of compliments for performers, and clapping at the end of the sequence.

Sample Rules

1. Watch quietly.
2. Don't laugh.

Figure 11.7 Taking time to calm down

3. Think of compliments.
4. Clap at the end.

H. Teach Children to Coach and Compliment Opponents and Other Groups

Similar to peer tutoring, when children are working in small groups, have them provide peer coaching and positive support. Emphasize they need to be supportive of both more highly and less skilled classmates. For example, when children are designing dance and gymnastics sequences, you can have two groups show each other their sequences, give each other feedback, assess each other's sequences using a checklist or rubric, and offer compliments (see **Figure 11.8**). In game lessons, you can stop the class and have the opponents teach each other how to improve their tactics.

Sample Content to Teach

- Give your opponents a thumbs-up when they make a nice play.
- Tell the group what you liked about their dance.
- Compliment your opponents on a good game.
- Shake hands at the end of a game.

I. Teach Children Criteria for Caring and Respect Within the Tasks of the Lesson

You need to think about lesson tasks and explicitly explain the criteria for judging whether children are appropriately caring for their partner's well-being. This means teaching children to modify tasks to ensure challenge and success for both partners. To teach this message, teachers can describe a scenario in which one partner sets up a task that is too difficult for the other partner and ask the children, "How will your partner feel? Are you caring about your partner's learning?"

In competitive games, being caring and respectful also means not being overly aggressive (e.g., fouling) and not taunting or constantly reminding your opponent that you have scored more points. You can be a caring opponent, yet still be competitive and play with as much effort as you can to score points. Being a caring, respectful opponent means being kind and gracious when you win or score, complimenting your opponent when he or she does well, and helping your opponent improve his or her game skills and tactics.

Showing you care about your classmates also includes tasks in which one child "sets up" the ball for the other's practice in an appropriate way, such as tossing a ball so your partner can practice catching or tossing a tennis ball so your partner can practice striking with a racket.

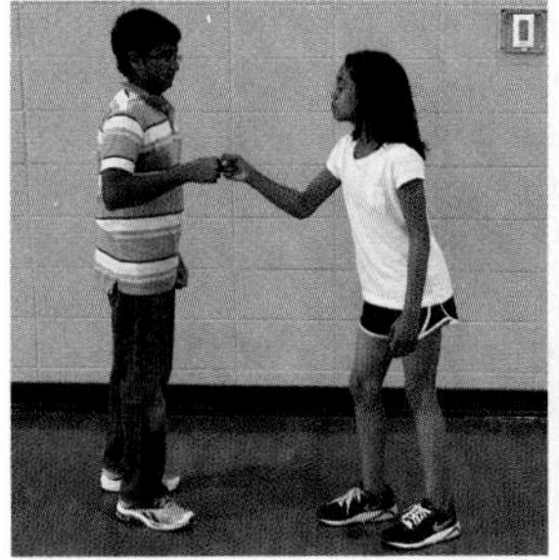

Figure 11.8 "You did great!"

Courtesy of John Dolly

Sample Criteria

Task: Partners practicing skills such as passing and catching or striking a ball back and forth

- *Criteria:* Be sure the force and speed of the ball are at a level that is developmentally appropriate for your partner. For example, passes must be catchable. Balls must be hit at a speed and to a location your partner can successful hit back.

Task: Challenge course or dance or gymnastics sequence

- *Criteria:* Select only those movements that both partners can do safely and confidently. A good movement is also one you both feel comfortable performing—it is not a good movement if it feels embarrassing or silly to one of you, even if it is a creative movement.

Sample Task

We thank Dr. Tim Hopper for this idea:

- When children are skilled enough to rally in a striking game, inform them that the task for the lesson will be to design boundaries and rules for each person so that no matter who you play, the game is even. Possible modifications

The Noodle Experiment

We learned about the noodle experiment at a "Yes, I Can!" volleyball clinic sponsored by Stan Kellner. In this activity, the entire class forms a circle around a garbage can. Ask everyone who they think is the best athlete in the class. (This part is important because it eliminates anyone giving the excuse that the outcome wouldn't happen if a better athlete performed the task.) That child comes forward and picks up a swimming pool noodle cut in half. Tell the child that he or she has 10 seconds to whack the garbage can as hard and fast and as many times as possible. The children on the outside circle have to remain perfectly quiet and count the number of whacks in their heads.

Then ask the selected child if he or she tried as hard as he or she could. The children who are first up typically say yes. (If not, send that child back to the circle and pick someone else, again with everyone on the outside circle remaining quiet.)

Then have the child repeat the 10-second whacking of the garbage can. This time, however, everyone on the outside circle should cheer the child on, saying things like, "Faster! Harder! You can do it—you're the best!" The scores always improve in this situation.

Then ask the students, "What did you learn from this experiment?" They typically reply, "Cheering someone on makes him or her better," "You want to try harder when someone is cheering for you," or "You may think you're doing your best, but you can be better with support from teammates."

Finally, pose the following question to the students: "We will be playing a game that will be hard for some of your teammates. How will you use what you learned today in that game?"

include smaller boundaries on the side of the less skilled player, so the more skilled player has to be very accurate, and different rules, such as letting the less skilled player hit after the ball bounces twice. Set children up with partners of differing abilities and have them figure out which rules and boundaries to use for each of them to have a good game with balanced scoring. Once they succeed and have played for a while, rotate partners and repeat the process.

Sample Discussion

- Why it is important to be willing to accommodate your partner's ability level without the teacher telling you to do so?
- What can you do if you and your partner (or individuals in your group) have very different ability levels?

Sample Objective

- Children will try to give a catchable toss to help their partners learn to catch, rather than pouting and hurrying their partners.

Collaboration

A. Teach Children to Listen to the Teacher and Respond Appropriately

Teaching children how to collaborate in groups and meet the CCSS standards for speaking and listening and National Standard 4 begins with learning to listen to the teacher's directions, do what the teacher said, listen to feedback on how to perform a skill, and try to perform as instructed.

Sample Questions

- Which two locomotor skills did I tell you to use as you travel about the space?
- What performance techniques are you supposed to use when you catch your beanbag?
- Turn to your assigned partner. One of you repeats what performance techniques I just told you to focus on when tossing the beanbag to your partner. Then the other person repeats what I said about catching the beanbag.

B. Teach Children to Ask and Answer Questions About the Teacher's Instructions

You also need to teach children to ask questions when they don't understand instructions or to clarify the information presented by the teacher or a classmate. They need to learn to listen carefully so they can answer questions about the information the teacher discussed.

Sample Questions

- Does anyone have a question about dribbling?
- It's important to ask questions if you're confused. Turn to your assigned partner. One of you asks the other a question about the cue I just taught you about throwing overhand. The other person answers the question.

C. Teach Children to Speak Audibly and Explain Their Ideas Clearly

To meet CCSS, children need to learn how to present information in ways their classmates can hear and understand. You can begin teaching this skill by asking for the children's opinions of task options in the lesson, such as which locomotor skill they found most exciting, which balance they found most challenging, or which ball they liked best.

Sample Question

- Which ball did you like the best for catching: the large foam, small foam, string, or yarn ball? Why did you like that one best?

D. Teach Children How to Listen Carefully to a Partner's Ideas, Care About a Partner's Opinions and Feelings, and Share a Decision

When children are ready for partner work, you need to teach them to listen to peers in the same way they listen to a teacher, to care about and respond to peers' opinions and feelings, and to share decisions with a partner.

Sample Content to Teach

- Listen attentively, smile, and make eye contact when your partner is talking.
- Ask for your partner's opinion.
- Find ways to incorporate your partner's suggestions.
- Think of something nice to say that tells your partner you value her or his ideas.
- Share the decision making.
- Pay attention to your partner's feelings, and respond with positive support.

Sample Tasks

- Sharing in the decisions, build two targets from the equipment in your basket for practicing throwing with accuracy. Decide together on two different distances to throw from, and use a jump rope to make a throwing line. Select two different-sized balls to use.

Sample Discussion

- What can you do when your partner gets upset at missing the target?
- How can you cheer up your partner when he or she feels sad?

E. Teach Children It Is Important for Both Partners to Contribute Ideas and Work on the Project

When children first begin partner work, it is common for them to work independently without discussing their ideas. It is also common for one person to do all of the work with the other not wanting to work, or wanting to contribute but not knowing how to engage in a collaborative discussion. You need to teach children they must discuss their ideas with each other and work together to complete the project. Recent research on children's perspectives on partner and group work found that children value a partner who does a fair share of the work and is conscientious (Ladd et al., 2014).

Sample Content to Teach

- Both partners must contribute ideas during the discussion.
- The discussion must be an exchange of ideas with each of you discussing your ideas and the ideas of your partner.
- Both of you must do your fair share of the work.
- The final product must include contributions from both of you.

F. Teach Children How to Be Good Group Members and Use Cooperative Group Processes so Their Group Work Demonstrates Caring

Once children begin group work, they need to learn social interaction skills that make group work collaborative. Teach children the qualities of a good group member and cooperative group processes, such as giving everyone a chance to talk, asking for others' opinions, and giving reasons for ideas. Slavin (2014) suggests children learn to be "active listeners," who look at the speaker, nod, summarize what the speaker said, and refrain from interrupting. The following is a set of procedures modified from Cohen (1994) for teaching cooperative group processes. You can explain and discuss these procedures with the class and post them on the wall for reference.

Group Process to Teach When You Disagree About the Rules of a Child-Designed Game

1. Everyone talks; everyone listens. (Each person gives his or her opinion, and everyone must listen.)
2. Everyone gives a reason for his or her opinion.
3. Discuss the consequences for each suggestion.
4. Agree to try one solution for a short period of time and then evaluate whether it works.
5. If everyone isn't happy with the rule, try a different solution for a short period of time.

Group Process to Teach for Designing a Dance or Gymnastics Sequence

1. Everyone talks; everyone listens.
2. Eliminate all critique during the brainstorming phase.
3. Try to build on classmates' ideas.
4. When making decisions about what to include, give reasons for your opinions.
5. The finished sequence must include at least one idea from each group member.

Sample Discussion

- What can you do when one person in your group won't talk?
- What makes a good group member?
- What makes a poor group member?
- Which kinds of actions ruin games?
- Which actions or attitudes can stop a group from coming up with lots of ideas?
- Which actions or attitudes can stop a group from making decisions?
- What steps can you take when you disagree?

Sample Rules for Group Work

- Listen to all ideas.
- Be responsible when the teacher is not looking.
- Never be satisfied. Always look for ways to improve.
- Let everyone contribute and give ideas.
- Don't be afraid to experiment.

G. Teach Children to Improve the Quality of Their Discussions

The following behaviors are based on the standards for speaking and listening from the CCSS. All are linked to developing better-quality discussions.

Sample Content to Teach

- Gain the floor respectfully.
- Talk one at a time.
- Listen carefully to understand what your peer is saying.
- Build on what other children say; elaborate on their ideas.
- Connect their ideas to other children's ideas.
- Provide and ask for additional explanations, details, or examples.
- Give reasons, evidence, and logical arguments for their own suggestions for designing games, dances, or gymnastics sequences.
- Provide examples from the group's experiences working on the game or sequence to enhance their own suggestions.

H. Teach Children to Persist When the Going Gets Tough

Research showed that children value group members who persist in contributing to the group assignment even when it gets hard (Ladd et al., 2014). Children need to be taught to persist when the going gets tough and remain focused on the task until it's complete.

Sample Feedback

- I know this is a challenging project, so you need to keep focusing on the task.

Sample Discussion

- What can you say to encourage a classmate to keep working hard when the task is difficult and your classmate is frustrated?
- What can you say or do to help your group focus on completing the task?

I. Teach Children About Individual Differences in Ways People Share Ideas and How to Respond Appropriately

It is also important to help children understand that people generate and communicate their ideas in different ways in group discussions. Some people think aloud and generate lots and lots of ideas publicly. If you don't like one of their ideas, they won't care; they'll simply give you another idea, and then another, for as long as it takes to come up with ideas their partner or the entire group likes.

Other people generate a lot of ideas privately and will tell you only ideas that they have critiqued and really like. These people will care very much if a partner or group member criticizes their ideas.

Neither approach is right or wrong—they are simply different ways in which people come up with and share ideas. Children need to be sensitive to whether other group members prefer to generate ideas publicly or privately.

Personal and Social Responsibility

A. Teach Children that Being Fair and Responsible Means Not Infringing on Classmates' Time, Personal Space, or Opportunities to Learn

Teaching young children about social responsibility begins with discussing fairness to others and their basic responsibility to not infringe on classmates' time, personal space, or opportunities to learn. This content links misbehaviors to the broader moral principle of fairness to others. For example, teach children how to travel about the physical education space without bumping into one another because bumping into other children infringes on their classmates' personal space. Teach children to identify actions that are unfair to others because these actions infringe on their classmates' opportunities to learn—for example, taking others' equipment, kicking others' balls, not returning equipment nicely, and talking to a partner when he or she is working. It also means teaching them that if they don't follow the class rules or the teacher's directions or are slow to settle down or put away equipment, they will be disrupting the class and infringing on everyone's time and opportunities to learn. Teach children not to infringe on a partner's opportunity to learn by teaching them how to share a center by sharing space and equipment equally.

Sample Discussion

- What should you remember when you share a center with a partner?
- Is it fair to take or kick your partner's ball? Why not?
- If you lose your ball, how can you get it back without disrupting your partner?

Sample Objective

- At the end of the lesson, children will know that being fair to their partner at centers means sharing space equally and not bumping into their partner.

Sample Class Rules

- Stray balls: Don't chase a ball by going into another group's space. Stop playing when a stray ball comes into your space.
- If it is not your equipment, do not touch it, unless you are going to pick it up and hand it directly to the owner.

B. Teach Children How to Practice Skills and Use Equipment Safely

Part of both personal and social responsibility within National Standard 4 is maintaining a safe environment for yourself and classmates. This means learning how fast you can travel without risking losing control and bumping into another child. It also means learning how to handle equipment safely, such as not hitting, kicking, or throwing a ball too hard or too close to classmates, being aware of the increase in the size of your personal space when you swing a racket or hit a ball with a bat, and ensuring that you have plenty of space between you and your nearest classmate. In addition, it means anticipating where a ball will travel in the air and land and making sure this pathway is clear of and safe for other children. Finally, it means recognizing skills and actions that are potentially unsafe for your developmental level, in particular, in gymnastics.

Sample Questions

- When you dribble fast, what do you need to do to be able to stop safely without falling down?
- When you throw the ball against the wall, what do you need to look for before you throw?

Sample Content to Teach

- Some of your classmates take gymnastics lessons after school. You will see them performing skills that are safe for them, but are not safe for someone who has not had the same experience and training. Ask me before you try a new skill or movement that you think might be unsafe for you.

C. Teach Children How to Carry, Set Up, and Put Equipment and Apparatus Away Safely

To meet Standard 4, children need to learn how to set up and put away equipment and apparatus sections safely and responsibly. Gymnastics apparatus, in particular, require children to work with a partner or group to get an apparatus out of storage, carry it to the needed location, and set it up safely. This is a major challenge for teachers because we need apparatus sections to be set up and taken down quickly to avoid losing precious lesson time. These time constraints mean children must all work at the same time and in the same space. Children typically enjoy carrying and setting up gymnastics mats and apparatus and, if given a choice, will race about the gym holding a mat over their heads and throwing it onto the stack of mats. You need to teach routines for setting up and putting away equipment and apparatus sections and set rules for doing so safely.

Sample Rules

- Always use two children to carry a mat. The mat must be carried (not dragged on the floor) at about waist height (not over your head).
- Balls need to be placed (not thrown) in the ball container.
- Walk when you are putting away the equipment, and wait patiently in line to stack the mat or enter the equipment room.

D. Teach Children to Take Responsibility for Their Actions

Taking responsibility for their actions means children need to learn about and anticipate the consequences of their behavior. For example, they need to learn it is their responsibility to be prepared for class so they don't miss opportunities to learn or disrupt the work of their group by not participating. They also need to learn to accept responsibility for their misbehaviors,

What the Research Says

Norms of Good Discussions

Classroom research on what contributes to good class discussions revealed that the following norms were important (Hadjioannou, 2007):

- Students' "opinions and ideas were welcomed and valued" (p. 392).
- Students listened "*attentively and respectfully* to the contributions of other members…participants invariably built on each other's ideas" (p. 392).
- Students "were *expected to express their opinions and ideas* about the issues at hand" (p. 392).
- Students' experiences and lives outside of school were legitimate topics and contributions.
- Students "acknowledged other participants, complimented their knowledge and their contributions, or assisted them in making their contributions more complete and effective" (p. 393).
- Students had "*the right to produce humorous comments* that were relevant to the conversation at hand and did not violate the rights of other members" (p. 393).

SAFETY AND LIABILITY 11.1

Increasing Safety and Decreasing Risk of Liability: Guidelines Relevant to Content in this Chapter

We discuss two broad guidelines for teaching children about safety and, more significantly, how to be personally and socially responsible for their own and their classmates' safety. See the following sections: ***B. Teach Children How to Practice Skills and Use Equipment Safely and C. Teach Children How to Carry, Set Up, and Put Equipment and Apparatus Away Safely***. Safety is part of National Standard 4, and thus a reasonably prudent teacher will ensure this standard is addressed thoroughly. Although to decrease risk of liability, you need to discuss safety information explicitly, you can initially have children generate this information themselves by thinking critically about potential safety problems within the skill practice task for themselves and their partners. Then discuss their ideas as a class. The goal is for students to become independent thinkers about safety and to become able to discern potential dangers in situations they encounter within and outside of school.

which means telling the truth and not blaming others for their predicament.

Sample Content to Teach

- Avoid blaming others and using "they made me" or "they told me to" statements.
- Always tell the truth.
- Be prepared for class by
  - Wearing sneakers
  - Wearing shorts under a dress
  - Bringing a note from your parents if you can't participate
  - Leaving jewelry at home
  - Going to the bathroom before PE

E. Teach Children to Take Turns Fairly

For most children, fairness is critical—whether that means having their fair share of cake for dessert or their fair share of time spent playing a game. Children sense whether their teachers, parents, and friends are treating them fairly. Learning about fairness is an early step in learning about social justice, thus allowing you to link behaviors to broader moral principles.

Although physical education teachers try to ensure that every child has equipment, sometimes children need to share. This process will go more smoothly if you spend time teaching young children about the importance of taking turns fairly and then have them practice taking turns (see **Figure 11.9**). You can deliver this lesson with whole-class teaching or in centers. Try to acknowledge children's likely affective responses directly by acknowledging that it's sometimes difficult to wait for your turn while your partner works with the equipment.

Figure 11.9 "You can go first."

Sample Content to Teach

- Would it be fair if your teacher let only the good readers have the books, or allowed only those students who are good at math to do math problems? The same is true in PE: Everyone needs a chance to play every position in the game.
- Turns need to be equal in number or time.
- You need to share equipment equally.
- Children feel bad when they don't get fair opportunities.
- Don't hog the ball.
- Listen to and carefully watch classmates, and intentionally pass the ball to someone who has not had fair chances to play.

F. Teach Children to Challenge Themselves Safely Without Disrupting Others

Teach children how beneficial—and fun—it is to challenge themselves and to try difficult tasks. Engaging in this kind of self-motivation is part of developing autonomy. Encouraging students to "do something hard," rather than "taking it easy," helps them understand both a work ethic and the satisfaction that comes from accomplishing a challenging task.

At the same time, children must respect the rights of others and not disrupt other children's practice. When children challenge themselves with game skills, they will be more likely to lose control of the ball. You need to help children understand the difference between losing control of the ball because you were trying hard and challenging yourself and losing control because you were off task or fooling around.

We find that children readily understand the difference between the two concepts. They can differentiate between making a "mistake" in the course of trying to learn and improve and simply misbehaving; they know when they cross the line.

Sample Task

- Dribble as fast as you can *without* losing control.

G. Teach Children to Take Responsibility for Their School's Property After School

Encourage children to have a sense of responsibility beyond themselves and their immediate class environment by teaching children to view their school as part of their community for which they are responsible.

Sample Content to Teach

- This is our school; respect its equipment and property.
- After school, don't smash bottles on the playground.
- After school, don't hang on the basketball hoops. If big kids do, remind them that this is our community and our school.
- No spitting.

H. Teach Children What Contributes to Being a Good Teammate and a Good Opponent

Building on what you've taught about working with partners, you need to teach children what attitudes and behaviors contribute to being a good teammate and opponent. This lesson is especially important in the competitive environment of games. Once you start teaching level 3 game content, the behaviors and attitudes of professional, collegiate, and high school athletes influence the kinds of behaviors and attitudes elementary school children think are appropriate in any game setting. You need to teach children specifically which behaviors by teammates and opponents are responsible, fair, and respectful—and which are not.

Sample Discussion (The answers below are direct quotes from a class of children.)

Teacher: As I look around at the games, I see some teams have a great game going and some are always stopping play and arguing. If you were on a team that seemed to keep the game going, can you tell us how you did that?
Children: We used teamwork.
Teacher: What do you mean by teamwork?
Children:

- We said no arguing about balls being hit out of bounds. If it was not clear who hit it, we would ask each other. If we could not tell, we dropped the ball between two opponents.
- When someone called a foul, we just did the consequence (like a free shot) without arguing.
- We made sure everyone had a chance.

Teacher: What makes a poor teammate or opponent?
Children:

- They brag when they win. We were *there*; we know—they don't have to rub it in.
- Someone who always wants it their way.
- Someone who only wants the best players on their team.
- Someone who always wants the ball, even if they're on your team or it's going right toward you and not them.
- Someone who wants to win no matter what and won't let everyone have the chance to play the fun and important positions, such as quarterback.
- Someone who just wants to pass the ball to their friends or to the "best players" or only to boys.
- Someone who takes the easy road and doesn't try or work hard.

Teacher: What makes a good teammate?
Children:

- Someone who lets everyone have a turn at the fun or important jobs.
- Someone who tries hard.
- Someone who doesn't yell if you don't succeed and doesn't make snide comments about your performance.
- Someone who encourages everyone to work hard.
- Someone who compliments you when you make a good play and understands when you make a mistake.

I. Help Children Learn to Interpret Other Children's Actions More Accurately and Resolve the Problem When They Think Someone "Cheated," Played Unfairly, or Intentionally Broke a Rule

One common occurrence when children design and play games is that they don't make the rules clear or complete. Sometimes two or three children will make a rule and not tell the other group members. Sometimes a child will break a rule that he or she didn't even know was a rule, only to find classmates becoming angry and reacting negatively. Sometimes children who play in community youth leagues will forget that those who don't participate in those programs are not aware of the rules that children in youth leagues take for granted.

Sample Ideas to Teach

- Before you start to play, check whether everyone knows the rules.
- If someone breaks a rule, ask if the person knew about the rule.

J. Teach Children to Self-Referee

One way to help children develop honesty and a sense of justice is to teach them to self-referee. Self-refereeing includes (1) learning to admit when they break a rule; (2) not believing that it's acceptable to cheat as long as they don't get caught; (3) not using negative body language to intimidate a child who called a violation or foul; (4) not questioning an honest call, (5) not pretending to be fouled; and (6) not trying to draw a penalty.

Sample Objective

- At the end of this lesson, children will have learned to recognize and call when they make a violation.

Sample Discussion

- Discuss and critique the way professional athletes act toward referees in games. Professional teams all agree on the rules but then have to hire someone to make them play by the rules they determined. Once the game begins, they argue with the referee and sulk if they don't get their way.

How mature is that? Isn't it more mature to learn how to call the rules fairly on ourselves?

K. Teach Conflict Resolution Strategies

Although the goal is to prevent conflicts by teaching caring, respect, collaboration, and social responsibility, conflicts sometimes develop. Goleman's book *Emotional Intelligence* (1995) contains an excellent description of the "Red Light, Yellow Light, Green Light" method of conflict resolution. This method has been shown to be effective in school settings. Two modifications of this method are described here:

Conflict Resolution Strategies for When Children Are About to Argue or Fight

Red Light

1. Stop, calm down, and think before you speak. Do not use name calling.

Yellow Light

2. State the problem and describe how you feel. Decide who has the problem.
3. Walk in the other person's shoes. Try to look at the problem from the other person's perspective.
4. Set a positive goal (e.g., we want to solve this problem and have fun playing the game).
5. Try to think of many possible solutions and the consequences of those solutions.

Green Light

6. Decide on a solution, make a plan, and try it out. If it doesn't work, try a different solution.

Conflict Resolution Strategies for Gameplay

Red Light

1. Stop, calm down, and think before you speak. Do not use name calling.

Yellow Light

2. Don't jump to conclusions: Find out the facts. What was the rule? Did you discuss the rule? Did everyone understand the rule the same way? Was this the only violation of the rule, or had this been happening in the game before?
3. Check your assumptions. Did you assume there was a rule not to go out of bounds, for example, or did you and your group actually make and discuss the rule?
4. Say how each of you feels.
5. Think of lots of solutions. Agree on the best plan.
6. Check whether everyone understands the rule.

Green Light

7. Go ahead and play your game.

L. Teach Children to Critique the Etiquette and Ethics They See in Different Sport Settings

Teach children to identify and critique demeaning sport behaviors they see in professional sports on television and in youth sports. Teach children to identify taunting behaviors that they see on television and to understand how this kind of behavior affects youth sports, high school sports, and physical education class. Hold a class discussion about the negative taunting behaviors displayed by some elite athletes and the ways such behaviors can be hurtful to children in physical education.

Teach children about which negative cultural norms are associated with sports and why they are detrimental in an educational setting. This lesson includes identifying "win at all costs" behaviors, such as the best players getting the most playing time, putting the weakest players in right field, publicly picking the best players first, and complaining when a team "has to have" a less skilled child, as well as highlighting a "physical education for all" educational model that puts children and learning first.

M. Identify and Critique Media Images

This strategy includes critiquing with the upper elementary school grades culturally limited images of the body on television and in magazines and advertisements that depict the so-called ideal man (e.g., big muscles, tall, suntanned) and woman (e.g., thin, big breasts). Describe how these images affect children's (and adults') feelings of self-worth and acceptability.

Valuing the Affective Aspects of Physical Activities

Most of us who major in physical education have enjoyed and value many positive experiences in sports, dance, gymnastics, outdoor adventure activities, or fitness workouts. National Standard 5 focuses on the affective domain and aims to ensure students recognize and value physical activities for the many positive experiences (e.g., self-expression, social interactions), feelings (e.g., enjoyment, challenge), and health benefits these activities can provide.

The word *affective* refers to feelings. We include both emotional and physical feelings in our definition of affective aspects of physical education, thereby eliminating any mind–body dichotomy. Affective goals aim to help children recognize and value the emotional and physical feelings that are part of participating in physical activities. They can include feeling joy, excitement, and total engagement in a physical activity; developing a sense of community within a team as you play a game; enjoying the satisfaction of persisting through to the end of a physically demanding workout; experiencing the joy of effort; and taking pride in successfully facing a challenge.

The affective domain also includes physical feelings, such as the positive feeling of being in control of your body movement in a dance and the feelings of power, strength, and flexibility in a fitness workout. Affective aspects of movement are commonly central to dance lessons in which children focus on the feeling of the movement and express feelings and ideas through movement. Lessons in this text designed to bring out this response include jellyfish floating, prancing ponies, angry waves crashing on jagged rocks, kangaroo mothers protecting their babies in their pouch (see **Figure 11.10**), and happily playing in the snow. Children enjoy being able to express their ideas and feelings.

A. Discuss and Help Children Value the Affective Aspects of Physical Activities

To meet the outcome for National Standard 5, you will need to engage children in discussing their feelings during and about physical activities. Discussing affective aspects with children helps them not only recognize the positive feelings they have,

Figure 11.10 Representing the feeling of a mother kangaroo protecting her baby

Figure 11.11 Representing herons stalking fish

but also differentiate and give definitions to different emotions. Children know when something feels good or bad, but their immature vocabularies limit their understanding. Describing and defining positive emotions will help build their vocabularies and help them appreciate in greater depth the value of physical activities. We list these points as lesson objectives designed to address National Standard 5.

Sample Affective Objectives

By the end of this unit, children will

- Appreciate both physical and emotional feelings when representing content in a dance lesson (such as anger, boredom, happiness, or experiences such as finding shelter from a storm, greeting a friend, hiding from a predator, or stalking fish like a heron) (see **Figure 11.11**).
- Appreciate the feeling of movement—both the emotional feeling and the kinesthetic feeling within their bodies.
- Recognize the feeling of excitement when doing movements such as leaping, running fast, chasing, jumping high, skipping high, or swinging on gymnastics apparatus.
- Enjoy challenging themselves.
- Understand and value the health benefits of physical activity.
- Appreciate the joy of effort.
- Value the satisfaction that comes from knowing they tried their hardest.
- Feel the joy in playing a game all out and challenging themselves to do their very best.
- Value the feeling of intensity and total involvement in a game or dance or gymnastics performance.
- Value the feeling of skillfulness, power, control, and/or precision while performing skills or fitness activities.
- Enjoy working with partners to express their ideas about the topic they selected for their dance.
- Appreciate the uplifting feeling of teamwork in a game or a well-executed dance or gymnastics group performance.
- Appreciate the excitement of playing in a game between equal opponents.
- Value the feeling of satisfaction that comes from persisting to the end of a physically demanding workout.

Sample Discussion

- How did you feel when you held that balance on the apparatus?
- How did it feel to jump off the springboard? Why did you think it was fun?
- What was your team's best moment? How did you feel?
- What was the best play of the day? Why did it work so well? How did you feel?
- When did you have your most positive feelings today? What did you feel?
- What activities did you enjoy the most?
- In what ways were your group's social interactions positive or negative?
- How did your muscles and body feel when you did that dance task (e.g., tense, relaxed, strong, soft, heavy, alert, slow, fast, smooth, jerky)?
- How did you feel in that dance task when we were darting quickly to avoid the imaginary monster (e.g., scared, nervous, excited, pressured, confident I could get away)?

Acknowledgments

We thank Robin Litaker for her ideas about teaching social and emotional skills. We thank Nate McCaughtry for his contributions to an earlier version of the framework.

Summary

Research shows that teachers recognize the importance of social and emotional goals. Within the social and emotional domains, there are four categories of goals for elementary physical education: (1) developing caring and respect for others; (2) developing collaboration skills; (3) developing personal and social responsibility; and (4) valuing the affective aspects of physical activities. Each category can be broken down into specific behaviors and attitudes.

Teachers use decision-making and cooperative-learning tasks to work on social and emotional goals. However, children will not automatically learn the behaviors and attitudes that support caring, respect, cooperation, and social responsibility through these types of tasks. For this reason, teachers need to teach explicitly the attitudes and behaviors they want children to learn.

Review Questions

1. When do sports build character, and how?
2. Discuss the implications for teachers of research on children's social and emotional development.
3. Select a social skill, attitude, or behavior. Write a task or activity you could use to teach it, and describe how you would define and discuss the desired social skill, attitude, or behavior with children.
4. What is the impact of student status on group work? As a teacher, how can you deal with issues of student status?
5. Describe how you might teach two of Hellison's five levels for teaching personal and social responsibility.
6. Describe behaviors and attitudes you can teach children about caring and respect, and provide details and examples to illustrate your ideas.
7. Describe the qualities of good group work that you need to teach children.
8. Why is teaching children impulse control important? Give an example of how you might teach impulse control.
9. Describe one conflict resolution strategy, or modify one from the text.
10. Which lessons can you help children learn by critiquing elite athletes' negative behaviors that they see on television and in media images of the body?
11. List the top five affective objectives for you personally as a participant in a physical activity of your choice.

References

Berk, L. E. (2010). *Development through the lifespan* (5th ed.). Boston: Pearson Education.

Brock, S. J., Rovegno, I., & Oliver, K. (2009). The influence of student status on student interactions and experiences during a sport education unit. *Physical Education and Sport Pedagogy, 14*(4), 355–375.

Byra, M. (2006). Teaching styles and inclusive pedagogies. In D. Kirk, D. MacDonald, & M. O'Sullivan (Eds.), *The handbook of physical education* (pp. 449–466). London: Sage.

Cohen, E. G. (1994). *Designing groupwork: Strategies for the heterogeneous classroom* (2nd ed.). New York: Teachers College Press.

Common Core State Standards Initiative. (2010). *Common core state standards for English language arts and literacy in history/social studies, science, and technical subjects.* Retrieved from www.corestandards.org

Dean, C. B., Hubbell, E., Pitler, H., & Stone, B. (2012). *Classroom instruction that works: Research-based strategies for increasing student achievement* (2nd ed.). Alexandria, VA: ASCD.

DeBusk, M., & Hellison, D. (1989). Implementing a physical education self-responsibility model for delinquency-prone youth. *Journal of Teaching in Physical Education, 8*, 104–112.

Dyson, B., & Grineski, S. (2001). Using cooperative learning structures in physical education. *Journal of Physical Education, Recreation and Dance, 72*(2), 28–31.

Ennis, C. D. (1994a). Urban secondary teachers' value orientations: Delineating curricular goals for social responsibility. *Journal of Teaching in Physical Education, 13*, 163–179.

Ennis, C. D. (1994b). Urban secondary teachers' value orientations: Social goals for teaching. *Teaching and Teacher Education 10*(1), 109–120.

Ennis, C. D., & Chen, A. (1995). Teachers' value orientations in urban and rural school settings. *Research Quarterly for Exercise and Sport, 66*(1), 41–50.

Erikson, E. H. (1950). *Childhood and society.* New York: Norton.

Freeman, W. H. (2012). *Physical education, exercise, and sport science in a changing society* (7th ed.). Burlington, MA: Jones & Bartlett Learning.

Gibbons, S. L., Ebbeck, V., & Weiss, M. R. (1995). Fair Play for Kids: Effects on the moral development of children in physical education. *Research Quarterly for Exercise and Sport, 66*, 247–255.

Goleman, D. (1995). *Emotional intelligence.* New York: Bantam Books.

Hadjioannou, X. (2007). Bringing the background to the foreground: What do classroom environments that support authentic discussions look like? *American Educational Research Journal, 44*, 370–399.

Hellison, D. (2003). *Teaching responsibility through physical activity* (2nd ed.). Champaign, IL: Human Kinetics.

Hellison, D., & Martinek, T. (2006). Social and individual responsibility programs. In D. Kirk, D. MacDonald, & M. O'Sullivan (Eds.), *The handbook of physical education* (pp. 610–626). London: Sage.

Iserbyt, P., Elen, J., & Behets, D. (2010). Instructional guidance in reciprocal peer tutoring with task cards. *Journal of Teaching in Physical Education, 29*, 38–53.

Ladd, G.W., Kochenderfer-Ladd, B., Visconti, K., Ettekal, I, Sechler, C., & Cortes, K. I. (2014). Grade-school children's social collaborative skills: Links with partner preference and achievement. *American Educational Research Journal, 51*, 152–183.

Locke, L. F., & Lambdin, D. (2003). *Putting research to work in elementary physical education: Conversations in the gym.* Champaign, IL: Human Kinetics.

McCaughtry, N. (2004). The emotional dimensions of a teacher's pedagogical content knowledge: Influences on content, curriculum, and pedagogy. *Journal of Teaching in Physical Education, 23*, 30–47.

McCaughtry, N., Barnard, S., Martin, J., Shen, B., & Hodges Kulinna, P. (2006). Teachers' perspectives on the challenges of teaching physical education in urban schools: The student emotional filter. *Research Quarterly for Exercise and Sport, 77*, 486–497.

Osher, D., Bear, G. G., Sprague, J. R., & Doyle, W. (2010). How can we improve school discipline? *Educational Researcher, 39*, 48–58.

Phillips, P. (1997). The conflict wall. *Educational Leadership, 54*(8), 43–44.

Romance, T. J., Weiss, M. R., & Bockoven, J. (1986). A program to promote moral development through elementary school physical education. *Journal of Teaching in Physical Education, 5*, 126–136.

Slavin, R. E. (2014). Making cooperative pearning Powerful. *Educational Leadership, 72*(2), 22–26.

Society of Health and Physical Educators (SHAPE). (2014). *National standards and grade-level outcomes for K–12 physical education.* Champaign, IL: Human Kinetics.

Theodoulides, A., & Armour, K. M. (2001). Personal, social and moral development through team games: Some critical questions. *European Physical Education Review, 7*(1), 5–23.

Vande Broek, G., Boen, F., Claessens, M., Feys, J., & Ceux, T. (2011). Comparison of three instructional approaches to enhance tactical knowledge in volleyball among university students. *Journal of Teaching in Physical Education, 30*, 375–392.

Wandzilak, T., Carroll, T., & Ansorge, C. J. (1988). Values development through physical activity: Promoting sportsmanlike behaviors, perceptions, and moral reasoning. *Journal of Teaching in Physical Education, 8*, 13–22.

Ward, P., & Lee, M. A. (2005). Peer-assisted learning in physical education: A review of theory and research. *Journal of Teaching in Physical Education, 24*, 205–225.

CHAPTER

12

Diversity

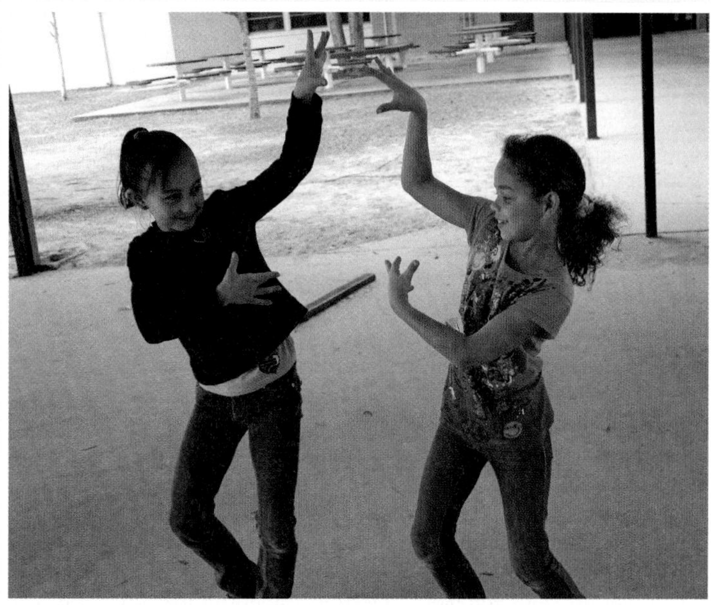

PRE-READING REFLECTION

1. Think about a time you were excluded. How did you feel?
2. Think about a time you were excluded, teased, or harassed because you were different in some way. How did you feel?
3. Think about a time you were included in a high-status group you wanted to be part of, but a friend was not included. How did you feel?

OBJECTIVES

Students will learn:

1. Physical education is committed to providing a learning environment that is inclusive, welcoming, and free from harassment to all children, regardless of race, gender, ability, disability, religion, ethnicity, sexual orientation, body size and weight, socioeconomic status, and nature of the child's family.
2. Public schools historically reflect cultural values of the white European middle class because this is the group in power, both within schools and within the broader educational and political communities. Consequently, children from different cultures and races can find some of the values in schools to be different from some of the values they learn in their families and ethnic communities. Understanding these cultural differences will make you a better teacher.
3. Cultural stereotyping means that a characteristic that may be an appropriate descriptor for one person or a group of individuals is assumed to be a characteristic of all members of that race or ethnicity. Stereotyping can lead to prejudicial behaviors and attitudes.
4. Inclusive, equitable classrooms share six characteristics:
   - Cultural sensitivity

- Caring about students' lives and about what they learn, demonstrated by setting high expectations and providing equal opportunities for all learners
- A curriculum that is relevant for diverse groups and is also connected to the lives of children
- Creation of an affirming, inclusive community in which diversity is respected, accepted, and valued
- Teaching that helps children become aware of injustice and take actions when they witness injustice
- Teaching that helps children acquire a future orientation that encompasses hope, joy, and a vision of a better tomorrow

KEY TERMS

Collectivistic cultural values
Cultural sensitivity
Duct tape and Velcro approach
Future orientation
Individualistic cultural values
Stereotyping

CONNECTION TO STANDARDS

In this chapter, we describe the research and issues that support the intention of the Society of Health and Physical Educators (SHAPE) to set a goal and design national standards and student outcomes that meet the needs of all children regardless of race, gender, ability, disability, religion, ethnicity, sexual orientation, body size and weight, and socioeconomic status. In addition, this chapter discusses ways to address National Standard 4.

Introduction

In this chapter, we discuss issues concerning diversity and ways teachers can effectively provide a just and inclusive classroom climate for all students. North American public schools are becoming increasingly more diverse ethnically and racially. It is estimated that in a few decades, the United States will become a majority–minority society, meaning there will be no majority racial or ethnic group. Even today, in states such as Hawai'i there is no majority racial or ethnic group. Creating a school system that provides equitable educational opportunities for children of all races, ethnic groups, and social classes has been, and will continue to be, a long-term goal in schools.

Multicultural diversity is only one type of diversity important to physical education. Because sport is a major part of our subject matter and provides disproportionate opportunities for males and able-bodied people, physical education teachers must also be concerned with providing equitable educational opportunities for females and for both boys and girls with disabilities. Moreover, as in all subject areas, physical education is committed to providing a classroom environment that is inclusive, welcoming, and free from harassment to all children, regardless of race, gender, ability, disability, religion, ethnicity, sexual orientation, body size and weight, socioeconomic status, and nature of the child's family.

In this chapter, we begin by discussing issues related to diversity and inequality that affect elementary physical education. This discussion will help you develop an awareness of possible issues you might face when teaching in increasingly diverse settings. Awareness is the first step in learning how to provide inclusive, culturally relevant, and equitable physical education programs. We then describe six characteristics of inclusive, culturally relevant, equitable classrooms.

Issues Related to Diversity and Inequality

Race, Ethnicity, and Social Class

Recognizing and understanding cultural differences will make you a better teacher. There is no doubt that during the course of your career, you will be teaching children from families, cultures, and social classes that differ from yours. Sometimes these differences may be difficult to recognize, even if you are trying your best to demonstrate **cultural sensitivity**—that is, an awareness of cultural differences and responding in ways that are affirming and equitable. Before you can create an inclusive, just, and caring community in your classes, you need to understand and value different cultural perspectives, values, and ways of knowing and seeing the world (see **Figure 12.1**).

This is not an easy task, because all people view the world from their own perspectives and often assume (inaccurately)

Figure 12.1 Children working together on an assessment
Courtesy of John Dolly

that everyone else has a relatively similar perspective. Let us give you a personal and noncontentious example. At the first family Thanksgiving dinner the first author's husband attended, he was surprised to find that we start the meal with ravioli, made from an old family recipe handed down from the small town in Italy from which our family immigrated. The pasta course is followed by turkey and other dishes traditionally associated with Thanksgiving in the United States. My husband was surprised because he took for granted what he thought was universal Thanksgiving fare, whereas having pasta as a first course is common practice for Italian families.

Although it is difficult to imagine anyone developing prejudices against eating delicious ravioli, a lack of understanding and valuing of different cultural values and behaviors can and does lead to discriminatory and prejudicial attitudes that are harmful to members of a minority culture. We know children who have two moms and others who have two dads (as you might now and almost certainly will when you become a teacher). We have family and friends who have experienced harmful prejudicial actions and attitudes from others because of their sexual orientation. To understand different cultural perspectives that others might hold, you will need to be open to understanding how ideas and ways to behave that seem correct, normal, and noncontroversial to you might be seen very differently from the perspectives of others.

Public schools have historically reflected the cultural values of the white European middle class. One reason is because the overwhelming percentage of teachers and administrators have been white and were not only successful in school but enjoyed school to the extent that they chose to work in school environments. Thus, they maintained the kind of environment and mainstream perspective that worked well for them. This white Western mainstream perspective of those in power, combined with a lack of diversity among teachers and administrators, can result in the culture of schools being different from the various ethnic and racial cultures of many children attending these schools. Consequently, children from different cultures and races may find some of the values in schools to be different from some of the values they have learned in their families and ethnic communities (Bazron, Osher, & Fleischman, 2005). This point is important because the conflict in values can make learning difficult and leave children confused about behavior and attitudes.

For example, Trumbull and Rothstein-Fisch (2008) describe how mainstream culture and, in turn, school culture encourage more **individualistic cultural values**, such as independence (e.g., working alone on assignments), individual achievement (taking tests individually, being graded on work individually, competition, succeeding as an individual), self-expression, and individual responsibility. Other cultures, in contrast, encourage more **collectivistic cultural values**, such as interdependence within the family, concern for group well-being and success, group responsibility, cooperation, modesty, and respect for elders. Trumbull and Rothstein-Fisch explain that their framework does not mean cultures are either completely individualistic or collectivistic, because all cultures have some of both values; the difference lies in the points of emphasis and how that emphasis transfers to school settings.

When teachers understand that the emphasis on individualistic values that pervades schools is linked to mainstream cultural values, they can appreciate that children from different cultures might not value individual achievement and competition to the extent that they value being part of a group, cooperative activities, and helping others. For example, Klug and Whitfield (2003) suggest that many Native American tribes value cooperation over competition; in this setting, when teachers use competition as a teaching method, it needs to be team competition focused on sharing and harmony. The goal of competition, then, is taking pride in a job well done, rather than winning and showing you're better than other children. Nevertheless, Klug and Whitfield also point out that you cannot generalize across Native American tribes. In addition, some Native American students like competition and do not prefer group work.

Understanding that other cultures might value collectivism more than individual achievement can also help teachers learn to build on the equally important cultural values children bring to physical education. For example, teachers can have children work in cooperative learning groups, encourage them to care about the success of their group, provide opportunities for them to help other groups to improve, and allow children to choose whether to play a cooperative or competitive game and choose whether to keep score.

What the Research Says

Cultural Differences

Raeff, Greenfield, and Quiroz (2000) used the following scenario as part of a research study. Before you read about what the research found, read the scenario and answer this question: What do you think the teacher should do? (Although the study used a classroom example, imagine a similar situation in a physical education setting.)

> It is the end of the school day, and the class is cleaning up. Denise isn't feeling well, and she asks Jasmine to help her with her job for the day, which is cleaning the blackboard. Jasmine isn't sure that she will have time to do both her job and Denise's. What do you think the teacher should do? (p. 66)

What was your initial idea, and how did you compare to the teachers and parents in the study? In one school, in which all the parents and children were European American, parents and teachers thought Jasmine's first responsibility was to complete her assigned job and that the teacher should find a third person to do Denise's job. In a second school, with Latino students and parents, 74% of the parents said Jasmine's first responsibility was to help Denise. The most important cultural value to these parents was helping others.

Now rethink the scenario and ask yourself these questions: What do you think the teacher should do? Who will benefit from the teacher's actions? Who, if anyone, might be hurt by the teacher's actions?

In addition, research shows that when teachers use group work with children from minority cultures, class management typically improves (Rothstein-Fisch & Trumbull, 2008). Management improves because group work builds on the children's strengths and prompts them to be concerned about the well-being of others within their group. In this environment, children encourage one another to make positive contributions to the group and not disrupt group harmony.

Recognizing different cultural norms also helps teachers better understand and avoid misinterpreting children's behaviors. For example, some behaviors, such as interrupting someone to comment on and contribute to her or his ideas, are common in some cultures but considered rude in others. For instance, you might assume that a child is being disrespectful if the child won't make eye contact with you when the two of you are discussing the child's misbehavior. In reality, the reverse might be true in that child's family and cultural community: Looking down when you are in trouble may be perceived as a sign of respect for an adult.

Stereotyping

A second issue is **stereotyping**, in which a characteristic that may be an appropriate descriptor of one individual is assumed to be a characteristic of all people of that ethnicity or race. For example, Cornelius (1999) describes five stereotypes of Native Americans that are pervasive in the elementary school curriculum, children's literature, and the media: "the Nobel Red Man or Nobel Savage, the Savage, the Vanishing Race, Living Fossils, and the media image of Generic Indians" (p. 3). Thus, stereotyping leads children to assume incorrectly that all Native Americans are a war-like, uncivilized, homogeneous group of people with a single set of cultural values, living in harmony with nature, and that they were only important in the past, rather than Native American families being important members of society living in the Americas today.

Some of the most pervasive and harmful stereotypes held by teachers are about poverty. Some teachers cling to the following misconceptions (Gorski, 2008):

- Poor people do not have a strong work ethic. (In fact, working adults who are poor work more hours than those who make more money. Many poor parents must work two or three jobs to support their families.)
- Poor parents don't value education and, therefore, don't get involved with schools. (In reality, the failure to participate may be due to lack of public transportation, lack of child care, and the need to work evenings.)
- Poor people disproportionately abuse drugs and alcohol. (In fact, drug use occurs across all social classes, and alcohol abuse rates are higher among wealthy people.)

Stereotyping leads to prejudicial and discriminatory behaviors and attitudes. For example, a negative and inaccurate stereotype of African Americans who play football is that they play instinctively as opposed to being good decision makers and, therefore, are best suited for positions such as running back and receiver rather than quarterback (Eitzen & Sage, 2003; Loy & McElvogue, 1970). Consequently, when children begin playing football at a young age, coaches may channel African Americans into these positions. It is only recently that this stereotype has begun to lessen as we have seen more and more collegiate and professional African American quarterbacks.

> **What the Research Says**
>
> Cultural Differences
>
> The following is an abbreviated version of a story told by a teacher in the book by Rothstein-Fisch (2003) and repeated in the book by Rothstein-Fisch and Trumbull (2008):
>
> Two boys were called into the principal's office. One looked down, and the other looked the principal straight in the eyes. The principal decided the boy who looked down was the guilty one and expelled him for a few days.
>
> The classroom teacher knew the boy who had been expelled and thought he was innocent. She also understood the cultural difference of looking down as a sign of respect in Latino families and how that could be misinterpreted in white cultures. So, she taught her entire class that there are cultural differences and that in some cultures, looking down is a sign of respect for adults, whereas in others, children are expected to look adults in the eyes. She then took the class on a field trip around the school, and they discussed which adults they should look in the eye and which they should avoid looking in the eye. She also taught them that if their approach was not working, to shift to the other approach.

Lack of Equitable Opportunities to Learn and Participate

A third major issue for physical education teachers related to ethnicity, race, and social class, which often interact and overlap, is the lack of equitable opportunities for learning and participating in physical activity. African American and Hispanic children are less active than white children (McKenzie, 2003; McKenzie, Sallis, Nader, Broyles, & Nelson, 1992; Simons-Morton et al., 1997; Trost, 2006). Different values also are assigned to activity within cultures. For example, often in Mexican cultures, it is not viewed as gender appropriate for girls to be active in the same ways as boys.

Children living in poor and working-class families have fewer opportunities to participate in physical activities after school and more often attend schools that have larger classes, poor-quality facilities, a lack of equipment, fewer certified teachers, and a less demanding curriculum (Darling-Hammond, 2006; Kozol, 1991, 2005; Ladson-Billings, 2006). "There is a 10-to-1 ratio in spending between the highest-spending and lowest-spending schools in the nation, and a 3-to-1 ratio within most states, with rich districts getting richer and the children of the poor more seriously disadvantaged each year" (Darling-Hammond, 2006, p. 13). Some urban environments lack parks and recreation programs, do not have enough indoor space to house physical activity programs after school, and are unsafe places for children to play actively outdoors. Rural communities often lack the financial or transportation resources to provide after-school programs for children.

Figure 12.2 Enjoying playing a game
Courtesy of John Dolly

Parents of middle- and upper-class children can afford to support their children's participation in youth sports and pay for lessons in activities such as tennis, gymnastics, swimming, dance, soccer, and golf. In contrast, for children who are members of working-class and poor families, physical education classes are often the only opportunity to learn and participate in physical activities (see **Figure 12.2**). Learning and participating in physical activities is "differentially distributed along the lines of social class, disability, race and gender" (Kirk, 2007, p. 131).

Thus, in terms of our goals for children to have physically active, healthy lifestyles, children from different races, ethnicities, and social classes will have different opportunities available to them for learning and participating in physical activities.

Gender

There is no doubt that the enactment of the federal legislation known as Title IX of the Education Amendments of 1972 resulted in tremendous increases in girls' opportunities to participate in sports. Nevertheless, research shows that girls continue to be less active than boys both in physical education classes and outside of school (McKenzie, 2003; McKenzie et al., 1992; Simons-Morton et al., 1997; Trost, 2006). Even within the same coeducational physical education classes at the elementary level, girls are less active than boys, and boys use disproportionate amounts of space and equipment (Nilges, 1998). Recess can also be a time when girls are less active than boys, with boys controlling the equipment and space for physical activity and girls left to play on the margins (Oliver & Hamzeh, 2010).

Title IX

Title IX, a piece of U.S. federal legislation enacted in 1972, states that in organizations receiving federal assistance—which includes most schools—no one can be denied benefits or be subject to discrimination on the basis of sex. Its greatest impact was calling for equal opportunities for girls and women to participate in sport programs. According to Sabo and Snyder (2013), since the passage of Title IX, girls' high school sport participation has increased over 1000% and women's collegiate participation over 800%.

In addition to disproportionate levels of physical activity, girls must deal with stereotypical and prejudicial beliefs that sports are a male domain linked to dominant forms of masculinity (e.g., having power, strength, big muscles). For example, football, basketball, ice hockey, baseball, wrestling, and soccer are viewed as sports where boys can showcase masculinity. Research shows that girls who enjoy and are skilled at sports can face name-calling and harassment questioning their femininity and sexual orientation (Oliver & Hamzeh, 2010). Likewise, boys who exhibit alternative forms of masculinity often face harassment, oppression, and taunting from peers and teachers alike (Tischler & McCaughtry, 2011).

Girls also face the prejudicial belief that boys are better at sports, which can result in boys not letting girls play, girls receiving fewer opportunities in games (e.g., fewer passes, fewer opportunities to shoot the ball), boys publicly degrading and trivializing girls' abilities, girls receiving fewer leadership opportunities, and girls standing on the sidelines watching while boys engage in physical activities (Nilges, 1998; Oliver & Hamzeh, 2010). Research on girls' and boys' interactions in coeducational classes shows that girls assume nonassertive roles, such as acquiescing to boys, giving up, and hanging back to avoid having to take part in the activity, while boys hassle girls by teasing, criticizing, and laughing at them; cutting ahead in line; and giving orders (Griffin, 1983, 1984).

Finally, research shows that teachers treat boys and girls differently in physical education classes. Teachers' conversations with girls tend to be more interpersonal rather than instructional, they speak in language that conveys the message that girls are less skilled in team sports, and they demonstrate lower expectations that girls will engage positively in physical education (Wright, 1997). In addition, teachers give boys more praise, more attention, and more verbal interactions than they give girls (MacDonald, 1990; Wright, 1997). All too often, we see physical education classes in which the boys play basketball or other active sports dominating the space, while the girls sit in the bleachers or walk around the track.

Sexual Orientation

A third issue related to diversity is sexual orientation, which often is the most highly charged diversity issue for teachers. This status results from the power and pervasiveness of homophobia in our society. Teachers and parents readily teach children that sexist and racist slurs and jokes are unacceptable, but they often ignore slurs, name-calling, jokes, and teasing about sexual orientation.

You cannot do justice to the issue of oppression without also including the oppression of lesbians, gay men, and bisexual or transgendered individuals (Gordon, 1994). As a teacher, you will teach children who have parents who are lesbians or gay men. In addition, although children rarely perceive their sexual orientation in elementary school, you will be teaching children who will later identify themselves as lesbian, gay, bisexual, or transgendered. Regardless of your beliefs about homosexuality, including your religious beliefs, you will need to treat children and their parents in respectful ways. Children with gay or lesbian parents should not have to defend their families, nor should they have to suffer harassment.

The use of anti-gay name-calling has increased dramatically in recent years. Today, even children in the youngest grades use terms such as "faggot," "dyke," and "sissy" to humiliate, ridicule, and hurt other children. Today, the term "gay" is used by children and adolescents to denote something that is extremely negative, disgusting, or disliked.

Not only has name-calling increased, but many teachers rarely challenge it. While teachers readily react to a child using racial slurs, they let comments such as "That's so gay" pass without acknowledgment. Thus, teachers give their tacit approval for children to degrade gays, lesbians, and transgendered people and to harass their peers with prejudicial comments. This behavior creates a hostile environment. Far worse, it has led to suicides and the murder of homosexual and transgendered adolescents. Stopping homophobic name-calling is not promoting homosexuality; it is ensuring students' safety and inclusion. The most important responsibility of schools and teachers is to keep all children safe, regardless of who they are.

Another issue with sexual orientation is the fact that children are pressured to behave according to strict sex-role stereotypes of masculinity and femininity. If they don't match these expectations, they risk being labeled gay. This perspective limits both boys and girls in the physical activities they might express interest in learning and the benefits of learning a wide range of physical activities as viable expressive and social activities (Gard, 2006). Although there is more leeway for girls to participate in traditionally male-dominated sports, such as soccer and basketball, than for boys to participate in traditionally female physical activities, such as dance and gymnastics, the pressure for both girls and boys to engage in gender-appropriate activities is based in prejudicial and oppressive attitudes toward homosexuality. As physical education teachers, we have to work hard at helping *all* students understand that physical activity of *all* types is for everyone. Boys and girls need to experience a variety of physical activities to develop their skills for whichever activities they might try across their lifespan (see **Figure 12.3**).

Obesity

Another issue related to diversity and oppression that is important in physical education is body shape and weight. Our field promotes health-related physical activity, which entails maintaining appropriate amounts of physical activity to enhance health and prevent disease. However, many people take a more narrow view and focus on physical fitness and being "in shape," meaning for males to have a body that is muscular but not fat and for females to be slender and toned. In the mass media, having a fit-looking body is associated with power, beauty, sexiness, popularity, and a good life. Unfortunately, this promotion of fit bodies also has contributed to the stigmatizing of overweight and obese people.

Figure 12.3 Enjoying a folk dance

Research shows that children and adolescents who are overweight or obese are often victims of prejudice, marginalization, oppression, and stereotyping (Puhl & Latner, 2007). Peers may tease and harass them. The social consequences of obesity are equally—if not more—detrimental to their well-being than the physical consequences.

In their comprehensive review of studies on how children and adolescents viewed overweight and obese peers, Puhl and Latner (2007) reported 3- to 5-year-olds labeling overweight peers as "mean, stupid, lazy, ugly, sloppy, loud, sad, and lacking friends." Six- to 12-year-olds claimed overweight peers were "ugly, selfish, lazy, stupid, lying, dirty, sloppy, cheats, mean, and less popular." Adolescents labeled overweight peers as "lazy, self-indulgent, sexually unskilled, unclean, and unattractive" (p. 563).

Although you might wonder whether this kind of peer pressure would help overweight and obese youth to lose weight, the research indicates that the reverse is true. That is, being the victim of harassment and weight bias and feeling dissatisfied with their bodies further contribute to obesity in young people (Puhl & Latner, 2007).

Even physical educators may demonstrate these negative biases. Research on the attitudes of physical education majors from one program found that they held strong, negative stereotypes and prejudices against obese people (O'Brien, Hunter, & Banks, 2007; Puhl & Latner, 2007). Physical education teachers have also been found to have anti-fat attitudes (Greenleaf & Weiller, 2005).

Although our field is committed to helping people develop healthy lifestyles, we also need to understand the causes of and potential ways to prevent obesity and to develop programs that make a positive contribution to the well-being of overweight and obese students. At the very least, we need to ensure that our attitudes do not contribute to the oppression and marginalization of overweight and obese people. We need to be part of the solution by making physical education a fat-friendly place, and by not being part of the problem.

Disabilities

Children with disabilities face some of the same prejudices as overweight and obese children. Part of the problem is that society's view of the body and sport can affect how we view disabilities. Cultural conceptions of the ideal body suggest that it is physically strong and perfectly proportioned. The epitome of sport is assumed to be male elite sport. The perspective that is taken for granted posits that biological qualities of the body lead to natural inequalities in sport performance (i.e., men perform better because they are naturally stronger and taller than women; athletes without disabilities perform better than

Figure 12.4 Athletes on the national championship wheelchair basketball team
Courtesy of John Dolly

athletes with disabilities) (DePauw, 1997). When only the most highly skilled male performances are considered the epitome of sport performance, this viewpoint can lead to inequalities and marginalization of women and people with disabilities in sport (DePauw, 1997). For example, far too often teachers do not hold high expectations that children with disabilities can achieve and succeed in physical education activities (Fitzgerald, 2006). In reality, individuals with disabilities—both physical and developmental—can participate in all sorts of activities and achieve high levels of prowess (see **Figure 12.4**).

Surveys of students with disabilities reveal that in physical education, they have fewer activity options, face discriminatory attitudes of teachers and peers, and attend schools with inaccessible programs and facilities (Fitzgerald, 2006). Other studies have found that students with disabilities spend less time practicing at an appropriate level, are less active, and have lower fitness levels and lower self-concepts than peers who are not disabled (Vogler, 2003).

In part, these inequitable practices are an outgrowth of the "medical model" of disability, which is the predominant model in schools. In the medical model, "the disabled person is regarded as having limited functioning that deems them to be deficient in some way" (Fitzgerald, 2006, p. 755). Those who critique the medical model claim that it does not direct attention toward the societal attitudes that limit the participation of people with disabilities and the lack of programs, the lack of accessible facilities, and the lack of teachers who have been trained to provide inclusive and equitable physical education programs.

The good news is that well-run programs offered by well-trained teachers with appropriate support can provide positive, effective physical education experiences for children with disabilities (Vogler, 2003). If we refuse to maintain a narrow view of achievement and refuse to view a child with disabilities as a child with limitations who can achieve only an impaired performance, then we will be able to offer physical education programs that are equitable and just (see **Figure 12.5**) (DePauw, 1997).

In summary, teachers work in increasingly diverse schools with parents and children who have the right to—and are not shy about demanding—equitable opportunities for all children. If you are aware of and attend to diversity issues, you will give all your students the best opportunities to learn in physical education and to develop the skills needed to participate in a range of activities throughout their lives.

Six Characteristics of Inclusive, Culturally Relevant, Equitable Classrooms

Teachers identify six characteristics as crucial for creating inclusive, equitable classrooms that work against discrimination and prejudice (Bigelow, Christensen, Karp, Miner, & Peterson, 1994; Flory & McCaughtry, 2011; Ladson-Billings, 1994, 1995a, 1995b):

1. Cultural sensitivity
2. Caring about students' lives and caring about their learning by setting high expectations and providing equal opportunities for all learners
3. Providing a curriculum that is relevant for diverse groups and connected to the lives of children
4. Creating an affirming, inclusive community in which diversity is respected, accepted, and valued

Figure 12.5 Child in a wheelchair contributing equally to the group dance
Courtesy of John Dolly

Culturally Relevant Pedagogy

Dr. Gloria Ladson-Billings is a researcher who has been interested in understanding why some teachers are very successful in teaching African American children from families with low income levels. Many schools have failed dismally to provide a quality education for this group of children. Ladson-Billings researched how teachers succeeded in teaching African American children from low-income families (1994, 1995a, 1995b).

To begin her work, Ladson-Billings first found excellent teachers by asking parents and principals to nominate those teachers whom they felt excelled in their work. Only teachers on both the parents' and principals' lists were asked to participate in the study. The students taught by these teachers consistently scored higher on standardized tests than students taught by other teachers.

To study the teachers, Ladson-Billings spent three years in their school watching them teach and interviewing them. When she began, she faced what she called a researcher's nightmare. She could not see common characteristics among the teachers' teaching methods. On the surface, their pedagogy differed greatly: some used a structured pedagogy, others did not, and some were even rigid. It was only after making extensive observations and meeting with the teachers as a group that Ladson-Billing realized she had to go beyond surface teaching strategies to identify a set of common beliefs and to determine how the teachers enacted those beliefs on a daily basis.

Ladson-Billings labeled these excellent teachers' common characteristics "culturally relevant pedagogy." All the teachers held high standards for excellence and saw it as their responsibility that students meet these standards. They absolutely insisted students learn and succeed. They supported and built on students' cultural competence. Within their classrooms, they built a community of learners. They taught students to think critically about the culture of power and to take action to promote social justice. They were proud of being teachers, were passionate about what they taught, and viewed teaching as a way of giving back to the community. Ladson-Billings' work has since been expanded on and replicated by many other researchers and teachers (e.g., Foster, 1993; Gay, 2002; Henry, 1992; Noblit, 1993).

5. Teaching children to be aware of injustice and to take action when they witness injustice
6. Helping children acquire a future orientation that encompasses hope, joy, and a vision of a better tomorrow

Cultural Sensitivity

Increase Your Knowledge of the Local Community and Your Students' Cultures

As a beginning teacher, you cannot expect to know the cultures of all children you will be teaching in your career—but you can certainly learn. When you first start working in a community, make an effort to learn about the community and the cultural backgrounds of the children in your classes. Figure out how what happens in the students' community affects what happens in your school and in your classes (Flory & McCaughtry, 2011).

Find out about the culture of your school. Ask parents, custodians, lunchroom personnel, teachers, and principals, "What are the values, goals, and philosophy of this school from your perspective?"

Extend your research to learn about the community. Visit community parks, recreational facilities, and community centers. Find out what programs and recreational opportunities are available for children and which children have access to these opportunities. Get to know the parents. Ask them about their neighborhoods, community, culture, and their children. Ask them about their goals for their children, neighborhoods, and community. Find out how they, their children, and the community feel about sports, dance, and other physical activities.

Once you know what after-school programs and parks are available for children, teach your children about these opportunities. One urban teacher we know takes his students on a field trip every year where he teaches them about the bus routes in their community. He takes them on the city buses, teaching them where and how to get on the bus and pay the fare and which bus routes will take them from their homes to parks and recreational facilities. Then he has the children participate in activities in those parks. The next day, the classroom teachers assign written journals for the children to reflect on their experiences and explain what physical activity means to them.

Work to Change Cultural Norms that Negatively Impact Students

Once you understand that cultural norms privilege some groups over others, you can work to become an agent of change. For example, we have never seen a kindergarten class (in schools without preschool) in which, *on average*, the girls throw overarm at a more mature level than the boys. *On average* means that some girls throw at more mature levels than some boys, but more boys than girls throw with a higher skill level. This difference results simply from the cultural norms that encourage boys to practice throwing with parents, siblings, and peers during the preschool years. These norms privilege boys when they enter school because boys get more practice opportunities than girls get. Of course, the more you practice, the more mature your throwing pattern will be.

Similarly, a related cultural norm suggests that sports are a male domain, whereas dance and gymnastics are female domains. Consequently, boys are encouraged to practice sport-related skills and participate in sports more than girls are. Conversely, girls are encouraged to engage in dance- and gymnastics-related activities more than boys. Again, the more you practice, the more skilled you become.

As physical educators, we can do a great deal to counteract these cultural norms. We can teach children that their ability to perform skills results from practice and instruction—not because boys are inherently better than girls or because some children are simply better athletes. We can also encourage girls to participate in sports. We can refuse to believe that boys are naturally better at sports and teach our children to have the same beliefs. Finally, we can help parents understand the importance of all forms of physical activity for both boys and girls.

Pay Attention to Messages on Bulletin Boards

Look carefully at the posters and bulletin boards in your school:

- Are there more boys pictured than girls?
- Are boys shown being active while girls are doing more passive activities?
- Do you have posters of elite male athletes, but not elite female athletes or elite athletes with disabilities?
- Are your posters reflective of the various ethnic groups represented in your school?
- Are there individuals with various body types engaged in physical activity in the posters, or are all the people stereotypically fit?
- Do your posters highlight both males and females doing activities such as aerobics or football, or are they perpetuating stereotypical activities for males and females?

Use Inclusive Language and Language that Does Not Degrade or Stereotype Cultural Groups

Pay attention to your word choices, and use inclusive language. Although younger generations speaking informally often use the phrase "you guys," to refer to both genders, this is not appropriate formal language for teachers because "guys" refers to only males. Use inclusive language: Say, "boys and girls," "folks," "everyone," or "you all."

Don't use stereotypical phrases, such as "sit Indian style" or "sit tailor style"; instead, say "sit with your legs crossed" or "sit crisscross apple sauce." Don't say, "You are acting like a bunch of wild Indians"; say, "You are wild and out of control." Avoid using the term "girl" to define certain movement patterns or equipment, such as "You throw like a girl," "girls' push-ups," "girls' basketballs," "girls' volleyball–height net," and "girls' rules." Say, "1v1 defense" (or "person-to-person") rather than "man-to-man." Especially avoid terms such as "sissy" and "wuss," as these terms are used to degrade someone by implying they are homosexual. (We will discuss name-calling later in this chapter.)

When children select team names, don't let them use Native American names. If your school mascot is Native American in origin, get it changed. In the past 10 years, most colleges and universities with Native American team names have changed the nickname or the mascot, except in instances where the local Native American tribe voted to have the university continue to use its tribal name.

Language varies in different contexts. The way you talk when you are with your friends and family might be very different from the more formal language you will need to use as a teacher. For example, terms that African Americans might use among themselves are inappropriate when used by white teachers. It is important for teachers to model formal English because it is the language of power—that is, it is the language used by people in positions of power in the workplace. Children need to be able to switch from the more informal language they use among friends to the language of power when they are in positions where they want to acquire power and influence, such as when they are on job interviews or in the workplace.

> **Y'all**
>
> An English professor from a southern state joked, "I don't understand why anyone would need to use the phrase 'you guys' when we have a perfectly good word in 'y'all.'"

Caring About Students' Lives and Caring About Their Learning by Setting High Expectations and Providing Equal Opportunities

Research provides strong support for teachers caring about students' lives inside and out of school and caring that students learn in physical education (Flory & McCaughtry, 2011; Owens & Ennis, 2005). This means caring about children's experiences, feelings, well-being, and safety; it also means caring about providing a quality education and believing that students can achieve and succeed (see **Figure 12.6**). Little dampens the prospects for achievement more than a teacher who doesn't care and doesn't believe that a child can be successful.

Research on excellent teachers of African American children has found that one common characteristic among these teachers was their belief that all their children could learn. In turn, they set high expectations, and they insisted all children meet those expectations (Ladson-Billings, 1994, 1995a, 1995b). If you believe girls are not as skilled as boys, you will convey these expectations in ways that you won't even recognize. If you believe that children with disabilities can't learn skills or participate in class, you will have them sit out rather than find meaningful ways to include them in physical activity. If you expect African American children to excel at certain activities (e.g., "White people can't jump," "Black people run faster") but not children of other ethnic backgrounds, your students will pick up on that attitude and your expectations will become a

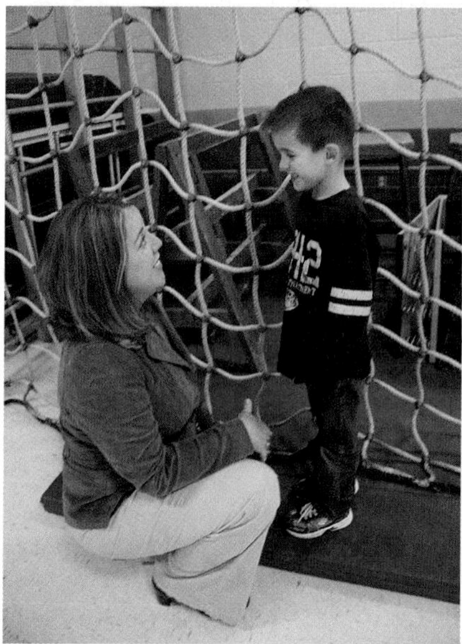

Figure 12.6 Caring about a child's life

self-fulfilling prophecy. Conversely, if you hold high expectations for all children, you will convey to them a more empowering message—that they can learn and find success in physical activities.

In addition, you need to critically examine what happens in your classes to see if all children are having equal opportunities to practice. Scan the class, asking yourself these questions:

- Are some children hogging the ball?
- Are some children hanging back and not participating in the team's play?
- Are some children spending all their time retrieving balls because the tasks are too difficult or because they're avoiding embarrassing situations?
- Are partners and groups treating each other fairly?
- Are boys excluding girls from playing on their team?

If you see these problems, ask the children whether everyone is getting equal practice time and why or why not. Then help them modify the task or change the rules of the game so that play and practice become more equitable.

Finally, pay attention to your feedback patterns:

- Do you give boys and girls equal amounts of feedback?
- Do you give positive feedback to more boys or girls?
- When you call on children to answer questions, do you call on the same children all the time?
- Do you call on more girls than boys?
- Do you have boys demonstrate more often than girls?

Although typically the classroom teachers are in charge of recess, physical education teachers often see what goes on in recess and can address recess issues in faculty meetings:

- Are the boys using more of the space and denying girls spaces for physically active play?
- Do boys and girls share equipment equitably?
- How do the children divide into teams?

Experienced Teachers Talk

Who Gets Your Attention?

We had read and discussed research that found teachers gave more feedback and attention to boys. We looked at our own teaching of coeducational gymnastics classes and found, to our chagrin, that this was true for us, too. Consequently, we worked hard at changing our behavior but found it was not easy. The boys got our attention because they were most likely to be having fun experimenting with skills that were not safe for them, asked for feedback to improve a skill, or tended to slip off task and begin using the gymnastics equipment to work on strength exercises. Every time they got on the parallel bars, they started doing dips (rather than the task assigned); the high bar was first a chinning bar. Boys demanded and got our attention by engaging in off-task behavior. They knew which buttons to push. What we learned was that giving equitable feedback and attention was not simply based on what the teacher did but on what students did to either demand attention or avoid contact. It was a much more complex issue than we had assumed.

Provide a Curriculum that Is Relevant for Diverse Groups and Connected to the Lives of Children

Battle Stereotypes

Research has shown that many children and adults hold stereotypical beliefs about physical activities. Specifically, they think that some activities, especially those highlighting strength, power, and aggressive competitiveness, are masculine, whereas others, especially those activities highlighting graceful movement, are feminine (Flintoff & Scranton, 2006; Gard, 2006). The dramatic increase in girls' and women's participation in sports since the enactment of Title IX has clearly helped change perceptions that sports are just for boys. Nevertheless, stereotypical beliefs about certain physical activities being more appropriate for one gender or the other persist.

For example, the following stereotypes are common in physical education:

- Boys should be in charge during sports lessons and can be rough, loud, argumentative, and insulting (even jokingly), whereas girls must be quiet, calm, nice, submissive, and not argue.
- Boys are good at sports.
- Sports are for athletic-looking boys.
- Gymnastics, dance, and jumping rope are for girls.
- Girls are weak; boys are strong.

As you can imagine, if we allow these stereotypes to go unchallenged, then we will limit the choices of physical activities children see available to them. We will also undermine beliefs about the possibility that they can succeed in a physical activity.

Unfortunately, research has found that when "females perceive an activity to be for males, they are unlikely to see themselves as competent in that activity, and therefore are unlikely to exert effort" (Solmon, Lee, Belcher, Harrison, & Wells, 2003, p. 275). In essence, stereotyping physical activities becomes a self-fulfilling prophecy. Girls think the activity is for boys, so they won't be any good at it; in turn, they don't work hard to learn. The boys work harder and practice more and, in fact, do become skilled while the girls don't. Thus, the stereotype is confirmed.

The good news is that teachers can change students' beliefs and convince students that they can be successful. To do so, teachers need to combat stereotyping of physical activities and teach students that the full range of physical activities is appropriate for them. Here are some suggestions for how to achieve this goal:

- Find examples in the media, such as photographs, posters, and videos, showing both genders and people with disabilities being skilled at and enjoying a physical activity.
- Tell students about how adolescent culture values boys who are skilled in dance, gymnastics, and breakdancing skills.
- Tell students about the value adolescent girls and adult women find in participating in basketball, softball, and soccer programs.

Why Are So Many Professional Hockey Players Born Early in the Year?

In *Outliers* (2008), Malcolm Gladwell describes a situation that at first glance has no logical explanation. He notes that the birthdays of elite ice hockey players follow this pattern:

- 40%: January–March
- 30%: April–June
- 20%: July–September
- 10%: October–December

Why would this discrepancy occur? After all, the month of your birth should not affect your achievement as an adult athlete.

Gladwell explains, however, that in Canada, children play on age-group teams, which are determined by year of birth beginning in January. As you know, there can be large differences in children's growth and development in one year's time. Consequently, children ice hockey players born in the first few months of the year are typically larger, stronger, and more physically mature than those born in the last few months of the year. When children are 8 and 9 years old, coaches select the best players for traveling all-star teams; at that age, the "best" players are typically those who are more physically mature. The all-star teams get better coaches and practice at least twice, if not three times, as often as regular teams. By adolescence, children who have been on traveling teams have had so much more practice and coaching that they are, in fact, better skilled. Inequitable opportunities for practice and coaching lead to the privileging of some children over others simply due to the month of their birth.

- Look up local sport leagues and ballroom, folk, and square dance clubs, and tell children about them.
- Encourage children to watch television programs including men dancing and women playing sports.

Teach children to stand up to stereotypes and to not let stereotypes influence what they want to do and enjoy. To do so, you can explain the history of sports and show how cultural norms have changed over time. Once it was believed that girls were frail and that competition was harmful to their sensitive natures—an idea that sounds absurd today. In class discussions, explicitly critique stereotypes. You can tell children stories about individuals who have refused to let stereotypes stop them. Most importantly, you can establish high standards for everyone regardless of the activity and insist that children meet these standards.

Teach a Foundation of Skills

Probably the best way you can battle stereotypes is to teach an inclusive curriculum in which all children achieve the grade-level outcomes of the National Standards. The goal of the elementary curriculum is to develop the foundational skills, knowledge, and confidence to enable children to enjoy a lifetime of healthful physical activity (SHAPE, 2014). In part, this means focusing on basic skills used across major sports and physical activities, such as catching, throwing, and striking. Team sports are popular activities for children and adolescents, with opportunities for participation being available in intramural, interscholastic, and community sport programs.

Elementary physical education, however, must prepare children for more than team sports. While adults can participate in basketball and softball leagues across much of the country, most adult forms of recreation center on fitness activities, social dance, tennis, racquetball, swimming, golf, and outdoor activities such as hiking. Consequently, the elementary program also needs to teach the skills that will support participation in individual sports, dance, outdoor activities, and fitness activities. If children are taught the skills and tactics of only basketball, soccer, and softball/baseball, it leaves them with a very narrow range of physical activities in which they have a background that will support further learning and participation as adults. Moreover, as Gard (2006) argues, our job is not to offer only those activities stereotypically associated with physical education as a male domain, but to expand the possibilities for all children.

Most significantly, elementary physical education needs to teach physical activities that are meaningful to all children. A curriculum that teaches only the major team sport skills is not respectful of the diversity among children in a school. As stated in the National Standards document, "SHAPE America also considers the traditional (and gendered) team sport curriculum to be a concern for the profession. The evidence clearly indicates that this type of competitive sport curriculum alienates many students, particularly girls and less-skilled students" (SHAPE, 2014, p. 10).

Favorite activities for many girls and African American boys are gymnastics and multiple forms of dance. One of the authors taught in a school with a 100% African American population. She found that 20% to 25% of second-grade boys could perform back handsprings—an advanced gymnastics skill the teachers could add to the lessons for those children ready to improve these skills because these teachers were skilled spotters and experienced gymnastics teachers. Even a cursory

Mirrors and Windows

A good metaphor to help guide curriculum is the idea of providing mirrors and windows. This concept originated in children's literature. The idea is to provide books in which children can see themselves mirrored in the story—that is, books about their culture. At the same time, you also want to provide books that serve as windows looking at other cultures (Purcell Cone, 2000).

The same metaphor works in physical education. You want to provide mirrors, which are physical activities important to the children prior to entering your program. At the same time, you must provide activities they have not yet experienced that represent windows for opening up a whole new world of physical activities that they can find meaningful.

glance at television offerings shows the popularity of hip hop, street dancing, social, and ballroom dance in music videos and competitions for adolescents and young adults. The physical education curriculum isn't about which activities the teacher enjoys; it's about what interests the kids.

It has been our experience that children will enjoy *any* well-taught physical activity. If the teacher is enthusiastic, makes connections to their lives, and explains how the activity can be appropriate, relevant, and enjoyable for them, then children will value the content.

What If I Have Only Limited Time per Week?

If your time with the children is limited, there are regional differences you might want to consider. Ask yourself, "What are the primary physical activities and recreational opportunities in my region of the country for children, adolescents, and adults?" Volleyball is a major sport for males and females in Hawaii, the West, and beach communities. Ice hockey is a major sport in New England and upper Midwest states, with recreational leagues available for males and females of all ages. Field hockey is a major sport for Pakistani and Indian boys and in the Northeast for girls; women can continue to participate in recreational field hockey leagues once they leave school. Many children play Rollerblade hockey with friends after school. Consequently, teaching children how to dribble, pass, and hit with hockey sticks is critical in those areas of the country or in ethnic communities in which hockey-type sports are important. In contrast, if you work in a different region of the country and have only a limited number of days per week for physical education, hockey skills are far less important.

Create an Affirming, Inclusive Community in Which Diversity Is Respected, Accepted, and Valued

Inclusion

Being sure that children feel included and respected in your class is critical. No one wants to feel excluded and unwanted. No one wants to be treated with disrespect. Unfortunately, children often do feel alienated in physical education. There is no doubt that children are sometimes mean and hurtful to other children, especially to children who are different in some way. To have a classroom where all children feel welcomed and valued, you must teach children how to be inclusive and respectful.

Research on teachers in urban schools in low-income areas revealed that successful teachers require students to get along and treat everyone with respect (Flory & McCaughtry, 2011). Their success at flattening student hierarchies (i.e., not letting students with high status and power dominate) and teaching students to behave respectfully has resulted in fewer discipline problems and more satisfied students.

One teaching strategy used to promote an inclusive classroom is class discussions. Following are several potential discussion topics:

- Ask the children to think about a time when they were excluded and to describe how they felt. Make a class list on one side of a poster board. Then ask students to think about a time when they were included and describe how that felt. Make a class list on the other side of the poster board. Post the list on the wall.
- Ask children to identify body language used by children that excludes other children or makes them feel excluded.
- Ask children to think about a time when they were excluded or left out because they were different in some way and to describe (verbally or in writing) how this experience felt. Alternatively, ask children to imagine how they would feel if they were excluded because they were different in some way and to describe these feelings.
- Ask children what they can do to make their class welcoming to everyone. Make a class list and post it.
- Ask children why it is important to include everyone, regardless of differences, and how that practice might benefit them in physical education classes as well as in school in general.

Teach Children to Value Diversity and Learn to Work Respectfully with Everyone

In addition to learning how to be inclusive, children need to learn the benefits of diversity and the ability to work respectfully with everyone. We live in a multicultural, diverse world, and to be educated and flourish, you need to understand diverse people and be able to work with people who are different from you. There are very few jobs in which people work in isolation. Almost all jobs require people to work collaboratively with people who have different talents, perspectives, values, knowledge, and beliefs. People who have different talents and perspectives may make different contributions to the task or job and contribute to a more productive product or environment.

Learning to appreciate diversity and to work respectfully and cooperatively with everyone begins in elementary school. To accomplish this goal, as a teacher you need to include partner and group work in your lessons and to explicitly teach the social, emotional, and attitudinal aspects of successful group work. To supplement your material, you can teach children these precepts:

- It can be fun to work with different people.
- You can learn interesting things from different people.
- Learning to work with different people is an important skill in the workplace.
- A good life skill is to learn to work productively with children of different genders, races, and ethnicities.

Selecting Partners and Groups

One of the best ways to teach children how to work with everyone is for the teacher to select partners and groups and to ensure that everyone gets the chance to work with everyone else. To help you understand why this is a valuable idea, we describe the experience of Dianna Bandhauer in selecting groups, including how, across a 10-year period, she came to believe that teachers should always select partners and groups.

Dianna's Story

When I first started teaching, I would say, "Get in a group," and I would specify the number of group members. I found that certain students would always be excluded. I would have to help them "beg" to be in a group.

Because no one should have to beg to be in a group, I started saying students could not tell a person no when they asked to be in a group unless they could give a reason that was related to class work, such as "When you work with me, I end up getting in trouble," or "When you work in a group, you argue all the time, and we lose playing time." They could not say anything hurtful or mean, such as "We don't like you."

I then noticed that students would sometimes see a student coming up to them and quickly turn their backs or even run away. I would hear reasons like "We already have five," or "Go ask them." I would see students still having to beg to be in a group. If one group member was willing to let them in the group, I would see the other members make faces at both of them. Because children were giving inappropriate reasons for not letting people in the group, I made a rule that if someone does not let you in a group, come tell me. This didn't work, either. Everyone blamed everyone else for not letting him or her in the group. No matter how much I tried to appeal to their sense of fairness, they just would not allow those children they deemed "social outcasts" in their group without some sort of resistance.

I then decided I would be responsible for forming all groups. I told the students that this was our class family and they needed to learn and expect to work with anyone. I would select groups in a variety of random ways, such as their birth month, birth dates (e.g., those born on the first through the fifth day of any month), a letter in their first name, a letter in their last name, and so on. It was funny watching them try to predict how I was going to group them because they were going to try to "bust" my system.

Initially some students resisted. If they made remarks or faces about any member of their group, I kept them with the same group until they finally realized this would be their group until the person they were treating badly told me that their group members had all stopped being mean.

In addition, I still saw them "picking" teams at recess. I made it a school rule that they were not allowed to pick teams at recess in a way that made someone be picked last. I asked the kids to tell me how they could pick teams. They suggested by birthday, such as January to May on one team and June to December on another; by a letter in their name; by clothing items, such as a shirt with buttons, a belt or no belt; and by the color of something they were wearing. I said they could stand by someone who was on their team yesterday, and then those two would be on opposite teams today. They also suggested the teacher select the teams.

I elicited the aid of the teachers to enforce the rule. If the children got caught picking teams, the game would be over and they would have to play something else.

Now I don't have to be so dramatic about the randomness of the groups. I can pick someone who is next in line, put skilled players together, or use the old random techniques. I still see a little resistance now and then. When I do, the class gets a 3-minute lecture on the rule that you must treat everyone

Class Discussions About the Benefits of Playing with Different Children

When you have children work with everyone in the class, you can help them learn to value this experience by discussing the benefits of working with someone new. It can also help if you discuss what wasn't good about their experience with their partners. Some children don't realize that they're behaving in ways that other children don't like. Once they hear their classmates discuss poor partner behaviors, they learn to change how they're acting. Following are children's answers to three questions during class discussions.

What Is Good About Working with Someone New?

- I found someone who was really interested in the activity and was good at cooperating.
- I learned to respect the ability of those I do not normally play with.
- I met some people who try harder than others.
- The girls were better than I thought.
- I learned some people are more competitive.
- It was nice because the new person welcomed me in a friendly manner.
- I found out that some people are more skillful than I thought.
- I found a new friend.
- You get good and different ideas from working with different people.
- I met people who were nicer than I thought.
- I learned people could do more than I thought they could.
- I found that your attitude influences others.

Is There Anything Negative You Discovered?

- Some people can't stand it when others make mistakes.
- Some people are rude.
- Some argue too much.
- Some make faces at a new partner.
- Some are not honest about the rules.
- Some people fool around and think it's funny.
- Some are less interested in the activity.
- Some people can't get along with you or someone in the group.
- Some are meaner than I thought they would be.
- Some don't pay attention to the assignment.
- Some yell at you.
- Some are too bossy.
- Some won't try.

What Do You Think You Can Do When Things Are Negative Between You and Your New Partner?

- Nicely tell them to stop doing it.
- Tell them how they're making me feel.
- Ask them what's wrong and why they don't want to try.
- Maybe they don't know what they're doing, so tell them nicely. Like, say, "You sound like you're yelling at me."
- If they're being bossy, ask them when it will be my turn to be bossy or if we can just work together.
- Say, "I'd rather not argue. Can we do this without arguing?"

SAFETY AND LIABILITY 12.1

Increasing Safety and Decreasing Risk of Liability: Guidelines Relevant to Content in this Chapter

In this box, we discuss specific guidelines built on information discussed throughout this text on professional standards of practice, negligence, and liability. The goals of these guidelines are to increase children's safety and decrease teachers' risk of negligence and liability.

- Following accepted professional practice and thus decreasing risk of liability requires that "the curriculum specifies equitable instruction and participation with regard to students' individual needs. Respect for diversity is taught and practiced" (National Association of Sport and Physical Education [NASPE], 2010, p. 5).
- Equitable opportunities are required by law. In 1975, the Education for All Handicapped Children Act (P.L. 94-142) was passed into law. It has been revised six times and has evolved into the Individuals with Disabilities Education Improvement Act (IDEA). What is critical about IDEA is that children can no longer be segregated from the general education curriculum based on a disability. Instead, children must be educated in the least restrictive environment based on an evaluation and the development of an individual education program. Teachers must differentiate instruction and modify equipment to meet the needs of all children, including children with disabilities, in the least restrictive environment.
- We discuss ways to differentiate instruction and modify equipment elsewhere in the text. In this chapter, we discuss these topics in the section ***Modifications: The Duct Tape and Velcro Approach***.

with respect even if you don't like them. In addition, because we so rarely have problems now, I have to bring up the topic of how children feel about being picked last or having to beg to be in a group and discuss it as something that happens in other schools. We then have a class discussion about why they think that is not right.

Modifications: The Duct Tape and Velcro Approach

For all children to feel included, you must modify activities to meet their diverse needs. It is critically important to modify activities so that all children are challenged and can be successful, and there are various ways to differentiate instruction to accomplish these goals. In this section, we talk about the issues of diversity related to inclusion and the attitudes you need to teach children that will support their willingness to work with diverse children and modify tasks to meet everyone's needs. We call this the **duct tape and Velcro approach** after the presentation of a recreational therapist that we heard at a conference. We tell his story here.

Several years ago, we attended a state convention session on therapeutic recreation in which the presenter was explaining how to modify equipment so that people with disabilities could enjoy outdoor adventure activities, including kayaking and Project Adventure ropes courses in which individuals climb up to high platforms, cross rope bridges, and slide down ziplines. We were impressed by his slides showing how he had found ways to modify equipment and work with peer assistants to enable children and adolescents with disabilities to enjoy challenging outdoor adventure activities. Although we regrettably do not remember his name, we never forgot his approach. He said, "With Velcro and duct tape, I can modify any equipment to make outdoor activities accessible."

When working with children with diverse abilities, not only do we find the duct tape and Velcro mindset helpful for us as teachers, but we also find it helpful to teach to the children. The duct tape and Velcro approach encourages you to never give up on finding ways to make games and activities inclusive. It is an approach that shouts, "We can figure out a way to make this work, and we won't let traditional ways of doing things get in our way or block our thinking!" If you teach children that it's fun and challenging to invent modifications, this perspective will help them view inclusion positively.

As an example, **Table 12.1** describes a set of fundamental locomotor patterns for children who use wheelchairs. You can integrate this content into your lessons to develop skills needed for children who use wheelchairs. Dr. Margaret Stran, a Paralympian in wheelchair basketball and a physical educator, helped us develop this list.

Name-Calling

Another important step in creating an inclusive environment is to stop actions that exclude and degrade children. At the top of this list is name-calling. When children call other children names, their intent is to degrade or hurt the other child. According to Gordon (1994), there are two kinds of name-calling. The first is what are known as the "four-letter words." The second is cultural and linked to race, gender, physical and mental abilities, or ethnicity; these names are meant to be insulting by implying that there is something wrong with a cultural group and that it is degrading to be part of or like that group.

Name-calling is a form of harassment, and one that can quickly escalate to violence. Schools and teachers are responsible for providing a safe environment free from harassment, so it is critical to stop name-calling. Name-calling, while common, is not something you should assume is simply part of childhood and will go away on its own.

Teach Children that Name-Calling Is Unacceptable

The first step in stopping name-calling is to teach children that name-calling is mean and hurtful. Children need to know that they always have the right not to like someone, but they do not have the right to be disrespectful and hurtful. Everyone has the right to be treated with respect. Consequently, name-calling is unacceptable.

Table 12.1 Fundamental Skills for Children Who Use Wheelchairs

Body Aspects	Space Aspects
Traveling on smooth and rough surfaces	Traveling forward and backward
Getting in and out of the chair	Traveling on straight, curved, and zigzag pathways
Traveling over curbs	Traveling on large and small curved and zigzag pathways
Wheelies	Traveling uphill and downhill
Tilts and hops	Maneuvering to travel sideways
Pushing with two and alternating hands	
Grasping, catching, and picking up objects still and while traveling	
Throwing, shooting	
Striking with hands, rackets, hockey sticks, foam plastic disks with handles, and children's golf clubs	
Dribbling with hands	
Kicking (using the chair frame, foam plastic disks with handles, hockey sticks, or plastic pipes attached to chair; you may need a larger ball)	
Effort Aspects	**Relationships Aspects**
Traveling and stopping	Stopping near and far from objects
Traveling at slow, medium, and fast speeds	Traveling under, over, around, and through objects
Accelerating and decelerating	Traveling in relation to moving objects such as balls
Traveling with bound and controlled free flow	

Although most of the time teachers deal with name-calling when it occurs, it helps to teach the children about this behavior before you need to deal with a name-calling incident. At the beginning of the year, have a class discussion about name-calling. Assume that children want to be good and want to learn how to be good (even though they sometimes misbehave and say hurtful things). In turn, it's your job to teach them how to treat other children in kind and caring ways—the same way that they want to be treated. In other words, teach the "golden rule": Do unto others as you would have others do unto you. The golden rule is, in one form or another, part of all major religions and is something parents and teachers spend considerable time teaching children. It is the basis for a civilized society.

Potential topics in the discussion of name-calling include these questions:

- How do you feel when someone calls you a name?
- How do you feel when you hear someone calling your best friend or your brother or sister a name?
- How do you feel when you call someone a bad name?
- How do you feel when someone calls you a bad name and the teacher says to ignore him or her?
- Why is name-calling bad?

It helps to remind children that people who are the frequent victims of name-calling will remember the hurt for a long time. In addition, name-calling can escalate into fighting.

What to Do When You Hear Name-Calling

The first step when you hear children engaging in name-calling is to interrupt and stop the behavior. You can say, "Excuse me," or "I don't like to hear that," or "I heard that—we don't allow name-calling in this school." If possible, discuss the incident with the children immediately. If this is not possible, tell the parties involved, "We will talk about this after I get the class working on the next task [or after class]."

In this discussion, you need to begin by finding out both sides of the story. Remember, you have heard only the tail end of a long incident, so start asking questions and listening non-judgmentally. Ask, "Why did you call him or her a name?" Children call each other names for a variety of reasons. For example, this behavior may result from an inability to communicate what is truly bothering them. Maybe the child stole his or her chips at lunch or shoved or kicked the name-caller, and the child retaliated by name-calling. Often students resort to name-calling because they are frustrated with the situation and do not have the appropriate social skills to talk to those who are upsetting them.

It is critical to get the whole story. You might need to check with the classroom teacher or other children to get the real details. Sometimes children who are victims of name-calling are persistently annoying or harassing classmates but do not recognize that they are doing so. Consequently, they may not have many friends and feel alienated. In these instances, you need to help that child learn to behave in ways that won't annoy other children.

The reverse also might be true. The children being called names might not be doing anything wrong, but other children don't like them because they are different in some way. Children may call them names because of their race, ethnicity, disability, economic status, lack of nice clothing, lack of a fashionable hairstyle, looks, size, or behaviors that don't match strict gender stereotypes, such as a boy who is not skilled at competitive team sports or a girl who is.

Once you find out the whole story, you need to take action. If both children are guilty of misbehavior, then you need to punish them both or ask if the problem is solved and no punishment is therefore necessary. Children need to know that even when provoked, they cannot retaliate and that you will not tolerate name-calling.

When Name-Calling Is Racist, Sexist, Ableist, or Homophobic

Times when children use racist, sexist, ableist, or homophobic slurs or jokes can be difficult for teachers. Such behavior typically takes you by surprise, and the situation between the children can be heated. First, you need to stop the behavior. It is essential that you do not remain silent, because your silence implicitly says that you support the name-calling and jokes. Stay calm and keep things light so your manner can defuse some of the tension. You are the adult, and your manner will remind the children that dealing appropriately with difficult situations means being calm but firmly in control.

Gordon (1994) explains that often children do not understand the name they are using—it's simply a bad name they've heard other children using and they know it's a bad name. She and other teachers suggest teaching children the meaning of the term, including why it is hateful. Wessler (2008) describes a program at one school with serious racial problems. In one group discussion, an African American girl explained the history surrounding the "n" word and the way it had been used to perpetrate humiliation and violence against African Americans. One white boy, who had been a leader in racist name-calling, said that her explanation helped him understand "how awful that word is" (p. 46). He then announced to his peers, "We need to change; we need to come together" (p. 46).

In all instances of name-calling, following up is the key. Ask the children if they are still having problems. Check with their classroom teachers or parents. Unfortunately, teachers won't be able to catch every instance of name-calling and other hateful behaviors—but if you don't try to catch and stop it, you won't catch anything. When you fail to stop name-calling, children will find schools to be hurtful places, and the destructive cycle of victims becoming bullies themselves will continue.

Cultural Stereotyping

Another behavior that works against inclusion and is disrespectful to peoples from diverse groups is cultural stereotyping. Stereotypes are often negative and prejudicial, such as "Obese people are lazy." Even when stereotypes are positive, such as "Asians are smart in mathematics," they are always oversimplifications and prejudice our thinking.

Teachers need to teach children about the problems of cultural stereotyping and not let them remain ignorant about different cultures. For example, many Americans know little about the countries of the African continent. Consequently, many children believe the stereotype that all Africans carry spears and wear costumes—a stereotype that children have seen on television. One of our colleagues, Dr. Seido Sofu, originally from Ghana, described stereotyping this way. He explained, "What if someone came to study the United States on only one evening, Halloween? That person would assume that all American children and many adults dress in strange costumes all the time, when in fact it only occurs on special occasions. The same is true in Ghana. Sometimes we dress in our traditional costumes for special occasions; however, we typically dress in much the same way as Americans in comparable climates."

Tales from School

Back in the '50s when I was in elementary school, we lined up every morning waiting for the principal to open the doors. I raced to school and tried to be first in line every day. There was a boys' line and a girls' line. When boys misbehaved, they were forced to stand in the girls' line. As a girl, I remember feeling deflated and inferior when this happened—embarrassed about being a girl. The biggest punishment the teachers could think of was to humiliate a boy by making him stand in the girls' line—a line I had raced each day to lead. Did the teachers mean to degrade the girls? I don't think so, but they did, and, at some level, we knew it.

Teach Children to Be Aware and to Take Action When They Witness Injustice

Most children have an acute sense of fairness and do not want to see other children treated unfairly. Even so, they do not always understand what constitutes injustice. Just as with cultural stereotyping, teachers need to teach children about injustices. Have a class discussion about behaviors and comments by asking questions such as these:

- Is it okay to tease a kid because he or she is fat?
- Is it okay to whisper behind a boy's back, telling everyone that he's "gay" because he's not good at sports?
- Is it okay to call a girl "butch" because she is good at sports?
- Is it okay for everyone to ignore a kid because he or she dresses in clothes that aren't stylish?
- Is okay to use racial slurs even if you heard them on television and they were made by a person of that race?
- Is it okay to use put-downs as jokes even if you hear comedians on television modeling that kind of humor?
- Is it okay to call someone a "retard" because he or she doesn't always know the answers or misses the ball sometimes?

A Story About Standing Up to Injustice: Strength in Numbers

Beyond responding individually, we need to help children not become silent bystanders when other children do hurtful things. Wessler (2008) tells a story that teachers can use to help children learn to stand up to injustices. The teacher holds up a pencil and then suddenly breaks it. Next, the teacher holds up a handful of pencils and tries to break those but can't. At this point, the teacher says, "There is no one student in this class who can't be singled out for mistreatment and bias. And that student can be deeply hurt or, like the pencil, broken. But all it takes is a small group of you to stick together and you become too strong to be broken" (p. 48).

Once children understand the injustice of name-calling, teasing, harassment, and hurtful jokes, you need to help them learn how to deal with these situations when they occur. Most instances of disrespect happen when teachers are not around (Wessler, 2008). We need to help children stand up to harassment and disrespect in all situations.

One way to start is to hold a class discussion on how to respond to put-downs and name-calling. Have the children make a class list of what they can say back to the name-caller. Here are some suggested responses (Gordon, 1994, p. 87):

- I don't think you intended to offend me, but you did.
- Who are *you* to be criticizing me?
- I'm not ashamed.
- I don't care.
- I'm just as different as you are.
- So what?

It's difficult for adults to stop inappropriate jokes and prejudicial comments among themselves, and it will be difficult for children as well. However, all of us can work to become allies of individuals who are being targeted. Have a class discussion in which students are asked to think of things they can say to stop someone from harassing someone else. Here are some starter suggestions:

- Did you know that is a really hurtful thing to say?
- I don't like to hear that kind of language.
- Hey, that wasn't very nice.
- No. [In response to the question, "Do you want to hear what I heard about Kanisha?"]
- Give him a break.
- Leave her alone.
- I don't like those kinds of jokes.

Physical Activity Barriers

In addition to social interactions, teachers need to know and help children learn about how they are being denied equal opportunities to participate in physical activities. Oliver and her colleagues have studied several ways to teach students in physical education how to critique their experiences and identify barriers to being physically active (Oliver & Hamzeh, 2010; Oliver, Hamzeh, & McCaughtry, 2009; Oliver & Lalik, 2004). Some of their suggestions are presented here.

Have a small group discussion and then combine ideas into a class list about the following questions:

- Identify times and places where girls, less-skilled children, and children with disabilities are denied equal opportunities to participate in games and physical activities.
- Identify things that prevent you from participating in games and physical activities. What might you do to make it so you have more chances to participate?
- List times you have wanted to participate in some physical activity but couldn't. Explain why you could not participate.
- If you could make the world perfect for all children to get fair chances to participate in games, dance, and other physical activities, what would you do?
- If you could make PE (or school) a happy, safe place for everyone, what would you change?

Acquiring a Future Orientation that Encompasses Hope, Joy, and a Vision of a Better Tomorrow

It can be very discouraging to think about the extent to which we live in a world that lacks social justice, equity, and respect for diverse peoples. Even when you think about only the children in your own school, sometimes the problems they face may seem overwhelming, and you may wonder if you can really make a difference. Children can feel this way, too. They may think, "This is how it has always been, and this is how it will always be." We disagree with this perspective: We think there is reason for being hopeful and for believing that teachers can make a difference.

Change Happens

In our own lifetimes, the authors of this book have witnessed great changes. For example, in 1965, schools kept children with physical disabilities segregated. One boy had one arm and used a prosthetic arm and hook. The principal explained that having him in a regular school would be disturbing for the other children, so they segregated him in a special education school.

In New York State, legislators considered girls so frail and sports so inappropriate for them that our varsity athletic seasons were limited to six games. (Of course, we competed in nine different sports in a year and consequently were always playing one sport or another.) Women coaches were viewed as the greatest volunteer organization since the Girl Scouts because they were not paid to coach, although men were. Things are different today because many individual teachers and coaches worked for change.

You Can Make a Difference

We have witnessed many teachers step up to the challenges they face with optimism and hope that they can make a difference—and they have, in fact, done just that. The longer you teach, the more skills you will develop, and the more you will be able to effect change in your school. Although you may not have the community and school contacts to create change in your school when you first begin to teach, once you have taught a few years, you can become a leader in your school. When all teachers work together to solve a problem such as exclusion, harassment, or bullying, they can make a difference in their school climate and in the lessons that children learn. Part of creating change in a school is political.

Even for beginning teachers, one way of creating change in a school is to make a difference in the lives of individual children. Research on gifted African American students who were underachieving found that they turned their lives around because an adult—often a coach/PE teacher, mother, grandmother, or other significant adult—believed in them and told them they could succeed (Hebert, 1995). This person served as a touchstone for their transformation to the road of success.

You Can Help Children Develop a Future Orientation

A considerable body of research indicates that teachers can develop a **future orientation** in children in which they can envision a different future for themselves—a future in which they are self-directed and can have careers that are meaningful to them and productive; a future filled with possibilities, and not dead ends (Husman & Lens, 1999; Kauffman & Husman, 2004). When students acquire a future orientation, it helps them understand the usefulness of what they are doing in school now. They learn that an education can give them the skills and knowledge to enable them to meet long-term goals.

To help children develop a future orientation, you need to do the following (see **Figure 12.7**):

- Talk positively about their future.
- Ask children what they want to be when they grow up.
- Talk to them about their goals and ways they can meet their goals simply through hard work at school.
- Work with children on being resilient and bouncing back from the problems they face.
- Tell them that they can work hard and be anything they want to be.

Recall that research shows that students who do not do well in school, and who think they are not smart and unable to succeed, believe that their intelligence and physical abilities are fixed traits. We know now that this perspective is a misconception: If children can adopt a growth mindset, they can and will get smarter, will increase their skill abilities, and will be able to succeed. We know one teacher who works with children who face difficult problems at home. She tells them that their community or home situations do not control them. They may have it harder than other kids, but that simply means they need to work harder to overcome the obstacles they face. They can develop resilience, and they can set and reach their goals.

The goal of creating a socially just and caring society might seem like an endless journey. However, all we need to do is to start the journey and take it one step at a time and one child at a time.

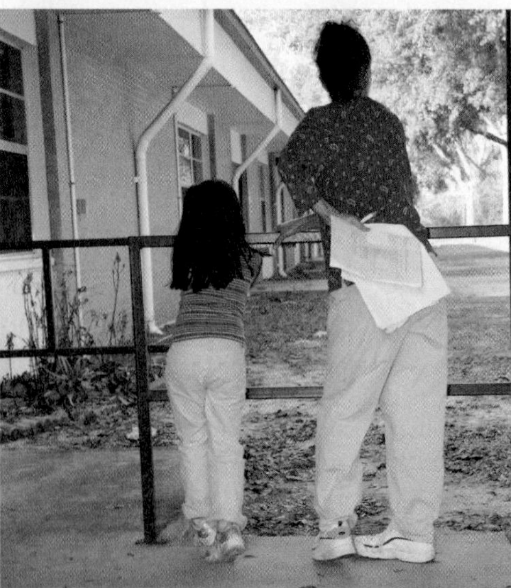

Figure 12.7 A child singing operatic-style and discussing her future as an opera singer with her teacher

Summary

It is critical for physical education teachers to create a learning environment that is equitable, inclusive, and culturally relevant to diverse learners. All children—regardless of race, gender, ability, disability, religion, ethnicity, sexual orientation, body size and weight, economic status, and nature of their family—need to learn in an emotionally safe and welcoming environment that is free from harassment.

Public schools have historically reflected the cultural values of the white European middle class. Consequently, children from different cultures and races may find some of the values in schools to be different from some of the values they have learned in their families and ethnic communities. Understanding these cultural differences will make you a better teacher.

Six characteristics of inclusive, culturally relevant, equitable classrooms are (1) cultural sensitivity; (2) caring about students' lives and caring about what they learn by setting high expectations and providing equal opportunities for all learners; (3) providing a curriculum that is relevant for diverse groups and connected to the lives of children; (4) creating an affirming, inclusive community in which diversity is respected, accepted, and valued; (5) teaching children to be aware of injustice and to take action when they witness injustice; and (6) helping children acquire a future orientation that encompasses hope, joy, and a vision of a better tomorrow.

Review Questions

1. Why do teachers need to understand and recognize cultural differences?
2. How do individualistic and collectivistic cultural values differ? Give examples to illustrate your answer.
3. Define cultural stereotyping, and explain why it can be problematic.
4. What are the issues and problems that girls face in coeducational physical education? Give examples of specific behaviors to support your answer.
5. Why do you need to be sensitive to issues related to sexual orientation and stop name-calling and jokes based on sexual orientation?
6. Discuss the implications of an anti-obesity bias.
7. What is the impact on people with disabilities of the cultural norm that assumes male elite sport is the epitome of sport performance?
8. Discuss how you can increase your cultural sensitivity.
9. Which teacher behaviors and attitudes do you need to examine to determine whether you are providing equal opportunities for all children?
10. How do sport stereotypes affect boys and girls in physical education?
11. What is an inclusive curriculum based on the goals of elementary physical education?
12. Discuss how you can teach children to be inclusive.
13. What is the "duct tape and Velcro approach"?
14. Why is it critical to stop and address name-calling? How can you achieve this goal?
15. How and what can you teach children about being aware of and then taking action when they witness injustice?

References

Bazron, B., Osher, D., & Fleischman, S. (2005). Creating culturally responsive schools. *Educational Leadership, 63*(1), 83–84.

Bigelow, B., Christensen, L., Karp, S., Miner, B., & Peterson, B. (Eds.). (1994). *Rethinking our classroom: Teaching for equity and justices.* Milwaukee, WI: Rethinking Schools.

Cornelius, C. (1999). *Iroquois corn in a culture-based curriculum: A framework for respectfully teaching about cultures.* Albany, NY: State University of New York Press.

Darling-Hammond, L. (2006). Securing the right to learn: Policy and practice for powerful teaching and learning. *Educational Researcher, 35*(7), 13–24.

DePauw, K. (1997). The (in)visibility of disability: Cultural contexts and "sporting bodies." *Quest, 49*, 416–430.

Eitzen, D. S., & Sage, G. H. (2003). *Sociology of North American sport* (7th ed.). Boston: McGraw-Hill.

Fitzgerald, H. (2006). Disability and physical education. In D. Kirk, D. MacDonald, & M. O'Sullivan (Eds.), *The handbook of physical education* (pp. 752–766). London: Sage.

Flintoff, A., & Scranton, S. (2006). Girls and physical education. In D. Kirk, D. MacDonald, & M. O'Sullivan (Eds.), *The handbook of physical education* (pp. 767–783). London: Sage.

Flory, S. B., & McCaughtry, N. (2011). Culturally relevant physical education in urban schools: Reflecting cultural knowledge. *Research Quarterly for Exercise and Sport, 82*, 49–60.

Foster, M. (1993). Education for competence in community and culture: Exploring the views of exemplary African-American teachers. *Urban Education, 27*, 370–394.

Gard, M. (2006). More than science? Boys, masculinities and physical education research. In D. Kirk, D. MacDonald, & M. O'Sullivan (Eds.), *The handbook of physical education* (pp. 784–795). London: Sage.

Gay, G. (2002). Preparing for culturally responsive teaching. *Journal of Teacher Education, 53*, 106–116.

Gladwell, M. (2008). *Outliers: The story of success.* New York: Little Brown.

Gordon, L. (1994). What do we say when we hear "faggot"? In B. Bigelow, L. Christensen, S. Karp, B. Miner, & B. Peterson (Eds.), *Rethinking our classroom: Teaching for equity and justices* (pp. 86–87). Milwaukee, WI: Rethinking Schools.

Gorski, P. (2008). The myth of the "culture of poverty." *Educational Leadership, 65*(7), 32–36.

Greenleaf, C., & Weiller, K. (2005). Perceptions of youth obesity among physical educators. *Social Psychology of Education, 8*, 407–423.

Griffin, P. S. (1983). "Gymnastics is a girl's thing": Student participation and interaction patterns in a middle school gymnastics unit. In T. J. Templin & J. K. Olsen (Eds.), *Teaching in physical education* (pp. 71–85). Champaign, IL: Human Kinetics.

Griffin, P. S. (1984). Girls' participation patterns in a middle school team sports unit. *Journal of Teaching in Physical Education, 4*, 30–38.

Hebert, T. P. (1995). Coach Brogan: South Central High School's answer to academic achievement. *Journal of Secondary Gifted Education, 7*, 310–323.

Henry, A. (1992). African Canadian women teachers' activism: Recreating communities of caring and resistance. *Journal of Negro Education, 61*, 392–404.

Husman, J., & Lens, W. (1999). The role of the future in student motivation. *Educational Psychologist, 34*, 113–125.

Kauffman, D., & Husman, J. (2004). Effects of time perspective on student motivation: Introduction to a special issue. *Educational Psychology Review, 16*, 1–7.

Kirk, D. (2007). The "obesity crisis" and school physical education. *Sport, Education and Society, 11*, 121–133.

Klug, B. J., & Whitfield, P. T. (2003). *Widening the circle: Culturally relevant pedagogy for American Indian children*. New York: Routledge Falmer.

Kozol, J. (1991). *Savage inequalities: Children in America's schools*. New York: Crown.

Kozol, J. (2005). *The shame of a nation: The restoration of apartheid schooling in America*. New York: Crown.

Ladson-Billings, G. (1994). *The dreamkeepers: Successful teachers of African American children*. San Francisco: Jossey-Bass.

Ladson-Billings, G. (1995a). But that's just good teaching! The case for culturally relevant pedagogy. *Theory into Practice, 34*(3), 159–165.

Ladson-Billings, G. (1995b). Toward a theory of culturally relevant pedagogy. *American Educational Research Journal, 32*, 465–491.

Ladson-Billings, G. (2006). From the achievement gap to the education debt: Understanding achievement in U.S. schools. *Educational Researcher, 35*(7), 3–12.

Loy, J. W., & McElvogue, J. F. (1970). Racial segregation in American sport. *International Review of Sport Sociology, 5*, 5–24.

MacDonald, D. (1990). The relationship between the sex composition of physical education classes and teacher–pupil verbal interaction. *Journal of Teaching in Physical Education, 9*, 152–163.

McKenzie, T. L. (2003). Health-related physical education: Physical activity, fitness, and wellness. In S. J. Silverman & C. D. Ennis (Eds.), *Student learning in physical education: Applying research to enhance instruction* (2nd ed.) (pp. 207-226). Champaign, IL: Human Kinetics.

McKenzie, T. L., Sallis, J. F., Nader, P. R., Broyles, S. L., & Nelson, J. E. (1992) Anglo- and Mexican-American preschoolers at home and at recess: Activity patterns and environmental influences. *Developmental and Behavioral Pediatrics, 13*, 173–180.

National Association of Sport and Physical Education (NASPE). (2010). *Opportunity to Learn: Guidelines for Elementary, Middle, and High School Physical Education: A Side-by-Side Comparison*. Reston, VA: Author.

Nilges, L. M. (1998). I thought only fairy tales had supernatural power: A radical feminist analysis of Title IX in physical education. *Journal of Teaching in Physical Education, 17*, 172–194.

Noblit, G. W. (1993). Power and caring. *American Educational Research Journal, 30*, 23–38.

O'Brien, K. S., Hunter, J. A., & Banks, M. (2007). Implicit anti-fat bias in physical educators: Physical attributes, ideology and socialization. *International Journal of Obesity, 31*, 308–314.

Oliver, K. L., & Hamzeh, M. (2010). "The boys won't let us play": 5th grade Mestizas challenge physical activity discourse at school. *Research Quarterly for Exercise and Sport, 81*, 38–51.

Oliver, K. L., Hamzeh, M., & McCaughtry, N. (2009). "Girly girls can play games/Las niñas pueden jugar tambien": Co-creating a curriculum of possibilities with 5th grade girls. *Journal of Teaching in Physical Education, 28*, 90–110.

Oliver, K. L., & Lalik, R. (2004). Critical inquiry on the body in girls' physical education classes: A critical poststructural perspective. *Journal of Teaching in Physical Education, 23*, 162–195.

Owens, L. M., & Ennis, C. D. (2005). The ethic of care in teaching: An overview of supportive literature. *Quest, 57*, 392–425.

Puhl, R. M., & Latner, J. D. (2007). Stigma, obesity, and the health of the nation's children. *Psychological Bulletin, 133*, 557–580.

Purcell Cone, T. (2000). Off the page: Responding to children's literature through dance. *Teaching Elementary Physical Education, 11*(5), 11–34.

Raeff, C., Greenfield, P. M., & Quiroz, B. (2000). Conceptualizing interpersonal relationships in the cultural contexts of individualism and collectivism. In S. Harkness, C. Raeff, & C. M. Super (Eds.), *New directions for child and adolescent development* (pp. 59–74). San Francisco: Jossey-Bass.

Rothstein-Fisch, C. (2003). *Bridging cultures teacher education module*. Mahwah, NJ: Lawrence Erlbaum.

Rothstein-Fisch, C., & Trumbull, E. (2008). *Managing diverse classrooms: How to build on students' cultural strengths*. Alexandria, VA: Association for Supervision and Curriculum Development.

Sabo, D., & Snyder, M. (2013). Progress and Promise: Title IX at 40 White Paper. Ann Arbor, MI: SHARP Center for Women and Girls.

Simons-Morton, B. G., McKenzie, T. J., Stone, E., Mitchell, P., Osganian, V., Strikmiller, P. K., et al. (1997). Physical activity in a multiethnic population of third graders in four states. *American Journal of Public Health, 87*, 45–50.

Society of Health and Physical Educators (SHAPE). (2014). *National standards and grade-level outcomes for K–12 physical education*. Champaign, IL: Human Kinetics.

Solmon, M. A., Lee, A. M., Belcher, D., Harrison, L., & Wells, L. (2003). Beliefs about gender appropriateness, ability, and competence in physical activity. *Journal of Teaching in Physical Education, 22*, 261–279.

Tischler, A., & McCaughtry, N. (2011). PE is not for me: When boys' masculinities are threatened. *Research Quarterly for Exercise and Sport, 82*, 37–48.

Trost, S. G. (2006). Public health and physical education. In D. Kirk, D. MacDonald, & M. O'Sullivan (Eds.), *The handbook of physical education* (pp. 163–187). London: Sage.

Trumbull, E., & Rothstein-Fisch, C. (2008). Cultures in harmony. *Educational Leadership, 66*(1), 63–66.

Vogler, E. W. (2003). Students with disabilities in physical education. In S. J. Silverman & C. D. Ennis (Eds.), *Student learning in physical education: Applying research to enhance instruction* (2nd ed.) (pp. 83–105). Champaign, IL: Human Kinetics.

Wessler, S. (2008). Civility speaks up. *Educational Leadership, 66*(1), 44–48.

Wright, J. (1997). The construction of gendered contexts in single sex and co-educational physical education lessons. *Sport, Education and Society, 2*, 55–72.

CHAPTER

13

Managing Behavior and Misbehavior

PRE-READING REFLECTION

1. Think of a teacher you know whom students respected as a good teacher and manager and as someone who was fair to students. Which qualities did the teacher have that led to his or her reputation? What did the teacher do and say? What did the teacher not do or say?
2. Think of a teacher you know who was a weak manager, did not hold students accountable for learning, and/or did not treat students fairly. Which qualities did the teacher have that led to his or her reputation? What did the teacher do and say? What did the teacher not do or say?

OBJECTIVES

Students will learn:

1. Children need a safe, welcoming school climate with predictable rules, routines, and social norms.
2. Teachers, administrators, and parents need to work to prevent bullying by increasing their awareness of when and how bullying occurs.
3. Teachers need to encourage students to report bullying and other problems.
4. Instructional, managerial, and social task systems affect teaching.
5. Positive student–teacher relationships contribute to strong management and the prevention of misbehaviors.
6. You can prevent misbehavior problems by optimizing teacher location, minimizing transition time, using teaching routines, presenting clear expectations, and speaking often, positively, but briefly.
7. Children need to learn how rules connect to broader moral standards.
8. When children break rules, teachers must make sure the children understand what they did wrong.

KEY TERMS

Classroom ecology
Instructional task system
Management task system
Reporting
Routines
Social task system
Tattling
Trading off

CONNECTION TO STANDARDS

This chapter focuses on National Standard 4: learning social and personal responsibility and respecting self and others. It also addresses meeting the Common Core and other State Standards (CCSS) for collaboration, listening, and respecting others.

Introduction

Developing the skills of an effective classroom manager is one of the most important tasks confronting undergraduates and beginning teachers for many reasons. More than 30 years of research shows that classroom management underlies good teaching (Marzano, 2003). Teacher effectiveness, as measured by both student achievement and an external rater's assessment (e.g., principals), is higher when the teacher is a strong classroom manager. Moreover, teachers themselves rate strong classroom management as critically important. Finally, when teachers have management problems, it can lead to burnout and lack of job satisfaction.

As a beginning teacher, you may observe excellent classroom managers. Perhaps it appears as if such teachers are simply teaching and not spending time on management and misbehavior. You might even be tempted to think such teachers have no management or misbehavior problems because the children are well behaved on their own. Don't be deceived! As Tannehill, van der Mars, and MacPhail (2015) note, it is a myth that good teaching does not require good management.

In this chapter, we describe effective teachers' management skills and misbehavior techniques that you can develop. In addition, we discuss how teacher–student relationships and the school climate affect management and misbehavior, often in subtle ways. This knowledge will help you interpret students' behavior and will prepare you to prevent problems as much as possible, rather than having to react to such issues after they occur. We also discuss dealing with misbehaviors and teaching students appropriate social behaviors that are central to National Standard 4 and the CCSS for listening and collaboration.

A Safe, Caring School Climate

Making the school climate safe and caring is, and historically always has been, a top priority for communities, parents, administrators, teachers, and students (Cornell & Mayer, 2010). It is often the focus of school and district policies and is a major part of administrators' jobs. Individual teachers working alone cannot control the total school environment because it arises from interactions among the community, parents, students, teachers, superintendent, principals, other administrative personnel, and district and school policies. Nevertheless, individual teachers can and do make many positive contributions to the school climate. When teachers band together, they can be a powerful force that can make a difference in creating a positive climate.

Social and Economic Conditions

First, however, we must acknowledge that many serious social and economic conditions affect children and their families that influence children's experiences at school and, in turn, the school climate. These factors include racism, classism, concentrations of poverty, homelessness, lack of medical care, inadequate nutrition, unsafe neighborhoods, school facilities that are inadequate and in disrepair, lack of financial support for instructional equipment, and lack of qualified teachers. These conditions certainly make the lives of children, families, and teachers more complex and difficult.

Some research has found that these conditions could lead some teachers to believe they can do little to change their school climate and improve both their programs and their students' responses to physical education (Chen, 1999; McCaughtry, Barnard, Martin, Shen, & Hodges Kulinna, 2006). These teachers feel burned out and adrift without administrative support. Other researchers have studied similar settings and found the reverse—that is, teachers who are successful in meeting the challenges of dealing with children who face difficult social and economic problems (Ladson-Billings, 1994; McCaughtry, 2004).

Despite the challenges and obstacles, we have confidence in teachers' abilities to learn to be effective in even the most difficult situations. It would be unrealistic—even foolish—to assume teachers can always be successful with all children in all schools. Nevertheless, we know of too many teachers and their students who have overcome incredible odds to succeed. Their stories leave us not only optimistic, but also aware of our responsibilities to do the best that we can do for as many

Classroom Management

"It is probably no exaggeration to say that classroom management has been a primary concern of teachers ever since there have been teachers in classrooms."
—Marzano, 2003, p. 4

Experienced Teachers Talk

Three Teachers on Management

Many people come and watch me teach, both teachers and undergraduates from the local universities. It makes me mad when they say the only reason my kids are well behaved is because my school is in [the suburbs]. When I taught in the inner city, my kids were just as well behaved—in fact, better behaved. It's not the kids. Teaching kids good behaviors is establishing a program itself, just like your PE program. You can't just go in and say, "These are the rules," and expect them to behave. Kids have to be taught behavior. I used to lifeguard, and if you don't do something to that pool every day, the chemicals get out of balance. Same thing with kids.

It makes me crazy when teachers watch me and say, "Well, I like what you are doing, and your kids are working so well in small groups, but my kids would never behave this way." I just say, "Well, I spent a lot of time teaching them how to work cooperatively." And, I think to myself, "Your kids are no different from mine." To be fair, I suppose it would be the same as me going up to a basketball referee and saying, "Well, this refereeing stuff wouldn't work in my school—the students and crowd wouldn't behave this way. It works here only because your students are different." The truth is I couldn't referee a high school game. I have no idea how to referee basketball, and I would lose total control of the game and crowd (I'd probably cause a riot), and it would be my lack of ability to ref that would be the problem. I would have to learn how to ref to make it work. I can learn how to ref, and obviously many people are good refs. It is the same with cooperative group work and getting kids to work in small groups. Many teachers have learned these skills and are very successful in all kinds of schools, but you have to be willing to work at it.

We get lots of teachers come to visit our program. They all say, "Oh, your kids are so well behaved." We don't think so. But we know what goes on all the time behind the scenes, so to speak, and how we all work hard on teaching social responsibility and teaching students how to have a safe school and a positive environment.

children as we can. Curwin, Mendler, and Mendler (2008) provide a good guideline: "Realize that you will not reach every child, but act as if you can" (p. 24).

Contributing to a Safe, Caring School with Predictable Rules, Routines, and Social Norms

No one wants to work in an unsafe environment where he or she is fearful about physical and emotional safety. No one wants to feel alienated, alone, and disliked. Children and teachers want to learn and work in a place that feels welcoming—one that is safe and in which they feel cared for, comfortable, and accepted. Creating this climate is critical for learning to occur.

A safe, caring school climate has predictable rules, routines, and social norms that children understand. No one wants to be unsure about how to behave appropriately or be mystified about what is or isn't acceptable behavior in the eyes of other children and teachers. Children want to understand what teachers expect of them. They want to be confident that they know and are capable of complying with the rules, routines, and social norms of the school (Curwin et al., 2008).

Sometimes it can be difficult to think that particularly disruptive students want a structured environment with rules and positive social norms because their actions seem to indicate the reverse. To give you a way to think positively and productively, Smith and Lambert (2008) use the analogy of an "invisible contract":

> Whenever students walk into the classroom, assume they hold an invisible contract in their hands, which states, "Please teach me appropriate behavior in a safe and structured environment." The teacher also has a contract, which states, "I will do my best to teach you appropriate behavior in a safe and structured environment."...When students act out, they are really saying, "We don't have the impulse control that you have. We are acting out so that you will provide us with safety and structure—be soft yet firm—so that we can learn the behavior we need to learn to be happy and successful" (p. 17).

Teaching Caring and Social Responsibility

One way we can improve the climate of schools is by encouraging students and teachers to care about and take social responsibility for their own and others' physical and emotional well-being (Owens & Ennis, 2005). Research shows that teaching social responsibility leads to decreases in disruptive behavior (Marzano, 2003; Osher, Bear, Sprague, & Doyle, 2010). Moreover, a caring, socially responsible climate is associated with positive social interactions, less antisocial behaviors, and less bullying (Gano-Overway, 2013; Weissbourd & Jones, 2012). Teaching social responsibility is important, and there are emotional behaviors and attitudes that apply well to managing misbehavior. Here, we build on those ideas and discuss ways you can address National Standard 4.

Discussing Safety

Another way you can help improve the school climate is by teaching children specifically what they need to do to contribute to a safe school and class. Start with class discussions about what makes a school and class safe. You can begin by asking, "How do you know when a school is safe? Let's make a list." If you don't get quick responses, say, "I will start you off by telling you some of my ideas. I think a school is a safe place when

- Kids get up in the morning and don't have a stomachache because they dread what they will have to face at school or on the bus.
- Kids are not afraid to walk by someone in the lunchroom because they know others won't tease or bully them because they are different.

Bad Choices

"I have never met a bad child. I have met kids who have made bad choices." —Experienced teacher

- Kids don't worry that someone will steal their lunch money.

What else can you add?"

Next, discuss what children need to do to make a school safe. Typically, this discussion needs to include the following behaviors:

- No fighting
- No bullying
- No making threats or intimidating other kids
- No name-calling or disrespecting others
- When someone is being hurt, speaking up or telling a teacher
- When someone is causing you problems and you can't work it out alone, getting a friend or a teacher to help you
- Banding together as a group and taking a stand against hurtful behaviors, harassment, and bullying

If the children do not discuss rules or ideas you know to be important, you need to add them to the list.

Although school safety is, of course, linked to preventing violence, research shows that lack of civility in daily interactions—in the form of teasing, exclusion, and hateful language, for example—contributes more to students feeling fearful and unsafe (Cornell & Mayer, 2010). Teachers can boost school safety by working on improving the ways children treat one another.

Bullying

Recently, teachers, administrators, and researchers have begun paying far more attention to bullying as an action that makes schools unsafe and contributes to serious academic and psychological problems for both victims and bullies (Swearer, Espelage, Vaillancourt, & Hymel, 2010). Olweus described bullying as follows:

> A student is being bullied or victimized when he or she is exposed, repeatedly and over time, to negative actions on the part of one or more other students (1993, p. 9)....Bullying also entails an *imbalance in strength* (or an *asymmetrical power relationship*), meaning that students exposed to negative actions have difficulty defending themselves. Much bullying is *proactive aggression*, that is, aggressive behavior that usually occurs without apparent provocation or threat on the part of the victim (2003, p. 12).

Cyberbullying is bullying via the Internet. This type of bullying is more common with adolescents than with elementary school or younger children. The negative effects are the same with cyberbullying, but bullying over the Internet allows the bully to remain anonymous (Gibbone & Manson, 2010).

On the negative side, research shows dramatic increases in the percentage of students victimized by bullies since the 1980s (Olweus, 2003; Swearer et al., 2010). On the positive side, it shows that the actions and attitudes of teachers and principals can effectively decrease incidents of bullying. A positive school climate in which students know that teachers care about and respect them regardless of their race, gender, ability, size, sexual orientation, and religion can help mitigate the negative effects of bullying (Gano-Overway, 2013; Swearer et al., 2010; Tenorio, 1994). Moreover, research has found that students want teachers and other adults to intervene to prevent bullying (Cooper & Snell, 2003; Garbarino & deLara, 2003).

Both boys and girls bully, with boys both bullying and being victims of bullies more frequently (Olweus, 2003; Swearer et al., 2010). Approximately 80% to 85% of victims are passive and 10% to 15% are aggressive, acting themselves in negative ways that can elicit bullying from others. Research suggests that children are more likely to become victims if they have disabilities; are obese, insecure, or anxious; or have a frail appearance and lack strength (Berk, 2010; Swearer et al., 2010), findings that have been replicated in physical education research (O'Connor & Graber, 2014). Research on gay, lesbian, bisexual, and transgender students reveals that 85% have experienced bullying (Kosciw, Diaz, & Greytak, 2008). Being a victim can lead to depression, problems adjusting to school, lack of self-esteem, withdrawal, and anxiety.

In one study, 28% of middle school students said they had been bullied in physical education (Gano-Overway, 2013), with locker rooms reported as the most prevalent place for bullying to occur (O'Connor & Graber, 2014). Most disturbing was that students reported their teachers ignored or made light of bullying unless it escalated to physical violence (O'Connor & Graber, 2014). In addition, they were afraid to report bulling to teachers or parents, and many students did not assist or defend friends who were victims of bullies. Other scholars have also noted the problems of teachers failing to act when they see or hear bullying and hurtful language (Weissbourd & Jones, 2012).

Research has yet to identify the most effective antibullying programs. Some school-wide programs reduce bullying in

Experienced Teachers Talk

Listening to Children

Kids are not used to adults being that available and that open to them. Trying to build trust with me is important. I tell them they can always come to me and say, "Miss Litaker, I think there is something you need to know." And I listen to them. Teachers need to listen to them. When adults don't take the time to listen to them, it enables the bullying to continue. The messages teachers are sending are that "the kid's tattling," "you should be able to fix it yourself," and "I don't have time for that." Kids don't think adults have time for them. In their heads, it is confusing. It's a mixed message.

Experienced Teachers Talk

Bullying

Bullying is a huge problem. When teachers think about bullying, they think about the big end of bullying, but it can be very subtle. I tell kids, "Any time someone says or does something that makes you uncomfortable or is hurting you or your feelings, it is bullying."...They don't have to put up with bullying.

some contexts but less so in other contexts. This mixed bag of results arises because the causes of bullying are complex and include individual characteristics, peer groups, families, student–teacher relationships, neighborhoods, and cultural norms (Swearer et al., 2010). Peer groups, in particular, can contribute to bullying because members of some peer groups perceive bullying to be a normal way to interact with one another.

Increasing Teachers' Awareness

To decrease bullying, teachers must become much more aware of incidents of bullying, harassment, and mean behaviors (Gibbone & Manson, 2010). You must pay special attention to what happens when teachers are not around, because bullying tends to increase when students are unsupervised (Swearer et al., 2010). You need to develop observational skills that tell you in subtle ways that something is wrong. Following is one teacher's account of how she acts on her hunches about bullying:

> If I suspect any problems in a class, I talk to small groups in PE while the kids are working. I ask, "Do you have any bullies in your class?" Then I speak to the person identified and tell him or her, "Several of your classmates perceive you as a bully. Do you know why?" Sometimes they know, but often they don't have a clue about the behaviors they are doing that other kids don't like. Between talking to other kids and the kid who is causing trouble, I find out exactly what the problems are. It might be kicking other kids in the lunchroom, saying mean things, or other behaviors. So, if it isn't too serious, I say to the kid, "You need to stop. I will follow up and find out if you have stopped, and if not, you will be punished." But, if someone has been causing harm, doing something serious, or behaving negatively over a long time, I get the guidance counselor, classroom teacher, and principal involved right from the start.

Here is another account of how and why a teacher and teachers in her school learned to address bullying proactively:

> We have learned over the years how important it is to stop kids from being mean to each other. A kid being mean is either bullying or a short step from bullying. We want to stop kids from being mean before it escalates into bullying.
>
> It happens every year, and it happens in places where teachers can't hear or see it, like on the bus, in line, at recess, during lunch, and after school. So I look for it now. I pay attention to what happens when the class lines up, and I try to notice if kids try to avoid a particular kid or don't want to be near someone.
>
> I ask the kid (who is being avoided) if he or she has noticed it. Never has the kid said no. They say, "Yeah," or "I'm used to it."
>
> Then we have a class discussion. There are two kinds of kids who get picked on or stigmatized. One is the nice, quiet kid who never does anything mean to anyone else. When it is the nice kid who is being picked on, I say to the class, "Janie's mother loves her. Do you think her mother would want you to treat her like that? What did she do to you? Janie would never do that to you, so what gives you the right to treat her like that when she has done nothing wrong to you? Being mean to Janie must stop, and I will find out if it does not stop. I will call her parents and ask them if it has stopped, and I will ask her. If it does not stop, there are levels of punishment that will happen until you do stop."
>
> I have learned that there must be consequences. If you just tell them to "stop being mean," they won't. The consequences I have used are
>
> 1. Call parents.
> 2. Sit by self at lunch.
> 3. Have the classroom teacher move his or her desk by the door.
> 4. Lose a class field trip, field day, or some fun activity.
>
> Another kind of consequence I use in physical education is to assign the bully to the bullied person until the bullied person tells me the mean actions have stopped, with each instance of bullying resulting in a consequence for the bully.
>
> The next time I see Janie, I ask, "How are things going?" I can't tell you how many times I have checked back and the child says, "Half of the class came up to me and gave me a hug and said they were sorry."
>
> The second kind of kid who is a victim is one who is aggravating other kids and usually the teachers, too. When I talk to that kid, I say, "If you tell me what is going on, I can help. But if you keep being mean to other kids, I can't help you. How can I help you from being picked on if you don't respect them? You have to start respecting them, too." I ask the class, "What do you think would happen if everyone treated him [or her] nicely, and no one was mean to him [or her]?" After we discuss that, I say, "Even if he [or she] is not nice to you, you can be nice to him [or her]. Give everyone a second chance." My rule is that you don't have to like someone, but you must treat them with respect. Then I follow the same set of consequences.

Bullying, harassment, and hurtful behavior are difficult problems without simple solutions. Teachers can, however, at least listen to students, and when they hear, see, or learn about problems, respond. Lack of action implies that you don't think bullying and being hurtful is wrong or that you don't care about the victim.

Increasing Students' Involvement in Stopping Problems: Tattling or Reporting?

A second critical way to decrease bullying, harassment, and children being mean is to teach children the importance of

Experienced Teachers Talk

Dealing with Bullies

A girl came up to me and said, "I think you need to know that X is being mean to Y." Y was going up to X and saying, "Will you be my friend?" two to three times a day. And X was being mean because he could not get Y to stop. I talked to X and said, "He is really getting on your nerves. I understand, but you need to get over it. You can't be mean to him." Then I talked to Y and got him to stop.

reporting incidents of negative behavior. In today's world, it is critical that children feel free to tell an adult when something is wrong. We need to know when children are being abused, bullied, or hurt by the behaviors of others. We must encourage children to tell adults, and we must be willing to act on what we hear.

At the same time, there are negative cultural attitudes toward what is called "tattling," and no child wants to be labeled a tattletale. We suggest discussing this issue with children and defining two different actions: tattling and reporting. **Tattling** means trying to get someone in trouble who is breaking a rule but not harming anyone (Cooper & Snell, 2003). **Reporting** means trying to keep someone or something (e.g., equipment) safe from harm.

You can't simply tell children the difference between reporting and tattling. Teachers often expect children to intuitively recognize the distinction, but they don't. Instead, we need to teach these concepts just as we teach any other complex content. We need to take the time to explain the importance of reporting problems to adults, reinforce the message frequently, make connections to incidents in their lives, and give them examples and non-examples. An experienced teacher explains it this way:

> You need to teach children that they are responsible for telling you if someone is being hurt. Over the years, I have learned to say it simply in kid terms and give them plenty of examples in multiple contexts. I tell them to tell me if someone is:
>
> - Hurting you [physically or emotionally]
> - Hurting someone else [physically or emotionally]
> - Tearing something up [damaging equipment]
>
> Sometimes they head over, but turn around before they even get to me, so I go back to them later and say, "What were you going to tell me?"

Another way to encourage children to tell teachers about problems is to have a "see me" clipboard at the side of the physical education space. When a student wants to talk to the teacher about an issue, the student puts his or her name on the "see me" clipboard. This practice cuts down on unnecessary complaints but ensures children know you care about what is happening and are willing to act on problems they observe.

Classroom Ecology

The **classroom ecology** is the work environment resulting from the teacher's tasks, the students' responses to those tasks, the social interactions among students, and the teachers' response to students' responses. As a K–12 student, you observed the classroom ecology of thousands of classes. You will find, however, that the view from the other side of the desk is more complex than you might imagine. A long line of research on what is called the "ecology of the classroom" has analyzed some of this complexity. When you understand how the classroom ecology works, it will be easier for you to anticipate and prevent problems with classroom management and instill a more positive class climate.

Led by Dr. Walter Doyle (2006) in education and Dr. Daryl Siedentop and Dr. Peter Hastie in physical education, classroom ecology research has shown that two kinds of task "systems" exist: instructional and management. The **instructional task system** comprises the set of tasks for learning the lesson content, including teachers' methods of holding students accountable for learning the content (Hastie & Siedentop, 2006). The **management task system** encompasses the set of tasks and accountability measures designed to create a smoothly running, nondisruptive work environment.

Accountability drives both task systems. Indeed, students will engage in only those tasks for which they are held accountable

Encouraging Children to Tell Adults About Problems

Here are several ways teachers encourage children to step forward and tell an adult when they know about bullying and other negative, potentially aggressive behavior:

- "I know some teachers discourage tattling. I think this is a mistake. What would happen to that teacher if a kid brought a gun to school and the other kids didn't report it because the teacher said not to be a tattletale?"
- "One time I asked a student why she never told me how terrible she was being treated by her classmates. She said, 'Our teacher doesn't want us to be tattletales.' She suffered needlessly for so long. At the beginning of the year, we have a class discussion on the difference between tattling and reporting harassment."
- "You have all heard about school shootings. They have studied what happens to make kids so unhappy and disturbed that they end up bringing a gun to school to kill other kids. One thing they found was that many of them were bullied as students. That's why we need to stop bullying. Another thing they found was that the killer almost always told someone they were going to do it beforehand, either in person, on the Internet, or in a note or letter. This is why it is critical that if you hear a rumor or you hear that someone is going to bring a gun to school, you need to tell someone. We want to have a safe school and to make the school safe you have to tell when you hear something, even if you think he or she is kidding.
- "Would you want to live in a world in which I make a rule that I can do any mean or hurtful thing I want, and you are not allowed to tell anyone? What kind of a world would that be? Would you feel safe in that world?"
- "When something happens in school and teachers are not told about it immediately, I ask that class, 'How many of you knew and didn't tell?' Then we have another discussion about why it's important to tell an adult when someone is doing something that hurts someone or harms property or equipment."
- "We adopt a zero-indifference policy. Don't ignore bullying or harassment. Be clear about what is acceptable. Say, 'I don't want that word used in my classroom; it hurts people's feelings, and it's not kind.' If you hear it and say nothing, it is telling the abuser you agree with what they are doing."

SAFETY AND LIABILITY 13.1

Increasing Safety and Decreasing Risk of Liability: Guidelines Relevant to Content in this Chapter

In this box, we discuss specific guidelines built on information discussed throughout this text on professional standards of practice, negligence, and liability. The goals of these guidelines are to increase children's safety and decrease teachers' risk of negligence and liability.

- Emotionally and physically harmful behaviors, such as bullying, harassment, hazing, discrimination, and intimidation, typically happen when students are out of the sight or hearing of teachers. Reasonably prudent teachers instruct students on rules and procedures prohibiting emotionally and physically harmful behavior to peers (Hart & Ritson, 2002). This instruction includes helping children understand how and why discrimination, name calling, bullying, and harassment are harmful and teaching children strategies for treating classmates equitably. These topics are discussed under the following headings: ***Contributing to a Safe, Caring School with Predictable Rules, Routines, and Social Norms***; ***Teaching Caring and Social Responsibility***; ***Discussing Safety***; ***Bullying***; and ***Rules and Values***.
- Supervision of all children all the time will not only decrease risk of liability, it is the basis for management. Putting your back against the wall or at the perimeter of the space to keep all children in view in front of you enables you to see safety and management problems and act quickly to stop their potential escalation. This is discussed under the heading ***Teacher Location***.
- Insist children tell you if they get injured. Then follow the school's procedures and complete the school's injury report forms. Keep these records. We recommend keeping a copy for yourself. We discuss this under the heading ***Injuries***.
- The routines and rules discussed in this chapter under the following headings are designed specifically to maintain a safe environment and decrease risk of liability: ***The Stop Routine***; ***The Stop-with-a-Ball Routine***; ***The Loose Ball Routine***; ***Carrying Gymnastics or Other Heavy Equipment***; and ***Entering and Leaving the Physical Education Area*** (which discusses the transfer of authority between the classroom teacher and the physical education teacher).
- "The use of corporal punishment makes physical educators and coaches vulnerable to litigation and should be avoided. This includes the prescription of exercise, such as laps and push-ups, for discipline or punishment purposes" (Hart & Ritson, 2002, p.55).
- A position statement by the National Association of Sport and Physical Education (NASPE) defines professional standards of practice clearly: "Administering or withholding physical activity as a form of punishment and/or behavior management is an inappropriate practice" (NASPE, 2009, p. 1).

by the teacher (Hastie & Siedentop, 2006). If the teacher holds students accountable for management but not learning, then the instructional task system is suspended. Students appear to be on task and well behaved but are not focusing on learning.

The suspension of the instructional task system is, unfortunately, all too common and has been well documented by research in physical education and classroom subjects (Ennis, 1995; McNeil, 1986; Rovegno, 1994; Siedentop, Doutis, Tsangaridou, Ward, & Rauschenbach, 1994). The management task system becomes more important to teachers than the instructional task system when school administrators and teachers assign the greatest value to control and well-behaved students. In turn, teachers respond with an unstated contract with students: "If you don't cause problems, even though the class is boring, I will not make you work hard or hold you accountable for learning difficult material." Hastie and Siedentop (2006) call this "trading off," "where teachers negotiate with students to produce the necessary cooperation in the managerial system by reducing the demands of the instructional system" (p. 216). Obviously, **trading off** learning for management is not in students' best educational interests.

How Negotiations Occur

When students and teachers trade off, they engage in subtle, often nonverbal negotiations about instruction and management task demands. The result is that students modify tasks in ways not intended by the teacher (Doyle, 2006; Hastie & Siedentop, 2006). Thus, the task assigned by the teacher is not the actual task done by the students. Sometimes students make tasks easier. If the task places them at risk of embarrassment, they may modify the task to make it less risky. They may also modify tasks to make them more fun, challenging, or less boring.

At the same time, teachers set standards for what they are willing to accept from students working on a task. If students have made the task easier and the teacher accepts this modification, the students have negotiated lower accountability standards. Thus, regardless of the task assigned, the actual instructional task is what the teacher holds students accountable for completing.

How to Improve Accountability and Maintain the Instructional Task System

Several techniques can help you improve accountability:

- Describe the task in detail, and set clear expectations so that students have no doubts about what you expect them to do. In research on students' perceptions, students reported that good teachers were clear and specific about what students needed to do and the criteria they needed to meet (Williams, 1993).

- Remember the slogan, "If you say it, get it." In other words, when you give a task and the criteria you will use for accountability, you must make sure the children meet the criteria. Do not move on until you get complete compliance. A simple example is telling children to gather in front of you and sit down. Once you make this statement, wait until all children have done just that before moving on.
- Watch for subtle signs of children testing you (i.e., trying to negotiate less accountability). This can be difficult to notice. Returning to the preceding example, perhaps children will gather in front of you, but one or two will stand in the back listening attentively. Unfortunately, they are testing you to see whether you will hold them accountable for doing what you said. When you repeat, "Sit down," they will respond by kneeling, again testing you. Be firm and persistent—if you say it, get it. Don't go on until all the children are sitting appropriately. Remember, children want teachers to pass their own tests; they want to know their teacher is consistent and fair. They are not intentionally trying to anger you, but rather are seeking the limits within which you work and the extent to which you will negotiate task demands.
- Differentiate instruction by providing choices for students so that they can work at the level of accountability that is right for them. Differentiating instruction is critical for preventing misbehavior because when students are afraid of failing, looking foolish, or losing their dignity, they are likely to be disruptive (Curwin et al., 2008).
- Teach children appropriate ways to modify tasks to make the tasks easier (ME) or more difficult (MD), along with ways to judge whether their choices are based on improving their learning or just trying to negotiate less work. You want children to be motivated to learn and enjoy the work; they will be more likely to do so if the tasks are not boring or frustrating for them.
- Follow the old armed forces rule of thumb: "Never give a command you know won't be obeyed." If the criteria for accountability are too hard, too risky, or potentially embarrassing, then students are likely to modify the task. Don't back yourself into a corner by making demands that are unrealistic.

The Social Task System

Research in physical education has also uncovered a social task system that can either support or disrupt the instructional and management task systems. The **social task system** consists of students' attempts to interact with their peers during the physical education lesson. Talking with peers is often part of group work in physical education, such as when groups or partners are designing dance, gymnastics, jump rope, and fitness routines, and when groups are designing games or planning game tactics. Moreover, there are times during physical education when students can talk with their friends without being off task, such as when they are carrying equipment out to the field.

Clearly, if students socialize instead of practicing, it can disrupt both the management and instructional task systems. However, research has shown that the student social system can contribute positively to the instructional task system in units such as Sport Education and Adventure Education (Carlson & Hastie, 1997; Hastie, 1996). In these activities, students work in groups to solve problems (in the same ways this text suggests). They play key leadership roles and take responsibility for their group completing the learning tasks assigned. Thus, the physical education content and student responsibilities for their groups successfully drive the management and instructional task systems.

One implication of the research is to allow for social time that does not disrupt the lesson. The social system is important to students, and physical education is one of the few times during the day in which children can talk with their peers. If there are times when children can work productively and talk, such as when they are gathering equipment, let them do so.

Student–Teacher Relationships

Research in both classroom and physical education settings suggests that positive relationships between teachers and their students are critical for management and handling misbehavior. At the heart of such relationships are respect, caring, being willing to listen, and maintaining the students' dignity at all times (see **Figure 13.1**) (Curwin et al., 2008; Wallace & Chhuon, 2014).

Several groups of researchers decided to ask students what made a teacher good at class management and handling misbehavior (Cothran, Kulinna, & Garrahy, 2003; Deiro, 2003; Williams, 1993). High on students' lists were teachers who treated students with respect. Rather than yelling, pulling rank, being authoritarian, berating students, and humiliating students, teachers who were successful in the eyes of students treated them like adults. They spoke with students in a respectful and considerate tone of voice. They took seriously what students had to say. When they talked with students, they listened carefully, assuming that the students had important information to contribute to the conversation. They treated students with dignity.

According to these research findings, students did not expect teachers not to punish them when they broke a rule.

Students believed good teachers held high standards and did not let students walk all over them. They were firm, but kind.

Figure 13.1 Listening and caring

Courtesy of John Dolly

Students' Dignity

"There is no better way to damage students' dignity than to embarrass them in front of their friends, scold them in public, or have them fail in front of the class." —Curwin et al., 2008, p. 30

In addition, teachers known to be good managers and disciplinarians let students know that they cared about them (Cothran et al., 2003; Deiro, 2003; Marzano, 2003; Williams, 1993). They took an interest in students' personal lives. They cared about students' learning, successes, problems, and who they were as people outside of class.

As Deiro (2003) noted, being a caring teacher does not require teachers to be permissive and sugar sweet. Teachers can show caring in many ways—for example, in brief comments before or after class or learning what students like to do in their free time and talking with them about it. Forging a personal connection and briefly chatting with a student each day about his or her life is effective in increasing the cooperation of a disruptive child (Bilmes, 2012).

Getting to know your students will also help you interpret their reactions. Researchers have found that students need to feel (1) connected to school; (2) competent enough to be successful; and (3) that they matter to others (Curwin et al., 2008). Students who feel disconnected will act out inappropriately so they will be noticed. Students who feel incompetent will give up; they think it is better not to try than to try, fail, and consequently look incompetent to peers. Students who feel they don't matter to anyone will act out by trying to take control and end up in power struggles.

Finally, teachers who are good managers and disciplinarians view incidents in which students misbehave as opportunities for teaching students about responsibility. They are nonjudgmental and understand that students make mistakes and can learn to face the consequences of their actions (Deiro, 2003).

Hellison (2003) suggests that you can expect ups and downs during the learning process, but he believes that it is critical to recognize each student as an individual with positive potential to learn to be responsible. When teachers assume the best about their students, it can help them contribute to the long-term improvement of their classrooms and students' development (Smith & Lambert, 2008).

TEACHING TIP

Advice from a Cooperating Teacher

Student teachers are often so worried about kids liking them and PE and having fun that they can't gauge the difference between that and keeping control. They are afraid to be the bad guy. They want the kids to like them, but the bottom line is your job is to keep the kids safe and to teach. For example, when a kid does something wrong, the student teacher gives the kid a second chance. Then the kid does it again, and they give the kid another chance. Then the kid does it again, and they give the kid another chance. Then things get out of control, and they have to stop the class to redirect. When they give kids too many chances, after three to four days it disrupts teaching. It's as if the kids are antelopes and you're the dying tiger. They sense your weakness.

Experienced Teachers Talk

Exceptionalities

Teachers take a lot of required courses on diversity, management, and exceptionalities, but sometimes teachers have an unwillingness to study certain behaviors and understand children with exceptionalities. I had children with autism in my classes, and it is really important to set the scene ahead of time. When I am going to change to a new unit, with a child with autism you must start the week before to set this up. You need to tell them, "When you come in next week, your partner won't be your partner. We won't be working on stations," so when they walk in and their world is turned upside down, they won't lose it.

Given the choice, we always want to prevent management and misbehavior problems rather than have to respond to such incidents after they occur. Many studies in physical education have outlined proven techniques for helping teachers prevent such problems. We describe these methods next.

An Ounce of Prevention Is Worth a Pound of Cure: Preventing Misbehavior Problems

Teacher Location

One of the oldest tricks in the book to prevent or halt off-task behavior is for the teacher to move very close to the offending child. Often that step is all it takes for the child to stop the misbehavior so that the lesson can continue without interruption.

Of course, a teacher can't be everywhere at once. The guideline for observing students—put your back against the wall or at the perimeter of the space and keep moving—works equally well with management. Researchers have noted that when teachers spend more time traveling around the perimeter and give high rates of enthusiastic feedback, students stay on task more often (van der Mars, Darst, Vogler, & Cusimano,

Experienced Teachers Talk

Making Time for Informal, Positive Interactions

I had a few children who frequently got in trouble in this one class. I decided to test an idea. I made one or two positive comments just before class or very early in the lesson to those children and found that their attitudes remained positive during the rest of the lesson (see **Figure 13.2**). It did not take a lot of time to talk to them, and what I said didn't have to be class related, and it worked.

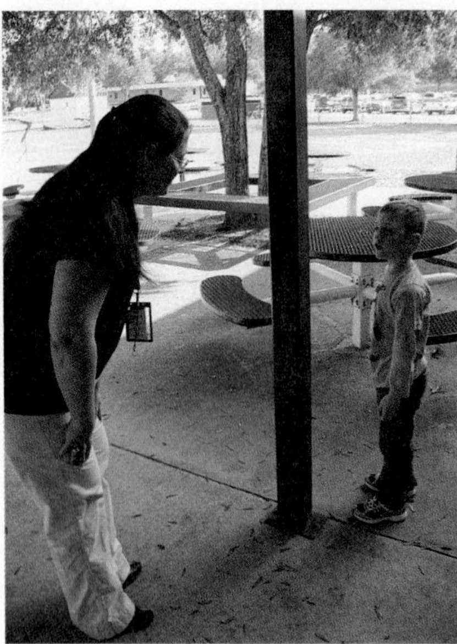

Figure 13.2 Taking time to teach a child about being self-responsible

1994; van der Mars, Vogler, Cusimano, & Darst, 1998). As you travel the perimeter, remember to scan and watch the children farthest from you—they move to the back to keep you from hearing or noticing them.

Organization Time

When students must stand around waiting while the teacher organizes the class or deals with paperwork, they are more likely to get bored, entertain themselves, and behave inappropriately. Thus, as teachers, we want to minimize the time students are not engaged in physical activity not only to increase practice and physical activity time, but also to prevent management problems. To do so, you need to plan efficient ways to deal with noninstructional tasks, such as the ones described here.

Taking Attendance

- *Inefficient:* Have children enter the lesson space in a line and then call names one at a time.
- *Efficient:* Make an attendance chart and assign students a permanent "attendance spot" at a wall or scattered in a grid. Just before the students enter class, assign them a skill to practice in their attendance spot. As the children practice, you can quickly take roll, deal with parent notes, and travel about the space commenting briefly on the children's performance or on some aspect of a child's life outside of class (see **Figure 13.3**).

> **Classroom Management**
>
> "The most effective classroom management comes in the form of strategies that prevent acting out before it occurs."—Smith & Lambert, 2008, p. 16

Figure 13.3 Taking attendance while children practice in a grid

Getting Equipment

- *Inefficient:* Have children select equipment from a bin or rack one at a time.
- *Inefficient and contributes to misbehavior problems:* Have children all race to grab equipment from the rack at the same time. This practice often leads to children bumping into each other and arguing over who gets which piece of equipment.
- *Efficient:* Have equipment out and available prior to class. Place equipment in 8 to 10 baskets or hoops (to prevent balls from rolling) spread around the sidelines or perimeter of the lesson space so children can all get their equipment simultaneously without bumping into each other.

Transitions

The transitions from one activity to another also take time that could otherwise be devoted to instruction. Different lesson activities often require different equipment, formations, and number of children in each group. For example, a lesson might include the following tasks: (1) all children in a scattered formation dribbling with their feet on different pathways; (2) partners starting at a goal line and dribbling and passing with their feet down the field; and (3) dribbling and kicking at soccer goals.

You need to know how to organize the transitions between such activities efficiently. In general, the fewer formation changes, the less time students will spend in transition. Try to plan activities that use the same formation and equipment. Try to minimize the number of times you have the children stop and wait for new instructions:

- *Inefficient:* At the end of an activity, have children put the equipment away, gather in front of the teacher, and sit and wait for everyone to finish. Then explain the next formation. Send the children to get the equipment for the next activity, get in the new formation, and sit and wait for everyone to finish. Demonstrate the new activity, and have the children begin practicing.
- *Efficient:* At the end of an activity, have the children stand with the equipment by their feet. Demonstrate the new activity in the new formation. Explain how to put away old equipment, get new equipment, get into the new

formation, and tell them to begin practicing as soon as they are in place and no other children are obstructing their practice space.

Overall, transitions need to be smooth and quick, so students maintain their focus on learning, rather than having time to get distracted or bored.

In addition, to prevent management problems, don't simply tell children where to go; you need to stand where you want the children to relocate and gesture as you demonstrate the new formation. When children change formations, they can easily become confused about where to go and how to line up. For example, if you say, "Line up on the end line," some children will not know which line is the end line. In addition, they won't know whether to spread out over the entire length of the line facing the middle of the space or whether to line up as if they were preparing to return to their classroom (where they will inevitably jockey for a position toward the head of the line).

Instead, tell *and* show students where to go. For example, before you end the previous activity, move and stand on the end line and say, "Stop and look at me. When I say 'Go,' line up on this end line [gesture with both hands pointing down the end line] and spread yourselves out equally from here [travel quickly down the line] to here, and face the center of the court [turn and point which way they will face]. Go." When you explain the new formation and demonstrate where you want the children to locate, you eliminate confusion and are able to change formations efficiently.

Routines

Routines are standard procedures you use frequently in class to organize and manage students, such as routines for lining up for a fire drill or getting out equipment. We cannot emphasize enough how establishing routines and teaching them to children will help you improve your class management. Research across a variety of school subjects, including physical education, has shown repeatedly that good teachers spend the first few days of school teaching and having the children practice class routines.

Without a doubt, the most important routine to teach is the "stop" routine. Children love to run and move, and the physical education space typically offers a wealth of temptation in this regard. Moreover, children can generate more speed and force than they can control. In other words, they can run at a faster speed than they can control. Children must learn how to stop immediately on the teacher's command. The following subsections provide suggestions for how to teach and practice a stop routine.

The Stop Routine

Select which command you will use. Many teachers simply use the terms "stop" or "freeze," whereas others use fun or catchy phrases related to their school mascot such as "Panthers, pause" (paws), play and then stop music, hit a drum, or use a "round-up" sign (making a lasso motion over your head). Some teachers clap once and have the children respond by clapping twice. Some hold up their hand, with the children responding by stopping and holding up their hands.

Tell the children the stop command, and then have them practice stopping. A suggested task progression follows for younger and older children.

Younger Children

1. *Walk and stop on spots.* [For kindergarten and first-grade children who are working with you for the first time, spread plastic spots about the physical education lesson space in a scattered formation. Have four to five more spots than children.] "Today we will work on walking and stopping in a scattered formation. When I say 'Go,' walk and stand on one of the spots with only one child per spot. There are plenty of spots, so if someone is on a spot you thought you might stand on, just look for another one. Do not touch anyone else as you are walking. Great job. Notice that you are in your own personal space, that is, the space around you that you can reach. You can't touch another child, and no one can reach into your personal space. Walk to another spot and stop. Look around and notice how you are all separated equally and no one is near any other child. We call this a scattered formation. When I say 'Go,' walk to a different spot, and stop with only one child per spot. Go. Stop. Go. Stop." [Continue several times until the children can do this easily.] (See **Figure 13.4A**.)
2. *Walk and step over spots, keep moving, and stop.* "Let's do the same task, but this time don't stop on the spot; just walk over it and keep moving to a different spot. Walk over that spot and keep walking from spot to spot [demonstrate while talking] until I say 'Stop.' This is called traveling and stopping in a scattered formation in general space. General space is the entire space in the gym (or physical education area). Go. Stop. Go. Stop." [Continue practicing until the children can do this easily. (See **Figure 13.4B**.)]

Older Children New to the Scattered Formation

1. *Stand in a scattered formation.* "Spread throughout the space so that you are not next to or touching anyone else like the children are in this illustration. [Hold up an illustration of a class in a scattered formation.] You should be standing in your personal space—that is, the space around you that you can reach. Look around and see if the class is spread out evenly in general space, which is the entire space in the gym (or physical education area). If you are not spread evenly in general space, fill the spaces. If there are clumps of children, separate. I see a clump here and a space here. See if you can move to fix that. This is called a scattered formation." [Continue several times until the children can do this easily.]
2. *Walk and stop while staying out of other children's personal space.* "When I say 'Go,' walk, and when you hear me say, 'Stop,' you must immediately stop moving, stand still, look at me, and listen. Do not stop in someone else's personal space. Walk. Stop. Walk. Stop."
3. *Walk while maintaining the scattered formation.* "Now walk about the space traveling to all areas of the space keeping the scattered formation as a class. Do not get in anyone else's personal space. Be very aware of your classmates. Try to keep evenly spread out with no clumps. Stop

(A)

(B)

Figure 13.4 (A) Kindergarteners stopping on poly spots (B) Kindergarteners traveling in general space guided by poly spots

immediately when I say, 'Stop.' Walk. Stop, Walk. Stop. [Continue practicing until the children can do this easily.] Do you know what you need to do with your body to stop safely? Great answers. Stop on both feet, feet apart for balance, and remain standing. [Some children will stop in an off-balanced position and then wave their arms (dramatically) as they fall to the floor.] We are going to practice walking and stopping still as if you were frozen. You are not allowed to 'freeze' and fall; you must remain standing." [Practice several times until all children are stopping perfectly and in a responsible manner.]

4. *Walk fast and stop.* "This time, walk faster and notice what is different about stopping when walking slow and fast. Walk. Stop. Walk. Stop. What is different in your body? [Takes more time, must move from leaning forward to standing upright, must position your feet in a slightly wider stance.] Great answers. Let's try again. Go." [Practice several times until all children are stopping perfectly and in a responsible manner.]
5. *Jog and stop.* You are doing such a good job at stopping without falling that I am going to challenge you by having you jog. What do you think you will need to do differently to stop from jogging? [It will probably take more time and space, lift the torso upright, move the feet in front of the hips, keep the feet wider apart in a stable base of support.] Great answers. Show me the stop position with your feet wide in a stable base [demonstrate while talking]. That's it. Let's practice again. Go." [Practice several times until all children are stopping perfectly and in a responsible manner.]
6. *Run at a moderate speed and stop.* [With older children or later in the year with younger children, we then practice jogging fast or running at a moderate speed working on their ability to stop quickly by lifting their torso and moving their feet in front of their hips to counteract the force of the run. During the earlier developmental phases, children lead with their heads; as they mature, they must learn how to shift from leaning forward while running to moving upright and changing direction by repositioning their torso and head. We explain how important this skill is both to their safety in class and to their abilities to play games and sports.]

The Stop-with-a-Ball Routine

When children are practicing with a ball, the stop routine some teachers use is to have children stop, sit, put the ball in their laps, and take their hands off the ball. Other teachers have them stop, stand still, and put the ball between their feet. Balls offer many temptations for children (and adults!), including dribbling, tossing, passing the ball around the waist, and sitting on the ball and bouncing up and down. Children also enjoy squishing foam balls, picking the foam out, pulling balls apart, peeling off the plastic covers, and pulling the yarn and rubber strings out of yarn and string balls. You can also teach them to stop and hold their ball without playing with it, but this will take more practice and monitoring.

The Loose Ball Routine

When children practice motor skills with balls, at times they will lose control and the ball will roll into other children's workspaces. This can be dangerous because the other group might not see the ball and might trip and fall over it. It can also be dangerous when children run into the space of another group to retrieve their ball. One routine to solve this problem is to have the children say, "Loose ball," as a signal for both groups to stop. Then one child walks and retrieves the ball, and play can continue. Another possible routine is for the child to say, "Loose ball," but not enter another group's area without their permission. The child then waits until play is finished before interrupting. In all cases, have children walk around and behind other groups to retrieve their equipment.

One dangerous response we see with loose balls is for someone to either kick or throw the ball back to the child or group who lost it. As you might imagine, kicked and thrown balls can go astray and disrupt even more children. To solve this problem, one routine is based on the idea that children cannot touch another child's or group's ball unless they pick it up, walk over, and hand it back to the original owner(s).

Bathroom Routines

You will need to establish bathroom routines. In our experience, these practices vary greatly depending on the school. Some gymnasiums have bathrooms. In other schools, the classroom teachers take their class to the bathroom before physical education. If your gymnasium has a bathroom, consider letting children decide when to use the facility. Leave a bathroom pass (some object) hanging in a prominent place. If no one is using the bathroom, a child can use the pass. Some teachers require children to ask permission first, whereas others know their children can self-regulate without much teacher monitoring.

In schools where children are to use the bathroom before and after physical education and a child asks to go during class, some teachers have the child sign a "time-out" sheet and let the child go to the bathroom. Then, when the PE teacher sees the classroom teacher, he or she informs the teacher that the child had to go the bathroom during PE and asks that the teacher ensure the child uses the bathroom before class next time.

Some children are physiologically not sensitive enough to anticipate accurately when they need or will need to go to the bathroom, and they suddenly realize they have an emergency. It is essential for teachers to be sensitive to this situation—it is humiliating for a child to have an "accident." One teacher we know says if children are doing the "pee dance," she sends them to the bathroom, no questions asked. We agree. If a child asks to use the bathroom, say yes.

Carrying Gymnastics or Other Heavy Equipment

You will also need to establish routines for moving heavy equipment. Typically, we demonstrate exactly how children are to carry and set up such equipment and establish rules such as "no carrying the mat over your head," "walk slowly," and "two children must carry each mat or piece of equipment."

Entering and Leaving the Physical Education Area

If possible, arrange for the classroom teachers to bring their classes to a designated location; the physical education teacher can then escort the children to the work area. The meeting place is where a "transfer of authority" routine must take place. The classroom teacher and the physical education teacher make eye contact to transfer authority (do not let classroom teachers drop the children off at the door and leave the area).

Meeting with the classroom teachers promotes communication about what you are teaching in physical education, how it might connect with the content they are teaching in the classroom, and how noninstructional issues, such as excuse notes, misbehavior problems, or other confidential information, will be handled. If possible, schedule five minutes between classes to allow for arrival and dismissal overlap.

Do not be afraid to ask classroom teachers to drop off and pick up their classes on time. If delays become a continual problem, keep a log and show the teacher in question how many times it happens. As a last resort, you can ask administrators to intervene.

For schools with multiple classes, you can have the children exit through one door while the children coming to physical education enter through another door. Alternatively, you can use different sides of the hallway. With multiple classes, ensure all classroom teachers remain with their classes until the physical education teachers are ready to transfer authority for everyone.

Ending Class by Lining Up

At the end of class, children need to learn to line up without pushing and remain quiet. We learned this fun technique from a colleague. When students line up to go in and they are noisy, we say, "Make a clapping line," and the children all clap. "Now make a shaking line"; the children shake their bodies. "Make a turn-the-wrong-way line"; the children turn around to face the other way. "Make a stamping line"; the children stamp their feet. "Now make a straight, quiet, shoulder-straight line." Using this method, the children will settle down without the teacher having to yell or speak negatively.

Water

Many schools allow children to bring water bottles to their classroom and to physical education. In physical education, they carry the water bottles to their work area. They may get a drink whenever they want, but it is not a "coffee break." We suggest the following rules for water bottles:

- You are not allowed to drink while walking in line (inside or outside).
- If you pour water on your head or on someone else, or share the drink with anyone, you are not permitted to bring water anymore.
- You can bring only water. (Students tend to bring sugary drinks, which attract ants and bees.)

Most teachers also allow children to get drinks at the end of class and, on extremely hot days, to drink from the fountain during class—especially if they did not bring water with them. The line walks to the drinking fountain. Students choose to stay in line or get a drink. Each child then counts for himself or herself, "1-2-3-4-5, good-bye, and stop." Those getting a drink go to the end of the line after their drink. This rule prevents pushing in line to get the child's spot back.

Lining up to get water can be a prime time for misbehavior. We know of one principal who figured out that most fights started while children waited in line for water. She then had drinking fountains installed in each classroom, which solved the problem.

Injuries

It is critical to insist that children tell you if they get hurt, no matter how slight the injury. Take notes, write down what the child says, and fill out the appropriate school forms for injuries. Note which other children might have witnessed the injury, what you did, and what the children had been assigned to do. Note whether the child was behaving appropriately or was off task when the injury occurred and what safety instructions you gave the children. Send your report to the appropriate school personnel. Keeping accurate injury records decreases risk of liability and provides protection for you if parents choose to file a lawsuit.

Practicing Routines

In the same way children must practice motor skills to learn them, so children must also practice class routines to master them. At the beginning of the year, have the children practice picking up and putting away the equipment at least five times. Practice the stop routines several times a day for the first week or two. Practice retrieving loose balls. Practice getting in a line without pushing or shoving.

Although you might worry that spending time practicing routines will unnecessarily take time away from learning, in the long term, these routines will actually increase the amount of learning time. This extra time becomes available because you will not have to remind children continuously what they should do every time you set a task. Children will know what to do, and you can spend your time on instruction.

Misbehavior

All teachers, even the best managers, will have to deal with misbehavior problems—they simply come with the territory. Of course, some schools have fewer problems than others do, but don't be discouraged when you must deal with students who break rules.

Curwin et al. (2008), who have studied misbehavior and successfully worked with teachers to improve school misbehavior, believe that there are three groups of students in a typical school:

- Seventy percent of students rarely break rules. They do not need a misbehavior plan.
- Twenty percent of students regularly misbehave. They need rules, consistent consequences, a teacher who sets clear expectations, and a teacher who discusses the reasons for rules.
- Ten percent of students cause chronic misbehavior problems. They have experienced school failure for many years, and many need professional help beyond what a teacher can provide.

Curwin et al. (2008) suggest, "The trick of a good discipline plan is to control the 20 percent without alienating or overly regulating the 70 percent and without backing the 10 percent into a corner" (p. 33). The following subsections present teaching techniques that research suggests will help you in dealing with misbehavior.

Rules and Values

Typically, teachers set four or five general class rules, often posting them permanently on a wall.

Setting rules, however, is not enough. Children need to understand that rules are not some arbitrary regulations set by teachers, but rather are connected to a set of values that make schools safe, welcoming, and productive learning places. They need to understand how rules are connected to broader moral standards (see **Figure 13.5**).

For example, one teacher has only three "rules" that are standards connected to broad values:

1. Always listen.
2. Always do your best.
3. Always treat people the way you want to be treated.

When problems arise, she discusses the specific situation in relation to one (or more) of the three standards. She explains:

> They sound simple, but you can teach and revert back to them daily—and I do. When two kids are arguing, I ask, "Were you listening? Really listening?" Kids get in arguments because they don't have the chance to talk it out. If someone is making fun of someone, I ask, "Are you treating people the way you want to be treated?" This becomes the culture in your gym. We don't have rules; we have standards. I tell them this, and I say that I try to live by these standards, too. This has always worked for me in [an inner-city school], in [a suburban school], and it works for me now as an administrator.

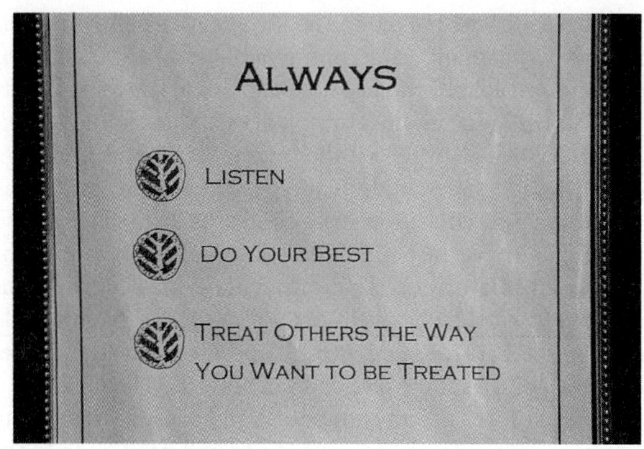

Figure 13.5 Standards

Courtesy of John Dolly

Many teachers begin the year with a class discussion in which they ask children to help determine class rules. As children identify rules, the teacher makes a list, and the class discusses how a specific rule connects to a broader principle, moral value, or positive social interactions.

The following is a sample list of broad rules and values (in italics) with possible discussion topics and more specific rules listed for each.

Treat Others with Respect by Listening Carefully

- Listen carefully to the teacher and respond appropriately.
- Listen carefully to your classmates and respond to what they said.
- Ask questions if you don't understand what the teacher or your classmate said.
- As you listen, try to understand the speaker's perspective. Try to see what happened from their point of view.

Always Doing Your Best Is Respecting Yourself

- Try new things without complaining.
- Say "I'll try," instead of "I can't."
- Try to do your best even if it is a new skill for you.
- Persist.
- Believe that you can learn if you work hard.

Respect the Class Community and Don't Infringe on Other Children's Right to Learn

- Follow directions the first time.
- Put equipment on the ground on the stop signal and during discussions.
- Listen quietly.

TEACHING TIP

Advice from a Cooperating Teacher About Rules

You have to work on management every day. Undergraduates seem to think you teach the rules on day one and students will know them. They won't. You have not given them a social context for the rules, why the rules are important, and what they mean in their lives or the lives of others.

- Wait until an appropriate time to talk with friends.
- Find good personal space for work or play.

Consequences

In most circumstances, you should try to avoid laying out a predetermined order of consequences for breaking rules. Curwin et al. (2008) recommend saying, "These are the consequences when you break a rule. One of these will happen, but there is no predetermined order. Either you or I will pick the most appropriate one, based on what will help you most." This approach enables you, or you and the child together, to select the consequences that will most assist a particular child in learning to be more responsible. Having a child sit out of physical education who *wants* to sit out is not a punishment. Including the child in the decision can help the child develop responsibility and better understand the reasons for rules.

When you don't use a predetermined order of consequences, you will need to reinforce the notion that being fair is not the same as being equal. If a child complains that his or her punishment was not the same as another child's, explain that you are willing to discuss his or her consequences and listen to other suggestions, but you are not willing to discuss other children, just like you will not talk about the child behind his or her back (Curwin et al., 2008). Finally, never threaten with a consequence you can't make happen.

The most important thing to remember about rules and consequences is that you must teach children how inappropriate behaviors are connected to broader values and moral standards. As one teacher said:

> Rules: there is more to it. It is not black and white. You don't just make a list of rules and consequences. That's superficial. That is not all that matters because the behaviors need to be taught. Consequences are not the end of the problem. Nothing takes the place of teaching them why they are in trouble and why their behavior is inappropriate. The misbehavior act itself doesn't change behaviors. It is what you say before, during, and after. You must help kids learn how to work through things.

TEACHING TIP

Advice for Young Teachers About Consequences

Every situation is different. You need to be consistent, but young teachers don't understand that being consistent does not mean "The first offense, X happens; the second offense, Y happens." There is a place and time for that, but for everyday dealings, you must look at the entire picture of what happened. A large part of the time, it started at lunch or the day before. Take the time to figure it all out. It's the same as taking an engine apart piece by piece. It takes time to take it apart until you are clear about what happened. Then you explain to the kid, "This is why you had that argument, and this is why what happened happened, and these are the consequences of what happened." This is teaching them about behaviors. If you work on this, you will get a reputation that kids can trust you. You are fair, and parents will know that you will take care of their children.

Experienced Teachers Talk

Be Clear About Misbehaviors

When you talk to a child, the child must be crystal clear about what they did to get in trouble. And there will always be another child involved. I tell them I will deal with that child, too. I tell both the child and parent this. You need to figure out exactly what happened, and then be sure the child and parents know why it happened, and then how to make sure it doesn't happen again.

> If you are willing to work on this daily, you won't have management problems. Just stop the lesson. Don't go back over the rules again and expect it to work. You need to teach them about the bigger values and standards and teach them how to behave, just as we teach them any other subject in school. If you have problems, you haven't instilled the standards in them.

Reinforcing Appropriate Behaviors

The best consequence you can use is to reinforce appropriate behaviors. When you see a problem, simply state the appropriate behavior, and praise those students who are engaging in the appropriate behavior. For example, you can say, "Look at how the children along this wall did a great job in setting up their cones and are ready to practice dribbling." This kind of statement will encourage the children who responded inappropriately to quickly get on task.

Tannehill et al., (2015) report that effective teachers frequently reinforce appropriate behaviors, praise success and improvement, and maintain a positive class climate. Unfortunately, the typical physical education class tends to have a slightly negative climate, with the teacher giving mostly negative performance feedback and insisting that children be quiet and listen. These researchers suggest that a positive climate is preferable, and doling out frequent praise will contribute to this environment. Studies show that students achieve less when the classroom climate is harsh and punitive, and when teachers ridicule students.

Not all teachers and researchers agree on the topic of praise. Many teachers believe in the positive effect of not only praise but also extrinsic rewards—that is, rewards such as gold stars, "happy" stickers, treats, special privileges, and extra free time. Other teachers believe, just as strongly, that extrinsic rewards and excessive praise counteract the development of children's abilities to regulate their own behavior in more mature ways and to value intrinsic rewards, such as pride in a job well done. Hellison (2003), who supports developing intrinsic motivation, suggests not using extrinsic rewards unless they are necessary, noting that this technique will be required for some students.

Ignoring Behaviors

Although you need to stop any behavior that is dangerous or will interfere with the lesson, sometimes children behave inappropriately to get attention. In this situation, ignoring the behavior works better than giving them the attention that they want. In addition, teachers learn that they can sometimes ignore tolerable behavior to maintain lesson momentum (Tannehill et al., 2015). Be sure, however, that you are consistent in which behaviors you ignore and by which children. Children will quickly pick up (before you do) if you tend to let some children get away with inappropriate behavior but not others. Children expect and need a consistent and fair teacher.

Telling Students to Stop and Change Misbehaviors

When you tell students to stop a misbehavior, be very clear and specific about what you want them to stop doing, what you want them to do instead, and why (Tannehill et al., 2015). With children, it can be very helpful to start by asking them if they know what they are doing wrong. You will be surprised how many have no idea that they are misbehaving or why their behavior is a problem.

Marzano's (2003) summary of research gives helpful suggestions on body language to employ when you discuss misbehavior with a student. When you speak, be assertive, not passive or aggressive. Stand upright and make eye contact. Remember, however, that making eye contact is considered disrespectful in some cultures, so do not expect all children to maintain eye contact (Curwin et al., 2008). Do not get into a huddle position, as this is a sign of camaraderie—not a sign of assertiveness. Speak deliberately and without emotion, and always listen to what the child says. Avoid ever touching a student during misbehavior.

You need to be realistic in your expectations for changing a student's misbehavior. It is unlikely that you will see miracles from students who have habitually been behaving inappropriately (Tannehill et al., 2015). Focus on making small improvements. As mentioned earlier, effective teachers find it helpful to think of times when they talk to disobedient students as an opportunity for developing self- and social responsibility. It is critical to deal with the student in a respectful manner that maintains the child's dignity.

Time-Outs

Having children take a time-out from participating in class is a misbehavior technique commonly used in physical education. Because most children enjoy physical activity, they view time-out as a punishment.

> **Experienced Teachers Talk**
>
> The Difficulty of Being Fair
>
> As a beginning teacher, I was certain I would be fair in applying rules. I knew how important it was to my peers and me that our teachers were fair, and I thought this would be simple. How wrong I was. I learned quickly that being fair was difficult and depended on the context and each student's situation. I still remember one day when two girls from two different classes asked to be excused from PE. I believed the story of the first girl and thought the circumstances were valid, so I said yes. I did not believe the story of the second girl, who offered what I thought was a weak and dishonest explanation, so I said no. A few days later, I learned I was completely wrong about both girls—the first had lied and the second had told the truth.

> **Experienced Teachers Talk**
>
> Exceptionalities and Management
>
> A boy with autism in my class said, "I can't dribble. Watch." But he could dribble, and then he lay on his stomach and had a fit. I said calmly, "You have two choices. You can get up and dribble, or you can take a time-out," and I walked away. With children with autism, you need to give them the choices and then walk away because they need time to digest their options.

Most teachers designate a space for time-out. The first time-out is short—about 2 minutes or less, with a maximum of 5 to 10 minutes, depending on the severity of the misbehavior. Be sure to ask children what they did wrong to deserve a time-out. Again, it will surprise you how many do not know what they were doing wrong. As a teacher, you want to be sure your students know exactly what they need to be doing differently when they rejoin the class.

Including Children in the Decision

Children can be included in the time-out decision. We find it helpful to ask children who are slipping into problematic behavior if they need a time-out. Sometimes they will tell you yes; at other times they will get back on task immediately. We also tell children that they can rejoin the class when they are ready to participate appropriately. Giving these decisions to children helps to develop self-regulation.

One suggestion we learned from an expert teacher is to teach children how to take a time-out. Like any behavior we want children to know, we can't assume they know how to

> **Experienced Teachers Talk**
>
> Time-Outs
>
> Sometimes with time-outs, we send a message that is unclear. We put a kid in time-out for not putting away the equipment fast enough, and we put a kid in time-out for hitting someone. The consequence to the kid is the same: a time-out. The message is, "Regardless of what you do here, here's what will happen." Ninety-nine percent of the time, you give a time-out because the kid was a little out of control. It's not a big deal. So I talk about being out of control. I tell them, "If you show me you have got your control back, I might let you back in before your bottom hits the floor." That's a chill-out time-out. Other time-outs for bullying, being mean, hurting someone—you kick it up a notch. I say, "You are going to time-out and sit there, sit out, and at the end of class, we are going to my office and calling your mom."
>
> You have to explain why they are sitting out. Say, "You are sitting out, and here's why." Make the distinction between a chill-out minute and "You have crossed the line when you went and mistreated Kendra." Kids need to know the difference. It's technically the same punishment, but with very different meanings.

do that behavior appropriately. We need to teach them. First, demonstrate a child who pretends he or she did nothing wrong, stomps over to the time-out space, sits and pouts, and tries to talk to other children while in time-out. Then demonstrate how to take a time-out appropriately by accepting responsibility for actions and using respectful body language.

Calling Parents

Do not be afraid to contact parents. They can be tremendously helpful, and they know their child better than you do. The main thing to remember is that you have to establish a relationship with the parents, just as you do with their children. You want them to know you have the best interests of their children at heart.

If you are worried about what to say, you can start the conversation with a statement such as "I'm having a problem with Fred in my class, and I need your help to get the situation resolved. This is what happened...." Alternatively, you might say, "I had a little problem with Louisa, and I need you to help me. This is not typical behavior for Louisa. I have never had a problem with her before. She is typically really good, but today she was unsettled. I don't know why. Is there something going on? Has something changed? Is she worried about something? I'm not trying to be intrusive, but this is not her typical behavior. I don't expect you to tell me any specifics—this is your personal business—but I need to know how to help her."

Call the parents before the student gets home from school. Children can be great storytellers at home and often leave out the part that includes what they did wrong. For major infractions or if their attitude warrants it, take time to have the student call the parent with you standing by. Dial the number and tell the parent his or her child is having trouble in class and the child is going to tell the parent about it—and then hand the phone to the student.

Keep your administration informed of any major problems. Parents tend to call the principal first; thus, if the principal knows what's going on, problems can be minimized. In addition, keep classroom teachers informed about rule infractions and misbehavior problems. Many of them are likely having the same problem and can share with you what they are doing.

Some teachers send form letters to parents about minor infractions. The "Sample Letter to Send Home to Parents" provides an example of this. We recommend that you don't sent emails. Most people write emails differently than letters. Because it's so easy to send an email, you might send one when you are angry and upset. Calling parents is typically more effective.

Experienced Teachers Talk

Working with Classroom Teachers

If you're having trouble with your class, don't send it back to the classroom teacher. When you do so, you're sending kids the message, "I can't handle you." You can tell the classroom teacher, but say, "I don't want you to do anything. I will deal with my misbehavior problems." When they bring the kids in, they will also warn you about problems kids are having, but it isn't fair to throw your misbehavior problems back on the classroom teachers.

Sample Letter to Send Home to Parents

Date: ____________

Teacher's Name: ____________________

School Phone Number: __________________

Dear Mom, Dad, and/or Grandparent [or other caregiver],

I have broken rules in my physical education class in a way that has disrupted learning. I was warned about the offenses, but I continued to break the following rules:

_____ Not prepared for class

_____ Talking when the teacher is talking

_____ Disrespectful to the teacher or my classmates

_____ Not stopping on the teacher's signal

_____ Failing to follow directions

_____ Not willing to cooperate with my classmates

_____ Not caring for or using equipment properly

I understand that if I don't bring this letter back by my next PE class, I will be provided with an alternative activity. I also want you to know that if my behavior does not improve, we will need to have a conference with my teacher. If you have any questions, please call the school to talk to my PE teacher.

_______________ _______________

Child's Name Parent/Guardian Signature

Point Systems

Some teachers give students points as a consequence for misbehavior. For example, they might use this system:

- Point 1: Warning
- Point 2: Short time-out
- Point 3: Longer time-out
- Point 4: Note home to the parents

Keep a point sheet at the side of the physical education space, and have children sign their names when they get a point. Children view the act of signing as a punishment, even if it is only a warning. If you use a point system, always reserve the right to assign as many points as you deem appropriate and be willing to listen to an alternative punishment that the child suggests.

In addition, with point systems, remember that once children have reached the limit of points, they have no reason to behave for the rest of the lesson (or the rest of the week if you use a weekly point system). One suggestion is to let them earn the removal of points by demonstrating exceptionally good behavior. This way, they will have reasons to try to maintain appropriate behavior.

Your Own Emotional Responses

There is no doubt that misbehavior and management problems can be upsetting to both teachers and students. You may feel frustrated and guilty, and even question your competence as a

It's Not About You

"Some adults have the attitude that the kid is doing it to them or they are doing it on purpose to get me upset. Kids don't do things to you. They are not trying to upset you. They want to be good and to know how to be good. It's not about you."—Experienced teacher

teacher. Many times, we have replayed a misbehavior situation in our heads and wished we had handled it better.

It is critical not to take students' misbehavior problems personally. Students misbehave for many reasons. Some crave attention; others are insecure; others act out their hostility to ward off things that are happening in their lives outside of school (Marzano, 2003). Remember, you don't know everything going on in a child's life. Try to find a way to meet all children's needs.

In his workshops on creating caring schools, Kohn (2003) found that he was more successful when teachers asked the right questions:

> Some teachers and administrators want to know, *How can we get these kids to obey? What practical techniques can you offer that will make students show up, sit down, and do what they're told?* Other educators begin from an entirely different point of departure. They ask, *What do these kids need—and how can we meet those needs?* (p. 27).

In any confrontation with a student, at the very least remember that someone must be the adult in the situation, and that adult is you. Remain positive, upbeat, and in control of your emotions and the situation. Use humor if possible (Curwin et al., 2008). Don't let students bait you into anger, as this means that they are controlling you, not the reverse. Don't hold a grudge. Respond with as much care and respect as you can (see **Figure 13.6**).

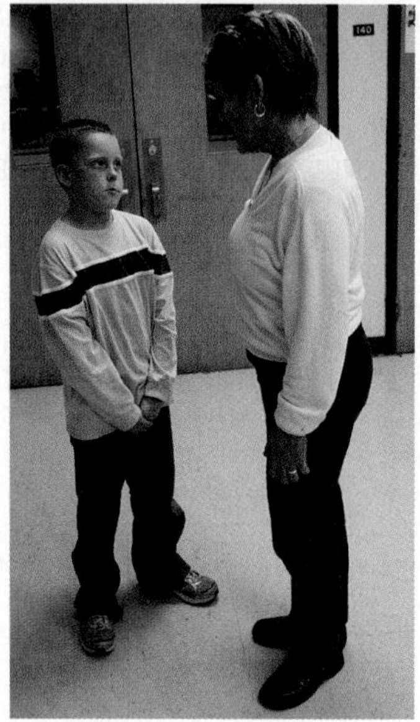

Figure 13.6 Responding with care and respect

Support from Other Teachers

Don't be afraid to seek help from other teachers, even other beginning teachers. In one research study, the beginning teachers periodically went out Friday evenings for drinks and snacks to talk about how things were going at school. They found their conversations very helpful. Their peers often had good ideas, and the teachers learned that they were not alone—other teachers had the same misbehavior problems they were having.

Summary

A safe, welcoming school climate has rules, routines, and social norms specifying appropriate behavior. Students understand what teachers and administrators expect. Bullying, however, creates an unsafe environment. Teachers can work to prevent bullying by increasing their awareness of when and how bullying occurs, teaching children what constitutes bullying, working with bullies and victims to stop the unwanted behaviors, and teaching children the importance of reporting bullying and other harmful behaviors to teachers.

Students will do only what teachers hold them accountable for doing. They will try to negotiate nonverbally and test teachers to see whether they can reduce the demands of working hard and learning. Teachers need to resist giving in to students' negotiations and to remain committed to student learning.

Positive student–teacher relationships contribute to strong management of behavior and misbehavior. The best way to deal with misbehavior problems is to prevent them from ever happening by using sound management techniques. These methods include setting clear expectations, keeping the lesson moving without students spending much time transitioning from one activity to another, and teaching routines so students know how to pick up equipment efficiently, stop on the teacher's signal, and enter and leave the physical education area.

Effective teachers set a small number of class rules and teach students why these rules are important and how the rules connect to important moral standards. When a student breaks the rules, the teacher must make sure the child understands what he or she did wrong. Consequences for breaking rules range from simply telling the child to stop to time-outs to phone calls to parents. Teachers should not take students' misbehavior problems personally. In any confrontation, they need to be positive, calm, and in control of their emotions and the situation.

Review Questions

1. How can you help children understand what makes a school feel safe and which rules need to be enforced?
2. What is bullying? What does research say about the negative effects of bullying?
3. Describe how teachers can help stop bullying.
4. How can you deal with a victim of bullying who is also aggressive toward other children?
5. What is the difference between tattling and reporting, and why is it critical for children to understand this difference? Why is it advisable for teachers *not* to tell children, "Don't be a tattletale"?
6. Describe three things you can tell children to encourage them to report possible problems and bullying to adults.
7. How and why do teachers trade off instruction that holds students accountable for learning for management and good behavior?
8. What is the social task system, and how can it be used in a positive way in physical education?
9. Which kinds of student–teacher relationships lead to strong management and reduced misbehavior, and which kinds do not?
10. Write a typical rule for physical education, and then explain how you would teach children how this rule connects to broader values and moral standards.

References

Berk, L. E. (2010). *Development through the lifespan* (5th ed.). Boston: Pearson Education.

Bilmes, J. (2012). Chaos in kindergarten? *Educational Leadership, 70*(2), 32-35.

Carlson, T. B., & Hastie, P. A. (1997). The student social system within sport education. *Journal of Teaching in Physical Education, 16*, 176–195.

Chen, A. (1999). The impact of social change on inner-city high school physical education: An analysis of a teacher's experiential account. *Journal of Teaching in Physical Education, 18*, 312–335.

Cooper, D., & Snell, J. L. (2003). Bullying: Not just a kid thing. *Educational Leadership, 60*(6), 22–25.

Cornell, D. G., & Mayer, M. J. (2010). Why do school order and safety matter? *Educational Researcher, 39*, 7–15.

Cothran, D. J., Kulinna, P. H., & Garrahy, D. A. (2003). "This is kind of giving a secret away...": Students' perspectives on effective class management. *Teaching and Teacher Education, 19*, 435–444.

Curwin, R. L., Mendler, A. N., & Mendler, B. D. (2008). *Discipline with dignity: New challenges, new solutions* (3rd. ed.). Alexandria, VA: Association for Supervision and Curriculum Development.

Deiro, J. A. (2003). Do your students know you care? *Educational Leadership, 60*(6), 60–62.

Doyle, W. (2006). Ecological approaches to classroom management. In C. Evertson & C. Weinstein (Eds.), *Handbook of classroom management: Research, practice, and contemporary issues* (pp. 97–125). New York: Lawrence Erlbaum.

Eickhoff-Shemek, J. M., Herbert, D. L., & Connaughton, D. P. (2009). *Risk Management for Health/Fitness Professionals: Legal Issues and Strategies.* Philadelphia: Wolters Kluwer/Lippincott Williams & Wilkins.

Ennis, C. D. (1995). Teachers' responses to noncompliant students: The realities and consequences of a negotiated curriculum. *Teaching and Teacher Education, 11*, 445–460.

Garbarino, J., & deLara, E. (2003). Words can hurt forever. *Educational Leadership, 60*(6), 18–21.

Gano-Overway, L. A. (2013). Exploring the connections between caring and social behaviors in physical education. *Research Quarterly for Exercise and Sport, 84*, 104–114.

Gibbone, A., & Manson, M. (2010). Bullying: Proactive physical educators' contribution to school-wide prevention. *Journal of Physical Education, Recreation and Dance, 81*, 20–24.

Halsey, J. J. (2005). Risk Management for Physical Educators. In H. Appenzeller, (Ed.). *Risk Management in Sport: Issues and Strategies*, (2nd ed.), (pp. 151-163). Durham, NC: Carolina Academic Press.

Hart, J. E., & Ritson, R. J. (2002). *Liability and Safety in Physical Education and Sport.* Reston, VA: National Association for Sport and Physical Education.

Hastie, P. A. (1996). Student role involvement during a unit of sport education. *Journal of Teaching in Physical Education, 16*, 88–103.

Hastie, P. A., & Siedentop, D. (2006). The classroom ecology paradigm. In D. Kirk, D. MacDonald, & M. O'Sullivan (Eds.), *The handbook of physical education* (pp. 214–225). London: Sage.

Hellison, D. (2003). *Teaching responsibility through physical activity* (2nd ed.). Champaign, IL: Human Kinetics.

Kohn, A. (2003). Almost there, but not quite. *Educational Leadership, 60*(6), 26–29.

Kosciw, J. G., Diaz, E. M., & Greytak, E. A. (2008). *The 2007 National School Climate Survey: The experiences of lesbian, gay, bisexual, and transgender youth in our nation's schools.* New York: GLSEN.

Ladson-Billings, G. (1994). *The dreamkeepers: Successful teachers of African American children.* San Francisco: Jossey-Bass.

Marzano, R. J. (2003). *Classroom management that works: Research-based strategies for every teacher.* Alexandria, VA: Association for Supervision and Curriculum Development.

McCaughtry, N. (2004). The emotional dimensions of a teacher's pedagogical content knowledge: Influences on content, curriculum, and pedagogy. *Journal of Teaching in Physical Education, 23*, 30–47.

McCaughtry, N., Barnard, S., Martin, J., Shen, B., & Hodges Kulinna, P. (2006). Teachers' perspectives on the challenges of teaching physical education in urban schools: The student emotional filter. *Research Quarterly for Exercise and Sport, 77*, 486–497.

National Association for Sport and Physical Education (NASPE). (2009). *Physical Activity Used as Punishment and/or Behavior Management.* Reston, VA: Author.

McNeil, L. M. (1986). *Contradictions of control: School structure and school knowledge.* New York: Routledge & Kegan Paul.

Nohr, K. M. (2009). *Managing Risk in Sport and Recreation: The Essential Guide for Loss Prevention.* Champaign, IL: Human Kinetics.

O'Connor, J. A, & Graber, K. C. (2014). Sixth-grade physical education: An acculturation of bullying and fear. *Research Quarterly for Exercise and Sport, 85*, 398–408.

Olweus, D. (1993). *Bullying at school: What we know and what we can do*. Cambridge, MA: Blackwell.

Olweus, D. (2003). A profile of bullying at school. *Educational Leadership, 60*(6), 12–17.

Osher, D., Bear, G. G., Sprague, J. R., & Doyle, W. (2010). How can we improve school misbehavior? *Educational Researcher, 39*, 48–58.

Owens, L. M., & Ennis, C. D. (2005). The ethic of care in teaching: An overview of supportive literature. *Quest, 57*, 392–425.

Rovegno, I. (1994). Teaching within a curricular zone of safety: School culture and the situated nature of student teachers' pedagogical content knowledge. *Research Quarterly for Exercise and Sport, 65*, 269–279.

Siedentop, D., Doutis, P., Tsangaridou, N., Ward, P., & Rauschenbach, J. (1994). Don't sweat gym! An analysis of curriculum and instruction. *Journal of Teaching in Physical Education, 13*, 375–394.

Smith, R., & Lambert, M. (2008). Assuming the best. *Educational Leadership, 66*(1), 16–20.

Swearer, S. M., Espelage, D. L., Vaillancourt, T., & Hymel, S. (2010). What can be done about school bullying? Linking research to educational practice. *Educational Researcher, 39*, 38–47.

Tannehill, D., van der Mars, H., MacPhail, A. (2015). *Building effective physical education programs*. Burlington, MA: Jones and Bartlett Learning.

Tenorio, R. (1994). Race and respect among young children. In B. Bigelow, L. Christensen, S. Karp, B. Miner, & B. Peterson (Eds.), *Rethinking our classroom: Teaching for equity and justice* (pp. 24–28). Milwaukee, WI: Rethinking Schools.

van der Mars, H., Darst, P. W., Vogler, E. W., & Cusimano, B. E. (1994). Active supervision patterns of physical education teachers and their relationship with student behaviors. *Journal of Teaching in Physical Education, 14*, 99–112.

van der Mars, H., Vogler, E. W., Cusimano, B. E., & Darst, P. W. (1998). Teachers' active supervision patterns and students' activity levels during fitness activities. *Journal of Teaching in Physical Education, 18*, 57–75.

Wallace, T.L., & Chhuon, V. (2014). Proximal processes in urban classrooms: Engagement and disaffection in urban youth of color. *American Educational Research Journal, 51*(5), 937–973.

Weissbourd, R., & Jones, S. (2012). Joining hands against bullying. *Educational Leadership, 70*(2), 26–31.

Williams, M. M. (1993). Actions speak louder than works: What students think. *Educational Leadership, 51*(3), 22–23.

CHAPTER

14

Planning

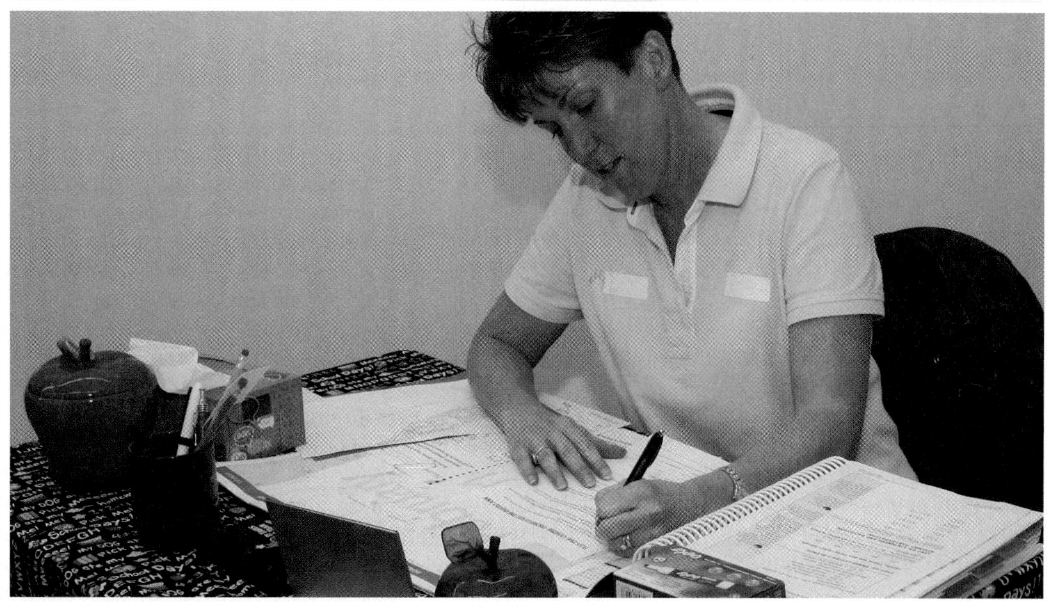

PRE-READING REFLECTION

1. What have you heard about planning from experienced teachers and other students? What do they say is easy? What do they say is difficult?
2. Imagine a week before school starts, you get a job teaching elementary physical education. What do you want to know about writing lesson, unit, and year-long plans?

OBJECTIVES

Students will learn:

1. Well-written lesson plans make you a better teacher.
2. Lesson objectives are sentences that state exactly what the children will learn and the specific ways they will improve movement, cognitive knowledge, thinking skills/motivation, and social skills.
3. Lesson plans have three parts: (1) introductory and warm-up activities; (2) content development; and (3) a culminating activity.
4. Lesson plans incorporate a progression of tasks, including (1) introductory/informing tasks; (2) extending tasks; (3) refinements; and (4) applying/assessing tasks (Rink, 2014).
5. Unit plans outline the major tasks and culminating activity for a set of lessons about a topic.
6. Year-long plans describe what you will teach each week for each grade across the school year.
7. K–5 physical education programs follow national, state, and/or district standards.

KEY TERMS

- Application tasks (A)
- Block plan
- Closure
- Content development
- Culminating activity
- Exploring tasks (E)
- Extending tasks (E)
- Informing tasks (I)
- Introductory and warm-up activities
- Lesson objectives
- Major learning outcome
- Refinements (R)
- Stem
- Unit objectives

CONNECTION TO STANDARDS

This chapter shows you how to start with National Standards and plan lesson, unit, grade level, and K–5 content that will ensure your program is standards-based and students' learning outcomes will meet the standards.

Introduction

Teachers write four types of plans:

1. K–5 program plans listing in broad terms what the children will learn in keeping with all of the national or state standards for K–5
2. Year-long plans listing what each grade will learn during the school year in keeping with the grade-level outcomes of national or state standards
3. Unit plans outlining what children will learn in a set of lessons related to one topic linked to one or more national or state standards
4. Lesson plans describing what children will learn and how they will learn it in one lesson linked to one or more national or state standards

Undergraduates spend most of their efforts mastering lesson and unit plans. You are not responsible for the development of the programs in the field placements in which you teach. However, as a teacher you will be responsible for setting goals for what students will learn as a result of your program by grade and across K–5. It is critical that you begin to think about planning like an expert teacher—that is, planning in relation to short-term and long-term goals for the learning outcomes of students aligned to the National Standards. We begin by describing lesson plans.

Lesson Plans

There is no doubt that a well-written lesson plan will make you a better teacher. We can't count the times we have watched undergraduates teach lessons and asked them if they knew why their teaching improved considerably over a previous lesson. Their response: "I did a more thorough or more detailed lesson plan," or "I spent much more time thinking about and writing this lesson plan." We know our teaching is better when we spend more time planning.

One issue you might encounter in the field is that some experienced teachers do not spend much time planning; others may tell you that only your professors care about lesson plans. There is a little element of truth to their claims: Some experienced teachers have taught the same lesson so many times they literally have it memorized word for word. However, good teachers will say that even with lesson plans that have consistently led to excellent lessons, they will carefully think about the current class and modify the lesson to meet the needs of the class and of individual children in the class.

In addition, and unfortunately, some experienced teachers do not spend much time planning. Consequently, their programs are weak, and they do not know if children have achieved the outcomes they desire for their program. When you do not plan lessons to meet specific objectives leading to specific learning outcomes that you assess, your program becomes recreational and is not aimed at meeting the national, state, or district standards for children's learning (Patton & Griffin, 2008).

Professors typically do care more about lesson plans because they recognize how important lesson plans are in the development of strong beginning teachers. In writing lesson plans, undergraduates learn about the details of the content they will teach the children, how to break this content down into a sequence of tasks, how to present information efficiently, how to organize the children, which teaching methods to use, how tasks might be modified if something goes wrong, how to anticipate the responses of the children, and how to assess whether the children have learned what you had planned to teach. Moreover, when undergraduates teach from well-written plans, they experience fewer management problems. Experienced teachers often forget what they didn't know when they were undergraduates and forget how lesson plans served as a teaching tool. Even student teachers forget what they didn't know about teaching but learned by writing lesson plans for their early field experiences.

There also is no doubt that writing lesson plans can be difficult and time consuming. Although we sympathize with those who complain about this burden, we know how important lesson plans are for your development as a teacher. You also need to remember that the ability to write an excellent lesson plan is a requirement for certification in most, if not all, states. Principals pay particular attention to the lesson plans of beginning teachers. Many even require both beginning and experienced teachers to submit their lesson plans in written form. If a child is injured in your class and the parents file a lawsuit, a written lesson plan provides necessary evidence about the content that you taught and the diligence of your teaching. Without a written lesson plan, you can be left with no support for your actions.

Finally, designing lesson plans can be an engaging, problem-solving process. Finding better ways to improve skill performance, teach tactics, or develop children's creative thinking is a challenge, and it is very satisfying when you succeed. Even after 20 years of collaborating, we still telephone each other to report, "I've got lead passes figured out. Wait until you hear what we did in the unit!" We also find it fun to think of different ways to capture children's attention—whether with an interesting story to help them remember a performance technique, a joke (only) young children think is hysterically funny for understanding what to do in a social situation, or a novel task that gets them engaged in learning.

Different Forms of Lesson and Unit Plans and Objectives

There have always been debates about the correct way to write lesson plans and lesson objectives. University teacher education programs, school districts, and even principals have preferences for certain formats, for example. The degree of specificity and the information that should be included in objectives also are widely debated (Rink, 2014). Some educators believe in including assessment criteria related to the product (e.g., hitting a target 8 out of 10 times), whereas others prefer including process-oriented criteria (e.g., children learning to push with their finger pads while dribbling).

In this text, we describe only one of a range of appropriate forms of lesson, unit, and program plans and objectives. You should be able to adapt these examples to the form required in your program or school. The form we use is geared to the elementary school level, the content taught in the K–5 grades, and how children's motor skills develop.

Do Your Homework

Before you plan objectives and lessons, we highly recommend you "do your homework" and study the content you will be teaching (see **Figure 14.1**). You can't possibly be an expert on all physical education content, but there are many sources that can help you learn more about the subject matter and how that subject matter is learned by children. For example, what do children find difficult or confusing; what immature movement patterns are you likely to observe; and, keeping in mind the children's developmental level of the skill you're teaching, which performance techniques are most important to learn and which can be saved for later? Even if you're an intercollegiate athlete in the content you're teaching, you probably don't remember initially learning the skills; the teachers and coaches you do remember were likely working with you at an advanced stage of your development. To teach physical education at the K–5 level, you need to study how beginners learn the content.

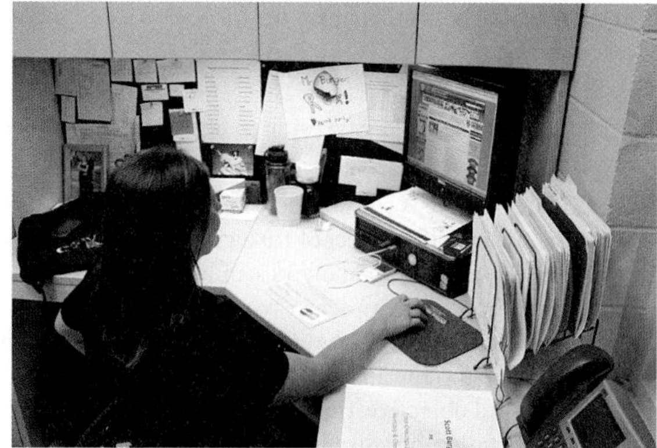

Figure 14.1 Studying content using the Internet

Courtesy of John Dolly

Lesson Objectives

A lesson plan begins with a list of lesson objectives, or intended learning outcomes for the lesson. **Lesson objectives** are sentences that state exactly what the children are expected to learn in the lesson. They are specific and detailed. Objectives are not what the teacher will do, but rather describe the content that the children will learn and the specific ways they will improve a movement, thinking, or social skill. Here is an example:

Objective: By the end of this lesson, the children will have learned to

- Catch a self-tossed playground ball by reaching for the ball and absorbing force by bending their elbows.

What makes this objective specific are the following phrases:

- Self-tossed
- By reaching for the ball
- Absorbing force by bending their elbows

This text identifies six types of objectives: (1) motor; (2) cognitive knowledge; (3) thinking skills; (4) motivation concepts; (5) social skills; and (6) affective. Motor objectives are the most important because physical activity is our most important domain. Learning to move skillfully and to appreciate the role of physical activity in our lives is our central purpose. The cognitive, thinking, motivation, social, and affective objectives are all derived from the movement content. Recall that all physical activities have motor, cognitive, thinking, social, and affective components that are important to teach. The National Standards for Physical Education include all these aspects.

Motor Objectives

Every motor objective includes a description of the movement the children will do and the specific criteria for improving or refining performance, consisting most often of a phrase or word that specifies the exact, detailed performance technique that is the focus of the lesson. The following are examples of inappropriately broad and appropriately detailed objectives for a kindergarten lesson:

Motor Objective: By participating in this lesson, the children will learn to

- *Inappropriately broad:* Throw overhand for force.
- *Appropriately detailed:* Start side to target when throwing overhand for force.

The first objective is considered too broad because it does not focus on any specific aspect of throwing. Thus, it does not set a specific learning outcome you can assess. It also is too broad because no child can learn to throw in one lesson—children learn to throw across the entire elementary grade span, so the objective is too broad for a single lesson plan.

In the second objective, the phrase "side to target" makes the objective detailed because it is a performance technique you plan to teach that will refine the children's performance. The intended outcome of your lesson is children who know to, and do, start with their side to the target when throwing for force (see **Figure 14.2**).

To write a motor objective aimed at improving skill performance, select a performance technique that the children are developmentally ready and need to learn. For example, the performance technique to rotate the hips before the shoulders in the forceful overarm throw is an important technique, but a waste of time for K–2 students because they are not ready to learn that performance technique in a lesson. It is simply too advanced for their developmental level. Write a motor objective by describing the movement and a developmentally appropriate performance technique the children are ready to learn.

The criteria for improving performance in a motor objective also can be to refine the quality of the movement. In dance, for example, children often move and gesture but do not perform what we typically refer to as skills. That is, they may rise to a high level, sink to a low level, stretch, curl, and end in a round shape. Put simply, dance is expressive. As a teacher, your goal is to teach children to express different movement qualities, such as gentleness, strength, and power. Write the motor objective by describing the movement and the movement qualities. For example,

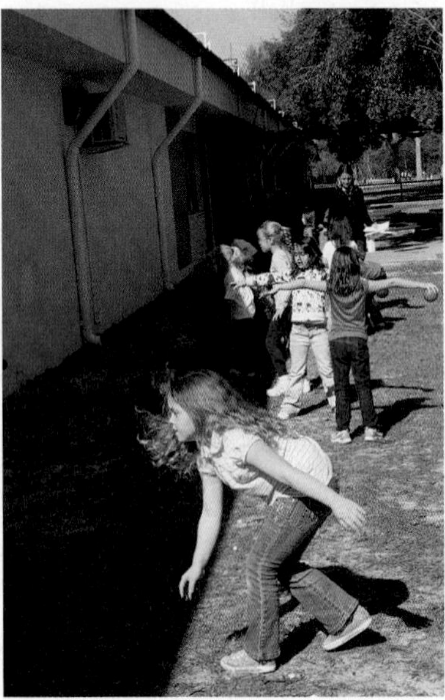

Figure 14.2 Kindergarten children working on "side to target" while throwing forcefully

Motor Objective: By the end of this lesson, the children will have learned to

- *Inappropriately broad:* Design a short sequence, including a beginning and ending shape, rising, sinking, stretching, and curling.
- *Appropriately detailed:* Design a short sequence, including a held beginning and ending shape; rising and sinking with soft, gentle force; and stretching and curling with strong force.

Thus, in every motor objective, there is a phrase describing *how* the children will refine their performance or the quality of their movements.

Movement Variety in Motor Objectives

Many motor objectives focus on both refining performance techniques and extending the variety of ways children perform the skill or movement. With the exception of a few closed skills, most skills in physical education are open skills, meaning they are performed in a variety of ways based on environmental conditions (e.g., game situations change). Consequently, most motor objectives need to include a phrase about the movement variety you expect children to learn or improve upon during the lesson. In the following objectives, the performance technique or movement quality is shown in italics and the movement variety in bold.

Motor Objectives with Movement Variety: By participating in this lesson, the children will learn to

1. Dribble with their hands *looking up* while **traveling on straight, curved, and zigzag pathways.**
2. Catch balls tossed by a partner **to their left and right sides** so they must *move to align themselves with the ball* to catch it.
3. Perform a **variety of curled, straight, wide, and angular shapes** while maintaining *light tension throughout their body.*

If it is easier or more helpful for you, you can write two separate objectives for the same skill, one describing the movement variety and one the skill refinement. For example,

Motor Objectives: By the end of this gymnastics lesson, the children will have learned to

- *Movement variety:* Balance on a variety of body parts.
- *Movement Quality/Skill Refinement:* Stay tight and point their feet/toes while balancing.

The Stem

Objectives are written as complete sentences and begin with what we call a **stem**—that is, a starting phrase that is the same for all objectives. Teachers, principals, and professors sometimes disagree with what is an appropriate stem. At the elementary level, teachers often use stems focused on improvement because the performance techniques for skills such as throwing, catching, and dribbling develop over years of practice. As a consequence, learning outcomes can be assessed on a continuum from less mature to more mature. We list sample stems here from which you can choose:

- At the end of this lesson, the children will have learned
- As a result of participating in this lesson, the children will improve their ability to
- As a result of this lesson, the children will have (created and perfected a dance sequence that includes)
- At the end of this lesson, the children will be able to
- The children will

Cognitive Knowledge, Thinking Skills, Motivation Concepts, Social Skills, and Affective Objectives and the Respective National Standards

Once you know your motor objectives, you should plan whatever cognitive knowledge, thinking skill, motivation concept, social skill, or affective objectives are appropriate to, and will support, the movement content the children will be learning. The children must be able to meet the objectives from other domains in the tasks, activities, or class discussions in relation to the motor objectives. For example, you should not plan an objective to improve cooperation unless cooperation is embedded in the physical activities of the lesson.

Cognitive knowledge objectives meet National Standards 2 and 3. They include knowledge about fitness concepts, such as cardiorespiratory endurance and muscle fitness; Laban movement concepts, such as levels, force, and shape; biomechanical principles that affect skill performance; tactical and strategic principles of games; choreographic and movement quality principles of dance and gymnastics; and learning and development principles affecting the learning process.

Thinking, motivation, and social objectives meet National Standards 2, 4, and 5. They include thinking, social, and affective aspects, such as making decisions with a partner about what movements to put in a dribbling routine, solving tactical problems with teammates, working cooperatively with peers to design a dance, being socially responsible during group discussions, and caring about the feelings of others during competitive situations.

Affective objectives deal with physical and emotional feelings during physical activities and meet National Standards 1 and 5. They include the kinesthetic feeling of different body components while performing skills and the emotional feelings expressed in dance. These objectives also include the feelings of power and strength experienced when doing fitness activities and the feeling of endurance experienced when running fast for a long time. In games, affective objectives include the feelings of challenge in playing all out, confidence when you know you will be successful, being engrossed when you are totally focused on the game, and the enjoyment and togetherness of team play.

As in the motor domain, the objectives from other domains are specific and detailed and describe what children will learn and how they will improve. They are an intended outcome of the lesson that you could assess. The following are sample objectives matched to the related motor objective.

Sample Cognitive, Thinking, Motivation, Social, and Affective Objectives Matched to a Motor Objective

Example One

Objectives

By the end of this child-designed folk dance lesson, the children will have learned to

Motor

1. Walk, hop, jump, slide, and skip, traveling in different directions, moving lightly to the beat of the music and stretching tall through the spine.

Cognitive Knowledge (Choreography Principle)

2. Design smooth transitions between different formations that do not require extra steps or jumps to shift positions.

Social

3. Listen to and encourage all group members to contribute ideas about the dance.

Example Two

Objectives

By the end of this gymnastics lesson, the children will have learned to

Motor

1. Balance in a variety of shapes while staying tight and pointing their feet.

Cognitive Knowledge

2. Understand that staying tight and pointing their feet allows for an improved aesthetic body line and increased balance and control.

Thinking Skills

3. Think creatively and design some original and unusual balances.

Motivation Concept

4. Appreciate that improvement in gymnastics is due to hard work and effort, not to natural ability.

Example Three

Notes: Game tactics by their very nature include movement, a decision, and cognitive knowledge. For example, the movement of a lead pass is to pass the ball ahead of the receiver so the receiver doesn't have to slow down or turn to catch the ball. The cognitive knowledge is that positioning the ball ahead of the receiver prevents the defender from intercepting and allows the receiver not to slow down and, thus, not let the defender catch up and be in a good defensive position. The decisions made during lead passes are deciding when the receiver is about to get free from the defender and be in an open passing lane and when to pass. Because tactics include movement, decision making (i.e., a thinking skill), and cognitive knowledge, you can combine labels for objectives.

Objectives

By the end of this games lesson, the children will have learned

Motor and Decision Making

1. To pass the ball ahead of the receiver, deciding when to pass so the receiver doesn't have to slow down or turn to catch the ball.

Cognitive Knowledge

2. That passing the ball ahead of the receiver prevents the defender from intercepting and allows the receiver not to slow down and the defender not to catch up and be in a good defensive position.

Example Four

Objectives

By the end of this creative dance lesson, the children will have learned to

Motor

1. Assume different body shapes (symmetrical, asymmetrical, thin, wide, round, twisted, pointy) representing leaves, holding each shape still.
2. Perform turning jumps, landing lightly, and travel quickly and lightly on circular pathways, expressing leaves swirling in the wind.
3. Swing and sway, expressing leaves falling off a tree using soft, slow, indirect movements (see **Figure 14.3**).

Affective

4. Increase their awareness of the kinesthetic feeling of movement (i.e., the tension in their muscles when they make shapes) by being aware of the feeling of stillness (when holding leaf shapes), swirling motion while traveling quickly, and swinging and swaying gently and slowly.

Creative Thinking Skills

5. Explore freely using images of autumn leaves to enhance their variety and the originality of their shapes.

Figure 14.3 Swinging and swaying to represent autumn leaves

Three Parts of a Lesson

A lesson plan has three major parts:

1. Introductory and warm-up activities
2. Content development
3. Culminating activity

Introductory and Warm-Up Activities

Introductory and warm-up activities prepare students for the lesson. When you introduce the lesson, you inform children about what they will be learning and why it is important. You also try to capture children's interest and build enthusiasm. As part of the introduction, you might review the previous lesson's content and explain how the new content builds on what they already know. You can discuss how the new content relates to classroom content or to the children's lives outside of school. You can tell stories, present interesting facts, or present a puzzling problem that students will get to solve during the lesson. Some teachers call this a *set induction.*

Warm-up activities warm up the children's bodies and get them physically active quickly. Many elementary school teachers like to start class with a simple activity—one that requires only a brief explanation to get all children moving as soon as they enter the physical education space. Children look forward to physical education, and they like becoming physically active as soon as they arrive. Whether you begin with a warm-up activity or an introduction to the lesson is up to you. Either order is appropriate. Decide which to do first based on what is best for your classes and the lesson you have planned.

The pattern often used to start classes in the past—having students run a lap and then complete some sit-ups, push-ups, and jumping jacks—does not meet the criteria for good introductory activities. These activities are not only boring for children, but they also do not relate to the content taught in the rest of the lesson. The main goal of the introduction is to introduce the purpose and importance of the content you will be teaching, get children excited about what they will learn, and warm up their bodies in ways that match the requirements of the content you will teach. If you start with traditional calisthenics, you are probably reinforcing the idea that fitness activities are something to dread rather than enjoy—a message our profession does not want to reinforce.

Content Development

The **content development** section is the heart of the lesson. In brief, your central duties during planning are to identify content that will enable children to meet your lesson objectives, break that content down into smaller parts, identify tasks for teaching that content, and arrange the tasks into a progression that *leads to learning.*

Rink (2014) developed a way to identify and label tasks that will help you understand how to build a sound progression of tasks for the content development section of your lesson. We have adapted her approach here.

Informing Tasks

Informing tasks (I) (introductory tasks) introduce new content and are the first tasks in the progression of tasks for your lesson. Typically, informing tasks are used at the beginning of your lesson and at the beginning of each new section that works on a different skill. These tasks give children just enough information to begin practicing. With informing tasks, the key is to not lecture or review excessive amounts of information beyond the children's attention and memory capabilities.

Extending Tasks

Extending tasks (E) are the progression of tasks that build from simple to more complex or from easier to more difficult. Extending tasks are the result of breaking the content down into smaller parts, resulting in a series of tasks that lead to students to learn the skill or movement pattern that is your objective. The following is an example of an informing task followed by a progression of extending tasks.

I Toss and catch a sponge ball with your assigned partner, keeping your tosses at chest height or slightly higher.

E Toss the ball chest high and slightly to the right of your partner [demonstrate with a child] so your partner will have to travel to the side to get in line with the ball to catch it.

E Now change to tossing to the left of your partner so your partner must travel to the side to get in line with the ball to catch it.

E Now toss the ball sometimes to the left and sometimes to the right. Receivers, get into the ready position [knees bent, hands open and in front], and be prepared to move to either the left or the right to catch the ball.

E Let's vary the pass. Toss the ball to the right or left of the catcher, but this time make the ball bounce once before the catcher catches it.

E This time, toss the ball high with a high narrow arch like this [demonstrate]. Stand farther away from each other than you have been doing. The first time, just toss without your partner trying to catch the ball. Watch how I toss the ball high, but it lands between my partner and me. My partner needs to run forward to get in line with the ball and catch it high. With your partner, first try tossing high and see if you can make the ball land halfway between you. Once you can do this consistently, then the receiver can try to catch it.

E Now try to bounce the ball so it is high and to the front, so that the receiver has to move forward to catch it. What do you need to do differently from bouncing to the right or left? [If the students do not raise the point of the increased force of the bounce, then tell them.]

E If you think you are ready, you may now try to travel backward one or two steps to catch the ball.

E We are going to repeat the same tasks, but this time at a low level. First roll the ball to the right, then roll it to the left, and finally toss it in front of your partner at a low level.

Notice how the progression began with the easiest catches—chest height and traveling to the left and right, then progressed to catching a ball after one bounce, which is more difficult because the height of the bounce is more unpredictable and the child must judge the timing of the bounce and the catch. Moving forward and backward to catch a ball tossed high has more complex perceptual demands, and catching at a low level is a more difficult movement pattern.

Exploring Tasks and Extending Movement Variety

Exploring tasks (E) are a subset of extension tasks. Exploring tasks are extending tasks that also ask children to explore and find different ways to extend their movement variety. For example,

E Explore dribbling on different pathways (i.e., straight, curved, and zigzag).

E Explore catching balls in all areas of your personal space.

E Explore making different round shapes. Now explore twisting into a variety of twisted shapes.

A progression of extending/exploring tasks in a gymnastics lesson on balancing on different body parts follows:

I I want you to get into the same position I am in. [Demonstrate a balance on hips with legs tucked and arms out.] We call this a balance because I am working hard to hold my body still. You have both small and large body parts on which you can balance. Can you tell me some large body parts? [Hips, belly, back, shoulders, sides].

E Explore balancing in a variety of ways on large body parts.

E Now explore trying to find a variety of ways to balance on your hands and feet.

E Explore balancing on your hands and feet with three parts touching the mat. You can balance on two feet and one hand, or on two hands and one foot.

E Now using just one hand and one foot, try to find different ways to balance on two body parts.

E Now alternate balancing on your hands and feet and balancing on a large body part. Try to explore a variety of balances.

Notice in this progression the tasks begin with the easier balances on large body parts and move to the more difficult small body parts. It is important to think about progressively increasing task difficulty and complexity related to the specific content of game, gymnastics, and dance lessons because progressions are necessary for safety.

Refinements

Refinements (R) work on improving movement quality or performance techniques. For example, if you say, "This time, I want you to swing your arms over your head when you take off for your jump," you are asking the class to focus on a performance technique (i.e., swing arms over head) that will improve their jumps. Here are other sample refining tasks appropriate for the sample extending tasks described above.

Extension Task	Refining Task
E Toss the ball to the right or left of the catcher, making the ball bounce once before the catcher catches it.	**R** Move and get in line with the flight path of the ball to catch.
E Explore dribbling on different pathways (i.e., straight, curved, and zigzag).	**R** Keep the ball in front and toward the dribbling-hand side.
E Explore balancing in a variety of ways on large body parts.	**R** Stay tight in all your muscles, including your core muscles.

As we discussed earlier, the most important refinement you intend children to learn is stated within the motor objective. Refinements are similar to giving whole-class feedback on skill performance. You anticipate children's responses in advance, and plan refining tasks based on your knowledge of which performance techniques will most likely improve performance at the children's level of development. You then make a decision about the actual refinements to assign based on your observations of the children's movement during the lesson. Don't focus on refining a performance technique children are already doing, even if the refinement was in your lesson plan.

Application/Assessment Tasks

Tasks that apply the content in a culminating activity, such as a dance, gymnastics sequence, game, or game-like task, are termed **application tasks (A)** (or assessment tasks). With such tasks, the children's focus of attention shifts from how to perform a skill to using the skill in different situations and broader contexts. Application tasks also include self-challenges, such as "Try to improve the number of times you hit the target," and self-competition tasks, such as "Each time you dribble, try to dribble the ball more times in a row without losing control." Again, the children's focus of attention shifts to applying the skill in a broader, more complex context. Assessment tasks give children the opportunity to assess their progress. Sample application tasks include the following:

- Jump as far as possible and have a partner put a chalk mark where you land; repeat jumping, each time trying to surpass your previous record.
- Design a jump rope routine with at least three different tricks.
- With a partner, design a dribbling routine.
- See if you can catch the ball from a rebound from the wall five times in a row.
- See if you can kick the ball in the goal three times in a row. Back up and try again. Keep backing up each time you score three times in a row.
- Play a 1v1 dribbling game with each of you having a ball and each trying to touch their opponent's ball.
- Play 3v1 and score one point each time your team passes five times in a row. The defender scores by touching the ball. Rotate defenders with every score.

Rink's (2014) system, used in her research, helped her label progressions that are effective versus ineffective in helping children's skill development. She found (supported by many other studies) that teachers who progressed from informing tasks immediately to application tasks were ineffective. In other words, they taught a new skill using an informing task and then after some practice had children use that skill in a game. Without the extending tasks that build the children's movement variety and ability to perform skills in different situations, and without refinements that focus on performance techniques, children learn less and their skills develop more slowly, if at all. To ensure you are providing adequate practice for children to learn and develop skills, the content development section of your lesson plan must consist predominantly of extending tasks and refinements.

Other Types of Tasks

You will typically include several other types of tasks in your lesson plan. Organizing tasks (**Org**) tell children which equipment to get, how to set it up, how to group themselves, and/or where to go in preparation for a movement task. Cognitive knowledge (**Cog K**) tasks are tasks in which the teacher either explains and defines a concept or, preferably, elicits children's understanding of the concept through questions. Social tasks (**Social**) describe social behaviors, such as "Be sure to share the decisions by asking for your partner's opinions about what to put in your gymnastics sequence." Thinking skill (**Th**) and motivation (**Mot**) tasks describe thinking skills to be used during the task or motivation concepts you will teach. Safety tasks (**Safety**) remind or tell children about the safety requirements of the activities. Finally, we use the task label **MD** (modification more difficult) to indicate planned modifications designed for individuals or groups of children who need more of a challenge and the task label **ME** (modification easier) to identify modifications designed to make the task easier for children who are not experiencing success. Examples are below.

Cognitive Knowledge

Cog K When you were the receiver, what were the clues you used to anticipate where the ball was going? Talk with your partner first, and then we will share what you learned.

Cog K Let's make two lists on the whiteboard of the characteristics of good offensive play and poor offensive play in the 3v1 keep-away task today.

Cog K In gymnastics there are three ways to land from a jump. The first is a spring-like landing when your legs are like springs and compress to absorb force and then immediately extend to jump again.

Thinking Skills

Th Without using names, compare and contrast how you adjusted the force you used to strike the ball in a cooperative rally (i.e., striking the ball back and forth as many times in a row as you can) when you had different partners.

Th Think critically about your dribbling, and decide which performance technique to focus on that will improve your dribbling.

Th Discuss with your teammates why the defense is intercepting your passes and how you can solve this problem.

Motivation Concepts

Mot The reason you are improving is your effort and hard work.

Mot The goal for today is to value your self-improvement and help your partner value her or his improvement, not to compare how you did with any other child.

Mot This is a challenging task, and it is important you persist and keep working hard. That is what leads to improvement.

Social Skills

Social Try very hard to be a good partner and toss the ball accurately.

Summary of Task Label Abbreviations

I	Informing tasks
E	Extending/exploring tasks
R	Refinements
A	Application/assessment tasks
Org	Organizing task
Cog K	Cognitive knowledge: Explains or defines a concept
Social	Social skill or concept
Th	Thinking skill
Mot	Motivation concept
Safety	Safety information or reminder
MD	Modification to make the task more difficult
ME	Modification to make the task easier

Source: Adapted and modified from Rink, J. E. (2014). *Teaching physical education for learning* (7th ed.). New York: McGraw-Hill.

Social What do you think you need to change so the task is fair for everyone?

Social When one of your classmates is trying hard but having difficulties, what can you say?

How to Write Tasks

Recall that the principles guiding task design include the importance of practice and designing tasks that provide maximum practice time, designing tasks for open and closed skills and part–whole learning, eliciting tasks, and designing tasks to differentiate instruction to accommodate individual differences. Here we discuss how to write tasks in lesson plans.

We recommend that you write tasks as if you are actually talking to the children. Write down exactly what you plan to say. Put teacher behaviors in [brackets]. When you ask a question, write in the answer or answers you want or expect from the children, again in [brackets]. This format will help you anticipate children's responses and recall the detailed aspects of the content.

The following are two examples of written tasks. The first is a set of tasks from a kindergarten lesson on tossing and catching. The second illustrates how to write an introductory discussion for a fourth-grade lesson on fielding.

Kindergarten Striking Balloons

I Stay in your personal space and strike your balloon straight up in the air using different body parts.

E Explore using as many different body parts as you can to strike the balloon up.

E Which body parts did you use? [Hands, feet.] Those are an excellent start. This time, try to discover different body parts you can use to strike the balloon straight up.

E Which body parts did you use? [Wrists, thighs, ankles, arms, elbows, shins, back of the hand, head.] You thought hard and discovered a lot of different body parts. Now, experiment and see if you can figure out what you need to do to strike the balloon straight up so you remain in your personal space.

Cog K What did you discover? [I had to hit it up, not forward.] What did you do to hit it up? [I put my body part under it and aimed up. I got under the balloon.]

R Excellent suggestions. Let's all work on striking the balloons with different body parts keeping in our personal space by getting the body part under the balloon and striking straight up.

Fourth-Grade Introduction to Dealing with the Pressure of Quickly Fielding and Throwing to a Base to Beat a Runner

Cog K Put your thumbs up if you have ever played in a baseball or softball game. What does the person usually do after catching a batted ball? [Throw it to the base.] Why do the fielders want the base player to catch the ball? [To make an out.] Describe how the fielder needs to catch and throw the ball. [The player needs to catch and then throw quickly because the runner will be safe otherwise.] How does it feel if you are the fielder trying to catch and throw the ball to the base quickly? [Scared, excited, worried, nervous, confident.] That is called pressure. Today we are going to work on dealing with the pressure to throw to beat the runner.

The reasons we suggest writing exactly what you plan to say to the children is that this process will help you think through the details of the content you are teaching. It will also help you learn how to say things efficiently, as you are unlikely to write a long lecture in your lesson plan. It takes fewer words to write what you will say to the children than to write what you as a teacher need to do and say. Finally, you are less likely to leave out important organizational comments.

Although you write what you plan to say, you do not need to memorize or read your words when you teach! You do not even have to say exactly what you planned. Your plan is a teaching tool. When you teach, speak naturally, while using your lesson plan as a guide.

Culminating Activity

It is critical for almost all lessons to have a **culminating activity** in which the children use the skills and movements they have practiced in more complex settings, application tasks, assessments, or centers.

We recommend that dance and gymnastics lessons end with sequences. Early in the unit and with younger children, these sequences will likely be very short (two to four skills or shapes). Toward the end of the unit and with older children, the sequences will be longer and require more time to prepare. The lessons at the end of the unit might begin with a short introductory activity and a short review, with most of the lesson then being devoted to the culminating activity of the unit—that is, a full gymnastics sequence or dance to be used for assessment.

In gymnastics, another appropriate culminating activity is to practice the theme on an apparatus. With this approach, after teaching themes such as balancing, rolling, and jumping on the floor mats, the teacher adds an apparatus, and the children practice those same themes in a more complex environment. Using apparatus is essential for extending children's movement vocabulary. In addition, children find apparatus work enjoyable and interesting. Thus, apparatus can help motivate children to work productively and independently.

The culminating activities for games lessons are typically application tasks or centers for younger children and game-like experiences or small-sided, modified games for older children. These games need to use the skills and tactics taught in the content development section of the lesson. In fact, the content development sections should include game-like experiences so that the transition to the culminating activity is only a small-step progression.

Teachers often use culminating activities to assess the outcomes of their lessons and units, because such activities are authentic activities for using the skills and concepts taught in lessons. Authentic activities are the reasons we teach skills in the first place. Thus, it makes sense to assess students' progress based on their performance on lesson and unit culminating activities.

Closure

At the end of the culminating activity is the lesson **closure** that occurs once the children have put away the equipment. This phase of the class is also an excellent time for making informal assessments of what each child learned during the lesson. Techniques for doing so include brief written assessments, peer discussions, and whole-class discussions.

In your closure, you can ask questions to

- Summarize and extend the learning process.
- Check for understanding.
- Help children connect lesson content to other content or their lives outside of school.
- Help children think critically or in greater depth about lesson content.
- Help children reflect on their feelings about the lesson and what it meant to them.

An excellent teacher will end a lesson knowing what every child learned or did not learn that day. An outside observer should be able to come into your class and ask, "What did the boy in the red shirt learn today? Which children had problems?" We know of one principal who, in part, evaluated student teachers by asking individual children who were walking back from physical education, "What did you learn today?" If the child did not readily respond with something specific, he talked with the student teacher.

Criteria for Lesson Plans

You can use the criteria identified here to evaluate whether you have written a good lesson plan. A good lesson plan achieves the following goals:

- Focuses on meeting the objectives for children's learning outcomes
- Includes motor objectives that describe specifically what children will learn
- Includes cognitive knowledge, thinking skill/motivation, social skill, and/or affective objectives that support the motor content of the lesson
- Consists predominantly of extending tasks and refinements
  - Extending tasks break the content down into a series of tasks organized in a logical progression aimed at learning outcomes safely
  - The progression of extending tasks shows that the teacher has anticipated how children will learn and progress and safety issues that might arise
  - Anticipated refinements reflect the performance techniques of the motor objective
- Includes instructions about safety
- Connects to previous lessons when possible
- Includes MD and ME tasks, indicating the teacher has thought about safety, differentiating instruction, possible problems, and planned task modifications
- Is detailed and specific
- Shows the teacher has engaged in a careful, thoughtful, and thorough planning process
- Demonstrates the teacher is knowledgeable about the subject matter

Scripted Lesson Plans

This section includes a sample lesson plan, followed by a sample plan for a center (or station) when the lesson consists of a set of centers. In this text, we have written scripted lesson plans. Scripted lesson plans are just one of many forms of lesson plans possible, however. We chose this form because when you read the plans, you can envision what the lesson would look like with a class of children. As you will see, we write questions to ask children and include the answers you can expect or want to hear in [brackets]. In addition, we illustrate how you can integrate thinking skills, motivation concepts, and social skills within the lesson plan.

Reviewing scripted lesson plans also gives you access to how teachers think about content and teaching. When you write a scripted lesson plan, you will be learning how to think like a teacher. Thus, these plans serve as teaching tools to help you learn about planning, content, teaching, and children's responses.

How to Use Scripted Lesson Plans

Scripted lesson plans are very detailed. When you use one, you do not memorize it or read it like a script. Instead, you observe

> **Experienced Teachers Talk**
>
> **Advice from a Long-Term Cooperating Teacher**
>
> Here is some advice from a teacher who has supervised many student teachers from several colleges and universities:
>
> Student teachers write their lessons, and they are very well-organized plans. Then they just focus on what they wrote down. They don't rehearse what to say or how to say it. It may sound silly, but you need to rehearse. It's just like mental practice before a game. Consequently, they talk too long, and they are not clear. They have problems anticipating and don't know what to do when things go wrong. They need to spend more time planning alternative strategies for when things go wrong. They can't answer kids' questions. They have not taken the time to think through different scenarios and will get caught when things go in a different direction, and then they don't know what to do next.

the children's responses and make decisions about whether the tasks are eliciting the movement responses and learning outcomes you want. Based on this information, you might decide to change the task, modify the environment, clarify the task, move on to the next task, or give children feedback. In short, the tasks you plan are the starting point for interactive teaching. Plans, however, can't predict every decision you will need to make because you can't predict children's responses on any given day. Scripted plans are only a guide.

In addition, scripted lessons are too long to read once the lesson begins. We recommend that after you write a scripted lesson, you create a brief outline of your tasks that you can put in your pocket and use as a quick reference if needed.

When writing a scripted lesson plan, we plan the left column first. This consists of the progression of informing, extension, and application/assessment tasks. The right column includes anticipated refinements, potential modifications to make the task easier or more difficult if the task we planned proves to be developmentally inappropriate for some or all children, and potential thinking skills, motivation concepts, and social skills we can teach if the need or opportunity arises. In essence, the right column is our best guess about how the children will respond.

SAMPLE PLAN 14.1

Scripted Lesson Plan for Dribbling: Grade 2

Dribbling while Traveling at Different Speeds, Dribbling and Stopping

Prerequisites

Before reading this lesson, you need to know the prerequisite capabilities of the children for whom we wrote it:

- Children must have developed the ability to travel safely, competently, and confidently while jogging fast in a scattered formation without bumping into anyone.
- Children must have developed a level of social responsibility such that they can be trusted to care about the well-being of other children while jogging fast in a scattered formation.
- Children must be able to control the ball while dribbling by pushing with their finger pads and not slapping the ball.
- Children must have learned how to dribble and change directions and pathways to avoid other children and obstacles. These skills include being able to dribble on an angular or curved pathway around cones (i.e., pretend defenders) without bumping into anyone.

These prerequisites are important because the lesson asks children to dribble while traveling at different speeds. They can't focus on traveling at moderate or faster speeds in a scattered formation if they haven't learned how to dribble and change directions and pathways to avoid other children.

Information Influencing Task Selection

Of the four major performance techniques to teach for dribbling, looking up is the most difficult and the last one to develop. Dribbling with the nondominant hand and a cross-over dribble are also challenging, and few children will practice these techniques without teachers reminding them or using tasks that elicit looking up. Dribbling at moderate or fast speeds in a scattered formation and the two "games" in the culminating activity elicit looking up. When teaching this lesson, the teacher will likely need to say "Look up" frequently and "Practice with your nondominant hand."

The decision to focus on the principle of learning and motivation to embrace challenging tasks was selected to help children both challenge themselves and reassure them that being challenged is a good thing and part of learning. Because this lesson is challenging, we offered a choice of easier and more difficult balls to dribble, while reminding children they could change to the other ball at any time.

Grade level: Second

Length of lesson: 40 minutes

Equipment

8-inch playgrounds balls that are not nylon bound (which are bouncy and easier to dribble) and 8-inch nylon-bound playground balls (which are less bouncy and more difficult to dribble): enough for each child to be able to select the appropriate ball for him- or herself

Objectives	Notes and Potential Interactive Decisions
At the end of this lesson, the children will have learned **Motor** 1. To dribble while traveling • At different speeds while looking up. • Stopping quickly by bending the knees and shifting from leaning forward to being upright. • At a speed that they can control.	**Alignment with Standards** This lesson addresses National Standards 1, 2, and 4.

(*continues*)

SAMPLE PLAN 14.1

Scripted Lesson Plan for Dribbling: Grade 2 (*continued*)

Cognitive Knowledge

2. That looking up is important for safety and tactics (to see defenders and teammates).

Thinking Skills and Motivation Concepts

3. To make decisions about switching hands and the appropriate speed to travel: one that challenges them but also ensures success and control.
4. That to improve dribbling it is important (and fun) to challenge yourself with difficult tasks.

Social Skills

5. That disrupting classmates and bumping into them is disrespectful and unfair because it takes away their chance to learn.

Observation Plan

1. Scan the entire lesson to see if all children are scattered and traveling at a safe distance away from one another.
2. Scan the entire lesson to see if all children are traveling at a speed they can control.
3. See if the children are looking up.
4. See if the children shift from leaning forward to being upright to stop quickly.

Introductory Warm-up Activity

Org	When you enter the gym, walk over to the baskets spread along the side wall, select your ball, walk carrying your ball, and get into a scattered formation.		
Mot	Select the ball that will best help you improve your dribbling by challenging you but also allowing you to succeed and control the ball.		
Cog K	What did you learn about the two types of playground balls? [Nylon-bound playground balls are more difficult to dribble; non-nylon-bound playground balls are easier to dribble.]		
I	Start by dribbling in place with your dominant hand. You may enter the gym.	**R**	[Talk as children are dribbling.] Heads up. Look up. Today we will focus on keeping your heads up looking up while you dribble.
Cog K	Stop. Dribbling with your nondominant hand is so much harder than your dominant hand. What would be the advantage of being equally good at dribbling with each hand? [You could use either side in a basketball game so you can protect the ball on either side.]		
E	Now switch and dribble with your nondominant hand.	**Mot**	[Talk as children are dribbling.] It's a challenge to dribble while looking up, but challenging yourself will help you improve.
Introduction **Mot**	I was very proud of your dribbling skills and ability to change directions last week. You are all pushing with your finger pads and dribbling at a waist-high level and to the front and side. You are ready to work on more challenging tasks and looking up while you dribble. To improve your dribbling, you need to challenge yourself. These are very exciting tasks to learn, and it is fun to challenge yourself with difficult tasks.	**ME/MD**	At any time during the lesson, you may change to the bouncier balls if you are not experiencing success or to the less bouncy ball if the tasks are too easy.

SAMPLE PLAN 14.1

Scripted Lesson Plan for Dribbling: Grade 2 (*continued*)

Content Development			
Review of Dribbling with Dominant and Nondominant Hand While Traveling			
E	Now travel about the gym in a scattered formation while dribbling with your dominant hand.	**Safety**	What do you have to do to be safe and not bump into someone else? [Look up.]
		R	Are you looking up? Can you see your classmates?
E	Now travel while dribbling with your nondominant hand.	**R**	Heads up and look up.
E	Now dribble about the space while switching hands, sometimes dribbling with your dominant hand and sometimes with your nondominant hand. You decide when to switch.	**Safety**	Why is it important to see your classmates? [So you don't bump into them and hurt them.]
		Social	But what if you just brush against them having fun—is that okay? [No.] It is unfair to disrupt your classmates' chances to learn.
		ME	[If you observe these movement patterns, a modification is needed.] I can see some of you find using your nondominant hand difficult and you are losing control of the ball. If you lost control of the ball, practice dribbling while walking or even while staying in one place, sometimes dribbling with your dominant hand and sometimes with your nondominant hand. You decide when to switch.
E	As you dribble about the space or in place, try to give each hand equal practice.	**Safety**	Are you paying attention to your classmates so you don't bump into them?
Explore Cross-over Dribbling in Place			
E	Now everyone dribble in place and try to find different ways to bounce the ball from one hand to the other in front of and behind your body and under different body parts.	**ME**	[Scaffold exploration by giving examples if children do not start exploring easily.] For example, you can try bouncing the ball from one hand to the other in front of your body, between your legs, behind your back, and under one leg.
Cog K	We call this a cross-over dribble because the ball crosses from one side of your body to the other.	**Mot**	I can see you are challenging yourselves. Great! When you challenge yourself, you will improve your dribbling.
Dribbling at Different Speeds			
E	When I say "Go," dribble about general space traveling a little faster. Only travel as fast as you can without losing control of the ball. If the ball bounces away from you, if the ball hits your foot, or if the ball bounces into someone, that is a problem. What should you do? [I went too fast—I needed to go slower]. Right. Go.	**R**	Look up to see where you are going.
Cog K	Has anyone ever seen a basketball game being played? When one team has the ball, what is the other team doing? [Trying to steal the ball away.] What would happen if you kept looking at the ball while you were dribbling during the game? [You would not see if defenders are near.] Who else wouldn't you see? [My teammates and if they are in a good place to score so I can pass to them.] Right. Another reason why you are learning to look up is so you will be able to use good tactics when you play games.		
E	Travel about general space using your dominant and nondominant hands and a cross-over dribble to change hands.	**R**	Which performance technique do you need to think about while dribbling? [Looking up.]

(*continues*)

SAMPLE PLAN 14.1

Scripted Lesson Plan for Dribbling: Grade 2 (*continued*)

E	Now let's try more of a challenge. Travel as fast as you can without losing control. You decide how fast you can go.	**Th**	What were some of the things you were thinking about when you were traveling fast? [Watching out for people, not losing control of the ball, not bumping into someone by changing direction when I saw someone ahead of me.]
Mot	Remember, it is fun and important for improving your skills to challenge yourself with difficult tasks.	**Cog K**	Why was going faster more challenging? [It takes the focus off the ball because you need to focus on where you are going.]
		ME	[If you observe a significant number of children are going too fast, then scaffold the decision-making process.] I see some of you had problems making a good decision about how fast to travel. Let's work on making this decision. Dribble while standing in one place and ask yourself, "Am I in control of my ball, or is the ball in control of me?" If you are in control, then you may walk; if not, stand in place. Weiyun made a great decision—she was in control, and she kept the ball in control while she walked. Now, if you are ready and able to control the ball at a faster speed, try walking faster or jogging. Did you make a good decision? Yes, I agree. No one bumped into anyone else, and no one lost control of the ball. Now travel as fast as you can without losing control.
Dribbling at Different Speeds and Stopping			
E	Explore dribbling at different speeds and then suddenly stopping and dribbling in place. You decide when to travel and when to dribble in place. Go.	**Th**	[If you observe children are not practicing stopping, stop the class.] Assess your decision making. Did you stop at least three times, or did you just keep dribbling? Try again, and this time practice stopping frequently.
R	What does your body have to do to stop quickly? Let's try to figure it out. Dribble traveling as fast as you can, but staying in control, and when I say "Stop," stop quickly. Pay attention to what your body is doing. Go. Stop. Go. Stop. Go. Stop.		
Cog K	Tell me what you discovered. [Lift your chest up, bring your feet in front of your hips, bend your knees, shift from leaning forward to being upright.]		
R	Dribble again and practice stopping suddenly.	**R**	Shift quickly from leaning forward to being upright to stop quickly.
		R	Make sure you give each hand equal practice.
R	What is the difference between stopping quickly when you are dribbling traveling fast and slow? Let's experiment. Dribble traveling slowly and stop suddenly, then dribble traveling fast and stop suddenly. Pay attention to the differences in your body positions. Go.		
Cog K	What did you discover? [When going faster: takes longer to stop, need bigger lean, need to bring feet more in front of me, need more knee bend, need feet farther apart.] Great answers.		
R	Try again, varying your speed. See if you can apply what you just learned, and stop as quickly when you dribble and travel fast as you can when you dribble and travel at a moderate speed.		

SAMPLE PLAN 14.1

Scripted Lesson Plan for Dribbling: Grade 2 (*continued*)

Culminating Activities

A	Let's play a game. Dribble traveling when I circle my finger like this [looks like a lasso], and then stop when I hold up my hand as a stop sign [demonstrate as you talk]. With my other hand, I will count off seconds and see how many seconds passed before you looked at my stop signal.	**R**	What are you going to have to do to play this game successfully? Right. You need to look up to see my signals. Go. [Change from finger circle to stop signal frequently.]
A	Try again, and see if you can break your record for stopping in the shortest amount of time.		
A	Let's add changes of speed. I have three cards, and I will hold up only one card at a time. Red means stop quickly and dribble in place, yellow means travel slowly, and green means travel as fast as you can while still in control of the ball. The game is to try to change speeds the instant I change cards. Go. [Repeat several times.]	**R**	What do you need to do to stop quickly [bend knees, shift from leaning forward to being upright].

Closure: Checking for Understanding

A	Go with your assigned partner and discuss why is it important to look up and how to stop suddenly. [Give the children time to discuss these issues.] Select one of your partner's best answers and be prepared to share with the class if I call on you.

SAMPLE PLAN 14.2

Plan for a Dribbling Center

Objectives

As a result of this center, the children will improve

Motor

1. Dribbling on different pathways looking up.

Social

2. Their sensitivity to the need of their partner to have a fair amount of space by looking up and not infringing on their partner's space.

Task

Working with your partner, put the cones anywhere you want in your area. Dribble on different pathways all around the cones any way you want. Be sure to look up to see whether you are letting your partner have a fair amount of space.

ME You can choose to practice dribbling while traveling slowly and focus on pushing with your finger pads rather than slapping the ball.

MD You can travel as fast as you want *as long as you control the ball.*

Questions to Ask

- [If children are sharing space]: What are you doing to share space fairly?
- [If children are infringing on space]: I see Tonya is staying in the corner of your space and doesn't have a chance to dribble around the cones. What is happening here?
- I see your dribbling has improved. Which performance technique were you working on?

Teaching Content Versus Covering the Lesson Material

Beginning teachers sometimes think a lesson plan means they *must* cover all the tasks in one lesson. A lesson plan, however, is simply your best guess as to what children can learn well within one class period. The goal is not to cover the content or get through your lesson plan; rather, the goal is for children to learn the content. The time it will take to achieve that goal is something you cannot know before you teach the lesson.

Accomplished teachers usually can predict (but not always) how much content each of their classes will learn in one lesson. It takes years before beginning teachers can make such estimates accurately. We recommend that beginning teachers not view their lesson plans as the precise amount of content they must cover in one lesson, but instead teach only as much content as the children can learn well. Then, begin the next lesson with a review and continue developing the content from the previous lesson.

The length of time it will take you to teach a lesson segment will vary depending on the children's ages and ability levels, your own experience, and the number of minutes allocated for physical education lessons. Again, teach only as much as you can teach well, and leave the rest for another day.

Unit Plans

Length of Units

The length of units for elementary-age children is different from what you experienced in high school. Many high school units are 10 weeks long. Current physical education scholars recommend high school students spend a minimum of 20 lessons on an activity such as a basketball unit or a health-related physical activity unit.

This span is far too long for the elementary school setting. First, children get bored, and weeks and months feel much longer to a child than to an adolescent. Remember back to how long the school year felt when you were in elementary school and how much shorter years feel as you get older.

Second, children need considerable repetition across the school year to master their basic skills. If they practice dribbling for only one six-week unit of 12 lessons in first grade, but then never repeat that skill until second grade, they will forget much of what you taught and their dribbling skill development will regress. They will learn more and dribble at a more mature level if they practice dribbling in four units of three lessons each spread across the school year.

Unit plans at the elementary level typically run from two to eight lessons, with a caveat: The younger the grade, the shorter the units. Kindergarten through grade 2 are far better served with two- to four-day units focused on one to three different skills per unit—for example, practicing throwing and catching for four lessons and then repeating those skills several times across the school year.

Major Learning Outcome

The process of planning a unit begins by determining the major learning outcome you want to achieve. A **major learning outcome** is a superordinate objective for the unit—it is your main goal for what you want the children to learn. It typically comprises the most important content within the culminating activity of the unit, such as the theme and concepts of the final dance or gymnastics sequence, the tactical skills of the game or game-like experience for older children, or the skill movement variety and quality for younger children. List the major learning outcome at the top of your list of unit objectives.

If possible, this major learning outcome should come directly from your state standards if your state standards are detailed enough. If not, the major learning outcomes for units should be linked to a broader state or national grade-level learning outcome. For example, the major learning outcomes for a unit on countertension and counterbalance, (which are two ways partners can balance together with each child partially supporting the weight of the other child) (**Sample Plan 14.3**),

SAFETY AND LIABILITY 14.1

Increasing Safety and Decreasing Risk of Liability: Guidelines Relevant to Content in this Chapter

In this box, we discuss specific guidelines built on information discussed throughout this text on professional standards of practice, negligence, and liability. The goals of these guidelines are to increase children's safety and decrease teachers' risk of negligence and liability.

- Written lesson and unit plans should follow a progression, or sequence, of tasks that build students' skill performance safely and competently (Halsey, 2005). Being able to provide written documentation of lessons and units is critical in liability lawsuits.
- The scope and sequence of the curriculum, unit plans, and lesson plans should follow standard professional practices, which are described in state and national standards and recommended scope and sequence documents, such as the *National Standards and Grade-Level Outcomes for K–12 Physical Education* (SHAPE, 2014) (Halsey, 2005; Hart & Ritson, 2002).
- Lesson and unit plans should include written instructions for both skills and safety. Safety is emphasized in teaching performance techniques (Halsey, 2005; Hart & Ritson, 2002).
- "Safety issues are identified in all lessons and are monitored continually during each lesson/activity" (National Association of Sport and Physical Education [NASPE], 2010, p. 9).
- A plan for what to observe begins with safety issues and then progresses to skill components.

SAMPLE PLAN 14.3

Sample Gymnastics Block Plan for Grade 5

Unit Objectives for Fifth-Grade Countertension and Counterbalance Unit

As a result of this unit, the children will

Major Learning Outcome

Perform a partner sequence that they have designed and refined on countertension and counterbalance, using a trapezoid, stacked mat, sturdy box, platform, or bench 12 inches in height as an apparatus.

Motor Objectives

Movement Variety Objectives

Learn to perform a variety of countertension and counterbalance movements on floor mats and apparatus

1. Using a variety of like and unlike body parts.
2. In a variety of shapes, with some shapes being original or unusual.
3. Rolling out of countertension and counterbalance in a variety of directions.
4. Connecting countertension and counterbalance with a variety of transitions using step-like actions, rolls, slides, and jumps.
5. Moving out of countertension and counterbalance using step-like actions, rolls, jumps, and slides, and moving directly into another counterbalance or countertension.
6. Rotating or spinning a countertension or counterbalance.

Refinement Objectives

Learn to

1. Stay tight and stretched throughout their bodies when performing countertensions and counterbalances.
2. Roll smoothly, staying tight and rolling to their feet without using their hands.
3. Keep their legs straight and land on their feet (not their knees) in step-like actions.
4. Jump while extending their knees explosively on take-off and keeping their toes pointed in the air.
5. Connect movements smoothly, using no extra steps during transitions.
6. Synchronize their movements with their partners' movements.

Cognitive Knowledge Objective

1. Understand that in a sequence, all the parts fit together logically, with fluid transitions and no extra steps, and end in the next counterbalance or countertension position, ready to begin the next movement.

Thinking Skills Objective

1. Think creatively to generate a variety of shapes and a variety of ways to use different body parts in countertension and counterbalance, finding some that are original and unusual.

Social Objectives

1. Share decisions, listen carefully to their partners' ideas, and care about their partners' opinions by
   - Asking for their partners' opinions.
   - Incorporating their partners' ideas.
   - Listening attentively, smiling, and making eye contact when their partner is talking.

Affective Objectives

1. Enjoy the feeling of being trusted to support a partner's weight.
2. Feel satisfaction and pride in designing an interesting sequence.

(*continues*)

SAMPLE PLAN 14.3

Sample Gymnastics Block Plan for Grade 5 (*continued*)

Day 1 Focus Countertension (CT) lowering into a variety of rolls (see).	Day 2 Focus Countertension (CT) with like and unlike body parts lowering into rolls.	Day 3 Focus Counterbalance (CB) with like and unlike body parts (see).
Major Tasks Countertension: • Both partners hold hands. • One partner creates a stable base, holds wrist to wrist with one hand, and slowly lowers the partner onto mat and into side roll. • One partner lowers the other partner into rolls in different directions holding one and two hands. • Both partners lower at same time and side roll. • Both partners lower at same time and roll in different directions and shapes. **Culminating Activity** Sequence: Design a short sequence of three different countertensions lowering into different rolls. Use rolls and step-like actions to transition back together without taking extra steps, and end in a position ready to begin the next countertension.	**Major Tasks** Countertension: • One partner lowers the other into a variety of rolls, starting by holding like body parts (e.g., hand to hand, hooking elbows). • Same as the preceding task, but start by holding unlike body parts (e.g., hands holding foot, hands holding knee). • Both partners lower into a variety of rolls starting with a variety of like body parts. • Same as the preceding task, but start with a variety of unlike body parts. • Apparatus: Repeat the major tasks above with each pair using a section of a trapezoid (or a stacked mat, sturdy platform, box, or low bench) to add about 12 inches of height. **Culminating Activity** Sequence: Design a short sequence of three different countertensions lowering into a variety of rolls. Use an apparatus. Use rolls, step-like actions, and jumps to transition between countertensions.	**Major Tasks** Counterbalance: • Back to back • With a variety of like body parts (e.g., hands, shoulders) • With a variety of unlike body parts Counterbalance with both partners lowering into a variety of rolls: • Back to back, lower to side rolls • Hands to back, lower to rolls • Starting with unlike body parts • Starting with like body parts • Apparatus: Repeat the major tasks above using an apparatus. **Culminating Activity** Sequence: Design a sequence of three different counterbalances lowering into rolls using rolls, step-like actions, and jumps to transition to the next counterbalance.
Day 4 Focus Counterbalance (CB) and countertension (CT) with a variety of different, original, and creative shapes.	**Day 5 Focus Design a final sequence of counterbalances and countertensions using an apparatus (stacked mats, trapezoid sections, sturdy boxes/platforms/benches about 12 inches in height).**	**Day 6 Focus Class show and teacher assessment.**
Major Tasks Cognitive knowledge: difference between plain, varied, and original and unusual shapes. Countertension with like and unlike body parts making varied and original shapes: • Lowering into rolls with different shapes or ending in different shapes • Lowering into slides or step-like actions making different shapes	**Major Tasks** • Select six (three each) of your most creative and interesting CTs and CBs lowering into rolls, step-like actions, jumps, and slides. • Design new CBs and CTs if necessary to add originality. • Arrange the CBs and CTs into a logical sequence that facilitates good transitions. • Design transitions to eliminate any extra steps between a CB and CT.	**Major Tasks** • Practice and perfect the performance techniques of the sequence. • The teacher assesses the sequences on originality, transitions, and movement quality using a rubric. **Culminating Activity** Show the sequences to the class, with several groups performing at once. Have the class give compliments to each group, explaining what was good about the sequence.

SAMPLE PLAN 14.3

Sample Gymnastics Block Plan for Grade 5 (*continued*)

Counterbalance with like and unlike body parts making varied and original shapes:

- Same as CT above
- Same as CT above
- CB transitioning immediately to a second CB or CT
- Trying different ways to rotate or spin the CB or CT

Culminating Activity

Select your three most original and creative CTs and CBs to show the class.

Culminating Activity

Practice and perfect the performance techniques.

Perform a dress rehearsal of the complete sequence with peer coaching using the rubric the teacher will use for the assessment.

is linked to the grade 5 learning outcome from National Standard 1: "Combines actions and balances to create a gymnastics sequence with a partner on equipment or apparatus" (Society of Health and Physical Educators [SHAPE], 2014, p. 28), and Grade 3 learning outcome from National Standard 2: "Employs the concept of muscular tension with balance in gymnastics" (SHAPE, 2014, p. 33).

Unit Objectives

Unit objectives are similar to lesson objectives except that unit objectives are broader and encompass more content (see **Sample Plan 14.3**). Unit objectives break down the major learning outcome into the motor, cognitive knowledge, thinking skill/motivation, social skill, and affective content on which you plan to focus. Because the culminating activity is most often the source of the major learning outcome and related unit objectives, teachers typically assess the unit culminating activity and design assessment tools based on some or all of the unit objectives. This technique ensures that your assessment is aligned with your objectives. Based on your major learning outcome, write your motor objectives and decide how many lessons will be in the unit.

Figure 14.4 Countertension leading into a roll and balance

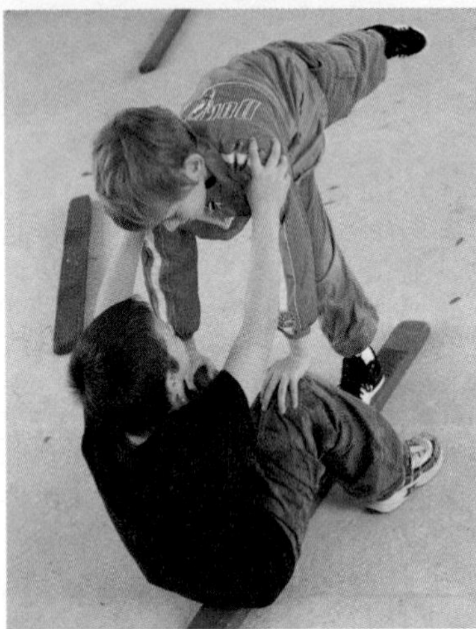

Figure 14.5 Counterbalances
Courtesy of John Dolly

Block Plan of Major Tasks

Once you define your major outcome and motor objectives, you can start planning the content and major tasks for each day of the unit. The most common form of unit plan is called a block plan. A **block plan** lists the major tasks and the culminating activity for the set of lessons in the unit (see **Sample Plan 14.3**). The content for each lesson is identified in a separate box. Teachers write unit plans before they write lesson plans because the block plan serves as an outline for each lesson.

To plan the major tasks of the unit, use top-down and bottom-up planning. Top-down and bottom-up planning is a process in which you build a progression by simultaneously considering the desired learning outcome, unit objectives, and culminating activity you want for the end of the unit, and ensuring a progression of content from simple to complex that begins with students' prior knowledge and experience. In other words, you think both top down from your objectives and bottom up from where students begin.

Following is a description of top-down and bottom-up planning for a unit plan. A similar process also works for lesson plans.

1. Start with the major learning outcome and what you envision to be the assessment and culminating activity, and write the motor objectives. Notice in Sample Plan 14.3, we choose to divide the movement variety and refinement aspects of the motor objectives. We could have combined these, but the objectives would be wordy and we would need to repeat the refinement objectives in several movement variety objectives.
2. Consider carefully the prior knowledge and experiences of the children. Ask yourself, "Have they learned this content? Are they ready to learn this content? What prior knowledge and skills do they have that will help them in this unit?"
3. Brainstorm and then figure out which skills and knowledge the students will need to learn to meet the unit objectives and successfully participate in the culminating activity. Use the Laban framework for games, dance, and gymnastics to help you identify appropriate content.
4. Break those skills and knowledge down into smaller, yet still meaningful, chunks. As you break down the content, you should begin to develop a sense of potential learning outcomes, objectives, and assessments for each lesson. Divide the content into the number of lessons in the unit, and decide on a progression of major tasks for each day, building from simple to complex or easier to more difficult content. List each lesson focus and the major tasks in each block of the block plan. For example, look at the major learning outcome and the movement variety objectives, and then compare these to the focus for each of the six lessons and the major tasks in Sample Plan 14.3.
5. Take a moment to reevaluate your planned culminating activity for the unit. Ask, "Is this activity reasonable to accomplish, and will it follow logically from the lessons? Will the children be successful with and prepared for the culminating activity with the time I have in the unit? Does it represent an important activity that will allow me to assess a substantive learning outcome for the unit?" If necessary, revise the culminating activity and intended learning outcome.
6. For your unit plan, plan intermediary culminating activities and assessments for each lesson in the unit that build to the culminating activity of the unit (see the culminating activities for each lesson in Sample Plan 14.3).
7. Consider the students' prior knowledge and the motor objectives, and write the cognitive knowledge objectives for the unit.
8. Consider the students' prior experiences and the thinking skills, social skills, and affective content that are part of the unit tasks. Write the thinking skill/motivation concepts, social skill, and affective objectives for the unit.
9. Plan the lessons.

Curriculum Scripts

In planning units, don't be swayed by traditional progressions that are called curriculum scripts. A curriculum script is a familiar progression taught year after year in the same way, regardless of the students' prior knowledge and experiences.

For example, the curriculum script for a basketball unit calls for students to stand in squads and dribble weaving to the left and right of cones in a straight line down the gym; practice chest passes, bounce passes, and overhand passes standing about 10 feet from a partner; practice lay-up shots and set shots; and then play five-on-five games.

A curriculum script includes a set of drills you accept uncritically as the "right" way to begin a unit or to teach and practice skills. Perhaps you learned these drills from coaches or teachers. Some traditional drills are tried and true—they work well. Others don't. Part of your job as a physical education teacher is to think critically about your prior knowledge and experience and to be open to new ideas. For example, think critically about the three-person weave drill in basketball. Students practice sending lead passes, which is important content, but they also follow their passes, which is not what you want them to do in a basketball game because this behavior draws the defender closer to the receiver and the ball. Even so, many teachers blindly accept the three-person weave because it is traditional content.

Most of the time, curriculum script progressions are ineffective. Some students already can perform the skills; for them, the tasks are developmentally inappropriate. (Why teach a cartwheel if most of the class can do it?) The repetition is an inefficient use of time and can lead to boredom and management problems.

Moreover, the traditional order of beginning with skills and then progressing to games can be detrimental to motivation and less effective for learning. Research on an approach called Teaching Games for Understanding found that for older children and adolescents, starting with small-sided games and game-like situations—rather than skills practiced in isolation—was more effective for motivating students and helping them to understand the purpose, meaning, and importance of the skill practices included later in the unit (Butler & Griffin, 2010; Oslin & Mitchell, 2006).

K–5 Programs and Grade-Level Plans

It is an awesome responsibility to decide which physical skills and activities children will learn across their entire elementary school career. This decision can feel overwhelming to beginning teachers. In this section, we show you how to get started planning what you will teach each grade within one school year and how to plan the total K–5 program.

K–5 Program Plans

A K–5 program plan outlines the major learning outcomes children will acquire from kindergarten through fifth grade. Such a program plan is a *vertical progression* because it shows how each grade's content builds on what children learned in the previous grade. Thus, you would plan the K–5 dance content; gymnastics content; content related to the skills and tactics of invasion, net/wall, field, and target games; and health-related physical activity content. A K–5 plan is the broadest and least detailed of the four types of plans.

K–5 plans must align with the National Standards for Physical Education and your state standards or programs of study. State K–5 standards are typically more specific than the National Standards. In addition, some districts and counties develop their own K–5 programs of study, which are even more detailed than the state and national standards. Most schools require teachers to base their K–5 program on state standards.

When you are a new teacher in a school, don't be afraid to backtrack on the K–5 plan and teach older grades content listed for younger grades if needed. You might find that children in the upper grades have not yet mastered the skills typically learned in a K–2 program; if so, you will need to go back and teach those skills to the older children. Assess the children's skill levels and prior knowledge, and begin at their level of development.

In designing your vertical program plan, we suggest you consider the following criteria.

Less Is More

A good K–5 program plan provides in-depth learning of the significant content in the physical education field. As we and many other teachers and curriculum writers suggest, you need to avoid teaching any and every physical activity you read about or see. If you don't limit activities to allow for in-depth learning of fewer skills and concepts, your program will become an exposure curriculum in which children experience many activities, but don't have the time to develop skills to a level of maturity that will support their participation in physical activities on a lifelong basis. An exposure curriculum is a mile wide and an inch deep. When you teach fewer activities in depth, the curriculum leads to more learning. In this case, less is more.

Each Grade Builds on Previous Grades

In a vertical curriculum, the content taught in each grade builds on the content the children learned in the previous grade. To plan this vertical progression, consider the children's prior knowledge and experiences and start new units at the learners' current developmental levels. Repeat work on major skills at each grade level, but ensure that the movement variety, performance techniques, and the use of the skill in application contexts become more difficult or complex. As noted earlier, teaching a curriculum script using the same tasks each year is inefficient, ineffective, and boring for students.

The Elementary School Years Represent a Unique Period in Children's Development

You also need to consider what is unique about students in elementary, middle, and high school, especially in relation to their social and emotional development. Many exciting programs have been developed for secondary students. For example, Project Adventure and the trust- and team-building activities that are part of that program are a perfect match for the social and emotional developmental needs of adolescents to establish peer group relationships, to work on personal relationships, and to learn more about their own personalities, feelings, and abilities to interact with peers.

Project Adventure is truly an outstanding program that can also be taught well in the elementary grades. However, if children have Project Adventure units during the K–5 years, they will be bored with this approach by the time they reach the age when the program is most powerful. How many times can you solve the challenge of the "electric fence" (in which a

Experienced Teachers Talk

Experiences of a Beginning Teacher

My first year was overwhelming in trying to decide what to do. I took a job just before school started, and the PE teacher before me did not teach skills. The kids ran laps and played kickball—he was a ball roller. So I wrote one plan for teaching K–2 skills and one for 3–5 skills. That's all I could manage for the first month in the time I had, with all the lesson plans and unit plans I had to write, too. It wasn't great, but it worked okay because the kids hadn't learned the skills anyway, and I had to start with the basics. I wish I had gotten the job at the beginning of the summer so I would have had time to plan.

group of students must get their entire group over a chest-high rope representing an electric fence that extends to the ground) before students will roll their eyes at you and say, "We did this before"? Every good idea developed for middle and high school students does not need to start at the elementary level. We need to leave some activities for middle and high school teachers.

Conversely, many activities that are excellent choices at the elementary level would be disastrous or silly at the secondary level because of children's differing cognitive, social, and emotional developmental levels. Elementary school games do not have to be modified versions of middle school games, nor do they need to "grow up" to look like middle school games. For example, dribble tag-type games, dribbling routines (like the one in *High School Musical*), and dribbling tricks are great elementary school activities for practicing dribbling skills and tactics, but they do not evolve into five-on-five basketball.

How to Plan the K–5 Program

After examining the courses of study and the state and national standards and referring to texts such as this one, we suggest you plan a progression for three grades—either K, 2, and 4 or 1, 3, and 5. After completing three grades, it is a simple matter to shift and adapt the content for the other three.

With experience, you will easily be able to plan for all grades at the same time. We also recommend that you begin with the games portion of the curriculum, because this is the area most familiar to beginning physical education teachers. We suggest that you develop your K–5 plan by following these steps:

Step One

Gather the national, state, and district standards to use as references. For each skill, brainstorm a list of variations of that skill and game-like experiences that you might teach. Use the Laban framework to help you generate ideas. Narrow your list to those experiences you believe are the most essential and significant content for children to learn. Take into consideration the number of lessons per week you teach each class. Below we give you a list resulting from our brainstorming of possible content to teach for catching K–5. Notice we organize the content using the four aspects of the Laban framework, which helped us generate content ideas. Also notice that the relationship aspect includes game tactics.

Brainstorm List of K–5 Content for Catching Using the Laban Framework

Body Aspects

- Left and right hands, both hands, with a glove, self-tossed, and from a partner
- Different-sized and -shaped balls
- While standing still and while moving
- With scoops or lacrosse sticks
- Bounce and catch
- Toss against wall and catch
- Combining catching and passing, catching and overhand throwing, catching and dribbling

Space Aspects

- In all areas of personal space; at high, medium, and low levels
- Near to you and extending far from you
- From different directions
- Balls traveling on different air pathways (from grounders to pop flies)

Effort Aspects

- Balls thrown with different amounts of force and speed

Relationships

- While defended
- Catching in a position that leads most directly to the next skill or movement for the game situation
- Cutting into a free space to catch a pass
- Cutting into the most advantageous space for the game situation and catching a pass
- Catching and throwing to the appropriate base ahead of the runner(s)
- Running a planned pass receiver route to allow you to catch a ball in an area free from defenders

Step Two

Determine the content for grades K, 2, and 4 (or 1, 3, and 5). Typically kindergarten and grade 1 focus on fundamental skills, grades 2 and 3 focus on varying those skills, combining skills, and using skills in game-like tasks, and grades 4 and 5 focus on tactical skills, tactics, game-like experiences, and modified, small-sided games. Below we list our decisions about catching for grades K, 2, and 4. Notice how we use our brainstorm list of content from step 1 to develop step 2 grade-level content.

Proposed Catching Content by Grade Level

Note: We deleted lacrosse because we teach in a school without such equipment and in an area of the country where lacrosse is not played. You may make a different decision based on where your school is located.

Catching

Kindergarten

- Both hands self-tossed
- Right and left hands self-tossed
- Different-sized and -shaped balls
- While standing still and while moving

Grade 2

- To the left and right, so you must move to catch ball tossed from partner

Grade 4

- From different directions (from behind or over the shoulder or head while traveling forward, from behind on a diagonal, from the side, from the front on a diagonal, from the front while traveling forward)
- Balls thrown with strong amounts of force and speed
- Apex of high balls
- While defended

- Balls traveling on different air pathways (from grounders to pop flies)
- In all areas of personal space; at high, medium, and low levels
- Near to you and extending far from you
- Combining catching and passing, catching and throwing, and catching and dribbling
- Balls thrown with moderate amounts of force and speed
- Cutting into a free space to receive a pass
- Catching and throwing to the appropriate base ahead of the runner(s)

Step Three

Determine the content for the other three grades. Check the vertical progression to confirm that you have taught the skills in the K–3 grades that the children will need to participate in the game-like situations in grades 4 and 5.

Step Four

Next, plan your gymnastics, dance, and fitness content by following the same procedure. If you are not very experienced in these areas, we suggest you use texts such as this one as your guide. Health-related physical activity (HRPA) and health-related fitness (HRF) are areas of the curriculum with different requirements.

Year-Long Plans

Your year-long plan describes what you will teach each week for each grade across the school year. Curriculum scholars refer to this type of plan as a *horizontal progression*. Begin by counting the weeks of school and the number of lessons per week. Multiply the weeks by the number of lessons and subtract the days off for holidays. This calculation identifies the number of lessons per grade in one year.

Deciding the Percentage of Time to Be Spent on Games, Dance, and Gymnastics

Next, you should decide how many lessons you will devote to games, dance, and gymnastics by grade. Many curriculum scholars suggest that you spend an equal percentage of time on each content area, especially in grades K–2. This division allows children to develop locomotor skills that will be used in combination with games skills in later units (e.g., jumping, leaping, and sliding while throwing and catching). It also helps children develop an excellent understanding of the Laban movement concepts in dance and gymnastics without having to worry about controlling a ball. For example, when they have explored knowing the range of their personal space in dance in the younger grades, children will be better able to explore catching balls in all areas of their personal space in the older grades. Finally, giving equal time to games, gymnastics, and dance provides a curriculum that is meaningful for both boys and girls, and for children of all races, ethnicities, abilities, and disabilities.

Other sources suggest that as children become older, teachers should increase the percentage of game lessons to accommodate the increased amount of tactical content children are developmentally able to learn. However, older children who have had a strong K–2 dance and gymnastics program will likely want to continue their work in these two areas, so the same percentage of time should be devoted to them as is allocated to games.

Selecting the Number of Lessons or Weeks for Each Skill/Content Unit

Your K–5 plan provides an excellent starting point for selecting the specific content for your year-long plan. Develop the year-long plan the same way, but be much more specific. Again, we suggest starting with games because it will likely be easier.

1. Decide and note how many lessons you will spend on games, dance, and gymnastics content across the school year.
2. Brainstorm a list of games skills, movement variety for games skills, tactical skills, tactics, game-like experiences, and/or games for one grade. Start with either a young age group (kindergarten or first grade) or an older age group (fourth or fifth grade). Use the Laban framework for games to help you identify content.
3. Considering the importance of the content, select the content for that grade for one year. During this process, your major learning outcomes should begin to emerge. Then decide how many lessons or weeks to spend on each skill, tactic, or game.
4. Decide how many units you will teach for each skill, tactic, or game situation. Remember, young children need shorter units and repeated practice of a skill in several units across the school year. For the K–2 grades, it is a good idea to combine two to three skills in a lesson, in particular if you have a shortage of equipment or space.
5. Repeat the process for two other grades so you end up with a year-long plan for games content in grades K, 2, and 4 (or grades 1, 3, and 5).
6. Repeat the process for gymnastics themes and dance lessons. With gymnastics, your decisions about the length of units will often be dictated by equipment and apparatus availability and storage. In many schools, the apparatus and mats are not easily accessible. Once you get the mats out and equipment set up, it is easier to have every grade working on gymnastics at the same time, even though the various groups will be working on different themes. In other districts, you may share equipment across schools and, therefore, will have little flexibility in scheduling.
7. Order your units across the school year. Weather is often the most important factor affecting your decision making in this area. In the north, activities such as kicking, punting, soccer tactics, and game-like situations need to be done in the fall or spring when classes can be taught outside. In the south, where many schools have no indoor physical education space, soccer-type activities should be done in the winter, both to keep children active and warm and because the heat in the fall and spring can negatively affect children's energy levels in endurance running activities.
8. Repeat the process for the other three grades.

For teachers with minimal indoor space, we recommend teaching dance lessons on rainy days when you must teach inside. Most of the dance lessons in this text can be done in limited space. Have your lessons planned and ready to go. Then, if it rains in the middle of an outdoor unit, you can simply switch to the next dance lesson in your year-long plan, returning to the original planned unit once the weather improves.

Sample Plan 14.4 illustrates a possible year-long plan for grade 3.

SAMPLE PLAN 14.4

Year-Long Plan for Grade 3

This year-long plan describes a physical education program that is administered three days per week. We have taken all lesson plans from the games, dance, and gymnastics content chapters of this text. This plan assumes the children know how to set up and work independently at centers, have developed the social skills needed to work with partners and small groups, have progressed beyond level 1 content in games and gymnastics, and have ample experiences with level 1 dance content in grades K–2.

August

Week 1—Creative dance: Body actions

Day 1: Review management routines. Body action learning experiences.

Day 2: Review management routines. Body actions; begin to develop individual sequences.

Day 3: Complete and refine sequences; have class show.

Week 2—Games: Refine throwing and catching

Day 1: Practice previously learned throwing techniques if needed (side to target, elbow up, thumb on bottom in backswing, rock and roll). Teach new techniques if students are ready: stepping straight to target, shuffle. Practice previously learned catching techniques if needed (reach, cover, and cradle). Teach new techniques if students are ready: ground balls fielded with legs apart and bottoms up, pinkies together for grounders, thumbs together with fingers up (not forward) for high balls.

Day 2: Use centers to practice techniques for throwing and catching.

Day 3: Continue rotating centers. Teacher assessment.

September

Week 3—Gymnastics: Refine jumping for height and distance, hopping, and five types of flight from feet

Day 1: Mini-lessons on five types of flight from feet and jumping for height and distance.

Day 2: Continue workshop, with children rotating centers.

Day 3: Continue workshop, with children rotating centers. Peer coaching and assessment.

Week 4—Games: Refine dribbling with hand

Day 1: Dribbling on different pathways. Practice previously learned dribbling techniques if needed (push with finger pads/don't slap the ball, waist high, ball to front/side, heads up/look up). New technique: on zigzag pathways, make a very sharp angle by bending the knee and pushing off with the foot extended beyond the hips. Practice previously learned ways to combine dribbling and shooting.

Day 2: Child-designed challenge courses dribbling on different pathways with shot on goal.

Day 3: Dribbling at different speeds; child-designed challenge courses dribbling at different speeds with shot on goal. Teacher assessment.

Week 5—Creative dance: Round, wide, thin, angular, and twisted shapes; rising/falling; swirling; turning jumps

Day 1: Autumn leaves lesson plan (integrated with science).

Day 2: *The Snowy Day* lesson plan, part 1 (integrated with children's literature).

Day 3: *The Snowy Day* lesson plan, part 2, ending in individual sequence. Peer coaching and assessment.

Week 6—Games: Striking with hands (light vinyl balls) over low nets, striking large light balls over high nets

Day 1: Techniques. Aligning to the side of where the ball bounces and hitting it after its apex; using a circular backswing for striking over low nets; getting under the ball for high-net striking.

Day 2: Centers to practice techniques for striking skills from day 1.

Day 3: Continue rotating centers. Teacher assessment.

SAMPLE PLAN 14.4

Year-Long Plan for Grade 3 (*continued*)

October

Week 7—Games: Dribbling with the feet

Day 1: Dribbling with the feet on different pathways; finesse shooting. Practice previously learned techniques if needed (use inside of the foot, outside of the foot; use laces while dribbling but not the toes; step to side and slightly behind the ball for shooting with inside of the foot; squash the bug position). Provide new cues if students are ready: lock ankle, point nonkicking foot at the goal, lean forward and step on kicking foot on follow-through; make really sharp angles to dodge imaginary defenders while dribbling on zigzag pathway.

Day 2: Child-designed challenge courses dribbling on different pathways with shot on goal.

Day 3: Dribbling at different speeds; child-designed challenge courses dribbling at different speeds with shot on goal. Teacher assessment.

Week 8—Folk dance: How to design a folk dance using formations, locomotor steps in a repeatable pattern, and gestures and actions to represent something

Day 1: Part 1, child-designed lesson plan using topics studied in the classroom social studies unit about their state.

Day 2: Part 2, work on child-designed folk dance in groups of two to four students.

Day 3: Practice and refine dance; peer coaching and assessment; class show for classroom teacher.

Week 9—Games: Introduction to net game structures and tactics with deck tennis rings or homemade paper rings

Day 1: Tactics for creating space. Toss and catch quickly, toss where opponent can't catch it, make opponent move. Game structures: learning when boundaries are too wide and too narrow for a good rally.

Day 2: Tactics for defending space. Getting back to central ready position, anticipating where the opponent will toss the ring by looking for clues.

Day 3: Tactics for creating space. Thinking ahead (while the opponent is moving to make a catch, think about where my next toss will be sent).

Week 10—HRF components and creative dance: Effort—wringing, slashing, scurrying, slithering

Day 1: *Where the Wild Things Are* dance lesson to teach HRF components: cardiorespiratory endurance, body composition, muscle fitness (strength, power, and endurance), and flexibility.

Day 2: Effort: *Invasive Species* integrating an informational text on a science topic taught in the classroom. Design a dance in groups of three.

Day 3: Practice and refine dance; peer coaching and assessment; class show of dances.

November

Gymnastics: Three-week unit on combining skills on floor mats and then adding apparatus (stacked mats, trapezoid sections, stable boxes, or platforms about 8 to 12 inches high).

Week 11—Gymnastics: Combining skills

Day 1: Combining jumping and safety rolls, jumping making different shapes, and rolling in different directions.

Day 2: Combining balancing on different body parts and in different shapes and rolling in different directions.

Day 3: Combining a variety of step-like actions and rolling in different directions. Peer coaching and assessment.

Week 12—Gymnastics: Combining skills using apparatus (stacked mats, trapezoid sections, wide benches, or short stable boxes about 8 to 12 inches in height)

Day 1: Balancing and rolling in different directions; on and off stacked mats/trapezoid sections at different levels and changing levels.

Day 2: Connecting two balances in different shapes on different body parts, on and off stacked mats/trapezoid sections at different levels and changing levels.

Day 3: Combining rolling and step-like actions on, over, and off stacked mats/trapezoid sections at different levels and changing levels. Peer coaching and assessment.

Week 13—Designing sequences

Day 1: Work on transitions, learning not to take any steps between movements. The end of the first movement is the exact starting position for the next movement. Begin designing individual sequences using stacked mats or trapezoid sections,

(*continues*)

SAMPLE PLAN 14.4

Year-Long Plan for Grade 3 (*continued*)

consisting of balancing, rolling, and using step-like actions in different ways, different shapes, and at different levels (based on content learned in gymnastics lessons 1–6).

Day 2: Work on making transitions fluid and smooth without hesitations. Finish designing the sequence. Begin to practice the sequence.

Day 3: Practice with peer coaching/assessment. Class show of sequences. Teacher assessment.

Week 14—Games: Introduction to invasion game structures and tactics with tag-type games

Day 1: Game structures: setting perfectly sized boundaries that are not too large (which favor the offense) and not too small (which favor the defense). Designing rules and consequences that are fair for both defense and offense. Offensive tactics for avoiding boundaries and defenders. Defensive tactics for using boundaries to constrain and trap runners.

Day 2: Game structure: designing tag games with bases, including rules and consequences needed for a base. Offensive and defensive team tactics for a base. Tactics: decoys, sacrifices, and blocking for scoring; concentrating the defense near likely places to score.

Day 3: Goal-oriented tag-type games. Tactics: zone and one-on-one defenses, blitzing, and picks. Teacher assessment.

December

Week 15—Creative dance: Mirror, match, contrast

Day 1: Mirroring, matching, and contrasting shapes with partner.

Day 2: Design a sequence with a partner.

Day 3: Refine the sequence with peer coaching/assessment. Show sequences with teacher assessment.

Week 16—Gymnastics: Jump rope

Day 1: Practice previously learned skills if needed (single and double jumps, figure eights, turning). Learn cross-arm swinging if ready.

Day 2: Long rope jumping. Practice previously learned skills if needed (front door, back door, jumping in and out alone and with partners). Learn tricks (e.g., turners jumping, push-up jumps, round-offs, squats, leap frog).

Day 3: In groups of four, design a long rope jumping sequence. Peer coaching/assessment. Class show of sequences.

Week 17—Games: Striking over low nets with hands or rackets (if ready) using large vinyl balls, progressing to smaller balls when ready

Day 1: Aiming by having the hand or racket face perpendicular and toward the partner. Cooperative rallies.

Day 2: Moving to align to the side to hit the ball as it's falling after the bounce. Cooperative rallies.

Day 3: Setting boundaries that work for you and your partner. Cooperative rallies. Rotate partners and change boundaries to work with new partner. Teacher assessment.

January

Week 18—Folk dance: Balkan countries, schottische, grapevine steps

Day 1: *Schottische*, modified *Poskok* (Serbia), modified *Kalamatianos* (Greece) (integrated with social studies).

Day 2: Grapevine, modified *Kalamatianos*.

Day 3: Child-designed sequence of folk dance steps including *schottische* and grapevine.

Weeks 19–21: Gymnastics

Consists of a two-week unit on matching, contrasting, and complementing; plus a one-week unit on varying speed.

Week 19—Gymnastics: Matching, contrasting, complementing

Day 1: Lesson on matching and contrasting; short partner sequence.

Day 2: Matching, contrasting, and complementary shapes; add to partner sequence.

Day 3: Add stacked mats or trapezoid sections using the tasks from lessons 1 and 2.

Week 20—Continue work on matching, contrasting, and complementing

Day 1: Arrange two or three stacked mats for your sequence. Brainstorm with a partner ways to match, contrast, and complement shapes and actions on your apparatus center.

Day 2: Design a partner sequence.

Day 3: Refine the sequence with peer coaching/assessment. Class show.

SAMPLE PLAN 14.4

Year-Long Plan for Grade 3 (*continued*)

Week 21—Clear changes in speed: Using mats and apparatus

Day 1: Lesson on different speeds. Develop a short individual sequence.

Day 2: Add apparatus, and repeat and modify tasks. Begin to develop the sequence while using both the floor and apparatus.

Day 3: Refine, practice, and show the sequence at different speeds.

February

Week 22—Creative dance: Effort—light, strong, heavy, sudden, sustained

Day 1: Animal haiku lesson plans from *If Not for the Cat* (integrating with children's literature): jellyfish, hummingbird.

Day 2: Cat and mouse, kangaroo, sloth.

Day 3: Rattlesnake, butterfly metamorphosis.

Week 23—Games: Batting

Day 1: Practice previously learned cues if needed (back foot pivot, front foot close, swing shoulder to shoulder). New techniques: head still, track ball to contact. Judging extension (ball near to you, down the middle, far from you). Practice at centers (e.g., batting tees, whiffle balls hanging from strings, partner soft toss, ball machines).

Day 2: Continue rotating centers with peer coaching/assessment.

Day 3: Continue rotating centers with peer coaching/assessment. Teacher assessment.

Week 24—Folk dance: Partners movements to meet and part (e.g., do-sa-do, star turns)

Day 1: Partners movements to meet and part (e.g., do-sa-do, star turns). Modified *Tarantella*.

Day 2: More authentic *Tarantella*; child-designed partner dance based on the story behind the *Tarantella* using energetic steps and partner movements to meet and part.

Day 3: Practice and refine the dance with peer coaching/assessment. Class show.

Week 25—Games: Throwing and catching as tactical skills for field games

Day 1: Tactical skill: Catch and throw in one motion quickly to target.

Day 2: "Runner beats the throw" game-like experiences.

Day 3: "Catching a batted ball" and "runner beats the throw" types of games. Teacher assessment.

March

Week 26—Creative dance: Bound flow, stretch and curl

Day 1: Prey-and-predator lesson plan, part 1 (integrating with science).

Day 2: Prey-and-predator lesson plan, part 2. Design a partner sequence.

Day 3: Practice and refine the dance with peer coaching/assessment. Class show of partner sequences.

Week 27—Games: Sending lead passes, cutting to receive a pass

Day 1: Sending lead passes (receiver does not need to stop, reach back, or slow down to catch), cutting on a straight pathway by making 45-degree angle toward the passer, running forward (not sliding), and accelerating.

Day 2: Techniques: making catchable passes, applying the right amount of force, judging the receiver's speed, catching in front of the body (not needing to turn to catch).

Day 3: Add a defender. Techniques: plant, razor, run. Cut again if the passer doesn't send the ball. The passer anticipates when the receiver will be free.

Week 28—Games: Continuation of week 27 invasion game tactics for passing and catching with hands

Day 1: Three-on-one keep away. Tactics: passing to open receiver, cutting into a space. Defender must guard receivers, never the passer.

Day 2: Same as day 1, working on recognizing an open passing lane.

Day 3: Same as day 1, trying to increase the number of successful passes in a row. Teacher assessment.

Week 29—Folk dance: Native American dance following grade 3 field trip to Moundville State Archaeological Park and Museum (prehistoric Native American site)

Day 1: Current intertribal steps: toe heel, canoe step, three-tap stomp, two-one-two-one, pawing. Snake dance as a whole class.

Day 2: Three-hop stomp, three-hop pivot. Design own freestyle dance.

(*continues*)

SAMPLE PLAN 14.4

Year-Long Plan for Grade 3 (*continued*)

Day 3: Refine and practice the freestyle dance. Creative dance lesson part 1: representing an animal from the prehistoric period important to a tribe from the state exploring ways to use current intertribal steps, combined with gestures and shapes to represent the animal.

April

Week 30—Continue Native American unit

Day 1: Practice free style dance. Creative dance lesson part 2: design individual dance representing an animal.

Day 2: Refine and practice individual dance. Dress rehearsal for powwow: grand entry, snake dance, freestyle dance, individual animal dance. Teacher assessment of individual dance.

Day 3: *Song Within Your Heart* powwow for parents.

Week 31—Games: Striking over high nets; practicing skills, cooperative rally tactics

Day 1: Techniques: using legs for force and arms to guide.

Day 2: Cooperative rallies. Techniques: moving to, aligning with, and getting under the ball.

Day 3: Cooperative 2v2 rallies. Tactics: covering the space, calling for the ball. Game structures: designing perfect boundaries and net height for cooperative rallies. Teacher assessment.

Week 32—Gymnastics: Over, under, on, off, through three-week unit with playground or larger apparatus set up as centers

Day 1: Following a leader on large apparatus centers. Rotate centers.

Day 2: Apparatus centers: traveling over, under, on, off, and through apparatus. Rotate centers.

Day 3: Select a center and design a short sequence of traveling over, under, on, off, and through the apparatus.

Week 33—Gymnastics: Levels, twisting, and turning (on apparatus centers)

Day 1: Levels: holding shapes and balances and doing skills at different levels on the apparatus centers. Rotate centers.

Day 2: Using different skills and actions to connect movements and shapes at different levels. Rotate centers.

Day 3: Twisting and turning to move on, over, under, off, and through the apparatus. Rotate centers.

May

Week 34—Gymnastics: Designing individual sequences on an apparatus center

Day 1: Select a center and brainstorm ways of traveling and balancing over, under, on, off, and through for your sequence. Select your best movements and put them into a sequence.

Day 2: Brainstorm ways to incorporate twisting, turning, and changing levels into your sequence as transitions or as major actions. Complete designing your sequence.

Day 3: Refine, practice, and show sequences. Teacher assessment.

Week 35—Games: Dribbling, passing, trapping a ball with the feet, invasion game tactics

Day 1: Dribbling with the feet. Tactics: shielding the ball. Child-designed challenge courses with defender in a one-on-one setup.

Day 2: Child-designed, keep-away type of game, 3v1 setup. Tactics: sending lead passes to open receivers; marking receivers and intercepting passes. Game structures: setting boundaries, rules, and consequences.

Day 3: Continue with day 2 content; with different groups. Teacher assessment.

Week 36—Summer fitness fun: Health-related fitness; using centers with soccer and gymnastics skills to illustrate the components

Day 1: HRF concepts: review cardiorespiratory endurance, muscle fitness (strength, power, endurance), and flexibility; Teach effects of exercising the cardiorespiratory system on the body, intensity levels, and the specificity principle. Teach half the centers.

Day 2: Teach the rest of the centers, and have children begin working at and rotating centers. Cardiorespiratory endurance sample centers using soccer dribbling, dribbling and shooting, one-on-one game-like tasks, and so on. Muscle strength, power, and endurance gymnastics centers using playground apparatus and other available gymnastics apparatus for climbing, swinging, balancing in strength positions, jumping for height and distance working on power and bone strength, traveling using the five basic types of flight for bone strength, and making shapes working flexibility.

Day 3: Continue rotating centers.

Summary

Creating and using detailed, carefully planned lessons will make you a better teacher. Lesson plans begin with a set of objectives stating specifically what children will learn in the lessons. In the introduction, you get children quickly engaged in a simple physical activity that relates to the lesson content. In addition, you capture children's interest in the lesson content and explain why the content is important and relevant to learn. The content development segment of the lesson then consists of a progression of tasks that focus on extending and refining children's motor skills. The culminating activity typically has children apply the skills in different situations.

Teachers also write unit plans, year-long plans for each grade, and a K–5 program plan, along with assessments that seek to determine whether the children have achieved learning outcomes based on state and national standards. All plans should be designed to meet national, state, and district standards for physical education. A good K–5 program plan provides in-depth learning of the significant content in the physical education field and avoids the creation of an exposure curriculum in which children experience many activities but don't have the time to develop skills to a level of maturity that will support their participation in physical activities on a lifelong basis.

Review Questions

1. Discuss why writing lesson plans is important for beginning teachers.
2. Write one motor objective, including both skill improvement/movement quality and movement variety, and one cognitive knowledge objective that works with this motor objective.
3. Write one motor objective, including both skill improvement/movement quality and movement variety, and one affective objective that works with this motor objective.
4. Write one motor objective, including both skill improvement/movement quality and movement variety, and one thinking skill objective that works with this motor objective.
5. Write one motor objective, including both skill improvement/movement quality and movement variety, and one social skill objective that works with this motor objective.
6. What are the two purposes of the introductory warm-up section of the lesson?
7. Write an informing task, three extension tasks, and one refinement for a short segment of a lesson teaching one open skill you know well (e.g., catching, dribbling). Do not use the examples from the chapter.
8. Select three criteria for a good lesson plan, and discuss why each is important.
9. What is a curriculum script, and why can it be a problem?
10. Why is "less is more" an important criterion for a K–5 program plan?

References

Butler, J. I., & Griffin, L. L. (Eds.). (2010). *More teaching games for understanding: Moving globally*. Champaign, IL: Human Kinetics.

Eickhoff-Shemek, J. M., Herbert, D. L., & Connaughton, D. P. (2009). *Risk Management for Health/Fitness Professionals: Legal Issues and Strategies*. Philadelphia: Wolters Kluwer/Lippincott Williams & Wilkins.

Halsey, J. J. (2005). Risk Management for Physical Educators. In H. Appenzeller, (Ed.). *Risk Management in Sport: Issues and Strategies*, (2nd ed.), (pp. 151-163). Durham, NC: Carolina Academic Press.

Hart, J. E., & Ritson, R. J. (2002). *Liability and Safety in Physical Education and Sport*. Reston, VA: National Association for Sport and Physical Education.

National Association for Sport and Physical Education (NASPE). (2010). *Opportunity to Learn: Guidelines for Elementary, Middle, and High School Physical Education: A Side-by-Side Comparison*. Reston, VA: Author.

Nohr, K. M. (2009). *Managing Risk in Sport and Recreation: The Essential Guide for Loss Prevention*. Champaign, IL: Human Kinetics.

Oslin, J., & Mitchell, S. (2006). Game-centered approaches to teaching physical education. In D. Kirk, D. MacDonald, & M. O'Sullivan (Eds.), *The handbook of physical education* (pp. 627–651). London: Sage.

Patton, K., & Griffin, L. L. (2008). Experiences and patterns of change in a physical education teacher development project. *Journal of Teaching in Physical Education, 27*, 272–291.

Rink, J. E. (2014). *Teaching physical education for learning* (7th ed.). New York: McGraw-Hill.

Society of Health and Physical Educators. (2014). *National standards and grade-level outcomes for K–12 physical education*. Champaign, IL: Human Kinetics.

CHAPTER

15

Assessment in Educational Games, Gymnastics, and Dance

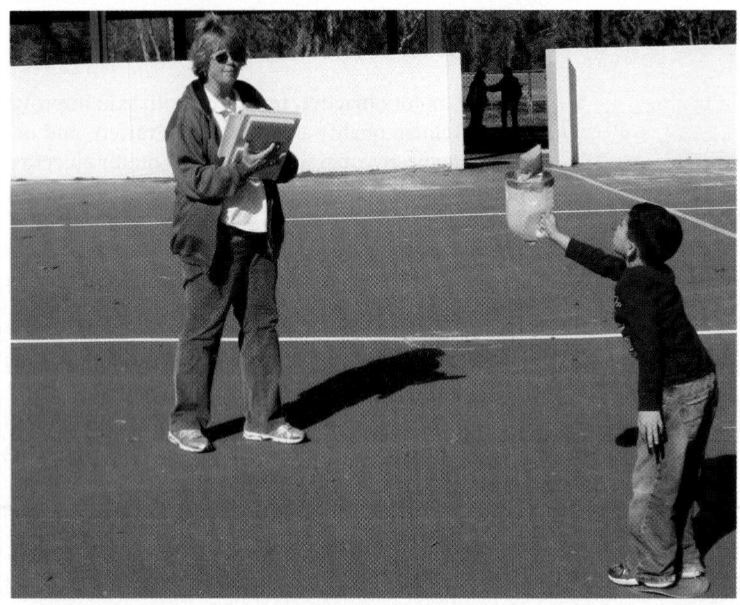

PRE-READING REFLECTION

1. Which assessments do you remember in physical education when you were in elementary school, middle school, and high school?
2. How did you feel about those assessments?
3. What do you think is the purpose of assessments for elementary physical education teachers?

OBJECTIVES

Students will learn:

1. Assessments let you know what children have learned and the extent to which they have met the intended learning outcomes.
2. Assessments need to be integrated into the teaching and learning process.
3. Assessments are valuable teaching tools that provide clear criteria for student performance and give students feedback on their progress.
4. Assessments must be matched to the developmental level of the children and focus on performance techniques that children can reasonably be expected to develop in a unit.
5. Peer assessments and self-assessments can be valuable learning experiences. Peer assessments are valuable for both the peer doing the assessment and the child whom the peer is assessing.
6. Peer assessments and self-assessments reinforce the criteria for the performance techniques and tactics you have taught, thereby supporting the development of self-regulation and independent learning.
7. Assessing students' social interactions provides feedback that helps students understand appropriate personal and social responsibility.
8. Affective assessments help teachers understand how children feel about physical activities, their motivation, and their experiences in lessons.

KEY TERMS

Aligned developmental feedback
Checklist
Exit slip
Formal assessments
Formative assessments
Informal assessments
PE Metrics
Quick card assessments
Rating scale
Rubric
Student journal
Summative assessments
Web-form graphic organizers

CONNECTION TO STANDARDS

This chapter describes how assessments are based on intended learning outcomes and objectives derived from state standards, the National Standards for Physical Education (National Standards) (Society for Health and Physical Educators, 2014), and the Common Core and other State Standards (CCSS) (Common Core State Standards Initiative, 2010). The process of designing standards-based summative and formative assessments is described and illustrated.

Introduction

During your years as a K–12 and college student, teachers assessed you many times through tests, papers, and projects. You have taken many standardized tests. Your grades in college and most classes in middle and high school were based on a variety of assessments. In the course of your educational journey, you have probably formed strong opinions about different types of assessments and know a lot about assessment.

In addition, we assume you will take or have taken a course on measurement, evaluation, and assessment, either within a department or college of education, which focused on assessment in schools and classroom subjects, or within a department or college of kinesiology, which addressed the entire field of kinesiology, from exercise science to sport management. In this text, we focus solely on assessment in elementary school physical education and the conditions under which most elementary physical educators work. We begin by reviewing four types of assessments.

Experienced Teachers Talk

Knowing What Every Child Learned

I went to the most awesome teacher workshop that focused on learning outcomes. One thing the presenter said made a big impression on me. He said, "If I come in and watch you teach a lesson, I want to be able to ask you at the end, 'Do you know if the boy in red learned anything today? Did he understand what you taught? Did he acquire the knowledge or not?'" His point was that we must know what every student learned or did not learn.

Summative, Formative, Formal, and Informal Assessments

Summative assessments: Occur at the end of a unit or grade level and assess what students have learned in that unit or across the school year.

Formative assessments: Occur before and during a unit to assess what students currently know, can do, and feel, their improvement on those fronts, and the extent to which they have learned the objective for your lesson or unit.

Formal assessments: Are planned, rely on criteria for making judgments, and yield results for every child that are recorded in writing or electronically.

Informal assessments: Have criteria for making judgments, but the results are typically not recorded. Teachers rely on informal assessments in every lesson. These ongoing assessments are critical to good teaching because they enable you to give students immediate feedback on their performance and understanding. Informal assessments include observing children's responses to assess the extent to which they are improving and checking for understanding by asking questions of individuals and partners. Formal, formative, and summative assessments, in contrast, give you information about what *every* child knows, can do, and feels. The problem with informal assessments is that it is very difficult to assess what each child has learned. We simply teach too many children to be able to rely on our informal assessments to accurately assess learning outcomes.

Why Elementary Physical Education Teachers Assess Students

Elementary physical education teachers assess children for three primary purposes. First, teachers plan the learning outcomes they want children to achieve and then use formal, summative assessments to assess the extent to which children have achieved those outcomes. This type of analysis is called assessment *of* learning (van der Mars & Harvey, 2010).

A second purpose also relies on formal, summative assessments. This purpose is for teachers to provide evidence that their programs are effective in meeting state and national standards. Schools today are increasingly being held accountable for student learning outcomes based on standards. The extent to which students meet those standards is used for evaluating teacher effectiveness (Rink, 2013; Ward, 2013). Teachers thus

What NASPE, the U.S. National Physical Education Professional Organization, Says About Assessment of Learning Outcomes

In today's education climate, there's no place in the school curriculum for a program area that can neither define the outcomes students should achieve nor measure the extent to which they have met those outcomes. Too many physical education programs have largely avoided doing both (NASPE, 2010, p. 9).

need to provide evidence of their effectiveness by formal, summative assessment of student learning.

In the same way that classroom subjects have standardized tests, elementary physical education now has standardized tests for assessing learning outcomes based on the National Standards. Called ***PE Metrics*** (National Association of Sport and Physical Educators [NASPE], 2010), these standardized tests include motor assessments for foundational skills, dance sequences, gymnastics sequences, and gameplay addressed in National Standards 1 and 2, in addition to written test items for National Standards 2 through 5 covering knowledge of principles, health-related physical activity, socially responsible behavior, and the affective value of physical activity. These assessments are both valid and reliable. In *PE Metrics*, each assessment is described, along with criteria for competence, an assessment rubric, a diagram of the test station, a score sheet, and directions to read aloud to students. The book comes with two DVDs that have videos of children at different levels of competence performing each motor assessment. You can use these assessments to demonstrate how the children in your school meet the criteria for learning outcomes established in state standards as well as the National Standards.

The third purpose, and in our opinion the most important at the elementary level, is to provide students with detailed, specific information about what you want them to learn in a lesson or unit and the extent to which students have met these learning outcomes; in other words, their progress and what they specifically need to work on to learn and master the content. This type of analysis is called assessment *for* learning (van der Mars & Harvey, 2010). Assessments become teaching tools and are integrated into the teaching and learning process.

Grading

Of course, teachers also assess students to help determine grades, in particular, at the middle and high school levels. In elementary physical education, some schools have letter grades for physical education on the children's report cards; however, most schools use a simple system of satisfactory (S), needs improvement (N), and unsatisfactory (U). Other schools send home report cards that are detailed progress reports for physical education, informing parents of the extent to which children have mastered or are still developing skills and tactics.

Assessing the Motor Domain

We begin our discussion of assessments with the motor domain, which includes our most important content, that is, skills and physical activities from the areas of games, gymnastics, and dance. This section on the motor domain is followed by discussions of cognitive, social, motivation, and affective assessment.

The Connection Between Standards and Assessments of Learning Outcomes

When teachers plan their programs, they start with state standards or the National Standards and then design grade-level learning outcomes to ensure students will meet the standards. Based on grade-level learning outcomes, teachers then design unit learning outcomes for each unit in each grade. Next, they create assessments based directly on unit and grade-level learning outcomes. Using this approach, teachers align their curricula to state standards or the National Standards. You will most likely rely on your state's standards because most schools require teachers to use those standards.

State standards are beneficial because they tend to be more specific than the National Standards and therefore give you more specific information on the grade-level learning outcomes children must meet and which you must teach and assess. In this text, we predominantly use the National Standards for Physical Education because most state standards are aligned with the National Standards. Throughout, we augment the National Standards with typical state standards with which we are familiar.

Summative Assessments Can Provide Evidence of Meeting Standards

Aligning your assessments to state standards and/or the National Standards is essential when you create summative assessments to provide evidence that your students have met those standards. These summative assessments also give you information about what your students have learned across a grade level or unit. You can use this information to identify gaps between what you have taught to meet standards and what the students, in fact, have learned. Then you can reflect on those gaps to figure out why and in what ways the students did not meet your expectations. These reflections will help you improve your curriculum and instruction and guide your future planning.

You will notice in our examples of summative assessments later in the chapter (see **Table 15.1** and **Assessments 15.2, 15.3,** and **15.4**) how the criteria for demonstrating competence are very specific and require the assessor to count the number of times an action is observed within a specific time limit. Criteria that are this specific and precise means the assessments must be videorecorded and evaluated by the teacher who is a trained evaluator. Check your school policies before videorecording children. The stringency of the assessment process ensures the results are evidence of student learning and teacher and program effectiveness.

Needless to say, formal, summative assessments *of* learning with stringent quantitative criteria are time consuming. It is unrealistic to think a teacher can assess all the skills, knowledge, and attitudes we teach using formal, summative teacher assessments. You would need to carefully select representative skills to assess (See **Figure 15.1**). However, these summative assessments are obviously important, especially if they are used to evaluate your teaching effectiveness and if the results affect your salary.

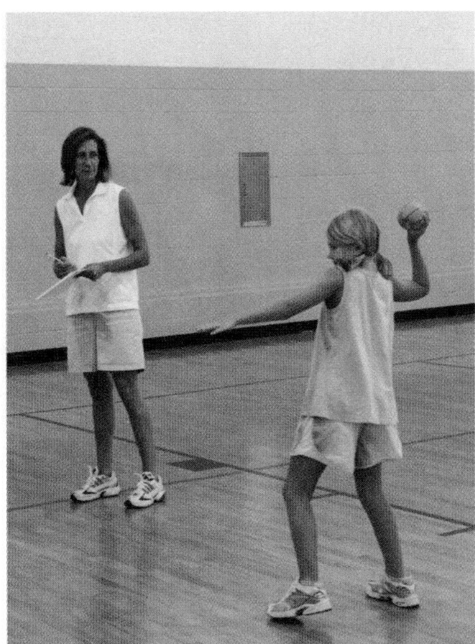

Figure 15.1 Assessing a significant skill
Courtesy of John Dolly

How to Use Formative Assessments as Instructional Tools

Regardless of the value of summative assessments, there is a critical need for formative assessments that are integrated into the teaching and learning process and used as teaching tools and as a means to provide students with ongoing feedback on their progress toward competent performance. We discuss how to use formative assessments as instructional tools next.

Teacher Assessments

The first way teachers use formative assessments as instructional tools is to share the assessment tool at the start of the lesson or unit that they will use at the end of the lesson or unit (Brookhart, 2013). This assessment describes the learning outcome and the exact criteria on which achievement will be assessed. When students know what they are expected to learn, they will focus on that content and learn more. Knowing the criteria on which they will be assessed before they begin the unit or lesson will help them understand the importance of the detailed, specific content presented. Knowing the criteria for assessment is particularly important with projects such as designing dance, gymnastics, jump rope, dribbling, or fitness sequences and routines. The assessment of sequences and routines is more complex than assessing skills because the criteria for competent performance can't be broken down into brief cues describing performance techniques, such as the performance technique "side to target" for assessing the overhand throw. The criteria for sequences are often multifaceted and abstract, requiring judgments such as whether a sequence has originality. An assessment tool, such as a rubric for assessing a dance sequence, will describe criteria for originality with specific, detailed descriptions of what both a sequence demonstrating originality and a sequence that does not demonstrate originality will look like.

When you share an assessment tool with students, it needs to be in language they understand and at an appropriate reading and vocabulary level. With younger children, you can describe the learning outcome and criteria for assessment in an abbreviated version of the assessment tool on a white board.

After sharing the assessment tool, you then need to check for understanding (Brookhart, 2013). You can have students discuss the assessment tool, learning outcome, and criteria with a partner and have them share any questions they have. With their partner or in a group, they can discuss and then practice assessing another pair or group using the assessment tool. As a class, you can discuss what the students can do to improve to their level of competent performance. When you

SAFETY AND LIABILITY 15.1

Increasing Safety and Decreasing Risk of Liability: Guidelines Relevant to Content in this Chapter

In this box, we discuss specific guidelines built on information discussed throughout this text on professional standards of practice, negligence, and liability. The goals of these guidelines are to increase children's safety and decrease teachers' risk of negligence and liability.

- Skill and fitness assessment tasks are like any other instructional task, and a reasonably prudent educator must anticipate safety issues and prepare students for test tasks in the same ways as they do for other tasks. This instructional preparation includes ensuring tasks are at developmentally appropriate levels for each child, teaching the movements using a progression of tasks, differentiating instruction, teaching safety procedures, and warning against inherent dangers.
- Written lesson plans need to include instruction of safety procedures and safe performance techniques during testing.
- Testing does not mean you can ignore measures to decrease liability risk and increase safety simply because you want valid, reliable test scores.
- Moreover, testing can be coercive, in that students want to perform well on tests and thus can feel pressured to perform in ways they ordinarily would not. Coercion to perform increases risks of liability and negligence.
- It is prudent to honor all parental notes excusing students from testing even if you question the truth of the claims.
- If a student asks to stop the test, it is prudent to do so.
- Because you have a duty to exercise reasonable professional care to prevent harm, you need to watch for overexertion, signs of unusual discomfort, movements that indicate distress, and performance techniques that are unsafe. Stop the testing if any of these conditions is evident.
- No test is worth a child being harmed or injured and the teacher sued; think, "safety first."

Appropriate Instructional Practice Guidelines for Elementary School Physical Education

Assessment Use

Appropriate Practice	*Inappropriate Practice*
Formative and summative assessments are an ongoing and integral part of the learning process for all students, including those with disabilities.	Assessment is rare and random, occurring only in the context of grading.

Variety of Assessments

Appropriate Practice	*Inappropriate Practice*
Teachers teach and assess all domains (cognitive, affective, and physical) systematically, using a variety of assessment techniques.	Teachers assess only physical fitness.
Assessments include clearly defined criteria that are articulated to students as part of instruction prior to the assessment (e.g., a rubric is provided and explained during instruction).	Assessments aren't clearly defined or don't relate to program goals and objectives.

Source: Reprinted from *Appropriate Instructional Practice Guidelines for Elementary School Physical Education*, with permission from the National Association for Sport and Physical Education (NASPE), 1900 Association Drive, Reston, VA 20191-1599. www.naspeinfo.org

assess their performance at the end of the unit or lesson, they will know what you will be looking for and will have prepared throughout the unit or lesson.

Peer Assessment

A second way to use formative assessments as instructional tools is to have peers assess and tutor each other. Studies indicate that students who participate in peer assessments understand the performance techniques used as the assessment criteria, are able to analyze their peers' performance correctly, and see their own skill and tactical learning increase as a result (Dyson, Linehan, & Hastie, 2010; Johnson & Ward, 2001) (see **Figure 15.2**). For example, when students used a rubric with detailed descriptions of performance levels for performance techniques and game tactics, the act of applying that knowledge to tutoring and assessing peers contributed to a deeper understanding and a stronger application of that knowledge in gameplay (Iserbyt, Elen, & Behets, 2010; Vande Broek, Boen, Claessens, Feys, & Ceux, 2011).

Many students are motivated to perform well when being assessed by their peers. Nevertheless, you will need to teach the children how to give constructive feedback to their partners.

Figure 15.2 Peer assessments
Courtesy of John Dolly

Byra (2004) suggests that you teach children to give specific feedback by having the observer state exactly what he or she saw in relation to the assessment criteria. For example, if the assessment is to watch whether the partner is dribbling waist high and pushing with the finger pads, the observer needs to say specifically, "I can see you are dribbling waist high. Way to go." In addition, Byra suggests teaching children to give all feedback—even corrective feedback—in a supportive way. For example, the peer assessor might say, "I can see you're really trying to push with your finger pads. Keep trying—you can do it."

Self-Assessments

Self-assessments have many of the same benefits that peer assessments have. Students learn which performance techniques they are expected to learn, and they can determine their progress in mastering those techniques. The widespread use of smartphones and tablets, which can serve as video cameras, offers teachers simple and easy ways for students to self-evaluate. After checking with your school policy, make a videorecording of a student performing a skill on the student's smartphone or, in schools that provide tablets for students, on his or her tablet. Armed with a rubric, which has been discussed in class, the student can self-assess his or her performance at home without using up valuable class practice time.

In summary, formative assessment can be built into the teaching and learning process. When you design an assessment tool, you select the criteria on which you will base your assessment. These criteria come directly from your intended learning outcomes and objectives and the specific content and performance techniques you teach. When you teach the performance techniques corresponding a particular objective, you simultaneously teach children the criteria on which they will be assessed. You can also write the cues on a whiteboard to help children remember the criteria and show them the rubric or checklist before you begin the lesson or unit. During and at the end of the lesson or unit, you ask the children about the performance techniques they need to demonstrate during an assessment. You may include peer or self-assessment of the performance techniques the children use in the skill. Following these procedures, your assessment becomes an integral part of the teaching and learning process and supports student learning.

Experienced Teachers Talk

Bingo Assessments

I tried the bingo assessment. This has been the single most effective way to get improvement in throwing. The level of work was inspiring.

Including Student Choice in Assessments

Research on motivation consistently reports that the extent to which students have choices and autonomy to make decisions leads to increased motivation, engagement, enjoyment, effort, persistence, and self-sufficiency (Bryan & Solmon, 2007; Johnson, Prusak, Pennington, & Wilkinson, 2011; Koka & Hagger, 2010; Prusak, Treasure, Darst, & Pangrazi, 2004; Shen, McCaughtry, Martin, & Fahlman, 2009; Standage, Duda, & Ntoumanis, 2003; Treasure & Roberts, 1995). One study examined a formative assessment aimed at facilitating learning within a mastery-oriented climate (Johnson et al., 2011). The assessment provided students choices in the level of difficulty of the assessment tasks and allowed students to repeat test items until they achieved a competent performance level. Students, in particular girls, reported the assessment was more motivating than traditional assessments.

Later in this chapter, we provide two examples of formative assessments in which students choose the assessment items and/or the level of difficulty. Each assessment item is set up as a center designed to engage and motivate students to practice with effort and persistence. George Kelly (2006) designed one such assessment using a bingo format, and we have adapted this format (see **Assessment 15.18**). Each bingo square is a challenging center. Children select their assessment centers as long as they complete a "bingo" line (horizontal, vertical, or diagonal). When the student successfully completes a center using the performance technique described, her or his partner circles "yes" and initials a box on the bingo card. Based on Johnson et al. (2011), we designed "Assessment Center Challenges," which give children choices about which level they want for assessment, along with extra credit for social responsibility (see **Assessment 15.19**).

Assessments Tools for the Motor Domain

Three types of assessments are well suited for the goal of assessing motor skills and physical activities. These assessment tools include explicit information on the criteria for assessing if learning outcomes are met. Because these assessment tools are shared with students, they can enhance learning. These tools are rubrics, checklists, and rating scales.

Rubrics

A **rubric** describes specifically and in detail levels of performance from beginner to competent performer for each component of the skill or physical activity students are expected to learn. Rubrics do not judge a performance as simply good or poor; they describe the movements you observe at each level of performance for an intended learning outcome.

In addition, rubrics do not include items related to whether the student included each aspect of the assignment; rubrics focus solely on student learning and describe what learning will look like (Brookhart, 2013). For example, let's say we assigned students to design a gymnastics sequence including at least three balances with a variety of interesting shapes held with a tight, stretched body. The task appears to have three components to assess:

1. The sequence includes at least three balances.
2. The balances have a variety of interesting shapes.
3. The balances are held with a tight, stretched body.

However, only two of these components are learning outcomes. To improve balancing, students need to learn to maintain tight muscles and stretch their torso and legs fully. An emerging performance level would be the student having a loose body with sagging in the torso and bent knees and ankles. In lessons, you would teach students how to stay tight and stretched, and if students did so, their balance would improve in ways that are significant to skillful gymnastics performance. Item 3 is thus an *intended* learning outcome.

Item 2 is a learning outcome. A criterion of the competent design of a gymnastics sequence is to include a variety of shapes. Students need to learn how they can vary the shape of their bodies while balancing. Designing interesting sequences is also a criterion of competent design and a characteristic of choreography students can learn and improve. Interesting sequences in gymnastics typically have a variety of different shapes—asymmetrical and unusual—and body positions or actions that take the observer by surprise. An emerging level of choreography would include plain or ordinary shapes, such as a tucked shape, an overabundance of symmetrical shapes, a lack of asymmetrical shapes, the repeated use of the same shape, and a lack of a variety of shapes. Thus, having a variety of interesting shapes is a learning outcome.

Designing a sequence that includes at least three balances is a requirement of the assignment. There is nothing to learn about the number of balances to include in a sequence other than following the teacher's directions. Having three balances is not a criterion of competent design, and there are no specific performance techniques you would teach related to the number three. Thus, including three balances is a checklist item discussed below rather than a rubric item. We provide a sample rubric for assessing the sequence of three balances (see **Assessment 15.1**).

In summary, rubrics provide students with clear descriptions of what they need to learn and a way to assess their current level of performance, in turn providing them with the information they need to improve. Rubrics can therefore be used to provide student feedback and reinforce the content taught.

Checklists

Similar to rubrics, checklists describe learning outcomes. Most often in physical education, a **checklist** is a list of performance techniques for skills that teachers have taught that are performance techniques critical to developing the mature movement pattern of the skill. Typically, checklists require a yes/no answer and assess whether the student is doing the performance

ASSESSMENT 15.1

Rubric for Assessing a Sequence of Balances with a Variety of Interesting Shapes

Level 1: Plain
Shapes of the balances are plain and symmetrical; legs are either tucked or straight. A tucked or straight shape is repeated.

Level 2: Varied
All three balances have different shapes. At least one shape is asymmetrical.

Level 3: Interesting
All three balances have different shapes. All shapes are asymmetrical. In all shapes, the legs are in interesting positions. At least one shape is unusual.

Balances Are Held with a Tight, Stretched Body

Level 1: Not There Yet
The body is loose, the torso sags, and the knees and ankles are relaxed and bent when they should be straight. The child has difficulty holding the body still in the balances.

Level 2: Emerging
The child is stretched tight enough to hold the balance for one second. The legs are almost straight, and it is evident the child is attempting to point the feet and toes, but the ankle is not fully extended. The body is partially stretched tight.

Level 3 Proficient
The legs are perfectly straight, stretched, and tight when they are supposed to be and tucked tight when they are supposed to be. The ankles are always extended with the toes pointed. The body is stretched and tight, and the balance can be held for three seconds.

technique or has yet to master the technique and needs more practice. Checklists can also be used with tally marks to count the number of times an action is observed, such as the number of times an offensive player appropriately cuts into an open space in a game-like situation. This approach to checklists is particularly valuable in assessing game play. Like rubrics, checklists provide detailed, specific information about intended learning outcomes and are used to provide feedback on performance and improvement. Thus, they can be a learning tool for students (see the sample checklist in **Assessment 15.5**).

Checklists can also be used to indicate whether the student has included all requirements of the assignment. Using checklists for this purpose is an efficient way to communicate with students and remind them of what they are expected to include in a project. Designing a rubric for checking whether a project includes all requirements is a waste of time when a checklist can serve the same purpose more efficiently without having to describe levels of performance.

Rating Scales

A **rating scale** is an elaboration of a checklist. Like checklists, rating scales describe performance techniques that are linked directly to student learning outcomes. Unlike checklists, rating scales also include a way to assess the extent to which a performance technique has been mastered or the developmental level of the performance. Rating scales often include assessing the frequency with which an important movement pattern or action is observed. Whereas a checklist with tally marks counts the number of times an assessor observes a movement, a rating scale uses scales that require a judgment, such as always, often, sometimes, or rarely (Brookhart, 2013). These subjective ratings can be quantified, such as by stating that "often" means more than 75% of the time, and "sometimes" means between 50% and 74% of the time. In our opinion, counting actions to determine accurately whether the student performed an action 74% or 75% of the time is not worth the teacher's time and that subjective scales are adequate. Rating scales as formative assessments should be easy to use. If they are not, you would be better served by a rubric.

Notice in our descriptions of rubrics, checklists, and rating scales, we have focused on describing learning outcomes. The descriptions are detailed and specific and provide clear information about what students have learned and what they have yet to master (see the sample rating scale in **Assessment 15.6**). We have not included any scales used for grading (i.e., a scale of A, B, C, D, and F) or any scales used to evaluate quality, such as excellent, good, fair, or poor. This is because scales evaluating quality or grades do not provide specific information the teacher or student can use to help the student achieve a learning outcome. What does a "B" tell you about what you need to learn?

Rubrics, checklists, and rating scales are the bread and butter of motor domain assessments because of their specificity and, in turn, their contributions to student learning. We describe how to create these assessments next.

Creating Motor Assessments: Rubrics, Checklists, and Rating Scales

Begin with the Standard and then Identify a Specific, Detailed Learning Outcome

To create an assessment, you begin with a state standard or a National Standard and identify a learning outcome that will meet that standard. In **Table 15.1**, we identify three grade-level learning outcomes for dribbling with the hand that address National Standards 1 and 2. We chose three grades to illustrate how the specific learning outcomes for a skill will change as students master the content in earlier grades and progress to more difficult content. Examine the three learning outcomes in **Table 15.1** and notice that each grade-level outcome is very specific and describes the detailed performance techniques children need to learn. In addition, notice that both the task and the performance techniques are different at each grade level.

Learning outcomes need to be very specific and detailed because they define what you will teach—for example, dribbling at a particular grade level—and become the criteria for assessing learning outcomes. Compare the descriptions of the performance techniques (i.e., the content to be taught and learned) for each grade in **Table 15.1** with the criteria for assessing competence in the summative assessments for these same learning outcomes in **Assessments 15.2, 15.3**, and **15.4**. Matching content taught with content assessed is critical because you should not assess content you have not taught. Moreover,

Table 15.1 Deriving Grade-Level Learning Outcomes from the National Standards

National Standard 1: Demonstrates competency in a variety of motor skills and movement patterns.

Relevant Part of National Standard 2: Applies knowledge of concepts and tactics.

Grade-Level Learning Outcomes for Dribbling with the Hand:

By the end of this year, the children will have learned to

Grade 1

Dribble continuously, controlling the ball within personal space, with one hand pushing with the finger pads.

Grade 3

While jogging, dribble keeping the ball waist high and in front and toward the dribbling-hand side (front/side), using a sharp, angular pathway when dodging cones in a scattered formation.

Grade 5

In a two-player dribble tag game with boundaries, protect the ball by keeping the body between the ball and the defender and avoid being trapped in the corners.

when children are practicing, self-assessing, assessing a peer, or performing as you assess them, they know exactly which performance techniques they need to demonstrate, and they have received feedback on those techniques during the lesson or unit. This form of assessment can motivate children and facilitate learning (Martin, Kulinna, & Cothran, 2002).

To create specific, detailed learning outcomes, you will need to study the content you will teach. This content will include both tasks and performance techniques. The content progression illustrated in grades 1, 3, and 5 is based on the progression of content that focuses on dribbling.

The learning outcome for grade 3 includes applying knowledge about the movement concept of pathways while dribbling, and the learning outcome for grade 5 includes applying knowledge of tactics. Both of these applications of knowledge are taken directly from National Standard 2.

Base the Assessment on the Specific, Detailed Content Identified in the Learning Outcome

The next task in creating an assessment is to determine the assessment task, the components of the skill or physical activity, the criteria on which each component will be assessed, and the performance levels that will identify whether the student has successfully achieved the learning outcome. The assessment task either matches the learning outcome or is a task for which the learning outcome is the primary skill or physical activity. The components you will assess and the criteria (e.g., the performance techniques that identify competent performance) are written into the learning outcome. When you're creating your assessment, you might realize there are too many or too few components included in the learning outcome. You can then revise the learning outcome accordingly. In the three summative assessments in **Assessments 15.2, 15.3,** and **15.4,** you can see that the criteria for each component match the descriptions in the learning outcomes in **Table 15.1**. There are four components of dribbling assessed in grade 1, three components assessed in grade 3, and three components assessed in grade 5. In the assessments, we identify three performance levels and quantify the criteria for determining performance level. We discuss how to determine performance level next.

ASSESSMENTS 15.2, 15.3, AND 15.4

Creating Assessments for Grade-Level Learning Outcomes from National Standards 1 and 2

Grade 1

Task: For 20 seconds, dribble

Components and Criteria

- Continuously without missing a dribble
- While controlling the ball within personal space (within 3 feet of a poly spot) without having to chase the ball to regain control
- With one hand
- By pushing with the finger pads

Performance Levels and Criteria for Scoring

Level 3: Competent = The entire time

Level 2: Nearing competent = Most of the time (losing continuity, not controlling the ball within personal space, touching with two hands, or slapping the ball two or fewer times)

Level 1: Emerging = Some of the time (losing continuity, not controlling the ball within personal space, touching with two hands, or slapping the ball three or more times)

Name	Dribbles Continuously	Remains in Personal Space	Dribbles with One Hand	Pushes with Finger Pads	Total

(*continues*)

ASSESSMENTS 15.2, 15.3, AND 15.4 (*Continued*)

Grade 3

For 20 seconds, jog, dribble, and dodge cones in a scattered formation while

Components and Criteria

- Keeping the ball waist high or lower
- Keeping the ball in front and toward the dribbling-hand side (front/side)
- Using a sharp, angular pathway when dodging cones

Performance Levels and Criteria for Scoring Waist High, Front/Side

Level 3: Competent = The entire time
Level 2: Nearing competent = Most of the time (going higher than waist or dribbling in front of body two or fewer times)
Level 1: Emerging = Some of the time (going higher than waist or dribbling in front of body three or more times)

Performance Levels and Criteria for Scoring Using Sharp Angular Pathways when Dodging Cones

Level 3: Competent = Always using a sharp, angular pathway when dodging cones
Level 2: Nearing competent = Most of the time using a sharp, angular pathway when dodging cones (on a rounded, angular pathway two or fewer times)
Level 1: Emerging = Some of the time using a sharp, angular pathway when dodging cones (on a rounded, angular pathway three or more times)

Name	Waist High or Lower	Front/Side	Sharp, Angular Pathway	Total

Grade 5

Play two 20-second rounds of a dribble tag game with one dribbler and one defender who tries to tap the ball. Switch roles after one round.

Criteria

- Stay within the boundaries.
- Protect the ball by keeping the body between the ball and the defender.
- Avoid being trapped in the corners.

Scoring

Level 3: Competent = Consistently
Level 2: Nearing competent = Most of the time (goes out of bounds or gets trapped in the corner one time, does not protect the ball two or fewer times)
Level 1: Emerging = Some of the time (goes out of bounds or gets trapped in the corner more than one time, does not protect the ball three or more times)

Name	Stays Within Bounds	Avoids Being Trapped in Corner	Protects the Ball	Total

Peers assessing dribbling on different pathways around cones

Courtesy of John Dolly

Determining the Number of Performance Levels

Determining the number of performance levels appropriate for the assessment is not an easy or straightforward task. Do not think you must have the same number of performance levels for all assessments or for all components of a skill within one assessment tool. Some components of skills will have a small number of levels of immature performance, whereas others will have more levels. For example, research has found that the action of the feet in the overhand throw for force has three progressive immature levels, whereas the action of the humerus has only two immature levels. The number of performance levels must reflect the reality of skill development. You should not try to manufacture artificial performance levels simply to keep the number of performance levels consistent across skills you assess or all components within a skill. Recent research has shown that when the number of levels of performance in a rubric was consistent regardless of the nature of the criteria and the component being assessed, the assessment was significantly less valid than when the rubric was modified to eliminate artificial performance levels and have the number of performance levels reflect the qualitative gradations of each component and criterion (Humphry & Heldsinger, 2014). The researchers claimed it is critical not to follow a consistent structure when creating a rubric for complex skills or tasks with many components because it is doubtful whether a rubric with a consistent structure can assess complex skills with any validity.

As you are considering the appropriate number of performance levels, you will be reviewing information on the description of immature patterns. The learning outcome describes the mature performance techniques you intend the children to learn. Taking all this information into account, you must then write a clear, specific description of each performance level from immature levels through to the mature, competent level. These descriptions are critical because they identify the components of the skill you are assessing and the relevant performance techniques and clearly differentiate the levels of performance. When students are assessed to be at an immature level of performance, they will understand both what they are doing that can be improved and what specific performance techniques to work on next to facilitate improvement to the next level.

Using Developmental Information to Delineate Performance Levels

When you describe performance levels for motor skills, base your descriptions on research on the development of motor skills and tactics as much as possible. We include research-based information on immature through mature performance levels for the following skills: skipping, hopping, jumping, catching, overhand throwing for force, forward rolling, hand dribbling, cutting into a space to receive a pass, and sending lead passes. When no research was available, we based descriptions of immature patterns on our experiences as teachers.

In addition to descriptions of immature through mature movement patterns, research shows that fundamental game skills and tactics take considerable practice and many years to develop. For example, children cannot learn how to throw overhand for force at a mature level of performance in a short span of time, nor will they learn to send lead passes consistently in game-like situations in one unit of instruction (MacPhail, Kirk, & Griffin, 2008; Roberton & Halverson, 1984; Rovegno, Nevett, Brock, & Babiarz, 2001).

Consequently, when designing assessments, you need to match the assessment to the children's developmental levels and determine the extent to which they can reasonably be expected to progress along the developmental continuum. For example, we know children will not develop differentiated rotation on the overhand throw (i.e., with the hips rotating forward before the shoulders) when they are throwing at immature level 1 with no trunk action or with a forward–backward movement. For children at level 1, the intended learning outcome and, in turn, the assessment and feedback need to focus on performance techniques that the children can develop in a unit and that will help them progress beyond level 1, such as assessing the performance technique to start with side to target. This is called **aligned developmental feedback**, which research has shown increases student learning more than specific feedback that is not aligned developmentally (Cohen, Goodway, & Lidor, 2012).

Sample Formative Assessments Using Developmental Information

The following examples of a checklist, rating scale, and rubric all incorporate information about immature patterns based on developmental research. (The developmental assessments used here for dribbling are based on the work of Wickstrom [1983] and Chen, Rovegno, Todorovich, and Babiarz [2003]. The developmental assessments for throwing and catching are based on the work of Roberton and Halverson [1984].)

Assessment of Gameplay

In this next section, we discuss assessing content that is more complex than assessing individual motor skills. We begin with gameplay. Assessing gameplay is probably the most difficult assessment, but it is critically important. Motor skill and cognitive tests cannot accurately assess children's use of skills in games or their tactical decision making. If you want to determine whether children have learned your objectives for gameplay, you need to assess them in the authentic contexts of gameplay.

The good news is that researchers have validated assessment tools for gameplay, which you can adapt for your situation

ASSESSMENT 15.5

Sample Checklist with Descriptions of Immature and Mature Performance Techniques

Dribbling with Hands in Place

Name	Immature Performance Level: Slaps ball, no pushing action, makes contact with ball using palm	Mature Performance Level: Pushes with finger pads
Mia	X	
Jill	X	
Bill		X

ASSESSMENT 15.6

Sample Rating Scale Using Performance Techniques Designed to Facilitate Development of the Level 1 Immature Patterns for Trunk, Humerus, and Leg Actions

Throwing Overhand for Force

Instructions to students: Throw a fleece, yarn, or soft foam ball to a wall as forcefully as you can five times.

3 = Always demonstrates the pattern (five times out of five trials)

2 = Usually demonstrates the pattern (two to four times out of five trials)

1 = Rarely demonstrates the pattern (zero or one time out of five trials)

Name	Side to Target, Point to Target	Make the T; Break the T (Elbow at Shoulder Height, Hand Away from Head)	Transfer Weight to Nonthrowing Side Foot (Opposite Foot)
Tennicka			
Carlos			
Grace			
Jenny			
Antoine			

and your objectives. *PE Metrics* (NASPE, 2010) include validated tools for assessing basketball defense, basketball offense, and soccer offense in fifth grade.

One of the most useful and adaptable tools is the Game Performance Assessment Instrument (GPAI), which was developed by Oslin, Mitchell, and Griffin (1998). The GPAI has not only been used in research, but has also been adapted to provide teachers with a valid and usable tool for assessing gameplay. **Table 15.2** summarizes the seven major components of gameplay that you can assess.

ASSESSMENT 15.7

Sample Rubric with Performance Levels Based on Developmental Research Findings

Lead Passing with the Hands and Cutting to Receive a Pass

Instructions to Class: In your assigned groups of three, the passer stands in a hoop, and the receiver stands about 15 feet away, with the defender close to the receiver and in between the receiver and the passer. The receiver dodges, feints, and cuts to get free from the defender, while running forward on a straight line on an angle to the passer. The passer sends a lead pass so that the receiver does not need to stop, twist back, or change stride to catch the ball in front of her or his body. The defender plays soft defense (allows the receiver to catch ball but makes the receiver work to get free).

Performance Levels for Cutting to Receive a Pass

Immature Pattern Level 1: Most of the time, the receiver jumps up and down behind the defender, or slides sideways a few feet in one direction and then reverses direction but stays behind the defender and does not get free.

Intermediate Pattern Level 2: Most of the time, the receiver cuts on a curved pathway, faces the passer, is just about to get free, and then reverses direction, cuts at a moderate speed with no movement or acceleration, and may turn to face the passer to catch the ball.

Mature Pattern Level 3: The receiver consistently fakes, feints, and dodges and accelerates quickly while running on a straight pathway on an angle toward the passer. Faces forward and catches the ball in front of the body.

Performance Levels for Sending Lead Passes

Immature Pattern Level 1: The passer throws behind the receiver or throws too late or too early. Most of the time, the pass is not catchable.

Intermediate Pattern Level 2: The passer sends the pass to the receiver, not ahead of the receiver, so the receiver needs to turn to catch the ball. Pass might be too forceful. Pass is catchable most of the time.

Mature Pattern Level 3: Consistently sends catchable lead passes with appropriate force ahead of the receiver so the receiver does not have to twist, slow down, or change stride to catch the ball.

Name	Developmental Performance Level of Cut	Developmental Performance Level of Pass
Lindsey		
Eric		
Joey		

Table 15.2 Games Performance Assessment Instrument Components and Coding Categories

Tactical or Skill Component	Appropriate	Inappropriate
Return to base or recovery position in net/racket games		
Adjust appropriately offensively or defensively in invasion, net/racket, and field games		
Make appropriate tactical decisions when you have the ball in invasion, net/racket, and field games		
Off-the-ball offensive support of teammate with the ball by getting open or in the right position to receive the ball in invasion, net/racket, and field games		
Guarding/marking an opponent in invasion games		
Off-the-ball support by covering or backing up a defensive teammate who is on the ball in invasion, net/racket, and field games		
	Efficient	**Inefficient**
Skill execution		

Source: Adapted from Oslin, J. L., Mitchell, S. A., & Griffin, L. L. (1998) and Mitchell, S. A. & Oslin, J. L. (1999).

To adapt the GPAI, select the component or components that match your intended learning outcomes. Your learning outcomes will be specific to one of the four game forms—invasion, net\wall, field, or target—and will be based on a small-sided, highly modified version of the game. For example, an appropriate "basketball" game modified for fifth grade is to play three offensive players versus two defensive players, with no dribbling, scoring by passing to a teammate over the end line, with no stealing the ball out of a player's hands, starting on a line ten yards from the end line, stopping play when the defense intercepts or the offense scores, and starting again at the starting line, rotating the players on defense to offense.

Your learning outcomes and the components you select will also reflect the gameplay performance level of the students. The two components appropriate for assessing beginners, which is the performance level of almost all elementary school children, are of the ball support cutting to get open to receive a pass and making an appropriate decision on when to pass and to whom. The other components are either irrelevant to invasion games or too advanced for children who are just learning to send and receive passes.

Next, you need to describe the specific criteria for determining competent performance for each component. These criteria will also need to reflect the developmental level of the students. You can assess each component by counting the number of appropriate and inappropriate tactical actions. **Assessment 15.8** illustrates this form of assessment using a peer assessor in a modified net game.

Mitchell and Oslin (1999) suggest that an easier scoring system, especially for invasion games is to use a scale from 1 to 5, with 1 being very weak performance and 5 being very effective performance. You would watch a student for several minutes and then make an overall assessment of that child on one component. Then assess another child in the group. There are many labels you can use for describing the gradations of a 1-to-5 scale, such as

- Level 1, level 2, level 3, level 4, level 5
- Beginning, emerging, capable, near competent, competent
- Not effective, occasionally effective, mostly effective, effective, very effective
- Beginner, novice, capable, proficient, competent

Gameplay can be difficult to assess live. You might need to videorecord the games and then assess each child within each team. If you want to assess the gameplay on a live basis, you could assess one component per lesson or one group per lesson.

Assessment of Gymnastics and Dance

In gymnastics and dance, we assess the quality of movement and the quality of students' sequence choreography. We also assess foundational skills, such as jumping, hopping, sliding, and galloping, using checklists and rating scales. In this section, we first discuss assessing movement quality, followed by assessing sequence choreography.

Assessing Movement Quality

Gymnastics, dance, and health-related fitness movements share a set of general characteristics defining movement quality. Similar to the role of learning performance techniques to improve the quality of the movement of a particular skill, learning these nine characteristics improves the movement quality of gymnastics, dance, and health-related fitness movements in general. In

ASSESSMENT 15.8

Level 3 Net Game Tactics (Peer Assessment in Groups of Three)

Game: 1v1 striking a light foam ball with a short-handled racket over a low net.

Instructions to Class (Peer Assessment): Watch partner A for 1 minute (teacher times the class) to see if he or she returns to the center baseline after striking the ball. Put a tally mark under the "Appropriate" or "Inappropriate" column. Then watch partner B for 1 minute. Next, watch partner A to see if he or she makes the appropriate tactical decision to hit the ball to the open space so the opponent has to move to hit the ball. Put a tally mark under the "Appropriate" or "Inappropriate" column for every hit. Then watch partner B. Next, we will rotate, and partner A will assess, while partners B and C play. Finally, partner B will assess, while partners A and C play. [Each child will have a score sheet like the one below.]

Partner A's Score Sheet
Name of partner A: ___________

Assessed by partner C: _______________

Partner A Versus Partner B (Assessment 1)

Assessment 1	Appropriate	Inappropriate
Returns to center base line after striking	//// //	////
Hits to open space so opponent must move to hit	////	//// //

Name of partner A: ___________

Assessed by partner B: _______________

Partner A Versus Partner C (Assessment 2)

Assessment 2	Appropriate	Inappropriate
Returns to center after striking	//// //// //	//
Hits to open space so opponent must move to hit	//// ////	////

other words, these characteristics apply to all skills and movement patterns. These nine characteristics are as follows. The first six apply to movement quality, and the remaining three apply to performance quality.

Movement Quality

1. Using appropriate amounts of tension, staying tight throughout the body in gymnastics, and having light, isometric tension in dance
2. Maintaining appropriate body alignment (e.g., legs straight, not hyperextended; toes pointed; knees aligned over toes)
3. Landing lightly with control over body parts and over flow of movement. Landings from jumps and leaps are light, with all body parts under control. When landing in place, the child controls the flow of movement, and the feet remain exactly where he or she landed.
4. Stretching or elongating the torso and body, head stretched tall, shoulders down, and chest up.
5. Using appropriate amounts of speed and force, strong and fast movements are strong and fast. Slow movements are slow. Gentle movements are soft. Traveling speed is not faster than the child's ability to control.
6. Engaging the core, maintaining isometric tension in the core to protect the back, movements are initiated from the torso, and the whole body is engaged in a coordinated way.

Performance Quality

7. Rhythm and tempo: The child or group moves to the beat of the music, and the movements are coordinated.
8. Concentration and engagement: The child or group appears totally engaged throughout the performance.
9. Well practiced until movements can be repeated accurately: The child or group can repeat the sequence with accuracy and precision.

These characteristics of movement quality are critical to competent performance in dance, health-related fitness movements, and gymnastics and for safety, in particular, in gymnastics. If children are not tight, land without controlling the flow of the movement, or their movements are too fast for them to control, they can get injured. We find most of our informal assessment and lesson feedback in gymnastics is about movement quality.

In **Table 15.3**, we describe the performance levels for each of the nine characteristics of movement quality. We created this table because most physical education majors have few experiences with dance and gymnastics and thus have problems describing levels of performance for rubrics and rating scales. The information in **Table 15.3** provides a detailed description for multiple components. When you design an assessment tool using this information, you will need to select portions of only one or two components to assess.

You can formally assess the movement quality of individuals during sequence performance or while they work on tasks during a lesson. Assessing movement quality during lesson tasks provides especially valuable feedback. To do formal lesson assessments, you would select one component of one characteristic to assess, such as "points toes" from "maintains appropriate body alignment." Using a simple rating scale, you can assess an entire class while you are teaching.

Table 15.3 describes the performance levels for each component of movement quality. This table is followed by a sample of a rubric for assessing the movement quality of a short first-grade dance sequence (see **Assessment 15.9**). We also include a sample assessment for giving students feedback on pointing their toes to conduct during a series of lessons (see **Assessment 15.10**). Notice that in both assessments, we select only a portion of one component of movement quality to assess. The portion we selected is both significant to movement quality in the particular task taught in the lessons and matched to the developmental level of the students. We also simplified the criteria.

Table 15.3 Performance Levels and Criteria for Assessing Movement Quality and Performance Quality

Movement Quality

Appropriate Amounts of Tension

Level 1: Not There Yet

The body is consistently loose.

Level 2: Emerging

The body is sometimes tight. Many body parts are tight.

Level 3: Proficient

The body is always tight. All body parts have the appropriate amount of tension.

Appropriate Body Alignment

Level 1: Not There Yet

Toes are almost always flexed and knees almost always bent. In most movements, the body parts are inappropriately aligned. Movements do not reach their full range of motion. Curled positions are open. The child does not appear to be kinesthetically aware of the position of most body parts.

Level 2: Emerging

Toes are often flexed and knees often bent. In many movements, the body parts are inappropriately aligned. Movements do not reach their full range of motion. Curled positions are open. The child does not appear to be kinesthetically aware of the position of many body parts.

Level 3: Proficient

Toes are almost always pointed; legs are mostly straight and aligned appropriately. Body alignment is appropriate most of the time. Movements come close to their full range of motion. The child appears to be kinesthetically aware of the position of body parts most of the time.

Level 4: Perfected, Exceptional

Feet and toes are always pointed and legs straight. Body parts are aligned appropriately all the time. The child is aware of the position of all body parts. Movements are done to their fullest range of motion. Splits and straddles are perfectly straight, and tucks are a tight ball.

Lands Lightly with Control Over Body Parts and Over Flow of Movement

Level 1: Not There Yet

Landings are flat-footed and heavy. There is little or no resiliency in the actions of the feet, ankles, and knees. The body lands with little control, and many body parts are out of control. The child may fall because there was no control over the flow of movement.

Level 2: Emerging

Jumps and leaps are low and landings somewhat heavy, with some control over some body parts. When trying to land in place, the child has some control over the flow of movement but takes several steps or jumps before the body is under control. Resilient landings are low with little extension of the ankles.

Level 3: Proficient

Jumps and leaps are high and landings light, with all body parts almost always under control. When trying to land in place, the child controls the flow of movement and remains still with the feet remaining exactly where they landed or on occasion takes one step or small jump. Resilient landings pop off the floor.

Stretched or Elongated Torso

Level 1: Not There Yet

The body is slouched, the back sags, the chest is sunken in, and the shoulders are hunched forward or shrugged.

Level 2: Emerging

The torso is stretched some of the time. The shoulders are sometimes down and back, with the chest up. The head is held high sometimes.

Level 3: Proficient

The body is stretched. The head is held high, the shoulders are down, the ribs are separated from the hips, and the chest is up.

Appropriate Speed and Force

Level 1: Not There Yet

Strong and fast movements are performed at medium speeds and force. Slow and gentle movements are performed at medium speeds and force. Traveling movements are too fast for the child to easily control.

(continues)

Table 15.3 Performance Levels and Criteria for Assessing Movement Quality and Performance Quality (*continued*)

Level 2: Emerging

There is a difference in the speed between slow and fast movements and between strong and gentle movements. Traveling speed is often within the child's ability to control.

Level 3: Proficient

Strong and fast movements are strong and fast. Slow movements are slow. Gentle movements are soft. Traveling speed is always within the child's ability to control.

Engages the Core

Level 1: Not There Yet

Core muscles are loose. Only part of the body does the movement. Gestures are done with the arms or legs only. The torso is not coordinated with the arms and legs.

Level 2: Proficient

Core muscles have tension. The core muscles are engaged and are part of the movement. Most of the time, the whole body is engaged in a coordinated way.

Level 3: Perfected, Exceptional

Movements are initiated from the core. Core muscles are tight. The whole body is engaged in a coordinated way.

Performance Quality

Rhythm and Tempo

Level 1: Not There Yet

In group sequences, individuals and the group have problems staying on the beat of the music. The group members do not coordinate the rhythm of their movements.

Level 2: Proficient

In group sequences, most individuals move in time with the beat of the music or in time with each other.

Level 3: Perfected, Exceptional

In group sequences, the entire group moves together to the beat of the music, and the movements are coordinated rhythmically.

Concentration and Engagement

Level 1: Not There Yet

The child or group does not appear to be engaged and seems to be just going through the motions.

Level 2: Emerging

Concentration is evident some of the time but seems to drift.

Level 3: Proficient

The child or group concentrates and is engaged during the performance.

Level 4: Perfected, Exceptional

The child or group appears totally engaged throughout the performance. The performance appears effortless. The group members appear to believe in their sequence.

Well Practiced Until Movements Can Be Repeated Accurately

Level 1: Needs Much More Practice

Sequence needs much more practice. In individual sequences, the sequence is different every time the student performs it. Sometimes he or she makes it up during the performance. In group sequences, children talk and look at one another for information about what to do next. Sometimes they make things up as they go along. The group members do not coordinate their movements. The group loses their formations.

Level 2: Needs More Practice

Sequence needs more practice. Some sections of the sequence can be repeated, but other sections change every time the child or group performs. In group sequences, formations get a little sloppy at times but can be regained.

Level 3: Well Practiced

Sequence is well practiced. The child or group can repeat the sequence with reasonable accuracy and precision. Each time the sequence is performed, body actions and skills are the same, but some body parts are in different positions. Formations are the same, but the relationship of group members to the formation varies slightly.

Level 4: Perfected, Exceptional

Sequence is very well practiced. The sequence can be repeated accurately, down to the last detail. Each time the sequence is performed, the body actions, skills, and positions of body parts are exactly the same. In group sequences, the entire group moves together precisely, and the formations are exact with precise relationships among group members.

ASSESSMENT 15.9

Rubric for Assessing the Movement Quality of a Grade 1 Dance Sequence

This rubric aligns with a dance sequence titled "The Thunderstorm."
Sequence Task: Design a sequence representing clouds using the movements we explored today. Start in a round shape held with soft tension, slowly move into two other soft, round shapes in a row, then travel slowly and gently on curved pathways, and end in a different soft, round shape.

Demonstrating the Appropriate Force and Speed

Level 1
Moves quickly or at a medium speed. Has soft force infrequently.

Level 2
Sometimes moves slowly and sometimes moves at a medium speed. Has soft, gentle force and tension most of the time.

Level 3
Moves slowly and with soft, gentle force throughout the entire sequence and holds the starting and ending shapes with soft tension.

Reasons for Assessing Sequence Choreography

In addition to assessing the fundamental skills of jumping, leaping, hopping, and skipping and movement quality, we strongly recommend that teachers assess the sequences children have designed, even in the youngest grades. Sequences are the essence of both gymnastics and dance and are also used with dribbling, jumping rope, and health-related fitness routines.

In gymnastics, the traditional approach was to assess specific required skills (e.g., backward rolls, headstands). This practice will create unsafe pressure for some children who are not ready to try difficult skills and can lead to serious injuries and be a liability risk for teachers. Students who were capable of more difficult skills got better grades. This method of grading can be discouraging and embarrassing to many students and establishes an ego-oriented class climate, rather than a mastery-oriented climate.

We suggest assessing child-designed sequences, which allow students to choose the movements and skills to include in their unique sequences and the teacher to base assessments on the quality of the performance and the quality of the choreography. Thus, assessing sequences accommodates individual differences. Research discussed earlier supports giving students choices in assessment and in the difficulty of the skills and movements they learn and practice. We have found that grading the difficulty of sequences is unnecessary at any grade level. Although it may seem counterproductive not to consider the difficulty of the skills as part of the grade, it has been our experience that students who learn skills that are more difficult also have higher performance and choreographic quality. Thus, rewarding students for the difficulty of their sequences is not necessary and ensures students' safety is not at risk.

ASSESSMENT 15.10

Quick Card Assessment of Movement Quality by the Teacher

Quick card assessments are an excellent way to improve the quality of students' movement. These tools assess only one performance technique over several class periods. This performance technique needs to be general and easy for children to correct. We suggest selecting one of the following in educational gymnastics: (1) tight body; (2) pointed toes; or (3) straight legs.

Use an index card or half of a sheet of paper for each child. On the front, write the child's name, the selected performance technique, and the dates of the assessments. On the back, write the child's name in large letters. If possible, use several different card colors. Rate each child each day on the following scale:

1 = Only sometimes
2 = Most of the time
3 = All the time

Name:
Pointed Toes
3/24
3/26
3/28
3/31
4/2
4/4

Although it might sound difficult to assess an entire class while you are teaching, you are looking for only one performance technique. The trick is first to look for and assess the children scoring 1 (only sometimes), because these children will be easy to see. Next, look for children scoring 3 (all the time), who are also easy to see. The remainder of the children will score a 2.

At the end of class, spread the cards grade-side down on a line. Children can look for their name and their color, turn the card over, and see their scores. Then have them drop their card in a box as they leave the physical education space.

If you repeat this assessment for several class meetings in a row, the children will know that they are being scored and will work to improve. The repeated assessments work well to encourage children to remember the performance technique more frequently during class until the technique becomes automatic.

Assessing sequences using rubrics and rating scales enables you to determine whether children have met state standards and/or the National Standards. Moreover, it provides necessary feedback to students about the extent to which they have achieved learning outcomes with regard to the quality of their sequence choreography. Prospective teachers sometimes ask, "Won't giving feedback on children's choreography stifle their creativity?" We don't think so. The goal of providing feedback is to help children create what they want to create and express what they want to express more effectively. Sharing the criteria for assessment and using peer coaching and self-evaluation with assessment tools will help children to improve their knowledge of choreography and their ability to apply that knowledge.

Elements of Sequence Choreography and Corresponding Levels of Performance

There are elements of sequence choreography that are appropriate for elementary grade levels. You will need to review more detailed information about these elements before you create a gymnastics or dance assessment. In this chapter, we list elements of choreography important for children's dance and describe levels of performance for each element. As with movement quality, we do this for you because few physical education majors have experience choreographing gymnastics and dance sequences, and thus it would be very difficult for you to describe either competent performance or levels of performance. These descriptions can serve as reference tools to help you design assessments.

Our list includes far too many elements for any one assessment or for any grade level—these are the elements you would teach once you have worked with your students across the elementary grades. Our goal was to list the elements and describe the performance level so you can more easily select which one or two elements you want to teach and assess as learning outcomes for your lessons and units. Next, we provide a brief description of the elements of choreography, followed by descriptions of performance levels, and two examples of rubrics derived from these performance levels. At the end of the chapter, we illustrate how to transform our performance levels into rubrics for different grade levels and different sequence tasks. The elements of choreography important for children's dance include the following:

- Sequences have a beginning, middle, and end.
- All parts fit together logically with fluid transitions: Movements are connected with transitions in which one movement leads to the next without the performer having to take extra steps.
- Originality: Shapes and movements are different and interesting with many asymmetrical shapes, a variety of body actions, and something in the sequence that is unusual.
- Expressing an idea: The sequence expresses and represents the idea, object, animal, feeling, story, or whatever is the topic theme of the dance.
- Contrasts and aesthetic highlights: The sequence has contrasts in several movement concepts, such as speed and levels, and an aesthetic highlight that captures the observers' attention.
- Relationships of body parts—line, focus, and clarity: Shapes and body parts form lines that focus or direct the observers' attention. The positions of all body parts are intentional and precise.

Table 15.4 Performance Levels and Criteria for Assessing Elements of Sequence Choreography in Gymnastics and Dance

Sequences Have a Beginning, Middle, and End
Level 1: Missing Parts
The sequence is missing a beginning or an ending shape held still. The sequence is missing parts of the middle that were assigned by the teacher as required components of the sequence, or the child creates a never-ending sequence.
Level 2: Complete
The sequence has a beginning, middle, and end.
All Parts Fit Together Logically with Fluid Transitions
Level 1: Stops and Steps
Performers do one movement but then stop. Many extra steps are taken between movements, formations, or parts of the sequence. Transitions are not planned. Performers seem to make it up as they go along. The sections of the sequence are disconnected, and the parts don't seem to fit together. Each person in the group seems to be working separately.
Level 2: Hesitations and Extra Steps
Many movements are connected with the performer having to take extra steps. Transitions between skills or body actions are mostly planned, but sometimes the order of skills is not logical and creates transition problems. Often the performer takes extra steps or hesitates. In group work, when the performers change formations, many group members take extra steps. Some transitions are abrupt and don't seem to be part of the sequence. Sometimes the order of formations is not logical and creates transition problems.
Level 3: Planned, Logical, and Only a Few Hesitations
Movements fit together logically. Most movements are connected with transitions in which one movement leads to the next without the performer having to take extra steps. Transitions between skills or body actions are planned, but a few times the performers hesitate. In group work, when the performers change formations, most do not take any extra steps. A few transitions are abrupt and don't smoothly connect the parts of the sequence.
Level 4: Smooth/Fluent
The sequence has a sense of unity and coherence from start to finish. Transitions are well planned (down to the last body part). They are not noticeable because they seem to be part of the sequence. The sequence is fluent and smooth. One movement leads to the next seamlessly with no extra steps or hesitations. Sections of the sequence seem to follow each other logically. In group work, when the formation changes, no one takes any extra steps. One formation leads to the next.

Table 15.4 Performance Levels and Criteria for Assessing Elements of Sequence Choreography in Gymnastics and Dance (*continued*)

Originality

Level 1: Plain

Shapes are plain and mostly symmetrical. The same shape is used several times. Only a few body actions are used. Combinations are ordinary and repeated. Starting and ending positions are most often on the children's feet in ordinary positions.

Level 2: Varied

Shapes have variety. Arms and legs are in different shapes and positions. Some shapes are asymmetrical. A variety of body actions is used. Body actions are combined in a variety of ways. Combinations start and end in a variety of shapes and positions.

Level 3: Original

Shapes and movements are different and interesting. There are many asymmetrical shapes. Symmetrical shapes, if present, are used only to make a statement. A variety of body actions and combinations is used, and some combinations are unusual. Starting and ending shapes are interesting and different. Something in the sequence is unusual.

Expressing an Idea

Level 1: Imitates

The individual or group imitates or pantomimes and presents a surface-level caricature.

Level 2: Nearing Representation

A few times the performers imitate, but sometimes they represent their ideas. Sometimes it is not clear what the performers are trying to express.

Level 3: Represents

The sequence expresses and represents the idea. Shapes and movements elaborate on the topic and are abstracted. The meaning is clear to the performers and observers.

Level 4: Represents Powerfully

The sequence effectively communicates a powerful statement about the idea or emotion of the dance. It captures the essence of the idea and is personally meaningful to performers and observers.

Contrasts and Aesthetic Highlights

Level 1: Repetitive

The sequence has no contrasts. There is sameness from start to finish. There are some good ideas, but they are repeated over and over. The sequence is predictable and seems to go on and on. If one person does a series of movements, then everyone else in the group does the same series in turn. If a movement is done to the left, it is then repeated to the right. The rhythm and speed are steady with no changes.

Level 2: Contrasts/Interesting

The sequence has a clear contrast in one of the following aspects: speed, levels, shape, force, pathways, movement versus stillness, directions, and relationships. The sequence is interesting to watch. Repetition is used only to make a statement.

Level 3: Aesthetic Highlights

The sequence has contrasts in several of the following aspects: speed, levels, shape, force, pathways, movement versus stillness, directions, and relationships. The sequence has clear aesthetic highlights that capture the observers' attention. It has a visual impact and/or emotional impact on the performer(s) and/or observers.

Relationships of Body Parts: Line, Focus, and Clarity

Level 1: Infrequent Clarity and Little Attention to Line and Focus

Shapes and movements are nondescript and vague with no identifiable lines or focus. Body parts do not relate to other body parts; in group work, the shapes of group members do not relate. Feet and toes are flexed and/or knees are bent, preventing a straight line in the legs. Body parts stick out of the intended line.

Level 2: Moderately Clear, Some Attention to Line and Focus

Shapes are moderately clear, and the positions of many body parts are planned and relate to one another forming lines that are easily recognized. During group sequences, the shapes of most individuals relate to one another and indicate a group focus.

Level 3: Clarity and Intentional Lines and Focus

In shapes and movements, the positions of all body parts are intentional and precise with all body parts related to the intended shape. Shapes and body parts form lines or indicate a group's focus that directs the observers' attention. All body parts contribute to the lines intended by the performers. All individuals contribute to the group shape, line, and focus.

ASSESSMENT 15.11

Rubric for Assessing the Choreography of a Grade 2 Dance Sequence

(This assessment is aligned with a dance sequence titled "When Autumn Leaves Fall.")

Sequence Task: Based on the movements you explored and the topic of autumn leaves, design a dance sequence that shows a variety of interesting, different, and unusual shapes representing autumn leaves. This is the structure of the dance:

1. Start with a shape that represents an autumn leaf on a tree.
2. Sway and change to a different leaf shape two times.
3. Fall and rise slowly two times, ending in a different leaf shape each time.
4. Travel on a circular pathway, swirling and turning like autumn leaves blowing in the wind.
5. Pause in a different leaf shape and slowly fall to the ground, ending in a different leaf shape.

On the white board, I have written what I will be looking for to assess the variety and originality of your leaf shapes [write the rubric on the white board].

Originality

Level 1: Plain
Shapes are plain and mostly symmetrical. Arms and legs often are straight.

Level 2: Varied
There are a variety of shapes. Arms and legs are in a variety of different positions. Many shapes are asymmetrical.

Level 3: Original
Shapes are very different and interesting. There are many different asymmetrical shapes. The arms, legs, and torso are in a variety of interesting and different positions. At least one shape is unusual.

ASSESSMENT 15.12

Rubric for Assessing the Choreography of a Grade 4 Gymnastics Sequence

(This assessment is aligned with a gymnastics sequence that includes matching, contrasting, and complementing shapes.)

Sequence Task: With a partner, design a sequence showing clear, identical, matching shapes, contrasting shapes that are totally opposite and as contrasting as is possible, and complementing shapes in which the partners' lines formed by all their body parts relate to and complement each other. Last lesson, we discussed the rubric's three assessment levels for line and clarity of shapes. These levels tell you what I will be looking for to show me you understand line and clarity when you match, contrast, and complement your partner's shapes. The rubric is posted on the wall.

Relationships of Body Parts to Shapes: Line and Clarity

Level 1: Shapes Are Vague, Lines Are Not Evident
Shapes are vague; it is difficult to recognize contrasting shapes because the shapes are too similar. It is difficult to recognize complementing shapes because the shapes are not clear. The partners' body lines on complementing shapes are not identifiable. Matching shapes have some body parts that are not in identical positions.

Level 2: Shapes Are Moderately Clear, Lines Are Identifiable
Observers can recognize matching, contrasting, and complementing shapes because the shapes are moderately clear. The positions of many, but not all, body parts are identical in matching shapes. Contrasting shapes are different but not totally opposite. The lines formed for complementary shapes are evident, but all body parts do not contribute to the line. Partners' lines partially relate to or complement each other.

Level 3: Shapes and Lines Include All Body Parts and Clearly Show Matching, Contrasting, and Complementing Shapes
Observers can easily recognize matching, contrasting, and complementing shapes because all shapes are clear. The positions of all body parts are identical in matching shapes. Contrasting shapes are totally opposite and as contrasting as possible. The lines formed by all partners' body parts in complementing shapes relate to and complement each other.

Examples of Rubrics Created from the Descriptions of Levels of Performance for Sequence Choreography

Assessments 15.11 and **15.12** illustrate how you can use the descriptions of levels of performance to create a rubric for assessing sequences. Notice we select only one element to assess, although other elements could apply as well. We also simplified the criteria for competent performance to match the developmental levels of the children. Finally, we made the criteria specific to the tasks.

Assessing the Cognitive, Social, and Affective Domains

In addition to the motor domain, state standards and the National Standards in physical education also include learning outcomes for cognitive knowledge, social behaviors, motivation, knowledge about the values of physical activity, and feelings associated with participation in physical activity. Consequently, you will need to assess what students know, value, and feel about the physical activities in the curriculum and also their social and motivational behaviors.

Cognitive assessments include assessing knowledge, such as children's knowledge of health-related fitness, nutrition, performance techniques, characteristics of movement quality, the application of movement concepts, tactics, and elements of choreography.

Assessing social responsibility and social interactions are also critical for teaching students about appropriate and inappropriate behaviors and giving them feedback on their actions. They need to know the specific criteria for appropriate behavior, and teachers need to know if children understand what they expect from them in terms of personal and social responsibility. Sometimes we assume children know the rules and what they should and should not do, when, in fact, they simply do not understand our expectations for social behaviors. Assessments will help you determine whether children understand your expectations for social interactions and social responsibility.

Teachers also need to know how children feel about physical activities, their experiences in lessons, and their motivation. Physical educators take seriously the goal for all children to find their experience in physical education meaningful and joyful. We hope this experience motivates them to engage in lifelong participation in healthful physical activities. Unfortunately, we know many adults who did not like physical education.

If we want to improve our programs to meet the needs of all children regardless of race, gender, ethnicity, body shape, sexuality, and ability, we need to find out how students are feeling and to what extent they are motivated. We need to know what overweight and obese children like and dislike about our classes. We need to know when children feel hurt, angry, or embarrassed. We need to know whether children are experiencing prejudice or discrimination.

Assessing motivation, social responsibility, and the affective domain gives you information on children's experiences that can help you improve your program. In particular, these assessments can help you identify possible problems, which you can then follow up by talking with the child.

We have already described rubrics, checklists, and rating scales, all of which are excellent tools for assessing learning outcomes in the cognitive, social, and affective domains. The following are additional assessment options.

Exit Slips

A popular, simple, quick form of assessment is an **exit slip** in which the students respond to a question or prompt from the teacher on an index card, slip of paper, or via their smartphones or tablets (Marzano, 2012). At the end of class, ask children one question, such as "Which performance cues did you learn today about dribbling?", "How hard did you work today?", or "How carefully did you listen to your group members and then respond to their ideas? Score yourself from 1 to 5, with 1 being 'I didn't work hard at all,' or 'I didn't really listen, and I never responded to their ideas,' and 5 being 'I worked hard,' or 'I listened and responded consistently all the time.'"

Student Journals

Another useful form of assessment is a **student journal** in which students respond to prompts from the teacher and write about what they learned or how they felt about the physical education lesson or unit (Mohnsen, 1998). You can keep student journals in a file in your office and then hand them out at the start of the unit to record what children know about the activity you are about to teach and what they want to learn; the children can then write in the same journals at the end of the unit to summarize what they learned (Woods, 1997). Often, classroom teachers are willing to have students write in journals about physical education experiences in their classroom as part of a writing lesson, especially when the unit integrates physical education and classroom content.

Web-Form Graphic Organizers

Web-form graphic organizers have the main topic written in a center circle; the concepts related to that topic are then written in circles surrounding this topic, with lines connecting the circles showing the relations among concepts. Webs give children a visual picture of the most important concepts they need to learn about a topic.

In physical education, webs are excellent graphic organizers for teaching, reviewing, and assessing cognitive information about performance techniques for skills and tactics. You can have children in pairs fill out a web at the start of a unit to assess what they remember from previous grades. You can fill out webs as a class to help the children summarize the important concepts and performance techniques associated with a skill or tactic and post these webs on the gymnasium walls or in the hallway. Finally, you can use webs as a summative assessment tool.

Quizzes

You can also use multiple-choice, true/false, and short-answer quizzes to assess knowledge of concepts related to National Standards 2, 3, 4, and 5. *PE Metrics* (NASPE, 2010) provide a test bank of multiple-choice questions for each of these standards. You would need to select questions that match the content you have taught. You can also create your own quizzes.

Many, if not most, schools have systems for sharing documents and assignments over the Internet with the results reported back to the teacher. Typically, with these systems you can create written assessments or assignments, sometimes including videos, and then the students take the test or complete the assignment at home or, in some districts, in class. These results are automatically sent back to you. You need to find out what system your school uses and then learn how it works.

If your school does not have such a system, you can use Google Drive to create your own system. In Google Drive, you can create a variety of assessments using Google Forms and also create surveys and track discipline referrals. Using the URL from the assessment you create in Google Forms, you can link the forms to a QR code using a QR code generator site. Print the QR code and have students scan the code with a QR scanning app on their smartphone or tablet. They take the test, and the results come back to your Google Drive as an Excel-style spreadsheet.

In addition, many apps for teachers allow you to ask a question and get an immediate student response. Both you and the students download the app on your devices. You create an account, enter students' names, and create questions. The students then sign in and answer the questions. Some examples of these apps include Kahoot, Socrative, Plickers, and EDpuzzle.

With technology changing rapidly, by the time this text is published there will be many new options for teachers. Many more schools will have systems for record keeping, assignments, tests, and grading, and these systems will be better than they are today. You will need to find out what is available at your school.

Sample Assessments

In the remainder of the chapter, we provide sample assessments. As you select and modify these assessments, we suggest you do the following:

- Make the performance criteria clear and then check whether the children understand the criteria so the assessment serves as a learning tool.

- Match the assessment to the content you teach (i.e., your objectives and the learning outcomes you plan for a unit).
- Remember the main purpose of the assessment is for you to know what each child can do, knows, and feels and to use that information to increase student learning and improve your teaching.

We include self, peer, and teacher assessments, all of which can be modified to be appropriate for a different assessor. We organize these assessments into three sections:

1. Assessments for games content from level 1 through level 3
2. Assessments for gymnastics and dance
3. Cognitive, motivation, social, and affective assessments

Assessments for Games Content: Levels 1, 2, and 3

ASSESSMENT 15.13

Level 1 Throwing Overhand for Force

Name	Side to Target	Make the T; Break the T
	Yes Not yet	Yes Not yet
	Yes Not yet	Yes Not yet
	Yes Not yet	Yes Not yet

ASSESSMENT 15.14

Level 1 Kicking and Receiving Passes with the Feet (Peer or Teacher Assessment)

Instructions to Class: In your group of three, two will kick and receive passes, and one will be the peer assessor and coach. You will rotate so everyone gets to be the coach and all of you are assessed twice.

Pass the soccer ball back and forth with your playing partner, trying to use *as few touches as possible* to control the ball before you pass it. Your peer coach will be counting how many touches it takes you to control the ball and position it for your pass and will put a tally mark under the column indicating you needed one touch to control the ball or two or more touches to control it.

I will time you and give you one minute to pass while the peer assessor watches partner 1. Then I will time you and give you one minute to pass while the same peer assessor watches partner 2. Do not score the receiver if the pass is not accurate. Then we will rotate peer coaches. Once you have all been the peer coach, compare what you found and discuss ways to improve. [Give every child a peer coach assessment form.]

Peer coach's name: __________

Partner 1: ____________________

Partner 2: ____________________

Name	One Touch to Control, then Pass	Two Touches to Control, then Pass
Partner 1		
Partner 2		

ASSESSMENT 15.15

Level 1 Catching (Peer or Teacher Assessment)

Instructions to Class: In your group of three, two will toss and catch the foam ball, and one will be the peer assessor and coach. You will rotate so everyone gets to be the coach and all of you are assessed twice.

Watch one person five times to see if he or she looks and reaches to catch the ball. Then watch the other person five times. Circle "yes" or "not yet" depending on whether your peers have learned to look and reach to catch the ball.

Once you have all been the peer coach, compare what you found and discuss ways to improve. [Give every child a peer coach assessment form.]

Peer coach's name: __________

Partner 1: ____________________

Partner 2: ____________________

Name	Look and Reach
Partner 1	Yes Not yet
Partner 2	Yes Not yet

ASSESSMENT 15.16

Level 2 Dribbling and "Push Pass" Shooting with a Floor Hockey Stick (Using a Puck or Ball Depending on Your Situation) (Peer Assessment)

Instructions to Class: Set up five cones in a row about 10 feet apart, and put a goal at the end of the row [demonstrate setup]. Dribble a puck/ball with a hockey stick, alternating to the left and then to the right of the cones. End with a push pass shot at the goal (two cones set 10 feet apart). Hold the stick with the nondominant hand on top and the dominant hand below. Use both sides of the stick. The peer coach watches to see whether you use both sides of the stick, counts how many cones you successfully dodged, and sees whether you scored a goal using a push pass (no slap shots). Repeat one time.

Name	Both Sides of Stick?	Tally Marks for Number of Cones	Scored Goal with "Push Pass" Shot?
	Yes No		Yes No
	Yes No		Yes No

ASSESSMENT 15.17

Level 2 Strike a Ball Over a High (5 to 6 Feet) Net Overhand (Peer Assessment)

Instructions to Class: In groups of three, one person is the peer coach while the other two strike a light ball over the net back and forth six times in a row, using an overhand pattern. The peer coach will watch for the following performance techniques: Did you get your body and forehead under the ball? Did you strike with your finger pads? Each of you will assess the other two. Then get together and compare scores and coach each other. Try the test again and see if you improve.

Peer coach's name: ___________________

Name	Body and Forehead Under the Ball	Contact with Finger Pads, Not Palm
	Yes No	Yes No
	Yes No	Yes No

ASSESSMENT 15.19

Bingo Assessment (Peer Assessment)

Your partner assesses the performance technique written in *italics* for each center and circles "yes" if you successfully used the technique or "not yet" if you haven't mastered it yet.

B	I	N	G	O
Tell the teacher about someone who said something encouraging or positive to you.	Make three fielding plays in a row with an *accurate, catchable* throw to the base. Catchable? Yes Not yet	Run through and past *first base, touching the front of the base* two times in a row. Yes Not yet	Complete five throws in a row to a partner from 40 feet, showing *weight transfer to your front foot.* Yes Not yet	Complete five throws past a cone 50 feet away, *taking a large step on the opposite foot.* Yes Not yet
Throw past a cone placed 60 feet away 3 times in a row, *using a shuffle.* Yes Not yet	Make three catches in a row on a medium pop-up, *with thumbs in and hands above head.* Yes Not yet	Throw and knock a cone off a box from 30 feet, *twisting your belly button toward the target.* Yes Not yet	Using an underhand toss, throw five times into a bucket 10 feet away, *pointing to the target on follow-through and stepping with opposite foot.* Yes Not yet	Throw into a bucket on its side from 30 feet and 60 feet, *stepping on a line directly toward the target.* Yes Not yet
Throw and hit the wall on the fly from 40 feet two times in a row, *using a shuffle.* Yes Not yet	Catch three balls in a game of "pepper," *using both hands.* Yes Not yet	Free space	Throw a ball and pop one balloon tied to a fence from 20 feet, *stepping on a line directly toward the target and finish with weight forward.* Yes Not yet	Knock a ball off a tee with a throw from 40 feet, *stepping on a line directly toward the target.* Yes Not yet
Stand between cones and move to catch three balls in row outside the cones, *using a cutback to align with the ball to catch it.* Yes Not yet	Run out a double, *starting turn before first base and leaving the base straight* two times in a row. Yes Not yet	Count how many throws/catches you can make in 15 seconds at the wall *using hands only to catch;* repeat two times, equaling or beating your record. Yes Not yet	Drop back and catch a ball tossed over your head three times in a row, *using a cutback to get in line with the ball.* Yes Not yet	Complete three catches in a row that require a short hop, *catching the ball out in front with both hands.* Yes Not yet
Catch two high pop-ups in a row, *with thumbs and hands above head.* Yes Not yet	Catch five high pop-ups in a row, *with thumbs and hands above head.* Yes Not yet	Throw 60 feet three times, using *the shuffle/tuck performance technique.* Yes Not yet	While playing first base, complete three catches in a row on medium-hard throws, *using the reach, catch, cradle technique.* Yes Not yet	Throw a ball through a hanging hoop from 40 feet, *stepping on a line directly toward the target.* Yes Not yet

Source: Based on format developed by Kelly, G. (2006, April). *Motivational strategies for a mastery environment.* Paper presented at the meeting of the American Alliance for Health, Physical Education, Recreation and Dance, Salt Lake City, UT.

ASSESSMENT 15.18

Level 2 Dribbling with Hands Protecting the Ball from a Defender, 1v1 (Teacher Assessment)

	Head and Eyes	Left and Right Hands	Protects the Ball
Name	**Level 1:** Looks at the ball **Level 2:** Looks up	**Level 1:** Dribbles with dominant hand only **Level 2:** Dribbles with both dominant and nondominant hand (whichever is appropriate)	**Level 1:** Back to opponent **Level 2:** Protects the ball by dribbling to the side opposite the opponent

ASSESSMENT 15.20

Assessment Center Challenge: Throwing Overhand for Force and Accuracy (Self and Peer Assessment)

Complete at least one level from each row. You select your level of difficulty. You may complete more than one task in any row. All throws are overhand for force aiming at a target. You can complete the tasks in any order. You do not have to start with level 1; you can skip around the levels. Have your partner watch one throw and assess whether you successfully used the performance techniques written in *italics* and then circle "yes" or "not yet." When you successfully complete the task, mark an X through the box, and have your partner initial the box. Social responsibility behaviors are for extra credit.

Your name: ____________________

Your classroom teacher's name: ________________

Level 1	Level 2	Level 3	Social Responsibility
Center 1: Throw and hit the big wall from 40 feet on the fly five times, *taking a large step on the opposite foot.* Yes Not yet	*Center 2:* Throw and hit the big wall from 50 feet on the fly five times, *taking a large step on the opposite foot.* Yes Not yet	*Center 3:* Throw and hit the big wall from 60 feet on the fly five times, *taking a large step on the opposite foot.* Yes Not yet	I did not interfere with other groups.
Center 4: Make five throws to a partner from 30 feet, *transferring weight to the front foot.* Yes Not yet	*Center 5:* Throw a ball and pop one balloon tied to the fence from 25 feet, *transferring weight to the front foot.* Yes Not yet	*Center 6:* Knock a ball off a tee, throwing from 40 feet, *transferring weight to the front foot.* Yes Not yet	Say something encouraging to a classmate; write in the margin what you said and to whom.
Center 7: Knock a cone off a crate, throwing from 20 feet, *stepping on a line directly toward the target.* Yes Not yet	*Center 8:* Knock a cone off a crate, throwing from 30 feet, *stepping on a line directly toward the target.* Yes Not yet	*Center 9:* Knock a ball off a tee, throwing from 40 feet, *stepping on a line directly toward the target.* Yes Not yet	I did not always go first.
Center 10: Hit a large target five times from the yellow line (about 30 feet), *twisting your belly button toward the target.* Yes Not yet	*Center 11:* Hit a large target five times from the red line (about 40 feet), *twisting your belly button toward the target.* Yes Not yet	*Center 12:* Hit a target five times from the white line (50 feet), *twisting your belly button toward the target.* Yes Not yet	I placed equipment in the proper location for the next group.
Center 13: Throw past a cone at 40 feet on the fly, *using the shuffle/tuck technique.* Yes Not yet	*Center 14:* Throw past a cone at 50 feet on the fly, *using the shuffle/tuck technique.* Yes Not yet	*Center 15:* Throw past a cone at 60 feet on the fly, *using the shuffle/tuck technique.* Yes Not yet	I demonstrated responsible behavior by remaining on task.
Center 16: Throw five times and hit the target on the fence from 30 feet, *stepping on a line directly toward the target.* Yes Not yet	*Center 17:* Throw a ball through a hanging hoop from 40 feet, *stepping on a line directly toward the target.* Yes Not yet	*Center 18:* Throw a ball into a bucket on its side from 60 feet, *stepping on a line directly toward the target.* Yes Not yet	I did not complain or whine to my partner for any reason.

ASSESSMENT 15.21

Level 3 Offense Tactics in 3v1 Games (Using Hands, Feet, or Hockey Sticks) (Teacher Assessment)

Game: Play keep-away with three offensive players versus one defender within boundaries appropriate for modified basketball, soccer, or hockey games. I will time you for two minutes. The defender must guard or mark players without the ball. I will watch to assess how well you execute two tactics:

1. Cut into an open space that supports the passer.
2. Send lead passes to an open receiver.

Watch one child for two minutes and assess their tactics using the following scale:

Level 5: Consistently successful

Level 4: Highly successful

Level 3: Successful

Level 2: Sometimes successful

Level 1: Not successful

Then have the children rest briefly, rotate who plays defense, and assess the second child.

Name	Cuts into Open Space that Supports the Passer	Sends Lead Passes to an Open Receiver	Total

ASSESSMENT 15.22

Level 3 Field Game Tactics: Deciding Who Should Field the Ball and Which Base to Cover (Teacher Assessment)

Instructions to Class: Play the game "Three Bases" we played last week. I am going to assess you on your decision making about who is the closest person to the ball when you're calling it and fielding it. I will also assess you on whether the person closest to the base (who is not fielding the ball) covers the bases.

After each play, place a tally mark for each player under the appropriate (A) or inappropriate (I) column.

	Decision to Field Appropriate Inappropriate		Decision to Cover Base Appropriate Inappropriate		Total Appropriate	Total Inappropriate
Name	**A**	**I**	**A**	**I**		
Harris	///	//	////	//	7	4
Elaine	///	///	////	/	7	4

Assessments in Gymnastics and Dance

ASSESSMENT 15.23

Skipping (Teacher Assessment)

Name: ________________

Circle the developmental level for legs and arms.

Skipping	Level 1: Immature	Level 2: Intermediate	Level 3: Mature
Legs	Skips on only one foot, steps on other, flat-footed	Alternates legs, flat-footed	Alternates legs, skips on balls of feet
Arms	Arms pump up and down	Arms swing sometimes	Arms swing in opposition or are used intentionally to gesture

ASSESSMENT 15.24

Hopping (Teacher Assessment)

Name: ________________

Circle the developmental level for legs and arms.

Hopping	Level 1: Immature	Level 2: Intermediate	Level 3: Mature
Legs	Swing (free) leg is held up and does not move very much	Swing leg pumps up and down in front of the body	Swing leg uses the full range of motion and thigh swings behind support leg
Arms	Used for balance	Pump up and down to assist in getting height	Arms swing in opposition to the swing (free) leg

ASSESSMENT 15.25

Jumping (Teacher Assessment)

Name: ________________

Circle the developmental level for arms and legs.

Jumping	Level 1: Immature	Level 2: Intermediate	Level 3: Mature
Arms at take-off	Inactive or swing backward	Swing partially forward	Start back and then swing fully forward to full extension over head
Legs at take-off	Knees and ankles remain bent, little force generated, might take off one foot at a time	Two-foot take-off, partial extension of knees and ankles, some force generated	Two-foot take-off, full extension of knees and ankles, strong force generated

ASSESSMENT 15.26

Leaping (Teacher Assessment)

Name: ____________

Leaping	No	Yes
Legs straight in the air		
Pushes off by extending knee and ankle		
Light landing		

ASSESSMENT 15.27

Full Turn (Teacher Assessment)

Name: ________________

Full Turn	No	Yes
Stretched tall through spine		
Remains vertical over supporting foot		
Shoulders down		

ASSESSMENT 15.28

Rubric Assessing the Movement Quality of a Kindergarten Gymnastics Sequence

(This assessment is aligned with a gymnastics sequence involving step-like actions at low levels.)
Sequence Task: Design a starting shape; travel taking your weight on your hands by springing off both feet keeping your feet low near the floor around the stacked mat (or trapezoid section); and finish in an ending shape controlling your body so you land lightly.

Landings and Controlling the Flow

Level 1: Emerging
Heavy landings, sometimes lacks control.

Level 2: Capable
Light landings and control most of the time.

Level 3: Competent
Light landings and control all the time.

ASSESSMENT 15.29

Rubric Assessing the Movement Quality of a Grade 1 Gymnastics Sequence

Sequence Task: Create a sequence of three different sideways rolls changing the shape of your legs on each roll. You also may choose to roll in different directions. In all rolls, point your toes and ankles. When you make a shape with one of both legs straight, keep your knees perfectly straight.

Appropriate Body Alignment

Level 1: Emerging
Toes and ankles often flexed; knees often bent (when they ought to be straight).

Level 2: Capable
Toes and ankles sometimes flexed; knees sometimes bent (when they ought to be straight).

Level 3: Competent
Toes and ankles always pointed; knees always straight at appropriate times.

ASSESSMENT 15.30

Rubric for Assessing the Movement Quality of a Grade 2 Gymnastics Sequence

(This assessment is aligned with a gymnastics sequence combining balancing on different body parts with different shapes and rolling.)
Sequence Task: Create a sequence combining balancing on different body parts in different shapes with rolling.

Appropriate Amounts of Tension

Level 1: Not There Yet
The body is consistently loose.

Level 2: Emerging
The body is sometimes tight. Many body parts are tight.

Level 3: Proficient
The body is usually tight. Most body parts are tight.

Level 4: Perfected, Exceptional
The body is always tight. All body parts have the appropriate amounts of tension.

ASSESSMENT 15.31

Rubric for Assessing the Movement Quality of a Grade 3 Dance Sequence

(This assessment is aligned with a dance sequence titled "Animal Haiku.")
Sequence Task: Design a sequence based on one of the haiku from today's lesson. You can create a butterfly metamorphosis dance, a rattlesnake dance, a cat-and-mouse dance, or a kangaroo-and-baby dance. Make your strong, fast, and firm movements strong, fast, and firm. Make your soft and slow movements soft and slow.

Demonstrates Appropriate Speed and Force

Level 1: Not There Yet
Strong and fast movements are performed at medium speeds and force. Slow and gentle movements are performed at medium speeds and force. Strong movements have little tension.

ASSESSMENT 15.31 (*Continued*)

Level 2: Emerging
There is a difference in the speed between slow and fast movements and between strong and gentle movements. Some strong movements have tension.

Level 3: Proficient
Strong and fast movements are strong and fast. Slow movements are slow. Gentle movements are soft. Strong movements have firm tension.

ASSESSMENT 15.32

Rubric for Assessing if Sequences Are Well Practiced Until Movements Can Be Repeated Accurately for a Grade 4 Dance Sequence

(This assessment is aligned with a dance sequence titled "Invasive Species.")
Sequence Task: In your group of three, design a dance representing one of the four invasive species: Asian long-horned beetles, hydrilla, yellow crazy ants, or cane toads. Practice your dance until you can repeat it accurately doing the same body actions with the same body positions in the same relationships to each other. I will watch your dance at least two times.

Level 1: Needs Much More Practice
Sequence needs much more practice. The sequence is different every time the children perform it. The children talk to and look at one another for information about what to do next. Sometimes they make things up as they go along. The group members do not coordinate their movements.

Level 2: Needs More Practice
Sequence needs more practice. Some sections of the sequence can be repeated, but in other sections, the body positions and their relationships to each other change every time the group performs.

Level 3: Well Practiced
Sequence is well practiced. The group can repeat the sequence with reasonable accuracy and precision. Each time the sequence is performed, body actions are the same, but some body parts are in different positions. The relationships of group members to each other vary slightly.

Level 4: Perfected, Exceptional
Sequence is very well practiced. The sequence can be repeated accurately, down to the last detail. Each time the sequence is performed, the body actions and body positions of the group members are exactly the same. The entire group moves together precisely with the same relationships among group members.

ASSESSMENT 15.33

Rubric for Assessing if Sequences Are Well Practiced Until Movements Can Be Repeated Accurately with Unison and Cannon Movements Performed in Rhythm for a Grade 5 Gymnastics Group Sequence

(This assessment is aligned with a gymnastics group sequence incorporating canon and unison movements and with **Assessment 15.34**.)
Sequence Task: Design a group sequence showing movements in canon and unison with fluent transitions, interesting and varied skills and body positions that bring out the aesthetic potential of cannon and unison, and an aesthetic highlight. *Practice your dance until you can repeat it accurately with the same body positions, unison sections are in perfect unison, and cannon sections are in perfect rhythm.*

Well Practiced Until Movements Can Be Repeated Accurately

Level 1: Needs Much More Practice
The group needs much more practice. The body positions are different every time the children perform it. The children talk to and look at one another for information about what to do next. Sometimes they make things up as they go along.

Level 2: Needs More Practice
The group needs more practice. Body positions vary in some sections every time they perform it.

Level 3: Well Practiced
The group appears to have practiced the sequence and can repeat it accurately. The body positions are the same with only slight variations.

Level 4: Perfected, Exceptional
The sequence is very well practiced and can be repeated accurately, down to the last detail. Body positions are exactly the same every time they perform.

(*continues*)

ASSESSMENT 15.33 (*Continued*)

Unison and Cannon Movements in Rhythm

Level 1: Not There Yet
In many unison sections, individuals do not move simultaneously. Students move in order but are not coordinated in rhythm in cannon sections.

Level 2: Proficient
Most individuals move simultaneously most of the time during unison and are coordinated in rhythm during canon parts of the sequence.

Level 3: Perfected, Exceptional
Unison sections are perfectly in unison, and canon sections are coordinated in perfect rhythm.

ASSESSMENT 15.34

Rubric for Assessing the Choreography of a Grade 5 Gymnastics Group Sequence

(This assessment is aligned with a gymnastics group sequence incorporating canon and unison movements and with **Assessment 15.33**.)
Sequence Task: Design a group sequence showing movements in canon and unison with fluid transitions, interesting and varied skills and body positions that bring out the aesthetic potential of cannon and unison, and an aesthetic highlight.

All Parts Fit Together Logically with Fluid Transitions

Level 1: Stops and Steps
Performers do one movement and then stop. Many extra steps are taken between formations. Transitions are not planned. Performers seem to make it up as they go along. The sections of the sequence are disconnected, and the parts don't seem to fit together. Each person in the group seems to be working separately.

Level 2: Hesitations and Extra Steps
When the performers change formations, many group members take extra steps. Some transitions are abrupt and don't seem to be part of the sequence. Sometimes the order of formations is not logical and creates transition problems.

Level 3: Planned, Logical, and Only a Few Hesitations
Movements fit together logically. Most movements are connected with transitions in which one movement leads to the next without the performers having to take extra steps. Transitions between skills or body actions are planned, but a few times the performers hesitate. When the performers change formations, most do not take any extra steps. A few transitions are abrupt and don't smoothly connect the parts of the sequence.

Level 4: Smooth/Fluent
The sequence has a sense of unity and coherence from start to finish. Transitions are well planned (down to the last body part). The sequence is fluent and smooth. One movement leads to the next seamlessly with no extra steps or hesitations. Sections of the sequence seem to follow each other logically. When the formation changes, no one takes any extra steps. One formation leads to the next.

Interest and Aesthetic Highlights

Level 1: Repetitive
There is sameness from start to finish. There are some good ideas, but they are repeated over and over. The same curled and straight shapes and the same skills are repeated. Formations are repeated. The sequence is predictable and seems to go on and on. There is neither a good match between skills and body positions nor for the aesthetic potential of cannon and unison.

Level 2: Interesting
A variety of skills with interesting shapes are included. Some skills, shapes, and formations are repeated. The sequence is interesting to watch. The skills and shapes of each section are well suited for cannon or unison.

Level 3: Aesthetic Highlights
A variety of skills with interesting shapes is included. If a skill is repeated, the ending and starting positions are different. No shape is used in more than one section. All formations are different. The skills and body positions used in each cannon and unison section highlight the aesthetic potential of cannon and unison and capture the observers' attention. The sequence has a visual impact and/or emotional impact on the performers and/or observers.

ASSESSMENT 15.35

Rubric for Assessing the Choreography of a Kindergarten Dance Sequence

Sequence Task: Create a sequence with a beginning shape you think is interesting, a middle with a pattern of repeating two of your favorite or best locomotor skills (e.g., gallop, jump, gallop, jump), and an ending shape you think is interesting.

Level 1: Missing Parts
The sequence is missing a beginning or ending shape held still. The sequence is missing parts of the middle that were assigned by the teacher as required components of the sequence, or the child creates a never-ending sequence.

Level 2: Complete
The sequence has a beginning, middle, and end.

ASSESSMENT 15.36

Rubric for Assessing the Choreography of a Grade 3 Dance Sequence

(This assessment is aligned with a dance sequence titled "Animal Haiku.")
Sequence Task: Design a sequence based on one of the haiku from today's lesson. You can create a butterfly metamorphosis dance, a rattlesnake dance, a cat-and-mouse dance, or a kangaroo-and-baby dance.

Expressing an Idea

Level 1: Imitates
The individual imitates or pantomimes and presents a surface-level caricature of the animal and its circumstances.

Level 2: Nearing Representation
A few times the performer imitates, but many times he or she represent ideas of the animal and its circumstances. Sometimes it is unclear what the performer is trying to express.

Level 3: Represents
The sequence expresses and represents the idea of the animal and its circumstances.
Shapes and movements are abstracted, not imitative. The meaning is clear to the performer(s) and observers.

Level 4: Represents Powerfully
The sequence effectively communicates a powerful statement about the animal and its circumstances.
Shapes and movements capture the essence of the animal and its circumstances.
The emotional character of the haiku is demonstrated in the sequence. The sequence is personally meaningful to the performer(s) and observers.

ASSESSMENT 15.37

Rubric for Assessing the Choreography of a Grade 5 Dance Sequence

(This assessment is aligned with a dance sequence based on sports and sport tableaux.)
Sequence Task: In groups of four or five, design a dance based on today's lesson on sport tableaux. Design at least three sport tableaux that represent a moment in sport and fluent transitions between them.

All Parts Fit Together Logically with Fluid Transitions

Level 1: Stops and Steps
Performers do one movement and then stop. Many extra steps are taken between movements, formations, or parts of the sequence. Transitions are not planned. Performers seem to make it up as they go along. The sections of the sequence are disconnected, and the parts don't seem to fit together. Each person in the group seems to be working separately.

Level 2: Hesitations and Extra Steps
Many movements are connected with the performers having to take extra steps. When the performers change formations, many group members take extra steps. Some transitions are abrupt and don't seem to be part of the sequence. Sometimes the order of formations is not logical and creates transition problems.

Level 3: Planned, Logical, and Only a Few Hesitations
Movements fit together logically. Most movements are connected with transitions in which one movement leads to the next without the performers having to take extra steps. When the performers change formations, most do not take any extra steps. A few transitions are abrupt and don't smoothly connect the parts of the sequence.

Level 4: Smooth/Fluent
The sequence has a sense of unity and coherence from start to finish. Transitions are well planned (down to the last body part). The sequence is fluent and smooth. Sections of the sequence seem to follow each other logically. When the formation changes, no one takes any extra steps. One formation leads to the next.

Expressing an Idea

Level 1: Imitates
The group imitates or pantomimes and presents a surface-level caricature of the main idea. The body parts of many group members frequently do not relate to those of other group members. There are few instances when the group makes a clear shape focused on the main idea.

Level 2: Represents
The sequence expresses and represents the idea. Group shapes are clear and well planned. Most of the time, the shapes of all individuals relate to and express the main idea. The main idea is clear to the performers and observers.

Level 3: Represents Powerfully
The sequence effectively communicates a powerful representation of the main idea. The positions of the body parts of all group members are planned in relation to expressing the main idea of each tableau. The sequence captures the essence of the idea and is personally meaningful to performers and observers.

ASSESSMENT 15.38

Peer Checklist for Whether the Sequence Has the Required Elements for a Grade 4 Gymnastics Sequence

Sequence Task: Design a sequence with two matching skills and two contrasting skills.

	Included the Elements of the Assignment (circle yes or no)
Matching skill 1	Yes No
Matching skill 2	Yes No
Contrasting skill 1	Yes No
Contrasting skill 2	Yes No

ASSESSMENT 15.39

Peer Assessment Checklist for Movement Quality in a Dance Sequence

Watch your partner's sequence and circle the best word for each item.

Ankles and feet	Flexed	Pointed
Knees	Bent	Straight
Body tension	Loose	Tight
Landings	Heavy	Light

ASSESSMENT 15.40

Peer Assessment Checklist of Choreography for a Grade 5 Dance Sequence in groups of four with two partners assessing two other partners

Sequence Task: Design a sequence with a partner on the topic of prey and predator showing a variety of relationships (e.g., apart, together, back to back, facing, side by side). Include original and interesting shapes and movements and an aesthetic highlight. Circle the words that best describes how much variety was in the relationships, and then circle *yes* or *no* to indicate whether the sequence included original, interesting shapes and an aesthetic highlight.

Relationships:
Little Variety Some Variety Lots of Variety

Original, interesting shapes: Yes No

Aesthetic highlight: Yes No

Cognitive, Motivation, Social, and Affective Assessments

ASSESSMENT 15.41

Web-Form Graphic Organizer Assessing Prior Knowledge of Batting

You and your partner have a blank web-form graphic organizer with the word "batting" in the center with a number of blank circles around it. Before we work on batting, I want to know what you remember about batting from previous grades. In each of the blank circles, write a performance technique you should try to use when you bat a ball.

ASSESSMENT 15.42

Catching with a Glove Exit Slip

If a new child came into your class in the middle of the year and I assigned you to teach her or him what you have learned about how to catch a ball with a glove, what would you say?

ASSESSMENT 15.43

Partner-Share Assessment

Ask the children a question about some content you have taught in the lesson. Partner 1 tells partner 2 the answer. Then, randomly select partner 2 children to tell you what partner 1 said. This technique allows you to assess what individual children have learned—information that you do not get when you have a group discussion at the close of a lesson. Then ask a second question and partner 2 tells partner 1 the answer.

Sample Questions

What makes a good transition?

How can you have contrast in a sequence?

What is a symmetrical shape?

What are the different directions in which you can roll?

ASSESSMENT 15.44

Partner Webs

Hand each pair a blank web with the main topic in the center and four to six bubbles to fill in connected to the center.

Sample Topics for the Center of the Web

Jumping and landing safely

What does a sequence need to include to be interesting?

Different formations

Performance cues for jumping

Different types of shapes

Performance cues for balancing

ASSESSMENT 15.45

Self-Assessment of Group Work

Put a check in the box that describes how often you had the following experiences or feelings in physical education this week when working in your group (designing games, dances, gymnastics, and/or jump rope sequences).

Name	Almost Always	Often	Occasionally	Never
Everyone listened to me.				
The group made decisions but did not include me in the decision.				
People made fun of my suggestions.				
People liked my suggestions.				
I made an important contribution to our (game, dance/gymnastics/jump rope sequence).				
I felt left out.				
I didn't like the ideas, but I didn't say so.				

ASSESSMENT 15.46

Self-Assessment of Motivation, Competence, and Having a Growth Mindset

Name_______________________________

Circle *yes* or *no* for each line.

When practicing today, I felt:

Yes No Challenged

Yes No Successful

Yes No Confused

Yes No Bored

Yes No Good about my improvement

Yes No Frustrated about my lack of improvement

Yes No Discouraged because I don't think I will ever be better

ASSESSMENT 15.47

Self-Assessment of Task Engagement

Name_______________________________

Put an X before the words describing how hard you worked on your gymnastics sequence today.

_____ Worked very hard the entire time

_____ Worked hard most of the time

_____ Worked hard sometimes

_____ Worked hard occasionally

_____ Did not work hard at all

ASSESSMENT 15.48

Peer Tutoring Self-Assessment on the Extent of Support in Your Role as a Tutor

Name_______________________________

Put a check in the box that describes how often you had the following experiences or feelings in physical education this week when assessing and tutoring your peer.

Name	Always	Usually	Sometimes	Rarely
I watched very carefully.				
I accurately completed the assessment form.				
I spoke positively.				
I encouraged my peer when he or she did not meet the criteria.				
I complimented my peer when he or she did meet the criteria.				

ASSESSMENT 15.49

Self-Assessment of Mastery Orientation, Self-Regulation, and Growth Mindset

Name________________________________

Put a check in the box that best describes what you thought when practicing today.

	Almost Always	Often	Occasionally	Rarely
I thought about the performance technique.				
I thought about what I needed to improve and worked on that.				
I worked hard.				
I never gave up even when it was difficult.				
I tried to do better than my classmates did.				
I compared how I was doing to my classmates.				
I worried about being the worst in the class.				
Negative thoughts kept coming into my head.				

ASSESSMENT 15.50

Assessing Feelings and Social Experiences in Physical Education

Name________________________________

Circle *yes* or *no* to tell me about your feelings and experiences in PE this week.

Yes No I was teased.
Yes No People made fun of me.
Yes No I enjoyed learning a new skill.
Yes No I had fun playing the dribbling game.
Yes No People laughed at me.
Yes No I worked hard.
Yes No My feelings were hurt.
Yes No I had fun making up the dance.
Yes No My partner liked working with me.
Yes No I was embarrassed.

ASSESSMENT 15.51

Exit Slip on Feelings During Physical Education for Grades K–1

Name________________________________

Instructions to Class: I gave you a picture with a circle face with two eyes and a nose. Draw a mouth that best shows how you felt in physical education today. You can draw a big smile if you were very happy, a small smile if you were happy sometimes, a straight line if you were not happy or sad, a small frown if you were unhappy or sad sometimes, or a large frown if you were unhappy today.

ASSESSMENT 15.52

Exit Slip on Feelings During Physical Education for Grades 2–5

Name________________________________

Did you feel happy in physical education today? When?

Did you feel sad in physical education today? When?

ASSESSMENT 15.53

Rating Scale on Confidence About Supporting Your Weight on Your Hands

Name________________________________

How confident are you supporting your weight on your hands? Circle how you feel.

Not confident; I need more practice at it.	I'm pretty good.	I'm a perfect 10 and ready for more difficult challenges.

ASSESSMENT 15.54

Rating Scale on Feelings about Lesson Activity [state the specific activity]

Name________________________________

Would you do the activity we did in class today in your free time? Circle how you feel.

I doubt it.	I might.	I would.	Yes, any chance I can get.

Summary

Assessments enable teachers to determine whether children have achieved the intended learning outcomes. When properly integrated into the teaching and learning process, assessments provide valuable feedback on students' performances. Peer assessments, self-evaluation, and posted criteria for assessments help children learn and contribute to children becoming self-regulated, independent learners. Well-designed assessments are matched to the developmental levels of the children and assess performance techniques and knowledge children can reasonably be expected to develop in a unit. In physical education, we assess content from the motor, cognitive, social, and affective domains that allows us to know what each child knows, can do, feels, and experiences.

Review Questions

1. What is the purpose for assessment *of* learning? What is the purpose of assessment *for* learning?
2. What are *PE Metrics*? How can they benefit you as a teacher?
3. How do you align your curriculum to the National Standards?
4. Why should your assessments match your intended learning outcomes?
5. What contribution can developmental information make to designing assessments?
6. How can assessments contribute to the development of self-regulation and independent learning?
7. Design two different assessments for a skill other than dribbling with the hand and throwing overhand for force, using the examples of assessments for dribbling and throwing in this chapter as a guide. Look up information on immature patterns and use this information when creating your assessment. Explain how you used the information.
8. Based on the Game Performance Assessment Instrument (GPAI) components (Oslin et al., 1998) described in this chapter, design an assessment for tactics within gameplay that is different from the assessments presented in this chapter.
9. Design a bingo assessment or assessment center challenge for a skill or tactic not described in the chapter.
10. Why are social and affective assessments important?

References

Brookhart, S. M. (2013). *How to Create and Use Rubrics for Formative Assessment and Grading.* Alexandria, VA: ASCD.

Bryan, C. L., & Solmon, M. A. (2007). Self-determination in physical education: Designing class environments to promote active lifestyles. *Journal of Teaching in Physical Education, 26*, 260–278.

Byra, M. (2004). Applying a task progression to the reciprocal style of teaching. *Journal of Physical Education, Recreation and Dance, 75*(2), 42–46.

Chen, W., Rovegno, I., Todorovich, J., & Babiarz, M. (2003). Third grade children's movement responses to dribbling tasks presented by accomplished teachers. *Journal of Teaching in Physical Education, 22*(4), 450–466.

Cohen, R., Goodway, J. D., & Lidor, R. (2012). The effectiveness of aligned developmental feedback on the overhand throw in third-grade students. *Physical Education and Sport Pedagogy, 17*, 525–541.

Common Core State Standards Initiative. (2010). *Common core state standards for English language arts and literacy in history/social studies, science, and technical subjects.* Available at http://www.corestandards.org

Dyson, B. P., Linehan, N. R., & Hastie, P. A. (2010). The ecology of cooperative learning in elementary physical education. *Journal of Teaching in Physical Education, 29*, 113–130.

Humphry, S. M., & Heldsinger, S. A. (2014). Common structural design features of rubrics may represent a threat to validity. *Educational Researcher, 43*, 253–263.

Iserbyt, P., Elen, J., & Behets, D. (2010). Instructional guidance in reciprocal peer tutoring with task cards. *Journal of Teaching in Physical Education, 29*, 38–53.

Johnson, M., & Ward, P. (2001). Effects of classwide peer tutoring on correct performance of striking skills in 3rd grade physical education. *Journal of Teaching in Physical Education, 20*, 247–263.

Johnson, T. G., Prusak, K. A., Pennington, T., & Wilkinson, C. (2011). The effects of the type of skill test, choice, and gender on the situational motivation of physical education students. *Journal of Teaching in Physical Education, 30*, 281–295.

Kelly, G. (2006, April). *Motivational strategies for a mastery environment.* Paper presented at the meeting of the American Alliance for Health, Physical Education, Recreation and Dance, Salt Lake City, UT.

Koka, A., & Hagger, M. S. (2010). Perceived teaching behaviors and self-determined motivation in physical education: A test of self-determination theory. *Research Quarterly for Exercise and Sport, 81*, 74–86.

MacPhail, A., Kirk, D., & Griffin, L. (2008). Throwing and catching as relational skills in games play: Situated learning in a modified games unit. *Journal of Teaching in Physical Education, 27*, 100–115.

Martin, J. J., Kulinna, P. H., & Cothran, D. (2002). Motivating students through assessment. *Journal of Physical Education, Recreation and Dance, 73*(8), 18–19, 30.

Marzano, R. J. (2012). The many uses of exit slips. *Educational Leadership, 72*(2), 80–81.

Mitchell, S. A., & Oslin, J. L. (1999). *Assessment in games teaching.* Reston, VA: National Association for Sport and Physical Education.

Mohnsen, B. (1998). Assessing and grading middle school students. *Teaching Elementary Physical Education, 9*(6), 13–15.

National Association for Sport and Physical Education (NASPE). (2009). *Appropriate instructional practice guidelines for elementary school physical education* (3rd ed.). Reston, VA: Author.

National Association for Sport and Physical Education (NASPE). (2010). *PE metrics: Assessing national standards 1-6 in elementary school*. Reston, VA: Author.

Oslin, J. L., Mitchell, S. A., & Griffin, L. L. (1998). The Game Performance Assessment Instrument (GPAI): Development and preliminary validation. *Journal of Teaching in Physical Education, 17*, 231–243.

Prusak, K. (2005). Assessing students in the task-involved motivational climate. *Teaching Elementary Physical Education, 16*(1), 11–17.

Prusak, K. A., Treasure, D. C., Darst, P. W., & Pangrazi, R. P. (2004). The effects of choice on the motivation of adolescent girls in physical education. *Journal of Teaching in Physical Education, 23*, 19–29.

Rink, J. E. (2013). Measuring teacher effectiveness in physical education. *Research Quarterly for Exercise and Sport, 84*, pp. 407–418.

Roberton, M. A., & Halverson, L. E. (1984). *Developing children: Their changing movement*. Philadelphia: Lea & Febiger.

Rovegno, I., Nevett, M., Brock, S., & Babiarz, M. (2001). Teaching and learning basic invasion game tactics in fourth grade: A descriptive study from situated and constraints theoretical perspectives. *Journal of Teaching in Physical Education, 20*, 370–388.

Shen, B., McCaughtry, N., Martin, J., & Fahlman, M. (2009). Effects of teacher autonomy support and students' autonomous motivation on learning in physical education. *Research Quarterly for Exercise and Sport, 80*, 44–53.

Society of Health and Physical Educators (SHAPE). (2014). *National standards and grade-level outcomes for K–12 physical education*. Champaign, IL: Human Kinetics.

Standage, M., Duda, J. L., & Ntoumanis, N. (2003). A model of contextual motivation in physical education: Using constructs from self-determination and achievement goal theories to predict physical activity intentions. *Journal of Educational Psychology, 95*, 97–110.

Treasure, D. C., & Roberts, G. C. (1995). Applications of achievement goal theory to physical education: Implications for enhancing motivation. *Quest, 47*, 475–489.

van der Mars, H., & Harvey, S. (2010). Teaching and assessing racquet games using "play practice" part 2: Integrating assessment into teaching. *Journal of Physical Education, Recreation and Dance, 81*(5), 35–43, 56.

Vande Broek, G., Boen, F., Claessens, M., Feys, J., & Ceux, T. (2011). Comparison of three instructional approaches to enhance tactical knowledge in volleyball among university students. *Journal of Teaching in Physical Education, 30*, 375–392.

Ward, P. (2013). The role of content knowledge in conceptions of teaching effectiveness in physical education. *Research Quarterly for Exercise and Sport, 84*, pp. 431–440.

Wickstrom, R. L. (1983). *Fundamental motor patterns* (3rd ed.). Philadelphia: Lea & Febiger.

Woods, A. M. (1997). Assessment of the cognitive domain. *Teaching Elementary Physical Education, 8*(3), 28–29.

CHAPTER

16

Teaching Large Classes and Teaching in Small Spaces

PRE-READING REFLECTION

1. Make a list of problems you anticipate you would face while teaching large classes of 40 to 80 children (the children have physical education five days a week).
2. What do you want to know about teaching large classes?

OBJECTIVES

Students will learn:

1. Research shows that teachers of large classes can be effective if they follow these guidelines:
   - Provide maximum amounts of skill practice.
   - Avoid large group games.
   - Use efficient, consistent management routines.
   - Teach children to self-regulate and learn independently.
   - Teach children to be socially responsible.
   - Use peer teaching and assessment.
2. An excellent, skill-based curriculum does not depend on class size.
3. With large classes, it is recommended to introduce content with whole-class teaching, but then have children practice content in centers.
4. Centers provide maximum practice opportunities and effective use of limited amounts of equipment and space.
5. Centers can be used to differentiate instruction.

CONNECTION TO STANDARDS

Although large classes do not meet guidelines promoted by the Society of Health and Physical Educators (SHAPE America), they are an unfortunate reality for many teachers. In this chapter, we offer teaching strategies for teaching large classes so that children in these classes can meet the National Standards for Physical Education (National Standards).

Introduction

In this chapter, we discuss large classes and teaching in small spaces. Some solutions to the problems that arise with large classes and small spaces are the same for both. We begin with large classes.

Teaching Large Classes

Unfortunately, many teachers face the reality of having to teach large classes. Due to low budgets, budget cuts, and pressure on principals to spend money on improving reading and mathematics scores, the problem of large physical education classes is likely to increase rather than decrease.

We want to say up front as loudly and clearly as we can that we do not support physical education teachers teaching more than one class of children at a time. The SHAPE America (National Association of Sport and Physical Education [NASPE], 2009) position on this point is equally clear. The association recommends that physical educators teach classes that are the same size as those taught by classroom teachers.

Having said that, we will do our best to help those teachers who must teach large classes to do an excellent job. Much of the material presented in this chapter is based on the research on teaching large classes and on our observations and research on Robin Litaker, who taught classes ranging in size from 70 to 115 children (typically with two aides) in inner-city Mobile, Alabama, and in a Birmingham, Alabama, suburb. Not only has Robin Litaker been the Alabama State Alliance of Health, Physical Education, Recreation, and Dance's "Physical Education Teacher of the Year," but she also has been the Alabama "Teacher of the Year," competing against teachers from all subject areas and grade levels. In addition, in this chapter we share what we have learned from experience both teaching large classes ourselves and helping undergraduates learn how to teach large classes.

Experienced Teachers Talk

Teaching Large Classes

If you must teach large classes, we suggest you try as best as you can to follow the advice of Robin Litaker:

> Just because you can do a good job with large classes doesn't make it right, but throwing up your hands and saying it can't be done is not doing right by the kids. You have to face it. Don't make an excuse. Figure out how to get it done. [For us in Alabama,] the good side is, we get the kids five days a week.

The Amount of Practice Is the Most Important Variable

First and foremost, remember that the amount of practice is the most important variable for learning skills. Individual feedback from a teacher to a child does not define teaching. Individual feedback is nice but not a necessary ingredient for learning. Silverman, Tyson, and Krampitz (1992) found that the total amount of feedback did not relate to student achievement; rather, practice was the important variable.

If you can find ways to provide maximum skill practice time, your students will learn. This translates into the following criteria:

- No large group games
- No long lines
- Every child (or pair, when appropriate) has a ball

The primary way that effective teachers of large classes provide maximum practice time is through centers, which we discuss in detail later in the chapter.

What the Research Says

Class Size

A considerable amount of research on elementary classroom subjects has shown that small classes lead to greater student achievement (Finn, Pannozzo, & Achilles, 2003). What is important for our discussion is why this relationship arises. Small classes have an advantage for the following reasons (Finn et al., 2003; Hastie & Saunders, 1991):

- Students are more cognitively engaged in learning.
- Students spend more time learning and have more practice opportunities.
- Students spend less time waiting and transitioning from one activity to another.
- Students are more visible to the teacher and can't hide in the corner or in a crowd and drift off task.
- Students exhibit less antisocial behavior.

However, research has also shown that physical education teachers can provide an amount of time for both learning and practice opportunities comparable to those delivered by teachers of small classes (Hastie, Sanders, & Rowland, 1999). What seems to be the most critical factor is not class size, but adequate amounts of equipment and maximum amounts of skill practice (Hastie & Saunders, 1991). To teach large classes successfully, you need to replicate what occurs more easily in small classes. We discuss suggestions for doing so in this chapter.

Acquire Equipment (Any Way You Can Do It)

Obviously, all children can't practice at the same time if you don't have enough equipment. Research supports the contention that lack of equipment has a negative impact on learning (Hastie & Saunders, 1991). Some schools are well equipped; others are not. If you are new to a school, ask parents for donations. Write grants. Hold fundraisers.

You also can use homemade equipment. One of us began her teaching career in a school with limited equipment. She taught punting with empty milk jugs and kicking using foam cubes she cut from an old foam mattress. You can make paper canes from tightly rolled newspapers to jump over. These paper canes can, in turn, be flattened and taped in a circle to become deck rings for teaching net games. Milk jugs with the ends cut off and duct tape covering the sharp edges make excellent scoops for teaching catching (see **Figure 16.1**). Collect plastic cups from stadiums after games to use as cones. You can make volleyballs out of old beach balls stuffed with Styrofoam packing peanuts held together with duct tape or balloons covered with a nylon web. You can make balance beams from 2-inch-by-4-inch boards (see **Figure 16.2**), 8- and 12-inch-diameter PVC pipe bolted onto 2-inch-by-4-inch bases (see **Figure 16.3**), and even an old garden hose.

If you don't have enough balls for every child, get out every piece of equipment you have and organize enough centers so that everyone can practice some skill. Some children might practice throwing old tennis balls, others catching beanbags, and others dribbling playground balls or any other skills. The critical point is to get every child practicing as much as possible.

Over time, you will be able to accumulate adequate amounts of equipment. It will take effort and persistence, but it can be done.

Figure 16.1 Milk jug scoops

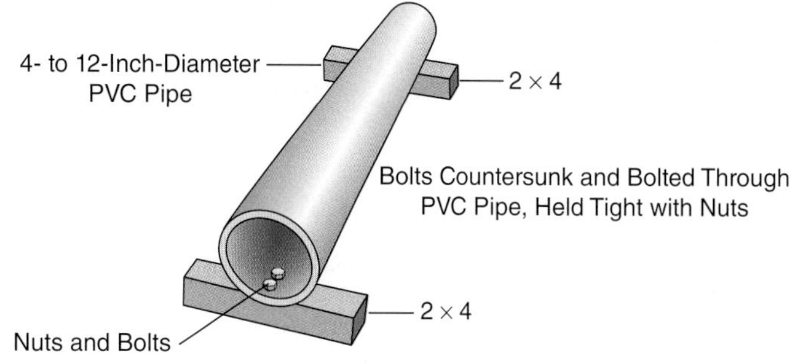

Figure 16.2 PVC pipe beam

Be Well Organized with Consistent Routines

According to the research, large classes spend more time transitioning from one activity to another (Hastie & Saunders, 1991). While a teacher of small classes can vary the routines or change formations within a lesson, a teacher of large classes should not.

With large classes, whenever possible you should use the same organizational formation (e.g., scattered the entire lesson or in partners facing each other) with all skill practices. Maintaining this consistency will save time and help you avoid confusion and management problems.

Try to rely on a small number of formations across the school year, and have children practice getting into these formations quickly. We were surprised to learn that a well-known football coach spent the first day of practice having the team practice the practice routines, rotating stations and moving efficiently to where they needed to be in each phase of practice. As consequence, however, his team wasted no time on organizational issues during the rest of the season.

As you plan your lesson, think very carefully about your organization. Plan exactly how you will describe what the children will do and where they need to go. Rehearse what you will say (experienced teachers do this, too). Make things as simple as possible.

Equipment must be spread out before the children enter the physical education space so they can pick up a piece of

Figure 16.3 Simple 2-inch-by-4-inch beam

SAFETY AND LIABILITY 16.1

Increasing Safety and Decreasing Risk of Liability: Guidelines Relevant to Content in this Chapter

In this box, we discuss specific guidelines built on information discussed throughout this text on professional standards of practice, negligence, and liability. The goals of these guidelines are to increase children's safety and decrease teachers' risk of negligence and liability.

- Supervision is more difficult with large classes simply because there are more children to supervise. You must actively scan for safety throughout the lesson.
- As in small classes, all instruction in large classes must be in keeping with professional standards. Students must receive instruction on how to perform skills, safety procedures, and warnings against inherent harm in physical activities. Tasks must be developmentally appropriate, taught in a sound progression, and in keeping with the scope and sequence of district, state, and national standards. Teachers must differentiate instruction to meet the needs of each child.
- Even with large classes or small spaces, a reasonably prudent teacher must ensure there is adequate space for children and equipment to move safely.

equipment without waiting or bumping into anyone. Lining up at the equipment room door is not an option. Arrange your equipment so the children won't get confused. For example, you can color-code classes and equipment baskets, setting up multiple baskets for each class. (We purchased cheap laundry baskets in different colors for this purpose.) You can even color-code balls if you have the funds.

Provide a Substantive Curriculum that Prepares Children for a Lifetime of Physical Activity

Whether you have large or small classes, you can teach substantive, important motor skills and activities to your students. Your curriculum does not depend on the number of children you teach. It should always focus on the most important skills and avoid fads.

Robin Litaker said, "With five days a week, I still thought I did not have enough time to teach. Five days a week isn't good if you don't take the time to develop a curriculum the way it needs to be developed. It is not good if you use time fillers." If you have a good curriculum with adequate equipment, your children will learn what they need to learn to support a lifetime of physical activity, whether you have large classes or small.

Use Tasks that Encourage Engaged Practice Time

Research indicates that children in small classes are more engaged cognitively in learning (Finn et al., 2003). To replicate this outcome in large classes, you will need to design motivating tasks. Research shows that children are motivated to practice when they find the task is challenging, interesting, novel, enjoyable, and/or demands their attention (Sun, Chen, Ennis, Martin, & Shen, 2008).

To ensure the children are cognitively engaged, you will need to provide a wide variety of tasks for practicing skills—you won't be able to do the same tasks over and over. You can find or devise many interesting tasks for practicing each skill you teach (see **Figure 16.4**). For example, literally hundreds of tasks for practicing dribbling are possible. Believe it or not, children will view the dribbling tasks as totally different if you make the following changes:

Figure 16.4 Children view practicing the same skill as totally different with minor changes in the task

- Add an imaginative element.
- Add a story behind the task.
- Change the equipment or equipment arrangement.
- Change the performance technique focus.
- Change the formation.

Teach Children to Learn Independently and Self-Regulate

At the heart of successfully teaching large classes are children who know how to learn in such an environment. In other words, these students are able to learn independently of a teacher's constant, individual attention. Children must learn that they need to think critically about their performance techniques while practicing and attempt to improve on their own. To teach children to self-regulate and learn independently, convey the following messages:

- The gym is a learning place in which you are responsible for working hard to learn.
- To learn motor skills requires persistence, effort, and challenging yourself. It has to come from you.

- To learn motor skills, you need to think about trying to improve one performance technique while you are practicing.
- You need to think critically about your performance techniques, and select those performance cues that will best help you learn.
- You need to be able to select equipment and modify the level of task difficulty so that you are challenged and successful.

The difference between small and large classes is that with large classes you must be certain the children understand the thinking skills and their responsibilities for making appropriate decisions. You can't get away with brief explanations and rely on individual feedback to keep children on track. Instead, you must teach critical thinking and self-regulation skills more thoroughly, more powerfully, and repeatedly.

For example, you can demonstrate a skill while thinking aloud, thereby showing the children how you are critiquing your performance. You can demonstrate a skill and ask children to assess which technique they would select if they were you. As always, you will need to check up on the children's thinking many times by asking them which performance technique they are thinking about at that moment.

Teaching children the disposition to work hard and persistently is equally important for developing independent learners. You need to convince them that you can't learn for them; rather, the learning effort has to come from them. Tell inspirational stories about athletes or children who were not initially successful but who never gave up and became champions. Tell stories about yourself when you were a child. Promote and post locker room slogans and mottoes about effort and hard work.

It may not be easy to teach children to work independently and take responsibility for their own performance, but it can be done if you persist. Most significantly, for teachers of large classes, it is necessary. Once children can work on their own, your life as a teacher will improve measurably. You will be free to work with individual children and small groups. You can be confident that the children have gained the ability to teach themselves physical skills activities—an ability that will last for the rest of their lifetimes.

Focus on Two to Three Performance Cues

For children to work independently and think about a performance technique while practicing, they must memorize and understand two or three performance cues for each major skill (see **Figure 16.5**). They can't rely on the teacher to constantly remind them, and they typically can't remember more than three cues. While a teacher of small classes can, over the year, teach more performance techniques, a teacher of large classes must be more selective.

To help children remember the performance cues, you can't simply show and tell the cues. Instead, you must make your presentation truly memorable. Tell a story, use a funny metaphor, or demonstrate the cue in a way they won't forget. For example, here is Robin's story for teaching kindergarteners that the same foot leads when galloping. It is a story that appeals to the humor of 5- and 6-year-olds (it won't work in middle school!):

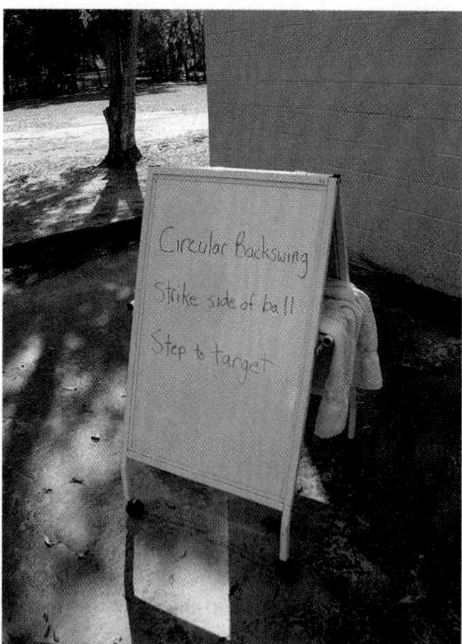

Figure 16.5 Writing cues on a whiteboard

> There was a kindergarten boy named Fred. Everyone liked Fred because he was kind to everyone and always cheerful and happy. But Sally liked Fred so much she had a crush on him. One day during recess, Sally tried to give Fred a big old kiss. Fred knew he was way too young to be kissing a girl, and any way he didn't want Sally to kiss him. So, he said no and ran away from her. Sally tried very hard to catch him, but Fred was faster. Every time Sally got close, Fred stayed ahead of her and got away. When I tell you to gallop, I want you to think about the story of Fred and Sally. Your front leg is Fred and your back leg is Sally. Fred always stays in front, and when Sally catches up, Fred moves ahead.

After you have taught performance cues, you will need to check for understanding frequently until you know every child can tell you the cues for whichever skill he or she is practicing. You will also need to review the cues more frequently than a teacher with small classes.

Teach Children to Be Socially Responsible in the Large Class Environment

Successful discipline relies not only on sound organization and routines, but also on teaching children how class rules are based on important broader values and moral standards.

We won't repeat information here, but we will emphasize that with large classes, it is even more essential to spend time teaching about appropriate behavior and social responsibility. This teaching will take time away from skills instruction, but it also will save time in the long run, as you won't have to deal with multiple discipline problems in every lesson.

If you see a discipline problem, you need to decide whether to stop the whole class or just deal quietly with the individual child or children involved while the rest of the children continue the lesson. We use the following criteria to make this decision:

- If several individuals are off task and you think they may have been confused about your directions, sit the whole class down and review the directions.
- If several children are off task and their out-of-control behavior seems to be spreading to other children, have the entire class sit down; use the incident as a teachable moment to discuss the behaviors and their connections to broader social values and moral standards. After teaching a few years, you will develop a storehouse of good stories to tell children to help them understand and remember why particular behaviors are inappropriate.
- If the rest of the class is working well and independently, you can decide to deal with the individuals who are causing the problem while the rest of the class keeps working. Be sure to talk with the misbehaving children with your back facing the wall and the children in front of you, so you can scan the rest of the class as you deal with the issue.
- If the problem is serious or if you discover it will take a long time for you to solve, have the children sit out and deal with the problem after class.

Use Peer Teaching and Assessment

Peer teaching and assessment is invaluable in large classes. It ensures that every child has someone watching her or him and attempting to offer helpful comments. You can devise checklists and rubrics for skills. These assessment tools will remind both children—the reviewed child and the reviewer—of the performance techniques they need to practice. The peer teachers will be able to provide feedback as to which performance techniques their peer performed well and which need more work. Game play research shows that when students are provided with a detailed rubric or checklist describing the movements and positioning of players for each game tactic, student learning increases (Iserbyt, Elen, & Behets, 2010; Vande Broek, Boen, Claessens, Feys, & Ceux, 2011). Requiring students to understand what to look for when assessing game tactics contributes to a deeper understanding and a better application of their knowledge of tactics in games. Both those assessing and those being assessed benefit.

To adhere to the imperative to have students active at least 50% of lesson time, have only one-quarter to one-third of the class assessing while the rest are practicing. Then rotate. You will need to hold students accountable for their assessments by having them sign their assessments and discussing the results with the person they assessed, who also must sign the assessment. For skills, you can design a simple checklist and have the students assess a limited number of skill components for a limited number of trials. Game play is difficult to assess. With game play, assign partners for assessing. They first discuss the assessment tool to make sure they understand what they are looking for and then together assess one team. They must sign their assessment sheets and discuss the results with the team. Depending on the tactics, you can divide the assessment into two parts; for example, one assessor watches off-the-ball play to see if the offense is cutting to receive a pass and supporting the passer or if they are standing still. The other can watch the passer and assess whether the passer is sending a lead pass to the best positioned receiver and to a receiver open in a passing lane.

Probably the best reason to use peer assessment with large classes is that it gives you relatively accurate assessment information about each child. Assessing 600 to 1,000 children by yourself is a daunting task, to say the least. Peer assessment can supplement teacher assessment and keep you better informed about the progress of your children.

Use Whole-Class Teaching for Introducing Content

For teaching large classes, we recommend using whole-class teaching to introduce content and then sending children to centers for extended practice. During whole-class teaching, try to include those tasks that you will later use as centers. This way, children will practice the center task under your guidance before they work more independently.

When you introduce the content, capture the children's attention. Your goal is to firmly imprint the information on the children's memories so that once you switch to centers, they will know the information well.

When using whole-class teaching with large classes, we recommend that beginning teachers initially rely on whole-class feedback. Scan the class and select the feedback needed by a majority of the children. Give that feedback and monitor the class, repeating the feedback until as many children as are developmentally ready to improve that performance technique are responding appropriately. Then move on to the next most needed feedback. By the end of the lesson, you will have provided the right feedback for almost all the children. This is not a perfect system, but it will get you started.

Differentiate Tasks and Feedback

If possible and if you know the children, differentiate instruction immediately, and provide task and feedback options. Recall that you can differentiate instruction by providing multiple practice tasks and letting the children decide which task to practice. For example, you might say, "Those children who are ready to practice dribbling with your feet at a slow or moderate speed, work on this half of the field. Those children who have experience and are ready for faster speeds and avoiding a defender, work on this half of the field."

To provide feedback options, scan the class and select two performance techniques on which many children need to focus. Say, "I can see some of you need to work on supporting your weight on your hands so your head doesn't touch the mat when you roll. Others need to work on staying tucked and rolling directly to your feet. You decide which performance technique is most appropriate for you."

Dealing with Limited Equipment

If you do not have enough equipment for everyone to practice the same skill simultaneously, teach two skills and divide the physical education space in half. Have half the children practice one skill and the other half practice the other skill.

Then have the children switch places, reminding them of the performance cues for each skill. If your equipment is even more limited, divide the class and space in thirds or fourths. Teach two new skills and practice two previously learned skills.

Buy equipment such as playground balls and vinyl balls that have multiple uses. Not only are basketballs and trainer volleyballs expensive, but they also get chewed up on playgrounds; thus you are very limited as to where and how you can use them. Regulation equipment is not a viable option for elementary schools with large classes.

Centers

Use Centers for Providing Maximum Practice Opportunities

Centers are sometimes called stations or circuits. We use the term *center* here because it matches the classroom terminology. Centers can solve many of the problems associated with large classes.

The first problem is limited equipment and limited space. With centers, some children can practice shooting at goals while others practice dribbling. Some centers may use only small amounts of space, enabling you to include other tasks that require larger amounts of space.

Centers also solve the problems of long lines and lack of practice and physical activity due to large group games. Children should never wait in line to practice the task assigned at a center. Set up enough centers so there are only two children at each center, and provide enough equipment at each center so both children can practice simultaneously. In the older grades, when you are working on tactics or game-like tasks, you can increase this ratio to one center for every three or four children as long as the task requires all of them to participate.

We met one teacher, new to her school, who had only three bags of equipment. We said, "Put it all out and design centers for the children to practice any skill the equipment allows." You can also include locomotor skill centers using no equipment.

Use Centers to Provide Varied Practice Opportunities

A good set of centers will include a variety of motivating practice tasks for each skill as well as centers at which to practice different skills. You can teach several skills in whole-class teaching and then set up centers for a few weeks for practicing those skills. As the year progresses, you can add new skills and repeat previously taught skills in a new set of centers, thereby allowing children to get the repetition needed to ensure mastery.

Baskets and Task Cards

In our recommended setup, each center has a laundry basket holding all small equipment. Moderate-sized equipment, such as balance boards, is placed next to the basket. Large equipment, such as gymnastics bars, mats, balance beams, and pitching machines, is set up before class begins.

Taped to the wall or, if the class is working outside, to the basket is a task card that briefly explains the task in a phrase or two (see **Figure 16.6**). With beginning readers, these phrases need to be simple, short reminders of what the teacher explained earlier that they were to do at that center.

You will have to take the time to explain and demonstrate the task for each center. It may seem like a lot for children to remember, but we find this is rarely a problem after kindergarten. We teach children to follow a three-step routine if they forget what to do at a center:

1. Read the task card.

Figure 16.6 Equipment basket and task card for a center

2. Ask their partner.
3. If neither can remember, then sit and raise their hands and the teacher will come over to them.

Management: Rotating Centers

We find that using centers also helps prevent management problems. Having children stop, settle down, rotate to a new center, and refocus their attention on a new task works to prevent the escalation of excitement and loss of control that can often occur when children practice enjoyable motor skills.

As with any other management routine, teachers need to teach children how to rotate from center to center. We suggest your rotation routine match the children's abilities to behave with self-responsibility.

With larger classes and younger children (or if you are a beginning teacher), break this process down into two steps. Tell the children to put all small equipment back into the center's basket and then sit down before they rotate. Stopping and sitting briefly gives the children a chance to regroup and calm down. It also allows time for the teacher to provide any whole-class feedback. Then have children point to the next center (see **Figure 16.7**); scan to see if they know where they are going. Rotate on your command, and set up any equipment,

Figure 16.7 Pointing to the next center: ready to rotate

Criteria for Centers

Good Task, Bad Center?

All "good" centers are also "good" tasks, *but* not all good tasks make good centers. Tasks that you might teach in a whole-class lesson must be modified to work in centers that will engage one or two children for approximately four minutes without teacher intervention. For example, don't plan a center at which children perform a skill "on signal" from the teacher—that is a task for whole-class teaching, not a center.

Engaging or Boring?

Ask yourself whether each of your centers will capture the children's interest. Will children think, "I can't wait to get to that center"? Will each center engage children in practicing vigorously, or will they get bored after just a few practice trials? Remember, children work at centers independently, and you can't rely on feedback or refining tasks to keep children on task.

Substantive, Important Content or Trivial and "Cutesy"?

Is each center working on important skills or content? Or is the center focused on trivial content that is simply a "cutesy" activity for fun? Ask yourself, "Why do I want the children to practice this content?" Is it meaningful, educational content? Will it meet one of the National Standards and an objective listed in the state course of study?

Challenge and Success? Developmentally Appropriate? Safe for All?

Will each center challenge children to improve their skills while at the same time providing opportunities for *all* children to experience success? Are any of your centers developmentally inappropriate for some students? Are your centers safe for all children? Will your centers tempt children to try a movement that is not safe?

Variety or Repetition?

Do your centers as a group provide a rich variety of ways to practice skills, or are they repetitious? Will children perceive each center as different and special or as the same old thing?

The "Me" Test

If asked, could you perform the movements required at each center? If you listened to someone else reading your task, would you know exactly what you had to do, or would you be confused? Would you *want* to do your center?

The Four-Minute Test

Is it likely that the children will willingly practice at your center for four minutes, or will they give up or get bored and look for something else to do?

such as scattering hoops about the space (see **Figure 16.8**). At that point, tell them to begin to practice at the new center (see **Figure 16.9**). In older grades and as children become better at self-responsibility, you can have children put away their equipment and rotate to the next center without stopping to sit. They can also be asked to put away the equipment at the end of the lesson or at the end of the day (see **Figure 16.10**).

If you will be using the same centers during the next lesson, have children rotate one last time at the end of class. Then tell them, "This is where you will start the next lesson."

Tactics, Game-like Experiences, and Gameplay Using Centers

Without a doubt, gameplay is the most difficult content to teach large classes. You can present information about tactics in the same ways you can with small classes, but it is much more difficult to actively monitor 10 to 20 small-sided games when children are first learning how to play.

A large part of this problem is social. The cultural model children have of social interactions in games comes from professional sports, collegiate sports, and elite age-group sports—all of which are highly competitive, focus on winning and losing,

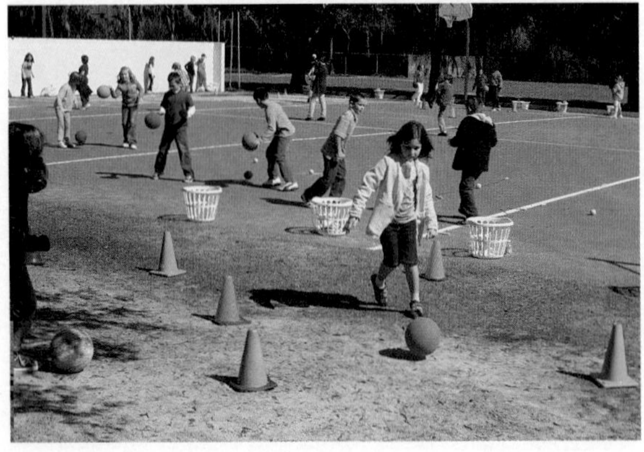

Figure 16.8 Working at centers

Figure 16.9 Quickly setting up centers

Figure 16.10 Putting centers away at the end of the day

and promote social interactions that detract from learning. Nevertheless, we find it is critical to hear what children say to one another and to be able to intervene during gameplay to help children understand tactics, especially invasion game tactics. Consequently, we offer the following suggestions for teaching tactics, game-like experiences, and games within centers.

Tactics and Game-like Experiences

Design game-like tasks for practicing tactics. Teach these tasks first through whole-class instruction, working on the task until the children know what they need to do and can coach one another. Then use these tasks as centers. For example,

1. Set up eight cones in a scattered formation, and balance four beanbags on top of four cones. Dribbling with the hand, play 1v1. Offense scores by dribbling and picking up a beanbag from a cone, then balancing it on a different cone. Defense tries to defend open cones and tap the ball. Design a fair way to switch roles. *Invasion game tactic:* Protect the ball by placing the body between the defender and the ball; dodge and dribble on angular pathways to get around the defender and score. Defense guards the open cones anticipating which cone is the likely goal and tries to tap the ball away from the dribbler.
2. With your partner, use cones, hoops, and jump ropes to design a challenge (obstacle) course for soccer dribbling. Have straight, curved, and angular pathways. Be sure your straight pathway is long enough for dribbling fast. One of you dribbles while the other is a defender in the angular-pathway section of the course. Then rotate. *Invasion game tactic:* Dribble on straight pathways when there is no defender and on angular pathways to get around a defender.
3. Stand 10 feet apart from a partner. Place a poly spot or hoop on the ground in between you. Toss a playground ball up at least higher than your head and try to have it bounce on the poly spot or in the hoop. Your partner must catch it after one bounce; then, from the location where the ball was caught, the partner tosses the ball above head height to bounce in the hoop or on the poly spot. *Net game tactic:* Anticipating the pathway of the ball and moving to get in alignment with it.

Modified 1v1 Games

In addition, you can teach students 1v1 games in whole-class teaching and then use these games as centers. For example,

1. Invasion game: Place poly spots about two yards away from the equipment basket and two yards apart from each other. The offensive player tries to toss a beanbag into the equipment basket; he or she must be standing on a poly spot to shoot. The offensive player can travel freely between poly spots. The defender guards the goal. *Invasion game tactics:* Shoot only when the basket is open; dodge and change direction quickly to get to a poly spot and shoot before the defender can cover the goal. Defense guards the goal by staying between the offensive player and the goal.
2. Invasion game: Set up four cones as boundaries of a square. One partner dribbles while the other tries to poke or touch the ball with one foot. Switch frequently so both partners get equal time on offense and defense. *Invasion game tactic:* While dribbling, avoid defenders and protect the ball with the body.
3. Net game: Set jump rope boundaries that are fair for both defense and offense. With your partner, throw and catch the deck ring over the net; throw the deck ring into open spaces so your partner can't catch it. *Net game tactics:* Throw into open spaces to the side, back, or front to make your opponent move to catch, creating a larger open space for your next shot. After tossing, move to the central ready position to cover as much space as possible.
4. Field game: Set up three bases in a triangle (first, third, home). Bat a ball off the tee, and run to first, third, and home before the thrower catches or collects the ball and throws at the target on the fence. *Field game tactic:* Hit the ball into open space. (You need a lot of space to use this center. Have the batter hit in a direction away from all classmates. Use a whiffle ball and plastic bat.)

Teacher-Coached Modified Games

Finally, you can have half or three-quarters of the students working in centers while you work with the rest of the class playing small-sided modified games, rotating the game groups after a set period of time. You would need to put your back against the wall to coach these groups so that you scan the rest of the class.

Another possibility is to include a four-person, small-sided, modified game as a center, such as 3v1 with the offense scoring a point when they complete five passes in a row. Each pair remains at the center for two rotations. When the class rotates centers, one new pair rotates into the 3v1 game, and the pair that has been there for two rotations rotates to the next center. You can easily coach one game and also work with students at the centers.

We recognize that it will take longer before all groups get the opportunity to work on gameplay when classes are large and this arrangement is used, but children will still be gaining important skill and game-like practice at the centers.

Teaching in Small Spaces

Teaching in small spaces has similar challenges to teaching large classes. Many schools in warm climates have no gymnasium and teachers teach outside, where there is plenty of space. When it rains, however, classes must remain indoors, often in a classroom or hallway. Both authors have worked in these situations, and we offer the following suggestions.

You can set up centers that require minimal space; for example, hitting a tennis ball up or down, remaining in personal space, tossing underhand into laundry baskets, three to four children in a small circle trying to volley a light plastic ball as many times in a row as they can, or throwing yarn balls at targets and for force at a wall.

Another suggestion is to teach dance when it rains or when you must be in a small space. The following are dance lessons that were originally designed to be taught in classrooms:

- Prey and Predators
- Sport tableaux (This lesson can be repeated using different themes that match what students are learning in their classroom or abstract themes, such as community, isolation, togetherness, support, power, caring, confusion, unity, justice, or freedom.)
- Animal haiku, jellyfish, kangaroo (remaining in personal space), sloth, and snake (modifying the jump to be a straight jump)
- Ashanti to Zulu: Ga Tribe dance, child-designed dances for other tribes
- Child-designed folk dances

Many dance themes can be taught effectively in small spaces; for example,

- Shape
- Body parts
- Sustained strong effort
- Sustained light effort
- Sustained heavy effort
- Matching, mirroring, contrasting, and complementing shapes
- Using body actions and gestures to represent topics such as modes of transportation (e.g., trains, planes, cars), machines, robots, magnets, undersea life, forest life, or insects
- Group shapes

In addition to dance, other cooperative group projects, such as dribbling routines (like in *High School Musical*) for older grades or sequences of catching or dribbling tricks for younger grades, take little room, but more importantly, students practice their skills and learn how to choreograph sequences.

Teaching Tactics and Gameplay in Small Spaces

For the older grades when you must be indoors in a small space and you are in the middle of a games unit, you can have two-thirds of the class play while the other third become peer coaches and peer assessors. As discussed earlier, research shows that peer assessment using a detailed assessment tool that describes the specific movements and positioning of players for game tactics facilitates the learning of both the peers assessing and the peers being assessed (Iserbyt, Elen, & Behets, 2010; Vande Broek et al., 2011).

Classroom Teachers and Centers

In some states, a certified physical education teacher teaches all physical education. In other states, the classroom teachers provide part of the physical education program. A common arrangement is for the physical education teacher to have the children one to three days per week and then be responsible for giving the classroom teachers lesson plans for the other days.

In response to the national call for improving the health of children and for dealing with obesity problems, more states have begun requiring children be physical active for at least 30 minutes five days per week. Consequently, many schools are now scheduling physical education (or physical activity) five days a week. Because it is unlikely that schools will be hiring the number of physical education teachers needed to teach these classes, we suspect classroom teachers will be teaching more physical education.

Having worked with classroom teachers for all of our careers, we have found that some classroom teachers will teach excellent physical education lessons, especially if they have some support and assistance from a good physical education teacher. Unfortunately, research reports that many classroom teachers perceive strong barriers to teaching physical education, including the following issues (Morgan & Hansen, 2008):

- Lack of training and knowledge about physical education
- Lack of confidence
- Lack of equipment and space
- Lack of time owing to the pressure to provide learning gains in reading and mathematics
- Lack of interest
- Lack of departmental and administrative support

When faced with such barriers, some classroom teachers do not provide a good physical education program. Typically, these teachers rely on large group games, which provide few practice opportunities, or recess.

Centers will help solve many of the barriers to providing excellent physical education that classroom teachers face. Because many classroom teachers think they lack the knowledge to teach skills, centers provide a way for them to provide lots of skill practice, with the physical education teacher providing the initial instruction.

For the situation in which the physical education teacher is responsible for providing lessons or guidance for classroom teachers, we offer four suggestions that have worked for us:

1. Design a set of centers for practicing the skills you have been teaching in your lessons and give these centers to the classroom teachers. Then have the classroom teachers monitor the children's practice at centers. This arrangement will ensure the children are getting plenty of skill practice in ways that support your program. It will also eliminate large group games and provide maximum amounts of physical activity. Print the performance cues on the bottom or back of the task card so the classroom teachers know what to look for and what to emphasize.
2. Have the classroom teachers teach dance—in particular, dance lessons that are integrated with classroom content. (Most of the dance lessons outlined in this text are integrated with classroom content and have been field-tested by many classroom teachers.) We have found that once classroom teachers have learned how to teach dance using children's literature as a stimulus for the dance, they tend to excel at designing new dance lessons for other books they use in their reading programs.
3. Have the classroom teachers teach health-related physical activity (HRPA) and health-related fitness (HRF) concepts,

and provide related physical activities for those concepts. Many classroom teachers have attended aerobics classes and are familiar with fitness activities. Moreover, they know how to teach scientific concepts. An excellent program developed by Catherine Ennis, called "Science, PE, and Me," provides HRPA lessons that incorporate scientific experiments and principles into the activities.

4. Have the classroom teachers teach target game skills, such as bowling and miniature golf. These skills are relatively easy for them to teach, compared to invasion, net, and field games.

Next are two sets of sample centers for gymnastics and games for classes of 70 children with a visual for where to set up each center.

Example of Gymnastics Centers for a Class of 70

When providing gymnastics centers for large classes, we include many dynamic balancing centers that are safe for children to practice independently, with a teacher or aide monitoring from the perimeter of the space. Centers for rolling require closer supervision.

In our example, we divide the space into three content areas: jumping, dynamic balancing, and rolling (see the map in **Figure 16.11**). Twelve centers for each content area are arranged in three rows in the physical education space in areas we call "Flight Town" (jumping) on the left side of the gym space, the "Kingdom of Balance" (dynamic balancing) in the middle, and the "City of Rock and Roll" (combining rolling with balancing, step-like actions, and jumping) on the right side of the gym space.

We further divide the space into horizontal color zones (green, blue, and red) that cross the content area zones. A child will work in one color zone until he or she has completed all centers in that zone. Thus, a child within one or two lessons will work on centers in, for example, the green zone Flight Town, the green zone Kingdom of Balance, and the green zone City of Rock and Roll. This organization gives the children variety in the centers and content area each day. The children then rotate to a new color and repeat the process.

We rely on stacked mats or trapezoid sections for equipment to add height. Aerobics boxes are a good substitute. A free way to make boxes that are safe and support children's weight is to ask the cafeteria workers to save #10 vegetable and fruit cans and the boxes in which they were delivered. Ask the workers to wash the cans. Then place the cans back in the box with all cans open and facing you in the same direction. Tape the box shut and turn it upside down, marking what used to be the bottom of the box and cans with the label "top." Thus, the platform on which the children stand is supported with six can bottoms and sides.

Center 1: Flight Town Green Zone

Name of center and task card: Jump for height, stick

Focus: Jumping for height off springboard; sticking landing

Equipment: Springboard, landing mat

Task: Do an easy approach jog, take off on one foot, land on two feet at the peak of the board, jump straight up reaching high with your arms to get height, land within three feet of the board, and stick your landing.

Performance cues: Reach with arms; bend knees to stick

ME Jump low.

MD Make a shape in the air.

Center 2: Flight Town Green Zone

Name of center and task card: Two in a row (distance, height, and roll)

Focus: Jumping for height and distance; safety rolls

Equipment: Two flat mats in a row

Task: Jump for distance, then immediately jump for height, land, and safety roll. You may do any roll you want (side, diagonal, forward, or back). Try to make different shapes with your legs when you roll.

Performance cues: Reach with arms in jump, bend knees to land, and smoothly transition into the roll.

ME Do only one jump and then safety roll, or do two jumps and leave out the roll.

MD Roll in different ways each time.

Center 3: Flight Town Green Zone

Center name and task card: Spiderman challenge course

Focus: Resilient jumping; five types of flight from feet (hop, jump, leap, two-to-one, one-to-two)

Equipment: Stacked mats, cones with canes, mats, long cane attached at one end to a high cone with the other end on the floor

Task: Set up equipment in any order in a line. Try different types of flight from feet (jump, hop, leap, two-to-one, one-to-two) over the stacked mats and canes. When you land on a mat, safety roll right to your feet.

Performance cues: Legs like springs; quick, light, resilient jumps

ME Spread obstacles farther apart.

MD Add turns in the air when you jump.

Center 4: Flight Town Green Zone

Center name and task card: Jump for height and stick

Focus: Jumping for height onto equipment

Equipment: One stacked mat, two stacked mats (or trapezoid sections) with flat mats on both sides for safety on landings and to prevent sliding of stacked mats

Task: Jump onto the stacked mat and land with a stick. Try different heights.

Performance cues: Reach with arms; bend your knees to stick.

ME Use one stacked mat.

MD Use three stacked mats.

(*continues*)

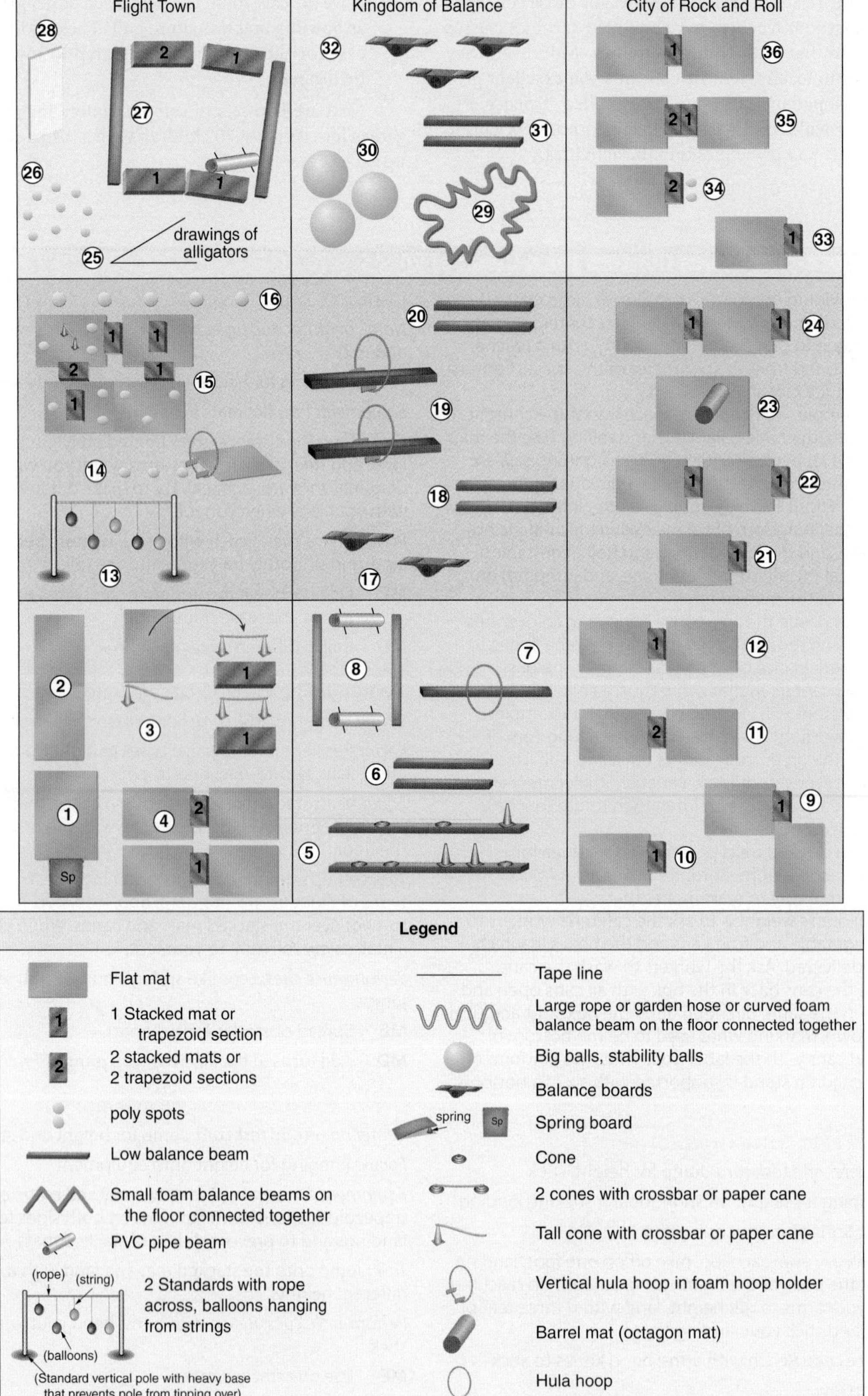

Figure 16.11 Map for gymnastics centers

Example of Gymnastics Centers for a Class of 70 (*continued*)

Center 5: Kingdom of Balance Green Zone

Center name and task card: I don't like spiders or snakes

Focus: Dynamic balancing while traveling over obstacles

Equipment: Any type of beam (low foam beam, big beam, or 2-inch-by-4-inch beam) and a variety of obstacles to put on the beam (e.g., beanbags, small cones, medium cones)

Task: Pretend the beanbags and cones are sleeping spiders and snakes. You don't want to step on a snake, because it will bite you. Most kinds of spiders and snakes are beneficial in that they kill harmful insects and rodents, but some are poisonous. In this task, travel down the beam while stepping carefully over the sleeping spiders and snakes.

Performance cues: Head up, eyes down

ME Put spiders and snakes farther apart.

MD Put spiders and snakes closer together and sometimes touching so you have step over two of them at once.

Center 6: Kingdom of Balance Green Zone

Center name and task card: Different locomotor steps

Focus: Dynamic balancing traveling in different ways

Equipment: Any type of beam; wide beam if possible

Task: Travel down the beam slowly, using different locomotor steps, such as galloping, skipping, jumping, and hopping.

Performance cues: Stretch tall with head up, but eyes on the beam.

ME Try low straight jumps.

MD Do several locomotor steps in a row; travel at a medium speed.

Center 7: Kingdom of Balance Green Zone

Center name and task card: Through the hoop

Focus: Dynamic balancing while traveling under and through obstacles

Equipment: Any type of beam; hoops (or jump ropes)

Task: Travel down the beam, pick up the hoop, and step through it. Then bring it over your head (like a jump rope) and then step through it again.

Performance cues: Watch your feet land on the beam.

ME Have a partner hold the hoop.

MD Jump over the hoop using the hoop like a jump rope. Or, do the same task with a jump rope.

Center 8: Kingdom of Balance Green Zone

Center name and task card: Walk the pipes and turns

Focus: Dynamic balancing while walking and turning

Equipment: PVC pipe and low beams placed in a triangle or square (PVC pipes that have been bolted onto 2-inch-by-4-inch cross supports; use pipes of various sizes from 3- to 12-inch diameters).

Task: Walk on the various-sized PVC pipe and low beams. Add different turns (turning on one foot, turning on two feet, turning on two feet at different levels, such as in a squat, mini-squat, or straight).

Performance cues: Stretch tall with head up but eyes on the beam.

ME Walk slowly with arms out.

MD Add full turns and jumps; walk faster.

Center 9: City of Rock and Roll Green Zone

Center name and task card: Roll on mat, step-like action on and off

Focus: Combining step-like actions and rolls

Equipment: Stacked mat with flat mats on one side and one end

Task: Explore different ways to roll on the stacked mat, and combine the rolls with a step-like action that travels off the mat. Explore step-like actions on the stacked mat combined with step-like actions or rolls off the stacked mat onto the flat mats.

Performance cues: Smooth transition; straight arms and palms flat during the step-like action; strong arms (bent) on the roll

ME Keep your feet low during the step-like action; roll sideways.

MD Try to stretch your feet to the ceiling. Do a different roll each time.

Center 10: City of Rock and Roll Green Zone

Center name and task card: Jump, land, roll, balance

Focus: Combining jumping, rolling, and balancing

Equipment: Aerobic box, stacked mat or trapezoid section, flat mat

Task: Stand on the stacked mat, jump reaching high to the sky, make a shape with your legs if you want, land on your feet, and gently take your weight into a roll on the mat, and without extra movements, end in a balance.

Performance cues: Land on your feet and bend your knees to absorb force; roll softly; stay tight in balance.

ME Do straight, low jumps and side rolls; balance on large body parts.

MD Make wide and twisted shapes in the air or do turning jumps. Vary your roll every time. Make hard-to-hold balances.

Center 11: City of Rock and Roll Green Zone

Center name and task card: Step-like action, roll, balance

Focus: Combining step-like actions and rolls

Equipment: In order—flat mat, two-layered trapezoid, flat mat

Task: Try different step-like actions over the trapezoid, land, and immediately, smoothly, and gently go into a roll. You may do any roll you want (side, diagonal, forward, or back) and try to make different shapes with your legs when you roll. End in a balance.

Performance cues: Straight arms and palms flat during the step-like action; strong bent arms on the roll

ME Keep your feet low during the step-like action; roll sideways.

MD Try to stretch your feet to the ceiling. Do a different roll each time.

(*continues*)

Example of Gymnastics Centers for a Class of 70 (*continued*)

Center 12: City of Rock and Roll Green Zone

Center name and task card: Jump, roll, jump, jump, roll

Focus: Combining jumping and rolling

Equipment: In order—flat mat, stacked mat, flat mat

Task: On the flat mat, jump and make a shape in the air, land, and roll to your feet. Immediately jump onto or over the stacked mat. If you jump over the stacked mat, land and roll on the flat mat. If you land on the stacked mat, jump again and land and roll on the flat mat. Try to make different shapes each time you jump. Roll in different directions or in different shapes.

Performance cues: Strong arms on the roll; point toes on jumps

ME Do side rolls and straight and tucked jumps.

MD Do a variety of rolls and wide and twisted shapes in the jumps. Try turning jumps.

Center 13: Flight Town Red Zone

Center name and task card: Jump high and tap the balloon

Focus: Jumping for height

Equipment: Several balloons hanging from strings at different heights, all above the children's reach

Task: Jump high and try to tap the balloon. Select a balloon at a height that challenges you.

Performance cues: Reach with your arms; bend your knees and explode.

ME Select lower balloons.

MD Select higher balloons.

Center 14: Flight Town Red Zone

Center name and task card: Minefield—jump, jump, and roll

Focus: Jump for distance and roll

Equipment: Three nonslip plastic poly spots, one vertical hoop held in a hoop stand, one mat

Task: Arrange the poly spots at a distance that is challenging for you but that also allows you to be successful. Start standing on the first poly spot, jump for distance onto the second poly spot, jump again for distance onto the third poly spot, and safety roll through the hoop onto the mat.

Performance cues: Reach with your arms; bend your knees to absorb the force of landing.

ME Do only one jump for distance, pause, and safety roll using a side roll.

MD Do three jumps for distance and vary the roll.

Center 15: Flight Town Red Zone

Center name and task card: Superman roof leap

Focus: Resilient jumping; five ways to get flight from the feet (hop, jump, leap, two-to-one, one-to-two)

Equipment: Stacked mats placed on mats making sure neither the stacked nor flat mats slide, stacked mats, trapezoid sections, flat mats, poly spots, cones with canes at different heights or hurdles representing buildings

Task: Arrange the equipment like buildings in a city, with different distances between each piece. Place flat mats where you plan to land on the floor. Try different jumps (jump, hop, leap, two-to-one, one-to-two), sometimes landing on the stacked mat, the trapezoid section, and the box, and sometimes going over a piece of equipment.

Performance cues: Legs like springs; quick, light resilient jumps

ME Move buildings closer together.

MD Move buildings farther apart.

Center 16: Flight Town Red Zone

Center name and task card: Dino jumps

Focus: Jumping for distance, hopping for distance

Equipment: Poly spots or dinosaur prints

Task: Pretend you are a velociraptor. Arrange the dinosaur prints in a line. Do two-to-one to two-to-one (hopscotch) jumps from print to print, traveling as far as you can on each jump. Repeat the task, but this time jump two-to-two. Repeat the task, but this time hop. Make the distance between the dinosaur prints challenging for you but also allowing you to succeed.

Performance cues: Arms swing up.

ME Move the dinosaur prints closer together.

MD Move the dinosaur prints farther apart.

Center 17: Kingdom of Balance Red Zone

Center name and task card: Partner balance boards

Focus: Countertension

Equipment: Balance boards

Task: Balance on a balance board with your partner, holding each other's elbows.

Performance cues: Maintain tension between you.

ME Hold shoulders.

MD Hold hands; try to "walk" the board (making the board travel by shifting your weight to one side and turning the other side of the board a few inches).

Center 18: Kingdom of Balance Red Zone

Center name and task card: Make and carry your own pizza

Focus: Stretching tall through the spinal column while walking on a beam

Equipment: Low, 2-inch-by-4-inch beam; two Frisbees per child; several small balls and beanbags

Task: Build a pizza you like by putting sausage, pepperoni, mushrooms, or extra cheese (small balls, beanbags, other very small equipment) on your pizza (Frisbee). Then walk on the beam while balancing your pizza in one hand.

Performance technique: Stretch tall.

ME Put fewer toppings on your pizza.

MD Use two pizzas, one in each hand; travel backward and sideways.

Center 19: Kingdom of Balance Red Zone

Center name and task card: Foot toss

Focus: Balancing on one foot while performing a second action

Example of Gymnastics Centers for a Class of 70 (*continued*)

Equipment: Low, 2-inch-by-4-inch beam; beanbag; hoop in vertical brace

Task: Put the hoop in the middle of the beam. Each partner stands at one end. Put the beanbag on your foot and toss it over the hoop so your partner can catch it.

Performance technique: Use "laces" and bend your kicking knee.

ME Toss the beanbag to a partner standing on the floor.

MD Toss the beanbag high; catch it with one hand; toss it through the hoop.

Center 20: Kingdom of Balance Red Zone

Center name and task card: Partner pass

Focus: Countertension

Equipment: Low, 2-inch-by-4-inch beam

Task: With a partner, walk on the beam from opposite ends, and change places with your partner in the middle by holding hands as you lean back to pass without falling off.

Performance technique: Maintain tension between you. Stay tight.

ME Touch the floor once. Hold shoulders.

MD Hold only one arm (hand, wrist, or elbow). Lean back.

Center 21: City of Rock and Roll Red Zone

Center name and task card: Jump and make a shape, land, and roll

Focus: Combining jumping and rolling

Equipment: Single stacked mat or box, flat mat

Task: Jump off the box, making different shapes in the air each time. Land on two feet every time, no matter which shape you made. Gently lower yourself into a roll.

Performance cues: Bend knees to absorb force; strong arms on roll

ME Do side rolls only.

MD Roll in different directions; make wide or twisted shapes in the air or do turning jumps.

Center 22: City of Rock and Roll Red Zone

Center name and task card: Two in a row—step-like, roll, step-like, roll

Focus: Combining step-like actions and rolls

Equipment: Two boxes, or two trapezoid sections, or two stacked mats and two flat mats in a row: trapezoid section, mat, trapezoid section, mat

Task: Try different step-like actions over the trapezoid section, land, and immediately, smoothly, and gently go right into a roll. Then, without taking any extra steps, do a second step-like action over the next trapezoid section, and roll again. You may do any roll you want (side, diagonal, forward, or back); try to make different shapes with your legs when you roll.

Performance cues: Smooth transition; straight arms and palms flat during the step-like action; strong arms (bent) on the roll

ME Keep your feet low during the step-like action; roll sideways.

MD Try to stretch your feet to the ceiling. Do a different roll each time.

Center 23: City of Rock and Roll Red Zone

Center name and task card: Roll the barrel

Focus: Combining jumping and rolling

Equipment: Flat mat, barrel (or any small round object, such as a foam ball) placed in the first section of the mat

Task: Taking a two-step approach, jump onto the mat in front of the barrel, and roll over the barrel. Alternatively, you can jump over the barrel and roll onto the mat.

Performance cues: Strong arms on the roll

ME Jump over the barrel and do side rolls.

MD Do a low-level dive roll over the barrel.

Center 24: City of Rock and Roll Red Zone

Center name and task card: Balance, roll, balance, balance, roll

Focus: Combining balances and rolls

Equipment: In order—stacked mat, flat mat, stacked mat, flat mat in a row

Task: Balance on the stacked mat, gently lower yourself into a roll on the floor mat, roll again if necessary, and end in a balance on the floor mat; transition without any steps to a balance on the stacked mat, and gently lower yourself into a roll on the second floor mat.

Performance cues: Stay tight; strong arms on rolls

ME Use side rolls.

MD Roll in a different way each time; balance on small body parts or upper body parts with your feet high.

Center 25: Flight Town Blue Zone

Center name and task card: Alligator swamp

Focus: Jumping and leaping for distance

Equipment: Two ropes (if on grass), or two taped lines in a horizontal V with the lines touching at one end and farther apart at the other, forming a swamp; place cut-out alligators in the swamp

Task: Stand in front of the swamp with the closed end on your right and the open end on your left, and jump over it. Select a place to jump the swamp by choosing a distance that is challenging but also lets you succeed. Repeat the task, but this time take a three-step approach to leap over the swamp.

Performance cues: Arms swing up on the jump; powerfully extend your knees and ankles on take-off for the leap. Bend your knees to absorb the force on landings.

ME Move to a location that is a shorter distance.

MD Move to a location that is a longer distance.

Center 26: Flight Town Blue Zone

Center name and task card: Froggie on the lily pads

Focus: Sticking landings on two feet and one foot

Equipment: Eight to 10 poly spots (lily pads) arranged in a scattered formation in a small area

Task: Using the five basic jumps (hop, jump, leap, two-to-one, one-to-two), travel from lily pad to lily pad. Stick your

(*continues*)

Example of Gymnastics Centers for a Class of 70 (*continued*)

landing so you remain perfectly still and your feet don't have to move for you to remain balanced on the lily pad.

Performance cues: Bend your knees.

ME Move the lily pads closer together and focus on two-foot landings.

MD Move the lily pads farther apart and try more one-foot landings.

Center 27: Flight Town Blue Zone

Center name and task card: Explore the city roofs

Focus: Five basic jumps to and from different levels

Equipment: A variety of beams (PVC ramps; PVC beams; 2-inch-by-4-inch beams; stacked mats; benches; single, double, and triple trapezoid sections)

Task: Imagine each piece of apparatus is a roof of a building. With your partner (or group), arrange the beams, trapezoids, and other equipment to form a city of roofs. Try to make some interesting angles when you connect the roofs. Have different levels so you have to jump for height, and leave some gaps between the roofs so you have to jump for distance. Then jump from roof to roof, jumping on and off different levels to explore the city. Try to stick your landings.

Performance cues: Eyes focused on the apparatus for landing

ME Move the roofs closer together.

MD Make bigger gaps between the roofs.

Center 28: Flight Town Blue Zone

Center name and task card: Make your mark; beat your record

Focus: Jumping for height

Equipment: Chalk and a wall that children can mark

Task: Holding the chalk in one hand, jump as high as you can and make a mark on the wall. Try to beat your previous record each time you jump.

Performance cues: Reach with your arms; explode from your legs.

ME Touch the wall with your hand.

MD Do two jumps in a row.

Center 29: Kingdom of Balance Blue Zone

Center name and task card: Amoeba

Focus: Dynamic balancing while traveling in different directions

Equipment: Ropes or hoses and various low beams, arranged in an amoeba-like circle; dribbling ball

Task: An amoeba is a tiny, tiny, one-celled organism, a living creature that lives in fresh and salt water. It is so small you can see it only by using a microscope. An amoeba moves by extending its lobes and looks something like these beams and ropes. Walk on the beams and ropes in different directions (sideways, forward, backward).

Performance cues: Stretch tall with head up but eyes on the beam.

ME Walk forward.

MD Add jumps and turns. Dribble a ball while walking.

Center 30: Kingdom of Balance Blue Zone

Center name and task card: Balance on the big ball

Focus: Balancing

Equipment: Big balls

Task: Try to balance as long as you can. Once you have mastered that skill, try making different shapes or balancing on different body parts.

Performance cues: Stretch and stay tight.

ME Have your partner hold your hands.

MD Try different shapes or body parts.

Center 31: Kingdom of Balance Blue Zone

Center name and task card: Travel in different directions, partner balance

Focus: Dynamic balancing while traveling in different directions

Equipment: Low beams, beanbags

Task: Travel up and down the beam forward, sideways, and backward.

Performance cues: Stretch tall with head up but eyes on the beam.

ME Walk forward and sideways.

MD With a partner, travel together while balancing a beanbag between two body parts (e.g., hands, elbows) without letting the beanbag fall.

Center 32: Kingdom of Balance Blue Zone

Center name and task card: Balance on different body parts

Focus: Balancing

Equipment: Balance boards

Task: Try to stand on the board and stay balanced as long as you can. Once you have mastered that skill, try balancing on different body parts or making different shapes (e.g., V sit, shin stand).

Performance cues: Stretch tall; stay tight.

ME Stay on your feet, and ask your partner to hold your hands.

MD Try turning and walking the board by leaning to one side, lifting the board and turning it a few inches.

Center 33: City of Rock and Roll Blue Zone

Center name and task card: Balance, roll, balance

Focus: Combining balances and rolls

Equipment: Stacked mat or trapezoid, flat mat

Task: Find different ways to balance on different body parts on the stacked mat. Gently, without taking steps, lower yourself into a roll on the mat, and end in another balance on a different body part.

Performance cues: Stay tight; strong arms on rolls

ME Do side rolls.

MD Try to balance with your feet high.

Center 34: City of Rock and Roll Blue Zone

Center name and task card: Jump, jump, jump, roll

Focus: Combining jumping and rolling

Example of Gymnastics Centers for a Class of 70 (*continued*)

Equipment: In order—two poly spots parallel to two stacked mats marking the take-off location, flat mat.

Task: Taking an easy approach, jog and assemble (one-to-two) onto the two poly spots marking the take-off location. Jump from two feet on the floor (on the poly spots) to two feet on the stacked mat. Jump as high as you can off the stacked mat, land on your feet, and safety roll.

Performance cues: Reach high to the sky; gently absorb force when you land.

ME Remove one stacked mat.

MD Make different wide or twisted shapes in the air, or do a turning jump.

Center 35: City of Rock and Roll Blue Zone

Center name and task card: Roll, balance, balance, roll

Focus: Combining balances and rolls

Equipment: In order—flat mat, stacked mat, two-layered stacked mat, flat mat

Task: Roll on the first mat and immediately, without taking extra steps, end in a balance on the stacked mat. Making only one movement, move into a balance on a different body part on the double stacked mat, then gently lower yourself onto the flat mat, and roll out to your feet.

Performance cues: Stay tight; strong arms on rolls

ME Do side rolls only.

MD Try hard-to-hold balances on upper body parts with your feet high.

Center 36: City of Rock and Roll Blue Zone

Center name and task card: Roll, step-like, roll

Focus: Combining step-like actions and rolls

Equipment: In order—flat mat, box or stacked mat, flat mat

Task: Start with a roll ending close to the box. Without any extra steps, do a step-like action over the box, and then immediately transition, without extra steps, into a different roll.

Performance cues: Straight arms and palms flat during the step-like action; strong bent arms on the roll

ME Keep your feet low during the step-like action; roll sideways.

MD Try to stretch your feet to the ceiling. Do a different roll each time.

Example of Outdoor Game Skill Centers for a Class of 70

We designed the centers described in this box for use with K–5 after each grade has had two weeks of whole-class teaching on dribbling with the hands in kindergarten and grade 1, dribbling variety (speeds, pathways, and directions) in grades 2 and 3, and dribbling tactics and games in grades 4 and 5. Thus, there are more centers for practicing hand dribbling than for any other skill. Dribbling with the feet, which was taught earlier in the year, is the second major skill and is revisited to help children understand the connections across invasion game movement concepts and tactics. For example, children dribble fast on straight pathways when there is no defender between them and the goal and dribble on zigzag pathways around defenders in both basketball dribbling and soccer dribbling. A few other skills are included to give children needed practice in throwing, catching, and striking.

Each center has three different color-coded task cards that are labeled with the grade. White is used for kindergarten and grade 1, yellow is for grades 2 and 3, and green is for grades 4 and 5. Center task cards are numbered and posted wherever you can—on portable boards, cones, walls, fences, or on the equipment baskets. The baskets are also numbered and hold equipment for the tasks for all grades. Organizing the equipment is easier if you list the equipment needed in each basket on the bottom of the task card.

These centers are planned for use outdoors in the last third of the year. You can set them up on a blacktop, a field, or a combination of the two. In one school, we taught the centers on a field with a service road (where a gate kept traffic out during the school day). We did the soccer dribbling on the field using small portable goals (with nets so the children did not have to chase balls after shooting a goal) and the basketball centers on the road. You also could do soccer centers shooting into goals made from cones against a fence and the basketball centers in the middle of the space.

All center equipment described here is intended for groups of two. If you have groups of three, you will need to add equipment to each basket. Use 8-inch nylon-bound playground balls for grades 2 to 5 and 8- to 10-inch non-nylon-bound playground balls for kindergarten and grade 1; the latter balls are bouncier and help younger children learn the pushing action. Use nylon-bound playground balls or slightly deflated (old) playground balls for dribbling with the feet.

Center 1

Equipment: Ten saucer cones, two dribbling balls for K–1 and two dribbling balls for grades 2–5

K–1: "Minefield"—Basketball dribbling (refining skill). Set up cones in a scattered formation. Dribble about the space avoiding the mines.

2–3: "Minefield"—Basketball dribbling tactics to avoid defenders (cones). Set up cones in a scattered formation. Dribble about the space using sharp, angular pathways to go around the defenders (cones).

4–5: "Minefield"—Basketball dribbling tactics to avoid defenders (cones). Set up cones in a scattered formation. Dribble about the space as fast as you can while maintaining control of the ball and avoiding the defenders. Make sharp, angular pathways around the defenders (cones). Use a crossover dribble.

(*continues*)

Example of Outdoor Game Skill Centers for a Class of 70 (*continued*)

Center 2

Equipment: Ten saucer cones, two dribbling balls

K–1: "Minefield"—Soccer dribbling (refining skill). Set up cones in a scattered formation. Dribble about the space avoiding the mines.

2–3: "Minefield"—Soccer dribbling tactics to avoid defenders (cones). Set up cones as pretend defenders in a scattered formation. Dribble about the space using sharp, angular pathways to go around the defenders.

4–5: "Minefield"—Soccer dribbling tactics to avoid defenders. Set up cones as pretend defenders in a scattered formation. Dribble about the space as fast as you can while maintaining control of the ball and avoiding the defenders. Make sharp, angular pathways around defenders.

Center 3

The tasks for grades 2–5 are designed to elicit looking up while dribbling.

Equipment: Two balls for hand dribbling, two small "gator-skin" balls

K–1: Catching (refining skill). Toss and catch the gator-skin ball. Try to toss the ball higher each time and still catch it.

2–3: Basketball dribbling (refining skill). Dribble one ball, toss the second ball about one inch, and then catch it at the same time as you dribble the ball with your other hand. You can also simply raise your hand to toss the ball but not release it until you are more confident about looking up from dribbling to watch the tossed ball.

4–5: Basketball dribbling (refining skill). Dribble one ball, and toss and catch a second ball at the same time, tossing it higher each time.

Center 4

Equipment: Small, portable soccer goal; ropes extending from the goal representing the endline; two dribbling balls; two cones

K–1: Soccer dribble and kicking (combining skills). Soccer dribble the ball about the space in front of the goal and then kick it into the goal.

2–3: Soccer dribble, pass, and shoot (combining skills). Partner A dribbles toward the goal and passes the ball to Partner B. Partner B dribbles and then passes the ball back to Partner A, who kicks it into the goal.

4–5: Soccer tactics for centering passes and shots. One child plays center attack and starts directly aligned with the goal. The center dribbles twice and passes to the wing, who is 10 yards to the side (near an imaginary sideline). The wing controls the ball and dribbles down the "field" while staying near the sideline, until he or she is about two yards from the endline. Then the wing "centers" the ball by kicking it parallel to the endline in front of the goal. The attacker shoots it in the goal, trying to deflect it in with one kick. Rotate positions.

Center 5

Equipment: Eight cones, two dribbling balls for kindergarten and grade 1, two dribbling balls for grades 2–5

K–1: Basketball dribble (refining skill). Set up cones in a scattered formation. Dribble (with your hand) around the cones.

2–3: Basketball dribble (on different pathways), crossover dribble. Set up cones as pretend defenders in a scattered formation. Dribble around the cones, alternating hands, with a sharp change of direction and a crossover dribble at each cone.

4–5: Basketball tactics for protecting the ball while dribbling. Play one-on-one using alternating hands and crossover dribbles.

Center 6

Equipment: Small, portable soccer goal; two dribbling balls

K–1: Soccer dribble and shoot (combining skills). Dribble in the space in front of the goal and shoot.

2–3: Soccer dribble and shoot (refining skills). Dribble and shoot from near, middle, and far distances from the goal.

4–5: Soccer dribble and shoot (refining skills). Dribble and shoot from near, middle, and far distances from the goal, each time dribbling in from a different angle.

Center 7

Equipment: Four ropes for boundaries, one hoop, two dribbling balls for kindergarten and grades 1–2, one dribbling ball for grades 3–5

K–2: Basketball dribbling (refining skill). Set up the ropes and hoop on the ground, making interesting pathways. Dribble following the pathways forward, sideways, and backward.

3–5: Basketball dribble "perfect boundary" task (tactics for protecting the ball). As you learned in class, using jump ropes set up two sideline boundaries that are the perfect size so both offense and defense have an equal and fair chance. Put the hoop in the middle. The offensive player dribbles and dodges the defender. The defender must keep one foot in the hoop (but can shift to the other foot at any time) and tries to tap the ball away from the offensive player.

Center 8

Equipment: Four ropes for boundaries, one hoop, one dribbling ball

K–2: Soccer dribbling (refining skill). Select a leader, and face each other. Both of you dribble, with the follower trying to mirror the leader. Switch leaders frequently.

3–5: Soccer dribble "perfect boundary" (tactics for protecting the ball). As you learned in class, using jump ropes set up two sideline boundaries that are the perfect size so both offense and defense have an equal and fair chance. The offensive player dribbles and dodges the defender. The defender tries to tap the ball away from the offensive player. The dribbler must stay within the boundaries. The defender must work at a level of defense that challenges but allows the offensive player to succeed (level 1: remain in place; level 2: travel about three feet; level 3: pest defender; level 4: soft marking; level 5: full marking).

Example of Outdoor Game Skill Centers for a Class of 70 (*continued*)

Center 9

The tasks for grades 2–5 are designed to elicit looking up while dribbling.

Equipment: Two dribbling balls for kindergarten and grade 1, two dribbling balls for grades 2–5, eight medium-height cones, four beanbags

K–1: Basketball dribble (refining skill). Dribble around cones while changing hands.

2–3: Basketball dribble (refining skill). Set up cones in a scattered formation, and balance four beanbags on top of four cones. Dribble and pick up a beanbag from a cone, and then dribble and balance the beanbag on a different cone.

4–5: Basketball dribble (tactics). Set up cones in a scattered formation, and balance four beanbags on top of four cones. Play 1v1. Offense scores by picking up a beanbag from a cone, then balancing it on a different cone. Defense tries to block offense from getting to a beanbag. Design a fair way to switch roles.

Center 10

Equipment: Two dribbling balls, four cones, four ropes, two hoops

K–1: Soccer dribble (refining skill). Set up hoops and cones in scattered formations. Dribble around each cone and each hoop in any order.

2–5: Soccer dribble (on different pathways). With your partner, design a challenge course for dribbling on straight, curved, and angular pathways. Be sure your straight pathway is long enough for dribbling fast.

Center 11

Equipment: Two dribbling balls for kindergarten and grade 1, two dribbling balls for grades 2–5

K–1: Basketball dribble (refining skill). Dribble in place five times, and then dribble while walking five times.

2–3: Basketball dribble (refining skill). Dribble continuously while you change positions (e.g., kneel, sit, lie down, roll over).

4–5: Basketball dribble (refining skill). Dribble continuously while you change positions (e.g., kneel, sit, lie down, roll over). If you want more of a challenge, try it with your eyes closed.

Center 12

Equipment: Small, portable soccer goal; five cones; two dribbling balls

K–1: Soccer dribble (refining skill). Set up cones in a straight line. Dribble around the cones using zigzag pathways.

2–3: Soccer dribble (on different pathways). Set up cones in a scattered formation. Start at the basket. Dribble around the cones (pretend defenders) with zigzag pathways, trying to make sharp angles. Then shoot at the soccer goal.

4–5: Soccer dribble (tactics). Play 1v1. Offense starts five yards to the left of the basket and must dribble the ball, stopping (with one foot) between the goal posts to score. Defense starts at the basket and must quickly recover to the goal-side position. Switch roles after each score.

Center 13

Equipment: Three boxes or crates, one broken hoop with each end placed in two large cones, two dribbling balls for kindergarten and grade 1, two dribbling balls for grades 2–5

K–1: Basketball dribble (refining skill). Set equipment any place you want. Dribble under the hoop and around the boxes and cones.

2–5: Basketball dribble (refining skill—dribble over and under obstacles). Set up an obstacle challenge course that includes dribbling under the hoop and over the boxes.

Center 14

The tasks for grades 2–5 are designed to elicit looking up while dribbling.

Equipment: Two dribbling balls for kindergarten and grade 1, two dribbling balls for grades 2–5, two small balls that bounce

K–1: Basketball dribble (refining skill). Select a leader. Dribble about the space following the leader. Change leaders frequently.

2–5: Basketball dribble (refining skill). Dribble one ball, and bounce and catch a second small ball.

Center 15

Equipment: Two beanbags, two poly spots

K–1: Tossing (refining skill). Toss the beanbag into the equipment basket.

2–5: Tactics for defending a goal and shooting, avoiding the defender. Place poly spots about two yards away from the equipment basket and two yards apart. The offensive player tries to toss the beanbag into the equipment basket; he or she must be standing on a poly spot to shoot. The offensive player can travel freely between poly spots. The defender attempts to stay between the offensive player and the goal.

Center 16

Equipment: Two hand dribbling balls for grades 2–5, two foam balls, one portable basketball goal with a low basket, two cones

K–1: Shooting (refining skill). Shoot the foam ball into the equipment basket.

2–5: Dribble and shoot (tactics to avoid defenders). Set up two cones as pretend defenders near the portable basketball goal. Dribble around the cones while avoiding the defenders, and then dribble straight to the basket and shoot. Grades 4 and 5 can choose to play 1v1.

Center 17

Equipment: Two hand dribbling balls for grades 2–5, one foam ball for K–1

K–1: Catching (refining skill). Play catch with a partner using the foam ball.

2–5: Basketball dribbling (refining skill). Follow the leader: One partner dribbles in different ways (left hand, right hand, under the legs, behind the back) and in different positions (sitting, kneeling, lying down), and the other mirrors or matches the leader's actions. Rotate leaders frequently.

(*continues*)

Example of Outdoor Game Skill Centers for a Class of 70 (*continued*)

Center 18

Equipment: Four cones, two soccer dribbling balls, two flag football flags

K–2: Soccer dribbling (refining skill). Set up four cones as boundaries of a square. Dribble anywhere in the square. Be sure to look up and avoid your partner.

3–5: "Knock-out"—Soccer dribbling (tactics to avoid defenders). Set up four cones as boundaries of a square. One partner dribbles while other tries to poke or tackle the ball. Switch frequently so both partners get equal time on offense and defense.

Center 19

Equipment: Four cones, two hand dribbling balls for kindergarten and grade 1, two dribbling balls for grades 2–5

K–1: Basketball dribbling (refining skill). Set up four cones as boundaries of a square. Dribble anywhere in the square. Be sure to look up and avoid your partner.

2–5: "Knock-out"—Basketball dribbling (tactics to avoid defenders). Set up four cones as boundaries of a square. Each partner dribbles while trying to tap the ball away from his or her opponent.

Center 20

Equipment: Four cones, two hoops, four ropes, two soccer dribbling balls

K–2: Soccer dribbling (refining skill). Set up the equipment any way you want and dribble around it.

3–5: Soccer dribbling (tactics to avoid defenders, tactics to steal the ball). Design your own one-on-one dribbling game using any of the equipment in the basket.

Center 21

Equipment: Four cones, two hoops, four ropes, two hand dribbling balls for kindergarten and grade 1, two dribbling balls for grades 2–5

K–2: Basketball dribbling (refining skill). Set up the equipment any way you want and dribble around it.

3–5: Basketball dribbling (tactics to avoid defenders, tactics to steal the ball). Design your own one-on-one dribbling game using any of the equipment in the basket.

Center 22

Equipment: One large, light plastic ball that children can strike up (like what occurs in volleyball), two balloons, net set at a height of six feet

K–1: Striking up (refining skill). Strike the balloon up. Count how many times you can strike it in a row.

2–5: Striking up (refining skill). Count how many times in a row you and a partner can set or bump the ball over the net.

Center 23

Equipment: Two dribbling balls for kindergarten and grade 1, two dribbling balls for grades 2–5, four poly spots

K–1: Basketball dribbling (refining skill). Arrange the four poly spots in a large square. Dribble fast to the first poly spot, dribble slowly to the second poly spot, dribble fast to the third poly spot, and dribble slowly to the fourth poly spot.

2–3: "Partner knock-out"—Basketball dribbling (tactics to avoid defenders, tactics to steal the ball). Put one poly spot on the ground, and play over and near that poly spot. Both partners dribble at the same time and try to tap each other's ball.

4–5: "Knock out one ball"—Basketball dribbling (tactics to avoid defenders, tactics to steal the ball). Put one poly spot on the ground. One person dribbles; he or she must stay *near* the poly spot. The other person tries to steal the ball. Keep score if you choose. Switch if the defender touches the ball. If you are not getting approximately equal time on offense and defense, change the rule for switching to make it fair for both of you.

Center 24

Equipment: Two large, light plastic balls that children can strike up (like what occurs in volleyball), net set at a height of six feet

K–1: Striking up (refining skill). Strike the ball up, let it bounce, and try to strike it up again.

2–3: Striking up (refining skill). Count how many times in a row you and your partner can set or bump the ball over the net. You can let the ball bounce once before striking it.

4–5: Striking up (refining skill). Count how many times in a row you and your partner can set or bump the ball over the net before the ball touches the ground.

Center 25

Equipment: Four hoops, four jump ropes, two dribbling balls for kindergarten and grade 1, two dribbling balls for grades 2–5

K–3: Basketball dribbling (refining skill). Arrange the four hoops in a square. Dribble anywhere you want in the square, and dribble five times in each hoop.

4–5: "Scoring square"—Basketball dribbling (tactics for defending goals, tactics for avoiding defenders). Arrange four hoops in a square, with jump ropes as boundaries. Use one ball. The dribbler tries to score by dribbling in any of the four hoops. The defender tries to tap the ball away. Rotate after three points are scored.

Center 26

Equipment: Six-foot-high net, one deck tennis ring, one yarn ball, four jump ropes

K–1: Passing and catching (refining skills). With your partner, throw and catch the yarn ball over the net.

2–3: Passing and catching (refining skills). With your partner, throw and catch the deck ring over the net as many times in a row as you can.

4–5: Net game tactics—Creating and defending space. Set jump rope boundaries that are fair for both defense and offense. With your partner, throw and catch the deck ring over the net; throw the deck ring into open spaces so your partner can't catch it.

Center 27

Equipment: Low basketball goal, two beanbags, two dribbling balls

Example of Outdoor Game Skill Centers for a Class of 70 (*continued*)

K–1: Tossing for accuracy (refining skill). Toss the beanbag into the equipment basket. Try shooting from different distances.

2–3: Shooting (refining skill). Practice shooting the ball from different distances.

4–5: Shooting (refining skill). Practice shooting the ball from different distances while your partner stands in front of you with hands up and near your face.

Center 28

Equipment: Two light, short-handled rackets, low net (one jump rope hung between two cones, or balance paper canes across three cones to form a low net), one vinyl ball

K–1: Striking over low nets (refining skill). Toss the ball to your partner, who lets it bounce once and then taps it with one hand back to you. Switch roles after three turns.

2–3: Striking over low nets (refining skill). With your hand, tap the ball underhand back and forth with your partner over the low net. Let the ball bounce at least one time before striking it back.

4–5: Striking over low nets (refining skill). With the rackets, strike the ball back and forth with your partner over the low net. Let the ball bounce at least one time before striking it back.

Center 29

Equipment: Low basketball goal, four hoops, two dribbling balls for kindergarten and grade 1, two dribbling balls for grades 2–5

K–1: Basketball dribbling (refining skill). Set up the four hoops any way you want. Dribble from hoop to hoop; when you get to a hoop, dribble around the hoop.

2–3: Basketball lay-ups (refining skill). Practice dribbling and, without stopping, take one step and shoot the ball so it rebounds from the backboard into the basket.

4–5: Basketball lay-ups from a pass (refining skills). Pass to your partner, run toward the goal, receive a pass back, and shoot without stopping.

Center 30

Equipment: Two light, short-handled rackets, low net (one jump rope hung between two cones, or balance paper canes across three cones to form a low net), one vinyl ball

K–1: Striking over low nets (refining skill). With your hand, tap the ball underhand back and forth with your partner. Let the ball bounce at least one time before striking it back.

2–3: Striking over low nets (refining skill). With your hand, tap the ball underhand back and forth with your partner over the low net. Let the ball bounce at least one time before striking it back.

4–5: Striking over low nets (refining skill). With the rackets, strike the ball back and forth with your partner over the low net. Let the ball bounce at least one time before striking it back.

Center 31

Equipment: Tin cans on cardboard boxes to serve as a target or a target that can be attached to a fence, six safety tee-balls (soft baseballs)

K–5: Overarm throw for force (refining skill). Set up the target and throw overarm as forcefully as you can at the target. See how far away you can move from the target and still hit it with the ball. You must throw as hard as you can (no moving close to the target and tossing the ball).

Center 32

Equipment: Six safety tee-balls; balloons attached to a fence; small, medium, and large cones set progressive distances away from fence that will challenge children in each grade

K–1: Overarm throw for force (refining skill). Stand behind the small cone and throw as forcefully as you can. Try to pop the balloons.

2–3: Overarm throw for force (refining skill). Stand behind the medium cone and throw as forcefully as you can. Try to pop the balloons.

4–5: Overarm throw for force (refining skill). Stand behind the large cone and throw as forcefully as you can. Try to pop the balloons.

Center 33

Equipment: Two ropes, one yellow medium foam ball (representing a bag of gold), four red poly spots (representing fire)

K–3: Leaping "river of fire" (refining skill). Set two ropes at a distance that you and your partner are challenged to leap. Have one end closer together (easier leap) and the other end farther apart (more challenging leap). Put the red poly spots in the middle, representing fire. Run and leap over the river of fire.

4–5 Lead passes—"River of fire pass and catch the bag of gold" (refining skill). Set two ropes at a distance that you and your partner are challenged to leap. Have one end closer together (easier leap) and the other end farther apart (more challenging leap). Put the red poly spots in the middle, representing fire. One person runs and leaps; when he or she is in the air, the other person tosses the jumper a gentle lead pass. Rotate.

Center 34

Equipment: Six safety tee-balls (soft baseballs); trash barrel on its side, representing a target for throwing to get someone out who is sliding into a base; small, medium, and large cones set progressive distances away from barrel that will challenge children in each grade

K–1: Overarm throw for force (refining skill). Stand behind the small cone and throw the ball overarm as forcefully as you can into the trash barrel on its side.

2–3: Overarm throw for force (refining skill). Stand behind the medium cone and throw the softball overarm as forcefully as you can into the trash barrel on its side.

4–5: Overarm throw for force (refining skill). Stand behind the large cone and throw the softball overarm as forcefully as you can into the trash barrel on its side.

Center 35

Equipment: Two plastic bats, two batting tees, two whiffle balls, three bases, target on a fence

(*continues*)

Example of Outdoor Game Skill Centers for a Class of 70 (*continued*)

K–1: Batting (refining skill). Using the plastic bat, practice batting the ball off the tee at the fence, focusing on the back foot pivot.

2–3: Batting (refining skill). Using the plastic bat, practice taking hands directly to the ball. Place one whiffle ball on top of the other, and place both on top of the tee. Hit the bottom ball only (the top ball should land on the tee).

4–5: Batting, running bases, and throwing (tactics to beat the runner, hit into open space). Set up the bases in a triangle (first, third, home). Hit off the tee, and run to first, third, and home before the thrower collects the ball and throws at the target on the fence.

Summary

Although research says small classes are associated with increased student achievement and teacher enjoyment, the unfortunate reality is that many teachers are assigned large classes. Large classes do not doom you to failure—you *can* successfully teach large classes. Many effective teachers of large classes provide whole-class lessons but rely on centers for practicing skills. Guidelines for teaching large classes include the following:

- Provide maximum skill practice opportunities.
- Avoid large group games or activities.
- Ensure that every child or pair has the equipment needed to practice the skill.
- Focus on the most important skills; avoid fads, time fillers, and "cutesy" activities.
- Ensure that centers are engaging and motivating (which are challenging, interesting, novel, enjoyable, and demand attention).
- Teach children to learn independently and self-regulate.
- Whenever possible, use only one organization pattern to avoid the time spent transitioning from one task to another.
- Teach children to be socially responsible within the large class environment.
- Use peer teaching and assessment.

Review Questions

1. Which six factors has research linked to the advantage of small class size? How can you apply these factors in large classes?
2. What is the single most important factor for facilitating children's learning?
3. Why is teaching children to learn independently and be self-responsible an important variable in physical education? Why are peer teaching and assessment valuable for large classes?
4. Describe how you can provide whole-class teaching to large classes.
5. What are five criteria for a good set of centers? Design three centers not described in this chapter for any skill.
6. Why does rotating centers help prevent management problems?
7. How can centers help classroom teachers?

References

Finn, J. D., Pannozzo, G. M., & Achilles, C. M. (2003). The "why's" of class size: Student behavior in small classes. *Review of Educational Research, 73*, 321–368.

Hastie, P. A., & Saunders, J. E. (1991). Effects of class size and equipment availability on student involvement in physical education. *Journal of Experimental Education, 59*, 212–224.

Hastie, P. A., Sanders, S. W., & Rowland, R. S. (1999). Where good intentions meet harsh realities: Teaching large classes in physical education. *Journal of Teaching in Physical Education, 18*, 277–289.

Iserbyt, P., Elen, J., & Behets, D. (2010). Instructional guidance in reciprocal peer tutoring with task cards. *Journal of Teaching in Physical Education, 29*, 38–53.

Morgan, P. J., & Hansen, V. (2008). Classroom teachers' perceptions of the impact of barriers to teaching physical education on the quality of physical education programs. *Research Quarterly for Exercise and Sport, 79*, 506–516.

National Association of Sport and Physical Education (NASPE). (2009). *Opportunity to learn: Guidelines for elementary school physical education.* Reston, VA: Author.

Silverman, S., Tyson, L., & Krampitz, J. (1992). Teacher feedback and achievement in physical education: Interaction with student practice. *Teaching and Teacher Education, 8*, 333–344.

Sun, H., Chen, A., Ennis, C., Martin, R., & Shen, B. (2008). An examination of the multidimensionality of situational interest in elementary school physical education. *Research Quarterly for Exercise and Sport, 79*, 62–70.

Vande Broek, G., Boen, F., Claessens, M., Feys, J., & Ceux, T. (2011). Comparison of three instructional approaches to enhance tactical knowledge in volleyball among university students. *Journal of Teaching in Physical Education, 30*, 375–392.

Health-Related Physical Activity

In this section, we discuss health-related physical activity (HRPA). We summarize the large body of research on HRPA, national guidelines for children, issues of obesity, and basic concepts about HRPA, health-related fitness (HRF), and nutrition. We also discuss creating healthy, active schools.

This section is child oriented. For adults, we think of HRPA as consisting of calisthenics, such as crunches, push-ups, and leg stretches, and continuous, high-intensity exercises, such as jogging, working on elliptical machines, aerobics, and lifting weights. Adults and even high school students typically use and enjoy these forms of movement as means to improve or maintain their physical fitness.

Most children, however, do not enjoy adult forms of exercise and calisthenics. In addition, the continuous nature and high intensity levels of these exercises do not match their physiological, emotional, or social developmental needs. For children, we take a much broader view of the forms of movement that work for enhancing health, such as physically active play, hopscotch, climbing on playground equipment, climbing trees, playing youth sports after school, riding bicycles, and physical education skill development lessons in games, dance, and gymnastics. While adults may go to a park to walk or jog, children go to a park to play.

Elementary physical education teachers can promote HRPA and teach children basic concepts about HRPA, HRF, and nutrition that will start them on the road to lifelong participation in physical activities and healthy eating habits. We believe they can do so in developmentally appropriate ways.

CHAPTER

17

Health-Related Physical Activity and Health-Related Fitness

PRE-READING REFLECTION

1. What do you do on a weekly basis for physical activity?
2. What do you like and dislike about health-related physical activity?
3. What motivates you to exercise?
4. Do you think your personal preferences will affect your decisions as an elementary physical educator, and if so, how?

OBJECTIVES

Students will learn:

1. A substantial body of research has documented the fact that physical activity is beneficial for health.
2. Research positively links physical activity to academic achievement, concentration, and attention. Increased time in physical education may help—and does not harm—academic performance.
3. Since the landmark 1996 U.S. Surgeon General's report, U.S. physical education professionals have shifted from a physical fitness approach to a health-related physical activity approach.
4. Physical fitness scores for children are predominantly related to maturation, age, and heredity.
5. Physical activity for children should be varied, developmentally appropriate, and enjoyable.
6. Knowledge of health-related physical activity (HRPA), health-related fitness (HRF), and nutrition can be integrated into physically active lessons in the areas of games, dance, and gymnastics.

KEY TERMS

ActivityGram

Body composition

Cardiorespiratory endurance
Components of fitness
Comprehensive School Physical Activity Program (CSPAPs)
Criterion-referenced tests
Dynamic stretches
Fitness model
FitnessGram
FITT
Flexibility
Frequency
Health-related physical activity model
Intensity
Muscle endurance
Muscle fitness
Muscle power
Muscle strength
MyPlate
Norm-referenced tests
Overload principle
Physical activity breaks
Progression principle
Specificity principle
Static stretches
Type of activity

CONNECTION TO STANDARDS

This chapter focuses on National Standard 3, including what concepts to teach and how to support children's acquisition of the knowledge, skills, and dispositions they will need to be physically active for a lifetime. The Common Core and other State Standards (CCSS) discussed in this chapter focus on acquiring domain-specific vocabulary.

Introduction

The Institute of Medicine (IOM) (2012a) released a report with a strong call to action:

> Schools are uniquely positioned to support physical activity and healthy eating and therefore can serve as a focal point for obesity prevention among children and adolescents. Schools can be leaders in reversing trends that have made a physically active lifestyles more difficult and high-calorie, nutrient-poor foods more accessible. Children spend up to half of their waking hours in school. In an increasingly sedentary world, schools therefore provide the best opportunity for a population-based approach to increasing physical activity among the nation's youth (p. 333).

The importance of physical activity and eating a healthful diet is being promoted by the U.S. government and governments internationally; organizations such as the American Heart Association, the National Football League, and the Society of Health and Physical Educators (SHAPE); celebrities; and, of course, physical education teachers and health professionals worldwide.

One reason for the current interest in health is that an ever-increasing body of research has clearly shown the relationship between physical activity, healthy eating, and decreased risk of diseases, whereas inactivity and overweight are related to increased risks of disease and obesity. The increase in obesity in both children and adults is a major concern of health professionals.

We live in a technological age characterized by trends that have contributed to increasingly sedentary lifestyles, as have changes in transportation and housing. Most children no longer bike or walk to school or spend much time playing outdoors after school. Rural and suburban communities rely on cars for transportation to work, shopping, and services. In low-income urban areas, people have less access to supermarkets and healthy, low-cost foods. High-calorie fast foods are cheap, easily accessible, tasty, and heavily advertised.

Research on the Benefits of Health-Related Physical Activity

In the 2000s, the benefits of physical activity for health have been well established by a substantial body of research. The Centers for Disease Control and Prevention (CDC) (U.S. Department of Health and Human Services [USDHHS], 2008, p. 9) summarizes the research by stating there is strong evidence that regular physical activity confers the following advantages:

- Lower risk of early death
- Lower risk of coronary heart disease
- Lower risk of stroke
- Lower risk of high blood pressure
- Lower risk of adverse blood lipid profile
- Lower risk of type 2 diabetes
- Lower risk of metabolic syndrome
- Lower risk of colon cancer
- Lower risk of breast cancer
- Prevention of weight gain
- Weight loss, particularly when combined with reduced calorie intake
- Improved cardiorespiratory and muscular fitness
- Prevention of falls
- Reduced depression
- Better cognitive function (for older adults)

For children, HRPA "builds healthy bones and muscles, decreases the likelihood of obesity and disease risk factors such as high blood pressure, and reduces anxiety and depression and promotes positive mental health" (CDC, 2013, p. 8). Physical activities that promote bone strength and growth in children include activities in which children generate power, that is, force with speed, and activities with impact with the ground. Moreover, evidence indicates that children maintain the bone mass developed through exercise into adulthood (American College of Sports Medicine [ACSM], 2004).

To date, most research on this topic has been conducted primarily on adults. The benefits of HRPA are far more difficult to demonstrate in children (Welk & Blair, 2008). One reason is that chronic diseases take many years to develop, and any benefit would depend on the child continuing to participate in physical activities through adulthood. Consequently, the goal for children is to acquire "the knowledge and skills to achieve and maintain a health-enhancing level of physical activity and fitness," as stated in National Standard 3 (SHAPE, 2014, p. 12).

The Link Between Physical Activity and Academic Achievement

In addition to identifying the physical benefits of HRPA, a body of research now confirms the positive link between physical activity and academic achievement. In 2010, the CDC issued a report summarizing the role of school-based physical activity in relation to academic achievement, academic behavior, and cognitive skills and attitudes. Across 23 years of research on physical education, recess, short physical activity breaks in the classroom, and before- and after-school programs, the CDC (2010) reported:

- There is substantial evidence that physical activity can help improve academic achievement, including grades and standardized test scores.
- The articles in this review suggest that physical activity can have an impact on cognitive skills and attitudes and academic behavior, all of which are important components of improved academic performance. These include enhanced concentration and attention as well as improved classroom behavior.
- Increasing or maintaining time dedicated to physical education may help, and does not appear to adversely impact, academic performance (p. 6).

Further research supports earlier studies and reports a link between fitness and higher attendance rates, fewer incidences of delinquency, and higher brain functioning (Hillman, Castelli, & Buck, 2005; Welk et al., 2010). The IOM (2012a) concluded there was a positive relationship between physical activity and academic performance.

Physical Activity and Brain Function

One possible underlying reason for the positive link between physical activity and academic achievement is that physical activity affects brain physiology by increasing the following factors:

- Cerebral capillary growth
- Blood flow
- Oxygenation
- Production of neurotrophins
- Growth of nerve cells in the hippocampus (center of learning and memory)
- Neurotransmitter levels
- Development of nerve connections
- Density of neural network
- Brain tissue volume (CDC, 2010, p. 9)

Researchers suggest that these changes can lead to a variety of cognitive and other benefits:

- Improved attention
- Improved information processing, storage, and retrieval
- Enhanced coping
- Enhanced positive affect
- Reduced sensations of cravings and pain (CDC, 2010, p. 9)

Thus, neuroscience research supports maintaining and increasing physical education in schools.

Recommendations for Physical Activity and Physical Education in Schools

Based on the research, the CDC (USDHHS, 2008, p. vii) developed guidelines for physical activity for children. These guidelines call for children to engage in a variety of activities:

- "Do 60 minutes (one hour) or more of physical activity daily."
- "Most of those 60 or more minutes should be either moderate- or vigorous-intensity aerobic physical activity at least three days a week."
- At least three days a week, children should do muscle strengthening activities and bone strengthening activities.

Table 17.1 shows examples of such activities by category for children. Research suggests that physical activities for children need to be developmentally appropriate, varied, and fun. As Corbin (2002) explains, children are not miniature adults; they are intermittent exercisers in contrast to the continuous forms of exercise typically enjoyed by adults, such as jogging. Intermittent exercise means children engage in highly vigorous movement, then rest, recover quickly, and move again. This pattern is in keeping with their physiological capabilities and their cognitive and emotional development.

In 2010, the U.S. Surgeon General responded to the research on the benefits of physical activity for health in a report titled *The Surgeon General's Vision for a Healthy and Fit Nation.* She set forth a series of recommendations for schools related to HRPA. This report states:

> To promote physical activity, school systems should
>
> - Require daily physical education for students in pre-kindergarten through grade 12, allowing 150 minutes per week for elementary schools and 225 minutes per week for secondary schools.
> - Require and implement a planned and sequential physical education curriculum for pre-kindergarten through grade 12 that is based on national standards.
> - Require at least 20 minutes of daily recess for all students in elementary schools.
> - Offer students opportunities to participate in intramural physical activity programs during after-school hours.

Table 17.1 Physical Activity Recommendations for Children

Moderate and Vigorous Aerobic Physical Activity: 60 Minutes or More Every Day	
Moderate aerobic activities: Hiking Skateboarding Walking to school Skating Bike riding (slow pace)	
Vigorous aerobic activities: Games involving running Jumping rope Bike riding (moderate to fast pace) Sports such as soccer, basketball, gymnastics, swimming, hockey, and tennis Martial arts	
3 Days per Week	
Muscle-strengthening: Climbing on playground equipment Swinging from hand to hand on an overhead bar Gymnastics (e.g., holding a balance on different body parts using core strength, hanging in a curled position from a bar) Raking the yard	
Bone-strengthening: Jumping Running Jumping rope Hopscotch Sports such as gymnastics, volleyball, tennis, and basketball	

Source: Data from U.S. Department of Health and Human Services (USDHHS). (2008). *Physical activity guidelines for Americans*. Washington, DC: Author. Retrieved from http://www.health.gov/paguidelines

- Implement and promote walk- and bike-to-school programs.
- Establish joint-use agreements with local government agencies to allow use of school facilities for physical activity programs offered by the school or community-based organizations outside of school hours (USDHHS, 2010b, p. 9).

Most recently, the IOM, part of the National Academy of Sciences, issued a report in 2013 aimed at improving policies and programs for school-based physical education and physical activity based on scientific evidence. The IOM recommended a whole-school approach. The IOM recommendations include previous recommendations for required time for physical education but also include stronger and more specific recommendations for physical activity time in schools, monitoring, policy, and equity. They recommend the following:

- 150 minutes per week of high-quality physical education at the elementary school level and 225 minutes for middle and high school.
- During physical education, 50% of the time children should be engaging in moderate to vigorous physical activity.
- Children should spend 60 minutes a day engaged in moderate to vigorous physical activity, with more than 50% of those minutes occurring during school hours through physical education, recess, and classroom physical activity time.
- All students should have access to before- and after-school programs, intramurals, and active transport.
- Education and health agencies should monitor policies and behavior in physical education and for physical activity in school settings. This includes assessing student achievement of physical education standards and monitoring the quality of physical education.
- Provide preservice and practicing teachers training to enable them to promote physical activity throughout the school day and across the curriculum.

In regard to government policies, the IOM (2013) wrote two strong recommendations:

> Federal and state governments, school systems at all levels (state, district, and local), city governments and city planners, and parent–teacher organizations should systematically consider access to and provision of physical activity in all policy decisions related to the school environment as a contributing factor to improving academic performance, health, and development for all children (p. 369).
>
> Because physical education is foundational for lifelong health and learning, the U.S. Department of Education should designate physical education as a core subject (p. 371).

Finally, the IOM recognized inequitable opportunities for physical activity in relation to race, ethnicity, economic status, gender, and immigrant generation. They recommended:

> Programs and policies at all levels address existing disparities in physical activity and that all students at all schools have equal access to appropriate facilities and opportunities for physical activity and quality physical education (p. 376).

The CDC (2013) and the American Alliance for Health, Physical Education, Recreation, and Dance (AAHPERD, now called SHAPE America) issued guidelines for establishing whole-school approaches similar to the IOM (2013) recommendations. We discuss their guidelines next.

Comprehensive School Physical Activity Programs

With the benefits of physical activity for children's health and academic achievement well established, governments and organization are seeking ways to increase physical activity in children's lives to the recommended level of 60 minutes a day. Because almost all children attend school, schools are potential sites for establishing programs that can positively affect children's health. SHAPE America and the CDC (2013) have called for these school-based programs to be comprehensive, whole-school programs and have provided guidelines for their establishment under the umbrella term "**Comprehensive School Physical Activity Programs (CSPAPs)**."

CSPAPs have multiple components that jointly aim to increase students' physical activity levels and develop the knowledge, skills, and dispositions to engage lifelong in physical activity (CDC, 2013). These components include quality physical education, before- and after-school programs, physical activity breaks, and recess.

Quality Physical Education

As discussed in the recommendation from the IOM (2013), children should have 150 minutes of physical education per week, with 50% of physical education time spent in moderate to vigorous physical activity taught by a qualified physical education teacher. Guidelines for appropriate practices include developmentally appropriate lessons focused on learning outcomes based on the National Standards for Physical Education (National Standards) and assessment of those learning outcomes (CDC, 2013; SHAPE, 2014). The content and instructional strategies ought to meet the needs of all children, regardless of gender, race, ethnicity, religion, sexual orientation, and socioeconomic status, in a positive, mastery-oriented learning environment, with opportunities for student autonomy and engagement in high-order thinking skills (CDC, 2013; National Association for Sport and Physical Education [NASPE], 2010a).

Before- and After-School Programs

CSPAPs include increased opportunities for children to engage in physical activities before and after school (CDC, 2013). These opportunities can be intramurals, physical activity clubs, sport camps open to all children, recreational active play, and active commuting to school.

Intramurals are within-school opportunities to play sports. They may consist of any sport modified to be developmentally appropriate with small-sized teams, modified equipment, and modified courts or fields and rules.

Physical activity clubs may focus on juggling, jump rope, fitness activities, walking, gymnastics, dance, or hiking. Such clubs can be set up simply for participation, or they can lead to a performance for classmates, the school, or the parent–teacher association (PTA). Some teachers have clubs such as jump rope teams that perform at local malls and at other schools.

Sport camps can be offered before or after school and typically include both instruction and developmentally appropriate gameplay. Sport camps and physical activity clubs can also be excellent fundraisers. You can charge a nominal fee to participants, while offering scholarships or finding donors to fund scholarships for children without the financial resources to participate. You can also approach local high school interscholastic teams to help provide instruction during sport camps and split the funds raised with the high school team.

Active Commuting to School

CSPAPs also include access to and the promotion of active commuting by walking or biking to school (CDC, 2013). For many reasons, many parents can't or don't allow children to walk, bike, or skateboard to school. Increasing the percentage of children living within one mile of school who commute actively to school is one of the goals of the *Healthy People 2020* initiative and the U.S. Surgeon General (USDHHS, 2010a, 2010b). Some promising programs along these lines include community-created safe routes to school and "walking school buses" in which children, accompanied by an adult, walk to school in a group. Although there is little research on the effects of active commuting to school, it certainly increases physical activity time and might contribute to preventing weight gain (Rosenberg, Sallis, Conway, Cain, & McKenzie, 2006).

During-School Programs: Recess

In some schools, time is set aside after lunch for physical activity clubs or intramurals; however, at the elementary school level, recess is the most common opportunity for additional physical activity during the school day. The CDC (2013) and the U.S. Surgeon General (USDHHS, 2010b) recommend that children have daily recess. Research shows recess is important for children's social development, cognitive skills, attitudes, and academic behavior (e.g., attentiveness, concentration, time on-task), and it plays a role in increasing children's physical activity time (CDC, 2010; CDC 2013).

Unfortunately, research indicates that children spend 65% of recess time being inactive (Babkes & Sinclair, 2004). In addition, boys tend to be more active than girls, and children with average body size are more active than children who are thin or larger. Worse, in some schools, recess is prime time for bullying, name-calling, and fighting.

Suggestions to increase physical activity during recess include the following (Babkes Stellino & Sinclair, 2008; Kahan, 2008; Verstraete, Cardon, De Clercq, & De Bourdeaudhuij, 2006):

- Provide ample game equipment (one piece for every one to three children).
- Make equipment developmentally appropriate.
- Have a recess activity board on which you list suggested activities for children with a range of interests and ability levels.
- Suggest success-oriented, noncompetitive activities.
- Have teachers or recess monitors promote and prompt physical activity.
- Paint court and game boundaries and targets.
- Ensure equitable use of space and equipment.

Some schools are now using structured recess in an attempt to prevent bullying and discipline problems. In structured recess, a recess coach teaches games and physical activities, such as hopscotch and jump rope. Structured recess is controversial because it denies children free, unstructured time, which is beneficial; in addition, some structured recess programs deny children the choice of activity. Other structured recess programs provide choices and successfully teach children cooperative games and traditional playground games and activities that children have not learned because they can't play outside after school.

> **What the Research Says**
>
> Intramurals
>
> In a review of research on intramurals and youth sports, researchers found that participation in these sport activities led to increased participation in sport activities as young adults (Bocarro, Kanters, Casper, & Forrester, 2008). The number of different sports (as opposed to the amount of time spent participating in them) predicted adult participation. Specifically, young adults who had not participated in sports as children were unlikely to participate as adults (Perkins, Jacobs, Barber, & Eccles, 2004). It seems that increasing intramural participation increases youth physical activity and can increase lifelong physical activity, because the more children and adolescents develop a level of competence that enables enjoyment in a range of activities, the more choices they have as adults.

During-School Programs: Physical Activity Breaks for Classrooms

Physical activity breaks are short, five-minute breaks in which children engage in physical activity in their classroom while being directed by the classroom teacher. They are often called "brain breaks." A number of research studies have provided solid evidence that classroom physical activity breaks enhance children's learning, attention, and on-task behavior (CDC, 2013; CDC, 2010[KK1]; Erwin, Beets, Centeio, & Morrow, 2014).

Physical activity breaks can be simple movement activities. For example, one simple activity is to put on music and have the children follow in a line behind the teacher (or a child leader) as he or she marches around the desks forward and backward, bending the knees to walk at a lower level, walking on "tip toes" and doing arm circles, lifting the knees high, and doing prancing steps. Children can also form lines of four that follow a child leader around the classroom while doing different locomotor steps and arm actions, changing leaders frequently.

Physical activity breaks can also reinforce educational outcomes from physical education. In physical education, you can have the children design a physical activity break with a partner. This can be a dance routine or a sequence of skills, such as jumping and hopping. Have the children work on their routines until they have them memorized and perfected. Then the classroom teacher can assign one pair a day to lead the classroom physical activity break. Physical activity breaks can also be taken directly from physical education lessons. For example, when the children learn a folk dance, you can also teach them a modified version that they can do in the space available in classrooms. Then, provide the music to the classroom teachers.

You can also design physical activity routines and teach these routines in physical education. Videorecord the children performing their routines and give copies of the DVD or video file to classroom teachers to play. In one school we know, the fifth-graders designed the physical activity break routines and the physical education teacher videorecorded their final product for use throughout the school. In another school, which had its own "television" network, different children performed physical activity break routines during morning announcements while the entire school joined in for a physically active start to the day.

A third type of physical activity break is one that integrates movement and classroom content. Many websites provide ideas, videos, and lesson plans for integrating classroom content with movement to create "brain breaks," which can be found via a simple Internet search. Dance sequences and learning experiences in which children portray vocabulary words can be used as brain breaks integrating movement and classroom content. For example, a dance sequence titled "Exploring the Haunted Ring of Stones by the Gnarled Old Tree" teaches the following vocabulary words: *gnarled*, *anguish*, *cauldron*, and *wring*. Once the children refine their dances and can repeat them with only a reminder from the classroom teacher of the order of the sequence movements (which you provide), the classroom teacher can use the sequence as a brain break that also reinforces the meaning of new vocabulary words.

Family and Community Involvement

Another component of CSPAPs is to involve the families and community in school activities. For families, the aim is to garner support for engaging with children in physical activity, attending programs, and volunteering to assist with physical activity programs in the school. One popular family activity is family fitness night in which a variety of formats and activities can be incorporated. Some have parents (voluntarily) join in with simple physical activities with their children. Others have children teach their parents what they have learned about the areas and principles of physical fitness and what they can do to maintain or improve fitness.

In addition, you can email or send home a newsletter discussing HRPA topics. In the newsletter, you might suggest family activities related to the topic and identify HRPA websites for children and families.

Community organizations can be well suited to provide physical activity programs after school or on weekends. Joint use of schools with community organizations is a way to share limited resources.

Teaching Children About Community Resources

It is also helpful to teach children about community resources available to them off school grounds. Check with your community recreation department and find out what programs are available for children in your school. Ask about youth sport seasons, and identify where and how children can enroll in these programs. Ask if funds are available to help children who can't afford the cost. Identify the locations of local parks. To publicize your findings, you can share all this information with children and parents in a newsletter. You can also create a display on the school walls promoting community recreational activities.

One teacher we know, who works in an urban environment, conducts a field trip each year to teach the children how to ride the city buses to each of the parks. After a fun day spent playing at the parks, the classroom teachers have the children write in their journals about their experiences.

The end of the school year is an important time to promote physical activity and community summer programs for children. Create a list of programs offered in the community, such as tennis and golf lessons, sport camps, snorkeling trips, wilderness hikes, and canoeing trips. Most community organizations advertise these summer programs in the newspaper just before school ends. Compile a list of the programs, giving the dates, estimated costs, and phone number to call for more information. Community organizations typically offer the same summer programs year after year. Once you create a list, you will simply need to update it each year.

Another way to promote physical activity over the summer or any vacation time is to send home a calendar on which you write suggested activities to do each day. For example, you might write: On June 15, take a 20-minute walk with your family; on June 16, jump rope; on June 17, tread water for 30 seconds, rest, and repeat.

Wellness Weeks

The concept of "Wellness Weeks," described by its originators in *Fitness for Life: Elementary School* (Corbin, Le Masurier, Lambdin, & Greiner, 2010), is an excellent example of a CSPAP. For one week, the whole school focuses on physical activity and nutrition. Wellness Weeks include the following (Corbin, Kulinna, Dean, & Reeves, 2013):

- Two five- to ten-minute brain breaks per day consisting of physical activity conducted by the classroom teacher, followed by a discussion of HRPA and nutrition. The children first learn the brain-break activities within physical education.
- Special nutritious meals are provided by the cafeteria staff and parents.
- Art and music teachers and librarians focus on nutrition and physical activity themes.
- Signs promoting wellness and physical activity before and after school are posted school-wide, and newsletters are sent to parents.
- Physical education includes discussions of nutrition and HRPA.
- An evening program is conducted for parents.

The Wellness Week program includes classroom lesson plans for each grade, physical education lessons, videos for classroom activity breaks, music, nutrition and physical activity signs, newsletters, and assessment tools for four wellness weeks across the school year (Corbin et al., 2010). Research has shown that the program is viewed as positive, valuable, and easy to implement by teachers, children, and parents, with a high commitment by schools to continue the program (Corbin et al., 2013).

Organizing a CSPAP

Organizing a CSPAP is not an easy task. There are several web-based programs and tools that can guide you through the process of organizing a CSPAP. NASPE designed a Director of Physical Activity (DPA) training and certification program to assist physical educators in taking on the responsibility of leading the CSPAP efforts (Carson, 2012). The "Let's Move! Active Schools" website provides a roadmap for developing an active school, and NASPE provides *Let's Move in School Physical Education Teacher Toolkit* and *101 Tips for Implementing a Comprehensive School Physical Activity Program.* In addition, there are books that provide detailed instructions of how to develop a CSPAP, including

Pangrazi, R. P., Beighle, A., & Pangrazi, D. (2009). *Promoting physical activity and health in the classroom.* San Francisco: Benjamin Cummings.

Rink, J. E., Hall, T. J., & Williams, L. H. (2010). *Schoolwide physical activity: A comprehensive guide to development and conducting programs.* Champaign, IL: Human Kinetics.

In brief, the process of organizing a CSPAP begins with a DPA and a committee, who together develop, implement, and assess components of the CSPAP. The DPA is typically a physical education teacher who has knowledge of designing and running physical activities and is an enthusiastic supporter of engaging students, staff, and families in physical activities (Carson, 2012; Erwin et al., 2014). One of the critical tasks for the DPA is to find an administrator who supports the CSPAP and work with this individual to get the time and financial resources for the program (Heidorn & Centeio, 2012). The DPA and the committee meet and do the following:

- Assess the current status of opportunities for physical activity within the school.
- Survey staff and students to see which components of a CSPAP are of interest, such as what physical activity clubs might the school sponsor or what before- or after-school activities students would like to have.
- Design a plan for which programs to develop and when to start each potential program.
- Recruit volunteer teachers and parents to supervise or direct the programs.
- Recruit a group of students interested in working on the programs.
- Organize fundraisers to purchase needed equipment.
- Promote the plan with staff, students, and parents.
- Connect with the community to explore possible alliances.
- Design and assess the programs and provide guidelines and assistance to volunteers.

Notice that this work is not done by the DPA alone, but with the help of committee members and volunteers. Organizing a CSPAP might sound overwhelming; however, being a DPA will give you the opportunity to have an important impact on your school and your students, which is one of the most satisfying aspects of being a teacher.

The Distinction Between Health-Related Physical Activity and Physical Fitness

Before the landmark 1996 U.S. Surgeon General's report (USDHHS, 1996), fitness experts recommended the adult exercise prescription model, referred to as the **fitness model**, for both children and adults (Corbin, 2002). This adult model focused on improving physical fitness with continuous, vigorous aerobic activities lasting for 30 minutes, performed three to four days per week. Today, by comparison, we promote a **health-related physical activity model** of moderate (to vigorous) physical activity lasting for 30 minutes most days of the week for adults and for 60 minutes every day for children.

This recommended shift from a physical *fitness* to a physical *activity* model reflects the findings from a large body of research on adults and children. Although it sounds counterintuitive, because we typically assume the process of physical activity leads to the product of physical fitness, experts point out that HRPA and physical fitness are very different (although both are linked to improved health) (McKenzie & Kahan, 2004). For children, the link between physical activity and physical fitness is weak (Corbin, Lambdin, Mahar, Roberts, & Pangrazzi, 2013; Trost, 2004). In other words, some children will score high on physical fitness tests but be inactive, whereas other children will be highly active but score low on physical fitness tests. Studies indicate that being physically active contributes less than 5% to children's scores on cardiorespiratory fitness tests (Trost, 1998, cited in Trost, 2006). In addition, research has yet to demonstrate strong relationships between fitness test scores on muscular strength, muscular endurance, and flexibility and health outcomes in children, although these relationships have been found for adults (Malina, 2014; Plowman, 2014). Consequently, for children, we view HRPA and physical fitness as distinct and only weakly related.

Physical fitness scores for preadolescent children relate predominantly to maturation, age, and heredity (Bouchard, 1993; Corbin et al., 2013; Pangrazi, 2000; Pangrazi & Corbin, 1990). Consequently, within a grade level, older children, children who are physically more mature, and children with genetic predispositions for physical fitness will score higher on physical fitness tests than their younger, less physically mature, and less genetically endowed classmates. Even three months of growth can make a difference in test scores (Pangrazi & Corbin, 2008).

Heredity also affects the extent to which fitness can improve through training (Bouchard, Dionne, Simoneau, & Boulay, 1992). Some children will have to exercise for a much longer period of time than others before they show any improvement in physical fitness (Malina, 2014). Moreover, children show little physiological training effects from aerobic exercise (Payne & Morrow, 1993). In other words, spending time trying to improve children's scores on cardiorespiratory endurance through aerobic training will have only a small impact. Whereas 95% of adults improve due to training, some studies of children younger than 10 show less than 5% improvement in aerobic power due to training (Morrow & Freedson, 1994; Welk, Eisenmann, & Dollman, J. 2006). Further, children can develop muscular strength in ways similar to adults, but they will not develop large, bulky muscles (Fisher, 2009). In general, there are wide variations across the age span in children's responses to training, with some children showing little physiological responses regardless of how hard they work (Malina, 2014).

Consequently, based on the research, the priority for children is to be physically active and develop motor skills, habits of physical activity, and dispositions to be physically active across the lifespan, rather than to spend the limited time available for physical education on cardiorespiratory endurance and muscle fitness training (Fisher, 2009). While genetics and maturation may influence which children can achieve high levels of physical fitness, all children can participate and benefit from a health-enhancing level of physical activity (Pangrazi, 2000). In addition, a priority for physical education is to ensure children acquire the knowledge of concepts about HRPA and HRF, guidelines for improving fitness, physical responses to physical activity, and the benefits of physical activity and physical fitness across their lifespan. We hope this knowledge will support children's engagement in physical activity not only in childhood but throughout adulthood.

Forms of Physical Activities

HRPA can take many forms. Experts agree that for children, the form of physical activity must be varied, developmentally appropriate, and enjoyable (USDHHS, 2008).

Varied Physical Activities

Children need, and enjoy, a variety of physical activities (see **Figure 17.1**). The first form required consists of moderate physical lifestyle activities, primarily active play, typically intermittent with phases of high activity and rest. Lifestyle activities also can include household chores and yard work.

Figure 17.1 Children need, and enjoy, a variety of physical activities

The second form of activiy important for children comprises opportunities in physical education and after school to participate in a wide range of vigorous aerobic activities and aerobic sport-related and recreational activities. These activities include skill development lessons, dance, youth sports, and recreational physical activities, such as skateboarding, biking, hiking, and skating.

The third form of activity includes activities directed at improving muscle fitness, that is, muscle strength, muscle endurance, muscle power (bone strengthening), and flexibility. Examples of these activities are jumping for strengthening bones, climbing on climbing walls for strengthening muscles, and activities that move joints through their range of motion for flexibility.

Developmentally Appropriate Physical Activities

Along with opportunities to participate in a variety of activities, these activities need to be developmentally appropriate. In the same way that we don't recommend older adults play tag and do cartwheels in a park, we don't recommend that children participate in adult forms of regimented physical activity.

Outside of school, children rarely engage in adult forms of high-intensity, highly regimented physical activity on a voluntary basis. Teachers and parents need not be concerned, however (Corbin & Pangrazi, 2008). The play-oriented intermittent activities children pursue match their physiological, cognitive, and emotional developmental needs and result in health benefits.

For elementary physical education, most experts suggest it is developmentally appropriate for teachers to focus on developing children's competence in motor skills in addition to motivational and social skills that will support their participation in whatever sports and physical activities they find enjoyable. This approach can increase levels of physical activity in childhood and physical fitness as adults. Research has shown that when children are proficient in motor skills (Barnett, Morgan, van Beurden, Ball, & Lubans, 2011; Lubans, Morgan, Cliff, Barnett, and Oakley, 2010; Malina, 2014; Stodden, Langendorfer, & Roberton, 2009; Stodden, True, Langendorfer, & Gao, 2013), competent in more than one activity, are skilled in their favorite sport, or play multiple sports (Castelli & Erwin, 2007), physical activity increases in adulthood, as does physical fitness. Being skillful is also linked to perceptions of competence, which in turn correlates with increased participation in physical activity (Crocker, Eklund, & Kowalski, 2000; Welk et al., 2006).

In addition to increasing childhood physical activity levels, competence in fundamental motor skills is a prerequisite for participation in physical activities throughout the lifespan (Clark, 2007; Welk et al., 2006). Seefeldt (1980) proposed a minimal level of proficiency in fundamental motor skills that children must acquire to allow for their subsequently enjoyable participation in adult forms of physical activity and active recreation. He labeled this threshold the "proficiency barrier." If children do not develop beyond this barrier, their options will be limited. Recent research is building support for the proficiency barrier (Stodden, et al., 2013).

Figure 17.2 Children enjoying an energetic dance

Enjoyable Physical Activities

Finally, the form of physical activity needs to be enjoyable for children (see **Figure 17.2**). Research on young children has shown that they do not enjoy regimented instructional methods and static stretching (Sanders & Graham, 1995). In addition, children tend to prefer skill-related physical education lessons to health-related lessons encompassing activities such as walking, jogging, or running and teacher-led exercises (McKenzie, Alcaraz, & Sallis, 1994). Children rank high-intensity aerobic activities as providing the lowest level of enjoyment. Finally, adult forms of fitness activities, which are neither interesting nor enjoyable for children, can be detrimental to motivation later in life (Chen, 2013; Chen & Liu, 2009).

Teaching Motor Skill Lessons from an HRPA Perspective

To teach motor skill lessons in ways that contribute to health, you will need to ensure that children are physically active during most of your lessons. A widely recommended goal is for children to be moderately to vigorously active during 50% of the lesson time (IOM, 2013). We know teachers can teach lessons with 50% or greater physical activity levels, but many do not (McKenzie & Kahan, 2004).

Teachers who succeed in meeting this goal minimize the amount of time children spend waiting in line and transitioning from one activity to another. They use a minimal number of organizational patterns, thereby saving the time it takes to switch a class from one formation to another. Recall that good physical education teachers are good managers who plan tasks and transitions while being mindful of the importance of giving children maximum opportunities to practice skills and be physically active (see **Figure 17.3**). In addition, such teachers maximize participation by having a ball available for each child or pair or small group if required by the task, such as striking

What the Research Says

The Potential for Student Choice and Child-Designed Games to Increase Physical Activity

In one study, researchers asked the physical education teacher to select girls who did not like physical education or physical activity to participate in the study (Oliver, Hamzeh, & McCaughtry, 2009). The researchers asked the girls to identify barriers for their participation in physical activity. The girls said they were "girly girls" and didn't want to mess up their hair, clothes, or nails; also, sometimes they liked to wear flip-flops. As the researchers worked with the girls, they found this "girly girl" identity was one the girls assumed only sometimes—for example, when they did not like the activities in physical education.

The researchers then worked with the girls to design games that "girly girls" would like. In the end, the girls designed a set of 21 games they enjoyed. For example, in the "Jump Band Game" (a game to play on days when they did not want to break their nails), two end jumpers and two center jumpers used jump bands in traditional ways, while the end jumpers also passed a ball back and forth trying to keep it away from the center jumpers. In "Color Tag Volleyball" (another game for days when the girls did not want to break their nails), two girls wearing flag belts passed a beach ball back and forth while two girls tried to steal their flags.

Of importance to physical educators, the 21 games the girls designed were highly active and some potentially could increase skill development. In other words, the girls did not design sedentary, low-activity games that would prevent them from messing up their hair or breaking their nails (as evidenced by the "Jump Band Game" and "Color Tag Volleyball"). As this study demonstrates, child-designed games can give children autonomy to design physical activities that are meaningful and enjoyable for them—even children who do not like physical education.

Figure 17.3 High activity levels during skill development lessons

What the Research Says

Motor Skill Development and Physical Fitness

Because longitudinal research following children through adolescence and adulthood is expensive and difficult, few studies conducted to date have addressed the impact of motor skill development in elementary physical education on adult participation in physical activity. Several studies, however, have shown that motor skill competence is associated with increased physical activity or fitness levels (Barnett et al., 2011; Castelli & Erwin, 2007; Lubans et al., 2010; Malina, 2014; Stodden et al., 2013).

For example, one study tested children's competence in dribbling and passing a basketball, striking a ball with a short-handled racket continuously over a low net, and overhand throwing for force, with the researchers then measuring the participants' levels of physical activity and physical fitness (Castelli & Valley, 2007). According to this research, children who were more competent and fit engaged in more physical activity. Another study showed a very strong association between competence in throwing, kicking, and jumping and higher levels of health-related fitness in adults (Stodden et al., 2009). Yet another indicated that competence in fundamental motor skills (running, vertical jumping, catching, overhand throwing, forehand striking, and kicking) was positively linked to time spent in organized physical activity as adolescents (Okley, Booth, & Patterson, 2001). A study of first-graders found that gross motor abilities were positively associated with an active lifestyle (Graf et al., 2004). Finally, a set of longitudinal studies showed that children who were competent in fundamental motor skills (throwing, catching, and kicking) at age 10 were more likely to be physically active, be physically fit, and have higher levels of perceived sport competence at age 16 (Barnett, van Beurden, Morgan, Brooks, & Beard, 2008, 2009). Thus, research supports the importance of motor skill development for increasing physical activity time and physical fitness.

a ball over a net with a partner. They use small-sided games (no more than 3v3) and set up enough centers or stations so that only two to three children are at a station at a time, with enough space and equipment provided for all children to practice at the same time.

One promising strategy to increase the amount of lesson time devoted to physical activity is "fitness infusion." As demonstrated in one study, it is possible to teach lessons that significantly improve skill performance and increase children's heart rates (Ignico, Corson, & Vidoni, 2006). With this technique, short bouts of high-intensity activity are interspersed, or infused, across the lesson. A meta-analysis of interventions aimed at increasing physical activity in physical education reported fitness infusion resulted in 61% more time spent in moderate to vigorous physical activity (Lonsdale et al., 2013).

Limiting the amount of time you talk also will increase children's physical activity. The rule of thumb at the elementary level is to talk briefly, but often. Children cannot process or remember more than one concept or performance technique at a time. Use children's physiology, which favors intermittent activity, to your advantage. Their need for brief periods of rest when activities are vigorous gives you enough time to present a new bit of information in a minimal amount of time. Providing maximum amounts of practice time is important for both skill development and health-related physical activity.

Fitness Testing

Fitness testing at the elementary school level has been a contentious issue for more than 20 years, especially since the shift from a physical fitness to an HRPA perspective. As discussed earlier, fitness test scores in children are predominantly linked to maturation, chronological age, and heredity, with training having only weak effects on scores (Bouchard, 1993; Bouchard et al., 1992; Pangrazi, 2000; Pangrazi & Corbin, 1990; Payne & Morrow, 1993). The weather, physical environment, nutrition, and cultural views of the testing situation can also influence test scores. In addition, because there is a weak relationship in children between physical fitness test scores and amount of physical activity, teachers and parents may inaccurately assume that a child who scores low is not physically active; such low scores may also discourage the child from physical activity or, even worse, lead to less self-esteem (Pangrazi, 2000). Fitness experts warn teachers that using physical fitness tests for grading, as a test of achievement, or as a way to determine whether the physical education program and teacher are effective is inappropriate (Corbin et al., 2013; IOM, 2012b).

In the recent past, different organizations sponsored different fitness tests—some were criterion referenced and some were norm referenced. **Criterion-referenced tests** indicate whether the student's score on a test meets the level of fitness recommended for health. **Norm-referenced tests** compare student's scores to each other and identify the percentile rank of one student compared to other students. Experts agree that fitness tests, if used, must be criterion referenced, not norm referenced (Pangrazi, 2000). Criterion-referenced tests are educational in that they inform students and their parents about the extent to which a child is at a health-enhancing level of fitness, whereas norm-referenced tests simply compare children's scores and do not provide information about whether those scores indicate positive health benefits (Corbin et al., 2013). In addition, norm-referenced tests can decrease motivation in low-performing children (Domangue & Solmon, 2010).

Recently, however, the establishment of the President's Council on Fitness, Sports, and Nutrition (PCFSN), a collaboration of organizations focused on health-related fitness, has been encouraging the elimination of multiple fitness tests and building consensus for fitness education (Corbin et al., 2014).

SAFETY AND LIABILITY 17.1

Increasing Safety and Decreasing Risk of Liability: Guidelines Relevant to Content in this Chapter

In this box, we discuss specific guidelines built on information discussed throughout this text on professional standards of practice, negligence, and liability. The goals of these guidelines are to increase children's safety and decrease teachers' risk of negligence and liability.

- Privacy laws about an individual's health require teachers to keep fitness assessment data confidential, in particular weight and body mass index (BMI). Keep records in a secure location.
- Some states' statutes specifically define the scope of practice for health and fitness instruction. Only medically certified professionals can diagnose and prescribe exercise programs to treat medical problems. Teachers are limited to teaching information about exercise programs for overall improvement of health-related fitness. Only certified dieticians can recommend nutritional intake for weight management. Physical educators are limited to providing "general nonmedical nutrition information," defined as
  1. "principles of good nutrition and food preparation;
  2. foods to be included in the normal daily diet;
  3. the essential nutrients needed by the body;
  4. recommended amounts of essential nutrients;
  5. the actions of nutrients on the body;
  6. the effects of deficiencies or excess of nutrients; or
  7. food and supplements that are good sources of essential nutrients" (Eickhoff-Shemek, Herbert, & Connaughton, 2009, p. 192).
- Limit teaching nutrition information to information from the "MyPlate" website, and avoid recommending diets or weight loss programs.
- Fitness assessment tests are like any other instructional task, and a reasonably prudent educator must anticipate safety issues and prepare students for tests in the same way they do for other tasks. This instructional preparation includes ensuring tasks are at developmentally appropriate levels for each child, teaching the movements using a progression of tasks, differentiating instruction, teaching safety procedures, and warning against inherent dangers.
- Written lesson plans need to include instruction of safety procedures and safe performance techniques for each test item.
- Testing does not mean you can ignore measures to decrease liability risk and increase safety simply because you want valid, reliable test scores.
- Moreover, testing can be coercive, in that students want to perform well on tests and thus can feel pressured to perform in ways they ordinarily would not do. Coercion to perform increases risks of liability and negligence.
- It is prudent to honor all parental notes excusing students from testing even if you question the truth of the claims.
- If a student asks to stop the test, it is prudent to do so.
- Because you have a duty to exercise reasonable professional care to prevent harm, you need to stop a student's participation in any fitness test or physical activity if a student appears to be ill, unduly stressed, working beyond a safe level of exertion or beyond their capabilities, or requests to stop.
- No test is worth a child being harmed or injured and the teacher sued; think, "safety first."

The PCFSN recommends all schools use the "FitnessGram" criterion-referenced test, and some states now require the use of this test. The FitnessGram software program, designed by the Cooper Institute, consists of fitness tests for educational purposes that support lifelong physical activity.

FitnessGram offers a battery of tests from which teachers can select to best meet their needs. These tests report whether children's scores are in what is termed the "healthy fitness zone" or need improvements in the following areas:

- Aerobic capacity
- Body composition
- Abdominal strength and endurance
- Trunk extensor strength and flexibility
- Upper body strength and endurance
- Hamstring flexibility
- Shoulder flexibility

The **FitnessGram** includes three questions about the number of days in the past week in which the child engaged in aerobic activity, strength activity, and flexibility activity. The **ActivityGram** assesses the amount and intensity of children's physical activity across a three-day period.

The FitnessGram/ActivityGram software generates a report for students and parents, along with suggested ways to improve, if needed. The main purpose of the FitnessGram/ActivityGram is to teach students how to self-test, interpret the test scores, and plan personal HRF programs (Corbin et al., 2014).

The Cooper Institute does not recommend formal testing before fourth grade because the criterion standards are not reliable in younger grades. In addition, the tests require reading levels, computer skills, and the ability to interpret results that younger children have yet to develop to the level that would permit accurate scoring, results consisting of meaningful information, and a developmentally appropriate educational experience (Corbin et al., 2013). FitnessGram guidelines state that when teachers include fitness testing in fourth and fifth grades, they need to ensure confidentiality and prevent students from comparing scores. In addition, it is critical to provide an emotionally and physically safe environment (Corbin et al., 2013).

Research clearly shows the danger that taking physical fitness tests can lead to children comparing their results with others, which may then decrease perceived competence and be a discouraging, embarrassing, and physically and emotionally uncomfortable experience. Consider these examples:

- In a survey of 1,505 schools in Texas, approximately 25% reported students having negative experiences taking the FitnessGram test. These outcomes included many children crying; students embarrassed performing in front of peers; teasing and taunting of students who tried hard and of those who performed poorly; and students refusing to take the test, complaining, and avoiding the test by being absent or bringing parental notes denying permission for the test (Zhu, Welk, Meredith, & Boiarskaia, 2010).
- Other students assigned to this fitness test swore at test administrators, hid in the bathroom, and viewed the test as punishment. One didn't eat for two days because of the body composition test, while another tried so hard on the test for cardiorespiratory endurance that she vomited (Martin, Ede, Morrow, & Jackson, 2010).
- One study found that children disliked and tried to avoid the mile-run test, and if they could, they would change it to make it more fun (Hoople & Graham, 1995).
- Another study gave students pre- and post-tests of intrinsic motivation, looking at their perceived interest, enjoyment, competence, effort, and pressure or tension (Whitehead & Corbin, 1991). The researchers gave the children a fitness test and then gave them bogus feedback not based on their actual performance. The researchers told some randomly selected students they were below the 20th percentile and others that they were above the 80th percentile. The students who were told they were below the 20th percentile had decreased levels of intrinsic motivation, whereas those told they were above the 80th percentile had increased levels.

When considering fitness testing, teachers must remember that fitness tests are not equivalent to providing a sound education about HRPA and HRF. Fitness testing at the elementary school level can support the HRPA and HRF content we teach; however, fitness tests alone do not constitute an HRF education. Teachers must decide if the tests are worth the time it takes to administer them and to prepare children to take the tests, for example, by teaching and having children practice the test items and to explain why an activity that is not typically valued by children can be personally meaningful and interesting. Teachers can provide lessons that integrate important HRPA and HRF concepts (e.g., the components of fitness, principles for improving physical fitness, how to meet physical activity guidelines) and teach children how to apply this knowledge to plan personal programs for improving physical fitness and physical activity levels without taking what little practice time they have away from practicing motor skills to administer fitness tests. **Sample Plan 17.2** at the end of the chapter gives you examples of how to integrate teaching the components of fitness into a dance lesson. Sample plans for this chapter on the text website provide examples of similar lessons for games and gymnastics.

Measuring and Promoting Physical Activity in Children During and After School

Many teachers want to measure children's physical activity levels during physical education and after school. Within school, you can videorecord lessons and count the number of minutes children are physically active. Check your school's policy on video recording lessons before doing so. This technique gives you information on your teaching but no feedback to children. Pedometers are popular ways to measure physical activity levels in children because they are relatively easy to use, although they have some limitations.

In addition to using the ActivityGram, you can design other forms of self-reports or journals for monitoring afterschool participation in physical activities. Although these reports are not likely to be very accurate, they can help children learn how to develop personal physical activity plans. For example, periodically during the school year, students can develop a physical activity plan for one week to meet the guidelines of 60 minutes of physical activity each day. They can record their activity in a log or on a checklist you provide them.

Physical education teachers have successfully used physical education homework to increase children's time in physical activity after school. The dilemma with homework is that children can view it as a chore and parents as an unnecessary intrusion into family life. If you choose to assign physical education homework, make it fun and something children (and parents) will want to do and can do in their home environment. Homework, like any task, needs to be differentiated to accommodate individual differences. With physical activity, make it time based (e.g., do 15 minutes of any fun physical activity you want), rather than distance or repetition based. The goal is for children to look forward to physical activity after school, not to dread it as one more homework assignment.

Overweight, Obesity, and the Role of Physical Education

Much as government agencies and the U.S. Surgeon General have called on schools to provide increased opportunities for physical activity, they are now asking schools, specifically including physical education, to be a focal point for the prevention of overweight and obesity (IOM, 2012a). Major reviews of research show that physical education alone cannot make a significant impact on childhood obesity (Casazza et al., 2013; Hoelscher, Kirk, Ritchie, & Cunningham-Sabo, 2013; Shirley et al., 2014). These same reviews, however, have found that physical education can play a role in the *prevention* of obesity.

Considerable progress has been made in addressing obesity, and, in some population groups, the prevalence of obesity is no longer increasing (IOM, 2012a). However, the IOM (2012a) also reports evidence that the problems of obesity are complex and multidimensional and that preventing obesity will require a systems approach that includes changes in society, the built environment, and policy and action at all governmental levels and from multiple sources, using multiple strategies, and addressing multiple dimensions.

This systems approach acknowledges that obesity and overweight are not an individual problem and responsibility, but rather a complex issue that includes the relationships among the individual, family, community, and society (Li & Rukavina, 2012). For example, community and societal changes have contributed to today's more sedentary lifestyle, such as physical and social environments with the following detrimental characteristics:

- Decreased access to healthy, affordable foods and beverages
- Decreased access to safe parks for outdoor physical activities
- Decreased access to indoor spaces and programs for physical activity
- Decreased walking and bicycling to school and work
- Increased access to and advertising of low-cost, energy-dense fast foods served in larger portions
- Increased time spent watching television and sitting at computers

This same multifaceted perspective is promoted by *Healthy People 2020*, which sets nationwide goals for improving health (USDHHS, 2010a).

Teaching About Obesity

There is probably no more dangerous a minefield for teachers to navigate than the issues of overweight and obesity. On the one hand, the position of the Academy of Nutrition and Dietetics, based on research at the elementary school level, is that interventions combining nutrition education and increasing physical activity might be effective in improving body fat measures and behaviors associated with overweight (Hoelscher et al., 2013). In addition, research indicates that physical activity programs alone can increase the amount of physical activity and reduce screen time for children. Parental involvement in nutrition and physical activity interventions has been shown to increase the effectiveness of such programs (Shirley et al., 2014). Teaching students about nutrition and healthy eating and promoting physical activity can be effective in improving their health-related behaviors (Hoelscher et al., 2013; Shirley et al., 2014; Tassitano et al., 2010; USDHHS, 2010b). Finally, programs that combined education about nutrition and physical activity, included parents, modified the environment, monitored children's behaviors, and lasted more than one year were found to be the most effective (Sobol-Goldberg, Rabinowitz, & Gross, 2013). On the other hand, when teachers and parents attempt to prevent obesity, they may inadvertently contribute to negative consequences, such as increases in guilt, shame, eating disorders, negative body image, stigmatization of overweight students, and inappropriate dieting behaviors that can lead to health problems, including problems with growth and bone health (O'Dea, 2005; Ogata & Hayes, 2014; Rukavina & Li, 2008). The position of the Academy of Nutrition and Dietetics is that we need to be concerned with the unintended negative consequences of programs for preventing obesity (Ogata & Hayes, 2014).

Unfortunately, we do not yet have a body of research that can inform teachers on the most effective curriculum and programs for preventing obesity. In fact, the IOM (2012a) recommended that states and departments of education establish standards for nutrition curricula, assessments for determining if students meet these standards, and training for teachers in teaching nutrition. (See this chapter's "Safety and Liability" box for additional guidance on appropriate curriculum topics.) We want to do all we can to help children lead healthy lives without doing harm and without engendering unintended negative consequences.

Keep It Positive: Don't Focus on the Negative Risks Associated with Inactivity and Obesity

Thus, we know that teaching children about healthful eating, health-related physical activity and fitness, and increasing their physical activity levels are important for children's health and might contribute to preventing obesity. Some research also suggests the focus needs to be positive, not on the risks associated with obesity, inactivity, or weight control. In 2010, the Surgeon General outlined her *Vision for a Healthy and Fit Nation* (USDHHS, 2010b). This vision signaled a shift in perspective from focusing on recommendations for weight and body mass index to focusing on the benefits of healthy nutrition, physical activity, and stress management for achieving "invigorating, energizing, joyous health" (USDHHS, 2010b, p. 12).

O'Dea (2005) summarized a body of research that shows when teachers and parents focus on weight or weight control or, even worse, make suggestions for dieting, their input can lead to poor body images, unhealthy dieting behaviors, and less physical activity. In addition, research shows that blame-the-victim, guilt-inducing messages are unsuccessful in weight control. For example, if you focus on the risks of obesity and inactivity (such as teaching children that overweight and inactive people are more likely to develop heart disease, diabetes, and colon cancer and to die earlier), children easily can assume that being overweight means you *are* unhealthy and it is the fault of the individual. Physically active overweight and obese people can be healthy (Brodney, Blair, & Lee, 2000) because the

What the Research Says

Watching Television and Computer Use

A Kaiser Family Foundation study by Rideout, Foehr, and Roberts (2010) reported that the average total media use among 8- to 18-year-olds is 7 hours and 38 minutes per day. That rate extrapolates to more than 53 hours per week—longer than many adults work in a week. Children spend less time with media, however, when parents set rules and limit media opportunities. Among youths, heavy users of media report a greater percentage of fair to poor grades, more boredom, and more unhappiness, and they get into more trouble than moderate and light media users.

health benefits of physical activity mitigate the negative health effects of obesity (Casazza, et al., 2013). Moreover, by emphasizing body weight and weight control, you can contribute to body dissatisfaction, low self-esteem, and feelings of helplessness.

Counteract the Message that the Goal of Exercise Is Looking Good

Owing to the pervasive advertisements in the media, especially on television and the Internet, for weight-loss programs, fitness equipment, and fitness programs, all focused on changing the shape of your body to be slender and toned (women) and muscular (men), children typically develop an understanding of the association between working out, dieting, and looking good. Even the language "get in shape," which we take to mean "improve fitness levels," actually refers to the shape of the body, not health-related physical fitness. The message that permeates the media is that everyone can achieve the "perfect" body if you buy the product, go on the diet, or participate in the fitness program. This is nonsense, of course. Even so, studies have shown that children and adolescents believe that being physically fit means looking good (Burrows, Wright, & Jungersen-Smith, 2002; Kulinna, 2004; Placek et al., 2001).

When we focus on appearance rather than health, we reinforce the idea that what is important about you is your appearance, rather than who you are and your health, happiness, and quality of life. Worse, when hard work is associated with looking good, the focus on body weight and shape reinforces inaccurate, negative stereotypes that overweight and obese people are lazy, unmotivated, unhealthy people who impose a burden on society.

Children's concerns with body shape and size go beyond obesity to include children who believe they are too thin, too frail, too short, too tall, or in any way different from the idealized body. As you probably know, this kind of perception is an issue with children and adolescents with bulimia and anorexia. We need to teach children to appreciate and respect the full diversity of body sizes and shapes, to resist peer pressure, and to refrain from making comments and teasing others about their body shape or size. We need to help children feel good about their bodies, their levels of motor competence, and their participation in physical activity.

Make Physical Education a Fat-Friendly Place: Stop Stigmatizing and Teasing

Our goal in physical education is for *all* children to feel safe and welcomed and to enjoy learning, but especially children who are overweight or obese. One consistently reported problem for overweight children is stereotyping, prejudice, social stigmatizing, and weight-based teasing by peers, parents, and teachers (Greenleaf & Weiller, 2005; O'Brien, Hunter, & Banks, 2007; Puhl & Heuer, 2010; Puhl & Latner, 2007). After a review of research studies, Puhl and Latner concluded that the evidence suggests weight-related teasing rather than actual weight is responsible for problems with emotional well-being, poor body image, unhealthy eating behaviors, body dissatisfaction, and thoughts of suicide. In addition, when overweight children are teased or criticized about their weight or athletic abilities by teachers and peers, it can lead to decreased engagement in physical activity and unhealthy weight control behaviors, which often lead to weight gain (Bauer, Yang, & Austin, 2004; Puhl & Heuer, 2010; Puhl & Latner, 2007).

We need to work against stereotyping, stigmatizing, and teasing and make physical education a fat-friendly, enjoyable, emotionally safe, and stress-free setting, regardless of the participants' body shape and size, if we want all children to be physically active. People of all weights can benefit from physical activity (USDHHS, 2010b). Children and adults who are overweight can be fit and healthy. For example, moderately fit obese men do not have increased mortality rates and have lower mortality rates than unfit men who are not overweight (Brodney et al., 2000).

When children—especially those who are overweight—leave our classes, we hope they think, "I love PE. Being physically active is fun, and it is good for my health. My PE teacher believes in me and has taught me I am good at skills, games, and all of the activities we do in PE. Everyone enjoys being active together, and no one is teased or left out" (**see Figure 17.4**). One study showed that overweight students felt cared about when teachers built a personal relationship with them, maintained a positive motivational environment, differentiated instruction, and gave students choices, and when they were supported by peers (Li, Rukavina, & Kim, 2011).

Puhl and Heuer (2010) conclude, "On the basis of current findings, we propose that weight stigma is not a beneficial public health tool for reducing obesity. Rather, stigmatization of obese individuals threatens health, generates health disparities, and interferes with effective obesity intervention efforts. These findings highlight weight stigma as both a social justice issue and a priority for public health" (p. 1). Assuming weight control is simply an individual responsibility under personal control has led to greater levels of stigmatizing and stereotyping overweight students as self-indulgent, lazy, and lacking self-control. The factors that contribute to obesity are complex and include social, cultural, economic, genetic, and lifestyle factors.

Avoid Recommending Treatments

In recent years, we have been inundated with news stories about which diet is the most effective to lose weight and what you

Figure 17.4 Happily working on trunk extension in a gymnastics lesson

Courtesy of John Dolly

should and should not eat. Adult dieting is common, and many teachers have used dieting to control their own weight. The problem for teachers is that diets that may be safe for adults are not safe for children and adolescents who are still growing. In addition, dieting in children and adolescents is more likely to lead to weight gain over the long term (Neumark-Sztainer, 2005). Research on physical education and home economic teachers found that 85% recommended low-calorie diets to overweight students, a practice that can be dangerous to students' health (O'Dea & Abraham, 2001). In addition, teachers provided their students with misinformation about nutrition and dieting. The researchers suggest that teachers leave the treatment of overweight and obese students to physicians and dietitians who are certified to provide such treatment. A child's health is a complex, multifaceted issue that physical education teachers are not trained to diagnose, much less treat.

Understand the Effects of Obesity on Performance and Differentiate Instruction

As we know, it is critical to differentiate instruction to accommodate individual differences in children. With obese students, this step is necessary especially when working on cardiorespiratory endurance. Obese children do not have the equivalent aerobic capacities of lean children. When running (or doing any cardiorespiratory activity), obese children must work at a higher percentage of their aerobic capacity. For example, an overweight student may be walking with a faster heart rate than another student who is running past that individual (Kirkpatrick & Burton, 1997). Consequently, you need to base tasks for overweight and obese students on the amount of time devoted to them, not on distance or speed, and focus on more moderate-intensity levels of activity.

What the Research Says

Overweight Students' Viewpoints

In a study in which the researchers conducted in-depth interviews with overweight students, Trout and Graber (2009) found that overweight students perceived physical education to be of little value, reported negative treatment by physical education teachers, and said they disliked their peers watching them. Examples of what students (names are pseudonyms) said include the following (see the paper for many more examples):

- Ben: "The teacher would [say,] 'Well, you might want to sit this one out. You might not want to do this one. It's a little too strenuous.' I'd just get passed off and sit around. I didn't want to…it bothered me because I actually wanted to be in the game and play the game, but he'd just tell me to sit out."
- Lucas: "You always want to be, like, at least up with the group to be able to jog with somebody, you know, but I was always slow so no one would jog with me….For me it was bad. I hated it. I hated PE."
- Brianna: "I hated [fitness tests]. I would make up every excuse possible not to be there that day. It was embarrassing. You'd be the first one out [on the Pacer test], and everyone would be, like, down on you and be like, 'Huh, they can't do it; they're overweight.'"

What the Research Says

Barriers to Participation in Physical Activity

Children in general, overweight children, and girls reported the following were barriers to their participation in physical activity:

- Weight-related teasing and weight criticism during physical activity, which led to lower participation and less enjoyment (Bauer et al., 2004; Faith, Leone, Ayers, Moonseong, & Pietrobelli, 2002; Puhl & Latner, 2007)
- Negative comments by physical education teachers (Bauer et al., 2004; Faith et al., 2002; Trout & Graber, 2009)
- Competition (Trout & Graber, 2009)
- Feeling self-conscious about their bodies (Zabinski, Saelens, Stein, Hayden-Wade, & Wilfley, 2003)
- Worrying about others watching their bodies (Trout & Graber, 2009)
- Physical discomfort and emotional torment during running (Trout & Graber, 2009)
- Allowing captains to choose teams (Cardinal, Yan, & Cardinal, 2013; Trout & Graber, 2009)
- Boys dominating the playground space during recess and free play (Oliver & Hamzeh, 2010)
- Negative and critical comments by boys toward girls (Oliver & Hamzeh, 2010)
- Boys not allowing girls to play (Oliver & Hamzeh, 2010)

Health-Related Fitness and Health-Related Physical Activity Concepts

In this section, we briefly discuss the meanings of key HRF and HRPA concepts. We begin with the components of HRF and then discuss teaching HRPA and HRF to children.

Components of Fitness

What our profession considers a component of fitness has periodically changed since the Greek and Roman eras. Recall that developing fitness once included components such as lifting and carrying heavy weights, similar to weight lifting today, and also skills such as throwing a discuss and activities such as wrestling. In the 1950s, fitness included both health-related and skill- and agility-related components. Since the shift to an emphasis on health-related physical activity, the **components of fitness** have been cardiorespiratory endurance, body composition, muscular strength, muscular endurance, and flexibility. Recently, the way we view the components of fitness has changed in two significant ways.

First, it is now well established that "components of fitness change as a function of growth, maturation, development, and interactions among the three processes" (Malina, 2014, p. 165). For example, bone-strengthening activities are important components of health-related fitness for children because these activities result in stronger bones, and there is evidence that this effect remains into adulthood (ACSM, 2004). Research has yet to find a strong link between flexibility and health in children; however, flexibility, agility, and balance are important for older adults as these components of health-related fitness contribute to improved independence, mobility, and reduction of falls (Corbin et al., 2014; Plowman, 2014). Muscle power, which we discuss next, has been linked to health improvements in children and older adults, but not young adults (ACSM, 2013; Corbin et al., 2014).

The second shift in the way we view the components of fitness is that musculoskeletal fitness, or **muscle fitness**, is now viewed as multidimensional, including muscular strength, muscular endurance, power, and flexibility. Plowman (2014) explains, "Balanced healthy integrative functioning of the musculoskeletal system requires that muscles be able to exert force or torque (measured as strength), exert force quickly (measured as power), resist fatigue (measured as muscular endurance), and move freely through a full range of motion (measured as flexibility)" (p. 177). The IOM (2012b) reported adequate evidence for the relationship between this multidimensional view of muscle fitness and health.

The addition of power as an important component of fitness resulted from the report from the IOM (2012b) review of research to determine which fitness test items should be used to assess physical fitness in youth. The IOM used stringent criteria requiring research evidence that each item was linked to an aspect of health in youth and that improvements in the test item led to improvements in a marker of health. The IOM identified only two muscle fitness tests with enough evidence of markers of health-related benefits for youth. These are the standing long jump as a test of power and tests of handgrip strength. The standing long jump was linked to bone health, and handgrip strength was linked to body composition (IOM, 2012b). Adequate evidence for tests of muscle strength, muscle endurance, and flexibility has yet to be established for youth, but these components of fitness have adequate evidence of health benefits for adults (ACSM, 2013). Fitness experts anticipate the IOM report will result in the addition of tests for power in our fitness test options (Corbin et al., 2014).

Cardiorespiratory Endurance

"**Cardiorespiratory endurance** is the ability to perform large-muscle, whole-body exercise at moderate to high intensity for an extended period of time" (IOM, 2012b, pp. 7–8). To improve cardiorespiratory endurance, individuals need to do physical activities that make their hearts beat faster and make them breathe harder. Cardiorespiratory activities include sustained activities, such as jogging, biking, and jumping rope at moderate or vigorous levels, and intermittent or interval training activities. Intermittent activities are high-intensity short bouts of exercise alternating with brief periods of rest or low-intensity activity. Highly active gameplay, such as modified 3v3 soccer, hockey, and basketball; tag and chase games (see **Figure 17.5**); and dancing are physical activities that can be used to develop cardiorespiratory endurance.

Muscle Fitness: Muscle Strength, Muscle Endurance, and Muscle Power

Muscle strength is "the ability of skeletal muscle to produce force under controlled conditions" (IOM, 2012b, p. 8). Lifting a heavy weight is an example of muscle strength. **Muscle endurance** is "the ability of skeletal muscle to perform repeated contractions against a load" (IOM, 2012b, p.8). **Muscle power** is "the peak force of a skeletal muscle multiplied by the velocity of the muscle contraction" (IOM, 2012b, p. 8). A jump for height and a jump for distance use muscle power in the legs, torso, and arms.

Figure 17.5 Enjoying a tag game

Children should develop muscle fitness in all major muscle groups, including the legs, arms, and core (i.e., abdominal, back, chest, buttock, and shoulder muscles). Children typically can develop adequate levels of muscle fitness for many muscle groups by practicing skills such as jumping, hopping, kicking, throwing, and skating and by participating in games such as modified soccer, hockey, and volleyball. Many gymnastics skills also develop muscle strength and endurance for the core and upper body (see **Figure 17.6** and **Figure 17.7**). Examples include climbing, hanging from the hands with the body held in a curled position, traveling on an overhead ladder using a hand-to-hand technique, balancing on one hand and one foot with the core muscles holding the body up resembling a plank, and balancing in shapes that requires the core muscles to contract to maintain balance. Muscle power activities develop bone strength in children, including hopping, jumping, jumping rope, hopscotch, running, and some gymnastics and sport skills that involve impact with the ground.

Flexibility

Flexibility is the range of motion of the joints and connected muscles. *Stretching* is a term used synonymously with *flexibility.* Children are naturally more flexible than adults and can usually maintain adequate flexibility through games, dance, and gymnastics activities (see **Figure 17.8**).

Three types of flexibility exercises are distinguished. **Static stretches** are stretches in which the muscle, ligaments, and tendons are stretched and lengthened in a held position. Although in the past static stretches were used during warm-up activities, current recommendations are to work on static stretches only after the body is warmed up or at the end of an exercise session.

Figure 17.6 Working on core strength and endurance during gymnastics lessons

Courtesy of John Dolly © Jones & Bartlett Learning. Photographed by Sarah Cebulski. © Jones & Bartlett Learning. Photographed by Christine Myaskovsky.

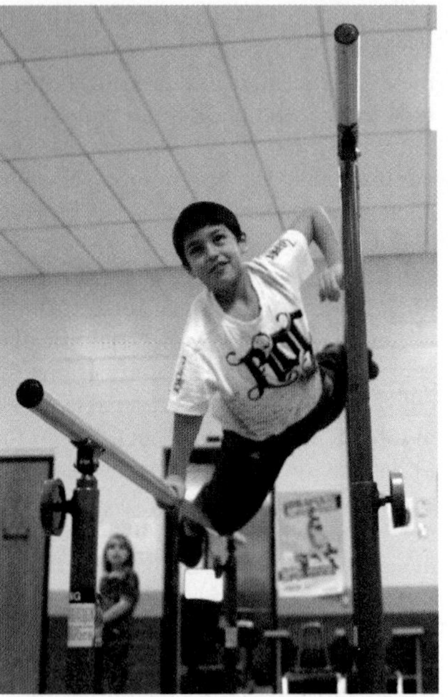

Figure 17.7 Working on arm strength in a gymnastics lesson

Courtesy of John Dolly

Because static stretching can be boring for children (Sanders & Graham, 1995) and is typically unnecessary for children's health, it is probably not a good investment of limited lesson time to work on static stretching other than for educating children about different types of flexibility exercises (Mally, 2006).

Ballistic stretches stretch the muscles by bouncing. This form of stretching is no longer recommended for any age group due to its potential for injury. **Dynamic stretches** slowly move the joints through their full range of motion to loosen the joint and eliminate any tension in the muscles. For example, in dance, dynamic stretches include drawing curved lines in all areas of your personal space. In gymnastics, children can stretch dynamically by slowly twisting and stretching to move from poly spot to poly spot on different body parts. Loosening the joints is considered an appropriate part of warm-up activities once the body has warmed up.

Body Composition

Body composition is the percentage of fat in the body in relation to the percentage of lean body tissue. For children, body composition is a controversial topic because it often is assessed by measuring skinfolds at the triceps and calf, teachers need training to obtain accurate measurements, measurements need to be taken privately, and the measurement process is time consuming.

Body mass index (BMI) often is used as a proxy for body composition because it uses a height-and-weight formula and, therefore, is simple to measure. However, for children, BMI is not reliably accurate as it can define muscular children as overweight when, in fact, they are not.

In addition, we know little about the effects of BMI measurements on children and their families' behavior, knowledge, and attitudes (Nihiser et al., 2007). The possibilities for contributing to weight stigmatization and measurement problems suggest measuring BMI in physical education needs to be either avoided or dealt with very carefully and confidentially,

Figure 17.8 Working on flexibility in a gymnastics lesson

Courtesy of John Dolly

while ensuring children and parents are given appropriate information to help them interpret the results accurately and respond in ways that are helpful and not harmful.

FITT

The acronym **FITT** is an easy way to remember four key principles of health-related physical fitness: frequency, intensity, time, and type.

Frequency and Time

Frequency refers to the number of recommended days of physical activity per week, and time refers to the recommended number of minutes devoted to such activity. For children, the current guidelines call for a minimum of 60 minutes or more of physical activity daily (USDHHS, 2008).

Intensity

Intensity is how hard you work. Intensity recommendations for cardiorespiratory endurance for children are to engage in moderate levels of physical activity daily and in vigorous intensity at least three days a week (USDHHS, 2008). Cardiorespiratory endurance intensity is measured by how fast your heart beats relative to your maximum heart rate. Heart rate can be difficult for children to measure accurately, but they can certainly feel the difference between a slow and a fast heart rate. Tell them to put two fingers under their ear and slowly move their fingers down their neck until they can feel their heartbeat.

An easy way to judge if you are doing moderate or vigorous physical activity is to think of a scale from 1 to 10, where 1 is the least amount of physical activity (such as sitting or lying down) and 10 is doing a physical activity with the most effort possible (such as sprinting as fast as you can). Moderate physical activity is a 5 or 6, and vigorous physical activity is a 7 or 8 (USDHHS, 2008). When you do moderate physical activity, your heart beats faster and you start to breathe harder and faster, but you can carry on a conversation. When you do vigorous physical activity, your heart beats a lot faster, you breathe much harder than normal, and it is more difficult to carry on a conversation.

Type of Activity and the Specificity Principle

The last T in the FITT acronym stands for **type of activity**. For children, the CDC (USDHHS, 2008) recommends four types of activities: vigorous physical activities, moderate physical activities, muscle strength and endurance activities, and muscle power activities for bone-strengthening.

The type of activity is important because of the **specificity principle**—that is, the idea that physiological changes in the body relate closely to the type of physical activity. For example, stretching exercises will not improve strength, and upper body strength exercises will not improve lower body strength. Thus, the type of activities you choose is important because different types of activities work on different areas of fitness.

The Overload and Progression Principles

The **overload principle** means that you must do more physical activity or work harder than you do at rest to improve your physical fitness. Your body adapts to an overload of work by becoming stronger or more flexible. To continue to improve in any area of fitness, you must follow the **progression principle** and work harder or longer than you did before. For both children and adults, the CDC recommendation is to increase the amount of overload gradually, as this approach lessens the risk of injury.

Performance Techniques

For safe and effective movement, it is important to teach children the performance techniques of movements used in fitness activities. Many fitness performance techniques originated from ballet and Olympic gymnastics performance techniques. For example, in relation to fitness these include:

- Appropriate body alignment, such as keeping the legs straight but not hyperextended when they are supposed to be straight and keeping the knees aligned with the feet (turned in or out to the exact same degree)
- Landing lightly with control over body parts and over flow of movement, such as landing lightly with resilient, spring-like landings in aerobic dance routines
- Elongating the spine, which is important in many fitness exercises and for healthy, everyday posture
- Engaging the core to support the spine and develop core strength, which are important in many health-related fitness activities and linked to a healthy back and preventing back pain
- Using appropriate speed and force, which means learning to travel only as fast and move only as forcefully as you can while still maintaining perfect control so you can stop the action or change direction safely.

Teaching HRPA Concepts

National Standard 3 and state curriculum standards recommend teaching children basic HRPA and HRF concepts. The intent is for children to acquire a sound knowledge base, which they can then enhance in middle and high school. In addition, the hope is that knowledge about HRPA and HRF will increase the amount of physical activity in childhood and lead to good health habits that will last a lifetime. Unfortunately, a review of research has found that students at the elementary, middle, and high school levels lack adequate HRF knowledge (Keating et al., 2009).

To date, research has not identified which HRPA concepts are developmentally appropriate to teach at the elementary school level and which we should leave for middle and high school, when students are cognitively and emotionally more mature, are better able to handle complex and negative information, and can understand how scientific knowledge is tentative and always evolving. For example, we don't know if teaching about risk factors of inactivity or obesity is helpful or—more likely—harmful for children, although such education can be helpful for adults. At the end of this section, we provide a list of commonly taught HRPA concepts that we believe are developmentally appropriate for elementary school children.

The problem with teaching cognitive content is that it can take time away from physical activity and make it difficult to meet the criteria of 50% of class time spent doing moderate to vigorous physical activity. Some fitness experts note that classrooms are better environments for teaching cognitive concepts and suggest that the limited time we have in the gymnasium and outdoors should be dedicated to motor skill development and physical activity (McKenzie, 2003). Research also has shown, however, that when teachers have taught HRPA concepts in constructivist-oriented, physically active lessons, children learned the information and were still physically active at least 50% of the time (Chen, Martin, Sun, & Ennis, 2007; Ennis, 2010). Moreover, they learned the scientific principles related to exercise physiology that explain why physical activity is beneficial and how intensity and heart rate contribute to improved cardiorespiratory endurance (Ennis, 2014). Teaching the scientific principles added situational interest (Chen, Darst, & Pangrazi, 2001) to the activities and contributed to a deeper understanding. At the end of this chapter, we provide a sample plan to illustrate how to teach concepts during skill development lessons (see **Sample Plan 17.2**).

Teaching HRPA concepts need not take long stretches of time. If you teach one major concept per lesson well through brief discussions, worksheets, and physically active experiments or illustrative tasks, and then build on and extend that knowledge across many lessons, children can learn critical HRPA concepts by the end of the elementary school years. For example, you can teach the different areas of fitness; repeatedly ask children to connect those areas to different activities in games, gymnastics, and dance lessons throughout the year; and periodically have children complete worksheets that require them to apply their knowledge. Worksheet assignments have been shown to be effective and critical for children's learning of health-related fitness concepts (Hong, Chen, Chen, Zhang, Loflin, & Ennis, 2011; Loflin, Chen, Hong, Chen, Zhang, & Ennis, 2011). Continue to build children's knowledge structures until they know the areas of fitness well and can identify a wide range of activities for working on each area. Simply defining the areas of fitness during one lesson will not lead to robust knowledge structures; this information must be repeated and reinforced to ensure long-term learning.

As with all content, you need to assess knowledge of HRPA at the conclusion of lessons or units and periodically across the year to determine whether the children have truly learned the concepts. In addition to teacher-designed cognitive assessments, you can use the *PE Metrics* (NASPE, 2010b) standardized tests for cognitive knowledge of National Standard 3 to assess your students' knowledge at grades 2 and 5 and to identify whether the children have met critical HRPA knowledge outcomes. You will also need to include questions from *PE Metrics* in the section related to the previous National Standard 4, which dealt with HRPA.

Children's Prior Knowledge and Misconceptions

You can plan more effective lessons if you are aware of children's current knowledge levels and the possibility of their holding misconceptions about the content you are about to teach. In general, children do not know much about health-related fitness and they often have misconceptions about this subject (Keating et al., 2009). Research shows that, in or by the end of elementary school (Burrows et al., 2002; Desmond, Price, Lock, Smith, & Stewart, 1990; Friedlander & Ennis, 2011; Kiefer, 2008; Kulinna, 2004; Merkle & Treagust, 1993; Placek et al., 2001),

- Students know exercise is good for you and improves health.
- Students have problems defining cardiorespiratory endurance, muscular endurance and strength, and flexibility.
- Students have problems identifying activities that can improve each area of fitness.
- Students inaccurately identify activities for improving cardiorespiratory endurance and strength.
- Students know little about FITT principles.
- Students do not know the guideline for children to be physically active 60 minutes or more per day.

The same research sources also report that popular culture and the media influence children's knowledge, such that they often believe the following misconceptions:

- Being fit is the same as looking good and being thin.
- If you are not overweight, you are fit.
- Girls should be slender and boys muscular.
- Spot reduction works (e.g., doing sit-ups will decrease abdominal fat).
- If girls lift weights, they will gain big muscles.
- To burn fat, you should wear extra clothes.
- No pain, no gain.
- If you are running out of breath, you are losing your energy.
- It is bad if your heart beats fast because you will lose your breath, run out of breath, or have a heart attack.

These kinds of misconceptions can be very difficult to change. Students do not simply drop their prior beliefs and whole-heartedly embrace the alternative explanations teachers offer. Thus, teachers need to find ways to help students recognize misconceptions, understand how misconceptions can develop, and offer more compelling information that students will accept as a better explanation. For example, the misconception about spot reduction has been around at least since the 1950s, despite scientific evidence that it is untrue.

There is no avoiding popular culture and the media. Nevertheless, two studies with upper-elementary-grade girls show you can help children learn to identify and critique cultural conceptions and identify and confront barriers such students experience in being physically active (Oliver & Hamzeh, 2010; Oliver et al., 2009). You can do this by having students collect and critique advertisements from print media and discuss the myths these advertisements promote. Students can discuss with partners and the whole group the barriers they experience to participating in physical activity and potential ways to overcome these barriers. They can also discuss in journals their positive and negative experiences with the social expectations and biases of others.

Overview of Key HRPA and HRF Concepts to Teach

This box summarizes key HRPA and HRF concepts that you can teach at the elementary school level.

A. Benefits

Physical activity and physical fitness are good for everyone's health, from children to older folks. Being active and fit helps the heart, lungs, muscles, and bones be stronger. For example, HRF helps children play longer, throw farther, dribble longer, kick farther, leap higher, and balance longer. If you build strong bones as a child, you will have stronger bones as an adult. Physical activity can enhance concentration and attention in school. Fit children feel better physically and emotionally. Physical activity should be a fun, healthy, lifelong habit.

B. Meeting the Guidelines for Physical Activity for Children

1. Children need to do
   - "60 minutes (one hour) or more of physical activity daily."
   - "Most of those 60 or more minutes should be either moderate- or vigorous-intensity aerobic physical activity at least three days a week."
   - "At least three days a week, children should do muscle strengthening activities and bone strengthening activities." (USDHHS, 2008, p. vii)
2. You can monitor the amount of physical activity you get by keeping a physical activity log and by wearing a pedometer.
3. You can increase the amount of physical activity you get by setting goals and making a plan for doing a variety of fun physical activities after school and on weekends. When you don't like a game or physical activity, modify it to make it work for you. Say positive things to yourself when you engage in physical activity. When you increase your physical activity, pat yourself on the back for your effort and success. Remember, it is your responsibility for improving your level of physical activity and fitness; no one can do it for you.
4. To participate in HRPA, you can go outside and play; go to a park and play; do physical activities with your parents, friends, or siblings; participate in youth sports; participate in activities offered by the town recreational department, YMCA, churches, temples, or boys and girls clubs; join martial arts or gymnastics clubs; join a swim team; or take dance lessons. You can also help with house and yard work, such as raking leaves.
5. Learn which opportunities you have for physical activity in your community.
6. Remember it is harder to be physically active
   - If your friends and family are not physically active.
   - If there are no indoor recreation facilities near your home.
   - If there are no outdoor spaces near your home that are safe.
7. Remember that if you have too much screen time (watching TV and using computers), this contributes to having less physical activity and more inactivity.
8. The goal of HRPA and HRF is to improve health. Media portrayals of the so-called "perfect body" set unrealistic standards and focus on looking good, rather than being healthy.

C. Cardiorespiratory Endurance

1. Cardiorespiratory endurance is the ability to perform whole-body exercise for a long time, working your heart and lungs.
2. Your heart is a muscle about the size of your fist located in your chest.
3. Your heart needs exercise for health.
4. When you work on cardiorespiratory endurance, you are able to move faster and for longer periods of time. When you move faster, your heart beats faster, you breathe faster and harder, and you sweat. These are positive signs of the effects of exercise; they are not negative signs that something is wrong. Moving faster and for longer amounts of time promotes a healthier heart.
5. You can feel your heartbeat by touching the carotid artery in your neck (or feeling the pulse in your wrist). To feel your carotid heartbeat, put your index and middle fingers under your ear and slide them down your neck slowly until you feel your heartbeat.

D. Intensity Levels

1. Intensity means the amount of effort you use during an activity.
2. There are two levels of intensity—moderate and vigorous—that exercise the cardiorespiratory system.
3. You are working at a moderate intensity level if your heart rate and breathing increase but you can still carry on a conversation. You are working at a vigorous intensity level if your heartbeat and breathing rates increase significantly and you have difficulty carrying on a conversation.

E. Moderate and Vigorous Activities for Building Cardiorespiratory Endurance

1. Moderate-intensity activities include walking or biking at a moderate pace to school, skateboarding, skating at a moderate pace, and hiking.
2. Vigorous-intensity activities include skating or biking at a fast pace or up hills, running, jumping rope, doing karate, and playing games that involve running, such as tag, soccer, hockey, and basketball (small-sided games).
3. Sedentary activities do not help you become physically fit because they do not increase your heart rate, breathing rate, muscular strength, endurance, bone strength, or flexibility. Examples include standing and sitting motionless, sitting and watching television, sitting and playing on the computer, playing board games, and reading.
4. Learn to rate different activities as sedentary, moderate, or vigorous.

(*continues*)

Overview of Key HRPA and HRF Concepts to Teach (*continued*)

F. Muscle Fitness

1. Muscle fitness has three components: strength, power, and endurance. Muscle strength means your muscles can exert force, muscle power means you can exert force quickly, and muscle endurance means your muscles can resist fatigue and repeatedly lift a weight.
2. Increasing your muscle fitness will help you perform skills better. You will throw farther, kick harder, and jump higher. Greater muscle fitness can also help you in emergencies. For example, muscle strength and power will help you pull yourself out of a window in a flipped bus or car.
3. Working on muscle power strengthens your bones. To strengthen your bones, you need to do activities in which you generate force quickly, such as jumping for height or distance and making contact with the ground with force, such as hopping, hopscotch, and modified games, such as volleyball, basketball, and racket sports.
4. The more you move and use the muscles of a body part, the healthier it is for your body. Using strong force as part of your physical activity will increase your muscle fitness. For example, in gymnastics, creating hard-to-hold shapes makes the muscles you are using stronger.
5. You need to develop muscle fitness in all the major muscle groups, including the legs, arms, and core (abdominal, back, shoulder, chest, and buttock muscles).
6. Learn to rate different activities as good or poor for muscle fitness for each major muscle group.

G. Flexibility

1. Flexibility means moving through the full range of motion of your joints and muscles.
2. Stretching increases flexibility. We work on flexibility when we stretch, twist, bend, arch, and circle our joints during different movements in dance and gymnastics lessons.
3. Flexibility allows you to make a wider variety of body shapes and improves dance skills such as leaping, many gymnastics skills, and sport skills such as punting.
4. Work to improve flexibility only after your body has warmed up.

H. Body Composition

Body composition is the percentage of fat versus lean body tissue (muscles, bones, and organs) in your body.

1. Keeping these percentages in a healthy zone has health benefits.

I. FITT

To increase muscle fitness, flexibility, and cardiorespiratory endurance, you have to apply the FITT principle:

1. Frequency: Daily
2. Intensity: Moderate to vigorous
3. Time: 60 minutes or more
4. Type: Moderate and vigorous aerobic activities daily; muscle fitness, especially bone strengthening, at least three times per week

J. Overload and Progression Principles

Overload means doing more physical activity than you do at rest. You have to be willing to challenge yourself physically to have a healthier heart and strong bones and muscles. When you overload, you become stronger. To continue to progress, you need to increase the workload and overload to a new, higher level.

K. Specificity Principle

Exercise helps improve only the specific area of fitness and muscle groups you are working. If you want to improve heart endurance, for example, you need to work the heart so it beats faster, and you need to work the heart longer. If you want to improve a muscle, you must work on that muscle. Doing a skill that uses only your legs will not help you improve arm strength. Hanging by your hands and traveling on an overhead bar will not improve your leg strength.

L. Making an After-School Plan

To improve cardiorespiratory endurance, muscle fitness for the major muscle groups, and flexibility, you can make a plan for after-school physical activity that includes activities specific for each area of fitness and each major muscle group. Even children who live in environments where they must remain inside due to lack of safe outdoor play areas can develop after-school plans. You will need to teach children examples of activities that can be done indoors and then teach them how to design their own activities and relevant after-school plans that work in their environment.

M. Water

Drinking a lot of water is important for your health. You want to be hydrated, not dehydrated. When you exercise, drinking water helps you replace the liquids you lose when you sweat.

N. Social Responsibility

When you are playing with others, both in and after school, it is important to help your peers by being supportive, encouraging, and focusing on everyone having fun. Eliminate all teasing. Never make fun of or comment on someone's weight; accept everyone's and your own body shape and size. What matters is not how you look on the outside, but how healthy you are. Everyone can be physically active and healthy.

Nutrition and Healthy Eating

In addition to physical activity, healthy eating is a lifestyle choice that can decrease your risk of disease. Unfortunately, multiple research studies report that children eat more solid fats and sugar and less whole grains, dairy, vegetables, and fruit than is recommended by the government guidelines and consequently are not getting nutrients such as calcium, fiber, potassium, and vitamin D, which decrease the risk of disease (Ogata & Hayes, 2014). Children have less control over what they eat than adults because children do not purchase or plan family meals or control the foods served at school. Even so, they can learn about healthy eating, and this knowledge can then influence their food choices and lead to healthier eating. The goal, as with physical activity, is to instill healthy eating habits in children at an early age, with the hope that these habits will continue through adolescence and adulthood.

In this section, we discuss basic nutrition concepts. Many Internet sites also offer nutrition information and lesson plans for children. The U.S. government site ChooseMyPlate.gov (http://www.choosemyplate.gov) describes the guidelines established for Americans and offers tips for healthy eating; interactive tools for tracking what you eat daily and weekly; menu planning; printable posters and signs with tips for children and families; activities, games, and assignments for children and families; and suggestions for teachers. The Health Canada site provides similar information and guidelines (http://www.healthcanada.gc.ca/foodguide).

Food Groups

MyPlate (see **Figure 17.9**) was developed by the U.S. Department of Agriculture (USDA) Food and Nutrition Service (2011). It illustrates the five food groups and the proportions of each to eat daily; notice that half the plate consists of vegetables and fruits, with the amount of vegetables being larger than the amount for fruits. Protein is only a small portion of the plate. Compare the size of the protein and vegetable portions on MyPlate with the amount of protein and vegetables that restaurants typically serve, and you can appreciate the value of MyPlate as a teaching tool. Next, we describe each food group and the MyPlate tips.

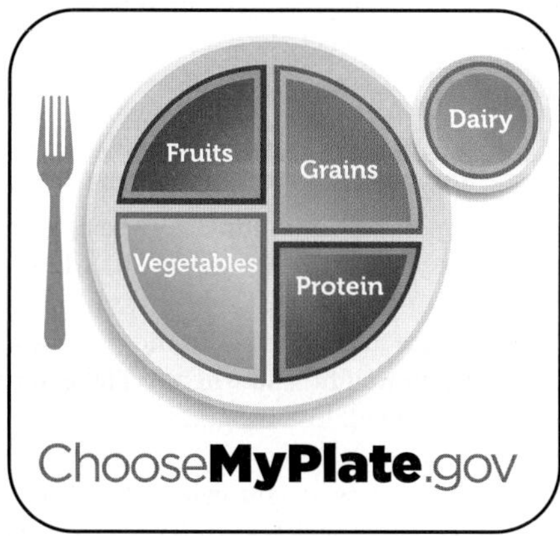

Figure 17.9 MyPlate

Source: Courtesy of the USDA

Grains: "Make Half Your Grains Whole"

The grains most often consumed in the United States are wheat, rice, cornmeal, and oats, which are typically baked, cooked, or processed into breads, cereals, tortillas, pastas, pancakes, biscuits, cornbread, crackers, pitas, and other grain products. MyPlate recommends that half the grains eaten daily be whole grains, such as brown rice, whole wheat, and rolled oats. You can tell whether a product is made of whole grains by reading the label and looking for the word "whole" before the name of the grain. Don't be fooled by products labeled as containing "wheat flour"; this term simply means flour, not whole-wheat flour.

Vegetables: "Vary Your Veggies"

Vegetables can be raw or cooked. They include the following choices:

- Dark green (e.g., broccoli, spinach, dark green lettuce, bok choy, collards)
- Red and orange (e.g., carrots, sweet potatoes, butternut squash, red peppers, tomatoes)
- Beans and peas (e.g., black-eyed peas, chickpeas, pinto beans, split peas)
- Starchy (e.g., corn, peas, potatoes)
- Other (e.g., asparagus, beets, bean sprouts, green beans, green peppers, okra, yellow squash, zucchini)

All vegetables are nutritious, but the vegetables with the most vitamins and lowest number of calories are dark green vegetables, carrots, and tomatoes.

Fruits: "Focus on Fruits"

Fruits can be fresh, canned, frozen, or dried (such as raisins, dried cranberries, and prunes). Juice, if it is 100% fruit juice, counts as a serving of fruit. Juice can be high in calories, however, and it does not contain the fiber that whole fruits have.

Milk: "Get Your Calcium-Rich Foods"

Milk products are important for children because they provide the calcium needed for bone growth and bone density. Milk products include milk, cheese, yogurt, puddings (made with milk), frozen yogurt, and ice cream. MyPlate guidelines recommend consuming skim or 1% milk, low-fat or fat-free yogurts, and low-fat cheese.

Meats and Beans: "Go Lean with Protein"

The meats and beans group is important because these foods are major sources of protein. It includes meat, poultry, seafood, eggs, dry beans, tofu, nuts, and seeds. MyPlate recommends eating a variety of proteins, including eating seafood at least once a week. For meats and poultry, MyPlate recommends choosing lean or low-fat options.

Oils

Oils are not a food group, but they are an important part of the diet. Oils are liquid at room temperature and are highly unsaturated (e.g., monounsaturated, polyunsaturated) and low in saturated fats. Fats are solid at room temperature and are more saturated. The term *saturated* refers to the chemical composition of a fat or oil and expresses the extent to which the molecules are "saturated" with hydrogen. Saturated fats, such as butter and the fat you see on meats, are linked with increased levels of "bad" (low-density lipoprotein [LDL]) cholesterol and can increase the risk of heart disease. Unsaturated oils come from vegetables (e.g., olives, corn, canola, soybeans). Oils are sometimes processed by adding hydrogen to them (i.e., making them "hydrogenated"), a process that increases the amount of trans fats, which in turn increases the level of LDL ("bad") cholesterol.

While some oil is essential to healthy eating, most Americans eat far more fats and oils than they need. Eating too much fat and oil can lead to increased weight. Unfortunately, fats and oils are often what make food taste good. Solid fats are in many of our favorite foods, such as ice cream, bacon, steak, regular ground beef, cookies, doughnuts, and pastries. Favorite, tasty foods are why many people have problems decreasing the amount of fat from their diet.

Nutrients: Carbohydrates, Proteins, Fats, Vitamins, Minerals, and Water

Foods provide nutrients for the body. Four categories of macronutrients have been identified: protein, fats, carbohydrates, and water. In addition, foods may contain a variety of micronutrients, including vitamins, minerals, and trace elements (Jeykendrup & Gleeson, 2010).

To get a general idea of how the body uses nutrients, imagine your body is a house. Proteins supply the materials for the walls, floor, and roof. For example, your muscles and organs are constructed mostly of proteins. We need protein not only for growth and for development in childhood but also throughout life for the repair and maintenance of body tissues.

Carbohydrates are like the wood you burn in the fireplace for heat or the electricity you use for lights and heat. Carbohydrates provide the energy your body burns for growth and daily living. They include simple sugars and complex carbohydrates, such as the starches in grains, beans, peas, and potatoes. Carbohydrates also include fiber, which is important for healthy digestion.

Fats are like the insulation of the house. They store energy and provide a layer of protection to prevent injury to vital organs. Fats also help with the absorption of the fat-soluble vitamins, A, D, E, and K, which are stored in fat.

Vitamins and minerals are like the key to the door. They don't provide energy to live, but without the keys (i.e., vitamins and minerals), you can't get in the door. You need vitamins and minerals for the chemical processes that enable your body to use the fats, carbohydrates, and proteins you eat. Critical vitamins and minerals include vitamin A, which helps protect your eyes, helps with night vision, and contributes to healthy skin and fighting off infections. Vitamin C helps with healing and healthy gums. Vitamin D and calcium contribute to strong bones and teeth. Iron is used in the process of carrying oxygen in your blood. Potassium is used in the muscles and nervous system. Sometimes when you have muscle cramps, this is due to too little potassium and calcium in your body and dehydration.

Water is the water in the house. Keeping your body well hydrated by drinking plenty of water is essential when exercising because you lose water from your body when you sweat.

As part of a healthy diet, you need all the nutrients in the same way your house needs walls, heat, insulation, water, and a key to get in the door.

Fiber

Fiber is a plant substance. Inclusion of increased amounts of fiber in the diet is associated with decreased risk of some cancers, cardiovascular disease, type 2 diabetes, and constipation (Jeykendrup & Gleeson, 2010). We get fiber from fruits, vegetables, and whole grains that include the bran. High-fiber foods also can help you feel full. Because they add bulk, they can help delay hunger between meals. Fiber is not digested, but it helps food move through the digestive tract.

Salt and Sodium

Fats, sweets, and salt are ingredients that make foods taste good. Unfortunately, Americans eat far more salt each day than is needed for good health. Salt is 40% sodium. The MyPlate guideline recommends a maximum intake of 2,300 mg of sodium per day. We get most of our sodium in processed foods, to which it is added to improve taste.

To decrease sodium consumption, don't add salt to foods. Read labels. Limit your consumption of high-sodium foods, such as bacon, hot dogs, salted chips, and luncheon meats. Rely on fresh fruits and vegetables without adding high-sodium sauces and dressings.

Principles of Healthy Eating: Moderation, Variety, and Balance

Nutritionists have long described three principles of healthy eating: moderation, variety, and balance. Moderation in eating means being reasonable, not going to extremes such as eliminating forever every food that is high in fat or sugar, and not eating any food in excess (Insel, Turner, & Ross, 2010). You can eat reasonable amounts of ice cream, candy, and cake—sometimes. Eating should satisfy hunger and not be a stressful experience of guilt and denial. You can have healthy eating habits and enjoy delicious meals with occasional special treats.

Variety means eating many different kinds of foods within and across each food group on a daily and weekly basis. Not only does variety prevent boredom, but it will help you get all the vitamins, minerals, proteins, trace elements, and other nutrients that are needed to ensure good health (Insel et al., 2010).

Balance means eating the right amount of food in the right proportions of carbohydrates, protein, and fat that your body needs to maintain your organs, repair and replenish cells, and be active in daily life (Insel et al., 2010).

Energy Balance

Energy balance means that your energy intake, that is, the food you eat, equals your energy expenditure, that is, the energy needed for basal metabolism (your body's basic physiological functions, such as repairing cell damage, building new cells, and growth), digesting food, and daily physical activity. When there is an imbalance and you take in more energy than you expend, you will gain weight, and when you take in less energy than you expend, you will lose weight.

For children, energy balance "supports normal growth without promoting excess weight gain" (IOM, 2013, p. 387). Energy imbalance is critical for understanding obesity. "A fundamental principle in the study of obesity is that changes in body weight are the direct result of a chronic, positive imbalance between EI [energy intake] and EE [energy expenditure]" (Shook, Hand, & Blair, 2014, p. 55).

On the surface, energy balance appears to be a simple concept meaning that to lose weight, you simply need to eat fewer calories and exercise more. This apparent simplicity has led to widespread misconceptions due to the fact that energy intake and energy expenditure are interdependent, and changes in intake or expenditures lead to compensation in the other (Hafekost, Lawrence, Mitrou, O'Sullivan, & Zubrick, 2013). In other words, when calorie intake is reduced, the body compensates by decreasing calories spent (e.g., by reducing basal metabolism), and when calories spent are increased through exercise, the body compensates by reducing energy expenditure and/or increasing calorie intake (e.g., by increasing hunger). For example, using the rule that 3,500 calories equals one pound of body weight and using the simplified energy balance equation of calorie intake minus calories spent equals the amount of weight loss, you would predict that an individual who spends an extra 100 calories per day by walking one mile for five years would lose 50 pounds; however, actual weight loss in such a case is about 10 pounds (Casazza et al., 2013). The compensatory mechanisms when an increase in calorie expenditure occurs protect against weight loss. Other research shows a workout at moderate intensity and a workout at high intensity can be equal in the number of calories expended but have different effects on the hormones that affect appetite and consequently cause increased food intake (Shook et al., 2014). Research on weight loss programs of dieting combined with exercise most often show short-term success but long-term failure to maintain weight loss. This long-term failure can be attributed to long-term compensation for weight loss by neural and hormonal factors (Hafekost et al., 2013). It appears that the compensatory mechanisms that protect against weight loss do more than the compensatory mechanisms that protect against weight gain. Hafekost et al. (2013) warn that promoting a simplified energy balance model that is unlikely to succeed in diet-and-exercise weight control programs is unproductive and can be discouraging to individuals trying to lose weight.

Calorie-Dense, Nutrient-Poor Foods

Calorie-dense, nutrient-poor foods are high in calories, sugars, and/or salt but low in healthy nutrients, such as dietary fiber, protein, vitamins, and minerals. Calorie-dense, nutrient-poor foods are also called "junk" foods or empty-calorie foods. Soft drinks, candy, and sweet snacks made with highly refined flour and lots of sugar are empty-calorie "junk" foods because they offer few to no nutrients and are high in calories. Highly salted, fried foods such as chips, pork rinds, Cheetos, and cheese puffs are frequently considered junk foods as well.

The problems with high-sugar, high-fat foods is that they fill children up and then they don't eat the nutrients they need for healthy eating. In addition, high-sugar foods and drinks contribute to dental cavities and weight gain.

Nutritionists recommend that teachers do not label foods as bad, good, or junk, because all foods can be part of a healthy diet. As discussed earlier, the key is moderation, variety, and balance, while limiting the intake of high-sugar foods and soft drinks. Calorie-dense, nutrient-poor foods can be eaten on occasion, but they should not make up the bulk of a child's diet. MyPlate educational materials label these foods "sometimes foods."

Fast Food

Fast food is food that can be purchased quickly, typically at a low cost. The fast-food industry has been heavily criticized in documentaries and in the press for its contribution to rising rates of obesity. The problem for families living in low-income, urban environments is that fast food from restaurants, convenience stores, and service stations is often the only food that is easily accessible.

When families rely on fast food for several meals per week, their overall pattern of nutrition is a problem. This pattern includes limited or no fruits, vegetables, and whole grains; high-calories sauces (e.g., dipping sauces, salad dressings, sauces on sandwiches and hamburgers); the prevalence of fried food; and large portion sizes. Recently enacted legislation in many states has required fast-food restaurants to post the calorie content and nutritional information for their products, which can help families make wise choices when purchasing these foods.

Reading Food Labels

Reading the information on food labels is one way for children to learn more about the foods they eat. For example, children can read labels and compare and contrast

- The extent to which two different foods provide the healthy nutrients of dietary fiber, protein, vitamins A and C, calcium, and/or iron
- The amount of sodium, total fat, trans fat, saturated fat, and/or cholesterol in two different foods
- The number of calories and total fat of several foods from different food groups

The Academy of Nutrition and Dietetics (2014) offers a guide for how to read food labels. They suggest you start with the serving size and the number of servings in the package. This information is critical because, using crackers as an example, it may appear that two different crackers have the same number of calories per cracker. However, the label on the first box states there are 100 calories in a serving of 15 crackers, whereas the label on the second box states there are 100 calories in a serving of only 10 crackers. Thus, crackers in the second box have more calories per cracker than the crackers in the first box. To know that the crackers in the second box have more calories, you need to look at both the number of calories and the serving size.

A second suggestion is to use the percent daily values to help you know how much of a particular nutrient fills your daily needs. The problem with daily food values are that they are based on a 2,000-calorie-per-day plan and the number of calories needed for an average adult male, which is not accurate for women or children. Nevertheless, the Academy of Nutrition and Dietetics (2014) suggests that when a percent of the daily value is 5% or less, you know that this food does not provide much of that nutrient. When the percent is 20% or higher, the food provides a good amount of that nutrient for one serving for one meal or snack for the day.

In addition, they suggest children learn that the list of ingredients on the package is in order from largest amount to smallest amount. Knowing which ingredient is largest can be helpful in making decisions about whether a food contributes to healthy eating. For example, if sugar or one of the forms of sugar, such as high-fructose corn syrup, corn syrup, sucrose, or honey is listed first or second, this means that the food is high in added sugars. **Figure 17.10** provides a sample food label.

Nutrition and Ethnicity

Different cultures worldwide have different diets and rely on different foods for their primary nutrients. For example, rice makes up the bulk of the diet in Southeast Asia, corn in South America, and cassava in parts of Africa (Insel et al., 2010).

Geography has traditionally influenced the foods that develop as part of a culture. For example, people who lived in cold climates kept fires burning all day long for heat. In turn, they prepared foods such as stews, soups, and jams that required long, slow cooking. People who lived where fuel was scarce developed ways to cook foods quickly, such as cooking fresh vegetables, seafood, and meats cut in small pieces quickly over high heat in woks in Southeast Asia. In addition, different foods were indigenous to different parts of the globe, as were different spices and seasonings. These traditional, geographically influenced foods became part of different cultures handed down from generation to generation.

The enormous variety of foods that developed across the globe has given people today a wondrous choice of foods to eat and enjoy. North American is a multicultural society and, as a result, many different ethnic foods are available.

This diversity has implications for teachers. When teaching about nutrition, we need to be sensitive to the cultural and physical environments in which children live and not promote only one set of foods or criticize foods associated with certain children's cultures. In addition, we can promote respect for diversity by teaching children about different ethnic foods and possibly making a variety of foods available for sampling.

Nutrition Facts

Serving Size 1/2 cup (120g)
Servings Per Container About 3.5

Amount Per Serving	
Calories 50	Calories from Fat 0
	% Daily Value*
Total Fat 0g	**0%**
Saturated Fat 0g	**0%**
Trans Fat 0g	
Cholesterol 0mg	**0%**
Sodium 10mg	**1%**
Total Carbohydrate 11g	**4%**
Dietary Fiber less than 3g	**12%**
Sugars 4g	
Protein 2g	

Vitamin A 280% • Vitamin C 8% • Calcium 4% • Iron 4%

Percent Daily Values are based on a 2,000 calorie diet. Your daily values may be higher or lower depending on your calorie needs:

	Calories	2,000	2,500
Total Fat	Less than	65g	80g
Sat. Fat	Less than	20g	25g
Cholesterol	Less than	300mg	300mg
Sodium	Less than	2,400mg	2,400mg
Total Carbohydrate		300g	375g
Dietary Fiber		25g	30g

Figure 17.10 Nutrition Facts (food label)

Overview of Nutrition Concepts to Teach

This box summarizes the nutrition concepts you can teach at the elementary school level.

A. The Five Food Groups

Children need to know the five food groups, be able to identify examples of foods from each food group, and understand that they should eat foods from the five food groups every day to get all the nutrients they need for health:

1. Grains (e.g., rice, breads, cereals, pastas, tortillas). Make half your grains whole grains.
2. Vegetables (e.g., carrots, broccoli, spinach, lettuce, tomatoes, sweet potatoes, bok choy, peas). Try to eat a variety of vegetables, especially dark green, red, and orange vegetables.
3. Fruits (e.g., oranges, apples, peaches, strawberries, plums, raisins, dried cranberries). Try to eat fruit every day.
4. Drink and eat calcium-rich foods (e.g., milk, yogurt, cheese) several times every day. Drink 2%, 1%, or skim milk. Eat low-fat or fat-free yogurt and cheese.
5. Eat protein every day (e.g., meat, poultry, eggs, dry beans, and nuts). Choose lean meats.

B. MyPlate

Children need to understand the meaning of MyPlate. They need to recognize the five food groups on MyPlate and understand the portion sizes recommended. Even before children learn fractions and percentages, they can understand that fruits and vegetables should cover half their plate. They also need to learn to select food for meals that meet the portion recommendations of MyPlate.

Overview of Nutrition Concepts to Teach (*continued*)

C. Variety, Balance, and Moderation

Children need to know it is important to eat a variety of foods within each food group. This will help them get all the nutrients they need, including vitamins and minerals. Moderation is the key. Don't think of foods as "good" or "bad." You can eat all foods as an occasional treat, but focus on eating healthy food. Eat a balanced diet, but if you need to prevent weight gain, pay attention to the number of calories you eat in a day.

D. A Calorie Is a Unit of Energy

In general, the number of calories in food tells you the amount of energy the food provides and the amount of energy you need to expend to use those calories. The equation isn't perfect. The body will compensate for weight loss by using fewer calories or increasing hunger. Our bodies have this compensation mechanism because many years ago, before there were cities and before there was agriculture, humans were hunters and gathers. They didn't plant food where they lived; rather, they traveled and searched for food and game. Some years, humans could not find enough plants and animals. In these lean years, humans who lost too much weight quickly starved to death, and those who lost less weight lived and passed on their genes to humans today. We don't need to hunt and gather food, but we still have the genes that protect us against lean years; only now those genes contribute to overweight and obesity.

E. Calorie-Dense, Nutrient-Poor Foods Versus Nutrient-Dense, Low-Calorie Foods

Children need to understand that some foods have a lot of calories (i.e., calorie-dense foods) and very few nutrients, so they are called empty-calorie foods. Examples are candy, cake, doughnuts, Cheetos, cheese puffs, and pork rinds. Eat these foods only occasionally. MyPlate calls these "sometimes foods." Other foods are low in calories and high in nutrients that are good for you, such as vitamins, minerals, fiber, and protein. Examples of nutrient-dense foods are vegetables, low-fat milk, fruit, whole-grain breads, cereals, and tortillas. For healthy eating, focus on the nutrient-dense, low-calorie foods. The problem with eating foods high in sugar and fat it that these foods can fill you up and not leave any room for healthy foods that give you the nutrients you need to be healthy.

F. Healthy Eating

Children need to understand how to improve their diet so that they eat a more healthy diet (USDHHS, 2010b):

1. Reduce and limit your intake of sodas and juices with added sugars (such as Gatorade).
2. Reduce and limit your intake of foods that are high in fat and/or high in added sugars.
3. Eat more fruits, vegetables, whole grains, and lean proteins.
4. Control the size of your portions.
5. Drink more water.
6. Choose low-fat or nonfat dairy products.
7. Avoid calorie-dense, nutrient-poor foods.

G. Self-Regulating Food Intake

Children need to learn to self-regulate the amount of food they eat based on what their body needs, not on the size of the plate or the size of the portions given. Self-regulation means they must pay attention to the difference between feeling hungry and feeling full and satisfied. Eat when you are hungry; stop when you are satisfied.

H. Compare and Contrast Snacks

Children need to learn to identify snacks that contribute to healthy eating and those that can undermine healthy eating. They need to learn to determine the number of calories, the number of empty calories, and the amount of sodium in processed, purchased snacks. It is also helpful for establishing healthy eating if children learn to make healthy snacks themselves.

I. Sources of Healthy Nutrients and Healthy Fats

Children ought to be able to identify foods that are high in fiber, calcium, and protein, which are connected to good health. Understanding the reverse is also important, that is, being able to identify foods that provide large amounts of fat, sugar, and salt and therefore need to be regulated. There are two kinds of fats: solid and liquid. Solid fats, like butter and the fat you see on meat, can make it harder for your heart to pump blood through your arteries and veins, which can get clogged, in part from eating too many solid fats. Liquid fats, like corn oil, olive oil, peanut oil, and canola oil, are better for your heart.

J. Food Labels

Children should be able to compare and contrast different foods based on information from the food label on the package and the ingredient list and determine which foods are more healthful choices.

K. Trying New Foods

Children need to know that sometimes it takes eight or more times of tasting a new food before they learn that they like it. We suggest a "two-bite adventure," in which children take two small bites of a food to try it out. You can keep a poster on the wall on which children report when they successfully learned to like a new food by using the two-bite adventure.

L. Appreciating Cultural Differences

Children need to understand and value cultural difference in what people eat.

MyPlate for Kids

The MyPlate website (http://www.choosemyplate.gov) offers excellent suggestions for teaching nutrition concepts to children, as well as lesson plans for grades 1–2, 3–4, and 5–6 (plus secondary school levels). These lessons are free to download or obtain through the mail. They include objectives; detailed lesson plans; lesson activities integrated with mathematics, English language arts, science, and health standards; handouts; posters; three original songs; and projects children can do with their families.

In addition, the MyPlate website provides information about nutrition and healthy eating. It offers a multitude of educational tip sheets (all free) for improving healthy eating, such as tips for making fruits and vegetables fun and tasty for kids, making healthy snacks, creating more healthy ways to celebrate special occasions, and grocery shopping.

Sample Plans

Next, we show two sample lesson plans. **Sample Plan 17.1** describes how children can design a brain break for their classroom based on the five food groups. We assumed the five food groups had been taught in previous classroom lessons; however, the dance lesson below could be modified to include teaching this information. **Sample Plan 17.2** illustrates how to integrate HRF concepts within a skill development lesson in dance. On the text website, we include two lesson plans for games and gymnastics, again illustrating how to embed HRF concepts into lessons. You may recall the more detailed explanations of the codes labeling the tasks in the lessons (adapted from Rink, 2014). In brief,

I = An introductory/informing task that introduces the first movement task in a progression of tasks.

E = An extending or exploration task that progresses from the introductory/informing task.

R = Refinements to improve the quality of the movement or the performance techniques of the children's movements.

Cog K = Presenting or asking about cognitive knowledge.

SAMPLE PLAN 17.1

Brain Break Nutrition Dance

Movement themes: Angular, round, wide, straight, and twisted shapes with strong force
Topic theme: The five food groups
Notes:

The following dance activity can be taught in physical education or in the classroom. The goal is to reinforce a previous lesson on the five food groups and/or to provide a movement activity for a lesson on the five food groups and design a brain-break dance.

Equipment: Hand drum, white board with the chants for each food group written.

Objectives

Children will learn

Motor

1. To make the angular, round, wide, straight, and twisted shapes, with strong force and firm tension, to the rhythm of a chant.
2. To jump making a straight shape in the air and landing with a stick (feet remaining in the location they landed).

Cognitive and CCSS

3. To design a brain-break dance about the five food groups.
4. Acquire and apply domain-specific words and phrases that are basic to a particular topic.

Potential Performance Techniques for Refinements

- Feel the tension.
- Be strong, powerful, and tight.

Introduction

I Today we are going to design a brain break for your classroom. With your assigned partner, identify the five food groups and give examples of food from each group. Does any pair need help? [If so, assign another pair to help.]

Content Development

I Each food group has a chant. You and your partner will design a short sequence for each chant.

SAMPLE PLAN 17.1

Brain Break Nutrition Dance (*continued*)

Dairy Chant

Cog K Let's start with dairy. Listen to the chant.

Beat 1	Beat 2	Beat 3	Beat 4
We	are	dairy	[pause]
We	are	dairy	[pause]
Milk	and cheese	yogurt	please
We	are	dairy	[pause]

E On your own, explore making different angular shapes each time I beat the drum.

R Move into each shape quickly, with strong force, and hold the shape with firm tension.

[Beat the drum three times, at a speed slower than the chant. Repeat several times, encouraging children to find many, varied, and some unusual shapes.]

E Put your best three shapes in a sequence. [Beat the drum slowly at first, and increase speed once the children have settled on their three choices.]

E You can change your shapes if you are not happy with your sequence.

R Practice your sequence until you can repeat it accurately, making the same shapes each time you do the sequence.

Note: For younger grades, you can stop here and use individual sequences. Skip ahead to the application task (A). The following tasks are for older grades after children have learned to work with a partner to design a short sequence.

E Show your sequence to your partner. Then combine the best elements from each person's sequence to make one partner sequence with three matching angular shapes. Each of you must contribute at least one shape.

R Practice your sequence until you match perfectly, that is, you both make the exact same shape with each body part in the same position.

A Let's try it to the chant. You make your three shapes every time I chant, "We are dairy." When we say "milk and cheese, yogurt please," hop in place and make different angular movements with your arms. [Try the dance to the chant; repeat several times.]

Dairy Dance: Angular Shapes

Beat 1	Beat 2	Beat 3	Beat 4
We (angular shape)	are (angular shape)	dairy (angular shape)	[pause]
We (angular shape)	are (angular shape)	dairy (angular shape)	[pause]
Milk and (hop and make angular arm gestures)	cheese (hop and make angular arm gestures)	yogurt (hop and make angular arm gestures)	please (hop and make angular arm gestures)
We (angular shape)	are (angular shape)	dairy (angular shape)	[pause]

A Now, you chant as you perform your sequence. I will beat the drum.

Note: Repeat the same process for designing the other four chants:

Veggie Dance: Round Shapes

Beat 1	Beat 2	Beat 3	Beat 4
We (round shape)	are (round shape)	veggies (round shape)	[pause]
Heal (round shape)	thy (round shape)	veggies (round shape)	[pause]
Orange (jump in a circle while circling arms over head)	red (jump in a circle while circling arms over head)	purple (jump in a circle while circling arms over head)	green (jump in a circle while circling arms over head)
We (round shape)	are (round shape)	veggies (round shape)	[pause]

(*continues*)

SAMPLE PLAN 17.1

Brain Break Nutrition Dance (*continued*)

Fruit Dance: Twisted Shapes

Beat 1	Beat 2	Beat 3	Beat 4
We (twisted shape)	are (twisted shape)	fruit (twisted shape)	[pause]
We (twisted shape)	are (twisted shape)	fruit (twisted shape)	[pause]
Great for (jump and twist)	snacks (jump and twist)	in your (jump and twist)	pack (jump and twist)
We (twisted shape)	are (twisted shape)	fruit (twisted shape)	[pause]

Protein Dance: Jump for Height, Straight Shape

Beat 1	Beat 2	Beat 3	Beat 4
We (jump for height, arms swing up, land, bend knees, arms down)	are	protein (jump for height, arms swing up, land, bend knees, arms down)	[pause]
Eggs (jump for height, arms swing up, land, bend knees, arms down)	meat	and beans (jump for height, arms swing up, land, bend knees, arms down)	[pause]
Building (keeping knees bent, jump low, stomp, extend elbows pressing palms out)	me (keeping knees bent, jump low, stomp, extend elbows pressing palms out)	building (keeping knees bent, jump low, stomp, extend elbows pressing palms out)	me (keeping knees bent, jump low, stomp, extend elbows pressing palms out)
We (jump for height, arms swing up, land, bend knees, arms down)	are	protein (jump for height, arms swing up, land, bend knees, arms down)	[pause]

Carbohydrate Dance: Wide Shapes

Beat 1	Beat 2	Beat 3	Beat 4
Car- (wide shape)	bo- (wide shape)	hydrates (wide shape)	[pause]
Car- (wide shape)	bo- (wide shape)	hydrates (wide shape)	[pause]
Ener-, (prance and wave arms side to side overhead)	gy and (prance and wave arms side to side overhead)	fiber (prance and wave arms side to side overhead)	too (prance and wave arms side to side overhead)
Car- (wide shape)	bo- (wide shape)	hydrates (wide shape)	[pause]

When the Brain Break Nutrition Dance is done in the classroom, the teacher can have each pair quickly teach their shapes and lead the chants.

SAMPLE PLAN 17.2

Where the Wild Things Are

The learning experiences here explain how to modify a dance lesson to focus on teaching children three components of fitness and how different dance movements work on each component. It meets the CCSS for domain-specific vocabulary acquisition. Following recommendations from language arts experts, we define each component when children need to know the definition in the lesson.

This lesson also integrates material from children's literature, which can extend children's understanding and appreciation of a story. As with all lessons using children's literature, it is better if the classroom teacher teaches the book to the children first, but this is not necessary. The lesson here assumes that the children have read the book, but the bracketed notes indicate what you can do if you are introducing the story to the children.

Prior to this lesson, the children learned the difference between moderate and vigorous intensity. To illustrate that teachers must review fitness concepts repeatedly, we ask questions to review moderate and vigorous intensity in the lesson.

SAMPLE PLAN 17.2

Where the Wild Things Are (*continued*)

Movement themes: Angular shapes and pathways, strong force

Topic theme: Sendak, M. (1963/1991). ***Where the wild things are.*** New York: Harper Collins. (We thank Dr. Teresa Purcell Cone (2000) for her suggestion to use this book for children's dance.)

Notes:

Equipment: Hand drum; tambourine; white board with the definitions of muscle fitness, flexibility, and cardiorespiratory endurance written in developmentally appropriate language

Objectives

By the end of this lesson, the children will have learned

Motor

1. To move their joints through their range of motion on curved pathways moving slowly.
2. To travel on zigzag pathways moving fast with firm tension.
3. To create angular shapes with strong tension.
4. To jump making big shapes in the air.

Cognitive and CCSS

5. The definitions of three components of fitness: muscle fitness, flexibility, and cardiorespiratory endurance, and how different dance movements work on each component.
6. Acquire and apply domain-specific words and phrases that are basic to a particular topic.

Potential Performance Techniques for Refinements

- Feel the tension.
- Be strong, powerful, and tight.
- Make big circles slowly, stretching through the full range of motion.

Introduction

I Do you remember the story you read in your classroom about Max in *Where the Wild Things Are*? Today, we will be doing a "wild things" dance. The best thing is that this dance is not only fun, but also healthy for your body because we will be working on physical fitness.

Content Development

Explore Stomping in General Space

I What happens at the beginning of the book? Great answers. Max is bad and is sent to his room without his supper. [Read the book showing the illustrations to the children through the pages where Max is sent to his room.] Let's start by warming up to the wild things dance by walking and stomping all about the space. Look like you are mad and pouting. Stomp all about general space. [Beat the hand drum at a walking pace.]

Cog K Are you moving with moderate intensity or vigorous intensity? Right, moderate. Great job remembering that concept. Moderate intensity is an appropriate intensity for warming you up for the wild things dance.

R Continue to walk and stomp. Make your entire body tight with anger, and stomp with strong force because you are being bad and sent to your room.

Cog K There are three components of fitness you will learn today. You have just been working on muscle fitness. Look at the white board. Muscle fitness means your muscles are strong and can exert force. Your muscles are also powerful and can exert force quickly, and your muscles can also resist fatigue and endure lots of exercise.

E Walk and stomp about the space again. Stomp with strong and powerful force. Feel the strong tension in your muscles because you are working on muscle fitness.

Explore Drawing Curved Lines with Hands (Curved Pathways in the Air) Doing Dynamic Stretching

Cog K Then what happens? Right. Vines grow all over Max's room. [Read the pages showing the children the illustrations of vines growing all over Max's room.]

I Standing in personal space, draw curved lines in space with one hand and arm as if you are vines growing. Make small curves, large curves, and curves all about your personal space—to your side and back, high and low. [Shake the tambourine as you demonstrate and as the children explore.]

R Don't forget to reach behind you by twisting your entire back through its range of motion while making vines behind and to the side of you. Make your vines as big as you can.

(*continues*)

SAMPLE PLAN 17.2

Where the Wild Things Are (*continued*)

E [Repeat these tasks with the other hand.]

E [Repeat these tasks with both hands.]

Cog K You have just been working on a second area of fitness called flexibility. Flexibility means stretching as you slowly move your body parts through their full range of motion.

R Circle one arm through its full range of motion, twisting your back so you can reach behind you, working on flexibility while you represent the vines growing in Max's room.

E [Repeat these tasks with the other hand.]

E [Repeat these tasks with both hands.]

Strong movements like wild things on the shore

Courtesy of John Dolly

Strong Movements, Deep Lunges, Curls, and Arches

E Max then sailed to where the wild things lived, and he saw the monsters on the shore roaring, gnashing their teeth, and showing their terrible claws. [Read the pages up to where Max finds the wild things on the shore.] Let's move the way wild things might dance. Reach out your arms and hands like claws, making your muscles very tight. Put a ferocious look on your face. Lift one leg high with tension in your muscles and take a big, strong step, bending your knee when you land like this [demonstrate walking with a high leg lift followed by a deep lunge]. Now walk about general space taking strong, powerful, giant steps, bending your knees, and showing your terrible claws. [Beat the hand drum at a slow pace.]

R Show through your movement and tension that you are a strong monster.

E Now turn into a monster that walks on hands and feet. Put your hands flat on the ground and take your weight on your hands, springing your legs to the side. Keep your feet low and travel sideways. [Repeat several times.]

E Other monsters travel low on the ground. Lie down on your belly and arch it so that your feet, claws, and face are up. Be tight, strong monsters. Make a monster face. [If you teach outside, you can use exercise mats or two carpet pads for each child in this section of the dance, or you can modify the movement to be on the feet leaning forward, arching and curling the back if your physical environment makes these movements inappropriate on the ground.]

E Now slowly roll onto your back and curl into a ball on your bottom with your head up and your legs up looking strong and ferocious. Pretend to eat your knees.

E Keep transferring your weight slowly from curled on your back or bottom to arched on your belly. [Repeat several times.]

Working on trunk extensions

Courtesy of John Dolly

Working on abdominals

Courtesy of John Dolly

Cog K Which areas of fitness have we worked as monsters on the shore? Right, muscle fitness.

Running on Zigzag Pathways, Stopping in Strong, Angular Shapes

I But Max tames the wild things, and they make him king. Max says, "Let the wild rumpus start!" [Read the pages up to the quote and show the children the illustrations of the rumpus.] When I say go, I want you to run as fast as you can safely on a sharp, angular, zigzag pathway [demonstrate as you explain]. Go. [Beat the drum fast and loud.]

SAMPLE PLAN 17.2

Where the Wild Things Are (*continued*)

E Stop and make an angular, sharp, pointy shape like a wild thing.

E Run again on an angular pathway as I beat the drum, and stop in an angular shape when you hear two fast, loud drum beats.

E This time when you stop, make three angular shapes in a row. Run fast. Stop in an angular shape 1, now 2, now 3.

E Make three more angular shapes by adding punches and kicks like a wild thing, making sure you stay within your personal space.

E [Repeat several more times, increasing the amount of time you have the children run and having them make a variety of angular shapes each time they stop. Check whether they are breathing hard. Then stop.]

Cog K You have just been working on a third area of fitness called cardiorespiratory endurance. Cardiorespiratory endurance is the ability to exercise for a long time working your heart and lungs. Which feelings in your body might tell you that you are working your lungs hard? [I'm breathing harder.] Yes, I can see you're breathing harder. If we took your heart rate, we would find that your heart is beating faster. When you breathe faster and harder and your heart beats faster, you know you're working cardiorespiratory endurance, which is very good for your heart and lungs.

E Let's run like wild things and check your heart rate. Go. [Let them run until you can see they are breathing hard or are fatigued.] Stop and put two fingers under your ear, and slide them down until you can feel your heart beating. Do you know what your heart is telling you? Thank you, thank you, you're making me stronger [speak in the rhythm of a heart beating].

E Run like wild things again. This time when you stop, make 10 different angular shapes, creating a different shape each time I count and beat the drum. Go. Stop.

R Be very tight in your muscles and make forceful, angular shapes with tension in your whole body and powerful punches and kicks like a wild thing. 1, 2, 3, 4, 5, 6, 7, 8, 9, 10.

Cog K Which area of fitness do you think you are working the most when you punch, kick, and make tight, angular shapes? Right. Muscle fitness. Which feeling in your body tells you that you are working on muscle fitness? [My body is tight; it feels strong; my muscles get tired.]

Short Run and Large, Forceful Jumps

E Move down to the end of the physical education space. What a great workout you all are doing. To represent wild things in another way, we are going to run a few steps down the space on a straight pathway, building up to a huge jump, thrusting your legs and arms in the air with strong, fast force. Run and jump when I beat the drum, making sure to bring your legs together before you land.

Safety Spread out so you are not in anyone's personal space. When you jump, be sure you are not near anyone else's personal space. Go.

E Let's do it again, but this time run and jump twice.

E This time, the wild thing is even bigger. Jump three times in a row, making different big shapes each time. Explode through your legs to get height in your jumps.

E [Repeat several times, giving the children just enough time to recover before running again.]

Cog K Which areas of fitness are you working? [Cardiorespiratory endurance when we run and jump; muscle fitness in jumping.] What are you making strong? [Heart, leg, and possibly arm muscles.] Great thinking. Do you know what else you are making strong? Your bones. When you run and jump, you are using power to jump and hitting the ground forcefully with your feet. This impact helps your bones to get stronger. When you work using power, you are helping your bones grow stronger.

Wild Rumpus

E Now make up your own wild rumpus dance. I will beat the drum for 30 seconds and you can do any wild movement you want, as long as you are safe and not invading anyone else's personal space. Go. Rest. Dance again. Stop and take your pulse. Is your heart beating fast or slow? [Repeat several times.]

Dynamic Stretching

E In the book, what happened after the wild rumpus? Right. Max got lonely and wanted to be where someone loved him best, so he sailed home. [Read the book, showing the illustrations to the children, until Max has sailed home.] Walk about the space drawing big ocean waves with your hands. Reach high and low. [Beat the tambourine at a walking pace.]

R Let the wild thing tension slowly drain from your body.

(*continues*)

SAMPLE PLAN 17.2

Where the Wild Things Are (*continued*)

E Stop and circle your arms gently like the waves.

E Now gently twist and swing your arms from side to side slowly.

E Curl forward, letting your hands hang near the ground, and stretch the back of your legs. Let all of the wild thing tension flow out of your fingers and feel the comfort of someone who loves you best.

E How does the book end? [Read the last pages.] You have eaten your supper; now lie down and rest. Relax every muscle in your body because the wild thing has left.

The wild rumpus

Courtesy of John Dolly

CCSS Closure Discussing and Assessing Domain-Specific Vocabulary

Cog K Go with your assigned partner. Discuss how your body felt when you were working on each of the three areas of fitness. You may refer to the definitions of the three areas of fitness on the white board. Then discuss how you might judge if the movements or skills you are doing are working on muscle fitness, flexibility, or cardiorespiratory endurance.

Fitness Assessment Sheet for Identifying Dance Movements and the Corresponding Areas of Fitness

Assessment: I have given you and your partner an assessment sheet and pencil. Discuss which section of the dance worked on which area of fitness. Draw a line from the dance movements in column 1 to the area of fitness in column 2. You may draw more than one line to any area of fitness.

Dance Movements	Area of Fitness
Max walking and stomping, being bad and mad because he was being sent to his room.	Muscle fitness
Moving like vines growing in Max's room	Flexibility
Monsters lunging, taking big steps and gnashing their teeth	Cardiorespiratory endurance
Wild rumpus dance	
Sailing home, moving arms in circles on ocean waves, bending so hands are near the ground	

Summary

Physical activity benefits everyone's health. Regular physical activity leads to the decreased risk of many diseases. In children, research also links physical activity to academic achievement, concentration, and attention. Increased time in physical education may help—and certainly does not harm—academic performance. U.S. federal guidelines call for children to be physically active for 60 or more minutes every day, and to participate in muscle and bone-strengthening activities on at least three days each week. Physical activities for children should be varied, developmentally appropriate, and enjoyable. Many factors facilitate health-related physical activity in children, especially participation in activities they enjoy, access to programs and play environments, and time spent outdoors. To meet the guideline of 60 minutes of physical activity a day, a whole-school approach is needed. In physical education, children need to be moderately or vigorously active more than 50% of the time. Teachers can promote physical activity and wellness in schools through physical activity breaks; recess; before-, during-, and after-school programs; active commuting; newsletters; family nights; and teaching that informs children about community resources.

Fitness tests, if used to assess children's physical activity levels, should be criterion referenced. The FitnessGram and

ActivityGram measurements are not recommended for children younger than fourth grade.

Today the government is asking schools to play a role in the prevention of overweight and obesity. The issue of obesity can be a dangerous minefield for teachers, because teachers' and parents' efforts to deal with overweight and obese children can have unintended negative consequences. Experts advise teachers to focus on teaching children about healthy eating and engaging in enjoyable physical activities and to leave the treatment of obesity to physicians and dieticians trained in the complex issues of children's health. In the social environment, teachers can and must work to eliminate stigmatizing overweight and obese children and weight-based teasing, which research has found to cause harm.

Teaching the cognitive concepts underlying HRPA, HRF, and nutrition can help children adopt lifelong habits of physical activity and healthy eating. Teachers can integrate these concepts into game, dance, and gymnastics lessons.

Review Questions

1. What are bone-strengthening activities, and why are they important for children?
2. What does research show about the impact of physical activity and physical education on academic achievement? What are the pros and cons of using these findings as an argument to gain support for physical education?
3. What are the CDC guidelines for physical activity for children? Describe one way you might teach these guidelines to children.
4. Explain the distinction between HRPA and HRF. What misconceptions have you heard about the purpose of engaging in HRPA?
5. What is intermittent activity, and how does it relate to children? How might you take advantage of this aspect of children's physiology in teaching skill development lessons?
6. Why might child-designed games prove successful in promoting physical activity for children who do not enjoy physical education?
7. Without using the example in the chapter on teaching the areas of fitness, describe how you might teach one HRPA concept across a unit or grade level.
8. What does research say about the relationship between motor skill development and physical fitness?
9. What are the recommendations for fitness testing at the elementary school level? Assuming you have a choice, would you perform fitness testing at the elementary level? Why or why not?
10. What is the dilemma that faces physical education professionals when teaching about obesity?
11. What has research shown to be barriers to physical activity participation?
12. How does obesity affect performance, and what are the implications for teaching?
13. Describe how you might teach the FITT concept to children.
14. What are typical misconceptions students have about HRPA and HRF?
15. What are the five food groups and the recommendations for each in terms of a balanced diet?
16. What is the difference between oils and fats?
17. What are the three principles of healthy eating?

References

Academy of Nutrition and Dietetics. (2014). *Shop smart—Get the facts on food labels.* Chicago, IL: Author.

American College of Sports Medicine (ACSM). (2004). Physical activity and bone health. *Medicine and Science in Sports and Exercise, 36*(11), 1985–1996.

American College of Sports Medicine. (2013). *ACSM's guide to exercise prescription and testing*, Philadelphia, PA: Lippincott, Williams, & Wilkins.

Babkes, M. L., & Sinclair, C. D. (2004). The nature of elementary school children's recess behavior. *Research Quarterly for Exercise and Sport, 75*(suppl), A56–A57.

Babkes Stellino, M., & Sinclair, C. D. (2008). Intrinsically motivated, free-time physical activity: Considerations for recess. *Journal of Physical Education, Recreation and Dance, 79*(4), 37–40.

Barnett, L. M., Morgan, P. J., van Beurden, E., Ball, K., & Lubans, D. R. (2011). A reverse pathway? Actual and perceived skill proficiency and physical activity. *Medicine and Science in Sport and Exercise, 43*, 898–904.

Barnett, L. M., van Beurden, E., Morgan, P. J., Brooks, L. O., & Beard, J. R. (2008). Childhood motor skill proficiency as a predictor of adolescent physical activity. *Journal of Adolescent Health, 44*, 252–259.

Barnett, L. M., van Beurden, E., Morgan, P. J., Brooks, L. O., & Beard, J. R. (2009). Does childhood motor skill proficiency predict adolescent fitness? *Medicine and Science in Sports and Exercise, 40*, 2137–2144.

Bauer, K. W., Yang, Y. W., & Austin, S. B. (2004). "How can we stay healthy when you're throwing all of this in front of us?" Findings from focus groups and interviews in middle schools on environmental influences on nutrition and physical activity. *Health Education and Behavior, 31*, 34–46.

Bocarro, J., Kanters, M. A., Casper, J., & Forrester, S. (2008). School physical education, extracurricular sports, and lifelong active living. *Journal of Teaching in Physical Education, 27*, 155–166.

Bouchard, C. (1993). Heredity and health-related fitness. *President's Council on Physical Fitness and Sports Physical Activity and Fitness Research Digest, 1*(4), 1–8.

Bouchard, C., Dionne, F. T., Simoneau, J. A., & Boulay, M. R. (1992). Genetics of aerobic and anaerobic performances. *Exercise and Sport Sciences Review, 20*, 27–58.

Brodney, S., Blair, S. N., & Lee, C. D. (2000). Is it possible to be overweight and fit and healthy? In C. Bouchard (Ed.), *Physical activity and obesity* (pp. 355–371). Champaign, IL: Human Kinetics.

Burrows, L., Wright, J., & Jungersen-Smith, J. (2002). "Measure your belly": New Zealand children's constructions of health and fitness. *Journal of Teaching in Physical Education, 22*, 39–48.

Cardinal, B. J., Yan, Z., & Cardinal, M. K. (2013). Negative experiences in physical education and sport: How much do they affect physical activity participation later in life. *Journal of Physical Education, Recreation and Dance, 84*(3), 49–53.

Carson, R. (2012). Certification and duties of a directory of physical activity. *Journal of Physical Education, Recreation and Dance, 83*(6), 16–19, 29.

Casazza, K., Fontaine, K. R., Astrup, A., Birch, L. L., Brown, A.W., Bohan Brown, M. M., et al. (2013). Myths, presumptions, and facts about obesity. *New England Journal of Medicine, Jan 31; 368*(5):446–54.

Castelli, D. M., & Erwin, H. E. (2007). A comparison of personal attributes and experiences among physically active and inactive children. *Journal of Teaching in Physical Education, 26*, 375–389.

Castelli, D. M., & Valley, J. A. (2007). The relationship of physical fitness and motor competence to physical activity. *Journal of Teaching in Physical Education, 26*, 358–374.

Centers for Disease Control and Prevention (CDC). (2010). *The association between school-based physical activity, including physical education, and academic performance*. Atlanta, GA: U.S. Department of Health and Human Services.

Centers for Disease Control and Prevention (CDC). (2013). *Comprehensive School Physical Activity Programs: A Guide for Schools*. Atlanta, GA: U.S. Department of Health and Human Services.

Chen, A. (2013). Top 10 research questions related to children physical activity motivation. *Research Quarterly for Exercise and Sport, 84*, 441–447.

Chen, A., Darst, P. W., & Pangrazi, R. P. (2001). An examination of situational interest and its sources. *British Journal of Educational Psychology, 71*, 383–400.

Chen, A., & Liu, X. (2009). Task values, cost, and choice decisions in physical education. *Journal of Teaching in Physical Education, 28*, 192–213.

Chen, A., Martin, R., Sun, H., & Ennis, C. D. (2007). Is in-class physical activity at risk in constructivist physical education? *Research Quarterly for Exercise and Sport, 78*, 500–509.

Clark, J. E. (2007). On the problem of motor skill development. *Journal of Physical Education, Recreation and Dance, 78*(5), 39–44.

Corbin, C. B. (2002). Physical activity for everyone: What every physical educator should know about promoting lifelong physical activity. *Journal of Teaching in Physical Education, 21*, 128–144.

Corbin, C. B., Kulinna, P. H., Dean, M., & Reeves, J. (2013). Wellness weeks: A total school approach for promoting physical activity and nutrition. *Journal of Physical Education, Recreation and Dance, 84*(6), 35–41.

Corbin, C. B., Lambdin, D. D., Mahar, M. T., Roberts, G., & Pangrazi, R. P. (2013). Why test? Effective use of fitness and activity assessments. In S. A. Plowman & M. D. Meredith (Eds.), *FitnessGram/ActivityGram Reference Guide* (4th Edition) (pp. 2-1—2-26). Dallas, TX: The Cooper Institute.

Corbin, C., Le Masurier, G., Lambdin, D., & Greiner, M. (2010). *Fitness for life elementary school program package*. Champaign, IL: Human Kinetics.

Corbin, C. B., & Pangrazi, R. P. (2008). Physical activity for children: How much is enough? In G. J. Welk & M. D. Meredith (Eds.), *FitnessGram/ActivityGram reference guide* (3rd ed.) (pp. 61–69). Dallas, TX: Cooper Institute. Retrieved September 1, 2010, from http://www.cooperinstitute.org/ourkidshealth/FITNESSGRAM?_Reference Guide.pdf

Corbin, C. B., Welk, G. J., Richardson, C., Vowell, C., Lambdin, D., & Wikgren, S. (2014). Youth fitness: Ten key concepts. *Journal of Physical Education, Recreation, and Dance, 85*(2), 24–31.

Crocker, P. R. E., Eklund, R. C., & Kowalski, K. C. (2000). Children's physical activity and physical self-perceptions. *Journal of Sport Sciences, 18*, 383–394.

Desmond, S. M., Price, J. H., Lock, R. S., Smith, D., & Stewart, P. W. (1990). Urban black and white adolescents' physical fitness status and perceptions of exercise. *Journal of School Health, 60*, 220–226.

Domangue, E., & Solmon, M. (2010). Motivational responses to fitness testing by award status and gender. *Research Quarterly for Exercise and Sport, 81*, 310–318.

Ennis, C. D. (2010). On their own: Preparing students for a lifetime. *Journal of Physical Education, Recreation and Dance, 81*(5), 17–22.

Ennis, C. D. (2014). The role of students and content in teacher effectiveness. *Research Quarterly for Exercise and Sport, 85*, pp. 6–13.

Erwin, H., Beets, M. W., Centeio, E., & Morrow, J. R. Jr. (2014). Best practices and recommendations for increasing physical activity in youth. *Journal of Physical Education, Recreation, and Dance, 85*(7), 27–34.

Faith, M. S., Leone, M. A., Ayers, T. S., Moonseong, H., & Pietrobelli, A. (2002). Weight criticism during physical activity, coping skills, and reported physical activity in children. *Pediatrics, 110*, e23.

Fisher, M. (2009). Children and exercise: Appropriate practices for grades K–6. *Journal of Physical Education, Recreation and Dance, 80*(4), 18–23, 29.

Friedlander, L., & Ennis, C. D. (2011). Examining students' naïve conceptions of exercise intensity [Abstract]. *Research Quarterly for Exercise and Sport, 82*(suppl), A-40.

Graf, C., Koch, B., Kretschmann-Kandel, E., Falkowski, G., Christ, H., Coburger, S.,... Dordel, S. (2004). Correlation between BMI, leisure habits and motor abilities in childhood (CHILT-Project). *International Journal of Obesity and Related Metabolic Disorders, 28*, 22–26.

Greenleaf, C., & Weiller, K. (2005). Perceptions of youth obesity among physical educators. *Social Psychology of Education, 8*, 407–423.

Hafekost, K., Lawrence, D., Mitrou, F., O'Sullivan, T. A., & Zubrick, S. R. (2013). Tackling overweight and obesity: Does the public health message match the science? *BMC Medicine 11*(1), 41.

Heidorn, B., & Centeio, E. (2012). The director of physical activity and staff involvement. *Journal of Physical Education, Recreation, and Dance, 83*(7), 13–19, 25–26.

Hillman, C. H., Castelli, D. M., & Buck, S. M. (2005). Aerobic fitness and neurocognitive function in healthy preadolescent children. *Medicine and Science in Sports and Exercise, 37*, 1967–1974.

Hoelscher, D. M., Kirk, S., Ritchie, L., Cunningham-Sabo, L. (2013). Position of the Academy of Nutrition and Dietetics: Interventions for the Prevention and Treatment of Pediatric Overweight and Obesity. *Journal of the Academy of Nutrition and Dietetics, 113*, 1375–1394.

Hong, D., Chen, A., Chen, S., Zhang, T., Loflin, J., & Ennis, C. D. (2011). Conceptual learning in a muscular fitness unit [Abstract]. *Research Quarterly for Exercise and Sport, 82*(suppl), A-42.

Hoople, C., & Graham, G. (1995). What children think, feel, and know about physical fitness testing. *Journal of Teaching in Physical Education, 14*, 408–427.

Ignico, A., Corson, A., & Vidoni, C. (2006). The effects of an intervention strategy on children's heart rates and skill performance. *Early Child Development and Care, 176*, 753–761.

Insel, P., Turner, R. E., & Ross, D. (2010). *Discovering nutrition* (3rd ed.). Burlington, MA: Jones & Bartlett Learning.

Institute of Medicine (IOM). (2012a). *Accelerating progress in obesity prevention: Solving the weight of the nation*. Washington, DC: The National Academies Press.

Institute of Medicine (IOM). (2012b). *Fitness measures and health outcomes in youth*. Washington, DC: National Academy of Sciences.

Institute of Medicine (IOM). (2013). *Educating the student body: Taking physical activity and physical education to school*. Washington, DC: National Academy of Sciences.

Jeykendrup, A., & Gleeson, M. (2010). *Sport nutrition: An introduction to energy production and performance* (2nd ed.). Champaign, IL: Human Kinetics.

Kahan, D. (2008). Recess, extracurricular activities, and active classroom: Means for increasing elementary school students' physical activity. *Journal of Physical Education, Recreation and Dance, 79*(2), 26–31, 39.

Keating, X. D., Harrison, L., Chen, L., Xiang, P., Lambdin, D., Dauenhauer, B., et al. (2009). An analysis of research on student health-related fitness knowledge in K–16 physical education programs. *Journal of Teaching in Physical Education, 28*, 333–349.

Kiefer, H. S. (2008). Myths and truths from exercise physiology. *Journal of Physical Education, Recreation and Dance, 79*(8), 23–25.

Kirkpatrick, B., & Burton, H. B. (1997). *Lessons from the heart: Individualizing physical education with heart rate monitors*. Champaign, IL: Human Kinetics.

Kulinna, P. H. (2004). Physical activity and fitness knowledge: How much 1–6 grade students know. *International Journal of Physical Education, 41*(3), 111–121.

Li, W., & Rukavina, P. B. (2012). Including overweight or obese students in physical education: A social ecological constraint model. *Research Quarterly for Exercise and Sport, 83*, 570–578.

Li, W., Rukavina, P., & Kim, J. (2011). Overweight or obese students' perceptions of caring in physical education [Abstract]. *Research Quarterly for Exercise and Sport, 82*(suppl), A-46.

Loflin, J., Chen, A., Hong, D., Chen, S., Zhang, T., & Ennis, C. D. (2011). Contribution of cognitive tasks to learning flexibility and nutrition concepts [Abstract]. *Research Quarterly for Exercise and Sport, 82*(suppl), A-46.

Lonsdale, C., Rosenkranz, R. R., Peralta, L. R., Bennie, A., Fahey, P., Lubans, D. R. (2013). A systematic review and meta-analysis of interventions designed to increase moderate-to-vigorous physical activity in school physical education lessons. *Preventive Medicine, 56*, 152–161.

Lubans, D. R., Morgan, P. J., Cliff, D. P., Barnett, L. M., & Oakley, A. D. (2010). Fundamental movement skills in children and adolescents: Review of associated health benefits. *Sports Medicine, 40*, 1019–1035.

Malina, R. M. (2014). Top 10 research questions related to growth and maturation of relevance to physical activity, performance, and fitness. *Research Quarterly for Exercise and Sport, 85*, 157–173.

Mally, K. K. (2006). Stretching and young children: Should we or shouldn't we? *Teaching Elementary Physical Education, 17*(1), 37–39.

Martin, S. B., Ede, A., Morrow, J. R., & Jackson, A. W. (2010). Statewide physical fitness testing: Perspectives from the gym. *Research Quarterly for Exercise and Sport, 81*(3 suppl), S31–S41.

McKenzie, T. L. (2003). Health-related physical education: Physical activity, fitness, and wellness. In S. J. Silverman & C. D. Ennis (Eds.), *Student learning in physical education: Applying research to enhance instruction* (2nd ed.) (pp. 207–226). Champaign, IL: Human Kinetics.

McKenzie, T. L., Alcaraz, J. E., & Sallis, J. F. (1994). Assessing children's liking for activity units in an elementary school physical education curriculum. *Journal of Teaching in Physical Education, 13*, 206–215.

McKenzie, T. L., & Kahan, D. (2004). Impact of the Surgeon General's report: Through the eyes of physical education teacher educators. *Journal of Teaching in Physical Education, 23*, 300–317.

Merkle, D. G., & Treagust, D. F. (1993). Student knowledge of health and fitness concepts and its relation to locus of control. *School Science and Mathematics, 93*, 355–359.

Morrow, J. R., & Freedson, P. S. (1994). Relationship between habitual physical activity and aerobic fitness in adolescents. *Pediatric Exercise Science, 6*, 315–329.

National Association for Sport and Physical Education (NASPE). (2004). *Physical activity for children: A statement of guidelines for children ages 5–12*. Reston, VA: Author.

National Association for Sport and Physical Education (NASPE). (2008). *Comprehensive school physical activity programs*. Reston, VA: Author.

National Association for Sport and Physical Education (NASPE). (2010a). *Opportunity to Learn: Guidelines for Elementary, Middle, and High School Physical Education: A Side-by-Side Comparison*. Reston, VA: Author.

National Association for Sport and Physical Education (NASPE). (2010b). *PE metrics: Assessing national standards 1–6 in elementary school*. Reston, VA: Author.

Netzer, C. T. (2006). *The complete book of food counts* (7th ed.). New York: Bantam Dell.

Neumark-Sztainer, D. (2005). Can we simultaneously work toward the prevention of obesity and eating disorders in children and adolescents? *International Journal of Eating Disorders, 38*, 220–227.

Nihiser, A. J., Lee, S. M., Wechsler, H., McKenna, M., Odom, E., Reinold, C.,... Grummer-Strawn, L. (2007). Body mass index measurement in schools. *Journal of School Health, 77*, 651–671.

O'Brien, K. S., Hunter, J. A., & Banks, M. (2007). Implicit anti-fat bias in physical educators: Physical attributes, ideology and socialization. *International Journal of Obesity, 31*, 308–314.

O'Dea, J. A. (2005). Prevention of child obesity: "First, do no harm." *Health Education Research, 20*, 259–265.

O'Dea, J. A., & Abraham, S. (2001). Knowledge, beliefs, attitudes and behaviours related to weight control, eating disorders and body image in Australian trainee home economics and physical education teachers. *Journal of Nutrition Education, 33*, 332–340.

Ogata, B. N., & Hayes, D. (2014). Position of the Academy of Nutrition and Dietetics: Nutrition guidance for healthy children ages 2 to 11 years. *Journal of the Academy of Nutrition and Dietetics, 114*(8), 1257–1276.

Okley, A. D., Booth, M. L., & Patterson, J. W. (2001). Relationship of physical activity to fundamental movement skills among adolescents. *Medicine & Science in Sports & Exercise, 33*, 1899–1904.

Oliver, K. L., & Hamzeh, M. (2010). "The boys won't let us play": 5th grade Mestizas challenge physical activity discourse at school. *Research Quarterly for Exercise and Sport, 81*, 38–51.

Oliver, K. L., Hamzeh, M., & McCaughtry, N. (2009). "Girly girls can play games/Las niñas pueden jugar tambien": Co-creating a curriculum of possibilities with 5th grade girls. *Journal of Teaching in Physical Education, 28*, 90–110.

Pangrazi, R. P. (2000). Promoting physical activity for youth. *Journal of Science and Medicine in Sport, 3*, 280–286.

Pangrazi, R. P., Beighle, A., & Pangrazi, D. (2009). *Promoting physical activity and health in the classroom*. San Francisco: Benjamin Cummings.

Pangrazi, R. P., & Corbin, C. B. (1990). Age as a factor relating to physical fitness test performance. *Research Quarterly for Exercise and Sport, 61*, 410–414.

Pangrazi, R. P., & Corbin, C. B. (2008). Factors that influence physical fitness in children and adolescents. In G. J. Welk & M. D. Meredith (Eds.), *FitnessGram/ActivityGram reference guide* (3rd ed.) (pp. 52–60). Dallas, TX: Cooper Institute. Retrieved September 1, 2010, from http://www.cooperinstitute.org/ourkidshealth?/-FITNESSGRAM_Reference Guide.pdf

Payne, V. G., & Morrow, J. R. (1993). Exercise and VO2 max in children: A meta-analysis. *Research Quarterly for Exercise and Sport, 64*, 305–313.

Perkins, D. F., Jacobs, J. E., Barber, B. L., & Eccles, J. S. (2004). Childhood and adolescent sports participation as predictors of participation in sports and physical fitness activities during young adulthood. *Youth and Society, 35*, 495–520.

Placek, J. H., Griffin, L. L., Dodds, P., Raymond, C., Tremino, F., & James, A. (2001). Middle school students' conceptions of fitness: The long road to a healthy life study. *Journal of Teaching in Physical Education, 20*, 314–323.

Plowman, S. A. (2014). Top 10 research questions related to musculoskeletal physical fitness testing in children and adolescents. *Research Quarterly for Exercise and Sport, 85*, 174–187.

Puhl, R. M., & Heuer, C. A. (2010). Obesity Stigma: Important Considerations for Public Health. *American Journal of Public Health, 100*, 1019–1028.

Puhl, R. M., & Latner, J. D. (2007). Stigma, obesity, and the health of the nation's children. *Psychological Bulletin, 133*, 557–580.

Purcell Cone, T. (2000). Off the page: Responding to children's literature through dance. *Teaching Elementary Physical Education, 11*(5), 11–34.

Rideout, V. J., Foehr, U. G., & Roberts, D. F. (2010, January 20). *Generation M²: Media in the lives of 8- to 18-year-olds.* Menlo Park, CA: Kaiser Family Foundation.

Rink, J. E. (2014). *Teaching physical education for learning* (7th ed.). New York: McGraw-Hill.

Rink, J. E., Hall, T. J., & Williams, L. H. (2010). *Schoolwide physical activity: A comprehensive guide to development and conducting programs.* Champaign, IL: Human Kinetics.

Rosenberg, D. E., Sallis, J. F., Conway, T. L., Cain, K. L., & McKenzie, T. L. (2006). Active transportation to school over 2 years in relation to weight status and physical activity. *Obesity, 14*, 1771–1776.

Rukavina, P. B., & Li, W. (2008). School physical activity interventions: Do not forget about obesity bias. *Obesity Reviews, 9*(1), 67–75.

Sanders, S., & Graham, G. (1995). Kindergarten children's initial experiences in physical education: The relentless persistence for play clashes with the zone of acceptable responses. *Journal of Teaching in Physical Education, 14*, 372–383.

Seefeldt, V. (1980). Developmental motor patterns: Implications for elementary school physical education. In C. H. Nadeau, W. R. Halliwell, K. M. Newel, & G. C. Roberts (Eds.), *Psychology of motor behavior and sport—1979* (pp. 314–323). Champaign, IL: Human Kinetics.

Sendak, M. (1963/1991). *Where the wild things are.* New York: Harper Collins.

Shirley, K., Rutfield, R., Hall, N., Fedor, N., McCaughey, V. K., & Kristyn Zajac, K. (2014). Combinations of Obesity Prevention Strategies in US Elementary Schools: A Critical Review. *The Journal of Primary Prevention, 36*(1), 1–20.

Shook, R. P., Hand, G. A., & Blair, S. N. (2014). Top 10 research questions related to energy balance. *Research Quarterly for Exercise and Sport, 85*, 49–58.

Sobol-Goldberg, S., Rabinowitz, J., & Gross, R. (2013). School-based obesity prevention programs: A meta-analysis of randomized controlled trials. *Obesity, 21*(12), 2422–2428.

Society of Health and Physical Educators (SHAPE). (2014). *National standards and grade-level outcomes for K–12 physical education.* Champaign, IL: Human Kinetics.

Stodden, D., Langendorfer, S., & Roberton, M. A. (2009). The association between motor skill competence and physical fitness in young adults. *Research Quarterly for Exercise and Sport, 80*, 223–229.

Stodden, D. F., True, L. K., Langendorfer, S. J., & Gao, Z. (2013). Associations among selected motor skills and health-related fitness: Indirect evidence for Seefeldt's proficiency barrier in young adults. *Research Quarterly for Exercise and Sport, 84*, 397–403.

Tassitano, R. M., Barros, M. V. G., Tenorio, C. C. M., Bezerra, J., Florindo, A. A., & Reis, R. S. (2010). Enrollment in physical education is associated with health-related behavior among high school students. *Journal of School Health, 80*(3), 126–133.

Trost, S. G. (1998). *The association between physical activity and cardiorespiratory fitness in children and adolescents: A meta-analytic review.* Report prepared for the University of South Carolina School of Public Health. Columbia, SC.

Trost, S. G. (2004). School physical education in the post-report era: An analysis from public health. *Journal of Teaching in Physical Education, 23*, 318–337.

Trost, S. G. (2006). Public health and physical education. In D. Kirk, D. MacDonald, & M. O'Sullivan (Eds.), *The handbook of physical education* (pp. 163–187). London: Sage.

Trout, J., & Graber, K. C. (2009). Perceptions of overweight students concerning their experiences in physical education, *Journal of Teaching in Physical Education, 28*, 272–292.

U.S. Department of Agriculture (USDA) Food and Nutrition Service. (2011). *MyPlate for kids.* Washington, DC: Author. Retrieved from http://www.MyPlate.gov

U.S. Department of Health and Human Services (USDHHS). (1996). *Physical activity and health: A report of the Surgeon General.* Atlanta, GA: Centers for Disease Control and Prevention.

U.S. Department of Health and Human Services (USDHHS). (2000). *Healthy people 2010* (Conference Education, in 2 vols.). Washington, DC: U.S. Government Printing Office.

U.S. Department of Health and Human Services (USDHHS). (2008). *2008 physical activity guidelines for Americans.* Washington, DC: Author. Retrieved from http://www.health.gov/paguidelines

U.S. Department of Health and Human Services (USDHHS). (2010a). *Healthy people 2020.* Washington, DC: U.S. Government Printing Office.

U.S. Department of Health and Human Services (USDHHS). (2010b, January). *The Surgeon General's vision for a healthy and fit nation.* Rockville, MD: USDHHS, Office of the Surgeon General.

Verstraete, S. J. M., Cardon, G. M., De Clercq, D. L. R., & De Bourdeaudhuij, I. M. M. (2006). Increasing children's physical activity during recess periods in elementary schools: The effects of providing game equipment. *European Journal of Public Health, 16*, 415–419.

Welk, G. J., & Blair, S. N. (2008). Health benefits of physical activity and fitness in children. In G. J. Welk & M. D. Meredith (Eds.), *FitnessGram/ActivityGram reference guide* (3rd ed.) (pp. 40–51). Dallas, TX: Cooper Institute. Retrieved September 1, 2010, from http://www.cooperinstitute.org/ourkidshealth/FITNESSGRAM?_Reference Guide.pdf

Welk, G. J., Eisenmann, J. C., & Dollman, J. (2006). Health-related physical activity in children and adolescents: A bio-behavioral perspective. In D. Kirk, D. MacDonald, & M. O'Sullivan (Eds.), *The handbook of physical education* (pp. 665–684). London: Sage.

Welk, G. J., Jackson, A. W., Morrow, J. R., Haskell, W. H., Meredith, M. D., & Cooper, K. H. (2010). The association of health-related fitness with indicators of academic performance in Texas schools. *Research Quarterly for Exercise and Sport, 81*(3 suppl), S16–S23.

Whitehead, J. R., & Corbin, C. B. (1991). Youth fitness testing: The effect of percentile-based evaluative feedback on intrinsic motivation. *Research Quarterly for Exercise and Sport, 62*, 225–231.

Zabinski, M. F., Saelens, B. E., Stein, R. I., Hayden-Wade, H. A., & Wilfley, D. E. (2003). Overweight children's barriers to and support for physical activity. *Obesity Research, 11*, 238–246.

Zhu, W., Welk, G. J., Meredith, M. D., & Boiarskaia, E. A. (2010). A survey of physical education programs and policies in Texas schools. *Research Quarterly for Exercise and Sport, 81*(3 suppl), S42–S52.

SECTION III

Educational Games

In this section, we discuss content and present Sample Learning Experiences and sample annotated lesson and unit plans for the games content area. Our approach focuses on children learning fundamental game skills, basic tactics, and developmentally appropriate game-like tasks and small-sided, modified games designed to practice skills and tactics.

Recently, the Teaching Games for Understanding (TGfU) approach, which was primarily developed for use in middle and high school physical education, has suggested exciting ways to identify and teach tactics—content that, to date, has not been done well at the elementary level. From our knowledge of game playing and ideas presented in TGfU, we start with the fundamental game skills and then use the Laban framework to help us teach children how to vary and adapt fundamental game skills so that, with development, they can be used tactically in game-like situations and modified, small-sided games. Teaching skills and tactics is critical for children's success in and enjoyment of gameplay—in particular for lower-skilled children. Skills, tactics, and developmentally appropriate modified, small-sided games designed to practice skills and tactics form a sound foundation for participating in sports in middle school and in community youth sport programs.

We begin in Chapter 18 with a discussion of the philosophy of the educational games curriculum designed for elementary schools. We organize content into four game categories:

1. Invasion games
2. Net/wall games
3. Field games
4. Target games

A three-level progression for teaching game content is proposed: At developmental level 1, children develop fundamental game skills; at developmental level 2, children develop fundamental skills into tactical game skills; and at developmental level 3, children learn to use tactical skills and tactics in child- and teacher-designed and -modified, small-sided games.

Invasion games content is covered in three chapters because these games are much more complex and extensive than net/wall, field, and target games. In Chapter 19, we describe content appropriate for developmental levels 1 and 2 for catching, passing, kicking, and trapping the ball with the hands, feet, or hockey sticks. Because passes and shots on goal must be accurate, we include target game content in Chapter 19 as a foundation for invasion games. In Chapter 20, we show you how to teach game structures, such as boundaries and rules, and how to teach children to design and modify their own games. We use tag as an example of an invasion game, describing a unit for teaching tag tactics and designing games. Children learn about game structures, basic tactics, and designing and modifying games most easily in tag games where they do not need to use ball skills. Knowledge of the effects of game structures on tactics and gameplay and ways to modify these structures are prerequisites for all other game play content presented in Chapters 21, 22, and 23. In addition, in Chapter 20, we describe how to teach content appropriate for developmental level 3 for modified invasion games and tactics using passing and receiving with the hands, feet, or hockey sticks.

In Chapter 21, we describe content appropriate for developmental levels 1, 2, and 3 for dribbling with the hands, feet, and hockey sticks. Chapter 22 focuses on content and lesson segments for developmental levels 1, 2, and 3 for net/wall games. We end the educational games section with Chapter 23, which contains content and lesson segments for developmental levels 1, 2, and 3 for field games.

We have organized the content based on invasion, net/wall, field, and target game categories because this structure helps children make connections, acquire a greater depth of understanding, and become more skillful games players. For example, in invasion games, tactics such as sending a lead pass to a teammate who has cut into an open space to receive a pass are similar regardless of whether children are using their feet, hands, or a hockey stick to pass the ball. When you teach the same tactic across different skills, you are teaching children to understand the connections among games and to transfer their knowledge from one game situation to another.

CHAPTER

18

Introduction to Educational Games

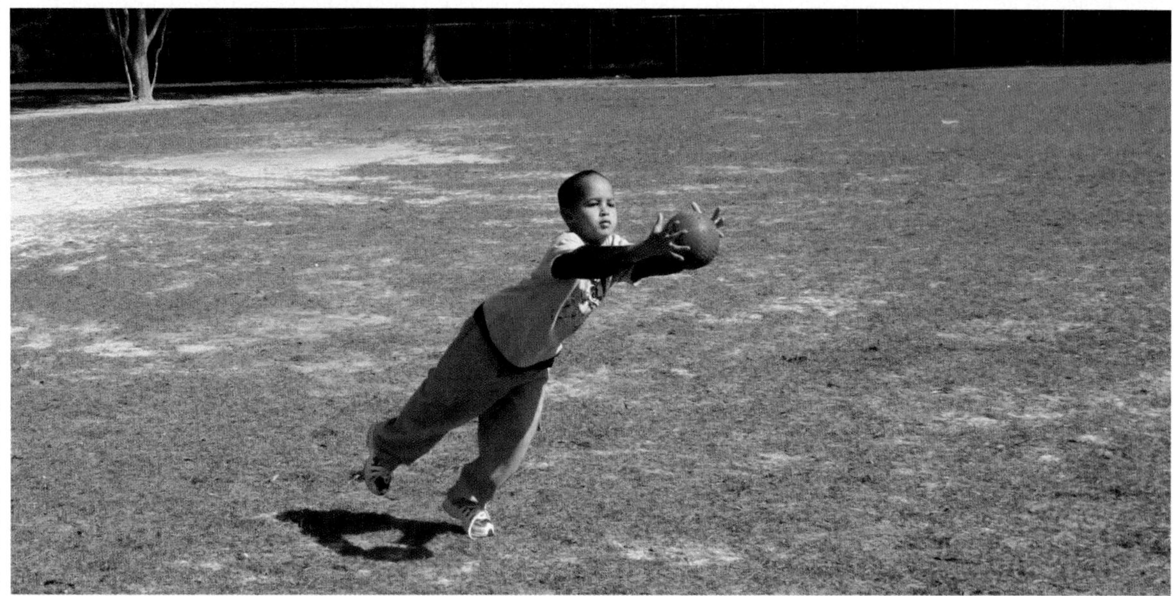

PRE-READING REFLECTION

1. What were your most positive and memorable game experiences from elementary school, and why are they memorable?
2. What were your most negative game experiences from elementary school, and why were they negative?

OBJECTIVES

Students will learn:

1. Educators think many traditional elementary physical education games are inappropriate for children.
2. SHAPE America supports specific guidelines for appropriate practice when teaching games; this text's educational games curriculum meets these guidelines (National Association for Sport and Physical Education [NASPE], 2009).
3. Educational games focus on developing skillful, versatile games players who can use appropriate tactics and understand game structures.
4. The content areas of elementary physical education include four game categories: invasion, net/wall, field, and target.
5. The specific content within each game category is based on the Laban framework and is organized in a three-level progression based on children's developmental levels in skill performance capabilities:
   - Children's Developmental Level 1: Fundamental skills
   - Children's Developmental Level 2: Tactical games skills
   - Children's Developmental Level 3: Using tactical game skills in modified gameplay

6. Games used in level 3 are designed and modified by the teacher and the children for the purpose of practicing skills and tactics.
7. A set of educational criteria is used to ensure gameplay meets the goals of the educational games curriculum.

KEY TERMS

Elimination games
Field games
Invasion games
Net/wall games
Target games

CONNECTION TO STANDARDS

The educational games content in this text focuses on children learning and practicing motor skills and basic tactics to achieve competence in performance. This focus on learning (as opposed to playing games and keeping children physically active) matches the focus of learning in the National Standards for Physical Education (National Standards). Games content specifically addresses all five National Standards. The extensive use of partner and group work in game tasks also provides an excellent context for meeting the Common Core and other State Standards (CCSS) for speaking, listening, and collaboration.

A Critique of Traditional and Recreational Games Programs

We begin with a quote from Dr. Kate Barrett, one of the developers of educational games. In this quote, she lists and critiques the wide range of conference session titles at the time she wrote the paper:

> The content of our field symbolizes what we stand for and what we have to offer the education of children. Our graduates will have to make decisions about what children will experience, in what sequence, and about how skillful they want children to become. These are tough decisions; never before in our history have we had so many directions from which to choose. For example, we can choose among:
>
> Adventure
> Aerobic exercise
> Aerobic dance
> American country dance
> Basic movement
> Basketball
> Basketball basics
> Bean bags
> Beginning ball skills
> Breaking up space sensibly
> Challenging climbing capacities
> Creative dance
> Creative movement
> Creative dramatics
> Educational dance
> Educational games
> Educational gymnastics
> Eyes and fingers in motion
> Fitness trails
> Folk dance for fun
> Football fantastics
> Fun with ropes
> Hoopnastics
> Huckleberry beanstalk
> Modern educational dance
> Movement/dance
> Movement/gymnastics
> Movement/games
> Parachute play
> Partner gymnastics
> Rhythmic movement for fun and fitness
> Rope courses
> Rope jumping
> Simple soccer skills
> Sittercises
> Softball strategies
> Sticks and wands
> Sticks, paddles, and things
> Tinkling for fun and fitness
> Tennis tactics
> Ultimate Frisbee
> Volleyball requisite skills
> Working in your own target zone
>
> How do you react to this list? My reaction is that any profession which defines its content to include so great a range needs to reevaluate its purpose for being and, ultimately, its justification as a required subject in a child's curriculum (Barrett, 1985, pp. 9–10).

A similar list of conference titles could easily be generated today, and Barrett's reaction remains highly pertinent. How can we justify our games program as an important and necessary part of the elementary school curriculum if we include any and every activity regardless of its educational outcomes for children?

The games portion of the elementary school curriculum is often, unfortunately, either a hodge-podge of recreational activities and children's games or a watered-down high school curriculum. When teaching a recreational activities and games curriculum, many teachers simply explain the game, and the children then play. This approach does not produce any substantial learning outcomes.

In a watered-down high school curriculum, teachers teach traditional sports skills and have children play regulation games as best they can. They do not teach children how to adapt skills to different game situations, nor do they teach the tactics of the game. Consequently, children do not learn the skills and tactics necessary to be skillful games players, and only the highly skilled children are successful.

Recommendations from Professional Organizations and the Professional Literature

In the United States, the Society of Health and Physical Educators (SHAPE) supports guidelines for elementary school physical education, describing both appropriate and inappropriate practices that support Barrett's and our own critique (NASPE, 2009). **Table 18.1** presents these guidelines related to game instruction.

Table 18.1 Appropriate Instruction Practice Guidelines for Elementary School Physical Education

Appropriate Practice	Inappropriate Practice
Teachers develop learning experiences that help students understand the nature of and the different kinds of competition. For example, students can elect to keep score or play for skill practice in selected situations.	Students are required to always keep score and participate in activities (e.g., relay races, elimination tag) that publicly identify them as winners or losers.
Teachers create a mastery- learning environment that encourages students to compete against previous personal performances or against a criterion score. Children are given opportunities to choose their competitive environment.	Teachers focus on production of full-scale competition and limit skill instruction (e.g., playing 11v11 soccer instead of emphasizing skill development through small-sided games).
Children are guided to understand that some students prefer competitive situations, while others do not; either preference is acceptable.	Children are made to feel that something is wrong with them if they don't enjoy competition.
The teacher uses small-sided games (e.g., 1v1, 2v2) or mini-activities to allow students ample opportunities to participate.	The teacher consistently uses only one ball for most activities that involve playing with a ball (e.g., soccer, softball). In the game situation, most players touch the ball only rarely.
The teacher allows students guided choices in matters such as equipment, rule modification, or type of skill practice (e.g., completing individual task sheets or small-group instruction).	The teacher controls the curriculum tightly, and children rarely have input regarding rules, activities covered, or equipment used for practice.
The teacher emphasizes critical-thinking and problem-solving tactics and strategies, using higher-order questions (e.g., those that deal with similarities, differences, efficiency, and effectiveness).	Activities are always taught command style, with no attempt to stimulate analysis or evaluation.
Teachers select, design, sequence, and modify games to maximize specific learning, fitness/skill enhancement, and enjoyment.	Teachers use games with no obvious learning purpose or goal other than to keep children "busy, happy, and good."

Source: Reprinted from *Appropriate Instructional Practice Guidelines for Elementary School Physical Education*, with permission from the National Association for Sport and Physical Education (NASPE), 1900 Association Drive, Reston, VA 20191–1599.

Scholars writing in the professional literature provide a similar critique. In a series of articles, Dr. Neil Williams (1992, 1994, 1996) described games belonging in the physical education "Hall of Shame," including the following:

- Dodgeball (also called Bombardment and Murderball)
- Duck, Duck, Goose
- Elimination tag games
- Giants, Elves, and Wizards (also called Crows and Cranes)
- Kickball
- Line Soccer
- Messy Back Yard
- Musical Chairs
- Red Rover
- Relay races
- Simon Says
- SPUD
- Steal the Bacon

In most Hall of Shame games, few children are active; most sit and watch. Some, such as dodgeball, are **elimination games**, meaning that as the game progresses, children are eliminated when they make a poor play. The less-skilled children are typically eliminated first, often intentionally, and their more highly skilled peers remain and get considerably more practice (and praise) than their classmates. Williams (1992) wrote,

> Elimination games are self-defeating, because the students who are in the greatest need of skill development are immediately banished, embarrassed, and punished, and then given no opportunity to improve. The next time they play, those students will be first out again.

Can you imagine a reading teacher taking the book away from a child who makes a mistake and letting only the best readers continue reading?

Gameplay and, in fact, all movement responses in physical education lessons are public. Children can easily see who is more skilled and who is less skilled. You will need to be sensitive to this issue and its effect on children. As Williams (1992) notes, many Hall of Shame games humiliate children by putting their low-skill ability on display. Relay races are a classic way to humiliate children. Everyone watches who is last and who "causes" his or her team to lose. Because children shout and cheer throughout the relay race, the class as a whole seems to be enjoying the races. You only need to watch the faces of those children who are last, however, to know why relay races belong in the Hall of Shame. (See also the "Student Tales" box on Hall of Shame activities.)

We agree with Williams that these games need to be eliminated from the physical education curriculum. Moreover, his articles were published in the *Journal of Physical Education,*

Student Tales

What Do Kids Think About Hall of Shame Activities?

We have talked about what physical education professionals think about games, but what do kids think? This answer can be surprisingly difficult to determine because the children who are highly skilled tend to be most happy with highly competitive elimination games because they are on positive display. They also tend to be the most vocal in voicing their opinions, whereas the quiet children who are miserable suffer in silence. It would take an incredible amount of bravery and self-confidence for a less-skilled child to complain to a teacher about the games the teacher selects. An experiment that we and others have performed is to have a classroom teacher teach a lesson including activities such as relay races, kickball, and other large-group games. At the beginning of the lesson, we assign each undergraduate (physical education or classroom major) to watch one to three children and then interview those children at the end of the lesson. We ensure that *every* child in the class is observed and interviewed. On the surface, the class appears to enjoy the lesson because the children yell and scream for their team to win. It is only when you watch and interview every child that you learn what really happened. We ask the children about their feelings during the lesson and their opinions about the activities. After the children leave, we compare answers. Rather than finding that most of the class liked the lesson, we discover that most did not—and a significant number of children were unhappy, embarrassed, and angry. As one undergraduate classroom teacher said, "I know what you have been telling us all semester, but it took a child to convince me."

The Case Against Dodgeball

The popularity of dodgeball on college campuses, along with its media exposure in the movie *Dodgeball* and on television, might lead you to wonder if you can modify dodgeball and teach it in physical education. Although you can modify dodgeball so it is not an elimination game, it remains inappropriate because it has a strong potential for physical and psychological harm—even if you use foam balls. Moreover, it has become a controversial game. NASPE (n.d.) has issued the following position statement: "Dodgeball is **not** an appropriate activity for K–12 school physical education programs." Consequently, if you have children learn dodgeball, regardless of any modifications you make, you will be acting in violation of a position statement by our national association. If a child gets hurt, you will be at risk for liability claims.

Recreation and Dance, which is the major journal for SHAPE America (see box "The Case Against Dodgeball"). Sanctioned by our national professional association, Williams' (1992, 1994, 1996) work stands as a powerful statement about the content of a safe, high-quality physical education program, and his suggestions continue to enjoy wide support. For example, Quinn and Carr (2006) argue that both physical education teachers and youth sport coaches need to stop using elimination games and abandon the "three Ls": laps, lines, and lectures. If you ignore the professional literature of national associations, you put yourself at risk for litigation and for negative evaluations of your program by administrators and parents.

Opinions from the Professional Literature About Competition

Competitive games that focus on keeping score and anointing winners and losers have been a contentious issue in elementary physical education for many years. Many physical education professionals believe we need to emphasize cooperation. To that end, they have developed a large number of cooperative games that are effective in teaching skills and cooperation in a physical education program (Grineski, 1996; Midura & Glover, 1999; Orlick, 1978).

We believe that what matters is whether a cooperative or competitive game is appropriate for a particular child at his or her physical, cognitive, social, and emotional developmental levels. Because you can teach skills and tactics in either cooperative or competitive games, you can differentiate instruction for different groups of children. To do so, you give children the choice to play a cooperative game, a competitive game, or a competitive game without keeping track of the score—a stance supported by NASPE's guidelines on appropriate practices.

It also is important to remember that competition and cooperation are interdependent, rather than mutually exclusive. Cooperation is a key component of positive competitive experiences and successful gameplay. Teammates who cooperate and interact positively form a more effective team. Cooperation between teams is also essential to make the games fair, balanced, and fun for both teams. A game is not fun if one team scores all the points and the other team is on defense the whole time. In such situations, the game or teams need to be modified.

You will need to monitor competitive games and recognize when competition is beneficial and when it is harmful. The following guidelines can help:

- Is the competitive environment detracting from learning and being physically active?
- Does any child feel incompetent or incapable?
- Do any children appear to be part of the game but are not actively participating in it?
- Is the competition contributing to an environment that is not emotionally or physically safe?
- Are the children enjoying gameplay and valuing the competition, or are they alienated, humiliated, and learning to hate PE?
- Do the children maintain a mastery orientation during competitive games? Do they feel good about their performance and effort in a well-played game regardless of the score? Do the children value the challenge of working hard against a good opponent?
- Are the children maintaining a cooperative, caring ethic during competitive games? Or are they engaging in

> **Student Tales**
>
> What Do Kids Think About Competition?
>
> A study of 10,000 students and their feelings about sport gives us considerable insight into what is important to them and how adults should respond (Ewing & Seefeldt, 1990). The study surveyed young people who were involved in competitive youth and school sports. Thus, the sample was biased toward children and adolescents who chose to participate after school and presumably did so because they wanted to play competitive sports. We know there is a significant decline in sport participation from age 10 to 18. The survey asked not only what children thought and felt, but also why they dropped out of sports.
>
> In brief, fun was the most important reason both boys and girls participated in sport. Not having fun was the second most important reason for dropping out. (The most important reason for dropping out was "I lost interest.") "To win" was the seventh most important reason boys participated in sport. Winning ranked behind improving skills, staying in shape, experiencing the excitement and challenge of competition, and being part of a team. Winning was twelfth on girls' lists, behind getting exercise, improving and learning new skills, being part of a team, feeling the team spirit, and experiencing the excitement and challenge of competition.
>
> Thus, in terms of competition, children do not rank winning and losing high on their list of importance, but they do give a high ranking to enjoyment and learning. Can 10,000 kids be wrong?

all-too-common youth sport behaviors such as yelling, "Hey, batter, batter, batter"?

- Do the children play poorly, but win and cheer (or gloat), claiming they were successful?
- Are the children focusing on learning, the enjoyment of the game, and the value and joy of effort?

Based on your answers, you should modify the competitive element of the games if needed and hold a class discussion on this issue. It is important to set up a mastery-oriented learning environment within competitive game structures and maintaining a cooperative, caring ethic by designing game rules to make competitive situations fair and enjoyable for all.

Goals of Educational Games

The educational games curriculum is different from a recreational or traditional sport curriculum and meets the National Standards and our professional organization SHAPE America's recommendations for appropriate practices (NASPE, 2009). Educational games focus on developing skillful games players with a deep understanding of substantive game skills, structures, and tactics associated with our major sports (see **Figure 18.1**). This curriculum is well supported by research and scholars from Australia, New Zealand, Canada, France, the United Kingdom, and the United States (Barrett, 1984; Belka, 2004; Grehaigne, Wallian, & Godbout, 2005; Griffin, Brooker, & Patton, 2005; Mauldon & Redfern, 1969; Werner, 2001). The goals are for children

1. To become skillful games players with versatile skills that they can adapt to different game situations.

> **SAFETY AND LIABILITY 18.1**
>
> **Increasing Safety and Decreasing Risk of Liability: Guidelines Relevant to Content in this Chapter**
>
> In this box, we discuss specific guidelines built on information discussed throughout this text on professional standards of practice, negligence, and liability. The goals of these guidelines are to increase children's safety and decrease teachers' risk of negligence and liability.
>
> - To increase safety and decrease liability risk, teachers should plan and follow a written curriculum with a progression or sequence of tasks to develop children's skills safely. The curriculum should be based on district, state, and national standards and guidelines. All tasks should be developmentally appropriate and modified to accommodate individual differences. Safety issues within tasks must be taught and students warned about potential dangers.
> - All students must always supervised while they are in the physical education space and during transit to this space. Teachers cannot leave the children alone to step into the hallway for any reason—even to deal with an emergency situation—without another qualified supervisor in the physical education space. Classroom and physical education teachers must communicate when they transfer supervisory duties from one to the other.
> - A reasonably prudent physical educator would follow the appropriate practice guidelines, such as those listed in **Table 18.1**, because these are part of a larger document published by our professional organization that helps define accepted professional practice.
> - Dodgeball and other "Hall of Shame" games are games a reasonably prudent teacher would not teach.
> - Reasonably prudent teachers organize tasks, equipment, and stations so students have adequate space and will not infringe on the space needed by others and will remain safe from collisions, loose or hit balls, and equipment usage, such as children swinging rackets and bats.
> - In any task or modified game, the teacher must plan for overflow space or space beyond the boundaries so that children will not run into a wall or other children if they go out of bounds or beyond the task boundaries.
> - Reasonably prudent teachers will check the grounds and floor to ensure the facilities are free from hazards and uneven or slippery surfaces. Teachers must report all hazardous conditions and ensure these conditions are repaired.

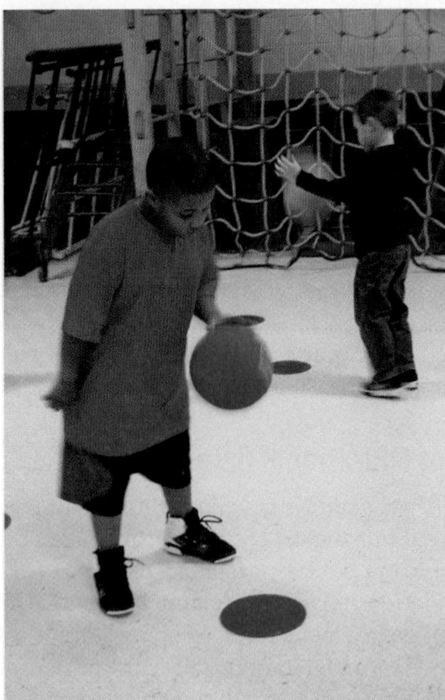

Figure 18.1 Learning skills

2. To understand tactical gameplay so that they can anticipate, think quickly, and make appropriate tactical decisions in game situations.
3. To understand game structures such as rules, consequences for breaking rules, boundaries, scoring goals, and scoring systems, as well as how these game structures influence gameplay and tactics.
4. To design and modify game structures to make games work well for all children in the group.
5. To value games content as meaningful and relevant to their lives.

The Four Game Categories

Within the educational games curriculum, we organize content into four game categories: invasion, net/wall, field, and target (Bunker & Thorpe, 1982; Ellis, 1983; Mauldon & Redfern, 1969; Werner, 1989). We categorize games based on similarities in tactics, with invasion games being the most complex tactically, followed by net/wall and field games; target games involve the least complex tactics at the elementary school level.

Invasion games include those games in which the offense and the defense play in the same space—that is, they invade the space of the other team to score. Sports that are invasion games include basketball, soccer, field hockey, ice hockey, team handball, lacrosse, football, and water polo. Although tactics vary when these sports are played at the elite level, for elementary-age children, the invasion game tactics we teach, such as cutting into open spaces to receive passes, are the same or similar whether using kicking skills or throwing and catching skills.

In **net/wall games**, a net separates the teams—an arrangement found in games such as volleyball, tennis, badminton, pickleball, table tennis, and deck tennis. Tactics such as hitting into open space where no defender can reach the ball and covering the space to prevent the ball or shuttlecock from hitting the ground or bouncing twice are the same or similar across all net games. Wall games such a racquetball, handball, and squash are grouped with net games because the tactics are the same or similar. Net/wall games usually use striking skills with the hands, forearms, or rackets.

Field games include major sports such as softball, baseball, and cricket. In field games, the offense hits a ball, usually with a bat, into a field space covered by defenders. The offense scores by running to bases ahead of a throw by the defenders.

Target games are typically individual sports focused on hitting a target, often using an implement. Target sports include golf, bowling, and archery. Because passing and shooting accurately are essential in invasion games, target games using tossing and kicking are foundational to invasion games. Thus, we teach practice tasks and child-designed target games using throwing, shooting, and kicking accurately to a variety of targets. We do not provide lesson plans for target games related to the skills used in golf, bowling, or archery due to the space limitations of most elementary physical education spaces.

Game Categories Help You Teach for Transfer

One of the benefits of organizing games content by game category is that it facilitates teaching for transfer—a concept that has some support in the research literature (Mitchell, Oslin, & Griffin, 2006). In educational games, we refer to units as focusing on invasion, net/wall, field, or target games. Then, for the focus of a unit, you select skills, movement concepts, and/or basic tactics that are important to that game category. Thus, you might teach an invasion game unit focused on two tactics, such as sending lead passes (with the hands) to open teammates and cutting into an open space to catch a pass. You can then easily transfer these tactics to units on sending lead passes and cutting to receive passes with the feet or a hockey stick. Teaching for transfer reinforces the movement concepts and tactics for children, helps them apply these concepts across games, and develops thinking games players who can use their knowledge flexibly across a range of game situations. **Table 18.2** gives several examples of tactics and movement concepts that can be transferred to other contexts.

When games are taught as separate sports at the elementary level, tactics are often taught narrowly or prescribed as rules that apply only to that sport. For example, young children are often taught the following rule in soccer: "Don't leave your assigned zone in a zone defense. You mark any offense player who comes into your zone." Children acquire some understanding of a soccer zone defense that is taught in a rule-like manner, but their understanding is narrow, and they are unable to adjust when the zone breaks down or the offense gets ahead of other defenders. Few students who learn this way can transfer their knowledge of tactics and movement concepts from one sport to another. Only the highly skilled players develop an understanding of tactics through many years of participation.

In contrast to teaching tactics narrowly as prescribed rules (see the "Parent Stories" box), teaching children how basic

Table 18.2 Transfer of Movement Concepts and Tactics Across Games

Game Category	Skills, Movement Concepts, and Tactics	Potential for Transfer
Invasion games: dribbling with the hands	Dribbling on angular and curved pathways around defenders Dribbling on straight pathways when there are no defenders between you and the goal	Soccer-type games played with the feet Hockey-type games played with floor or field hockey sticks Lacrosse cradling Running with a football
Invasion games: passing and receiving with the hands (e.g., team handball, basketball-type games)	Sending lead passes to open teammates Cutting into an open space to receive a pass	Soccer-type games played with the feet Hockey-type games played with floor or field hockey sticks Lacrosse Football-type games
Invasion games	Basic defensive position is between your opponent and the goal	All invasion games
Net/wall games: volleyball	Striking the ball to the open space between defenders to score or force the defenders away from a strong defensive position	All other net/wall racket games
Net/wall games: badminton	Recover to the central ready position that allows you to cover most effectively the space in which the offense can hit to score	All other net/wall games; sometimes called the base position in tennis-type games

Parent Stories

The son of one of our friends played youth soccer. His coaches taught him not to leave his defensive zone. In a game when an offense player broke free and was dribbling unopposed to score, his father yelled, "Sayon, go and mark him; stop him from scoring." His son looked at him, exasperated, and said, "Dad, I'm doing it right. My coach said I was not to leave my zone."

tactics cross game categories provides a broad-based games education (Thorpe & Bunker, 2010).

This approach develops children's tactical game skills and enhances their ability to make tactical decisions in unpredictable game environments in which no two tactical situations are precisely the same—a practice that is supported by motor learning theory (Davids, Button, & Bennett, 2008).

Identifying Content and Ordering It in a Progression

To identify potential content within each of the game categories, we use the movement concepts from the Laban framework adapted to games, along with our knowledge of sports and games. We then organize the content in the following progression, which we based, in part, on Dr. Judith Rink's (2014) four-step progression and Dr. Kate Barrett's (1977) three-phase process of games teaching. The progression of content is directly connected to children's level of developing competent skill performance.

A child at developmental level 1 is a beginner and just starting to learn the fundamental skill. A child at developmental level 2 has learned to control the ball in simple situations, such as dribbling with the hand in place, and is ready to practice the skill in a variety of ways and situations. A child at developmental level 3 can vary the skill in a variety of situations and can control the ball to the extent that he or she does not have to concentrate on performance techniques and thus can shift attention to focus on using the skill in tactical situations.

1. *Developmental Level 1: Fundamental Game Skills.* At this level of development, children learn the basic skill techniques that enable children to control the ball most of the time in simple situations (see **Figure 18.2**).
2. *Developmental Level 2: Tactical Game Skills.* At this level of development, children learn (a) how and why to vary and adapt fundamental game skills using movement concepts from the Laban framework; (b) how to combine skills; and (c) how to use skills and basic tactics in game-like situations with a cooperative ethic (see **Figure 18.3**). Children continue to focus on performance techniques for improving ball control, now in a variety of game-like situations, and learn how, when, and why skills are varied in relation to these situations.
3. *Developmental Level 3: Using Tactical Game Skills in Modified, Small-sided Gameplay.* Children at this level of development learn to use tactical game skills and tactics in teacher- and child-designed and -modified, small-sided games (see **Figure 18.4**). We define games as having boundaries, rules, scoring goals, scoring systems, and a cooperative/competitive structure.

Our framework differs from Rink's progression in two major ways. We eliminated her stage 4 only because it typically applies to the secondary school level. We also moved varying the skill using concepts from the Laban framework from

Figure 18.2 Developmental level 1: Fundamental game skills

Figure 18.4 Developmental level 3: Using tactical game skills in modified gameplay

Courtesy of John Dolly

Rink's stage 1 to our level 2a, in recognition of the connections between movement concepts and tactics and our theoretical view that movement patterns of skills emerge from the relations among individual, task, and environmental constraints.

Figure 18.5 illustrates this progression. It shows level 1, fundamental game skills, in the center. Content appropriate for developing level 2 expands and builds on level 1. Content appropriate for developing level 3 expands and builds on levels 1 and 2. **Table 18.3** provides examples of the progression using dribbling with the hand.

Content appropriate for developing performance at the three levels is not a step-like progression. Instead, as the dashed lines in **Figure 18.5** imply, you go back and forth between levels depending on what the children need to learn. For example,

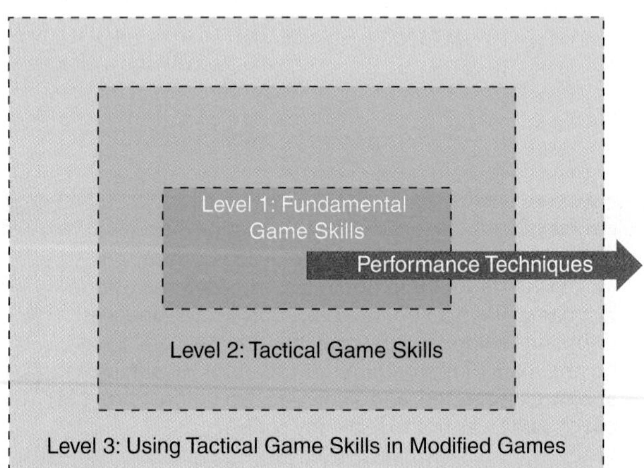

Figure 18.5 Model of progression of games content

Figure 18.3 Developmental level 2: Tactical game skills

you might set a task appropriate for developing the capability at level 2 to strike a ball with a racket back and forth over a low net with a partner and observe that some children cannot maintain a rally because they cannot control the direction of the ball. Thus, for those children, you would change the assignment to practice a task in keeping with developmental level 1.

In addition, some level 2 tactical game skills are not relevant to children until children have experience playing level 3 games. For example, children do not understand the value of drop shots, lobs, dinks, and clears in net games until they have played net games and understand the tactic of hitting to an open space to score.

Different Fundamental Game Skills Develop at Different Rates

Some fundamental game skills develop relatively quickly, whereas others take considerably more time to evolve. For example, striking backhand with a racket and an overhead strike with a racket typically still need practice as level 1 fundamental skills in the fourth and fifth grades. Thus, the three-level

Table 18.3 Examples of Level 1, Level 2, and Level 3 Using Dribbling with the Hand

Level	Content	Performance Techniques
Developmental Level 1: Fundamental Game Skills • Learning the most basic performance techniques that enable the children to control the ball most of the time	*Sample Developmental Level 1 Content for Dribbling* • Dribbling with dominant/nondominant hand in place while walking and while jogging • Controlling the ball by dribbling at an appropriate level and pushing with appropriate force and in the appropriate direction	*Performance Techniques Taught in Developmental Level 1 Lessons* • Push with finger pads • Waist high • Ball to front/side
Developmental Level 2: Tactical Game Skills Learning (a) how and why to vary and adapt fundamental game skills applying movement concepts from the Laban framework; (b) to combine skills; and (c) to use skills and tactics in game-like situations	*Sample Developmental Level 2 Content and Tactics for Dribbling and Combining Dribbling with Other Skills in Game-like Situations (Tactics in Italics)* Level 2A • Dribbling on different pathways because you need to learn how *to feint, fake out, dodge*, and *drive by defenders* (cones or noncompetitive defenders) • Dribbling at different speeds, accelerating and stopping quickly, and changing directions because you need to learn how *to feint, fake out, dodge*, and *drive by defenders* (cones or noncompetitive defenders) Level 2B • Combining dribbling and passing; combining dribbling and shooting Level 2C • Practicing dribbling in a 1v1 situation, learning to *put the body between the ball and a defender to protect the ball* (pretend or noncompetitive defender)	*Performance Techniques Taught in Developmental Level 2 Lessons* • Head up/eyes up *to see defenders and teammates.* • Wide V-shaped bounce when doing a crossover dribble; dribbling on zigzag and curved pathways • When combining dribbling and shooting, transferring the ball to the shooting position within one step
Developmental Level 3: Using Tactical Game Skills and Tactics in Modified, Small-sided Games • Learning to use tactical game skills in child- and teacher-designed and -modified games with boundaries, rules, scoring goals, scoring systems, and a cooperative/competitive structure	*Sample Developmental Level 3 Modified Games for Dribbling* • 1v1 dribbling games with scoring goals, rules, boundaries, and an active defender • Dribble tag-type games • 2v2 games with dribbling, shooting, and passing *Developmental Level 3: Tactics* • In dribble tag, use teammates as blockers • Know that you can pass the ball to a teammate close to the goal faster than you can dribble the ball there yourself • Dribble when no one is open and everyone is standing still	*Performance Techniques Taught in Developmental Level 3 Lessons* • Dribbling fast and low while driving by defenders

progression varies based on children's capabilities with particular skills, tactics, and game-like situations.

Developmental Level 1: Fundamental Game Skills

At developmental level 1, children learn the most basic performance techniques associated with the skill—techniques that enable them to control the ball most of the time. Teaching focuses on two to four techniques that are appropriate at immature performance levels *and* are important for gaining ball control. For example, in teaching dribbling with the hand, you focus on pushing with the finger pads rather than slapping the ball, as this technique is essential for ball control (see **Figure 18.6**). You teach dribbling while looking up—a more difficult performance technique—later, as part of level 2 tasks, when children learn why they need to look up in game-like situations.

With this approach, children need not learn and master all the performance techniques of the mature movement pattern of the skill before they progress to level 2 and learn to vary and adapt skills to game-like situations. Instead, they simply need to be able to control the ball safely.

At developmental level 1, children practice in simple situations (e.g., standing in place or while jogging) and in situations in which the environment does not vary much, if at all. For example, dribbling with the hand while standing in place (with no defenders) is a practice task appropriate for developmental level 1. If you have children try to develop movement variety or play in game-like situations in which the environment changes (i.e., level 2) and one child's skills regress to the point where the game-like situation falls apart or he or she becomes emotionally upset, then the task is inappropriate for that child. In this scenario, the child needs more practice in tasks appropriate for level 1.

Figure 18.6 Kindergarteners learning to control the ball who are not ready for level 2 tasks; poly spots provide orientation for personal space

Children at developmental 2C learn to use skills in game-like situations (played with a cooperative ethic) and to make decisions about what to do and when.

As in developmental level 1, the focus in level 2 is learning to control the ball; now, however, the context varies, and children learn why skills must change in relation to game-like situations. For example, children learn that the reason they practice dribbling on zigzag pathways is to be able to avoid defenders. As part of the content taught at level 2, we use cones as pretend defenders or defenders playing at a low intensity, thereby allowing the child with the ball to succeed and understand the meaning of skill variations in games.

The red arrow labeled "performance techniques" in **Figure 18.5** illustrates that you teach skill techniques across the elementary school years. Recall that developing mature performance techniques takes many years of practice. Typically, you teach only one or two new techniques in any one lesson or unit. The techniques you teach, however, become increasingly more difficult. At developmental level 1, you focus on techniques that help children gain control of the ball. At developmental levels 2 and then 3, you work on techniques that are more difficult and linked to performing the skill in more complex and difficult game-like situations. The extension of the line beyond level 3 in **Figure 18.5** implies that children will continue to work on techniques in middle school, high school, and beyond.

Table 18.3 presents a sample progression of skill techniques to teach for dribbling. It illustrates how these tasks increase in difficulty as children become better able to adapt fundamental game skills in increasingly more complex, game-like situations.

As game-like situations become more complex, however, you might have to review techniques that children mastered in less complex situations. Sometimes when children practice in situations that are more complex, their techniques will regress to immature patterns. For example, dribbling waist high is a performance technique that children easily master at level 1 when standing still or walking. Once you have children dribble at fast speeds to avoid a defender in level 2, however, they sometimes bounce the ball at a high level (Chen, Rovegno, Todorovich, & Babiarz, 2003). Consequently, they will need to focus again on dribbling waist high to be able to maintain control in the new and more complex game-like situation.

Developmental Level 2: Tactical Game Skills

At developmental level 2, the focus is on developing fundamental game skills into tactical game skills. At developmental level 2A, children learn how and why to vary and adapt fundamental game skills using movement concepts from the Laban framework. At developmental level 2B, they learn how to combine skills such as catching and then immediately throwing a ball.

Developmental Level 2A: Using Movement Concepts from the Laban Framework to Vary Skills

At developmental level 2A, children start working on National Standard 2 by applying movement concepts to vary skills. Recall that most skills used in games are open skills in which the movement pattern is adapted to changing environments (Rose & Christina, 2006). For example, in invasion games, children need to be able to pass and catch balls in a wide variety of ways, such as passing balls over different distances and catching balls at different levels (movement concepts from the space aspect of the Laban framework). *Thus, your practice tasks to develop movement variety are, in essence, game-like situations.*

We label skills appropriate for developmental level 2 "tactical game skills" because the kinds of variability and adaptability children need to develop are determined by the tactical context of games. For example, children need to be able to dribble while changing speeds (a concept from the Laban framework) to fake out and drive around defenders, but dribbling at a high level (another concept from the Laban framework) is not relevant because it leads to loss of control and an easy steal by a defender. Thus, not all movement concepts are relevant for a particular skill.

You don't select movement concepts randomly, nor do you simply teach them as context-free content preceding their application to motor skills. You select movement concepts to apply to the manipulative skills because the movement variety the movement concept generates is directly connected to how skills are used in game-like contexts. For example, hitting a ball with a bat is taught only at a medium level, whereas rolling a bowling ball occurs only at a low level. Throwing and catching balls at high, medium, and low levels, however, are all part of various games. Thus, the movement concept of levels is relevant to teach with some motor skills but not others.

Developmental Level 2B: Combining Skills

At developmental level 2B, children learn how to combine skills. Dribbling, stopping, and shooting are not the same as dribbling and smoothly, in one movement, transitioning to shooting. When you teach children to combine skills, you need to teach the transitional movements between skills, which begin in the first skill and continue to the second skill (Rink, 2014). For example, dribbling and then shooting and catching a ground ball and then throwing to first base both include transitional movements. The body position in catching a fly ball with no runners on base is square to the ball because there is no need to transition quickly to throw. The body position when you must catch and throw immediately to a base to stop a runner is to catch with the opposite foot to the throwing hand in front. Thus the preparation for the throw begins before the catch in this situation. In short, you don't simply have students combine skills; you must teach them how and why to do so.

Developmental Level 2C: Using Tactical Game Skills in Game-like Situations

Across developmental level 2, your focus is on children learning to control the ball in game-like situations but not on playing games, keeping score, or winning and losing. Game-like situations consist of an authentic game environment that allows children to practice and learn the appropriate movement responses and decisions about what to do and when. These game-like tasks help children learn why the movement patterns of skills are varied in different tactical situations and start the process of developing quick-thinking games players.

Although game-like situations are not games per se, *the children will most often perceive them as games.* We hear children saying, "We played a great basketball game today." They did not play regulation 5v5 basketball. Rather, partners practiced dribbling while protecting the ball in a 1v1 situation. The perception that level 2 tasks are games is natural, however, and we do not discourage it.

The Importance of Developmental Level 2 Content

Some teachers neglect level 2 content, even though it is the most important aspect of developing children's competence in gameplay. In fact, level 2 tasks are often the focus of high school and intercollegiate team practices for that very reason (Belka, 2004). At developmental level 2, children develop versatile skills and the ability to make decisions about why, how, and when to adapt skills to different game situations. For example, they learn why and how to dribble on zigzag and curved pathways to fake out and drive by defenders, and when to dribble fast on straight pathways (when there is open space between them and the goal). As motor learning research suggests, teachers need to set tasks that allow children to explore different movement patterns for skills in relation to game-like situations (Renshaw, Chow, Davids, & Hammond, 2010).

In level 2, children also learn to attend to the relationships between what they see within authentic contexts and what this environment means for the movement pattern of the skill. As we know, perception and action are coupled (Gibson, 1979/1986). Motor control research and theory indicate that, when performing motor skills, there is information in the environment, which learners perceive, that specifies movement patterns to achieve the goals of the task (Davids et al., 2008). For example, in striking a ball with a partner over a net with a racket, children need to learn to perceive where the ball will bounce, how high it will bounce, and how fast it is moving—and, consequently, where to position themselves and what timing and force of swing will be needed to make contact with the ball with the racket.

Not only do children need to learn about the relationships between perception and action, but they also need to understand the relationships between offensive and defensive players in space. For example, when dribbling, they need to learn how close they can get to a defender before that defender can steal the ball. When passing, they need to learn how far ahead of the defender the receiver needs to be to receive a lead pass. Research shows that tactical game skills are relational skills; that is, they are fundamentally concerned with making decisions about the appropriate movement response in relation to the positions of offensive and defensive players and the game situation (MacPhail, Kirk, & Griffin, 2008; Rovegno, Nevett, Brock, & Babiarz, 2001).

Research findings suggest that children need to learn even the most basic relational aspects that may be so obvious to adults that we don't realize that we need to teach them. For example, in one study, fourth-grade children were throwing passes that were too forceful and too high for the receiver to catch (Rovegno et al., 2001). The children's verbal explanations indicated that they needed to be taught that part of the passer's goal and responsibility is to send receivers a pass that is catchable because the receiver is on the same team and passers want their team to keep possession of the ball.

Introducing Basic Tactics

You start introducing basic tactics at developmental level 2. The following are examples of these tactics:

- *Invasion games:* To send a lead pass, throw the ball into the space ahead of the moving receiver.
- *Net/wall games:* Recover to the central ready position or base position after you hit the ball to be in a strong defensive position.
- *Field games:* Throw to the base ahead of the runner to put the runner out.

In teaching tactics, it is important that students not only learn to make appropriate tactical decisions, but also acquire cognitive knowledge of the tactics at a conscious level (Rink, 2010). As Rink explains, learners need a language in which to think about the range of tactical options and to decide which tactics they need to employ. In the same way that we describe performance techniques, describing tactics allows children—in particular, low-skilled children—to remember tactics during practice.

Like learning motor skills, learning tactics is a process that occurs over time. Children might successfully execute a tactic one instance and struggle with it the next. Research shows that when children understand and can discuss a tactic at a conscious level, simple prompts or reminders by teachers can be enough to help children make appropriate tactical decisions more frequently (Rovegno et al., 2001).

If children have spent considerable time developing tactical game skills in game-like situations, they can make the transfer to level 3 games. Even so, you will often include level 2 tasks in level 3 lessons when the need arises for children to learn a new tactic that will help them improve gameplay. Teaching tactics using level 2 tasks after children have played a game allows children to understand the meaning and relevance of tactical game skills to gameplay and gain additional, necessary practice in less complex, game-like situations (Bunker & Thorpe, 1982; Mitchell et al., 2006). For example, children might be working on the tactic of giving the passer multiple options in a level 3 game when you observe that they pass and just stand still, thus leaving the new passer with fewer receiver options. In this situation, you might stop gameplay and teach a "give and go" as a level 2 tactical game skill. You would then return to gameplay and have the children work on the give-and-go in their games.

The ability to use a tactic is highly dependent on the ability to control the ball in a variety of ways. Research shows that if students have not learned skills to a certain level of proficiency, they will not be able to improve their ability to play games, nor will their skills and tactical decision making transfer to gameplay (Holt, Ward, & Wallhead, 2006). Although research has not shown what level of skill development is necessary before students can successfully use tactics in games, research suggests that some tactics can probably be used once children can control the ball in a variety of situations, whereas other, more advanced tactics will require further skill development (Lee & Ward, 2009).

Figure 18.7 Level 2 practice task

Developmental Level 3: Using Tactical Game Skills in Modified, Small-sided Gameplay

Level 3 focuses on children learning how to use tactical game skills and tactics in teacher- and child-designed and -modified games. As noted earlier, we define games as having boundaries, rules, scoring goals, scoring systems, and a cooperative/competitive structure. A cooperative/competitive structure means you cooperate with teammates to compete against opponents by scoring in some way. You can choose not to keep track of the score, or you can devise a scoring system that reinforces the use of tactics (e.g., score 1 point if you catch the ball over the end line and 2 points if you catch a lead pass on the run over the end line); in any event, the underlying cooperative/competitive structure remains. Target sports, such as golf and archery, do not have the same kind of competitive structure because you perform these sports in an individual manner. The challenge in such sports is specifically to get the best score; any competition is with yourself, for example to try to improve on your personal best.

Thus, we draw a line between level 2 game-like situations and level 3 games with the addition of all game structures. For example, a 1v1 activity can be a game-like practice task appropriate for developmental level 2, but, if you add boundaries, consequences for breaking rules, and a competitive scoring system, it becomes a game appropriate for level 3.

Game Structures Add Complexity

The addition of all game structures adds considerable complexity to physical education tasks. At level 2, the child is still focused on controlling the ball and learning how, when, and why to adapt skills in a variety of game-like situations (see **Figure 18.7**). At level 3, the decision making is more complex because the game is more unpredictable and there are more factors to think about. In this environment, children need to be able to control the ball to the extent that they can also attend to the evolving game situation with multiple offensive and defensive players.

Moreover, game structures make level 3 more complex because they increase the social demands on children. For example, in a competitive game with scoring, children must manage the competitive environment in ways that support all children learning and having positive experiences in physical education regardless of the score. Because of differences in children's social development levels, competitive games (keeping track of the score) can be a stressful, negative experience for some children and can overpower the many other values of gameplay, such as learning, challenge, and enjoyment.

The decision about when to add all game structures can be difficult. It is not unusual to see some children working happily and productively in a level 2 game-like situation and think that the time is right to progress to level 3. When you add rules, consequences, and scoring systems to the same task, however, you may find the children start arguing about the score and become unproductive and flustered. In the upper elementary grades, experienced teachers shift back and forth between developmental levels 2 and 3 based on the needs of individual children. Learning when to shift is part of the art of teaching that you will develop with experience and reflection on your children's learning.

The Benefits of Modified, Small-Sided Games

Child- and teacher-designed and -modified small-sided games are the backbone of the level 3 curriculum in the upper elementary grades and the only games taught to children in this age group. Modified games are beneficial for the following reasons:

- *Modified games help teachers accommodate individual differences.* Just like shoes, one size of boundary does not fit all children. One set of rules and one set of scoring structures will not be developmentally appropriate for all children. In games, as in all areas of physical education, you need to differentiate instruction by modifying games for different children.

- *Modified games provide maximum practice opportunities.* Modified games at the elementary level are small-sided games (typically no more than three children per team) and therefore provide maximum practice opportunities and amounts of health-related physical activity (see **Figure 18.8**). There are few (if any) aerobic opportunities in 9v9 softball games, by comparison, and even fewer opportunities for children to practice the full range of skills used in field games. Thus, small-sided games provide better conditions for learning skills and tactics.
- *Modified games enable teachers to structure the game situation to highlight particular tactics and game skills.* For example, playing a 3v3 basketball-type game with no dribbling requires children to work on cutting and passing. Some physical educators call these "conditioned" games because they set conditions for children to learn and practice particular skills and tactics.
- *Modified games simplify the content.* Modified games allow teachers to break gameplay down into manageable chunks of information that children can learn within a lesson or unit. Regulation sports are simply too complex for young children to play well. To play these sports at later ages, they will need a solid background learning the skills and tactics in small-sided, modified games.

What Makes a Modified Game Educational?

In designing or selecting modified games for level 3, we use a special set of educational criteria to determine whether the game is appropriate for a lesson or unit. These criteria apply across game categories and are interdependent. To evaluate a modified game, ask the following questions:

1. *Will the children learn worthwhile, substantive content?* Are the skills and tactics of the game valuable learning outcomes that are worth spending lesson time developing?
2. *Are the children learning?* Are the children's skills and tactics improving through gameplay? Have the children developed the skills and tactics to a level needed to play the game successfully? Will the children understand the tactics so that the game is a meaningful activity in which they think and make tactical decisions (rather than a silly, fun game in which they simply run around)?

Figure 18.8 Level 3 modified game practice

3. *Is there maximum participation?* Is there opportunity for all children to be involved 100% of the time? If not, is there a legitimate need for rest? Will each child get plenty of practice at each position?
4. *Will all students be successful and challenged?* Is the game developmentally appropriate? If not, can you modify aspects of the game to make these aspects either more or less difficult or complex for individual students?
5. *Is the game emotionally and physically safe for all children?* Have the children developed the self-esteem and social responsibility needed for the game so that all children will feel confident, empowered, and able to play "all out" without fear of humiliation? Is the physical environment safe, or are there dangerous aspects of the game during which children could get hurt?

Child- and Teacher-Designed Games

Games can be designed or modified by the teacher, by the children, or, most often, by the teacher and the children together (Allison & Barrett, 2000). Having children participate in designing and modifying games is a curricular option we cherish for many reasons. Probably the most important reason for taking this road is that having children experiment and solve problems while designing and modifying games helps them acquire in-depth knowledge of game structures and tactics that is meaningful to them as opposed to seeing boundaries and rules as arbitrary and disconnected to tactical gameplay (see the "Experienced Teachers Talk" box).

Child-designed games also help develop thinking and social skills through group work. Putting children in groups requires them to learn how to cooperate and make decisions, how to explain and justify their ideas, and how to consider the needs and opinions of others. These collaborative skills are all required in the CCSS.

Moreover, designing their own games gives children the power to be in charge of their games and work independently from teachers. They will be able to design games exciting and challenging to them (Almond, 2010). In one research study at the second author's school, the first author interviewed one of the older classroom teachers. She explained why she liked the physical education program:

> Our first couple of years here we had recess…[it] was an exercise in [saying], "No, stop chasing; [leave] him alone," or watching kids just stand around looking at each other and talking. Well, recess kind of was legislated away from us for a little while….We reinstated recess, and suddenly it was like an explosion of activity. Nobody just stands and talks. They're all doing something. They're all inventing things….I can't believe these kids are any different than other kids…or different than the ones years ago, but these kids have less trouble finding something to do when they're given free time….The only difference that I can see is that they've been taught how to [design games] in PE, and I think that's a positive result. They love it…and they're all friends when they're done, and it's their game. They somehow make up the rules…and I'm not breaking up fights, and I'm not forced to go over to somebody and say, "Come on…I want you to do something. Don't just stand here and look at each other" (Classroom teacher).

The Important Role of the Teacher in Level 3 Gameplay

When children begin playing games, it is easy for beginning teachers to slip out of the role of a teacher and become a referee and scorekeeper. You need to maintain your role as a teacher. It helps to remember that children will not learn tactical content by simply playing games. Tactics and their relationships to rules, boundaries, scoring goals, and scoring systems need to be taught explicitly.

Thus, we teach basic tactics in levels 2 and 3. Although tactics might sound like advanced content needed only by highly skilled students, even the simplest games have tactics that children need to learn. If you have ever watched a whole class of kindergarteners without knowledge of tactics playing tag, you will notice that children run all over the place—but some children do not know they are supposed to avoid the taggers, some children try to get tagged, and some huddle in the corner. There is a difference between playing tag and learning how to play tag. When you play tag, you get kids running around screaming and having fun. *When you teach tag, you get kids having fun while learning the basic skills and tactics of invasion games.* When children understand basic tactics, they understand where to go and what to do. Average and less-skilled children particularly value learning tactics (Mitchell et al., 2006), because it enables them to play good games with competence and confidence.

The tactical content of invasion, net/wall, and field games comes directly from our major sports, such as basketball, soccer, tennis, and baseball/softball. Consequently, children who have learned tactical game skills in modified games will be well prepared to play sports in secondary school.

> **Experienced Teachers Talk**
>
> **A Teacher's First Experience with Child-Designed Games**
>
> This is so funny. I had an aide and another teacher in here, and we were doing all teacher-designed games in games—you know, the lead-off activities were movement-oriented, then the teacher designed the game....And I said, "You know, it's about time we break the rules. The literature says they can do it; let's see if they can [design their own games]."...And so we did it. We went out there, and the first thing that happened (that was like total shock!) was there was no yelling. The aide said, "I wonder if they're having any fun because they're not screaming anymore." We had nine [classes]—five classes from fourth [grade] and four from fifth [grade]. They did kicking. When we got to the place where *we* would have made up the game,...we said, "Now you can make up your game, and it has to have these elements (I don't remember, but it had to have kicking, the ball had to stay [with]in the boundar[ies], and it was up to you whether or not you kept score), or you can come and we will show you a game to play." And these are kids who had only, ever in their whole life, *only* played games that we had made up. No one picked that game in any class! In not one single class! No one said, "We want to play the game that you want to teach to us." I couldn't believe it; I mean, we laughed for a week (Rovegno & Bandhauer, 1997, p. 147).

Summary

Teachers, researchers, and our professional organizations have criticized many traditional elementary physical education games as inappropriate and have recommended guidelines for educational games that teachers can trust to be in the best interests of children.

We divide educational games into four game categories: invasion, net/wall, field, and target. In this text, we organize games content in a three-level progression. Children at developmental level 1 learn fundamental skills. Children at developmental level 2 focus on developing fundamental skills into tactical games skills by learning (a) how, when, and why to vary and adapt skills using movement concepts from the Laban framework; (b) how to combine skills; and (c) how to use skills and tactics in game-like situations. Children at developmental level 3 learn to use tactical game skills and tactics in modified, small-sided gameplay. Teaching children how to design and modify games helps them acquire an in-depth understanding of game structures (e.g., rules, boundaries, scoring systems) and gameplay.

Review Questions

1. Why are "games and activities" and "watered-down high school" curricula inappropriate for elementary-age children?
2. Describe who benefits and who is harmed by elimination games.
3. What are the goals of educational games?
4. Why is it beneficial to organize skills and tactical content by game category? Give an example not from the text to illustrate your answer.
5. Discuss the focus of content appropriate for children at developmental level 1. How do you know when a child is ready for level 2 work?
6. Discuss the focus of content appropriate for children at developmental level 2, and explain why it is important.
7. What differentiates level 2 content from level 3 content? Why is level 3 content more complex?
8. Give four reasons why modified games are beneficial. In your opinion, why do you think some elementary physical education teachers do not modify games?
9. Evaluate dodgeball and kickball against the five criteria for judging whether a game is educational.
10. Discuss the benefits of child-designed games.

References

Allison, P. C., & Barrett, K. R. (2000). *Constructing children's physical education experiences: Understanding the content for teaching.* Boston: Allyn & Bacon.

Almond, L. (2010). Forward: Revisiting the TGfU brand. In J. I. Butler & L. L. Griffin (Eds.), *More teaching games for understanding: Moving globally* (pp. vii–x). Champaign, IL: Human Kinetics.

Barrett, K. R. (1977). Games teaching: Adaptable skills, versatile players. *Journal of Physical Education and Recreation, 48*(7), 21–24.

Barrett, K. R. (1984). Educational games. In B. J. Logsdon, K. R. Barrett, M. Ammons, M. R. Broer, L. E. Halverson, R. McGee, & M. A. Roberton (Eds.), *Physical education for children: A focus on the teaching process* (2nd ed.) (pp. 193–240). Philadelphia: Lea & Febiger.

Barrett, K. R. (1985). The content of an elementary school physical education program and its impact on teacher preparation. In H. Hoffman & J. E. Rink (Eds.), *Physical education professional preparation: Insights and foresights* (pp. 9–25). Reston, VA: American Alliance for Health, Physical Education, Recreation and Dance (AAHPERD).

Belka, D. E. (2004). Combining and sequencing game skills. *Journal of Physical Education, Recreation and Dance, 75*(4), 23–27, 52.

Bunker, D., & Thorpe, R. (1982). Model for the teaching of games in secondary schools. *Bulletin of Physical Education, 18*(1), 5–8.

Chen, W., Rovegno, I., Todorovich, J., & Babiarz, M. (2003). Third grade children's movement responses to dribbling tasks presented by accomplished teachers. *Journal of Teaching in Physical Education, 22,* 450–466.

Davids, K., Button, C., & Bennett, S. (2008). *Dynamics of skill acquisition: A constraints-led approach.* Champaign, IL: Human Kinetics.

Ellis, M. (1983). *Similarities and differences in games: A system for classification.* Paper presented at the AIESEP Conference, Rome, Italy.

Ewing, M., & Seefeldt, V. (1990). *American youth and sports participation: A study of 10,000 students and their feelings about sport.* North Palm Beach, FL: Athletic Footwear Association.

Gibson, J. J. (1979/1986). *The ecological approach to visual perception.* Boston: Houghton Mifflin.

Grehaigne, J. F., Wallian, N., & Godbout, P. (2005). Tactical-decision learning model and students' practices. *Physical Education and Sport Pedagogy, 10,* 255–269.

Griffin, L. L., Brooker, R., & Patton, K. (2005). Working towards legitimacy: Two decades of teaching games for understanding. *Physical Education and Sport Pedagogy, 10,* 213–223.

Grineski, S. (1996). *Cooperative learning in physical education.* Champaign, IL: Human Kinetics.

Holt, J. E., Ward, P., & Wallhead, T. L. (2006). The transfer of learning from play practices to game play in young adult soccer players. *Physical Education and Sport Pedagogy, 11,* 101–118.

Lee, M., & Ward, P. (2009). Generalization of tactics in tag rugby from practice to games in middle school physical education. *Physical Education and Sport Pedagogy, 14,* 189–207.

MacPhail, A., Kirk, D., & Griffin, L. (2008). Throwing and catching as relational skills in games play: Situated learning in a modified games unit. *Journal of Teaching in Physical Education, 27,* 100–115.

Mauldon, E., & Redfern, H. B. (1969). *Games teaching: A new approach for the primary school.* London: Macdonald & Evans.

Midura, D. W., & Glover, D. R. (1999). *The competition–cooperation link: Games for developing respectful competitors.* Champaign, IL: Human Kinetics.

Mitchell, S. A., Oslin, J. L., & Griffin, L. L. (2006). *Teaching sport concepts and skills: A tactical games approach* (2nd ed.). Champaign, IL: Human Kinetics.

National Association for Sport and Physical Education (NASPE). (n.d.). *Position on dodgeball in physical education.* Reston, VA: Author.

National Association for Sport and Physical Education (NASPE). (2009). *Appropriate instructional practice guidelines for elementary school physical education* (3rd ed.). Reston, VA: Author.

Orlick, T. (1978). *The cooperative book of games and sports.* New York: Pantheon Books.

Quinn, R., & Carr, D. (2006). Developmentally appropriate soccer activities for elementary school children. *Journal of Physical Education, Recreation and Dance, 77*(5), 13–17.

Renshaw, I., Chow, J. Y., Davids, K., & Hammond, J. (2010). A constraints-led perspective to understanding skill acquisition and gameplay: A basis for integration of motor learning theory and physical education praxis. *Physical Education and Sport Pedagogy, 15,* 117–137.

Rink, J. (2010). TGfU: Celebrations and cautions. In J. I. Butler & L. L. Griffin (Eds.), *More teaching games for understanding: Moving globally* (pp. 33–47). Champaign, IL: Human Kinetics.

Rink, J. E. (2014). *Teaching physical education for learning* (7th ed.). New York: McGraw-Hill.

Rose, D. J., & Christina, R. W. (2006). *A multilevel approach to the study of motor control and learning* (2nd ed.). San Francisco: Benjamin Cummings.

Rovegno, I., & Bandhauer, D. (1997). Psychological dispositions that facilitated and sustained the development of knowledge of a constructivist approach to physical education. *Journal of Teaching in Physical Education, 16,* 136–154.

Rovegno, I., Nevett, M., Brock, S., & Babiarz, M. (2001). Teaching and learning basic invasion game tactics in fourth grade: A descriptive study from situated and constraints theoretical perspectives. *Journal of Teaching in Physical Education, 20,* 370–388.

Thorpe, R., & Bunker, D. (2010). Preface. In J. I. Butler & L. L. Griffin (Eds.), *More teaching games for understanding: Moving globally* (pp. xi–xv). Champaign, IL: Human Kinetics.

Werner, P. (1989). Teaching games: A tactical perspective. *Journal of Physical Education, Recreation, and Dance, 60*(3), 97–101.

Werner, P. (2001). More tactical approaches to playing games. *Teaching Elementary Physical Education, 12*(1), 6–7.

Williams, N. F. (1992). The physical education hall of shame. *Journal of Physical Education, Recreation and Dance, 63*(6), 57–60.

Williams, N. F. (1994). The physical education hall of shame, part II. *Journal of Physical Education, Recreation and Dance, 65*(2), 17–20.

Williams, N. F. (1996). The physical education hall of shame part III: Inappropriate teaching practices. *Journal of Physical Education, Recreation and Dance, 67*(8), 45–48.

CHAPTER

19

Invasion Games: Catching, Passing, Kicking, and Receiving with Hands, Feet, and Hockey Sticks: Levels 1 and 2

PRE-READING REFLECTION

1. Think of one performance technique that would apply across two or more passing or receiving skills.
2. Think of two tactics that would apply across more than two invasion games.
3. Think of two or more skills that would transfer across more than two invasion games.

OBJECTIVES

Students will learn:

1. In teaching invasion game skills, teachers should use a variety of tasks while paying close attention to designing developmentally appropriate environmental constraints.
2. Level 1 content focuses on two to four of the important performance techniques related to the fundamental skills critical to ball control.
3. Level 2 content focuses on developing fundamental skills into tactical game skills by (a) using aspects of the Laban framework to vary and adapt skills; (b) combining skills; and (c) using skills and tactics in game-like situations.
4. Modifying levels of defense intensity is critical in game-like situations, as the ability of children to perform offensive skills is slower to develop.

KEY TERMS

Block tackling
Cutting to receive a pass
Fundamental game skills
Lead pass
Passing lane
Tactical game skills
Target hands

CONNECTION TO STANDARDS

This chapter addresses National Standard 1 for demonstrating competence in a variety of motor skills, National Standard 2 for applying knowledge of strategies and tactics, National Standard 4 for exhibiting personal and social responsibility, and National Standard 5 for recognizing the value of physical activity for enjoyment and challenge. It also addresses the Common Core and Other State Standards (CCSS) for speaking, listening, collaboration, and domain-specific vocabulary.

PROGRESSION OF CONTENT

Level 1: Fundamental Game Skills

Catching

- A variety of self-tossed balls and objects
- Tossing and catching with one and two hands
- Self-tossed balls tossed to different levels
- With scoops
- A ball tossed to a wall
- A partner's pass

Passing with the hands

Self-tossing and catching different balls
Throwing different-size balls with one and two hands at large targets

Passing/shooting and receiving/trapping with the feet or hockey stick

Receiving/trapping a ball with feet or hockey stick
Passing/kicking or push passing to a wall and receiving/trapping the rebound
Passing/kicking or push passing to and receiving from a wall using as few touches as possible
Passing/kicking or push passing to and receiving from a partner
Passing/kicking or push passing to and receiving from a partner using as few touches as possible
Shooting with feet or hockey stick into a large goal

Level 2: Tactical Game Skills

Level 2A: Catching, Passing, Receiving, and Shooting While Varying Body, Space, Effort, and Relationships to Objects

Catching in a variety of ways

- Moving to catch a variety of balls in different areas of personal space
- Moving and reaching to catch a variety of balls in all areas of personal space
- Catching tricks
- Child or partner designed sequence of caching tricks

Passing/shooting with one and two hands at a variety of targets

- At different-size targets
- From different distances
- On different air pathways (straight and rainbow)
- To knock medium and small targets off a perch
- In child-designed centers, passing to and shooting at different targets
- Shooting with hands into adjustable youth basketball hoops set at a low height
- Shooting at youth basketball hoops against a level 3 pest defender
- Passing a variety of balls over different distances using the right amount of force
- Receiving balls with different amounts of force
- Receiving balls from different directions

Passing and receiving with the feet or hockey stick

- Moving to receive a ball/puck with the feet or hockey stick
- Moving to receive and, using as few touches as possible, immediately passing with the feet or hockey stick
- Passing balls/pucks over different distances using the right amount of force
- Receiving balls with different amounts of force
- Receiving balls from different directions
- Child-designed challenge courses for passing, receiving, and dribbling in different directions

Shooting with the feet or hockey stick

- Shooting into a goal with accuracy, keeping the ball low for safety
- Shooting from different directions
- Shooting from different angles
- Child-designed centers for practicing shooting from different directions and angles
- Shooting with force and accuracy
- Shooting while discovering the relationship between the angle of the shot and the amount of space to aim at in the goal

Level 2B: Combining Receiving, Passing, and Shooting

- Moving to catch and immediately pass from in all areas of personal space
- Child-designed centers or challenge courses for combining shooting at targets, receiving, and passing
- Child-designed target games

Level 2C: Using Tactical Game Skills in Game-Like Situations

- 2v1 cutting to receive lead passes against a low-intensity defender. Tactics introduced:
  - Send a lead pass into the space ahead of the receiver.
  - Make the pass catchable/receivable. The receiver is your teammate.
  - To receive a pass, cut into an open space called a passing lane.
  - Fake, feint, and dodge, and then accelerate on a straight pathway to get free.
  - Cut on an angle toward the passer.
- 2v1 cutting to receive lead passes against a low intensity defense. Tactics introduced:
  - Rely on short passes.
  - Pass only if the receiver is free and in a passing lane.
  - Target hands.
  - If you don't get the ball, cut again.
- Sending lead passes to a receiver who is running child-designed pass patterns.
- Sending lead passes over different distances and from different directions to a receiver who is running child-designed pass patterns.
- Sending and receiving lead passes in a 3v1 situation.
- Sending and receiving lead passes in groups of three with a distraction.

Figure 19.1 Progression of Content

Introduction

This chapter is organized around two basic ideas: (1) understanding level 1 and 2 content essential for the teaching of invasion games; and (2) visualizing what this content might look like when *actually* being taught in different lesson situations. Recall that the purpose of level 1 work is to learn two to four of the most important performance techniques of the fundamental skill that will enable children to control the ball most of the time. In level 2A, you focus on having children vary and adapt this fundamental skill by using concepts from the Laban framework. In level 2B, you focus on combining skills. Using skills and tactics in game-like situations is the focus of level 2C.

In level 1, each section begins with a detailed description of the content in a suggested progression for teaching each of the fundamental skills. We then discuss content progressions for level 2. In **Skills Box 19.1** (p. 370), "Technical Reference Information for Teachers About Skills," we provide technical reference information that teachers need to know to be effective in helping children develop skills. This material suggests what teachers should aim to observe in children's performances, thereby helping you select developmentally appropriate content for refining skills.

At the end of the chapter, we provide sample plans written to bring alive the content discussed earlier by giving it context. These sample plans will help you visualize the process of teaching level 1 and 2 content. When you read them, imagine yourself being the teacher. Using the descriptions of the content and the sample plans, you can learn to transform content for your lesson and unit plans.

FYI

Sample Plans in this Chapter

Level 1

Catching a variety of self-tossed balls

Kicking: Passing to and receiving from a partner (on the text website)

Level 2A

Catching various balls in different areas of personal space (on the text website)

Moving to catch in different areas of personal space

Moving and reaching to catch in different areas of personal space (on the text website)

Child-designed sequence of catching tricks

Level 2B

Catching and in one motion quickly passing (on the text website)

Child-designed challenge courses or centers (on the text website)

Child-designed target games

Level 2C

2v1 cutting to receive lead passes against a low-intensity defender

Sending and receiving lead passes in a 3v1 situation

Level 1: Fundamental Game Skills

Principles of Teaching Level 1 Fundamental Game Skills

We begin by briefly listing the principles of teaching that are applied to level 1 **fundamental game skills**. These principles are supported by research on learning, as discussed in other chapters (Davids, Button, & Bennett, 2008; Rink, 2014). Here, we make the principles specific to fundamental game skills.

Control and Accuracy

Know whether your primary goal is for children to develop force or accuracy. In invasion games at the elementary school level, the goal is usually to develop control and accuracy first, owing to the importance of accurate passing in gameplay and control of the ball while dribbling. (Only with the overhand throw for force and batting in field games do teachers initially focus on force.) You will need to modify tasks to ensure that children can engage in control and accuracy practice without having to contend with balls passed with more force than they can handle. As children's abilities to pass and catch develop, they can increasingly practice level 2 tasks, in which the more game-like environment demands more force.

Modifications

Observe the effects of the task and environmental constraints on the skill movement patterns. Modify the tasks to be more difficult (MD) or easier (ME) when needed, so as to ensure that children are practicing the performance techniques and tactical decisions that are the objectives of your lesson. For example, children cannot practice catching if their partners cannot pass accurately. In this instance, you would work on performance techniques for passing accurately or have the passer move closer to the receiver.

Types of Modifications

In level 1, the following modifications are typically most relevant for differentiating instruction:

1. *Balls.* In general, softer and larger balls are easier to catch and receive in hockey; lighter balls are easier to kick and shoot; and bouncier balls are easier to manage when dribbling with the hand and harder to control when dribbling with the feet.
2. *Size of Space.* Typically, smaller is easier because children need to generate less force and, therefore, can practice control and accuracy. The longer the pass, the more difficult it is to pass accurately.
3. *Speed.* Slower is easier.

Catching

Teaching catching begins either with self-tosses or at home with a willing parent sending a perfectly aimed toss directly to the child. We then progress to catching with scoops, self-tosses to a wall, catching tricks, and catching from a partner's toss.

Young children need to explore catching a variety of balls (see **Figure 19.2**). Give them many opportunities to practice

Figure 19.2 Self-tossing a variety of balls

Figure 19.3 Catching with an immature pattern, in part elicited by the size of the ball

with different types of balls and objects (e.g., beanbag creatures), from large to small with different shapes and textures. In the process of exploration, they will learn how the size, shape, and texture affect how they grasp the ball with their fingers and hands and how far apart to adjust their hands. Have them compare and contrast catching different balls and objects. Focusing on catching a variety of balls and objects begins to build the variability and adaptability needed in levels 2 and 3, when children must perform skills in a variety of ways to meet the demands of different game situations.

If children appear hesitant or lacking in confidence, soft foam balls, beanbags, and yarn balls eliminate the fear of a ball hitting the child in the face. They also are easiest to grasp.

As children's catching skills develop, your goal is to teach them to catch with their hands without trapping the ball with their arms or against the chest. There is a difference, however, between the immature pattern of trapping the ball and the practice of catching the ball with the hands and then trapping it because of the task or environment (see **Figure 19.3**). For example, the task to catch a very large ball will elicit trapping the ball against the chest, which in this task is not an immature movement pattern. Catching balls thrown to a low level or from behind (e.g., catching a football just before it hits the ground) will also bring out the movement pattern to catch with the hands and then trap the ball against the chest.

Passing with the Hands

A pass with the hands is a throw. To prevent confusion between an overhand throw for force, we will call all passes "tosses" or "passes." The movement pattern of the toss depends on the amount of force required by the task and environmental constraints. For example, the size and shape of the object, the available space, and the distance of the toss all require changes in the movement pattern due to the changes in force needed to account for these variables. In an overhand throw for force, children need to start with their side facing the target, step on the opposite foot, and generate force using the entire body, as in throwing footballs or throws used in field games. Passes in invasion games often need far less force than a throw in softball-type games, such that children can generate enough force with a quick extension of the elbows and wrists. Many passes in invasion games are two-handed tosses in which the passer starts by facing the receiver or in a variety of positions depending on the game situation. These tosses include overhead passes, underhand passes, and passes starting at chest level. In such a case, the goal is accuracy, which is enhanced by the fingers pointing to the target on release of the ball.

When teaching the overhand throw for force, you work on force before accuracy even in the youngest grades. We do not recommend initially teaching children the forceful overhand throw and catching at the same time because throwing with force makes the ball too difficult to catch. You can, however, teach catching and passing together, because passing focuses foremost on accuracy, which is necessary for practicing catching. Teach the overhand throw separately by having children throw balls such as yarn and foam balls as forcefully as they can at a wall.

SAMPLE LEARNING EXPERIENCES 19.1

Level 1: Catching

Catching

1. Catching a Variety of Self-Tossed Balls and Objects

Explore catching self-tossed balls and objects of various sizes, textures, and shapes while catching with both hands. Toss the ball accurately so you don't need to travel to catch it. If tosses are inaccurate, toss the object to a lower height. When your tosses are accurate and you are catching successfully, increase the height of your toss. Change to a different ball (or object) when I say change. Learning experiences are listed here in a progression from easier to more difficult:

- Small soft balls (e.g., yarn, squishy foam, fleece, rubber string balls) and small objects (e.g., beanbags, creature beanbags, fleece beanbags, foam jacks, fleece cubes)
- Medium balls (e.g., vinyl, foam, playground)
- Large balls (e.g., beach, larger playground)
- A variety of balls, sometimes letting the ball bounce once and sometimes catching it on the fly
- Alternating small and large balls, comparing and contrasting the catching movement pattern
- Alternating soft and hard balls, comparing and contrasting the catching movement pattern
- Traveling slightly to the left, right, forward, and on forward diagonals to catch the ball after one bounce and after no bounces
- Small hard balls (e.g., four-inch whiffle balls, tennis balls, soft tee-softballs, soft tee-baseballs)

2. Tossing and Catching with One and Two Hands

Explore catching a variety of balls (as outlined in the previous list):

- With two hands tossed by two hands
- With two hands tossed by one hand
- With one hand tossed by two hands
- With one hand tossed by one hand

3. Catching Self-Tossed Balls Tossed to Different Levels

- Intentionally vary the level of the toss, comparing and contrasting the catching movement pattern required.
- Catch different self-tossed balls tossed to different levels. (See the list of tasks for different balls under point 1.)

4. Catching with Scoops

Explore self-tossed beanbags and small soft balls by catching them with scoops. Scoops are particularly helpful for teaching children how to give to absorb force because they must give so the ball doesn't bounce out of the scoop (see **Figure 19.4**):

- Catch on the fly.
- Catch after the ball bounces once on the ground.
- Travel slightly to the left, right, forward, and on forward diagonals to catch balls after one bounce and after no bounces.
- Catch with the left hand and then with the right hand holding the scoop.

5. Catching a Ball Tossed to a Wall

Explore tossing balls to a wall and catching the rebound:

- Catch on the fly.
- Catch the ball after one bounce on the ground.
- Catch different-sized balls.
- Catch balls at different distances from the wall.

6. Catching a Partner's Pass

Explore catching with two hands balls and objects of various sizes, textures, and shapes passed from a partner who sends accurate underhand passes:

- See the list of tasks under point 1.
- Explore your catching range by seeing how far you can be from your partner and still catch the ball consistently.

SAMPLE LEARNING EXPERIENCES 19.1

Level 1: Catching (*continued*)

Sample Questions to Ask

- What did you do to catch successfully? [Reach and give; watch the ball go into your hands.]
- How do you have to move your body and body parts to "give" to absorb force? [Bend the elbows; bend the knees.]
- Compare and contrast catching different balls (e.g., different sizes, textures, shapes).
- Why was it harder to catch a ball tossed high with a scoop? [You have to get in line, give a longer distance, and watch the ball go into the scoop.]
- Which ball was easiest for you to catch? Why do you think that is?
- Did your partner affect your ability to catch? How hard did your partner pass the ball? Did your partner pass the ball in your catching range?
- Compare and contrast tossing and catching balls to yourself and catching balls tossed from a partner.

Figure 19.4 Learning to "give" to absorb force when catching
Courtesy of John Dolly

When teaching catching, you will need to focus first on self-tossing a ball with accuracy (see **Figure 19.5**). In general, children's initial attempts to toss a ball straight up tend to be inaccurate, so they cannot practice catching simultaneously. We typically use the learning experiences described in **Sample Learning Experiences 19.2** to start a lesson and unit on either passing or catching.

As with catching, children need to explore tossing a wide variety of balls at targets of different sizes at different distances. They also need to explore passing in different ways, such as with two hands, one hand, overhead, overhand, underhand (see **Figure 19.6**), and underhand rolling. As they explore and discuss the effects of different task constraints, they will learn about the relationships among the distance to the target, the force needed, and the movement pattern of the pass.

Kicking Passes and Shooting

With kicking, we require passes and shots to remain on the ground in elementary school settings. It takes many years for children to acquire the ball control necessary for kicking balls to different levels, although these are important skills in soccer. In elementary schools, however, safety must be your overriding concern.

Another reason to keep passes on the ground is that most often you are simultaneously teaching the difficult skills of receiving and trapping the ball. It is easier for beginning-level receivers to control a pass on the ground than to have to stop and control a ball coming in the air. (You can safely teach kicking to different levels in centers in which children kick toward a fence or wall.)

When they begin learning these skills, children need extensive time to explore dribbling, passing, and maneuvering the ball using different parts of the foot. The goal of exploring is to help children become familiar with the many different things they can do with the ball with their feet and the variety of ways they can maneuver the ball. This movement variety becomes critical later on when children practice in game-like and game situations. The foot actions children explore when dribbling and kicking short passes are similar. Consequently, we often combine dribbling and passing with the feet within one lesson and unit. In addition, children must learn passing

Figure 19.5 Mature pattern: catching a self-tossed whiffle golf ball

Figure 19.6 Tossing underhand for accuracy

SAMPLE LEARNING EXPERIENCES 19.2

Level 1: Passing with the Hands

Passing with the Hands

1. Self-Tossing and Catching Different Balls

Explore self-tossing and catching different balls while tossing the balls with two hands to a low level. You can increase the height of the toss as long as you continue to toss accurately and are successful at catching the ball. You can use a variety of balls for this task:

- Small soft balls (e.g., yarn, squishy foam, fleece, rubber string balls)
- Medium balls (e.g., vinyl, foam, playground)
- Large balls (e.g., beach, large playground)
- Small hard balls (e.g., four-inch whiffle, tennis, soft tee-softballs, soft tee-baseballs)

2. Tossing Different-Sized Balls with One and Two Hands at Large Targets

Explore tossing different balls with one and two hands to large targets on a wall or fence (e.g., a hoop tied on a fence, a target taped on the wall):

- Different balls (see the preceding list)
- With one and two hands:
  - Underhand with one or two hands, depending on the size of the ball
  - Underhand rolling with one or two hands, depending on the size of the ball
  - Overhead and from the chest with two hands
  - Overhand with one hand
  - Experiment to discover which size of ball works best with one or two hands

Sample Questions to Ask

- Which ball was easiest to pass/throw accurately?
- Which kind of pass with one or two hands was easiest and hardest to throw accurately?

and shooting skills with both their dominant and nondominant foot. From the start, teachers should encourage children to practice passing, receiving, and dribbling skills with each foot for an equal amount of time.

The parts of the foot used most often for kicking passes are the inside, outside, and laces. The most basic and important skill to master is kicking with the inside of the foot, as this is the most accurate way to pass and shoot. When kicking for power, you make contact with the ball with the laces.

With beginners, it helps to slow down the speed of the ball. You can do so by either deflating balls or using older playground balls that cannot maintain their air pressure.

Push Passes with Hockey Sticks

At the elementary level, the only pass or shot we teach (and allow) in hockey (field hockey and floor hockey) is the push pass (see **Figure 19.7**). Hitting the ball/puck involves lifting the stick in preparation and follow-through—a movement that can easily get out of control, such that the stick hits another child in the face.

In field hockey, you make contact with the ball only with the flat side of the stick. In floor hockey, you make contact with the ball/puck with both sides of the stick. Thus, in passing in floor hockey, you pass from both the forehand and the backhand sides, with your nondominant hand at the top of the stick and your dominant hand lower on the stick.

Like kicking skills, the skills of passing and dribbling or stick handling with hockey sticks take time to develop. Because of the length of the hockey stick, the ball/puck is far from children's hands. Consequently, children need plenty of time to explore ways they can travel with, send, and receive a ball/puck with the stick before progressing to game-like situations.

Receiving with the Feet or Hockey Stick

In soccer- and hockey-type games, receiving means gaining control of a ball sent to you. To do so, you must absorb the force of the ball by giving with or cushioning the ball by moving the stick head or foot slightly back, which absorbs the force of the ball. The aim is to gain control of the ball or puck in as few touches as possible (see **Figure 19.8**), keep it close to you, and then immediately pass, dribble, or shoot. Sometimes receivers use a one-touch reception in which they deflect the ball off their foot or stick in a pass or shot without having to stop the ball.

Figure 19.7 Push pass

Courtesy of John Dolly

SAMPLE LEARNING EXPERIENCES 19.3

Level 1: Passing, Shooting, and Receiving/Trapping with the Feet or Hockey Stick

1. Receiving a Ball With the Feet or Hockey Stick

Working with a partner, roll a ball accurately with light force so your partner can receive the ball with the inside of the foot or hockey stick face. If you can pass with your feet or hockey stick accurately, you may do so. Give your partner equal practice with the left and right feet and with the forehand and backhand sides of a floor hockey stick.

2. Passing (Kicking) or Push Passing to a Wall and Trapping the Rebound

Starting with a stationary ball, pass with the inside of the foot or push pass with a hockey stick at a wall, trap the rebounded ball with the sole of your foot or receive it with your hockey stick, stopping it still, and pass it to the wall again.

- If kicking, use both dominant and nondominant feet.
- Explore kicking and receiving with different parts of the foot.
- If using a floor hockey stick, use both the forehand and backhand sides.

3. Passing or Push Passing to and Receiving from a Wall Using as Few Touches as Possible

Continuously pass or push pass a ball at a wall so it rebounds back to you using as few touches as possible to control the ball between passes. (The items in the bulleted list in point 2 also apply.)

4. Passing or Push Passing to and Receiving from a Partner

Receive and pass a ball/puck using the foot or hockey stick with a partner. (The items in the bulleted list in point 2 also apply.)

5. Passing to and Receiving from a Partner Using as Few Touches as Possible

Receive and pass a ball/puck using the foot or hockey stick with a partner. (The items in the bulleted list in point 2 also apply.)

6. Shooting with the Feet or Hockey Stick into a Large Goal

Starting as close as you need to succeed, use your feet or hockey stick to shoot to a goal made with two cones placed five feet apart against a fence or wall. Keep the ball low for safety.

Sample Questions to Ask

- Were you able to stop the ball most of the time?
- Why do you think you were successful? [Absorbed the force.]
- What was hard about receiving the ball?
- What are some performance techniques you could think about to help you improve? [Reach and give; cushion the ball.]
- What happens in hockey when the puck or ball gets close to your feet? [It is difficult to control.]

Figure 19.8 Gaining control of the ball

Level 2: Tactical Game Skills

Principles of Teaching Level 2 Content

The following principles of teaching specifically apply to level 2 content.

Develop Movement Variety

The goal for level 2 is to transform children's fundamental game skills into **tactical game skills**. At this level, teachers have children explore using movement concepts from the body, space, effort, and relationship aspects of the Laban framework to vary the movement pattern of the fundamental game skill. For example, children learn to pass different-sized balls with one and two hands over different distances using different amounts of force.

To develop movement variety, you need to provide a wide variety of tasks for practicing each skill. For example, you can change the movement pattern required by the task (e.g., throw underhand, overhead, or overhand), the ball, the target, the equipment arrangement, or the distance between children. Using a variety of tasks both increases children's learning (Davids et al., 2008) and enhances their motivation.

Further, as research on motor control suggests, it is important to teach children to adapt skills in a variety of ways in game-like situations that are within the children's motor, cognitive, emotional, and social developmental capabilities (Davids et al., 2008). These more authentic situations help children learn to make tactical decisions related to when and why they need to use particular movement patterns (Rovegno, Nevett, Brock,

& Babiarz, 2001). For example, they learn when to send the ball to a running receiver and discover that sending it ahead of the receiver is important to prevent the defender from intercepting the ball.

Integrate Target Games

We integrate target games with level 2 invasion game content. Being able to pass and shoot accurately is critical in invasion games; thus, these target games serve as the foundation for invasion games. Target games—in particular, child-designed target games, centers, and challenge courses—provide excellent opportunities for children to practice passing and shooting with the hands, feet, and hockey stick and to design inventive targets, scoring systems, and rules. As with all child-designed games, with this approach children have a voice in the content they practice as well as autonomy; research on motivation indicates that both of these aspects are crucial for increasing engagement. Moreover, when children construct their games and centers, this experience facilitates learning. We include descriptions of child-designed learning experiences within the chapter and two sample unit segments at the end of the chapter.

Make Connections

Make connections between performance techniques, movement concepts, and tactics. This kind of linkage helps children understand the relevance of what you are teaching. For example, you need to be able to pass balls in different directions, to different levels, with different amounts of force and speed, and to different areas of the receiver's personal space (all movement concepts from the Laban framework) because different passes are required in different game situations to prevent defenders from intercepting the pass.

Modify the Number of Players

The fewer the players, the more practice and physical activity each child gets. In addition, with fewer players the decisions are less complex; for example, 2v1 situations are less complex than 3v2 tasks. Having fewer players allows you to break down the decision making of tactical game skills into smaller chunks. For example, in passing, you can focus first on sending a lead pass to a receiver. This activity uses just two players, and the passer focuses on sending the ball ahead of the receiver. Next, you can add a defender on the receiver. Now the passer must also anticipate whether the receiver is about to get free and make the appropriate decision about when and where to pass.

Modify the Equipment

As with level 1 content, level 2 game-like situations and even game play in level 3 requires modified equipment to bring out the most mature patterns the children have developed. For example, some children are fearful or lack confidence to catch a regulation basketball, but play competently with a foam ball. In a study of 9- to 11-year-old boys playing basketball, the researchers found that when the weight of the ball was less than the weight of a regulation basketball, the children could shift attention away from ball handling skills and onto gameplay, completing more passes and more receptions. The games were better (Arias, Argudo, & Alonso, 2012). As always, modifying equipment to get the practice and games working well will facilitate learning.

Use Defenders for Authenticity, But Modify the Levels of Defensive Intensity

When children are learning tactical game skills, a defender can help them understand the tactic and perceive why they need to vary and adapt a skill. Put simply, the defender makes the task more authentic (Davids et al., 2008; Rovegno et al., 2001). The defender provides important information that children need to understand to elicit the movement patterns and decision making you are trying to teach. In other words, with a defender providing authenticity, the children understand more easily the tactical meaning of the skills they are practicing. For example, when a defender is marking/guarding them, they understand better why they need to dodge to get free from the defender and cut into open space to receive a pass.

A child who plays defense at the level of intensity of which elementary children are capable, however, will make the task and environment too difficult and will hamper learning of the offensive tactical skill. Children's abilities to move without the ball (e.g., run fast to intercept a pass or cover a defender) are more advanced than their ability to control the ball while dribbling, to send accurate passes, and to catch or receive passes.

To establish an appropriate learning environment, you need to match the intensity level of the defense to the capabilities of the offense. Consequently, we teach children five levels of defensive intensity and require them to use the level of defense appropriate to the individual whom they are guarding/marking:

- *Level 1: Feet still, arms still.* The defender remains still and in place (see **Figure 19.9**). Depending on the game-like task, the defender stands on either the goal side or the ball side of the offensive player.
- *Level 2: Feet still, arms move.* The defender can wave her or his arms but must remain in place. This type of defense is used in level 2 invasion game-like tasks with passing and shooting with the hands.

Figure 19.9 Level 1 defense on inbound pass in 3v3

Courtesy of John Dolly

- *Level 3: Feet move, can't touch the ball.* The defender can apply pressure, jump up and down, wave hands, and travel with the offensive player, but cannot use her or his hands, feet, or hockey stick to touch the ball. We often call this kind of defensive player a "pest defender" because he or she buzzes around like a pesky fly.
- *Level 4: Soft guarding/marking.* The defender can move both arms and can travel while guarding the offensive player but most of the time allows him or her to make the play successfully.
- *Level 5: Full guarding/marking.* The defensive player is not restricted and plays competitive guarding/marking with a no-contact rule.

With elementary-age children, we also use pretend defenders in physical education programs. A pretend defender is a cone, hoop, or other obstacles the children know represent defenders. Typically, children will not select an appropriate level of defense unless you and/or a classmate insist. Remind the children that this is physical education, and reinforce the message that its purpose is for all children to get fair chances to learn. Scan the class for children arguing or getting angry; when those problems crop up, one potential source of conflict is that the defense is too strong. You also can ask children if they believe their opponent is using an appropriate level of defense. Once children learn they are entitled to ask or demand that a classmate use an appropriate level of defense, they will work with the teacher so that the games and task work well to facilitate learning for every child in the group.

Teaching children about the five levels of defense is also helpful when you divide the class into groups that stack the offense with more players (such as in 2v1 and 3v2 situations) and there is an extra child. If the numbers do not work out perfectly, you may wind up with one group having equal numbers of players on offense and defense. In this case, you can limit the defender on the passer to level 1 or 2 defense, thereby maintaining the needed offensive advantage.

Have Children Practice with Different Partners

A teaching technique we use frequently across level 2 lessons is to assign partners, have children practice a game-like task, and then switch partners several times to practice the task again. We then have a class discussion focusing on what they learned about tactics and skills with different partners.

There are also important social reasons for changing partners several times during a lesson. When the children know you will assign and switch partners, the problem of some children being ignored and isolated disappears. This practice also helps prevent children from thinking they are entitled to play only with their friends or only with children whom they think are "good enough" for them. An important life skill children need to develop is the ability to work with different people (whether they like them or not). If children know you will

SAFETY AND LIABILITY 19.1

Increasing Safety and Decreasing Risk of Liability: Guidelines Relevant to Content in this Chapter

In this box, we discuss specific guidelines built on information discussed throughout this text on professional standards of practice, negligence, and liability. The goals of these guidelines are to increase children's safety and decrease teachers' risk of negligence and liability.

These guidelines refer to specific tasks and performance techniques to teach to increase safety for tasks within the lesson content of this chapter.

- Equipment: The safest ball to use when you are indoors or in a crowded space is a yarn ball, which does not roll fast or far and is soft.
- For all tasks, teach children to be socially responsible and safe by not chasing balls that inadvertently roll into another group's space and by stopping play when a stray ball comes into their space.
- Push passing with hockey sticks: In both floor and field hockey, start passes and shots with the stick touching the ball—don't allow even an inch of backswing. When running without the ball or puck, keep sticks on or near the ground.
- In floor hockey, use foam hockey sticks.
- With soccer kicking, require passes and shots to remain on the ground in elementary school settings. It takes many years for children to acquire the ball control necessary for kicking balls to different levels, although these are important skills in soccer. In elementary schools, however, safety must be your overriding concern.
- In soccer and hockey, teach block tackles. Tackling means taking the ball away from the dribbler. There is no body contact. Even in regulation games, students must tackle only the ball, not the opponent. We recommend teaching **block tackling** in which the defender blocks the ball with the stick or foot, positioning the body to the side of the offense so the foot of the defender aligns with the foot and ball of the offense. Otherwise, they will kick or hit their opponent with the hockey stick or collide.
- When teaching catching, focus first on how to perform a safe, effective toss for the catcher to catch. If the task is for the catcher to travel to the side to catch, the tosser is responsible for ensuring that there is plenty of open space to the side for the receiver to catch the ball. If the task is to catch a high ball tossed behind the receiver, the tosser is responsible for making sure there is space behind the receiver before tossing the ball.

switch partners frequently, they are usually willing to work with anyone.

Finally, it is important that boys and girls work with each other. Such interactions can help children learn through experience about inaccurate gender stereotypes.

Teach the Cognitive Dimensions of Tactics

In teaching tactics, you must teach several cognitive dimensions, all of which add complexity to the learning process. These elements include teaching children

1. To think, make decisions, and move at the same time.
2. To appreciate the different tactical options for tactical situations, allowing them to discover which tactical option is most appropriate.
3. To see perceptual clues within the movements of teammates and opponents, such as clues that tell them their teammate is about to get free from a defender. These clues will help them decide what to do and when to do it.

To learn to see perceptual clues, it helps to stand behind them and coach them when to pass the ball. Tell the children what you are seeing (e.g., "He is about to get free," "She is going to reverse directions"), and say "Ready! Pass!" when the time is right.

Progression for Level 2 Tactical Game Skills

We organize passing and receiving content into three progressive sections:

- Level 2A: Using concepts from the Laban framework to vary catching, passing, receiving, and shooting
- Level 2B: Combining passing and receiving
- Level 2C: Using tactical game skills in game-like situations

Level 2A: Using Concepts from the Laban Framework to Vary Catching, Passing, Receiving, and Shooting

We begin level 2 work by teaching children how to vary and adapt level 1 skills using concepts from the body, space, effort, and relationship aspects of the Laban framework. For example, children learn to catch in all areas of personal space, including catching balls thrown high, low, to the left, to the right, and in every area in between. Critical, too, is the ability to catch a ball coming from the side, on a diagonal, and from behind. Movement variety is necessary because children must reach around defenders to the sides, high, and low to catch and because passes can be inaccurate. The environment of invasion games is such that versatility in catching balls anywhere within reach is a valuable skill.

In level 2, children also need to learn to catch balls that are of different sizes and shapes, such as footballs. Moreover, the other passing and receiving skills using the feet or hockey sticks discussed in this chapter require children to be able to vary their movement pattern using movement concepts from the Laban framework. In learning to vary movement patterns, some performance techniques remain the same, such as giving by bending the elbows to absorb force in catching. Other performance techniques change, however, such as catching with the thumbs together when catching a ball at a high level, but catching with the pinkies together when catching a ball at a low level. Thus, when you apply movement concepts to the fundamental skill pattern, it will help if you think of the experience as almost like teaching the children a new skill.

Level 2B: Combining Skills

In level 2B in this chapter, we focus on sample learning experiences for combining passing and receiving (see **Sample Learning Experiences 19.8**). We also include some learning experiences for combining dribbling, shooting, passing, and receiving; however, the bulk of these combinations are discussed later, with dribbling.

Level 2C: Using Tactical Game Skills in Game-Like Situations

In level 2C, we focus on the most basic tactics for sending and receiving a **lead pass**. **Table 19.1** describes these tactics. Most of these tactics cross invasion games, so you can teach them whether you are teaching a lesson using hockey skills, kicking skills, or catching and passing with the hands.

When learning to send lead passes against a defender, initially we do not allow defenders against the passer. Therefore, you will not see 2v2 or 3v3 game-like situations—these are too difficult for children at level 2. At this age, children literally cannot see the open receiver. We do not focus on defense other than to say "Guard/mark the receiver," because children's defensive abilities develop far in advance of their abilities to get free and send lead passes; defense does not require moving while controlling a ball. We teach defensive tactics in level 3 and do not worry if the defense is weak or out of position in level 2 because it allows for practice of the more difficult offensive skills.

In addition, it is important to remember that passing and receiving are relational skills; that is, the pass occurs in relation to what the receiver does, and the reception occurs in relation to the location from and the force with which the passer passes (MacPhail, Kirk, & Griffin, 2008; Rovegno et al., 2001). When you understand the relational aspects of passing and receiving, you will be better able to interpret children's responses and design lesson tasks. For example, a good passer can bring out more mature, successful receptions; likewise, a good receiver who cuts and signals in an appropriate space can help the passer develop the ability to perceive the clues as to when and where to pass.

The reverse is also true. A less skilled passer and receiver will bring out less mature receptions and passes from each other. For example, the immature pattern of running away from the passer directly to the goal and then standing in the goal signaling for a pass will elicit the immature pattern to send a long pass that is beyond the range of the passer and too difficult to catch. At the elementary level, the long pass is a poor tactic due to the children's skill capabilities, and one that leads to a breakdown in successful gameplay. The long pass, of course, is an important tactic at more advanced levels. We describe the immature movement patterns for passing and **cutting to receive a pass** and performance techniques in **Skills Box 19.1**.

Sample Learning Experiences for Level 2

SAMPLE LEARNING EXPERIENCES 19.4

Level 2A Catching in a Variety of Ways

1. Moving to Catch a Variety of Balls in Different Areas of Personal Space

With a partner, explore moving to catch a variety of balls in all areas of personal space. As a peer coach, learn to provide accurate passes for the catcher in each situation.

Different Areas Within Personal Space

- Medium level to the left and right sides
- High and low levels
- High and low diagonals to left and right

Variety of Balls

- Yarn balls and beanbags
- Medium and small foam balls
- Medium and small playground balls
- Whiffle and tennis balls
- Footballs designed for children

2. Moving and Reaching to Catch a Variety of Balls in Different Areas of Personal Space

With a partner, explore catching a variety of balls that the passer tosses so that the receiver must not only move but also reach to catch. As a peer coach, learn to provide accurate passes for the catcher in each situation:

- Different areas within personal space (see the list given in point 1)
- A variety of balls (see the list given in point 1)

3. Catching Tricks

Explore and invent different catching tricks. Challenge yourself to extend the range of ways you can toss and catch.

- Catch the ball after one bounce on the ground.
- Toss, clap, and then catch; toss; clap two, three, four, or more times; and then catch.
- Toss, clap under one leg, and then catch.
- Put your hand on the wall, reach under your arm, toss the ball over that arm, and catch it with the same hand; switch hands.
- Toss, do a full turn, and either catch after letting the ball bounce or catch on the fly.
- Toss and catch with one hand under one leg.
- Catch a ball off the wall thrown by a partner.

4. Child- or Partner-Designed Routines of Catching Tricks

- *Child-designed tricks.* Children design their own catching tricks by tossing the ball in the air or toward a wall. As the culminating activity of the lesson, put the children in groups of four. Each child teaches her or his trick(s) and tries the tricks invented by other group members.
- *Child-designed body part sequence.* With a partner, design a sequence (routine) for touching different body parts before you catch. For example, you can start with one body part and add another body part each time, such as tossing and touching your head, or tossing and touching your head, shoulders, knees, feet, and so on. Teach your sequence to another pair and learn their sequence.
- *Child-designed sequence of tricks.* Develop a sequence of tossing and catching tricks. For example, toss and perform one action, and then catch; toss and perform two actions, and then catch; and so on. As the culminating activity of the lesson, teach your sequence to a partner.

SAMPLE LEARNING EXPERIENCES 19.4

Level 2A Catching in a Variety of Ways (*continued*)

- *Partner sequences.* With a partner, design a sequence of tossing and catching tricks. As a culminating activity, teach your sequence to another pair.

Reaching to catch

Courtesy of John Dolly

Catching a variety of balls in different areas of personal space

SAMPLE LEARNING EXPERIENCES 19.5

Level 2A Passing/Shooting with One and Two Hands at a Variety of Targets

1. At Different-Sized Targets

Explore tossing to different-sized targets on a wall or fence:

- Use large, medium, and small targets with different balls (yarn balls, beanbags, medium and small foam balls, medium and small playground balls, whiffle and tennis balls, footballs designed for children) that are tossed with one and two hands.
- Experiment to discover which size of ball works best for you at different size targets
- Experiment to discover whether tossing with one or two hands works best at different sizes of target.

2. From Different Distances

Explore passing to a partner from different distances:

- Pass different balls (see the list given in point 1) with one and two hands from cones placed at different distances (e.g., 5, 10, 15, and 20 feet).
- Experiment to discover at which distance your passing becomes inaccurate.
- Experiment to discover at which distance you need to use an overhand throw to reach the target.

3. On Different Air Pathways (Straight and Rainbow)

Explore shooting and passing to a partner on different air pathways (from straight to a high "rainbow"):

- Toss different balls (see the list given in point 1) with one and two hands to a partner, large targets, and into baskets or boxes.
- Experiment to see which pathway gets the ball to the target most quickly or most successfully.

4. To Knock Medium and Small Targets Off a Perch

Explore tossing different balls to knock small and medium-sized targets off a perch (see **Figure 19.11**):

- Toss different balls (see the list given in point 1) with one and two hands, focusing on accuracy by trying to hit different targets on a perch.
- Use different kinds of targets on a perch:
  - Cones and plastic bowling pins on boxes
  - Balls on deck rings on boxes
  - Playground balls (six or eight inches) perched on tall cones

(*continues*)

SAMPLE LEARNING EXPERIENCES 19.5

Level 2A Passing/Shooting with One and Two Hands at a Variety of Targets (*continued*)

- Experiment to discover which ball works best when focusing on medium and small targets.
- Experiment to discover whether passing with one or two hands works best when focusing on medium and small targets.
- Experiment to find at which distance your passing becomes inaccurate with medium and small targets.

5. Child-Designed Centers Passing to Different Targets

With a partner, design a center to practice passing different balls to different targets. [Put out a wide variety of balls and potential targets. Assign each pair an area against a fence or wall if possible.] Refine your center until you think it is a good center to help you and your partner improve. As a culminating activity, teach your center to your classmates and rotate practicing at each center.

6. Shooting with the Hands Into Adjustable Youth Basketball Hoops Set at a Low Height

Shooting at a basketball hoop is a fundamental throw adapted to be a level 2 skill specific to basketball-type games. With equipment made for children, you can teach shooting starting in the youngest grades. We use adjustable youth plastic baskets and set them a few inches higher than the children can reach (about five feet high) so they cannot simply walk up and drop the ball into the basket.

- *Shooting from different distances.* Experiment to discover (1) the range at which you are accurate, (2) the range at which your shooting is accurate at least half of the time, and (3) the range at which you can rarely succeed. Compare and contrast your movement patterns when shooting at different distances.
- *Shooting from different angles from a close distance.* Explore using the backboard so your shot hits the backboard and then goes into the hoop.
- *Shooting from different angles from farther away.* Experiment to discover which angles are easier and which are more difficult.

7. Shooting at Youth Basketball Hoops Against a Level 3 Pest Defender

Practice shooting with the hands with a level 3 defender who waves arms and jumps up and down but does not block the shot.

8. Passing a Variety of Balls Different Distances Using the Right Amount of Force

- With a teammate, explore passing a variety of balls different distances:
  - Medium foam balls
  - Yarn and small foam balls
  - Medium and small playground balls
  - Footballs designed for children
- Compare and contrast the different movement patterns you need to pass over short, medium, and long distances.
- Experiment to discover the longest distance over which you can pass accurately.

9. Receiving Balls with Different Amounts of Force

- Explore receiving and passing balls with different amounts of force.
- Experiment to learn how to adjust your body actions when you receive a ball with different amounts of force, such as how quickly you need to travel to get in line with the ball and how you need to adapt your speed and distance to absorb the force of the ball.
- Experiment to find the amount of force you and your partner can successfully control.

10. Receiving Balls from Different Directions

Explore receiving from a diagonal forward, from the side, from a diagonal back, and from the back. Experiment to learn how to adjust your body actions when you receive a ball from different directions.

Sample Questions to Ask

- Which ball was easiest to pass accurately?
- Compare and contrast the impact of different sizes of balls on your passing techniques.
- Why did your ball miss the target?
- What helped you improve your accuracy?
- What makes the ball go too high or too low? [Releasing it too late or too early.]
- What did you do that made your shot successful?
- What was difficult about shooting? How might you solve this problem?
- What happens to shots that don't follow a rainbow pathway?
- Can you hit the backboard any place if you want the ball to rebound into the hoop? Where are the best places?

Figure 19.10 Catching with a partner

Figure 19.11 Tossing at different targets

SAMPLE LEARNING EXPERIENCES 19.6

Level 2A: Passing and Receiving with the Feet or Hockey Stick

1. Moving to Receive a Ball/Puck with the Feet or Hockey Stick

With a peer coach, explore moving to receive a ball with the feet or hockey stick. Learn to move to the left and to the right so that you line up behind the ball to receive it with the feet or hockey stick, control it, reposition to pass, and pass it back to your peer coach. The peer coach remains stationary. Decide a fair way to switch roles.

2. Passing Balls/Pucks Over Different Distances Using the Right Amount of Force

- With a teammate, explore passing over different distances.
- Compare and contrast the different movement patterns you need to kick or push pass for short, medium, and long distances.
- Experiment to discover the longest distance over which you can pass accurately.

3. Receiving Balls with Different Amounts of Force

- Explore receiving and passing balls with different amounts of force.
- Experiment to learn how to adjust your body actions when you receive a ball/puck with different amounts of force, such as how quickly you need to travel to get in line with the ball/puck and how to adapt the speed and distance you need to absorb the force of the ball/puck.
- Experiment to find the amount of force you and your partner can successfully control.

4. Receiving Balls from Different Directions

Explore receiving from a diagonal forward, from the side, from a diagonal back, and from the back. Experiment to learn how to adjust your body actions when you receive a ball/puck from different directions.

5. Child-Designed Challenge Courses for Passing, Receiving, and Dribbling in Different Directions

With a partner, design a challenge course to practice passing, receiving, and dribbling with feet or hockey sticks. [Make available plenty of cones, jump ropes, hoops with stands, and other potential targets for the children to use in their obstacle courses.] Refine your challenge course until you think it will challenge you and your partner to improve. As a culminating activity, teach your challenge course to your classmates, and rotate to practice on other students' courses.

SAMPLE LEARNING EXPERIENCES 19.7

Level 2A: Shooting with the Feet or Hockey Stick

1. Shooting Into a Goal with Accuracy While Keeping the Ball Low for Safety

Shoot with accuracy with the feet or a hockey stick. Set up a line of cones about five feet apart down the middle of the field to serve as goals. Each pair of children uses one goal, with the partners positioning themselves on opposite sides of the goal approximately 10 to 15 feet away from the goal. They alternate kicking or push passing goals. The receiver stops the shot and shoots back.

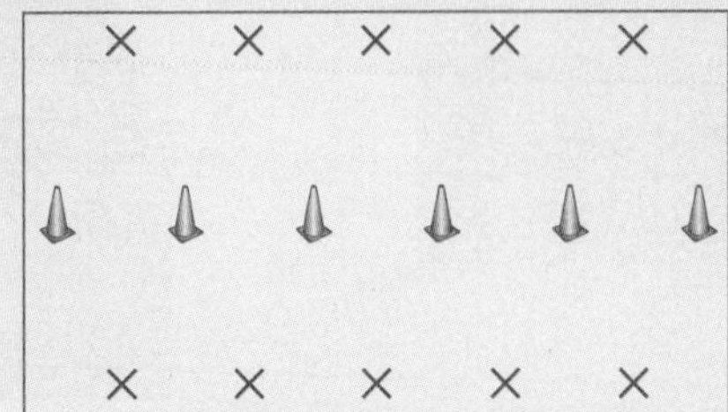

Five sets of partners at opposite sides of shooting goal

2. Shooting from Different Distances

Explore shooting from different distances. Experiment to discover (a) the range in which you are accurate; (b) the range in which your shooting is accurate at least half of the time; and (c) the range in which you can rarely succeed. Compare and contrast shooting at different distances with hands, feet, or hockey sticks.

3. Shooting from Different Angles

Explore shooting from different angles (in front of and to the left and right sides of the goal). Experiment to discover which angles are easier and which are more difficult.

4. Child-Designed Centers for Practicing Shooting from Different Directions and Angles

With a partner, design a center to practice shooting from a variety of angles and distances. Set up your center at a wall or fence. Have at least five shots at your center, and decide on an order in which the shots should be completed. Decide whether you will include just dribbling, just passing, or both.

5. Shooting with Force and Accuracy

Practice shooting with force and accuracy with the feet while keeping the ball low for safety. Practice shooting using the laces, kicking with strong force but keeping the ball at a low level. Place two cones against a fence or wall to serve as a goal. Have one goal per child. Class discussion question: Will the children who kept the ball low please give us tips on how they did so?

6. Shooting to Discover the Relationship Between the Angle of the Shot and the Amount of Space to Aim at in the Goal

With a partner, set up an experiment in which you shoot with feet or a hockey stick, and try to discover the relationship between the angle of the shot and the amount of space available in the goal. Set up two cones spaced six feet apart for a goal, and spread out five poly spots in a line parallel to the goal line. Shoot from each of the poly spots and notice the amount of space available in the goal. Discuss what you notice with your partner, and try to summarize what you discover.

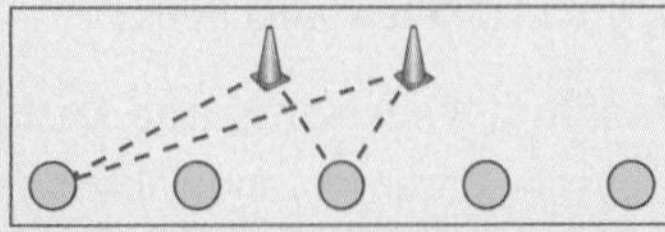

Cones as goals with poly spots to learn the effect of shooting from different angles

Sample Questions to Ask

- Which performance technique were you thinking about to improve your skill? Were you successful in getting better?
- At which distance were you most successful in shooting? Go back and practice shooting at other distances.
- When moving to receive a ball, which clues helped you anticipate where the ball was going?
- How did you know you were in a good shooting range?

SAMPLE LEARNING EXPERIENCES 19.8

Level 2B: Combining Skills

1. Moving to Catch and Immediately Pass from All Areas of Personal Space

Explore moving to catch in and immediately pass from all areas of personal space. The peer coach sets up the practice. The peer tosses the ball, remains stationary, and then catches the return pass. Practice in all areas of personal space and with a variety of balls. Decide a fair way to switch roles.

Different Areas Within Personal Space

- Medium level to the left and right sides
- High and low levels
- High and low diagonals to the left and right

Variety of Balls

- Yarn balls and beanbags
- Medium and small foam balls
- Medium and small playground balls
- Whiffle and tennis balls
- Footballs designed for children

2. Child-Designed Centers or Challenge Courses for Combining Shooting at Targets, Receiving, and Passing

With a partner, design a challenge course or center combining shooting at different targets, passing, receiving, and dribbling in different ways (e.g., in different directions, on different pathways, using different amounts of force, at different speeds). [Make available plenty of cones, jump ropes, hoops and hoop stands, and a variety of equipment that can be potential targets and obstacles.] You can also make up a story about your challenge course or center or pretend it is in a special place like a forest, cave, or outer space. Refine your challenge course or center until you think it will help you and your classmates improve your shooting, receiving, and passing. As a culminating activity, teach your challenge course or center to your classmates, and rotate working at different challenge courses or centers.

3. Child-Designed Target Games

In assigned groups (of two, three, or four), design a target game that includes shooting, passing, and receiving. Design a scoring system. You can assign points for hitting different targets, sending accurate passes, or any other action you want. Your game can be cooperative or competitive. You can keep track of the score or not. You can arrange the equipment in any way you want. You can also make up a story about your game or pretend your game is in a special place like a forest, a cave, or outer space, or that it's part of a board or video game. Experiment playing your game, and then refine it until it is a good game and helps you improve your skills. As a culminating activity, teach your game to your classmates, and rotate playing other groups' games.

Sample Questions to Ask

- How do you play your game?
- Are there any parts of your challenge course or game that need to be improved?
- I see you changed your game. What led you to make changes?
- Did you have any problems in your game? Did you have to add any rules?
- What ruins a game?
- What do you like best about your game or challenge course?

SAMPLE LEARNING EXPERIENCES 19.9

Level 2C: Using Tactical Game Skills in Game-Like Situations

1. 2v1 Cutting to Receive Lead Passes Against One Defender Playing with Low Intensity

Place a hoop and poly spot approximately 15 to 20 feet apart. Place two poly spots on 45-degree angles towards the left and right of the passer and about 15 feet from the receiver. The passer stands in the hoop. The receiver stands on the spot. The defender stands in front of the spot between the receiver and passer and plays level 1 defense. The receiver feints, dodges, and fakes out the defender (plant, razor, run) and cuts into the space on a 45-degree angle toward the passer (which would be towards one of the two poly spots, see illustration labeled "Diamond formation for practicing cutting and passing"). The passer sends a lead pass. Because of the level 1 defense, the passer will see when the receiver is free and will start to learn to anticipate when to send the pass. After the passer can successfully send lead passes, have the defender play level 2 defense, and then

(*continues*)

SAMPLE LEARNING EXPERIENCES 19.9

Level 2C: Using Tactical Game Skills in Game-Like Situations (*continued*)

level 3 defense. This progression will challenge the receiver to learn how to feint, dodge, and quickly accelerate to get free. The following tactics are introduced:

Lead Passes

- Send a lead pass into the space ahead of the receiver
- Make the pass catchable/receivable

Cutting to Receive a Pass

- To receive a pass, cut into an open space called a **passing lane**
- If a defender is covering you, fake, feint, dodge, and then accelerate (explode) on a straight pathway to get free
- Cut on an angle toward the passer

Receiver
Defender
Passer

Diamond formation for practicing cutting and passing

2. 2v1 Cutting to Receive Lead Passes Against Low-Intensity Defense

The passer stands in a hoop. The receiver starts approximately 15 to 20 feet away. The defender marks/guards the receiver and stands ball side and directly in front of the receiver. He or she plays level 3 or 4 defense, depending on the abilities of the passer and receiver. Receivers and passers must be challenged yet be able to succeed most of the time. Explore dodging and cutting on different pathways and directions. Experiment to see which work best for you. The following tactics are introduced:

Lead Passes

- Rely on short passes
- Pass only if the receiver is free and in a passing lane

Cutting to Receive a Pass

- Target hands
- If you don't get the ball, cut again

Passer standing in a hoop sending a lead pass

3. Sending Lead Passes to a Receiver Running Student-Designed Pass Patterns

In this activity, the passer sends lead passes to a receiver running a student-designed pass pattern. In groups of three (two players on offense, one defender), explore designing and running pass patterns like in football. Design a variety of pass patterns, and experiment to see which work best. Use an eight-inch foam ball or a football designed for children—whichever matches the passing and catching abilities of the pair on offense. Rotate after every pass.

a. The defender plays level 3 defense (no touching the ball). The passer and receiver plan a different pass pattern each time. The defender tries to stay on the receiver and does not know the pass pattern.
b. The defender plays level 4 defense (lets the receiver be successful most of the time but intercepts at times). The passer and receiver plan a different pass pattern each time.
c. Switch groups and try to devise new pass patterns and ways to get free from the defender. The defender plays level 4 or 5 defense—whichever supports more improvement for each pair of passer and receiver.
d. As a class, share different pass patterns and ways to get free from defenders. Switch groups and try new ideas.

4. Sending Lead Passes Over Different Distances and from Different Directions to a Receiver Running Student-Designed Pass Patterns

In this activity, the passer sends lead passes over different distances and from different directions (side, behind, diagonal behind, diagonal in front) to a receiver running a student-designed pass pattern. Repeat tasks (a) to (d) from activity 3, but this time intentionally explore passing over different distances and then receiving from different directions.

5. Lead Passes in a 3v1 Situation

In a 10-foot-by-10-foot space for hand passing and a 20-foot-by-20-foot space for passing with the feet or a hockey stick, play three offensive players versus one defender. The defender can only mark/guard the receivers. Cut in all directions within the space and send lead passes. Support the passer by having two receivers always trying to be open and cutting on an angle to the passer, who is not marked/guarded. Playing 3v1 is difficult for children. Passers often cannot see which of the two receivers is open, and many times both receivers move behind the defender. It is an excellent task for improving getting open and sending lead passes.

SAMPLE LEARNING EXPERIENCES 19.9

Level 2C: Using Tactical Game Skills in Game-Like Situations (*continued*)

6. Lead Passes in Groups of Three with a Distraction

In a 20-foot-by-20-foot space for hand passing and a 30-foot-by-30-foot space for passing with the feet, children in groups of three cut in all directions within the space and send lead passes, trying to receive the ball and pass quickly. Assign each child a number. Number 1 must pass to number 2, number 2 must pass to number 3, and number 3 must pass to number 1, in that order. Once the children can successfully perform this task, add another group to the space to perform the same task independently of the first group. Then, the children must not only find their assigned receiver but also avoid bumping into the other group that is also trying to pass in order to teammates. If the children stand still, modify the task to move the ball from endline to endline.

Sample Questions to Ask

- How does a target hand help the passer?
- What helps you dodge and fake out a defender?
- How does a good lead pass help prevent an interception?
- Which perceptual clues do you use to let you know the receiver is about to become free and, therefore, it is time for you to pass the ball?
- Which pass patterns worked best and why?
- What do you think will happen when we add a third offense player?
- Do you predict there will be any change in your tactics when playing 3v1 in contrast to playing 2v1?
- I have seen free receivers wide open, but the passer sent the ball to a guarded/marked receiver. Why does this happen? [They pass only to their friends. They pass only to the boys.] How can we prevent it?
- Why do people put up a target hand when they are not open? [By mistake; they thought they were open when they were not; they forgot they were supposed to signal for the ball only when they are open.]
- Did everyone get a fair chance to play every position?
- What happens if you cut and see the defender's back—that is, the defender is in front of you? [You cut the wrong way.]

Table 19.1 Basic Tactics for Level 2C Passing and Receiving

Teach First	Teach Second	Teach Third
When Are You an Offensive Player? When Are You a Defensive Player? You are on offense when your team has the ball. You are on defense when your team does not have the ball. *When Are You on the Ball? When Are You Off the Ball?* There are two kinds of offensive players: those who have the ball (called on-the-ball players) and those who do not have the ball (off-the-ball players). Offensive off-the-ball players have many important roles; they don't just stand and watch. They are responsible for supporting the passer by moving and cutting into spaces to receive passes and spreading out to create space for themselves and teammates. There are two kinds of defensive players. The first kind is defenders who are guarding/marking the person with the ball; they are called on-the-ball defenders. The second kind is off-the-ball defenders, who guard/mark off-the-ball offensive players.	*Lead Passes* Send a lead pass into the space ahead of the receiver so the receiver does not have to change stride or speed to catch the ball. Make the pass catchable/receivable (not too forceful or with too much speed for your teammate to control the ball). Your partner is a teammate, and it is a good pass only if it is within your receiver's ability to catch the ball. *Cutting to Receive a Pass* To receive a pass, cut into an open space called a passing lane. A passing lane means there are no defenders in the lane between you and the passer. Be sure the passer will not have to pass over the head of a defender. If a defender is covering you, fake, feint, dodge, and then accelerate (explode) on a straight pathway to get free (see **Figure 19.12**). Cut on an angle toward the passer so the passer can send a short pass. *Defense* Keep a wide body shape to help block the offensive players' space.	*Lead Passes* Rely on short passes because long passes are too difficult for both the passer and the receiver in the elementary school grades. Pass only if the receiver is free and in a passing lane and there are no defenders between you and the receiver. Don't pass over the head of a defender. *Cutting to Receive a Pass* Show **target hands**. When you are free, stretch your arm and hand out to make a "target hand." This gives the passer a target and tells the passer you are free. If you don't get the ball, cut again. Keep trying, and don't give up.

Figure 19.12 Cutting to get free

SKILLS BOX 19.1

Technical Reference Information for Teachers About Skills

In this feature box, we describe movement patterns, from least to most mature, for invasion game skills. This technical information is not a description of lesson tasks or recommended content, but rather is meant to help you see immature patterns and, based on what you see, make decisions about content development and feedback.

Although it is important for teachers *to know well* (internalize) this material, you should not teach children everything you know. Rather, when focusing on improving performance techniques (i.e., advancing skill level), you should carefully limit the amount of information given to children. The most important guideline for teaching performance techniques is to *tell them what they need to know, when they need to know it*. Developing the ability to apply this guideline should be a goal for all teachers, as it is an essential ingredient to becoming an effective teacher.

Based on your knowledge of technical information, in level 1 lessons you select which two or three performance techniques are both developmentally appropriate and will help children acquire control over the ball. Teach these performance techniques one at a time. Writing the performance techniques on a whiteboard and having children select which performance technique they will focus on helps develop self-regulation. In level 2 game-like tasks and level 3 modified game tasks, you select and teach only technical information that children need and are ready to learn within the task and environment you set.

Although the technical information describes the movement patterns from least to most mature, it is unrealistic to assume that all children at the elementary level will progress to the most mature level. For many children, achieving this level of skillfulness takes much practice and instruction (Clark, 2007).

Thus, in this section, we describe, for example, the mature performance techniques of skills even though children might not develop every skill to a mature level in the time you have. In addition, the performance technique might not be relevant or meaningful to the tasks you are teaching. For example, the techniques for the follow-through of the chest pass are not necessary or meaningful to first-graders tossing to large targets. We repeat: Tell the students what they need to know, when they need to know it.

Catching

Immature Movement Patterns

In this chapter, we discuss catching passes in invasion games but not catching as it is performed in softball and baseball. There are slight variations in the techniques and movement variety emphasized in different game forms.

The following list describes immature through mature catching patterns based on the research of Roberton and Halverson (1984). The accompanying figure illustrates an immature catching pattern.

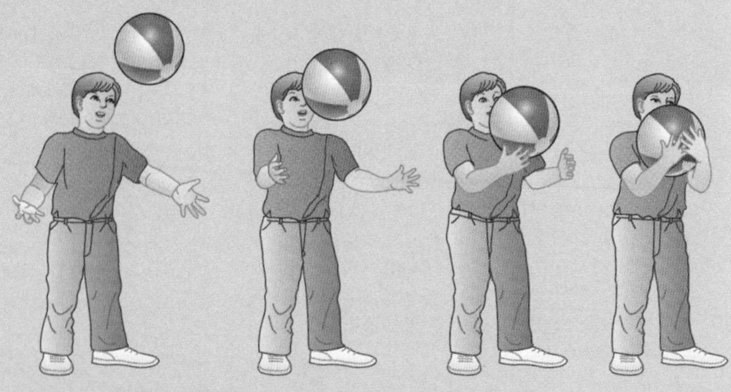

Immature pattern of trapping a ball

Modified from Wickstrom, R.L. (1983). Fundamental Motor Patterns (3rd edition). Philadelphia: Lea & Febiger.

SKILLS BOX 19.1

Technical Reference Information for Teachers About Skills (*continued*)

Catching

Arm, Hand, and Head Actions

Immature Patterns

- Arms are stretched wide.
- Sometimes the ball bounces off the arms, which do not move.
- Sometimes the child closes eyes and turns head to the side.

Intermediate Patterns

- Catches with arms rather than hands
- Traps ball against chest

Mature Patterns

- Catches ball with hands
- Reaches toward the ball, then "gives" to absorb the force of the ball by bending the elbows toward the body

Alignment with the Pathway of the Ball Tossed to the Side, High and Behind, and in Front of the Child

Immature Patterns

- Remains in place

Intermediate Patterns

- Reaches for the ball but the feet remain in place

Mature Patterns

- Moves feet to align the whole body in relation to the flight pathway of the ball

Potential Refinements

Basic Techniques When Children Are at Developmental Level 1

- Reach and give (by bending the elbows and bringing the hands toward the body) to absorb force.
- Watch the ball into your hands.
- Catch with your hands, not your arms.

More Advanced Techniques When Children Are at Developmental Level 2

- Travel to be in line with the ball.
- Thumbs together when the ball is high (moose antlers); pinkies together when the ball is low

More Advanced Techniques When Children Are at Developmental Level 3

- Catch the ball away from the defender; don't turn to face the passer. (This performance technique is for catching an accurately thrown lead pass.)
- Catch and follow through by smoothly moving the ball into position to immediately pass, dribble, or shoot.

More mature pattern for catching a high ball (moose antlers)

Courtesy of John Dolly

Passing/Tossing with the Hands

Immature Movement Patterns

Underhand Rolling

- Standing upright
- Releasing the ball too high

Underhand Throwing/Passing

- Releasing the ball too early or too late

Two-Handed Passes (Such as a Chest Pass)

- Sticking the elbows out with the fingers behind the ball
- Not pointing the hands toward the target on the follow-through

Potential Refinements for Underhand Rolling

Basic Techniques When Children Are at Developmental Level 1

- Bend knees; opposite foot in front
- Swing arm back and then forward and low, releasing the ball near the ground.
- Point fingers toward the target on release.

Potential Refinements for Underhand Toss

Basic Techniques When Children Are at Developmental Level 1

- Arm back, swing forward; the arm swings straight back in preparation and then swings forward to toss ("tick, tock")
- Point toward target; to aim, point to the target on the follow-through.

More Advanced Techniques When Children Are at Developmental Level 2

- Release forward; make sure the arm swings forward to toss, not to the side.
- Opposite foot forward; step on the opposite foot

(*continues*)

SKILLS BOX 19.1

Technical Reference Information for Teachers About Skills (*continued*)

More Advanced Techniques When Children Are at Developmental Level 3

- Aim the ball so the receiver can catch it in the most advantageous position to then do what is needed in the game situation (e.g., pass, dribble, shoot).

Potential Refinements for Two-Handed Passes

Basic Techniques When Children Are at Developmental Level 1

- Point fingers toward the target on release

More Advanced Techniques When Children Are at Developmental Level 2

- Hold the sides of the ball with thumbs behind and elbows down; push the ball by extending arms and snapping wrists
- Follow through with thumbs down.
- Make the pass catchable; don't pass with too much force for the receiver.
- Send the ball ahead of a moving receiver.

More Advanced Techniques When Children Are at Developmental Level 3

- Aim the ball so the receiver can catch it away from the defender and in the best position to catch and then immediately pass, dribble, or shoot.

Passing a Football

Immature Movement Patterns

Passing a football has many similarities to throwing a small ball overhand for force, as in baseball and softball. Both types of throws start with the side to the target and the elbow up. During the throw, the step is on the opposite foot directly toward the target, and there is differentiated rotation that begins with the belly button rotating toward the target.

There are also differences between these throws, of course. When throwing a football, the grip is on the laces, with the pinkie back in preparation and rotating to the front during the throw. The point on the ball initially points away from the target, rotates as the trunk rotates, and points toward the target on release.

In throwing a football, the wrist snap ends with the fingers parallel to the target. If students snap the wrists with the fingers under the ball, they will get a "whirly bird." If they snap the wrist toward the target (as in a baseball throw), they will get a wobbly pass instead of a spiral.

Potential Refinements for Passing a Football

Basic Techniques When Children Are at Developmental Level 1

Preparation

- Side to target and elbow up

More Advanced Techniques When Children Are at Developmental Levels 2 and 3

Preparation

- Hold the ball on its laces (if the ball is not too big)
- Palm away (pinkie in back)

Action

- Step on the opposite foot on a line directly toward the target
- Pinkie rotates to the front, wrist snap, fingers end parallel to target
- Belly button rotates toward target

Passing a football

Courtesy of John Dolly

Passing and Shooting (Kicking) with the Inside of the Foot

Immature Movement Patterns

Preparation

- Stepping either too far in front or too far behind the ball
- Side facing the target rather than turning the hips square to the target
- Little or no backswing

Action

- Loose "floppy fish" ankle on contact

Potential Refinements for Passing with the Inside of the Foot

Basic Techniques When Children Are at Developmental Level 1

Preparation

- Step to side and slightly behind ball, with the nonkicking foot pointing toward the target.
- Thigh, knee, and foot turn out to the side so the inside of the foot is square to the target (like squashing a bug).

Contact

- No "floppy fish" (make contact with the center of the ball with the heel down, toe up, and ankle locked tightly)

SKILLS BOX 19.1

Technical Reference Information for Teachers About Skills (*continued*)

More Advanced Techniques When Children Are at Developmental Levels 2 and 3: Contact

- Transfer weight forward (don't lean back or get underneath the ball).
- Keep your pass on the ground.

Follow-Through

- Follow through, then step on the kicking leg with the whole body moving forward to generate force.

Kicking with the Laces for Power

Immature Patterns (Wickstrom, 1983)

Preparation

- Little or no backswing
- Stepping too far behind the ball (or too far in front)

Action

- Kicking with the toe
- Leaning back (not over the ball)
- Kicking *at* (then retracting the leg) rather than *through* the ball

Immature pattern: too far behind the ball

Follow-Through

- Flexing the ankle on the follow-through
- Flexing the knee on the follow-through

With development, there is an increased range of motion of the backswing as well as an increased whipping action of the leg. In addition, as children develop, they begin to focus on transferring their weight forward to the kicking leg on the follow-through to gain more power by putting the whole body behind the shot.

Mature pattern: "squash the bug"

Potential Refinements for Kicking with the Laces for Power

Basic Techniques When Children Are at Developmental Level 1

Preparation

- Step to the side and slightly behind the ball with the nonkicking foot pointing toward the target.
- Big backswing and whip leg forward

Immature pattern: flexing the ankle on follow-through

Action

- Kick with the laces with the toe pointed.
- Kick the center of the ball (to prevent loft).

Follow-Through

- Point the toe during follow-through (not flexed to form a basket).

(*continues*)

SKILLS BOX 19.1

Technical Reference Information for Teachers About Skills (*continued*)

More Advanced Techniques When Children Are at Developmental Levels 2 and 3

Preparation

- Hips are square to target.
- Keep head down and look at the ball.
- Knee and body are over the ball.

Follow-Through

- Momentum carries the body forward; land on the kicking foot so you drive the ball with your whole body contributing to the power.

Push Passes and Shooting with Hockey Sticks

Potential Refinements for Push Passes and Shooting with Hockey Sticks

In both floor and field hockey, start passes and shots with the stick touching the ball—don't allow even an inch of backswing. This is for safety. With floor hockey, you pass and shoot from the forehand and backhand sides.

Grip

- In field hockey, the left hand is at the top of the stick and the right hand below; the hands are apart, with the thumbs pointing to the ground. (Place the stick on the shoulder, hold it like a baseball bat, slide the hands apart, and put the stick on the ground.) In floor hockey, the nondominant hand is at the top.

Preparation

- The left shoulder points in the direction of the pass and the left foot is in front; for a backhand pass in floor hockey, the right shoulder points in the direction of the pass.

Action

- Both hands push the stick forward, with the bottom hand providing most of the force because it pushes for the longest distance.
- Push toward the target.
- The angle of the stick faces the direction of the pass or shot.

Follow-Through

- Follow through to the target.

Receiving Balls with Feet or Hockey Sticks

Immature Movement Patterns

Preparation

- Reaching with foot or stick, not moving in line with the ball
- Holding the hockey stick like a broom

Action

- Keeping the foot/stick still or jabbing forward rather than giving backward to absorb force
- Stepping on the ball (while trapping it with the foot)
- Taking the eyes off the ball as it arrives

Control

- Beginners will often need two to four touches before they have the ball under control and can pass or shoot (or turn toward the goal in soccer)

Potential Refinements

Basic Techniques When Children Are at Developmental Level 1

- Extend and align the foot or stick to meet the ball.
- Give, be like a sponge, make a soft cushion for the ball, and absorb the force.

More Advanced Techniques When Children Are at Developmental Levels 2 and 3

- Move to the ball.
- Receive with the nondominant or dominant foot, depending on the game situation.
- Receive with the field hockey stick in regular or reverse stick position, depending on the game situation.

Block Tackles

Tackling means taking the ball away from the dribbler. There is no body contact. Even in regulation games, you must tackle only the ball, not the opponent. We teach tackling so children know how to steal the ball safely. Otherwise, they will kick or hit their opponents with the hockey stick.

Immature Movement Patterns

- Floppy foot
- Aligning directly in front of the player with the ball, rather than the ball

Basic Techniques When Children Are at Developmental Level 1

- Position the inside of the foot or the face of the stick in line with the ball. [Be sure to emphasize that the child's foot or stick remains in line with the ball.]
- Align your body to the side front of your opponent, not directly in front.
- Keep your ankle flexed and your foot firm, or hold the stick firmly.

More Advanced Techniques When Children Are at Developmental Level 2

- When you make contact with the ball, you match the force and intensity of the dribbler.
- Keep your knees bent, and be in a balanced position.

Shooting at Youth Basketball Hoops

Immature Movement Patterns

- Throwing directly at the hoop
- Using only the arms to generate force

SKILLS BOX 19.1

Technical Reference Information for Teachers About Skills (*continued*)

Potential Refinements for Shooting at Youth Basketball Hoops

Basic Techniques When Children Are at Developmental Level 1

- Serve a pizza—to duck's head. These two cues mean starting with ball in the palm face up, like you are carrying a pizza over your head, with the elbow up and in front. Then make a duck's head by extending the arm straight up to shoot and extending the wrist until it looks like a duck's head on the follow-through. The fingers are parallel to the ground (don't "drown the duck" by pointing the fingers downward).
- The ball travels in a "McDonald's arch" (or "rainbow") path.

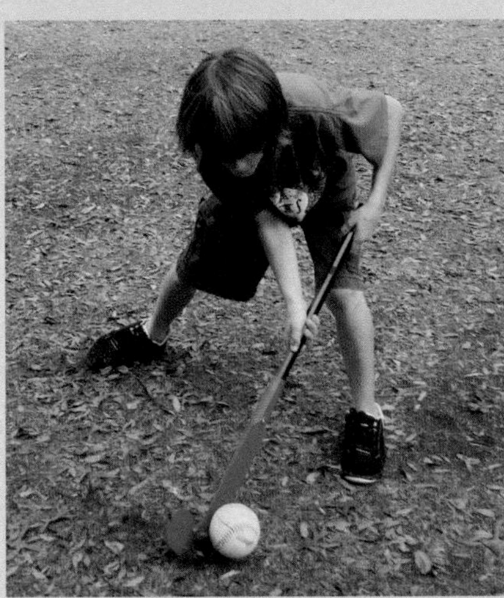

Receiving a hockey pass

More Advanced Techniques When Children Are at Developmental Level 2

- Shoot one-handed with a helper hand; keep the elbows in (the helper hand elbow is close to the other elbow).
- Bend your knees and extend them as you shoot; the power comes from the legs.

More Advanced Techniques When Children Are at Developmental Level 3

- If you want it to go in, it has to spin.
- If shooting right-handed, keep the right foot slightly in front. If shooting left-handed, keep the left foot slightly in front.

(A)

(B)

(A) Preparation for shooting: serve a pizza (B) Follow through

Lead Passes

Level 2 Immature Movement Patterns

- Passes go behind the receiver so the receiver has to stop, turn, slow down, or reach back to receive the ball; passers throw the ball where they see the receiver, not in the open space ahead of the receiver where the receiver is running.
- Passes are not catchable; passes are too forceful or too long in relation to receiver's ability.

(*continues*)

SKILLS BOX 19.1

Technical Reference Information for Teachers About Skills (*continued*)

- The receiver gets free but the passer passes too late, letting the defender catch up, or the passer thinks the receiver must be completely open with no defender near.
- The passer throws when the receiver is covered and the passing lane is blocked.

Potential Refinements for Lead Passes

- Send catchable passes; send passes that are easy to receive with the feet or hockey stick.
- Send the pass to the space ahead of the running receiver.
- Send short passes.
- Try to anticipate when receiver will be free.

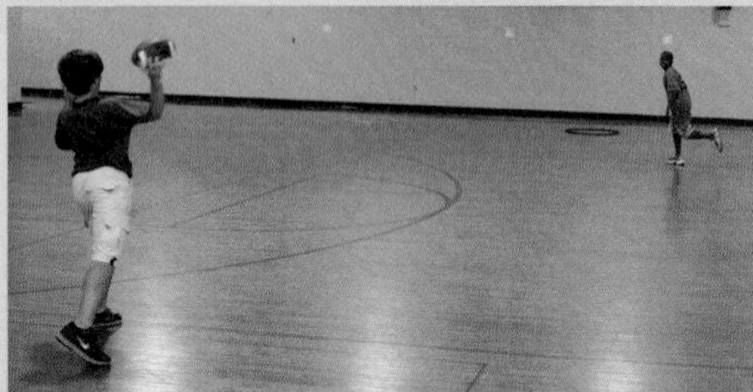

Immature movement pattern: throwing behind the receiver

Cutting, Catching, and Receiving

Level 2 Immature Movement Patterns

- Jumping up and down or shuffling a few feet sideways, then reversing back and forth, remaining behind the defender
- Sliding sideways on a curved pathway ("banana cut"), facing the passer to catch
- Changing direction slowly (not quickly); moving at a moderate speed with no acceleration to get free
- For hand passing, not using target hands (reaching forward with one or both hands to provide a target for the passer and to indicate the receiver is free) or using target hands when the receiver is not free

Running too far away from the passer and ending up outside of the passer's throwing, kicking, or hitting range for an accurate pass

Immature pattern: sliding sideways on a curved pathway

Immature cutting pattern: contributes to immature throw

SKILLS BOX 19.1

Technical Reference Information for Teachers About Skills (*continued*)

- Research shows that one immature pattern of children cutting to receive a pass is to slide sideways while always facing the passer or to run forward and then turn to face the passer to catch the ball; sometimes children stop running as soon as they face the passer (Rovegno et al., 2001). The mature pattern is to continue to run forward, catching the ball from the side or side diagonal.

Immature throw: over defender to receiver who is not free

This does not mean children should never turn to face the passer—some game situations will require this behavior. A child at an immature level, however, can catch a ball only while facing the passer. Mature catchers have the full range of catching options available; it is this capability we aim to develop with level 2 tasks.

Mature cutting pattern

Potential Refinements for Cutting, Catching, and Receiving

- "Plant, razor, run": Plant or jab your foot and fake with your body; make a V cut on razor-sharp angles to dodge a defender; accelerate and run fast to get free from the defender.
- Run forward on a straight pathway (don't slide sideways on a banana pathway).
- Run on an angle toward the passer so the passer can send a short pass.
- Use target hands when cutting and free; point with one or two hands in the direction you are cutting to indicate to the passer you are free.
- Plan by thinking ahead—before you receive the ball, anticipate your first touch (in soccer and hockey) so you can protect the ball from defenders or be in a good position to pass or shoot.

Skills for Children in Wheelchairs

Potential Refinements for Children in Wheelchairs

Children in wheelchairs require some changes in the movement patterns of skills. Here we describe differences in performance techniques for these children.

Dribbling

The child puts the ball in her or his lap and pushes the wheels twice. (In wheelchair basketball, there is no double-dribbling rule.) Although the child can also dribble continuously, it is important to roll with speed; having both hands on the wheels contributes to speed.

Throwing

Preparation

- Turn the chair fully side to target. (Consistently starting with the side to the target increases accuracy because the child does not need to make adjustments in the arm action to compensate for the smaller rotation of the chair when starting partially side to target. In addition, in gameplay, the side to target position protects the ball by having the chair between the defender and the ball.)
- Keep the throwing arm back, with the ball resting in the palm for medium- and large-sized balls (for small balls, the palm can face back).

Action

- Throw the ball (overhead pattern); with the nonthrowing hand, pull the opposite wheel back, causing the chair to rotate to help generate force.

Follow-Through

- Fingers toward the target

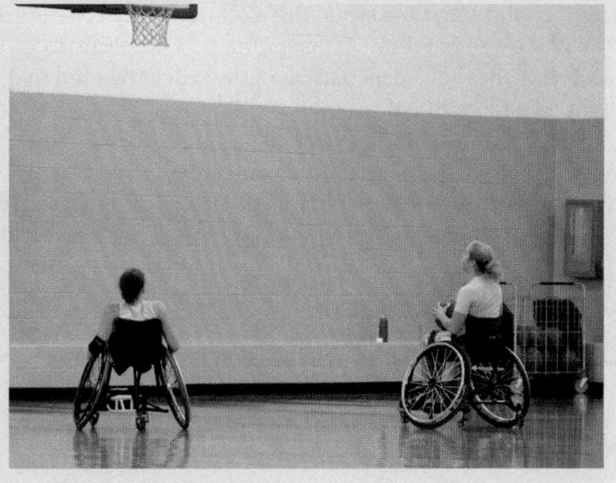

(*continues*)

SKILLS BOX 19.1

Technical Reference Information for Teachers About Skills (*continued*)

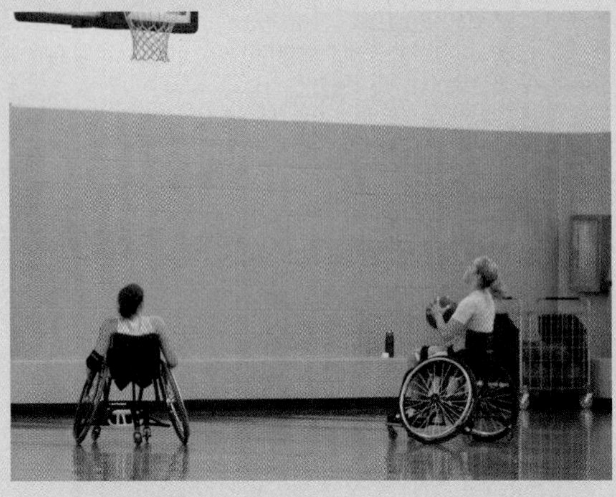

Shooting

Courtesy of John Dolly

Shooting at Youth Basketball Hoops

- Hook shots are used extensively because the action is the same as the throw except that you aim higher (children need to learn to shoot with both hands).
- Shooting techniques from the front are the same, except when the child is farther from the hoop; in this scenario, the child starts the motion from near the lap to have a longer distance to generate force.

Soccer Striking

The chair (footplate and side metal frame) is used to strike the ball. Striking is done by turning side to target, pulling on the wheel with the front hand, and pushing on the opposite wheel with the back hand, causing the chair to rotate and strike the ball.

Soccer Receiving

Use the front of the footplate, metal frame, or wheel to stop the ball. Use very large balls so the ball doesn't get trapped under the footplate. If the child has strong balance capabilities, the hand can be used to receive the pass.

Power Soccer

Children in powered wheelchairs have a square plastic cover or metal frame guard attached around the footplate for striking and stopping the ball. The child strikes the ball by rotating the chair.

Goalkeeping

Playing goalkeeper is an excellent position for a child in a wheelchair because the chair represents a large obstacle.

Source: Adapted and simplified from Roberton, M. A., & Halverson, L. E. (1984). *Developing children: Their changing movement.* Philadelphia: Lea & Febiger.

Summary

Invasion game skills are performed in a variety of ways. Children need to first develop the fundamental skill in simple situations, continuing to work on this skill until they can control the ball most of the time. At that point, they are ready to work on varying the movement pattern of the skill in relation to different game-like situations.

We begin teaching movement variety by using concepts from the Laban framework that are relevant to invasion games. We then combine skills. Next, we add defenders but limit the intensity of the defense to enable children to develop the more difficult offensive skills of sending lead passes and cutting into open spaces to receive the pass.

Game-like situations for level 2 tasks are similar across invasion games with the hands (e.g., basketball, team handball), feet, and hockey sticks (both floor and field hockey). Consequently, as a teacher, you can use similar tasks to help children understand the connections and application of tactics across invasion games.

Review Questions

1. Why is it important to focus on only two to four rmance cues when children are developing fundamental skills?
2. Why is movement variety an important focus of level 2 tactical game skills?
3. Describe how you can teach children to make a connection between a movement concept and a tactic. Do not use the examples from the text.
4. What are the five levels of defense? Why do you need to teach them to children?

5. Why is it valuable to have children practice with different partners?
6. Describe three ways to vary catching using concepts from the Laban framework, and then discuss how those concepts are linked to invasion sports.
7. Describe how you can teach children the tactics for sending lead passes.
8. Describe how you can teach children the tactics for cutting to receive a pass.
9. Describe two immature patterns for the following skills:
   a) Catching
   b) Kicking with the inside of the foot
   c) Receiving/trapping with the feet
10. Describe two immature patterns for lead passes.
11. Describe two immature patterns for cutting to receive a pass.

References

Arias, J. L., Argudo, F. M., & Alonso, J. I., (2012). Effect of ball mass on dribble, pass, and pass reception in 9–11-year-old boys' basketball. *Research Quarterly for Exercise and Sport*, 83,407–412.

Chen, W., Rovegno, I., Cone, S. L., & Cone, T. P. (2012). An accomplished teacher's use of scaffolding during a second grade unit on designing games. *Research Quarterly for Exercise and Sport*, *83*, 219–234.

Clark, J. E. (2007). On the problem of motor skill development. *Journal of Physical Education, Recreation and Dance*, *78*(5), 39–44.

Davids, K., Button, C., & Bennett, S. (2008). *Dynamics of skill acquisition: A constraints-led approach*. Champaign, IL: Human Kinetics.

MacPhail, A., Kirk, D., & Griffin, L. (2008). Throwing and catching as relational skills in games play: Situated learning in a modified games unit. *Journal of Teaching in Physical Education*, *27*, 100–115.

Rink, J. E. (2014). *Teaching physical education for learning* (7th ed.). New York: McGraw-Hill.

Roberton, M. A., & Halverson, L. E. (1984). *Developing children: Their changing movement*. Philadelphia: Lea & Febiger.

Rovegno, I., Nevett, M., Brock, S., & Babiarz, M. (2001). Teaching and learning basic invasion game tactics in fourth grade: A descriptive study from situated and constraints theoretical perspectives. *Journal of Teaching in Physical Education*, *20*, 370–388.

Wickstrom, R. L. (1983). *Fundamental motor patterns* (3rd ed.). Philadelphia: Lea & Febiger.

Sample Plans for Levels 1 and 2 Passing and Receiving

In this section, we annotate plans written to bring alive the content discussed in this chapter so you can imagine how it might look in actual learning environments. As you read these lesson segments, imagine you are the teacher and think about what is happening and how you might react. You could develop some of these plans into full lesson plans and others into a series of lessons for a unit.

In the annotated plans we include objectives, tips for teaching, an observation plan, and potential interactive decisions such as refining tasks and tasks for teaching social responsibility and thinking skills. Although we cannot predict accurately which refining tasks your class of children will need or whether you will need to devote lesson time to teaching social responsibility, we include these tasks here to give you examples of how you might respond on your feet if the need for them arises.

To make interactive decisions you must observe the children's responses. Consider whether the task or environmental constraints are having a positive or negative effect. If the task is not working to elicit the performance techniques or tactical decisions you want children to learn, then modify the task.

In addition, based on your observations you may decide a child or a class needs to work on performance techniques. Follow the guideline to "tell them what they need to know, when they need to know it." Children do not need to hear about every performance technique that applies to a skill; that is far too much information for them to remember at one time. Instead, recognize that they can think about only one performance technique at a time, and that many performance techniques are beyond the capabilities of children at immature levels. For example, the techniques for snapping the wrists and following through with thumbs down in a chest pass are not needed when children are learning to toss balls in the lower elementary grades. Tell children about those techniques only when they need to know them.

FYI

Summary of Task Label Abbreviations

I	Informing tasks
E	Extending/exploring tasks
R	Refinements
A	Application/assessment tasks
Org	Organizing task
Cog K	Cognitive knowledge: Explains or defines a concept
Social	Social skill or concept
Th	Thinking skill
Mot	Motivation concept
Safety	Safety information or reminder
MD	Modification to make the task more difficult
ME	Modification to make the task easier

Source: Adapted and modified from Rink, J. E. (2014). *Teaching physical education for learning* (7th ed.).New York: McGraw-Hill.

SAMPLE PLAN 19.1

Level 1: Catching a Variety of Self-Tossed Balls

Level 1: Catching a Variety of Self-Tossed Balls	Notes and Potential Interactive Teaching Decisions
Standards	
This unit addresses National Standards 1, 2, and 4 and CCSS for vocabulary acquisition.	Children can take from one to three lessons to learn this content.
Objectives	
The children will learn to **Motor** 1. Catch self-tossed beanbags and balls of various sizes and degrees of softness, catching with both hands by reaching and giving. 2. Self-toss accurately by pointing fingers up. **Thinking Skills and Cognitive Knowledge** 3. Think about a performance technique while practicing. 4. Remember and think about the performance techniques "reach and give" to catch. **CCSS** 1. Understand that the metaphors "reach for the baby," and "bring the baby gently to bed" can help them reach and give to catch better. 2. Compare and contrast the different qualities of balls and the actions when catching the balls.	*Equipment:* One beanbag, yarn ball, six-inch foam ball, and poly spot for each child. If you have limited equipment or space, you can divide the space into three sections and teach one performance technique for three different skills by having the children rotate. For example, the children might practice catching in the middle of the space, throwing overhand for force with yarn balls against a wall at one end, and jumping at the other end. **Observation Plan**  1. Scan to be sure children are spaced far enough apart for safely tossing and catching. 2. See whether tosses are accurate (which is a critical task constraint). 3. Scan elbows to see whether the children reach with extended arms and then bend the elbow to absorb force. 4. When children toss balls, scan to see whether they are catching with their hands or trapping the ball against their chests.
Org Before class, scatter poly spots about the space. For every four children, have an equipment basket or hula-hoop holding four of each of the following (or whatever balls you have): beanbags, yarn balls, six-inch foam balls, string balls, beanbag critters, and fleece balls. Spread the baskets about the edge of the space.	
Introduction	
I Today we will learn two amazing ideas for being great at catching a ball. Have you ever had an amazing idea you wanted to share with others? I am excited to share some amazing ideas about catching with you today. **Org** Get a beanbag from one of the baskets of equipment along the wall and go stand on a poly spot.	
Content Development	
Self-Tossing Accurately **I** Hold the beanbag in the palm of your hand, toss it, and catch it in your personal space. [Demonstrate.] Toss the beanbag straight up so it falls straight down to your hands and you don't need to move from your personal space to catch it.	**R** Stop. I noticed a lot of you tossed the beanbag and it wasn't close enough to catch. Why did that happen? [I threw it too high or too hard.] [Demonstrate tossing it to a height that is appropriate for most of the children.] That was a toss at a height I could catch. Watch this. [Demonstrate tossing higher and missing.] What was the problem? [It was too high.] What else might cause the beanbag to be too far away to catch? [You need to make it go straight up.] How do you make it go straight up? [Point your fingers up.] Let's see if you're right. Go try it. Make sure your tosses come right back down so you can catch and stay on your poly spot.

SAMPLE PLAN 19.1

Level 1: Catching a Variety of Self-Tossed Balls (*continued*)

E Toss and catch again, tossing only as high as you can accurately. **Th** When you practice a skill, you need to think about one performance technique while you are practicing. As you toss, think about fingers pointing up.	**R** Stop. Does the beanbag go up when your fingers go up? [Yes.] The performance technique you need to think about is to point your fingers toward the target on release. We will use this technique a lot when you get to play catch with a friend. Our target today is straight up above your hand. Practice tossing the beanbag up and let it fall to the ground; see if it lands directly in front of you. Go.
Teaching Performance Techniques for Catching **I** I know all the amazing ideas that will help you be great at catching. Do you want to know what they are? How many do you think there are? [Children will say any number that comes to mind, such as thousands, millions, 20, or 50.] Today, you are going to learn two. **Cog K** Think of the beanbag as a baby. Toss the baby up and reach for the baby. [Demonstrate as you talk.] **E** You try it.	*Note:* The metaphor of a baby is age appropriate for young children and helps them understand the meaning of reaching and absorbing force with the catch. In addition, metaphors can also help children remember performance techniques. **R** I see many great reaches but some of you are not reaching your arms past your heads and your elbows are still bent. Don't reach out to give the baby a hug; reach high and try to reach for the baby as soon as you can. Practice some more.
Cog K The next amazing idea is to catch the baby and bring it to bed. [Demonstrate catching the beanbag and then giving by bending the elbows to absorb the force and bring the beanbag toward your body]. So you reach for the baby, then catch the baby, and because the baby is falling fast, you need to gently bring it to bed. We don't want the baby to fall out of the bed. We call bringing the baby to bed "giving." **E** You try it. Toss the beanbag, reach for the baby, catch it, and bring it safely to bed.	[Another metaphor many teachers use is to be like a sponge and absorb or soak up the force of the ball, or to be like a pillow or cushion and absorb the force of the ball.]
Cog K Let's shorten the performance technique to "reach and give." Repeat that with me, "Reach and give." **Th** Let's practice again. To help you remember to think about cues as you practice, say the cues aloud each time you toss and catch the beanbag. Use your soft inside voice. Go.	**R** Observe the children to see which performance technique they are having problems with and give a refining task or individual feedback. Work on one performance technique at a time. For example, if they are not bending their elbows, have them focus on giving gently to put the baby to bed. If they are reaching but not fully extending, work on reaching.
Varying the Ball **E** One of the fun things about practicing catching is that you can practice using different balls and objects. (see **Figure 19.13**). Take your beanbag back to the same basket and pick up a ball or object, whichever you think you will enjoy the most. Then go back to your spot and practice tossing and catching. **R** What are your cues? Right. Reach and give.	**R** Observe the children to see if they are trapping the ball against their chest, rather than catching it with their hands. If so, spend time having them focus on catching with their hands rather than trapping the ball.
E Now take your ball back to the same basket and pick up a different ball you think you will enjoy. Then go back to your spot and practice tossing and catching, while calling out each time, "Reach and give."	**R** Scan first the accuracy of the children's tosses; second, their elbows in reaching and then bending to give; and third, if they are trapping the ball on their chests. Give appropriate feedback or refining tasks.
Culminating Activity	
E Now return the ball to the basket and select your favorite ball or beanbag. This time, try to toss your favorite ball or beanbag higher by using more force. See how high you can toss and catch it without having to leave your spot.	**R** Continue to work on the performance technique that the children are having difficulty performing.
E Now try tossing it low using light force and then tossing it high using strong force.	

(*continues*)

SAMPLE PLAN 19.1

Level 1: Catching a Variety of Self-Tossed Balls (*continued*)

<table>
<tr>
<td>

Potential CCSS Discussions for Closure

The Meaning of Metaphors

Put your equipment away and come sit in front of me. Who can tell me one of the amazing performance techniques to use to be a good catcher? Satache. Right. Reach for the baby. What is the other important performance technique? Kayla. Right, give. Reach for the baby, catch the baby, and gently bring the baby safely to bed. Why do you think I used the idea of a baby to help you learn to catch? [If we pretend the ball is like a baby, we will be sure to catch it and not drop it. When we put a baby in a bed we do it gently, and we need to gently catch the ball.]

</td>
<td>

Notes: These are three potential discussion topics that address CCSS. Understanding metaphors, making connections to their lives outside of school, and comparing and contrasting experiences are also important thinking skills that young children need to develop and that help them begin to understand movement variety.

Sample Assessment

4 = Always demonstrates reach and give (more than 90%)

3 = Usually demonstrates reach and give (50% to 84%)

2 = Sometimes demonstrates reach and give (50% to 74%)

1 = Rarely demonstrates reach and give (less than 50%)

</td>
</tr>
<tr>
<td>

Making Connections to Real Life

What parts of your body reach and then bend when you catch? [Arms reach, elbows bend to give.] Let's see if we can think of different times in your life when you use the same reach with your arms and bend with your elbows to give. [Reaching to pick a leaf or fruit off a tree, reaching for a book off a shelf, reaching for a toy off a shelf, reaching on the counter for an apple, reaching for a can out of the cabinet for my mom, giving a friend a high five.]

Comparing and Contrasting According to Categories

Let's practice comparing and contrasting how things are alike and how they are different. How are the balls and beanbags alike? Let's discuss color. Now compare texture and softness. Finally, compare size. Now discuss how they are different. Start with color. Now texture and softness. Now size. Compare and contrast what your hands had to do when catching the large foam ball and the beanbag.

</td>
<td>

Name	*Score for "Reach and Give"*
Alissa	2
Niko	1
Kono	1

Sample Assessment

Have student circle pictures that show correct catching. Put an X on those that are not correct.

</td>
</tr>
</table>

Figure 19.13 Choosing from a variety of balls and objects

SAMPLE PLAN 19.2

Level 2A: Moving to Catch in Different Areas of Personal Space

Level 2A: Moving to Catch in Different Areas of Personal Space	Notes and Potential Interactive Teaching Decisions
Standards	
This unit addresses National Standards 1, 2, and 4 and CCSS for collaborating.	
Objectives	
The children will **Motor** 1. Learn to catch balls in different areas of personal space by traveling to get in line with the ball. **Cognitive Knowledge and Thinking Skills** 2. Remember and think about the performance technique to travel to get in line with the ball. **Motivation** 3. Improve their growth mindset by attributing success to effort rather than ability. **Social** 4. Be socially responsible by trying hard to send accurate passes within their partner's range, checking to see if there is plenty of space for their partner to move to catch. **CCSS** 5. Participate in collaborative conversations with diverse partners explaining their ideas and listening carefully to their partner's ideas.	These tasks will take from one to three lessons. *Equipment:* The safest ball to use when you are indoors or in a crowded space is a yarn ball, which is soft and does not roll fast or far when missed. Yarn balls are also easy to catch. You might want to start with small foam or playground balls, but have yarn balls in the baskets for children who need to use an easier-to-catch ball or if you decide the entire class needs to revert to the yarn balls because they are not as successful as you anticipated. *Prerequisites:* Knowing the performance techniques to (1) reach and give; (2) when the ball is high, thumbs together; and (3) when the ball is low, pinkies together. **Observation Plan**  1. Observe whether the children are setting up the necessary task constraint to toss safely and accurately. If not, work on that first. 2. Scan to see whether tosses are within the range of each child to travel to catch but not have to reach. 3. Scan to see whether catchers' feet are moving to get into position or whether the children are standing in place or simply reaching.
Introductory Activity	
Reviewing Catching Techniques **Org** I am going to assign you to partners. After I do, walk to one of the equipment baskets (laundry baskets) on the side of the space, and select a sponge ball (high density so it bounces) and then find a space. **I** Toss and catch the ball with your partner, keeping your tosses at chest height or slightly higher. **Cog K** Do you remember your catching performance techniques? Discuss with your partner what they are. [Call on several pairs until you get the correct answers: reach and give; when the ball is high, thumbs together; when the ball is low, pinkies together.] **Th** Keep tossing and catching but make sure you are thinking about one of the performance techniques.	**R** Some of you have tossed the ball inaccurately; others are tossing perfectly aimed balls. Discuss with your partner what you need to do to make the ball go exactly where you want it to go. Listen carefully to your partner and explain your ideas, too. [Point your fingers toward the target.] **Th** Ask several children what they are thinking about while they are tossing and catching.
Content Development	
Moving to the Right and Left to Catch **Mot** You have worked very hard. Because of your efforts, you are ready to move on to more difficult catches.	

(continues)

SAMPLE PLAN 19.2

Level 2A: Moving to Catch in Different Areas of Personal Space (*continued*)

Cog K When you play catch or have to catch a ball in a game, do you think the ball will come right to you every time? [No.] You are correct; it doesn't. So, what do you think you will have to do? [Travel to get it.] Great answers.

E Toss the ball chest high and slightly to the right of your partner so your partner will have to travel to the side to get in line with the ball to catch it. [Demonstrate with a child.] Be sure the receiver is in a ready position before you toss. Go.

Mot You are working hard, and your effort is helping you improve.

E Now change to tossing to the left of your partner. Work on accurate tosses when you are the tosser and getting in line with the ball as the catcher.

E Now toss the ball sometimes to the left and sometimes to the right. Receivers, get into the ready position [knees bent, hands open and in front], and be prepared to move to either the left or the right to catch the ball.

Safety Discuss safety with your partner. What do you think the tosser needs to do before they toss to a space in which their partner must move? [Give the children a minute to talk, and then call on a few pairs.] What did you decide the tosser needs to do? [Check if there is plenty of space for the receiver to catch the ball.] Right.

Potential Refinements for Tossing Accurately

R What is the technique to make accurate tosses? Right. Point your fingers toward the target.

R Tossers, right now we are just working on tossing so your partner has to move to catch. I saw some of you tossing so your partner had to both move and reach. That is a great skill, but we will be working on that later. For now, toss it within their range to be able to move quickly to catch it.

Potential Refinements for Catching

R I see some of you standing in place and reaching for the ball. Which performance technique should you try to use? [Move to get in line with the ball.] Right answer. Now try hard to be in line with the ball when you catch it.

Catching Bounced Balls Moving to the Left and Right

E Let's vary the pass. Toss the ball to the right or left of the catcher, but this time make the ball bounce once before the catcher catches it.

Tossing or Bouncing the Ball High, Traveling Forward and Backward to Catch

Org I am going to have you switch partners with another pair. [Quickly point to groups of four and have them switch partners.]

E This time, toss the ball high with a high, narrow arch like this. [Demonstrate.] Carita is my partner, and we will stand farther away from each other than you have been doing. This first time I want her to stand still and not try to catch the ball. Watch how I toss the ball high, but it lands between Carita and me. For her to catch the ball, she needs to run forward to get in line with the ball and try to catch it high. With your partner, first try tossing high and see if you can make it land halfway between you. Once you can do this consistently, then the receiver can try to catch it. Go.

E Now try to bounce the ball so it is high and to the front, so that the receiver has to move forward to catch it. What do you need to do differently from bouncing to the right or left? [If they do not raise the point of increased force of the bounce, then tell them.]

Social Work very hard to be a good partner and toss the ball accurately.

Mot Compliment your partner when you see your partner trying hard to improve.

R Continue asking questions about performance techniques, both to ensure that children remember these techniques and to encourage them to think about their techniques when practicing.

E If you think you are ready, you may now try to travel backward one or two steps to catch the ball.

Safety Discuss with your partner what you think is the most important thing for you as the tosser to do if you are tossing the ball so high your partner has to move back a couple of steps? [Call on several pairs.] Right. Make sure there is space behind your partner before you toss the ball. Safety comes first! You are responsible for your partner's safety.

ME If you need more practice catching while moving forward, you can continue to practice that. Go.

SAMPLE PLAN 19.2

Level 2A: Moving to Catch in Different Areas of Personal Space (*continued*)

Catching Balls Rolled to the Left and Right and then Tossed at a Low Level to the Left and Right **Org** I am going to have you switch partners with a different pair. [Quickly point to different groups of four and have them switch partners.]	
E When I say, "Go," we are going to repeat the same tasks, but this time at a low level. First roll the ball to the right, then roll it to the left, and finally toss it in front of your partner at a low level.	**R** With your partner, compare and contrast how you position your hands when you catch a ball at a low level and a high level. Listen carefully to your partner. [Your pinkies are together and your fingers point down for a low ball and your fingers point up with your thumbs together for a high ball.].
Catching Balls Tossed on a Diagonal to the Right and Left at High and Low Levels **E** [Repeat the same tasks, but have children make tosses to the diagonal right and left at high and low levels.]	**R** Continue putting feedback in the form of questions to improve critical thinking and help children believe in their capabilities to be independent learners. **Mot** You are working very hard. Your hard work will make you great catchers.
Culminating Activity	
Org I am going to have you switch partners with a different pair. [Quickly point to different groups of four and have them switch partners.]	
Cog K Let's discuss how you make your partner travel to catch without tossing it out of their range. Talk with your partner and come up with at least two things you could tell someone who has not had this lesson to help them learn their partner's range.	*Notes:* Give the children a brief time to talk. Then call on several children to report one of their ideas.
E You have been practicing tossing the ball to different places in your partner's personal space so they need to travel to catch. Now vary your tosses but don't tell your partner where the ball will be going. Be sure, however, that you always toss the ball within your partner's range to be able to move to get in line and catch the ball. You are *not* playing a game. In this task, you are the coach trying to help a player get better at catching. Go.	**Mot** We have talked about this topic before. Can you make yourself smarter? [Yes.] How? [By working hard.] Can you make yourself an athlete? [Yes.] How? [By working hard.]
Cog K When you were the receiver, what were the clues you used to anticipate where the ball was going? Talk with your partner first, and then we will share ideas. [Arm movements, body movement, eyes.]	
E I'm going to have you switch partners once more. [Quickly point to different groups of four and have them switch partners.] Practice moving to catch without the passer telling you where the ball is going. Try to pay attention to the clues that let you know where to move.	**Social** Tossers, try really hard to send accurate passes so your partner can practice traveling to catch the ball.
Closure **Th** **CCSS** With your partner and without using names, compare and contrast how you adjusted your tossing when you had a different catcher. Listen carefully to your partner, and explain your ideas, too.	Have the children talk first with their partners, and then call on several children to share what they discussed.

SAMPLE PLAN 19.3

Level 2A: Child-Designed Sequence of Catching Tricks

Level 2A: Child-Designed Sequence of Catching Tricks	Notes and Potential Interactive Teaching Decisions
Standards	
This unit addresses National Standards 1, 2, 4, and 5 and CCSS for vocabulary acquisition.	
Objectives	
The children will learn to **Motor** 1. Toss and catch in a variety of ways. **Thinking Skills** 2. Think creatively and design a sequence of catching tricks. **Social** 3. Be respectful audience members. **Affective** 4. Appreciate the challenge and enjoyment of designing and practicing a sequence of catching tricks. **CCSS** 5. Understand the meaning of domain-specific words and phrases, including those that signal precise actions that are basic to designing sequences, specifically, "think creatively and explore."	**Observation Plan**  1. Scan to see if children have enough space to work safely. 2. Observe whether each child is trying a variety of catching tricks. 3. Observe whether children need to refine performance techniques relevant for their tricks. This may mean refining the toss or the catch.
Content Development	
Explore and Invent Catching Tricks **I** We have been exploring and practicing different catching tricks in previous lessons. Today, think creatively and explore or invent as many different catching tricks as you can. Invent at least some unusual tricks. This half of the class work at the wall, and this half of the class work in the middle of the space.	**Cog K/CCSS** [Write what is in italics on the whiteboard.] *"Think creatively and explore" means to try many ideas, try a variety of ideas, and find some unusual ideas.* When I say, "Think creatively and explore," this means I want you to 1. Try to do many different catching tricks. For example, try some tricks in which you do actions while the ball is in the air, and some in which you toss the ball from different positions, such as from under your leg or while kneeling. 2. Try to do a variety of catching tricks. For example, experiment with different actions while the ball is in the air. 3. Try to invent some unusual tricks. These can even be weird!
E Let's share some of your ideas. You decide whether you want to share your ideas. Children in the center can show some ideas first. [Give the children about 30 seconds.] Now children at the wall can show their ideas.	
Cog K Wow. I saw many different ideas. Some were even unusual. [Switch locations for both groups, and repeat the task to explore. Ask the children to then show their ideas if they choose.]	*Notes:* Research shows that being critical of children's creative efforts too early in the creative process can lead them to limit their ideas owing to fear of negative judgments. Try to encourage them to start by brainstorming without judging their ideas. *Refining Catching* Watch the children and help them refine their performance techniques when needed.

SAMPLE PLAN 19.3

Level 2A: Child-Designed Sequence of Catching Tricks (*continued*)

E You have seen many ideas, a variety of catching tricks, and you have invented ideas yourself. Now choose five different tricks and put them in a sequence. Start by selecting two tricks and practicing them in a row. Then add a third trick, and practice trick 1, trick 2, and trick 3 in a row until you feel confident. Then add a fourth trick, practice, and then add a fifth trick. Decide whether you want to use the wall for some or all of your catching tricks. If so, find a personal space at the wall. If you don't want to use the wall, find a personal space in the center of the general space. Begin and design a rough draft of your sequence.

Affective

Many children like catching trick sequences because these sequences are both challenging and enjoyable. For your sequence, select tricks you enjoy the most and at least one challenging trick.

R Now, take some time to refine your sequence and make any changes. You will have 10 minutes to finish your revisions.

Refining Sequence Choreography

Give the children plenty of time to select their tricks and put them into a sequence. You will probably need to scaffold the process of refining the selection of tricks and the order in the sequence. Periodically stop the children and remind them that they can change their sequence. Some sample refining tasks follow.

R Remember, just like in dance, your first sequence is just a starting point. You can make changes in the sequence if you like.

R Stop. You are free to change your sequence. You can change the order of your catching tricks to make your transitions smoother. You can change your tricks. You can change the number of times you do an action within the trick, such as clapping two times instead of one time. You can change the ball you selected.

R Remember in your classroom how you write a sentence and then you edit that sentence? Sequences are like sentences. You can edit the sequence.

E Once you have decided on your sequence, practice it until you have it memorized and can perform it to the best of your ability.

R Think about the performance techniques you learned for catching. Check on your performance of each trick and see whether you are using those performance techniques.

R How did knowing the performance techniques for catching help you successfully complete your sequence without dropping the ball?

Culminating Activity

Option 1

A Anyone who wants to show her or his catching sequence to the class may do so. This third of the class will go first. This third will show second, and this third will show last. Watch carefully, and be prepared to offer a compliment to classmates or describe a trick they did that you would like to try to show you appreciate their creativity, hard work, and skill. [Have the children give compliments after each group performs.]

Option 2

A Show and teach your sequence to your assigned partner. Each of you should try your partner's sequence.

Notes: With small classes, you will need to assign members of the audience to watch specific children to be sure someone is watching each child.

Social Let's review respectful audience behavior. What are the rules?

1. Pay attention
2. No laughing or talking
3. Clap
4. Give compliments

CCSS Closure

With your partner, discuss the meaning of the phrase "think creatively and explore." [Select several pairs to share their ideas with the class.]

Affective Closure

Tell your partner which tricks you enjoyed the most and which you found most challenging.

SAMPLE PLAN 19.4

Level 2A: Child-Designed Target Games

Level 2A: Child-Designed Target Games	Notes and Potential Interactive Teaching Decisions
Standards	
This unit addresses National Standards 1, 2, and 4 and CCSS for collaborating and presenting.	
Objectives	
The children will learn to **Motor** 1. Catch passes and pass and shoot accurately at a variety of targets. **Thinking Skills** 2. Think creatively and design a target game to practice catching, passing, and shooting in a variety of ways. **Social** 3. Consider all group members' feelings about whether the game should be cooperative, competitive, or competitive without keeping track of the score. 4. Be socially responsible and safe by not chasing balls that inadvertently roll into another group's space and by stopping play when a stray ball comes into their space. **CCSS** 5. Participate in collaborative conversations following agreed-upon rules that everyone talks, listens, asks for classmates' opinions, builds on their ideas, and tries out ideas before eliminating any. 6. Present their game to the class, giving relevant details and expressing ideas clearly.	These unit tasks will take 3 to 4 days, depending on the extent to which you want children to play other groups' games. This unit is appropriate for grades 1 through 3, depending on the children's abilities to work cooperatively in groups. This unit is similar to Sample Plan 19.3, except that the goal is to design a game with a scoring system. However, the game is not a complex invasion game. Instead, children design a target game in which they construct targets and plan a game in which they can score points for catching and accurate passing, tossing, and/or shooting. We always leave children the option of designing a game that is competitive, cooperative, or competitive without keeping track of the score. *We thank Theresa Purcell Cone for inspiring this unit. It is an adaptation of a unit she designed and taught for second-graders, which then became the focus of a research study. See Chen, Rovegno, Cone, and Cone (2012) for a description of Purcell Cone's teaching and unit, along with theoretical support for this and similar units.*
Introduction	
A Today you're going to take all of the different ways you have been learning to catch, toss, and shoot at different targets, and pass to partners, and design a target game. A target game is a game that includes one or more targets.	**Observation Plan**  1. Scan the entire unit for safety to ensure that children set up their game so passes and shots, if missed, will not fly into other groups' spaces. 2. During the design phase, scan to see whether students are discussing productively or whether they are arguing or looking at each other but not generating ideas. 3. During the practice phase, scan to see whether each child is getting an equal opportunity to play each role in the game.
Cog K Let's start by making a list on the whiteboard of the different ways you have been practicing catching and passing, tossing, and shooting at different targets.	
Content Development	
I I have put out all the equipment you can use to build targets, obstacles, and boundaries. I also put out a wide variety of balls, beanbags, and other objects you can toss and catch safely. You can select whatever equipment you like for your game.	Include as many balls, beanbags, and other objects for tossing and catching as are available. In addition, set out equipment that children can use to construct targets or obstacles to toss over, such as foam cylinders, cubes, cones of all sizes, boxes, hoops and ropes to tie hoops to a fence, wall targets, and poly spots.

SAMPLE PLAN 19.4

Level 2A: Child-Designed Target Games (*continued*)

Th To get started, in your assigned group of three people, brainstorm different ways you can shoot in a game. Experiment setting up different targets for your game, and begin to design your game. Now brainstorm different passes and catches you might include with equipment that you can use for passing and catching.	**R** You will have plenty of time to change and refine your game, add or delete skills, and change your equipment and the construction of targets. Right now, the goal is to get started and experiment without thinking you have to stick with your first ideas forever.
Social When you set up your game, try to arrange your targets so that balls that miss the target won't go into another group's space. What are the class rules about stray balls? [Don't chase a ball into another group's space. Stop playing when a stray ball comes into your space. If it is not your ball, don't touch it unless you are going to hand it back nicely.]	If the children have not learned rules or a class management routine for how to deal with stray balls, now is a good time to teach them.
Cog K You can have many different scoring systems in target games. Can anyone think of one? [You can score points for hitting the target. You can score different numbers of points for hitting more or less difficult targets. You can lose points if you miss an easy target completely.] Those are good ideas. You can add a scoring system to your game if you want. You can have a cooperative scoring system in which you all work together to score as many points as possible. You can have a competitive system in which you compete against others in your group or against yourself by trying to improve your score each turn. You can also decide not to keep track of the score.	**Social** Both cooperative and competitive games are okay. What you must do is decide which you prefer and which your group members prefer. Consider one another's feelings, and design a scoring system that everyone in your group finds acceptable. [If some groups are not being productive, you can ask one of the groups that is being productive to give the class tips on how they are working together to design their game.]
Lesson 2 **E** Start today by setting up and playing the game you were working on in the last lesson. **R** Then refine your ideas. You can make changes in equipment, in the way you construct targets, or even in the skills you use. You can add or delete sections. You can change any rules and modify your scoring system. Refine your game until the three of you are satisfied. **E** You can also make up a story about your game. You can pretend it is played in a special place, like a forest, a cave, or outer space. You can pretend it is a board game, like Candyland, or a sport or video game. Come up with a name for your game.	**R** I can see you made some changes. Tell me about them. **Social** Is everyone getting a chance to contribute ideas? *Notes:* Children in grades 1 through 3 often design elaborate equipment setups with a large amount of equipment for target games. We allow this practice because it gives the children ownership of their game and makes the game engaging for them. When they get older, they tend to design games with less elaborate equipment setups. In addition, their games become more sport-like, in part because you have taught older children tactics and skills in game-like situations and the child-designed games evolve from that content.
E Finish refining your game.	**R** Practice playing your game, trying to improve your skill performance.
Lesson 3 **A** Today, as a group, you will present your game to your classmates. Then one person will stay to be the teacher while the others rotate to try your classmates' games. Each time we rotate, a different group member goes back to be the teacher to show your classmates how to play your game. **Social/CCSS** First, decide as a group how you will present your game to your classmates. You must both describe and demonstrate your game. Every group member must contribute to the presentation, so plan how you will do this.	**R** Plan which details you will present. Make sure they are important details that will help your classmates understand your game.

SAMPLE PLAN 19.5

Levels 2A and 2C: Two Sample Tasks to Supplement a Level 2C Unit on Lead Passes

Passing to a Rolling Hoop (Outdoor Task)

Org Go with your assigned partner, and when I say "Go," pick up two hoops, two poly spots, one cone, and one foam ball. Set up the equipment in a diamond formation like this. [Demonstrate as you explain.] The passer stands in a hoop at the bottom. The receiver stands by a cone at the top. The two poly spots are at the left and right sides on about a 45-degree angle toward the passer.	**Observation Plan**  1. Scan first to see whether the groups have adequate space to work safely. 2. Scan second to see whether the children can roll the hoop successfully and accurately. 3. Scan to see whether the passer is sending the ball ahead of the hoop at the moment of ball release.
I First, you need to practice rolling the hoop. Receivers, put both hands on top of the hoop with your fingers open. Put a little pressure on the hoop and push it with your hands, aiming it so it rolls over one of the poly spots. Once you can roll the hoop accurately, the passer tries to throw the ball through the rolling hoop or at the top of the hoop as it rolls toward the poly spot. You have to throw the ball ahead of the hoop so that the ball and the hoop intersect or meet.	**Cog K** Watch the hoop rolling, and time your pass so it goes through the hoop. Where do you think you need to throw the ball to be successful? [Toss the ball to the space ahead of the hoop because it takes time for the ball to travel and the hoop won't be at the same place as it was when you released the ball.] [You might need to demonstrate this by hand-rolling the hoop and cueing the children when to pass it. Give the children plenty of practice, because sending passes ahead of a moving player is a difficult task to learn.]

Sending a Lead Pass to a Receiver

E Great effort. Now let's try it with a real receiver. Receivers, start behind the cone, which is now a pretend defender. Plant your foot, do a quick feint on a razor-sharp angle that fakes out the defender, and then run forward toward the poly spot. The shorthand cue is "plant, razor, run." You will receive the pass *while you are running*.	**Observation Plan**  1. Scan to see whether the passer is sending the ball ahead of the receiver so the receiver can catch it on the run without having to stop or reach back to catch it.
Cog K This is called a lead pass because the passer leads the receiver by sending the pass ahead of the receiver so that the receiver does not have to stop, slow down, or reach back to catch the ball. [Demonstrate several times.] Notice when I cut for the pass, I held one arm out in front of me. This is a signal to the passer that I got free from the defender. Reaching forward indicates I want to catch the ball in front of me. We call this "target hands." Go back to your space and try it.	**R** Passers, send the ball ahead of the receiver. **R** Passers, do you want the receiver to catch the ball while on the run or while standing still on the poly spot? [On the run.] Receivers, if you get to the spot and the passer has not sent the ball yet, what should you do? [Start over.] It is critical that you don't practice running to the spot and then stopping to catch the ball. You are practicing lead passes and catching on the run.

SAMPLE PLAN 19.6

Level 2C: 2v1 Cutting to Receive Lead Passes Against a Low-Intensity Defender

Level 2C: 2v1 Cutting to Receive Lead Passes Against a Low-Intensity Defender	Notes and Potential Interactive Teaching Decisions
Standards	
This plan addresses National Standards 1, 2, and 4 and CCSS for vocabulary acquisition.	

SAMPLE PLAN 19.6

Level 2C: 2v1 Cutting to Receive Lead Passes Against a Low-Intensity Defender (*continued*)

Objectives

The children will learn to

Motor and Cognitive

Passers:

1. Send catchable passes (not too forceful for the receiver).
2. Send the ball ahead of the receiver so the receiver does not have to stop, reach back, or face and point their fingers at the passer to catch the ball.

Receivers:

3. Plant the foot, feint quickly on a razor-sharp angle, and run forward into an open space (plant, razor, run).
4. Run on a straight pathway.
5. Explode (accelerate fast to get away from the defender).

Motivation

6. Value self-improvement and not view tasks as a chance to show you are more skilled than your classmates.

Social

7. Understand the social responsibility in teamwork by sending passes that are catchable in relation to the receiver's abilities.

CCSS

8. Acquire domain-specific words and phrases including those that signal spatial and temporal relationships, specifically "lead passes" and "target hands."

These unit tasks will take four to six lessons. You will also need to practice these tasks in later lessons as a review. Sending lead passes and cutting to get free for a pass are difficult content for children.

We teach lead passes with the hands first because the children have greater control over accuracy with hand passing. After they know the techniques and are having success, it helps to repeat lead passes with the feet and then with hockey sticks. This practice reinforces the concepts and helps them learn the connections among invasion games. You can easily modify the lesson tasks presented here for passing with the feet or hockey sticks.

Equipment: One hoop, one cone, and one eight-inch foam ball for each group of three children. Divide the gymnasium into grids so each group has a square or half of a rectangle in which to work.

Observation Plan

1. Scan to see if there is enough space for each group to work safely.
2. Scan to see whether the passer is sending the ball ahead of receiver so the receiver can catch it on the run without having to stop or reach back to catch the ball.
3. Scan to see whether the receiver is feinting and running on a straight line at about a 45-degree angle.
4. Scan to see whether the children are using immature patterns, including jumping up and down behind the defender or cutting on a curved "banana" pathway rather than running straight.

Content Development

Sending a Lead Pass to a Receiver Who Cuts to Get Free from a Level 1 Defender in a 2v1 Situation

Cog K Does anyone know what a lead pass is? Today, you will learn the answer.

Org In your assigned group of three, set a hula hoop in the corner of your assigned square and a cone at least one giant step in from the opposite corner. The passer stands in the hoop with a foam ball. The receiver stands in front of the cone, and the defender stands in front of the receiver. The defender, for now, will be a level 1 defender, which means you can't move your feet or arms; just stand still.

I Receivers, fake out the defender and cut on an angle toward the passer. Passers, watch carefully, and anticipate when the receiver will burst free from the defender. Then, send a pass so the receiver catches it on the run. [Demonstrate.] [Practice several times in each role before defining the performance techniques.]

R Think back on your practice experiences and try to describe specifically what a great lead pass looks like. [The ball is sent ahead of the receiver; it leads the receiver. The receiver does not have to stop, slow down, reach back, or turn and face the passer, reaching toward the passer to catch the ball.]

R Now, describe how the receiver can fake out the defender. [Plant your foot, do a quick feint or dodge on a sharp angle to fake out the defender, and then run forward on an angle toward the passer.]

(*continues*)

SAMPLE PLAN 19.6

Level 2C: 2v1 Cutting to Receive Lead Passes Against a Low-Intensity Defender (*continued*)

Cog K The shorthand cue is "plant, razor (because you are making a sharp, angular pathway), run." You will receive the pass *while you are running*. **Cog K** Notice that when I demonstrated cutting for the pass, I held one arm out in front of me. This is a signal to the passer that I got free from the defender and I want to receive the ball ahead of me. We call this "target hands."	
Mot Your goal for today is to value your self-improvement and help your partners value their self-improvement, too. Compliment your partners when you see they have improved.	**R** Receivers, which performance techniques are you thinking about just before and while cutting? [Plant, razor, run. Fake out the pretend defender by pretending to go one way and then dodging and running the other way.]
E Receivers, be sure to vary the direction in which you run. Sometimes go to the left and sometimes to the right. **Mot** Raise your hand if you have improved today. Raise both hands if both you and your partners have improved.	**R** Why should the passer try to send a catchable pass? [The receiver is a teammate. You want to send a pass that is catchable for the person catching it so our team keeps possession of the ball.] How much force should you use to pass? [You can't throw the ball too forcefully because the receiver won't be able to catch it.] If the receiver does not catch the ball, ask yourself, "Did I send a pass that was catchable?" **R** Receivers, I know it is difficult, but try to catch the ball while you are running forward. Sometimes beginners turn their entire body to face the passer and point their fingers toward the passer. Try not to do this. Instead, show your target hand and catch the ball in front of you while you are running forward, not sliding sideways.
Sending a Lead Pass to a Receiver Who Feints and Dodges to Get Free from a Level 2, 3, and then 4 Defender **E** If your group is having success, you may now let the defender play level 2 defense (wave arms, feet still). This will make it harder to see the receiver get free.	**R** Receivers, plant, razor, run quickly, and accelerate fast so you really explode on your cut. **R** Passers, why should you send the ball ahead of the moving receiver? [Because the defender will catch up.]
E If your group is successful at level 2, then try a level 3 defense (a pest defender who can move the feet but the arms stay down). Receivers, the defender is going to try to stick with you to prevent you from getting free. What do you think you need to do? [Explode, accelerate fast, do several feints or dodges before cutting.] Great answers. Passers, this task is much harder. You really need to watch carefully and anticipate when the receiver will be free so you can get the ball to her or him before the defender catches up. Sometimes you will have only a brief time to pass when the receiver gets free before the defender can move into position. **Mot** Pat yourself on the back for focusing on self-improvement and not on how you compare to your classmates. **MD** For those of you who are ready for more of a challenge, the defender can play level 4 defense. Remember, soft guarding means most of the time you let the receiver get free but sometimes you can intercept the ball.	**R** Receivers, how can you get away from the defenders? [Fake them out, run fast.] Right. Some of you are sliding back and forth behind the defender and you are never exploding to get free. If this applies to you, try to think of this cue: "Explode!" **R** Receivers, I noticed some of you are cutting on a curved pathway rather than running straight. We call this a "banana cut." No banana cuts. Run forward on a straight pathway. **R** Passers, don't pass over the head of the defender. Wait until the receiver is free. **R** Receivers, sometimes you got free but the passer had problems. What do you think you should do? [Just cut again in a different direction. Don't give up. Keep cutting until you get free and the passer sends you the ball.] **R** Try to cut toward the passer; get in front of the defender. Don't stay behind the defender. **R** Passers, work on your anticipation. Watch for the receiver's burst of speed, so you can see when the receiver is about to get free. Send your lead pass then, so the pass gets to the receiver when he or she is free.

SAMPLE PLAN 19.6

Level 2C: 2v1 Cutting to Receive Lead Passes Against a Low-Intensity Defender (*continued*)

Potential Questions to Ask to Bring Closure to These Tasks	
CCSS Within your group, discuss the meaning of "lead pass" and "target hands." Be specific and detailed. List the key points on a sheet of paper. 1. What was most difficult about cutting to get free to receive a pass? 2. What was most difficult about sending lead passes? 3. When you were successful, what did you do to get free? 4. When you sent a perfect lead pass, what did you think about during the task? **Mot** Remember there are always some people who are more and less skilled than you are. What is important? [Focusing on self-improvement.]	

SAMPLE PLAN 19.7

Level 2C: Sending and Receiving Lead Passes in a 3v1 Situation (Hands, Feet, or Hockey Sticks)

Level 2C: Sending and Receiving Lead Passes in a 3v1 Situation (Hands, Feet, or Hockey Sticks)	Notes and Potential Interactive Teaching Decisions
Standards	
This plan addresses National Standards 1, 2, and 4 and CCSS for collaborating.	
Objectives	
The children will learn to **Motor and Cognitive** *Passers:* 1. Anticipate and pass the ball ahead of the receiver. 2. Pass only if the receiver is in a passing lane. **Receivers:** 3. Plant, razor, run—explode. 4. Cut into a passing lane. 5. Recognize the situation and reposition if both receivers cut into the same space. **Motivation** 6. Persist and work hard even when the task is difficult. **Social** 7. Modify the intensity level of defense in relation to each classmate's ability level. **CCSS** 8. Engage effectively in small-group collaborative discussions with diverse individuals on fairness in practicing game-like tasks, following agreed-upon rules for listening carefully and making sure everyone contributes.	These unit tasks will take two to four lessons. The tasks are easier to introduce by using passing with the hands; an excellent progression is to teach the same lesson first with the hands, then with the feet, then with hockey sticks. This practice will help children understand the connections among invasion games and reinforce the tactics. In addition, research shows that cutting and passing with three offensive players is easier to introduce with a defender rather than without one. The defender adds necessary authenticity and helps the offense understand the importance of receiving on the run and passing only to teammates who are free. Because there is only one defender, one receiver can always get free. Insist that the defender *never* guard/mark the passer, or else it will be too difficult for the passer to see the receivers get free. Don't worry if the defense is weak and doesn't succeed. These tasks are intended to teach offense only.

(*continues*)

SAMPLE PLAN 19.7

Level 2C: Sending and Receiving Lead Passes in a 3v1 Situation (*continued*)

Content Development

Reviewing Performance Techniques

Cog K Let's review what you learned in our 2v1 practices about sending lead passes to a receiver who had to feint and cut to get free from the defender. [See the previous unit tasks.] What makes a good lead pass? [The receiver does not have to stop running or slow down to receive or trap the ball; the ball is delivered ahead of the receiver.] What makes a good cut? [Explode, plant, razor, run; straight pathway, not curved; get free from the defender, show target hands when free.]

Forecasting How 2v1 will Change in a Game Situation

Th What do you think will change if we make it a 3v1 situation? [Various answers. Elicit the following response if the children do not mention it: Someone will always be open.]

Social/CCSS Discuss in your group of four what will make this practice task fair and an equally good learning experience for all group members. [Everyone gets to catch and send passes; everyone spends the same amount of time on defense.] Remember, everyone talks and everyone listens. Then discuss what you think you will need to do to make the practice fair. [Modify the level of defense based on individual capabilities; don't pass to the same person; pass to everyone so they get a fair chance to play.]

Observation Plan

1. Scan to check if there is enough space for each group to work safely.
2. Scan to see whether the defender is marking the passer. If so, remind the children that defenders can only mark receivers.
3. Scan to see whether the receivers are getting into passing lanes.
4. Scan to see whether the passer is kicking lead passes.

Org I will put you in groups of four. After I do, take four cones and set up boundaries like this. [Demonstrate.] [If you teach indoors or in a crowded space, have a grid set up before the lesson begins.]

I Play "keep away" with three people on offense and one defender. The offense tries to pass the ball as many times in a row as they can without the defender touching it or without the ball going out of bounds. The defender cannot mark the passer. The defender must try to mark the receivers. The four of you should decide in which order you will rotate and when to rotate so that everyone gets the same amount of practice on offense and defense.

E Because today is a practice day, don't send a pass unless the receiver is cutting into a free space. This way, you will practice your cutting to get free.

R Sometimes the defender successfully marks both receivers at the same time. What suggestions can you make for the offense so this doesn't happen? [Stay far apart from each other. Don't cut into the same space. If you start to cut into the same space, one of you should reposition and cut to a different space.] Great suggestions. Go back and try them.

CCSS/Social Stop and discuss whether your practice has been fair for everyone. Then discuss what you need to do differently to make the practice an equally good learning experience for all group members.

What are the rules for a good discussion? [Everyone talks; everyone listens.]

R Receivers, what should you do if you don't get the pass? [Keep trying. Cut again into a different space.]

R Passers, how do you know if the receiver is free? [The receiver is an arm's length or more ahead of the defender; the defender is marking another receiver.] Try to anticipate when receivers are about to get free and pass the ball ahead of the receiver.

R Receivers, what are your performance techniques? [Plant, razor, run. Really explode to get away from the defender.]

Mot This is a challenging task, and it is important that you persist and keep working hard. That is what leads to improvement.

Social When one of your classmates is trying hard but having difficulties, what can you say? [Keep trying hard; your hard work and persistence will pay off. Don't give up; this is difficult, and working as hard as you are, you will succeed.]

SAMPLE PLAN 19.7

Level 2C: Sending and Receiving Lead Passes in a 3v1 Situation (*continued*)

Passing Lanes

Cog K Stop. I am going to teach you a name for an open space called the "passing lane" that will help you understand when you are free. A passing lane is like a tiny road, or a lane, between the passer and the receiver, where no defender is already or is about to run into that lane. Therefore, the ball can be passed in the passing lane and won't be intercepted by the defender. Receivers, you are free when there is a passing lane between you and the passer. Try to imagine this lane. Passers, send the ball only when you have an open passing lane to the receiver.

R Passers, what is a passing lane? [An open lane between the receiver and me.] What do you do if you don't see a receiver in a passing lane? [Don't pass. Receivers will try to cut into a passing lane.]

Social Which level of defense should you use? [One that is best for the person I am marking so he or she is challenged but can still succeed.]

Org I am going to reorganize your groups so you can play with different people. Then figure out a fair way to rotate positions and play 3v1 again.

Rotate groups several times, so children get the experience of playing with different people.

Culminating Activity

Cog K Let's make two lists on the whiteboard of the characteristics of good offensive play and poor offensive play.

[Have children discuss this topic in pairs and then share their suggestions as you write on the whiteboard.]

R Now take one of those suggestions and see if you can improve in the last five minutes of class. Go back with your groups and play again. I will call out when you should rotate defenders so everyone gets an equal amount of time to practice on offense.

CCSS Closure

Discuss the extent to which you made successful changes in your practice so it was an equally good learning experience for all group members. Then discuss why you think in your group or in some other group the practice wasn't initially an equally good learning experience for everyone. What can happen that would contribute to group practice not being fair?

Extending the Content in Later Lessons

Attending to where the other receiver is cutting:

E We are going to practice 3v1 again. This time, I want the members of the offense to concentrate on cutting and repositioning in relation to one another. If it is a bad pass and goes out of bounds, which rule could we use? [The closest person goes and gets the ball.] That's a good suggestion. Let's all use it. Defenders, remember you can't mark the passer; you can mark only receivers. I will tell you when to rotate to defense. Number yourselves 1 through 4. Number 3 is defense first.

A Sample Peer (or Teacher) Assessment

Assign groups of five. One child assesses one group member. Then rotate until each child has assessed one group member. The child doing the assessment watches one group member for one minute (the teacher times the class). The peer puts a tally mark under the *yes* or *no* column for each pass and cut.

Name: ____________________

	Yes	No
Sends lead pass	____	____
Cuts into open space	____	____

R What did you discover last lesson? [Receivers: Cut into a passing lane; don't cut into the same space because the defender can mark both of you; stay away from each other so the defender can't mark both of you at the same time; reposition if you get too close to each other.]

Perceptual Clues

Cog K Stop. Let's discuss as a group what was happening when the passer was most successful. Which perceptual clues helped you anticipate when the receiver was about to be open? [I could see she was running faster than the defender; I could see the receivers were separated, and I passed to the one who was away from the defender.] What did the receivers do to help the passer? [Avoided the defender; didn't cut into the same space.]

A This time, practice some more and count how many continuous passes you can make.

R How many continuous passes were you able to make before the play broke down? When you had many successful passes in a row, what did the offense do well? What can the offense do to improve? What did the defense do? [Played an appropriate level of defense and did not mark the passer.] I will change groups so you can practice with different people. Then play again.

CHAPTER 20

Invasion Games: Designing and Modifying Games and Tactics for Tag and Passing, and Receiving with the Hands, Feet, and Hockey Sticks: Level 3

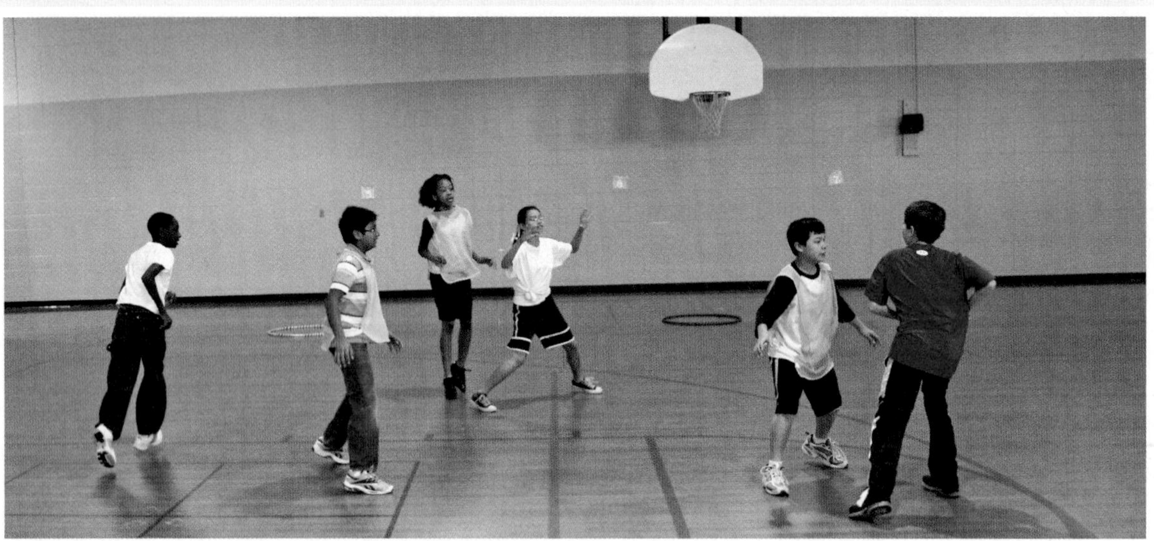

PRE-READING REFLECTION

1. How do you think children will respond if you have them design games in physical education? For example, will they be able to design a game? Will they like doing so?
2. Do you remember a physical education teacher teaching you tactics in any sport? Do you remember a coach teaching you tactics? Compare and contrast your experiences with each and speculate on why there were differences.

OBJECTIVES

Students will learn:

1. All invasion games have game structures (e.g., boundaries, rules and consequences for breaking rules, scoring goals, scoring systems).
2. Teaching children how to modify and design games makes rules and tactics meaningful and relevant to them and teaches them how game structures affect tactics and gameplay.
3. Invasion games include different skills (e.g., throwing, kicking, dribbling) but use the same or similar basic tactics.
4. Basic tactics of offense should be taught before tactics of defense.
5. Tactics should be taught by asking questions that require children to think critically and solve tactical problems.

KEY TERMS

Game structures
"Goldilocks Principle"
Play–discuss–play cycle

CONNECTION TO STANDARDS

1. This chapter addresses National Standard 1 for demonstrating competence in a variety of motor skills, National Standard 2 for applying knowledge of strategies and tactics, National Standard 4 for exhibiting personal and social responsibility, and National Standard 5 for recognizing the value of physical activity for enjoyment and challenge.
2. This chapter also addresses the Common Core and other State Standards (CCSS) for speaking, listening, collaboration, and domain-specific vocabulary.

PROGRESSION OF CONTENT

Level 3: Using Tactical Game Skills in Small-Sided Modified Gameplay

Level 3A: Game Structures and Tactics Related to Tag-Type Games

- Design appropriate size boundaries for tag-type games
- Tactics: Protect your flag, avoid defenders, and use boundaries tactically on offense and defense
- Design rules and consequences for breaking rules, and a scoring system in tag-type games
- For offensive support block and help trapped teammates
- For defensive support double team
- Design tag-type games with bases as safety-zones
- Use bases tactically on offense and defense
- Design goal-oriented tag-type games and set scoring goals
- For offensive support use picks and decoys
- Use offensive tactics for beating a person-to-person defense
- Use defensive tactics for person-to-person defense
- For defensive support cover for other defenders

Level 3B: Tactics for passing and receiving games with one endline scoring goal in 3v1, progressing to 3v2 modified games

- On offense, as a team move the ball closer to the scoring goal.
- Adapt level 2 offense tactics to rely on short, lead passes and to cut into passing lanes from keep-away to goal-oriented games.
- On defense, deny space by using a wide base of support with hands in a ready position and moves to block passing lanes.

Level 3B: Tactics for when to pass, dribble/run with the ball, or shoot in games with a single, center scoring goal in 1v1, 3v2, and progressing to 3v3 modified and child-designed games

- Shoot when you have an open shot; if not, pass to a teammate who does.
- Pass to an open teammate closer to the goal rather than running with or dribbling the ball. Dribble or run when no one is open closer to the goal.
- Receive and pass quickly to deny time for the defense to reposition.
- The defender stays on the goal side of the assigned offense player.

Level 3C: Tactics for passing and receiving games with an endline scoring goal for each team in 3v2, progressing to 3v3 modified and child-designed games

- Support the passer, with all receivers trying to get free. Cut multiple times until you get free. Cut away from the goal toward the passer if the passer needs support.
- Pass and then cut quickly.
- Spread out to create space. Reset the offense when you are ineffectively bunched in front of the goal.
- Defenders play person-to-person defense.

Level 3C: Tactics, and modified and child-designed 3v3 games with an endline scoring goal for each team, focusing on when to pass, dribble/run, or shoot

- Shoot when you have an open shot; if not, pass to a teammate who does.
- Pass to an open teammate close to the goal rather than running with or dribbling the ball. Dribble or run when no one is open closer to the goal.
- Receive and pass quickly to deny time for the defense to reposition.
- The defender stays on the goal side of the assigned offense player.

Level 3D: More advanced defensive tactics for passing and receiving games

- Switch quickly from offense to defense.
- Commit to intercepting the ball only if you are sure you will succeed.
- Contain the dribbler and time when you try to steal the ball.
- Defensive support: Back up a teammate and shift when scoring is imminent.
- Play closer to your assigned offense player when he or she is closer to the ball or goal.

Figure 20.1 Progression of Content

Introduction

In this chapter, we discuss teaching children how to design and modify game structures, such as boundaries, rules, and scoring goals. We initially use tag to do so because children play tag without balls; thus, you can focus on game structures and design games without the children's ball-handling skills being a constraint. At the same time that we teach children about designing game structures, we also teach tag tactics, which are basic tactics that apply to invasion games. We then discuss teaching passing and receiving tactics in modified games appropriate for children at developmental level 3.

FYI

Sample Plans in this Chapter

Level 3B

Tactics for when to pass with the hands, run with the ball, or shoot at one central target goal

Passing and receiving with the feet in goal-oriented modified games with an endline scoring goal (on website)

Level 3C

Goal-oriented passing and receiving using endline goals for each team working on supporting the passer and resetting the offense

Child-designed lead passing games (using the hands, feet, or hockey sticks)

Child-designed games for the tactics of when to pass, dribble or run with the ball, or shoot (on website)

Level 3D

Defensive support and decisions about whether to intercept or position oneself between the receiver and the goal (using feet or hockey sticks) (on website)

Before we discuss teaching game structures and tactics, we discuss a set of principles specific to teaching developmental level 3 invasion gameplay.

Principles of Teaching Gameplay for Children at Developmental Level 3

We begin with two principles related to safety. Both are common problems you will encounter when teaching invasion games.

At the Elementary Level, Invasion Games Are Not Contact Sports

At the elementary level, invasion games are not contact sports. We know invasion sports like basketball, soccer, lacrosse, Gaelic football, and team handball are contact sports, in that contact (sometimes considerable contact) is legal and part of the game. Nevertheless, we do not allow any contact between children during games at the elementary level: contact is a foul. The reason for this is that minor and even incidental contact can lead to children fighting, being injured, arguing, and having hurt feelings. Many schools have a "zero tolerance" policy for fighting, and you don't want what one child perceives as a legitimate block with the shoulder in a kicking game to end up in a fight that gets both children suspended.

More significantly, children tend to have contact in invasion games because they are not controlling their bodies or they are attempting a movement that they are not skilled enough to perform safely. Our goal is to teach children to be skillful games players. It takes much more skill to steal the ball without contact than it does to steal the ball by shoving the ball handler. We explain to children that at their level, they need to focus on skill alone, not body contact. There is no justifiable need to teach body contact at the elementary level. (When children need to use body contact to play in after-school leagues, they will learn it quickly.)

One problem with contact being a foul is that some children will foul intentionally to prevent a score. We suggest as a penalty simply awarding the point to the other team; alternatively, we allow children to create a consequence for breaking the no-contact rule, such as a free shot at the goal. After you have been at a school for a number of years and the children have learned to self-regulate and modify their games, you will find that when children have incidental, unintended contact they will create a "held whistle" rule, similar to that found in field hockey and soccer, in which the children call the foul but play continues if it is to the advantage of the team fouled. However, for beginning teachers new to a school, we recommend a strict no-contact rule.

At the Elementary Level, Don't Allow Kicking or Hitting Balls to High Levels

Another safety issue is the problem of children kicking or hitting balls to high levels. In passing and receiving with the feet or hockey stick, we require passes to be on the ground, and we don't allow kicking the ball over the heads of defenders or goalkeepers—although these are important skills and tactics for advanced players who play on teams after school. At the elementary level, where children typically have a wide range of ability levels, we believe keeping the ball on the ground is necessary for safety. In addition, because trapping the ball with the feet or hockey stick is very difficult, we want children to send those types of passes that are the easiest to receive.

The Issue of Long-Bomb Passes at the Elementary Level

In sports such as football and basketball, "long bombs" ("rainbow" passes) over defenders' heads are excellent passes. However, in elementary school physical education, long bombs are considered immature patterns because the receiver is simply running toward the goal, and the passer is simply trying to throw the ball to the goal or up in the air because the defender is closing in. Neither passer nor receiver understands the importance of maintaining possession of the ball, nor has the pair learned that passing and cutting to receive a pass are relational skills—that is, the force and distance of the pass must be *in relation* to the passer's ability to throw accurately and the receiver's ability to catch the pass. Sending a long bomb over the head of a defender is difficult, risky, and rarely leads to catchable passes at the elementary level (see **Figure 20.2**). Consequently, we don't teach or allow children to throw long bombs, explaining they will learn these skills in middle and high school, once their passing and catching abilities are stronger. If you allow these passes too early in gameplay development, children will stop using short passes, and the games will fall apart.

Use Ability Grouping When Needed

We find it is sometimes necessary to group children by ability level in invasion games—in particular, in tag-type games. A child who can't run fast can never tag a fast runner, so the game is embarrassing and discouraging for the slower child and boring for the fast runner—a situation that works against our goals to help all children value and participate in physical activity.

In soccer-type games, children with after-school experience can dominate play to the extent that the less-skilled children never get opportunities to practice passing because the more highly skilled children tackle and steal the ball quickly.

SAFETY AND LIABILITY 20.1

Increasing Safety and Decreasing Risk of Liability: Guidelines Relevant to Content in this Chapter

In this box, we discuss specific guidelines built on information discussed throughout this text on professional standards of practice, negligence, and liability. The goals of these guidelines are to increase children's safety and decrease teachers' risk of negligence and liability.

- We discuss two principles of modified game play related to safety. Both are common problems you will encounter when teaching invasion games. First, at the elementary level, invasion games are not contact sports. Some invasion sports, like basketball, soccer, and lacrosse, are contact sports, in that contact is legal and part of the game. Nevertheless, we do not allow any contact between children during games at the elementary level: contact is a foul. Children tend to have contact in invasion games because they are not controlling their bodies or they are attempting a movement that they are not skilled enough to perform safely. Our goal is to teach children to be skillful, safe games players. It takes much more skill to steal the ball without contact than it does to steal the ball by shoving the ball handler.
- Second, in passing and receiving with the feet or hockey stick, require passes to be kept on the ground, and don't allow kicking the ball over the heads of defenders or goalkeepers—although these are important skills and tactics for advanced players who play on teams after school. At the elementary level, where children typically have a wide range of ability levels, we believe keeping the ball on the ground is necessary for safety.
- When children design games, they must learn that rules are needed for games to be safe. Safety and consideration of teammates is the number-one responsibility.
- The first rules children must make when designing games are safety rules. For example, they need to create rules for using equipment safely (e.g., rules to prevent swinging hockey sticks high or throwing balls near opponents' faces). In tag-type games, they must make safety rules such as no pushing or shoving, no hitting anyone's hands, and grabbing the flag without grabbing clothes or yanking on them. In hit-the-pin-type games, they must make rules for not throwing the ball hard at the defenders' legs.
- For all invasion games, they need to set rules against diving for loose balls.

Don't announce that you are arranging groups by ability—just do it.

Use Defenders to Contribute Authenticity and Facilitate Learning

When dividing tactical content into smaller chunks, it is usually important to include defenders who play at a level of intensity that matches the ability level of the offense (recall that there are five levels of defensive intensity). Research has revealed that the addition of defenders as a task constraint elicits more tactically appropriate and skilled cutting and passing (Rovegno, Nevett, Brock, & Babiarz, 2001). The defenders add authenticity; consequently, children better understand the meaning and relevance of tactics. Moreover, motor learning theory supports the importance of setting tasks with as much authenticity as possible for the developmental level of the children (Davids, Button, & Bennett, 2008).

For example, research analysis of the task to have children cut and pass in groups of three without a defender showed that these scenarios produced few good cuts and few lead passes, even though the children could perform those tactics in other situations. The teachers told the children to run and cut into an open space, catch a lead pass, and then immediately look to pass to a teammate cutting into a space. Cutting and passing in groups of three seemed to be a reasonable progression leading to cutting and passing in a 3v1 situation—but it wasn't. When working in groups of three, the children passed to teammates standing still, who then ran with the ball because they remembered the teachers' instructions to run into a space. The teachers then had to spend considerable time reminding children of the task. The task was meaningless to the children; it was simply one more school task teachers assigned.

In contrast, when the teachers added a defender, so that the children played 3v1, the meaning of cutting to get free from a

Figure 20.2 Long bombs rarely work at the elementary level

Courtesy of John Dolly

defender and cutting into open space was readily evident to the children. Thus, the 3v1 task constraints worked well for eliciting more skilled cutting and sending lead passes. The teachers did not have to spend time repeatedly explaining what children should do and why because the task constraints made this information obvious. Defenders added authenticity to tasks, which in turn made the tactics meaningful and relevant to the children.

Teach Anticipation

We have heard people say you can't teach anticipation. We disagree: Not only can you teach children how to anticipate what is likely to happen in gameplay, but it also is critical to do so. Knowing what to anticipate helps children perceive which actions the game situation allows and then make an appropriate tactical decision (See box, "The Wayne Gretzky Story"). To teach anticipation, ask children questions about what they need to perceive to give them clues about what will happen next. For example, have them ask themselves:

- What can I look at to tell me if the receiver is going to get free?
- If I get the ball, what am I going to do? Pass? Shoot? Dribble? Which perceptual clues will tell me which action is best?
- When the receiver gets free and I send the pass, where will the defenders likely be positioned?
- After I pass this ball, where is the best place for me to run?
- My teammate has just started to cut. After he or she cuts, where will there be an open passing lane for me?
- Which clue tells me the receiver is open?

Sometimes, successfully teaching anticipation takes no more effort than simply reminding children that they need to anticipate what will happen next and giving them opportunities to predict (even guess) what will happen. The more they guess and compare their guesses to what actually happened, the better their predictions will become. If you discuss what might happen and what they need to observe, then they will respond by learning to think ahead and read how the game situation is evolving.

The Impact of the Environmental Constraint of a Scoring Goal

In level 3, we add scoring goals, and both tag and passing and receiving games become goal-oriented. The change to goal-oriented gameplay is a major challenge for children. In passing and receiving games, the change to goal-oriented gameplay elicits two relational immature patterns. The receivers cut directly toward the goal while running away from the passer, who then tries to send long passes to get the ball near the goal in one pass (MacPhail, Kirk, & Griffin, 2008; Rovegno et al., 2001). Passing and receiving are relational and develop together—passers send long passes, in part, because receivers run toward the goal without regard to ball location. Although research shows that children can learn the importance of short passes and cutting toward the passer in level 2, the new goal-oriented task and environmental constraints tend to bring out less mature patterns. Consequently, you need to begin units on goal-oriented gameplay by teaching the children how to adapt tactical game skills, such as sending short passes learned in level 2, to a new environment.

Recognize that Learning Invasion Game Tactics Takes Time

Gameplay is complex, and it takes time for children to master the passing and receiving skills and tactics used in invasion gameplay. To be successful, children must understand and see the relationships among defenders, offensive teammates, and the scoring goal. In other words, they need to learn the relational aspects of tactical skills. Studies of passing and receiving games with fourth-grade children found that children made significant learning gains across a 12-lesson unit but had not mastered the content (Rovegno et al., 2001). Thus, educators must respect this content as difficult but developmentally appropriate for grades 3 to 5.

Recognize that Cognitive Understanding Comes Before Consistency in Performing Tactics in Gameplay

Research also shows that children acquire a cognitive understanding of the tactics and know what they are supposed to do before they are actually able to use these tactics in games (MacPhail et al., 2008; Rovegno et al., 2001; Sanchez-Mora Moreno, Garcia Lopez, Sagrario Del Valle Diaz, & Solera Martinez, 2011). Even when they begin to use tactics successfully, they will not be able to do so consistently. Game situations—even in simple games—are too unpredictable and complex for children to master gameplay quickly. Thus, teaching gameplay tactics is one of physical education teachers' most important and challenging tasks.

Teaching Game Structures and Designing Games

We begin teaching level 3 games by teaching children about game structures using tag. **Game structures** include boundaries, rules, consequences for breaking rules, scoring goals, scoring systems, a competitive/cooperative structure, the number of players, and the equipment and skills used.

The meaning and importance of game structures are obvious to adults—for example, you play inside a boundary line, and if you go out, you have broken a rule; boundaries are necessary to keep gameplay contained. Children, however, do not perceive game structures as either important or meaningful. Game rules to children are simply more rules imposed by adults and are no different from the rule to walk quietly in lines in the hallway. It is not uncommon to see children play a game and ignore boundaries. Research suggests that even secondary school students do not have an in-depth understanding of game structures and their impact on gameplay (Casey & Hastie, 2011).

The Wayne Gretzky Story

Here is a story we tell children to help them value the ability to predict and anticipate:

Has anyone ever heard of Wayne Gretzky? He is one of the all-time greatest ice hockey players. He once said, "A good hockey player plays where the puck is. A great hockey player plays where the puck is going to be." What do you think that means? Yes, great players plan ahead and anticipate where the puck is going to be and when it will be there. Gretzky did not follow the puck to the goal—he met it there.

Typically, we begin level 3 lessons on game structures with third-graders. By third grade, most children have reached a level of social and emotional development sufficient to support working in groups and playing small-sided competitive games. In third grade, we typically teach only boundaries, rules, consequences for breaking rules, basic scoring, and basic tag tactics. In fourth and fifth grades, we teach more complex rules, consequences for breaking rules, scoring systems, tag team tactics, and invasion games using passing and receiving.

Teach Game Structures Through Child-Designed and Child-Modified Games

To help children understand the meaning and relevance of game structures, we use child-designed and child-modified games. Research suggests student-designed games are an effective way to teach these structures (Casey & Hastie, 2011). As children design and modify their own games, they experiment with game structures, such as different-sized boundaries, different ways to score, and different rules, and they experience the results of those changes.

Game structures have much more meaning when children design them to solve a problem in their game. For example, a game gets boring, dangerous, and/or falls apart when members of the offense can plant themselves in front of the goal and just shoot and shoot. Rules such as the establishment of a zone in which the offense cannot step, an offsides-type rule, or a three-second-type rule (like in basketball) will solve the problem. When teachers lecture and children memorize rules, however, rules don't have meaning or relevance. For example, we have found that even some secondary students think the three-second rule in basketball applies to the defense. Children need to understand why a rule exists and what problem it solves.

When child-designed games are used to help children learn about game structures, students simultaneously learn how to modify games. We then can spiral back to this knowledge throughout the games curriculum to help children modify games to accommodate their individual differences, to solve problems with their game structures, and to make their games more challenging and enjoyable.

When Teaching Game Structures, Teach the Related Tactics

Not only do we teach game structures using child- and teacher-designed games, but we also simultaneously teach the basic tactics related to the specific game structures taught in the lesson. For example, when we teach children how to design appropriately sized boundaries, we teach them tactics related to boundaries, such as how defenders use boundaries to constrain the offense and limit where the offense can run or dribble. When children understand how boundaries are used tactically in games, they understand boundaries as more than an arbitrary area within which they must stay, but as an integral part of games. Their knowledge becomes both deeper and more connected to tactical gameplay.

Use a Play–Discuss–Play Cycle

In all level 3 lessons, we use a **play–discuss–play cycle**. In this cycle, children make decisions about their game structures or tactics and then play the game for several minutes. At that point, they stop to discuss the game structures or tactics briefly, make any needed modifications, and then play again. This play–discuss–play cycle continues throughout the lesson. Be sure the children spend more time playing than discussing, however.

It is our experience that when children first learn to design or play games and with large classes, the teacher must control the timing and content of the play–discuss–play cycle. Scan the entire class. When you see social or game problems, stop the class and have the children gather in their groups to discuss what you identify as critical topics. You might say, for example:

- What problems are you having with your game?
- I noticed one team had the ball most of the time. How can you change your game to make it fair?
- Can any team share how they solved the problem of the offense bunching in front of the goal and not being able to score because all of the defenders were there, too?
- Which defensive tactics did you use to prevent the offense from scoring? (See the "Teaching Tip" box for other suggestions.)

During small-group discussions, make sure all children get a chance to have input (see **Figure 20.3**). You can assign one child to be an "inclusion monitor" who monitors the discussion to see if everyone participated and, if not, asks for opinions or ideas from those who did not participate. When we teach outside, sometimes we have the children come into a central area and sit or stand in their groups around a hoop facing each other (see **Figure 20.4**). This arrangement allows the teacher to monitor the discussions.

The ultimate goal is for the children to stop their games on their own when they recognize problems, hold a group discussion with everyone contributing, solve their problems, and play again without teacher intervention. This outcome tends to happen after you have been at a school for many years and the children are well versed in making group decisions and the process of designing and modifying games.

TEACHING TIP

Teaching Children How to Change the Rules

One potential problem arises when a child frequently stops the game to make or change a rule. If this behavior is occurring in one group, try to discover whether the game is working for that child, and why or why not. If the game is not the problem, you might need to restrict the children in that group to making one rule change each. You also need to tell children that they have the option to ask the teacher for help. Give them some examples of when they might need to do so. For example, they might need the teacher's help if they are trying hard to solve their game problems, but their solutions never seem to work; if their discussions are not productive or efficient; or if they have to stop their game frequently. Children might also need help if their group has a majority vote but the minority has a strong belief that the solution is not fair. It is critical to consider not only the number of people who believe in one solution, but also the depth and strength of the feelings of those who have a minority opinion. Arriving at consensus helps children feel like their views matter.

Figure 20.3 Group discussion that is not working

Help Children Design Good Games that Work Well

After you give children a task to design a game or after you assign a modified game to practice tactics, you and the children need to focus first on the game's structures. The goal is to get a good game working. Research shows that until children have a good game, their game environment will not facilitate learning tactical game skills and tactics (Rovegno et al., 2001).

Figure 20.4 Play–discuss–play cycle using hoops to organize discussion groups

The following criteria are used for judging whether a game is working well:

1. There is balance between offense and defense.
2. Time spent playing on offense and defense is roughly equal.
3. All children within a group understand and agree on the rules and scoring system.
4. The game has flow.

There Is Balance Between Offense and Defense

Designing and modifying games to ensure a balance between offense and defense is critical at the elementary level, because at this age children's defensive abilities are greater than their offensive abilities. Consequently, you need to find ways to limit the defense so that games can be balanced.

One approach in invasion games that meets this goal is to have more children on offense than defense and to play 2v1, 3v1, and 3v2 games. You can also have a neutral offensive player who switches teams when possession of the ball changes. For example, four children might form themselves into two teams of 2v2 with a fifth child joining the team when they are on offense. In this scenario, the children rotate to fill the role of the neutral offensive player.

A second approach is to limit the intensity of the defense by using the five levels of defense (see the next "What the Research Says" box for support for using the levels of defensive intensity). In brief, these levels are as follows:

- *Level 1: Feet still, arms still.* The defender remains still and in place.
- *Level 2: Feet still, arms move.* The defender can wave her or his arms but must remain in place.
- *Level 3: Feet move, can't touch the ball.* The defender can apply pressure, jump up and down, wave hands, and travel with the offensive player, but can't use her or his hands, feet, or hockey stick to touch the ball. We often call this a "pest defender."
- *Level 4: Soft guarding/marking.* The defender can move both arms and can travel, guarding the offensive player but most of the time allows him or her to make the play successfully.
- *Level 5: Full guarding/marking.* Competitive guarding/marking with a no-contact rule.

You will likely need to require children to use the level of defense appropriate to the individual whom they are guarding/marking because children tend to automatically play level 5, full-intensity defense.

You also can set the level of defense for different situations within the game or for different individuals. A child with a disability might need defenders to work at level 1. A team that can't get a good game started because of problems with the first inbound pass will benefit from setting level 1 defense on the inbound pass only.

A final way to balance teams is to establish a rule that if one team gets ahead by 3 or 4 points, the two teams must meet and the team that is ahead must explain what they have been doing to succeed and what the other team could do better. Then the teams trade one or two players and begin the game again.

What the Research Says

Levels of Defensive Intensity: The "Goldilocks Principle"

Research shows that the quality of students' practice improves when teachers monitor and modify the levels of defensive intensity (using the five levels of defense) (Nevett, Rovegno, Babiarz, & McCaughtry, 2001; Rovegno et al., 2001). A high level of defense (level 5) constrains the development of passing and cutting to receive a pass. When the passers and receivers have less skill ability and the defenders are fast runners and play high-intensity defense, the receivers cannot get free and passers cannot successfully send passes. Consequently, the offensive players get frustrated and have few practice opportunities.

In contrast, when the passers and receivers have higher skill abilities and the defenders are slow and play with low intensity, receivers do not have to run fast into open space or work hard to get free from defenders. In this scenario, the offense simply tosses the ball back and forth. There is no practice of cutting into an open space and no practice in sending lead passes.

When the level of defense is just right, the defenders challenge receivers and force them to cut appropriately to get free but enable them to succeed in doing so. Good practice opportunities require a good game with a balance between offensive abilities and the level of intensity of the defense, which the researchers refer to as the **"Goldilocks Principle."** Just like Goldilocks, who did not want her porridge to be either too hot or too cold, but just right, the level of defense cannot be too intense or too slack, but needs to be just right—that is, challenging yet also allowing for success.

Time Spent Playing on Offense and Defense Is Roughly Equal

Research shows that for student-designed games to be good games, there must be an approximately equal amount of time spent playing on offense and defense, along with ways for the defense to gain possession that are not too difficult (Casey & Hastie, 2011). There is something wrong with a game in which one team is always on defense. If the problem is not due to a lack of balance between offense and defense, the culprit is likely the change of possession rule, or the lack of such a rule. There needs to be a fair change of possession rule enabling the defense to get the ball and become the offense in a reasonable amount of time. In addition, the rules governing how the defenders can gain possession cannot make the change of possession too difficult.

All Children Within a Group Understand and Agree on the Rules and Scoring System

Typically, when children argue as they are playing child-designed games, the problem arises because some or all of them are confused about the rules. Sometimes a few children make a rule but don't discuss the rule with all group members. Sometimes children—especially those who participate in youth leagues after school—assume that everyone knows rules such as you can't go out of bounds, you can't run with the ball, or you can't touch a ball with your hands. You will need to teach children that it is not a rule unless they have made it a rule and *everyone* hears and understands it.

At other times, children argue because the scoring system of the game is more competitive than they can manage emotionally. You can teach children how to view competition from a mastery orientation, focusing on learning and respecting their classmates' rights to learn in a positive emotional climate. At the same time, we always give children the choice to design cooperative, competitive, or competitive games without keeping track of the score.

The Game Has Flow

If a game has flow, it doesn't stop frequently. Lack of flow may be due to many causes:

- Boundaries are too small, so the ball goes out of bounds frequently.
- The children's skills are not developed enough to successfully complete passes or strike a ball back and forth over a net in a rally.
- The equipment makes gameplay too difficult (e.g., volleyballs are too small and heavy, preventing rallies and game flow).
- Change of possession rules are too difficult (e.g., change of possession occurs on the spot and immediately after an interception when the children have not learned tactics to change from offense to defense quickly).

First Work on Getting Good Games, then Teach Tactics

Good games provide the task and environmental constraints to help children develop skills and tactics. Research shows, however, that it is difficult to get games working and keep them working well (Rovegno et al., 2001). You need to monitor games throughout the lesson, and if the games are not working, assist children in making modifications so that the games become and remain a good learning environment for achieving your lesson objectives. Focus the play–discuss–play cycle on game structures until the children have developed good games (see **Figure 20.5**). Then shift the children's attention to the tactics they are using and ways to improve tactical gameplay—which are your primary objectives.

The Role of the Teacher in Child-Designed and Child-Modified Games

We need to say up front that the phrase "child-designed games" can be misleading. It seems to imply that the children design the game without teacher input. Nothing could be further from the truth: Teacher input is critical and extensive.

Determine and Focus on Lesson Objectives

First, as the teacher, you determine the lesson objectives, including deciding which game structure and tactical content

Figure 20.5 A good game

to teach the children. You also set the task, selecting the goal of the game, skills, tactics, and equipment. Setting the task narrows and guides which kinds of games children design. For example, if you give them a choice of balls, one of which is a football, and tell children to design a game to practice lead passes and running pass patterns, you will end up with games that resemble football game-like situations.

Once children begin playing, you must ensure that the game provides practice of the lesson objectives. For example, if you are teaching children how to design boundaries that provide fair opportunities for both the offense and defense, and the children design boundaries that are too large for the defenders to ever tag the runner in tag games or to ever get the ball in passing and receiving games, you will need to intervene. You can then help the children modify their boundaries so that they will work on your lesson objectives.

Observing Gameplay: Teaching "Under the Influence"

Second, you observe the games the children design, interpret what you see, and then must decide what to do next. This process comprises the observation, interpretation, and decision making cycle (Barrett, 1984).

The phrase "teaching under the influence" was a joke made by undergraduates in a research study that required them to observe students' gameplay and then design the next lesson to solve the most important problems the students exhibited during their games (Alexander & Penney, 2005). In other words, they had to observe their students to see what they needed to learn next. Thus, the novices were teaching "under the influence" of student learning.

Teaching gameplay under the influence requires you to observe children's responses in relation to the task constraints (i.e., the game the children design), environmental constraints (e.g., playing area, equipment), and individual constraints (children's motor, cognitive, and affective capabilities). Recall that the relations among task, environment, and individual constraints determine children's movement responses and, in turn, what they learn. Research on children learning gameplay indicates that environment and task constraints that are either too easy or difficult will negatively affect children's learning (Rovegno et al., 2001). Thus, when children design games, teachers must monitor the task and environmental constraints and intervene if they are not seeing the movement responses they want the children to learn. For example, you will need to observe to see:

- If the environment is causing a problem, such as whether the endlines are too far apart so that the children are getting frustrated because they can't score.
- If the task is a problem, such as when some children are consistently on defense because, in a child-designed game, the children did not design a rule for how the teams change possession of the ball or change from offense to defense in tag. Without teacher intervention to ensure equal opportunities for both offense and defense, children might not recognize the problem.
- If individual capabilities are problems, such as when some children are less skilled and rarely send a successful lead pass. In such cases, the game has no flow and stops often. To solve this problem, the group can set a rule that whoever is defending when that child is trying to pass must play level 1 defense, meaning the defender stands still and does not wave her or his arms to try to prevent the pass. This criterion adds a small amount of defensive pressure but allows less skilled passers more time and space to see the receivers.

Lessons using child-designed games are like any other lesson; once you observe a problem, you decide how to respond.

Guiding Children's Decisions, Giving Feedback, and Guiding Discussions

Thus, the third role of the teacher during child-designed games lessons is to intervene. You might help children modify their game, give feedback, provide explanations and demonstrations, or guide a class or group discussion. Children do not have the range of knowledge about the rules and procedures of different sports that you have, so they might not be able to generate rules to solve the problems with their games (see **Figure 20.6**). You will often have to describe and suggest options for rules, scoring systems, and scoring goals.

Our experience with beginning teachers when they have children design games (including our own experiences when we first started using child-designed games) and the research suggest that sometimes, beginning teachers are afraid to intervene with the children's games (Rovegno, 1998; Rovegno & Bandhauer, 1994). Some teachers think they are not supposed to intervene. Others think children should learn only on their own through experimentation. Still others do not want to stifle creativity. These are worthy concerns: After all, we want children to learn by exploring and experimenting, which includes sometimes making mistakes. Nevertheless, at times children will design games that have little chance of facilitating lesson objectives. Sometimes their group discussions will hit a stumbling block. At other times, children will be confused about the task or the content. Part of constructivist teaching is monitoring and guiding the children's explorations. These actions will facilitate, not harm, children's learning (see the next "What the Research Says" box for support for teacher intervention).

It can be a challenge to know how to intervene when you are first learning to teach using child-designed games. Our fail-safe technique is to observe the group, stop them, and say, "Tell me about your game." Between what you see and what you hear the children say, you will be able to figure out if the game needs

Figure 20.6 Solving problems with child-designed games

modifications or if the children need additional explanations about game structures or feedback on their tactics.

Improving Your Observations

You can improve your ability to observe by creating an observation plan (Barrett, 1984). Try to anticipate how children will respond in the games, and decide what to look for that will tell you what you need to do next. The following examples suggest what you might plan to observe in child-designed game lessons. *When children are designing or modifying games, look for these behaviors:*

- Are children getting along or arguing?
- Does the game flow, or does the game stop frequently?
- Are all children in a group looking at each other, or are some having a private conversation and leaving other children out?
- Is everyone active, or are some children standing and not contributing to gameplay?
- Are children observing the boundaries or ignoring them?
- Is there body contact or no body contact?

When children are practicing tactics in their games, think about the specific tactics that are your lesson objective and look for evidence that the children understand the tactics. For example,

- Are the children are protecting their flag in tag?
- Are the children using the boundary to try to trap the runner?
- Are the children double-teaming to get the flag of an opponent?

Learning Experiences for Teaching Game Structures, Designing Games, and Tag Tactics

In this section, we describe in detail learning experiences for a unit introducing game structures. We simultaneously teach children how to design and modify games and the tag tactics of those games, showing the children how to put all the pieces together. We teach this unit outdoors where there is ample space. (If you don't have outdoor space, you can use 1v1 dribbling to teach game structures.)

If you are new to a school or if the children have never designed games, you can teach the entire unit in grades 6, 5, and often 4. The older the children are, the faster they will progress through the unit. With grades 3 and 4, observe the children's responses and stop the unit when it becomes developmentally inappropriate. For example, do not progress further in the unit if the children are frustrated, arguing, or upset about scoring; if their games do not work well; or if their skills are not mature enough to allow for the practice of tactics.

Before describing the unit, we briefly discuss prerequisite level 1 and 2 content we teach in earlier grades.

> **What the Research Says**
>
> **Expert Teachers' Assistance During Tasks in Which Children Make Decisions**
>
> Research on constructivist expert teachers indicates that expert teachers not only intervene when children design games, centers, or practice tasks, but also provide explicit information and guidance (Rovegno, Chen, & Todorovich, 2003). A handy way to think of this assistance is the "three Cs." First, the teachers provide *clarification* about possible options, suggest possible rules, and list categories of rules children need to consider. Second, they describe the *criteria* for good and poor decisions—for example, telling children what is unacceptable in regard to safety. Third, they monitor the children's decisions and provide a *critique* of the decisions—for example, they critique decisions that might hamper safety, fairness, and appropriate skill practice.

Level 1 Tag Content

Level 1 tag content includes the following:

- Chasing
- Fleeing
- Traveling quickly on angular pathways to change direction
- Dodging

We don't teach separate lessons for level 1 tag content for several reasons. Children even as young as 2 years old begin to play chasing and fleeing games with adults and older siblings. They even figure out at a very young age that they can get closer to an adult who can't run fast than they can to one who can respond more quickly. Very young children also play chasing and fleeing games at recess, before school, and after school. We believe our job in physical education is to help children improve their abilities to chase, flee, and dodge.

We introduce level 1 content first in dance, by teaching children how to travel on angular pathways, including traveling quickly while making sharp angular changes in direction by leaning in the opposite direction and pushing off a planted foot with knees bent. A lesson titled "The Thunderstorm" is appropriate for first-graders and illustrates one way to teach this content, with lightning serving as the stimulus for moving quickly on angular pathways.

We then teach dodging and traveling quickly on angular pathways in level 2 dribbling tasks while having children dodge cones (pretend defenders).

Level 2 Tag Introductory Activities

We teach the level 2 content for tag as introductory activities for other lessons or as part of health-related fitness lessons. We provide three examples here. These games are energetic but do not have enough depth of content to serve as the basis for an entire lesson. Consequently, when we teach tag as a game, we begin with level 3 content.

- *Touch Knees.* Face your partner and get into a ready position with knees bent, feet apart, and hands ready. Count how many times you can touch your partner's knees in 30 seconds (I will time you), while at the same time trying to prevent your partner from touching your knees. Here are the rules for the game:
  Touch—don't slap—your partner's knees. Touch only your partner's knees. You may not push their hands away.
- *Touch Toes.* Same as "touch knees," but try to touch your partner's toes.
- *Triangle Tag.* In your assigned group of four, one person is the tagger. The other three hold hands in a circle, with one person designated as the person to tag. The other two members of the circle are defenders who try to prevent the tagger from tagging your teammate. The tagger may not touch anyone except the designated person to tag. What do you think the tactics of this game will be? [To block the tagger by rotating the circle to keep the defenders' bodies between the tagger and the designated person to tag.] Right. We call this tactic *blocking.* [Rotate so each child gets to play each position.]

Game Structure and Tactic Content

Table 20.1 describes the content of game structures that we teach to children. Using this information, you can design unit and lesson objectives. We introduce much of this content in the first tag unit. You will continue to teach additional game structures across grades 3–5, as children become more skilled in designing and playing games.

We organize the tactics in four progressive levels: level 3A tag tactics, and levels 3B, 3C, and 3D for passing and receiving

Table 20.1 Level 3 Game Structure Content

Game Structure Content	Examples and Suggestions
Players, Skills, and Equipment • Games have different numbers of players on a team. • Games have different equipment and skills. • Equipment and skills affect the type of game you design and the tactics you use.	
Perfect-sized Boundaries • Boundaries that are too small favor the defense. • Boundaries that are too large favor the offense. • Design perfect-sized boundaries that provide equal, fair opportunities for both offense and defense.	
Rules • Rules make games fun and fair. • Respect for rules is imperative because ignoring rules ruins games. • Rules are needed for safety.	• You need rules to prevent body contact. • Create rules for using equipment safely (e.g., rules to prevent swinging hockey sticks high or throwing balls near opponents' faces).
• Rules can be (and are often) changed to make games better. (This is true of sports, too.)	• Change or modify your rules if your game is not fair. • Take care to change rules at fair times (e.g., don't stop the game to change a rule just before the other team is about to score). • If you don't all agree, use a majority vote to make or change a rule.
Make rules for the following elements: • Boundaries • Scoring • Violations that ruin the game • Violations for actions that are not part of the task given by the teacher	For example, if the teacher says to make up a game using only passing and catching, you need a rule against running with the ball.
Make rules for when and how teams change possession of the ball (e.g., when the ball is intercepted, stolen, dropped, or goes out of bounds) and rules for free balls (e.g., when someone misses a pass) that ensure both teams get equal opportunities to play offense and defense.	Base change of possession rules on your ability to switch from offense to defense quickly. If you can do this quickly, your change of possession can be immediate and on the spot of the interception, for example. If you are just learning gameplay and need time to switch from offense to defense (or the reverse), devise a system that gives you more time, such as stopping play and taking possession at the endline or stopping play and taking possession on the nearest sideline.

Table 20.1 Level 3 Game Structure Content (*continued*)

Game Structure Content	Examples and Suggestions
Some games need rules for special situations: • Bases • A no-play zone • A no-standing-still zone	For example, tag games using bases need rules to limit the runner's time on base or the number of players who can be on a base. Some games need rules for having a no-play zone around a base or goal to prevent the offense or defense from having too much of an advantage (e.g., to prevent the defense from bunching up and completely covering the goal area). Some games need rules for having a no-standing-still zone to prevent the offense from planting themselves in front of the goal.
Consequences for Breaking Rules • When you break a rule, there are consequences that give the advantage to your opponents.	Consequences commonly used in invasion games: • Giving the ball to the opposing team • Awarding points • Losing tries • Moving a player to a position that gives the opponent an advantage • Awarding penalty shots or plays
• Some consequences are inappropriate in physical education.	• Having someone sit out is inappropriate, because the goal in physical education is for all children to practice, learn, and stay active, which a child can't do while sitting out. • Doing exercises such as jumping jacks, push-ups, or any punitive activities not related directly to the game is inappropriate. (Try to imagine a professional basketball player who is called for a traveling violation having to stop and do push-ups on the court, and you will understand why we recommend this restriction. Just because students are children doesn't mean they won't feel they have lost their dignity when given a public punishment.)
Scoring Goals and Scoring Systems • Invasion games have scoring goals. • You can design different types of scoring goals.	For example, basketball hoops and goal cages may be used for • Passing to a teammate over the endline (as in football) • Shooting a ball into a basketball hoop or target on the wall • Shooting a ball into a wide goal on the ground (e.g., cones, portable small soccer goals) • Knocking a pin down • Passing to a teammate who cuts into one or more hoops behind the endline • Dribbling with the feet and balancing the ball on one of several saucer cones over the endline
• The type and number of goals influence the tactics of the game.	For example, having two hoops in which you can pass to a teammate to score gives you more options on offense, and the defense will need to figure out how to defend two goals.
• Goals need to be the perfect size for your game and the number of players.	Very large goals make it too easy to score, and very small goals make it too hard to score. However, small goals allow you to play a good game without a goalkeeper.
• Games can assign different numbers of points to different scoring actions.	For example, in archery you score more points if you shoot the arrow in the center of the target. You need to decide the point system for your game (e.g., 1 point for passing the ball to a teammate over the endline, 5 points for kicking it into the goal, 1 point for intercepting a pass).
Competition and Cooperation • Invasion games have a competitive structure, in that the goal is to outwit and outplay your opponent and score points in some way (even if you do not keep track of the score).	
• Invasion games have both competitive and cooperative aspects. • You can decide to play a competitive game and keep score, a competitive game and not keep score, a cooperative game while trying to beat your own record, or a cooperative game and not keep score.	When you work *with* teammates, you are cooperating. When you play *against* another team, you are competing. Cooperative games, such as trying to kick passes with a partner as many times in a row without missing, can also have competitive aspects. You can try to beat your own best score, or you can try to beat the score of other individuals or pairs.

Student Tales

What Children Think

Rick: We make up our own game.

Researcher: How do you feel about that?

Rick: I like it a lot better because we get to make up our own rules and how we want to play.

Researcher: So you like that better than when the teacher does it.

Rick: Yup.

Researcher: Do you ever have any troubles when you make up your own games? Ever fight with each other?

Rick: No. We just get on it.

games. This progression reflects research on the development of children's passing and receiving in games. These basic tactics are developmentally appropriate at the elementary level. If the children have physical education only a limited number of days per week, however, it is unrealistic to think you will be able to teach all this content. In such a case, you will need to select the tactics your children are ready to learn and the invasion games (e.g., basketball, soccer, floor hockey, field hockey, football) that are most important for children to learn in your community and area of the country.

Table 20.2 describes the level 3A tactics we teach in tag-type games (which include tag with flags, dribble tag, and football-type games). Children's gameplay in passing games (with hands, feet, or hockey sticks) rarely is skilled enough for the more advanced tag tactics to be important. If they become important, you can easily help children transfer their knowledge of these tactics to the passing and catching games. The tactics are, of course, important in regulation invasion sports, so introducing them prepares children for learning the major sports in middle and high school. In addition to game structures, these tactics become the basis for your unit and lesson objectives.

Sample Learning Experiences

We divide the tag unit into four parts. Each part requires one to three lessons. We teach this unit outside where there is plenty of space. The initial tasks won't work as well if the children are

Table 20.2 Level 3A Tactics for Tag Games

Tactics to Teach First	Tactics to Teach Second
Protect the Flag You can protect your flag by turning your body, doing jump spins, or keeping the flag between the boundary and your body. *Avoid Defenders* To avoid taggers, run on different pathways, changing direction quickly, changing speeds, running fast, and using body feints. *Use Boundaries Tactically* • Boundaries work like a defender by denying space, constraining the offense. Defenders try to force the offense into the corner by running at them and constraining space, cutting off their likely avenue of escape, and shifting if the offense shifts. • Offensive players try to stay away from the boundaries, especially the corners, to avoid defenders trapping them. *Use Bases (Safety Zones) Tactically* • When on offense, if you are about to be tagged and can't score, going to a base (safety zone) is the next best option. • When on defense, you must guard both the base and the scoring zone. *Offensive Support: Blockers and Helping Trapped Teammates* • Run behind a blocker to avoid being tagged. • If you lose your flag, you can block for teammates. • Sometimes you need to help players who are trapped or who have lost their flags by trying to steal the flag from those players trapping your teammate. *Defensive Support: Double-Teaming* • "Double-teaming" involves two defensive teammates working together to stop one offensive player. Two defenders are better for trapping an offensive player because they deny more space in which the offensive player can escape.	*Offensive Support: Picks and Decoys* • In tag, decoys and sacrifices can enable some runners to score. • Run by a teammate who "blocks" your defender so your defender must stop and run around the block. We call this a "pick" in basketball. *Offensive Tactics for Beating a Person-to-Person (1 on 1) Defense* (We typically do not teach a zone defense at the elementary level unless children try to do a zone defense in their tag games. If they do so, we help them if necessary.) • To beat a 1 on 1 defense, use picks and blockers. • Two offensive players crossing pathways can counteract a 1 on 1 defense by confusing the defense and forcing them to take time to shift positions around each other or to shift the players they are defending. *Defensive Tactics for a Person-to-Person Defense* • In person-to-person defense, each defender guards one person on the other team—1 on 1. • Select the person whom you will guard ahead of time based on matching abilities. • Tag (pull the flag) by watching the runner, anticipating his or her direction, and watching eye and body movements. • Stay with the person you are guarding until he or she loses the flags, unless your team needs you to double-team someone. • Try to cut off the angle on which the offense will run to score. • Avoid "doggie chases the tail" (running behind the runner in a circle and never changing your pathway). Doggie chases the tail will not result in pulled flags. *Defensive Support: Covering for Other Defenders* • If a teammate gets beat and his or her opponent is about to score, go off your opponent and try to stop the person about to score. • If you get beat, run back and help a teammate.

constrained to a small space. You will need to group the children by their ability to run quickly, because slower runners will never be successful against children who are faster.

Below is an outline of the content we teach for designing games and tag tactics that is described in **Sample Learning Experiences 20.1 to 20.4.**

Part 1

- Learning to design fair boundaries that don't favor the offense or defense
- Tactics for protecting your flag and using boundaries tactically

Part 2

- Learning to design rules, consequences for breaking rules, and scoring systems
- Tactics for offensive support and defensive double-teaming

Part 3

- Learning to design tag games with bases as safety zones
- Tactics for using bases on offense and defending bases on defense

Part 4

- Learning to design tag games with scoring goals
- Tactics for scoring and defending scoring goals

FYI

Summary of Task Label Abbreviations

I	Informing tasks
E	Extending/exploring tasks
R	Refinements
A	Application/assessment tasks
Org	Organizing task
Cog K	Cognitive knowledge: Explains or defines a concept
Social	Social skill or concept
Th	Thinking skill
Mot	Motivation concept
Safety	Safety information or reminder
MD	Modification to make the task more difficult
ME	Modification to make the task easier

Source: Modified from Rink, J. E. (2014). *Teaching physical education for learning* (7th ed.).New York: McGraw-Hill.

SAMPLE LEARNING EXPERIENCES 20.1

Level 3A: Designing Boundaries, Tactics for Protecting your Flag, and Using Boundaries Tactically

Objectives

Children will learn

Motor and Cognitive Knowledge

Game Structures

1. Boundaries of the wrong size can be a reason a game is not working; boundaries that are too large favor the runners (offense); and boundaries that are too small favor the taggers (defense).
2. For a game to work, it has to provide reasonably even opportunities for defense and offense. If the offense gets out immediately or if the defense rarely thwarts the offense, the game has no suspense and no excitement, and is not at the appropriate level of challenge to foster learning for both teams.

Game Tactics

3. To fake out and dodge taggers by running on different pathways, changing direction quickly, changing speeds, running fast, and using body feints.
4. To protect their flag by turning their body, doing jump spins, and keeping the flag between the boundary and their body.
5. To look at the tagger and select a pathway away from the tagger's intended direction.
6. To tag runners by watching them and anticipating their pathway.
7. To avoid the boundary on offense and to use the boundary to trap and corner a runner on defense.

Thinking Skills

8. To identify and solve problems with game structures.

Social

9. To listen to everyone's suggestions and respond respectfully to their opinions.

(continues)

SAMPLE LEARNING EXPERIENCES 20.1

Level 3A: Designing Boundaries, Tactics for Protecting your Flag, and Using Boundaries Tactically (*continued*)

Content Development

Identifying Problems with Boundaries that Are Too Large

I Today, you are going to be playing tag and learning how to identify problems in games, solve these problems, and design your own tag games. I am going to put you in groups of four. Put on a flag ("flag football" flags), decide on an order for each of you to be a tagger, find a large space on the field, and play tag. I will call out when to switch taggers. [This game is designed not to work well, thereby allowing children to experience the problems with boundaries that are too big. Without boundaries, the defense (tagger) will have a very difficult time catching the offense (runners). After the children have all been chasers, have a problem-identification and problem-solving discussion.]

Th Stop, come in, and stand in front of me. I saw many problems with this game. That's okay—the games were supposed to have problems. Our goal today is to learn how to identify and then solve problems in games.

1. What are the problems with this game? [I couldn't catch anyone. They just ran so far away that I got tired chasing them, and no one else was nearby to chase.]
2. What could you add to give the tagger a better chance to tag the runners? [Boundaries.]
3. Do you think it is a fair game if you have to chase someone you can never catch? [No.]

Identifying Problems with Boundaries that Are Too Small

E Great answer. Pick up three cones each (12 total for each group) to form boundaries. As a group, you will now experiment with boundaries of different sizes to see what effect this has on the game. You just played with a boundary so big it was in the next county! Now set a boundary that is too small and play several rounds.

Solving Problems with Boundaries: Perfect Boundaries

Th Stop. Who had an easier time with small boundaries—the tagger or the runners? Who had an easier time when you played with a huge boundary? What would be a perfect boundary? [One that gives an equal chance to both the tagger and the runners.]

E Now design a perfect boundary for your group and play several rounds of tag. I will call out when to rotate taggers.

Cog K Stop. Summarize what you learned about the size of boundaries. [Boundaries of the wrong size can be a reason a game is not working; boundaries that are too large favor the runners (offense); and boundaries that are too small favor the tagger (defense). For a game to be fair, fun, and exciting, it has to have equal opportunities for defense and offense.]

Identifying and Solving Tactical Problems

E Play again, and pay attention to the tactics you use to tag and avoid the tagger tagging you. See what you can learn about tactics by paying attention.

Cog K Stop. Discuss within your group which tactics you used to keep the tagger from pulling your flag and what you did when you were the tagger.

Social Before you do, tell me some behaviors that make good group discussions. [Everyone listens, no one interrupts, no one is bossy, and everyone gets to give an opinion.] What are some behaviors that ruin group discussions? [Making fun of someone's idea, saying someone's idea is stupid or bad.] Great insights. In your discussions today, focus on everyone listening and responding respectfully to everyone's ideas and opinions.

Cog K Now, we will go around and have each group share one tactic. [Call on groups until you have elicited the following: fake out and dodge taggers by running on different pathways, changing direction quickly, changing speeds, running fast, and using body feints; protecting your flag by turning your body and doing jump spins; looking at the tagger and selecting a pathway away from the tagger's intended direction; tagging by watching the runners and anticipating their pathway.]

R Discuss with your group which ideas you think you most need to improve. Play again, and see if you can improve your tactics.

Boundary Tactics

E As you play, pay attention to the tactics you use in relation to the boundaries. See what you can discover by paying attention.

Cog K Stop. Let's discuss boundary tactics. What did you learn? [The tagger can trap a runner in the corner, where it is easier to get the flag. When I run near the boundary, the tagger has an easier time getting my flag because I have less space for escape. It is harder for the tagger when I turn so my flag is toward the boundary, and I protect it with my body. When I am a tagger, I can force a runner toward the boundary or corner giving the person less space to run.]

SAMPLE LEARNING EXPERIENCES 20.1

Level 3A: Designing Boundaries, Tactics for Protecting your Flag, and Using Boundaries Tactically (*continued*)

Cog K Would one group like to volunteer to demonstrate how to trap a runner in the corner? Janika's group will do so. [Students demonstrate.] [Set up a second demonstration if needed, so children get to see the principle of staying an equal distance from the sideline and endline and cutting off likely avenues of escape. Then verbally repeat how to trap a runner so children can both see and hear the tactical principle and understand it on a conscious level (Rink, 2010).]

Culminating Activity

R I am going to switch your groups. Play again. See if you can improve your boundary tactics.

Th Talk to your current group and discuss the differences and similarities in your tactics compared to your first group. How did you adjust to those differences?

SAMPLE LEARNING EXPERIENCES 20.2

Level 3A: Designing Rules, Consequences, and Scoring and Using Tactics for Offensive Support and Defensive Double-Teaming

Objectives

Children will learn

Motor and Cognitive Knowledge

Game Structures

1. Rules make games fun and fair. Respect for rules is imperative because ignoring rules ruins games.
2. Rules are needed for safety.
3. Rules can be (and are often) changed to make games better.
4. When you break a rule, there are consequences that give the advantage to your opponents.
5. Some consequences are inappropriate in physical education, such as having someone sit out or doing exercises such as jumping jacks and push-ups. Consequences must be sport-like (e.g., get your opponent's flag, help the offense, lose a tag).

Tactics

6. Blocking: To avoid being tagged, you can run behind a blocker.
7. Sometimes you need to help players who are trapped or who have lost their flags by trying to steal the flag from those players trapping your teammate.
8. "Double-teaming" is using two defenders for trapping an offensive player.

Thinking Skills

9. To identify and solve problems with game rules.

Social

10. To interpret other children's actions more accurately and resolve problems when they think someone has "cheated."

Content Development

Safety Rules

Cog K Today, we will be designing tag games again. All games have rules, and if you break those rules, there are consequences. The first rules you must make are safety rules. Which safety rules do you think might be important for tag? [No pushing or shoving, no hitting anyone's hands, no grabbing clothes and yanking on them.] Okay. Those are great rules for a start. I will put you in groups of four [or six].

Th Quickly design a tag game and try it out. Decide on these rules:

- What the boundaries will be
- Whether you will play 2v2 or 3v1 (or 4v2 or 3v3)

(*continues*)

SAMPLE LEARNING EXPERIENCES 20.2

Level 3A: Designing Rules, Consequences, and Scoring and Using Tactics for Offensive Support and Defensive Double-Teaming (*continued*)

- How many flags each of you will wear
- How you will change taggers

Problem Solving to Avoid Elimination

Th Stop. [Stop the games relatively quickly.] I saw some problems with your games. What problems did you see? [I was tagged quickly and then just stood around watching; it was boring.] Right. In physical education, we want everyone to participate all the time. Can you participate if you are eliminated from the game? [No.] If you are not playing, can you practice your skills and tactics and improve? [No.] You all know that PE is the chance for all of you to learn and improve, because we have talked about this subject before. The first problem I want you to fix with your game is elimination. Decide

- What happens when someone is tagged and when someone loses all of her or his flags. You must figure out a way for that person to continue to play.
- If you will have a scoring system, what it will be, and if you will keep track of the score.

E Play again. [Watch to see if the games are working. If you see problems, work with that group; if the problems are widespread, stop the class.]

Cog K Stop. These games are working much better. Let's share ideas about how you solved your problems. What were some of your rules? [When you are tagged, you lose a flag, join the chasers, give the chaser one of your flags, or become "it."]

Problem-Solving Rules for Boundaries

Th Now focus on rules for boundaries. Which problems did you have with boundaries? [They were too small/large. It was hard to see. Some people run out of the boundary.] Why were some people running out of bounds? [They couldn't see the boundary, they forgot, we didn't make a rule against running out of bounds.] What can you do to fix these problems? [Change the size of the boundary, add more cones so you can see the boundary better, use jump ropes in addition to cones, have a penalty for going out of bounds.] Good ideas.

E Decide on how to fix your problems and play again.

Identifying Problems and Solutions for Fairness Rules

Social Stop. Now discuss anything that has happened in your game that didn't feel fair or anything that *might* happen in a tag game that you would not consider fair. [Give the class time to discuss these issues within their groups.] Without giving names, share with the class some of the ideas you discussed about what doesn't seem fair. [People bumping into each other, guarding their flags with their hands, pushing the tagger's hands away, pulling their shirt down over their flags, rolling on the ground, holding their flag belt with their hands, people cheating.]

Interpreting "Cheating" Behaviors

Social Try to remember that if you don't make a rule about something and if you don't tell everyone in your group about the rule, then it isn't cheating. Set some rules and consequences for breaking the rules for flag guarding, body contact, and any other action you think isn't fair. Be sure everyone hears the discussion and knows the rules. Remember, not everyone plays games in a league after school. Maybe you take for granted that everyone knows a certain rule, but, in fact, your teammates and opponents might never have heard of the rule before.

E Decide on how to fix your problems and play again.

E We are now going to focus on tactics.

Identifying and Solving Tactical Problems

Cog K Start by discussing the tactics you are using to tag and avoid the taggers successfully. [Let them discuss in their group.] Let's share with the class. [Elicit information about two or three of the tactics listed below. Select one tactic you think children most need to learn. Have one group demonstrate or set up a demonstration on how to use the tactic and then discuss the tactic, providing explicit information about how it works (see **Figure 20.7**).]

- Using a blocker
- Blocking for teammates
- Helping trapped teammates
- Double-teaming

E Play again and practice the tactic (see **Figure 20.8**).

[Using the play–discuss–play cycle, repeat this process several times until the children have learned the tactics listed above.]

SAMPLE LEARNING EXPERIENCES 20.2

Level 3A: Designing Rules, Consequences, and Scoring and Using Tactics for Offensive Support and Defensive Double-Teaming (*continued*)

Figure 20.7 Discussing tactics

Figure 20.8 Playing the game again

Culminating Activity

Social As a class, we are going to make two lists on the whiteboard about rules and behaviors. The first list will be what makes games fair and fun, and the second will be what ruins games. Discuss these issues with your assigned partner, and then you can tell the class some of your partner's ideas. [Give the children time to talk with their partners.] Now let's put our ideas together. When I call on you, tell me one thing your partner said about what makes games fair and fun. [Call on children until there are no new ideas.] What ruins games? [Continue calling on children you have not called on before.]

SAMPLE LEARNING EXPERIENCES 20.3

Level 3A: Designing Tag Games with Bases as Safety Zones and Using Offensive and Defensive Tactics for Bases

Objectives

Children will learn

Motor and Cognitive Knowledge

Game Structures

1. Locating a base near a boundary limits its use by the offense; locating a base in the middle makes it harder for the defense to guard the base.
2. Rules need to be made to limit how long a runner can stay on a base, when the runner can return to a base, and how many runners can be on a base.
3. In some games, a zone needs to be added around bases or goals to keep offense or defense from getting too close and having too much of an advantage.

(continues)

SAMPLE LEARNING EXPERIENCES 20.3

Level 3A: Designing Tag Games with Bases as Safety Zones and Using Offensive and Defensive Tactics for Bases (*continued*)

Tactics

(In addition to any previous objectives children need to review)

4. Bases or safety zones add options for the offense to outmaneuver the defense and add responsibilities for the defense to defend the base and chase the runners.
5. It is best to score, but if you are about to be tagged, going to a base (a safety zone) is the next best option.

Thinking Skills

6. To identify and solve problems with bases in tag games.

Affective

7. To appreciate the excitement of playing a game between equal opponents. [Be sure to group children by ability during the children's games.]

Content Development

Forecasting Game Structure Problems

Th Today we will be designing tag games with bases. Forecast how your tag games will change if you add a base on which runners can be safe. Predict if there will be any problems. [If children do not predict problems, have them add a base and try the game. Often children will forecast that too many players will get on the base at once, stay on the base too long, or simply hover near the base.]

Solving Problems to Get the Game Working Well

Th Design a tag game with a base or bases, and devise rules you think might solve anticipated problems. What are some rules you always must include? [Rules for safety, no body contact, boundaries, flag guarding, how to score, and if you want to keep track of the score.] Right. Decide on the number of flags each of you will wear.

I Once you have designed your rules and consequences for breaking rules, try out your game.

Th Use your problem-solving skills to identify any problems you had with bases. [Some people stayed on the base the whole time, most of their team stayed on the base, people would jump off and then immediately back on, the defense surrounded the base so runners could never get off.] What can you do to solve these problems? [Make a rule that runners can be on the base for only three seconds; make a rule that you can go on the base only once during each round; make a rule that only one person can be on the base at one time; if someone gets on the base, you must get off; the defense must stay one arm's length away from the base.]

E Discuss in your group what rules you want to add about bases, and then play your game.

Cog K Stop. I noticed some groups have their base in the middle and some in a corner or near the endline. What difference does it make where you locate your base? [Putting the base in the corner gives the advantage to the chasers.] Why? [Because it denies the runners space to get away once they get on base, allowing the defense can trap them.] What if you put the base in other locations? [Putting the base in the middle is harder on the defense. Putting the base on the sideline is harder on the offense but not as hard as putting the base in the corner.]

R Discuss with your group what you might do to improve your game by adding another base or changing the location of your base. You might also want to revise your rules for different bases. Then play.

Th Stop. Use your problem-solving skills to identify problems you are having with your games. [Once you lose your flag, there isn't much you can do to help your team. The game is over quickly because we can steal the flags quickly.] Those are problems. What suggestions do you have to solve the problems? [Once you lose your flag, block for your teammates. Put captured flags on the base and allow the other team to recapture them. Put captured flags over the endline so the other team can take them back.] In your groups, discuss these suggestions and come up with your own to solve the problems with your games.

E Play your game again.

Affective You have designed and are playing great games, with both teams having equal chances on offense and defense. How do you feel when you play a game with opponents who are equal to you? [Various positive answers.]

Identifying Successful Tactics

Cog K Stop. Now, in your group, share with each other the tactics you are using that are successful. [After one to two minutes, share ideas with the class. Try to elicit the following:]

- On offense, if you are about to be tagged and can't tag someone on the other team, going to a base (safety zone) is the next best option.

SAMPLE LEARNING EXPERIENCES 20.3

Level 3A: Designing Tag Games with Bases as Safety Zones and Using Offensive and Defensive Tactics for Bases (*continued*)

- On defense, you must both guard the base and try to tag runners.
- You can assign some children to guard the base and some to chase in general space.
- Players with two flags can try to entice the defense away from the base.
- Block for your teammates if you don't have a flag.

R Great suggestions. Discuss with your teammates which tactics you need to practice the most, and work on them. Play your game again and see if you can improve your tactics. [Using the play–discuss–play cycle, repeat this and the previous task several times until the children have learned the tactics.]

Extending the Content in Future Lessons

Cog K Stop. Let's summarize what you have learned about tactics and bases. [Select one or two of the following questions that best capture what you think the children learned during the lesson.]

Potential Questions to Ask

- What would make it harder to get on base? What would make it easier to get on base?
- What would be different if the base were in a different location? What were your team tactics?
- What did you do on defense to deny space to the offense? What did you do to cover space the offense wanted?
- What did you do on offense to create space? How did you get the defenders to move out of position?
- What do you think about when you are off the base and the tagger is starting to come after you?
- As a tagger, how do you decide which runner to chase?
- What are all the jobs you have to do on defense?
- What might be jobs you could do on offense that would help your team?

R Play your game again, and work on improving those tactics. [Using the play–discuss–play cycle, repeat the task above several times by asking different questions and working on different tactics.]

Culminating Activity Options

Option 1

A I am going to assign you a new group. Design a new game or use one of the games your group members played in the first part of the lesson [or last lesson]. Then, play the game while working on one of the tactics you think will help you improve your gameplay. Be sure to share with your new teammates what really worked in your last group.

Option 2 to Meet CCSS

A Teach your game to the class. Plan how to present your game so all group members have a role in the presentation. Speak clearly and audibly. Then we will try different groups' games.

SAMPLE LEARNING EXPERIENCES 20.4

Level 3A: Designing Goal-Oriented Tag Games with Scoring Goals Using Tactics for Defending Goals and Scoring

Notes: In these learning experiences, children design goal-oriented tag games. Having a goal is a major adjustment for the children, and the resulting tag games will more closely resemble invasion sports and their tactics.

Objectives

Children will learn

Motor and Cognitive Knowledge

Game Structures

1. In goal-oriented invasion tag games, you score by crossing a goal line in your opponent's end of the field without losing your flags or by stealing equipment or flags located in your opponents' goal area.

(*continues*)

SAMPLE LEARNING EXPERIENCES 20.4

Level 3A: Designing Goal-Oriented Tag Games with Scoring Goals Using Tactics for Defending Goals and Scoring (*continued*)

Tactics

2. The importance of planning team tactics and how to plan a particular tactic related to a particular defense or offense.

Offense

3. To beat a 1 on 1 defense, use picks and blockers.
4. Two offensive players crossing pathways can counteract a 1 on 1 defense by confusing the defenders and forcing them to shift their positions around one another or to change the players they are defending.
5. Decoys and sacrifices can enable some runners to score.

Defense

6. Use boundaries to deny space, double-team to trap the offense, and use person-to-person (1 on 1) defense.
7. With 1 on1 defense, you select the player whom you will guard ahead of time based on matching abilities.
8. If you get beat, run back and help out a teammate.
9. If a teammate gets beat and his or her opponent is about to score, go off your opponent and try to stop the person about to score.

Thinking Skills

10. To identify and solve problems in designing goal-oriented games.
11. To think critically about tactics and devise ways to improve them.

Social

12. Good sportsmanship means congratulating opponents on a good play and a good game.

Content Development

Forecasting as Part of Problem Solving

Th In the next few lessons, we will be designing goal-oriented tag games in which the runners have to cross from one endline or their side of the court to the other endline without getting tagged. Forecast how your tag games will change now that you have a goal. [We won't have as many places to run; the other team will know we need to run to the goal; on defense, we will know when the other team is in a dangerous area for scoring and when they are in an area in which they probably won't score.] Predict if there will be problems you have not encountered before with rules and boundaries.

Designing a Goal-Oriented Tag Game

I Using saucer cones for boundaries, design a goal-oriented game in which you must score using endlines. Discuss your options for ways to score and select the one you like best. I put out cones in case you want to score by stealing the cone and running it back across the centerline.

Identifying and Solving Problems to Get the Game Working Well

Th Stop and identify any problems in your games. What changes in the boundaries, rules, and consequences can you make to improve your game? Are you happy with your scoring system? Are your goal areas too big or too small? Do you need to have more than one goal? Decide whether you want to keep track of the score. Revise your game if needed.

E Play again. [You might need to repeat this problem-solving task several times, using the play–discuss–play cycle until the games are working well.]

Identifying and Solving Tactical Problems

Notes: These learning experiences might take several lessons.

Th Stop. Now that your games are working well, let's work on tactics. Get together with your teammates and plan your team tactics. Think critically about and discuss what has worked well and what hasn't. Think about your opponents' speed. Do they do the same thing every time? Then decide what you will try to do in this round of tag.

E Play again.

Social Tell me some things you can do to show good sportsmanship. [Various answers. Select one idea presented by a child on which to focus.] Let's take the suggestion to congratulate your opponents on a good play and a good game, and work on that today.

SAMPLE LEARNING EXPERIENCES 20.4

Level 3A: Designing Goal-Oriented Tag Games with Scoring Goals Using Tactics for Defending Goals and Scoring (*continued*)

Cog K Stop. I am seeing some great offensive tactics. Share with your classmates which tactics your team has used successfully to score. [Elicit and discuss one or two of the offensive tactics listed in the objectives. If some children do not understand a tactic, demonstrate and explain how it works.]

R Play again and see if you can improve by using the tactics your classmates suggested. [Repeat this process several times, using the play–discuss–play cycle until the children learn all of the offensive tactics listed in the objectives.]

Potential Questions to Ask

- Which tactics did you use to avoid the tagger? Which tactics did you use to tag a runner?
- What were your team's offensive tactics?
- What did you do on offense to create space? How did you get the defenders to move out of position?

Cog K Stop. Now let's focus on defense. Share with your classmates which tactics worked on defense. [Elicit and discuss one or two of the defensive tactics listed in the objectives. If some children do not understand a tactic, demonstrate and explain how it works.]

R Play again and see if you can use the tactics your classmates suggested. [Repeat several times, using the play–discuss–play cycle as needed until children are successfully using the defensive tactics listed in the objectives or described in more detail in **Table 20.2**.]

Sample Questions to Ask

- What did you do on defense to deny space to the offense? What did you do to cover space the offense wanted?
- How do you play a 1 on 1 defense?

Culminating Activity

A I am going to switch your team to play against a team from another group. Use one of the games you already designed, or design a new game that has elements of both your games. Play your new game.

Cog K What did you learn from playing against a different team? How did you have to adjust your tactics to deal with different players?

Extending the Game Structures in Future Lessons

E If you want, you can add bases to your game. Do all players need to have access to the base? [Yes.] What modifications do you need to make for you classmate in a wheelchair? Decide how many bases you want and where to place them. What did you learn in previous lessons about how the placement of the base affects the defense and offense?

Potential Assessments for the Unit

ASSESSMENT 20.1

Tactical Gameplay

Tactic	Consistently	Most of the Time	Sometimes	Rarely
On offense, avoids being trapped by the boundaries				
On offense, uses the base only when necessary				
On defense, remains with assigned opponent unless another opponent is about to score				
On defense, when beat, immediately gets back to help teammates				

ASSESSMENT 20.2

Social Responsibility

Check the appropriate box about how you felt during group discussions.

	True	Sometimes True	Sometimes False	False
I didn't think my group listened to my ideas.				
We cared about everyone's opinion.				
My group ignored me.				
People in my group interrupted me.				
People in my group interrupted others.				
Everyone listened to everyone else.				
We didn't listen to some people.				
One person never talked.				
We didn't listen carefully.				
We encouraged each other to share ideas.				

Teaching Invasion Games for Passing and Receiving with the Hands, Feet, or Hockey Stick

The tag learning experiences provide an excellent introduction to invasion games with passing and receiving balls. Through the tag learning experiences, children come to understand game structures, basic tactics, and how to design and modify games. They also become familiar with lesson routines, such as the play-discuss-play cycle and problem-solving tasks. Finally, they begin to develop collaborative social and group interaction skills. You now build on these skills and knowledge and add the complexity of ball-handling skills.

We start by describing in **Table 20.3** the basic tactics of invasion games with passing and receiving balls. We organize these tactics into three progressive levels: 3B, 3C, and 3D. We based this progression on research examining the development of children's passing and receiving skills in games. When teaching level 3 tactics, you will also need to review the tactics from level 2.

We have described the tactics in language you can use with children. Often children "discover" tactics in the level 2 game-like situations and level 3 modified gameplay that you set as tasks. Even so, it helps if you also reinforce what they learn with clear verbal descriptions (Rink, 2014). The verbal descriptions are particularly helpful for low-skilled children who have little experience playing youth sports after school.

Table 20.3 describes far more tactical content than you can teach in a typical school with physical education two days a week. There are, however, some schools with physical education five days a week, and you will have some children with youth sport experiences who are ready and able to learn more advanced tactics. Notice that we recommend a focus on offensive tactics, leaving many defensive tactics for Level 3D. You might find, however, that in your situation, you need to teach more defensive tactics.

Table 20.3 is followed by sample learning experiences for Levels 3B, 3C, and 3D. Then, we provide reference information for teachers about the development of game tactics, describing movement patterns from least to most mature and performance techniques to teach. You are likely to observe these movement patterns when children begin gameplay.

The chapter ends with annotated plans to help you visualize what it might look like to teach gameplay and design level 3 lesson and unit content. We also show you ways you can integrate the teaching of thinking skills, social responsibility, and the CCSS.

Overview of the Progression

Below is an outline of the progression described across **Sample Learning Experiences 20.5 to 20.20.**

1. Level 3B: 3v1, then 3v2; one endline
   - Pass to teammate over the endline to score
   - Start midfield or midcourt with each new possession
   - Cut toward the passer; no long bombs (see **Figure 20.2**).
2. Level 3B: 1v1, when to run or shoot
   - Toss beanbag into hula hoop to score
   - Shooting allowed only when one foot touches a poly spot
3. Level 3B: 3v2, "hit the pin" in the center circle
   - When to pass or shoot
   - Pass quickly to shift the defense
4. Level 3B: 3v2, 3v3, hit the pin in the center circle
   - When to pass, run/dribble, or shoot
   - Pass quickly to shift the defense
5. Level 3C: 3v2, then 3v3, passing and receiving with two endline scoring goals
   - Score by passing to a teammate over the endline or cutting into one or two hula hoops
   - Multiple receivers getting open
   - Not getting bunched in front of the goal
6. Level 3D: Shifting to defense
   - Getting back quickly to be between offense and the goal

Table 20.3 Tactics for Levels 3B, 3C, and 3D Goal-Oriented Passing and Receiving Games

Level 3B	Level 3C	Level 3D
Tactics for Games with One Endline Scoring Goal On offense, as a team, move the ball closer to the scoring goal: • In games with scoring goals on the endline, the offense cuts and passes to move the ball down the court/field, closer to the scoring goal. Adapt the following level 2 offense tactics from keep-away to goal-oriented games: • Rely on short lead passes. • Cut into passing lanes. • When on defense, deny space to the offense. • Deny space by using a wide base of support with your hands in a ready position. Deny space by moving to block passing lanes. *Tactics for When to Pass, Dribble/Run, or Shoot in Games with a Single, Center Scoring Goal* When to run/dribble, pass, or shoot: • Shoot when you have an open shot on goal; if not, pass to a teammate who does. • Pass to an open teammate close to the goal rather than running with or dribbling the ball. • Dribble or run when no one is open closer to the goal. • Receive and pass quickly: Time is an enemy of the offense and a friend of the defense. • Receive and then pass quickly to deny time for the defenders to reposition themselves. Passing makes the defense shift (around the pin in "hit the pin" or around the goal in a game with a central goal). If the defense does not shift quickly, your team has created space for an open shot. • Straight, direct passes are quicker than high, loopy passes. The defender stays on the goal side of the assigned offense player: • Stay between the offensive player and the goal; you are responsible for marking/guarding and the goal. • Stay close to your opponent.	*Tactics for Passing and Receiving Games with Scoring Goals at Each End* When off the ball, support the passer: • Support the passer, with all receivers trying to get free. • Cut multiple times until you get free. • Cut away from the goal toward the passer if the passer is trapped and can't pass closer to the goal. This is called *offensive depth* (Wilson, 2002). Pass and then cut quickly: • Time is an enemy of the offense and a friend of the defense. • After you pass, don't stand, watch, and not think about what support the passer needs. Cut into a passing lane. • "Give and go"/wall pass: Pass the ball to a receiver and then run fast by your defender; your teammate can send a lead pass right back to you. A "give and go," called a "wall pass" in soccer, is a good way to beat your defender. • When off the ball, spread out to create space (width). Reset the offense when you are ineffectively bunched in front of the goal. • If offensive players get too close together, one defender can easily guard/mark two offensive players. When the offense spreads apart using the width of the field/court, the defenders must spread apart to guard/mark them. This gives the offense more space in which to cut. • When you get bunched near the goal and don't score, reset the offense by spreading out and trying again. • Avoid running into spaces occupied by offensive teammates because you will bring your defender with you. Defenders play person-to-person defense: • Person-to-person (or one-on-one) defense means you guard one person *even if that person does not have the ball.* Don't chase the ball.	*More Advanced Defensive Tactics for Passing and Receiving Games* Switch quickly from offense to defense: • When your team loses possession, switch quickly to defense and run to be goal side of your opponent as fast as possible. Commit to intercepting only when you are sure you will succeed: • On defense, try to intercept the ball if you are *sure* you will succeed. Otherwise, stay on the goal side of the receiver and try to steal the ball. Block the dribbler's pathway to the goal. Be close enough to slow the dribbler down but not so close that he or she can easily dodge you. Try to steal the ball when your opponent doesn't protect the ball well or makes a mistake. Defensive support: Back up a teammate and shift when scoring is eminent: • Guard/mark your offensive player. If another offensive player beats his or her defender and is about to score, however, you need to shift to that player and prevent the score. (We don't teach this tactic until children are skilled at staying with the person they are assigned to defend. Otherwise, they just run around chasing the ball because they think their teammate is always in trouble.) Play closer to your assigned offense player when he or she is closer to the ball or goal: • The closer the opponent is to the ball and goal, the closer you must be to your opponent. The farther the opponent is from the ball and goal, the farther you can be from your opponent. The reason you position yourself farther away from your opponent is to be closer to the goal so you can shift over to back up another defender when necessary and to crowd the space in front of the goal, thereby denying the offense space.

Sample Learning Experiences for Levels 3B, 3C, and 3D

SAMPLE LEARNING EXPERIENCES 20.5

Level 3B: Passing and Receiving with One Endline Scoring Goal—3v1 and 3v2

Notes: **Table 20.3** lists a suggested progression of tactical content for level 3B that you can use for lesson and unit objectives. Here, we outline how to teach these tactics and suggest modified games that provide an environment designed to facilitate practice of the tactics. Based on this outline, you can design units that will require four to six lessons to teach.

In these learning experiences, we focus on offense and stack the offense (i.e., have more offensive players) because children's offensive tactical game skills are not as developed as their defensive abilities. Recall that 3v1 situations are more difficult than you might imagine. Passers often can't see which of the two receivers is actually open, and many times both receivers move behind the defender.

Passing and Receiving Games with One Endline as a Scoring Goal

1. Modified 3v1 Game

I Today we will be playing 3v1, that is, three offensive players versus one defender. We will be passing and receiving using the hands. You cannot run with the ball or dribble. Your team scores by passing to a teammate over the endline. The defender cannot steal the ball from or mark/guard the passer; the defender can only intercept passes. The game will start with an inbound pass at midcourt/midfield.

Forecasting Tactical Problems to Solve

Th

- How is this game different from the 3v1 keep-away that we played in previous lessons? [We have to move down the field/court. We must travel as a team, using passing to get close to the goal to score.]
- How can you do that? [We have to keep repositioning ourselves closer to the goal. We have to look for a receiver closer to the goal.]
- Which tactics do you think will be the same as in 3v1 keep-away? [Cut to get open; cut into a passing lane; send passes that my teammate can catch/receive easily; don't make passes too hard; if I don't get the pass, cut again; keep trying to get open.]
- What do you think will work better: many short passes or one long pass to the endline? [Short passes.]

Designing the Game

E Before you play, design the following:

Boundaries: Try to determine perfect boundaries, and set the boundaries using saucer cones. [Be alert for groups that set the endline too far from the starting line and get frustrated because they can't score. In that case, you will need to intervene to ask the children questions about their boundaries and discuss what happens when boundaries are too large. If you must teach inside, you will have to set up a grid of boundaries, giving teams as much room as your space allows.]

Rules: You must have a rule that there is no running with the ball or dribbling. You need to determine a change of possession rule. As always, you must set a no-contact rule.

Consequences: You determine consequences for breaking the rules.

E Play the game.

Getting the Game Working Well

Th I see some problems with your change of possession rules. Use your problem-solving skills and select a rule that will work best for your group. You also need to determine if you want a scoring system and if you want to keep track of the score. Here are some options:

- Have the defender give the ball back if he or she successfully intercepts a pass. Each group gets one to three opportunities to score, and then switch defenders.
- If the defense touches the ball or the ball touches the ground, the offensive team must start over at the endline. Decide how many chances the offense has to score before rotating defenders.
- If the defense touches the ball or the ball touches the ground, the defender joins the offense, a new defender rotates in, and the game begins back at the endline.
- Use a scoring system that provides ways for the defense to score. Rotate defenders after three total scores by the offense and defense.

E Play the game testing your change of possession rule and scoring system, if you have one. [Use the play–discuss–play cycle to modify the games until the games are working well. Then discuss how to solve tactical problems, and critique and improve the children's tactical decisions.]

SAMPLE LEARNING EXPERIENCES 20.5

Level 3B: Passing and Receiving with One Endline Scoring Goal—3v1 and 3v2 (*continued*)

Thinking Critically to Identify Tactical Problems and then Solve Those Problems

R Now that your game is working well, let's work on improving your tactics. Think critically about your tactics.

Sample Questions to Ask

[Select one question to ask, and then have children play again. Then ask another question in the next discussion phase.]

- What were your best passes? Why did they work? [Short passes, because they are easier to receive and you are less likely to drop the ball or lose control of the ball with your feet or stick. We got closer to the goal and scored. We did a bunch of passes in a row without anyone missing.]
- How did your team maintain possession of the ball? [By sending catchable passes, by passing it quickly before the defense got to me, by passing only to open teammates.]
- Did everyone participate equally, or did some teammates dominate the game?

R Decide what you need to do to improve, and play again.

2. Modified 3v2 Game

I Today we will play 3v2. You score by passing to a teammate over the endline. Defenders cannot steal the ball from or mark/guard the passer; defenders can only intercept passes. The game will start with an inbound pass at midcourt/midfield.

Forecasting Tactical Problems to Solve

Th

- How will adding a second defender change the game? [It will make it harder to score, we will need to cut more times and keep trying to get free, we will need to pass quickly before the defenders can shift to cover both receivers.]
- Which tactics do you think will be the same as in 3v1? [Cut to get open; cut into a passing lane; send passes that my teammate can catch/receive easily; don't make passes too hard; if I don't get the pass, cut again; keep trying to get open; don't send long bombs; cut toward the passer.]

Designing the Game, Getting the Game Working Well

E Before you play, your group needs to design the following:

Boundaries: Try to determine perfect boundaries, and set the boundaries using saucer cones.

Rules: You must have a rule that there is no running with the ball or dribbling. You need to determine a change of possession rule. As always, you must also set a no-contact rule.

Consequences: You determine consequences for breaking the rules.

Scoring: Decide whether you want a scoring system and if you want to keep track of points. Some options for scoring for the defense are

- Scoring a point for touching the ball
- Scoring more points for intercepting a pass
- Scoring even more points for successfully passing to the other defender.

Level of Defense: You need to determine the appropriate level of defense so that the offense is successful most of the time. If receivers get frustrated because they can never get free, have the receiver make this decision.

E Play the game, testing your boundaries, rules, and scoring system, if you have one. [Use the play–discuss–play cycle to modify the games until the games are working well. Then discuss how to solve tactical problems, and critique and improve the children's tactical decisions.]

Thinking Critically to Identify Tactical Problems and then Solve Those Problems

R Now that your game is working well, let's work on improving your tactics. Think critically about your tactics.

Potential Questions to Ask

[Select one or two questions to ask, and then have children play again. Then ask one or two other questions in the next discussion phase.]

- How did you keep the defense from getting the ball? [By passing it quickly before they got to me, by passing only to open teammates.]
- Why was an offensive player open? [He or she dodged and cut into an open space.]
- Why was the defense caught out of position? [After the pass, the defender didn't shift to the new receivers.]
- Did everyone participate equally, or did some teammates dominate the game?

SAMPLE LEARNING EXPERIENCES 20.6

Level 3B: Tactics for When to Run or Shoot—1v1

Motor and Cognitive Objectives

Children will learn

1. On defense, to deny space by using a wide base of support with your hands in a ready position.
2. On defense, to block the shot by moving their hands and body to be between the shooter's hands and the hula hoop goal.
3. On offense, to shift quickly to the left and right, moving their hands to different levels and running and changing direction quickly between poly spots to get an open shot at the hula hoop goal.

Introduction: Selecting the Game

I I am going to demonstrate three games. Then you and your partner decide which game you want to practice. Select the game that best challenges you but also allows success.

A. 1v1 Tossing a Beanbag into a Hula Hoop on the Ground

- One hula hoop on the ground is the scoring goal.
- The offensive player must have one foot on a poly spot set one and a half yards away from the hoop and tries to toss the beanbag in the hoop to score.
- The defender is positioned between the offensive player and the hoop goal and tries to block the toss.

B. 1v1 Offense Can Run with the Beanbag, Two Poly Spots from Which to Shoot

- One hula hoop goal on the ground is the scoring goal.
- The defender is positioned between the offensive player and the hoop goal and tries to block the toss.
- Set up two poly spots about two yards apart and one and a half yards away from the hoop.
- The offensive player must have one foot on a poly spot to shoot.
- The offensive player can run with the beanbag from one spot to the other and tosses the beanbag into the hoop to score.

C. 1v1 Offense Can Run with the Beanbag, Two Hoop Goals

- Place two hula hoop goals about two yards apart on the ground for scoring. The defender tries to position him- or herself between the offensive player and the most likely hoop goal.
- Set up two poly spots about two yards apart and one and a half yards away from the hoops.
- The offensive player must have one foot on a poly spot to shoot.
- The offensive player can run with the beanbag from one spot to the other and shoot at either hoop.

Content Development

Potential Questions to Identify Tactics

Th Before you play, let's forecast possible tactical problems.

- What will the defender have to do? [Stay between the offense and the goal, watch the offense and move when the offense moves, anticipate where the offense is going to move and try to block the shot.]
- What should be the shape of the defender? [Wide to block the most space, in a wide ready position to be able to move quickly.]
- When should you shoot in game A? [When I can toss the beanbag by the defender; when the defender's arms are up, I can toss low; when the defender's arms are low, I can toss higher; when I can reach to the side and toss before the defender moves to block the shot.]
- When should you shoot in games B and C? [When I have an open shot and the defender is not blocking me.]
- How can you get an open shot? [By running from spot to spot to get the defense out of position, changing directions in the middle, fake tossing to the hoop and running to the other spot.]

Designing Game Rules and Getting the Game Working Well

I Select your game, set up your equipment, and play. Figure out a fair way to change from offense to defense so you both get equal chances to try to score. Decide if you want to keep track of the score.

Mot Stop. Are you both challenged and successful? If not, how can you modify your game? You don't need to play the same game when you are on offense, and you don't have to have the same distance between the poly spots and goal for both of you; one can have the goal closer and the other farther away. [One person can be offense using game B and the other can use game C. Move the poly spots farther apart to make it more difficult or closer together to make it easier. Move the hula hoop farther away to make it more difficult or closer to make it easier.]

E Modify your game to make it a perfect challenge for both of you, and play again.

Improving Tactics

Th Stop. Talk with your partner. Discuss what tactics you used when you were successful.

SAMPLE LEARNING EXPERIENCES 20.6

Level 3B: Tactics for When to Run or Shoot—1v1 (*continued*)

E I will assign you a new partner. Select your game. Play. Then modify your game until both of you are challenged and successful.

Th Discuss with your new partner what tactics you used when you were successful. Then we will share successful tactics with the whole class.

SAMPLE LEARNING EXPERIENCES 20.7

Level 3B: Tactics for When to Pass, Dribble/Run, or Shoot in Games with a Single, Center Scoring Goal—3v2 and 3v3

Notes: In level 3B, we also teach children how to make decisions as to whether they should pass, shoot, or dribble/run with the ball. Before this content is introduced, children need to have mastered level 2 content for combining dribbling and shooting and dribbling and passing. **Table 20.3** describes the tactics on which to base lesson objectives for when to pass, dribble/run, or shoot.

These learning experiences are designed for passing with the hand but can easily be modified for passing and receiving with the feet or hockey stick. Have one central cone or pin for hand-passing games and two central cone goals for passing and receiving with the feet or hockey stick from which the children can score from either side.

With hit-the-pin games, the children will learn through the play–discuss–play cycle that they need to set a "no-play" boundary around the pin in which neither the offense nor defense can go. They also will learn to set a no-play boundary when using two cones as one central goal in soccer- or hockey-type games. Without this rule, the defense will soon figure out they can huddle around the central goal, making it impossible for the offense to score. This behavior can lead to dangerous throws or kicks by the offense to intimidate the defense.

Motor and Cognitive Objectives

[Notice how the objectives come directly from **Table 20.3**.]

Children will learn to

- Shoot when they have an open shot on goal; if not, to pass to a teammate who does.
- Pass to an open teammate close to the goal rather than running with or dribbling the ball.
- Dribble or run when no one is open closer to the goal.
- Receive and then pass quickly to deny time for the defenders to reposition themselves.
- Use straight, direct passes that are quicker than high, loopy passes.
- On defense, to stay goal side of the offensive player.

Content Development: 3v2 Hit-the-Pin Passing with Hands

I Today we are going to work on tactics for when to pass and when to shoot. We will play with

- Three offensive players versus two defenders.
- Passing with hands only.
- One center goal (a cone or plastic bowling pin on a crate), which you hit with a foam ball to score.
- The first pass cannot be a shot on goal.
- The defense can intercept and block shots.

Set up and play your game.

Identifying and Solving Problems with Game Rules: Getting the Game Working Well

Th Stop. Use your problem-solving skills to identify problems with your game rules. [The defense bunches up around the pin, and we can't hit the pin without hitting their legs.] How can you solve that problem? [We can set a boundary around the goal that no one can cross—a no-play zone.]

E Design a no-play zone boundary, a no-contact rule, consequences for breaking rules, a scoring system if you want, and a change of possession rule for rotating who plays defense. Decide what level of defense you need to make your games balanced between offense and defense. Play again. Use the play-discuss-play cycle until your game is working well.

Identifying and Solving Tactical Problems

Cog K Stop. Let's work on tactics:

- Where do you think the defenders should position themselves? [Between the offensive players and the goal.]
- When should you shoot, and when should you pass? [Shoot when you have an open shot on goal. If you don't, pass to a teammate who does.]

(*continues*)

SAMPLE LEARNING EXPERIENCES 20.7

Level 3B: Tactics for When to Pass, Dribble/Run, or Shoot in Games with a Single, Center Scoring Goal—3v2 and 3v3 (*continued*)

E Play and work on tactics.

Cog K Stop. Tell me how to solve the following tactical problem:

- How can you get the defense out of position? [Receive and pass quickly to deny time for the defenders to reposition themselves (time is an enemy of the offense and a friend of the defense). Pass the ball quickly around the pin to make the defense shift. If they do not shift quickly, the offense has created space for an open shot or a receiver to cut to the goal.]

Extending the Content in Future Lessons

3v3 Hit-the-Pin

Once the children have a basic understanding of how to play hit-the-pin, you can progress to three options for 3v3 hit-the-pin games:

1. Passing with the hands, can run with the ball
2. Passing with the hands, can dribble the ball (no running with the ball)
3. Passing and dribbling with the feet or hockey stick; shooting from either side of the goal

The tactical problems to solve remain the same, with the addition of two issues: when to run and when to pass or shoot. The increase to three defenders counterbalances the option to run or dribble the ball. Practicing tactical decisions with one central goal (rather than two endline goals) allows children to focus on the tactics of when to pass, dribble/run, or shoot without having to also contend with tactics of traveling down the field/court to score and to shift quickly from offense to defense.

Designing the Game, Getting the Game Working Well, Improving Tactics

Use the play–discuss–play cycle to first design and modify the game. Once the games are working well, discuss how to solve tactical problems, and critique and improve the children's tactical decisions.

Potential Questions to Identify and Solve Tactical Problems

- When should you pass, and when should you run with the ball? [Pass to an open teammate close to the goal rather than running with the ball. Run when no one is open closer to the goal.]
- When should you shoot? [Only when you have a clear shot.]
- If you don't have a clear shot, what should you do? [Look for a teammate who does.]
- Which travels faster, a pass or you running with the ball? [Pass.] Can you dribble to the goal faster than you can pass to a teammate who is closer to the goal? [No.]
- When should you run (or dribble)? [When no one is open, when everyone is standing still.]
- Why is time an enemy of the offense and a friend of the defense? [If you give the defenders time, they can get into a good position to prevent you from scoring or making easy passes.]
- How can the defense force the offense to take more time? [Stay with the person you are guarding/marking. Stay between that person and the goal.]
- On offense, how can you create space to shoot? [Receive and then pass quickly to deny time for the defenders to reposition themselves. Make several quick passes to get the defense out of position. Pass the ball around the pin quickly so the defense can't get in position to prevent a clear shot.]
- Which travels faster: a straight, direct pass or a high, loopy pass? [Straight, direct pass.]
- After you pass, what should you do? [Quickly cut or reposition yourself to support the new passer.]
- Which body shape is best for guarding? [Wide.] Why? [Takes up more space.]

SAMPLE LEARNING EXPERIENCES 20.8

Level 3C: Goal-Oriented Passing and Receiving Games with Endline Scoring Goals for Each Team

Notes: Level 3C has a considerable amount of content that takes time for children to learn. It is important that you don't try to include too much content in one lesson and that you base lesson objectives on problems children are having in their games. Children find tactics easier to understand after recognizing problems or having successes in their game (see **Figure 20.9**). You can anticipate teaching several units on this content. It helps when children repeatedly learn about the tactics across different types of invasion games using different skills.

SAMPLE LEARNING EXPERIENCES 20.8

Level 3C: Goal-Oriented Passing and Receiving Games with Endline Scoring Goals for Each Team (*continued*)

Figure 20.9 Mature cutting and passing with two hula hoops as scoring goals
Courtesy of John Dolly

Progression for Increasing the Complexity of Games Across the Unit

Three game structures change as you progress to more complex games and games requiring more mature passing and receiving skills.

1. *Increase in number of defenders from two to three:* When there are three offensive players, having two defenders allows one offensive player to be free. Three defenders are much more difficult because all offensive players are guarded and must get free by dodging and feinting.
2. *Change of possession from endline to on the spot:* Starting from one endline with each change of possession allows the children time to adjust to the switch from offense to defense and to set up in a similar situation each time. Progressing to change of possession on the spot with no stopping of play makes the game more complex.
3. *Change of possession to drop balls as free balls:* Starting with dropped balls becoming free balls is more complex than dropped balls remaining in the possession of the offense or automatically being given to the defense because which team recovers the ball is unpredictable and children must learn to react quickly.

Research shows that not setting the appropriate change of possession rule for each group's abilities can be a primary reason why games fall apart, thereby preventing achievement of learning outcomes (Rovegno et al., 2001). We suggest you initially set the following rule for all groups, and then apply it only to those groups who need this option: if the ball is dropped, intercepted, or successfully stolen, play stops and the other team gains possession at their endline. The threat of losing possession will contribute to children working hard to send short passes only to open teammates, which is one of your major objectives. As children improve gameplay and to maintain game flow, you can give children the option that if the ball touches the ground but the offensive player was unguarded and he or she can catch the ball before it bounces twice, the game can continue.

Progression of Games

1. In passing and receiving games with the hands, no dribbling or running with the ball; in passing and receiving games with the feet or hockey stick, dribbling is allowed.
2. In passing and receiving games with the hands, allow dribbling (such as in basketball-type games) or running with the ball (such as in football-type games).
3. Design games in which children select which combination of skills to use in their game (such as games with passing with the hands and feet, or games with passing and dribbling with the hands and feet).

Level of Defense

Children need to use a level of defensive intensity based on the capabilities of the child they are marking/guarding to make their games balanced between offense and defense. Arguing or children getting frustrated because they never get the ball or can never pass successfully signals that their decision about level of defense is not working.

We find it helpful to set a level 1 defense (hands still, feet still) on the passer making the first pass to start play at the endline. The first pass can be difficult because the defenders have ample time to get in good defensive positions.

Scoring Zone

When you teach 3v3 soccer- and hockey-type games, sometimes a child will drop back and stand in the goal. To help solve this problem, set up a scoring circle or square approximately 10 to 15 feet around the goal in which the offense must be to shoot. With this arrangement, there is no need for defenders to worry about the offense kicking the ball in the goal from a long distance away. In addition, you can make the goals small, have two or three goals, and/or tell the children that they can't play goalkeeper when their team has the ball.

(*continues*)

SAMPLE LEARNING EXPERIENCES 20.8

Level 3C: Goal-Oriented Passing and Receiving Games with Endline Scoring Goals for Each Team (*continued*)

Content Development Outline

1. Start by having children design the rules, consequences for breaking rules, and the scoring system and decide whether to keep track of the score. Then have them play their game and figure out what level of defensive intensity they need to employ.
2. Once the game is working well, work on tactics.

Potential Questions to Identify Tactics Needed for the Game

Cog K Now that your game is working well, identify the tactics you need to play this game well.

- What do you need to do when you are off the ball on offense to help your team keep possession of the ball? [Support the passer, with both receivers trying to get open. Cut again if you don't get the pass; keep trying to get open. Cut on an angle toward the passer so the passer can make a short pass.]
- What do you need to do when you are on the ball on offense? [Look for receivers closer to the goal. Pass quickly, and then immediately cut for another pass. Don't stand around and watch.]
- What do you need to do on defense? [Guard/mark my assigned player. Stay on the goal side of her or him.]

Potential Questions to Identify and Solve the Tactical Problem of a Lack of Open Receivers

Notes: After children begin work on level 3B gameplay, we find it helpful to teach them a "give and go"/wall pass. Play the game first. Ask children questions to help them recognize the problem of passers standing still after they pass. This discussion will help the children understand the context for, and value of, a "give and go." Then, you can stop the game and teach a "give and go" as a level 2 practice task. Finally, have the children play the game again and try to apply the "give and go" in game situations (see **Sample Plan 20.2** and **Figure 20.10**).

R I noticed the passer was having problems finding open receivers. Why do you think this is happening? [We are standing still too often. Not all of us are cutting into open spaces. After we pass, we watch the game and don't cut to receive another pass.]

Cog K I am going to teach you a "give and go" (see **Sample Plan 20.2**).

R Play again, and work to improve the number of receivers cutting by trying to include a "give and go."

Figure 20.10 Give and go

Courtesy of John Dolly

SAMPLE LEARNING EXPERIENCES 20.8

Level 3C: Goal-Oriented Passing and Receiving Games with Endline Scoring Goals for Each Team (*continued*)

Potential Questions to Identify and Solve the Tactical Problem of the Offense Bunching Up in Front of the Goal

R I noticed you are getting bunched up in front of the goal and can't score. Why can't you score? [The defenders are all there covering us. We are not free because the defenders are all there. The defenders have us trapped.]

Cog K What can you do to solve this problem? [Spread out, then try again to score. Have one person cut away from the ball so the trapped passer can pass the ball away from the trap. Don't run into a space where one of my teammates is already positioned.]

R Play again, and try to improve by not getting bunched up in front of the goal. If you do, spread out and try again.

Potential Questions to Ask During the Play–Discuss–Play Cycle

- What should you do after you pass the ball? [Support the new passer by getting open in a passing lane, reposition and cut into a passing lane, cut for a "give and go."]
- How can your team keep possession of the ball? [By passing quickly, by making short catchable/easy-to-receive passes, by getting open to receive a pass, by cutting into a passing lane.]
- How can you help or support the passer? [By having both teammates get free, by cutting back if the passer is trapped and can't pass toward the goal or shoot.]
- What is the most important thing to do when you tackle (in soccer- and hockey-type games)? [Do it safely! Don't kick your opponent. Only touch the ball. Keep your stick low.]
- Why is a 3v2 situation hard for defenders? What was your plan? [It is easy to get confused. You have to switch to a different receiver after the pass. The teacher had a rule not to guard/mark the passer, so we played one-on-one with the receivers.]
- When you were guarding well, what were some of the clues that let you know what the receiver was going to do? [I looked at the receiver's body position. I looked at what was the best open space to use and anticipated the receiver would see it, too. I looked at where the receiver was looking.]
- Will this game work if your teammates can't make accurate passes? [No.]

SAMPLE LEARNING EXPERIENCES 20.9

Level 3C: Games with an Endline Scoring Goal for Each Team Focusing on When to Pass, Dribble/Run, or Shoot

Notes: Once children are skilled at tactics for when to pass, dribble/run, or shoot with one central goal (**Sample Learning Experiences 20.7**), and once they are skilled at tactics for passing and receiving with two endline scoring goals (**Sample Learning Experiences 20.8**), you can combine these games. Playing with two endline scoring goals and having the option to dribble or run with the ball can elicit a regression in the children's use of appropriate passing tactics. For example, if they are playing a basketball-type game with two goals, children may revert to a pattern in which the player who gets the rebound dribbles down the court and shoots even if he or she is well guarded and has teammates who are free and in a better position to shoot. We regularly see adults demonstrating this behavior, too. It is difficult to overcome the culture of recreational and playground basketball where even skilled adults tend to ignore passing opportunities in favor of the chance to dribble and shoot.

Consequently, when we shift to two-goal games in which running/dribbling is allowed, we encourage children to design games using multiple skills. For example, children can design a game that includes dribbling with the feet, passing with the feet or hands, and shooting with the feet or hands, with a ball kicked in the goal being worth more than a score using the hands. Not only do children find games with multiple skills engaging, but such games also allow you to focus on particular tactical situations. The following are sample games.

Sample Games

1. 3v3with two endline goals; passing, receiving, and dribbling (with hands, feet, or hockey sticks)
2. 3v3 with two endline goals and flag-football flags; passing foam footballs with the hands; can run with the ball
3. 3v3 with two endline goals and flag-football flags; dribble with the feet; pass and shoot with the hands or feet; convert a ground ball to the hands using feet; no dribbling with hands; no running
4. 3v3, with children selecting any combination of skills

(*continues*)

SAMPLE LEARNING EXPERIENCES 20.9

Level 3C: Games with an Endline Scoring Goal for Each Team Focusing on When to Pass, Dribble/Run, or Shoot (*continued*)

Designing Game Structures

Scoring Goal Options: Ways to score goals are decided by the children alone or by the teacher and children together. Possible options include the following:

- Passing to a teammate over the endline
- Passing to a teammate cutting into one to three hula hoops on the endline
- Dribbling/running over the endline
- Dribbling the ball onto a saucer cone
- Shooting into basketball-type goals or portable soccer-type goals

Boundaries: Some games will require a scoring circle in which the offense must be before shooting. This rule, along with the use of a very small goal, eliminates the need for a goalkeeper. Other games might require a no-play zone.

Change of Possession: Change of possession needs to be matched to the children's capabilities of maintaining the flow of the game and shifting quickly from offense to defense. If they don't shift quickly to defense, the offense simply dribbles down and then scores. It is not a good game because the offense is now overpowering the defense. Make the change of possession easier by stopping play, starting over at the end line or a pass from the sideline, and have dropped balls remain in the possession of the offense. Progress to allowing play to continue immediately after an interception, from the spot the interception occurred, and allowing dropped balls to be free balls when children are able to do so successfully and maintain a good game. When playing football-type games, you can specify that a change of possession occurs after a certain number of downs (attempts to pass or run with the ball until an opponent pulls the flag of the ball carrier).

Lesson Outline

1. Start by having children design the rules, consequences for breaking rules, and a scoring system and decide whether to keep track of the score. Then have them play their game and figure out what level of defensive intensity they need to employ.
2. Once the game is working well, work on tactics.

Potential Questions to Start the Lesson and Identify Tactics

- When should you run (or dribble)? [When no one is open; when I am open, the scoring goal is open, and I will be able to dribble/run in and score.]
- When should you shoot? [Only when you have a clear shot.]
- If you don't have a clear shot, what should you do? [Look for a teammate who does.]
- Which travels faster—a pass or you running with the ball? [Pass.] Can you dribble to the goal faster than you can pass to a teammate who is closer to the goal? [No.]
- How can you use boundaries to help on defense? [Try to trap the offense in the corner or near the sidelines by running toward them and constraining space, cutting off their likely avenue of escape, and shifting if the offense shifts.]
- Repeat other questions from earlier units if necessary.

Additional Questions to Identify Problems with Tactics

- Why is time an enemy of the offense and a friend of the defense? [If you give the defenders time, they can get into a good position to prevent you from scoring or making easy passes.]
- On offense, how can you create space to shoot? [Receive and then pass quickly to deny time for the defense to reposition.]
- After you pass, what should you do? [Quickly cut or reposition.]
- What should you do if you get bunched up in front of the goal? [Reset the offense by spreading out, and have someone cut back away from the goal to get the passer out of the trap.]

SAMPLE LEARNING EXPERIENCES 20.10

Level 3D: More Advanced Defensive Tactics for Passing and Receiving Games

Notes: Because there is a considerable amount of difficult content in level 3C, most elementary programs will not progress to level 3D within the time available in physical education. Level 3D focuses on defensive tactics, which make offensive gameplay more difficult. If children's offensive skills and tactics develop to the point that they can manage more skilled defenders, then working on defensive play is appropriate. **Table 20.3** describes the level 3D defensive tactics that form the basis for lesson and unit objectives.

Motor and Cognitive Objectives

By the end of this unit, the children will have learned

1. When their team loses possession, to switch quickly from offense to defense and get back goal side of their opponent as quickly as possible.
2. On defense, to intercept the ball if they are sure they will succeed. Otherwise, stay on the goal side of the receiver.
3. In games with dribbling, if they can't intercept, to block the dribbler's angle to dribble in and shoot a goal and to time when they try to steal the ball by stealing it when their opponent doesn't protect the ball well or makes a mistake.

Content Development

Identifying More Advanced Defensive Tactics for Passing and Receiving Games

I Today we will be playing the same 3v3 game we played in the last lesson but this time we are focusing on defense. The game was passing and receiving with your feet, with dribbling allowed, and scoring by passing to a teammate over the endline. Today, change of possession occurs immediately on the spot where the ball was intercepted or tackled.

Potential Questions to Identify Tactical Problems to Solve

Cog K

- What impact do you think having a change of possession occurring immediately and on the spot will have on the defense? [We will have to get back fast. We will need to pay attention so we can start getting back immediately and guarding our opponent. This will make the game harder for the defense.]
- How can you anticipate when you need to switch from offense to defense? [Watch the pass; if the defense intercepts it, then switch immediately. Remind myself to think ahead and try to figure out what will happen next. Remind myself not to waste time after we lose the ball, but to get back on defense as quickly as I can.]

Designing Game Structures

I Before playing, decide whether to keep track of the score, and decide on the level of defense needed to make your games balanced between offense and defense.

Identifying Problems with Tactics for Getting Back on Defense

Th Use your problem-solving skills and discuss with your teammates what you were doing when you didn't switch to defense quickly. [I was feeling bad that we didn't score. All I was thinking about was playing offense. I forgot.]

R Play again and concentrate on improving how fast you can get back on defense.

[Repeat until the children are getting back into defensive positions reasonably quickly.]

Potential Questions to Identify Problems with Tactics for Intercepting

Cog K

- In hockey- and soccer-type games, when should you attempt to intercept a pass to your opponent, and why? [Only when you are sure you can get it. Because if you can't intercept, your opponent will be open to dribble in and shoot.]
- What should you do if you don't think you can successfully intercept? [Stay between your opponent and the goal. Block the dribbler's angle to dribble in and shoot. Try to steal the ball. Try to steal the ball when your opponent doesn't protect the ball well or makes a mistake.]

E Play again, and work on tactics for intercepting or remaining goal side of your opponent.

SKILLS BOX 20.1

Technical Reference Information for Teachers: Least to Most Mature Patterns for Passing and Receiving in Level 3 Modified Games

In this Skills Box, we provide reference information about the development of game tactics, describing tactical movement patterns from least to most mature. You are likely to observe immature movement patterns when children begin gameplay. Knowing what to expect and what to look for will help you observe children more astutely when you teach them and enable you to better respond to the children's learning progress.

When you observe immature movements, remember that such behavior does not mean the children were not listening to you or were not trying to perform the skill or tactic in the ways you told them to. Rather, it simply means they are in the *process* of developing the complex, mature patterns and will do so over time, with plenty of practice, and continued teacher guidance. As physical education teachers, it is our job to help children move through this process from immature patterns to higher levels of performance while respecting that this process takes time. The information presented here is based on research on the development of tactics (MacPhail et al., 2008; Rovegno et al., 2001).

Passing

Immature Movement Patterns

- Sends very long passes (long bombs) over defenders (when such passes are beyond the capabilities of the passer to throw accurately or the receiver to catch).
- Sends the ball when the receiver is not free.
- Passes to the same person every time even if he or she is guarded.
- Tosses the ball "up for grabs" (just to get rid of it) when there is no receiver in the area.
- Holds the ball too long or does not see who is open; waits until the receiver is totally open before passing and misses opportunities to make quick or more advantageous passes.
- Doesn't recognize that one arm's-length distance from the defender is enough for the receiver to be free.

Potential Refinements

- Send catchable lead passes to the space ahead of the running receiver.
- Use short passes to move the ball down the field/court.
- Do not use long bombs.
- Look for receivers cutting toward you.

Cutting and Receiving

Immature Movement Patterns

These movement patterns apply to the receiver:

- Cuts away from the passer, often going directly toward the goal, until the receiver is out of range of the passer's ability to throw an accurate pass or the receiver's ability to catch a long pass. This immature pattern occurs in all invasion games, but especially in football-type games.
- Cuts into a space that is guarded (often runs behind a defender) and does not recognize a potential passing lane.

Mature dodge and fake; cut toward passer

- Cuts too close so the passer can hand the ball off.
- Target hands: Does not look at the passer and show target hands or shows target hands when not free.

Potential Refinements

- Cut on an angle toward the passer so the passer can send a short pass.
- Reposition yourself as a receiver, and try again if you don't get the pass.
- Don't keep running to the passer for a hand-off.

Passing and Cutting

Immature Movement Patterns

- Passers standing still after they pass or running to a space without thinking whether it is a space that will either support the passer or advance the ball down the court or field.
- Passers not picking up perceptual clues to help them anticipate the receiver getting free.
- Passers getting angry inappropriately when receivers miss the ball without considering whether the pass was catchable or easy to receive with the feet or hockey stick.

SKILLS BOX 20.1

Technical Reference Information for Teachers: Least to Most Mature Patterns for Passing and Receiving in Level 3 Modified Games (*continued*)

Two girls in green pinnies mature cutting with target hands

Immature pattern: offense bunched too close together

- Receivers not cutting back (away from the goal) to help a passer who is trapped and can't find an open receiver.
- After an unsuccessful attempt to score, offensive players standing bunched around the goal and not resetting the offense by spreading out to create space to cut in and try to score again.
- On defense, everyone chasing the ball rather than marking/guarding their assigned opponents.

Potential Refinements

- Which perceptual clues will tell you that the receiver is about to get free? [Target hand signal, running faster than the defender, getting an arm's length ahead of the defender, a burst of acceleration, a quick dodge that fools the defender.]
- Scan the field. Try to anticipate where and when receivers are going to cut. What are the perceptual clues? [The receivers get in a ready position. They look at me.]
- Pass and immediately cut into a passing lane or into a position to support the passer.
- Ask yourself, "If I get the ball, what am I going to do after I pass?"

More Advanced Defensive Tactics

Immature Movement Patterns

- Not shifting quickly from offense to defense.
- Trying to intercept every ball, even when there is little chance of success, so that defenders chase the ball rather than mark/guard their assigned offensive players.
- When on defense, not shifting to back up a teammate who got beat and whose assigned offensive player is about to score.
- When on defense and the opponent successfully gets by them, not getting back quickly to back up the other defenders. (Even varsity high school players have problems getting back quickly on defense.)
- Diving in too quickly to steal the ball, allowing the dribbler to dodge the defender easily, rather than the defender timing the tackle when it is likely to be effective or containing the dribbler.

Potential Refinements

- Keep the entire game situation in mind and be prepared to shift to prevent an imminent score.
- Don't try to intercept the ball unless you are certain you can succeed. Don't chase the ball.
- Get back on defense quickly.
- Don't dive in; time your tackle to steal the ball from a dribbler.

Backing up on offense and defense

Summary

Game structures for invasion games include boundaries, rules and consequences for breaking rules, scoring goals, scoring systems, and a competitive/cooperative structure. Although the meaning and relevance of game structures are obvious to adults, they are not obvious to children. Teaching children to design game structures helps them develop in-depth knowledge of games, which they can then use to modify games to make their games fair and exciting. As they learn to design tag-type games, children also learn basic tactics that apply across invasion games.

The various invasion games played at the elementary school level involve different skills (e.g., throwing, kicking, dribbling) but use the same or similar basic tactics. As a consequence, you can help children acquire more in-depth knowledge of games and tactics by teaching them the connections among different games.

We focus first on offensive tactics at the elementary level, because children's defensive capabilities are stronger than their abilities to pass accurately and cut into appropriate passing lanes to receive the ball. We break down invasion game tactics into smaller chunks and play modified games designed to practice those tactics. As much as possible, we teach tactics by asking questions that require children to think critically and solve tactical problems. This process helps develop their tactical thinking during gameplay.

Review Questions

1. Why is the presence of defenders helpful for assisting children in understanding tactics?
2. How can you teach anticipation?
3. What consequences are inappropriate in physical education and why?
4. Why is it important to teach game structures?
5. Why are child-designed games more helpful in teaching game structures than lecturing about the rules? Link your answer to what you learned in this or another course about how children learn.
6. What are the teacher's roles in teacher- and child-designed games, and why are these roles important?
7. What is a fail-safe question to ask children when you are not sure about what feedback and guidance to give them to improve their game structures?
8. You are teaching a lesson and the children are engaging in body contact typical of the youth or professional sport that uses the skills and tactics you are teaching. What should you do, and why?
9. What is the play–discuss–play cycle?
10. Children are playing a lopsided game in which one team rarely gets the ball. Give suggestions you can make to help the children balance the offense and defense.
11. What is the "Goldilocks Principle," and why is it important?
12. Discuss two boundary tactics and describe how you can teach them.
13. Why is a perfect boundary important?
14. Describe how you can teach children to use blockers, picks, or decoys in a game of tag.
15. What do you think are the two most important tactics for person-to-person defense to teach children and why?
16. Describe two immature patterns of level 3 passing, and write tasks that you can use to help children improve each pattern.
17. Describe two immature patterns of level 3 cutting to receive a pass, and write tasks that you can use to help children improve each pattern.
18. Why is time an enemy of the offense and a friend of the defense?
19. Describe two immature patterns for offensive support and resetting the offense, and write tasks that you can use to help children improve each pattern.
20. What is a "give and go"?
21. Describe the decision-making tactics that are appropriate when you have the opportunity to intercept the ball.
22. Why does the defender stay farther away from the assigned offensive player the farther the pair are away from the soccer or hockey goal?
23. Which tactical content do you teach children for knowing when to pass, dribble/run, or shoot?

References

Alexander, K., & Penney, D. (2005). Teaching under the influence: Feeding games for understanding into the sport education -development-refinement cycle. *Physical Education and Sport Pedagogy, 10*, 287–301.

Barrett, K. R. (1984). The teacher as observer, interpreter, and decision maker. In B. J. Logsdon, K. R. Barrett, M. Ammons, M. R. Broer, L. E. Halverson, R. McGee, & M. A. Roberton (Eds.), *Physical education for children: A focus on the teaching process* (2nd ed.) (pp. 295–355). Philadelphia: Lea & Febiger.

Casey, A., & Hastie, P. (2011). Students and teacher responses to a unit of student-designed games. *Physical Education and Sport Pedagogy, 16*, 295–312.

Davids, K., Button, C., & Bennett, S. (2008). *Dynamics of skill acquisition: A constraints-led approach.* Champaign, IL: Human Kinetics.

MacPhail, A., Kirk, D., & Griffin, L. (2008). Throwing and catching as relational skills in game play: Situated learning in a modified games unit. *Journal of Teaching in Physical Education, 27*, 100–115.

Moreno, D. S. M., Lopez, L. M. G., Diaz, M. S. V., & Martinez, I. S. (2011). Spanish Primary School Students' Knowledge of Invasion Games. *Physical Education and Sport Pedagogy, 16*, 251-264.

Nevett, M., Rovegno, I., Babiarz, M., & McCaughtry, N. (2001). Changes in basic tactics and motor skills in an invasion-type game after a 12-lesson unit of instruction [Monograph]. *Journal of Teaching in Physical Education, 20*, 352–369.

Rink, J. (2010). TGfU: Celebrations and cautions. In J. I. Butler & L. L. Griffin (Eds.), *More teaching games for understanding: Moving globally* (pp. 33–47). Champaign, IL: Human Kinetics.

Rink, J. E. (2014). *Teaching physical education for learning* (7th ed.). New York: McGraw-Hill.

Rovegno, I. (1998). The development of in-service teachers' knowledge of a constructivist approach to physical education: Teaching beyond activities. *Research Quarterly for Exercise and Sport, 69*, 147–162.

Rovegno, I., & Bandhauer, D. (1994). Child-designed games: Experience changes teachers' conceptions. *Journal of Physical Education, Recreation, and Dance, 65*(6), 60–63.

Rovegno, I., Chen, W., & Todorovich, J. (2003). Accomplished teachers' pedagogical content knowledge of teaching dribbling to third grade. *Journal of Teaching in Physical Education, 22*, 426–449.

Rovegno, I., Nevett, M., Brock, S., & Babiarz, M. (2001). Teaching and learning basic invasion game tactics in fourth grade: A descriptive study from situated and constraints theoretical perspectives. *Journal of Teaching in Physical Education, 20*, 370–388.

Wilson, G. E. (2002). A framework for teaching tactical game knowledge. *Journal of Physical Education, Recreation and Dance, 73*(1), 20–26

FYI

Summary of Task Label Abbreviations

I	Informing tasks
E	Extending/exploring tasks
R	Refinements
A	Application/assessment tasks
Org	*Organizing task*
Cog K	*Cognitive knowledge: Explains or defines a concept*
Social	*Social skill or concept*
Th	Thinking skill
Mot	*Motivation concept*
Safety	*Safety information or reminder*
MD	Modification to make the task more difficult
ME	Modification to make the task easier

Source: Modified from Rink, J. E. (2014). *Teaching physical education for learning* (7th ed.).New York: McGraw-Hill.

Sample Plans for Level 3 Passing and Receiving Games

In this section, we annotate plans written to bring alive the content discussed earlier by describing how it might look in actual learning environments. Some of these plans could be the basis for a lesson plan, whereas others describe units comprising several lessons.

As you read these plans, imagine you are the teacher and consider what is happening and how you might react to it. Think about which level 2 skills and tactical content and which knowledge about designing game structures the children must learn prior to (or must be added to) these lesson segments.

As with all annotated plans in this text, we illustrate how you might integrate social responsibility, thinking skills, and motivation content into lessons. We recommend beginning teachers select only one thinking skill or social skill to teach in addition to the primary motor and cognitive knowledge objectives. As you gain experience, you will be able to integrate thinking and social skills as the need arises.

Although you cannot predict which refinements you will need, good teachers plan anticipated refinements based on their experience and knowledge of likely immature movement patterns.

SAMPLE PLAN 20.1

Level 3B: Tactics for When to Pass with the Hands, Run with the Ball, or Shoot at One Central Target Goal

Level 3B: Tactics for When to Pass with the Hands, Run with the Ball, or Shoot at One Central Target Goal	Notes and Potential Interactive Teaching Decisions

Standards

This plan addresses National Standards 1, 2, and 4 and CCSS for collaboration.

Objectives

The children will learn

Motor and Cognitive Knowledge

Offense:

1. To get free from a defender and shoot only when they have a clear shot.
2. If they don't have a clear shot, to pass to a teammate who does.
3. To receive and then pass quickly to deny time for the defenders to reposition themselves.
4. That straight, direct passes are quicker than high, loopy passes.
5. To pass the ball quickly around the pin to make the defense shift, and if they do not shift quickly, to take the open shot.

Defense:

6. To position themselves on the goal side of the opponent.

(See additional objectives below for when the game changes to allow running with the ball.)

Thinking

7. To forecast what will happen tactically in game situations.
8. To think critically about tactics and select which tactic needs the most improvement.
9. To recognize and solve problems with games that need a no-play zone.

Social

10. To not hog the ball, but rather pass to teammates who are free, giving all classmates a chance to improve their gameplay.
11. To peer coach in a supportive way to help classmates improve.
12. To ensure all group members contribute to discussions about rules and tactics.

CCSS

13. To engage effectively in small group collaborative discussions with diverse partners on topics, expressing their own ideas clearly.

Notes: We begin teaching when to run/dribble, pass, or shoot with 3v2 hit-the-pin–type games in which children are allowed to use their hands to pass or shoot but cannot run with or dribble the ball. Once the children understand how to get free from defenders and shoot only when they have an open shot, we add the rule that the person with the ball can run. The target in the middle of the playing space can be a cone or plastic bowling pin on a crate.

Org Divide the class into groups of 3v2. Provide each group with one soft, six- to eight-inch foam ball, a cone or plastic bowling pin, crate, and saucer cones for boundaries. The children set the cone target in the center of their space.

Observation Plan

1. Watch whether children throw the ball hard at defenders' legs and any other safety problems.
2. Watch whether the defense clusters around the goal, making it impossible to score.
3. Watch whether the children are passing to an open player or taking a shot when a defender is in between them and the goal, blocking the shot.

SAMPLE PLAN 20.1

Level 3B: Tactics for When to Pass with the Hands, Run with the Ball, or Shoot at One Central Target Goal (*continued*)

Content Development

I Today we are going to play 3v2 keep-away, but now adding one central scoring goal. The game is called hit-the-pin. The offense scores by hitting the cone with the ball. The offense can't run with the ball. The first pass can't be a shot on goal.

Notes: If necessary, demonstrate how to set up the game with one group of children. Set up the offense in an outside circle formation surrounding the cone, with the defense in an inside circle formation also surrounding the cone.

Th Within your group, forecast how adding a central goal will change the game of keep-away. [It will be harder for the thrower; it will be more fun; you will have to think about scoring and whether your teammates are open.]

Cog K Remember when you forecast, you try to generate many and varied predictions for how the game will change when you add a target goal.

Social/CCSS Make sure everyone in your group forecasts at least one prediction.

Th Now forecast any problems the central goal might cause.

[If they can't think of any problems, let them play even though you know some teams on defense will practically sit on the pin.]

Getting the Game Working Well

Safety/Social Before you start, I have one rule that you must include in your game. When the offense does not have a clear shot, you are not allowed to throw the ball hard at the goal to intimidate the defense or at the defenders' legs. If you do, the ball goes to the defense and you lose a point (if you are keeping score). Safety and consideration of your teammates is your number-one responsibility. Set safety rules first. Then decide all other rules and consequences and your boundaries.

A Design and play your game.

Safety Stop the games immediately if you see children throwing the ball hard at the defenders' legs. Discuss the importance of safety rules. Otherwise, stop the games once the defenders discover the tactic to surround the goal with their legs.

Th Use your problem-solving skills and identify any problems with your games. [The defense is just standing around the pin, and we have no fair way to hit it.] Right. So what can you do to solve this problem? [Make a rule that they can't do that. Set up a no-play zone around the goal that no one can enter.] That sounds like a good idea. You decide how large your no-play zone needs to be to make the game fair and fun for both offense and defense.

E Play again, and experiment until you figure out the perfect size for the no-play zone.

Th Stop. Are there any other problems with rules, consequences, and boundaries? If so, find ways to solve those problems and then play again.

Improving Tactics

Potential Questions to Identify Tactical Problems with Defense

Cog K

- In this game, what are the responsibilities of the defense? [The defense both guards the target and tries to steal the ball.]
- The offense seems to be scoring easily. Why? [They pass to someone who is open and has a clear shot. We were just chasing the ball.]
- What happens when you all chase or guard the ball? [We leave people and space for scoring open.]
- Defenders, where is the best location for you to be in relation to the person you are guarding? [Between that person and the goal, so if the opponent catches the ball, he or she won't have an open shot.] Excellent answers.

Notes: You may need to demonstrate the relationship among the defenders, the offensive players, and the goal. Set up one group with all defenders in the appropriate positions.

R Defenders, work hard at staying on the goal side of the offense.

(*continues*)

SAMPLE PLAN 20.1

Level 3B: Tactics for When to Pass with the Hands, Run with the Ball, or Shoot at One Central Target Goal (*continued*)

R Discuss possible defensive tactics. Decide which will help you improve the most. Plan your tactics and play again.

Th Stop. Think critically about your defensive positions. What problems did you have?

Social Both offense and defense discuss this topic together, and give each other suggestions for improving on defense. When you give suggestions, do so in a supportive way.

Potential Questions to Identify Tactical Problems on Offense

Cog K

- Now let's focus on offense. What are your tactics when you are on offense? [Cut into an open space to shoot. Shoot if no one is there to block your shot. Get free from the defender.]
- What do you look for to know where to run to be in a good place to shoot? [See where the defense is standing. See where there could be an open shot at the goal and run there.]
- You are working very hard to think about and solve tactical problems in games.

R Play again, focusing on getting free and in a position to have an open shot at the goal.

Notes: When working on offensive tactics, scan the groups to see which problems the children are having. Stop the games and ask the children to identify the problems. Then select one to discuss and practice. By using this play–discuss–play cycle and selecting different tactics to discuss and practice, you can teach the children all the tactics that are in your unit objectives. You will need to decide during the lesson if the class is ready to discuss another tactic or if they need more discussion and practice of the one you just discussed. Obviously, this process takes several lessons.

Th What are you not doing successfully? [We are not getting open and not running into open spaces. We are standing around waiting for the ball.] Yes. I have seen that. You need to cut to get open in this game, just as you did in your other keep-away games.

R Play again, and work on cutting to get free.

Cog K Is it easier to guard someone who is moving or someone who is standing still? [Standing still.] What does that imply for the offense? [We must always be cutting and repositioning ourselves.] Should you ever stand still? [No. If we don't get the pass, we need to cut again.] Right.

R After you passed the ball, what did you do?

Social Has everyone participated equally, or did some teammates dominate the game? If so, discuss in your groups what you can do to make this practice session fairer for everyone.

Th Think critically about your tactics. When is the defense intercepting you? [When we send high passes.]

Cog K Does the offense or the defense benefit from long, slow, high, loopy passes? [Defense.] Why? [It gives them time to set up.] Yes, you have discovered a critical principle: Time is an enemy of the offense and a friend of the defense. Why do you think this is so? [If you give the defense time, they can get in a good position to prevent you from making easy passes.] What can you do on offense to take very little time? [Catch and pass quickly.] Why is it important to catch and pass quickly? [Because the defense can't get into position fast enough.] What else can you do to take very little time on offense? [Send direct, straight passes, not high, loopy passes.] Why is a straight lead pass difficult to intercept? [Because the defense can't catch up and intercept it.] Excellent thinking.

R Play again, focusing on catching and passing straight passes quickly.

Notes: The left column describes each of the tactics and children's responses typically encountered in lesson segments on hit-the-pin. The order of presentation of these tactics is not predetermined, but rather based on the problems typically seen in lessons. Your children might have different problems or need to learn the tactics in a different order.

Social/CCSS Get together with your group and peer coach the offense in a supportive way. Discuss each of the tactics related to the idea that time is the enemy of the offense and the friend of the defense. Be sure everyone contributes to the discussion. Try to help your classmates improve.

Cog K What else can you do to help your team take less time on offense? [Look around when you don't have the ball and think about what you will do when you get the ball.]

R Play again, trying to improve how you use time on offense and defense.

Social Is everyone on your team getting an equal number of opportunities to score? If not, why not? Are your teammates not getting open to receive passes, or are they open and people are not passing to them? Figure out what you can do to solve this problem.

SAMPLE PLAN 20.1

Level 3B: Tactics for When to Pass with the Hands, Run with the Ball, or Shoot at One Central Target Goal (*continued*)

Th I see that the defense is getting into position to prevent you from having an open shot. Use your problem-solving skills to figure out what you can do to get the defense out of position. [Pass the ball around the no-play zone quickly, and shoot before the defenders can reposition themselves.]

R Try that and see if it works.

R You are scoring more often now. What did you do to improve? [Passed quickly around the no-play zone.]

Modifying the Game to Extend the Unit Content

Additional Motor and Tactical Objectives

Children will learn

Offense:

1. That you can pass the ball to a teammate close to the goal faster than you can run (or dribble) the ball there yourself.
2. To run (or dribble) when no one is open in a more advantageous position (everyone is guarded), everyone is standing still, and the scoring goal is guarded.

Defense:

3. To play person-to-person defense by staying on the goal side of the assigned offensive player.

Notes: At this point in the unit (or sooner if the children were successfully getting free in 3v2 passing only), you add the rule that children can run with the ball. This extension allows you to work on the main unit object, which is learning when to pass, run/dribble, or shoot. If your children are ready, you can shift to a 3v3 format: Once the offense can run, the game becomes more difficult for the defense.

Observation Plan

1. Watch whether children throw the ball hard at defenders' legs and any other safety problems.
2. Determine whether there is a balance between offense and defense. If not, have the children solve the problem. They can decide to play 3v2 or change the level of defensive intensity.
3. Watch whether children hog the ball by running and trying to score every time they receive a pass or whether they pass to teammates who are open and in a position to score.
4. Determine which offensive tactics need improving from previous lessons.

Th Now we will be playing hit-the-pin, but the offense can run with the ball. Forecast how the game will change now that the offense can run with the ball. [It will be more fun, it will be harder for the defense, some people might hog the ball.]

Social In your small-group discussions, encourage everyone to contribute. What can you say to someone who is quiet? [What do you think, Cary?]

Getting the Game Working Well

A In your group of six, divide into two equal teams, and set up your space to play hit-the-pin. Design the safety rules, rules for boundaries, rules for change of possession, a scoring system if you want, and the boundaries of the no-play zone. Use the play–discuss–play cycle, and experiment with your game to see if you have perfect boundaries and all the rules you need to make the game safe, fair, and balanced between offense and defense.

Th Use critical thinking and problem solving and decide if your game is working well. Do you have any problems with rules and boundaries? Does anything feel unfair? Solve the problems by modifying the rules or boundaries.

Social/CCSS Did everyone on your team contribute to the rules or express an opinion about the rules?

(*continues*)

SAMPLE PLAN 20.1

Level 3B: Tactics for When to Pass with the Hands, Run with the Ball, or Shoot at One Central Target Goal (*continued*)

Improving Tactics *Potential Questions to Identify Tactical Problems on Offense* **Cog K** Now that you have played the game briefly, what choices do you have on offense? [Shoot, run, pass.] Discuss in your group when and why shooting, running, or passing is the best choice. Then we will share the answers. [Shoot only if you have a clear shot. Pass if a teammate has a clear shot. Run if everyone is covered.] **R** Play again, and see if you can make better decisions about when to run, pass, or shoot.	
Th Stop. I have seen some missed opportunities to score. Think critically to figure out when this is happening. [When the passer runs with the ball and a teammate is in a position to score.] What travels faster—a ball or a runner? [The ball.] **R** Play again, and work on passing to a teammate who is in a position to score, rather than running with the ball.	**Social** Get together with your group and peer coach the offense. Discuss the decisions about when to run, pass, or shoot. Make sure everyone understands the tactics. Try to help your classmates improve.
Potential Questions to Identify Tactical Problems on Defense **Th** Think critically about your gameplay. What problems are you having on defense? [We are getting confused where to go; we are chasing the ball.] What can you do to improve your defensive tactics? [We can plan who we are responsible for guarding. We can play one-on-one defense, which will make it harder for the offense to have someone open.] You are working very hard to think about tactics. **R** Play again, and work on your defensive tactics.	**Social** Get together in a group and peer coach the defense. Tell them in a supportive way what they could do better to prevent you from scoring.
Suggestions for Bringing Closure to this Series of Tasks **Cog K** Let's share what you learned about tactics. Partner A, discuss what you learned about offensive tactics; partner B, discuss what you learned about defensive tactics. I will then call on partner A to share one point discussed by partner B. Next, I will call on partner B to share what partner A suggested. I will keep a list on the whiteboard.	**Possible Assessment for Hit-the-Pin with Hand Passing and Running with the Ball (Teacher Assessment)** Makes appropriate decision to pass, run with the ball, or shoot. 4 = Always (more than 90%) 3 = Usually (50–84%) 2 = Sometimes (50–74%) 1 = Rarely (less than 50%) *Name* *Score* Myra 2 Kwok 3 Hope 4
Extending the Unit to Pass, Dribble, or Shoot **A** Today, we are going to continue working on hit-the-pin, while learning the tactics of when to pass, dribble, or shoot. Instead of being allowed to run with the ball, you can now dribble only to travel. Predict how this new rule will change the game. [It will be harder because it is harder to dribble the ball than to run with it.]	

SAMPLE PLAN 20.1

Level 3B: Tactics for When to Pass with the Hands, Run with the Ball, or Shoot at One Central Target Goal (*continued*)

Extending the Unit to Pass, Dribble, or Shoot with the Feet or Hockey Stick

A Today, we are going to play a game similar to hit-the-pin. We will be using only kicking skills. You will have a center goal made by two cones. You can score by shooting from either side. Do you think you will need a no-play zone? [Varied answers.] Design your game rules, try the game, and see. If you need a no-play zone, set one up, experimenting with how large it needs to be to make the game work well.

SAMPLE PLAN 20.2

Level 3C: Supporting the Passer and Resetting the Offense

Level 3C: Goal-Oriented Passing and Receiving Using Endline Goals for Each Team, Working on Supporting the Passer and Resetting the Offense	Notes and Potential Interactive Teaching Decisions
Focus Passing with the hands (can be modified to feet or hockey sticks).	*Notes:* The tasks in these lesson segments will take from four to six lessons. Children need considerable practice before they can use these tactics consistently in their games. To maintain their motivation, you can switch groups several times and then have a class discussion comparing what they learned from different groups.

Standards

This plan addresses National Standards 1, 2, and 4 and CCSS for vocabulary acquisition.

Objectives

The children will learn to

Motor and Cognitive Knowledge

1. Support the passer, with all receivers cutting multiple times.
2. Reset the offense when they end up bunched ineffectively in front of the goal.
3. Pass and immediately cut to receive a return pass ("give and go").

Thinking Skills

4. Think critically to identify and then solve tactical problems.

Social

5. Be concerned about the problems facing passers and work to be a supportive teammate.

CCSS

6. Acquire and use accurately the domain-specific phrases "supporting the passer" and "give and go" that signal precise actions.

Game Progression

Start the unit with a 3v2 format, rotating the defenders and starting from one endline with each change of possession. Then progress to a 3v2 game, with a roving, neutral offensive player, allowing scoring at both ends. Have the game stop with every change of possession, and start with a pass from the endline or sideline. Once the children understand and are reasonably successful with the tactics, play 3v3 while working on the same objectives. In the 3v3 situation, you and the children together will have to modify the level of defensive intensity for different individuals and groups and will need to start possession with a pass from the endline or sideline with a level 1 defender on the inbound pass.

Observation Plan

1. Scan for safe distances between groups and unsafe behaviors such as diving for loose balls due to lack of safety rules prevent these behaviors.
2. Watch whether offensive players are standing still or trying to get free.
3. Watch for moments when children are bunched around the goal. Use this as a teachable moment.

(continues)

SAMPLE PLAN 20.2

Level 3C: Supporting the Passer and Resetting the Offense (*continued*)

Content Development

Potential Questions to Identify Tactics for Supporting the Passer

Cog K/CCSS Today in our 3v2 games, we are going to focus on what we call "supporting the passer." That means when you are on offense, not only do you think about scoring, but you also always think about the passer's needs. When you are a passer, what do you need from your off-the-ball teammates? [Getting free, cutting more than once in case I don't get the pass off, cutting so I have to make only short passes, having more than one person free.] Right. Those actions support the passer.

Decisions to Make in Designing Games

If your children have been designing games in other units, you should not need to remind them of the following decisions. You can list the decisions on a whiteboard to remind them about the game structures they need to design.

- Set rules for safety (e.g., no diving for loose balls), no dribbling, and what happens if a ball goes out of bounds or is dropped or intercepted.
- Set perfect boundaries.

A Design a 3v2 passing game, play it, and try to think about how you can support the passer when you are off the ball on offense.

- Decide whether you want to score by passing over the endline, into one hoop, or into two or more hoops on the endline.
- Determine a change of possession rule and how you will rotate defenders. [Don't play defense too long because you can get too tired, and then the game won't be fun for either team.]
- Set up a scoring system for the offense and, if you want, for the defense (e.g., if defenders touch or intercept the ball).
- Decide whether to keep track of the score.

Supporting the Passer

R Stop. I can see you are having some problems supporting the passer. I will time you. Play for two minutes and see if you can discover when or where on the court/field/playing area the passer is having problems making a quick pass.

Th Stop. Think critically and figure out when and why passers had problems sending quick, short passes. [When we got down to the goal, we'd be in the goal, and the defense would crowd around covering us. Sometimes in midcourt/midfield, there was only one receiver open.] Excellent observations.

Cog K Let's deal with one issue at a time. Start with the problem of having only one person free. One reason there is only one receiver free is that the passer sends a pass and then stands and watches the rest of the action. You need to have multiple receivers getting free. What do you think the passer should do? [Pass and then quickly cut or reposition to cut.]

R Play and try to improve supporting the passer with multiple receivers cutting into open passing lanes.

Getting the Game Working Well

Th [You can skip this task if you have observed all of the children's games and talked with all of the groups about whether their games are working well.] Stop. Think critically about your boundaries, rules, and scoring goals. Discuss your critique within your group. Ask yourselves, "Do we need to make any changes in the game to make the game fairer? Do we have a fair system for rotating defenders quickly? Are the boundaries the right size? Do we have the right number of goals?" Make any necessary changes in your games, and play again.

SAMPLE PLAN 20.2

Level 3C: Supporting the Passer and Resetting the Offense (*continued*)

Give and Go

Cog K/CCSS Let's stop our games. I am going to teach you a tactic that we call a "give and go." A "give and go" means you pass the ball, that is "give" the ball to an open receiver, cut immediately toward the goal, that is "go," and receive the pass back.

I will demonstrate. One person, Nikko, is the passer and stands here. A second person, Pedro, is the defender and stands in between the passer and the goal. A third person (me) cuts to a position on an angle (about a 45-degree angle) to the side and ahead of the passer. Nikko sends me the ball and then quickly sprints by Pedro. I then send the ball back to Nikko. Why do we call this a "give and go"? [Nikko "gives" (sends) the ball to the passer and then "goes" quickly, cutting to get the ball back.] I will assign groups of three, and each of you practice the "give and go" until you feel like you have it mastered.

E Return to your original groups and play your game again. Try to use the "give and go" as a tactic. Passers think ahead, "I need to support the passer by passing and immediately cutting for a possible return pass."

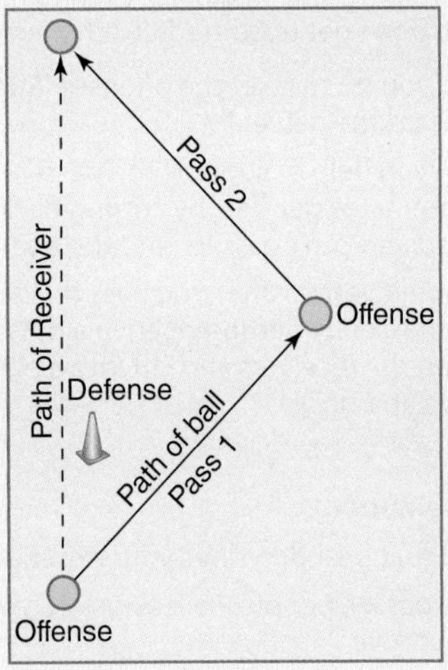

Give and go

Example of Teaching a Tactic in a Level 2 Task in the Middle of a Level 3 Lesson

Many times in teaching games, you will recognize that the class needs more practice on a skill using a level 2 game-like task or needs to learn a new tactic using a level 2 task. Here is an example of how you can incorporate this learning.

Linking the Content to Soccer

Cog K In soccer, we sometimes call the "give and go" a "wall pass." Can anyone guess why? Right [The receiver is just like a wall. The dribbler passes the ball, and the receiver one-touches it on an angle ahead back to the original passer, just as if the passer had sent the ball rebounding off a wall.]

Mot You thought hard to figure out the answer.

Cog K Have any teams managed to include a "give and go"? Share the secrets of how you succeeded.

R Has your group improved today on supporting the passer? Discuss quickly what you have been doing better.

Extending the Content in Future Lessons

Potential Questions to Identify Problems and Solutions to Getting Bunched Around the Goal: Resetting the Offense

Cog K In the last lesson, I asked when and where passers had problems sending a pass. The problem we worked on last lesson was having multiple receivers getting free, with the passer sending the pass and then immediately cutting, maybe getting a "give and go" pass. Do you remember the other problem you mentioned? Right. Sometimes the offense was bunched in the goal area.

Notes: Typically, working on multiple passers getting free and the "give and go" tactic takes two or more lessons. The second lesson starts where the class ended in the previous lesson. In the second lesson, require all groups to use two hula hoops on the ground as scoring goals. You score by passing to a teammate who cuts into one of the two hoops over the endline. Several groups might have used this scoring option in the previous segment. Using two hoops is easier than using one hoop because two hoops elicit a spreading-out of the offense.

(*continues*)

SAMPLE PLAN 20.2

Level 3C: Supporting the Passer and Resetting the Offense (*continued*)

Let's demonstrate this problem with a group. Here we have the passer, Anna Maria, about 10 feet from the goal; both receivers, Sydney and Julie, are bunched around the hoop. Is it easy or hard to defend Sydney and Julie? [Easy.] Why? [Because one defender can cover both of them; with two defenders, they won't have a chance to catch a pass.] Let's figure out how to solve this problem. Julie got free and made a great cut into the hoop, but the passer didn't pass the ball to her. What happens next? [Her defender, Tomas, catches up.] Sydney cuts near the goal, too, and her defender, Aaron, catches up. Can you see how both defenders can easily intercept the ball? What else is a problem? [There is no place to go.] Right. The defense has denied you space. You have no place to go to get free because you are in the goal and the defenders are blocking you. How can you create space? [We have to spread apart and get away from the defenders.] Good problem solving. We call this "resetting the offense."

Learning to avoid bunching around the goals and figuring out ways to fix this problem when it occurs take many days of practice and teacher guidance. You can keep children motivated by assigning new groups and designing new games. Then have a class discussion in which the children share what they learned playing with different teammates and opponents. When the class is supporting the passer reasonably well and not betting bunched around the goal, change to one hoop for scoring.

E Play your game. If you bunch up, someone say, "Reset the offense." You should then spread apart and try to support the passer by multiple receivers getting free to receive passes.

R You can't simply stand in the goal jumping up and down and hope the defense forgets you are there! What do you need to do? [Spread out, support the passer, and try again.]

Mot Sometimes you make great cuts but don't score. This happens all the time in games, even to high school athletes. Don't get frustrated. Just try again.

Cog K Let's talk more about where you should go when you are bunched and need to reset the offense. Where could you go to create space for you or your teammate? [Cut to the sides or back away from the goal; cut back so the passer can send you a "give and go" pass.] How will this create space? [The defenders will have to follow us because we might cut into the other hoop, and they will need to be close to us to intercept a pass.] Nice job solving a tactical problem. Play again, and see if you can solve this problem when it occurs in your game.

R What do you do to reset the offense? [Spread out, cut back toward the passer.]

R How can you help or support the passer? [By having both teammates get free, by cutting back if the passer is trapped and can't pass toward the goal or shoot.]

R What should you do after you pass the ball? [Support the new passer by getting open in a passing lane, reposition the receivers and cut into a passing lane, cut for a "give and go."]

CCSS Closure

Have partners discuss the definitions of "give and go" and "supporting the passer." Then discuss ways to support the passer. In a whole-class discussion, call on pairs to list the tactics for supporting the passer on a whiteboard.

Possible Assessment

Circle the word that best describes your experience today:

When I was the passer, people were aware of my position and tried to be supportive.

Always *Often* *Sometimes* *Never*

When I was a receiver, I remembered to think about the passer's situation and was supportive by cutting into a free space and resetting when we got bunched around the goal.

Always *Often* *Sometimes* *Never*

Sample Plan for Child-Designed Games

The next sample plan is a template that shows how you can teach child-designed games for invasion game units. You can substitute different tactics and skills and, with slight modifications, adapt the plan to that content. The following outline summarizes the discussion about how to teach children to design games described earlier in this chapter.

Outline of Content

1. Typically, the teacher decides the skills for the game (e.g., throwing and catching, dribbling with hockey sticks). As children acquire skills, tactical knowledge, and game design experiences, we shift to having the children select the skills.
2. Use a play–discuss–play cycle as many times as necessary to have children decide on game structures (i.e., boundaries, number of players on each team, rules and consequences for breaking rules, number and kinds of scoring goals, scoring systems, whether the game is cooperative or primarily competitive, and whether to keep track of the score).
3. Initially let children brainstorm and experiment freely as they explore different possibilities for their game structures.
4. Next, have children think critically and solve problems with the game structures until they have a good game that works well.
5. Still using the play–discuss–play cycle, focus on having children think critically and solve problems with their game tactics. Work on appropriate refining content to help them improve their skills and tactics.

SAMPLE PLAN 20.3

Level 3B or 3C: Child-Designed Lead Passing Games

Level 3B or 3C Child-Designed Lead Passing Games (Using the Hands, Feet, or Hockey Sticks)	Notes and Potential Interactive Teaching Decisions
Standards	
This unit addresses National Standards 1, 2, and 4 and CCSS for collaboration.	
Objectives	
The children will learn to **Motor and Tactical Decision Making** 1. Design a good game that works well. 2. Appropriately use invasion game tactics relevant to lead passes and other aspects of their game. **Thinking Skills** 3. Think critically about and solve problems related to their game design. 4. Think critically about and solve problems related to their tactics. **Social Responsibility** 5. Work cooperatively with a group to design a game, think critically about their game design and tactics, and solve problems related to their game design and tactics. **CCSS** 6. Engage effectively in small-group collaborative discussions with diverse partners on topics, building on others' ideas and expressing their own clearly.	**Prerequisites** *Knowledge of game structures:* Children should have learned how to design game structures in a tag unit (see **Sample Learning Experiences 20.1 to 20.4** for suggestions on how to teach this content) or in 1v1 dribbling games. *Knowledge of tactics for lead passes:* You can teach this lesson any time after children have learned the tactics for lead passes in levels 2 and 3A. *Tips for beginning teachers:* When you have children design games, you obviously can't predict the exact rules they will set or the tactics of the games. The uncertainty might appear overwhelming, yet units and lessons on child-designed games are easier than they appear, and the rewards are great. Children enjoy inventing games. Through game invention, their knowledge about game structures (i.e., rules, procedures, boundaries, goals, scoring systems) and tactics develops. Moreover, they have ownership over their games and grow in their ability to solve problems they face playing games in recess and outside of school.
Introduction	
Cog K We have been working on the tactics of passing and receiving in games. Discuss with the person next to you as many tactics as you can remember.	[Watch the children and stop partner discussions when many partner groups appear to have exhausted their ideas.]
Each set of partners tell me one tactic, which I will list on the whiteboard.	[Keep calling on partners until you have all the tactics you have taught written on the whiteboard.]

(*continues*)

SAMPLE PLAN 20.3

Level 3B or 3C: Child-Designed Lead Passing Games (*continued*)

Content Development

A I have assigned you to a group of four to five children. In your group, create a game where the focus is sending lead passes.

Game Design Decisions

I have listed the game design decisions you need to make on the white board.

Balls and Skills

You can see in the equipment baskets that you can choose which equipment you will use. You can choose from a variety of balls. You can choose skills using the equipment provided (e.g., hockey sticks, scoops, or your hands and feet) to send and receive lead passes. You can decide how many balls you will use in your game. Your game must focus on lead passes. You will work on improving your ability to send lead passes to open receivers.

Scoring Goals

You need to decide on goals. Will you have target goals? Will you have one, two, three, or more goals? How large or small will your goals be? Where will you locate your goals in your playing space?

Selecting the Tactical Focus

You can select a different tactic that is closely related to recent lesson objectives. We selected lead passes as an illustration because this is a basic tactic used in all invasion games with the hands, feet, or hockey sticks.

Selecting the Skill

Although we have illustrated this unit by having the children select whether the skill for sending lead passes will be using the hands, feet, hockey sticks, or scoops, if you are new to child-designed games, it will be easier to restrict the children to only one skill (e.g., throwing passes with the hands, kicking passes).

Presenting the Task

This lesson starts with more teacher talk than most lessons. This long introduction is included because it can be helpful to suggest options for each of the decisions the children must make. The more you teach child-designed games with your classes, the less they will need you to give them suggestions.

Scoring System

You need to decide what kind of scoring system you will use and whether you will keep track of the score. Will your game be cooperative or competitive against opponents? Will you be able to score different numbers of points for different actions, such as making a certain number of lead passes in a row and for scoring at different goals?

How the Game Is Played

Decide the procedures for your game. Decide on the rules that determine how to play your game. For example, your game rules might state that you can send lead passes only with your feet, with no dribbling. Alternatively, you might decide to use scoops and beanbags to send lead passes. Maybe your game will allow dribbling with the feet and running with the ball in your hands, with lead passes being made with either hands or feet. You have many choices.

Safety

As always, the most important rules are for safety. Think carefully about the equipment you have selected, and design appropriate safety rules.

Boundaries

You will need to set boundaries and determine rules about boundaries.

Consequences

Decide on the consequences for rule violations and the ball going out of bounds.

Change of Possession

You need to decide how the change of possession will occur. You will need to make sure that the change of possession procedure ensures that everyone gets a fair turn on offense and defense and that everyone is active in the game.

Game Design Decisions (Listed on Whiteboard)

[To help children remember your assignment, list on a whiteboard the following decisions they need to make:]

- Balls and skills
- Goals (number of goals, location, type of goal)
- Cooperative or competitive game
- Scoring system
- Whether to keep track of the score
- How the game is played
- Safety rules
- Boundaries and boundary rules
- Rules and consequences for breaking rules
- Change of possession rule and procedure

Observation Plan

1. The games are safe.
2. There is balance between offense and defense.
3. Time spent playing on offense and defense is roughly equal.
4. Social interactions are positive.
5. The game flows.
6. The children are practicing lead passes (the objectives of the lesson).

As you observe the children's games, try to keep in your head (or write on a note card) the criteria for a good game discussed earlier.

SAMPLE PLAN 20.3

Level 3B or 3C: Child-Designed Lead Passing Games (*continued*)

A Go with your group, brainstorm ideas for your game, explore these ideas, and design an initial game.	*Notes:* Give the children time to design and play a few rounds of their initial game before starting the play–discuss–play cycle.
Getting the Game Working Well **R** Stop. Remember the procedures we follow in all lessons in which you design games. Your initial game is simply a place to start. The rules are not chiseled in stone. Now meet with your group and make changes in your game to see if you can improve it. You can change the skill, goals, scoring, boundaries, or any other element you want.	*Notes:* Don't hesitate to help struggling groups. One sign of problems is one person "messing up" the game. When you see that, intervene and help the children identify the problem (e.g., not listening to ideas, not following established rules, not getting turns) and make a rule or find a way to solve the problem.
R [Continue using the play–discuss–play cycle so the children can critique their game structures and solve problems in their games until it is a good game that works well. This can take an entire class period with younger children or children who are less experienced in designing games. Take as much time as the process requires. Children are learning important information about how games work and how to work cooperatively in groups.]	*Notes:* When you first observe a group, it can be a challenge to understand their game. When we are not sure what to say, we make a simple request: "Tell me about your game." As the children describe their game, you will be able to figure out if there are any problems they have not recognized. You can then ask them questions or bring the problem to their attention. You also can offer suggestions. **Social/CCSS** Is everyone in your group contributing ideas and expressing an opinion? **Social/CCSS** Listen carefully to your classmates' ideas and try to build on them. Try to use each other's ideas as a springboard for new ideas. Remember that sometimes an idea doesn't sound great at first, but it can be built into a great idea if all of you try to do so.
Improving Tactics **Th** Now that you have good games, let's work on improving your lead passes. Think critically about your tactics, and discuss in your groups when you have been successful and when you have not been successful sending lead passes. Try to identify the problem and figure out a solution. Are there some rules in your game that are preventing practice of lead passes? Are receivers standing still rather than cutting for a lead pass?	*Notes:* You may need to do several play–discuss–play cycles before the children have lead passes working in their game. Be alert to game structures that are hampering the practice of lead passes, and help the children solve the problem. **R** What do you need to do to send a good lead pass? [Send it in front of the receiver so he or she can catch the pass on the run.] When you had problems sending the pass so the receiver could catch it on the run, what happened? [I sent it to where the person was, rather than to where the person was going to be.]
[Continue using the play–discuss–play cycle to improve lead passes until the children are successful.]	

(*continues*)

SAMPLE PLAN 20.3

Level 3B or 3C: Child-Designed Lead Passing Games (*continued*)

Th You are doing such a good job with your lead passes! Now let's work on the other tactics in your game. Think critically about your games, and discuss in your group which tactics you are using, when you are successful, and when you are not successful.

R Play again, and try to improve on those tactics.

Potential Questions to Ask

- What was your best play? Why did it work? What do you have to do to make it happen again? If you were the defender, what can you do to keep the "best play" from happening again?
- What was the worst play of the day? Where did it break down? How can you avoid that mistake?

Social Both teams talk together. Your goal is to help both teams improve. If you have been successful on defense, peer coach the offense so they can improve. It you have been successful on offense, peer coach the defense.

Social Make sure everyone in the group contributes to the discussion. Listen carefully and build on each other's ideas.

[Continue using the play–discuss–play cycle to improve the offensive or defensive tactics until the children are successful playing a good game in which the offense and defense are balanced.]

Notes: It is a challenge to predict the tactics for child-designed games. However, once you understand the game, you will know the tactics and be able to help children identify these tactics and how to improve their gameplay.

Observation Plan

1. Observe the game and note when the ball changes possession. If it was after a score, did the defenders do a good job challenging the offense, or do the children need to improve their defense?
2. If the change of possession occurred before a score, note whether it was due to problems with offensive tactics or the change of possession rule about free balls.
3. If the offense cannot score, note whether they need to improve their offensive tactics or whether the group needs to limit the defensive intensity.

Closure Options

CCSS

- Discuss how to encourage everyone to participate in the group discussion. Discuss examples of when one person built on the idea of another person. Discuss how you can encourage each other to build on ideas presented to the group.
- Have a class discussion on what children learned about lead passes.
- Have a class discussion on what children learned about designing good games.
- Discuss what made the games fun and whether the children would teach this game to friends or their siblings at home.

Potential Assessment

Developmental rubric for sending lead passes:

Developmental level 1: Throws behind the receiver. Throws too late or too early. Throws to a receiver who is not free. The pass is seldom catchable (less than 50% of the time).

Developmental level 2: Sends the pass ahead of or to the receiver. The pass might be too forceful. The pass is usually catchable (50–85% of the time).

Developmental level 3: Consistently sends catchable (appropriate force and placement) lead passes ahead of the receiver so the receiver does not have to twist, slow down, or change stride to catch the ball most of the time (85–100% of the time).

Name	*Developmental Level*
Kyung-Sook	2
Connell	3
Emma	2

CHAPTER 21

Invasion Games: Dribbling with the Hands, Feet, and Hockey Sticks: Levels 1, 2, and 3

PRE-READING REFLECTION

1. Think about dribbling in soccer, basketball, field hockey, and floor hockey games. What is similar about dribbling across those games?
2. What is the purpose of dribbling in games?

OBJECTIVES

Students will learn:

1. When teaching level 1 dribbling, focus on two or three performance techniques.
2. Level 2 content includes the following elements:
   - Varying and adapting the basic dribbling pattern by changing pathways, directions, speeds, levels, and relationships
   - Combining dribbling with shooting, passing, and receiving
   - Learning to use skills and dribbling tactics in game-like situations
3. Challenge courses are beneficial for practicing level 2 content.
4. Level 3 includes learning to use tactical game skills and basic invasion game tactics in dribbling games.
5. Child-designed dribbling games are excellent means of teaching children about game structures and tactics.

KEY TERMS

"Ball, me, defender" position

Challenge courses

Double dribble

Stick handling (ball control)

CONNECTIONS TO STANDARDS

1. This chapter addresses National Standard 1 for demonstrating competence in dribbling, National Standard 2 for applying knowledge of movement concepts, strategies, and tactics, National Standard 4 for exhibiting personal and social responsibility, and National Standard 5 for recognizing the value of physical activity for enjoyment and challenge.
2. This chapter also addresses the Common Core and other State Standards (CCSS) for speaking, listening, collaboration, domain-specific vocabulary, and reading.

FYI

Sample Plans in this Chapter

Level 1
Dribbling with the feet
Dribbling with the hand (on the website)

Level 2A
Dribbling on different pathways

Level 2B
Combining dribbling, pivoting, passing, and shooting (on the website)

Level 2C
Dribbling while protecting the ball against a defender in game-like 1v1 situations

Level 3
Dribbling, passing, and shooting against a defender in 2v1 situations (on the website)

PROGRESSION OF CONTENT

Level 1: Fundamental Game Skills

Dribbling with the Hands

- Pushing with two hands to bounce and catch the ball
- Dribbling in place with the dominant hand and nondominant hand
- Dribbling while walking, progressing to jogging easily
- Level 1 dribbling tricks

Dribbling with the Feet, Floor Hockey Sticks, or Field Hockey Sticks

- Explore dribbling with different parts of the feet while walking
- Dribbling with the feet while jogging easily
- Dribbling with a floor or field hockey stick (called stick handling or ball control) walking, progressing to jogging easily

Level 2: Tactical Game Skills

Level 2A: Applying Movement Concepts from the Laban Framework to Vary Skills

Dribbling with the Hands, Feet, or Hockey Sticks

- Dribbling on different pathways
- Dribbling while accelerating and stopping quickly and changing directions
- Dribbling at different speeds

Dribbling with the Hands

- Hand dribbling varying the level (low and medium) and over, under, and on obstacles
- Hand-dribbling tricks for eliciting looking up
- Dribbling tricks following a leader and dribbling routines

Level 2B: Combining Dribbling, Shooting, Passing, and Receiving

- Combining dribbling and shooting with the feet or hockey sticks
- Combining dribbling and shooting with the hands
- Combining dribbling and shooting while changing speeds, pathways, and directions
- Receiving lead passes and shooting with the feet or hockey sticks
- Combining passing, receiving, pivoting, and shooting
- Combining dribbling, passing, and shooting

Level 2C: Learning Tactical Game Skills in Game-like Situations

- Dribbling while protecting the ball against pretend defenders
- Dribbling changing speeds, directions, and pathways to avoid pretend defenders
- Dribbling 1v1 protecting the ball against a level 3 "pest: defender
- Dribbling 1v1 protecting the ball against a level 4 defender (soft defense)
- Dribbling focusing on protecting the ball and avoiding multiple level 4 defenders
- Shooting at and defending soccer- and hockey-type goals
  - Shooting against a goalkeeper, exploring the offensive and defensive relationships of the goalkeeper's distance to the shooter and the amount of space available for shooting
  - Dribbling and shooting against a goalkeeper while exploring the amount of space for shooting at different angles.
- Dribbling, passing, and shooting 2v1 against a level 3 pest defender.

Level 3: Using Tactical Game Skills in Small-Sided, Modified Gameplay

- Designing boundaries, rules, and consequences for breaking rules for 1v1 dribbling games
- Using tactics for protecting the ball and avoiding defenders in 1v1 dribble tag–type game
- Using boundaries tactically in 1v1 dribble tag–type games
- Designing 1v1 dribbling games with scoring goals and a scoring system
- Using tactics for defending goals and scoring in 1v1 dribbling games
- Designing small-sided (2v2) team dribbling games
- Using offensive tactics for dribbling and passing in 2v2 dribbling games
- Using defensive tactics for dribbling and passing in 2v2 dribbling games

Figure 21.1 Progression of Content

Introduction

In this chapter, we discuss levels 1, 2, and 3 dribbling with the hands, feet, and hockey sticks and related invasion games and tactics. In level 1, we describe how to set tasks and the environment and introduce performance techniques to help children gain control of the ball.

In level 2A, we describe tasks for varying dribbling using movement concepts from the Laban framework. In particular, we include tasks involving dribbling using different pathways, directions, and speeds, as these are the movements required for later practice in game-like situations. In level 2B, we discuss combining dribbling with shooting, passing, and receiving; in level 2C, we explore the use of developmentally appropriate basic tactics related to dribbling in invasion game-like situations.

The movement concepts and tactics are used in ways that are the same or similar whether the children are dribbling with the hands, feet, or hockey sticks. Thus, level 2 lessons are excellent choices for helping children understand the connections across invasion games. You reinforce the concepts and tactics you teach related to dribbling with the hands when you apply the same concept or tactic to dribbling with the feet or hockey sticks. This reinforcement helps children acquire more in-depth, well-connected knowledge and develops their tactical decision making in game situations (Thorpe & Bunker, 2010).

In level 3, we discuss dribbling games and related invasion game tactics. We show you how to teach children to design and modify dribbling games. **Figure 21.1** summarizes content taught when children are at developmental levels 1, 2, and 3.

Level 1: Fundamental Dribbling Skills

Principles of Teaching Level 1 Dribbling

Dribbling with the Hands

Dribbling with the hands is a skill used in basketball—but it is also more than that. Dribbling is the basis for children's games such as dribble tag, and, perhaps more significantly, children enjoy trick dribbling and designing dribbling routines. The dribbling routine in *High School Musical* is familiar to many children. You have probably seen trick-dribbling entertainers in halftime performances at basketball games. Many years ago, Fred "Curly" Neal of the Harlem Globetrotters was famous for his trick dribbling.

We discuss performance techniques and cues for dribbling in **Skills Boxes 21.1** and **21.2**, which includes far more information than you will need to teach in level 1. Remember the guideline to "tell them what they need to know, when they need to know it." Children do not need the teacher to tell them about all of the performance techniques of skills as beginners. For example, they don't need to hear "Keep your eyes up while dribbling," because this requirement interferes with learning how to control the ball by pushing with the finger pads. Children can't think about more than one performance technique at a time.

In level 1, we focus on only those performance techniques that help children gain ball control. We begin with pushing the ball with the finger pads, not slapping with the palm. We use the terms "finger pads" or "fingerprints" to reinforce this message. Otherwise, if you say, "Dribble with your fingertips," children will follow your directions literally and attempt to dribble using just the very tips of their fingers. Tasks such as a two-handed push to bounce the ball and then catch it help elicit the desired pushing action.

Figure 21.2 The hand is like a spider

To help children learn the pushing action and remember the performance techniques, you can tell stories or use metaphors. The following examples are taken from a study on expert teachers (Rovegno, Nevett, Brock, & Babiarz, 2001):

- Spread your fingers so your hand looks like a spider, with finger pads on the ball (see **Figure 21.2**).
- The top of the ball is like an egg: If you slap it, it will break, but it is a magic egg that doesn't break on the floor.
- Don't flop your hand up and down; you should not have "cooked spaghetti" wrists.

To help with ball control, we then focus on dribbling waist high and diagonally to the front and side of the dribbling-hand side (front/side). You can have children experiment pushing the ball with strong force so it bounces head height to see how hard it is to control a ball that is dribbled too high.

Dribbling with the Nondominant Hand

Although teachers try to get children to practice dribbling with their left and right hands, children prefer practicing with their dominant hand. This tendency is easy to understand because dribbling is enjoyable, and they are far more successful with their dominant hand. In a study of 105 third-graders, only one child dribbled with his nondominant hand unless the teacher set a task requiring practice with the nondominant hand (Chen, Rovegno, Todorovich, & Babiarz, 2003). Consequently, we recommend focusing on dribbling with the right and left hands from level 1 onward, so children enjoy and become competent dribbling with either hand.

Making Performance Techniques Relevant

As research on motivation suggests, performance techniques must be relevant to children. To help them understand the relevance, you can link techniques to gameplay even though children at level 1 will not be ready for game-like situations, much less gameplay. For example, explain that they need to learn to keep a soccer ball close to their feet *because* if they don't, when they play games in older grades, the defense will steal it. Once they understand the reason, they will be more likely to practice trying to keep the ball close to their feet rather than kicking it hard and chasing after it (which is fun for children). Following are the connections you might emphasize between hand dribbling and dribbling tactics:

- You need to learn to dribble to the front/side *to protect the ball from a defender on the other side.*
- Dribble waist high or lower *to make it harder for defenders to steal the ball.*
- Look up *to see teammates, defenders, and the basket. You can plan your tactic if you can see what is going on around you.*

Balls for Dribbling

We teach dribbling using playground balls. There are two kinds: Some are rubber and bouncier, whereas others have nylon-bound bladders, which make them harder to dribble. If some children are having problems pushing the ball, give them a rubber playground ball or, if available, a larger playground ball. If others are very successful, give them a nylon-bound ball, which will further develop their ability to ride and push the ball, as this type of ball bounces more like a basketball. Most teachers do not have the budget to purchase single-game balls, such as basketballs (especially leather balls, which quickly become damaged when used on playgrounds). If you have basketballs, these balls will be too heavy and hard to bounce for your beginning dribblers.

Dribbling with the Feet

To dribble with the feet, you kick the ball with the inside, outside, and instep (laces) of the foot, and sometimes (when under close attack from an offensive player) with the heel and sole of your foot to pull the ball backward. Throughout this text, we will refer to the instep as the "laces" because this term is clearer to children.

When you are near defenders, the goal is to control the ball while keeping it close to your feet. When you have a long, open space with no defenders, the goal is to dribble fast with a looser dribble, pushing the ball ahead with your laces and then sprinting to push the ball again without having to slow down.

When teaching dribbling with the feet, it is important to give children plenty of space and to let them explore how to move the ball with different parts of the feet while keeping the ball close to them (see **Figure 21.3**). Playground balls that are slightly deflated do not travel as fast and are easier for beginners to control. Balls that are too difficult to control are task and environmental constraints that inhibit learning.

Figure 21.3 Dribbling with the feet in a scattered formation

Dribbling with Floor and Field Hockey Sticks

In field hockey, you can touch the ball with only the flat side of the stick. To do so, hold the left hand at the top of the stick, with the "V" between the thumb and fingers aligned with the edge of the stick. Then turn the stick so that the flat side faces forward. The right hand grasps the stick a little less than halfway down its length.

To teach field hockey dribbling, called **stick handling** or **ball control**, start by having children explore pushing the ball about the space as they walk, while keeping the flat side of the stick on the ball. Have them experiment to find where the ball is easiest to push in relation to their body. They will discover it is easiest to control the ball by keeping the ball to the right side and slightly in front of their feet so the right palm and the back of the left hand are facing forward. If you are teaching on a playground, in a gym, or on a field with very short grass, the children can push the ball with the stick while maintaining continual contact as they run forward. If you are teaching on grass, the children will have to tap the ball forward, keeping it close to the stick.

With floor hockey, you can touch the ball with both sides of the stick. Tell the children this, and then have them explore pushing the ball or puck about the space, keeping it close to them and trying to push it with both sides of the stick (see **Figure 21.4**). If needed, teach them to turn the blade about 45 degrees and push the ball or puck forward. Then have them lift the stick blade over the ball or puck and push it with the other side, keeping the ball or puck within the width of their feet.

An easy way to teach children how to grip a floor hockey stick is to have them hold it like a baseball bat—that is, resting on their shoulders, with their nondominant hand on top. They should then put the stick edge on the ground and slide the dominant hand down the stick.

Child-Sized Sticks and Environmentally Appropriate Balls and Pucks

For both floor and field hockey, find a ball that works on the surface you have for teaching. This quality is critical to set the

Figure 21.4 Dribbling with a floor hockey stick

SAFETY AND LIABILITY 21.1

Increasing Safety and Decreasing Risk of Liability: Guidelines Relevant to Content in this Chapter

In this box, we discuss specific guidelines built on information discussed throughout this text on professional standards of practice, negligence, and liability. The goals of these guidelines are to increase children's safety and decrease teachers' risk of negligence and liability.

- Purchase foam floor and field hockey sticks to ensure everyone's safety. If you must use plastic or wood sticks, have the students wear eye goggles.
- With floor hockey, use a plastic puck or bean bag on the gymnasium floor. With both field and floor hockey outside, you need a ball that doesn't bounce, is three to four inches in diameter (larger than a regulation field hockey ball), is soft (for safety reasons), and doesn't roll too fast on the playground or too slowly on the grass.
- Many dribbling tasks require children to dribble in general space in a scattered formation. If children have not learned the stop routine and how to safely work while traveling in a scattered formation, then you need to teach this content first without a ball.
- Children must learn they are responsible for dribbling at a speed that is challenging but also safe. Safe means they can control their speed and body and stop quickly. Safe also means they don't trip and fall, don't run into anyone else, can stop before hitting the wall or another person, and don't lose the ball so it doesn't roll on the floor out of their control for others to trip over.

task and environmental constraints you need to elicit and to allow for the dribbling and passing actions you want children to develop. If the environment doesn't work, the children will struggle to learn.

You want a ball that doesn't bounce, is three to four inches in diameter (larger than a regulation field hockey ball), is soft (for safety reasons), and doesn't roll too fast on the playground or too slowly on the grass. With field hockey, you can use softballs if you can't purchase hockey balls designed for beginners. With floor hockey, you can use a plastic puck or bean bag on the gymnasium floor.

We recommend purchasing foam floor and field hockey sticks to ensure everyone's safety. If you must use plastic or wood sticks, you can have the students wear eye goggles. Children also need sticks that are short enough for them to dribble using the appropriate movement patterns. When adult-length sticks are used, this task constraint elicits children holding the stick like a broom and trying to sweep the field hockey ball or puck about the space. The adult-sized field hockey sticks we have purchased all needed to have at least 12 inches sawed off the end to make the sticks an appropriate length for children.

Sample Learning Experiences

In this section, we describe sample level 1 learning experiences for dribbling. You can use these ideas to build lessons, along with performance techniques discussed in **Skills Boxes 21.1** and **21.2**. Skill development is our primary goal and something that you must keep in mind as you think about potential learning experiences.

We suggest starting learning experiences by giving the children a task that elicits—or at least allows for—the desired movement response. Observe the children to see if the task and environmental constraints are working. Based on that information, decide whether you need to teach or review specific performance techniques (see **Skills Boxes 21.1** and **21.2** for descriptions of performance techniques). Tell the children what they need to know, when they need to know it. If you begin by lecturing about a performance technique, you may be wasting time because the children might already know and can do it. Alternatively, you may select a performance technique that is beyond the capabilities of the children at their level of development.

SAMPLE LEARNING EXPERIENCES 21.1

Level 1 Dribbling

Dribbling with the Hands

1. Pushing with Two Hands to Bounce and Catch the Ball

- Bounce the ball by pushing the ball down with both hands, and then catch it.
- Explore pushing with different amounts of force to bounce the ball to different levels and then catch it.
- Explore pushing with one hand (the other hand can be a helper hand on the side of the ball) using different amounts of force to bounce the ball to different levels and then catch it. Give both hands equal practice.

(continues)

SAMPLE LEARNING EXPERIENCES 21.1

Level 1 Dribbling (*continued*)

2. Dribbling in Place with the Dominant Hand and Nondominant Hand

- Remaining in your personal space, try bouncing the ball as many times in a row as you can. This is called dribbling.
- Give both hands practice.
- Try to increase the number of times you can bounce the ball without missing it or having it bounce out of your personal space.

3. Dribbling While Walking, Progressing to Jogging Easily

- Give both hands practice.
- Try to increase the number of times you can bounce the ball and keep it with you without losing control of it. If you have problems keeping the ball with you, practice dribbling in personal space.
- Dribble while jogging easily.

4. Level 1 Dribbling Tricks

- In personal space, explore dribbling the ball once, then letting it bounce once without touching it, then dribbling it once again.
- Dribble once at a medium level, and then push forcefully, trying to make the ball bounce high. Then catch it.

Sample Questions to Ask

- What did you do to dribble successfully?
- Which cue did you think about when you dribbled?
- Why would you want to practice dribbling with both your right and left hands?

SAMPLE LEARNING EXPERIENCES 21.2

Level 1 Dribbling

Dribbling with the Feet or Hockey Stick

1. Explore Dribbling with Different Parts of the Feet While Walking

- Explore dribbling while walking and using different parts of the foot. Which parts did you use?
- Explore using any part of your foot you heard a classmate identify that you didn't try yet. Which part of the foot gave you the most control?
- Try dribbling while walking using the inside and outside of the foot and the laces.
- Intentionally practice with both the dominant and nondominant foot.

2. Dribbling with the Feet While Jogging Easily

- Dribble using the inside of the foot.
- Intentionally practice with both the dominant and nondominant foot.
- Dribble using the inside and outside of the foot and the laces.

3. Dribbling with a Field or Floor Hockey Stick While Walking, Progressing to Jogging Easily

- *Field hockey:* Explore pushing the ball about the space, keeping the flat side of the field hockey stick on the ball. Don't let the ball come off your stick.
- Travel forward, and experiment to find where in relation to your body it is easiest to maintain control of the ball.
- *Floor hockey:* Explore pushing the puck or beanbag while traveling about the space, keeping it close to you, and trying to push it sometimes with one side of the stick and sometimes with the other side.
  - Travel forward, and experiment to find where in relation to your body it is easiest to maintain control of the puck or beanbag.
- *Field and floor hockey:* Dribble while jogging easily.

SAMPLE LEARNING EXPERIENCES 21.2

Level 1 Dribbling (*continued*)

Sample Questions to Ask

- Where in relation to the body is it easiest to control the field hockey ball while jogging? [To the front and slightly to the side of the right foot.] The floor hockey puck? [In front.]
- Which performance cue did you think about while dribbling?
- Which performance cues do you still need to work on to improve?
- Which part of the foot worked best for you? Which part gave you the most control?
- Which is easier for you—dribbling with the inside of the foot, the outside of the foot, or the laces? Why?
- What happens in hockey when the ball gets too close to your feet? [Can't keep it going forward, trip over it, lose it, can't see where you are going.]

Level 2: Tactical Game Skills

Principles of Teaching Level 2 Dribbling

In level 2, you work to transform fundamental skills into tactical game skills. The focus is still on children learning to control the ball, but now dribbling is practiced as an open skill. The contexts vary, and children learn to adapt their movement patterns in a variety of ways.

We organize level 2 dribbling into three progressive levels: 2A, 2B, and 2C. Most learning experiences at each level can be modified for dribbling with the hands, feet, and hockey sticks.

In level 2A, children explore and practice content derived from the body, space, effort, and relationship aspects of the Laban framework in relation to cones, hoops, or other obstacles. These tasks include the following:

- Dribbling on different pathways (straight, curved, and zigzag)
- Dribbling while accelerating and stopping
- Dribbling while changing directions
- Dribbling at different speeds
- Dribbling (with the hands) while varying the level from low to medium
- Dribbling (with the hands) in different body positions and with the ball in different relationships under and around the body and body parts

In level 2B, you teach children how to combine dribbling with shooting and with passing and receiving. You continue to have children vary dribbling by using movement concepts from the Laban framework.

In level 2C, you begin giving children opportunities to use their developing tactical game skills and tactics in game-like practice situations against defenders. Because the children's tactical skills are still developing, you control the intensity level of the defense.

Invasion game tactical content is predominantly approached from the relationship aspect of the Laban framework, albeit blended with content from the other three aspects: body, space, and effort. For example, players on both the defense and the offense move *in relation* to each other's movements and will, while dribbling, have to change directions and speeds—the dribbler to fake out and drive by the defender, and the defender to stop the dribbler from getting by.

A "Double Dribble" Is Not an Error with Young Children

Research shows that when children are first learning to dribble at a fast speed and while making a sharp, angular change in pathway with a crossover dribble, they sometimes use their nondribbling hand to assist in keeping control of the ball (Chen et al., 2003). This behavior is part of the learning process and is the same as spotting in gymnastics or using a kickboard or flotation support when learning to swim—that is, touching the ball with the nondribbling hand, which is technically **a double dribble**, is a temporary scaffold that children will not use once they have mastered the skill. This scaffold allows them to work at a more advanced level while learning the movement pattern with a temporary assist. Consequently, we recommend not calling double dribble as a violation for children who are developing their dribbling skills, as this can slow down the developmental process.

Challenge Courses

Challenge courses are an important task we use frequently in level 2 dribbling lessons and units. With this task, children design an obstacle course or center that challenges them to vary the basic skill and improve performance techniques. Obstacles can represent defenders. After children's skills have improved, you can add defenders to their challenge courses playing at intensity levels 2 to 4. In brief, the levels of defensive intensity are as follows:

- *Level 1: Feet still, arms still.* The defender remains still and in place.
- *Level 2: Feet still, arms move.* The defender can wave her or his arms but must remain in place.
- *Level 3: Feet move, can't touch the ball.* The defender can apply pressure, jump up and down, wave hands, and travel with the offensive player but can't use her or his hands, feet, or hockey stick to touch the ball. We often call this a "pest" defender.

SKILLS BOX 21.1

The Performance Technique of Looking Up While Dribbling with the Hands

In level 2, when children can control the ball most of the time, we add the performance technique of looking up, which is necessary for dribbling in a variety of ways. Dribbling without looking at the ball is the performance technique that takes the most time to develop. Consequently, you must work on looking up while dribbling across several years of the physical education program. In a study of 105 third-graders dribbling, researchers noted that the children rarely looked up. As constraints theory predicts, the children looked up only immediately after the teacher said, "Look up," or when the task constraints elicited looking up (Chen et al., 2003). The tasks that were used for this purpose included the following:

- Dribbling fast (Children were worried about where they were going.)
- Dribbling in a crowd (Children needed to see where classmates were moving.)
- Dribbling with one hand while doing a skill with the other hand such as tossing a ball, which they needed to see
- Dribbling while following a leader
- Dribbling when there was a defender

Learning to look up is so difficult that when tasks required children to look up, the other components of the skill regressed to levels that were more immature. Thus, when the children looked up, they slapped the ball more, their palms contacted the ball more, and the height and distance they pushed the ball became more inconsistent, and consequently, they lost control of the ball more often. With plenty of practice, however, this tendency toward regression will disappear.

Tasks that elicit looking up

- *Level 4: Soft guarding or marking.* The defender can move both arms and can travel guarding the offensive player but most of the time allows him or her to make the play successfully.
- *Level 5: Full guarding or marking.* Competitive guarding/marking is used, but with a no-contact rule.

To design challenge courses, children work in groups of one to three, with partners being the most common arrangement (see **Figure 21.5**, **Figure 21.6**, and **Figure 21.7**). One requirement you set is that their challenge courses challenge them to improve their skills. Another requirement is that they cannot stand in line waiting for one child to finish; in other

Figure 21.5 Dribbling challenge center

Figure 21.6 Dribbling challenge course: dodge the basket and dribble over and under the hoops

words, all children should be able to practice on the challenge course at the same time. The second child starts in the middle or as soon as there is space. Before designing challenge courses, children need to have had experiences in varying the body, space, effort, or relationship aspect of dribbling that is the focus of the challenge course.

Tips for Teaching Challenge Courses

We offer two tips for teaching challenge courses. First, we find it helps to list your assigned requirements (e.g., include straight, curved, and angular pathways) on a whiteboard. Thus, the children can see your requirements without having to ask you repeatedly what they need to include in their challenge course.

Second, when you first use challenge courses, you may need to teach relevant thinking and social skills. If you see children are arguing, designing their own challenge course while ignoring their partner, or sitting and thinking rather than having productive discussions, it can help to demonstrate the appropriate thinking and social skills by designing a challenge course while you talk aloud about your thinking.

For example, you might demonstrate with an aide or a child and say, "Keely, the teacher said we could select only six pieces of equipment. What do you want? [Keely responds, 'I want to use three jump ropes.'] Okay. I want to use one hoop and two cones. Is that okay with you? [Keely responds, 'Sure, let's try it.'] What do you want to do first? [Keely responds, 'Let's set the ropes up in a curved pathway.'] Okay. Let's set that up. [Set up ropes together.] Now we need to have a place to dribble straight and on angular pathways. We could use the cones first, end with the hoop, do angular pathways until after the hoop, and then we can dribble straight back to the beginning of the ropes. How does that sound to you? [Keely responds, 'Great. Is this a good place for the cones?'] Yes, and the hoop can go here. [Keely responds, 'Let's try it, and see if it works or if we need to change things.'] Okay. You start, and I will start once you get beyond the ropes."

To extend lessons with child-designed challenge courses, you can have students explain and demonstrate their course to their classmates. Then have the class rotate to try the challenge courses of other groups.

Dribbling Tricks, Following a Leader, and Dribbling Routines

Because dribbling takes many years of practice and instruction before children have mastered the skill, you need to use a variety of developmentally appropriate tasks to maintain motivation. Dribbling tricks, playing follow the leader (see **Figure 21.8**), dribbling in different positions, bouncing the ball under and around the body, and designing group dribbling routines are excellent tasks for doing so. Children today are still familiar with the dribbling routine from *High School Musical*. Moreover, these tasks give children the opportunity to learn to work cooperatively and creatively to design their own tricks and routines.

Figure 21.7 Challenge course dribbling on different pathways

Figure 21.8 Playing follow the leader

Basic Tactics for Dribbling

In levels 2C and 3, you will be teaching tactics for dribbling in game-like situations with defenders (as opposed to using cones as pretend defenders). We begin with protecting the ball by placing your body between the ball and the defender, and avoiding defenders. These tactics are so basic that adults sometimes do not recognize that children need to learn them.

Low-skilled children, in particular, can benefit from instruction on tactics (Mitchell, Oslin, & Griffin, 2006). Children of all skill levels also need to be able to discuss tactics with their teammates and need both a language to do so and knowledge of tactics at a conscious level (Rink, 2010). **Table 21.1** describes the basic dribbling tactics we teach across levels 2 and 3.

Table 21.1 Basic Dribbling Tactics

Taught First and Discussed Throughout Level 2	Taught After Children Begin Level 3 Gameplay
Protect the Ball • Protect the ball by placing your body between the ball and the defender. In hand dribbling, hold the off-ball arm up and keep the ball to your side. In dribbling with the feet, keep the ball to your side or initially turn your back on the defender; this maneuver is called "shielding" in soccer. You will eventually have to turn to dribble toward your goal. Shielding is against the rules of field hockey. ***Avoid Defenders*** • Avoid defenders by changing speeds, directions, and pathways; by stopping quickly and then accelerating; by accelerating and then quickly stopping; and by using body feints to fake out, dodge, and drive by the defender. ***Tactics for Dribbling and Shooting at Soccer- and Hockey-Type Goals*** • The closer you dribble to a wide goal, the more space you have to shoot because the angle on which you can shoot is wider. • The widest angles and, therefore, the largest amount of space for shooting are directly in front of the goal. As you move to the sides, the angle gets narrower. ***Tactics for Defending Soccer- and Hockey-Type Goals*** • As a goalkeeper, the farther you move from the goal toward the shooter to pressure one offensive shooter, the less space the player will have to shoot because you have cut off a lot of space in the angle for shooting. However, if you get too close to dribbling players, they can easily dodge you and have an easy score. Eventually, if they get too close to the goal, you have to commit to blocking the shot or stealing the ball.	***Use Boundaries Tactically (in Dribble Tag–Type Games)*** • Boundaries work like a defender by denying space. • Defenders try to force the offense toward the boundary or trap them in the corner by running at them and cutting off their likely avenue of escape. • Offensive players try to stay away from the boundaries, especially the corners, to avoid being trapped. ***Offensive Player Dribbles to the Goal Until the Defender Commits, then Passes to an Open, Off-the-Ball Teammate*** • If there are no defenders in front of the goal, dribble the ball as close as you can and shoot. If there are one defender and two players on offense, try to dribble the ball as close as you can to the goal as if you're going to shoot. Look like you mean it. Keep the ball until the defense commits to guarding/marking you. Then pass to your teammate who has a free pathway to score. • If you are off the ball, run fast toward the goal, but stay in your own passing lane. Do not get in the way of your teammate or move so close that the defender can defend both of you at the same time. Be prepared to receive the pass and shoot quickly once the defense commits to the dribbler. • Avoid trying to steal the ball from your own teammate. (We know this sounds amusing, but it happens at the elementary school level.) ***Defender Stays on the Goal Side of the Offensive Player Whom the Defender Is Marking/Guarding*** • Stay between the offense and their goal. • Keep a wide body shape to help block their space. • When the offense is dribbling, try to block their pathway. • Try to herd the offense away from the scoring goal. ***Defender Blocks the Dribbler and Tries to Steal the Ball Without Being Dodged by the Dribbler*** • Your first responsibility in games is to block the dribbler's pathway to the goal, thereby slowing the offense down. Immediately run to the dribbler. Steal the ball when the dribbler makes a mistake or does not protect the ball. Don't commit too early to stealing the ball if the dribbler protects it well because the player can then easily drive by you for an easy score. • If the dribbler gets close enough to the goal to score, you must commit and go after the ball, whether it is well protected or not. Your intention is to force the offense to pass and possibly make a mistake. If the dribbler does not pass, try to block the shot. • If two offensive players are playing against one defender, try to stay on the goal side of and pay attention to both the dribbler and the person without the ball, covering both if possible (e.g., if the two offensive players are too close together) until your teammate gets back to guard/mark her or his offensive player. • If you successfully force the pass, try to intercept it; if you can't, shift and guard/mark the new person with the ball. Again, your first responsibility is to slow the offense down, giving your teammates who were beat time to get back to guard/mark free offensive players (at this point, you have traded which player you are assigned to guard/mark). If all else fails and the offense is about to shoot, try to block the shot or steal the ball.

SAMPLE LEARNING EXPERIENCES 21.3

Level 2A: Applying Movement Concepts from the Laban Framework to Vary Skills

Here, we list sample learning experiences for level 2A lessons on dribbling with the hands, feet, or hockey sticks. You can connect these learning experiences to the basic tactics. To help you do so, we describe the connection between the skill as varied, using aspects from the Laban framework, and the tactic. When you make these connections, you help children understand the meaning and relevance of the learning experience and, in turn, their motivation.

1. Dribbling on Different Pathways (Space Aspect)

Making Connections to Tactics: You learn to dribble on zigzag and curved pathways to feint, fake out, dodge, and drive by defenders (relationship aspect) and on straight pathways to allow you to travel fast in open space to score.

A. Everyone has a ball. Dribble in a scattered formation, exploring ways to avoid classmates intentionally.

B. Dribble in a scattered formation, dribbling on different pathways (zigzag, curved, and straight).
- Intentionally dodge classmates using curved and zigzag pathways.
- Starting on the edge of the PE space, plan your pathway, and dribble across the space.
- Dodge cones (pretend defenders) scattered about the space. Use zigzag and curved pathways to dodge the cones and straight pathways when you are open.
- Add cones so the cones are closer together, requiring tighter zigzag and curved pathways.

C. Half the class remains stationary in a scattered formation, dribbling in place (dragging the ball forward and back with hockey sticks); the other half of the class dribbles, feints, dodges, and fakes out stationary players dribbling on different pathways. With hand dribbling, stationary dribblers can reach out and try to touch the ball. The teacher calls for a switch in roles every 30 seconds.

D. Design a challenge course for practicing dodging and driving by pretend defenders (e.g., cones, hoops) using zigzag and curved pathways and dribbling fast on straight pathways.
- Show and teach your challenge courses to your classmates.
- Rotate, and practice at other children's challenge courses.

E. With a partner, design a challenge course with a pathway. The leader dribbles, and the follower tries to pass the leader. Vary the time of the leader's head start so the task is challenging but allows for the follower to sometimes catch up.

Sample Questions to Ask

- Why is it important to be able to dribble on different pathways?
- How did your challenge course help you improve your dribbling?
- Which performance techniques were more important when you dribbled on a straight pathway? [Look up, waist high, push the ball forward.] Which were more important when you dribbled on a zigzag pathway? [Plant foot and make a sharp, angular change of pathway.]
- When you were chasing your partner on your challenge course, which pathway was the most difficult and which was the easiest for you to get closer to the leader?
- Think critically about how you moved around the cones. Were your pathways sharp enough?
- Now that you have done a challenge course for dribbling with the hands and a hockey stick, compare and contrast the movements (or compare and contrast feet versus hockey stick or feet versus hands).

Dribbling on curved and angular pathways to avoid pretend defenders

Dribbling on curved and angular pathways around cones in a more difficult crowded space

(continues)

SAMPLE LEARNING EXPERIENCES 21.3

Level 2A: Applying Movement Concepts from the Laban Framework to Vary Skills (*continued*)

2. Dribbling While Accelerating and Stopping Quickly (Effort Aspect) and Changing Directions (Space Aspect)

Making Connections to Tactics: You learn to dribble while accelerating and stopping, and changing directions to fake out, dodge, and drive by (pretend) defenders (relationship aspect).

A. Dribble and stop on my signal. When dribbling with the feet or hockey sticks, keep the ball close to you so you can stop quickly.

B. In a scattered formation, explore dribbling, stopping, and changing directions avoiding classmates:
   - The scattered cones about the space serve as fake defenders.
   - Practice accelerating in a burst of speed to drive by the cones.

C. Design a challenge course with obstacles for practicing dribbling and stopping quickly, changing directions, and accelerating.

D. Working with partners, play follow the leader, with the whole class dribbling in a scattered formation. Following your partner, try to stop and accelerate as quickly as your partner. Either switch roles on my command or decide on your own a fair way to switch roles.

E. Scatter poly spots about the space. Every child with a ball starts on a poly spot. Children dribble and touch as many spots as they can in 30 seconds while dodging classmates. Count the number of spots. After a brief rest, children repeat the activity while trying to increase their scores.

Sample Questions to Ask

- What makes it easy to stop suddenly?
- Why would you want to stop in a game?
- What did you think about to help you accelerate quickly?
- Compare and contrast stopping when you are dribbling slowly versus quickly.
- Think back to your challenge course to practice accelerating and stopping quickly in hand dribbling. How do you think that will compare or contrast to hockey dribbling (or dribbling with feet)?
- When you increased your score dribbling from poly spot to poly spot, what did you do that helped you improve? [Moved faster, kept control of the ball with light taps instead of kicking and chasing after it.]

3. Dribbling at Different Speeds (Effort Aspect)

Making Connections to Tactics: You learn to dribble fast to drive to score, dribble while changing speeds, and accelerate as a feint to fake out and drive past defenders (relationship aspect).

A. Practice dribbling traveling fast in open space. Explore dribbling straight in open space, traveling as fast as they can without losing control of the ball and while using the laces or hockey stick to push the ball forward on a straight pathway (i.e., a loose dribble).

B. Dribble at different speeds in scattered formation while avoiding classmates:
   - Change speed on my command.
   - Decide on your own when to change speed.

C. With a partner, design a challenge course and designate certain sets of obstacles for changing speeds and dribbling at fast, medium, and slow speeds.
   - Show and teach your challenge courses to your classmates.
   - Rotate, and practice at other children's challenge courses.

D. Red light, yellow light, green light: Dribble while looking up at the teacher. When I hold up a green card, dribble fast. A yellow card means dribble slowly, and a red card means dribble in place.

Sample Questions to Ask

- Why would you want to change speeds in a game?
- Compare and contrast how you push the ball while dribbling with the hand at different speeds. [The faster you go, the farther in front you need to push the ball.]

4. Hand Dribbling Varying the Level (Low and Medium) (Space Aspect) and Dribbling Over, Under, and On Obstacles (Relationship Aspect)

Making Connections to Tactics: You learn to change dribbling levels from medium to low to protect the ball from defenders (relationship aspect).

SAMPLE LEARNING EXPERIENCES 21.3

Level 2A: Applying Movement Concepts from the Laban Framework to Vary Skills (*continued*)

A. Explore dribbling at low and medium levels. Bounce the ball faster at low levels:
- In place
- While traveling
- Traveling on different pathways
- While following a leader

B. Dribble while traveling over, on, and under obstacles:
- Over low and medium hurdles, cones, jump ropes hung between cones, and so on
- Walking and/or dribbling the ball on wide balance beams, a series of aerobic steps, large ropes, and so on
- Under broken hoops with each end stuck in large cones forming an arch, high hurdles, and so on

C. Explore dribbling at low levels:
- Around your feet, dribbling the ball on different pathways
- Changing to kneeling, sitting, and lying down
- At very low levels

D. Dribble around cones, dribbling low when near the cones to protect the ball from the pretend defender and at medium levels when open.

E. Design a challenge course for dribbling under, over, around, and on obstacles (e.g., balance beams, broken hoop placed in two large cones, hoops, jump ropes, boxes, cones, low hurdles).
- Show and teach your challenge course to your classmates.
- Classmates rotate and practice at other children's challenge courses.

5. Hand Dribbling Tricks for Eliciting Looking Up (Body Aspect) (see Skills Box 21.1)

A. Challenging centers and dribbling tricks:
- Dribble with one hand, and toss and catch a small ball with the other hand.
- Dribble two balls at once.
- Dribble with one hand, and bounce and catch a small ball with the other hand.
- Dribble with eyes closed.
- Dribble with one hand as you pick up and carry beanbags balanced on cones to other cones.
- Dribble with one hand as you toss another ball to the wall and catch the rebound.
- Dribble while walking on a low beam.

Sample Questions to Ask

- Which dribbling technique did you select to work on to improve?
- When did you have the most trouble controlling the ball?
- What is the best part of your challenge course?

6. Dribbling Tricks Following a Leader and Dribbling Routines

A. "Challenge me:" Dribbling tricks following a leader, dribbling in different body positions with the ball in different relationships under and around the body and body parts. Explore different dribbling tricks, such as dribbling under the legs, under one leg, around the body, behind the back, and in front with a crossover dribble, while changing body positions (e.g., kneeling, lying down) and at very low levels. Invent your own dribbling tricks. With your assigned partner, play "Challenge me." One partner is the leader, who does a series of different dribbling tricks; the other partner follows the leader. Switch roles every minute, and switch partners after three or four turns. When you are leader, do dribbling movements that challenge your partner but that your partner can succeed in doing.

B. Design a sequence of dribbling tricks.

C. Design a partner or small group dribbling routine: *High School Musical*. In groups of two or three. Have you seen *High School Musical*, and do you remember the dribbling routine? Design your own dribbling routine. Suggestions for scaffolding the design process or a list from which students select at least three elements:
- Dribbling in unison
- Changing formations
- Trick dribbling actions (discussed previously)

(*continues*)

SAMPLE LEARNING EXPERIENCES 21.3

Level 2A: Applying Movement Concepts from the Laban Framework to Vary Skills (*continued*)

- Dribbling while traveling and exchanging balls by passing, rolling, or putting the ball on the ground
- Having some children dribble two balls at once while their other group members do different locomotor actions

Sample Questions to Ask

- When following the leader, should you do tricks that are too difficult for your partner? [No.] Why not?
- Which dribbling tricks did you both like the most?
- What are different formations you can use for your dribbling routine?
- Which parts of your dribbling routine did you like the most, and why?

SAMPLE LEARNING EXPERIENCES 21.4

Level 2B: Combining Dribbling, Shooting, Passing, and Receiving

In level 2B, we teach children how to combine dribbling and shooting. In dribbling with the feet or hockey sticks, this combination is easier: The child simply kicks or pushes the ball with more force while aiming at a target.

Combining dribbling and shooting with the hands is more difficult because the child must take the ball from dribbling at a low or medium level to a high-level shooting position. Simultaneously, the child must stop running, get in a stable position, and shoot or continue running, get airborne, and shoot like in a layup shot. We suggest you teach combining dribbling and shooting first and then add passing and receiving.

1. Combining Dribbling and Shooting with the Feet or Hockey Sticks

A. Dribble straight, and then kick or push pass at a hula hoop target on a fence or wall.

B. Explore shooting at different targets, such as knocking down pins, hitting a line of cones placed in side-by-side positions, and shooting between cones.

C. [Set up at least 15 different targets around the physical education space.] Dribble across the space on different pathways, changing directions to dodge classmates, and then shoot at a target. Retrieve your ball, and then dribble and shoot at a different target. Continue until you have shot at each target.

2. Combining Dribbling and Shooting with the Hands

A. Try dribbling to the basket and shooting. Work on making a smooth transition between dribbling and shooting without slowing down your momentum.

B. Experiment shooting with and without the use of the backboard.

C. Shoot with left and right hands.

D. Shoot from different locations on the sides and in the center.

E. Stop the dribble farther from the basket, and shoot from different distances.

3. Combining Dribbling and Shooting While Changing Speeds, Pathways, and Directions

A. Set up several cones (pretend defenders) at different distances from the basketball/soccer/hockey goal. Starting about 20 feet away from one cone, dribble toward the goal, pull up when hand dribbling or dodge the cone when dribbling with feet or hockey stick, and shoot before the pretend defender can reach the ball. Repeat at each cone.

B. Design a challenge course in which you dribble fast while changing speeds, pathways, and directions to get around several obstacles. End by shooting at a target (e.g., basketball hoop, cone, bowling pin, hula hoop). Vary the way you feint and drive by each pretend defender.

4. Receiving Lead Passes and Shooting with the Feet or Hockey Sticks

A. Set up 10 to 12 goals per 25 children using cones (e.g., two red, two yellow, two purple). With a partner, decide which color goal to dribble and pass to and at which to shoot. Dribble and send lead passes back and forth. When you get to the cones, shoot. Then decide which color goal to shoot at next.

5. Combining Passing, Receiving, Pivoting, and Shooting

A. The partner dribbles and passes the ball to the shooter, who has her or his back to the basket or goal. The shooter catches or receives the ball with the feet, pivots to the basket/goal, and shoots. When the pair is using hockey sticks, the shooter receives the ball while facing the goal, controls it, and shoots. The shooter gets the rebound and dribbles back, and the partners switch roles.

SAMPLE LEARNING EXPERIENCES 21.4

Level 2B: Combining Dribbling, Shooting, Passing, and Receiving (*continued*)

6. Combining Dribbling, Passing, and Shooting

A. Set up 10 to 12 youth basketball hoops per 25 children. With a partner, dribble toward a basketball hoop; just before you get to the hoop, send a lead pass to your partner, who takes one step and shoots. Change roles, and select a different hoop.

Sample Questions to Ask

- Did anyone think about a dribbling performance technique when you were playing? If so, what was it?
- Why is keeping the ball close to you important when dribbling with the feet or hockey stick?
- What helped you combine hand dribbling with shooting at a basket to make your action smooth and continuous?
- What did you think about just before you changed from dribbling to shooting at the soccer/hockey goal?
- We are going to do the same dribbling task as last class, but today we will be dribbling and shooting with the hands rather than the feet. What do you think is going to be different?

SAMPLE LEARNING EXPERIENCES 21.5

Level 2C: Using Tactical Game Skills in Game-like Situations

Although across level 2, children have been practicing against cones as pretend defenders, once they can combine skills, they are ready to work specifically on the level 2 basic tactics (see **Table 21.1**). We begin with cones and then add human defenders. The focus of these learning experiences is to improve tactical dribbling skills and tactics for protecting the ball. When dribbling with the hands, it is important to put your body between the defender and the ball, dribbling to the side. Likewise, when dribbling with the feet, it is important to shield the ball against defenders by putting your body between the defender and the ball, and turning your side and back to the defender. Although defense is not the focus on the 1v1 learning experiences described here, you should teach the defenders to stay on the goal side of the dribbler, trying to contain the dribbler by blocking the dribbler's pathway to the goal, thereby slowing the offense down.

1. Dribbling While Protecting the Ball Against Pretend Defenders

A. Children dribble by cones or hoops that serve as pretend defenders, all the while protecting the ball. The class dribbles in a scattered formation, first with cones spread apart and then after adding cones so the cones are closer together. With hand dribbling, when children get to a cone, they should use a crossover dribble so the ball remains protected.

B. Half of the class does not have a ball, but rather stands with one foot touching a cone and plays level 2 defense (waving hands with hand dribbling and reaching out with the feet or the stick with soccer or hockey dribbling, but not stealing the ball). Dribblers concentrate on getting into a **"ball, me, defender" position** (where a dribbler puts him- or her body between the ball and the defender) to shield the ball. You can then allow the defenders to try to touch the ball. Finally, with dribbling with the hands or feet, you can have the defenders continue to dribble their own ball in place and also try to touch the ball of the dribblers. Rotate roles every 30 seconds.

2. Dribbling Changing Speeds, Directions, and Pathways to Avoid Pretend Defenders

A. Children design a challenge course for dribbling while changing speeds, directions, and pathways to avoid cones that serve as pretend defenders. Add one human defender to increase the difficulty level. Children choose a level of defense that challenges them but also allows them to succeed. They decide whether the defender will be allowed only to guard/mark the offensive player at the end (attempting to block the goal) or whether the defender is allowed to challenge the offensive player in the middle or throughout the entire challenge course.

3. Dribbling 1v1 Protecting the Ball Against a Level 3 "Pest" Defender

A. Children play 1v1 in a 20-foot-by-30-foot space for controlling the ball with the feet or hockey sticks, and in a 10-foot-by-20-foot space for dribbling with hands, with one defender and one dribbler starting at their own endlines. The offense tries to dribble to the opposite line, while the defender runs to the offensive player and tries to contain the dribbler by blocking the pathway to the goal. The defender can't touch the ball. The dribbler must feint and drive by the defender by changing speeds, directions, and pathways. Children switch roles when the offensive player dribbles over the endline.
   - Rotate so that all children get the chance to play against as many different partners as is reasonable during the time for the lesson.
   - Progress to level 4 defense (i.e., soft guarding/marking, allowing the offense to succeed most of the time). The defense tries to contain the dribbler and steal the ball when the dribbler does not protect the ball well.
   - Have a class discussion without sharing names on what the students learned by playing against different opponents.

(*continues*)

SAMPLE LEARNING EXPERIENCES 21.5

Level 2C: Using Tactical Game Skills in Game-like Situations (*continued*)

B. Children play 1v1 while staying close to a poly spot (within four to five feet) for one minute with a level 3 pest defender/peer coach (who does not touch the ball). The pest defender tells the dribbler when he or she needs to shield or protect better by calling out "shield" or "protect."

C. Children play 1v1 while staying close to a poly spot with a level 3 defender (can move feet but cannot use hands) and then a level 4 defender (soft marking/guarding) and peer coaching. When playing at level 4, count how many times the defender can touch the ball in one minute. Alternate roles after one minute (the teacher keeps track of the time).
- Have a peer coaching discussion, telling your partner how to improve.
- Rotate so that all children get the chance to play against as many different partners as is reasonable during the time for the lesson.
- Have a class discussion without sharing names on what the students learned.

4. Dribbling Focusing on Protecting the Ball and Avoiding Multiple Level 4 Defenders

A. Children dribble while focusing on protecting the ball and avoiding the defenders. Use five or six different colored balls, evenly distributed among the children. Have the children with, for example, the yellow balls put their balls on the side; they then have 30 seconds to try to touch as many balls of dribblers as they can with their hands, feet, or sticks (whichever is appropriate). Then switch so children with a different color ball become defenders. Continue until children with all colors have had a chance to be defenders.

Sample Questions to Ask

- How does changing the pathway and direction of the ball help you avoid the defender?
- How does changing speeds help you get around a defender?
- What was the dribbler doing when the defender successfully touched the ball?
- When you prevented the defender from touching the ball, which tactic did you use?
- Did you use the same tactics every time? If not, which other tactics did you use?
- How does changing hands help you avoid the defender?
- In playing 1v1, did you have to adjust your level of defense, and if so, why?
- Without using names, compare and contrast the different people you challenged today. Describe what they did.
- Without using names, describe someone who was easy to defend and easy to get by on offense. What did that person do?
- Without using names, describe someone who was hard to defend and hard to get by on offense. What did that person do?
- What feels different when you dribble without a defender versus a level 3 pest defender?
- What did you feel and do differently on offense with a level 4 defender?
- Last class we practiced 1v1 dribbling with the feet. Today we will practice 1v1 dribbling with hockey sticks. Predict what changes, if any, you will have to make in your tactics.

1v1 dribbling

SAMPLE LEARNING EXPERIENCES 21.5

Level 2C: Using Tactical Game Skills in Game-like Situations (*continued*)

5. Shooting at and Defending Soccer- and Hockey-Type Goals

A. Children shoot against a goalkeeper, while exploring the relationship of the goalkeeper's distance to the shooter and the amount of space available for shooting (for soccer- and hockey-type shooting). Experiment by having one shooter play against a goalkeeper while varying the distance between the goalkeeper and the shooter. Shoot from a stationary position about 15 feet in front of a 10-foot-wide goal. The keeper starts by standing on the goal line and then moves a step closer to the shooter after each shot, until the keeper is about three feet from the shooter. Then the shooter and keeper switch roles. Shooters should aim for the low corners of the goal.

B. Children dribble and shoot against a goalkeeper, while exploring the amount of space for shooting at different angles. Play 1v1, with the offensive player dribbling in a 30-foot-by-30-foot space and shooting from various positions. Experiment to learn the amount of shooting space available at different angles. Keepers move to the appropriate spot to block as much of the goal as possible from shots taken at different angles. Switch roles, and then discuss with your partners what you learned. Come up with a principle describing the ease of shooting from different angles and blocking shots from different angles.

Sample Questions to Ask

- How does the position of the foot or stick affect the direction of the ball when you are shooting?
- Why should the goalkeeper not stand on the endline?
- What happens when the goalkeeper moves toward the dribbler?
- How does your angle affect the amount of space you have to score?
- In which location do you have the most space for your shot? In which do you have the least amount of space?

6. Dribbling, Passing, and Shooting 2v1 Against a Level 3 Pest Defender

A. One offensive player dribbles the ball toward the goal. The other offensive player runs in a passing lane toward the basket but is not so close to the dribbler that the defender can guard both offensive players. The dribbler dribbles to the goal until the defender commits to trying to touch the ball. Just before the defense closes in, the dribbler passes the ball to his or her open, off-the-ball teammate, who tries to dribble and shoot. The defender stays goal side of the dribbler, contains the dribbler, and tries to touch the ball without committing too early. The children rotate roles and give each other feedback on how to improve.

Level 3: Learning to Use Tactical Game Skills and Tactics in Modified Dribbling Games

Dribbling games include 1v1 dribbling games in which the defender simply tries to touch the ball and then to steal the ball. We progress to 1v1 dribbling and shooting at goals, dribble tag, and dribble team games. Once children have experience in level 3 dribbling games, they are ready to learn more advanced tactics for making decisions on when to dribble, pass, and shoot to beat a defender.

Dribbling games are excellent opportunities for having children design games and, in turn, learn about game structures, such as boundaries, rules, and scoring systems, and the ways that game structures affect game tactics. Child-designed games also give children a voice in the games they play and expand the opportunities to teach cooperative group work and social responsibility.

We begin teaching level 3 dribbling games with a unit on teaching children about game structures, ways to design dribbling games, and the related basic tactics. You can also teach children to design games using tag, which allows children to focus on game design and tactics without having to deal with ball control. Typically, we teach this unit in grade 3. If the children have not learned how to design games, you can teach this unit in grades 4, 5, or 6.

We divide the dribbling unit into four parts: (1) designing boundaries and tactics for protecting the ball, avoiding defenders, and boundaries in 1v1 games; (2) designing scoring goals and scoring systems and the related tactics for 1v1 games; (3) designing small-sided team dribbling games and the related tactics; and (4) designing dribbling and passing games and the related tactics. If you teach the tag unit first, you can begin the dribbling unit with part 2. Each part can take one or more lessons, depending on the children's dribbling capabilities, level of self- and social responsibility, and the length of your lessons. Parts 3 and 4 may consist of three or four lessons each, depending on whether you want children to teach their games to classmates.

You may need to devote class time to teaching children how to work cooperatively and productively with a partner. These are excellent units for prompting class discussions on responsible behavior in games.

SAMPLE LEARNING EXPERIENCES 21.6

Level 3: Designing Boundaries, Tactics for Boundaries, and Protecting the Ball

These learning experiences focus first on understanding the impact of boundaries on games by learning how to design perfect-sized boundaries. Next we focus on tactics for using boundaries on defense and protecting the ball.

1. Experimenting with Boundaries that Are Too Wide and Too Narrow

A. Go with your assigned partner. Get one ball, one hoop, and eight saucer cones (or jump ropes) for boundaries. Set the endlines about 20 feet apart. The dribbler dribbles from one endline to the other, attempting to get by the defender, who must keep at least one foot in a hula hoop set in the middle. Experiment first with side boundaries that are wide, with at least two yards between the edge of the hoop and the sideline.

B. Now experiment with side boundaries that are too narrow, with less than one yard between the hoop and the sideline.

Sample Questions to Ask

- What was the problem with boundaries that were too large? [Defense could never get the ball. It was boring, not challenging.]
- What was the problem with boundaries that were too small? [Offense could not pass the defense without going out of bounds because the defender blocked all the space. It wasn't fair. Offense started to foul to get by the defender.]
- Summarize what you learned about how the boundaries affect offense and defense. [Boundaries that are too large favor the offense; boundaries that are too small favor the defense.]
- How would you describe perfect boundaries? [Boundaries that challenge and give a fair, equal chance to both offense and defense.]

2. Designing Perfect Boundaries and Related Rules

A. Experiment to find perfect-sized boundaries for you and your partner to have a good game.

B. Design rules and consequences for fouling, going out of bounds, and change of possession. You must include a no-contact rule.

C. Repeat the play–discuss–play cycle until you have a good game.

Sample Questions to Ask About Game Structures

- What problems are you having with your game?
- How can you make your game better?
- What did you decide about changing possession?
- Did both of you have a fair and equal chance to play offense and defense?

3. Tactics to Protect the Ball and Use Boundaries to Constrain the Offense

A. Play your game, and pay attention to how you can use boundaries when you are on defense. Also pay attention to how to protect the ball.

Sample Questions to Ask About Tactics

- How did you protect the ball? [I put my body between the ball and the defender.]
- Which tactics did you use on offense? On defense?
- Which tactics did you use when you were near the boundaries on defense and offense? [Tried to contain the dribbler near the boundary; tried to avoid the boundary when I had the ball.]
- After you played for a few minutes, how did you make adjustments to your opponent's ability to play offense or defense?
- How did you avoid the defender? [Changed pathways, speeds, went in other direction, faked him or her out.]

B. Then help your partner improve by discussing which tactics worked and which didn't work.

SAMPLE LEARNING EXPERIENCES 21.7

Designing a Scoring System, Rules, and Consequences for Breaking Rules

1. Play "partner knock-out."

Both of you dribble, and at the same time try to tap your partner's ball out of bounds. Using the play–discuss–play cycle, decide on perfect-sized boundaries, rules, consequences for going out of bounds and breaking the no-contact rule, and a scoring system. You must include a no-contact rule. Decide whether you want to keep track of the score.

2. Once you have a good game, peer-coach each other.

Discuss which dribbling and boundary tactics worked and how each of you can improve your tactics.

3. Share with the class how and when to tap the ball away with hands.

Sample Questions to Ask About Tactics

- How did you avoid contact when you tapped the ball away from your partner? [Put my body between my partner and my ball.]
- How and when should you tap the ball away with your hand? [When I can touch the ball without touching my partner; when my partner doesn't protect the ball.]
- Which body actions did you use to control your own ball while you tapped your partner's ball? [Stayed low, held nondribbling hand up, dribbled to the side away from my partner, changed hands, kept changing positions.]
- What are some hints for helping someone protect their ball?

Sample Question to Ask About Social Responsibility

- How can a person ruin a game? [Grabbing, running with the ball, not honoring a call.]

SAMPLE LEARNING EXPERIENCES 21.8

Designing and Playing 1v1 Games with One or More Scoring Goals and Tactics for Defending and Scoring Goals

These learning experiences are designed for grades 4 and 5, assuming the children have mastered the content in **Sample Learning Experiences 21.6** and **21.7**.

Using the play–discuss–play cycle,

1. Design a 1v1 game

In this game, you score goals by dribbling into or through a scoring goal or goals.

A. Experiment with different types and sizes of scoring goals.
B. Decide how many hoops, cones, poly spots, or other items to use as scoring goals and where to locate the goals.
C. Experiment and decide on a scoring system, which can include a different number of points for different goals, and decide whether you want to play a cooperative game or a competitive game. Decide whether you want to keep score.
D. Decide whether you want to use two balls (both partners dribbling at once) or one ball.
E. Set up a perfect-sized square boundary.
F. Establish rules and consequences for breaking those rules. You must include a no-contact rule.

2. After you get a good game working, discuss tactics for defending goals and scoring.

Peer coach each other.

3. Rotate Partners

After the children have designed their games and peer-coached one another, rotate partners. Teach your new partner your game. Then design a new game using the best parts of each of your games. [You can rotate partners several times across lessons.]

Sample Questions to Ask About Tactics (in Addition to Previous Questions)

- What were successful defensive tactics? [Getting between my partner and the goal, staying low with head up and a wide shape, watching for when I could tap the ball, trapping the dribbler in the corner.]
- Tell us some ways to successfully score. [Pretend to go in one direction, then quickly change direction and dodge the defender; pretend to go for one goal, and then switch to a different goal.]
- Without using names, compare and contrast how different people used offensive and defensive tactics. What did they do? Then explain how you adjusted your play in response.

(*continues*)

SAMPLE LEARNING EXPERIENCES 21.8

Designing and Playing 1v1 Games with One or More Scoring Goals and Tactics for Defending and Scoring Goals (*continued*)

Sample Questions to Ask About Social Responsibility

- What are some of the problems with refereeing yourselves? [Sometimes other people don't honor a call. It can be hard to referee and play because you need to look at your partner and watch the boundaries. Sometimes things happen quickly, and you are not sure what happened.]
- Have you ever seen professional athletes who foul and then pretend they didn't and argue with the referee? What do you think about that situation? How would you feel in PE if that happened here?
- Is it fun to win if you cheat?

Figure 21.9 Dribbling game

SAMPLE LEARNING EXPERIENCES 21.9

Designing and Playing Team Tag Games and Team Tactics for Defending and Scoring Goals

1. [For grades 4 and 5.] In groups of four, design a dribbling game.

- It can be a dribble tag game or not. If you design a dribble tag game, you can use as many flag-football flags as you want.
- You can use as many balls as you want.
- Experiment with and decide on the number of people on a team (3v1 or 2v2).
- Decide on the number and location of scoring goals (e.g., hoops, poly spots, endlines) and a scoring system.
- Experiment and set perfect-sized boundaries.
- Decide on rules and consequences for breaking rules. You must include a no-contact rule. Make sure your change of possession rule is fair so that everyone gets equal time to play offense and defense.

2. After you have a good game working, discuss tactics.

Sample Questions to Ask About Tactics

(Also see the previous questions. Tactics will depend on the game the children design.)

- What did you do on defense to support other teammates? [We double-teamed, we assigned each of us to guard one person on the other team, and we stayed with that person.]
- What did you do as a team on offense that was successful? [One of us was a decoy so others could score. We blocked for each other. We changed position quickly to fake out the defenders.]

Sample Questions to Ask About Social Responsibility

- What makes a good opponent?
- How do you want opponents to treat you?

SAMPLE LEARNING EXPERIENCES 21.10

Designing and Playing Games Using Dribbling and Passing and Team Tactics for Defending and Scoring Goals and for Intercepting Passes

1. [For grades 4 and 5.] In groups of four, design a game with both dribbling and passing.

- It can be a dribble tag game or not. If you design a dribble tag game, you can use as many flag-football flags as you want.
- You can use as many balls as you want.
- Experiment with and decide on the number of people on a team (3v1 or 2v2).
- Decide on the number and location of scoring goals (e.g., hoops, poly spots, endlines) and a scoring system.
- Experiment and set perfect-sized boundaries.
- Decide on rules and consequences for breaking rules. You must include a no-contact rule. Make sure your change of possession rule is fair so that everyone gets equal time playing offense and defense.

2. After you have a good game working, discuss tactics.

Sample Questions to Ask About Tactics

- What did you do on defense to support other teammates? [We assigned each of us to guard one person on the other team, and we stayed with that person.]
- What did you do as a team on offense that was successful? [We passed when our teammate was free and dribbled when he or she was not free. We worked hard to get free for a pass.]

SKILLS BOX 21.2

Technical Reference Information for Teachers About Dribbling

In this feature box, we describe technical reference information for teachers related to dribbling, including immature movement patterns you are likely to see and descriptions of the mature performance techniques. Reference information is not a list of recommended content to teach, but rather information to inform your observations and decisions about lesson content.

Teachers must know well the content they are teaching and the various ways that children learn it. As a teacher, however, you don't tell children everything you know. Instead, you start by designing tasks and an environment that will elicit or allow for the movement responses you want children to learn. In addition, you limit the amount of information you provide at one time. *Tell children what they need to know, when they need to know it, to improve their levels of performance.* Learning to apply this guideline is important for becoming an effective teacher, as it focuses your teaching on what your children need to learn.

Dribbling with the Hands

Wickstrom (1983) described the following continua from immature to mature patterns of dribbling. These patterns also were reported by Broderick and Newell (1999), Chen et al. (2003), and Deach (1951, cited in Wickstrom, 1983).

Hand and Wrist Component

Immature Movement Patterns

- Slapping the ball, hitting it with the palms
- Extending the fingers upward
- Using excessive wrist action

Mature Movement Patterns

- Riding the ball up and pushing it down
- Contact is with the finger pads, with the fingers spread and curved downward

Consistent Force, Direction, and Positioning of Ball Component

Immature Movement Patterns

- Inconsistent direction of force (e.g., some bounces are chest high and some thigh high; sometimes children push the ball so far in front it takes two bounces before they can run and catch up; sometimes the ball is not pushed far enough in front so they have to catch it behind them)
- Problems judging the timing of the bounce (e.g., sometimes children miss the ball)
- Dribbling the ball directly in front (sometimes kicking it by accident)

Mature Movement Patterns

- Waist high
- Front/side (in front of the body and on the dribbling-hand side)
- Child controls force and direction of the push

Body and Head Position Component

Immature Movement Patterns

- Leaning forward from the hips with the head over the ball
- Knees almost straight

Mature Movement Patterns

- Upright with the knees bent
- Head up, eyes looking at the game situation

(*continues*)

SKILLS BOX 21.2

Technical Reference Information for Teachers About Dribbling (*continued*)

Potential Refinements for Hand Dribbling

Basic Techniques When Children Are at Developmental Level 1

- Push the ball with the finger pads or fingerprints; don't slap the ball.
- Dribble waist high.
- Dribble to the front/side.

More Advanced Techniques When Children Are at Developmental Level 2

- Look up, head up

Immature dribbling pattern

Mature dribbling pattern

Dribbling with the Feet

Immature Movement Patterns

- Kicking the ball too far away using too much force (beyond the child's control)
- On a fast, loose dribble in open space, kicking the ball with the toes (not the laces)
- Kicking only with the dominant foot

Potential Refinements for Dribbling with the Feet Keeping the Ball Close (Such as While Being Defended Closely)

Basic Techniques When Children Are at Developmental Level 1

- Light touch
- Keep it close

More Advanced Techniques When Children Are at Developmental Level 2

- Bend knees for balance.
- Head up when possible.
- Use body feints (frequently change pathways, direction, and speed).

Potential Refinements for Dribbling with the Feet Fast in Open Space

More Advanced Techniques When Children Are at Developmental Level 2

- Use the laces.
- Push the ball ahead, sprint several steps, then push the ball again.
- Head up, look for defenders and receivers.

Dribbling with Hockey Sticks

Immature Movement Patterns

- Gripping the stick like a broom
- Letting the ball get too close to the feet
- Swinging the stick like a golf club rather than pushing the ball or tapping it with a small backswing

Potential Refinements for Dribbling with Hockey Sticks

- Keep the stick on the ground and the stick face low at all times.
- Hands apart
- Push or tap only.
- Knees bent

Mature movement patterns dribbling with floor hockey stick

SKILLS BOX 21.2

Technical Reference Information for Teachers About Dribbling (*continued*)

Level 2: Changing Directions and Pathways While Dribbling with the Hands, Feet, or Hockey Sticks

Dribbling while making a quick, sharp, angular change in direction is a difficult skill. Children may need more help and information on planting the outside foot, bending the knee, leaning in the opposite direction, and pushing off.

Immature Movement Patterns

- Rounding a zigzag pathway, thereby making it curved.
- Maintaining a constant speed rather than doing a burst of acceleration

Mature movement pattern dribbling with the feet on an angular pathway

Crossover Dribble with the Hands

Immature Movement Patterns

- Bouncing the ball with a narrow V rather than a wide V, so the ball does not travel the necessary distance
- Inconsistent force and direction

Crossover dribble

Potential Refinements

- Plant the outside foot to the side and push off.
- Bend your knees and extend forcefully to push off.
- Lean in the direction you want to go.
- For a crossover dribble, start with your dribbling hand out to the side so when you dribble to cross in front of your body, you make a wide V-shaped pathway with the ball.

Dribbling with the Hands Against a Defender (Chen et al., 2003)

Immature Movement Patterns

- Keeping the back toward the defender and dribbling in front of the body. Children may seem to be hovering over the ball to protect it.
- Dribbling only with the dominant hand, turning whichever way is necessary to do so.

Potential Refinements

- Turn your head to watch the defender and watch the action of the game.
- Keep the ball out to the side, and turn your body enough to protect the ball by putting your body between the defender and the ball.

Dribbling with the Feet or Hockey Stick Against a Defender

It is much more difficult to learn to control a ball with the feet or hockey stick than with the hands. Consequently,

(*continues*)

SKILLS BOX 21.2

Technical Reference Information for Teachers About Dribbling (*continued*)

you will need more practice at level 1 and level 2 with a defender who cannot touch the ball. It is also *much easier* to tackle the ball—that is, to steal the ball by poking or kicking it away from the dribbler in soccer- and hockey-type games. Throughout level 2 tasks, you will need to monitor the children carefully and be prepared to limit the intensity of the defense.

Immature Movement Patterns

- Hitting or kicking the ball too hard and, therefore, too far away.
- Changing directions and speeds slowly (rather than explosively). Children may not use body feints.
- Looking down the entire time.
- Remaining upright rather than bending the knees and using fast, small steps to change directions quickly.
- Relying too much on turning the back on the defender.
- When dribbling fast in open space, the dribble becomes kicking or, in hockey, pushing and chasing the ball without maintaining possession.
- When dribbling with the feet, using only the dominant foot and kicking with the toes rather than the laces.

Summary

Although performance techniques for dribbling with the hands, feet, and hockey sticks differ, many of the same movement concepts from the body, space, effort, and relationship aspects of the Laban framework are used to vary and adapt the fundamental dribbling skill so children develop tactical game skills. In addition, the basic tactics are the same or similar across all these sports. Teaching these similarities across dribbling with the hands, feet, and hockey sticks and across game-like situations helps children acquire an in-depth knowledge of games.

Review Questions

1. (a) How can you make performance techniques relevant? (b) Invent a metaphor, story, or image to teach one of the performance techniques for dribbling.
2. What is a challenge course, and why is it valuable?
3. Discuss two tactics for dribbling when on offense, and describe how you might teach them to children.
4. (a) Discuss the defensive tactics for containing the dribbler and trying to steal the ball without committing too early; and (b) describe how you might teach them to children.
5. (a) Describe three ways to vary dribbling by using concepts from the body, space, or effort aspects of the Laban framework; and (b) discuss how those concepts are linked to invasion sports.
6. Describe how to have children explore the relationship of the goalkeeper's distance to the dribbler and the amount of space available for shooting.
7. What are three immature patterns for (a) dribbling with the hands; and (b) dribbling with the feet?

References

Broderick, M. P., & Newell, K. M. (1999). Coordination patterns in ball bouncing as a function of skill. *Journal of Motor Behavior, 31*, 165–188.

Chen, W., Rovegno, I., Todorovich, J., & Babiarz, M. (2003). Third grade children's movement responses to dribbling tasks presented by accomplished teachers. *Journal of Teaching in Physical Education, 22*(4), 450–466.

Deach, D. F. (1951). Genetic development of motor skills of children two through six years of age. *Dissertation Abstracts, 11*(1), 287–288.

Mitchell, S. A., Oslin, J. L., & Griffin, L. L. (2006). *Teaching sport concepts and skills: A tactical games approach* (2nd ed.). Champaign, IL: Human Kinetics.

Rink, J. (2010). TGfU: Celebrations and cautions. In J. I. Butler & L. L. Griffin (Eds.), *More teaching games for understanding: Moving globally* (pp. 33–47). Champaign, IL: Human Kinetics.

Rink, J. E. (2014). *Teaching physical education for learning* (7th ed.). New York: McGraw-Hill.

Rovegno, I., Nevett, M., Brock, S., & Babiarz, M. (2001). Teaching and learning basic invasion game tactics in fourth grade: A descriptive study from situated and constraints theoretical perspectives. *Journal of Teaching in Physical Education, 20*, 370–388.

Thorpe, R., & Bunker, D. (2010). Preface. In J. I. Butler & L. L. Griffin (Eds.), *More teaching games for understanding: Moving globally* (pp. xi–xv). Champaign, IL: Human Kinetics.

Wickstrom, R. L. (1983). *Fundamental motor patterns* (3rd ed.). Philadelphia: Lea & Febiger.

FYI

Summary of Task Label Abbreviations

I	Informing tasks
E	Extending/exploring tasks
R	Refinements
A	Application/assessment tasks
Org	Organizing task
Cog K	Cognitive knowledge: Explains or defines a concept
Social	Social skill or concept
Th	Thinking skill
Mot	Motivation concept
Safety	Safety information or reminder
MD	Modification to make the task more difficult
ME	Modification to make the task easier

Source: Adapted and Modified from Rink, J. E. (2014). *Teaching physical education for learning* (7th ed.).New York: McGraw-Hill.

Sample Plans for Levels 1 and 2 Dribbling

In this section, we annotate plans to help you understand and imagine what the content discussed in this chapter might look like in an actual teaching environment. We include objectives, observation plans, and potential interactive decisions about skill and tactic refinements and teaching social responsibility and thinking skills. Of course, we cannot predict which of these elements you will need to teach. As you read the tasks and potential decisions, think about what is happening in the lesson, imagine you are the teacher, and consider how you might respond.

The annotated plans also illustrate the practice of asking questions as an instructional technique. Here, we illustrate how to give feedback in the form of a question, including discussion-starter questions that assume children always know something about the topic you are about to teach (this is particularly true in elementary physical education where we teach skills that take years of practice to master), questions that check for understanding, and questions that extend children's thinking and knowledge. Brackets enclose answers based on actual answers we have gotten from children who have worked in learning environments in which teachers ask questions and expect children to think about what they are learning during lessons. These answers give you an idea about what sort of task engagement and learning outcomes we are seeking.

We also include refining content for motor objectives based on our experiences teaching these lessons. This refining content will need to change based on the developmental levels of the children you teach.

To make interactive decisions, you must observe the children's responses. First, consider whether the task or environmental constraints are yielding the responses you want. If they are not, think about how you might change the task or environment. Then, decide whether the children need to perform refining tasks or learn new information.

SAMPLE PLAN 21.1

Level 1: Dribbling with the Feet

<table>
<tr><th>Level 1 Dribbling with the Feet</th><th>Notes and Potential Interactive Teaching Decisions</th></tr>
<tr><td>

Standards

This plan addresses National Standards 1, 2, and 4 and CCSS for vocabulary acquisition and reading.

Objectives

The children will learn

Motor and Cognitive Knowledge

1. To dribble with the feet, keeping the ball close by tapping with light force.
2. To read and remember that cues for dribbling are to tap lightly and keep the ball close.

Social

3. That being socially responsible means watching out for classmates and not bumping into them.

CCSS

4. To identify new meanings for familiar words and apply them accurately.
5. To read with sufficient accuracy and fluency to support comprehension.

</td><td>

Notes: With young children, this set of tasks will take from two to four lessons before they acquire the ability to keep the ball close while traveling at a slow speed.

Equipment: One playground ball per child (or soccer ball, foam ball, or slightly deflated/dead playground ball).

Observation Plan

1. Watch the force of the children's kicking actions first for safety and then to focus on skill development.
2. Scan the entire lesson to see if all the children are scattered and traveling at a safe distance away from one another.

</td></tr>
</table>

(continues)

SAMPLE PLAN 21.1

Level 1: Dribbling with the Feet (*continued*)

Introduction	
CE Sometimes words have two different meanings. Think of the word "boot." You can boot up your computer. What else does the word "boot" mean? [You can put boots on your feet.] In school, sometimes you have your desks in a row. When else can you row? [You can row a boat, or braid rows in your hair.] The word "row" has several meanings. So does the word "rock." What meanings can you identify? [Grandma rocks in a rocking chair, we rock in gymnastics, and you can throw a rock in a lake.] How about the word "bolt"? What happens in a thunderstorm? [Bolts of lightning.] What other meanings can you think of for "bolt"? [Bolt two boards together, bolt by running home fast.] Today we are going to work on a skill that has different meanings. The skill is dribbling. "Dribble" means bouncing a ball with your hand. But it also means kicking a ball with your feet or tapping a ball with a hockey stick. Did you ever put too much milk in your mouth and it dribbled out the corner? Today, we will work on dribbling with your feet.	*Notes:* You can find many opportunities to integrate what you teach in physical education with classroom subjects. This introduction is a simple example of integrating physical education with literacy.
Content Development	
Performance Techniques: Keep the Ball Close and Tap Lightly	
Org Walk over to one of the hula hoops spread around the PE space and pick up a playground ball. Spread out in a scattered formation. **Cog K** I have written two cues for dribbling on the whiteboard. Let's read them aloud together: 1. Keep the ball close; 2. Tap lightly. Think about these cues when you practice dribbling. **E** In your personal space, explore moving the ball on the ground using different parts of your left and right feet while *keeping the ball close to you.* **R** Stop the ball with your foot. What are the cues for dribbling written on the whiteboard? [Keep the ball close; tap lightly.]	**Safety** If children have not been taught about personal and general space at the beginning of the year and how to safely work while traveling in a scattered formation, then you need to teach this content first without a ball.
E If you have been successful keeping the ball close to you, travel at a walking speed in general space and explore tapping the ball using different parts of your foot. If not, stay in your personal space while you explore.	**Social** What did you learn about traveling in a scattered formation at the beginning of the year? [Don't bump into anyone. Stay out of other children's personal space. Watch out for classmates, and change where you are traveling so you don't bump into anyone.] Excellent answers. When you do that, you are showing me you are responsible.
Cog K When I say "Explore," I want you to think creatively and try to find as many different parts of your foot as you can use successfully to move the ball on the ground. Keep dribbling.	**R** What do you need to do to keep the ball close to you? [Tap it only a short distance. Tap it lightly.][If no child says, "Tap it lightly," ask, "Which will work better to keep the ball close—kicking it hard or tapping lightly?"]
Cog K Which parts did you use? [Call on as many children as necessary until they have identified all the parts of their feet that can be used to maneuver the ball.]	

SAMPLE PLAN 21.1

Level 1: Dribbling with the Feet (*continued*)

E Explore again, this time trying to use any part of your foot you heard a classmate identify that you didn't try yet. **E** Explore with both your left and right feet.	**R** Are you thinking about keeping the ball close? **R** If the ball is not staying close to you, what do you think you need to do differently? [Tap it lightly, don't kick it hard.]
Cog K Does anyone know which parts of their foot soccer players use? Yes, in different situations they might use all the parts of their foot. That is one reason why you need to practice moving the ball in different directions with different parts of your foot. You need to be comfortable playing with the ball and making it go where you want.	
Cog K Does anyone know which part of the foot soccer players use most often? The inside of your foot. This is the inside of your foot. [Touch the inside of your foot.] **E** Now try walking about the space using the inside of both your left and right feet to make the ball move forward, but don't let it get far from you. **R** Keep the ball close.	**Social** In physical education, it is important to be responsible and care about your classmates. What is one way to show me you care and are responsible? [By not bumping into anyone, by not kicking anyone else's ball, by not cutting in between someone and their ball.] Excellent answers.
Cog K Anyone know why you want to keep the ball close to you? [So you don't lose the ball, so it doesn't trip anyone else, so you can practice your skills, so when you play games no one can take the ball away from you.]	
R Dribble again, and remember the cue to keep the ball close. **E** This time, you can increase your speed as long as you can keep the ball close. If the ball gets too far away from you, slow down.	**R** Which kind of force is necessary to keep the ball close? [Light force] **R** Are you thinking about the force you are using while you are dribbling?
E Give both your left and right feet the same amount of practice.	**R** Remember from our dance lesson last week that we practiced light and strong force. You know what light force means in dance; now use it with your game skills. Tap the ball with light force.
Social How can I know that you are a responsible person? [I don't bump into anyone.]	
Extending the Content in Later Lessons	
E Dribble about the physical education space at a walking speed or slightly faster, dribbling with the inside of your foot.	**R** Which performance cues should you think about while dribbling? [Keep the ball close, tap with light force.]
E Now, explore dribbling with different parts of your foot again.	
Cog K Which parts of your foot did you use? [Various answers.] Which parts were most difficult for keeping the ball under control? [Various answers.] **E** Experiment to see if you notice which parts of the foot are easier or more difficult to use to control the ball.	

(*continues*)

SAMPLE PLAN 21.1

Level 1: Dribbling with the Feet (*continued*)

Cog K	What did you discover? [Various answers.] [Larger parts are easier, smaller parts like the heel or big toe are harder to use to control the ball.] Can anyone guess why?	**Cog K**	[If you don't have many answers, you can offer the following explanation:] Let's look at this shoe and soccer ball to see if I can help you see why some parts of your foot would give you more control over the soccer ball. [Hold a shoe up and touch it with the toe, then heel, then inside, then laces, then outside.] So what did you notice? [Various responses.] Did you notice that only a very small part of the shoe touched the ball when you kicked with the rounded toe or heel rather than the flat parts like the inside of your shoe? Which do you think will give you more control—the large parts of your feet or the small tip of your shoes?
E	Dribble again, this time increasing your speed. Don't go faster than you can travel while still keeping the ball close to you, but use the larger parts of your foot like the inside, outside, and laces.		

Potential Questions to Bring Closure to These Tasks

1. What did you enjoy the most about dribbling with your feet?
2. What was most challenging?

SAMPLE PLAN 21.2

Level 2A: Dribbling on Different Pathways

Level 2A: Dribbling on Different Pathways	Notes and Potential Interactive Teaching Decisions
Standards This plan addresses National Standard 1, 2, 4 and CCSS listening and collaboration. **Objectives** The children will learn to **Motor and Cognitive** 1. Dribble on straight, curved, and zigzag pathways, making a sharp, angular change on zigzag pathways by planting and pushing off the outside foot. **Thinking** 2. Think critically about their dribbling performance techniques and select one on which to focus. **Social** 3. Work cooperatively with a partner to design a challenge course. **CCSS** 4. Listen carefully to partners' ideas and build on them.	These learning experiences will take from two to four lessons. *Equipment:* For every two children, a minimum of three hoops, four cones, and four jump ropes. **Observation Plan**  1. Scan for safety to be sure children maintain an appropriate distance from peers and do not bump into each other. 2. Watch whether the children are making clear distinctions between straight, curved, and zigzag pathways. 3. Watch whether the children travel on sharp angles when they use zigzag pathways.

SAMPLE PLAN 21.2

Level 2A: Dribbling on Different Pathways (*continued*)

Introductory Activity

Review Performance Techniques

I	For warm-up today, I want you to dribble about general space. As a review, what should you do to dribble skillfully? [Push the ball, use finger pads, dribble to the front and to the hand side, keep my head up so I can look around, dribble waist high.] Excellent. You remembered the performance techniques. As you dribble, monitor and think critically about your performance. Go.	**Cog K**	By "monitor and think critically," I mean I want you to think about what your body is doing and compare your body actions to what skillful dribblers do. For example, ask yourself, "Did I use my finger pads, or did I slap the ball with my palm? Did I keep my head up? Was my wrist firm? Did I dribble to the front and side?"
Th	Now think back on your dribbling and make a decision about the one technique that will most help you to improve.	**R**	Ask several children which performance technique they selected to improve. This will allow you to check for understanding and remind students that they are responsible for self-regulation.
R	Dribble again, and work on improving that one technique. Go.		

Content Development

Dribble on Different Pathways

Cog K	Today we are going to work on dribbling on different pathways. We worked on pathways in dance. What are the different pathways? [Straight, zigzag, curved.]		
E	Explore dribbling on different pathways.		
Cog K	When I say "Explore," it means I want you to try each pathway several times.		
E	Give both right and left hands equal practice.		
Cog K	Stop. Imagine you are in high school and you are playing a basketball game. You get the ball, and no one is between you and the basket. Which pathway do you think would be best to dribble on—straight, curved, or angular—and why? [Straight because I can get to the basket quickly before any defenders can get back and stop me.] When in a basketball game do you think you would dribble on angular and curved pathways? [When I need to get around defenders, so they can't take the ball away from me.]		*Notes:* Making the connection between pathways and tactics helps children understand the reasons why they are learning to dribble on different pathways.
E	Now pretend you are in a basketball game. Sometimes there are no defenders and sometimes there are many defenders. Make a decision about which pathway is best. Practice dribbling on straight pathways and on zigzag and curved pathways around pretend defenders. Don't forget to use both your left and right hands.		
R	As you dribble, try to figure out what you need to do with your body to make a sharp change in pathway.		
Cog K	What did you figure out about what you need to do with your body to make a sharp change on a zigzag pathway? [Change hands, push the ball across my body, bend knees, plant and push off foot, make the angle sharp, shift my weight.] Those are all good suggestions for different performance techniques.	**CCSS**	Write each performance technique on a whiteboard. Children can then refer to the board to assist in making the decision about which technique to practice. Using text as part of your lessons helps children improve reading skills.

(*continues*)

SAMPLE PLAN 21.2

Level 2A: Dribbling on Different Pathways (*continued*)

R Make a decision about the one technique that will most help you to improve, and think about it when you dribble on sharp angular pathways.	**R** Ask several children which performance technique they selected to check for understanding and to reinforce the importance of self-regulation and being self-responsible for learning.
E Now dribble on straight, curved, and zigzag pathways, challenging yourself to dribble as fast as you can without losing control of your ball or body.	**Social** You are responsible for dribbling at a speed that challenges you to do the best that you can, but at the same time is a safe speed for you. **Social** How do you know that your speed is safe? [I don't trip and fall, I don't run into anyone else, I can stop before I hit the wall or another person, I don't lose the ball, my ball doesn't get loose and roll on the floor for others to trip over.] **Th** How do you know when you are challenging yourself? [It is difficult to do the task, but I can do it if I concentrate and try hard.]
Dribbling on Different Pathways Around Obstacles **E** I have scattered hoops about the space. Now dribble on different pathways, and when you come to a hoop, pretend it is a defender. Which type of pathway should you use to get around the defender? [Curved, zigzag.] Right. When you have no defender in front of you and you can travel faster, which pathway do you use? [Straight.] Go.	**R** Select only one performance technique to work on as you dribble while avoiding the pretend defenders. Molly, what are you thinking about? Seneca, what are you thinking about? Great choices. Everyone select her or his own performance technique that you think will help you the most.
E I have added a bunch of cones to the space, so now you have to dodge many more defenders. Go.	**R** Did you make an improvement in your dribbling? What did you do better? Bo, what did you improve? [My angles were sharper.]
Challenge Courses **A** Today we are going to design challenge courses with a partner. Using cones, jump ropes, and hoops, design an obstacle course that challenges you to practice and improve dribbling on different pathways. On the whiteboard is your assignment. It says, "Have some straight, some zigzag, and some curved pathways, and use your right and left hands when you dribble. Use the hoops and cones that are on the floor and the hoops, cones, and jump ropes in the equipment baskets around the physical education space."	**Social** You have worked with partners in physical education and in your classroom. Tell me some of the things you and your partner need to do to work cooperatively together. [Listen to each other; build on each other's ideas, share decisions; don't be bossy; don't do all the work yourself; ask your partner's opinion; cooperate; be sure you both like the challenge course; be sure the course is challenging, but not so hard that your partner can't do it.] *Notes:* When children design challenge courses, sometimes they use too much equipment, and it takes a long time to set up. Depending on your schedule, you can let them experiment and know that they will figure this out given time. If you have limited time, limit the children to no more than 10 pieces of equipment.
E Once you get your initial challenge course designed, figure out how both of you can practice in the course at the same time. There should be no more than a five-second wait before each of you starts the course. We want to be physically active as much as possible. Go. **R** Discuss with your partner whether you need to improve any part of your challenge course. Is any section too difficult for one of you? Is any section too easy? Do you both like all sections? You can edit your challenge course just as you edit sentences in your classroom.	**Social** Are you cooperating with your partner? If not, what can you do to improve the way you are working together? **R** I see some great challenge courses. As you are practicing, critique your performance. Make a decision about one technique to focus on to improve your performance.

SAMPLE PLAN 21.2

Level 2A: Dribbling on Different Pathways (*continued*)

Culminating Activity

A Now that you have your challenge courses perfected, let's share your courses with classmates. [You can have the children share with the whole class or with another pair.] Then we will rotate and you can work on improving dribbling on other pairs' challenge courses.

Th I am so proud of how much work you put into your challenge course and how hard you practiced to improve your dribbling. Everyone can learn skills if they work hard.

Potential Questions to Bring Closure to These Tasks

Cog K and CCSS Talk with your partner about the following questions.

Motor and Cognitive Knowledge

1. How does the pathway affect the speed of dribbling?
2. Make real-life connections and identify where outside of physical education you travel on straight, curved, and zigzag pathways.

Social

1. Give examples of when you considered one of your partner's ideas and changed your idea about the challenge course to make it better for your partner.
2. Give an example of when in the past few days you considered the ideas of others at home or in your classroom.

Tips for Teaching

After the children discuss their ideas, ask several pairs to share their ideas.

Each of these questions addresses one of the CCSS. We suggest selecting only one question per lesson due to time constraints and the need to have children physically active 50% of lesson time.

You can extend the lessons by having children present their challenge courses to the class (another CCSS) and let the children try each other's courses.

SAMPLE PLAN 21.3

Level 2C: Dribbling Protecting the Ball Against a Defender in a 1v1 Situation

Dribbling Protecting the Ball Against a Defender in a 1v1 Situation

Standards

This plan addresses National Standards 1, 2, and 4 and CCSS for comprehension.

Objectives

The children will learn to

Motor and Tactical Knowledge

1. Shield the ball while dribbling against a defender by positioning their body between the defender and the ball.

Social

2. Recognize when their partner needs peer coaching based on a peer assessment checklist and then offer coaching in a supportive way.
3. Know when they are being socially responsible by dribbling close enough to their poly spot to allow their partner an equal opportunity to touch or steal the ball and to avoid infringing on the space of other pairs.

Notes and Potential Interactive Teaching Decisions

Notes: These tasks can take two to three lessons and can be modified easily for dribbling with the feet.

Equipment: One ball per pair, one poly spot to define the playing space for each pair of children.

Teaching Tip: The poly spots, scattered about the gym, define the playing space for each pair of children. Each pair of children must stay within four to five feet of their poly spot. When you scan and see children who are too far from the spot, simply say, "Oops, too far from the dot—give the ball to your partner." The children will quickly learn to recognize when they are dribbling too far away from the poly spots. You can also set up a grid or boundaries for each pair, but this arrangement takes more time and is more difficult to monitor because the children feel free to dribble close to the boundary and, therefore, possibly too close to another pair.

Write the potential refinements on a whiteboard so children can read and remember the appropriate performance techniques.

(*continues*)

SAMPLE PLAN 21.3

Level 2C: Dribbling Protecting the Ball Against a Defender in a 1v1 Situation (*continued*)

CCSS

4. Describe key ideas and details from information presented through text and visual observations of movements.

Potential Refinements

"Ball, me, defender:" Put my body between the ball and the defender.

Content Development

A Today, we are going to play 1v1. One person dribbles. The defender tries to touch the ball, while the dribbler tries to prevent the defender from touching the ball. I will time you and tell you when to switch roles. Go with your assigned partner and get a poly spot. Find enough space for you both to move around the dot without infringing on the space of other groups. The dribbler must stay near the poly spot. Defenders, use level 4 defense (soft guarding/marking; letting your partner succeed most of the time but sometimes touching the ball). Level 4 defense puts pressure on you and helps you learn how to avoid the defender without being overwhelmed.

Observation Plan

Scan for both safety and fairness to see whether all of the children are

1. Staying within four to five feet of their poly spot. Make sure poly spots are scattered far enough away from each other to ensure one pair will not inadvertently bump into another pair.
2. Shielding the ball.
3. Using both their dominant and nondominant hands (or feet if dribbling with the feet).

Cog K Now that you have both had a chance to be the dribbler, discuss what you did to prevent the defender from touching the ball. [Let children discuss this topic briefly and then share ideas with the class.]

Cog K What were some of the things you discussed that the dribbler needed to remember? [Use body to block/shield; "ball, me, defender"; arm out to guard; keep eyes on defender.]

Social Is it fair to dribble far from your poly spot if your partner is about to touch the ball? [No.] That's correct. Be socially responsible and allow your partner a fair chance to touch the ball. Stay about four to five feet from the dot.

R Play again and see if you can use the suggestions of your classmates to improve. [Teacher continues to time how long each child is the dribbler.]

ME Stop. I am going to modify the game. This time, the defender can't touch the ball but instead is a peer coach. Help your partner by calling out, "Shield," or "Protect" when you see you can touch or steal the ball.

MD If you and your partner want, you can count the number of times the defender touches the ball in one minute. Or, you can continue playing without keeping track of the score.

E We are going to modify the game. This time, possession changes when the defender touches the ball or grabs it (hand dribbling) without touching the dribbler.

Social If you are able to steal the ball all the time, then peer-coach your partner by saying "Protect" (or "Shield" when dribbling with the feet), and don't steal the ball.

Org Whoever has the ball now remains in place, and the other partner points to the nearest new partner in a clockwise direction from you. [Gesture showing a clockwise rotation.] See if anyone else is pointing at that partner; if not, then you may rotate.

R Practice protecting the ball playing with your new partner.

SAMPLE PLAN 21.3

Level 2C: Dribbling Protecting the Ball Against a Defender in a 1v1 Situation (*continued*)

R I noticed many of you are protecting (shielding) the ball, but you are dribbling only with your dominant hand.

Cog K Do you think it is important to use both dominant and nondominant hands and why? [I might need to use my nondominant hand because the defender is on the other side; it will give me more moves I can use to protect the ball and get away from defenders.] Try to use both hands equally.

R [Repeat, rotating partners frequently, practicing protecting the ball.]

Teaching Tip: During this practice task with hand dribbling, you will see the developmental pattern for the child who is dribbling to stop, catch the ball, and then start dribbling again. This pattern emerges due to the pressure of having a defender and the need for the child to look up, making ball control harder. Do not call this a double-dribbling violation unless the child is highly skilled and is catching the ball to gain an unneeded advantage. Rather, remember it is a developmental pattern that will improve with practice. Simply encourage children to try to dribble continuously with one hand.

Culminating Activity

A Peer/Self-Assessment

Discuss with your partner how each of you protected the ball and the extent to which you used your dominant and nondominant hand/foot. Then put a check mark in the appropriate line for each.

Name: ____________________

Protected the ball:

_____ Always

_____ Most of the time

_____ Sometimes

_____ Rarely

Used dominant and nondominant hand/foot:

_____ Equally

_____ Mostly used dominant hand/foot

_____ Exclusively used dominant hand/foot

Potential Questions to Bring Closure to These Tasks

Did anyone defend against someone who made it difficult to touch the ball? Tell us what they did. [Call on many children.]

What did good defenders do? [Call on many children.]

How did your thinking change when you played against a good defender?

CHAPTER

22

Net/Wall Games: Skills, Tactics, and Modified Games: Levels 1, 2, and 3

PRE-READING REFLECTION

1. Make a list of all of the net, wall, and striking games, recreational activities, and fun challenge tasks (e.g., hacky sack) that you can think of.
2. Think of one performance technique that would apply across two or more striking skills.
3. Think of one tactic that would apply across more than two net/wall games.

OBJECTIVES

Students will learn:

1. Net/wall units focus on teaching children to strike a variety of balls with a variety of body parts and rackets over low nets, over high nets (five to six feet), and to a wall.
2. You can progressively increase the difficulty of the equipment with younger children by using larger, lighter balls and rackets and with older children by using junior-sized rackets and trainer balls.
3. Teaching children to rally successfully is critical for teaching net/wall skills and tactics.
4. For successful rallies and games, you must differentiate instruction by providing children with a choice of different balls, rackets, net heights, boundary sizes, and rules.

KEY TERMS

Central ready position

Open space

CONNECTION TO STANDARDS

1. This chapter addresses National Standard 1 for demonstrating competence in a variety of motor skills, National Standard 2 for applying knowledge of strategies and tactics, National Standard 4 for exhibiting personal and social responsibility, and National Standard 5 for recognizing the value of physical activity for enjoyment and challenge.
2. This chapter also addresses the Common Core and other State Standards (CCSS) for speaking, listening, collaboration, and domain-specific vocabulary.

PROGRESSION OF CONTENT

Level 1: Fundamental Striking Skills

Striking a Variety of Balls with Different Body Parts and Rackets

- Strike a balloon up with the hands, trying to make consecutive hits
- Strike a balloon up with different body parts, trying to make consecutive hits
- Strike a beach ball up with the hands, trying to make consecutive hits
- Strike a beach ball up with different body parts, trying to make consecutive hits
- Strike a vinyl ball up with the hands, progressing to different body parts and trying to make consecutive hits
- Strike a balloon up with a foam lollipop paddle or other very light paddle, trying to make consecutive hits
- Strike a beach ball with the dominant hand off a tee to a wall, progressing to a vinyl ball
- Self-bounce and strike a beach ball with the hand to a wall, progressing to a vinyl ball
- Strike a beach ball with the hand to a wall as many times in a row as you can, progressing to a vinyl ball
- Strike a light ball with a light paddle or racket off a tee to a wall, progressing to a self-bounce and then to striking as many times in a row as you can

Level 2: Tactical Striking Skills

Level 2A: Striking in a Variety of Ways, Progressively Increasing the Difficulty of the Equipment and Focusing on the Tactic of Consistency

Keep-It-Up Rallies Without a Net

- Keep-it-up with a partner using balloons or light balls
- Keep-it-up alone using different body parts with one bounce
- Keep-it-up with a partner using different body parts
- Keep-it-up in groups of three, progressing to groups of four, using different body parts

Cooperative Rallies with a Partner Over a Low Net

- Cooperative rally striking with the hands without a net
- Cooperative rally striking with the hands over a low net or rope
- Cooperative rally with a light racket and a large, light ball over a low net or rope
- Cooperative rally with the hand to a wall, alternating hits with your partner
- Cooperative rally with a light racket and a four-inch whiffle, bouncy foam, or trainer tennis ball

Cooperative Rallies Over a High Net

- Cooperative rally with a partner striking a very light ball over a high (six-foot) net with different body parts as many times as you can in a row; experiment striking with different amounts of force to different levels
- Cooperative rally with a partner striking light balls over a high (six-foot) net with different body parts as many times as you can in a row progressively using heavier balls; experiment striking with different amounts of force to different levels
- Cooperative rally in groups of four (two people on each side of the net), striking a ball over the net as many times in a row as you can

Level 2B: Tactics Striking to Open Space and Covering Space in Game-like Situations with a Cooperative Ethic

- Toss and catch deck rings, sending deck rings to open space
- Toss and catch deck rings, recovering to the central ready position on defense
- Toss to an open space, making your partner move to strike the ball
- Strike to an open space, making your partner move to strike the ball
- Strike and recover to the central ready position and anticipating the placement of the ball
- Anticipate the line of flight of the ball working alone
- Anticipate the line of flight of the ball working with a partner

Level 3: Using Tactical Game Skills in Modified Gameplay

Designing and Modifying Game Structures

- Designing net/wall games tossing and catching deck rings over a high (six-foot) net: understanding boundaries, scoring systems, rules, and serving rules
- Designing net/wall games striking with different body parts over a low (three-foot) net: understanding boundaries, scoring systems, rules, and serving rules

Tactics for Creating and Covering Space

- 1v1 Creating space by shot placement to the sides tossing and catching deck rings
- 1v1 Creating space by shot placement deep and short (deck rings or striking balls)
- 1v1 Moving closer to the net for a wider angle and space for shots
- 2v2 Passing to a teammate closer to the net for a wider angle and space for shots (using deck rings); progress to striking skills when ready; progress to 3v3 when ready
- 2v2 Covering space using different formations; progress to 3v3 when ready

Figure 22.1 Progression of Content

FYI

Sample Annotated Unit Segments at the End of this Chapter

Level 1
Striking a beach ball up with different body parts, trying to make consecutive hits

Level 2A
Striking using a variety of balls, rackets, and net heights, focusing on the tactic of consistency

Level 2B
1v1 tossing and catching deck rings, sending rings to open space

Introduction

Net/wall games include popular lifelong sports, such as volleyball, tennis, badminton, and racquetball, and a host of leisure outdoor and beach activities, such as paddleball and *sepak takraw* (volleyball with the feet). The skills of net/wall games are striking skills, including striking with rackets or paddles and different body parts. The popularity of these games makes it important to ensure children develop the skills and tactical knowledge that will support continued learning and participation throughout their lives, which is why these skills are prominent in National Standards 1 and 2.

At the elementary level, we focus on teaching children how to strike a variety of balls with a variety of body parts and rackets over low and high nets and to a wall. This variety provides a sound foundation for participation in net/wall games across the lifespan. **Figure 22.1** summarizes the content progression across the K–5 grades.

Children's learning of net/wall games differs in two critical ways from their learning of invasion games. First, striking skills take many more hours and years of practice at levels 1 and 2 before children can control the ball enough to engage in competitive level 3 games. Second, the tactics of net/wall games at the elementary level, compared to invasion games, are fewer in number and easier for children to learn. Children enjoy level 2 cooperative rallying (without scoring) in game-like situations, which feel like games, so the addition of competition is not needed for motivation or for helping children understand level 3 tactics.

Principles of Teaching Net/Wall Skills and Games

Two principles of teaching are absolutely critical for successfully teaching net/wall skills and games: (1) modifying the equipment, court, and rules; and (2) fostering successful rallies.

Modifying the Equipment

No games for children require modified equipment more than net/wall games. Regulation volleyballs are too hard, too small, and too heavy, and they hurt children's forearms when children practice their striking skills. In addition, the regulation volleyball net is too high for children.

Likewise, adult rackets are too heavy, the handles too long, and the face of the racket too far away from the body when elementary-age students hit the ball, which makes eye–racket coordination and racket control difficult. Tennis balls are too small and too heavy, and they bounce and travel too fast for children at the elementary level. It is critical to modify the equipment to slow the game down so children have more time to perceive ball flight and position themselves to return shots (Harvey & van der Mars, 2010).

Moreover, equipment affects performance techniques both negatively and positively. A tennis racket that is too heavy will affect wrist angle and swing. A study of modifying tennis racket size and ball compression reported that the smallest racket and the lowest-compression ball produced the best striking performance (Buszard, Farrow, Reid, & Masters, 2014). A low-compression ball travels slower in the air and bounces lower. The combination of the low-compression ball and small racket brought out a swing from low to high and striking the ball in front of and to the side of the body. Both these performance techniques are techniques we want children to learn.

The good news is that there are many ways to modify the equipment, nets, and court sizes to accommodate children's size, strength, and skill levels. **Table 22.1** orders equipment, nets, and participants on a continuum from easiest to most challenging (also, see box "Homemade Volleyballs and Rackets"). It serves as a guide to help you design task progressions, moving across the continuum as children's abilities increase.

Modifying the Court

In general, a smaller court is easier. To accommodate individual differences, you can have different-sized boundaries on either side of the net (see **Figure 22.2**), allowing lower-skilled and higher-skilled children to play together with equal challenge and success.

Figure 22.2 Different-sized boundaries to accommodate individual differences

Table 22.1 Ways to Modify Equipment, Nets, Court Sizes, and Participants

	Easiest ←		→	Most Challenging
Balls for striking with different body parts	Balloons Weighted balloons	Nylon-webbed balloons Beach balls	Vinyl balls Packing-peanut beach balls	Trainer volleyballs
Rackets	Hands	Hand rackets (worn like a glove) Lollipop foam paddles Nylon rackets (purchased or homemade)	Junior-sized plastic paddleball/pickleball rackets Junior-sized, light racquetball rackets	Junior badminton rackets Junior tennis rackets
Balls for striking with rackets over low nets	Balloons	Beach balls Vinyl balls	Whiffle balls	Foam indoor tennis balls, medium and small sizes Trainer tennis balls
Nets	None	Lines Jump ropes	Jump ropes hung between cones Domes with poles as standards strung with a rope or net	Rope or nets tied between chairs For high nets, ropes or nets tied between standards
Participants	Alone to self Alone off a tee	Alone to a wall from self-bounce or toss	Partners, with one partner tossing	Partners, both striking Groups of three or four

Modifying the Rules

Many rules in net/wall games need to be modified as children are developing striking skills. For example, you might eliminate the rules that specify only three hits per side and only one tap or strike in a row per person in high-net games. You also might let the ball bounce twice in low-net games. Make the serve easy to return by using a toss or underhand serve.

You will even need to modify different rules for different children. For example, children in wheelchairs will need extra

Homemade Volleyballs and Rackets

Packing Peanut–Stuffed Beach Ball Volleyball

A surprisingly good ball for striking over high nets (as in volleyball) can be made for little cost. Ask parents to donate old beach balls, bags of Styrofoam packing peanuts, and at least one roll of duct tape. Slit open the beach ball and stuff it with as many peanuts as you can. Place duct tape over the slit to close the hole.

Balloon Stuffed with Nylon Hose

Pushing nylon hose into a balloon and then blowing it up creates a heavier balloon with an appropriate amount of weight. A balloon alone can be too light and slow.

Nylon-Webbed Balloons

Tying nylon hose in a web around a blown-up balloon also adds an appropriate amount of weight to a balloon. Cut off the leg of panty hose. Cut off the foot, and save it to tie the "doughnuts" together. Start at one end of the leg and roll it into a doughnut (wear long sleeves; put the nylon over your sleeve and roll it down your arm). Each doughnut will be attached to four other doughnuts, by connecting them at the 12, 3, 6, and 9 o'clock positions. You can get large quantities of defective hosiery from manufacturers at a very low cost (about 300 pairs for $10). You also can dye the hose using regular fabric dyes before making the webs.

Homemade Nylon Rackets

Using a rounded wire coat hanger, stretch nylon hose over the hanger to form a rebound surface. Compress the wire hook and wrap it with the ends of the nylon hose.

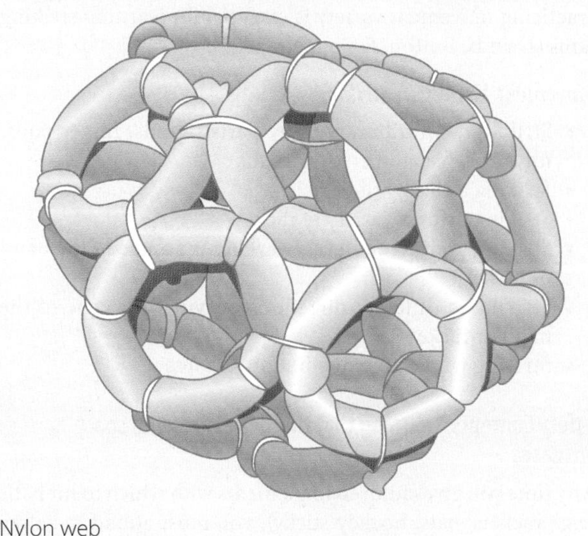

Nylon web

SAFETY AND LIABILITY 22.1

Increasing Safety and Decreasing Risk of Liability: Guidelines Relevant to Content in this Chapter

In this box, we discuss specific guidelines built on information discussed throughout this text on professional standards of practice, negligence, and liability. The goals of these guidelines are to increase children's safety and decrease teachers' risk of negligence and liability.

- Whenever children hit balls with implements (e.g., rackets, bats, hockey sticks), they need to learn (1) the size that their personal space increases and, consequently, that they must be farther away from other children; and (2) to check the space behind them so that they don't hit another child with their backswing.
- Children also need to be taught to be aware when setting up a center or a practice task to anticipate the flight pathway of their hit balls. They then need to set up the task so that the ball does not hit another child or roll into the space of another child or group and thus become a tripping hazard.
- Children need to learn to stop play if a ball rolls into their area so they don't trip on the ball. Then they can safely hand the ball back to the child responsible for it.

bounces and a small-handled racket so the child can hold the racket *and* push the wheel at the same time.

Getting Successful Rallies

One of the joys of net/wall games is a rally. Even in elite competitive play, what is exciting is seeing great rallies and not knowing when a rally will end by a well-placed shot. Nothing is more boring than playing a net/wall game in which the ball is served and never returned or is returned only once.

In turn, nothing is more important in teaching net/wall games than teaching children to rally successfully. Rallies enable children to practice their skills in authentic contexts. Moreover, once children can rally, you can begin teaching tactics and a variety of shots.

Movement Variety

As with all content areas, the striking skills for net/wall games are open skills that require children to respond with a variety of movement patterns. As research in motor learning suggests, practicing movement variety is essential for learning striking skills (Davids, Button, & Bennett, 2008).

Movement Variety in Striking

- Striking with different body parts (hands, finger pads, forearms, feet and ankles, thighs)
- Striking a variety of balls
- Striking using a variety of rackets
- Striking to different levels, varying the angle of the hand or racket
- Striking in different directions, varying the angle of the hand or racket
- Striking with different amounts of force

Safety Concepts: Learning that the Size of Personal Space Increases

Any time you give children implements with which to hit balls (e.g., rackets, bats, hockey sticks), you must attend to safety issues. Children need to learn that the size of their personal space increases when they use an implement such as a racket and, consequently, they must be farther away from other children. Moreover, because children must focus on the flight of the ball, they will not be watching their backswing. You will have to remind them to check the space behind them before they begin practicing.

Level 1: Fundamental Striking Skills

We begin teaching striking for high-net games by having children tap balloons, weighted balloons, and light balls with their hands. The goal is for them to strike a balloon or ball up as many times in a row as they can—that is, to rally with themselves, while working on getting the body and/or body parts under the ball to strike up. For low-net games, we begin by having children strike a ball at a wall with their hands from a tee, with a self-bounce, and then with light rackets, working on being able to contact the ball, positioning to the side of the ball with their side to the target, and controlling the direction of the ball.

We teach children how to strike a variety of balls with different rackets and different body parts. This emphasis on movement variety forms a solid foundation for learning striking skills (Davids et al., 2008). In addition, it prepares children to play whatever net/wall games they choose as they develop across their lifespan.

The tasks listed in this section are appropriate, in progression, for units across the lower elementary grades. In the upper elementary grades, when children progress to using heavier rackets and faster balls (e.g., junior tennis racquets and trainer tennis balls), you will also need to use level 1 tasks for practicing these more advanced skills.

Each learning experience or set of learning experiences will take from one to three lessons. If you have limited equipment, you can design a set of striking centers and have children rotate to each center. With both whole-class teaching and centers, you need to provide equipment options and teach the children to choose which ball is most appropriate for them.

SAMPLE LEARNING EXPERIENCES 22.1

Level 1: Fundamental Striking Skills

Striking a Variety of Balls with Different Body Parts and Rackets

1. Striking a Balloon/Weighted Balloon Up with the Hands, Trying to Make Consecutive Hits

Explore

A. Striking using both hands, just the right hand, and just the left hand.

Experiment

A. To find the most effective relationship of your hands and body to the balloon in order to strike straight up.
B. To find the amount of force needed to strike high and low.

2. Striking a Balloon Up with Different Body Parts (e.g., Forearms, Head, Thighs, Feet), Trying to Make Consecutive Hits

Experiment

A. To find the most effective relationship of your hands and body to the balloon in order to strike straight up.
B. To find the amount of force needed to strike high and low.

Explore

A. How many different body parts can you use to strike the balloon without letting it touch the ground?
B. Striking the balloon up as many times as you can in a row using one body part. Try forearms, feet (laces), inside of the foot, outside of the foot, thighs, elbows, head, palms, and back of the hand.
C. Striking with a different body part each time you strike the balloon.
D. Striking the balloon, alternating two different body parts. Explore different combinations of body parts (e.g., foot and hand, head and laces, thigh and inside of foot, forearm and head).
E. How many different parts of your body can you use to tap the balloon without repeating a body part?

3. Striking a Beach Ball Up with the Hands, Trying to Make Consecutive Hits

Explore

A. Striking using both hands, just the right hand, and just the left hand.

Experiment

A. To find the most effective relationship of your hands and body to the ball in order to strike straight up.
B. To find the amount of force needed to strike high and low.

4. Striking a Beach Ball Up with Different Body Parts (e.g., Forearms, Heads, Thighs, Feet) Trying to Make Consecutive Hits

Experiment

A. To find the best relationship of your hands and body to the ball to strike straight up.
B. To find the amount of force needed to strike high and low.

Explore

A. How many different body parts can you use to strike the ball without letting it touch the ground?
B. Striking the ball up as many times as you can in a row using one body part. Try forearms, feet (laces), inside of foot, outside of foot, thighs, elbows, head, palms, and back of hand.
C. Striking with a different body part each time you strike the ball.
D. Striking the ball, alternating two different body parts. Explore different combinations of body parts (e.g., foot and hand, head and laces, thigh and inside of foot, forearm and head).
E. How many different parts of your body can you use to strike the ball without repeating a body part?

5. Striking a Vinyl Ball Up with the Hands, Progressing to Different Body Parts and Trying to Make Consecutive Hits

Experiment

A. To find the most effective relationship of your hands and body to the ball in order to strike straight up.
B. To find the amount of force needed to strike high and low.

(*continues*)

SAMPLE LEARNING EXPERIENCES 22.1

Level 1: Fundamental Striking Skills (*continued*)

Explore

A. How many different body parts can you use to strike the ball without letting it touch the ground?

B. Striking the ball up as many times as you can in a row using one body part. Try forearms, feet (laces), inside of the foot, outside of the foot, thighs, elbows, head, palms, and back of the hand.

C. Striking with a different body part each time you strike the ball.

D. Striking the ball, alternating two different body parts. Explore different combinations of body parts (e.g., foot and hand, head and laces, thigh and inside of foot, forearm and head).

E. How many different parts of your body can you use to strike the ball without repeating a body part?

6. Striking a Balloon Up with a Paddle, Trying to Make Consecutive Hits

A. Use a foam lollipop paddle or other very light paddle. Use a circular backswing every time you hit the balloon. Do not strike with the racket starting at shoulder height.

7. Striking a Beach Ball with the Dominant Hand Off a Tee to a Wall, a Suspended Parachute, or a Vertical Gymnastics Mat

A. Start side to target slightly behind and to the side, circle the dominant arm back and down, start swing low, and swing up and forward.

B. Progress to a vinyl ball.

8. Self-Bounce and Striking a Beach Ball with One Hand to a Wall

A. Turn side to target, toss a beach ball in front of your front hip, let it bounce, circle arm back and down, start swing low, and swing up and forward. You can catch the rebound or let the ball bounce once or twice and try to strike it again.

B. Progress to a vinyl ball.

9. Striking a Beach Ball with the Hand to a Wall as Many Times in a Row as You Can

A. Turn side to target, position slightly behind and to the side of the ball; after the peak of the bounce, hit the ball on its way down, circle arm back and down, start swing low, and swing up and forward. Let it bounce once or twice.

B. Progress to a vinyl ball.

10. Striking a Light Ball with a Light Paddle Off a Tee to a Wall (see Figure 22.3)

A. Start side to target slightly behind and to the side, circle paddle back and down, start swing low, and swing up and forward.

B. Progress to a self-bounce (see **Figure 22.4**).

C. Progress to striking as many times in a row as you can. Let it bounce once or twice.

Sample Questions to Ask

- What helped you be successful in striking the ball or balloon several times in a row?
- What did you think about to make the ball go straight up? [Got underneath it, extended my arms straight up.]
- Which body parts were easier to use?
- Which parts worked best in your combinations?
- Which ball worked best for you?
- Which performance cues did you think about while striking the ball off a tee?

Level 2: Tactical Striking Skills

Once children can control a tapped ball and strike it consecutively to themselves, you can begin teaching level 2 content. In level 2, we continue using a variety of balls, rackets, and body parts. In addition, we begin work on tactics.

Tim Hopper proposes teaching three progressive tactical principles when teaching net/wall games (Hopper, 1998; Hopper & Bell, 2000):

1. *Consistency.* The goal of this principle is for students to be able to return the ball more times than their opponent does.
2. *Placement.* The goal of this principle is for students to know where they are on the court (player placement) and where to strike (ball placement).
3. *Power and spin.* The goal of this principle is for students to understand how to change the tempo of the game by adding power and spin shots.

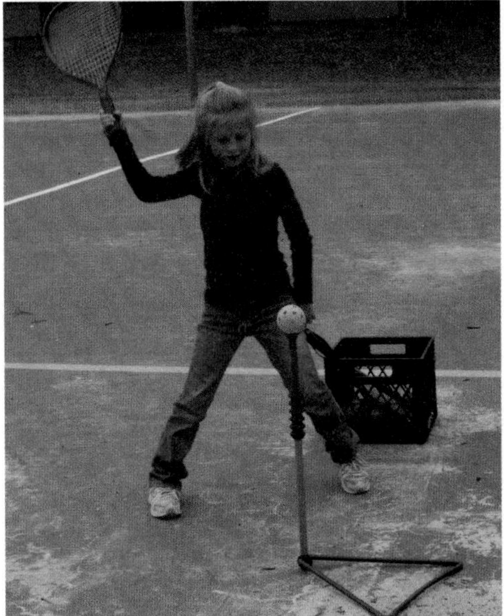

Figure 22.3 Striking a ball off a tee

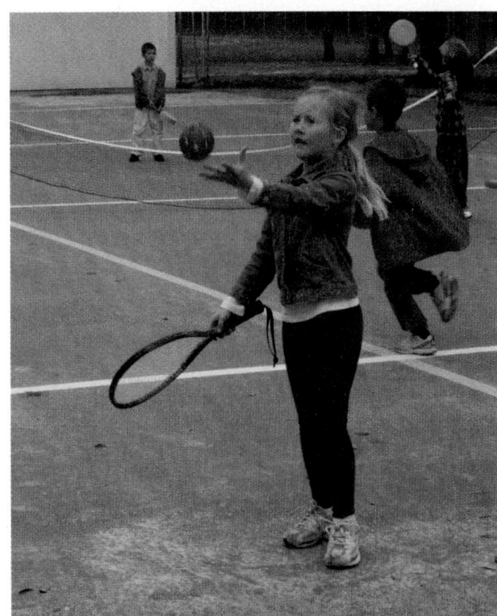

Figure 22.4 Striking with a light racket from a self-bounce using different types of rackets and balls

Table 22.2 Net/Wall Tactics

Level 2A: Consistency (Typically Introduced in Grades 2–5)

- Hit and return the ball inbounds. Try hard to get to every shot.
- Hit and return the ball inbounds more times than your opponent does. (This tactic is typically introduced in grades 4 and 5 if children are ready for competitive games.)

Level 2B: Positioning and Ball Placement (Typically Introduced in Grades 3–5)

Offense

- Send the ball to an open space. In high-net games, such as volleyball or deck-ring tennis, you score when the ball or deck ring lands on the floor. In racket games, you score when the ball bounces twice. An **open space** is the space between the defender and the boundary or between defenders.
- Open spaces change based on defenders' positions. When defenders cover the center space, open spaces are typically near the sidelines, corners, very close to the net (or wall), or at the far back end of the court.

Defense

- Recover to the central ready position. To deny the offense the most space, position yourself in the center. In tennis-type and one-wall handball-type games, this is just behind the baseline and is called the *base position*. In badminton-type games, the central ready position is in the middle of the court because the shuttlecock does not bounce. In racquetball-type wall games with four walls, it is the center of the court, with both players trying to control the same spot. In volleyball-type games, the players' positions vary depending on the number of players and the size of the court. In all net/wall games, stand in a ready position with weight on the balls of the feet, knees bent, and feet shoulder-width apart, ready to move quickly. Quickly recover/return to the central ready position after you hit.

Level 3: Positioning and Ball Placement (Typically Introduced in Grades 4–5)

Offense (Listed in a Progression)

- Create space by shot placement to the side by forcing the defender to shift near the sideline on every shot, creating a space too large to defend on the subsequent shot. When you hit near the sideline, your opponent must shift far to the side. On the next shot, send the ball to the opposite side so the opponent might not have enough time to run across to get the shot.
- Create space by shot placement deep and short. Such shots force the defender to shift his or her court position up and back, creating space and requiring the defender to hit difficult shots in return. Shots sent close to the net typically are called *drop shots*; shots sent deep typically are called *lobs* or *clears*.
- The closer you are to the net, the wider the angle of possible shots. As a consequence, you have a larger space in which to hit the ball. (See **Figure 22.11** later in this chapter, which shows how standing closer to the net gives you a wider angle and more space.)
- Pass to a teammate closer to the net. In volleyball-type games with two or three individuals on a team, you try to pass to a teammate who has moved close to the net to take advantage of the wider angle of possible shots.
- Hit to an open space that requires the defense to hit a difficult shot (e.g., a backhand shot in racket games).

Defense

- Anticipate and decide as early as you can where your opponent will hit the next shot.
- Use the back of the court to give you more time to address the ball. If your opponent forces you out of a good defensive position, hit a high, deep shot to give you enough time to get back in position.
- Cover space using different formations. With 2v2 and 3v3 games, use a formation that denies the most scoring space. With partners, this formation can be up-and-back or side-to-side. In groups of three, it can be a triangle with one or two players up or back.
- Reposition formations based on the game situation. When your teammate moves to strike the ball in a tennis-type game, move to deny the new space that this shot has created. In a volleyball-type game, move to receive a pass closer to the net.

We typically don't progress to teaching power and spin at the elementary level except with older children who participate in net/wall sports after school.

For the elementary level, we divide tactics into three levels: levels 2A, 2B, and 3. **Table 22.1** describes net/wall tactics in language children can understand. These tactics, along with performance techniques, form the basis for your motor objectives for levels 2 and 3 lessons.

Level 2A: Striking in a Variety of Ways, Progressively Increasing the Difficulty of the Equipment and Focusing on the Tactic of Consistency

In level 2A, we focus on the tactic of consistency by teaching cooperative rallies and encouraging children to strike the ball back and forth as many times as they can. At the same time, we teach children how to use a variety of balls and rackets, progressively increasing the difficulty of the equipment. For example, children in second grade might practice rallies with foam lollipop paddles and beach balls. Third-graders might use small, light racquetball rackets and vinyl balls, and fifth graders might use junior tennis rackets and trainer tennis balls. As you increase the difficulty of the equipment in the upper elementary grades, you can begin to teach the more specific performance techniques associated with the volleyball, tennis, and racquetball skills discussed in **Skills Box 22.1**.

We cannot emphasize enough that, if you set the environment and task constraints (e.g., equipment, boundaries, skills) to match the capabilities of each child, your children can learn to rally cooperatively with a partner. Be willing to modify anything to get good rallies working.

You will have to differentiate instruction and provide different equipment choices for different children. Provide an appropriate variety of equipment, and teach children how to select equipment that will enable each pair to strike the ball back and forth successfully. Children might even have to use a different racket than their partner or have different rules—for example, "the higher-skilled child must strike the ball after one bounce, while the lower-skilled child can have one or two bounces."

When we are teaching in a new setting, we get out all the available balls and rackets, test every combination so we know the options, and then help the children make decisions about which ball and racket will work best for them. Later in this chapter, we describe a unit with centers that allow children to experiment with different balls, rackets, and net heights and then decide which they prefer. Another excellent task to teach children how to modify equipment is to have children rally a few minutes with different partners. With each new partner, the pair experiments with the equipment until they have a good rally.

Each of the learning experiences described in this section can take from one to four lessons. Be sure to provide options for equipment so children can use the weight of a ball appropriate for them. During the lessons, work on performance techniques appropriate for the ability level of the children.

Motivation and Social Objectives

The learning experiences described here are excellent opportunities to focus on motivation to persist and keep trying even if the skill is difficult and on having a growth mindset—that is, believing you can learn and improve through effort (rather than assuming success is due to ability).

In addition, social objectives for cooperation and caring about partners are critical. With all cooperative rallying tasks, the purpose is to hit the ball as many times in a row as you can. Consequently, for children to be able to rally, they need to care about their partners and work diligently to send shots that are returnable—that is, within reach, not too forceful, and at an appropriate height. To do so, they need to get the body part striking the ball in the appropriate relationship with the ball (e.g., directly under, under on a slight diagonal, and/or behind) and strike with the appropriate amount of force.

SAMPLE LEARNING EXPERIENCES 22.2

Level 2A: Striking in a Variety of Ways, Progressively Increasing the Difficulty of the Equipment, and Focusing on the Tactic of Consistency

Keep-It-Up Rallies Without a Net

1. Keep-It-Up with a Partner Using Balloons/Weighted Balloons

A. Try to strike the ball up as many times in a row as you can using balloons.

Experiment

B. To find the most effective relationship of body parts to the balloon in order to strike in such a direction and to such a height that your partner can return the shot.

C. To find the amount of force needed to get the balloon high enough that your partner can get under it.

Explore

A. Using just the left hand, just the right hand, and two hands.

B. Using different body parts (e.g., different parts of the hands, arms, and feet; head; thighs).

SAMPLE LEARNING EXPERIENCES 22.2

Level 2A: Striking in a Variety of Ways, Progressively Increasing the Difficulty of the Equipment, and Focusing on the Tactic of Consistency (*continued*)

C. Selecting two different body parts and alternating striking with each.
D. Striking with different amounts of force to different levels.

Progress to

- Nylon-webbed balloons
- Beach balls or other very light balls

2. Keep-It-Up Alone Using Different Body Parts and with One Bounce

A. Working alone, explore keep-it-up with one bounce between strikes using a bouncy vinyl ball.

Experiment

B. To find the most effective relationship of the body parts to the ball in order to strike it up repeatedly.

Explore

A. Using different body parts.
B. Selecting two body parts and alternating striking with each.
C. Striking with different amounts of force to different levels while keeping the ball up.
D. Designing a combination of striking with three body parts (e.g., left hand, right thigh, left foot). Repeat this sequence as many times in a row as you can.

As a culminating activity, ask several children if they are willing to demonstrate their combinations. Then have the class practice those combinations.

3. Keep-It-Up with a Partner Using Different Body Parts

A. Explore keep-it-up with a partner using different body parts with one bounce and/or no bounces between strikes using vinyl balls.

Experiment

B. To find the most effective relationship of body parts to the ball in order to hit a returnable shot and rally consistently with your partner.

Explore

A. Using different body parts.
B. Getting under the ball and striking up using the finger pads.
C. Alternating getting under the ball and striking up using the finger pads and one other body part.
D. Using the inside of the forearms, sometimes letting the ball bounce and sometimes hitting it on the fly.
E. Alternating using the inside of the forearms and one other body part, sometimes letting the ball bounce and sometimes hitting it on the fly.
F. Striking with different amounts of force to different levels, finding which level makes it easy for your partner to return the hit.
G. Designing a sequence of striking using three different body parts with one and/or no bounces. Repeat the sequence as many times as you can in a row. As a culminating activity, show your sequence to another pair, and try each other's sequence.

Progress to

- Trainer volleyballs if and when ready

4. Keep-It-Up in Groups of Three Using Different Body Parts

A. Explore keep-it-up in groups of three, using different body parts with one bounce and/or no bounces. The group selects a ball that they all can use successfully.
B. After exploring, select one to three body parts, and decide whether to allow one or no bounces.
C. As a culminating activity, show your game to another group, and then try their game.

Progress to

- Groups of four if and when ready

(*continues*)

SAMPLE LEARNING EXPERIENCES 22.2

Level 2A: Striking in a Variety of Ways, Progressively Increasing the Difficulty of the Equipment, and Focusing on the Tactic of Consistency (*continued*)

Playing keep-it-up striking with different body parts

Cooperative Rallies with a Partner Over a Low Net or Rope

Set boundaries, if needed due to gymnasium space, that help children to rally successfully (not too large or too small).

1. Cooperative Rally, Striking with the Hands, Without a Net, Using a Vinyl or Beach Ball, Letting the Ball Bounce One or More Times

A. Try to hit the ball so your partner can easily return it.
B. See how many times you can hit the ball in a row without missing.
C. Try to use both left and right hands.

2. Cooperative Rally, Striking with the Hands Over a Low Net/Rope

A. Strike a vinyl ball or beach ball with your hands back and forth over a low net or rope, letting the ball bounce once or twice.
B. Aim the ball so your partner can easily return it.
C. Experiment with how high you need to strike the ball so it bounces to a height that is easy for your partner to return. Discuss with your partner the height of the bounce that is easiest to return.
D. Experiment with the relationship between the direction of your swing and the angle of your hand on contact and the resulting height of the ball's flight and bounce. Discuss what you discover with your partner.
E. Based on what you discover, try to see how many times you and your partner can hit the ball in a row without missing.
F. Try to use both left and right hands.

3. Cooperative Rally with a Light Racket and Large, Light Ball Over a Low Net or Rope

A. Strike a large, light ball with a light racket (lollipop paddles, hand rackets, or light, junior-sized racquetball rackets) over a low net/rope, letting the ball bounce once or twice. Aim the ball to your partner's forehand side.
B. Experiment and discuss with your partner how high you need to strike the ball so it bounces to a height that is easy for your partner to return.
C. Experiment with the relationship between the direction of your swing and the angle of the face of your racket on contact and the resulting height of the ball's flight and bounce. Discuss what you discover with your partner.

SAMPLE LEARNING EXPERIENCES 22.2

Level 2A: Striking in a Variety of Ways, Progressively Increasing the Difficulty of the Equipment, and Focusing on the Tactic of Consistency (*continued*)

D. Based on what you discover, try to see how many times you can hit the ball in a row without missing.
E. If you are rallying successfully, try to hit backhands.
F. Challenge yourselves to hit the ball lower and closer to the net height and still rally successfully.

4. Cooperative Rally with the Hand to a Wall, Alternating Hits with Your Partner

A. Strike a large, light ball to a smooth wall with your hand, alternating with your partner and letting the ball bounce once or twice. Aim so your partner can hit the ball with her or his dominant hand.
B. Experiment by hitting the ball to different heights on the wall, and discuss with your partner which height results in easy shots to return.
C. Based on what you discover, try to see how many times you can hit the ball in a row without missing.
D. Challenge yourselves to strike with more force and still rally successfully, keeping the ball within the boundaries.

5. Cooperative Rally with a Light Racket and a Four-Inch Whiffle, Bouncy Foam, or Trainer Tennis Ball Over a Low Net/Rope, Letting the Ball Bounce Once or Twice

A. Using the appropriate direction of the swing and angle of the face of the racket, aim so your partner has an easy shot to return.
B. Experiment and adjust the force of the swing to the new speed of the ball so you and your partner can rally successfully.
C. Experiment and adjust your boundaries so they are not too large or too small.
D. If you are rallying successfully, try to hit backhands.
E. Challenge yourselves to strike the ball lower and close to the net height and still rally successfully.

Sample Questions to Ask

- Which body parts were easier for you to use?
- Which parts worked best for you in your combinations?
- What happens when you take a big circular backswing swing at the balloon with your hand? With a paddle? [The balloon goes higher. You can hit it harder.]
- What helps you make continuous strikes up? [Hit the ball/balloon high, strike it on the bottom, swing upward, follow through upward.]
- How do you make the balloon go forward? [Hit it on the side, aim the face of the racket forward.]
- What helped you time the hit? [Say, "Bounce one, hit two."]
- Which performance cue do you think can help you improve the most during this task?
- What do you think you did when the ball hit the net? [My racket face was pointed down. My swing was aimed down. I did not get under the ball enough.]

Striking a beach ball with hands over a line

Striking a heavier ball with the hands over a rope

Striking whiffle balls with paddles over a rope net and low net

Courtesy of John Dolly

(*continues*)

SAMPLE LEARNING EXPERIENCES 22.2

Level 2A: Striking in a Variety of Ways, Progressively Increasing the Difficulty of the Equipment, and Focusing on the Tactic of Consistency (*continued*)

- What can you do to keep the ball inbounds? [Turn my side to the net. Hit the ball in front of my hip.]
- What height of the ball after the bounce is easiest to hit with a racket? [Front hip height as the ball is starting to come down.]

Cooperative Rallies Over a High Net or Rope

For high-net tasks, set the net above the children's reach. If necessary, due to gymnasium space considerations, have children set boundaries that allow them to rally successfully as many times in a row as they can—with the area being not too large for children to cover the space and not so small that it is hard to hit within the boundaries.

1. Cooperative Rally with a Partner Striking a Very Light Ball Over a High Net with Different Body Parts as Many Times as You Can in a Row

A. Use a beach ball or nylon-webbed balloon to volley as many times as you can in a row (see **Figure 22.5**).

Experiment

B. Striking with different amounts of force to different levels, finding which level makes it easy for your partner to return the hit.

Explore

A. Using different body parts.
B. Selecting two or three body parts.
C. Getting under the ball and using the finger pads.
D. Using the inside of the forearms.
E. Using the finger pads and the inside of the forearms.

2. Cooperative Rally with a Partner, Striking Light Balls Over a High Net as Many Times as You Can in a Row Progressively using Heavier Balls

A. Cooperative rally with a partner using as many hits as you need on your side of the net to keep the rally going (in other words, you can tap the ball to yourself to get it under control and then tap it over the net).

Experiment

B. Striking with different amounts of force to different levels, finding which level makes it easy for your partner to return the hit.

Explore

A. Using different body parts.
B. Selecting two or three body parts.
C. Using the finger pads.
D. Using the inside of the forearms.
E. Using the finger pads and the inside of the forearms.

Progress to

- Trainer volleyballs, if and when ready (see **Figure 22.6**)

3. Cooperative Rally in Groups of Four, Striking a Ball Over the Net as Many Times in a Row as You Can

A. Have two people on each side of the net. Select a ball that everyone in the group can use successfully. Volley as many times in a row as you can.

Explore

A. Using different body parts.
B. Using the finger pads.
C. Using the inside of the forearms.
D. Using the finger pads and the inside of the forearms.

Sample Questions to Ask

- What level of hit made it easiest for the group to maintain a rally?
- What was the appropriate amount of force to use to hit the ball to the level that made it easiest for the group to maintain a rally?
- To get the ball to go in an upward direction, where do your hands have to be?
- How do two hands help you volley the ball better?
- What causes the ball to go backwards?

Figure 22.5 Cooperative rally with a beach ball

Figure 22.6 Cooperative rally with a trainer volleyball

Level 2B: Tactics Striking to Open Space and Covering Space

When children can consistently rally with a partner, we progress to level 2B. In level 2B, we introduce the tactics of positioning and ball placement, first using throwing and catching skills and deck tennis rings. Deck tennis rings are rubber rings approximately six inches in diameter that children typically throw like a Frisbee over a net placed at a height of five feet. We use deck rings because children can control the deck ring well enough to send the ring to a space, but they can't aim the ring so accurately that it is too difficult for the defense to catch it. You can easily make lightweight deck tennis rings with newspaper (see box, "Homemade Deck Tennis Rings"). The ethic remains cooperative; thus, the focus is not on hitting a shot your opponent cannot return, but rather on learning to control the ball, see and hit to an open space, and move to an open space to return a shot. On defense, the focus is to learn the center ready position and to recover to this position after every shot. After introducing the tactics with deck rings, we repeat the learning experiences using striking skills over low and high nets, giving children much needed time to practice striking skills.

In level 2B, you will need to have the children create boundaries. Initially, have them create boundaries they can easily defend, but progress as soon as possible to having them create "perfect" boundaries. Perfect net/wall boundaries are a challenge to cover but allow successful rallies.

Progressively Increasing the Difficulty of the Equipment

In level 2B, you continue to progressively increase the difficulty of the equipment as children are ready to move on to more complex skills. Typically, it is counterproductive to focus on hitting balls to open spaces on the day you introduce more difficult equipment, such as tennis balls and junior tennis rackets, because this equipment makes striking difficult for children and they simply need to work on consistency. You must be prepared to shift back to level 1 tasks as necessary. For example, learning the tennis backhand using a tennis ball and a junior tennis racket takes considerable practice with level 1 tasks, such as striking off a tee and striking to a wall, and then with level 2 tasks, such as rallying while focusing on consistency. Even with children in the fourth and fifth grades, you will spiral back and forth between levels 1, 2, and 3, depending on striking skill and equipment.

> **Homemade Deck Tennis Rings**
>
> You can easily make rings out of tightly rolled newspaper. Take two sheets of newspaper. Start at one corner, and roll the pages into a tight tube about three-quarters of an inch in diameter. (The trick to doing so is to start with a tiny roll that is less than one-eighth of an inch in diameter.) Tape the rolled paper at the end corner. Then, while pressing the roll flat, form it into a ring (overlapping the ends of the roll) about six inches in diameter. Tape all overlapped areas. If you tape the entire roll, it will last for years.

Level 3: Using Tactical Game Skills in Modified Gameplay

In level 2, children work on cooperative rallies and rallies with a competitive structure in which they learn to hit the ball to open spaces and recover to the central ready position. Children typically perceive these rallies as games. In level 3, children design and play modified games with scoring systems and rules about serving, change of serve, and rotation. As always, children choose whether to keep track of the score.

In addition, level 3 includes tactics to create space by shot placements to the sides, front, and back of the court. We also introduce team tactics during this time.

Once children begin playing level 3 net/wall games with striking skills, you will need to deal with serving. This can be done with a toss to get the game going. You can also teach serving techniques for striking; **Skills Box 22.1** briefly summarizes underhand volleyball serve performance techniques. In addition, you and the children will need to modify the serving rules so the children can successfully get the ball over the net

SAMPLE LEARNING EXPERIENCES 22.3

Level 2B: Tactics for Striking to Open Space and Covering Space

Tactics for Striking to Open Space and Covering Space in Game-like Situations with a Cooperative Ethic

1. 1v1 Tossing and Catching Deck Rings, Sending Rings to Open Space

A. Toss the ring back and forth, tossing to an open space and making your partner move to catch it. Open space is the space between your partner and the boundaries. After you catch the ring, you must toss it back from where you caught it. No running with the ring is allowed. Set up boundaries with your partner to create an area of a size you think you can cover.

B. Rotate partners. After the children are successful, rotate partners many times. Playing with many partners helps children learn how to adjust to a variety of throws and tactics.

Sample Questions to Ask

- Where are open spaces? [Where my partner is not standing.]
- How do you see an open space? What does an open space look like to you?
- How can you anticipate where your partner will send the ring? [Watch the ring, look at my partner's eyes and body motion.]
- When do you think about where you are going to throw? [When I catch the ring.] When do you think is the best time to think about where you are going to throw? [The earlier the better. As soon as you toss a shot, think about the next shot.]
- What did you learn by working with different partners? [Some people found different open spaces. Some used mostly the sides, but others used the corners, just over the net, and near the endline.]

2. Tossing and Catching Deck Rings, Recovering to the Central Ready Position on Defense

A. Toss the ring over the net to open spaces so your partner must move to catch it.

Sample Questions to Ask

- When you are the receiver, where do you think is the best place to stand to cover the most space, denying it to your partner? [In the center of the area where the partner can send the ring.]
- So, what do you need to do after you toss the ring? [Get back to the central area in the ready position as fast as I can.]
- We call that the **central ready position**.
- After you catch the ring, you must toss it back from where you caught it. No running with the ring is allowed.
- Set up boundaries with your partner to create an area of a size you think you can cover.

B. Rotate partners many times.

Sample Questions to Ask

- Why is it important to return quickly to the central ready position? [If I don't, there will be a big space where my partner can toss the ring.]
- Without using names, what did you notice about the play of different people? How did you adjust to those differences? What made some people hard to play against? [Threw it hard, made me run all over, threw it as soon as they caught it.] What made some people easier to play against? [Could not catch the ring, took too long to decide where to throw, looked at the spot for some time before throwing there, watched me catch the ring and did not return to the middle.]
- What did you notice about the size of the boundaries? How did you adjust to those differences?

Notes: The next three learning experiences are appropriate for developing into a unit on striking with a racket over a low net. However, you can easily modify them for a unit on striking with different body parts (including setting and forearm passes) over a high net. In either case, you must provide options for equipment that enable each pair to rally successfully.

3. Tossing the Ball to an Open Space, Making Your Partner Move to Strike the Ball Back for You to Catch It

A. You decide when to rotate roles, but the maximum number of turns you can take in a row is five. (Children working hard on this task have problems remembering how many turns they have taken.) Each of you selects a ball and a racket with which you can succeed. Set a boundary (with floor tape, cones, plastic lines, or other items) that you think you can cover.

4. Striking the Ball to Open Spaces so Your Partner Must Move to Return Your Shot

A. Try to strike the ball back and forth as many times as you can in a row. Each of you selects a ball and a racket with which you can succeed. Set a boundary (with floor tape, cones, plastic lines, or other items) that you think you can cover.

5. Strike and Recover to the Central Ready Position and Anticipating the Placement of the Ball

A. Try to strike the ball back and forth as many times in a row as you can. Each of you selects a ball and a racket with which you can succeed. Set a boundary (with floor tape, cones, plastic lines, or other items) that you think you can cover.

After you strike the ball, immediately return to the center of the court behind the endline.

SAMPLE LEARNING EXPERIENCES 22.3

Level 2B: Tactics for Striking to Open Space and Covering Space (*continued*)

B. Because the best time to strike a ball is after the ball bounces, reaches its apex, and starts to drop, you need to be far enough back so you are in the location where you will most likely receive the next shot.

C. Get into an alert, ready position, and be prepared to move to the left or right depending on where your partner hits the ball.

Notes: For a volleyball-type unit, the central ready position is in the middle of the court because you strike the ball before it bounces

Sample Questions to Ask

- What do you need to do to be a good tosser for your partner? [Aim the ball to the partner's side in open space. When your partner is using a racket, be sure to toss it so it bounces high enough to hit.]
- When do you decide where you are going to try to hit the ball? [As soon as possible after you hit the previous shot.]
- What can you watch to get clues about the probable flight path of the ball? [Watch your opponent's body motion, eyes, and racket position and motion.]
- Why does returning to the middle of the space help you deny space? What happens if you are slow to get there? Why do people watch their shot instead of moving back to the center?
- How does knowing about the "apex" of the bounce help you? [It is easier to strike the ball just after the apex, watching for the apex helps you track the ball.]

6. Anticipating the Line of Flight of the Ball Working Alone

Here we discuss variations on the "Castle Game" (see **Figure 22.7**). We are grateful to Dr. Tim Hopper for teaching us the Castle Game (Hopper, 2003; Hopper & Bell, 2000). The Castle Game tasks (see **Figure 22.8**) help children learn to move after they strike a ball and to judge the line of flight of the ball.

A. Stand about five feet away from a hula hoop (or a poly spot for older children). Toss a playground or vinyl ball up at least higher than your head so it bounces once in the hoop. Run around to the other side of the hoop and catch the ball before it bounces a second time. Without traveling with the ball, immediately toss it again from the location where you caught the ball.

Progressive Modifications (Hopper, 2003)

B. From a self-bounce in place, strike the ball underhand so it bounces in the hoop. Run around the hoop (reposition yourself), and catch the ball before it bounces a second time.

C. Self-toss the ball up, and set the ball so it bounces in the hoop. Run around and catch it.

D. Self-toss the ball up, and use a forearm pass to make the ball bounce in the hoop. Run around and catch it.

E. Design your own game using different body parts to strike the ball. Try different combinations of body parts.

7. Anticipating the Line of Flight of the Ball Working with a Partner

A. Stand 10 feet apart from a partner. Place a poly spot (or hula hoop if you think the spot is too difficult) on the ground in between you. Toss a playground ball up at least higher than your head, and try to have it bounce on the poly spot or in the hoop. Your partner must catch it after one bounce; then, from the location where the ball was caught, your partner should toss the ball up and try to bounce it on the poly spot for you to catch before a second bounce. Repeat this sequence as many times in a row as you can.

Because children must return the shot from the location where they caught the ball, the receiver learns to judge the likely flight of the ball and to move into position to catch it after one bounce. Aligning with the ball is a difficult component of net/wall game skills for children to develop.

Progressive Modifications

B. Use a small cone instead of a poly spot (the "castle"). Throw the ball down, trying to knock the cone castle over.

C. Self-toss a vinyl ball or trainer volleyball, and set the ball so it bounces on a poly spot, bounces in a hoop, or hits a cone representing a castle.

D. Self-toss a vinyl ball or trainer volleyball, and do a forearm pass so it bounces on a poly sport, bounces in a hoop, or hits a cone representing a castle.

E. Play the game while striking with different body parts.

F. Play the game using only striking skills (e.g., striking with the palm or forearm passing back and forth) without catching the ball.

G. Design a cooperative scoring system that awards points for hitting the castle or based on the number of times in a row the pair can toss/strike the ball in/on the hoop/poly spot and then catch it.

(*continues*)

SAMPLE LEARNING EXPERIENCES 22.3

Level 2B: Tactics for Striking to Open Space and Covering Space (*continued*)

H. For children ready for a competitive game, design a scoring system for knocking down the castle or not catching the ball after one bounce.

I. Design your own castle game. For example, you can use different body parts to strike the ball, a racket, one or two bounces, different castle targets, and different scoring systems.

Sample Questions to Ask

- Where should you be to catch or strike the ball? [Aligned behind the line of flight, behind and under it to forearm pass, aligned to the side for a forehand stroke.]
- What can help you get to the ball before the second bounce? [Don't stand in place after you hit. Immediately run to the other side to catch the ball.]
- What should you do after you toss or strike the ball? [Quickly run into position to catch it.]
- Is it easier or harder to catch the ball when you toss it high? [Easier because it gives me more time to run to the other side to catch it.]

Figure 22.7 Modifications of the Castle Game

Figure 22.8 Class of children playing the Castle Game

on their serve but not make the serve too difficult to return. For example, sometimes children need to use a toss to serve rather than striking the ball because some types of balls are too difficult to serve over high nets or over low nets that are too far away. Some balls also are too difficult to return when served with strong force from a long distance.

We begin with a set of sample learning experiences 22.4 to teach children how to design net game structures while throwing and catching deck rings and playing in a 2v2 format. These learning experiences serve as a template for planning units on volleyball striking skills over high nets. We then provide a template for designing net/wall games over a low net, striking with different body parts. These learning experiences can be adapted to plan units on striking with rackets.

SAMPLE LEARNING EXPERIENCES 22.4

Level 3: Designing and Modifying Game Structures

Designing Net Games Tossing and Catching Deck Rings Over a High (Six-Foot) Net: Understanding Boundaries, Scoring Systems, Game Rules, and Serving Rules

1. Designing Boundaries

A. Today we will work on designing a net game: Take a deck ring and jump ropes; you will use the jump ropes for boundaries. Find a space across one of the nets I set up for you [five to six feet high]. Experiment first with narrow boundaries and then with wide boundaries. Notice when the boundaries get so narrow that keeping a rally going is difficult. Notice when the boundaries are so wide that the ring can be tossed in bounds but is impossible to catch.

B. Then set perfect-sized boundaries, just as you learned to do in tag games.

2. Designing the Scoring System

C. Now decide on a scoring system: Many different scoring systems are used in net games, and these systems have changed over the years. The old rules in volleyball were that you scored only when your team served, a game was 15 points, and you needed to win by 2 points. If there was a tie, you kept playing until one team was ahead by 2 points. Now you can score no matter which team serves.

You also have to decide when to change which team gets to serve. In tennis, you serve an entire game. In racquetball, you keep serving until you lose a point, and then your opponent gets to serve.

Design your own scoring system and play a game.

D. Stop. Think critically and discuss whether you like the scoring system or want to change it. Make changes and play again.

3. Setting Rules for Running with the Ring

E. I noticed that there were some problems in your deck ring game. What seemed unfair to you? [The opponent would run up to the net and then toss it over.] Right. That shot isn't fair because there is no defense you can possibly use. What rule do we need to set to prevent that? [No running with the ring.] Right. You must toss the ring from wherever you caught it.

4. Designing Serving Rules

F. I noticed you are having problems returning the serve. Why? [It's too hard. The opponents are standing right by the net, and we can't possibly cover all that space, so we never get a rally going.] Right. That's why in tennis- and volleyball-type net games, you must serve from behind the baseline. In badminton, racquetball, and one-wall handball, you stand behind a service line in the middle of the court. This leaves you enough of an angle to make a shot but not so much that your opponent can never return the serve. Some games have a serving box in which the ball must bounce (tennis, racquetball, handball). Decide on a rule for serving that gives both teams a fair chance to score.

5. Designing Rotation Rules

G. What other rules do you think you need to make serving fair? Is it fun and fair if the same person serves all the time and some people never get to serve? [No.] In net/wall games, there is always a system for fairly rotating who serves. You have many options. In volleyball, the players rotate in a clockwise circle so everyone gets to serve and play front and back. In tennis, one person serves the entire game; then one person on the other team gets to serve. In the next game, the serve goes back to the

(*continues*)

SAMPLE LEARNING EXPERIENCES 22.4

Level 3: Designing and Modifying Game Structures (*continued*)

first serving team, and the second partner serves. In doubles badminton, it is even more complex. One person serves until the team loses a point. Then both players on the other team (one at a time) get to serve until their team loses a point. Then it goes back to the original serving team, and this time both players get to serve. Obviously, there are many fair ways to rotate serves in various sports. You design a system for rotating serve that you think is fair.

6. Revising Games

H. Let's share the rules you designed. [Call on different groups to show and describe their games. Ask the children to discuss what they liked about different systems.]

I. Play your game again, making any changes based on the rules you liked from listening to other groups.

7. Teaching Tactics

Once children have designed games and edited those games until they work well, you then progress to helping them learn and improve on the tactics in the game. See the Sample Learning Experiences later in this section and the Sample Plans at the end of the chapter to help you plan how to teach these tactics.

Designing Net Games Striking with Different Body Parts Over a Low (Three-Foot) Net: Understanding Boundaries, Scoring Systems, Rules, and Serving Rules

1. Designing the Initial Game

A. Today you are going to design a striking game using different body parts to strike a ball over a low net. First, let's explore striking with different body parts and types of balls. In your assigned group of four, get a rally working over a low net by striking a vinyl ball using different body parts.

B. This time, rally and let the ball bounce once, bounce twice, or hit it on the fly.

C. Now, explore rallying using different types of balls (e.g., nylon-net balloons, packing peanut–filled beach balls, beach balls, trainer volleyballs).

D. Design a striking game. As a group, make the following decisions:

- Select which ball to use.
- Decide which body parts to use. You can select specific body parts, you can decide to allow only two different body parts, or you can use any body parts.
- Decide whether you want a rule for the number of bounces or hitting the ball on the fly.
- Set perfect boundaries.
- Decide on a scoring system and a fair way to rotate serving.

2. Modifying Serving Rules

E. I noticed you had problems returning the serve (or getting the serve over the net). How can you modify the serve or service rules so you can all get a serve over the net that the other team has a reasonable chance to return? Discuss this problem. Come up with a solution. Play your game and then, using the play–discuss–play cycle, modify your game until you have a great game.

SAMPLE LEARNING EXPERIENCES 22.5

Level 3: Tactics for Creating and Covering Space

Tactics for Creating Space

The first set of learning experiences helps children learn the tactics of creating space by hitting to open spaces to the sides, close to the net, deep, or over their opponents' heads. These tactics are easiest to learn using deck rings; later, you can progress to using striking skills (see **Figure 22.9**). As children learn these tactics, they will simultaneously be learning drop shots, clears, lobs, and dinks (depending on whether you are doing racket games over low nets or volleyball-type games). To accommodate the individual differences between partners, the size of boundaries does not have to be the same on both sides. The number of bounces, number of hits per side, and rackets used do not have to be the same for each player, either.

SAMPLE LEARNING EXPERIENCES 22.5

Level 3: Tactics for Creating and Covering Space (*continued*)

Equipment Progression

- Deck tennis rings over a high net (five to six feet)
- Striking a vinyl ball with the hands over a low net, letting the ball bounce once
- Striking with light rackets over a low net, letting the ball bounce once
- Striking with large, light balls over a high net

1. 1v1 Creating Space by Shot Placement to the Sides: Tossing and Catching Deck Rings

A. Toss the ring over the net as close as you can to the side boundaries. When your opponent catches it right next to the boundary, is there a lot of space between her or him and the other sideline? Yes. You created that space for your next shot. If you toss the next shot way over to the other side, your partner will have a long way to run. Go play the game and work on creating space. The rules are the same: After you catch the ring, you must toss it back from where you caught it. No running with the ring allowed. Set up boundaries with your partner to create an area of size you think you can cover.

B. Rotate partners many times. [These learning experiences can be modified and used with striking skills over low or high nets using easy-to-strike equipment.]

Sample Questions to Ask

- What did you do when you successfully tossed the ring and it landed on the ground before your partner could catch it? [I tossed it close to the sidelines. I tossed it as soon as I caught it.]
- Why did that work? [My partner had a long way to run and didn't have time to get to the other side of the court.]
- When do you make the decision about where to toss the ring? [You can't wait until you catch the ring and then look around because by then your partner will have had enough time to get to center. You need to decide before you catch the ring where to toss it next so you can catch and toss in one motion.]

2. 1v1 Creating Space by Shot Placement Deep and Short (Tossing and Catching Deck Rings or Striking Balls)

A. With your partner, set narrow, deep boundaries and rally by tossing/hitting to an open space, trying to make your partner move to catch the ring/hit the ball.

B. With the boundaries narrow and deep, where are the open spaces? [Deep and near the net.] When you throw/hit a ring/ball close to the net, we call it a *drop shot* (see **Figure 22.10**). When you throw/hit a ring/ball high and deep, we call it a *clear* in some games or a *lob* in others.

C. Rally again, working to keep your drop shots very close to the net, and make your clears high and deep.

Sample Questions to Ask

- What do you have to do to get the ring/ball in the back of the court? [Toss/hit it higher than my opponent can reach.]
- Compare the amount of force you use on a drop shot and on a clear/lob.
- How does the force of your swing affect the shot? How much force do you use to send the ring/ball deep? [Strong force.] How much force do you use to send the ring/ball just over the net? [Light force.]
- How large is your swing, and how much speed do you use to swing the racket when striking the ball deep? [Large, fast.] How large is your swing when striking the ball short, just over the net? [Short.]

(*continues*)

Figure 22.9 Striking so your partner must move to the side to return the shot

Courtesy of John Dolly

SAMPLE LEARNING EXPERIENCES 22.5

Level 3: Tactics for Creating and Covering Space (*continued*)

- How does the direction of your swing affect the shot? [The ball goes in the same direction.]
- Which types of shots can you use to toss/hit a clear? [The answers will vary depending on equipment but can include overhand, underhand, Frisbee toss, sets, and forearm passes.]
- If you can't score on a shot, how can you create as much space as possible for your next shot? [Hit it high and deep to a corner or short and to a corner.]
- If your opponent forces you out of a good defensive position, what do you think you can do to gain more time to get back into a central ready position? [Hit a high, deep shot.]

3. 1v1 Moving Closer to the Net for a Wider Angle and Space for Shots

A. Experiment with your partner. Set a square boundary on both sides of a low net. Rally by striking a large, light ball (e.g., vinyl ball) using your palms, letting the ball bounce once within the boundaries before returning the shot. First, position yourself behind the baseline and try to make your partner move side to side to return your shot.

B. Now, one of you positions yourself approximately two yards from the net. Rally again, and try to make your partner move to return your shot. For this experiment, don't use lobs or clears. You can hit the ball on the fly without letting it bounce. Switch roles.

C. In which position did you have more space to place your hit? [When I was closer to the net.] I will draw this for you on the whiteboard (see **Figure 22.11**). You can see that the closer you are to the net, the wider the angle you have in which you can hit the ball.

D. Go back to your court, rally, and work on hitting to open spaces while making your partner move to return the shot. How do you think you can apply the tactic of getting closer to the net to give yourself a wider angle for your shots? [You could run up to the net and hit the ball before it bounces. You can move up if your partner hits a short shot.]

4. 2v2 Passing to a Teammate Closer to the Net for a Wider Angle and Space for Shots (Using Deck Rings)

Passing to a Player Closer to the Net

A. Play 2v2 tossing and catching deck rings. What do you think will change now that you have two people on each team? [It will be harder to find open spaces. You don't know what they are thinking.] Based on what you learned about angles, where do you have the most open space into which you can throw a ring to score? [Close to the net because the angle is widest there.]

   In our games today, you can pass the ring to each other before you send it back over the net. Let's start by exploring which tactics you can use once the first person on your team catches the ring. Think to yourself, if my teammate catches the ring, what can I do to toss the ring so it is difficult to return? Remember the rule that you must toss the ring from wherever you catch it; no running with the ring is allowed. Go with your assigned group of four and set boundaries for the area you think you can cover. Divide into two teams, discuss possible tactics, and play.

B. Stop. Which tactics did you discover that made it difficult for the other team to catch the ring? [After one person caught the ring, the other ran to the net. We then passed the ring to the person close to the net and sent it over to an open space.

Figure 22.10 Drop shot using light force

Courtesy of John Dolly

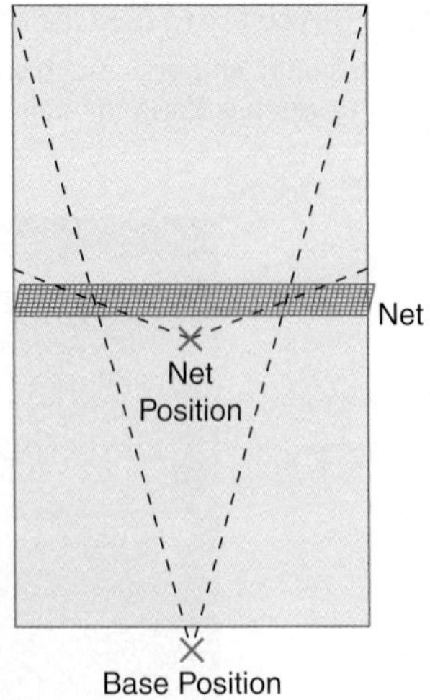

Figure 22.11 Possible angles for a shot from the base line and the net

SAMPLE LEARNING EXPERIENCES 22.5

Level 3: Tactics for Creating and Covering Space (*continued*)

We passed and shot quickly. We did not give the other team much time to reposition themselves. We did not stand around watching; we were always moving.]

C. Go back to your court, play again, and work on passing to a player who runs quickly to a position close to the net.

Communication

D. What problems are you having? [Sometimes we don't know who is supposed to catch the ring and who is supposed to run to the net for the pass.] Can any group share a way to solve that problem? [We called who was going to catch the ring.] We call this *communicating*. You need to communicate with each other so the ring does not drop in between you. What can you say to communicate? [Mine. I got it.]

Using More Difficult Skills and Equipment

Repeat the preceding tasks in a volleyball-type game using light, easy-to-control balls for striking over high nets, such as webbed balloons, vinyl balls, and trainer volleyballs. If children can't get a rally working, modify the rules to include one bounce and/or two taps in a row by one person and make the boundaries smaller. You also can progress to 3v3 when the children are ready.

5. 2v2 Tactics for Covering Space Using Different Formations

These learning experiences can be modified for badminton-type games using junior badminton rackets and for tennis-type games using rackets and balls appropriate for children's abilities to rally successfully.

Designing the Game and Getting the Game Working

A. Play 2v2 using volleyball striking skills with a high net (five to six feet). In your assigned group of four,
   - Select a ball for volleyball that all of you can successfully set and forearm pass. [Provide as many options as you have, including beach balls, vinyl balls, packing peanut–stuffed beach balls, nylon-net balloons, and trainer volleyballs.]
   - Set perfect boundaries.
   - Decide whether you want to require that all balls must be hit on the fly or whether one bounce is allowed if needed.
   - Decide whether you want to allow someone to hit the ball twice in a row if needed to get it under control.
   - Set up scoring and serving rules, and decide whether you want to keep track of the score.
   - Then rally. If you can't get a good rally that is challenging but allows everyone success, then change the rules or the equipment until you can. You might need to have different rules for different children, in the same way that we used different levels of defense for different children when we played invasion games.

Sample Questions to Ask to Get the Games Working Well

- Is there any way you can make this game better?
- Does everyone feel the game is fair and fun?
- Do you have any problems? How can you solve them?
- Are the boundaries too wide or too narrow, too long or too short?

Tactics for Covering Space Using Different Formations

B. Now that you have good games, experiment with different formations you can use to cover space on defense. What choices do you have? [We can stand side to side. One of us can be close to the net, and the other can be behind.] Let's start by experimenting with side-to-side.

C. Pay attention to how this formation works on offense and on defense, and in which situations. Later, we will compare and contrast side-to-side with the up-and-back formation.

D. Now, everyone play using an up-and-back formation and see how it works in different situations.

E. What did you learn in your experiment? Which formation worked best on offense and in which situations? Which formation worked best on defense and in which situations?

Rotate Teams to Play Different Pairs and Progress to 3v3 When Ready

F. Predict what will happen when we add a third player to each team.

G. Experiment with different formations.

H. Then compare and contrast which formations worked best and in which situations.

(*continues*)

SAMPLE LEARNING EXPERIENCES 22.5

Level 3: Tactics for Creating and Covering Space (*continued*)

Sample Questions to Ask

- When the opponents are side to side, where are the open spaces? [Close to the net and deep.]
- Why is a shot to the center difficult when you are playing in a side-to-side formation? [You don't know who should move to the ball. You think your partner is going to get it.]
- When you played a good team, what did they do that made them good? Besides not being able to hit the ball over the net, which tactics make a team weak? [Hit it right to me, didn't move to receive the ball, didn't recover to a good position to cover space, moved too late.] What advice would you give them to help them be more successful?

SKILLS BOX 22.1

Technical Reference Information for Teachers About Striking Skills

In this section, we describe technical information about immature and mature movement patterns for striking skills. This technical information informs your observations of children's movement patterns and helps you make decisions about which lesson content is appropriate and which performance techniques the children need and are ready to learn. More than any other skills, the performance techniques of the most mature movement patterns of striking skills are well beyond the needs and capabilities of children in the younger grades.

Because striking skills take many years to develop, we work on performance techniques while increasing the difficulty each year during the K–5 grades. We begin teaching level 1 striking skills by having children explore striking balloons, beach balls, vinyl balls, and other light balls with different body parts and light rackets. We focus on a few basic performance techniques that transfer across striking actions, such as getting the body part under the ball to strike it up. As children acquire the ability to strike a ball back and forth over a net continuously in level 2 rallies, which typically occurs by third grade, we progressively teach the more advanced techniques of skills, such as a forearm volleyball pass and a tennis forehand. In level 3, we teach techniques that are more difficult still, such as those related to a tennis serve.

The more advanced performance techniques of volleyball skills and tennis/racquetball strokes are information you need to know as a teacher but not what you start teaching children in kindergarten. Many advanced performance techniques are not meaningful, necessary, or helpful when children are first introduced to striking skills. Once children can rally cooperatively and understand basic tactics, the more advanced techniques then become meaningful, and you can teach them to either individuals or the class as a whole.

Remember the key guideline when teaching elementary-age children: *Tell them what they need to know, when they need to know it.* Begin with a task designed to get children practicing the skill, and set task and environmental constraints to elicit the performance techniques you are after. Then, based on your observations, teach the children whichever performance technique is most important. Knowing which performance techniques children need and when to teach them is a hallmark of effective teaching and an ability all teachers need to develop.

Striking Over a Low Net with the Hands or Racket

Immature Movement Patterns for Striking Over a Low Net with the Hands or Racket

Grip

- Holding the racket with the V between the thumb and index finger behind the racket.
- Pointing the index finger down the racket shaft (not wrapped around the grip).

Preparation

- Standing in place and reaching to hit the ball rather than moving the feet to position the body sideways to the ball.

Action

- Hitting down on top of the ball.
- Swinging too early or too late.
- Using an underhand swing when a sideways swing is more appropriate.
- Wrists rotated backward so the face of the racket is sideways.

Follow-Through

- Partial or no follow-through.

Reaching to hit rather than moving the feet

SKILLS BOX 22.1

Technical Reference Information for Teachers About Striking Skills (*continued*)

Using an underhand swing when a sideways swing would be more appropriate

Potential Refinements for Striking a Ball Over a Low Net with Hand or Racquet

Such content includes striking a ball off a tee to a wall, striking from a self-bounce, and so on.

Basic Techniques When Children Are at Developmental Level 1

- Handshake grip.
- Turn side to target, position slightly behind and to the side of the ball.
- After the apex of the bounce, hit the ball on its way down.
- Circle hand or racket back and down, start swing low, swing up and forward, follow through high.
- Hit the side of the ball (not its bottom).

More Advanced Techniques When Children Are at Developmental Level 2

This content includes cooperative rallies.

Preparation

- Track the ball; keep eyes on the ball at contact.
- Assume the ready position: Start in and return to the ready position—knees bent, feet shoulder-width apart, and weight on the balls of the feet. Be ready to move.
- Recognize that the direction of your swing and angle of the face of your hand, racket, or other body part will make the ball go in the same direction.

More Advanced Techniques When Children Are at Developmental Level 3

Swing

- Keep the non-racket shoulder pointing to the net at the start of the backswing.
- Squeeze the racket on contact, and keep a firm wrist.
- Step toward the net, transfer your weight forward, and hit the ball opposite the front hip.
- Keep the racket face perpendicular; swing from down to up. At contact, the arm and the racket form an L shape.

Follow-Through

- Follow through by turning to face the net and swinging the racket up and across the body.

Mature pattern moving to hit

Courtesy of John Dolly

End of follow-through

Courtesy of John Dolly

(*continues*)

SKILLS BOX 22.1

Technical Reference Information for Teachers About Striking Skills (*continued*)

Striking a Ball High

Immature Movement Patterns for Striking a Ball High

- Not getting underneath the ball.
- Bringing the hands up by the shoulders and dropping the elbows, so as to swat the ball with a downward swing.
- Partial or no follow-through.

Set/Overhead Pass

Immature Movement Patterns for Set/Overhead Passes

- Hands apart above the head, elbows bent, and arms swinging forward and down rather than straight up.
- Uses only the arms to generate force; does not use the legs.
- Hits with the palms of hands.
- Hands too low.

Immature movement pattern of the set/overhead pass

Backhand

Courtesy of John Dolly

Forearm Pass

Immature Movement Patterns for Forearm Passes

- Swings arms too high.
- Bends elbows.
- Bends forward at hips rather than bending knees.
- Hits with hands rather than forearm platform.

Immature movement pattern of the forearm pass

Immature movement pattern of the forearm pass

SKILLS BOX 22.1

Technical Reference Information for Teachers About Striking Skills (*continued*)

Underhand Serve

Immature Movement Patterns for Underhand Serves

- Stands straight before contact.
- Bends elbow on contact and follow-through.
- Nondominant hand holding the ball moves forward as the striking arm moves forward, striking with knuckles.

Striking a Ball High with Different Body Parts

Potential Refinements for Striking a Ball High to Self or Over a Five- to Six-Foot Net with Different Body Parts

Basic Techniques When Children Are at Developmental Level 1

- Get the body part or racket under the ball.
- Swing the body part in the direction you want the ball to go.
- For overhead hits to yourself, get your body and hands under the ball, and extend your arms up.

More Advanced Techniques When Children Are at Developmental Level 2

- Set: Hands over hairline, thumbs point to eyes, fingers spread, curved hands, hands form a window above forehead. Cue: Thumbs point to eyes.
- Set: Contact on finger pads, and extend arms up like Superman. Cue: Superman.
- Forearm pass: Thumbs parallel, heels of hands together.
- Forearm pass: Flat platform (rotate arms in so elbows face ground).

More Advanced Techniques When Children Are at Developmental Level 3

Set

- Bend and extend the knees to generate force.
- Face the target.

Forearm Pass

- Keep the knees bent and arms parallel to the thighs; extend the knees and lift the arms using a small striking action.
- The platform moves toward the target.

Underhand Serve

- With the non-hitting-side foot in front, lean forward; the striking arm swings back. Toss the ball with the nondominant hand in front and to the striking-arm side.
- Step and transfer weight forward, swing the hitting arm forward, hit with a firm palm or fist, and then stand up.

Ready position for the set

Ready position for the forearm pass

Underhand serve

Striking with a Racket for Children in Wheelchairs

- The serve, forehand, and backhand patterns are the same whether sitting or standing. However, the racket handle must be small enough for the child in a wheelchair to hold the racket and push the wheel at the same time. The racket is not set on the lap while traveling.
- In wheelchair tennis, the ball is allowed to bounce twice, including the second bounce being outside the court.

Theory in Practice: Using Stories and Metaphors

One way to explain the arm action of the set is to use a story and image that children enjoy and find easy to remember. The cue is "Slurp and burp." Pretend the ball is a two-liter bottle of soda. Hold the bottle high so it will pour into your mouth and you can gulp the soda down. If it is too far back, the soda will spill on your head. If it is too far forward, it will spill on your shirt. What happens when you gulp down soda? Right—you burp. This time, the burp starts from your toes, knees, whole body, and arms, and you end up straight pointing up with both hands. So the cue to remind you how to set is "Slurp and burp."

(*continues*)

SKILLS BOX 22.1

Technical Reference Information for Teachers About Striking Skills (*continued*)

Volleyball for Children in Wheelchairs

- For setting, the overhead serve, and the forearm pass, the performance techniques are the same. However, these techniques vary depending on the child's balance capabilities, which are highly individual. Children with less advanced balance capabilities can use one hand to strike while keeping the other hand on the wheel for balance. Children may need to throw and catch light balls rather than strike them.
- For an underhand serve, hold the ball with one arm (elbow and forearm) resting on the lap to help with balance. The hand holding the ball is to the side, and the hit is from a held ball or a toss, depending on the child and the ball.

Summary

In the elementary school years, lessons and units on net/wall skills, game-like situations, and games focus on teaching children to strike a variety of balls with different body parts and rackets to a wall, over low nets (approximately three feet), and over high nets (five to six feet). We also teach children how to vary the movement patterns to strike to different levels, with different degrees of force, in different directions, and using the appropriate relationships of their body, body parts or racket and the ball. This variety provides a sound foundation for children to participate in a range of lifelong sports and leisure outdoor and beach activities.

Teaching children to rally is critical and requires that you modify the equipment. Adult-sized rackets and regulation-size and -weight balls are not proportionate to children's size, strength, and skill levels. A wide range of modified equipment is now manufactured for the smallest kindergarteners to the largest fifth-graders. As children grow and gain skill, we increase the difficulty of the equipment, progressing toward more adult-sized and -weight rackets and balls.

Striking skills take many years to develop, but the tactics of striking games are comparatively easy to learn. We focus first on the tactic of consistently returning the shot and then address the tactics of striking to open spaces and covering space on defense.

Review Questions

1. Why is it critical to modify equipment for net/wall games?
2. What rules for a low-net game and equipment options should you design and provide for a child in a wheelchair who is paired with a child not in a wheelchair?
3. Why do you need to reteach children about personal space during striking lessons?
4. (a) Describe net/wall game defensive tactics; and (b) write a task for each that has children experiment with different options to understand these tactics.
5. Describe an open space, and explain how you might teach this concept to children.
6. Describe in language a child can understand how you create space in net/wall games.
7. Describe how you can teach children the tactics to create space.
8. Explain and diagram why the closer you are to the net, the more space you have on offense.
9. When teaching level 2 striking using keep-it-up tasks, what are five ways to vary the task?
10. Write a level 2 task for cooperative rallying over a high net and one potential refining task to help children improve their performance technique.
11. Write a level 2 task for cooperative rallying over a low net and one potential refining task to help children improve their performance technique.
12. What are the basic game structures of net/wall games that you teach children when they are designing games?
13. What are the different 2v2 and 3v3 formations that are possible, and how can you teach children these formations?
14. What are two performance cues for striking over high nets that cross several skills?
15. What are three performance cues for striking over a low net that also apply to striking with the hands or a racket?

References

Buszard, T., Farrow, D., Reid, M., & Masters, R. S. W. (2014). Modifying equipment in early skill development: A tennis perspective. *Research Quarterly for Exercise and Sport, 85*, 218–225.

Davids, K., Button, C., & Bennett, S. (2008). *Dynamics of skill acquisition: A constraints-led approach*. Champaign, IL: Human Kinetics.

Harvey, S., & van der Mars, H. (2010). Teaching and assessing racquet games using "play practice" Part 1: Designing the right games. *Journal of Physical Education, Recreation and Dance, 81*(4), 26–33, 54.

Hopper, T. F. (1998). Teaching games for understanding using progressive principles of play. *CAHPERD, 64*(3), 4–7.

Hopper, T. F. (2003). Four Rs for tactical awareness: Applying game performance assessment in net/wall games. *Teaching Elementary Physical Education, 14*(2), 16–21.

Hopper, T. F., & Bell, R. (2000). A tactical framework for teaching games: Teaching strategic understanding. *CAHPERD, 66*(4), 14–19.

Rink, J. E. (2014). *Teaching physical education for learning* (7th ed.). New York: McGraw-Hill.

FYI

Summary of Task Label Abbreviations

I	Informing tasks
E	Extending/exploring tasks
R	Refinements
A	Application/assessment tasks
Org	Organizing task
Cog K	Cognitive knowledge: Explains or defines a concept
Social	Social skill or concept
Th	Thinking skill
Mot	Motivation concept
Safety	Safety information or reminder
MD	Modification to make the task more difficult
ME	Modification to make the task easier

Source: Adapted and Modifed from Rink, J. E. (2014). *Teaching physical education for learning* (7th ed.).New York: McGraw-Hill.

Sample Plans For Levels 1, 2, and 3 Net/Wall Skills and Games

In this section, we expand on the sample learning experiences to help you imagine how the content in this chapter might be taught in actual school environments. As you read these plans, imagine you are the teacher, and think about how you might respond on your feet while teaching the content.

We include potential interactive decisions, such as performance techniques to teach if your observations of the children's movements suggest they need to learn a particular technique at a particular moment. Effective teachers begin by giving children tasks that are likely to elicit the performance techniques needed. If the children are already using a particular performance technique, then it is a waste of time to teach it. If not, then decide which performance technique is most important. Teach what they need to know, when they need to know it.

We also include teaching thinking and social skills to illustrate how you might integrate these skills into lesson segments. We suggest beginning teachers plan to teach only one social or thinking skill that relates directly to the lesson content. As you gain experience, you will be able to teach both thinking and social skills within lessons when the need arises, such as when a class misbehaves or groups do not work cooperatively on tasks. These "teachable moments" occur often in school settings, and you will learn how to capitalize on them over time.

SAMPLE PLAN 22.1

Level 1: Striking a Beach Ball with Different Body Parts

Strike a Beach Ball Up with Different Body Parts, Trying to Make Consecutive Hits

Standards

This plan addresses National Standards 1, 2, and 4 and CCSS for vocabulary acquisition.

Objectives

Children will learn

Motor

1. To strike a beach ball up with different body parts, getting the body part under the ball and making consecutive hits.

Cognitive Knowledge

2. That to strike a ball up, you must strike directly underneath it.

Creative Thinking

3. To explore by trying to use many varied body parts to strike.

Thinking Skill: Self-Regulation

4. To think about one performance technique while striking.

Social

5. To show they care for classmates by not interfering with their classmates' work, such as by walking through or striking a ball into their classmates' personal space.

Notes and Potential Interactive Teaching Decisions

Notes: Children can take from three to five lessons to learn this content. Using beach balls or other light balls is typically a progression from striking with balloons, which travel at a very slow speed. Other light balls include nylon-webbed balloons, balloons with nylon hose inside, and light plastic balls.

Observation Plan

1. Scan for safety to see if children are remaining in personal space and if not is it due to lack of space, striking too forcefully, or striking forward or to the sides rather than straight up.
2. Watch to see if they get the body part directly under the ball.
3. Watch to see if individual children are exploring different body parts.

(*continues*)

SAMPLE PLAN 22.1

Level 1: Striking a Beach Ball with Different Body Parts (*continued*)

CCSS

6. To acquire and accurately use conversational, general academic, and domain-specific words and phrases, including those that signal precise actions.

Content Development

I Pick up a beach ball from one of the hula hoops spread around the edges of the physical education space, find a personal space, and try to strike the ball straight up in the air using your hands. **E** Experiment to see if you can figure out what you need to do to hit the ball straight up.	**Social** If the ball travels out of your personal space, walk to catch it without interfering with another child's work. Show you care about your classmates by walking back to your space while avoiding other children's personal space, and begin again.
Th What did you figure out? [To hit the ball straight up, you need to get your hand directly underneath the ball.] **R** Right. Think "underneath" every time you strike the ball.	**MD/ME** If you are successful in keeping the ball in your personal space, try to strike it as many times in a row as you can. Alternatively, you can catch it and start over if it doesn't go straight up, or you can simply throw or catch the ball.
E Explore striking sometimes with your left hand, sometimes with your right hand, and sometimes with both hands.	**R** To hit the ball straight up, your palm must face straight up. The ball goes in the direction your palm faces and the direction of your tap.
E Explore striking the ball with different body parts. **CCSS** When I say, "Explore," I want you to find many body parts and varied body parts for striking the ball. "Many" means "a lot." "Varied" means "different." So explore and try to find a lot of different body parts that can be used for striking the ball.	**Scaffolding Exploration** If necessary, you may need to scaffold children's exploration. Examples: • Which body parts do you think you can use to strike the ball? [Forearms, head, thighs, different parts of the feet, palms, back of hand, and so on.] • I see many students using their hands. What about your feet or parts of your leg? What other parts might you try?
E Explore striking with a different body part each time you strike the ball.	**R** What do you need to do to hit the ball straight up? [Get the body part directly underneath the ball.]
E Try to strike the ball up as many times as you can in a row using one body part. Then try again but using a different body part. Then change to another body part. [Repeat several more times.]	**E** Try forearms, feet (laces), inside of the foot, outside of the foot, thighs, elbows, head, palms, and back of the hand.
E How many different body parts can you use to strike the ball without letting it touch the ground?	**Th** Are you thinking about your movement while you are moving? What do you need to think about? [Get the body part underneath the ball.]
E Explore striking the ball by alternating two different body parts.	
E Explore different combinations of body parts to strike the ball (e.g., foot and hand, head and laces, thigh and inside of foot, forearm and head).	**Th** Are you trying to use many different combinations of body parts?

Culminating Activity

A Here is a fun challenge: See how many different parts of your body you can tap with the ball without repeating a body part.

CCSS Closure

Sit with your partner and discuss how you explored striking and the meaning of the word "explore." Next,

- Tell her or him which body parts you used.
- Discuss which were your two favorite body parts to use to strike and why.
- Discuss which body parts were most difficult and which were easiest to use to strike.

Potential Assessment

On the slip of paper, write your name and draw a smiley face if you never interfered with another classmates' personal space. Draw a neutral face with a straight line for a mouth if you made an honest mistake and hit the ball into someone else's personal space. Draw a face with a frown if you didn't work hard to stay in your personal space.

SAMPLE PLAN 22.2

Level 2A: Cooperative Rally with a Partner Comparing and Contrasting a Variety of Balls, Rackets, and Net Heights

Cooperative Rally with a Partner Comparing and Contrasting a Variety of Balls, Rackets, and Net Heights	Notes and Potential Interactive Teaching Decisions
Standards This plan addressed National Standards 1, 2, and 5 and CCSS for speaking, listening, and collaborating. **Objectives** Children will learn to **Motor** 1. Strike a variety of balls with a variety of rackets standing side to target, swinging from low to high. 2. Recover to a central ready position after every hit. **Thinking Skill** 3. Compare and contrast striking with different balls, rackets, and net heights.	*Equipment:* Have six centers set for every 24 children (two pairs per center sharing the space). At four centers, set nets at five feet. Have two wall centers. Each center focuses on different balls and rackets. For teachers with large classes, add more centers or more space at each center. *Prerequisite knowledge:* Understanding that the direction of your swing and the angle of the face of your hand, racket, or other body part will make the ball go in the same direction.
Social 4. Share space safely, paying attention to how the racket increases the amount of personal space needed for each child. 5. Show they care about their partners by working hard to hit returnable shots. **Affective** 6. Appreciate the enjoyment and challenge of working with different balls, rackets, and net heights. **CCSS** 7. Engage effectively in a range of collaborative discussions with diverse partners and within a whole class, building on others' ideas and expressing their own clearly.	**Observation Plan**  1. Scan whether the children are a safe distance apart when they swing their rackets. 2. Watch for the circular backswing/follow-through-high sequence. 3. Watch for recovery to the ready position after every hit.
Lesson 1: Different Rackets and Different Balls	
I In the next four lessons, you will be practicing your striking skills at centers by experimenting with a variety of balls, rackets, and net heights. At the end of the lesson, be prepared to compare and contrast striking at the different centers. As you can see, I have six centers set up. When I say "Go," get with your assigned partner. I will send two pairs to each center. When you get to each center, pick up one racket from the equipment basket each and one ball between you and your partner. At the net centers, get on opposite sides of the net and try to strike the ball over the net as many times in a row as you can. At the wall centers, strike one ball to the wall, alternating between you and your partner hitting the ball. Try to aim so the ball bounces at your partner's forehand side. Go to your first station.	**Social** You will need to share the space. What do you need to remember about sharing space when we play striking games? [Be careful not to swing my racket when another person is nearby. My personal space is much bigger because it includes the racket, so I need to have more space available before I swing.]

(*continues*)

SAMPLE PLAN 22.2

Level 2A: Cooperative Rally with a Partner Comparing and Contrasting a Variety of Balls, Rackets, and Net Heights (*continued*)

Net Center 1: Coat hanger nylon stocking paddles and balloons. Low net. *Net Center 2:* Junior tennis racket with trainer tennis balls (high-density foam, medium size). Low net. *Wall Center 3:* Small, light racquetball rackets with vinyl balls. *Net Center 4:* Small, light racquetball or plastic rackets with high-density foam ball. Low net. *Wall Center 5:* Lollipop foam paddles with whiffle balls. *Net Center 6:* Striking Koosh balls with Koosh rackets (or other available rackets and balls). Low net.	**R** Use a circular backswing for every hit. Don't be tempted to simply hold the racket out in front and tap the ball from there. **R** Everyone, stop and get in the ready position. Excellent—you remember what that is. Be sure to start and return to the central ready position before every hit. **E** Does the ball always come to your racket side? What did you do when it went to your other side? We call that side your backhand side. Do you know why? The back of your hand faces the ball.
E Stop. Put your equipment back. Stand by the equipment basket, and point to your next center. Great job—everyone is pointing to the correct center. Rotate, and explore the next set of equipment. [Continue rotating through all six centers.]	**Social** Work really hard to send your partner a returnable shot. What can you do to hit a returnable shot? [Don't hit it too hard, aim to the partner's forehand side.]
Sample Questions to Ask **Th/CCSS** Talk to your partner, and compare and contrast the centers based on these questions: • What was different and what was the same at the centers? • At which center did you have your best rallies? • Which equipment was most challenging to use? Why do you think it was the hardest? [Length of racket, speed the ball moves, weight of the ball.] • Did you hit the ball the same way with each racket? • Which center did you enjoy the most?	After the children have discussed each topic, you can call on several groups to share their answers.
Th Tomorrow we are going to use whiffle balls with all the racquets. Can anyone predict what is going to happen?	
Lesson 2: Same Ball, Different Rackets	
I Today, you will practice striking at the same six centers using different rackets but using whiffle balls at every center. Be prepared to compare and contrast what you learn. **E** [Rotate as in lesson 1 until the children have experimented at each center.]	*Notes:* Set up the same six centers but use only whiffle balls. Objectives and observation plan remain the same unless the children are ready to focus on more advanced performance techniques. If so, write new motor objectives for this lesson.
Sample Questions to Ask **Th/CCSS** Compare and contrast the different rackets with the same ball: • What was the same and what was different with the different rackets? • With which racket did you have the most control? • Which racquet was the most challenging to use? • Which did you enjoy the most?	Have a whole-class discussion, or have the children discuss these questions in pairs or in groups of four and then share their responses with the whole class.
Th Tomorrow we will play using nets of different heights. Predict what you think will happen. How will you have to change your swing for different net heights? [If the net is high, we will have to hit more underneath the ball, and angle the racket upward more. When the net is low, we will have to hit the side of the ball.]	

SAMPLE PLAN 22.2

Level 2A: Cooperative Rally with a Partner Comparing and Contrasting a Variety of Balls, Rackets, and Net Heights (*continued*)

Lesson 3: Different Net Heights

I Today, we have six centers with nets at different heights. Everyone will start with vinyl balls and light rackets. We will rotate through the centers twice today. The second time, you and your partner will select your racket and ball. [Have the children rotate until they have experimented at each center.]	*Notes:* Again, add different lesson objectives and modify the observation plan if needed. *Equipment:* Set up six centers with nets of different height: very low nets, low nets, medium-height nets, high nets, and diagonal nets. Start with all children playing with vinyl balls and junior-sized, short-handled rackets (such as light, small racquetball rackets). Have a variety of rackets and balls available for the second rotation.
E Now that you have tried each center, select the racket that you want to use. You do not have to use the same racket as your partner. For example, I might choose a foam paddle, and you might choose a junior tennis racket. You and your partner will select a ball together. [Have the children rotate until they have experimented at each center.]	**R** Remember, the face of your racket and its relationship to the ball affect the direction of the ball's flight. If your racket is under the ball with the face diagonally up, the ball will go up over a high net. If the face is toward the top of a low net and you hit the side of the ball, your ball will go over the low net.
Sample Questions to Ask **Th/CCSS** • With your partner, compare and contrast your experiences with different net heights: • What was the same and what was different at each net height? *Class Discussion* • Put your thumbs up if you liked the low net. Who wants to share why? [It was fast.] • Put your thumbs up if you prefer the high net. Who wants to share why? [Hitting it high is fun. It allows you to hit the ball far, and then it's challenging to move quickly enough to get to the ball.] • Put your thumbs up if you liked the middle-height net. Who wants to share why? [You can use different amounts of force, and the challenge is to decide the right amount of force for the game situation.] • Put your thumbs up if you liked the slanted net. Who wants to share why? [You don't know if it will go to the high side or low side. I liked the challenge of the unknown.]	Give partners time to discuss, and then have a whole-class discussion. We have provided answers we have heard from children. Your class might respond very differently. Call on several children for each question.

Lesson 4: Children Select Racket, Ball, and Net Height

Additional Thinking Skill Objective Children will improve their ability to critique their striking movement pattern, and select one performance technique on which to focus.	*Notes:* Again, add different lesson objectives and modify the observation plan if needed. *Prerequisite knowledge:* Because this is a level 2A unit, the children will have been taught and can remember both basic and more advanced performance techniques for striking with rackets (see **Skills Box 22.1** for a list of performance techniques). Here you are asking them to continue to work on performance techniques they have learned but not yet mastered.
I Today you will select your racket, ball, and net height. You do not have to use the same racket as your partner. Go with your assigned partner, select your equipment and net height, and begin rallying.	**R** As you practice, critique your striking, and select one performance cue on which to focus that you think will best improve your skill.

(*continues*)

SAMPLE PLAN 22.2

Level 2A: Cooperative Rally with a Partner Comparing and Contrasting a Variety of Balls, Rackets, and Net Heights (*continued*)

Sample Questions to Ask

- Why did you select the racket, ball, and net height you did?
- What do you need to do to have a good rally?
- Which performance techniques did you select to focus on during your rallies?
- What do you need to do to become more skilled at striking?
- What did you enjoy most about your games?

SAMPLE PLAN 22.3

Level 2B: 1v1 Sending Deck Rings to Open Space

1v1 Tossing and Catching Deck Rings, Sending Rings to Open Space

Standards

This plan addresses National Standards 1, 2, and 4 and CCSS for vocabulary acquisition.

Objectives

Children will

Motor

1. Learn to toss a deck ring into open space.

Cognitive Knowledge

2. Understand that open space is the large space where their opponent is not standing and is typically between their opponent and the sidelines, endline, and/or net.

Thinking Skill

3. Learn to solve tactical problems of shooting into open space.

Social

4. Recognize that the goal of the games is for each child to improve and consequently cooperate with their partner to set boundaries that are the right size (i.e., challenging but allowing for success) based on the ability of the person on that side of the net.

CCSS

5. Acquire and accurately use domain-specific words and phrases, including those that signal spatial relationships, that is, open spaces in net game contexts.

Notes and Potential Interactive Teaching Decisions

Equipment: One deck tennis ring per pair, one five-foot net per pair, or plenty of space for several pairs to share a larger net.

Observation Plan

1. Scan to see if there is enough space between groups so if a child steps over the boundary there won't be a collision with other children.
2. Watch whether the children are sending the ring into open space or tossing it directly to their partner.
3. Decide whether the boundaries are large enough, allowing the children to see and send the ring into open space, or if they are too small, constraining the tosser to sending the ring to the receiver because it is too difficult to aim toward the narrow space between the receiver and the sideline.

SAMPLE PLAN 22.3

Level 2B: 1v1 Sending Deck Rings to Open Space (*continued*)

Content Development: Learning the Skills

I Using a Frisbee-like toss, explore with your partner tossing and catching the ring with both left and right hands.

E Now practice the same skills over a net set at five to six feet.

E Explore different ways to toss the ring, including underhand, sidearm, and overhand, and different ways to catch it, including with two hands (one on top and one underneath), left hand, right hand, and reaching a hand through the center.

Notes: To start the unit, you need to spend time teaching children the skills of tossing and catching deck rings. These skills are easy to master, as they are simply variations on skills that children have been practicing since kindergarten.

Cog K What were the different flight pathways of the ring? [Sometimes high, sometimes just over the net, sometimes faster and to the side.] What effect did this have on your ability to catch? [It was easier to catch the ring when it was tossed high because I had time to get there. It was easier when I could use two hands to catch the ring and harder when I had to reach to the side with one hand.]

Th Think critically about when you had problems catching and when you were successful.

Cog K Which performance techniques might help you catch the ring more skillfully?

R Practice again, and focus on one performance technique you think will most improve your tossing or catching.

R/Cog K Typically, you need to elicit the following performance cues. The answers will depend on the child's problems: Watch the ring. Quickly align with the flight path of the ring. Catch with two hands if possible.

Org Set up boundaries with your partner to create an area of a size you think you can cover when tossing and catching deck rings. You may need to set different-sized boundaries for each of you. Stand in the middle of your boundaries.

Social What is the purpose of PE? [For us to learn.] What is the purpose of today's game? [For us to improve.] Some people might need more boundaries of a more challenging size, and others might need boundaries of a less challenging size. You must help each other determine the size of boundaries that will best help each of you improve—even if you have a larger boundary on one side and a smaller one on the other side.

Sending the Ring to Open Space

Cog K/CCSS Today you will learn what open space means and then apply your knowledge to tossing and catching with your partner. Look at your partner and the boundaries. I am going to tell you to toss your ring into an open space so that so your partner must move to catch it. Before I do, where are the open spaces? [The spaces between my partner and the sidelines, endline, and net that my partner can't reach with her or his hands while standing in the middle.] Tossing to open space is a tactic in net games used to score by making it harder for your opponent to catch the ring and to make your opponent move out of the central ready position.

E Toss the ring back and forth, tossing the ring to an open space, making your partner move to catch it. After you catch the ring, you must toss it back *from where you caught it*. No running with the ring is allowed.

Notes: This task sounds easy, but it is difficult for children to learn to toss to a space rather than directly to their partner as they have been doing in previous lessons. This task might take an entire lesson.

ME If children are having problems seeing open space, you can stop the class and use a whiteboard to illustrate open space. Draw a court, net, and two players in the center of their sides of the court.

Who can write an "X" in an open space on this court? Excellent, Mahal drew an "X" over to the side. Who can draw another one?

Juan drew one in the back corner. Excellent. [Continue until the children have drawn "Xs" in all open spaces.]

Notice that the open space is the space between the defender and the boundaries and net.

(*continues*)

SAMPLE PLAN 22.3

Level 2B: 1v1 Sending Deck Rings to Open Space (*continued*)

E Go back and play your game, trying to throw to the open spaces every time.	**R** Where are open spaces? [Where my partner is not standing.] **R** As soon as you toss a shot, think about where your opponent is moving and where you might toss your next shot.
Cog K Why do you want to make your opponent move to catch the ring? [He or she is more likely to miss. If my opponent moves to one side far enough, he or she might have problems getting to the other side if I send my next shot there.] **Th** How can you anticipate where your partner will send the ring? [Look at the ring. Look at my partner's eyes and body motion.]	
E One partner stay in place, and the other rotate clockwise to a new partner. Play again.	Rotate many times during the lesson so the children can work with different partners.
CCSS Closure • Discuss with your partner the definition of open space and how you use open space in the context of net games. [The space between my opponent and the sidelines, endline, and net. You use it to score and to draw your opponent out of the center so there is a larger open space in which to send the next shot.] • Now we will have a class discussion. I will call on you. Which tactics did you use on offense? [Aimed for open spaces; as soon as I tossed, I watched to see where my opponent was moving and planned my next shot.] • What did you learn by working with different partners? [Some people found different spaces. Some used mostly the sides, but others used the corners, just over the net, and near the endline.]	

CHAPTER

23

Field Games: Overhand Throw, Batting, Catching with Gloves, and Modified Games: Levels 1, 2, and 3

PRE-READING REFLECTION

1. Think about softball/baseball. What problems can you anticipate in teaching these games in physical education?
2. Contrast and compare catching and throwing in the game environments of invasion games and the field games of softball and baseball: How are they different? How are they the same?
3. Try to imagine and list possible implications for teaching.

OBJECTIVES

Students will learn:

1. The major field games are softball and baseball.
2. When teaching the forceful overhand throw, children should be instructed to throw the ball with as much force as possible to elicit their most mature throwing pattern.
3. To teach force before accuracy.
4. To teach children to catch balls thrown at different levels (grounders to fly balls) and to their right and left.
5. To teach children to combine catching and quickly throwing.
6. In batting lessons and field games, to rely on batting tees.
7. The importance of modifying field games to be played by three to five children.

KEY TERMS

Apex

CONNECTION TO STANDARDS

1. This chapter addresses National Standard 1 for demonstrating competence in a variety of motor skills; National Standard 2 for applying knowledge of movement concepts, strategies, and tactics; National Standard 4 for exhibiting personal and social responsibility; and National Standard 5 for recognizing the value of physical activity for enjoyment and challenge.
2. This chapter also addresses Common Core and Other State Standards (CCSS) for speaking, listening, collaboration, domain-specific vocabulary, and reading.

PROGRESSION OF CONTENT

Level 1: Fundamental Game Skills

- Throwing yarn balls at a wall forcefully
- Throwing yarn or other soft balls at very large targets forcefully
- Catching with a glove a ball tossed by a partner
- Batting off a tee at a fence

Level 2: Tactical Game Skills

Catching at Different Levels

- Bear claws (medium), alligator hands (low), and moose antlers (high)
- Vary the level
- Vary the distance, speed, and level

Catching at Different Levels and to the Left and Right, Moving to Align Body with Ball

- Moving to the right and left to catch grounders
- Increasing the force of the grounder
- Catching at a high level: learning to see the apex
- Catching balls at different levels
- Catching a ball tossed high to the left and right
- Varying the height and direction
- Varying the height and direction: catching with a glove
- Challenge: catching as many times as you can

Combining Catching and Quickly, in One Motion, Throwing to a Target

- Exploring catching a grounder and immediately throwing
- Exploring catching a ball thrown at chest height and immediately throwing
- Bing, bang, boom: combining catching and throwing forcefully and accurately to a target

Catching a Ball Rolled or Thrown from the Side and, in One Motion, Turning and Quickly Throwing

- Catching a ball thrown from the dominant side
- Catching a ball thrown from the nondominant side
- Increasing the distance
- Using gloves and harder balls
- Catching balls at different levels
- Catching balls in the face of pressure from a runner

Combining Catching, Touching a Base, and then Throwing

- Clockwise and counterclockwise squares
- Counterclockwise with a turn
- Tagging a pretend runner

Level 3: Using Tactical Skills in Modified Gameplay

- Tactic: Throw quickly to beat the runner. Game: Beat the runner.
- Tactics: To beat the runner, cover and tag the base, runner runs past first base. Game: Field and throw to first base to beat the runner.
- Tactics: Deciding who should field the ball and which bases to cover. Game: Three bases.
- Tactic: Hitting to spaces. Game: Home run derby.
- Tactics: Deciding whether to run for the double and whether to throw the runner out at first or second base. Game: Run for the double.
- Child-designed throwing and catching field game: Tactics vary with each game.

Figure 23.1 Progression of Content

Introduction

In this chapter, we discuss softball skills, tactics, and field gameplay. Softball is a lifetime sport. With numerous youth and adult leagues for all age groups found across North America, softball is among our most popular lifetime activities.

We also describe how you can solve the problems of minimal practice opportunities in 9v9 (or 10v10) softball/baseball. As you might imagine, if you play the regulation game, few fielders will get the opportunity to catch and throw the ball, other than the pitcher and the catcher (Oslin, 2004). In addition, there are only limited opportunities to bat. The regulation game limits practice opportunities so extensively that children could play regulation softball in a 15-lesson unit and, if in the outfield, never catch a ball, bat fewer than 10 times, and possibly never run to a base. Children cannot develop throwing, catching, and batting skills and learn the most basic tactics without extensive practice, which the regulation game prevents.

Level 1: Fundamental Skills

In level 1, we focus on the overhand throw for force, catching with a glove, and batting off a tee. During level 1 learning experiences, we work on basic performance techniques to help children begin to develop the coordination pattern of the skills. We discuss these performance techniques in **Skills Box 23.1**, along with sample metaphors and stories you can use to capture children's attention and help them remember the performance techniques. We also suggest which performance techniques to teach when children are at developmental levels 1, 2, and 3.

FYI

Sample Plans for Teaching Performance Techniques and Sample Centers

Level 1

1. Throwing unit: side to target, "make the T, break the T"
2. Batting unit: where to stand, how to grip; back foot pivot, front foot closed

Level 2

1. Catching balls at different levels with a glove: bear claws, alligator hands, and moose antlers
2. Catching at different levels and to the left and right, moving to align body with ball (see text website)

Levels 1 and 2 Centers

1. Throwing centers
2. Batting centers

These suggestions will help you decide where to start. Of course, you will need to observe your children carefully to know which refinements and new performance techniques they are ready to learn. We also provide sample plans at the end of this chapter to illustrate how you might teach these techniques in actual lesson situations.

You can teach performance techniques for throwing, catching, and batting in whole-class lessons focused on one or two performance cues per lesson, with all the children practicing the same tasks. You will need to design a wide variety of practice tasks, however, because performance techniques for throwing, catching, and batting take considerable amounts of practice, and children are not likely to be motivated to practice the same tasks over and over. In addition, the inclusion of a variety of practice conditions facilitates learning (Davids, Button, & Bennett, 2008). Consequently, at the end of this chapter, we describe sample centers for children to practice these skills. If you have ample equipment, you can use these centers as whole-class practice tasks.

For grades K–2, the first units you teach for throwing, catching, and batting typically consist of two or three lessons each, focusing on performance techniques. You then continue working on these skills—in particular, throwing and catching—in six to eight additional lessons across the school year.

If you do not have adequate amounts of equipment or space, especially for batting, you can have children practice all three skills in centers within a longer unit, dividing the content as follows:

- Day 1: Teach one or two performance cues for throwing, and use centers to practice throwing.
- Day 2: Teach one or two catching cues, followed by throwing and catching centers.
- Days 3–6: Teach one or two batting cues, and use throwing, catching, and batting centers.

Based on your observations of the children, you can then plan which new performance cues the children are ready to learn for the remainder of the unit or in future units across the school year.

In addition, centers are helpful for assessing children's throwing, catching, and batting skills. Stay at one center for assessment while you scan the children working at other centers to ensure they are on task. Peer assessments are also viable at centers and helpful for improving children's throwing, catching, and especially batting.

Teaching the Overhand Throw for Force

The following suggestions will help you teach throwing.

Make the Task and Environment Elicit a Forceful Throw

Recall that task and environmental constraints influence the movement pattern of the skill (Newell, 1986). A key principle of learning supported by constraints theory and research on motor learning is to be sure the task and environment elicit the *most mature pattern the child can perform* at that point in time (Davids et al., 2008; Roberton & Halverson, 1984). This concept has important implications for teaching throwing:

- *Have children throw as forcefully as they can in all tasks for practicing the skill.* If children do not throw as forcefully as they can, they will not use their most mature pattern and will instead practice immature movement patterns. For example, if we asked two skilled softball players to stand 10 feet apart and throw a ball back and forth, they would throw the ball using the same arm, wrist, and hand actions as employed when throwing darts at a dartboard. That is, they would not wind up and throw like an outfielder trying to reach the catcher at home plate, which would be their most mature pattern. With this task, the environment constrains their throwing action, as constraints theory predicts (see **Figure 23.2**). Practicing a dart-throwing motion will not improve players' throws across the infield or from the outfield.
- *Don't practice slow-motion or moderate speed throws.* Throwing in slow motion doesn't help children develop mature techniques for throwing because mature techniques can be learned only when children throw as forcefully as they can. When children throw with force, they practice the authentic timing and coordination at their developmental level, which is essential for successful learning (Davids et al., 2008).

  Throwing at a moderate speed to practice performance techniques is not helpful, either. For example, teachers may say, "Practice stepping on your opposite foot," and give a task requiring the child to throw a short distance at a moderate speed. Because the child does not need to step to generate force to throw a short distance at a moderate speed, the child steps simply because the teacher said to step; this step is not coordinated with other body components, however, nor is it a long step in line with the target that the child needs to practice. The child does not need to take a long step to meet the task demands (it would actually be counterproductive), so the child is not improving on either the step action or its coordination with the other components.

Figure 23.2 Task constraints elicit less mature throwing patterns

- *Select balls that are safe for your tasks and environment and allow for forceful throwing.* Initially, have children throw using yarn or small foam balls at a wall (see **Figure 23.3**). With this setup, children can throw as forcefully as they can, and the ball will not rebound far from the wall. If a child is inaccurate or stands too close to the wall and the ball hits the child, yarn and foam balls are the safest balls. If you don't have an appropriate wall, you can have children throw across a field to a partner. Space the children far enough apart that the catcher can retrieve the ball after a bounce.

Teach Force Before Accuracy

If you try to teach accuracy at the same time as you teach force, children will tend to focus on accuracy and drop their elbow, shifting to a more immature pattern (with the humerus positioned in the dart-throwing motion) to hit the target. As a consequence, they will not practice their most mature pattern and will not improve their throwing techniques or coordination of body components.

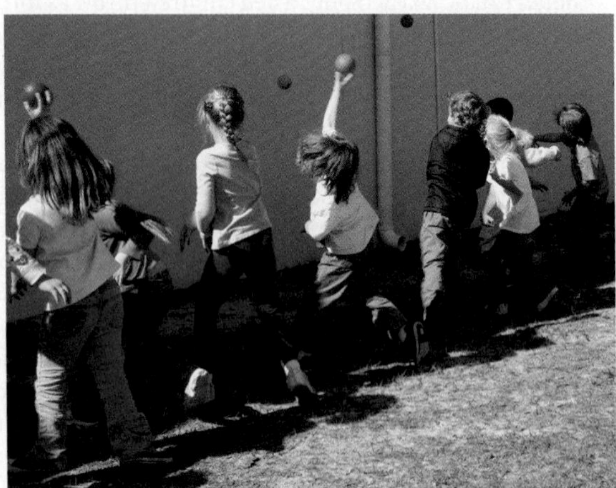

Figure 23.3 Kindergarteners throwing forcefully at the school wall

What the Research Says

Teaching Throwing

In a study of teaching beginners the overhand throw, when students were told to increase the speed of the ball and practiced throwing as forcefully as they could, the beginners improved faster than when they were taught trunk rotation (Southard, 2006). In fact, teaching trunk rotation and practicing at less than maximum speed were found to be detriments to the development of the hand and forearm action needed for an overhand throw. In studying this issue, Southard (2006) concluded that the most important thing teachers should do is to encourage beginners to increase the speed of the ball and the force of their throw.

Targets can be effective for teaching the overhand throw if they are very large or require force to reach, such as throwing at a bunch of balloons tied to a backstop and trying to pop the balloons. As children improve, you can use targets to a greater extent, thereby working on accuracy and force at the same time. Initially, however, you should focus on force alone.

In Level 1, Do Not Work on Throwing Forcefully and Catching in the Same Task

Because beginners need to practice throwing with as much force as possible, you will not be able to work on catching, as this skill requires an accurate throw. In addition, if children are too close together and the throw is forceful, the catcher is at risk of injury and will learn to be afraid of catching balls.

Do Boys Throw Better than Girls?

Of all the skills we teach in physical education, none is more misunderstood in relation to gender than the forceful overhand throw. Both of the authors of this book, having taught preschoolers and kindergarteners for more than 30 years, can tell you that, on average, boys will throw at more mature levels than girls. The key phrase here is "on average." Many girls will throw at higher levels than many boys. The best thrower in the class often is a girl, and the least skilled often is a boy.

The reasons for this difference are cultural. Parents and siblings are more likely to encourage preschool boys to play throw and catch. Moreover, playing catch is more often part of neighborhood boys' cultures. Consequently, when preschoolers enter school, boys have had, on average, far more

SAMPLE LEARNING EXPERIENCES 23.1

Level 1: Throwing, Catching, and Batting

- Throwing yarn balls at a wall forcefully
- Throwing yarn or other soft balls at very large targets forcefully
- Catching with a glove a ball tossed by a partner
- Batting off a tee at a fence

practice throwing. In today's video game generation, however, more boys are throwing at less mature levels. As you know, the amount of practice is the single most important variable accounting for skill development.

Teachers can and do change this inequity. They do so by teaching throwing, giving boys and girls plenty of practice, and actively counteracting stereotypes. Only after puberty do boys develop the advantages of upper body strength and a higher center of gravity that enable elite male athletes in throwing sports, on average, to throw farther than elite female athletes. The key phrase, again, is "on average." Averages do not mean anything in physical education because our goals are to help every child develop skills to their highest capabilities.

What's Wrong with "Throwing Like a Girl"?

For many years, physical education teachers have fought to ban the phrase "throwing like a girl" because children and adults used the phrase to humiliate the boy to whom they directed it. In addition, this phrase implies that all girls throw poorly. When people say, "You throw like a girl," what they are seeing is the child throwing at an immature level—in particular, with level 1 trunk, humerus, and forearm action. We correct folks when they use this phrase by saying, "Oh, I think you mean the child is throwing like a beginner, because you know there are many girls who are very skilled throwers," or "Oh, which girl do you mean—Dot Richardson or Jennie Finch?"

Teaching Catching for Softball/Baseball

The game environment of softball/baseball differs from the game environment of invasion games. In invasion games, children catch passes from teammates who are trying to throw catchable passes. In this setting, children need to absorb less force across a shorter distance because the balls are larger and generally thrown with less force. In softball-type situations, by comparison, children catch balls batted with strong force, grounders that bounce, and balls thrown with strong force in attempts to beat the runner to the base. The reach-and-giving action to absorb the force of the ball is more important and needs to occur across a longer distance from the reach toward the body. Consequently, in field game units, we focus on children learning to catch with gloves balls that have been thrown or batted with force.

You may recall our descriptions of learning experiences for introducing catching in invasion games and teaching the following level 1 content. This content also can be modified for field game lessons:

- Catching a variety of self-tossed balls
- Catching self-tossed balls so you have to move to get in line with the ball to catch it
- Catching with scoops
- Tossing to a wall and catching
- Catching tricks

In teaching catching in a field game unit, you may also find it helpful to recall the following annotated lesson segments on catching in invasion games discussed elsewhere:

Level 1

- Exploring catching a variety of self-tossed balls

Level 2

- Moving to catch in different areas of personal space
- Moving and reaching to catch in different areas of personal space (see text website)
- Catching various balls in different areas of personal space (see text website)
- Child-designed sequences of catching tricks

Issues with Gloves

The major concern of teachers related to purchasing gloves is their cost and the possibility of theft. You can purchase less expensive "soft hands," which are commercially produced foam rubber, flat gloves that promote the covering and cradling action used in catching a softball with a glove. You can purchase softball gloves in a variety of ugly colors and mark them with the school name and phone number, which will help identify school property and prevent theft. To get donated gloves, circulate a notice with your community's Parks and Recreation Department adult softball leagues asking for donations. Leave a donation box at their fields. Finally, you can purchase several kinds of soft softball balls designed to be caught with bare hands. We typically start using gloves in second grade classes.

Teaching Batting

Batting is a complicated skill. Numerous performance techniques influence children's abilities to hit a round ball with a round bat. It is important for teachers to understand all aspects of batting, even though you would never attempt to teach everything you know because it would be more information than the children could remember or use. (We discuss this information later in the chapter, in **Skills Box 23.1**.) Your knowledge of batting will help you observe the problems with each child's performance techniques and teach the most important and appropriate refinements to increase each child's success rate.

In teaching batting in levels 1 and 2 and in level 3 field games, we primarily use baseball/softball tees, in which the ball is positioned on a flexible pole set at the appropriate height for a child to bat (see **Figure 23.4**). You can make a batting tee by placing a ball on a cone on a large box set at the appropriate height for the children.

Batting tees enable children to work on the performance techniques of batting without having to also deal with a moving ball. By making multiple batting tees available, you can have many children practice this skill at the same time. In addition, they can practice without having to rely on a peer being able to pitch an accurate ball, which is beyond the capabilities of beginning throwers. Even self-tossing a ball and then hitting it is a difficult skill for children. Once children have learned to toss accurately, you can have children practice batting from a soft toss from a partner who stands to the side of the batter, well out of line of where the ball will be hit. Soft-toss or pitching machines that use softballs and whiffle balls also are excellent options for teaching batting if your budget allows for their purchase.

Figure 23.4 Batting tee

Batting in Different Directions

We don't teach batting in different directions at the elementary level because it is an advanced skill. For example, the timing of the hip rotation and the location of the pitch combine to allow batters to hit to the opposite field (left field for right-handed batters and right field for left-handed batters). To hit to the opposite field off a tee, the child would need to stand at a 9 o'clock or 3 o'clock position (directly opposite the ball); that is not the position in which they need to practice batting—between 8 o'clock and 7 o'clock for right-handed batters and between 4 o'clock and 5 o'clock for left-handed batters. See **Skills Box 23.1** for a description of teaching batting techniques.

Level 2: Tactical Game Skills

In level 2, we develop the fundamental skills into tactical game skills by focusing on the following tasks:

- Catching at different levels and moving in different directions to catch
- Throwing forcefully with accuracy
- Combining catching and quickly, in one motion, throwing

As in invasion games, catching balls at different levels and in all areas of personal space reflects how catching occurs in field games. In addition, it is important to teach children how to catch a ball and quickly throw to a target—it is an essential part of defensive tactics.

SAFETY AND LIABILITY 23.1

Increasing Safety and Decreasing Risk of Liability: Guidelines Relevant to Content in this Chapter

In this box, we discuss specific guidelines built on information discussed throughout this text on professional standards of practice, negligence, and liability. The goals of these guidelines are to increase children's safety and decrease teachers' risk of negligence and liability.

Equipment and Spacing

- Select balls that are safe for your tasks and environment. Yarn and foam balls are the safest balls.
- Use plastic bats.
- Make sure that when a lefty and a righty are batting on a tee near each other, they have sufficient room.
- Teach children that their personal space is much larger when they bat and that they must be responsible for ensuring no one is near their personal space when batting.
- Teach children to tell the batter where they are, rather than assuming the batter knows their location, and to make sure they put plenty of distance between the batter and themselves.
- In batting games, in particular, children cannot judge the distance they need to be from the batter. You need to set a physical boundary like cones or a fence behind which they must stand.
- Teach children the rule to stay at their tee unless they are moving forward (not sideways) to pick up balls.
- Insist that children never throw the bat after they hit and are running to a base.

Organization of Games

- Set up a safety zone in the center in which no one plays. Four to eight fields of play consisting of a triangle with a safety zone boundary on each side radiate from the safety zone. Bases for each field are well inside the safety boundary zone so runners will not collide with fielders, runners, or batted balls from other games.

Teaching Safety Procedures

- **Sample Plans 23.1** and **23.2** illustrate teaching safety procedures for classes throwing at a wall and retrieving their balls and batting from a tee.

SAMPLE LEARNING EXPERIENCES 23.2

Level 2 Catching at Different Levels and Combining Catching and Throwing

Catching at Different Levels

1. Bear Claws, Alligator Hands, Moose Antlers

A. *Bear claws:* The thrower tosses the ball chest high. Performance techniques for the catcher include keeping the thumbs up and fingers pointing toward the thrower like bear claws.

B. *Alligator hands:* The thrower rolls the ball. The catcher reaches with the glove palm up, uses the throwing hand to cover the ball, and then gives by bending the elbows ("reach, cover, cradle").

C. *Moose antlers:* The thrower tosses the ball high. The catcher keeps the thumbs together and places the hands up like moose antlers to catch.

Bear claws

Courtesy of John Dolly

2. Ground-ball Freeze (Peer Coaching)

Partner A rolls the ball to partner B. Partner B catches the ball and freezes as soon as he or she covers the ball. Partner A checks whether partner B is catching the ball out in front with the finger of the glove on the ground and covering the ball.

3. Vary the Level

Partners toss the ball to each other, as the teacher calls out the level (high, medium, low). Sometimes the teacher calls for a "surprise"—the thrower can then toss the ball to any level.

4. Vary the Distance, Speed, and Level

Partners move farther away from each other, throw and roll the ball harder, or have the ball take a small hop (bounce).

Catching at Different Levels and to the Left and Right, Moving to Align Body with Ball

1. Moving to the Right and Left to Catch Grounders

The thrower rolls the ball to the right and left of the catcher. The catcher needs to anticipate where the ball is rolling and immediately move in line with the ball.

2. Increasing the Force of the Grounder

The thrower rolls the ball faster.

The catcher also runs toward the ball to catch it.

3. Catching at a High Level: Learning to See the Apex

A. Draw a parabola on a whiteboard and explain that its highest point is the **apex**. Toss the ball up and have class say "now" when they think the ball is at its apex. Learning about the apex can dramatically improve children's abilities to catch pop fly balls.

B. Practice catching pop fly balls while looking for the apex.

4. Catching at Different Levels

The thrower throws grounders, chest-high tosses, fly balls, and pop-ups.

5. Catching a Ball Tossed High to the Left and Right

The thrower tosses the ball high to the catcher's left and right so he or she has to move in alignment with the ball to catch it.

6. Varying the Height and Direction

A. The thrower rolls or tosses the ball to the left and right of the catcher so that he or she has to move to catch it. The thrower asks the catcher at which level he or she wants to receive the ball—low, medium, or high.

B. Progress to having the thrower not tell the catcher where the ball will be thrown.

7. Varying the Height and Direction Catching with a Glove and a Soft Tee Ball

A. The thrower tosses the ball high to the catcher's left and right so he or she has to move in alignment with the ball to catch it.

B. The thrower rolls or tosses the ball to the left and right of the catcher so that he or she has to move to catch it. The thrower asks the catcher at which level he or she wants to receive the ball—low, medium, or high.

C. Progress to having the thrower not tell the catcher where the ball will be thrown.

(*continues*)

SAMPLE LEARNING EXPERIENCES 23.2

Level 2: Catching at Different Levels and Combining Catching and Throwing (*continued*)

8. Challenge: Catching as Many Times as You Can

A. Count how many catches you can complete before a miss, with the thrower varying the height and direction of the throws.

B. Move farther apart, and count how many catches you can complete before you miss, with the thrower varying the height and direction of the throws.

Sample Questions to Ask

- Have you ever seen a baseball game? Does the ball always stay at chest height during the game? Does it ever go low? High? When?
- Why do you think you need to learn how to move to catch a ball? [In games, the batter hits the ball and tries to keep it away from the fielders. Sometimes your teammates will try to throw the ball to you, but they will not be perfect, and you will need to be able to move to catch the ball.]
- If you hold your glove like a plate when catching a fly ball and the ball hits it, where is it going to roll? [Into your face.] That's why you practice using the moose hands position.
- Why do you think we use two hands to catch fly balls when you know it is possible to use just one? [You can make a quicker throw—as you cover the ball and absorb force with the cradle, you also can be moving your hand and body to get into position to throw. It helps you control the ball.]
- Why is it a bad idea to put your free hand behind the glove? [The force of the ball could make your hand force the ball to rebound, and it will fall out of the glove.]
- What happens if the catcher is too close to the apex? [It goes over the head of the catcher.] What happens if the catcher is too far away from apex? [The ball drops in front of the catcher.]
- Does the position of your thumb change when you are catching with a glove (e.g., do you turn your thumb down)? [No.]

Combining Catching and Quickly, in One Motion, Throwing to a Target

1. Exploring Catching a Grounder and Immediately Throwing

- Think about what body actions and positions you need to catch and immediately throw quickly.
- The end of the catching cradle becomes the beginning of the preparation to throw.
- Catch with your glove foot forward. As you cradle the ball, quickly turn your side to the target.
- The turn is so fast it is like a "pop."

2. Exploring Catching a Ball Thrown at Chest Height and Immediately Throwing

Children catch a ball thrown to chest height, experimenting with whether any performance techniques change.

3. Bing, Bang, Boom

"Bing" means that partner A rolls the ball to partner B; "bang" means that partner B catches the rolling ball and quickly throws it to partner A; "boom" means that partner A catches the ball and quickly throws it back to partner B. The partners repeat the sequence, but this time partner B rolls the ball to start the "bing, bang, boom" process.

Sample Questions to Ask

- Which body actions help you catch and immediately throw? [The end of the catching cradle becomes the beginning of the preparation to throw. Catch with your glove foot forward. As you cradle the ball, quickly turn your side to the target. The turn is so fast it is like a "pop."]
- What happens if you don't turn side to target? [You won't get enough force.]
- What do you think will help you improve? [Turn quickly].

Catching a Ball Rolled or Thrown from the Side and, in One Motion, Turning and Quickly Throwing

Equipment

Tape targets to a wall or fence. Use balls appropriate for your setting (yarn balls if you are inside or soft tee balls if you are outside with plenty of space). Set a yellow poly spot straight in front of the target and far enough away to elicit a forceful overhand throw. Set two red poly spots on diagonals, one to the left and one to the right.

1. Catching a Ball Thrown from the Dominant Side

The thrower stands on the yellow poly spot with side to the target. The roller (with the ball) stands on the red poly spot, facing the thrower (the right poly spot for right-handed throwers and the left poly spot for left-handed throwers). Roll the ball to your partner, who catches it and, in one smooth action, quickly throws to the target. [Switch roles.]

SAMPLE LEARNING EXPERIENCES 23.2

Level 2: Catching at Different Levels and Combining Catching and Throwing (*continued*)

2. Catching a Ball Thrown from the Nondominant side:

The roller switches to the other red poly spot on the nondominant side of the thrower.

3. Increasing the Distance

Spread farther apart and away from the target.

4. Using Gloves and Harder Balls.

Repeat task above but increase the difficulty of the equipment using gloves and harder balls for students ready to do so.

5. Catching Balls in the Face of Pressure from a Runner

Use a third poly spot as a base and have the roller run to the base to be the target and catch the ball.

Combining Catching, Touching a Base, and Throwing

Counterclockwise rotation forces more of a turn for children who throw right-handed, whereas clockwise rotation forces more of a turn for children who throw left-handed.

1. Clockwise Square

In groups of four with four poly spots for bases in a square, practice throwing the ball in a clockwise direction (throwing from home to third to second to first). Catch the ball, and, in one smooth, quick motion, touch your base (right-handed throwers with the right foot, so the left foot can step toward the target as you step on the base, and the reverse for left-handed throwers), and throw the ball to the next base. If you miss a good throw, you chase the ball. If you make a poor throw, you chase the ball.

A. How many throws and catches can you make before a drop?

B. How fast can you get the ball to travel around the square?

2. Counterclockwise Square

Same as in number 1, but the ball travels in a counterclockwise direction.

3. Counterclockwise with Turn

Same as in number 1, but the ball travels outside of the square in a counterclockwise direction. When you catch the ball, step on the base with your throwing-side foot, spin around, and then step with side to target, and throw to the next base. This activity is more difficult because you can't see the target the entire time, but the response is quicker and can give you power in your throw.

4. Tagging a Pretend Runner

Same as in number 1, but when you catch the ball, bend down and tag the base as if you are tagging a runner, and then quickly throw to the next base.

Sample Questions to Ask

- Has anyone ever played in a baseball or softball game? What do the players usually do after they catch a batted ball? [They throw it to the base.] Why do they want the base player to catch the ball? [To make an out.] Describe how the fielders need to catch the ball. [They need to catch and then throw quickly because the runner will be safe if they don't.]
- How does it feel if you are the fielder catching the ball and trying to throw it to the base quickly? [Various answers.] That is called pressure.
- Which performance techniques are important for catching and immediately throwing? [Turn so quickly it is like a pop. Turn; don't twist without a turn. In one motion, cradle and bring the ball into position to throw while turning side to target.]
- Compare and contrast catching a ball coming from your left and coming from your right side. What is the same, and what is different? Which is more difficult, and which is easier, and why? [Nondominant is more difficult because I have to turn before I throw.]
- Which performance cues help you throw fast and accurately? [Make sure to turn side to the target, step on a line to the target.]
- Which performance cues help you catch? [Reach, cover, and cradle.]

Level 3: Using Tactical Game Skills in Modified Field Gameplay

The major problem with teaching field games is modifying the games so children get ample practice opportunities at each position (Mitchell, Oslin, & Griffin, 2006). We do this in two ways. First, we use only small-sided games. Second, instead of children waiting to bat, we have all children except the batter and the runners play in the field.

To organize field games, set up four to eight fields of play depending on the game. In the center is a safety zone in which no one plays. Batters are located just beyond the safety zone, hitting away from the center. Each field of play consists of a triangle with a safety zone boundary on each side. Bases for each field are well inside the safety boundary zone so runners will not collide with fielders, runners, or batted balls from other games. **Figure 23.5** illustrates how to set up four fields of play. You can make the triangles narrower and set up more fields depending on the space available.

When you design modified game lessons and units, start with the game. Observe the games and determine whether the children are not being successful because they need more practice of the skills. If so, stop the game, and set up practice tasks. Starting with the game can help children understand how skills are used in games (Mitchell, Oslin, & Griffin, 2003).

At the beginning of a game lesson, you can put out different kinds of balls (e.g., tennis, whiffle, foam, soft tee balls), and have the students line up behind the kind of ball they want to throw and catch. Then you can group children based on the ball they like. Ensure students modify their rules to keep the games active.

The "Basic Field Game Tactics" box describes basic field game tactics. Softball and baseball tactics can be complex and always depend on the number of runners on base and the number of outs. We focus on those basic tactics that you can teach at the elementary level in modified games if you have ample time for physical education each week.

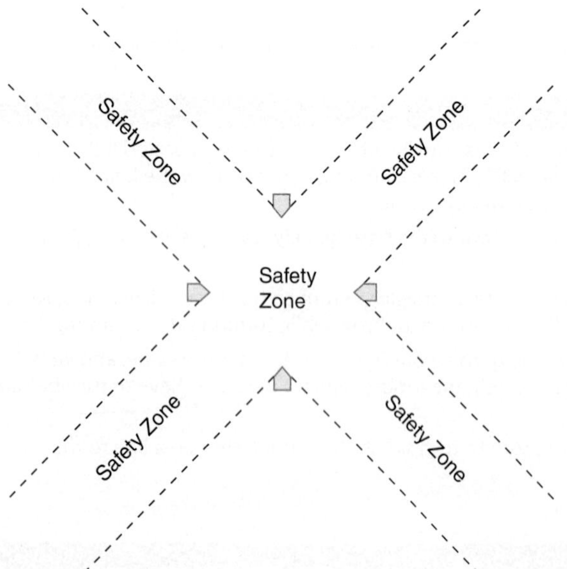

Figure 23.5 Organization for four fields of play

Sample Learning Experiences for Level 3: Using Tactical Game Skills in Modified Field Games

We do not include any sample plans for level 3 at the end of the chapter. Consequently, the sample learning experiences presented here include motor and tactical decisions, and objectives for each set of learning experiences for each game.

Basic Field Game Tactics

Offense

- *Hit to the space between fielders.*
- *Where the ball is hit determines how many bases you can touch.* If the ball is hit to the infield, typically you can run only to first base. If the ball goes into the outfield, you can probably make it to second, but you must make this decision by looking at where the ball is retrieved in the outfield.
- *Run past first base; do not stop on the base.* If you hit an easy grounder and know you are likely to be thrown out at first base, run as fast as you can, touch the base while running straight ahead, and slow down only after you touch the base.
- *Banana- or question mark–shaped run to the base; leave it straight.* If you might possibly be able to run to more than one base, start to make the turn before the base by running on a banana pathway (curving to your right). Leave the base running straight.
- *Fly ball: stay on base.* If you are on base and the ball is hit in the air, stay on base. A fly ball might be caught.
- *Run on grounders.* If a teammate is on a base behind you, you must run on a grounder.
- *Don't run ahead of other base runners.*
- *If the fielder misses the ball, try to take an extra base.*

Defense

- *Throw to the base ahead of the runner.* Throw the ball fast (without an arc) so it will get to the base before the runner. You can throw the ball to a base faster than you can run it to the base.
- *Throw to the base ahead of the runner who is closest to scoring.*
- *The fielder closest to the ball fields the ball.* Other fielders cover the bases closest to them. This tactic will change depending on where the ball is hit and where the runner is.
- *If you catch a fly ball, tag the runner out.* If the runner leaves the base and you catch the ball on the fly, throw the ball to the base to tag the runner out.
- *Cover the space, not the base.* The first-base and third-base players stand closer to the center of the field of play. If you have a shortstop and a second-base player, they cover the spaces in between. No one stands on a base waiting for the batter to hit. Move to your base if the throw to make an out is coming to you.

SAMPLE LEARNING EXPERIENCES 23.3

Catch and Throw Quickly to Beat the Runner

Motor and Tactical Objectives

Children will learn

1. To catch and throw quickly to beat the runner.

Potential Refinements

- Which performance cues can help you throw accurately? [Side to target, step on a line toward the target, keep weight on front foot.]
- You are having problems catching the ball. Which performance cues will help you improve? [Use two hands; reach, cover, cradle; catch the ball out front (reach); pinkies in for a low ball; thumbs in for a high ball; legs apart for grounders; move in line with the ball.]

Organization

Children work in groups of three. Set up four cones in a square—two blue and two red, forming the sides of the square. Use foam, tennis, or soft tee balls.

Play Initial Game: Beat the Runner

A. Have the children play the following game.

Runner A starts at a blue cone, says "Go," and runs to the other blue cone and back. Fielder B stands at a red cone. Fielder C stands at the other red cone. When runner A says go, fielder B throws the ball to fielder C, and fielder C throws it back to fielder B, trying to beat runner A. Rotate roles.

Modifying the Game to Get It Working Well

B. Using the play-discuss-play cycle, modify the game to get it working well.

Sample Questions to Ask

- Is your game too challenging or too easy for the fielders and the runner?
- What makes a game fair and fun? [When both offense and defense have equal opportunities to succeed. When everyone is challenged but can succeed.]
- How can you improve your game so it is fair and fun for everyone? [We can move the bases farther apart to make it harder for the runner or closer together to make it easier for the runner. We could do the same thing for the fielders.] Modify the distances between your cones to make the game perfect for both the runner and the fielders. You might have to experiment with different distances.

Improving Tactics

C. Now play your game and focus on the tactics. [Use the play-discuss-play cycle to work on the tactic until children understand and can apply the tactics in the game.]

Sample Questions to Ask

- What can you do to beat the runner? [Catch and throw quickly, make fast throws, make straight throws without an arc.]
- Your throwing has improved. What do you think made the difference?

SAMPLE LEARNING EXPERIENCE 23.4

Throw to the Base to Beat the Runner, Cover and Tag the Base, Runner Runs Past First Base

Motor and Tactics Objectives

Children will learn

1. To cover space on defense and to decide appropriately who should field the ball and who should cover bases.
2. To hit to spaces and run past first base.

(*continues*)

SAMPLE LEARNING EXPERIENCE 23.4

Throw to the Base to Beat the Runner, Cover and Tag the Base, Runner Runs Past First Base (*continued*)

Potential Refinements

- Which performance cues can help you throw accurately? [Side to target, step on a line toward the target, keep weight on front foot.]
- You are having problems catching the ball. Which performance cue will help you improve? [Use two hands; reach, cover, cradle; catch the ball out front (reach); pinkies in for a low ball; thumbs in for a high ball; legs apart for grounders; move in line with the ball.]

Organization

Children work in groups of three. Set up a cone for home plate, a poly spot for first base, and another cone for third base; the last cone serves as a boundary but is placed only 15 feet away from first base (the angle of the triangle at the home cone will be 30 to 40 degrees). Let students select the type of ball (yarn, foam, soft tee).

Play Initial Game: Field and Throw to First Base to Beat the Runner

A. Have the children play the following game.

The runner rolls the ball between the cone and first base spot and runs to first base. One fielder fields the ball, while the other fielder becomes the first-base player, runs to first base, turns, and prepares to catch the ball. The fielder throws the ball to the first-base player, who catches the ball and reaches back with her or his foot to try to tag the inside of the base before the runner gets there. The runner touches and runs past first base.

Modifying the Game to Get It Working Well

B. Using the play-discuss-play cycle, modify the game to get it working well.

It will not take the runners long to figure out that if they roll the ball only a few inches they will always beat the fielders. When this happens, stop the games and have a class discussion. Although as a teacher, you could have added a distance rule before the children played the game, the goal is to get students to think tactically and then to be able to solve a problem when the rules of the game are not fair for both offense and defense.

Sample Questions to Ask

- What is the problem when the runner rolls the ball only a few inches? [It is a great tactic, but the game becomes boring because the fielders don't have a fair chance to get the runner out.]
- What makes a game fair and fun? [When the offense and the defense have equal opportunities to succeed.]
- What rule can you add to the game to make the game fair and challenging for both the fielders and the runner? [Set a distance beyond which the ball must roll.]

Improving Tactics

C. Now play your game and focus on the tactics. [Use the play-discuss-play cycle to work on the tactics until children understand and can apply the tactic in the game.]

Sample Questions to Ask About Tactics

- Where should the runner roll the ball? [To the spaces between the fielders and the boundaries.]
- Where should the fielders position themselves? [Apart, not on a base but equally covering the space between the boundary and the base.]
- How can you avoid confusion about who should field the ball? [The fielder who is closer to the ball calls, "I got it," and fields the ball.]
- Students tend to run to the base to tag the runner rather than throw the ball to the fielder so they can tag the base. When this happens, ask them if they can throw the ball to the base faster than they can run. [Yes.]

Adding Batting and Designing a Scoring System

D. Play the same game, but have the runner bat a ball off a tee.

If children in a group want to add scoring, have them decide on a scoring system and a rule for foul balls (when the ball rolls out of bounds).

Play, and use the play-discuss-play cycle to work on the tactics.

SAMPLE LEARNING EXPERIENCES 23.5

Deciding Who Should Field the Ball and Which Bases to Cover

Motor and Tactics Objectives

Children will learn to

1. Cover space on defense and to decide appropriately who should field the ball and who should cover bases.
2. Hit to spaces.

Potential Refinements

- Which performance cue did you think about when you batted?
- Were you thinking about a performance cue that helped you improve catching and quickly throwing?
- You are having problems throwing accurately. Which performance cue will help you improve?
- What do you need to do to catch and quickly throw a fast ball on a straight, not arced, air pathway? [Be sure to turn side to target before throwing. Catch, and, as you give, bring the ball up to throwing position. Make the catch and throw one motion.]
- Your catching of fly balls has improved. What are you doing or thinking that has made the difference?
- Why is it better to hit line drives? [Hardest to field, less likely to make an out.]

Organization

Provide a whiffle ball and plastic bat. Put out three bases—first, third, and home. Set up a batting tee in front of home plate. There are three fielders and one hitter.

Initial Game: Three Bases

The batter hits the whiffle ball with a plastic bat off the tee. Gloves are not needed because of the whiffle ball. The batter runs to first, third, and home. The fielders throw to all three bases (order does not matter) trying to beat the batter.

Rules the Children Design

A. Before they play, have the children decide whether to rotate after one or two hits and how to rotate so all children play all positions equally.

Predicting Tactics in Initial Group Discussion

B. Before you play the game, have a group discussion about where you think the fielders should stand and what they should do to cover the bases.

C. Then play one round of the game so each person gets to bat and play each fielding position.

Modifying the Game to Get It Working Well

D. Have a class discussion about the rules and distances between the bases. Modify the game to get it working well.

Sample Questions to Ask

- Are there any problems with the game setup and rules? Is your game safe? Are there rules you need to keep the game safe?
- Do you need to make any changes to the distance between your bases so the batter and fielders have fair opportunities to score? If so, change the distance, and experiment until you have perfect distances. You might need to edit your game several times until you have it working well.
- If you want to design a scoring system, you can do that, too.

Improving Tactics

Play the game again while working on tactics—that is, making good decisions about where to hit and who covers the bases.

Sample Questions to Ask About Tactics

- Where should the fielders stand to cover the space? [Evenly spaced and covering the space, but not standing on a base.]
- When did the hitter's hit get by you? [When we stood on first and third base rather than covering spaces. When we did not cover the space evenly.]
- How do you know who fields the ball and who covers first, third, and home base? [The person closest to the ball calls, "I got it," and fields the ball. The other two fielders go to cover whichever base is closest to them in the most efficient way. This will vary depending on where the ball is hit.]
- Where should you hit? [To spaces.]

(*continues*)

SAMPLE LEARNING EXPERIENCES 23.5

Deciding Who Should Field the Ball and Which Bases to Cover (*continued*)

Adding a Base for Runners

Game: Four Bases for Runners, Three for Fielders

Modify the game so the batter hits the ball and runs to all four bases in order. The three fielders field the ball and throw to first, third, and home (staying out of the runner's pathway for safety), trying to beat the runner home. Rotate positions after each hit.

SAMPLE LEARNING EXPERIENCES 23.6

Hitting to Spaces

Motor and Tactics Objectives

Children will learn to

1. Bat line drives.
2. Hit to spaces.

Thinking Skill (Self-Regulation)

3. Select a performance cue to practice that will improve their batting.

Potential Refinements

- Which performance technique did you think about when you batted? [Hip speed is bat speed, front foot closed/back foot pivot, eyes at contact.]
- You are having problems hitting the ball over the cone. Which performance technique will help you improve?
- You have improved your batting. What are you doing or thinking about that has made the difference?
- See if you can figure out which performance technique you need to use to hit the ball within the boundaries.

Organization

Use one tee, four whiffle balls, one plastic bat, six cones, and two to four players. Place six cones in an arc (a semicircle where all cones are located the same distance from home base) just past what would be second base. The outside two cones are the boundary.

Play Initial Game: Home Run Derby

One person bats, and all remaining players are behind the outfield cones. Each batter gets to hit three balls, trying to make them go over the cones. Every ball that goes over the cones on the fly is a home run. Any ball caught on the fly takes a home run away from the batter.

Predicting Tactics in Initial Group Discussion

Where should you try to hit the ball? [To a space.]

A. Play one round, rotating positions until everyone has had one chance to bat.

Modifying the Game to Get It Working Well

B. Using the play-discuss-play cycle, modify the game to get it working well.

Sample Questions to Ask

- In your groups, discuss the distance the cones are from the tee. Are the cones too far away so batters can't score, or are they too close so fielders can't cover the spaces?
- Discuss the boundaries. Are the outside cones too close together so the batter can't score, or are they too far apart so the fielders can never catch a ball?
- Decide on perfect boundaries and a perfect distance from the cones to home plate for your group. Decide whether you need to have different boundaries for different classmates.

C. Play the game again and evaluate your decisions about boundaries and the distance of the cones to the batters. You may need to experiment a few times until you have a game that works well for everyone in your group—that is, so each of you is challenged but also has opportunities to be successful.

SAMPLE LEARNING EXPERIENCES 23.6

Hitting to Spaces (*continued*)

Modify the Game to 2v2 or 3v3 with Infielders and Running Bases

D. Divide into two teams with two or three children on a team. [If you put too many players on a team, it constrains the amount of thinking and moving each child will do.] Fielders are all in the infield. The batter hits and runs to the base. Balls hit past the cone are home runs (whether it is a missed grounder, line drive, or fly). Fielders try to get the runner out.

Rules the Children Design

- Batter hits a pitched ball or ball off a tee
- When to switch (e.g., after two outs, after each person has batted twice)
- What to do if all batters are stuck on base with no one left to hit
- Four or three bases

Modifying the Game to Get It Working Well

E. Using the play-discuss-play cycle, modify the game to get it working well.

Improving Tactics

F. Play the game again while working on tactics, including making good decisions about where to hit, where to cover space, and who covers which bases.

Sample Question to Ask about Tactics

- How did you work as a team to get the batter out? [The fielder closest to the ball caught it; the person closest to the base ahead of the runner ran to the base.]
- How did you cover space on defense? [Spread out and evenly covered the space.]
- How did you decide which base to throw to get the runner out? [The base ahead of the runner.]

SAMPLE LEARNING EXPERIENCES 23.7

Deciding Whether to Run for the Double and Whether to Throw the Runner Out at First or Second Base

Motor and Tactics Objectives

Children will learn to

1. Cover second base on a hit to the outfield.
2. Tag a runner out at second base.
3. Decide whether the fielders can get the runner out at first, get the runner out at second, or hold the runner at first.
4. Decide whether they can run safely to second, need to hold at first, or run fast past first to beat the throw.
5. Run for a double using a "banana" pathway to first base and a straight pathway off.

Potential Refinements

- How should the runner approach first base to make a straight run to second?

Organization

Children work in groups of four. Use poly spots for home, first, and second base. The batting tee is placed on the pitcher's mound (the space where the pitcher would play).

Initial Game: Run for the Double

The defense consists of one outfielder and one infielder (who stand between first and second base). The runner stands at home plate. The batter hits the ball off a tee placed on the pitcher's mound, hitting the ball to the outfield (the batter does not run). When the ball is batted, the runner must try to get a double off the hit. The batter and the runner change places and play one more round. Then the fielders come up to be the batter and the base runner. The runner is out if he or she does not make it to second before the fielders get the ball to second.

(*continues*)

SAMPLE LEARNING EXPERIENCES 23.7

Deciding Whether to Run for the Double and Whether to Throw the Runner Out at First or Second Base (*continued*)

Improving Tactics

A. Play the game while working on tactics, including how and when to run for a double, where to hit, who fields the ball, and who covers the base.

Sample Questions to Ask About Tactics

- When and why should you use a "banana" pathway when running to first? [Only when the ball is hit to the outfield and you think you can get to second base before the ball.]
- How and why is the "banana" pathway better? [It is a faster way to turn because you don't have to stop and change directions.]

Adding a Fielder

You are doing such a good job that you are ready to try a more difficult game. This game has three fielders and one batter/runner. Move the tee to home plate. The batter hits the ball and runs. The three fielders must make tactical decisions about whether they can get the runner out at first, get the runner out at second, or just hold the runner at first. Rotate after each hit so the batter becomes a fielder and a fielder becomes the batter.

B. Play the game working on the tactical decisions.

Sample Questions to Ask About Tactics

- As the runner, how do you decide whether you can run to second or whether you need to stay at first for a single? [See where the ball was hit, and decide whether the fielders can throw it to first quickly or if I can make it to second.]
- As a fielder, how do you know whether the play should be at first or at second? [It depends on where the ball was hit and if we have time to throw the runner out at first.]

SAMPLE LEARNING EXPERIENCES 23.8

Child-Designed Throwing and Catching Field Game

Motor, Tactics, and Thinking Skill Objectives

Children will learn to

1. Design a game that works on the skills and tactics of field games.
2. Make appropriate tactical decisions in the games they design.

Social

3. Work cooperatively with peers, listening to everyone's ideas and opinions.

Equipment

Put out a variety of balls, bats, poly spots, gloves, and tees.

Designing the Game

I Today you are going to design your own field games. It must be a throwing-and-catching game. In your assigned groups of four, make the following decisions:

- Which kind of ball will you use? (If group members don't want to use same ball, you can play for a short time with one ball, and then use a different ball.)
- Will you use gloves?
- Will you have running? Do you need bases?
- What will be your rules and consequences for breaking rules?
- Will you have a scoring system?
- Will you keep track of the score?

Social Before you start, what are some things you need to do to be a cooperative, productive group? [Make sure everyone participates equally. Make sure everyone has a chance to contribute ideas to the game. Listen to everyone's opinions.]

SAMPLE LEARNING EXPERIENCES 23.8

Child-Designed Throwing and Catching Field Game (*continued*)

Excellent answers. Before you begin playing, you need to tell me about your game so I can arrange the playing space for all groups in a safe way.

Sample Questions to Ask to Get a Good Game Working

- Is your game fair for both offense and defense?
- Is everyone active in your game?
- Which skills are used in your game? Did you include both throwing and catching, which was a requirement for all games?
- Did you solve any problems with rules, boundaries, or scoring that came up in your game?

Sample Questions to Ask About Tactics

- Tell me how to play your game.
- What are the offensive tactics?
- What should you try to do on defense?

Note to Teachers

Here are some sample games that children designed as a result of this lesson.

1. A group of four designed a throwing-and-catching game like four square (a popular playground game). Each player stood on a base. If a player dropped a ball, he or she moved to the lowest base. If a player made an uncatchable throw, he or she also moved to the lowest base.
2. A group of three designed a game called "Three Bases." The thrower threw the ball between two bases and tried to run to all three bases before the catcher fielded the ball and threw it to hit the fence (requiring a long throw). Sometimes the throw required a relay.
3. A group of three set three cones in a row perpendicular to the wall. Two runners each had a base. The thrower stood at the first cone, threw the ball at the wall, and tried to catch the ball before runners touched the wall and got back to their base. If the thrower won, the thrower had to move back to the next cone. The players switched roles if the thrower got to the third cone or a runner won.
4. Three players each stood on a base and threw to one another. A fourth player was in the middle trying to disrupt the throw. You went in the middle if you made a bad throw or if a good throw was dropped.
5. Each of five group members had five cones arranged in a line perpendicular to a wall (five total lines of cones). Each child stood at her or his first cone and threw a 6-inch rubber ball, baseball-size foam ball, or tennis ball. If the child caught the ball, he or she moved to the second cone. The first child to make it to the fifth cone was the winner.

SKILLS BOX 23.1

Technical Reference Information for Teachers

In this feature, we describe technical information about immature movement patterns and mature performance techniques for the overhand throw for force, catching in field games, and batting. When you observe immature patterns, it does not mean the children are not trying to perform the skill the way you said to do so. Rather, it simply means they are in the process of developing the mature pattern and need more experience in a range of practice tasks designed to elicit improved performance and feedback aligned to their developmental level.

The performance techniques for batting, in particular, are complex. As a teacher, you need to know the content you teach in depth, but you do not tell the children everything you know. Don't overload your students with information because there is only a limited amount of information that will help them at any one point in time. The information you share must be linked to the developmental level of components of the skill. Telling children what they need to know, when they need to know it, is a hallmark of an effective teacher and something you should strive to master early in your career.

Overhand Throw for Force

We begin with a list describing the developmental patterns for throwing simplified and adapted from research by Roberton and Halverson (1984). Immature, intermediate, and mature patterns are described.

Next, we provide a suggested progression of refinements for throwing. As always, you will need to adjust the performance techniques you teach based on your observations of the developmental level of each child.

For each performance technique, we present a sample story or several images and metaphors you can teach children to help them remember the technique. We encourage you to invent your own stories and cues that the children in your setting will find meaningful.

(*continues*)

SKILLS BOX 23.1

Technical Reference Information for Teachers (*continued*)

Mature pattern

The development of throwing takes time. Children need a lot of practice throwing in order to develop more mature throwing patterns.

Overhand Throw for Force

Trunk and Leg Actions and Transferring Weight

Immature Patterns

- Stands with body facing target
- Throws with arm action only or bends forward at the waist

Immature patterns, both girls: humerus feet, and trunk; girl wearing purple shirt: most immature pattern for feet

SKILLS BOX 23.1

Technical Reference Information for Teachers (*continued*)

- Does not step or transfer weight from back foot to front throwing-hand foot
- Holds ball in nondominant hand
- Starts with feet too wide apart and can't step

Intermediate Patterns

- Steps on same-side-as-throwing-arm foot (*homolateral* foot)
- Steps on opposite-side-of-throwing-arm foot (*contralateral* foot) with a short step
- Stands side to target but doesn't transfer weight from back foot to front foot
- Stands side to target, rotates truck to face target with hips and shoulders, rotating as a unit (called *block rotation*).
- Over-rotates (belly button past target) and back leg flings forward
- Transfers weight from back foot to front foot
- For right-handed throwers, steps on a line to the left of the target; for left-handed throwers, steps on a line that is to the right of the target

Mature Patterns

- Starts side to target and steps on contralateral foot with a long step
- Steps on a line directly toward target
- Hips rotate toward the target before shoulders (called *differentiated rotation*)
- Transfers weight to finish with weight forward on front foot
- Pulls the non-throwing-side elbow back and tucks the glove under the arm

Arm Action

Immature Patterns

- Lifts hand near ear; elbow is bent in an acute angle less than 90 degrees
- During the throw, the elbow remains bent in an acute angle, and the humerus is either up by the ear or down by the ribs

Intermediate Patterns

- Backswing starts on a circular, upward, and back pathway
- During the throw, the humerus is initially in line with the shoulders horizontally and forward and back (table-and-door plane), and the elbow is bent 90 degrees or more
- Before the trunk has rotated to face the target, the humerus has moved forward (breaking the door plane) so that the elbow is in front of the trunk pointing toward the target

Mature Patterns

- Backswing starts on a circular, downward, and back pathway, and the palm faces away from the target before the forward motion of the arm begins
- Humerus remains in a line with the shoulders until after the trunk faces the target.
- During the throw, the hand comes through last.

Potential Refinements for the Overhand Throw

Basic Techniques When Children Are at Developmental Level 1

- *Throw the ball with as much force and speed as you can.*
- *Side to target, point to target.* Having children point with one finger of the nondominant hand helps them remember to start with their throwing hand back and their entire side (from ankle to hips to ribs) to target. This technique aims to improve the immature patterns for the initial foot position and trunk action.
- *"Make the T, break the T."* Put arms straight out, making a T (with side to target). Break the T by bending the back elbow and bringing the forearm perpendicular to the ground, with the palm facing back. This body position gets the humerus aligned with the shoulder and aims to improve the immature patterns for the humerus and elbow angle. The goal is to help children at least start in and understand the mature position, although many will continue to drop their humerus or try to generate force by pointing their elbow up with the ball behind their head until they have practiced enough to develop the mature pattern. Other cues and metaphors that can help are "High five," "No local calls, only long distance" (i.e., a local call would be holding the phone—the ball—to your ear and letting the humerus drop below the horizontal; the joke is that a long-distance call would mean holding the phone away from the ear in the humerus-aligned position), "No pizza" (which means don't hold your hand down by your shoulder like a waitperson carrying a pizza to the table), "No puppets talking in your ear" (hand close to the head with finger pointing at head), and "No chicken wings" (elbow down).
- *"Rock and roll, step and throw."* This cue refers to stepping on the nonthrowing foot, while shifting the weight from the back foot to the front foot. In the mature pattern, the child has 80% of the weight on the back foot at the start of the throw and then steps and shifts the weight to the nonthrowing foot.
- *No helicopters.* This cue helps to constrain the common response of children to turn in a circle with their arm straight out to throw.

More Advanced Techniques When Children Are at Developmental Level 2

- *Palm away, thumb down and away.* These cues elicit the more mature circular backswing pattern. The hand curves down and back to end facing the back. The size of the backswing depends on the task and the environment. In a throw from the outfield, throwers use a big, circular backswing. An infield throw requires a much shorter backswing, and the catcher tossing back to the pitcher needs little backswing at all. Other cues are "Palm to _______" (fill in the blank with a landmark behind the child); "If you are the pitcher, show the ball to center field"; and "High five." Have students look back; they should see the back of their hand.
- *Long step, step on line to target.* These cues elicit progress to the mature pattern of the feet. Stepping on a straight line toward the target helps with accuracy. You can draw a line to help develop this action.

(*continues*)

SKILLS BOX 23.1

Technical Reference Information for Teachers (*continued*)

- *Shuffle on line to target.* A shuffle is a step–feet together–step sequence (or one slide). Having children shuffle helps elicit the contralateral, long step. When children shuffle before they throw, it is difficult for them to then step on the homolateral foot. This technique also keeps their shoulder pointing at the target. If a child is having problems stepping on the same foot as the throwing arm, you can teach the shuffle earlier to help with development. A cue for shuffling is "Cut the grass," which keeps the child low and traveling forward, not up and down.
- *Twist and throw, belly button twists to target.* These cues refer to the immature patterns of the trunk action. The aim is to help children learn to twist their hips to face the target. "Explode belly button to target," "Where your belly button points is the direction the ball will go," and "No backward twisting; only forward," are other performance techniques that can help.

More Advanced Techniques When Children Are at Developmental Level 3

- *Air pocket.* Hold the ball in your fingers so there is an air pocket between the palm and the ball. In addition, the middle finger and the thumb should line up with each other.
- *Elbow pull, tuck the glove.* As the throwing arm comes forward, pull the front elbow and tuck the glove under the arm. This cue increases force production by helping rotate the trunk for power. Tucking also helps keep the trunk from over-rotating.
- *Finish with weight forward.* This cue encourages children to lean over, with chest to knee, head toward the ball, and eyes parallel to the ground. Although you may see softball and baseball players bringing their back foot forward at the end of the throw, if you teach this technique to students at the elementary level, the children will turn too early and not have differentiated rotation, causing them to lose force and accuracy. They need to learn to keep the back foot back and twist the body. As they improve, they can end in a fielding position after release. Possible cues are "Belly button to target," and "Twist; back foot stays in back."

Kindergarten class practicing "make the T, break the T"

Catching in Field Games

Immature and Mature Patterns

There are immature and mature patterns for catching in general. This information also applies to catching in softball-type situations. Here, we list typical immature patterns we see when children catch grounders and fly balls thrown with force.

*Immature Patterns for Catching Grounders (see **Figure 23.6**)*

- Fingers point up; child tries to trap the ball when it gets under his or her body
- Child squats with bottom down
- Fingertips point down on the ground
- Prepares and catches ball with elbows already bent near feet
- Minimal or no bending of the elbows to absorb the force of the ball

Immature Patterns for Catching Fly Balls

- Holds the glove palm up as if holding a plate (missed balls will travel straight toward the nose)
- Runs too close to the thrower so the ball goes over the catcher's head
- Does not align with the flight path of the ball

Potential Refinements for Catching

The major difference in the performance technique for catching in field games is to catch with the nondominant hand with (or without) a glove and to cover the ball with the dominant hand on top. In addition, children must absorb more force than when they catch passes; thus reaching forward and then absorbing force by bringing the glove back (giving or cradling) becomes more critical.

Basic Techniques When Children Are at Developmental Level 1

- *Reach, cover, cradle.* When you catch balls hit or thrown with force, you need to really reach for the ball because you need space to absorb the force. Then cover the ball like covering a baby with a blanket. Then you cradle the baby by bringing the ball toward your body while bending your arms. You don't want to let the baby fall out of the bed. Pull the ball toward your trunk without trapping it against your chest.
- *Look at the ball.*

More Advanced Techniques When Children Are at Developmental Level 2

- *Align your body with the ball.*
- *Watch the ball into your glove/hands.*
- *Quick hands.* As soon as the ball hits the glove and the throwing hand covers the ball, start to separate the hands for the throw. This is the reason you don't catch with one hand (unless you are playing first base) or put the throwing hand behind glove.

Additional Techniques for Grounders

- *Feet apart, bottom up, flat back.*
- *Back of fingers (not fingertips) on the ground.*
- *Catch the ball out front, not near the feet.*

SKILLS BOX 23.1

Technical Reference Information for Teachers (*continued*)

(A)

(B)

(A) Common immature pattern: starting with the ball toward the target (B) Teacher told her to turn around

Additional Techniques for Fly Balls

- *Chest height: Thumbs up, bear claws.* (Your fingers are pointing toward your partner and your thumbs point up.)
- *High balls: Moose antlers, Mickey Mouse ears.* (Your thumbs are together, with your hands above your head. It looks like your hands are moose antlers or Mickey Mouse ears but held slightly in front of the head. Look over the fingers or the glove to catch the ball, not under them.)

More Advanced Techniques When Children Are at Developmental Level 3

- *Glove foot (slightly) forward.*

Batting

Potential Refinements for Batting

Basic Techniques When Children Are at Developmental Level 1

Preparation

- Stand between the 8 o'clock and 7 o'clock positions (for right-handed batters) or between the 4 o'clock and 5 o'clock positions (for left-handed batters), close enough to the tee that the fat part of the bat hits the ball. Draw or imagine a clock around the batting tee with 12 o'clock facing where the pitcher would stand and 6 o'clock being where the catcher would squat. Right-handed batters stand between 8 o'clock and 7 o'clock, and left-handed batters stand between 4 o'clock and 5 o'clock (slightly back toward the catcher).
- Grip the bat with the pencil hand on top, with hands together. [Pencil hand is a term kindergarteners understand to be their dominant hand before they learn the word "dominant."]
- Start with feet parallel (no "duck feet"), placed twice the shoulder width apart (called the *power pyramid* or *athletic stance*; see **Figure 23.7**). You can demonstrate and say, "This is standing in line to buy lunch [feet barely shoulder-width apart]. This is playing sports [the power pyramid with feet twice the shoulder width]."

Swing and Finish

- Back foot pivot, front foot closed (see **Figure 23.8** and the **Teaching Tip** box, "Why 'Front Foot Closed and Back Foot Pivot' Is an 'Absolute' for Good Hitting"). Pretend your back foot is squishing a bug (the back foot pivots). The knee turns toward the pitcher and the heel toward the catcher. Swing, and finish with the front foot remaining closed (pointing toward the base, with the outside of the foot facing the pitcher). Check your feet after the swing.
- Swing shoulder to shoulder (tattoo to tattoo): Pretend to put a tattoo on each shoulder. You might have one shoulder say, "I love the cat," and the other say, "I love the dog." When batting, swing from tattoo to tattoo. More specifically, start with the bat back (toward the catcher) and the hands held up slightly higher than the shoulder, approximately a fist-length away from the body. The elbows are relaxed but not touching the body. Many children drop their elbow next to their body when swinging. As a result, many teachers and youth league coaches tend to say, "Get your elbow up." However, this instruction can lead to children holding their elbows parallel to the ground. This stance will cause the batter's muscles to tighten, making the swing less effective and often leading to pop-ups. Swing the bat from shoulder to shoulder, ending with the hands up and in at the end of the swing, just as in the starting position.

More Advanced Techniques When Children Are at Developmental Level 2

Preparation

- 40/60: Weight is 40% on the front leg and 60% on the back leg with knees bent.

(*continues*)

SKILLS BOX 23.1

Technical Reference Information for Teachers (*continued*)

Swing and Finish

- Eyes on ball at contact. If you want to whack it, track it. You can't hit what you can't see. Watch the ball make contact with the bat (technically you can't see the ball hit the bat, but the eyes should look at the point of contact). As the ball is hit, the eyes look at the ball even as the shoulders continue to rotate. Thus, the chin starts at the left shoulder (for right-handed batters) with eyes looking at the pitcher; it finishes at the right shoulder looking at the ball at contact. (The opposite is true for left-handed batters.) Many children will look at a ball moving toward them, but continue to look at the pitcher even at contact. Instead, they should turn their head (slightly) to continue watching the ball, then hold it at contact during follow-though. A potential cue is "Don't look up until you hear the roar of the crowd" (see the **Teaching Tip** box, "Stride, Balance, and Finish)."
- Belly button rotates to pitcher (not first or third). The shoulders turn to squarely face the pitcher.
- Head stays in the middle. You want limited head movement, with the chin staying behind the front knee.

More Advanced Techniques When Children Are at Developmental Level 3

Preparation

- The knob of the bat points toward the plate, with the bat at a 45-degree angle. When children begin with the knob pointing at the catcher, it takes longer for the bat to get to the ball.
- Load up (sometimes called trigger). Loading up is a slight twist away from the pitcher prior to swinging forward. Once a famous baseball player was asked what made him such a good batter. His response: "When the pitcher shows me his bottom, I show him mine." Here is a story you can tell to your students: Two cars are going to race. Which one will win—the car that has its motor running with the driver ready to push on the gas pedal, or the car that has its engine stopped so the driver has to start the car after the race officials signal "Go"? That is why we need to load up for the swing before you hit the ball.

Swing

- Rotate hips quickly to face the pitcher. The hips rotate quickly to face the pitcher so as to generate more force. Hip speed is bat speed because the hips take the hands to the ball.
- Hands to the ball/compact swing. The left thumb (for right-handed batters) moves in a diagonal across the chest to the ball. The hands never swing farther away from the body than the ball.

Figure 23.6 Girl using mature pattern; two boys using immature patterns

Figure 23.7 Power pyramid stance

Figure 23.8 Back foot pivot, front foot closed

TEACHING TIP

Why "Front Foot Closed and Back Foot Pivot" Is an "Absolute" for Good Hitting

Select a talented student or a large student. Using a metal bat, have the student hold the bat at contact with hands over front foot, top hand palm up, bottom hand palm down, arms straight, both feet straight head, and front foot closed; the back foot is not pivoted, however.

"I am going to show you how important front foot closed and back foot pivot are to hitting. I am going to use my pinkie to try to push the bat the batter is holding. Do you think the batter will be able to keep the bat from moving since he is using both hands and I am just using my pinkie? Look at the batter's feet. There is no back foot pivot. Is this the strongest position? [No.] Watch, I am going to push the bat back with my pinkie [the bat moves easily back]. Now let's try it with the back foot pivoted and the front foot pivoted. I will use my pinkie again. Notice the batter was still not able to hold the bat in position. Now the batter will do front foot closed and back foot pivot. Look, I can't move it at all. You can try this experiment at home with your dad, with you mom, or with a coach—just use your hand instead of a bat. They will not be able to overpower you if they do not have front foot closed and back foot pivoted.

"What do you think will happen if you try to hit a 30- or 40-mile-per-hour pitch and you do not use front foot closed and back foot pivot? Yes, it will be a foul ball or a weak infield hit. I have seen a bunch of foul-ball home runs in my day. Do you know what they call them? Strike one. Have you ever heard someone say, 'Nice hit. Straighten it out'? Maybe they should be saying, 'Front foot closed, back foot pivot.'"

TEACHING TIP

Stride, Balance, and Finish

- *Stride:* There is always controversy about whether to teach stepping (striding) into the ball. Both methods are acceptable, but we do not mention the stride. If children choose to stride, we encourage them to make this step soft and short (three to six inches) or to pick up their foot and put it down in place. Anything longer or bigger than that will cause head movement.
- *Balance:* Rich Luppino from the United Sport Academy stresses that the key to hitting is balance. Nothing that the batter does should have a negative effect on balance. Balance is a result of performance techniques that allow the batter to finish the swing with front foot closed, back foot pivoted, eyes on ball at contact, and limited head movement.
- *Finish:* At the end of every *Oprah* magazine, Oprah Winfrey writes about "What I know for sure." What we know for sure is that if you do not have a good finish, the swing will not be as effective as it could be. Starting in the youngest grades, we concentrate on the finish with front foot closed, back foot pivot. To help teach these performance techniques, find pictures in sport magazines that illustrate each phase of the hit. Place these pictures on a bulletin board or use laminated cards so students can see the performance techniques at a mature level.

SKILLS BOX 23.2

Performance Techniques for Children in Wheelchairs

Catching with a Glove

When catching a high ball, the performance techniques for children with and without wheelchairs are the same. For most children in wheelchairs, catching a low ball with a glove is done to the side, with the other hand placed on the wheel for balance. Children with strong balance capabilities can catch in front.

Batting

If the child in a wheelchair has strong balance capabilities, the batting action is the same as for the child not in a wheelchair. Most children in wheelchairs hold the bat with one hand and use the other hand on the wheel to assist with balance. Children in wheelchairs should learn to bat with the dominant-hand shoulder starting toward the pitcher to enable a greater range of motion and consequently provide more force (i.e., a right-handed child bats lefty and a left-handed child bats righty).

Summary

The predominant field games in the United States are softball and baseball, with softball being one of the most popular recreational sports for adult men and women. The skills of throwing overhand for force, catching balls batted or thrown with force, and batting take years of practice and instruction before children acquire the mature pattern.

To develop the coordination pattern of throwing, you need to set tasks so children throw forcefully, thereby eliciting their most mature throwing. Teach force before accuracy. Work on throwing forcefully and accurately once children have acquired the basic coordination pattern.

With catching, teach children to catch balls (with gloves, if possible) thrown at different levels (grounders to fly balls), progressing to catching balls thrown with more force. In addition, teach them to combine catching and, in one motion, quickly throwing.

In batting lessons and field games at the elementary level, we rely on batting tees. Batting tees allow multiple children to practice simultaneously on performance techniques without having to deal with a moving ball. Tees also solve the problems related to beginning throwers' inability to pitch accurately. Field games are all modified to be played by three to five children.

Review Questions

1. Why is it critical for children to practice force before accuracy in the overhand throw for force?
2. What movement variety is important to teach children for catching balls, and why?
3. (a) Describe three immature or intermediate patterns for the trunk, leg, and transferring weight and three for the arm actions of the forceful overhand throw; (b) for each pattern, write a task, and develop a performance cue that will help children improve; and (c) invent a story, metaphor, or interesting phrase to teach children so they will remember the cue.
4. (a) Describe two immature patterns for catching; (b) for each pattern, write a task, and develop a performance cue that will help children improve; and (c) invent a story, metaphor, or interesting phrase to teach children so they will remember the cue.
5. (a) Describe two immature patterns for batting; (b) for each pattern, write a task, and develop a performance cue that will help children improve; and (c) invent a story, metaphor, or interesting phrase to teach children so they will remember the cue.
6. Based on your reading of **Sample Learning Experiences 23.3** to **23.8**, invent and describe a modified field game that uses the skills or tactics of field games and can be played by three to five children.

References

Davids, K., Button, C., & Bennett, S. (2008). *Dynamics of skill acquisition: A constraints-led approach.* Champaign, IL: Human Kinetics.

Mitchell, S., Oslin, J., & Griffin, L. (2003). *Sport foundations for elementary physical education: A tactical games approach.* Champaign, IL: Human Kinetics.

Mitchell, S. A., Oslin, J. L., & Griffin, L. L. (2006). *Teaching sport concepts and skills: A tactical games approach* (2nd ed.). Champaign, IL: Human Kinetics.

Newell, K. M. (1986). Constraints on the development of coordination. In M. G. Wade & H. T. A. Whiting (Eds.), *Motor development in children: Aspects of coordination and control* (pp. 341–360). Amsterdam: Martinus Nijhoff.

Oslin, J. (2004). Developing motor and tactical skills in K–2 physical education: Let the games begin. *Teaching Elementary Physical Education, 15*(3), 12–14.

Rink, J. E. (2014). *Teaching physical education for learning* (7th ed.). New York: McGraw-Hill.

Roberton, M. A., & Halverson, L. E. (1984). *Developing children: Their changing movement.* Philadelphia: Lea & Febiger.

Southard, D. (2006). Changing throwing pattern: Instruction and control parameter. *Research Quarterly for Exercise and Sport, 77*, 316–325.

FYI

Summary of Task Label Abbreviations

I	Informing tasks
E	Extending/exploring tasks
R	Refinements
A	Application/assessment tasks
Org	Organizing task
Cog K	Cognitive knowledge: Explains or defines a concept
Social	Social skill or concept
Th	Thinking skill
Mot	Motivation concept
Safety	Safety information or reminder
MD	Modification to make the task more difficult
ME	Modification to make the task easier

Source: Adapted and modified from Rink, J. E. (2014). *Teaching physical education for learning* (7th ed.).New York: McGraw-Hill.

Sample Plans for Levels 1 and 2 Field Game Skills

In this section, we illustrate how to teach performance techniques for overhand throwing, batting, and catching with a glove in field games at levels 1 and 2. In addition, we describe centers for having children practice throwing overhand for force and batting. The lesson segments indicate how to integrate key objectives for social responsibility aimed at teaching children how to work safely and responsibly when they throw and bat using force.

SAMPLE PLAN 23.1

Level 1: Throwing

Throwing

Standards

This plan addresses National Standards 1, 2, and 4 and CCSS for listening and speaking.

Objectives

Children will learn to

Motor

1. Throw overhand for force, starting with side to target.
2. Throw overhand for force, starting with the humerus aligned with the shoulders, and the forearm at a 90-degree angle ("Make the T, break the T").

Social

3. Be socially responsible by looking to make sure no one is in front of them before throwing.

CCSS

4. Describe key ideas from information presented orally about safely and being responsible.

Notes and Potential Interactive Teaching Decisions

Equipment and organization: One poly spot with a yarn or foam ball on it for each child; spots spread apart in a line approximately 10 to 20 feet (depending on the children's age) from a wall. If you don't have a wall, use a field with cones set very far away to elicit throwing forcefully.

Notes: The first lesson segment focuses on starting side to target. The second lesson segment, for a second lesson, focuses on "make the T, break the T."

Social and safety goals: This is an excellent lesson segment for working on social and safety goals. The aim is for the children to throw and retrieve their balls at their own pace, showing both self-responsibility and social responsibility. You might have to work on this aspect of the lesson step by step, especially if you do not know the children well. If so, break the ball retrieval routine down into the following steps, progressing as soon as the children show you they can work safely and responsibly:

1. Throw on the teacher's command. Remain standing on the poly spot. Retrieve on command.
2. Throw on the teacher's command, look for others, and safely retrieve ball. Stand on the spot, and wait for the teacher's command to throw again.
3. Throw and retrieve at your own pace, making sure no other child is standing between you and the target before throwing.

Observation Plan

1. Scan the entire class to see if the students are throwing and receiving safely and responsibly.
2. Look at the starting positions of the children, and check for side to target and "make the T, break the T."

Content Development

Org Everyone, walk and stand on one of the poly spots. Pick up the yarn ball on the poly spot in the hand you draw with, and face the wall. **I** When I say "Go," throw the yarn ball as hard as you can at the wall. The wall in front of you is your target. Remain standing on your poly spot. Go.	**Safety/Social** When I say "Go," you will retrieve your ball. What safety rules do you think we need to have for retrieving your ball? [Don't run. Don't bump into anyone. If someone crosses in front of you, stop so they can get by you.] Great suggestions. Retrieve your ball. Let's try that again, and see if you can throw and then safely retrieve your ball. [Repeat this activity until the children are working with self-responsibility.]
R Now I want to share some secrets that will help you improve your throwing. First, you need to learn about the best starting position. To start, point your finger of the hand without the ball at the wall and turn that same side to the wall like I am doing. The wall is your target. [Demonstrate.] Be sure you are holding the ball in the hand you draw with and that you are pointing to the target with your other hand and side. The cue is "Point to target, side to target." This gets you into a great starting position. Practice throwing at the wall, thinking about the cue "Point to target, side to target" every time before you throw. Throw as hard as you can. Go.	*Notes:* Repeat this activity many times, giving individual feedback as needed until the children consistently point to the target with their side to the target each time. Observe their hands. It is likely that some children will get confused about which hand is their dominant hand, and some will hold the ball in the same hand with which they are trying to point at the wall. In addition, some children who are left-handed might observe their right-handed classmates and think they need to face the same direction as everyone else. You might need to mention that children who are right-handed will face the door (or another landmark), and children who are left-handed will face a different landmark.

(*continues*)

SAMPLE PLAN 23.1

Level 1: Throwing (*continued*)

Lesson Two

R [This lesson segment will be in a second lesson plan within the unit. Start the second lesson with a review of pointing to the target and side to the target.] You are all working so hard, and you have done a great job pointing to target and side to target. Now, I will teach you another secret that will help you improve your throws. This cue is "Make the T, break the T." [Demonstrate.] Do this with me. For your starting position, make a T-shape like I am making. This is called "make the T." Then break the T by bending your throwing-arm elbow. Notice I have the ball hidden from the target. Don't let the target see what is coming. Let's practice that. "Make the T, break the T," and throw.

Repeat this activity many times, giving individual feedback as needed.

R Don't drop your elbow; keep it up so you can still have the T from elbow to elbow.

R Are you thinking about "Make the T, break the T" before you throw?

Social/Safety I am really proud of you because you are being so responsible. No one has bumped into anyone. No one has been running to retrieve her or his ball. I think you are ready to be given even more responsibility. You will now be allowed to throw, retrieve, go to your spot, and throw again without waiting for me to tell you to throw. What rules do you think we need now? [Don't throw if anyone is in front of you. Don't throw if people are walking over to your target area to pick up their yarn balls; wait until they have their balls before throwing.] Are you ready to handle this responsibility? Continue practicing. [Give feedback on performance cues and social responsibility as needed.]

CCSS Closure

We are going to make two lists on the white board. On one side, I will write safe behaviors you tell me are important in physical education lessons on throwing. On the other side, I will list the behaviors that are not safe. Talk with your assigned partner, and identify behaviors that are safe and not safe. I will call on pairs to share one answer with the rest of the class until we have a complete list.

SAMPLE PLAN 23.2

Level 1: Batting

Batting	Notes and Potential Interactive Teaching Decisions
Standards This plan addresses National Standards 1, 2, and 4 and CCSS for vocabulary acquisition. **Objectives** Children will learn to Motor 1. Bat while standing between 7 o'clock and 8 o'clock if batting right-handed or between 4 o'clock and 5 o'clock if batting left-handed. 2. Grip the bat with the pencil hand on top. 3. Bat while pivoting the back foot on the ball of the foot with the heel up and the knee bent so the heel points back toward where a catcher would stand.	*Equipment and organization:* Provide a plastic bat, five or six whiffle balls (if possible), and a batting tee for every child. (You can make a tee by placing a cone on a cardboard box.) Spread the tees out in a straight line so children cannot possibly hit balls at one another or hit one another with the bats. *Notes:* The first lesson segment focuses on where to position in relation to the batting tee and how to grip the bat. On another day, teach the lesson segment on back foot pivot.

SAMPLE PLAN 23.2

Level 1: Batting (*continued*)

Social

4. Be self-responsible, and ensure that no one is near their personal space while batting.
5. Be self-responsible by not leaving their tee unless it is to walk forward to retrieve balls.

CCSS

6. Acquire and use accurately the domain-specific phrase "back foot closed, front foot open" that signals precise actions.
7. Identify real-life connections between words and their use.

Observation Plan

1. Make sure all children are far enough apart to ensure safety.
2. Scan the children for the entire lesson for safety.
3. See whether the children are positioned appropriately in relation to the tee.
4. Check their grips.
5. If there is enough time, check whether their back foot is pivoted.

Starting Position in Relation to the Tee

I Today you will begin to learn how to bat. Here is a picture of a clock. [Draw a clock in the dirt around a tee.] You are going to imagine a clock around your batting tee. Twelve o'clock is facing the pitcher, and 6 o'clock is facing the catcher. If you bat left-handed, you should stand between 4 o'clock and 5 o'clock. If you bat right-handed, you should stand between 7 o'clock and 8 o'clock, like this. [Demonstrate.]

I Go to your tee, make sure you are standing in the appropriate position, and practice swinging the bat. [Check that children are at the correct clock positions and are far enough away from the tee. Sometimes you will have to draw a line in the dirt to help some children understand where to stand.]

Safety Before you go to your tee, what do you think you need to remember about safety? [Don't hit anyone with the bat. Don't be too close to anyone when you swing or you might hit someone by mistake. Look before you swing to see if anyone is near. If you are near someone who is about to swing, tell them, "Don't swing now; I am too close."] Those are great suggestions. Remember when you practiced striking with a racket, you learned that your personal space was much larger. The same thing happens when you bat. You are responsible for making sure no one is near your personal space when you swing. [Set up the tees prior to class to ensure batters remain a safe distance away from one another.]

Safety Your starting position is looking good. Now you can put a ball on the tee and hit it. You have five balls you can hit. After you hit them all, you can then retrieve your balls. For safety, do you think you should retrieve a ball that rolled in front of another child? No. That would not be safe. You are not allowed to move sideways away from your tee. When you run out of balls, you must go forward and get a ball.

E Hit your five balls, and then wait by your tee.

Org Now everyone retrieve all of your balls.

Grip

R Let's talk about the grip. Put your pencil hand on top. Check your grip, and practice hitting again.

Notes: With kindergarteners, this is probably all you can practice during the first lesson. With first-graders, you can probably teach one more performance cue.

Lesson Two

Lesson segment for a second lesson plan in the unit.

Back Foot Pivot

Cog K Watch me: I am going to show you a very important cue, which we call "back foot pivot." When you swing, your back foot moves just like you are squishing a bug, like this. [Demonstrate.] Without swinging the bat, show me your back foot squishing a bug. Really squish that bug by pivoting on the ball of your foot. I see a lot of dead bugs! What is the word we use in physical education to describe squishing the bug with your back foot? [Pivot]

(*continues*)

SAMPLE PLAN 23.2

Level 1: Batting (*continued*)

R Walk back to your tee, pick up your bat, check your starting position, check your personal space, and practice a few swings without the ball on the tee. Which cue do I want to you practice? Right. Back foot pivots to squish the bug. Go.

R Hit the balls, checking each time to see if you did back foot pivot. [Walk up and down the line checking for safety and back foot pivot. Scan the class frequently.]

CCSS Closure

With your assigned partner, discuss what "back foot pivot" means. What is a real-life connection to back foot pivot? [Squish the bug.] Can you think of any other real-life actions like the pivot?

Extending the Content in Future Units

Motor Objectives

Children will learn to

1. Bat by keeping the front foot closed while pivoting the back foot.

Review Back Foot Pivot

I Let's start by reviewing what you learned last year. What does "squish the bug" mean? Right, you pivot your back foot as you hit the ball. When I say "Go," walk to your tee, stand between 7 o'clock and 8 o'clock if you bat right-handed and between 4 o'clock and 5 o'clock if you bat left-handed. Look at your back foot after each swing to see if you have squished the bug (back foot pivot).

Safety Do you remember the ways you are responsible for safety when we work on batting? [You are responsible for making sure no one is near your personal space when you swing. Don't hit anyone with the bat. Don't be too close to anyone when you swing or you might hit someone by mistake. Look before you swing to see if anyone is near. If you are near someone who is about to swing, tell them, "Don't swing now; I am too close." No moving away from the tee unless you go forward to retrieve the balls.] [Set up the tees prior to class to ensure batters remain a safe distance away from one another.]

Front Foot Closed

E Today we are going to learn another part of hitting. It is called "front foot closed." When you swing the bat, your front does not pivot like your back foot. Instead, it stays just like it was when you started, pointing to the tee. It looks like this. [Demonstrate a swing showing front foot closed, back foot pivot.] Try to bat using front foot closed.

R Look down after every swing to check that you have back foot pivot, front foot closed. You will not know if you are in the right position for sure unless you *look*.

SAMPLE PLAN 23.3

Level 2: Catching Balls at Different Levels with a Glove: Bear Claws, Alligator Hands, and Moose Antlers

Catching Balls at Different Levels with a Glove: Bear Claws, Alligator Hands, and Moose Antlers	Notes and Potential Interactive Teaching Decisions

Standards

This plan addresses National Standards 1, 2, and 4 and CCSS for comprehending and vocabulary acquisition.

Objectives

Children will learn to

Motor

1. Appropriately position their hands and glove when the ball is rolled, tossed at chest height, and tossed to a high level.

Observation Plan

1. Scan the entire class to see if the children are spaced far enough apart from other pairs to give them plenty of room to move.
1. Watch whether they use "bear claws" at chest level.
2. Watch whether they use "alligator hands" for grounders.
3. Watch whether they use "moose antlers" for fly balls.

SAMPLE PLAN 23.3

Level 2: Catching Balls at Different Levels with a Glove: Bear Claws, Alligator Hands, and Moose Antlers (*continued*)

Social

2. Be a caring partner by rolling and tossing accurately.
3. Be a caring partner by complimenting their partners.

CCSS

4. Describe actions with relevant details, expressing ideas clearly.
5. Make real-life connections between appropriate body actions to catch and animals.

Thumbs Up, Bear Claws **I** Go with your partner, and toss the ball back and forth at chest height. **Th** Did anyone notice where your fingers were pointing when you caught the toss? Try tossing and catching again, and pay attention to where your fingers were pointing.	**Potential Introduction** **Cog K** Have you ever seen a baseball game? Does the ball always stay at chest height during the game? Does it ever go low? Does it go high? When? To learn the skills of softball and baseball, you need to learn to catch at different levels.
Cog K Where were your fingers pointing? Right, your fingers were pointing toward your partner. Notice when I demonstrate this how my thumbs point up. We call this, "thumbs up, bear claws." **R** Practice with your partner, making sure your thumbs are up.	*Notes:* Repeat this activity many times. Children need a lot of practice simply tossing and catching balls tossed easily.
Alligator Hands **E** Now we are going to work on catching balls at a low level. Stand about 10 feet from your partner, and be sure no other partners are within 10 feet of you. Let's start by practicing rolling the ball directly to your partner so your partner doesn't have to move. Keep your feet wide apart and your bottom up (you don't want to look like a frog squatting on a log). Notice your hand position.	**Getting Smooth-Rolling Balls to Allow for Successful Catching (if Needed)** **R** I can see a lot of you rolling bouncing balls. Let's review how to roll a ball so it doesn't bounce. Watch Pia roll the ball to Fatima. What did she do to keep it rolling smoothly? Right. She bent her knees, swung her throwing arm straight back, and released the ball when her hand was near the ground. Her follow-through was pointing directly at her target. Right now we want smooth rolls; later we will make the ball bounce. Go back and practice again, making sure you roll a smooth ball to your partner.
Cog K How did your hand position change when catching a low ball? [Various answers.] When the ball is low, you use "alligator hands." With alligator hands, you start with your glove down and out front and your non-glove hand up to protect your face from a bad hop. When you catch the ball, the non-glove hand covers the ball like an alligator chomping and swallowing the ball. The cue is "Reach, cover, cradle." **R** Practice that with your partner.	**Potential Peer Assessment** **A** Let's play a game called "Ground-Ball Freeze." Partner A rolls the ball to partner B. Partner B catches the ball and freezes as soon as he or she covers the ball. Partner A checks to make sure partner B is catching the ball out in front with fingers on the ground and covers the ball. [Repeat numerous times.] **MD** If you need more of a challenge, you can move farther away from each other, roll the ball harder, or have the ball take a small hop.
Thumbs Together, Moose Antlers **E** Now we will practice catching balls at a high level. When the ball is above your head, you want your thumbs to be together. We call this "Moose hands" because it looks like your hands are like moose antlers. [Alternatively, you can call this cue "Mickey Mouse ears."]	**Getting an Accurate Toss** Tossers, work hard to toss the ball high and accurately. This is difficult. Aim your fingertips right at your partner's moose antlers. [Watch for children throwing in ways that make the ball impossible to catch. If they do, stop the class, and have a discussion about helping others learn by making challenging but catchable tosses.]

(*continues*)

SAMPLE PLAN 23.3

Level 2: Catching Balls at Different Levels with a Glove: Bear Claws, Alligator Hands, and Moose Antlers (*continued*)

Potential Culminating Activity

E Now, let's practice all these cues. I will call out the level, and the catcher has to remember the hand position. [Call out "High," "Medium," and "Low," varying the order.]

E Now, for fun, I will sometimes say "Surprise," and the tosser can toss the ball at any level and surprise the catcher. [Call out "High," "Medium," "Low," and "Surprise," varying the order.]

CCSS Closure

Get with your assigned partner, and one of you describe what you do and the animal cue for catching a ball at a high level. Then the other partner, describe what you do and the animal cue for catching a rolling ball. Then both of you describe what you do and the animal cue for catching a ball at chest level.

Social Let's have a brief discussion.

What makes a caring partner? [Someone who tries to throw the ball accurately. Someone who doesn't throw it too hard or too high. Someone who compliments your hard work. Someone who doesn't complain. Someone who is nice. Someone who encourages you. Someone who does the assigned task and doesn't get me in trouble. Someone who works together to share and try new ideas.]

What makes a lousy partner? [Someone who laughs at you. Someone who makes faces when you miss. Someone who doesn't try. Someone who hogs the ball. Someone who doesn't listen to your ideas.]

Sample Throwing Centers

When working with centers, the ideal is to have only two or three children at each center. Based on your prior observations, you can list the performance techniques children need to practice on a whiteboard or on the center's task card. Another suggestion is to have the children (or you and the children together) select one performance technique that each child needs to practice. If you have just taught the children a new performance cue, then have them focus on that technique in the centers. You then can differentiate instruction for any child who is more advanced and ready to work on a different cue. We list possible performance cues for each center, but you will have to modify these choices for your children.

Center 1: Throw to Wall

Equipment: Yarn, fleece, or soft foam sport balls in baskets placed 15 to 30 feet away from a wall or fence.

Task: Throw as hard as you can against the wall. Retrieve the ball, and start at the basket again.

Performance technique: Point to target/side to target.

Center 2: Throw to a Very Large Target

Equipment: Tape or tie a large target (squares of paper taped together, laminated posters, squares of fabric) on a wall or fence. Put a ball in a basket located 15 to 30 feet away. Depending on whether you are working in an indoor or outdoor space, you can use yarn, foam, or dead tennis balls.

Task: Throw as hard as you can to the square and get the ball to come straight back.

Performance technique: "Rock and roll, step and throw."

Center 3: Pop the Balloons

Equipment: Tie a bunch of blown-up balloons to a backstop, or tape them on a wall at eye level, making a large target. Have a basket with soft tee balls or safe tee balls behind a line of cones (about 15 feet for kindergarteners and farther away for children in older grades).

Task: Throw as hard as you can, and try to bust the balloons. (The fun of popping a balloon elicits throwing hard across many practice trials.)

Performance technique: Point to target/side to target.

Center 4: Aerobic Throwing

Equipment: Set out baskets with one ball per child in each group. Set up different-colored cones in a line at 20 feet, 30 feet, 40 feet, and 50 feet away from the basket. Pick distances that challenge the children to throw far, but also allow the children to succeed.

Task: Throw the ball as far as you can. (All group members throw at the same time.) Run to retrieve your ball. Take turns being the teacher. (The "teacher" throws, too.) When everyone is ready, say "Throw."

Performance technique: "Make the T, break the T."

Social: You are responsible for safety. What must you do at this station to be safe? [Wait until the coast is clear for everyone before you say, "Throw," when you are the teacher. Wait until everyone is safely back by the basket before throwing again.]

Task: Throw as hard as you can at the pitch back.

Performance technique: Long step, on line to target.

Center 5: Throw Hard at a Target

Equipment: Set up several plastic bowling pins, cans, or cones on a crate or box. A basket with balls appropriate for the space set far away from the target to elicit forceful throws.

Task: Throw as hard as you can, and try to knock the cones off the box.

Performance technique: Shuffle, on line to target.

Center 6: Multiple Targets

Equipment: Hang multiple milk jugs, whiffle balls, and other objects from strings attached to a rope hung between standards or from playground equipment. Set a basket with balls far from the targets to elicit a forceful throw.

Task: Throw as hard as you can, and try to hit one of the targets.

Performance technique: Finish with weight forward.

Center 7: Throw Through a Hoop

Equipment: Set a hula hoop in a brace that holds it upright, tie a hoop to a fence, or hang the hoop from playground equipment. Place a basket with balls far away from the hoop to elicit a forceful throw.

Task: Throw as hard as you can, trying to throw the ball through the hoop.

Performance technique: Palm away, thumb down and away.

Center 8: Tag Out Barrels

Equipment: Place barrels or clean garbage cans on their side, with the opening facing the thrower. Place a basket of balls located at about the distance from second base to home plate.

Task: Throw the ball to home plate, low enough for the catcher to tag the runner.

Performance technique: Finish with weight forward.

Sample Questions to Ask During Throwing Practice at Centers

- Why do you think the ball went way high? [My elbow was too low. I was holding the ball like an ice cream cone instead of palm away. My hand dropped behind my head. My weight was not on my front foot.]
- How do you generate more force? [Make my hips and arm move faster; take a larger step; shuffle; finish with a body lean; and have a larger, circular backswing. Use my whole body, not one part at a time. Make a T, break the T. Twist and throw.]
- Why is the ball always missing the target to the left? [I did not step directly toward the target; belly button not pointing at the target; side not to the target; turning, not twisting, toward the target; over-rotating.]
- Compare and contrast what happens when you throw to a high level and a medium level.

Sample Batting Centers

Each of the following batting centers is designed to work on a particular aspect of batting, which is noted as the performance cue.

Center 1: Check, Check, Bat

Equipment: Batting tee, several whiffle balls, plastic bat, clock drawn in the dirt around the batting tee (or on a large sheet of paper under the tee).

Task: Check whether you are standing between 8 o'clock and 7 o'clock (right-handed batters) or between 4 o'clock and 5 o'clock (left-handed batters). *Check* whether your pencil hand is on top and your hands are together. *Bat* the ball at a fence or wall.

Performance techniques: Stand between 8 o'clock and 7 o'clock (right-handed batters) or between 4 o'clock and 5 o'clock (left-handed batters). Pencil hand on top, hands together.

Center 2: Check the Finish

Equipment: Batting tee, several whiffle balls, plastic bat.

Task: Bat the ball at a fence or wall, and hold the finish. Look down, and check for back foot pivot, front foot closed.

Performance technique: Back foot pivot, front foot closed.

Center 3: Partner Check, Head Stays in the Middle

Equipment: Batting tee, several whiffle balls, plastic bat.

Task: Bat the ball at a fence or wall. The partner watches the batter's head to see if it stays in the middle. The partner gives a thumbs-up sign when the batter succeeds.

Performance technique: Head stays in the middle.

Center 4: Partner Soft Toss

Equipment: Whiffle balls (can use different sizes, including baseball, softball, and golf ball size), poly spot (home plate), plastic bat.

Task: Soft toss. The partner stands facing the batter, at a 45-degree angle from the batter (not in the line of flight) and soft-tosses the ball over the poly spot. The batter tries to hit the ball.

Performance technique: Front foot closed, back foot pivot.

Center 5: Two Balls

Equipment: Batting tee, two whiffle balls, plastic bat.

Task: Stack two whiffle balls on top of each other on the tee. Swing, and try to hit only the bottom ball. If you do it correctly, the top ball will drop down near the tee, and sometimes it will even land on the tee.

Performance technique: Eyes on ball at contact.

Center 6: Over the Obstacle

Equipment: Tee; five whiffle balls; plastic bat; obstacle like a hula hoop in a brace, a hoop placed on a low wall or fence, or a wall of high cones (three feet if possible) set 20 to 30 feet away.

Task: Try to hit the ball over the obstacle.

Performance technique: Belly button rotates to target.

Center 7: Toss and Call

Equipment: Poly spot or base, two whiffle balls or two-inch pool noodles of different colors (cutting a swimming pool foam noodle into two-inch pieces is an inexpensive way to make balls).

Task: The batter stands at 7 o'clock for right-handed batters and at 5 o'clock for left-handed batters. The pitcher stands at a 45-degree angle to the side of the poly spot and soft-tosses (pitches) two noodles of different colors at the same time toward the batter's front knee and the poly spot. When the pitcher releases the noodles, he or she calls out one color. The batter tries to hit that color.

Performance technique: Eyes on ball at contact.

Center 8: Whiffle Golf Ball

Equipment: Whiffle golf ball, plastic bat, poly spot (home plate).

Task: The partner stands at a 45-degree angle from the batter and soft-tosses a whiffle golf ball over the poly spot. The batter tries to hit the ball.

Performance technique: Eyes on ball at contact.

Sample Questions to Ask During Batting Practice at Centers

- Why did you miss the ball? [I wasn't looking at it. I didn't track it until contact.]
- How do you generate force? [Back foot pivot, front foot closed; belly button rotates to pitcher; load up; hips rotate quickly to face pitcher; swing shoulder to shoulder.]
- Which performance technique are you thinking about before you start to swing?
- You have improved your swing. What did you do differently?

SECTION IV

Educational Gymnastics Content

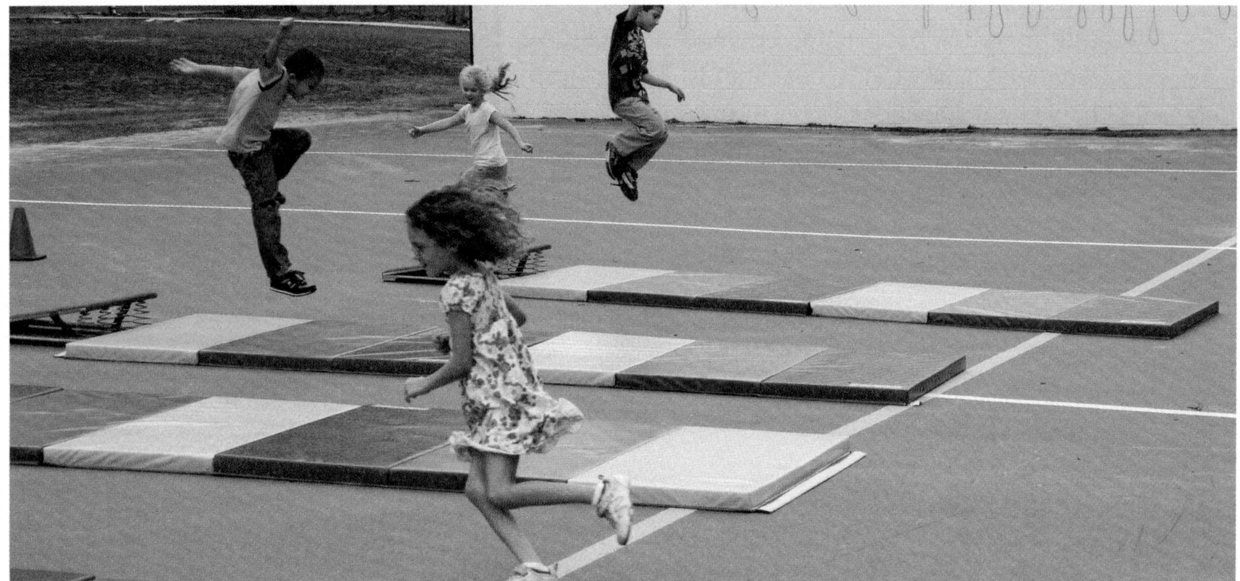

In this section, we provide comprehensive information about the content of educational gymnastics. While educational gymnastics is part of the National Standards, is covered in *PE Metrics*, and is beloved by many girls and boys, few conference sessions and texts are available from which teachers can acquire the information needed to teach this content (Baumgarten & Pagnano-Richardson, 2010).

In Chapter 24, we describe the goals and benefits of educational gymnastics. We point out how educational and Olympic gymnastics differ, clarify educational gymnastics' connections to the National Standards, and highlight safety considerations when teaching gymnastics. We also discuss different ways teachers can design apparatus centers and various introductory warm-up activities.

Chapter 25 focuses on the major learning outcomes in educational gymnastics and dance—namely, quality sequences and movement quality (i.e., skillful performance techniques). Elements of quality sequence choreography include structure, transitions, originality, expression of ideas, contrast and aesthetic highlights, line, focus, and clarity. Movement quality includes elements such as tight muscles, light landings, stretched torsos, straight legs, and pointed feet. In addition, we describe how to teach children to design sequences in both gymnastics and dance.

Chapters 26, 27, and 28 describe the content of educational gymnastics lessons and units. Chapter 26 addresses the five foundational skills (rolling, balancing, steplike actions, flight from feet, and dynamic balancing) that serve as content appropriate for children at level 1 and considers how to combine those skills in developmental levels 2 and 3. To help teachers who are new to educational gymnastics, we provide detailed, annotated lesson/unit plans and lesson segments for teaching. Chapter 27 explains how to use movement concepts as the focus of lessons along with sample lesson segments. Chapter 28 focuses on partner and group work. This section ends with Chapter 29, which describes technical information for teachers, including the performance techniques and likely immature patterns for the basic, named gymnastics skills (e.g., forward and backward rolls, cartwheels, handstands, headstands). This is information that teachers need to know about specific skills because it informs their teaching of educational gymnastics. We also provide intra-skill progressions for teaching these skills to individuals or small groups when this content is appropriate.

References

Baumgarten, A., & Pagnano-Richardson, K. (2010). Educational gymnastics: Enhancing children's physical literacy. *Journal of Physical Education, Recreation and Dance, 81*(4), 18–25.

CHAPTER

24

Introduction to Educational Gymnastics

PRE-READING REFLECTION

1. What are your prior experiences with gymnastics? Were these experiences positive or negative, and why?
2. Have you ever watched people performing gymnastics skills and wished you could perform those skills yourself?
3. What are your concerns about learning how to teach educational gymnastics to elementary school children?
4. What skills, knowledge, and attitudes do you think you need to develop to be able to teach gymnastics to elementary school children?

OBJECTIVES

Students will learn:

1. Even though you might not be a skilled gymnast, you can learn to be a great teacher of educational gymnastics.
2. Gymnastics is significant, important, and fun for children.
3. Educational gymnastics aims to teach children how to perform a range of gymnastics movements skillfully in a safe, productive learning environment.
4. Educational gymnastics is designed for schools and is different from Olympic gymnastics.
5. Content development focuses on extending children's movement variety and improving performance techniques. Culminating activities include working on apparatus and designing sequences.

KEY TERMS

Educational gymnastics

Educational gymnastics themes

Olympic gymnastics

CONNECTION TO STANDARDS

In this chapter, we describe how educational gymnastics meets each of the five National Standards. Common Core and other State Standards (CCSS) for speaking, listening, and acquiring domain-specific vocabulary can also be met through educational gymnastics lessons. All sample plans in this section include an example of how you can meet one of the CCSS.

Introduction

Most prospective teachers have little or no experience with gymnastics (Baumgarten & Pagnano-Richardson, 2010; Placek et al., 1995). Consequently, some may begin required courses in gymnastics while worrying that they will not enjoy gymnastics or become competent gymnastics teachers. Once you *teach* gymnastics in elementary schools, however, you will discover that children—regardless of race, gender, or ability—think gymnastics lessons are fun and meaningful. Children's enjoyment is contagious, and soon teachers find they not only enjoy teaching gymnastics, but also can develop competence in teaching it.

Why Teaching Gymnastics Is Important

Gymnastics is one of the content areas included in the National Standards (Society of Health and Physical Educators [SHAPE], 2014) and *PE Metrics* (National Association for Sport and Physical Education [NASPE], 2010), the U.S. physical education profession's set of nationally validated assessment tools. As you know, physical education is for all children. Teachers have an obligation to include gymnastics in their program to meet the needs of all children—boys and girls and children from different races and ethnicities (see box, "Children's Opinions"). Indeed, some children say gymnastics is their favorite activity (see **Figure 24.1**).

In addition, "the body awareness and control developed in gymnastics settings can contribute to the acquisition of sport skills and help children develop safety skills that are useful in both play and sport (e.g., safe landings)" (Nilges, 2000, p. 6).

Figure 24.2 Gymnastics skills are used in a variety of physical activities

It is easy to find places where children use gymnastics skills outside of school. Children show their prowess by incorporating gymnastics into street dancing (see **Figure 24.2**). Trampolines are ubiquitous in rural and suburban yards. Children use gymnastics skills in climbing and swinging on playground apparatus. Gymnastics is part of skateboarding, snowboarding, and skiing (see **Figure 24.3**). Televised competitions in rope

Figure 24.1 Children enjoying gymnastics

Figure 24.3 Gymnastics skills are used in a variety of physical activities

jumping and cheerleading show participants incorporating gymnastics skills into their routines. Obviously, helping children learn gymnastics skills provides a sound basis for their participation in many other activities.

Can I Teach Gymnastics if I Can't Perform the Skills?

It seems logical to think you need to be proficient in a skill to teach it. Certainly, it is helpful to have personal experience performing skills because it can contribute to your subject-matter knowledge; nevertheless, you don't need to be more skilled in gymnastics than the children you are teaching. Few gymnastics coaches can perform the skills they teach their athletes. What teachers and coaches must have is knowledge of their subject matter and knowledge of how to teach it.

What Is Educational Gymnastics?

Most people are familiar with **Olympic gymnastics**, which we define as the sport of gymnastics as performed in the Olympics. This chapter describes **educational gymnastics**—a form of gymnastics designed for school settings to meet educational objectives.

Educational Gymnastics and the National Standards

The aim of educational gymnastics is for *all* children (not just the ones with abilities to excel in gymnastics) to learn a wide variety of gymnastics movements, experience success, learn content valuable and enjoyable to them, and work in a safe, productive learning environment (Baumgarten & Pagnano-Richardson, 2010; Nilges-Charles, 2008). In addition, educational gymnastics offers excellent opportunities to help children develop abilities related to creative thinking, critical thinking, problem solving, and decision making, which are important goals for all subject areas in today's society (Resnick, 2010), and to develop social responsibility and collaborative skills while working with partners and small groups in designing sequences.

More specifically, in terms of the National Standards for Physical Education (SHAPE, 2014), the goals of educational gymnastics are to help all children to accomplish the following:

Standard 1

- Develop competency in a variety of gymnastics skills performed in a variety of ways, such as rolling in different directions and in different shapes and balancing on different body parts. Movement variety is highly valued in educational gymnastics, not just for individual children but across all children in a class (Nilges-Charles, 2008). We don't expect children to perform the same skills in the same way. Competency also includes learning appropriate performance techniques, such as pointing feet and toes, maintaining tension in the body, and landing lightly.

Standard 2

- Learn and apply movement concepts from the Laban framework to develop movement variety, such as jumping while making different shapes in the air and balancing at different levels.

Figure 24.4 Gymnastics skills are used in a variety of physical activities

Courtesy of John Dolly

- Learn and apply elements of quality sequence choreography.
- Learn and apply principles of movement quality to improve performance.
- Develop critical-thinking, creative-thinking, problem-solving, and decision-making skills to help apply movement concepts to gymnastics skills and acquire movement variety and improve performance techniques.

Standard 3

- Understand how gymnastics can contribute to muscle fitness (strength, endurance, and power) and flexibility (Langton, 2007).
- Understand how engaging in gymnastics-related activities after school, such as playing on playground equipment, jumping rope, and practicing gymnastics skills, can be healthy, enjoyable physical activities that contribute to health-related fitness (see **Figure 24.4**).

Standard 4

- Understand and demonstrate personal and social responsibility in working safely when setting up and putting away apparatus and working safely on apparatus.
- Demonstrate cooperative behaviors when speaking and listening with a partner and in small groups in designing sequences. This goal also addresses the CCSS.

Standard 5

- Appreciate the value of gymnastics for health, enjoyment, challenge, and self-expression.

Thus, educational gymnastics offers you multiple opportunities to address the National Standards, and the goals of educational gymnastics are in keeping with these standards.

Children's Opinions

The following quotes are taken from a research study in which children of different ability levels were interviewed about their perspectives on physical education (Rovegno, 2010).

Katie (fifth-grade girl, low ability): I'm not as athletic as some of the people are, but I enjoy PE because we get to do things with our friends in groups, like gymnastics. We do a lot of gymnastics....We get to do different things on the mats. We get to tumble. We get to do cartwheels—basically everything but things [that are] too difficult because the teachers don't want you to get hurt.

Researcher: So how do you feel about sequences?

Katie: I like them the best, doing sequences in gymnastics. All of my friends are like me, and they can do the same things.

Researcher: What do you do in gymnastics?

Kaylee (first-grade girl, low ability): Sometimes we do symmetrical and asymmetrical.

Researcher: How do you feel when you do that?

Kaylee: Terrific.

Researcher: Terrific? How come?

Kaylee: Because it's fun.

Sam (second-grade boy, low ability): Somersaults are very good because that's part of self-defense. If it's a tall guy that has his legs wide open—somersault.

Alexis (fourth-grade girl, low ability): I think gymnastics is probably the funnest for me.

Misconception Alert

When learning about a new curricular approach, a commonly used technique is to contrast the new approach with a traditional approach. Research shows that looking for only differences, and not for similarities, can lead to misconceptions about the new approach, however (Rovegno, 1992b, 1993b). When they focus on differences, learners perceive a false dichotomy between the new and old and incorrectly assume that nothing in the old approach will be part of the new approach. Consequently, they miss some critical features of the new approach. For example, in educational gymnastics, teachers ask children questions, present problems to solve, and give children opportunities to make their own decisions about which movements to perform. This has led to the misconception that in educational gymnastics, you "don't tell children what to do," which is an inaccurate statement. In educational gymnastics, you give information and frequently tell children what to do!

The Differences Between Olympic and Educational Gymnastics

Educational gymnastics will be new to many undergraduates and in-service teachers. Consequently, we describe its characteristics here by comparing and contrasting it with Olympic gymnastics. Although the contrast can be helpful in acquiring an initial understanding of educational gymnastics, there are many similarities between educational and Olympic gymnastics, and simply focusing on the differences can lead to misconceptions (see box, "Misconception Alert").

Specific Skills Versus a Broad View of Skills

The content taught in Olympic gymnastics consists of specific skills from the four Olympic events for women (floor, vault, balance beam, and uneven parallel bars) and the six events for men (floor, vault, rings, parallel bars, high bar, and pommel horse). In an Olympic gymnastics lesson, the teacher would teach a set of skills. For example, one lesson might be on egg rolls, log rolls, forward rolls, and back shoulder rolls; another lesson might cover handstands, headstands, and cartwheels. Unlike in educational gymnastics, in Olympic gymnastics, all children tend to learn the same skills at the same time (Belka, 1993).

In educational gymnastics, we base lessons and units on themes (Nilges-Charles, 2008). **Educational gymnastics themes** are groups of skills organized around a common action, movement concept, or both. For example, rolling is a theme that includes all the rolls with names, rolling skills that have no names, and any other rolling action. Balancing in different shapes is a theme that includes balancing (a skill of controlled stillness) and different shapes (a movement concept).

Consequently, in educational gymnastics, instead of teaching only rolls with names (e.g., forward rolls, backwards rolls), we teach the *theme* of rolling. When children work on the theme of balancing, they learn to balance on a variety of body parts while making a variety of shapes. Many, but not all, children will learn headstands and handstands, which are balances. All children, however, will understand that whatever balance they perform, that balance is part of a theme called balancing. Thus, the aim in educational gymnastics is not simply to teach specific skills, but rather to teach broader movement themes, such as rolling and balancing—in all their wondrous variety.

Educational Gymnastics Includes a Range of Teaching Strategies

Typically, in traditional Olympic gymnastics lessons, teachers present information about how children should perform skills and have children practice those skills to a specified form. In educational gymnastics, teachers also present information about skill performance and have children practice; however, the organization of content into themes requires the use of additional inquiry-oriented teaching strategies. For example, when teaching a unit on the theme of balancing on a variety of body parts in different shapes, teachers will include exploration tasks, decision-making tasks, and problem-solving tasks, along with refinements and presenting explicit information.

Sample Exploration Tasks

- Explore different ways to balance on large body parts. What are large body parts? [Hips, belly, side, back.]
- Explore different ways to balance on at least two small body parts. (For today, just to be safe, you cannot balance on your head, although that is a small body part.)

Sample Decision-Making Task

- You have been balancing on many different body parts. Now select and practice three balances you can do safely but with which you need more practice in staying tight and holding the balance for three seconds.

Sample Problem-Solving Task

- You have been working on balancing on different body parts and in different shapes for the past two lessons. Now your task is to design an interesting sequence of three balances that you can hold for three seconds each using appropriate performance techniques. Which characteristics did we discuss earlier that make a sequence interesting? [Have a variety of balances; include at least one balance that has an unusual shape.]

Sample Refinements

- When you balance, hold the balance still for three seconds.
- When you balance, keep your muscles tight.

Themes Result in More Beginning-Level Skills

One benefit of teaching using themes is that children can learn a far greater variety of skills. If teachers restrict the skills they teach to just Olympic skills, they will quickly run out of simple, safe skills that they can teach to large groups of children with diverse ability levels. For example, beginning balancing skills taught in Olympic gymnastics include scales, V sits, headstands, and handstands. For beginners, and especially for overweight children, headstands and handstands can be beyond their ability to learn safely. In educational gymnastics, those students ready for the challenge can learn handstands and headstands; at the same time, all children will have the opportunity to practice balancing on a variety of body parts, making a variety of shapes at their own ability level.

Educational Gymnastics Accommodates Individual Differences

In traditional Olympic gymnastics lessons, teachers typically have all students learn the same skill at the same time. This approach can be a problem because the class is bound to include high-skilled children, who have mastered the skill already (and are bored), and low-skilled children, who are not ready to learn the skill and would be at risk for injury when trying to perform it. Thus, teaching everyone the same skill at the same time does not accommodate individual differences. In addition, low-skilled children can be embarrassed in front of their classmates if they fail to master the same skills their classmates perform with ease.

When you organize educational gymnastics by themes, it becomes easier to differentiate instruction, challenging all children to improve their skills while simultaneously ensuring that they experience success. When a teacher presents tasks based on a theme, all children can work on the same task at the same time, but they don't have to work on exactly the same skill. For example, if you teach a lesson on the theme of balancing on different body parts, one child might work on balancing on the hips, while another might balance on the forearms—a far more difficult skill. Thus, children choose which movement to do and can work at their own developmental level and be successful. Research indicates that the potential for success is critical. As Solmon (2006) explains, "If individuals do not believe they can be competent, or successful, then they are likely to withhold, or withdraw, effort. For this reason, it is very important for teachers to structure the learning environment so students are able to experience some level of success" (p. 16).

Moreover, guidelines for appropriate and inappropriate practices supported by our professional organization, SHAPE America, discuss the use of gymnastics themes to help teachers accommodate children's individual differences (see **Figure 24.5**). **Table 24.1** presents these guidelines for gymnastics.

More Numerous but Less Expensive Apparatus Options

Olympic gymnastics apparatus includes balance beams, uneven parallel bars, vaulting platforms, high bars, parallel bars, pommel horses, and rings. Unfortunately, schools rarely can afford the cost of Olympic apparatus.

Educational gymnastics takes a broader view of the kinds of apparatus you can use (see **Figure 24.6**). Educational gymnastics uses inexpensive, even homemade, apparatus and equipment readily available in many schools and through catalogs. This includes equipment such as cones, jump ropes, hoops, crates, and canes, as well as larger apparatus, such as playground equipment, sturdy gymnastics benches, aerobic boxes,

Figure 24.5 Themes allow choice and accommodate individual differences

Courtesy of John Dolly

Table 24.1 NASPE's Appropriate Instructional Practice Guidelines for Elementary School Physical Education: Educational Gymnastics

Appropriate Practice	Inappropriate Practice
Lessons develop skills appropriate to children's abilities and confidence in balancing, rolling, jumping and landing, climbing, and transferring weight. Children practice on equipment designed to match their gymnastics abilities and confidence.	Teachers require all students to perform the same predetermined stunts and routines while the rest of the class sits and watches. Predetermined stunts require extensive teacher direction and spotting because they're too difficult for many of the children.

Source: Reprinted from *Appropriate Instructional Practice Guidelines for Elementary School Physical Education* (3rd ed.) with permission from the National Association for Sport and Physical Education (NASPE), 1900 Association Drive, Reston, VA 20191-1599.

inexpensive 2×4 beams, foam trapezoids, stacked mats, and swinging ropes.

Olympic gymnastics uses only one piece of apparatus for routines. In contrast, teachers of educational gymnastics combine different pieces of apparatus and arrange apparatus in different ways to encourage versatile and skillful movement. For example, in educational gymnastics, children might work on a balance beam with a two-layered trapezoid placed under it, a stacked mat positioned at an angle, and several floor mats as one connected "piece" of apparatus.

Figure 24.6 Educational gymnastics uses a wide range of apparatus

Courtesy of John Dolly

Summary of the Benefits of Educational Gymnastics

- Helps teachers accommodate the individual differences of students
- Supports children in working on different skills at their ability level
- Includes a wide variety of beginning-level skills
- Has many apparatus options
- Incorporates less expensive equipment and apparatus
- Promotes maximum practice time because children do not wait in long lines

Maximum Practice Opportunities and Physical Activity Time

When Olympic gymnastics is taught poorly, children stand in long lines, and the teacher spots each child one at a time. This approach is problematic for two reasons. First, to learn skills, children need many opportunities to practice the skill at a high engagement level (Rink, 2004; van der Mars, 2006). Second, physical activity is important for achieving health-enhancing levels of fitness—which doesn't happen when children spend time standing in lines.

In educational gymnastics, teachers provide enough mats, equipment, and apparatus centers so children will not need to stand in long lines waiting their turn. Ideally, each child should have his or her own equipment. When this arrangement is not possible, a good rule of thumb is to have a maximum of two or three children sharing a mat, equipment, or apparatus center.

Many schools do not have enough apparatus or mats to allow two to three children to all work at the same time on the same task on similar apparatus centers. For teachers in these settings to provide maximum practice opportunities, they must set up a variety of apparatus and equipment centers about the gymnasium and have children rotate to each center. Each center will be different and might even focus on a different task and theme. For example, children might be working on rolling in different ways at several different centers. At other centers, they might be practicing steplike actions over trapezoid sections. At still other centers, children might be jumping for height; working on challenge (obstacle) courses by hopping, jumping, leaping, and rolling over obstacles; and balancing and traveling in different ways on 2×4 balance beams and benches. We have successfully taught and observed gymnastics classes with as many as 80 children using centers. We summarize the benefits of educational gymnastics in the box, "Summary of the Benefits of Educational Gymnastics," illustrates the progression and provides an overview of educational gymnastics content.

Educational Gymnastics and Safety

There is nothing more important for you to think about during gymnastics lessons than children's safety. Teachers can use several teaching techniques to ensure safety and protect themselves from being held liable for injuries.

Know that children are attracted to gymnastics apparatus (including mats) and, consequently, that you must always supervise the apparatus or lock them in a secure location. Apparatus attract children like magnets attract iron filings. You must always actively supervise the physical education space when you have pieces of apparatus or mats set up. This means you cannot leave the space for any reason (even an emergency) if children are present. Simply telling them to get off the apparatus and sit on the floor is not enough. Apparatus are legally considered "attractive nuisances," meaning they are so attractive to children that adults must assume children will get on the apparatus despite having been told not to do so. In an emergency, call the principal or another teacher to come immediately to assist you or have a child get another adult come to the gymnasium. In between classes, lock the gymnasium.

Make sure the apparatus and mats are maintained and set up appropriately and safely (Nilges & Lathrop, 2000). This mandate means confirming that any adjustments for height are locked in place and all knobs tightened. Check for worn, torn, or damaged apparatus or mats, and remove these from use. Confirm that the mats are set up without overlaps or gaps that create an uneven surface that can cause falls or sprained ankles. Have the custodian clean the mats regularly with appropriate cleaning solutions. For mats with strings tacking the layers together, be sure the knotted side is down. If you teach on a concrete surface, make sure the mats do not slide on the floor. Check the apparatus arrangement to ensure that children will not cross pathways and will have plenty of overflow room when they finish the task, which requires keeping apparatus away from walls or other obstacles on both the ends where children will get on and off each piece of apparatus.

Teach children to stop safely. Teach children that when you say "Stop," they must do so safely, which might mean completing the gymnastics movement or dismounting from the apparatus (Nilges & Lathrop, 2000).

Assign tasks that allow children to choose which movements they do, and insist that children select only those skills that they can do safely, competently, and confidently. This point is a key factor in making educational gymnastics both developmentally appropriate and safe for children at all skill levels. For example, if you assign a task in which children must jump, making a shape in the air, land, and roll in different ways, lower-skilled children can practice a straight jump, land, and do a sideways roll, varying the shape of their legs or body each time they roll sideways. High-skilled children can practice wide jumps (e.g., straddle jumps) with half-turns, land, and roll backward, ending in a wide (e.g., straddle) position. In addition, children should learn that when they make decisions about which skills to perform, they should work at their own ability level and do only those skills that they can do safely, competently, and confidently. You must insist that children adhere to this policy at all times and repeat these instructions frequently. Children can be trusted to make sound decisions about what they should and should not do *if you teach them to do so.* It is a good idea to videotape the first gymnastics lesson so you will have evidence that you have taught children the safety rules and taught them explicitly that they are permitted to attempt only skills that they can do safely and competently (see box, "Sample Safety Rules for Educational Gymnastics," for potential rules to teach children in language they will understand).

A few children will make poor choices every so often. Scan the class continuously; if a child is making a poor choice, tell

SAFETY AND LIABILITY 24.1

Increasing Safety and Decreasing Risk of Liability: Guidelines Relevant to Content in this Chapter

In this box, we discuss specific guidelines built on information discussed throughout this text on professional standards of practice, negligence, and liability. The goals of these guidelines are to increase children's safety and decrease teachers' risk of negligence and liability.

Here, we discuss general guidelines, whereas in the boxes in the content chapters, we give you specific information about tasks and skills.

- To increase safety and decrease liability risk, teachers should plan and follow a written curriculum with a progression, or sequence of tasks, to develop children's skills safely. The curriculum is based on district, state, and national standards and guidelines. All tasks are developmentally appropriate and modified to accommodate individual differences. Safety issues within tasks are taught, and students are warned about potential dangers.
- A reasonably prudent educator inspects the apparatus for safety every day it is used, makes sure apparatus are reliable, maintained, and repaired when necessary, and checks to see if all mechanisms for locking the equipment in place are set and working.
- Children are taught how to set up, use, and put away apparatus safely and the inherent dangers in using, setting up, and putting away the apparatus.
- The teacher supervises the physical education space at all times when the gymnastics apparatus are set up and secures the space (lock, chain, etc.) when children and supervisor are not present.
- The teacher makes sure any area under a piece of apparatus from which a child could fall or any landing area is covered with a mat and the mats do not overlap, and he or she organizes the apparatus and mats such that children will not cross paths or collide while practicing.
- Finally, the teacher ensures that children are spotted when trying a difficult or new skill by a qualified spotter of adequate size and strength to spot the child.

the child he or she is not ready to perform the skill. In addition, sometimes children will misbehave and attempt to do a skill that is not safe for them. Typically, teachers know their children and can anticipate which children are likely to behave inappropriately.

When teaching unfamiliar classes, you need to anticipate possible responses that might not be safe and set rules for safety before giving a task. For example, if you ask children to balance on different body parts and you don't know the class, tell the students they cannot balance on their heads in a headstand without your permission.

Never teach a skill to an entire class, group, or individual unless you are certain they are all ready and able to learn the skill. Once you are certain, use a progression to teach the skill. A progression comprises a series of subskills that are easier than the terminal skill you will eventually be teaching. The subskills break down elements of the complete skill and build up to the terminal skill in a step-by-step fashion. When you teach a progression, insist that children continue to practice each subskill without moving on to the next subskill or terminal skill until the child has mastered the subskill and is doing so safely and confidently. There are several progressions for education gymnastics. Most of the time, progressions for learning specific skills are appropriate for use only with individual children or with a small group of children with similar abilities.

Even more importantly, *do not require that children learn particular skills for a grade* or base grades on skill difficulty. Children who want good grades might feel pressured to attempt a skill that is not safe for them. This practice can lead to injuries and problems with liability.

Emphasize good performance techniques at all times. To ensure safety, teachers need to insist that children perform gymnastics movements skillfully with appropriate performance techniques and maintain control over their bodies at all times. For example, demand that children land softly on their feet, and do not allow them to fling their bodies through the air and land on their knees or whatever body parts hit the ground first. Injuries can happen when children don't control the flow of their movement and are loose rather than tight.

Sample Safety Rules for Educational Gymnastics

Here are some sample safety rules you can teach and post on the wall. These rules break down safety procedures into language appropriate for children.

- If in your head you are saying to yourself, "This might not be safe," or "I don't think I can do that," then don't do it.
- When you look around and see someone doing something you would like to try, discuss it with the teacher first.
- Before you get on any piece of apparatus or do any movement, plan how you will safely get off the apparatus and how you will return safely to your feet after you do the movement.
- Don't do anything you don't know how to do safely, confidently, and competently.
- Unless you were assigned partner work, only one person can be on the apparatus at a time.

FAQs: Frequently Asked Questions and Misconceptions

Is It True that in Educational Gymnastics You Don't Tell Children What to Do?

No. Research shows this is a common misconception (Rovegno, 1993a, 1993b, 1998). As discussed earlier, in educational gymnastics, you use inquiry-oriented teaching strategies, such as asking questions, setting problem-solving tasks, and providing tasks in which children make decisions. You also demonstrate, give feedback, and provide explicit information telling children precisely what to do.

Moreover, in exploration and problem-solving tasks, such as having children design a sequence including a balance, jump, and roll, teachers are telling children what to do. Although teachers don't tell children precisely which jump, balance, and roll they must perform, they require children's sequences to include some type of jump, balance, and roll. In addition, the teacher identifies criteria for skillful performance and the quality of the choreography, provides guidance and feedback on these criteria, and holds children accountable for practice and learning.

Will Children Learn Skills such as Round-offs and Forward Rolls?

We find that most students learn most of the basic gymnastics skills, such as cartwheels, round-offs, and forward rolls. The key is that educational gymnastics does not require all children to learn these skills at the same time. We believe this flexibility is essential for safety. As you will recall, rates of childhood obesity have increased. Consequently, more children are at risk when learning some gymnastics skills, such as headstands and backward rolls. No skill is sacred. We should never risk a child's welfare simply because a skill has traditionally been included in gymnastics programs. If a child is developmentally ready and wants to learn a particular skill, then we teach it.

What About Spotting—Isn't It Necessary?

The biggest problem with spotting is that there is often only one teacher for 25 or more children. Teachers can spot only one child at a time, which results in long (boring) lines in which children are awaiting their turn, lack of physical activity, lack of practice opportunities, and children being put on display in front of their classmates. Too often, we have seen gymnastics club teachers spot by heaving and throwing children through a skill the child is not ready to learn—a practice we consider unsafe. Due to the limited time allotted to physical education, most of the skills we teach in educational gymnastics are basic skills that do not require spotting in order to be safe.

Sometimes, however, spotting is necessary. There are some skills, such as a handstand forward roll, that some children will want (and are ready) to learn. These skills can be learned safely but require some spotting on children's initial attempts. If teachers choose to teach these skills, they need to organize the class so all children are working productively while the teacher

monitors the class and at the same time works on the side with students needing assistance. In addition, sometimes spotting can help children learn the feeling of a particular movement. Thus, we sometimes use spotting as a scaffold for learning.

Children Ask Me to Teach Them Back Handsprings—What Do I Do?

Children ask us that question, too. This is an important question because the back handspring is important to children for two reasons.

First, children see athletes and dancers performing back handsprings on television and think it would be a fun skill to learn. One of us taught part-time in a school in which 100% of the children were African American, 95% of their families lived in poverty, and 20% of the second-grade boys could do a back handspring. They had taught themselves because they saw it on television and they saw older boys doing it (see **Figure 24.7**). Unfortunately, they did not use important performance techniques that would ensure safety. Because we had multiple teachers, we solved this problem by having one teacher teach the children in small groups after class how to perform back handsprings safely. At the same time, we believe that teachers should not feel obligated to teach skills that require one-on-one instruction, especially if you do not have multiple teachers and teachers' aides. You can say to children that those skills are better learned in a gymnastics club or in a before- or after-school program. Even in before- and after-school programs, however, we require children to first master all of the prerequisite skills to a back handspring, including a handstand, backbend from a stand, cartwheel, round-off, and a front handspring.

Second, the back handspring and other gymnastics skills are the basis for other physical activities. Many children want to participate in these activities but do not have the financial resources for club gymnastics lessons. For example, cheerleading is important to many adolescents, and being a cheerleader can be a position of power within high school cultures. Research has shown that racial inequities exist in cheerleading squads and that these inequities are often due to African Americans not having access to gymnastics lessons (Adams & Bettis, 2003; Bettis & Adams, 2003). Although the purpose of physical education is not to prepare children for athletics, teachers cannot ignore equity issues that affect children in schools. Teachers can help in this regard by advocating for or providing before- or after-school programs and working with the parent–teacher association (PTA) to provide resources or opportunities for children without financial resources. In general, however, educational gymnastics does not aim to teach skills that require one-on-one teaching and spotting.

Three Segments of Lessons and Units

As discussed in the chapter on planning, lessons typically include three segments: (1) introductory and warm-up activities; (2) content development; and (3) culminating activities. In this section, we provide information about each segment specific to educational gymnastics.

Introductory and Warm-up Activities

In gymnastics lessons, locomotor skills make excellent introductory activities. First, they warm up the body with appropriately vigorous movement. Second, after you have taught the locomotor skills, children need to practice these skills to the stage of automaticity—that is, until they can perform the movements without thinking about them. Children also need

Figure 24.7 A self-taught back handspring

Courtesy of John Dolly

Sample Introductory and Warm-up Activities

(Many of these activities can also be used for infusing short bouts of vigorous activity within gymnastics lessons.)

Level 1

- *Different directions:* Jog easily forward and sideways to as many places in the gym as possible. Now walk while stretching tall on your toes, going forward, backward, and sideways about the gym.
- *Zigzag pathway over rope:* Put one jump rope on the floor making a straight line, hop or jump in a zigzag pattern over the rope using springlike landings (i.e., resilience), and then gallop lightly around your rope. Repeat.
- *Locomotor skills and jumping:* Travel using any locomotor skill and jump. Sometimes take off and land on one foot, and sometimes take off and land on two feet. Use springlike landings, and travel lightly, stretching tall through your spine.
- *Run and leap:* Run, run, run, leap, repeat. Stretch tall through your spine when you leap, and keep your legs straight with feet pointed.
- *Run and perch:* Run, run, hold a high balance on one foot, staying tight and stretched, start to fall, and run again.
- *Human pogo stick* (requires paper canes spread about the space): Travel lightly using any locomotor pattern about the space. On my signal, go to a free cane and jump over and back like a human pogo stick, really popping up in the air using your ankles. On my signal, change and jump sideways over and back. Travel again to a new cane. Now think of different ways to be a human pogo stick over the cane.
- *Follow the leader:* Travel about the space using different locomotor patterns. One partner leads and the other follows both the pathway and the locomotor pattern. Switch lead roles frequently. Be sure to stretch tall as you travel.
- *Stuck together* (requires hoops scattered in general space): Face your partner and slide about the gym. Be very aware of other partners working. Turn back-to-back and slide about the gym staying close together. When you see a free hoop, run around the hoop, and then slide around the hoop. Travel again in general space. If you want, hold your partner's hands lightly. Be in control of your movements so you stay together without having to pull on each other's hands.
- *Three big springlike jumps:* Travel on your feet using different locomotor patterns. Take off from one foot, land on two feet, and do three big springlike jumps in a row. Pop off the floor on each jump.
- *Twisted jump, spin, side roll* (requires mats scattered about the gym): Jog, do a twisted jump with a controlled spin down to the mat, roll sideways gently up to your feet, and jog again.
- *Rodeo horses* (requires crates, large cones, or other obstacles resembling barrels): Pretend you are a rodeo horse and you need to gallop around the barrels as fast as you can. Be very aware of all the other horses galloping around the gym. Only go as fast as you can control your movement.
- *Skipping (or galloping) with balls* (requires many cones spread about the gym, plus one foam ball per child): Skip around the cones following any pathway you want. Be sure you are aware of where other children are skipping. As you skip, pass the ball around your waist.

Level 2

- *Different directions:* Jog easily forward and sideways to as many places in the gym as possible. Every so often, jog backward slowly, while looking behind you to see where you are going. Now, stretch tall, and walk on your toes forward, backward, and sideways about the gym.
- *Jumping over low obstacles* (requires jump ropes, low cones, and poly spots scattered in general space): Using different locomotor patterns, travel about the space, stretching your head to the ceiling. When you come to a free jump rope, do zigzag jumps or hops over the rope with springlike jumps. When you come to a free low cone, jump over the cone making different shapes, and land lightly. When you come to a free spot, put one hand on the spot, and run around your hand.
- *Three steps and hop (schottische):* Take three steps and then hop, doing a high hop while extending through your toes and reaching toward the ceiling with your arms. Land softly and continue.
- *Gallop and leap:* Do three gallops, do one step, and then leap. Repeat three times, and then switch the lead leg. Keep your gallops light, with your body stretched tall. Keep your legs straight on the leap.
- *Jump making shapes:* Travel using any locomotor pattern, jump, and make different shapes in the air each time you jump, and use springlike landings.
- *Three big springlike jumps in different shapes:* Travel about the space in different ways, and do three big springlike jumps in place, with different shapes in the air during each jump. Travel again.
- *Three big springlike turning jumps:* Travel about the space in different ways, and do three big springlike jumps, adding one turn (half or full) in at least one jump.
- *Three big resilient jumps, shapes, and turns:* Travel in different ways, and do three big resilient jumps. Have each jump be a different shape or add a turn in the air.
- *Hot dog skiing:* Jump while twisting your feet on the diagonals, pretending to be slalom skiing. Bend your knees to absorb force, and extend through the ankles when you jump.
  - On my signal, do a high jump while making the shape of an "X".
  - On my signal, jump far to one side and then far to the other side, as in skiing moguls.
  - On my signal, jump, and do a full turn.
  - On my signal, jump, arch your body, and aim to touch your toes to the back of your head.
- *Locomotor skills and body actions* (requires hoops scattered about the gym, with some held vertically in a foam hoop brace in front of a mat, some flat on a mat, and some flat on the floor):
  - Travel from hoop to hoop using different locomotor skills. When you get to a flat hoop on the floor, do springlike jumps in and out of the hoop, varying the direction of your jumps (forward, backward, and sideways).

Sample Introductory and Warm-up Activities (*continued*)

- Travel to another hoop, and slide around it, sometimes facing in and sometimes facing out.
- When you get to a free flat hoop on a mat, take your weight on your hands in the hoop, and then spring your feet in the air to land (with control) in a different place outside the hoop.
- When you get to a hoop in a brace, travel through the hoop using rolling or steplike actions. Land gently.

- *Locomotor skills and steplike actions on hands and feet* (requires mats scattered about the space): Travel fast in general space, and jump over a corner of a mat while stretching your arms to the ceiling to help you gain height. When you come to a free mat with no child on it, transfer your weight across the mat in a new way each time, with your hands and feet touching the mat and supporting your weight.
- *Jumping over low canes* (requires paper canes elevated about 6 inches set on small cones or a brace):
  - Jump over the cane forward, backward, and sideways. Explode from your ankles.
  - Straddle the cane. On four counts, do bounce, bounce, bounce, jump half-turn, and then straddle the cane again. Repeat multiple times. If you want a challenge, try a full turn in the jump. Extend through your ankles to get height.

Level 3

- *Gallop, turning leap:* Do three gallops, do one step, take off on one foot, and do a turning leap or jump in the air, landing softly on one or two feet. Repeat.
- *Jog, turning leap, steplike movement* (requires mats scattered about the gym): Jog, jog, jog, do a turning leap (called a "cat leap"—take off on one foot, bend knees in the air, and turn) before the mat, and then do a steplike movement on the mat, while taking your weight on your hands and keeping your arms straight.
- *Varying speed* (requires mats scattered about the gym): Travel fast by jogging, skipping, or galloping. Do three big springlike jumps with different shapes in each, take your weight onto the mat gently, and do two slow-motion, continuous rolls on the mat.
- *Hopping on stepping stones* (requires 10 poly spots for each group of three children; groups should be scattered about the gym, with their spots placed two to three feet apart): Hop from spot to spot as if you were hopping on rocks across a stream. Share spots equally with your partners.
- *Review three ways of landing as a warm-up* (requires mats scattered about the gym): Travel about general space, and using an easy approach jog, take off on one foot, and land on two feet. When you come to a free mat, gently take your weight onto the mat, roll, and come up to stand. Continue when you are in a free space—jump, land softly, and stick (freeze for three seconds balanced on your feet) or land, and spring away. Repeat.
- *Combining movements* (requires mats scattered about the gym): Travel about the gym from mat to mat. When you come to a free mat, combine two movements—one with your feet in the air and one roll. Repeat.
- *Running turned into a log roll* (requires mats scattered about the gym; one child per mat): Put one hand on the mat and run around your hand, with your feet going farther and farther away until you log roll.

to practice locomotor skills to develop speed, height or distance, agility, and accuracy. You can combine locomotor skills with other gymnastics movements that the children have learned in previous lessons. The "Sample Introductory and Warm-up Activities" box lists sample introductory activities, arranging them in three levels based on children's ability. These suggestions assume you have taught these locomotor skills in previous lessons.

Content Development

Content development focuses on extending the variety of gymnastics movements and refining performance techniques (Rink, 2014).

Progression from Floor to Apparatus

One rule of thumb for the content development segment in gymnastics is to start work on floor mats and then move to apparatus. Starting with floor work enables children to learn new movements safely while low to the ground, thereby avoiding the added challenge of height that apparatus typically bring.

Of course, no rule of thumb applies to all situations. Children can learn a few skills more easily using a low apparatus. For example, it is easier to learn a cartwheel following a progression that starts with a stacked (folded) mat or trapezoid section and then progresses to performing the skill on the floor.

Progression from Individual Work to Partners and Groups

A second progression we use in gymnastics is for the children to start work as individuals, then build to partner and group work.

Culminating Activity: Apparatus and Sequences

The culminating activity for gymnastics lessons is practicing the theme on an apparatus, developing sequences, or both.

Sequences

Sequences are the essence of gymnastics. Both Olympic gymnastics and educational gymnastics aim to develop children's abilities to combine skills, transition smoothly from one skill to the next, and move with continuity of flow. Sequences are also essential for developing children's creative and critical-thinking processes and choreographic abilities. Teaching sequences is a very important consideration.

Apparatus

Using apparatus is essential for extending children's movement variety. For example, when you add a stacked mat (a folded-up

Figure 24.8 Simple apparatus

Courtesy of John Dolly

sectional mat) or an aerobic box to a lesson on jumping, children can learn how to jump off, over, and onto an obstacle. In addition, children find apparatus work enjoyable and interesting; thus, apparatus can help motivate children to work productively and independently.

In this text, we describe tasks using low-cost educational gymnastics apparatus that teachers can purchase from catalogs. Few schools have Olympic gymnastics apparatus or educational gymnastics apparatus such as trestles, ropes, climbing apparatus, springboards, gymnastics benches, and vaulting apparatus. Consequently, we focus on lesson activities that rely on mats, stacked mats (folded-up sectional mats), trapezoids, and aerobic boxes. We also rely on inexpensive and homemade equipment, such as hoops, cones, spots, paper canes, and ropes. We include some activities using low 2×4 beams that can be easily homemade or purchased for a reasonable price (see **Figure 24.8**). Finally, we include some lessons for those teachers who have large apparatus or playground apparatus.

Because they have only limited pieces of apparatus at their disposal, most teachers arrange these items into apparatus centers to ensure maximum participation opportunities, which are critical for learning (NASPE, 2009; Rink, 2004; van der Mars, 2006). We use the term "center" rather than the traditional "station" because "center" is the term used in elementary classroom settings and children will be familiar with it. We always set up enough pieces of apparatus and equipment centers so there are only two or three children per center and then have the children rotate centers. If you have 25 children in a class, set up at least 12 centers. If you have 70 children in a class, set up 35 centers.

We find children can practice at five to 15 centers in a lesson, depending on the complexity of the task and themes. For large classes (60 or more students), children will rotate through all of the centers in five to 10 lessons. Most of the time, when teachers are assigned very large classes (with teachers' aides), they also see their children five days per week; thus, one set of centers will be used for one to two weeks.

Centers are recommended for use as culminating activities after children have learned all the movements used in the centers. Teach the content of centers first as whole-class tasks, making sure the children know the performance techniques to practice. This structure will help children understand what you expect them to learn at each center and will support their ability to work independently.

Different Types of Centers

Several types of centers are used in gymnastics. They include basic centers, challenge courses, malls, villages, and schools.

Centers

The most basic center organization is to set up centers around the physical education space in order. With this arrangement, children start at one center, and the teacher rotates all children at the same time. Each center can have several pieces of apparatus and equipment.

Center Guidelines

1. Assign a maximum of two to three children per center.
2. Teach one or two performance techniques during whole-class teaching, and post relevant performance cues at each center.
3. Teach children to think critically about their own performance, and select the one technique that they think will most help them improve.
4. Emphasize that the purpose of physical education is to learn and improve and that this drive must come from the children themselves—they need to learn to learn independently without the teacher telling them what to do every single minute.

Three Sample Centers

Focus: Traveling on Hands and Feet

Equipment: One section of a trapezoid with mats on both sides.

Task Card: [Posted on gym wall] Hands and feet, zigzag pathways.

Task: When you get to this center, travel on, over, and down the trapezoid, making zigzag pathways. Find different ways to travel on your hands and feet, taking your weight on your hands on and over the trapezoid.

Performance Techniques:

Keep your arms straight and elbows locked.

Keep your palms flat.

ME (modification to make task easier): If this center is too difficult, keep your feet low when you take your weight on your hands.

MD (modification to make task more difficult): If you need more of a challenge, try to stretch your legs toward the ceiling when you take your weight on your hands.

Focus: Jump, Land, Roll

Equipment: Stacked mat, mat.

Task Card: Jump, land on feet, and roll, ending in a balance.

Three Sample Centers (*continued*)

Task: When you get to this center, jump off the stacked mat onto the flat mat, land softly on your feet, roll in any way you like, and transition without taking any steps to end in a balance in an asymmetrical shape. In other words, your roll should end in a balance.

Performance Techniques:

Land on your feet from your jump.

Use strong arms when you roll.

ME: Work on rolling sideways; make a symmetrical shape in the balance.

MD: If you need more of a challenge, roll a different way each time, or balance on an upper body part.

Focus: Traveling on Different Pathways and in Different Directions

Equipment: Several large ropes or old garden hoses.

Task Card: Pathways and directions.

Task: When you get to this center, set up straight, curved, and zigzag pathways with the rope (or hose) in a way that you think will help you improve. Walk while balancing on the rope and following the pathway. Then explore walking in different directions—forward, backward, and sideways.

Performance Techniques:

Stretch tall.

Stay tight.

ME: Set up mostly straight pathways with only a few large curves, and walk forward.

MD: Set up all three kinds of pathways, and walk backward and sideways.

Teach children how to modify centers (to make them either easier or more difficult) so the task can accommodate individual differences and allow each child to be challenged and successful. Have children work at a center until you observe that their efforts are declining. Then have them rotate to the next center.

Challenge Courses

Challenge courses are obstacle courses that the children design. We call them "challenge" courses because we explain that their purpose is to challenge children to improve their skills.

Malls

A mall is a set of four to six centers that is used by a total of eight to 10 children (see **Figure 24.9**). The children decide when to change centers and can go to any center within their mall—just like going to stores at a mall. The teacher rotates children from mall to mall after they have had sufficient time to practice at the centers within their mall.

Mall Guidelines for Children

1. Select the centers you think will help you improve.
2. Share centers if there is enough room.
3. You cannot wait in line for any center; if the center is busy, come back later.
4. Be fair to others; move on to a new center if others want a turn.
5. Repeat your favorite centers only after you have completed all centers.

Villages

A village is like a mall but includes streets and sidewalks (beams, old hoses, ropes, lines on the gym floor) connecting the different centers, which are like stores within a village. Set up as many villages as you need so children can share the space in each store without having to wait in lines. (See the sample village in the box, "Sample Village: The Balance Village.")

Village Rules for Children

1. If a store is full, go to a different store.
2. Keep moving on the sidewalks.
3. You cannot pass any child going in the same direction (no cutting ahead).

Sample Gymnastics Challenge Course

Focus: Balance on Different Body Parts

Equipment: Two hoops, two poly spots, three mats, one trapezoid section, one box

Task Card: Balance challenge course.

Task: Set up the equipment, mats, and small apparatus in a row, in any order you and your partner choose. Balance on a different body part on each piece of equipment and apparatus, and connect these balances with any roll or steplike action. For example, you can start with a hoop (balancing on a big body part), then a poly spot (balancing on a small body part), then a hoop, the box, and the trapezoid, and end by balancing on a spot. In your transitions between balances, move immediately from or to the balance without taking any steps to start or at the end of the roll or steplike action.

Performance Techniques:

Stay tight in your balance.

Make smooth transitions by thinking about the body position and level where one action ends and the next begins.

ME: Balance only on large body parts or with large bases.

MD: Try some challenging balances on small body parts.

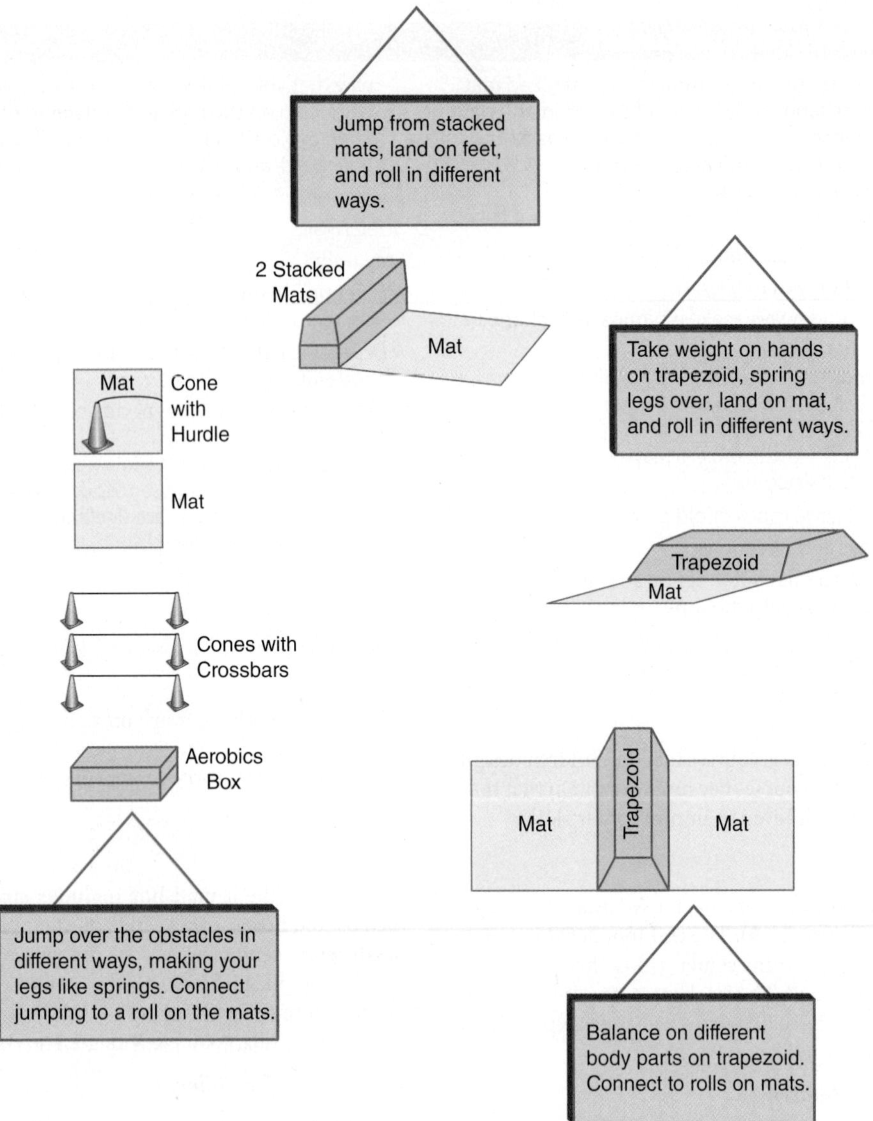

Figure 24.9 Gymnastics mall

4. Try to pass someone traveling toward you by holding hands and trying to step around each other without falling off the sidewalk.

Schools

A school is a set of centers arranged in a progression from easy to difficult. Children progress from grade to grade when they have mastered the movements in the lower grade. Schools most often are centers that increase in height as children progress. For example,

- Grade 1: Jump onto one stacked mat.
- Grade 2: Jump onto two stacked mats.
- Grade 3: Jump onto three stacked mats.

A Final Note for Beginning Teachers

Most undergraduate students have little experience with either gymnastics or teaching strategies in which students make decisions, solve problems, or explore movement options. Consequently, teaching educational gymnastics will be a new but exciting challenge.

Research on beginning teachers shows that some beginners are afraid they will lose control of the children if children make decisions about which content to practice; in reality, however, teachers find that the management techniques they learned for teaching more familiar content work just as well in gymnastics (Rovegno, 1992a, 1993a, 1998).

Sample Village: The Balance Village

Each village has at least five stores that branch off the main circular street and sidewalks. The streets consist of low balance beams, and the sidewalks are made from large ropes or old garden hoses. Connect beams and ropes together on a curved pathway. Assign 10 to 12 children to a village. Children travel on the streets and sidewalks (using dynamic balancing) from shop to shop, stopping when they want. The shops are as follows:

1. *Spots Galore:* This store consists of 8 to 10 poly spots set about three feet apart. Balance on small body parts on each spot. Transition from balance to balance by using rolls and steplike actions without taking any steps in between. The position of your balance should be the starting position of your roll or steplike action. End the roll or steplike action in a new balance without stopping or taking any steps.
2. *The Gap:* This store consists of four to six cones of different heights. Balance in different ways over each cone without touching the cone. Transition between the balances using rolls, steplike actions, or other balances; you should not take any steps in between balances.
3. *Great Balls of Fire:* Balance on your belly on large balls (designed to support the weight of a child) and try to hold the balance as long as possible.
4. *The Mattress Store:* This store consists of several trapezoids (or low boxes or stacked mats) set on angles close together. Balance on different body parts, and change from trapezoid to trapezoid without touching the floor. Transition between balances by going directly from one balance into the next without taking any steps, rolling, or using steplike actions.
5. *Hoop Haven:* This store consists of five to eight hoops set approximately one foot apart. Balance in large shapes on different body parts in each hoop. Transition between balances by going directly from one balance into the next without taking any steps or by using steplike actions.
6. *Balance Board Shop:* Balance in different ways on balance boards.

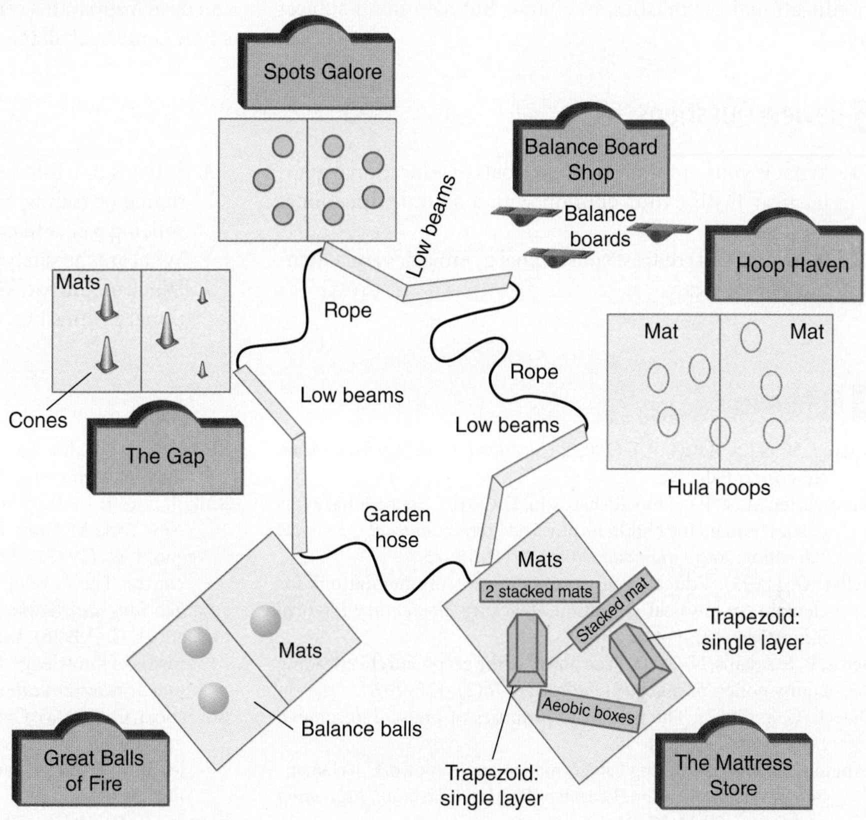

Other beginning teachers do not give effective feedback because lessons focus on themes that encompass a variety of skills that children can perform in different ways. In fact, this is only a temporary issue that you can quickly correct with careful planning of potential refining tasks, feedback, and an observation plan.

Finally, observing a class of children, all of whom are doing different movements at the same time, can tax the observational abilities of even the most willing newcomer. Even so, it is exciting to see the different movements children will invent.

The good news is that teachers who persist with educational gymnastics report they are grateful because they no longer have to deal with the problems of long lines, bored high-skilled children, and low-skilled children who face embarrassing and unsafe situations. In addition, they do not have to confront children who intentionally disengage because it is easier for children to say, “I am performing poorly because I am not trying and don’t care,” than it is to say, “I am trying hard and can’t do this” (Dweck, 2007). Teachers report they value educational gymnastics because it gives them a way to teach that matches their philosophy and provides a way to deal with the diverse ability levels in their classes. Once they learn how to teach educational gymnastics, they never go back to traditional gymnastics teaching.

To help beginners get their feet wet, we include scripted, annotated tasks for the content development and culminating activity segments of lessons and units for children at developmental level 1. Once you have studied or planned your own lessons based on these detailed suggestions, you will be ready for children at developmental levels 2 and 3. In levels 2 and 3, we present the major tasks for the content development segment of lessons and units with options for culminating experiences.

Summary

Educational gymnastics differs from Olympic gymnastics and is designed for schools using safe, inexpensive equipment and apparatus. By focusing lesson content on themes, rather than specific skills, educational gymnastics lessons accommodate the individual differences of children and enable teachers to ensure maximum practice opportunities. Safety is the single most important concern for teachers (not only in educational gymnastics, of course, but also in all subject areas).

Gymnastics lessons have three segments. First is introductory activities. Locomotor skills make excellent introductory activities. Second, content development focuses on extending the variety of gymnastics movements and refining performance techniques (Rink, 2014). Third, the culminating activity for gymnastics lessons is practicing the theme on apparatus, developing sequences, or both. With limited equipment, teachers can design apparatus centers in many different ways, including single centers, challenge courses, villages, malls, and schools.

Review Questions

1. What is your opinion about the goals of educational gymnastics? Justify your opinion with a sound educational argument.
2. Compare and contrast educational gymnastics and Olympic gymnastics.
3. What is the difference between teaching a lesson with the theme of rolling and teaching a forward roll, backward roll, log roll, and egg roll?
4. What are the safety guidelines for educational gymnastics?
5. What are the two kinds of culminating activities in educational gymnastics, and why is each important?

References

Adams, N. G., & Bettis, P. J. (2003). *Cheerleader: An American icon.* New York: Palgrave.

Baumgarten, A., & Pagnano-Richardson, K. (2010). Educational gymnastics: Enhancing children's physical literacy. *Journal of Physical Education, Recreation and Dance, 81*(4), 18–25.

Belka, D. (1993). Educational gymnastics: Recommendations for elementary physical education. *Teaching Elementary Physical Education, 4*(2), 1, 4–6.

Bettis, P., & Adams, N. (2003). The power of the preps and cheerleading equity policy. *Sociology of Education, 76*(2), 128–142.

Dweck, C. S. (2007). The perils and promises of praise. *Educational Leadership, 65*(2), 34–38.

Langton, T. (2007). Applying Laban's movement framework in elementary physical education. *Journal of Physical Education, Recreation and Dance, 78*(1), 17–24, 39, 53.

National Association for Sport and Physical Education (NASPE). (2009). *Appropriate instructional practice guidelines for elementary school physical education* (3rd ed.). Reston, VA: Author.

National Association for Sport and Physical Education (NASPE). (2010). *PE metrics: Assessing National Standards 1–6 in elementary school.* Reston, VA: Author.

Nilges, L. M. (2000). Teaching educational gymnastics: Feature introduction. *Teaching Elementary Physical Education, 11*(4), 6–9.

Nilges, L. M., & Lathrop, A. H. (2000). Eleven safety tips for educational gymnastics. *Teaching Elementary Physical Education, 11*(4), 10.

Nilges-Charles, L. M. (2008). Assessing skill in educational gymnastics. *Journal of Physical Education, Recreation and Dance, 79*(3), 41–51.

Placek, J. H., Dodds, P., Doolittle, S. A., Portman, P. A., Ratliffe, T. A., & Pinkham, K. M. (1995). Teaching recruits' physical education backgrounds and beliefs about purposes for their subject matter. *Journal of Teaching in Physical Education, 14*(3), 246–261.

Resnick, L. B. (2010). Nesting learning systems for the thinking curriculum. *Educational Researcher, 39*, 183–197.

Rink, J. E. (2004). It's okay to be a beginner. *Journal of Physical Education, Recreation and Dance, 75*(6), 31–34.

Rink, J. E. (2014). *Teaching physical education for learning* (7th ed.). New York: McGraw-Hill.

Rovegno, I. C. (1992a). Learning to teach in a field-based methods course: The development of pedagogical content knowledge. *Teaching and Teacher Education, 8*, 69–82.

Rovegno, I. C. (1992b). Learning a new curricular approach: Mechanisms of knowledge acquisition in preservice teachers. *Teaching and Teacher Education, 8*, 253–264.

Rovegno, I. C. (1993a). Content knowledge acquisition during undergraduate teacher education: Overcoming cultural templates and learning through practice. *American Educational Research Journal, 30*, 611–642.

Rovegno, I. C. (1993b). The development of curricular knowledge: A case study of problematic pedagogical content knowledge during advanced knowledge acquisition. *Research Quarterly for Exercise and Sport, 64*, 56–68.

Rovegno, I. C. (1998). The development of in-service teachers' knowledge of a constructivist approach to physical education: Teaching beyond activities. *Research Quarterly for Exercise and Sport, 69*, 147–162.

Rovegno, I. C. (2010). *Children's perspectives on physical education.* Unpublished manuscript, University of Alabama, Tuscaloosa.

Society of Health and Physical Educators (SHAPE). (2014). *National standards and grade-level outcomes for K–12 physical education.* Champaign, IL: Human Kinetics.

Solmon, M. A. (2006). Creating a motivational climate to foster engagement in physical education. *Journal of Physical Education, Recreation, and Dance, 77*(8), 15–16.

van der Mars, H. (2006). Time and learning in physical education. In D. Kirk, D. MacDonald, & M. O'Sullivan (Eds.), *The handbook of physical education* (pp. 191–213). London: Sage.

CHAPTER

25

Sequence Choreography and Movement Quality in Gymnastics and Dance

PRE-READING REFLECTION

1. What do you believe teachers should assess in gymnastics and dance?
2. Should teachers grade children's creative products, such as dance sequences? Why or why not?

OBJECTIVES

Students will learn:

1. The major learning outcomes in gymnastics and dance are quality sequences and movement quality.
2. Basic elements of sequence choreography include structure, transitions, originality, expressing ideas, contrast and aesthetic highlights, line, focus, and clarity.
3. The three phases of designing sequences are (a) exploring and experimenting; (b) selecting and arranging; and (c) refining and practicing.
4. Characteristics of movement quality and skillful performance techniques are (a) having the appropriate amount of tension; (b) appropriate body alignment (e.g., pointing the toes); (c) landing lightly with control over body parts and flow of movement; (d) a stretched or elongated torso; (e) appropriate speed and force; and (f) engaging the core.
5. Characteristics of quality performances include (a) accuracy in rhythm and tempo; (b) concentration and engagement; and (c) being well practiced until movements can be repeated accurately.

KEY TERMS

Aesthetic highlight
Asymmetrical shapes
Clarity
Elongate the spine
Engaging the core
Focus
Imitation
Line
Originality
Representation
Symmetrical shapes
Transitions

CONNECTION TO STANDARDS

This chapter addresses National Standard 2 for the application of principles of sequence choreography and movement quality in gymnastics and dance and National Standard 5 for the value of physical activity for enjoyment and self-expression (Society of Health and Physical Educators [SHAPE], 2014). Common Core and other State Standards (CCSS) are connected to the grade-level major learning outcomes for sequences.

Introduction

In this chapter, we discuss the major learning outcomes in gymnastics and dance: quality sequences, which range from short combinations of skills to longer routines, and movement quality. We describe the elements of quality sequence choreography and movement quality that physical education teachers should teach and assess.

We also describe the process of designing sequences, beginning with short, simple combinations of skills and movement concepts in kindergarten, building to longer gymnastics and dance group sequences in grade 5. Throughout history, performers and spectators have been drawn to the artistry and creativity of gymnastics and dance sequence choreography. As educators, we must ask, "Why should the highest skilled among us and professional choreographers be the only ones to enjoy some of the most meaningful experiences gymnastics and dance can offer—that is, designing you own dance and gymnastics choreography to express an idea?" The value of physical activities for self-expression is a component of National Standard 5. We need not reserve the delights of self-expression, creating gymnastics and dance sequences, and experiencing artistry in movement solely for elite-level gymnasts and dancers.

We believe having a clear idea about sequences as major learning outcomes for the K–5 grades and the principles to teach that apply to these outcomes will help you set lesson and unit objectives to address National Standards 2 and 5. These objectives, in turn, will guide your planning and teaching.

Basic Elements of Sequence Choreography

For the elementary grades, we teach six elements of choreography (Rovegno, 1988; Rovegno & Bandhauer, 2000; Stinson, 1982)

- Sequences have a beginning, middle, and end
- All parts fit together logically with fluid transitions
- Originality
- Expressing an idea
- Contrasts and aesthetic highlights
- Relationships of body parts: line, focus, and clarity

These elements are listed in a loose progression, which means we tend to teach the first elements first and in younger grades, with the later elements appropriate only in the upper elementary grades when students have had considerable experience designing sequences. The term *loose progression* means this is not a step-like progression in which you must master an element before you progress to the next element. Rather, we revisit elements across the elementary grades and match the element of choreography to the movement concepts that are the theme of the sequence. For example, matching, contrasting, and complementing shapes is an appropriate theme for grades 3 and above. The most relevant components of choreography to help students understand and improve the extent to which their shapes match, contrast, and complement each other are line and clarity, from the element titled relationships of body parts: line, focus, and clarity, which is an element we typically would not teach before students design group sequences in fourth or fifth grade.

Sequences Have a Beginning, Middle, and End

The most basic element of choreography is the structure—that is, the notion that sequences have a beginning, middle, and end. The beginning and end are shapes that are held still. With younger children, sequences are short. For example, a sequence for younger children might be to start in a curled shape (beginning); then gallop and leap (middle); and finally end in a curled shape (end). With older children, sequences are longer with more complex elements. Typically the teacher sets the order of sequence components, identifies skills and movement concepts students need to include in their sequence, or specifies the number of skills or movement components in the sequence. The following tasks to design a sequence are examples of how teachers can specify sequence components.

- Design a partner sequence with beginning and ending shapes with the middle including at least two matching, two contrasting, and two complementing shapes and skills.
- Design a sequence with the following in order: (1) a beginning shape; (2) jump and land at a low level; (3) rise and sink; (4) travel on a circular pathway; and (5) an ending shape.

In teaching sequences, you are likely to see the following immature patterns.

Immature Patterns

- The sequence is missing a beginning or an ending shape held still.
- The sequence is missing parts of the middle that were assigned by the teacher as required components of the sequence.
- Children create a never-ending sequence.

Although designing sequences structured with a beginning, middle, and end seems like an easy element to teach, children need teacher guidance in applying this element to their sequences. We describe one way to teach sequence structure below, labeled the "I, we, you" method. **Table 25.1** describes several other teaching strategies for introducing sequence structure to children.

The "I, We, You" Method

First, the teacher (i.e., "I") designs a sequence and teaches it to the children, illustrating the beginning, middle, and end segments. Second, the teacher and children together design a sequence (i.e., "we"). You can do this in several ways. For example, you might design and teach the children a sequence and have the children change one part. Alternatively, you might design a sequence and offer children a limited number of choices for each segment. For example, you might say, "Start in a balance on one leg; you can position your free leg any way you want. Then smoothly and gently take your weight down to the mat, and do two sideways rolls across your mat, showing two different leg shapes (see **Figure 25.1**). End in a shape on the mat kneeling on one or both shins."

Having learned a sequence designed by the teacher and having designed one with the teacher, the children are now ready to design their own sequence (i.e., "you"). The teacher assigns a simple sequence task for the children, and the children design their sequence.

TEACHING TIP

Teaching Sequencing and Patterns in the Down Times

Here is a fun game, called "Guess the Pattern," for teaching kindergarteners about sequencing and patterns that you can introduce during the down time when they line up to return to class. At the end of class during the first three months of school when the children are lined up and waiting for their classroom teacher, have them stand in line in a pattern. For example, have the first child cross her arms and the second put his arms at his sides. Then continue this pattern down the line—crossed, straight, crossed, straight, and so on. When their classroom teacher arrives, he or she has to guess the pattern. The children use thumbs up if the teacher is right and thumbs down if he or she is wrong (this part is especially fun for kindergarteners). Each time you play the game, make the pattern more difficult—for example, long pants, shorts, shorts, long pants, shorts, shorts, long pants, and so on, or has a zipper, doesn't have a zipper, has a zipper, and so on. The children enjoy it when their classroom teacher can't figure out the pattern. Then, when you teach patterns and sequencing in gymnastics and dance or the classroom teacher teaches patterns in math or sequencing in literature, the children will already know what the terms *pattern* and *sequencing* mean.

Table 25.1 Teaching Strategies for Introducing Sequences

Label	Description
I, we, you	1. Teacher designs and teaches a sequence. 2. Teacher and children design a sequence together. 3. Child designs a sequence.
I list the actions; you create the variations.	Teacher presents a list of actions, such as the following: • Beginning shape at low level • Big jump • Locomotor skill • Turn and sink • Ending shape at low level Child adds variations, shapes, and gestures.
I do half; you do half.	Teacher creates the first half of the sequence. Child creates the second half of the sequence.
I teach the steps; you add the formations and pathways.	Teacher designs steps of the dance to music. For example: • Four steps forward, four steps backward (repeat three times) • Eight slides left, eight slides right • Seven steps in a circle, turn and sink Children in groups of three add the formations, gestures, and pathways.

Figure 25.1 Sideways roll showing different leg shapes

Courtesy of John Dolly

All Parts Fit Together Logically with Fluid Transitions

In a sequence, all parts fit together in a logical order. The child doesn't stop and then start a new part that seems unrelated to the previous part. The parts make sense in relation to one another. **Transitions** are the movements between skills, shapes, and formations. A high-quality sequence consists of a series of movements that transition and flow one after the other as if they were one continuous movement (Nilges, 1999). Skills fit together seamlessly and logically, without the presence of hesitations or extra steps, and the elements of the sequence make sense in relation to one another. The only time the child pauses is to hold a balance (in gymnastics) or a shape (in dance) intentionally.

You can teach older children that not only do the parts fit together, but also the entire sequence has a sense of unity and coherence from start to finish. One way to understand unity and coherence is to imagine the opposite. Imagine a grandmother wearing an outfit with colors that look terrible together in a style designed for 13-year-olds. For the outfit to work aesthetically, the colors would need to look pleasing together, and the style would need to look right on an older woman. When a sequence has unity and coherence, there is a sense of wholeness. You don't view the parts as separate; you see a unified whole.

Sequencing words to write a sentence and sequencing ideas to tell a story are major parts of the literacy curriculum. Consequently, patterns and sequencing are critical skills for children to understand. You can support the development of sequencing skills in classroom subjects by teaching children that in gymnastics and dance sequences, all parts fit together, just as the words of a sentence or the parts of a story fit together.

Teaching Transitions in Gymnastics

Other than at the most elementary beginning level, teaching skills in combinations helps children develop fluent transitions (Doering, 2006). It is not enough, however, to have children practice combining skills; they need to learn how to do the transition between the skills. One way to teach transitions is to demonstrate (or have a child demonstrate) first a poor-quality transition by doing a roll, hesitating, standing up, taking several steps, and then doing a cartwheel. Then demonstrate a good-quality transition by doing a roll, stepping out one foot at a time, and from the squat position at the end of the roll, immediately, without hesitation, doing a cartwheel (see **Figure 25.2**). The following are immature patterns you are likely to see as children learn how to transition from one skill to the next.

Immature Patterns

- Taking several walking steps between every skill
- Standing up and pausing in between every skill
- Doing one movement, stopping, and walking back to the starting spot to perform the second movement

Figure 25.2 Forward roll with step out to a cartwheel

- Arranging skills based on the order in which they thought about the skills, rather than arranging skills so the transitions are logical and continuous

To have children practice transitions, you can give them tasks that require continuous movement. For example, you might assign this task: "Start in a balance, tip the balance by shifting your weight, and roll immediately from that balance position. Explore several ways to roll immediately out of a balance."

In addition, throughout lessons, you should give performance feedback on children's transitions when needed.

Sample Performance Techniques to Teach for Transitions

- The ending position of one skill is the starting position of the next skill.
- Think ahead—anticipate which movement you will do next before you have to start it.
- Instead of ending a skill on two feet, land on one foot (walk out) and then step on the other foot as the start of the next skill.
- Don't take any steps between movements. Where your feet land is where the next skill starts; don't readjust your foot placement between skills.
- Keep your movement continuous. Don't have any hesitations between the skills—flow like a river.

Teaching Transitions from One Formation to the Next

In gymnastics and dance, transitions during partner and group work from one formation or group shape to another can be difficult for children. To teach this content, you can assign children to groups of three or five, and have them figure out how to move from a circle to a line (e.g., follow a leader) and then from a line to a V (e.g., the center person does the movement three times, the next two do the movement twice, and the two children at the ends of the line do the movement once) (see **Figure 25.3**). Then have them explore changing to other formations.

Originality

Originality means the movements are varied, different, interesting, or unusual. Teachers sometimes label original movements "creative." For a sequence to be original, it must have lots of variations in shape, speed, levels, and directions and some different or unusual movements or combinations. (Not every movement needs to be original, however.) Immature patterns you will see include the following.

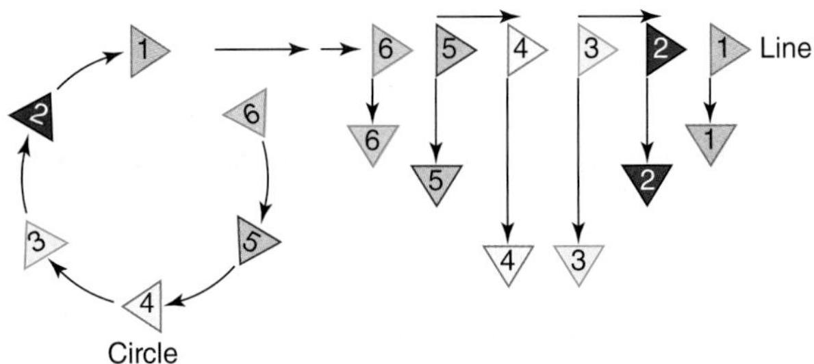

Figure 25.3 Changing formations from a circle to a line and from a line to a V

Immature Patterns

- Using the same shapes over and over
- In gymnastics, using the same tucked shape throughout
- Relying exclusively on symmetrical shapes
- Repeating the same skills over and over, such as a forward roll and cartwheel in gymnastics
- Designing combinations that are ordinary and repeated
- Creating starting and ending positions that are most often plain shapes with the child standing

A more mature original sequence would use a wide range of different shapes and as many different skills or body actions as possible and would start and end in interesting shapes on different body parts.

Three Levels: Plain, Varied, and Original

To teach children the idea of originality, we explain that there are three levels of originality: (1) plain; (2) varied; and (3) original. We illustrate this concept by having children make shapes (see **Figure 25.4**). We tell children to stand with their arms out to the side, and explain that this is a plain shape. To illustrate a varied shape, we have them change the shape of their arms. We explain that a varied shape expands on a plain shape by moving one or two body parts. To illustrate an original shape, we tell the children to twist at the hips, and have each leg and arm make a different shape twisting or turning in a different direction. Alternatively, we have them hold a still shape after moving their arms and legs into positions that no one else will think to do.

We then have children design short sequences by beginning in an original shape, traveling using a locomotor skill, jumping in an original shape, and then ending in an original shape. We repeat this process several times, having the children create different original shapes.

TEACHING TIP

Three Stories: Plain, Varied, and Original

I am going to tell you three stories to help you understand plain, varied, and original:

This is a *plain* story: "Yesterday, we went on a class trip. We packed our lunches. It was fun, and we came back at 2:30."

The next story takes the plain story and adds a *variety* of interesting elements: "Yesterday, we went on a class trip to the Georgia Aquarium, where you can actually pet sea creatures. We saw whale sharks, otters, and stingrays. We ate lunch at the park and saw the fountains. We came back at 2:30."

The last story is *original* and unusual: "Yesterday was the most exciting day of my life. The adventure began at the Georgia Aquarium, when I reached into the 'touching tank' and petted a stingray. Then, I tried to pet the shark, and my ring got caught on its tooth, and I was pulled into the tank. I thought I was going to be lunch!"

Now that you have heard the beginning of the original story, do you want to know what happened to the kid? That's what originality does for your sequence and for the stories you write in your classroom: It captures the interest of the audience.

(A)

(B)

(C)

Figure 25.4 (A) Plain shapes (B) Varied shapes (C) Original shapes

Courtesy of John Dolly

We also teach children about symmetrical and asymmetrical shapes. With beginners, **symmetrical shapes**—in which both sides of the body are the same—tend to dominate, especially in gymnastics. Their overuse can lead to sequences that are predictable and uninteresting. We explain that a sequence can have some plain and symmetrical shapes if they intend to use this format but that in general,

- **Asymmetrical shapes**, shapes in which the positions of body parts on both sides are different, should dominate.
- Children should not use the same shape more than once in a sequence (unless they intentionally repeat the shape to make an aesthetic statement).
- They should include as wide a variety of body actions as possible.
- When they repeat a body action, the shapes should vary (in other words, children should not do a tucked roll more than once. Each time they roll, they should vary the shape of their legs).

Expressing an Idea

We typically have children design dance sequences to express an idea or feeling or tell a story. For example, children might design a sequence representing the movements of a jellyfish, the feeling of being bored or angry, or the life cycle of a butterfly. With the introduction and growing popularity of shows such as *Cirque du Soleil* and *Pilobolus*, the boundaries between gymnastics and dance have become blurred. Recognizing that trend, children also might want to express an idea in a gymnastics sequence (although this is not necessary).

To express their ideas effectively, children need to understand the difference between representation and imitation. **Representation** means taking the main idea, abstracting it, and transforming it into movement. By abstracting, we mean taking an idea (about, for example, a feeling, object, animal, person, or event) and focusing on one portion that captures the essence of the idea—what is most essential. Representing an idea is thus not trying to portray an exact duplicate of the idea, nor is it pantomiming the movements associated with the idea. Representing an idea means expressing what that idea means to you.

Imitation, by comparison, is a surface-level characterization. For example, standing straight with the arms circled overhead is a static, surface-level characterization of a tree (see **Figure 25.5A**). To represent a tree, children might swing and sway different body parts in different ways, representing the movements of branches in the wind (see **Figure 25.5B**). Immature patterns you are likely to see include children

- Imitating
- Pantomiming
- Using obvious or stereotypical shapes or actions, like using the index fingers at the side of the head as horns to portray a horned animal
- Using symmetrical, plain shapes

Contrasts and Aesthetic Highlights

Contrasts

Contrasts add interest to choreography and keep sequences from being monotonous (Pollatou, Savrami, & Karadimou, 2004). Contrasts take observers by surprise and keep them wondering what will come next. Children can use the following movement concepts to provide contrasts in sequences:

- Changes in level (low, medium, high)
- Abrupt changes from traveling to stillness
- Abrupt changes in speed (fast and slow)
- Obvious contrasts in shape (e.g., changing from a big, wide shape to a small, round shape)
- Abrupt changes in force from strong to gentle
- Changes in relationship between partners, among group members, or with props, equipment, or apparatus

To help children understand contrasts, teachers can design lessons on matching and contrasting. Examples include "matching, mirroring, contrasting, and complementing shapes" in dance and "matching, contrasting, and complementing shapes" in gymnastics. Immature patterns you are likely to see include the following:

- Repeating the same movements or shapes
- Having no changes in speed, level, or force but maintaining a sameness from start to finish
- Moving in predictable ways (if a movement is done to the left four times, it is repeated to the right four times)

(A)

(B)

Figure 25.5 (A) Imitating a tree (B) Representing trees swinging and swaying in the wind

Aesthetic Highlights

An **aesthetic highlight** is a part of the sequence that stands out as distinctive, exceptional, or particularly interesting. It takes you by surprise and captures your attention; it is the high point of the sequence. Frequently, aesthetic highlights consist of a contrast of some kind or a particularly unusual movement or original idea.

An effective way to teach children about impact and aesthetic highlights is to discuss these concepts when children show their sequences to their classmates. We ask children to identify what, in their opinion, was the highlight of the sequence and what they found most interesting. Even children in the youngest grades can readily identify aesthetic highlights.

Relationship of Body Parts to Shapes: Line, Focus, and Clarity

Line

Line in gymnastics and dance refers to the lines formed by intentionally positioning several body parts (see **Figure 25.6**). For example, you might form a diagonal line by aligning one leg pointing to the lower corner of the gym, with the spinal column, head, and both arms pointing to the upper corner of the gym. Two children can form an "O" and one child can form a "C."

To form aesthetically pleasing lines, children need to stand back, metaphorically, and look at the shape of their body from the perspective of an observer. The relationship of every body part is important to the shape. For example, if the head sticks out of the line that other body parts make, this disruption will detract from the line.

Focus

Similar to line, **focus** in gymnastics and dance means that body shapes and body parts focus the observers' attention on a particular point in space (see **Figure 25.7**). For example, two children making a round shape while facing each other would focus the observers' attention on the middle of the pair.

To teach focus, have children explore making different group or partner shapes with different foci. For example,

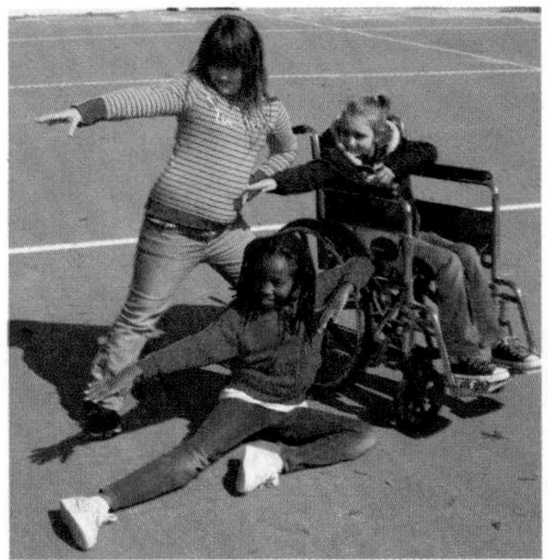

Figure 25.6 Children making shapes with clear lines

(A)

(B)

(C)

Figure 25.7 (A) Inward focus (B) Diagonal focus (C) Upward focus

Task: With your partner, create a shape that directs the observers' attention

- To the ceiling
- To the door
- To the floor
- To a space in the center of the group

For learning experiences addressing focus in dance, have children work on group shapes: angular, flat, round, and straight.

Clarity

Clarity refers to being precise and making a definite, repeatable movement or shape. Clarity requires that children know the exact shape they want to make and the position of every body part necessary to create that shape. The more precisely they can position their body parts, the clearer the shape.

Immature Patterns

Beginners are typically not aware of the precise positions of their body parts. They tend to focus on a few body parts but not attend to the position of other parts. Body parts stick out of the intended line. They have a vague idea of the movement and shape they want to perform but do not attend to the details. This fuzziness explains why children can have problems repeating a sequence exactly the same way each time. When they try to repeat a shape, it does not look the same because several body parts are in different positions.

Children can improve the clarity of their movements with practice. One task that is helpful for developing clarity is to have them teach their sequence to a partner, who in essence becomes a human video recorder who tries to reproduce the sequence exactly. As the partners watch each other and discuss the sequence, they learn where they were not clear and discover how to be more precise.

Recognizing Immature, Intermediate, and More Mature Elements of Sequence Choreography

In **Table 25.2**, we summarize the immature, intermediate, and mature performance levels you will see as children develop their abilities to choreograph sequences. Our intent here is to provide an instructional tool to help you know what to look for and identify ways children have improved along the developmental pathway.

Three Phases of Sequence Design

In this section, we discuss the process of designing sequences. Typically, sequences are the culminating activity of a lesson or unit. Thus, the sequence builds on the content progression of the lesson. For every sequence, the teacher sets a task describing exactly what the sequence should include. Most of the time for young children, we tell them the sequence components and the order.

Sample Sequence Tasks

- Create a sequence with a beginning shape you think is interesting, a middle with a pattern of repeating two of your favorite or best locomotor skills (e.g., gallop, jump, gallop, jump), and an ending shape you think is interesting.
- Create a sequence of three different sideways rolls, changing the shape of your legs on each roll. You also may choose to roll in different directions.

When designing sequence tasks, keep sequences very short for younger children and give them guidance. Younger children have less developed memory capacities and abilities to work independently for long periods compared to older children. Although younger children enjoy sharing their creations, they prefer not to be critiqued by their classmates. They also enjoy giving their sequences names, such as the "Manatee Sequence."

Older children who have more developed cognitive and social skills can design longer and more complex sequences. They enjoy putting their ideas in a sequence they can show their teacher and classmates. In particular, older children enjoy working with a partner or group.

The process of designing sequences incorporates three phases: (1) exploring and experimenting; (2) selecting and arranging; and (3) refining and practicing. You need to break down and teach this process in the same way that you break down and teach other thinking processes. It is our experience that it takes time for children to master the three phases; during this time, you will need to reinforce frequently what you have taught them about each phase.

Table 25.2 Observing and Identifying Performance Levels of Elements of Sequence Choreography in Gymnastics and Dance

Sequences Have a Beginning, Middle, and End
Level 1: Immature (Missing Parts)
The sequence is missing a beginning or an ending shape held still. The sequence is missing parts of the middle that were assigned by the teacher as required components of the sequence, or the child creates a never-ending sequence.
Level 2: Mature (Complete)
The sequence has a beginning, middle, and end.
All Parts Fit Together Logically with Fluid Transitions
Level 1: Immature (Stops and Steps)
Performers do one movement but then stop. Extra steps are taken between movements, formations, or parts of the sequence. Transitions do not look planned. Performers seem to make it up as they go along. The sections of the sequence are disconnected, and the parts don't seem to fit together. Each person in the group seems to be working separately.
Level 2: Intermediate (Hesitations and Only a Few Extra Steps)
Many movements are connected, although a few times the performer takes extra steps. Transitions between skills or body actions seem to be planned, but sometimes the order of skills is not logical and creates transition problems. Often the performer hesitates. In group work, when the performers change formations, many group members take extra steps. Some transitions are abrupt and don't seem to be part of the sequence.
Level 3: Mature (Smooth, Fluent, Logical)
Movements fit together logically. The sequence has a sense of unity and coherence from start to finish. Movements are connected with transitions in which one movement leads to the next without the performer having to take extra steps. Transitions between skills or body actions are planned, fluent, and smooth. Sections of the sequence seem to follow each other logically. In group work, when the formation changes, no one takes any extra steps. One formation leads to the next.
Originality
Level 1: Immature (Plain)
Shapes are plain and mostly symmetrical. The same shape is used several times. Only a few body actions are used. Combinations are ordinary and repeated. Starting and ending positions are most often on the children's feet in ordinary positions.
Level 2: Intermediate (Varied)
Shapes have variety. Arms and legs are in different shapes and positions. Some shapes are asymmetrical. A variety of body actions are used. Body actions are combined in a variety of ways. Combinations start and end in a variety of shapes and positions.
Level 3: Mature (Origina)l
Shapes and movements are different and interesting. There are many asymmetrical shapes. Symmetrical shapes, if present, are only used to make a statement. A variety of body actions and combinations is used and some combinations are unusual. Starting and ending shapes are interesting and different. Something in the sequence is unusual.
Expressing an Idea
Level 1: Immature (Imitates)
The individual or group imitates or pantomimes and presents a surface-level caricature.
Level 2: Intermediate (Represents)
The sequence expresses and represents the idea. Shapes and movements elaborate on the topic and are abstracted.
Level 3: Mature (Represents Powerfully)
The sequence effectively communicates a powerful statement about the idea or emotion of the dance. It captures the essence of the idea and is personally meaningful to performers. The meaning is clear to observers.
Contrasts and Aesthetic Highlights
Level 1: Immature (Repetitive)
The sequence has no contrasts. There is sameness from start to finish. There are some good ideas, but they are repeated over and over. The sequence is predictable and seems to go on and on. If one person does a series of movements, then everyone else in the group does the same series in turn. If a movement is done to the left, it is then repeated to the right. The rhythm and speed are steady with no changes.

(continues)

Table 25.2 Observing and Identifying Performance Levels of Elements of Sequence Choreography in Gymnastics and Dance (*continued*)

Level 2: Intermediate (Contrasts/Interesting)
The sequence has a clear contrast in one of the following aspects: speed, level, shape, force, pathway, movement and stillness, direction, and relationship. The sequence is interesting to watch. Repetition is used only to make a statement.
Level 3: Mature (Aesthetic Highlights)
The sequence has several contrasts in speed, level, shape, force, pathway, movement and stillness, direction, and/or relationship. The sequence has clear aesthetic highlights that capture the observers' attention. It has a visual impact and/or emotional impact on the performer and/or observers.
Relationship of Body Parts to Shapes: Line, Focus, and Clarity
Level 1: Immature (Infrequent Clarity and Little Attention to Line and Focus)
Shapes and movements are nondescript and vague with no identifiable lines or focus. Body parts do not relate to other body parts; in group work, the shapes of group members do not relate. Feet and toes are flexed or knees are bent, preventing a straight line in the legs. Body parts stick out of the intended line.
Level 2: Intermediate (Moderately Clear, Some Attention to Line and Focus)
Shapes are moderately clear, and the positions of many body parts are planned and relate to one another, forming lines that are easily recognized. During group sequences, the shapes of most individuals relate to one another and indicate a group focus.
Level 3: Mature (Clarity and Intentional Lines and Focus)
In shapes and movements, the positions of all body parts are intentional and precise, with all body parts related to the intended shape. Shapes and body parts form lines or indicate a group's focus that direct the observers' attention. All body parts contribute to the lines intended by the performers. All individuals contribute to the group shape, line, and focus.

Phase 1: Exploring and Experimenting

In phase 1, children explore, invent, discover, and experiment with movements associated with the theme of the sequence. This phase almost always begins during the content development section of the lesson as the teacher gives exploration tasks. We tell children this phase is for "body brainstorming." *Body brainstorming* means trying to generate (while moving) as many ideas as possible (a storm of ideas) without criticizing these ideas. The goal is to generate the following (Schlichter, 1986):

- Many ideas
- Varied ideas
- Some unusual and original ideas
- Elaborations on these ideas

Once you assign the sequence task, children experiment with the best ideas they have generated during exploration tasks by adapting those ideas to the requirements you have set for the sequence. Teachers can help children in phase 1 by asking questions, providing feedback, or making suggestions.

Sample Questions and Feedback

- Have you found some unusual or original ideas?
- You don't have to keep an idea that just doesn't work.
- I can see that you have several rolls in a curled shape. Can you think of other shapes you might use?
- The shape looks good, but it would be even better if you put your left arm more in line with your right leg like this.

You might wonder if you should help children design sequences. In fact, children benefit from teacher guidance in all three phases. Providing guidance, critiquing their work, and providing feedback will not stifle their creativity. Rather, by doing so, you will help children discover their own preferences, better understand the choreography process and elements, and design sequences that they find aesthetically pleasing.

> TEACHING TIP
>
> **Brainstorming**
>
> Beginners sometimes try to sit and think about movement ideas. Teachers need to encourage them to explore while moving. A phrase that can help them is "Think while you move, and move while you think."

Phase 2: Selecting and Arranging Ideas

When children begin phase 2, they use critical thinking skills to evaluate the quality of their ideas. Suggest that they select those movements they think are most original. If possible, they should include at least one unusual shape or movement. A second suggestion is to include their favorite movements and those they enjoy performing the most.

Next, children need to arrange the selected movements in order and add transitions. In gymnastics, one way to break this process down is to have children experiment with different ways to transition into and out of skills and to experiment with arranging the skills in different orders. The order of skills needs to allow for the easiest and best transitions. For example, the transition out of some skills, such as a backbend, is limited and difficult. Children can put these skills at the end of the sequence.

Children also need to think critically about the sequence as a whole and determine whether it includes contrasts and at

SAFETY AND LIABILITY 25.1

Increasing Safety and Decreasing Risk of Liability: Guidelines Relevant to Content in this Chapter

In this box, we discuss specific guidelines built on information discussed throughout this text on professional standards of practice, negligence, and liability. The goals of these guidelines are to increase children's safety and decrease teachers' risk of negligence and liability.

- In gymnastics and dance, sequences are often used for grading. Consequently, there is the potential for coercion from group members, partners, and from the individual to perform skills that are too difficult and not safe. Do not include the difficulty of the skills in a sequence as a criterion for grading. Teach students that their group or partner sequence must be within the developmental capabilities of all group members and that they are responsible for considering their peers' skill capabilities when they design a gymnastics or dance sequence to ensure the sequence is safe for everyone.
- Teach children to select for their sequences only those skills that they can perform well and are within their developmental capabilities.
- Performing with movement quality and appropriate performance techniques are two of the most important ways to increase safe participation. A reasonably prudent teacher focuses on movement quality throughout every lesson, teaches students the performance techniques that contribute to movement quality, and explicitly and repeatedly teaches students about movement quality. The elements of movement quality all contribute to safety. For example, to land safely, children must land lightly with control over their body parts and over the flow of movement, or they might fall or be injured. Using appropriate speed and force contributes to children's control over their movement. Children can and do generate more force and speed than they can control safely, and they must be taught to use only as much force and speed as is safe for them. Appropriate amounts of tension also contribute to control over the movement and body and can help to reduce injuries. Appropriate body alignment, especially when performing repetitious fitness exercises, is important for preventing injuries. Finally, a stretched and engaged core also contribute to control over the body and, in turn, safety.

least one aesthetic highlight. If not, they can add movements, rearrange skills, or change the shape, level, speed, force, or direction of one of their skills. As in phase 1, offer children guidance and feedback to help them analyze how their arrangements are working and identify choreography qualities they need to add or improve.

Sample Questions and Feedback

- You seem to be having problems moving from the balance to the steplike action without taking extra steps. How do you think you can solve that problem?
- The leap in the middle of your sequence is very dramatic and forceful—it looks like a highlight of your sequence.
- You might feel like you are doing one part fast and one part slow, but it looks like the same speed to me. When and how can you change your speed so I can see the difference?
- Have you included several changes in level?

Phase 3: Refining and Practicing

Phase 3, in which children refine and practice their sequences, is critical. Children need many opportunities to practice so they will be able to master the skills and perform the sequence with confidence and competence. To do so, children need to practice to the stage of automaticity—the point at which they do not have to think consciously about which movement comes next and at which they feel confident about the quality of their performance (see **Figure 25.8**).

Aesthetic Performance Experiences

Refining and practicing sequences is also important to enable children to have aesthetic experiences. If children perfect their sequence to the point at which they can perform it with ease and confidence and are physically, cognitively, and affectively engrossed in their performance, they can experience the joy and personal meaning of artistic, athletic performances—a joy well known to athletes (see **Figure 25.9**). Aesthetic experiences also can contribute to National Standard 5. It seems reasonable to assume that if we want children to engage in lifelong physical activities, we need to provide experiences that are meaningful, joyful, self-expressive, and engaging at the elementary level.

Theory in Practice: Constructivism Metaphors, Stories, and Images

Some children will change a sequence every time they perform it by doing different skills or changing the order. They need to understand that once they determine the final sequence and are ready for assessment or sharing with peers, the skills should not change. Telling the following story can help:

You go to a library and check out *Goldilocks and the Three Bears*. When you read it, you discover that Goldilocks runs away from the bears at the end of the book. A couple of weeks later you think, "That was a good book. I will check it out again." This time when you read it, will Goldilocks go on a bike ride with the three bears? If you check it out again a couple of weeks later, will she go swimming with the bears this time? If that did happen, then the story would have to have different titles, like *Goldilocks and the Bears Go Swimming*. We want your sequence to be like a book that does not change every time you go to the library.

Figure 25.8 Part of a well-practiced sequence

Showing and Observing Sequence Performances

Both informal and formal sequences are possible (Allison & Barrett, 2000). Children do not practice informal sequences to the extent that they practice formal sequences, nor are informal sequences shared with peers. In contrast, children practice formal sequences until they are ready to share their work with classmates.

Teachers need to decide when to offer children opportunities to show their sequences to their classmates. Performing sequences in front of their peers takes time, of course, so teachers need to weigh the benefits of showing their work against the time children could be engaged in physical activity. This balancing act is especially problematic for teachers who see their classes only one or two days per week. To save time, organizational patterns we have used frequently are (1) to have children show their sequences to a partner or small groups with many sequences performed at once; and (2) to divide the class in half or thirds and have multiple groups perform simultaneously.

Figure 25.9 Performing with confidence and engagement

Letting Children Decide Whether to Show Sequences

We believe it is essential that children be permitted to decide without penalty whether they will show their sequence to classmates. You can't possibly know if there are serious, personal reasons why one child on a particular day does not feel comfortable performing. Most of the time, most children want to share what they have created and worked hard to master.

Sometimes, one child within a group does not want to show her or his work to classmates, but the rest of the group does. To help prevent this problem, we suggest having children tell you that they will not want to show their sequence before partners and group assignments are finalized. This practice enables you to make other group assignments or help the children design a sequence in which the person who does not want to show does not have an integral part. Another solution is to allow children to show their sequence with an invisible partner.

Having a Good Seat in the House and Audience Behavior

Before showing sequences, "set the stage" so every child has an unobstructed view of the children performing. We begin by asking children to review appropriate audience behavior. Children readily identify behaviors that are inappropriate and hurtful. These pre-show discussions are critical because it can be devastating to children if other children laugh or tease them about their performance. We insist children show respect by not laughing, pointing, or talking during the performance and by clapping and offering compliments to their classmates after the performance. Public compliments can be very important to children, especially if their classroom teachers do not praise their work in other subject areas.

Sample Rules for Audience Behavior

- Pay attention.
- Be respectful—no laughing or talking.
- Clap.
- Give compliments.

Guidelines for Observing

Before the performance starts, the most frequent guideline we set is for observers to find something they like in another child's sequence. We tell children to try to identify the aesthetic

Kids Like Compliments

One day when one of us was teaching, there wasn't enough time for compliments after the performance. After class, one of the students was visibly upset and said, "Where were our compliments today? That's what I like best about showing."

highlights—that is, moments they think are special, particularly interesting, or exceptional, or that touch them emotionally in some way.

We limit discussions after performance to compliments by saying, "Which compliments can you give to these performers?" We find that younger children readily notice aesthetic highlights but often express their compliments in general terms by saying, "I liked it," "I liked the whole thing," or "They looked good." To help children be specific, you can ask, "What specifically did you like about the sequence?" Older children with more developed language skills are more able to be specific in what they liked and why.

You can help children improve their aesthetic perception by guiding their attention. For example, you might give the children the following instructions:

- Be ready to discuss what you felt when you watched the performance.
- Be ready to discuss what the sequence made you think about.
- See if you can identify contrasts in level or speed during the sequence.
- Be ready to talk about the different shapes you saw.
- Watch and be ready to tell us which were the best transitions and why they were good.
- Be ready to talk about the most interesting and unusual ideas you observed.
- Did the sequence include the three elements in the task: beginning shape, matching action, and ending shape?
- Be ready to talk about your emotional response to the sequence.

(A)

(B)

Figure 25.10 (A) Being tight (B) Tucked tight

(A) © Jones & Bartlett Learning. Photographed by Christine Myaskovsky. (B) Courtesy of John Dolly

Movement Quality and Performance Quality in Gymnastics and Dance

Movement quality and performance quality are critical in gymnastics, dance, and fitness exercises. Simply performing the skill is not enough—the quality of the movement matters. In this section, we discuss nine general characteristics of movement quality and performance quality in educational gymnastics and dance that apply across skills and themes. In the content chapters, we present specific performance techniques for skills.

Appropriate Amounts of Tension

Gymnastics: Tighten Up!

Gymnasts maintain a certain amount of muscular tension (isometric contractions) at all times, which they create through moderate isometric contractions of the muscles. We simply refer to this state as "being tight." It is especially important to stay tight through the legs, abdomen, and buttocks (see **Figure 25.10**).

It takes a considerable amount of experience before children maintain tension consistently and automatically. Most of the time, you need to remind children to stay tight.

Sample Performance Cues

- Stay tight.
- Tighten up.
- Squeeze your legs together.

Dance: Light, Anti-gravity Exertion

Dancers also maintain tension at all times through isometric muscle contractions. This tension, which is called *light, anti-gravity exertion* (Preston-Dunlop, 1980), contributes to kinesthetic awareness (see **Figure 25.11**). To feel this tension, start with no tension in your arm muscles. Then contract your muscles just enough to be able to lift your arms, feel light tension, and hold them still while maintaining an awareness of the feeling in your muscles.

Sample Performance Techniques

- Feel tension in your muscles.
- Make your muscles feel alive.
- Tighten your muscles a little so you are holding still and can feel every muscle.

Immature Patterns

- Loose body parts
- Relaxed throughout the entire body

Appropriate Body Alignment: Legs Straight, Toes Pointed

In gymnastics, fitness, and dance, children learn to perform skills with appropriate alignment of body parts. Most often, this means teaching them to

- Keep their legs straight (but not hyperextended) or tuck the legs tight
- Point the toes

(A)

(B)

Figure 25.11 (A) Showing stronger tension (B) Showing light, anti-gravity tension

(A)

(B)

Figure 25.12 (A) Inappropriate alignment in a scale (B) Appropriate alignment in a scale

- Keep the head in line with the spine
- Keep the knees aligned with the foot (turned in or out to the exact same degree) when the knees are bent

Partially flexed feet and bent knees (when the legs should make a straight line) are the most common immature patterns for children. Another immature pattern is sticking the buttocks out when children are trying to make a straight line between their leg and torso—for example, when balancing on one leg in a scale (see **Figure 25.12**).

It takes many years of practice before children will remember to point their feet and keep their legs straight automatically (see **Figure 25.13**). Teachers need to use the performance cues "Point your feet" and "Legs straight" frequently throughout the elementary school years. Using introductory activities that focus on the use of the feet and have children intentionally pointing and flexing their feet can be helpful.

Sample Learning Experiences

- Pretend your feet are glued to the floor, and then "peel" your foot off the floor slowly, starting from the heel to the arch to the ball, and ending with the tip of your toes, letting your toes come off the floor last. Then, reverse the process—toe, ball, arch, and heel.
- Walk toe–heel about the gym using the Native American dance step "toe–heel," pretending you are traveling silently through the forest, trying not to be heard by forest creatures.
- Bounce up and down like a pogo stick, working on extending your ankles fully and landing lightly ball–heel.
- Let's play a game like "Simon Says." Sit with your legs straight, and I will call out one of four possibilities: "Flex both feet," "Point both feet," "Point right and flex left," or "Flex right and point left," mixing up the order. [Make the game more difficult by having the children look up and not watch their feet.]

(A)

(B)

Figure 25.13 (A) Inappropriate alignment in a leap
(B) Appropriate alignment in a leap

Immature Patterns

- Ankles flexed
- Knees bent
- Hips stick up and out of the line from the leg to the shoulders
- Head down or not in alignment with the spine
- Movements do not engage full range of motion (curled positions are open, not tightly tucked; in straddles and splits, the legs are not in a line parallel to the ground)

Landing Lightly with Control Over Body Parts and Flow of Movement

Skillful landings are light, with control over the body and the flow of movement that comes from flight or transferring weight. When landing skillfully, the child must absorb the force by bending the ankles, knees, and hip joints, maintaining tension in the muscles and resisting gravity. The flow of movement is controlled and stopped. In a skillful landing, the body is balanced over the feet. The arms don't wave, the torso doesn't bend, and the feet don't jump to different locations; in other words, body parts are under control.

For children, we typically translate controlling the flow of the movement, which is Laban's terminology, as controlling their bodies and body parts. Control is important for safety. In skills such as rolls, children need to control their movement as they transfer their weight onto the floor softly and silently, rather than crashing hard and slapping body parts on the mat, making thumping sounds.

Two types of landing are used in educational gymnastics. One type of landing is stable, in which the child lands, bends her or his knees, and stands still. This is called a *stick* in gymnastics, meaning the feet are stuck to the mat. The second type consists of light, resilient, spring-like landings, which are most common in fitness. In a resilient landing, the child should land lightly with spring-like, resilient legs and, in some gymnastics skills, such as a round-off, immediately pop off the floor again into a jump or other skill (see **Figure 25.14**). Locomotor steps, such as skipping and galloping, and skills such as round-offs have resilient landings.

Immature Patterns

- Landings are flat-footed and heavy.
- Knees and hips are not bent to absorb force; landings are stiff-legged.
- There is little or no resiliency; feet, ankles, and knees don't extend quickly.
- Body weight is allowed to sag and drop with heaviness; the body lands with little control most often because there is little tension in the muscles to absorb the force of the body from flight.
- Many body parts are out of control and flopping all over the place.

Sample Performance Techniques

- Land lightly.
- Land softly and gently.
- Pop or spring away.

Figure 25.14 Second-graders learning resilient jumps

Courtesy of John Dolly

- Absorb the force.
- Bend your knees.

Stretched or Elongated Torso

In gymnastics, dance, and fitness exercises, children need to **elongate the spine**, creating as much space as possible between each vertebra (see **Figure 25.15**). To do so, the child stretches his or her head high as if he or she is a puppet with a string running up the spine through the top of the head lifting and stretching the child tall. The ribs are separated from the hips (not sagging), the shoulders are down (not shrugged up near the ears), and the chest is up (not sunken in). The buttocks and abdominal muscles are tight, and the pelvis is tilted back, meaning there is less arch in the lumbar (lower-back) region. Children should maintain an elongated back throughout all movements, even when arching or curling the back.

Elongating the spinal column is important not only in gymnastics and dance, but also in fitness exercises and for healthy, everyday posture. You might remember a parent, guardian, or other adult saying, "Stop slouching; stand up straight." In the armed forces, recruits learn early to stand at attention with their shoulders down and back, back stretched, and head up. Proper alignment of the spine and muscle strength in the core areas of the body (i.e., the torso) to support the spine are important for a healthy back.

Immature Patterns

- The body is slouched, the back sags, and the chest is sunken in.
- The shoulders are hunched forward or shrugged.
- The head is out of alignment with the spine.

Sample Performance Techniques

- Stretch through your spine.
- Pretend you are a puppet, and there is a string coming from the top of your head pulling you toward the ceiling.
- Tighten your tummy, and squeeze your gluteus muscles (i.e., your bottom).
- Keep your shoulders down and back.

Figure 25.15 Stretched and tight

Courtesy of John Dolly

Appropriate Speed and Force

In dance and gymnastics, tasks sometimes require children to move with or express strong or light force and tension at fast or slow speeds. Children typically move with force somewhere in the middle of the continuum from light to strong and at a medium or fast speed. You will need to help children learn to move at the ends of the light–strong continuum and the slow–fast continuum. In addition, children can and do generate more speed and force than they can control—for example, springing too high into a roll or running too fast to stop before they bump into a classmate. We typically tell children to go only as fast as they can while still maintaining perfect control; in other words, they should be able to stop or change direction safely.

Sample Performance Techniques

- Make the light movements as light as a feather.
- Make the fast movements fast.
- Make the slow movements slow.
- Show strong tension throughout your entire body.
- Show strong force in your jump.

Immature Patterns

- Strong and fast movements are performed at medium speeds and force.
- Slow and gentle movements are performed at medium speeds and force.
- Traveling movements are too fast for the child to easily control.

Engaging the Core

Engaging the core means that the muscles in the torso (the rectangular area from your shoulders to your hips) are part of the action (see **Figure 26.16**). *Moving from the core* means that any action of the arms, head, and legs originates from the core muscles. Beginners, especially in dance, tend to move just their arms and legs without engaging their core. For example, a beginner performing a strong jabbing movement will punch with strong force in the arm, but the tummy and hips will be loose, and there will be little or no force generated from the hips and legs. This also is true for beginners performing game skills—for example, throwing using the arms with little coordination with the torso and legs. Working on core strength and engagement is important in many health-related fitness activities and is linked to preventing back pain.

> TEACHING TIP
>
> **Contrast: Control and No Control**
>
> One way we teach children about control is by making a contrast: We tell them that they can determine whether they have control or whether gravity has control by the sounds that their body parts make. For example, "Hold your arms out to the side and let them drop. When the arms hit your sides, they make a noise. This is the sound of gravity controlling your movement. Now hold your hands out, and, as fast as you can, bring your arms to your sides without making a sound: This is you controlling your movement."

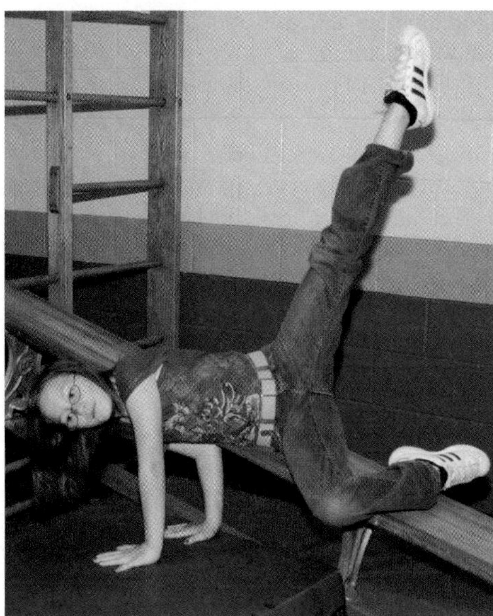

Figure 25.16 Engaging the core

Pencil Legs

Keeping the legs straight with feet and toes pointed is a critical performance technique for almost all gymnastics and dance skills. One way we teach this technique is by using a metaphor as a performance cue. We say, "Your legs and feet should be straight and end in a point, just like a pencil. When I give the performance technique 'Pencil legs' or 'Sharpen your pencils,' you know that I am reminding you to point your feet and toes or keep your legs straight."

Immature Patterns

- Only part of the body does the movement.
- Gestures are done with the arms or legs only.
- The torso is not coordinated with the movements of the arms and legs.

Performance Quality

In addition to the elements of movement quality, a quality performance of a sequence includes three other elements: (1) accuracy in rhythm and tempo; (2) concentration and engagement, and (3) being well practiced until movements can be repeated accurately.

Accuracy in Rhythm and Tempo

A requirement of a quality performance, especially when moving to music, is accuracy in the rhythm and tempo. When the rhythm and tempo are accurate, the entire group moves together to the beat of the music, and the movements are coordinated rhythmically.

Learning to move to the rhythm and tempo of music takes practice. Children who have had multiple experiences listening and dancing to music during their preschool years will be better able to move accurately to the beat of the music. Children with less experience will need more practice.

Some children (and even some teachers) have problems moving to the beat of the music. What is important to remember is that moving to the beat of the music is a learned skill that you can improve with practice. When helping children learn to move to the beat, select simple music with a strong, steady underlying beat that matches the melody. Beginners often move in time with the singers or the melody. If the music is more complex, and the underlying beat and rhythm of the melody differ, beginners can sometimes have problems. Have children practice clapping, walking, marching, or doing simple arm actions to the beat of this music—first following the teacher and then on their own.

Immature Patterns

- Individuals and groups have problems staying on the beat of the music.
- Individuals and groups move in time with the melody, not the underlying beat.
- Group members do not coordinate the rhythm of their movements.

Concentration and Engagement

Another characteristic of a quality performance is the concentration and engagement of the performers. To perform well, children must concentrate and focus their attention on their movements. In a good performance, children fully engage physically, cognitively, and affectively in the performance (Stinson, 1982). This feeling of total engagement is a meaningful aesthetic experience, a valuable outcome of the performing arts, and one reason the performing arts have had universal appeal historically and across cultures.

Immature Patterns

- Does not appear to be engaged
- Seems to be just going through the motions
- Concentration drifts

Sequences Are Well Practiced Until Movements Can Be Repeated Accurately

After children design a sequence, one of their final tasks is to practice the sequence until they can reproduce the movements accurately each time they perform. Younger children can learn short sequences, whereas older children can manage much longer sequences that take several lessons to design and practice until the sequence can be repeated accurately.

By "accurately," we mean the positions of all body parts, relationships among group members, formations, shapes, and timing are exactly the same every time the sequence is performed. To achieve this level of accuracy takes considerable practice, persistence, concentration, and cooperative group work. The amount of practice is worth the time because in their quest to make each performance identical, children improve their movement quality, clarity of shapes, and body alignment, such as pointing toes and keeping legs straight. In addition, practicing a sequence until it is the best performance of which the children are capable also supports increased feelings of engagement, confidence, enjoyment, and a sense of pride. Aspects of the affective domain such as these are the focus of National Standard 5.

Immature Patterns

- The sequence is different every time it is performed.
- The children make up the elements of the sequence during the performance.
- Children talk to and look at one another for information about what comes next.
- Body positions and shapes change with each performance.

In **Table 25.3**, we summarize what you will see as children's movement quality develops and improves. To assist you in your observations, we break development down into three performance levels.

Table 25.3 Observing and Identifying Performance Levels of Movement Quality and Performance Quality

Movement Quality
Appropriate Amounts of Tension
Level 1: Immature
The body is consistently loose.
Level 2: Intermediate
The body is sometimes tight. Many body parts are tight.
Level 3: Mature
The body is always tight. All body parts have the appropriate amount of tension.
Appropriate Body Alignment
Level 1: Immature
Toes are mostly flexed, and knees often bent. In many movements, the body parts are inappropriately aligned. Movements do not reach their full range of motion. Curled positions are open. The child does not appear to be kinesthetically aware of the position of many body parts.
Level 2: Intermediate
Toes are mostly pointed; legs are mostly straight and aligned appropriately. Body alignment is appropriate most of the time. Movements come close to their full range of motion. The child appears to be kinesthetically aware of the position of body parts most of the time.
Level 3: Mature
Feet and toes are pointed, and legs straight. Body parts are aligned appropriately. The child is aware of the position of body parts. Movements are done to their fullest range of motion. Splits and straddles are straight, and tucks are in a tight ball.
Landing Lightly with Control Over Body Parts and Flow of Movement
Level 1: Immature
Jumps and leaps are low, and landings heavy and often flat-footed. Resilient landings are low with little extension of the ankles. The child may fall because many body parts were out of control. When trying to land in place (i.e., stick), the child has some control over the flow of movement but takes several steps or jumps before the body is under control.
Level 2: Intermediate
Jumps and leaps are at a medium height, and landings are strong or with too much force (not heavy and loose but also not light and resilient). When trying to stick a landing, the child tries hard but must take several jumps or steps to land, and the arms and trunk move in various ways to help the child balance over the landing place.
Level 3: Mature
Jumps and leaps are high, and landings are light, with body parts under control. When trying to land in place, the child controls the flow of movement and remains still, with the feet remaining exactly where they landed; on occasion, the child takes one step or small jump on the landing. There are no extraneous movements of the arms and trunk to help the child balance over the landing place. Resilient landings pop off the floor.
Stretched and Elongated Torso
Level 1: Immature
The body is slouched, the back sags, the chest is sunken in, and the shoulders are hunched forward or shrugged.
Level 2: Intermediate
Sometimes, or during certain movements, the torso is stretched and the shoulders are down and back, with the chest up. The head is held high sometimes.
Level 3: Mature
The body is stretched. The head is held high, the shoulders are down, the ribs are separated from the hips, and the chest is up.
Appropriate Speed and Force
Level 1: Immature
Strong and fast movements are performed at medium speeds and force. Slow and gentle movements are performed at medium speeds and force. Traveling movements are too fast for the child to easily control.
Level 2: Intermediate
There is a clear difference in speed between slow and fast movements and between strong and gentle movements. Traveling speed is most often within the children's ability to control.
Level 3: Mature
Strong and fast movements are strong and fast. Slow movements are slow. Gentle movements are soft. Traveling speed is always within the child's ability to control.
Engages the Core
Level 1: Immature
Core muscles are loose. Only the extremities do the movement, with little or no core involvement. Gestures are done with the arms or legs only. The torso is not coordinated with the movements of the arms or legs.

Table 25.3 Observing and Identifying Performance Levels of Movement Quality and Performance Quality (*continued*)

Level 2: Intermediate

Core muscles have tension. The core muscles are often engaged and part of the movement. Most of the time, the whole body is engaged in a coordinated way.

Level 3: Mature

Movements are initiated from the core. Core muscles are tight. The whole body is engaged in a coordinated way.

Performance Quality

Rhythm and Tempo

Level 1: Immature

Individuals and the group have problems staying on the beat of the music. The group members do not coordinate the rhythm of their movements to each other or to the music.

Level 2: Intermediate

In group sequences, most individuals move in time with the beat of the music or in time with each other.

Level 3: Mature

In group sequences, the entire group moves together to the beat of the music, and the movements are coordinated rhythmically.

Concentration and Engagement

Level 1: Immature

The child or group does not appear to be engaged and seems to be just going through the motions. Concentration is evident some of the time but seems to drift.

Level 2: Intermediate

The child or group concentrates and is engaged during the performance.

Level 3: Mature

The child or group appears totally engaged throughout the performance. The performance appears effortless. The group members appear to believe in their sequence.

Movements Are Clear and Can Be Repeated Accurately

Level 1: Immature

The shapes of the body and/or body parts are vague and vary; thus, the sequence is different every time it is performed. Sometimes the child makes the sequence up during the performance. In group sequences, children talk to and look at one another for information about what to do next. Sometimes they make things up as they go along. The group shapes and shapes of group members are hard to determine and vary; thus, the sequence is difficult to repeat accurately. Group members do not coordinate the timing or shape of their movements. The group loses their formations. The sequence needs much more practice.

Level 2: Intermediate

Some sections of the sequence can be repeated, but other sections change every time the child or group performs. Sequence needs more practice, and the child or group needs to work on planning and making precise shapes and formations that they can repeat accurately. In group sequences, formations get a little sloppy at times but can be regained.

Level 3: Mature

The sequence is well practiced. The child or group can repeat the sequence with reasonable accuracy and precision. Each time the sequence is performed, body shapes, actions, and formations are the same. In group sequences, the entire group's movements are coordinated precisely.

Grade-Level Learning Outcomes for Sequences

We end this chapter by presenting what we believe are essential learning outcomes for sequences by grade level. Table 25.4 lists our suggestions and the most important element of choreography, movement quality, or performance quality connected to the grade-level outcome to assess. We also list potential CCSS you can address in the unit.

Experienced Teachers Talk

Teaching Children How to Practice a Sequence

A developmental characteristic of young children is that they approach the task of memorizing by repeating each part over and over, but they do not practice the parts in a sequence. For example, if you tell a young child to practice a sequence with a balance, roll, and jump repeated three times, he or she will practice the balance three times, then the roll three times, and then the jump three times. Thus, while children do practice the movements, they do not memorize the sequence of movements and transitions. You need to help young children learn how to memorize and practice sequences effectively.

I learned about this developmental pattern as a graduate student while studying development. Unfortunately, I wish I had known this earlier in my career when I was coaching gymnastics and yelled across the gym at a second-grader, "Laurie, I told you to practice your floor routine." The child yelled back (rightly so), looking at me with disgust, "I am." She was practicing each skill, one at a time. I did not recognize this behavior as a developmental pattern, and I had not taught her how to practice.

Table 25.4 Suggested Grade-Level Learning Outcomes for Sequences and Potential Connections to CCSS

Grade-Level Sequence	Element of Choreography, Movement, or Performance Quality and Potential CCSS
Kindergarten	
In dance, create a sequence of two locomotor skills and/or two of the following nonlocomotor movements (stretch, curl, twist) in a repeated pattern with fluid transitions. You can also include one of the following movement concepts: speed, direction, or level. For example, Two locomotor skills • Gallop, leap, gallop, leap Two nonlocomotor movements • Twist, curl, twist, curl Two locomotor skills at different speeds • Walk slowly, slide quickly, walk slowly, slide quickly Two locomotor skills in different directions • Jump forward, walk backward, jump forward, walk backward Two nonlocomotor movements at different levels • Stretch high, twist low, stretch high, twist low	***Element of Choreography*** Fluid transitions ***CCSS (Modified to Be Task Specific)*** With prompting and support, identify the locomotor skills, nonlocomotor movements, and movement concepts in your sequence.
Grade 1	
In both gymnastics and dance, create and perform a sequence with beginning, middle, and ending shapes.	***Element of Choreography to Assess*** Sequences have a beginning, middle, and end. ***CCSS (Modified to Be Task Specific)*** Compare and contrast the locomotor and nonlocomotor skills and movement concepts in your sequence with a peer's sequence.
Grade 2	
In both gymnastics and dance, create a sequence with varied movements and at least one original, unusual, or especially interesting movement.	***Element of Choreography to Assess*** Originality ***CCSS (Modified to Be Task Specific)*** Describe key ideas or details from information presented visually: Observe a peer's sequence, and describe the key movements or shapes that are original, unusual, or especially interesting.
Grade 3	
In gymnastics, create and perform a sequence in which all parts fit together logically with fluid transitions.	***Element of Choreography to Assess*** All parts fit together logically with fluid transitions. ***CCSS (Modified to Be Task Specific)*** Observe a peer's sequence, and in a supportive way, discuss with appropriate facts and relevant descriptive details the extent to which his or her transitions were fluid.
Create and perform a dance sequence expressing an idea. Then present and discuss the meanings of the sequence and the specific ways you expressed your idea.	***Element of Choreography to Assess*** Expressing an idea ***CCSS (Modified to Be Task Specific)*** Report on the meaning of and how you expressed your ideas in your dance sequence with appropriate facts and relevant descriptive details.
Grade 4	
In dance, with a small group, design a folk dance representing a country or historical time period you have been studying in your classroom. Design fluid transitions between each section. In gymnastics, create and perform a partner sequence matching, contrasting, and complementing shapes and actions.	***Elements of Choreography to Assess*** Expressing an idea All parts fit together logically with fluid transitions. ***CCSS (Modified to Be Task Specific)*** Observe and discuss in a supportive way another group's folk dance. Discuss how they represented their country or historical time period using relevant, descriptive details.

Table 25.4 Suggested Grade-Level Learning Outcomes for Sequences and Potential Connections to CCSS (*continued*)

	Element of Movement Quality to Assess Relationship of body parts to shape: line and clarity ***CCSS (Modified to Be Task Specific)*** Observe another pair's sequence, and compare and contrast the key movements and shapes you used to demonstrate matching, contrasting, and complementing.
Grade 5	
Design and perform a small-group sequence in gymnastics on cannon and unison and in dance on group shapes or group relationships, with each group member contributing at least one idea and everyone building on each other's ideas. Have at least five formations or group shapes, and design fluid transitions between each section of the sequence.	***Elements of Choreography and Performance Quality to Assess*** All parts fit together logically with fluid transitions. Interest and aesthetic highlights Sequence is well practiced until movements can be repeated accurately. Rhythm of cannon and unison ***CCSS (Modified to Be Task Specific)*** Engage effectively in a collaborative discussion, building on others' ideas and expressing your own ideas clearly.
In gymnastics or dance, design and perform a partner or small-group sequence that shows contrast, an aesthetic highlight, and attention to line and focus.	***Elements of Choreography to Assess*** Contrast and aesthetic highlights Relationship of body parts to shape: line, focus, and clarity ***CCSS (Modified to Be Task Specific)*** Observe another pair's sequence. Report on their use of contrast and aesthetic highlights using appropriate facts and relevant descriptive details to support your opinion.

CCSS were modified by the authors to include physical education vocabulary and be task specific. These standards were adapted from the Common Core State Standards Initiative. (2010. *Common core state standards for English language arts and literacy in history/social studies, science, and technical subjects.* Retrieved from www.corestandards.org.

Summary

Basic elements of sequence choreography include the following: (1) Sequences have a beginning, middle, and end; (2) all parts fit together logically with fluid transitions; (3) originality; (4) the expression of ideas; (5) contrast and aesthetic highlights; and (6) relationships of body parts, including line, focus, and clarity. The three phases of designing sequences are (1) exploring and experimenting; (2) selecting and arranging; and (3) refining and practicing.

Movement quality and performance quality include (1) appropriate amounts of tension; (2) appropriate body alignment; (3) landing lightly with control over body parts and flow of movement; (4) a stretched or elongated torso; (5) appropriate speed and force; (6) engagement of the core; (7) rhythm and tempo; (8) concentration and engagement; and (9) the sequence being well practiced until movements can be repeated accurately.

Review Questions

1. (a) Discuss immature and mature characteristics of transitions, originality, expressing ideas, and line. (b) Describe how you can help a beginner improve transitions in gymnastics.
2. What is an aesthetic highlight?
3. How can teachers guide children in each of the three phases of the choreographic process? List two questions or feedback statements appropriate for each phase.
4. Describe what it means to have the appropriate amount of tension in gymnastics and in dance.
5. What does it mean to "stick" a landing? Give an example of a resilient landing.
6. Describe what you can say to a class of children to help them understand how to elongate their backs. (Do not use any examples from the text.)
7. Describe three characteristics of quality performances.

References

Allison, P. C., & Barrett, K. R. (2000). *Constructing children's physical education experiences: Understanding the content for teaching.* Boston: Allyn & Bacon.

Common Core State Standards Initiative. (2010). *Common core state standards for English language arts and literacy in history/social studies, science, and technical subjects.* Retrieved from www.corestandards.org

Doering, N. (2006). Using stories to teach flow in educational gymnastics. *Journal of Physical Education, Recreation and Dance, 77*(1), 38–43.

Nilges, L. M. (1999). Refining skill in educational gymnastics. *Journal of Physical Education, Recreation, and Dance, 70*(3), 43–48.

Pollatou, E., Savrami, K., & Karadimou, K. (2004). Introducing aesthetic features in gymnastics skills. *Teaching Elementary Physical Education, 15*(2), 36–37.

Preston-Dunlop, V. (1980). *A handbook for modern educational dance* (rev. ed.). Boston: Plays.

Purcell, T. (1994). *Teaching children dance: Becoming a master teacher.* Champaign, IL: Human Kinetics.

Rovegno, I. (1988). The art of gymnastics: Creating sequences. *Journal of Physical Education, Recreation, and Dance, 59*(2), 66–69.

Rovegno, I., & Bandhauer, D. (2000). Teaching elements of choreography. *Teaching Elementary Physical Education, 11*(5), 6–10, 34.

Schlichter, C. L. (1986). Talents unlimited: Applying the multiple talent approach in mainstream and gifted programs. In J. Renzulli (Ed.), *Systems and models for developing programs for the gifted and talented* (pp. 21–44). Mansfield Center, CT: Creative Learning Press.

Society of Health and Physical Educators (SHAPE). (2014). *National standards and grade-level outcomes for K–12 physical education.* Champaign, IL: Human Kinetics.

Stinson, S. (1982). Aesthetic experience in children's dance. *Journal of Physical Education, Recreation, and Dance, 53*(4), 72–74.

CHAPTER 26

Foundational Gymnastics Skills and Combinations

Courtesy of John Dolly

PRE-READING REFLECTION

Before reading this chapter, rate yourself on the following items. Then, after reading the chapter, and after you have taught educational gymnastics lessons in field experiences, rate yourself again.

1. How much experience have you had teaching gymnastics of any kind?

   1 2 3 4 5

   None — A lot
2. How confident are you about teaching educational gymnastics lessons to children?

   1 2 3 4 5

   Not confident at all — I am confident and ready to go!
3. How do you think children will respond to educational gymnastics lessons?

   1 2 3 4 5

   They will hate it. — They will love it.

OBJECTIVES

Students will learn:

1. In level 1 of educational gymnastics, we teach the foundational gymnastics skills: balancing, rolling, flight from feet, steplike actions, rocking, and dynamic balancing.
2. In level 2 of educational gymnastics, we teach children how to combine the foundational skills using smooth transitions and how to design short sequences that feature beginning and ending shapes.
3. In level 3 of educational gymnastics, we teach more difficult combinations and longer sequences.

KEY TERMS

Balance
Dynamic balancing
Weight bearing

CONNECTION TO STANDARDS

This chapter addresses all five national standards but focuses primarily on National Standards 1 and 2. Because we include partner work, the chapter also addresses the Common Core and other State Standards (CCSS) for speaking, listening, comprehension, and collaboration. In addition, we address standards for vocabulary acquisition.

PROGRESSION OF CONTENT

Level 1: Exploring and Varying Foundational Skills

Balancing

- Weight bearing (beginning balancing for grades K–1) and stillness
- Balancing on different body parts
- Balancing in different shapes

Rolling and Rocking

- Safety rolling using side rolls
- Side rolls varying the shape of the legs
- Rocking on different body parts and in different directions

Transferring Weight

- Traveling across a flat mat on hands and feet, belly facing up and down
- Taking weight on hands on a stacked mat, keeping the body low and curled, and transferring weight from feet to hands to feet
- Taking weight on hands on a stacked mat, keeping the body low and curled, sometimes springing off and landing on one foot and sometimes landing on two feet

Flight from Feet

- Learning the basic patterns of the jump, hop, leap, *assemblé*, and *sissone*

Dynamic Balancing

Jumping Rope

Level 2: Combining Skills with Smooth Transitions; Extending Movement Variety on Mats and Low Apparatus; Short Sequences

Rolling and Rocking

- Rolling on different body parts
- Rolling in different shapes, from different shapes, ending in different shapes
- Combining rolling and rocking
- Rocking and rolling at different speeds (slow to medium)
- Rocking on the back and coming to the feet
- Rolling in different directions

Flight from Feet

- Three ways to land: stick, pop up (resilient), safety roll
- Jumping and hopping for height and distance
- Jumping in different shapes (straight, wide, curled, twisted, angular, symmetrical, asymmetrical)
- Combining jumping and rolling/rocking
- Jumping on, over, and off low apparatus (e.g., stacked mats, aerobic box)

Rolling and Jumping

- Combining a low, straight jump and rolling, then jumping higher
- Combining jumping with rolling, varying the shape in the jump, roll/rock, or both
- Three ways to land from a jump

Balancing and Rolling

- Balancing on like and unlike body parts
- Balancing on upper body parts
- Balancing in inverted positions
- Combining balancing and rolling, starting the roll from the position of the balance
- Combining rolling and balancing by ending the roll in a balance
- Combining balancing on different body parts and in different shapes and rolling in different shapes and directions
- Balancing under and on apparatus
- Rolling on and off apparatus
- Combining balancing and rolling
    - At different levels on an apparatus
    - Moving to and from different levels on an apparatus

Transferring Weight (Steplike Actions)

- On hands and feet traveling around the stacked mats, keeping the body low and curled
- On hands and feet at low levels on and over stacked mats or single trapezoid sections
- On hands and feet on and over stacked mats, traveling on different pathways (straight, curved, zigzag)
- Steplike actions over and on stacked mats, springing legs to medium and high levels
- Steplike actions on, over, and off low apparatus

Designing Short Sequences

Level 3: More Difficult Combinations; Extending Movement Variety on Low, Medium, and High Apparatus; Longer Sequences

Transferring Weight (Steplike Actions)

- Steplike actions using different body parts (e.g., shins, forearms)
- Steplike actions taking the feet to a high level
- Steplike actions at different levels on an apparatus
- Steplike actions moving to and from different levels on an apparatus

Combining Steplike Actions and Rolling

- Combining steplike actions and rolling
- At different levels on an apparatus
- Moving to and from different levels on an apparatus

Combining Balances

- Overbalancing to a new balance
- Twisting, stretching, and curling to a new balance or other skill
- At different levels on an apparatus
- Moving to and from different levels on an apparatus

Combining Balances and Steplike Actions

- At different levels on an apparatus
- Moving to and from different levels on an apparatus

Flight from Feet

- Jumping onto, off of, and over apparatus of increasing heights
- Jumping while twisting and turning
- Several high resilient jumps in a row, making different shapes
- Combining flight with steplike actions
- Combining balances and flight from hands or feet

Combining Multiple Foundational Skills

- Extending the movement variety of each skill, using a variety of transitions, and working on low, medium, and high apparatus

Designing Longer Sequences

Figure 26.1 Progression of Content

Introduction

This chapter and the following two chapters discuss the content of educational gymnastics. All this content is designed primarily to meet National Standards 1 and 2 but may also address National Standards 3, 4, and 5. We suggest beginning teachers start by teaching content from this chapter. As you gain experience, you will easily be able to teach lessons from Chapter 27 on "Using Movement Concepts as Themes" and Chapter 28 "Partner and Group Work."

Progression

We organize gymnastics content into three ability levels, for children at developmental level 1 (beginners and immature movement patterns) to level 3 (mature movement patterns). When children are at developmental level 1, we teach the foundational skills of educational gymnastics (Nilges-Charles, 2008), consisting of balancing (i.e., holding a position of controlled stillness that is hard to hold, so that the child needs to concentrate and maintain tension in the body to remain balanced), rolling (i.e., transferring weight onto adjacent body parts or body parts moved to be adjacent), transferring weight, called *steplike actions* (i.e., taking weight on hands and feet or other body parts to travel in steplike ways as in a cartwheel), flight from feet (i.e., loss of contact with a supporting surface as in jumping, hopping, and leaping), rocking (i.e., transferring weight onto adjacent body parts in one direction and then back to the original position), and dynamic balancing (e.g., walking on a balance beam). We suggest children learn the foundational skills to the extent that they can perform them safely without losing control of their bodies before progressing to level 2 content.

In teaching the foundational skills across levels 1 to 3, we use movement concepts from the Laban framework (e.g., shape, speed, force, direction, and level) to extend the variety of ways children can perform the skills. In educational gymnastics, we label the components of the movement concept of shape straight, round, wide, angular, and twisted. In contrast, Olympic gymnastics defines shapes with more specific terms. You can also use these named terms in educational gymnastics. **Table 26.1** links the components of shapes to the named shapes from Olympic gymnastics. To assist you in developing children's movement variety and incorporating movement concepts into your teaching, we provide sample plans with suggestions for which movement concepts to use with each of the foundational skills.

As you teach, of course, you need to observe your children and decide which movement concepts they need to address to a greater or lesser extent. There is no one right answer. For example, if your children are not using a variety of levels, integrate moving at different levels into the lesson. If your children are doing uninteresting, symmetrical shapes, integrate asymmetrical shapes and originality into the lesson.

One aspect of level 2 content is the combination of two foundational skills, with children working on the transitions between skills, along with more extensive use of the movement concepts from the Laban framework to develop movement variety. Children develop short sequences with starting and ending shapes (Nilges-Charles, 2008). Children work on mats and low apparatus and design short sequences with beginning and ending shapes. Learning to combine skills is so critical to developing competence in gymnastics that we start teaching how to combine skills as soon as the children are ready for level 2 work. For all combinations, students need to learn to use continuity of flow in the transitions between skills. This means they do not stop, hesitate, take steps, or shift the position of body parts before or after the transition. For example, when combining a balance and a roll, the child starts the roll from the position of the balance.

In level 3, we teach more difficult combinations and focus on combining multiple skills; extending movement variety on low, medium, and high apparatus; and creating longer sequences. **Figure 26.1** summarizes this progression.

Chapter 27 explores another aspect of level 2 and level 3 content, using the movement concepts as the major theme. In these lessons, the children still perform the foundational skills, but their main focus is on the movement concept. For example, a lesson on traveling at different speeds would use the skills of rolling, steplike actions, and jumping to explore moving at different speeds. Chapter 27 lessons can be more difficult for beginning teachers to plan and teach, but they are excellent tools for increasing children's movement variety.

Chapter 28 discusses level 2 and 3 content for partner and group work. Whether children are ready for partner and group work depends on their social development. These lessons are excellent opportunities to teach social responsibility. Older children, in particular, enjoy partner and group work; consequently, that factor motivates their engagement in the tasks. Finally, when you teach in a school with few pieces of apparatus, partner and group work provides ways to extend the movement variety of the foundational skills and combinations of skills.

Figure 26.2 illustrates the progression and provides an overview of educational gymnastics content.

Descriptions of Foundational Skills and Developmental Patterns

Balancing and Weight Bearing

When children **balance**, they support their weight on one or several body parts and hold that position still. Balancing implies positions that are hard to hold. By "hard to hold," we don't mean the child attempts a difficult or advanced skill, but rather that the child needs to concentrate and maintain tension in the body to remain balanced.

A precursor to balancing is weight bearing. **Weight bearing** means that children support their weight on one or several body parts in a position of momentary, rather than sustained, stillness. All balances are weight-bearing skills, but not all weight bearing is balancing because *weight bearing* does not imply *hard to hold*.

For younger children only (pre-kindergarten and kindergarten ages) with no gymnastics experience, we teach weight bearing before balancing. In teaching weight bearing, children focus their attention only on the part of the body supporting their weight.

Table 26.1 Categories and Named Shapes in Gymnastics

Category	Named Shapes
Round/curled	Tuck: both knees bent, bent at hips (body parts drawn into belly button) Arch: making a C shape by curving the back backward (body parts extended away from belly button)
Straight	Layout: whole body straight (body parts extended away from belly button while straight from head to toe)
Wide	Straddle: legs straight and extended to each side (body looks like an upside-down Y or, if flexible, a T; body parts extended away from belly button in a side-to-side manner) Split: one leg straight forward, the other straight back; legs will be in a perfectly straight line called a split
Angular	Pike: bent at hips, both legs straight Stag: front leg is bent, back leg is straight back; alternatively, one leg is bent to the side and the other leg is straight to the other side Double stag: legs are split, with both knees bent Wolf: pike with both knees together, but one knee bent (see **Figure 26.3**)
Twisted	Body parts rotated around the belly button

The aim is for them to experience supporting their weight on a wide variety of body parts and to know which parts can support their weight safely and which cannot (such as kneecaps and elbows). We teach weight bearing first on the floor and then apply it to apparatus such as climbing and playground equipment.

Once children progress to balancing, you will need to remind them to find hard-to-hold balances, or else their balances will become simply weight-bearing positions. We typically teach balancing content first on the floor mats, then on stacked mats or trapezoid sections, and finally on any large apparatus

Level 1	Exploring and Varying Foundational Skills		
	Balancing Rolling and rocking Weight transfer (steplike actions) Flight from feet Dynamic balancing Jumping rope		
Level 2	**Combining Skills with Smooth Transitions, Extending Movement Variety (Chapter 26)**	**Using Movement Concepts as Lesson Themes (Chapter 27)**	**Partner and Group Work (Chapter 28)**
	Combining rolling and rocking on different body parts, in different directions Combining jumping and rolling while making different shapes with the legs Combining balancing on different body parts with different shapes with rolling in different directions and shapes Designing short sequences with beginning and ending shapes	Over, under, on, off, and through Symmetrical and asymmetrical shapes Different levels Different speeds Designing short sequences with beginning and ending shapes	Copying and following a leader Matching, mirroring, contrasting, and complementing shapes with a partner Group work: canon and unison Designing short sequences with beginning and ending shapes
Level 3	**Combining steplike actions and rolling**	**Traveling with symmetry and asymmetry**	**Countertension combined with rolling**
	Connecting balances Combining multiple skills Designing longer sequences Using a variety of transitions in sequences	Twisting and turning Stretching, curling, and twisting to take you some place Advanced shape Designing longer sequences	Countertension using like and unlike body parts Counterbalancing Pairs balancing Group timing Designing longer sequences

Figure 26.2 Overview and Progression of Gymnastics Content

> **FYI**
>
> **Sample Plans at the End of this Chapter**
>
> **Level 1**
> 1. Weight bearing and stillness
> 2. Balancing on different body parts
> 3. Balancing making different shapes
> 4. Safety rolling using side rolls
> 5. Steplike actions at low levels on different pathways
> 6. Jumping, hopping, and other types of flight from feet
> 7. Jumping for distance and height, focusing on take-offs
> 8. Hopping for distance and height, focusing on take-offs
> 9. Jumping, focusing on landing
> 10. Sample centers for flight from feet: level 1
> 11. Sample centers for flight from feet: levels 2 and 3
> 12. Dynamic balancing lesson segments
> 13. Sample centers for dynamic balancing
>
> **Level 2**
> 1. Combining rolling and rocking on different body parts and in different directions
> 2. Combining jumping and rolling, making different shapes with the legs
> 3. Combining balancing on different body parts with different shapes and rolling
> 4. Combining rolling and balancing, varying direction and shape
>
> **Level 3**
> 1. Combining steplike actions and rolling
> 2. Combining balances

Figure 26.3 Wolf jump

Courtesy of John Dolly

available. In addition, children can explore balancing totally supported on a mat, partially supported by a piece of apparatus and partially on a mat, or totally supported on a piece of apparatus (all body parts supporting the body are on the apparatus).

Balancing is also a topic that can be integrated with science principles. See the box, "Integrating with Science: Biomechanical Principles".

Movement Variety and Combinations

This section identifies the movement concepts and combination you can use to help children learn to balance in a variety of ways. By applying movement concepts, children can find literally hundreds of developmentally appropriate ways to balance (see **Figure 26.4**). When children apply movement concepts to balancing, they are working on National Standards 1 and 2.

Balancing can be combined with all other foundational skills; however, some combinations, such as balancing and rolling, are easier, whereas others, such as balancing and flight, are more difficult and are level 3 work.

Level 1

- Weight bearing and stillness
- Balancing on different body parts
  - Balancing on large and small body parts
- Balancing in different shapes (wide, straight, round, angular, twisted)

Figure 26.4 Balancing on different body parts and in different shapes

SAFETY AND LIABILITY 26.1

Increasing Safety and Decreasing Risk of Liability: Guidelines Relevant to Content in this Chapter

In this box, we discuss specific guidelines built on information discussed throughout this text on professional standards of practice, negligence, and liability. The goals of these guidelines are to increase children's safety and decrease teachers' risk of negligence and liability.

- A reasonably prudent teacher teaches content in a progression from beginning developmental levels to advanced. We suggest children learn the beginning-level foundational skills to the extent that they can perform them safely without losing control of their bodies before progressing to more advanced content.
- In educational gymnastics, students select the skills to practice within a theme. Teach children they must select only those skills they can do safely, confidently, and with control. Teachers must monitor students' selections and modify selections when children select skills that are too difficult for them. The same principle applies when designing partner and group sequences. Select only those skills that all children in the group can do safely, confidently, and with control.
- Teach skills and movements first on a floor mat before progressing to apparatus.
- Teach students they can support their weight on a wide variety of body parts and to know which parts can support their weight safely and which cannot (e.g., kneecaps and elbows).
- Teach safety rolling as a way to land and safely absorb and control the force of the landing.
- Sideways rolls are the only rolls that beginners can learn safely. Forward and backward rolls can be difficult skills to learn and are dangerous for low-skilled children, obese children, and children with poor arm strength. Never teach forward and backwards rolls to whole classes, nor require children to learn them. Always give children the option to roll sideways.
- Don't allow children to support their weight on their head without your permission, and give permission only to those children who have learned how to do a headstand safely.
- When sharing a floor mat, teach children how to pay attention to the location of their feet and other body parts so that they do not bump into a partner.
- Using strong arms (bent arms pushing against the mat to support the weight of the body) is important for protecting the head during forward and backwards rolls.
- When supporting your weight on your hands with straight arms, spring your feet off the floor only to a height at which you can do so safely and confidently.
- When teaching jumping for distance, jumping over a rope can be dangerous on a floor, but it works in the grass. To mark lines on a floor, use chalk; floor tape; thin, plastic, movable lines that don't slip; or non-slip mats with lines on them.
- When setting up cones for hopping or other locomotor skills multiple times for distance, be sure cones don't cross into the paths other children's cones, and leave some overflow space behind each cone in case you continue traveling once you reach your cone.
- Master skills on a line on the floor before you try them on a very low beam. Master them on a very low beam before progressing to a higher beam.
- If you jump on a low beam, keep your eyes focused on the beam for landing; make sure your feet land on the beam. If you are slightly off center, land with your feet on the beam and then safely step or jump to the ground.
- When you jump and make a shape in the air, land with your feet together (not spread far apart) about shoulder-width apart, and bend your knees and hips to absorb the force.
- When you jump, land with your knees facing forward or backward, but never sideways, because that puts too much stress on the sides of your knees.
- When you are exploring different movements within a theme, do only movements in which you are perfectly in control, safe, and confident.
- When you are progressing from a mule kick to a handstand, learn to cartwheel out (bail out) by turning out of a handstand if you kick too high and are going over. Do not, under any circumstances, go over into a back bend or go over onto your back. Land on your feet, and don't fall.

Mats and Apparatus

- Teach children how to set up, arrange, and put away the gymnastics mats and apparatus. When carrying mats, watch where you are going, walk slowly, make sure two children carry each mat, and no lifting the mat over your head. Arrange mats around apparatus so the mats cover the entire space but don't overlap. Use thicker landing mats for dismounts and jumping from the springboard.
- Teach children how to carry or move each piece of apparatus you have (safety procedures will vary depending on the piece of apparatus).

What the Research Says

Balance

Research suggests that balancing and dynamic balancing might be among the most important skills to develop. For older adults, balance is considered a component of health-related fitness because it has a direct impact on health—in particular, in preventing injuries (Claxton, Troy, & Dupree, 2006; Corbin et al., 2014; Plowman, 2014). The ability to maintain balance when negotiating obstacles and traveling on uneven surfaces can help prevent falls.

Research also suggests that when children develop the ability to balance, this ability can be maintained into adulthood. A follow-up study on this topic was conducted on adults aged 30 to 33 who had participated in an experimental study when they were in elementary school (Trudeau et al., 2000). In the original study, the experimental group had elementary physical education five days a week, while the control group had elementary physical education one day a week. The adults in the experimental group were significantly better at maintaining balance on one leg even 20 years after the original study.

Finally, researchers are beginning to elucidate the role of movement in learning and brain development. Notably, balancing activities stimulate the integration of the visual, motor, and tactual sensory systems, thereby supporting the development of neural pathways in young children (Stevens-Smith, 2006).

Level 2

- Balancing on four, three, two, and one body part(s)
- Balancing on like and unlike body parts (e.g., forearm and shoulder, shoulder and hand)
- Balancing on upper body parts (e.g., shoulders, forearms, head, hands, and chest)
- Balancing in inverted positions (with hips higher than the head)
- Combining balancing and rolling, starting the roll from the position of the balance
- Combining rolling and balancing by ending the roll in a balance
- Combining balancing on different body parts and in different shapes and rolling in different shapes and directions
- Balancing under and on an apparatus
- Combining balancing and rolling
    - At different levels on an apparatus
    - Moving to and from different levels on an apparatus

Level 3

- Combining balances with other balances
    - Overbalancing to a new balance
    - Twisting, stretching, and curling to a new balance
    - At different levels on an apparatus
    - Moving to and from different levels on an apparatus
- Combining balancing with steplike actions
    - At different levels on an apparatus
    - Moving to and from different levels on an apparatus
- Combining balances and flight from feet and hands

Immature Movement Patterns

Level 1 beginners tend to be loose throughout their body. They rarely stretch their torso, and they flex their feet and bend their knees. In level 2, children tend to be loose in body parts that are not their immediate focus of attention; they rarely control the free body parts (the parts on which they are not balancing); and they do not attend to the aesthetic alignment of body parts. For example, when they balance on one leg in a scale, they lower their back leg and torso so that their bottoms stick out, rather than forming a more pleasing straight line or arch (see **Figure 26.5**). The connections between balances and other skills often include extra steps and hesitations.

The ability to stay tight and stretched without actively thinking about it takes many years to develop. Consequently, you will need to continue to use related refining tasks and performance techniques for staying tight and stretched in levels 2 and 3.

Potential Refinements

Level 1

- Stay tight.
- Point your feet and toes.
- Keep your legs straight.
- Place free body parts in a purposeful (planned) position. No body parts should be flopping about like a dishrag.

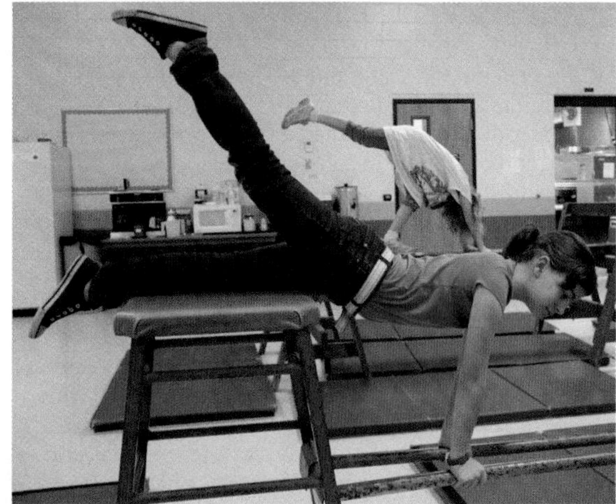

Figure 26.5 Girl in the foreground has appropriate body tension and alignment with the head, hips, and leg in an aesthetic, curved alignment; child in the background has inappropriate alignment with the hips out of line with the foot and head, with loose tension

Courtesy of John Dolly

Integrating with Science: Biomechanical Principles

You can teach your students four biomechanical (i.e., physics) principles of balancing, possibly integrating this content with classroom science lessons.

1. The larger the base of support, the more stable the balance.

The base of support is either the body part supporting the weight or the area between the body parts that support the weight. Lying on your back would be a large base of support. Supporting your weight on two hands and two feet spread apart uses a large base of support. Large bases are more stable. Balancing on your hands, however, represents a small base of support because the hands are small, and the area between the hands is small.

2. The lower the center of gravity, the more stable the balance.

The center of gravity is the point in the body around which all of your weight is equally balanced. When you stand, the center of gravity is located in the hips or lower-torso region. When you bend your knees while keeping your feet flat on the floor, you lower your center of gravity and become more stable than when your legs are straight.

3. The center of gravity must be over the base of support.

For a person to remain in a balance, the center of gravity must be over the base of support. If the center of gravity shifts beyond the base of support, you will "overbalance" and fall unless you perform another action.

4. Body parts in a triangular or square shape are more stable than body parts in a line; the amount of stability relates to the direction of force.

Sitting on a bicycle that is not moving is more difficult than sitting on a tricycle that is not moving; a three-legged stool is less stable than a four-legged chair. The same principles apply in balancing. Balancing on your hands and shins is very stable. By comparison, extending one leg back in a knee scale is less stable; picking up one hand and doing a one-handed knee scale is the least stable position. Children achieve stability in a headstand by making a triangle between their two hands and head (rather than by having their head and hands in a line, which would be less stable). A headstand with three body parts in a triangle is more stable than a handstand with two body parts in a line.

Similarly, if your feet are wide apart to the sides and someone pushes you from the front or behind, you would not be stable because your base of support is narrow from front to back. However, if the force came from the side, you would be stable because the base of support is wide sideways.

Level 2 (Continue Reinforcing Level 1 Performance Techniques)

- Stretch through your spine.
- Be tight in the core, especially the abdominal muscles.
- Go for three solid counts of stillness.
- Show good control going into and out of every balance—no flopping or falling.
- Use continuity of flow in the transitions between skills (e.g., rolling and then, without stopping, ending in a balance)

Level 3 (Continue Reinforcing Level 1 and 2 Performance Techniques)

- Pay attention to the lines that your body parts make. Don't let a body part stick out and ruin a line you like.
- Pay attention how each body part contributes or detracts from the total shape you are trying to make.

Rolling and Rocking

Rolling means transferring weight onto adjacent body parts, such as lying on your belly and transferring weight to your side and then to your back in a log roll. Rolling also means transferring weight onto body parts that can be brought close together to be adjacent, such as rolling sideways curled into a ball with bent knees, making the shins adjacent to the sides of the thighs.

Rocking is another foundational skill that is so closely related to rolling that we typically teach these two skills together. Rocking means to transfer your weight in one direction onto an adjacent body part and then to transfer your weight back to your original position.

Rolling and Safety

In level 1, safety rolls are taught first using side rolls (Ratliffe, 2000). *Safety rolls* are rolls that start from a stand (see **Figure 26.6**) or, if students are developmentally able, immediately follow landing from a jump. Safety rolls are also used to recover from a fall. Children are typically familiar with safety rolls from movies and TV, where they often see these skills used in fight scenes and chase scenes. We differentiate instruction by giving children who are more experienced the option of safety rolling in different directions.

Movement Variety and Combinations

For level 1 beginners, rolling offers far fewer options for movement variety than balancing does. The problem is that sideways rolls are the only rolls that beginners can learn safely and easily. Although you can roll in different directions, forward and backward rolls can be difficult skills to learn and are dangerous for low-skilled children, obese children, and children with poor arm strength. Although many years ago we found more children were ready and able to learn forward and backward rolls, with the increased percentage of overweight and obese children, we find we can no longer teach these skills to all children and ensure safety. This issue arises because in forward and backward rolls, children must hold their body weight off their heads and necks with their arms—and some children do not have the arm strength to do so. Consequently, to prevent

Figure 26.6 Safety roll

possible injuries (and liability problems), we never teach these skills to whole classes, nor do we ever require children to learn them. With rolling, it is essential that teachers always give children the option to roll sideways.

The progression of movement variety content for rolling and rocking and combining rolling and rocking with other skills is summarized next.

Level 1

- Safety rolls from a stand using side rolls
- Side rolls varying the shape of the legs (e.g., tucked in an egg roll, straight in a log or pencil roll, wide, straddled, V, split, one leg bent and the other straight)
- Rocking on different body parts (e.g., back, belly, hands and shins, feet, hands and feet, forearms and shins)
- Rocking in different shapes (round, straight, twisted)
- Rocking in different directions (backward and forward, side to side, on a diagonal)

Level 2

- Rolling on different body parts
- Rolling in different shapes
- Rolling from different starting shapes and positions (e.g., tuck, lunge, straddle, pike)
- Rolling and ending in different shapes
- Combining rolling and rocking, varying the shapes and body parts
- Rolling and rocking at slow and medium speeds
- Rocking on the back and coming to the feet (first with, and then without, hands)
- Rolling in different directions (listed in order from least to most difficult)
  - Forward diagonal (traveling forward but over the shoulder)
  - Backward diagonal (traveling backward but over the shoulder)
  - Forward
  - Backward
- Combining a low, straight jump and rolling, progressing to jumping higher
- Combining jumping, making different shapes with the legs in the air, with rolling
- Combining jumping with rolling, varying the shape in the jump, roll/rock, or both
- Three ways to land a jump
- Combining rolling and balancing (balancing on different body parts and in different shapes, rolling in different ways)
  - Starting the roll from the position of the balance (see **Figure 26.7**)
  - Rolling or rocking and ending in a balance
  - At different levels on an apparatus
  - Moving to and from different levels on an apparatus
- Rolling and rocking on and off different apparatus (e.g., stacked mats) at different levels

Level 3

- Combining rocking and rolling with steplike actions
  - Steplike action leading to a roll or rock
  - Rolling or rocking and then immediately moving into a steplike action
  - At different levels on an apparatus
  - Moving to and from different levels on an apparatus

Immature and Mature Movement Patterns

In this section, we describe the immature and mature patterns of named skills, side rolls, forward rolls, and back rolls. Don't be confused—we are not advocating that you teach these specific

Figure 26.7 Combining rolling out of a balance in an asymmetrical shape

rolls for the theme of rolling. Instead, we advocate having children select and vary the ways they roll. When children vary their rolls, however, you will see the same immature patterns and, in turn, teach the same performance techniques and cues as the named skills.

Side Rolls

In our experience, the most frequent immature patterns are as follows:

Immature Patterns for Side Rolls and Its Variation, Tucked Side Rolls ("Egg Rolls")

- Open up their tuck when they are on their backs
- Roll onto their kneecaps or belly rather than their shins

Straight Side Rolls (Log or Pencil Rolls)

- Bend the knees
- Cross the legs
- Separate the legs
- Flex the toes
- Have loose bodies

Motor development research has identified developmental characteristics of the forward roll, which informed our descriptions of immature patterns (Roberton & Halverson, 1984).

Figure 26.8 illustrates the immature pattern of a tucked side roll, **Figure 26.9** illustrates the mature pattern of a forward roll, **Figure 26.10** illustrates the immature pattern of a forward roll in which the tuck opens up, and **Figure 26.11** illustrates the immature movement pattern of the forward roll using the hands to push off the mat to stand. The following list summarizes the most frequently observed immature rolling patterns based on this research and our own experiences teaching children.

Figure 26.8 Immature movement pattern of a tucked side roll

Figure 26.9 Mature movement pattern of the forward roll

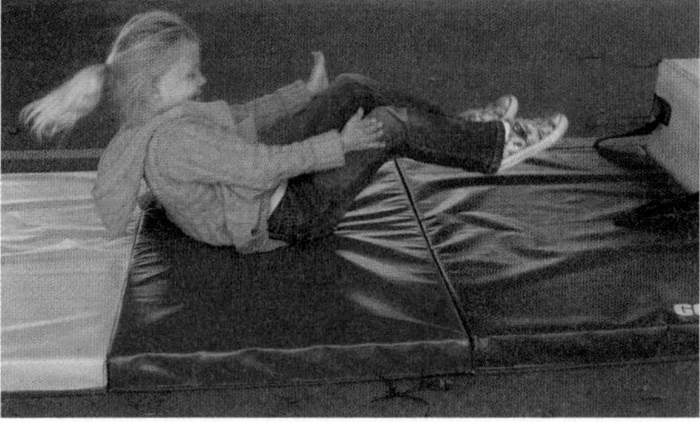

Figure 26.10 Immature movement pattern of the forward roll opening up the tuck

Figure 26.11 Immature movement pattern of the forward roll using hands to push off the mat to stand

Immature Patterns for the Forward Roll and Its Variations

- Children land on their heads or put a considerable amount of weight on their heads.
- Their hands and arms do not support their weight, and sometimes one elbow collapses to the side.
- They crash onto their backs because they are not round.
- Sometimes they push off their feet one at a time, rather than simultaneously.
- Their push-off is incomplete, and their legs never straighten while piked at the hips before tucking again to stand.
- On their backs, they open the tuck; sometimes they remain lying down.
- They use their hands to roll to a stand.
- At the end of the roll, they don't tuck their heels close enough to their hips to allow them to roll to their feet.

There has been no research on back rolls, so here we describe the immature patterns we have seen frequently in our own experiences.

Immature Patterns for the Backward Roll and Its Variations

- Children roll onto their heads, and their arms collapse, rather than pushing using strong arms to allow the head to pass through.
- Their palms rotate, rather than landing flat on the mat.
- The force from their arms is inadequate to lift their weight.
- They push with their arms either too early or too late.
- They end by crashing on their shins, rather than by landing on their feet.

Potential Refinements

Based on typical immature patterns, we find the following performance techniques and cues helpful:

TEACHING TIP

The Difference Between Straight Arms and Strong Arms

Children can get confused about the difference between *straight* arms and *strong* arms.

Straight arms are critical for all steplike actions and handstands. It takes less strength to support the body's weight in steplike actions with straight arms because children do not have to hold their weight off the ground using their arm muscles; instead, the weight is supported by the bones, and the arm muscles simply keep the arm straight.

Strong arms are bent arms used to hold the weight off the head while rolling. We teach children strong arms by imitating a weight lifter.

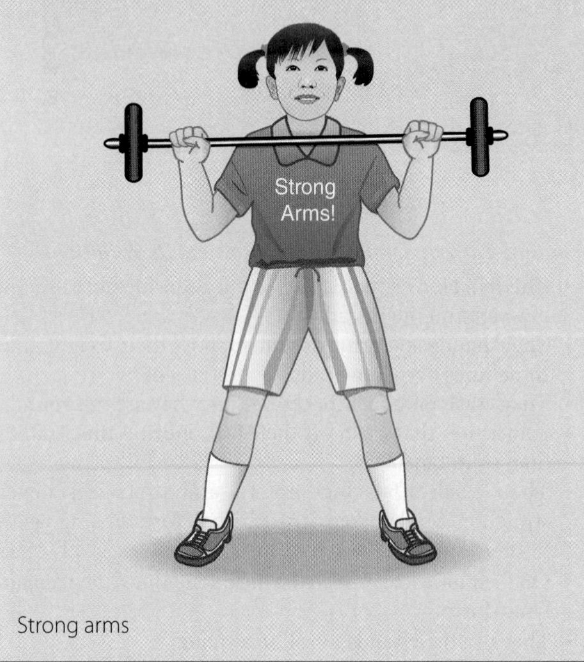

Strong arms

Performance Techniques and Cues for Safety Rolls and Side Rolls

- Take your weight gently onto the floor; smoothly transfer your weight
- Tuck tight, knees to chest, and be round like a ball (egg roll)
- Straight like a pencil; pencil legs (log roll)
- Legs together

Generic Performance Techniques and Cues that Work for Most Rolls

- Strong arms (arms are bent and supporting the weight of the body; see **Teaching Tip** box, "The Difference Between Straight Arms and Strong Arms")
- Keep your weight off your head
- Knees to forehead (Masser, 1993)
- Roll right to your feet

Transferring Weight or Steplike Actions

Transferring weight, often called *steplike actions*, is a way to transfer weight to nonadjacent body parts using a process such as stepping or walking (Belka, 2000). You are probably familiar with the cartwheel and round-off, which are commonly observed steplike actions.

You can do steplike actions using many different body parts, but the most important and frequently used parts are the hands and feet (see **Figure 26.12**). Often we refer to steplike actions as traveling on hands and feet.

It is critical for level 1 beginners to learn different ways to support their weight on their hands, first at a low level with their torso and legs in a curled position, and then in this curled position traveling at a low level around and over a stacked mat. We find that it is easier for children to learn most steplike actions on a stacked mat (or a low box on a mat). With this setup, they do not have to bend very low, and they are more likely to keep their hands flat on the mat. Once they have mastered this skill, we progress to steplike actions on a flat mat on the floor.

As children gain skill and confidence, they begin to spring their legs higher off the ground, straighten their knees, and stretch their legs toward the ceiling. Steplike actions such as cartwheels and round-offs begin to emerge more frequently. At this point, depending on the skill level of the students in the class, you can integrate progressions for teaching a cartwheel and round-off using a stacked mat.

Movement Variety and Combinations

Level 1

- Travel across the flat mat on two hands and two feet with the belly facing down and then up. Try again, this time switching from belly down to belly up halfway across the mat.
- Take your weight on your hands on a stacked mat, keeping the body low and curled, transferring your weight from feet to hands to feet.
- Take your weight on your hands on a stacked mat, sometimes springing off and landing on one foot and sometimes landing on two feet.

Level 2

- Take your weight on your hands and feet traveling around the stacked mat, keeping the body low and curled.
- Take your weight on your hands on the stacked mat, and spring your feet on and over the stacked mat.
- Take your weight on your hands on and over the stacked mat and then a flat mat, traveling on straight, zigzag, and curved pathways.
- Take steplike actions traveling on your hands and feet over and on the stacked and then a flat mat, springing your legs to medium and high levels.
- Take steplike actions on, over, and off a low apparatus.

Level 3

- Steplike actions using different body parts (e.g., shins, forearms)
- Steplike actions taking the feet to a high level
- Combining steplike actions with rolling/rocking
- Combining steplike actions with balancing and jumping
- Transferring weight from slow to medium speeds
- Steplike actions at different levels on an apparatus
- Steplike actions moving to and from different levels on an apparatus
- Steplike actions remaining on, springing over, and dismounting off of an apparatus set at different levels

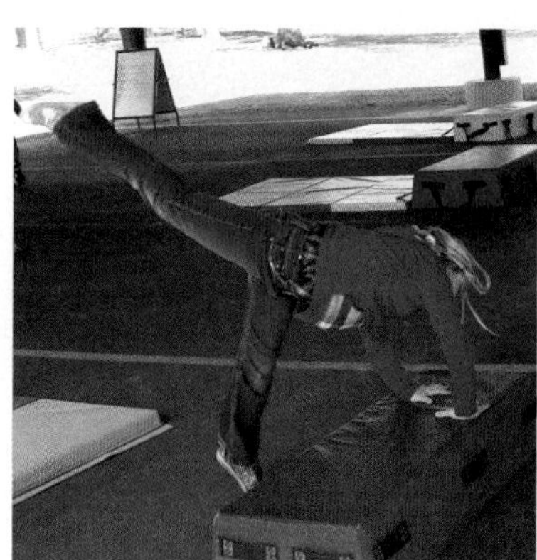

Figure 26.12 Steplike action (mini-cartwheel) over a trapezoid

Immature Movement Patterns

Beginners tend to bend their arms during steplike actions, rather than keeping them straight with elbows locked. Beginners also frequently land heavily with a thump, sometimes on their knees or shins, rather than lightly on their feet. In addition, beginners often take their weight on their hands using a sprinter's "track start" position (weight on the fingers, palms off the mat) rather than the mature pattern with the weight on their palms flat on the mat (see **Figure 26.13**).

As beginners gain confidence in taking their weight on their hands and begin to use straight legs in the air, performance techniques and cues for keeping their knees straight and feet pointed become important. In addition, in level 2, children need to develop more stable landings—that is, landings in which their feet land and "stick" to one spot, and the child remains still or balanced. Finally, by level 3, they need to learn to land resiliently—for example, being able to pop off the floor in round-offs.

Potential Refinements

Level 1

- Straight arms, lock elbows
- Palms flat
- Land lightly on feet, not knees

Level 2

- Place hands one at a time (hand–hand)
- Stay tight; maintain tension in your muscles to control your body when it is supported by your hands and in landings.
- Stretch your feet toward the ceiling.
- Body straight and stretched, legs straight

Level 3

- With resilient landings, spring and pop off the mat.
- Be tight in the core, especially the abdominal muscles.

Figure 26.13 Steplike action over stacked mats: Right hand in immature "track start" position and left hand in mature palms-flat position

Flight from Feet

Flight is weight transfer where there is a loss of contact from a supporting surface, such as the floor or an apparatus. In elementary educational gymnastics, we focus on flight from feet. In level 3, some children can work on flight from hands. There are five ways to perform flight from feet:

- *Jump:* two-foot take-off, land on two feet (2–2)
- *Leap:* one-foot take-off, land on the opposite foot (1–opposite)
- *Hop:* one-foot take-off, land on the same foot (1–same)
- *Assemblé:* one-foot take-off, land on two feet (1–2)
- *Sissone:* two-foot take-off, land on one foot (2–1)

Other skills we teach are jumping for height, jumping for distance, and consecutive hopping for distance. There are three ways to land from flight:

- *Jump and land with a stick:* Sticking a landing means that children bend their hips, knees, and ankles to absorb force and then straighten to stand in a perfectly still position while the feet remain in the exact location where they first made contact with the mat. The feet "stick" to the mat and don't move.
- *Resilient landings:* With resilient landings, children bend their hips, knees, and ankles, compressing and extending them quickly like a spring. They pop off the floor.
- *Land and safety roll:* In a safety roll, children land and absorb force by bending the hips and knees and taking their weight onto the floor and rolling.

Figure 26.14 Jumping making different shapes

Courtesy of John Dolly

Movement Variety and Combinations

Level 1

- Flight from feet: learning the basic patterns of the jump, leap, hop, *assemblé*, and *sissone*

Level 2

- Three ways to land: stick, pop up (resilient), safety roll
- Jumping and hopping for height and distance
- Jumping in different shapes (straight, wide, curled, twisted, angular, symmetrical, asymmetrical) (see **Figure 26.14**)
- Combining jumping and rolling/rocking
- Jumping on, over, and off of a low apparatus (e.g., stacked mat, aerobic box) (see **Figure 26.15**)

Level 3

- Jumping onto, off of, and over apparatus of increasing heights
- Jumping while twisting and turning
- Several high resilient jumps in a row making different shapes
- Combining flight with steplike actions
- Combining flight with balances

Figure 26.15 Jumping off apparatus of different heights

Courtesy of John Dolly

The Importance of Jumping and Hopping for Distance and Height

Jumping for distance and height are two of the most important skills we teach. Jumping works to develop muscle power, which means using strong muscular force with speed for the extension of the body joints. Muscle power and increases in scores on the standing long jump have been shown to improve children's bone density—a health benefit that lasts at least into young adulthood (American College of Sports Medicine, 2004; Institute of Medicine, 2012). The United States Department of Health and Human Services (USDHHS) recommends children do bone strengthening movements at least three days a week (2008). Presumably, hopping for distance and height, which is also produced by muscle power, also contributes to bone density.

Moreover, skill in jumping for height is critical to many sports and dance. We need to ensure children get plentiful practice and instruction in jumping across all grade levels.

Immature Movement Patterns for Jumping

Motor development researchers have identified developmental patterns for jumping, as illustrated in **Figure 26.16** and **Figure 26.17** and summarized next (Roberton & Halverson, 1984).

The immature jumping movement patterns we see most often in gymnastics are as follows:

Immature Take-off

1. Incomplete extensions in the hips, knees, and ankles at take-off
2. Either holding the arms out to the side or only partially swinging the arms forward and upward, stopping at about shoulder height at take-off

Mature Take-off

1. Arms swing down and back, then forward and upward forcefully to reach a full extension
2. Full extension of the hips, knees, and ankles

Figure 26.16 Immature movement pattern of jumping
Source: Modified from Wickstrom, R. L. (1983). *Fundamental motor patterns* (3rd ed.). Philadelphia: Lea & Febiger.

Immature Flight

1. Hips, knees, and ankles remain partially flexed

Mature Flight

1. Body is fully extended in the air

Immature Landing

1. Landing on stiff legs with only a slight bending of the knees or bending the knees without resisting the force of the body and then collapsing to the floor

Mature Landing

1. Knees extend to prepare for landing, and when the feet land, the knees bend to absorb the force.

When children exhibit immature patterns, we find it most helpful to focus on the arm action at take-off, a forceful leg action at take-off, and absorbing force with the knees on landing. We try to work on take-offs and landings on separate days.

Potential Refinements

Level 1 Take-off and Flight

- Arms back, knees bent
- Two-foot take-off, extend fully
- Swing your arms high, reach toward the sky
- Explode

Level 1 Landings

- Land on your feet
- Bend your knees when you land
- Absorb the force by bending your knees

Level 1 Resilient Landings

- Pretend your feet and legs are springs that compress and then send you back into the air (Nilges, 1999)

Level 2 Sticking

- Pretend your feet have glue on the bottom that helps you stick to the floor (landing with a stick)
- Land softly

Level 3 Resilient Landings

- Extend your knees and ankles forcefully
- Pop quickly and forcefully

Immature Movement Patterns for Hopping

Motor development researchers have identified developmental sequences for hopping, as illustrated in **Figure 26.18** (Roberton & Halverson, 1984).

Figure 26.17 Mature movement pattern of jumping

Source: Modified from Wickstrom, R. L. (1983). *Fundamental motor patterns* (3rd ed.). Philadelphia: Lea & Febiger.

Immature Movement Patterns for Hopping

- Child holds the swing leg in front and still as if it is a table on which you could place a tea cup
- Arms are held out and used for balance (not to generate force)
- Arms pump up and down to generate force

Mature Movement Pattern for Hopping

- Arms move in opposition to the legs
- Knee and ankle extend on take-off
- Swing leg (with knee bent) goes through the full range of motion (lifting high and extending behind the support leg)

Figure 26.18 Less and more mature movement patterns of hopping: Girl in pink has more mature leg action than the boy wearing stripes, but both are using their arms to help generate force

Courtesy of John Dolly

Potential Refinements

Hopping for distance has a unique status: It is the rare skill for which demonstrations and explanations of the performance techniques of the mature pattern—especially the arms moving in opposition and the swing leg moving through its full range of motion—are detrimental for most learners (Roberton, Halverson, & Harper, 1997).

We suggest teaching children that a hop is taking off one foot and landing on the same foot. Then, give them many opportunities to practice hopping while using eliciting tasks to increase their skillfulness and versatility. For example, have them hop for distance, hop for height, hop in different directions on poly spots close together on the floor, and hop over very low obstacles. "Use your arms to help" is the only performance technique we emphasize because it is general and applies to several developmental levels.

More mature patterns of the arms and legs will emerge as children are able to add force and hop for distance. This is an example of a motor development principle, namely, that changes in task constraints (i.e., increased force in hopping for distance) can elicit more mature patterns (Renshaw, Chow, Davids, & Hammond, 2010).

Dynamic Balancing

Dynamic balancing means traveling on a narrow surface without falling. This skill is most often associated with traveling on balance beams. Teachers can purchase or ask a parent to make a variety of different, low-cost dynamic balance apparatus using 2×4 lumber, PVC pipes, large ropes, and old garden hoses. We find dynamic balancing tasks to be most beneficial for younger children or when teaching very large classes. When such tasks are assigned, it is essential to have a large number of safe stations available for children's use.

Movement Variety

Movement variety options include dynamic balancing while engaging in the following activities:

Level 1

- Traveling on different apparatus, such as beams, PVC pipe beams, inclined beams, very narrow beams, stepping stones (sturdy plastic domes), thick ropes, and garden hoses
- Traveling on different pathways by arranging beams, thick ropes, stepping stones, or old garden hoses as different pathways

Level 2

- Traveling on beams using different locomotor skills, such as walking, galloping, and skipping
- Traveling while reaching to the left and right to place or retrieve beanbags or balls balanced on cones
- Traveling in different directions (forward, sideways, backward)
- Traveling over and through obstacles (beanbags, small and medium cones, hula hoops) while on a beam

Level 3

- Different ways of turning on the beam, including turning on two feet, two feet in a squat, one foot turning on your left foot turning outward toward the right and on your left foot turning inward towards the left, one foot turning on your right foot outward and inward, and one foot turning with the free leg in different positions (e.g., bent, straight and high, in front, behind)
- Jumping on the beam and making different shapes
- Jumping over obstacles, through hoops used like a jump rope, and while jumping rope

Potential Refinements

The following performance techniques and cues are used for dynamic balancing:

Level 1

- Maintain tension, stay tight

Level 2

- Stretch tall through the spinal column
- Head up, eyes looking down at the beam

Level 3

- Bend knees to lower the center of gravity to regain lost balance
- Counteract a shift in the center of gravity by moving a body part in the opposite direction

Jumping Rope

Jumping rope has long been a favorite activity during childhood and has grown into an activity with highly skilled rope jumpers doing routines and difficult tricks in nationwide competitions and shows. We discuss here the basic jumping-rope techniques, a progression for teaching these techniques, and some of the variety of ways children can jump rope. The Internet is a very good source for demonstrations of jumping-rope tricks and routines.

Single Rope

Progression

1. Select a rope of a length that when you stand on it, the handles come up to your armpits.
2. Waterfall grip: Wrap your hands and fingers around the handle so the rope drapes over your hands like a waterfall, not out of the bottom like a faucet.
3. Starting position: Stand with the rope behind your legs and your arms stretched out in front of you at waist height.
4. Turn, lift, trap: From the starting position, circle the hands down and back, then turn the rope over your head, lift your toes, and trap it under your feet. This task is used to help children acquire the timing of the jump. Keep your elbows by your side as you turn the rope.
5. Turn, lift, trap, heels up, turn again: Repeat task 2, but after the rope is trapped, lift up your heels moving the rope from beneath your feet, turn it again, lift, and trap it again under your feet.
6. Turn, and when you would lift your toes, instead jump over the rope.

Potential Refinements

- Keep the elbows by your side; don't reach over your head with your hands
- Jump at a low level

Movement Variety Level 1

- Jump one time for each turn of the rope
- Jump two times for each one turn (the second jump is like a bounce)
- Jog over the rope, springing from one foot to the other in place and at a low level

Movement Variety Level 2

- Hop over the rope
- Jump backward (in place) while swinging the rope in the other direction
- Land
  - Feet apart sideways, feet together, repeat
  - Feet apart, left foot in front and right foot back; reverse: right foot in front and left foot back
  - Feet crossed, feet apart; repeat crossing with other leg in front
  - Toes and feet turned in, toes and feet turned out; repeat
  - Touch toes. Jump and land on one foot with the toes of the other foot touching the ground behind you. Then reverse feet.
  - Touch heels. Jump and land on one foot with the heel of the other foot touching the ground in front of you. Then reverse feet.
- Figure 8: Swing the rope in a circle first to one side of your body and then to the other making a figure 8 but not jumping over the rope. Keep your hands together. Then open your hands, and jump over the rope.
- Half–figure 8 (single circle) and jump.
- Skier (twist at the waist so feet turn and land first to one side then the other)
- Crisscross: Cross your hands in front of you so far that your hands are out to the side and your elbows touch, turn the rope from this position, jump, uncross hands, and jump normally, and then crisscross again.

Partner Skills

- Jump with one rope, one partner turning, and both jumping:
  - Face to face
  - Back to front
  - Side to side
  - Side to side facing in opposite directions, one jumping forward and one jumping backward
- Jump with two ropes, partners side to side, with each partner holding the inside handle of their partner's rope and both turning the outside handle of the rope he or she is jumping, and the inside handle of the rope the partner is jumping. Jump over the ropes in unison.
- Jump with two ropes, partners side to side facing opposite directions, one jumping forward, and one jumping backward, each holding the inside handle of the partner's rope.

Long-Rope Jumping

First, teach the children how to turn a long rope. Beginners tend to pull on the rope or stand too far apart so the rope does not hit the ground or go over the jumper's head. Turners must make big circles with the rope, making an arch or "rainbow" at the top, and hear the rope hit the ground at the bottom each time. The turners must also match each other's arm circles and timing. The rope is turned counterclockwise.

Long-Rope Progression

1. Rope on the ground, jump side to side over the rope.
2. Tick tock: Turners swing the rope up and down in a quarter-circle, making the shape of a smile and hitting the ground every time (but not circling the rope overhead). Jumper jumps over the rope each time it hits the ground.
3. One time: Jumper stands in the middle. Turners turn the rope one full turn and the jumper jumps one time and then stops.
4. Two times: This time the turners turn the rope two times, and the jumper jumps two times.
5. Repeated jumps: Starting from standing in the middle the turners turn, and the jumper jumps multiple times.
6. Run in the front door and out the back. Turners turn. Jumper starts diagonally on the left side of one turner. When the rope hits the ground, the jumper runs in chasing the rope and continues running out without jumping.
7. Run in the front door and jump. When the rope hits the ground, the jumper runs in chasing the rope, stops in the middle, and starts jumping.
8. Run in the back door and jump. From a diagonal on the right side of one turner, the jumper runs in when the rope is at the top and starts jumping.

Group Patterns

J-Space: Four jumpers in two lines start from a diagonal on the left side of each turner. The first jumper runs in the front door from a diagonal on the left side of one turner, jumps once on the first turn of the rope, and runs out on the right side of the other turner. The first jumper runs around that turner and gets in line behind the fourth jumper. A second jumper does the same but starts from a diagonal on the left side of the other turner, jumps on the third turn of the rope (leaving a "space" turn of the rope), and gets in line behind the third jumper. The third jumper repeats what the first jumper did, and the forth jumper repeats what the second jumper did. The pattern continues. More difficult patterns include the following:

- Jumping each turn of the rope leaving out the space
- Two jumpers jumping the same turn

Long and Short Ropes Jumpers can jump a short rope inside a long rope and do various tricks.

Possible Modifications for Children with Disabilities

You can modify educational gymnastics for children with disabilities matching the modifications to each child's capabilities. Following are some suggestions.

Balancing

For children in wheelchairs, set up equipment such as an overhead bar, overhead ladder, or gymnastics bridge, from which they can hang. If the chair has armrests, they can also work on balancing on their hands on the arms of their chairs. Alternatively, they can grab a side support structure (e.g., stall bars, a pole, sturdy fence, doorframe, chair), and balance on a side wheel (see **Figure 26.19**). Some can learn wheelies (tipping back and balancing on the large wheels; see **Figure 26.20**). Some children with balance capabilities can balance forward on the casters (the little wheels in front on the wheelchair) with

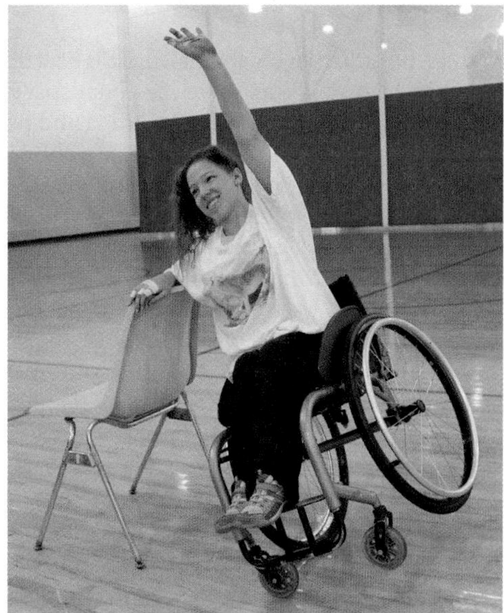

Figure 26.19 Balancing on one side of a wheel
Courtesy of John Dolly

Figure 26.21 Balancing forward
Courtesy of John Dolly

one hand or two hands on the ground and two wheels in the air (see **Figure 26.21**). Some children in wheelchairs can also learn how to balance in pairs(see **Figure 26.22**).

Children who use crutches can work on balancing in different ways on and off apparatus using no, one, or two crutches. They might also be able to work on balancing on their crutches or walkers with their body in different positions.

Jumping

For children in wheelchairs, jumping can be doing a wheelie and tapping the front wheel on the ground. In addition, jumping can be wheeling off or over low objects such as two- to three-inch foam floor beams. This skill is important for users of wheelchairs because of the need to learn to manage curbs.

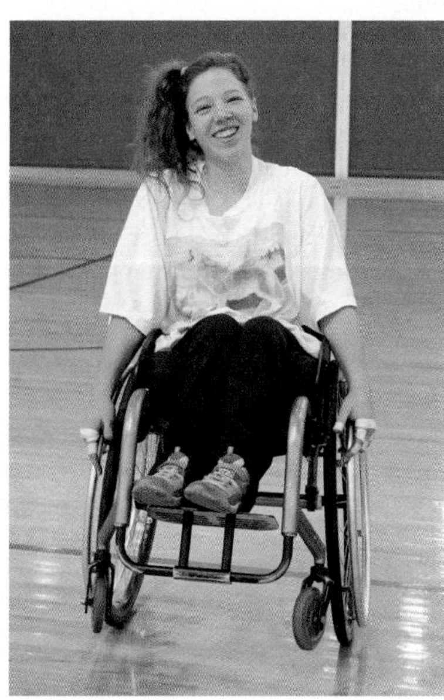

Figure 26.20 Wheelie
Courtesy of John Dolly

Traveling at Different Speeds and Stillness

Traveling and stopping needs no modification because it is an important skill to practice for all children with the capabilities to move. Traveling at different speeds and then stopping is also an important skill regardless of the mode of traveling. Different locomotor skills can be modified to include using the hands to push or tap the wheels or armrests in rhythm or in different ways.

Traveling on Different Pathways and in Different Directions

All mobile children need to learn to travel on different pathways and in different directions, as this sort of navigation is part of daily living. You can teach this content by using obstacle courses or simply designing a set of tasks through which the children

Figure 26.22 Pairs balancing
Courtesy of John Dolly

explore traveling on different pathways and in different directions. You can also purchase roller racers (large plastic seats low to the ground with wheels and bicycle handle bars that you pull and push with your hands to make the racer roll), and have children travel on different pathways.

Making Different Shapes (Symmetrical, Asymmetrical, Curled, Wide, Twisted, Angular, Straight) When Balancing

Have the child make the shape with her or his upper body. Give the child (depending on strength) a fitness bars, two canes, two plastic poles, two plastic rackets or Frisbees (which add interesting angles to shapes), peacock feathers, or light (juggling) scarves to make different shapes with different arm positions.

Fundamental Skills

For every child, regardless of capabilities, there is a set of important skills for traveling and maneuvering about space, which will differ by child. These skills can be learned and practiced in educational gymnastics lessons. For example, children with physical challenges can engage in traveling on the floor using arms, rolling over, reaching to grasp in different areas of personal space, propelling a wheelchair up an incline and controlling it down an incline, turning, pulling on a handrail to travel, and traveling backward. Use whatever equipment you have to design a set of skills for a child with disabilities to practice—even if those skills are not the same as the skills you are teaching in a particular lesson. The goal of gymnastics is for all children is to learn how to maneuver their bodies in a variety of ways.

Summary

Balancing, rolling, flight from feet, steplike actions, rocking, and dynamic balancing are the foundational skills that form the level 1 content of educational gymnastics. Once children have mastered these skills, they learn how to combine and use them on apparatus in levels 2 and 3. Each foundational skill and combination of skills can be performed in a variety of ways. Teachers use movement concepts from the Laban framework to help children develop this movement variety.

You can expect to see immature movement patterns in beginners in educational gymnastics. Knowing these likely movement patterns will help you anticipate which refinements you will likely need to use in lessons. Performance techniques such as "point your feet" and "stay tight" need to be reinforced across many lessons, as these techniques can be difficult to perform consistently.

Review Questions

1. What is the difference between balancing and weight bearing?
2. Describe how you can vary and extend balancing tasks.
3. Identify one of the four biomechanical principles described in the chapter, and describe how you can integrate it into a gymnastics lesson. Do not use examples from the chapter.
4. What are safety rolls?
5. Describe how you can vary and extend rolling tasks.
6. Describe four typical immature patterns for rolling. Describe how you can teach a performance technique that will help children improve on each immature pattern. Invent at least one image, story, metaphor, or clever/fun cue (not already found in the chapter) for teaching one of the performance techniques.
7. Describe three typical immature patterns for steplike actions. Describe how you can teach a performance technique that will help children improve on each immature pattern. Invent at least one image, story, metaphor, or clever/fun cue (not already found in the chapter) for teaching one of the performance techniques.
8. Label and describe the five different ways to perform flight from the feet.
9. Describe the three ways to land a jump.
10. Describe two immature patterns for the arms and legs in the take-off phase and one immature pattern for the arms and legs in the flight and landing phases of the standing long jump.
11. Describe how you can teach a performance technique that will help children improve on each immature pattern. Invent at least one image, story, metaphor, or clever/fun cue (not already found in the chapter) for teaching one of the performance techniques.
12. Describe how you can vary and extend jumping tasks.
13. What is dynamic balancing? Describe three performance techniques for improving children's performance of this skill.

References

American College of Sports Medicine. (2004). Physical activity and bone health. *Medicine and Science in Sports and Exercise, 36*(11), 1985–1996.

Belka, D. E. (2000). Teaching step-like actions. *Teaching Elementary Physical Education, 11*(4), 15–18.

Claxton, D. B., Troy, M., & Dupree, S. (2006). A question of balance. *Journal of Physical Education, Recreation, and Dance, 77*(3), 32–37.

Corbin, C. B., Welk, G. J., Richardson, C., Vowell, C., Lambdin, D., & Wikgren, S. (2014). Youth fitness: Ten key concepts. *Journal of Physical Education, Recreation, and Dance, 85*(2), 24–31.

Institute of Medicine. (2012). *Fitness measures and health outcomes in youth.* Washington, DC: National Academy of Sciences.

Lemov, D. (2010). *Teach like a champion: 49 techniques that put students on the path to college.* San Francisco: Jossey-Bass.

Masser, L. S. (1993). Critical cues to help first-grade students' achievement in handstands and forward rolls. *Journal of Teaching in Physical Education, 12*, 301–312.

Nilges, L. M. (1999). Refining skill in educational gymnastics. *Journal of Physical Education, Recreation, and Dance, 70*(3), 43–48.

Nilges-Charles, L. M. (2008). Assessing skill in educational gymnastics. *Journal of Physical Education, Recreation, and Dance, 79*(3), 41–51.

Plowman, S. A. (2014). Top 10 research questions related to musculoskeletal physical fitness testing in children and adolescents. *Research Quarterly for Exercise and Sport, 85*, 174–187.

Ratliffe, T. (2000). Teaching rolling actions. *Teaching Elementary Physical Education, 11*(4), 11–13.

Renshaw, I., Chow, J. Y., Davids, K., & Hammond, J. (2010). A constraints-led perspective to understanding skill acquisition and game play: A basis for integration of motor learning theory and physical education praxis. *Physical Education and Sport Pedagogy, 15*, 117–137.

Rink, J. E. (2014). *Teaching physical education for learning* (7th ed.). New York: McGraw-Hill.

Roberton, M. A., & Halverson, L. E. (1984). *Developing children: their changing movement.* Philadelphia: Lea & Febiger.

Roberton, M. A., Halverson, L. E., & Harper, C. J. (1997). Visual/verbal modeling as a function of children's developmental levels in hopping. In J. E. Clark & J. H. Humphrey (Eds.), *Motor development research and reviews* (*Vol. 1*, pp. 122–147). Reston, VA: National Association for Sport and Physical Education.

Schlichter, C. L. (1986). Talents unlimited: Applying the multiple talent approach in mainstream, and gifted programs. In J. Renzulli (Ed.), *Systems and models for developing programs for the gifted and talented* (pp. 21–44). Mansfield Center, CT: Creative Learning Press.

Stevens-Smith, D. (2006). Balancing with the brain in mind. *Teaching Elementary Physical Education, 17*(5), 28–33.

Trudeau, F., Espindola, R., Laurencelle, L., Dulac, F., Rajic, M., & Shephard, R. J. (2000). Follow-up of participants in the Trois-Rivieres growth and development study: Examining their health-related fitness and risk factors as adults. *American Journal of Human Biology, 12*, 207–213.

U.S. Department of Health and Human Services (USDHHS). (2008). *2008 physical activity guidelines for Americans.* Washington, DC: Author. Retrieved from http://www.health.gov/paguidelines

Sample Plan Segments

Here we provide sample plans. For level 1, we annotate these plans and include objectives, notes, and potential interactive decisions, such as refining tasks and tasks for teaching social responsibility and thinking skills. Although we cannot predict accurately which refinements your class of children will need or whether you will need to devote lesson time to teaching social responsibility, we include these tasks to help you visualize how you might respond on your feet to the real-life conditions you encounter. When you read these annotated plans, imagine you are the teacher.

Outstanding teachers plan carefully by anticipating which movement responses children are likely to make, which thinking skills will need to be taught to support children's learning of skills, and what each class will need to learn to develop social responsibility. They also plan the questions they will ask and which children they will call on to respond (Lemov, 2010). In addition, outstanding teachers make contingency plans in case the task they assigned does not work as they had anticipated. Here, we do so by planning ways to modify tasks to be easier (ME) or more difficult (MD). Planning potential interactive decisions is particularly important for undergraduates, because you cannot know the children you will be teaching in the same way as a teacher who works with those children every day and across many years.

In addition, in several level 1 lessons we illustrate how to scaffold exploration. We also illustrate how to introduce the following four aspects of designing sequences:

1. Designing sequences is a three-step process of brainstorming (exploring), selecting movements, and practicing to perfection (see **Sample Plan 26.2**).
2. Creating original and unusual shapes is important. (See **Sample Plan 26.3**).
3. Transitions (see **Sample Plan 26.14**, "Combining Rolling and Rocking on Different Body Parts and in Different Directions"; **Sample Plan 26.16**, "Combining Balancing on Different Body Parts with Different Shapes and Rolling"; and **Sample Plan 26.17**, "Combining Rolling and Balancing While Varying Direction and Shape").
4. Transitions and scaffolding the experimental phase of designing sequences (see **Sample Plan 26.19**, "Combining Balances").

FYI

Summary of Task Label Abbreviations

I	Informing tasks
E	Extending/exploring tasks
R	Refinements
A	Application/assessment tasks
Org	Organizing task
Cog K	Cognitive knowledge: Explains or defines a concept
Social	Social skill or concept
Th	Thinking skill
Mot	Motivation concept
Safety	Safety information or reminder
MD	Modification to make the task more difficult
ME	Modification to make the task easier

Source: Adapted and Modified from Rink, J. E. (2014). *Teaching physical education for learning* (7th ed.).New York: McGraw-Hill.

SAMPLE PLAN 26.1

Weight Bearing and Stillness

Lesson Theme: Weight Bearing and Stillness	Notes and Potential Interactive Teaching Decisions
Standards This plan addresses National Standards 1, 2, 4, and 5 and CCSS for speaking and listening. **Objectives** Children will learn to **Motor** 1. Support their weight on a variety of different body parts, staying tight and in control of the flow of the movement while transferring their weight from one body part to another. **Cognitive** 2. Apply the concept that staying tight helps you control your body. **Thinking Skill** 3. Explore by trying to find a variety of body parts on which to support their weight. **Affective** 4. Appreciate the feeling of bearing weight on different body parts. **Social** 5. Show they respect others by not touching or bumping into them and sharing equipment fairly. **CCSS** 6. Listen carefully and be able to repeat another child's answers to questions.	*Notes:* This plan is designed for ability level 1, pre-kindergarten or kindergarten children new to gymnastics. *Prerequisites:* Ability to travel safely in general space and stop, gallop at a basic level, and skip at a basic level. If you are in a school where the children have not learned the management routine to travel and stop in general space, you must teach this content during the introductory activity. If the children have not had lessons on galloping or skipping, you can substitute other skills or teach one of these skills. **Observation Plan**  1. Scan the class during the entire lesson for safe distance between children. 2. Scan for children being tight and in control of the movement. 3. Scan for children bearing weight on unsafe body parts.
Introductory Warm-up Activity	
Locomotion in General Space **I** When I say, "Go," spread apart and travel by walking about general space without touching anyone else. When I say, "Stop," see if you can stop immediately without falling. Go. Stop. [Repeat several times.]	**Potential Refinements** *Locomotion During Introductory Activity* • Jog, gallop, and skip lightly. *Weight Bearing* • Stay tight. Feel which body part is supporting your weight. • Control your body so you can stop at any time.
E As you walk and when you stop, look around to see if you and all of your classmates are spaced evenly about the space in a scattered formation. Walk. Stop. [Repeat several times.]	**Potential Social Tasks** **Social** How do you show respect for your classmates when traveling in general space? [By being careful not to bump into anyone else.]
E Let's travel about general space again, but this time you can jog, skip, or gallop. Go. Stop. [Repeat several times.]	**Social** I noticed some of you were excellent at avoiding others. Could you share some tips on what you did? [Looked and moved in a different direction, looked for open space and moved there, stopped.] **CCSS** Sara, would you tell us what Jason's tip was? [Repeat with a few other children.]

SAMPLE PLAN 26.1

Weight Bearing and Stillness (*continued*)

E Now change your locomotor step frequently. You decide when to change. [Repeat.]	**R** Jog, gallop, and skip lightly so your feet don't make any sound when they hit the floor.
Content Development	
Exploring Weight Bearing on Different Body Parts **Org** Go with your assigned partner for this week, take out a mat, and as a class, arrange the mats scattered about the gym.	**Safety** We have discussed taking out the mats before. I see you need a review. What do you need to do to make sure you are being responsible for your own and all other children's safety? [Watch where I am going, walk slowly, make sure two children carry each mat, no lifting the mat over our heads, cooperating with my partner in deciding where to locate our mat.] What sort of things do you need to do to protect the mats? [Don't drag them, don't yank out a mat from the bottom of the stack, and be sure the mat has the correct side up.] Why is this important? [So we won't get hurt, so we don't tear up the equipment.] **CCSS** Tucker, would you please tell us what Sawyer said about taking out the mats? [Repeat a few times with other children.]
I Each of you sit on your part of the mat with your feet flat on the floor in front of you like this. [Demonstrate.] **Cog K** You are supporting your weight on your bottom and feet. In other words, your bottom and feet are bearing your weight. We call this weight bearing in gymnastics.	**R** Now tighten your muscles. This will help you be in control of your body and be safe. **R** Let's review what it means to tighten your muscles. Squeeze your fingers into a fist like this. [Demonstrate.] Now squeeze your arms as close to your sides as you can. You should be so tight that if I came over and tried to pull your arm away from your body or tried to open your fist, I would not be able to succeed. *Notes:* You can demonstrate with several children, trying to move their arms away from their sides. If they are tight, do not pull any harder than they can resist. After you do this with a few children, all of them will tighten their arms and fists.
E Keeping at a low level, move and support your weight on a different body part. Then hold still. **Safety** Although your head is a body part, don't go on your head today.	**Social** Be aware of where your partner is moving so you don't bump into each other with stray body parts. **Affective** Concentrate on feeling, from the inside, the body part that is supporting your weight. For example, if you are supporting your weight on your shins, concentrate on how your shins are feeling.
E Travel again onto a different body part. Hold still, and feel your weight on your body part. [Repeat several times.]	**Social** When you were traveling on the mat, how did you keep from bumping into your partner? [I looked at him. I paid attention. I thought about her personal space.] How is paying attention when you are moving different from when you just sit and listen to a story? [When I move, I have to think about not bumping into anyone because I could hurt them.] Are you responsible for your classmates' and your safety? [Yes.]
E Explore traveling and supporting your weight on a variety of different body parts. **Th** When I say, "Explore," I want you to try out as many safe body parts as you can. Try to think of many different body parts.	**Scaffold Exploration If Needed** **E** Let's do several weight-bearing positions in a row. Start with your weight on one body part. Hold still. Change to another body part. Hold still. Change again. Change. Change. Change. See if you can support your weight on many different body parts. [Repeat many times.]

(*continues*)

SAMPLE PLAN 26.1

Weight Bearing and Stillness (*continued*)

Cog K Which body parts did you use in supporting your weight? [Various answers.] That's great. I heard many different body parts.	
Culminating Activity: Equipment	
Org When I say, "Go," one partner get five poly spots, and arrange them in a scattered formation on your mat. The other partner, get four hoops, and arrange them on the floor around your mat, touching the edge of your mat. Go.	
E Explore traveling, supporting your weight on a different body part on each spot or in each hoop. Hold still, and then travel to another spot or hoop. [Let children explore for several minutes.]	**Social** Show that you care for your partner by sharing equipment fairly. **R** I see you are working very hard to control your movement. How are you doing it? [I'm tight. I'm not going too fast. I am thinking about how I move.]
Th Discuss with your partner, what was different about supporting your weight on the spots and in the hoop. [The spots were harder because they are smaller; they were more fun; I could not use as many body parts because there was less room. The hoop had more room; I could use more body parts.]	**CCSS** Cassidy, would you please tell us what J.J. said?
Closure *Peer Assessment and Coaching* **A** To end the class, show your partner how you traveled and did weight bearing on different body parts on the spots and hoops. Partner A goes first, while partner B pays careful attention to see if partner A is tight and in control. Go. [Give the children enough time to travel to several spots and hoops.] Stop. Partner B, how did you know whether partner A was tight and had control over his or her body? [They looked tight, they seemed like they could stop when they wanted to stop.] Now, talk to your partner, and tell her or him when you see tightness and control and when you think he or she could improve. [Repeat several times, reversing roles.]	*Notes:* One assessment focuses on the objective for performance techniques, and the second addresses the social objectives.
Partner Share Assessments **A** Discuss with your partner how you can show classmates you respect them when you are moving, like today when you were doing weight bearing. [Not bumping into them, sharing equipment fairly.] [Call on several children to tell what their partner said.]	*Notes:* Plan to call on children. Don't have children raise their hands (Lemov, 2010). This adds an element of accountability because students know they must be prepared to answer and not rely on classmates who raise their hands.

SAMPLE PLAN 26.2

Balancing on Different Body Parts

Theme: Balancing on Different Body Parts	Notes and Potential Interactive Teaching Decisions
Standards This plan addresses National Standards 1 and 2 and CCSS for vocabulary acquisition. **Objectives** Children will learn to **Motor** 1. Balance on a variety of body parts, staying tight and pointing their feet. **Cognitive Knowledge** 2. Define and use the three-step process of designing short sequences, that is, exploring or brainstorming, selecting the best ideas, and finally practicing the sequence. **Thinking Skill** 3. Explore and to understand the meaning of the word *explore* as trying many, varied, and some unusual ideas (Schlichter, 1986). **CCSS** 4. Acquire and use accurately the domain-specific phrases describing the process of designing sequences: exploring/brainstorming, selecting the best ideas, and practicing the sequence.	*Notes and Special Features:* This lesson is appropriate for children at ability level 1, typically those in kindergarten and grade 1. However, it works for children of any grade who do not have experience with educational gymnastics. This set of learning experiences might take several lessons. We also wrote this lesson plan for teachers who are newcomers to educational gymnastics. In it, we label and illustrate how to scaffold exploration massively, moderately, and lightly. You scaffold only as much as the class you are teaching needs. In the introductory activity, we show you how to define a movement concept within a gymnastics context. This lesson also illustrates how to teach children the three-step process of designing sequences.
Introductory Warm-up Activities	
Locomotor Skills Working on Pointing Toes **I** Explore galloping forward and sliding sideways high and lightly about general space while trying to point your toes in the air.	**Observation Plan**  1. Scan the class during the entire lesson to see whether children are maintaining a safe distance from one another. 2. Scan for pointed toes and tight bodies. 3. Scan to see on which body parts children are balancing.
R Work on a smooth transition between sliding and galloping by not stopping or hesitating between the locomotor skills. [Demonstrate.]	
Cog K In which direction did we slide? [Pause and give children time to think. Then call on a child.] [Sideways.] In which direction were we moving when we galloped? [Forward.] Can anyone think of another direction in which we can travel? [Backward.] There are three main directions: forward, sideways, and backward.	**Potential Refinements** • Be tight. • Point feet. (Extend ankles and toes. You can also use the phrase "point toes.") • Make the transition between the gallop and slide smooth without hesitating.
E Now walk forward on the balls of your feet with your ankles extended. Now walk backward, looking over your shoulder to be sure you don't bump into anybody. Now walk sideways. Now you choose which direction to walk on your toes. Be sure to travel in all three directions.	**R** Point your feet.

(*continues*)

SAMPLE PLAN 26.2

Balancing on Different Body Parts (*continued*)

Content Development

Explore Balancing on Different Body Parts **I** Get into the same position I am in. [Demonstrate a balance on hips with legs tucked and arms out.] We call this a balance because I am working hard to hold my body still.	**R** Look at this big rubber band. It is not doing much right now. If I put some tension on it, then it can do some great work. What are some of the things a rubber band can do that is helpful? What happens if the rubber band is too big for the job and can't stay tight? [Put a rubber band around your arm and let it fall off.] Today, you are going to be like a tight rubber band when you balance.
Massive Scaffolding of Exploration **E** Which body part am I balancing on? [Hips.] Yes. Follow me. I want you to try to balance on another body part. [Demonstrate as you give the next tasks.] Now I am balancing on my side, now hands and shins, now belly. Do these with me.	**R** To hold your balance still, you need to be tight. Tighten up your stomach muscles. Tighten your legs. Hold still.
Cog K Which body parts can you balance on? [Hips, belly, back, shoulders, shins, forearms, hands, and feet. If anyone answers "head," tell them that is an accurate answer, but for today, they are not to balance on their heads because it might not be safe for them.]	**Safety Alert** **Safety** Some children will say, and will try to balance on, the points of their elbows and kneecaps. Teach the whole class that it is not safe to balance on these body parts. Some children will attempt to balance on their heads. If you know your children's capabilities, you can allow those who are competent and confident with headstands to perform these balances. If you do not know the children well, or if a child is not ready to balance on his or her head, tell them that they may not balance on their heads at this time.
E When I say, "Go," I want you to select a body part on which you can balance. Go.	**R** Make sure you can feel tension in your muscles. Staying tight will help you balance and keep still.
E Now balance on another body part. Go. Now another—go. [Repeat several more times.]	**R** When you balance, point your ankles and toes.
E I have not seen anyone balance on his or her side. Let's all try that.	
Cog K Today we have been focusing on two performance cues. What are they? [Point your toes and ankles, and stay tight.]	
Moderate Scaffolding *Balancing on Hands and Feet* **E** Now try different ways to balance on your hands and feet.	**ME** You can balance on your hips and two hands, or on your belly and two hands.
E Change to another balance on your hands and feet. Change again to a different balance on your hands and feet. [Repeat several times.] Change, change, change again.	**R** Which performance cues are you thinking about? [Tight. Point toes.]
E Now explore balancing on your hands and feet with three parts touching the mat. You can balance on two feet and one hand, or on two hands and one foot. Go. Change. Change. [Repeat several times.]	**ME** Keep balancing on two hands and two feet. **ME** Try balancing on your hips and one hand, your side and two hands, or your back.
E Now using just your hands and feet, try to find different ways to balance on two body parts.	**R** Are you working on your performance techniques? **ME** Balance on any two body parts.
E Sometimes when balancing on your hands and feet, you have your belly facing the mat and sometimes your back. Try balancing on your hands and feet sometimes with your belly and sometimes with your back facing the mat. You decide. Go. [Repeat several times.]	**R** If you are having problems staying still, what do you think you need to do? [Stay tight, point toes.] Great answers.

SAMPLE PLAN 26.2

Balancing on Different Body Parts (*continued*)

Light Scaffolding

Balancing on Large and Small Body Parts

Cog K You have both small and large body parts on which you can balance. Can you tell me some large body parts? [Hips, belly, back, shoulders, and so on.] How about some small body parts? [Hands, feet, shins, forearms.]

Safety Alert

Safety Possible answers that lead to a safety discussion: elbows or knees. Why do you think it is not safe to balance on the tips of your elbows or your kneecaps? [It hurts. They are not big enough to get a stable balance.] Great answers. You are right, it can hurt. Instead, balance on your shins or forearms.

E Explore balancing on a variety of large body parts.

MD Encourage children to balance with their feet high or to balance on upper body parts.

E Now explore balancing on a variety of small body parts.

ME Limit small body parts to hands and feet only.

E Now alternate balancing on a small body part with balancing on a large body part. Think of as many different balances as you can.

Affective Which do you like the most, balancing on large or small body parts, and why? [Various answers.] Show me your three favorite balances in a row.

Possible Integration with Science: Biomechanics

Which was more difficult? When is balancing on small body parts difficult, and when is it easy? [It is hard when the body parts are close together. It is easy when they are far apart.] Yes, the answer relates to the science or biomechanical principle that the wider your base of support, the more stable the balance. That is why four small body parts spread far apart form a more stable base than two body parts, and why one large body part is more stable than one small body part.

Balancing with Different Body Parts Highest

E Now, explore balancing on different body parts while holding different body parts highest in the air. [Demonstrate.] Right now, I am balancing on two hands and one foot while my other foot is the highest body part.

R Try to move smoothly and continuously between balances, stopping only when you are holding a balance.

E Try a balance you like, and see if you can change the body part that is highest.

E Try to explore different balances in which your foot or feet are the highest body parts.

R Be sure your base is very stable and tight if your feet are high in the air.

Possible Accommodations for Individual Differences

MD [More difficult task you might use when you are teaching older children who are ready for a challenge.] If you are ready for a more difficult challenge, that means you are perfectly in control of all your balances. If you feel confident and know you can do a more difficult balance safely, try different ways of balancing on upper body parts (shoulders, chest, forearms, and one shoulder). Keep one foot on the ground until you are certain you can hold both feet high. If you are not ready for a more difficult challenge, continue working on balancing on different body parts while holding different body parts highest. All of you must work on skills you can do safely.

Notes: Possible Accommodations for Children with Gymnastics Experience

MD We often find a group of children in a class who have had gymnastics experience, especially when we are teaching this lesson to older children in a school in which the teacher has not done very much educational gymnastics. To differentiate instruction, we use the task in the left column to allow them to explore more difficult balances. Children with Olympic gymnastics experience have rarely been given the chance to explore and create their own balances. Consequently, you need to scaffold exploration for them at a level of difficulty that engages and excites them.

Balancing on Different Body Parts

Cog K Now let's go back to the original task. When I say, "Go," I want you to explore different ways to balance on different body parts. Before you do, let's discuss the word *explore*. What does *explore* mean? [Try different ideas.] Yes. When you explore, I want you to try to find

- Many ideas (lots of ways to balance)
- Varied ideas (lots of different kinds of balances)
- Some unusual or original ideas (some balances that are very different and unusual)

This task on the left illustrates explicit teaching of what it means to explore. You cannot assume children will know what you expect them to do when you say, "Explore." You need to teach them what you mean explicitly, and repeat your explanation in several lessons.

(*continues*)

SAMPLE PLAN 26.2

Balancing on Different Body Parts (*continued*)

E Show me balances on all the different body parts you can. [You can call aloud the different body parts you see to help promote variety.] Explore and experiment freely. Try out your ideas; try to discover different ways you can balance.	**E** When you explore, don't criticize yourself; just brainstorm—come up with a storm of ideas as you move. You can have fun discovering different ways to balance. Don't worry if you make a mistake; just experiment freely.
Culminating Activity: Designing Short Sequences	
A Next you will design a short sequence that consists of three different balances on three different body parts. **Explicit Teaching of the Choreographic Process** When you design a sequence, step 1 is exploring as many different balances as you can. We call this step *brainstorming* or *exploring*. We just completed step 1. The next step is to select your three best balances. These should be your most creative balances, the balances that you think are most interesting, and the balances you can perform the best. Then put these three balances in a sequence. A sequence means that you do one balance, then the second, and then the third, putting them together in a row. Let's do this together. Everyone select one balance and do it. Go. Now select a second balance on a different body part and do it. Go. Now select a third balance on a third different body part and do it. Go. Let's do the sequence again. Ready? Do your first balance, second balance, and third balance. [Repeat several times.]	
R When we design sequences, the first balances you select might not be the ones you really wanted to select. Or maybe you might try the balance, and then decide you would rather do a different balance. You can change your sequence now if you want. Try out your new ideas, or, if you are happy with your first ideas, keep practicing on your own without my telling you when to change to the next balance. [Let the children practice several times.] **E** Make your final selections.	**R** What were the performance techniques you needed to use? [Point toes, stay tight.] Have you been thinking about them while you were performing your sequence?
Cog K/CCSS Let's review. What was the first step in designing a sequence, Jamal? [I don't know.] Carrie? [Brainstorming.] Jamal, what is the first step in designing a sequence? [Brainstorming.] What is step 2, Fredriko? [You select which balances you want in your sequence.] The last step in designing sequence is to practice until you have your sequence perfected, and you can repeat the same movements every time. So the three steps are brainstorm, select, and practice to perfection. Repeat as a class. [Brainstorm, select, practice to perfection.] **R** Practice now.	*Notes:* This set of questions is an example of "no opt out" (Lemov, 2010). Children need to know that you expect them to engage in class by paying attention and answering questions. If they think they can opt out by saying, "I don't know," they will not engage with the content to the level you want. **R** Sometimes, children practice one time and think that they have it perfect. You might need to guide practice by saying, "Everyone get in her or his starting position. When I say 'Go,' practice your sequence. Go." Do this several times.

SAMPLE PLAN 26.2

Balancing on Different Body Parts (*continued*)

Closure: CCSS Informal Assessment

A Go with your assigned partner. Partner A, tell partner B the three steps in designing a sequence. Partner B, tell partner A correct or not correct and give partner A another chance to answer if he or she is incorrect. If partner A is still incorrect a second time, then partner B should help him or her remember the steps.

Another Possible Assessment: Scrap Exit Assessment of Affective Domain

A Pick up a scrap exit ticket and pencil from one of the boxes at the side of the gym. You will see three faces. Circle the one that best shows how you felt today when you were exploring trying to think of different body parts on which you could balance. There are no right or wrong answers. What I want to know is how you felt. Did you feel happy or excited? Did you enjoy the challenge of having to think of different ways to balance? If you had happy feelings and liked exploring, circle the smiling face. Or were you confused, worried, or embarrassed? If you felt bad today, circle the frowning face. If you felt in between, or sometimes happy and sometimes bad, circle the middle face. Turn in your exit slip to me as you exit the gym.

SAMPLE PLAN 26.3

Balancing While Making Different Shapes

Theme: Balancing While Making Different Shapes

Standards

This plan addresses National Standards 1, 2, and 4 and CCSS for vocabulary acquisition.

Objectives

Children will learn to

Motor

1. Balance in a variety of shapes while staying tight, pointing their feet, and keeping their legs straight.

Thinking Skill

2. Think critically about their skills and select one performance technique to work on during the lesson.

Creative Thinking and Cognitive Knowledge of One Principle of Choreography

3. Think creatively, explore, and understand the meaning of original and unusual balances.

Social

(If using culminating activity 2)

4. Be a respectful audience.

CCSS

5. Identify real-life connections between words and their use.
6. Follow agreed-upon rules for audience behavior and discussions.

Notes and Potential Interactive Teaching Decisions

Notes:

These learning experiences are appropriate for children at developmental ability level 1, typically those in kindergarten and grade 1. If children are new to educational gymnastics, these learning experiences also work well with grade 2. Prerequisites are galloping and other locomotor skills you use in the introductory activity. You can substitute jogging or walking fast if children have not learned any other locomotor skills. We planned offer two options for a culminating activity. Option 1 is for kindergarten and grade 1; option 2 is for older beginners. You can also use option 1 on day 1, and then on day 2, review content development tasks and end with option 2. This set of learning experiences will take one to three days.

We scripted this set of tasks to illustrate how to integrate critical thinking skills into a lesson.

We illustrate how to teach the choreographic principle of originality.

Observation Plan

1. Scan for safe traveling in general space without moving into anyone else's personal space.
2. Scan for tight bodies during balances.
3. Look at which shapes children make and assess whether they are plain or original.

(*continues*)

SAMPLE PLAN 26.3

Balancing While Making Different Shapes (*continued*)

Introductory Warm-up Activity	
I Gallop about the gym, and when I say, "Hold," stretch tall on the balls of your feet, reach for the ceiling, and try to stay still and balanced. Then gallop again. Gallop, hold, gallop, hold. [Repeat using different locomotor skills, such as skipping, sliding, and jogging.]	**Potential Refinements** • Stay tight. • Point your feet. **R** When you stretch tall, which performance technique will help you keep balanced? [Stay tight.] So, what should you think about every time you try to stay still and balanced? Everyone answer aloud. [Stay tight.]
Content Development	
Balancing in Curled Shapes **I** Everyone sit curled up like me [demonstrate], grab your shins, and try to balance on your bottoms. We call this a round or a curved shape. Relax. **CCSS** What other things are round or curved? [Call on several children.] Yes, balls, balloons blown up, pumpkins, the moon. What letters are round or curved? [O, C.] Yes, some letters have both round lines and straight lines. What are some of those? [D, P, R, Q, B.]	**ME** If you can't curl your legs, you can keep them straight on the mat, and make curled shapes with your upper body or arms. **ME** If you are in a wheelchair, I have given you two scarves and two short swimming pool noodles [cut to be 12 inches long] [or peacock feathers, lollipop paddles, short dowels, plastic canes, paper canes, or other equipment] that you can use to make different shapes. *Notes:* See the section on modifying balancing activities for children with disabilities earlier in this chapter.
E Sit and balance again in a round shape. Move your arms and legs slowly, and make a different round shape. Now make another round shape. [Repeat.]	
E Let's try balancing on lots of different body parts making lots of different round shapes. Try another round shape. Change to another body part and curled shape. Change again. Great, I see you exploring many ideas. I see some of you on your sides, back, shins, belly, and feet.	**R** There are two performance cues we have learned in previous lessons in gymnastics. What are they? [Point your feet; stay tight.] Think critically about your movements, and choose the one technique you think will most help you improve today. When you make a shape, think about your technique. **R** [Check with individual children which technique they selected.]
Balancing in Wide Shapes **Cog K** Another shape you can balance in is a wide shape. Stand on two feet like me; stretch your arms out to the side. We are making a big, wide shape that is easy to hold. **CCSS** What other things have wide shapes like we are making now? [Stars, starfish, gingerbread people, leaves, cookies, pies, the letter X] **E** This wide shape is not a balance because it is not hard to hold. Let's make it harder. Balance on one foot while making a big wide shape that is harder to hold.	
E Now explore moving your arms and free leg and making different wide shapes that are hard to hold.	**R** Which performance technique did you select? Think about that while you are making wide shapes.
E Now explore balancing in wide shapes on your hands and feet. You can try two hands and two feet, one hand and two feet, two hands and one foot, or one hand and one foot. When you explore, try to move your free body parts to different positions all around your personal space. This makes different shapes.	**R/Th** Think critically about your balances, and decide whether you want to change your focus to point your feet or stay tight, or you can continue working on the same technique you have been focusing on so far. **R** See if you can hold each balance for three seconds.

SAMPLE PLAN 26.3

Balancing While Making Different Shapes (*continued*)

Explicitly Teaching Creative Thinking: Creating Unusual and Original Shapes **Cog K** Some shapes you make are plain. For example, everyone balance on two hands and two feet with feet apart and with your belly facing the mat. This is a plain shape. However, if you cross one arm under your chest or if you reach way back and try to cross your arm over your back, those are unusual and original shapes.	
E Explore different ways of balancing on your hands and feet, trying to make unusual or original shapes.	**R** Focus on the performance technique you selected.
E Now let's extend the task and try balancing on different body parts while making wide shapes. On which other parts might you balance? [Belly, hips, back, forearms and shins, sides.]	**R** If you are having problems staying still, what might you do to improve? [Stay tight, point your feet.] If the technique you are using is not helping, focus on a different performance technique.
E How do you make many different and unusual shapes? [By moving your free body parts in many different positions.] Continue balancing on different body parts trying to find some unusual shapes.	
Alternating Wide and Curled Balances **E** Now explore balancing by alternating balancing in wide shapes and balancing in curled shapes. Think to yourself as you move, "wide shape, curled shape, wide shape, curled shape."	
E Try to make a different wide shape and a different curled shape every time. **E** This time, try to make an unusual wide shape followed by an unusual curled shape.	**R** See if you can hold each balance for three seconds, staying perfectly still and thinking about your performance technique.
Culminating Activity Option 1: Equipment	
Galloping and Skipping, Curled and Wide Balances and Jumps **Org** When I say, "Go," walk over to the wall and pick up two hoops and two poly spots. As a class, spread them out evenly about the gym. Then, stand in your personal space in a scattered formation.	**Org** Check whether the hoops and spots are scattered evenly. *Notes:* Before class, spread hoops and spots around the space next to the walls.
E When I say, "Go," gallop about the space, going around the hoops and spots. Go. **E** Stop. This time, gallop, and when you see an open spot, stop and a balance in a curled shape. When you see an open hoop, stop and balance in a wide shape. Go.	**Social** What do you have to do to work cooperatively as a class in this task? [Watch classmates, and avoid them. Don't bump into anyone. If someone is in a hoop, move to another hoop.]
E Try to do a different balance each time that you stop on a spot or hoop. Move your free body parts in unusual positions.	**R/Th** Today you have been thinking critically and selecting your own performance techniques. What did you choose? [Call on several children.] You can stay with the same one technique or choose a different one. I want you to select the one performance cue that you think will most help you improve.
E This time, skip about the space, and when you come to a spot, jump over it while making a curled shape in the air. When you come to a hoop, stop and balance in a wide shape.	**MD** If you want a challenge, make each balance a difficult balance.

(*continues*)

SAMPLE PLAN 26.3

Balancing While Making Different Shapes (*continued*)

E Let's try the reverse. When you come to a hoop, jump and make a wide shape in the air, then bring your feet together to land on your feet in the hoop. Then skip to a spot, and balance in a curled shape. **E** Now, you make the decision about what to do when you get to a hoop or spot. Sometimes jump, and sometimes balance. Try to make a variety of wide shapes and a variety of curled shapes. Every so often, make an unusual shape.	
Culminating Activity Option 2: Equipment and Sequences	
Org Walk over to the wall, and pick up two hoops and one spot, bring them back to your space, and set them up in a line close together, but not touching—hoop, spot, hoop.	
Three Balances in a Row **E** Explore different ways to balance in a big, wide shape in or over the first hoop, make a curled shape on the spot, and end in a wide balance in or over the second hoop.	**R/Th** Today you have been thinking critically and selecting your own performance techniques. Which one did you choose? [Call on several children.] You can stay with the same technique or choose a different one. I want you to select the one performance technique that you think will most help you improve.
E Reverse direction, and try a different wide balance in or over the first hoop, a different curled balance on the spot, and a different wide balance in or over the second hoop. Make sure at least one balance is unusual or original. [Repeat task several times.]	**MD** If you want a challenge, make each balance a difficult-to-hold balance.
Create a Sequence of Favorite Balances **A** Now pick your favorite three balances and put them together into a sequence that you can repeat exactly the same way over and over. **R** Try to move directly from one balance to the next with just one step or movement. Don't stand up or take two or three steps between balances. If you need to move your hoops and spot closer together so you need to take only one step or movement between balances, you may do so.	**R** Practice the transitions so they are the same each time you practice your sequence. **R** Work on making your sequence a "perfect 10" by thinking about your performance technique as you move.
Show the Sequence to a Partner **A** When you feel confident about your sequence, show it to your assigned partner for the week. Partners, give the performers a compliment, telling them what you thought they did best.	*Notes:* We typically don't use this or the following tasks in kindergarten and grade 1.
Peer Assessment **A** I have given you a peer assessment sheet so you can help your partner improve her or his sequence. Watch your partner's sequence, and circle the answers that describe your partner's sequence. Then discuss what you saw with your partner, and try to help her or him improve.	**Sample Peer Assessment Tool** Name of performer: ____________ Name of peer helper: ____________ Three different balances: Yes No One unusual balance: Yes No Only one step or movement in between balances: Perfect Good Not Yet

SAMPLE PLAN 26.3

Balancing While Making Different Shapes (*continued*)

Show Sequence to Class (If Child Wants to Show)

A If you would like to show your sequence to the class, you may. All partner As can show first. Partner Bs will show second.

Social/CCSS What are the rules for good audience behavior? [Sit quietly and respectfully, don't talk, watch, clap at the end, give compliments at the end.] Let's watch those who want to show their sequence.

Closure: Potential Assessment

A/CCSS I will hand out a blank web and pencils to you and your partner. In the middle, write "good audience behavior." You and your partner should then fill in different characteristics of good audience behavior in all the bubbles connected by lines to the center of the web. At the bottom of the web is a smiling face and a frowning face. Circle the face that represents whether your classmates were a good audience when you performed.

Notes: If the children have not discussed good audience behavior in the classroom or in physical education, take the time to extend the discussion until you know through questioning that all children understand how you expect them to behave. This is a good time to link the discussion to the moral standard to always treat people the way you want to be treated.

SAMPLE PLAN 26.4

Safety Rolling Using Side Rolls

Lesson Theme: Safety Rolling Using Side Rolls

Standards

This plan addresses National Standards 1, 2, and 4 and CCSS for vocabulary acquisition.

Objectives

Children will learn to

Motor

1. Move from a stand to gently rolling sideways, and then return to a stand.
2. Jump, land, and smoothly transfer from feet to rolling.
3. Control the speed of the roll.
4. Use strong arms while rolling.

Cognitive

5. Understand the importance of landing safely in gymnastics

Social

6. Care about the safety of their classmates by not bumping into them and by sharing space fairly.

CCSS

7. Identify real-life connections between words and their use.

Notes and Potential Interactive Teaching Decisions

Notes: This lesson is appropriate for children at ability level 1 (all grades). It introduces rolling to children and, if they are ready, teaches them how to land safely and roll after a small jump. We teach sideways rolling because this skill is a safe roll for all children. We include possible modifications for rolling in different directions if you need to differentiate instruction. When undergraduates teach this lesson in field experiences to a class of older children without previous experience with educational gymnastics, they often discover that some children within the class have had previous gymnastics experiences. Allowing them to roll in different directions accommodates their more advanced ability levels.

Prerequisite: At least one lesson on skipping. The children can be skipping at an immature level, and you can use the warm-up as a time for additional needed practice.

(*continues*)

SAMPLE PLAN 26.4

Safety Rolling Using Side Rolls (*continued*)

Introductory Warm-up Activity	
I Let's warm up today by skipping about the space. Try to travel to all areas of the gym.	**R** Skip higher. Think about extending your ankles and swinging your arms high.
E Alternate skipping and bouncing in place like a human pogo stick. Skip, then bounce, skip, then bounce. You decide when to change from skipping to bouncing and back to skipping. Start with small bounces.	**R** Extend your ankles to help you bounce and skip.
E This time, bounce higher, now higher.	**R** Extend your ankles as if you are a human pogo stick.

Content Development

Org Go with your assigned partner, pick up a mat with one of you at each end, and place the mats in a scattered formation about the gym. Then sit on your mat. [Use one mat per child if possible, or have two children share one mat, with both practicing at the same time on half of the mat. When you progress to the stand–roll–stand sequence, have each pair start on one side of the mat. In most situations, there is no need to start at the end of the mat and go one at a time.]

Potential Refinements

- Control the speed of your roll.
- Stay tight to help you control your speed.
- Make the transfer from the stand or jump smooth and continuous.
- Land on your feet from the jump.
- Use strong arms on all rolls.

Making Connections

Cog K/CCSS Put your thumbs up if you have ever watched TV and seen a stuntman or stuntwoman in a chase scene jump from some tall object, land, roll, get up, and keep right on running. These people were doing what we call safety rolling. Safety rolling helps you land from a jump and safely control the force by rolling.

Can you think of other times you see safety rolling? [Parachutist landing and then rolling, fight scenes on TV where the actor moved quickly to avoid being hit and rolled right back up again.] Actors, stuntmen, and stuntwomen have practiced many years to do the kinds of safety rolling you see on television. Today we are going to learn safety rolling for beginners because it is important to always be safe in gymnastics.

Observation Plan

1. Watch the speed of the children's movements, and make sure they are moving at a safe speed they can control.
2. Watch whether any child leans too far forward during the jump and is not focused on landing on the feet first.
3. Watch for strong arms protecting the head.

Transferring Weight

I Start sitting like me. Slowly and with control, transfer your weight onto a different body part that is next to the one you are on. Transfer to a second body part. [Demonstrate as you talk the children through this task.] Now transfer to another body part that is next to the one you are on. Now transfer to another body part.

Social What do you need to do to show you care about your classmates' safety? [Stay on my section of the mat. Make sure I don't bump into my partner. Be especially careful of stray body parts.]

R Keep your bodies tight so you can control your weight as you transfer from one body part to another.

E Each time I say, "Transfer," I want you to transfer your weight to a different body part. Transfer, transfer, transfer. [Repeat several times.]

R Make sure you can feel inside your muscles that you are tight and in control of your body's movement.

Social Be very aware of your partner so you don't bump into him or her.

Rolling Sideways

Cog K What we have been doing is called rolling. Most of you have been rolling sideways.

SAMPLE PLAN 26.4

Safety Rolling Using Side Rolls (*continued*)

E Continue rolling, but roll sideways only. [Repeat several times.] **R** Keep your body curled, elbows bent, and palms flat. When your palms make contact with the mat, push against the mat. This helps to keep your head safe. When your arms are bent and pushing on the mat to keep your head safe, we call this technique *strong arms.*	**Social** What are some of the things you can do to make sure you don't bump into anyone? [Look around, move slowly, pause and let your partner roll by you, reverse your pathway and roll into an open space, look for open spaces.] **ME** Throughout this entire lesson, if you can't roll, you can slide down the mat by pulling or pushing with your arms or legs.
E This time, as you roll sideways, sometimes curl in a round shape, and sometimes roll in a straight shape. You decide when to be curled and when to be straight. You will also need to decide when to keep rolling in a straight pathway and when to reverse or go on a different pathway to stay on your mat.	**R** Don't forget—strong arms. **R** Stay round and tight so you can roll smoothly. *Note:* If tall children are sharing a small mat and doing straight rolls, they will have to start after their partner has traveled halfway across the mat.
Cog K Some of the rolling movements we do in educational gymnastics have names. The rolls you have been doing have names. **CCSS** One is an egg roll; the other is a log roll. Which do you think is which? Why do you think these rolls have names? [That's what they look like!] **R** When you do egg and log rolls, you can put your arms in a variety of positions to make your roll interesting and different. But first learn the strong-arms position (palms pushing on the mat when you roll); then when you have control and tight curled or straight bodies, you can work on varying your arms and body position.	*Note:* We suggest beginners use strong arms with palms flat on the mat in side rolls because this technique prepares them for more difficult forward and backward rolls, where it is critical to use strong arms. **R** One problem I am seeing with your egg rolls is that some of you are rolling on your kneecaps. That can hurt. When you do an egg roll, stay tucked tightly and roll on your shins.
Stand, Roll, Stand **E** Stand on the balls of your feet and stretch your arms toward the ceiling, being as tall as you can be. Next, slowly and gently take your weight down onto the mat, roll sideways, and come right back up to a stand. If you are sharing a mat with a partner, both of you start on one side of the mat, and each of you stay on your half of the mat. You can roll at the same time if you are careful and don't allow any body parts in your partner's personal space.	**R** Make the transition to the floor and back up smooth, gentle, and one continuous movement.
Cog K What you just did was a safety roll from a stand.	
E Let's practice safety rolls. Stand, roll, and come right back up to a stand again. [Repeat many times.]	*Notes:* It is important to have children work on rolling up to a stand with side rolls because this activity prepares them for the more mature pattern of rolling to a stand in forward and backward rolls. You want coming up to a stand to be a habit.
Modification to Differentiate Instruction and Accommodate More Experienced Children **MD** You can also do safety rolls in different directions. What are the different directions in which you can travel? [Forward, backward, sideways.] Yes, in gymnastics rolling, we also have diagonal forward and diagonal backward. For those of you who have experience with gymnastics, who have learned different rolls, and who are confident and sure you will be safe, you can try to stand, roll in different directions, and come up to a stand again. If you have complete control over your side rolls and you are ready to try a different roll, a forward diagonal roll is a good choice. To perform a forward diagonal roll, do a sideways egg roll but roll on a diagonal, going over one of your shoulders.	**R** For all rolls, use strong arms to protect your head. **R** Control your speed; don't roll so fast you make a thump on the mat. **Making Connections to Science** The following story is intended to help children appreciate the importance of strong arms: Did you know your neck is the same size as your thigh, but your neck has open tubes for breathing and eating and bones that move? Your thigh has a solid bone in the middle, so it is stronger for holding your weight. This is why it is so important to use strong arms to support your weight when you roll.

(*continues*)

SAMPLE PLAN 26.4

Safety Rolling Using Side Rolls (*continued*)

Jump, Land, Roll, Stand

E Using whichever roll you feel most safe and confident doing, add a straight jump. To start, do a small one-inch jump straight up while stretching your arms toward the ceiling, land on your feet, slowly and gently take your weight onto the floor, and then roll. Roll right back up to a stand, as you have been doing all during this lesson. Be sure to land on your feet before starting your roll. [Repeat several times.]

Immature Patterns and Safety Alert

This might seem difficult to believe, but when beginners first learn to connect a jump with a roll, some children jump and start leaning to begin their roll while they are still in the air before they land safely on their feet. Some even land on their knees. To prevent this problem, emphasize "land on your feet and then slowly take your weight down to the floor."

R Land on your feet before you roll.

MD/ME If you are perfectly in control of your roll and are safe and confident, you can start to jump higher. If you are nervous or flopping on the mat, practice the stand–roll–stand sequence until you have it perfected.

R Use strong arms to protect your head.

R Control the speed of your movement so you are safe and in control of your body.

R Make the transition from jump to roll smooth, continuous, and controlled.

Culminating Activity for Classes Able to Be Socially Responsible

E Everyone walk about the space. If you see a free mat, go to the end, stand, do a safety roll, and come to a stand. Walk about the space again.

Social Watch to make sure no one else is about to stand, roll, and stand on the mat before you start.

Silent Commandos

E You were perfect in being responsible for your and other classmates' safety. Let's make the task even more fun. Jog easily about the space. If you see a free mat, go to the end, jump, land on the mat on your feet, and do a safety roll. Come up to a stand, and then continue jogging.

CCSS Why do you think we call this "silent commandos?" [You pretend you are commandos on a raid. Because you move silently doing safety rolls as if you were on a commando raid.] Good answers. Also, try to move stealthily. Does anyone know what stealthily means? [sneakily, secretly, quietly, cautiously] Good descriptions. Now be silent, stealthy, commandos.

Notes: This is an exciting, engaging task for children who are socially responsible and have mastered the management routine of working safely in a scattered formation. Even older children who are at level 3 enjoy revisiting silent commandos, varying the shapes of their jumps and doing different rolls.

Social Make sure no one else is about to jump, land, and roll on the mat before you start.

Notes: This is also an energetic task. If you have taught health-related fitness (HRF), now is a good time to review the concepts and ask children on which area of fitness they have been working. Alternatively, you can integrate HRF concepts into the lesson from the beginning and have children take their pulse several times and compare their heart rates during different tasks.

SAMPLE PLAN 26.5

Steplike Actions at Low Levels on Different Pathways

Theme: Steplike Actions at Low Levels on Different Pathways

Standards

This plan addresses National Standards 1, 2, and 4 and CCSS for vocabulary acquisition.

Objectives

Children will learn to

Motor

1. Travel using a variety of steplike actions on their hands and feet with straight arms and flat palms.
2. Travel lightly and stretched tall using a variety of locomotor patterns on straight, curved, and zigzag pathways, accurately demonstrating the pathway.

Notes and Potential Interactive Teaching Decisions

Notes:

This lesson is appropriate for level 1 beginners (kindergarten and grades 1–2).

The tasks can take two to four days depending on the age of the children and the amount of review they need during the content development segment of your lessons.

This set of learning experiences includes an example of how to introduce the movement concept of pathways.

We describe two different options for culminating activities, which you can use for different lessons.

One of these lessons also includes an example of apparatus stations set up in a mall as the culminating activity.

SAMPLE PLAN 26.5

Steplike Actions at Low Levels on Different Pathways (*continued*)

Thinking Skill

3. Self-regulate their thinking about one performance technique while moving.

Social

4. Share space and apparatus stations fairly.

CCSS

5. Acquire and use accurately conversational, general academic, and domain-specific words and phrases, including those that signal spatial relationships.
6. Identify real-life connections to words and their use.

Observation Plan

1. Observe the distance between the children and make sure they have plenty of room for safety when their feet are in the air.
2. Listen and look for soft landings.
3. Look for flat palms and straight arms.

Introductory and Warm-up Activities

Review and Integration of an HRF Concept

Cog K/HRF Does anyone remember why we warm up? Yes: To get our bodies ready for physical education lessons. Why do we call it a "warm-up"? [Because we move so that our hearts start to pump more blood and our bodies get warmer.]

Potential Refinements

Locomotor Skills

- Travel lightly and stretch tall when you skip, gallop, or slide.

Steplike Actions

- Straight arms, lock elbows
- Palms flat

Locomotor Skills: Skip, Gallop, and Slide

I Let's get warmed up by traveling about the space while galloping. Freeze in a straight shape on the balls of your feet, reaching high toward the ceiling, when I say, "Balance high." Go.

Safety Call "Balance high" randomly or for safety whenever you see children beginning to generate too much speed.

R What do you need to do to balance? [Stay tight.]

E Now change to sliding.

R Be sure to travel throughout the entire space, moving to all parts of the gym—don't get stuck traveling in a circle.

E Now change to skipping.

R Be sure you are alternating legs.

Definition of Pathways

Cog K/CCSS How many of you have ever walked on a beach just after it has rained or been raked (or walked in new snow) and then looked back? You can see your footprints behind you. Your footprints show the pathway you took. We travel on pathways in physical education, too, but you can't look back and see your footprints because the floor is hard. So, in PE we pretend that we did something you won't be allowed to do at home—we pretend we have stepped in a can of paint with both feet. As you walk about general space, imagine that you can look back and see where you have stepped. You can travel on three different types of pathways. Can anyone guess what one of these might be? [Curved] Good answer.

Notes: Call on several children. If the children identify one of the three pathways, work on that. Then ask for another pathway and work on that. Then ask for the third. If the children cannot identify the pathways, then tell them.

Traveling on Different Pathways

Cog K/CCSS Let's travel on curved pathways, which look like this. [Demonstrate.] Which letters look like curved pathways? [S, C, O, and so on.]

I Walk about the space on curved pathways. They can be small curves or large curves.

Social Sometimes it is hard to share space. What can you do when you are following your pathway and you realize you are about to bump into someone else? [Stop to let the other person pass, slow down, change your pathway.]

(*continues*)

SAMPLE PLAN 26.5

Steplike Actions at Low Levels on Different Pathways (*continued*)

Cog K/CCSS What is another type of pathway? [Like the letter Z.] Excellent. We call those kinds of pathways zigzag or angular pathways. **E** Now walk on zigzag pathways. Zigzag pathways are like the letter Z with sharp points and sharp changes like this. [Demonstrate.] Go.	**R** Be sure you make a sharp angle when you do a zigzag, like this. [Demonstrate.]. Don't round your zigzags like this. [Demonstrate a rounded zigzag, reiterating that it is not a zigzag, but rather a curve.]
Cog K/CCSS What is the last type of pathway? Let me give you a hint. Think about letters. [Straight.] Correct. In which letters do you use a straight line? [T, I, X, L, and so on.] When you travel on a straight line, you are traveling on straight pathways. In the gym, you can do only short straight pathways because you can't walk through the walls. **E** Walk on straight pathways, pause, turn, and then start on another straight pathway. Go.	
Combining Locomotor Skills and Pathways **E** Now that you know the three different pathways, explore traveling on curved, straight, and zigzag pathways by sliding about the space.	**R** Make your zigzag pathways have really sharp angles.
E Now try skipping. Explore traveling on curved, straight, and zigzag pathways. You choose when to change pathways.	**R** Skip lightly. **R** Stretch tall.
E Now try traveling sometimes skipping, sometimes galloping, and sometimes sliding on curved, straight, and zigzag pathways. You choose when to change pathways and when to change locomotor skills, but be sure to practice all of them.	**R** Travel lightly while stretched tall.
Content Development	
Org Go with your assigned partner and carry two mats, one at a time, placing them in a scattered position in the gym. Then each of you sit on one mat.	**Social** Review rules for carrying mats if necessary.
Travel on Hands and Feet **Cog K** Instead of traveling on your feet, now you will travel transferring your weight from your hands to your feet. Sometimes we call these movements *steplike actions* because you take steps, but you use only your hands and feet. Today we will focus on steplike actions traveling on hands and feet. **R** The most important thing to remember when you transfer your weight to your hands is to lock your elbows straight—take an imaginary key and lock your elbows now. [Demonstrate pretending to lock elbows straight by turning a key in your elbow.] **E** Explore traveling across your mat, transferring your weight from your hands to your feet and back to your hands again.	**Scaffolding Exploration If Needed** **E** Try steplike actions sometimes with your belly facing the mat, sometimes facing the ceiling, and alternating facing up and down. **E** Try steplike actions traveling sideways, backward, and forward. **R** What's the performance cue you need to think about as you travel on your hands? [Lock elbows.]
Taking Weight on Hands with Body Curled **E** Starting from a stand, try taking your weight on your hands by putting your palms flat on the mat, with elbows locked, and springing your feet off the mat only one inch and landing back on your feet.	**R** Scan the class, and give individual feedback to those children using "track start" hand positions rather than flat palms. See the description and photograph of "track start" hands earlier in this chapter. **ME** Take some of your weight on your hands, but don't spring off your feet.

SAMPLE PLAN 26.5

Steplike Actions at Low Levels on Different Pathways (*continued*)

E Try again over and over until you feel comfortable transferring your weight onto your hands and back to your feet.	**MD** If you feel safe and confident, you can lift your feet higher, but for now still keep them low.
Teaching Self-Regulation **Th** It is important to think about one performance technique or cue while you are moving. Select the one cue you think will best help you improve today, and think about that cue while you move. As you take your weight on your hands, say to yourself, "Straight arms," or think, "Elbows locked," or think, "Palms flat." When you finish the move, ask yourself, "Did I keep my arms straight? Did I think about one performance technique?"	
E Explore traveling across your mat with steplike actions, sometimes taking your weight on your hands and then shifting your weight back to your feet. Stay at a low level.	**R** Which cue are you thinking about to improve your steplike actions? [Lock elbows, palms flat, straight arms.] **ME** Take some of your weight on your hands, but don't spring off your feet.
E Explore traveling and taking your weight on your hands; land sometimes on two feet and sometimes on one foot.	**MD** If you feel safe and confident, you can lift your feet higher, but for now still keep them low.
Culminating Activity: Stacked Mats	
Stacked Mats/Trapezoid Sections/Benches **Org** Go with your assigned partner, stack one of your mats, and put it across the center of the flat mat so there is space on the flat mat on both sides of the stacked mat. [Demonstrate with two children.]	**R** Throughout this next section of the lesson, frequently ask children which performance technique they have selected. Ask if they are thinking about the technique when they practice.
E You and your partner share a stacked mat. Stand to the side, put your palms flat on the stacked mat, take your weight on your hands, and spring your feet off the floor about one inch.	**R** Make sure you think about "elbows locked" or "palms flat" while you are practicing. **ME** Take some of your weight onto your hands, but don't spring off your feet.
E If you feel safe and confident, you can take your weight on your hands and spring your feet up a little higher, but still keep them at a low level.	**R** When you finish your skill, do you check whether you were thinking about your performance technique when you practiced?
E If you feel safe and confident, you can take your weight on your hands and spring your feet up, sometimes taking off from one foot or two feet and sometimes landing on one foot or two feet. Keep your feet at a low level.	**R** Continue working on flat palms and elbows straight. It might take some children several lessons to master the palms flat technique, although it will be easier for them to do so on the stacked mat.
On Different Pathways **E** This time, take your weight on your hands on the stacked mat, but instead of landing in place, make your feet land to the side. Then continue traveling on a straight pathway down the stacked mat and back.	**Social** What do you need to do to be fair to your partner? [Share the stacked mat equally.] **ME** You do not have to travel; you can remain in place.
E This time, travel on a straight pathway down the mat and on a curved pathway around the end of the mat. As you travel, sometimes land on one foot and sometimes on two feet.	

(*continues*)

SAMPLE PLAN 26.5

Steplike Actions at Low Levels on Different Pathways (*continued*)

E Explore different ways to take your weight on your hands and spring your feet on and over the stacked mat on a zigzag pathway down the mat. Keep your feet as low as necessary for you to be safe, in control, and confident. **E** Sometimes take off one foot at a time, and sometimes take off on two feet together. Sometimes land on one foot at a time, and sometimes land on two feet together.	**ME** You can travel on your feet on a zigzag pathway.

Culminating Activity: Equipment Mall

Org We are going to set up an equipment mall. In your space, scatter four hoops, three jump ropes (each in a straight line), two canes each placed on two small cones, and two stacked mats on flat mats. Be sure you have an area in front of and behind each piece of equipment for take-offs and landings.	**Org** Organize children in groups of four to six, with each group working in about a 15-foot-by-15-foot space. Demonstrate with one group how to set up the mall. Then check all malls to ensure that the children have arranged them properly.

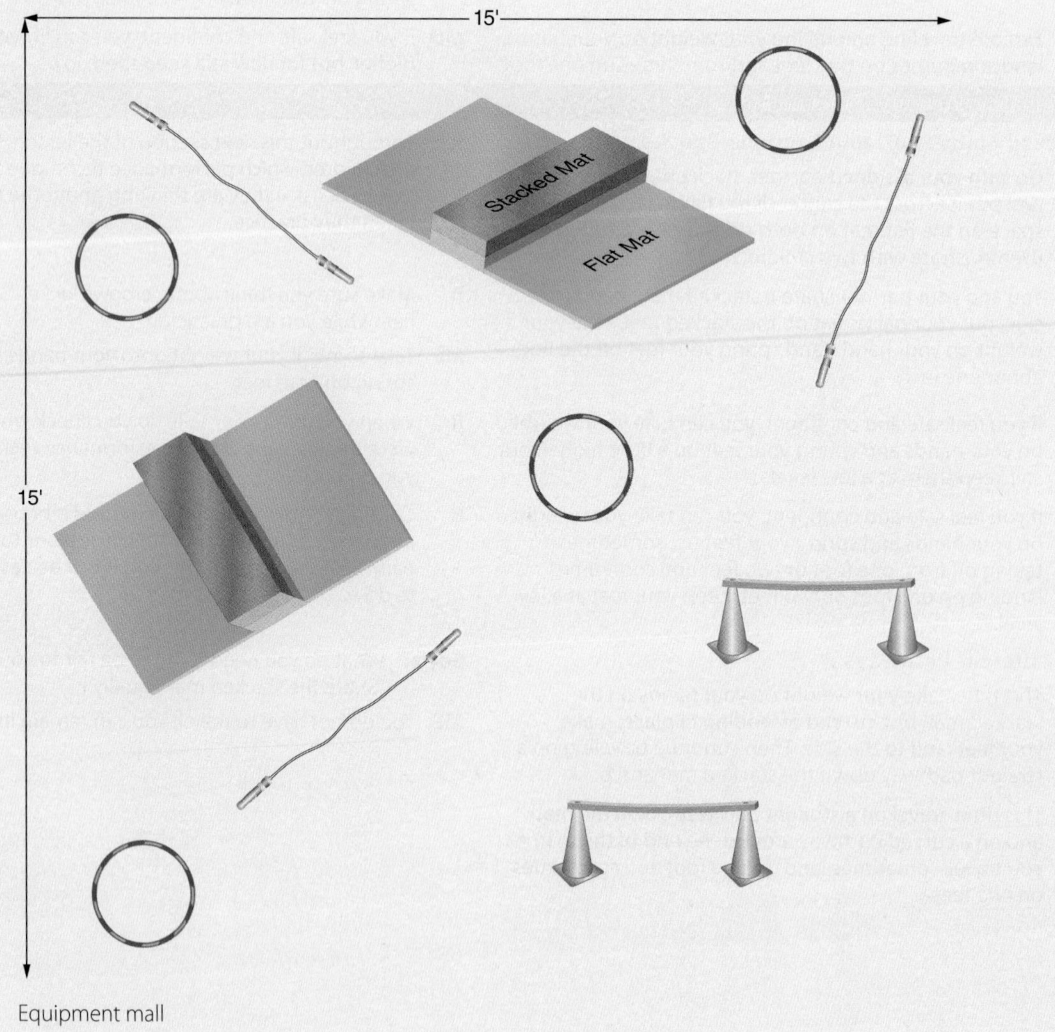

Equipment mall

SAMPLE PLAN 26.5

Steplike Actions at Low Levels on Different Pathways (*continued*)

A You have made an equipment mall. Just like in a real mall, you get to go to different stores (or centers) within your mall. At each mall store, practice traveling with steplike actions on different pathways. Here are the specific tasks for each store (i.e., center):

Ropes

E Explore traveling on your hands and feet going over the rope and then back on a zigzag pathway for the length of the rope. Sometimes take off on one foot at a time, and sometimes take off with two feet together. Sometimes land on one foot at a time, and sometimes land with two feet together. Sometimes take off on one foot, and land on the other.

Hoops

E Explore different ways to reach into the hoop, take your weight on your hands, and spring your feet to a different position around the hoop. Sometimes take off on one foot at a time, and sometimes take off with two feet together. Sometimes land on one foot at a time, and sometimes land with two feet together. Sometimes take off on one foot, and land on the other. You can also take your weight on your hands outside of the hoop and land on your feet in the hoop, twist and put your hands in a different place, and spring outside of the hoop. Travel on curved pathways.

Stacked Mats

E Explore traveling down the stacked mat on a zigzag pathway while taking your weight on your hands and feet. Sometimes take off on one foot at a time, and sometimes take off with two feet together. Sometimes land on one foot at a time, and sometimes land with two feet together. Sometimes take off on one foot, and land on the other.

R Select one performance technique to think about as you practice. Which performance techniques might you select? Right—locked elbows, straight arms, or palms flat.

MD If you need more of a challenge, take your weight on your hands, and spring your feet a little higher while still remaining safe with controlled, light landings.

ME Travel on your feet.

Rules for Equipment Malls That Make Them Fair and Fun for Everyone

- Go to a free center. (Don't wait in line.)
- Share time fairly with your classmates. (Don't stay at one center too long).
- You select which center and which performance techniques will most help you improve today.
- At each center, try to think while you move about one performance technique.

Rules of the equipment mall

Flight from Feet

In these descriptions of learning experiences, we discuss teaching jumping, hopping, and other types of flight from feet. These learning experiences are organized differently from previous sample plans. Because flight skills are energetic, and children can get over-tired and disengage, we typically teach jumping, hopping, and flight from feet within a lesson that includes other content. Consequently, we present lesson segments for introducing the content. In some lesson segments, we include suggestions only for content development. At the end of this section, we present centers (or stations) appropriate for children at ability levels 1, 2, and 3. As always, you can use centers as a whole-class task if you have adequate amounts of equipment and pieces of apparatus.

During their elementary school years, children need lots of practice in jumping and hopping in multiple lessons every year because the mature patterns take years to develop. Moreover, jumping uses muscle power and is linked to improved bone strength. In addition, jumping is an important skill in games, gymnastics, and dance. Including jumping centers for review and additional practice across the year in units on other game, gymnastics, or dance content is one way to increase the amount of practice children have jumping.

SAMPLE PLAN 26.6

Jumping, Hopping, and Five Types of Flight from Feet

Five Types of Flight from Feet	Notes and Potential Interactive Teaching Decisions
Standards These learning experiences meet National Standards 1 and 2 and CCSS for vocabulary acquisition. **Objectives** Children will learn **Motor** 1. To perform the five types of flight from feet with resilient landings, extending through the ankles and popping off the ground. **Cognitive Knowledge** 2. The names of the five types of flight from feet. **CCSS** 3. Acquire and use accurately conversational, general academic, and domain-specific words and phrases, including those that signal precise actions.	*Notes:* We begin teaching jumping, hopping, and other types of flight from feet by teaching the basic patterns and working on resiliency. The basic pattern is a prerequisite for teaching jumping and hopping for height and distance. In this lesson segment, we also describe one way to teach the appropriate terminology. You can introduce the terminology in different lessons or even at different grade levels. For example, you might teach the terms for jumping and hopping in pre-kindergarten and kindergarten and save the other terms for older grades.
Introductory and Warm-up Activities	
Why Jumping Is Important **Cog K** In the next month, we will spend several lessons on jumping. Jumping is important for your health. Do you know why? Jumping helps build strong bones. Jumping is part of the muscle power area of fitness. In addition, think of all the sports you know, and tell me when being a good jumper would be important. [Basketball, volleyball, track and field, gymnastics, ice skating, soccer, softball/baseball, football, and so on.] Yes, jumping is part of lots of sports. Jumping is an important skill for you to develop.	**Potential Refinements** • Be light and springy. • Pop. • Make your ankles and knees like springs.
Exploring Flight from Feet **I** Explore traveling about the space while jumping and springing in the air. Sometimes land on one foot, sometimes on two feet. Sometimes take off from one foot and sometimes from two feet.	**R** Be light and springy.
Content Development	
Cog K/CCSS You just explored the five different ways you can get flight from your feet. Now I will teach you their names. Does anyone know the name of this action? [Demonstrate a jump.] Right answer. A *jump* is a two-foot take-off with a landing on two feet. Can anyone guess what this action is called? [Demonstrate a leap.] A *leap* is a one-foot take-off with a landing on the opposite foot. What is this? [Demonstrate a hop.] A *hop* is a one-foot take-off with a landing on the same foot. For the last two, I will have to teach you French because the terms were first developed in France.	**Do Bunnies Hop?** Do you want to know a great fact of nature? Have you ever heard someone say, "Do a bunny hop" or "Hop like a bunny"? Do you want to know a surprising fact? Don't tell the bunnies about this! Bunnies don't hop; they jump. This is one of the surprising facts of nature, and now you know! Bunnies don't hop. A friend of ours, Robin Litaker, told us this fact—and now we are telling you.

SAMPLE PLAN 26.6

Jumping, Hopping, and Five Types of Flight from Feet (*continued*)

Assemblé [a-sahm-BLAY] means "assembled or joined together." An *assemblé* is a one-foot take-off with a landing on two feet. We also call it "1 to 2."

Sissone [see-SAWN] is a two-foot take-off with a landing on one foot. We also call it "2 to 1."

Org Walk over to the wall and pick up a paper cane, hoop, and jump rope. Scatter the equipment throughout the space, then stand in your hoop.

Resilient Jumps **E** Let's work on springlike jumping. Start by jumping up and down in your hoop.	**R** Be light and bouncy.
E Now jump out of your hoop, jump over to your paper cane, and jump back and forth over the cane.	
E Now travel to your rope and jump side to-side, traveling down the rope.	**ME** Jump over your rope forward. Jump side to side, but don't travel down the rope.
Leaping **E** Let's practice leaping. Jog easily about the space. When you come to a free paper cane, take off from one foot and land on the other foot, and continue jogging.	**R** Make your ankles like springs to help you get height on your leap.
Assemblé, Sissone **E** Now travel about the space practicing *assemblés* and *sissones*—that is, 1 to 2 and 2 to 1. This is like hopscotch.	**R** Really try to pop off the floor.
Hop **E** Finally, let's hop. Lift one knee up and see if you can spring off one foot and land on that same foot. Travel about the space hopping. **E** If you are ready for a challenge, when you come to a free hoop, see if you can hop into or out of the hoop. When you come to a free rope, try to hop over the rope.	**ME** You can hop once and pause. Or, you can hop once. Pause, and hop again. **MD** Alternatively, you can hop several times in a row into and out of the hoop and from side to side as you travel down the rope. **MD** Try hopping consecutively on the other foot. **R** Use your arms to help you gain height on your hop. **ME** If you get too tired and start to lose your balance, change legs or jog to the next piece of equipment.
E Let's go back to the original task. Travel about the space exploring the five different ways to get flight from your feet and using the equipment in different ways.	
Closure: CCSS Informal Assessment **A** With your assigned partner, discuss the names of the five different ways to get flight from feet. Raise your hand if the two of you cannot remember one of the terms, and I will help you. [Give the children time to talk. Then call on children randomly, demonstrating the movement as you ask the question.] [Repeat until the children answer correctly every time.] **Connection to HRF** **A** Let's do a heart rate check. Take your pulse. Is your heart beating fast? Is jumping (the way you have been doing) a good exercise for working on cardiorespiratory endurance? How do you know? [I am breathing faster, my heart rate is faster.] So jumping can work more than one area of fitness: muscle power and cardiorespiratory endurance.	**Asking Questions** Continue rapidly and repeatedly asking the questions, changing the order using the "cold call" technique. *Cold call* means calling on children regardless of whether they raise their hands. If a child gives an incorrect answer or says, "I don't know," ask another child or give the right answer yourself. Then come back to the original child, and ask the same question again. These questioning techniques are called "no opt out" and "right is right" and lead to improved engagement and learning (Lemov, 2010).

SAMPLE PLAN 26.7

Jumping for Distance and Height, Focusing on Take-offs

Jumping for Distance and Height, Focusing on Take-offs	Notes and Potential Interactive Teaching Decisions
Standards These learning experiences meet National Standards 1 and 2 and CCSS for reading. **Objectives** The children will learn to **Motor** 1. Jump for height and distance by swinging arms high, bending knees, and exploding on take-off. **Thinking Skill** 2. Think about one performance technique while jumping to improve the take-off. **Motivation** 3. Decide what distance to jump so that they are challenged but also successful **CCSS** 4. Determine the meaning of words and phrases in a text relevant to jumping. Describe the connection between steps in a technical procedure in a text and their observations.	*Notes:* Because you will be teaching jumping multiple times, we suggest you select only one performance technique for each lesson segment. Recall that for children to improve upon immature patterns, they must practice the skill with full force. Children can quickly tire when jumping as far or as high as they can. For this reason, jumping centers can be excellent additions to other lessons in which you set up centers. In this lesson segment, we focus on take-offs. Teachers need to teach children both how to generate force to jump high and to absorb force to land safely. We discuss landings in another lesson segment. **Potential Refinements** List the following cues on a whiteboard so children have them available as a reference: • Swing your arms back, and swing your arms high to the sky (for height). • Swing your arms back, lean forward, and swing your arms over your head (for distance). • Bend your knees and explode off your feet.
Org Get with your assigned partner. Pick up two jump ropes (or chalk, plastic strips, floor tape, or some other line-making equipment), and go to one of the colored strips of paper taped on the wall. First, work together to set up two plastic lines arranged in a V on the floor away from the wall. Then, one of you will practice jumping for distance over the lines, and the other partner will practice jumping for height using the colored strips of paper. Then we will switch.  Jumping for distance © Jones & Bartlett Learning. Photographed by Christine Myaskovsky.	**Safety Alert** **Safety** Jumping over a rope can be dangerous on a floor, but it works in the grass. When we teach this lesson on a floor, we use chalk to mark the lines, floor tape, thin plastic movable lines that don't slip on the floor, or non-slip mats with lines that don't slip on the mat. You will need to experiment to find safe equipment for your setting.

SAMPLE PLAN 26.7

Jumping for Distance and Height, Focusing on Take-offs (*continued*)

Content Development

E When you jump for distance, it is called a standing long jump. In this jump, you try to jump as far as you can. Stand behind the plastic line and do a standing long jump over the other plastic line. You decide where to stand to jump. **Mot** Select a distance that is challenging to you, but one you can successfully make without landing on the line. Experiment until you find the right distance.	**R** Do you know how to increase your distance or height? [Swing your arms back in preparation for the jump, and then forcefully swing them straight over your head to point to the ceiling. Bend your knees in preparation, and then really explode by forcefully pushing against the ground and extending your knees. Extend your legs on take-off all the way through your ankles so your body is straight in flight.]
E Now the other partner goes to the wall. Stand sideways next to one of the strips of colored paper (or large measuring tape on the wall). Jump up, and try to touch the wall as high as you can.	**Th** If you think about one performance cue while you jump, it will help you improve. You can't effectively think of more than one performance cue at the same time while you are performing the skill. First, think about swinging your arms for three jumps. Then, switch performance cues, and think about bending your knees and exploding off your feet.
CCSS/A When you are ready for your peer to watch you, take an assessment form and pencil from one of the boxes. Discuss with your partner the meaning of each item. Watch your partner and describe what you saw your partner do in relation to each item. Then fill out the assessment form.	**Peer Assessment of Partner** Swings arms over head: Yes No Bends knees and explodes: Yes No

SAMPLE PLAN 26.8

Hopping for Distance and Height, Focusing on Take-offs

Hopping for Distance and Height, Focusing on Take-offs	Notes and Potential Interactive Teaching Decisions
Standards These learning experiences meet National Standards 1 and 2 and CCSS for vocabulary acquisition. **Objectives** Children will learn to **Motor** 1. Hop for distance, doing several hops in a row and using arms to help. 2. Hop for height, swinging arms up, and exploding off the foot. **Thinking Skill** 3. Persist in trying to hop for distance consecutively. **CCSS** 4. Acquire and use accurately conversational, general academic, and domain-specific words and phrases, including those that signal precise actions.	*Prerequisite:* Children need to have acquired the basic hopping pattern of being able to hop consecutively and maintain their balance. **Potential Refinements** • Use your arms (consecutive hops for distance). • Swing your arms up, and explode off your foot (hopping for height). • Lean forward when hopping for distance, and stay more upright when hopping for height.

(*continues*)

SAMPLE PLAN 26.8

Hopping for Distance and Height, Focusing on Take-offs (*continued*)

Content Development	
Org When I say "Go," you and your assigned partner pick up two cones and set them up in the gym parallel to the side walls about 10 feet apart, like this. [Demonstrate with two cones.] You will be hopping from one cone to the other.	**Safety** What do you think you need to check to be sure your setup is safe? Great thinking. You need to be sure your cones don't cross the line of other children's cones. Also, leave some overflow room behind each cone in case you continue traveling once you reach your cone.
E Let's practice hopping by trying to hop from cone to cone using consecutive hops. **Th** Doing many hops in a row is challenging, but you can learn to do it if you keep trying and persist. Learning comes from your effort.	**R** Use your arms to help you.
A If you are hopping easily and in control, count the number of hops it takes to get from one cone to the other.	
MD If you are hopping easily and in control, try to decrease the number of hops between cones by making each hop longer. **ME** If you need to work on hopping continuously, then keep on doing that, and do not work on increasing the distance of each hop.	**ME** You can move the cones closer together if you want. **MD** You can move the cones farther apart to give you more of a challenge if you want.
Cog K/CCSS Now let's try hopping for height. Compare and contrast hopping for height and distance. What do you think will be the same, and what do you think will be different? [You won't lean forward, you will be more upright.] Right. Also, use the performance techniques for your arms like you did when you jumped for height. **E** Start at your cone, walk several steps, and then do one hop, trying to hop as high as you can. You are not hopping for distance—you will land close to where you took off. Instead, you are hopping for height.	**R** Swing your arms to the ceiling to help you get height, just the way you did when you jumped for height. **R** Explode off your foot by extending it forcefully.

SAMPLE PLAN 26.9

Jumping, Focusing on Landing

Jumping, Focusing on Landing	Notes and Potential Interactive Teaching Decisions
Standards These learning experiences meet National Standards 1, 2, and 5 and CCSS for vocabulary acquisition. **Objectives** The children will learn to Motor 1. Land from a jump with a stick, bending the knees to absorb force. 2. Land resiliently, by extending through the ankles and popping off the ground. 3. Land on the feet, then taking weight gently and slowly onto the floor in a safety roll.	*Prerequisites:* Ability to perform the basic pattern of jumping Previous lesson on safety rolling Previous lesson on resilient landings and the five types of flight from feet

SAMPLE PLAN 26.9
Jumping, Focusing on Landing (*continued*)

Thinking Skills

4. Think about one performance technique while landing to improve their jumps.

Social

5. Be responsible by sharing space and equipment fairly.

CCSS

6. Acquire and use accurately conversational, general academic, and domain-specific words and phrases, including those that signal precise actions.

Content Development

Org You and your assigned partner pick up and carry one mat. As a class, make sure the mats are scattered about the space evenly. Then, you and your partner get two red, orange, or yellow hoops and two blue spots; scatter them about the space on the floor, not on a mat. Then sit on a mat.

Cog K When you jump high or far, you have to control all of that force when you land. In gymnastics, there are three ways to land. The first you have already learned—springlike landings. With this kind of landing, your legs are like springs. They compress to absorb force and then immediately extend to jump again.

Reviewing Resilient Landings

E Using any locomotor pattern you want (e.g., jog, skip, gallop), travel about the space. When you come to a free hoop, jump into the hoop by doing any of the five types of flight from feet (jump, hop, leap, *assemblé*, *sissone*), and immediately spring away. Think about the red, yellow, and orange hoops as representing hot beds of coal—you want to spring away before your feet burn.

Social When you travel about the gym as a group, what do you have to do to be a responsible person? [Watch where I am going; don't hog equipment; don't go so fast I bump into anyone, even by mistake; don't try to cut ahead of someone who is about to use a piece of equipment.]

R Pop quickly and forcefully.

R Pop—it's hot!

Learning to Stick a Landing

Cog K The second type of landing is a stuck landing. When you stick a landing, you bend your knees to absorb force, your feet stick to the floor, and you stand up perfectly balanced without your feet having to shift even the tiniest bit. In Olympic gymnastics, all of the dismounts off apparatus end with a stick.

I Do a low jump in the air, land, and try to stick the landing.

E Now jump a little higher, and try to stick the landing.

R Bend your knees to absorb the force.

R Bend your knees and freeze.

E Excellent sticks. You are ready to try traveling, jumping, and sticking. Using any locomotor skill, travel about the space. When you come to a free blue spot, jump and land on the cool, soothing, icy spot. Keep your feet frozen for three seconds, and then travel away.

R Work very hard not to let your feet move even the tiniest bit after you land.

R Stick, and remain still and balanced on the cool blue spot.

R Pretend your feet have glue on the bottom that helps you stick to the spot.

(*continues*)

SAMPLE PLAN 26.9

Jumping, Focusing on Landing (*continued*)

Reviewing Safety Rolls **E** The third way to land is a safety roll, which you have learned before. When you come to a free mat jump, land on your feet at the edge of the mat, do a safety roll up to your feet again, and continue traveling.	**R** Land on your feet. **R** Gently take your weight onto the mat.
E Let's put all of the landings together. Using any locomotor pattern you want, travel about the space. When you come to a free hoop, jump into the hoop by doing any of the five types of flight from feet (jump, hop, leap, *assemblé*, *sissone*). The hoop is hot! Immediately spring away. When you come to a free blue spot, jump and land on the cool, soothing, icy spot; stick with your feet frozen for three seconds, and then travel away. When you come to a free mat, jump, land on your feet at the edge of the mat, do a safety roll up to your feet again, and continue traveling.	**Th** I have written three cues on the whiteboard to help you remember to think about one performance technique every time you land. If you think about a cue for every landing, you will improve. • Pop—it's hot! • Bend your knees and freeze. • Gently roll on the mat. **MD** Challenge yourself to jump as high as you can and land safely and skillfully.
CCSS Closure With your partner define the three ways to land from flight, and then compare and contrast the performance techniques you use for each type of landing.	

SAMPLE PLAN 26.10

Sample Centers for Flight from Feet: Level 1

The following sample jumping centers are suggestions for culminating activities for lessons in which flight from feet is taught or reviewed.

Center 1: River of Fire

Focus: Leaping.

Equipment: Two chalk lines, plastic lines, or masking tape lines on a V angle (because children might land on the line, use whatever equipment will not slip or slide and is safe for the surface of your teaching space); red spots or orange, red, and yellow small cones, or any colored equipment to represent fire.

Task: Imagine the cones between the lines make up a river of fire. Take a running start, and leap over the river of fire.

Performance Techniques:

- Swing your arms to help you get height.
- Use a resilient landing, and jog to slow your speed to a walk.

ME: Go over the river where the banks are close together.

MD: Go over the river where the banks are farther apart.

Center 2: Jump for Height

Focus: Jumping for height.

Equipment: Three different stations:

1. Tape a large ruler on the wall.
2. Tape a series of colored squares vertically on the wall. Alternatively, you can give children chalk to mark the wall when they jump. (Caution: Some chalk can stain certain surfaces.)

SAMPLE PLAN 26.10

Sample Centers for Flight from Feet: Level 1 (*continued*)

3. Suspend balloons or light, soft balls from strings.

Task: Stand sideways to the wall and jump, reaching as high as you can with one arm. Try to jump as high as you can.

Performance Techniques:

- Swing your arms down and then up forcefully.
- Explode off the floor.

ME: Jump next to the wall, but don't worry about touching it with your hand.

MD: Jump twice in a row.

Center 3: Over the Alligator Pit

Focus: Jumping for distance.

Equipment: Two chalk lines, plastic lines, or masking tape lines on an angle (because children might land on the line, use equipment that will not slip or slide and is safe for the surface of your teaching space). If the gym floor is slippery, use mats. Arrange paper alligators or similar creatures between the lines.

Task: Starting from a stand, jump over the alligator pit and land on two feet.

Performance Techniques:

- Really swing your arms back and then forward forcefully.
- On take-off, extend your hips, knees, and ankles completely and explosively.

ME: Jump across where the pit is narrow.

MD: Jump across where the pit is wider.

Center 4: Hopping for Distance

Focus: Hopping for distance.

Equipment: Four cones in a line, in two different colors. Outside cones mark overflow space (so children can slow down and not bump into a wall); inside cones mark hopping distance.

Task: Start at the red cone, and use an easy-approach jog to the yellow cone (about five feet). Then hop, trying to make each hop as long as you can to the next yellow cone (10 to 20 feet, depending on the ability level of the children). Finally, jog slowly to the red cone (about five feet used as overflow space), and stand behind it.

Performance Techniques: Research indicates that teaching performance techniques for hopping can cause problems for children. Simply telling children to hop for distance can be the most helpful way to elicit more mature patterns. We suggest telling children to use their arms to help, which is a performance technique that works for children at several developmental levels and is not specific enough to cause problems.

ME: Keep the yellow cones close together, and simply have children hop but not try to hop for distance.

MD: Move the yellow cones farther apart.

Center 5: Gallop, Step, Step, and Hop for Height

Focus: Combining galloping and step-hopping for height.

Equipment: Four cones in a line, in two different colors. The outside cones mark overflow space; the inside cones mark traveling distance.

Task: Gallop and step (step–together–step), then take a step on the other leg and hop, trying to hop as high as you can. Practice leading with one leg and then the other.

Performance Techniques:

- Gallop light and high
- Resilient landings
- Head high, stretch for the sky

ME: Just gallop one way, and come back using an easy jog and step-hops.

MD: Gallop and then leap, *assemblé*, leap, or hop. Then, in a row, try to do a second of the five types of flight without hesitating.

(*continues*)

SAMPLE PLAN 26.10

Sample Centers for Flight from Feet: Level 1 (*continued*)

Center 6: Jumping Ice Floes

Focus: Jumping for accuracy and sticking.

Equipment: Hoops scattered about the space but close enough for children to jump from one to the next.

Task: Imagine we all went to sleep and woke up and the gym was now the Arctic Ocean. Several ice floes have formed in the water. To travel to catch fish, you need to jump from ice floe to ice floe. They are very slippery, so when you land, you need to stick and land perfectly balanced on two feet.

Performance Techniques: Bend your knees to absorb the force.

ME: Move the hoops closer.

MD: Move the hoops farther apart.

Center 7: Hop the Stepping Stones

Focus: Hopping for accuracy. (This task can also be used for the five different types of flight from feet.)

Equipment: Spots scattered between two lines or ropes.

Task: Hop across the stream, hopping from stepping stone to stepping stone.

Performance Techniques:

- Eyes on your feet for landing accurately
- Resilient landings

ME: Move the spots closer together.

MD: Move the spots farther apart.

Center 8: Slalom Skiing

Focus: Jumping. (This task can also be used for the five different types of flight from feet.)

Equipment: Two parallel lines of plastic spots on a mat, or for level 3 jumpers, aerobic boxes (flat, no height).

Task: "Slalom" ski jump from side to side—that is, from spot to spot. (Level 3: Jump from aerobic box to aerobic box.)

Performance Technique: Resilient landings

ME: Move the spots/boxes closer.

MD: Move the spots/boxes farther apart.

SAMPLE PLAN 26.11

Sample Centers for Flight from Feet: Levels 2 and 3

These centers, in general, are more difficult than the previous set of centers described and are designed for children at ability levels 2 and 3. Set up 10 jumping centers per 20 children, with children working in pairs. You may want to repeat these centers for several days to give children lots of practice in jumping.

Prerequisites: Lessons on how to jump on a springboard, safety rolling, jumping for height and distance, hopping for distance

Introduction to "The Airport"

Today the gym is an airport, and you are going to flight school. An airport is a perfect place to work on jumping because jumping is flight, and an airport is all about flight—but what flies at an airport are airplanes. Does anyone know of anything we might see at an airport? [Hangars, planes, pilots, runways, passenger terminals, lines of people.] Today we will set up hangars, runways, and passenger terminals. Our airport is the best airport in the world because there are no lines. People who are traveling don't like lines at the airport, and we don't like lines at our airport either. If you see a line, just go to another hangar, runway, or passenger terminal. Although it is important to practice jumping at each center, a good decision is to practice at the centers with the skills you most need to improve.

SAMPLE PLAN 26.11

Sample Centers for Flight from Feet: Levels 2 and 3 (*continued*)

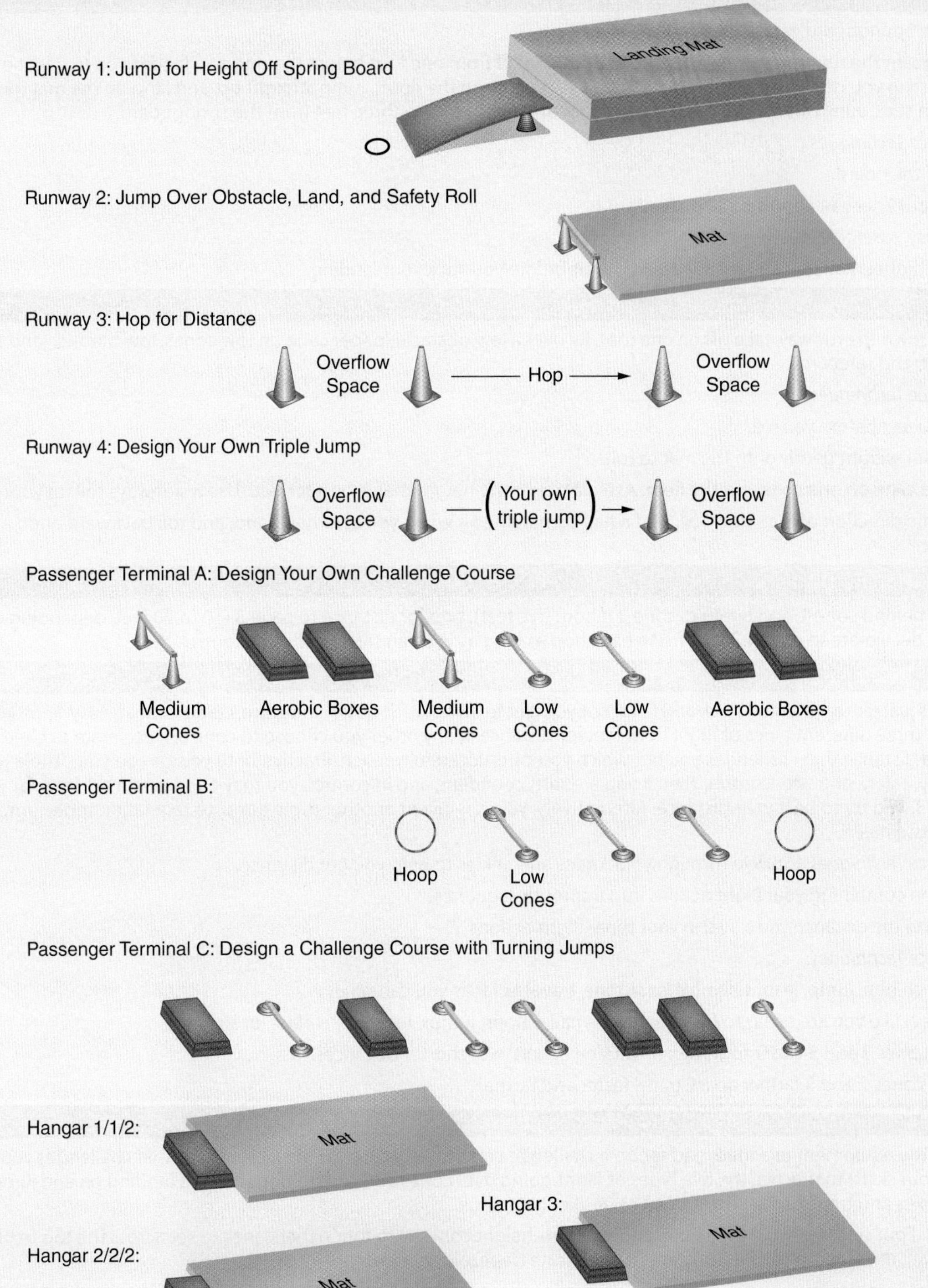

Organization of airport: 10 centers for practicing flight from feet

(continues)

SAMPLE PLAN 26.11

Sample Centers for Flight from Feet: Levels 2 and 3 (*continued*)

Runway 1: *Assemblé*, Jump High, and Stick

Equipment: Springboard, mat.

Task: Jog down the runway, "hurdle" (*assemblé*) by taking off from one foot before the ring and landing on two feet on the springboard (if you don't have a springboard, tape two spots on the floor), jump straight up, and land on the mat (or landing mat) with a stick. Jump for height, not distance, and land about two to three feet from the springboard.

Performance Techniques:

- Pop off the board.
- Bend your knees to absorb force on landing.

ME: Jog easy, *assemblé* low, jump low.

MD: Jump higher making different shapes in the air before you stick your landing.

Runway 2: Run, *Assemblé*, Parachute Land, Roll

Task: Run down the runway, take off on one foot, fly over a low obstacle (paper cane on low cones, low hurdle), land on two feet on the mat, and safety roll.

Performance Techniques:

- Land on *feet* before you roll.
- Take your weight gently onto the mat to roll.

ME: Set the cane on one cone and the floor. *Assemblé* over the height that is best for you. Use a sideways roll for your safety roll.

MD: Vary the direction of the safety roll. Add a half-turn in the air when you *assemblé*, land, and roll backward or do a back shoulder roll.

Runway 3: Hop for Distance

Task: Start behind cone 1, accelerate to cone 2 (about five feet), hop for distance to cone 3 (10 to 20 feet, depending on ability level), and decelerate to cone 4. Try to make each hop as long as you can safely and with control.

Runway 4: Design Your Own Triple Jump

Task: This is just like an event in track and field, but you get to invent it. Start behind cone 1, and with an easy-approach jog to cone 2, do three different types of flight from feet for distance in any order you choose to cone 3. Decelerate to cone 4. Move cone 3 to a distance that challenges you but which you can successfully reach. Practice until you can do your "triple jump" confidently, safely, and with control. Then if you are safe, confident, and in control, you may choose to mark how far you go with cone 3, and try to beat your distance. Alternatively, you can invent another triple jump. (A regulation triple jump is a hop, leap, and *assemblé*.)

Performance Techniques: Explode through your knees and ankles to help you get distance.

ME: Work on combining your flight actions into a smooth sequence.

MD: Work on the distance you travel in your three flight actions.

Performance Techniques:

- With each hop, jump, leap, *assemblé*, or *sissone*, travel as far as you can *safely*.
- If you feel like you are going to fall, then take smaller hops, jumps, leaps, *assemblés*, or *sissones*.

ME: Move cones 2 and 3 closer together; travel slower and over shorter distances.

MD: Move cones 2 and 3 farther apart; travel faster and farther.

Passenger Terminal A: Challenge Course Over "Suitcases"

Task: Take the equipment provided, and set up a challenge course (i.e., your own obstacle course that challenges you to improve your skills) to practice the five types of flight going over cones and canes (luggage) and landing on and jumping off aerobic boxes and trapezoid sections. Work on resilient landings.

Equipment: Four sets (eight cones) of low- and medium-height cones with four paper canes to set across the top to be obstacles to jump over, three aerobic boxes (or stacked mats), one trapezoid section.

Performance Techniques:

- Use arm swings for height.
- Make your legs like springs.

ME: Leave as much space between the suitcases as you need.

MD: Put the suitcases close together so you have to do several jumps in a row.

SAMPLE PLAN 26.11

Sample Centers for Flight from Feet: Levels 2 and 3 (*continued*)

Passenger Terminal B: Following Visual Signs

Task: In an airport, you have to be able to follow signs so you don't get lost. One partner, set up two hoops and three paper canes set on low cones, in any order. The other partner, make up a footwork pattern using the five types of flight, going over or in the hoops and over the canes on low cones. The other partner must copy the footwork pattern exactly. Switch roles.

Performance Techniques: Your legs have turned into springs.

ME: Make a simple sequence that is easy to remember. If your partner has problems, make the sequence easier.

MD: Make a more complex sequence that changes flight actions each time.

Passenger Terminal C: Getting Turned Around

Task: Sometimes in an airport, you get turned around and become lost. Design a challenge course (an obstacle course that challenges you to improve your skills) that includes at least three turning jumps or *assemblés*. Work on resilient landings, and always land facing forward or backward, never sideways, because landing sideways can hurt your knees. Start standing on an aerobic box.

Equipment: Four sets (eight cones) of low cones with four canes, three aerobic boxes, one trapezoid section (or stacked mats).

Performance Techniques:

- Use arm swings for height.
- Make your legs like springs.

ME: Use fewer turning jumps; leave a lot of space between the equipment.

MD: Use more turning jumps, and try some full turns. Put the equipment close together so you have to do several jumps in a row

Hangar 1/1/2 (One-Foot Take-off, One-Foot Landing/Take-off, Two-Foot Landing, Safety Roll)

Task: Approach with an easy jog, take off from one foot, land on a trapezoid (one or two layers) on one foot with a resilient landing, immediately spring into the air, land on two feet on a flat mat, and safety roll.

Equipment: Short space for approach, one- or two-layer trapezoid set widthwise, flat mat on other side for landing.

Performance Techniques: Land on your *feet* before you roll, and roll softly.

ME: Use a one-layer trapezoid; jump lower.

MD: Use a two-layer trapezoid; jump higher.

Hanger 2/2/2 (Two-Foot Take-off, Two-Foot Landing/Take-off, Two-Foot Landing, Safety Roll)

Task: Approach with an easy jog, *assemblé* (take off from one foot) on the floor, and land right in front of trapezoid on two feet. Jump from two feet to two feet onto a two-layer trapezoid. Stick the landing for two seconds. Jump, land, and do a safety roll on the mat.

Equipment: Short space for approach, two-layer trapezoid set widthwise, flat mat on other side for landing.

Performance Techniques:

- Land on your *feet* before you roll.
- Roll softly.

ME: Use a one-layer trapezoid; jump lower.

MD: Use a two-layer trapezoid; jump higher.

Hanger 3: Three Jumps and a Stick

Task: Approach with an easy jog, then *assemblé* and land on the floor in front of the trapezoid on two feet with a resilient landing, immediately jump onto the trapezoid with another resilient landing, immediately jump for height, and land on two feet with a stick.

Performance Techniques: Bend your knees and squeeze your muscles tight to stick.

ME: Set the trapezoid widthwise; jump lower.

MD: Set the trapezoid lengthwise; jump higher.

Dynamic Balancing

As in the previous section, we organize the content for teaching dynamic balancing in lesson segments and centers that are included in other gymnastics lessons. Children practice dynamic balancing on balance beams and other similar apparatus, but schools typically have limited amounts of such apparatus. Centers are labeled as level 1, 2, or 3. We are indebted to Robin Litaker, of the Hoover, Alabama, public schools, for the ideas for many of these centers.

Social Responsibility at Centers

The following questions can serve as the basis for class discussions on social responsibility during centers:

1. How many turns are fair?
2. When is someone being an equipment hog?
3. How do you know when you need to share and when you need to go to a different center to give other children a turn?
4. How can you politely tell others it is time for them to share?

SAMPLE PLAN 26.12

Dynamic Balancing Lesson Segments

Dynamic Balancing Lesson Segments	Notes and Potential Interactive Teaching Decisions
Standards These learning experiences meet National Standards 1 and 2 and CCSS for vocabulary acquisition.	
Motor Objectives The children will learn dynamic balancing on various pieces of apparatus and in a variety of ways: 1. Stretching tall through the spinal column. 2. Maintaining tension (staying tight). 3. Keeping the head up with eyes looking down at the beam. 4. Bending the knees to lower the center of gravity to regain lost balance. 5. Counteracting a shift in the center of gravity by moving a body part in the opposite direction.	
CCSS The children will compare and contrast domain-specific words or phrases to understand their meaning.	
Introducing Dynamic Balancing Techniques for Centers	
Cog K Today you will be working on dynamic balancing at some of the apparatus centers. In the dynamic balancing centers, you will explore many different ways to travel on beams. **CCSS/Cog K** What is the difference between dynamic and static balancing? [Static balancing is being still on a base of support in a position that is hard to hold; dynamic balancing is traveling while remaining balanced on a narrow surface or a small base of support.] **I** Let's prepare for the centers by practicing while walking on a line on the floor performance techniques that will help you maintain your balance. **Org** Find part of a line in the gym where you can walk back and forth. We will call this your personal beam.	
Stretch Tall **R** Start by stretching tall. We have worked on this technique in dance. Walk to the end of your personal beam, turn, and walk back.	**R** Feel like you are a marionette like Pinocchio with a string attached to the top of your head. The puppeteer is pulling the head string toward the ceiling.

SAMPLE PLAN 26.12

Dynamic Balancing Lesson Segments (*continued*)

Head Up, Eyes Down **R** As you stretch your head toward the ceiling, you need to look down so you can see the beam. Don't tip your head forward. Keep your head up but your eyes down. Walk on your personal beam again.	
Stay Tight **R** What is the one performance technique we emphasize the most in balancing? Right. Stay tight. Staying tight is important in dynamic balancing, too.	**R** As you walk, maintain light tension in your muscles the whole time so you can feel your muscles and the positions of your body parts.
Bending Knees to Lower the Center of Gravity **R** When you are walking on a beam and you start to lose your balance, lower your center of gravity. How can you do that? [Bend your knees.] Try walking on your personal beam, and start to tip slightly to one side. See if you can bend your knees and tighten up to remain on your beam.	**Cog K** Who remembers what their center of gravity is? Right, it is the point that is the center of the weight of your body. Are you more stable if your center of gravity is closer to the floor or higher up? Right, the lower your center of gravity, the more stable you are (assuming the size of your base of support is the same).
Counteracting a Shift in the Center of Gravity by Moving a Body Part in the Opposite Direction **E** Put one foot in front of the other, and reach over to the side. Keep reaching until you know that if you reach one more inch you will fall off your line beam. Experiment to see if you can find a way to reach even farther to the side without falling from your personal beam. [Children will find that when they stick their hips or a leg out to the opposite side, they will be able to reach a little farther.]	**R** Move a body part to the opposite side when you start to lose balance.

SAMPLE PLAN 26.13

Sample Centers for Dynamic Balancing

Level 1

Center 1: Walk the Beam

Focus: Head up, eyes looking down at beam while walking.

Equipment: Low 2×4 or PVC beam.

Task: Walk from one end of the beam to the other.

Performance Techniques: Keep your head up but eyes looking at the beam.

ME: Walk on a line on the floor.

MD: Travel in different directions.

Center 2: Beanbag Walk

Focus: Head up, eyes looking down at beam while traveling.

Equipment: Low 2×4 or PVC beam, several beanbags and small cones.

Task: Walk from one end of the beam to the other while balancing a beanbag on your head.

Performance Techniques: Keep your head up but eyes looking at the beam.

ME: Walk without the beanbag. Hold the beanbag with one finger until you gain confidence.

MD: Put a small cone on top of the beanbag.

(*continues*)

SAMPLE PLAN 26.13

Sample Centers for Dynamic Balancing (*continued*)

Level 2

Center 3: Ice Cream Cone Carry

Focus: Staying tight while walking on a beam.

Equipment: Low 2×4 or PVC beam, two small cones, and two small foams balls per child.

Task: Put a ball on a small cone like an ice cream cone. Then walk on the beam while balancing your ice cream cone in one hand.

Performance Techniques: Stay tight as you walk. Feel the tension in your arms, torso, and legs.

ME: Just carry the cone.

MD: Use two ice cream cones, one in each hand.

Center 4: Protect the Swan Eggs

Focus: Counteracting a shift in the center of gravity.

Equipment: Low 2×4 or PVC beam, three medium to large cones on one side of the beam about six inches beyond the arm reach of the children, three cones on the other side with three yarn balls balanced on top.

Task: Pretend the yarn balls are swan eggs, and you are one of the parents. Your job is to protect the eggs from predators who want to eat them. Walk down the beam, and reach over to pick up the swan egg from one cone that is exposed to predators. As you lean over, your center of gravity will move. If it goes too far from the beam, you will fall. To prevent that, move your hips or a leg in the opposite direction to counteract the weight of your torso. Then carefully transfer the egg to the cone on the other side of the beam, which you have hidden from predators.

Performance Techniques:

- Bend your knees to lower your center of gravity.
- Stay tight.

ME: If you are having problems reaching the egg without falling, move the cone closer to the beam.

MD: If you need more of a challenge, move the cone farther from the beam.

Center 5: Pathways and Directions

Focus: Traveling on different pathways and in different directions.

Equipment: Several very thick ropes or old garden hoses.

Task: Make straight, curved, and zigzag pathways with the rope (or hose) in any way you want. Walk on the rope following the pathway. Then explore walking in different directions: forward, backward, and sideways.

Performance Techniques:

- Stretch tall.
- Stay tight.

ME: Make mostly straight and only a few large curves; walk forward.

MD: Make all three kinds of pathways, and walk backward and sideways.

Center 6: Through the Hoop

Focus: Traveling over, under, and through obstacles.

Equipment: Any kind of beam, hoops (or jump ropes).

Task: Travel down the beam while stepping through the hoop and bringing it over your head (like a jump rope) and then stepping through it again.

Performance Techniques: Watch your feet land on the beam.

ME: Have your partner hold the hoop.

MD: Jump over the hoop. Alternatively, do the same task with a jump rope.

SAMPLE PLAN 26.13

Sample Centers for Dynamic Balancing (*continued*)

Level 3

Center 7: Travel Using Different Locomotor Skills

Focus: Traveling on different beams using different locomotor skills.

Equipment: This center can be done on a variety of beams, listed here in order from easiest to most difficult:

1. Benches
2. Padded regulation beams at floor level
3. 2×4 beams with four-inch side up
4. 2×4 beams with two-inch side up
5. Low regulation beams
6. PVC pipe beams
7. High beams

Task: Travel on the beam while experimenting with different locomotor skills—for example, walking, galloping slowly, sliding, skipping, jumping, and hopping. Make sure you select skills that you feel safe and confident doing.

Performance Techniques:

- Stretch tall.
- Eyes down.

ME: Travel slowly.

MD: As you gain confidence, increase your speed gradually.

Center 8: Explore the City Roofs

Focus: Traveling on different pathways, levels, and directions.

Equipment: Select from a variety of beams (PVC ramps; PVC beams; 2×4 beams; stacked mats; benches; single, double, and triple trapezoid sections).

Task: Imagine each piece of apparatus is the roof of a building. With your partner (or group), arrange the beams, trapezoids, and other apparatus to form a city of roofs. Try to make some interesting angles when you connect the roofs. Have different levels and some gaps between the roofs. Then travel from roof to roof on different pathways, levels, and directions exploring the city.

Performance Techniques:

- Keep eyes focused on the apparatus for landing.

ME: Keep the roofs close together.

MD: Leave gaps between the roofs.

Center 9: Half- and Full Turns

Focus: Turning.

Equipment: Low beam.

Prerequisite: Lesson on turning.

Task: Explore different ways to turn on the beam. Start with half-turns on two feet. Then try half-turns on one foot, practicing turning both to the left and to the right and with both left and right feet. If you have experience turning, you can also try full turns. Start practicing on a line on the floor. When you feel safe and confident, work on the low beam.

Performance Techniques:

- Watch for and focus on the end of the beam after you turn.
- Lead with your shoulders to turn.
- Stay tight and stretched tall.

ME: Work on a line on the floor.

MD: Work on full turns.

(*continues*)

SAMPLE PLAN 26.13

Sample Centers for Dynamic Balancing (*continued*)

Center 10: Turning at Different Levels

Focus: Turning at different levels.

Equipment: Low beam.

Task: Explore half-turns on two feet at different levels: standing, bending your knees, and squatting.

Performance Techniques: Try to keep your back straight and head up when you are in a squat position.

ME: Work on a low beam with turns on two feet.

MD: Work on a higher beam, and then try lunge positions and squats with one leg extended on the beam.

Center 11: Jump While Making Shapes

Focus: Jumping while making different shapes.

Equipment: Any low, wide beam; bench; aerobic box; and/or stacked mats.

Task: Starting on the floor and then progressing to the beam when you are certain you can work safely and confidently, jump while making different shapes (tucked, wide, straight, twisted, and angular). You also can try jumps that are done so often that they have names:

- Tuck: both knees bent, bent at hips.
- Pike: bent at hips, both legs straight.
- Straddle: legs straight and extended to each side so your body looks like an upside-down Y.
- Stag: front leg is bent and back leg is straight back; alternatively, one leg is bent to the side, and the other leg is straight to the other side.
- Split: one leg straight forward, the other straight back. If you are flexible, your legs will be in a perfectly straight line called a split.
- Double stag: legs are split with both knees bent.
- Wolf: pike jump with both knees together but one knee bent.

Performance Techniques:

- Keep eyes focused on the beam for landing; make sure your feet land on the beam.
- If you are slightly off center, land with your feet on the beam, and then safely step or jump to the ground.

ME: Start with straight jumps, then tucked.

MD: Try two or three jumps in a row.

Center 12: Jump Over

Focus: Jumping over obstacles.

Equipment: Any low, wide beam; bench; aerobic box; or stacked mats, jump ropes, hoops, low and medium cones, beanbags.

Task: Set any of the cones or beanbags you want on the beam. Travel down the beam while jumping over the cones and beanbags.

Performance Techniques:

- Keep eyes focused on the beam for landing; make sure your feet land on the beam.
- If you are slightly off center, land with your feet on the beam, and then safely step or jump to the ground.

ME: Start with the beanbag until you have mastered that jump and feel safe and confident. Then jump over a cone.

MD: Do several jumps in a row.

Sample Abbreviated Plans for Levels 2 and 3

In levels 2 and 3, we suggest tasks for content development and culminating activities for units on themes combining the foundational skills. We also suggest possible performance techniques you can use to guide your observations and feedback or to design refining tasks. These abbreviated plans are not annotated and do not include objectives other than CCSS.

SAMPLE PLAN 26.14

Level 1: Rocking on Different Body Parts and in Different Directions and Level 2: Combining Rocking and Rolling

CCSS Objective

Identify new meanings for familiar words.

Potential Refinements

- Stay tight and round when you rock and roll.
- Use strong arms when you roll.

Content Development

Introducing Rocking

Cog K Some words have different meanings. For example, you can go bowling and bowl a bowling ball, or you can eat cereal from a bowl. The same is true for the word *rock*. What different meanings can you think of for the word *rock*? [Pick up a rock from the dirt, rock-and-roll song, rock in a chair]. Put your thumbs up if you have ever sat on a rocking chair. What action do you do? [You rock back and forth.] Raise your hand if you want to share a special time when you rocked on a rocking chair. [Call on one child or more if the story was short.] What does a rocking chair look like, and what allows you to rock? [Some are like swings, and others have curved legs so the chair can rock back and forth.] We can also rock in gymnastics. Rocking is similar to rolling but when you rock, you start to roll in one direction and then stop before you finish, and roll back to your staring position.

Rocking in Different Directions and on Different Body Parts

I Stand like me with your feet apart. Rock side to side on your feet. This is one way of rocking in gymnastics.

E Explore changing the location of your feet and rocking on your feet in different directions [forward and back, diagonally]. Change again.

E There are many other body parts on which you might be able to rock. Explore rocking on different body parts.

R If you are rocking on your belly or back, which shape do you need to make your body? [Round.] Right. It must be round and tight like the curved legs of a rocking chair.

Level 2: Rocking on Hands and Shins and Transitioning to a Side Roll

E Rock side to side on your hands and shins like me. [Demonstrate.] Start slowly, increase the size of your rocks, and finally rock so big that the rock takes you directly into a sideways roll.

E Explore rocking on your hands and shins increasing the size of your rocks, then rolling sideways in different ways, varying the shape of your legs.

E Starting on your hands and shins, explore varying the direction of your rock. You can rock on the diagonals or forward and back. Increase the size of your rock until it takes you directly into a roll.

Rocking on Different Body Parts Transitioning into a Roll

E Let's take the same idea of rocking several times and transitioning directly into a roll, but this time explore rocking on different body parts. As you rock on different body parts, increase the size of your rock until it takes you into a roll. [Give the children a lot of time to explore this theme. Scaffold different ways to rock and then roll if needed (e.g., rocking on the hands and feet in different directions; rocking on the back and belly in different directions; rocking on the feet in different directions; rocking on a shin and one foot; and/or rocking on the hips. Large forward and back rocking actions on the belly leading to rolls is an advanced move that children who have experience with gymnastics enjoy learning in this lesson.)]

Connecting a Roll to a Rock

E Try the reverse. Explore different ways to start with a roll that leads you into rocking on different body parts and in different directions.

E You can continue working on that task or try this. Do only half a roll before you rock. This task requires you to have a lot of control over the speed of your rolls and your weight transfer. For example, if you roll forward or forward/diagonal over your shoulder, you will need to stop in the middle of the roll on your back and then rock.

Culminating Activity Option 1: Sequence

A Now put your best three ideas into a sequence. Do three different rocking movements, increasing the size of the rocking until it takes you into a roll.

R Work on your transitions. Try to have each roll lead to the next rock so your entire sequence consists of connected skills, with each rock leading to the next roll and each roll leading to the next rock.

(*continues*)

SAMPLE PLAN 26.14

Level 1: Rocking on Different Body Parts and in Different Directions and Level 2: Combining Rocking and Rolling (*continued*)

A Show your sequence to a partner. Pick the best ideas from both of your sequences and make one new sequence.

Social Be sure you select rocks and rolls that both of you feel safe and confident doing.

Culminating Activity Option 2: Apparatus

E Get one trapezoid section or a stacked mat. Explore different ways of rocking on the stacked mat that take you to a roll on the floor mat.

R You need to be very careful when you transition between the rock and roll so you don't fall off the trapezoid. You must use strong arms to control the transition and roll so you protect your head.

E Now try rocking on the floor into a roll on the trapezoid.

A Create a sequence using the stacked mat. Do three different rocking movements, increasing the size of the rocking until it takes you into a roll.

R Work on your transitions. Try to have each roll lead into the next rock so that your entire sequence consists of connected skills, with each rock leading to the next roll and each roll leading to the next rock.

SAMPLE PLAN 26.15

Level 2: Combining Jumping and Rolling While Making Different Shapes with the Legs

CCSS Objective

With a partner, determine the meaning of domain-specific words and phrases in a new context.

Performance Techniques Written on Whiteboard

- Roll gently.
- Land on your feet before you roll.
- Use strong arms in all rolls.
- Swing your arms toward the sky (in jumping).

Org With help from a partner, get a mat each, and spread the mats in a scattered formation about the space.

Content Development

CCSS Discussion

On the whiteboard, I wrote four performance techniques. Discuss with your partner what each of these performance techniques mean when you combine jumping and rolling. You are responsible for thinking about the relevant performance technique when you practice the skills today.

Stand, Roll, Stand

I Let's start today's lesson by reviewing and practicing "stand, roll sideways, stand" [see the level 1 lesson on safety rolling]. At the end of your mat, start stretched tall on the balls of your feet with your hands reaching high toward the ceiling. Then slowly and gently take your weight onto the mat, roll sideways, and roll right back up to a stand.

E Now that you have more experience rolling, I know many of you can roll in different directions. This time, start stretched tall on the balls of your feet with your hands reaching high toward the ceiling. Then slowly and gently take your weight onto the mat, roll in a way that is safe for you, and roll right back up to a stand. What are some of the ways you can roll? [Sideways, forward diagonal, backward diagonal, forward, and backward.] How else can you vary your roll? [Change the shape of your legs.] Remember to roll only in directions and shapes that you can perform well, safely, and confidently.

R For all rolls, use strong arms to protect your head and neck.

Jump, Land, and Roll While Varying the Roll

E Start standing; add a small, straight jump that includes reaching up before you roll; land on your feet; and gently and smoothly go into a roll of your choice.

R It is critical to remember to land on your feet before you start to roll. [Repeat multiple times.]

SAMPLE PLAN 26.15

Level 2: Combining Jumping and Rolling While Making Different Shapes with the Legs (*continued*)

MD If you want, you may choose to jump as high as you want as long as you safely absorb force of the jump when you land, land on your feet, and smoothly go into your roll.

E Explore jumping and rolling in different directions and shapes.

ME Remember, you can always use side rolls. Try to vary the shape of your legs in the side roll.

E Explore jumping straight, landing on your feet, doing two different rolls in a row, and ending in an ending position of your choice.

E Jump, land, and roll two times, intentionally varying the shape of your legs in each roll. End in a creative ending position.

Jump While Making Different Shapes, Land, and Roll

Safety When children first explore making different shapes in the air during jumps, they tend to land with their feet in whatever shape they made in the air. This is not a safe way to land. It is critical to emphasize that they make the shape in the air and then bring the legs together before they land from the jump.

E What are the different shapes you can make? [Straight, wide, round, angular, twisted.] Explore making different shapes in your jump. Be sure to bring your feet back together and land on your feet before you roll. For your first attempts, use the roll that you are most confident performing.

E Jump while varying the shape, and vary the roll each time.

Safety Be sure you always land either forward or backward, but never sideways—landing sideways can hurt your knees.

E If you want to land and roll backward or on a back diagonal, what will you have to do in the air? [Do a half-turn.]

Culminating Activity: Apparatus

A/Fitness Infusion

Let's play a round of "silent commandos" to get your heart beating faster and work on cardiorespiratory endurance. We call this "silent commandos" because you move silently and stealthily, doing safety rolls as if you were on a commando raid. Everyone jog about the space. If you see a free mat, go to the end, jump, land on the mat on your feet, and do a safety roll. Come up to a stand, and then continue jogging. Watch to make very sure no one else is about to jump, land, and roll on the mat before you start. You may use straight jumps or make a different shape when you jump. You may roll in any direction that is safe for you. [Play until you see the quality of the children's movements decrease indicating they are getting too tired to play safely.]

Org With your assigned partner, put two mats together. Stack one or get a trapezoid section, and set it up at the end of a mat so you can jump from the trapezoid and have enough space to land on the mat and roll without interfering with another pair.

E Start on the trapezoid, do a straight jump, land on your feet, and safety roll.

E If you are perfectly in control, safe, and confident, you may vary the shape of your legs in the jump.

E If you are perfectly in control, safe, and confident, you may vary the rolls.

E Finally, you may vary both the shape of the jump and the roll. Try to do a different jump and different roll each time.

SAMPLE PLAN 26.16

Level 2: Combining Balancing on Different Body Parts with Different Shapes and Rolling

Notes: The content in this and the following theme can take three to four lessons to develop.

CCSS Objective

With a partner, determine the meaning of domain-specific words and phrases in a new context.

Performance Techniques Written on Whiteboard

- Stay tight and stretched when you balance.
- Use strong arms when you roll to protect your head.
- Make transitions smooth without hesitations.
- For transitions, the ending position for one skill is the starting position for next skill.

(*continues*)

SAMPLE PLAN 26.16

Level 2: Combining Balancing on Different Body Parts with Different Shapes and Rolling (*continued*)

Content Development

CCSS Discussion

On the whiteboard, I wrote four performance techniques. Discuss with your partner what each of these performance techniques mean when you combine jumping and rolling. You are responsible for thinking about the relevant performance technique when you practice the skills today.

Review and Extend Balancing on Different Body Parts and in Different Shapes

I We will begin by reviewing balancing on different body parts. Try to explore balances you have not tried before. Focus on hard-to-hold balances.

MD For those of you who are ready for more of a challenge, work on balancing on upper body parts [shoulders, hands, forearms, and chest] with one foot on the floor for support.

MD If you are confident, and your balances are tight and stretched, you may work on balancing on upper body parts with both feet high.

ME Work on balancing on your back and belly or on two hands and two feet.

E Now concentrate on varying the shape of your legs. Try bending one or both legs and straddling or splitting your legs.

Combining Balancing and Rolling

I Our main focus today is combining balancing and rolling. *[Optional teaching of a specific combination.]* Let's try a fun, safe example. Try a knee scale–side log roll–knee scale sequence. You do this by balancing on two hands and one shin, with your free leg stretched behind. This is a knee scale. Then log roll sideways with a straight body, and end in another knee scale. [Repeat several times.]

MD If you want an additional challenge, do the knee scale without hands, log roll, and go up to the second knee scale without hands.

R What is critical when you combine skills is to transition between them smoothly, moving with continuity from balance to roll to balance without hesitation. Try it again, and work on continuity.

Balance and Roll Out

E Find a balance you are comfortable doing, and roll out directly from that balance. From your balance, tip or lean in one direction, and then roll. You may use any roll you can do safely and confidently, but make sure the roll starts directly from the balance.

E Now explore balancing on different body parts and finding ways to roll out of the balance. [Scaffold this exploration if the children are not using a variety of body parts or if they are sitting and thinking, rather than thinking while moving. For example, suggest balancing on hips, hands and feet, one foot, one shin and one foot, back of the shoulders, hand and front of one shoulder, and so on.]

E What do you have to do to initiate the roll? [Lean over, over-balance, push off the mat with one body part such as hands, move a free body part away from the base of support to cause a loss of balance leading into a roll.] Yes, these are great answers. If you have not tried one of these ways, try it. [You may need to provide light scaffolding by reminding children of ways to initiate the loss of balance and roll.]

Culminating Activity: Apparatus, Sequences

Balance on Different Body Parts

E Get a stacked mat or trapezoid section. Explore different ways to balance on different body parts. You can balance completely on the stacked mat or partly on the stacked mat and partly on the floor mat.

E Try finding different balances, with one part of your body on the floor mat and one part on the stacked mat.

MD If you are ready for a challenge, try to have your feet be the highest body parts.

E Vary the shape of your legs and the body parts on which you are balancing.

Balance and Roll Out

E Now find different ways to balance and roll out. You can roll on the stacked mat or on the floor mat.

E Try to vary (1) the rolls, (2) the body parts on which you balance, (3) your shape, and (4) whether you are on or partially on the stacked mat.

Sequences

A Using the stacked mat, design a sequence of four different balances connected by rolls emphasizing a variety of shapes and body parts.

SAMPLE PLAN 26.17

Level 2: Combining Rolling and Balancing, While Varying Direction and Shape

Notes: The content in these tasks can take three to four lessons to develop. We illustrate how to integrate teaching a specific skill (mule kick/handstand) through the use of a progression.

CCSS Objective

With a partner, determine the meaning of domain-specific words and phrases in a new context.

Performance Techniques Written on Whiteboard

- Stay tight and stretched when you balance.
- Use strong arms when you roll to protect your head.
- Make transitions smooth without hesitations.
- For transitions, the ending position for one skill is the starting position for next skill.

Content Development

Review Balance and Roll Out

I Today, we will be working on rolling and ending in a balance. Let's start by reviewing what we did in the last lesson. Find different ways to balance on different body parts, and roll out of that balance.

Teaching a Specific Skill: Balancing Skill Using a Progression

I You have been working so hard. You are tight, stretched, and your bodies are in control. You are ready to work on a mule kick and a handstand. A mule kick is almost a handstand, but you don't remain balanced on your hands. You kick one leg at a time, switch legs in the air, and land on your mat in a lunge. A handstand is a vertical balance on your hands, with your body straight and your feet pointing toward the ceiling. You hold the balance for one to three seconds (or longer if you want). You will learn the mule kick/handstand through a progression of subskills. It is just like school: You can't go to second grade until you pass first grade. In a progression, you can't move to the next subskill until you master the previous subskill.

Mule Kick/Handstand Progression

Subskill 1: Weight on hands, tuck position. Stand at the edge of your mat. Squat down; transfer your weight from your feet to your hands; with curled body, spring your feet one inch off the floor; land on your feet; stand; and stretch your arms toward the ceiling. [Repeat until mastered.]

R Keep your elbows locked; that means straight like this. [Demonstrate as you speak.] [Repeat the refining task throughout the remainder of the lesson if and when needed.]

R Be sure your palms are flat on the mat and you are not in the track-start position. [Demonstrate both palms flat and the immature track-start hand placements.] [Repeat the refining task throughout the remainder of the lesson if and when needed.]

Subskill 2: Weight on hands, switch feet. If you feel safe and confident and you have mastered the first subskill, you can work on subskill 2. Stand on the edge of your mat with one foot slightly in front of the other, transfer your weight to your hands, spring your feet off the floor a few inches, switch legs in the air, and land one foot at a time with the other foot in front.

Subskill 3: Lift your feet a little higher. If you are safe and confident and have mastered the previous task, you may move on to this next task. Do the same subskill, but spring your feet a little higher each time. Do not go any higher than about 24 inches. [Gesture with hands to show 24 inches.]

R Be sure to look at the mat between your hands.

Subskill 4: Mini-mule kick. If you are ready to move on, stand in a lunge with your front knee bent and your back leg straight, like this. [Demonstrate.] Reach your arms toward the ceiling. Put your palms down and kick one leg up just a little, then the other leg. Switch legs in the air, and land in a lunge with your hands pointing to the ceiling.

R Be sure to land on your front foot and stand up in a lunge. Don't land on your knees.

R Land one foot at a time.

R When you land, reach for the ceiling.

Subskill 5: Full mule kick. If you are safe and confident, kick higher and higher until you are kicking waist high and then chest high.

R [Repeat refining tasks for subskill 4.]

(*continues*)

SAMPLE PLAN 26.17

Level 2: Combining Rolling and Balancing, While Varying Direction and Shape (*continued*)

Subskill 6: Cartwheeling out. If you have mastered the previous task, practice how to "cartwheel out" or turn out of a handstand if you kick too high and are going over. Kick up at least chest high, pick up one hand and move it into a cartwheel, and twist your feet down. *Do not, under any circumstances, go over into a back bend or go over onto your back.* Land on your feet, and don't fall.

R Land on your feet.

Terminal skill: Full handstand. Once you can cartwheel out perfectly every time, you can practice full handstands.

Cartwheeling out
Courtesy of John Dolly

R Stretch through your back, and hollow out. "Hollow out" means to tilt the top of your pelvis back so you have less arch in your back, and your spinal column is as stretched and as straight as you can make it.

Cog K The mule kick is not technically a balance because you do not stay still for one to three seconds. Even so, because it is a subskill for a handstand, we will count it as a balance in this class.

Roll and End in a Balance

E Let's go back to the main theme for today: combining rolling and balancing. You started by reviewing balancing and rolling. Now work on the reverse. Start with a roll that ends in a balance. Be sure there are no extra steps between the roll and the balance. End your roll in your balance or on the body part that is the base of your balance.

E Explore different ways to vary the roll ending in a balance. How can you vary a roll? [Roll in different directions and different shapes, make different shapes of the legs.]

E Now roll and end in a balance, exploring as many different balances as you can. Try to vary the body parts on which you balance.

E Roll and end in a balance, exploring ways to vary the shape of your balances. [You may need to scaffold different shapes (wide, straight, round, angular, twisted, symmetrical, or asymmetrical) if you do not see enough variations.]

Balance, Roll, Balance

E Now put them together. Start in a balance, roll out, and end in a balance.

E Explore different balances and rolls.

E Now explore the reverse: roll, balance, and roll.

SAMPLE PLAN 26.17

Level 2: Combining Rolling and Balancing, While Varying Direction and Shape (*continued*)

Culminating Activity

Roll and End in a Balance

E With a stacked mat or trapezoid section, explore different ways to roll and end in a balance. Be sure there are no extra steps between the roll and the balance. End your roll in your balance position. You can be on the stacked mat, on the floor mat, or on both at the same time.

E Try to vary the rolls, the body parts on which you balance, your shape, and whether you are on the stacked mat or partly on the stacked mat and partly on the floor mat.

Balance, Roll, Balance, and Reverse

E Now explore different ways to put these moves together. Start in a balance, roll out, and end your roll in a second balance. Then explore the reverse: Start with a roll to a balance, and then roll out.

Sequences

A Using the stacked mat, design a sequence of four different balances connected by rolls, emphasizing a variety of shapes and body parts.

SAMPLE PLAN 26.18

Level 3: Combining Steplike Actions and Rolling

Notes: This set of tasks illustrates how to integrate the teaching of thinking skills and a specific skill (cartwheel) through the use of a progression. This set of tasks (and the companion set on the text website) might take three to four lessons to teach, depending on the amount of time for your lesson and the skill level of the children.

CCSS Objective

Refer to details and examples in text written on a whiteboard, drawing inferences about improving performance.

Performance Techniques Written on Whiteboard

- Use strong arms on rolls.
- Roll to your feet without using your hands to help.
- Straight arms on steplike actions.
- Palms flat on steplike actions.
- Legs straight and straddled wide and high on steplike actions.

Content Development

The Difference Between Strong Arms and Straight Arms

Cog K Two terms that can be confusing are *strong arms* and *straight arms*. When I say, "Strong arms," I want you to bend your arms like a weight lifter and push against the floor to protect your head while you roll. When I say, "Straight arms," I want you to lock your elbows to keep your arms straight when you do steplike actions. It actually takes less strength to support your weight on straight, locked elbows than it does on bent arms. Today we will be working on combining steplike actions and rolls.

Org Using partners to help set up, get mats, and place them in a scattered formation.

Review Steplike Actions

I Begin by reviewing and exploring different steplike actions taking weight on your hands.

R Are your elbows locked and arms straight?

(*continues*)

SAMPLE PLAN 26.18

Level 3: Combining Steplike Actions and Rolling (*continued*)

Teaching Self-Regulation

Th Whenever you do a movement in sports or in gymnastics, you want to be thinking about that movement in your head. Of course, your head can't think about every itty-bitty part of the movement, or it might split in half, and all the thoughts will go flying off into space. Your head needs to focus on one part of the movement. The best thing to do is to select one of the performance techniques and think about it when you do the movement. If you practice over and over, eventually you will master the performance technique and be able to think about a different part of the movement. Select one performance technique for the next task. I wrote the performance cues on the whiteboard. You need to decide which performance technique is most important for you at your level of development.

Combine Steplike Actions and Rolls

E Explore taking your weight on your hands, spring and twist your feet to a different position, land, and immediately roll. Keep your feet low—only 1 to 3 inches off the floor. Check to make sure that you have room on your mat before you start.

E Explore different ways to vary the shape or direction of your rolls.

MD If you feel safe and confident, you can lift your feet higher and higher, up to about two feet. [Gesture with hands what is two feet or demonstrate.] Lift your feet only as high as you can lift them safely, confidently, and in control of your body. You are not in control if you bend your arms, land on your shins, or fall. You are in control if you are tight, land softly on your feet, keep your arms straight and palms flat, and land where you intended to land.

Combining Steplike Actions Over Stacked Mats and Rolls

Org With a partner, get a stacked mat or trapezoid section each, and put it in the center of your mat. [If you do not have enough mats, have the partners stack one of their mats, place it on the other flat mat, and share the space.]

E Now, using a stacked mat, explore different ways of doing steplike actions over the stacked mat and immediately lower into a roll.

Cartwheel Progression

E You have worked very hard, and consequently you are landing on your feet and keeping your elbows locked. I think you are ready to work on the mini-cartwheel and cartwheel progression.

Potential Refinements

- Elbows straight
- Palms flat
- Land facing back where you started
- Legs straight and straddled in the air (for subskill 4 and higher)

Subskill 1: Weight on hands, spring feet over. Stand to the side of the stacked mat/trapezoid single section. Put your hands on the trapezoid to one side, put your weight on your hands, and, while keeping your feet at a low level, spring your feet to the other side.

Subskill 2: Stand, spring over, stand. If you feel safe and confident, and you have mastered the first subskill, you can now work on subskill 2. Start standing to the side of the stacked mat. In one motion, put your hands on the trapezoid to one side, spring your feet over at a low level, and stand with your hands stretched toward the ceiling.

Subskill 3: Lunge, spring over, lunge. If you feel safe and confident, and you have mastered the previous subskill, you can now work on subskill 3. Start in a lunge (front leg bent, back leg straight), with one foot in front of the other. If your left leg is in front, put your hands to the left; if your right leg is in front, put your hands to your right. Push off your front foot, and spring your back leg and then your front leg one at a time over the trapezoid. End standing with one foot in front of the other in a lunge, reaching your hands to the ceiling. If your left leg was in front at the start, your right leg will be in front at the end, and vice versa. Decide whether you prefer putting your hands to the left or right, and continue practicing that one way (see **Figure 26.11**).

Subskill 4: Mini-cartwheel. This is the same as subskill 3, but keep the legs straight and lift the legs higher each time. Be sure to end in lunge. Only go higher if you are safe and confident, have your elbows locked, and are landing in a stable lunge on your feet. Practice at the height that is safe for you.

Subskill 5: Progression on floor mat. If you feel safe and confident, and you have mastered the mini-cartwheel over a stacked mat, you can now work on a flat mat. If not, keep using the stacked mat. Push your stacked mat to the side, and do subskills 3 and 4 but on a floor mat.

Terminal skill: Full cartwheel. Stretch your legs toward the ceiling straddled wide apart so you look like an old-fashioned "cart" wheel! The rhythm is hand, hand, foot, foot. Hands and feet land on a straight line.

SAMPLE PLAN 26.18

Level 3: Combining Steplike Actions and Rolling (*continued*)

Combining Steplike Actions Over Stacked Mats and Rolls

E Let's go back to the main theme of our lesson: combining steplike actions and rolls. Using your stacked mat, explore different ways of doing steplike actions over the stacked mat, and immediately lower into a roll.

E Extend the task: this time, combine steplike actions and rolling onto, over, and off the stacked mat.

Culminating Activity Sequence with Stacked Mat

A Create a sequence that includes four combinations of steplike actions and rolls. Vary the shape or direction of the rolls. Vary landing on one foot or two feet.

SAMPLE PLAN 26.19

Level 3: Combining Balances

Notes: In this set of tasks, we illustrate moderate scaffolding of the experimental phase of designing a sequence.

CCSS Objective

Recount an experience with appropriate facts and relevant descriptive details speaking clearly.

Potential Refinements

- Stay tight and stretched in balances.
- Move only one body part to transition.
- Do only one movement to transition.

Introductory Warm-up Activity

I Run lightly about the space, and when I say, "Hold," stop perched on the ball of one foot with your head stretched toward the ceiling and the other leg back. Start to fall forward but before you do, quickly recover, and run again. [Repeat.]

Content Development

Review Balancing on Different Body Parts While Making Different Shapes

I The major focus of this lesson is on different ways to get into and out of balances, which link the balance to another movement. We will explore a variety of ways to connect balances with good transitions. Begin by reviewing and practicing balancing on different body parts making different shapes. [Give lots of time to explore.]

Balance to Balance

E Now explore ways to transition from one balance directly to another balance. Get into your first balance, and then over-balance—that is, lean and stretch your body in one direction until you lose your first balance and carefully land in a second balance. Try to do this by moving only a few of your body parts to establish the next balance. [Give lots of time to explore.]

Balance and Twist, Leading into a Different Skill or Other Balance

E Explore different ways to balance that will allow you to hold the balance, then twist your body and over-balance into another balance or another skill. You can twist your arms at your elbows and shoulders like this. [Demonstrate.] You can also twist your legs at the hip. Most of the time in gymnastics, we twist at the waist. *Twist* means that the top part of your torso faces in one direction while you move at your waist so your hips face a different direction. To twist in a balance, keep one part of your body facing the original direction, and then twist (usually at your waist or one leg) until part of you faces a different direction. Then go into another balance or skill. [Give the children lots of time to explore. There are many variations.]

Balance and Rock or Roll

E Now let's review different ways to link balances using rolls or rocks. Hold a balance, and then from that position, over-balance and immediately go into a roll or rock. Then explore rolling and rocking to end in a balance.

(*continues*)

SAMPLE PLAN 26.19

Level 3: Combining Balances (*continued*)

Balance and Steplike Actions

E You can also come out of a balance by putting a foot or other body part down and immediately doing a steplike action. Review and explore different ways to balance, moving immediately into a steplike action. Then explore steplike actions that end in balances.

Balance and Springing Off Hands or Jumping

E A final way to link a balance with another movement is to jump or spring off the body part on which you are balanced. If you balance on your feet, then jumping is a relatively easy transition, but springing off your hands is more challenging. Explore different ways to jump or spring out of your balance. Try to achieve flight directly from your balance. You might need to swing your free leg or arms to help you get flight from a balance or bend your arms so you can get a good push-off.

Exploring Different Sequences of Balances (Moderate Scaffolding)

E Let's explore different sequences of balances. Select two balances, and find two different ways to link those balances with good transitions.

E Find a balance with your feet high, and then do three different continuous linking skills (e.g., rolls, steplike actions) to end in the exact same balance.

E Balance with your feet high, transition to a balance with your head high, and transition back to a balance with your feet high.

E Select three different balances, and link them using the same linking movement—for example, balance 1, steplike action, balance 2, steplike action, balance 3.

E Select one balance, and find three different ways to link it to the exact same balance.

Culminating Activity

Stacked Mats

E Explore different ways to connect balances using two or more stacked mats, trapezoids, and/or boxes set at different levels and positioned on angles.

Sequences Using an Apparatus or on the Floor

A Today you will be designing a sequence with a stacked mat showing different ways to link four balances. Select the most interesting balances, combinations, and transitions that you can do smoothly with the fewest extra movements, and put them together into a sequence.

CCSS Closure

With your assigned partner, describe the three ways you connected your balances. Be clear and specific in describing your movements, explaining the type of connection, how you performed it, and how it was a smooth transition between balances.

CHAPTER

27

Using Movement Concepts as Themes

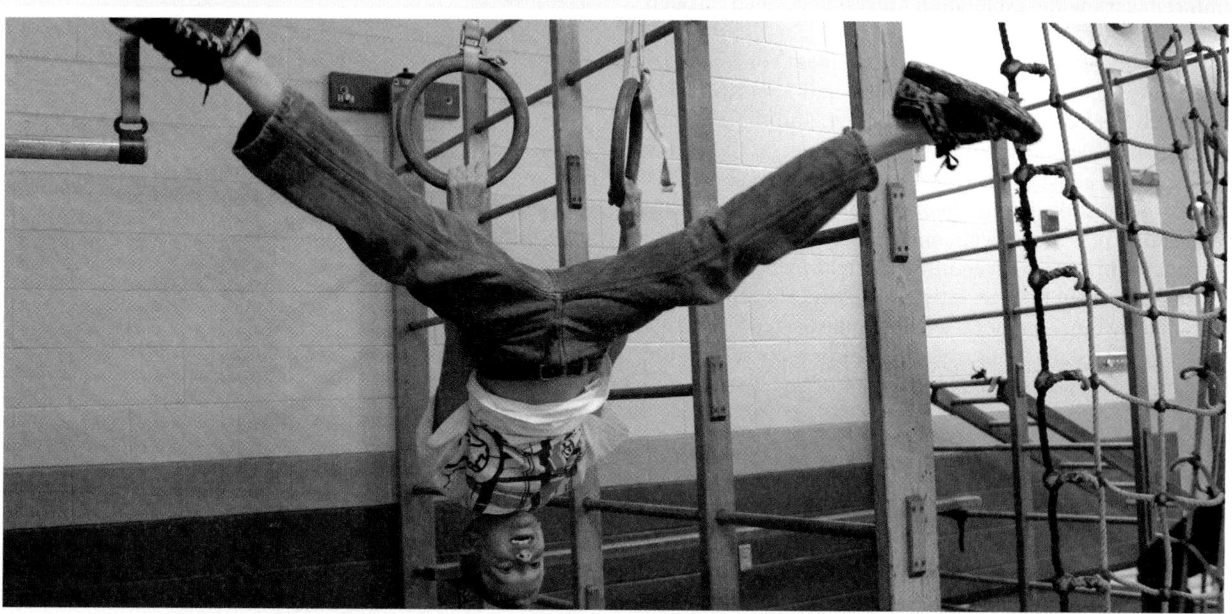

OBJECTIVES:

Students will learn:

1. Lessons with movement concepts as the theme require children to be able to readily apply level 1 balancing, rolling, jumping, and steplike actions.
2. Lessons with movement concepts as the theme shift children's attention from the foundational skill to the movement concept.
3. In these lessons, different children perform different foundational skills requiring different refinements.
4. Learning to use different levels and speeds helps children improve the quality of their sequences by adding contrast.
5. Learning asymmetry helps children improve the originality and interest of their sequences.

Introduction

In this chapter we show you how to use movement concepts from the body, space, effort, and relationship aspects of the Laban framework as the major theme of lessons. This approach stands in contrast to Chapter 26, an approach which uses the foundational skills and combinations of skills as themes. Using movement concepts as themes requires children to readily apply the foundational skills of balancing, rolling, jumping, and steplike actions. To do so, the foundational skills must be familiar parts of their movement vocabulary. It is critical to note that children do not need to be able to perform advanced skills before learning the content in this chapter; they simply need to be ready to move to level 2. Children also need to be comfortable using the exploration process developed through level 1 work.

Consequently, we organize the movement concepts presented in this chapter by ability levels 2 and 3. **Figure 27.1** lists the content discussed in this chapter, and the **FYI** box lists the sample lesson and unit segments found at the end of the chapter. The division between levels 2 and 3 is somewhat arbitrary because once children of any ability level understand the meaning of a movement concept, their teachers can use that concept in lessons. In addition, as children become more skilled, they benefit from revisiting movement concept themes and exploring those themes at a more sophisticated level using more advanced skills. Thus, you can use concepts such as on, off, over, and under with children in both kindergarten and fifth grade. In fifth grade, however, the children would work with partners at more difficult apparatus stations, performing more difficult skills than would kindergarteners.

FYI

Sample Plans in this Chapter

Level 2

1. Over, Under, On, Off, Through (includes examples of challenge courses and improving clarity)
2. Asymmetrical and Symmetrical Shapes (includes an example of teaching sequences that have a beginning, middle, and end, and in which all parts fit together)
3. Different Levels (includes an example of teaching contrast as an element of sequence choreography)
4. Different Speeds

Level 3

5. Twisting and Turning
6. Stretching, Curling, and Twisting to Take You Someplace

Using Movement Concepts as Themes Shifts Children's Attention

The aim of lessons with movement concept themes is to teach children how to apply these movement concepts to their

PROGRESSION OF CONTENT

Level 1 Foundational Skills

(Described in Chapter 26)

- Balancing
- Rolling and rocking
- Steplike actions
- Flight from feet
- Dynamic balancing

Level 2

On, Off, Over, Under, and Through

- Different ways to get on and off apparatus
- Traveling on, over, under, and through apparatus
- Supporting weight on and under apparatus using different body parts

Shapes

- Symmetrical and asymmetrical shapes

Different Levels

- Traveling and supporting weight at different levels
- Foundational skills on and off apparatus set at different levels
- Changing levels on apparatus using different foundational skills
- Changing levels for contrast

Different Speeds

- Varying the speed of foundational skills from slow to moderately fast
- Accelerating and decelerating
- Changing speeds for contrast

Level 3

Stretching and Curling

- Stretching and curling to travel
- Stretching and curling to change levels
- Stretching and curling to change the base of support

Twisting and Turning

- Twisting and turning jumps
- Twisting to transfer weight
- Twisting to change the base of support and balance
- Twisting to change levels on apparatus
- Turns and spins on feet and different body parts on the floor

Combining Stretching, Curling, and Twisting to Change Levels, Locations, and Positions

More Advanced Movements On, Off, and Under Apparatus

- Flight onto apparatus, landing balanced
- Flight off apparatus, landing with a stick, safety roll, or resilient jump
- Flight (vaulting) over apparatus
- Rolling, balancing, steplike actions, and jumping onto apparatus
- Swinging actions

Advanced Shapes (e.g., arches, straddles, splits)

Figure 27.1 Progression of Content

gymnastics movements. Although the theme is the movement concept, the children will use the foundational skills to explore that theme. For example, if the theme is levels, the children will explore the idea of moving at different levels while using the skills of rolling, jumping, steplike actions, and balancing.

This teaching approach shifts the children's attention from the foundational skills to the movement concept. It is important to remember that all aspects of the Laban framework are always in effect to one degree or another. Regardless of whether a lesson focuses specifically on levels as an element of space, children will always be moving at some level. Children will be at high levels when jumping, whereas they will be at low levels when rolling. If the lesson focuses on jumping and rolling, the children's attention will be on those skills. If the lesson focuses on the theme of levels, the children's attention will shift to levels. This is a subtle but important difference. In the latter case, children will still be jumping and rolling, but they will have a heightened awareness of their level in space and will be learning how to intentionally apply different levels to their gymnastics work.

Advice for Newcomers to Educational Gymnastics

Teaching lessons based on a movement concept theme poses an exciting challenge. What is exciting about these lessons is seeing how they extend movement variety and improve the quality of children's sequences. The challenge is to envision which movements the children will be doing and figure out which skill refinements they need. In a lesson focused on a movement concept such as speed, some children will be rolling, others jumping, and still others performing cartwheels, round-offs, and other steplike actions. Thus, you must be able to give performance feedback to children performing very different skills.

Any sense of being overwhelmed by children's diversity of skills is a temporary issue. As you feel more comfortable with educational gymnastics, you will learn how to refine performance techniques regardless of theme. We suggest you approach these lessons with an adventurous spirit, being open to new ideas and willing to try new ways of teaching content. No one can learn a new approach instantly. It takes time, trial, and error, as well as being willing to suspend judgment throughout the professional development process.

On, Off, Over, Under, and Through

We have children explore on, off, over, under, and through in relation to small equipment, large apparatus, and partners. These themes are important for teachers who have access to large educational gymnastics apparatus, such as trestles, ladders, arches, bars, Swedish boxes, and climbing bars, and for teachers with playground apparatus available. You can design different lessons for different apparatus, thereby extending children's movement variety. For example, using hoops in vertical braces brings out different actions in going over, under, and through than using a bar or a medium-height beam. Bars and beams will support a child's weight as he or she travels over it, whereas a vertical hoop won't.

Sample Movement Variety for Younger Children

- Finding different ways to get on and off different pieces of apparatus
- Traveling on, over, under, and through apparatus
- Traveling on apparatus set at different levels and inclines
- Supporting their weight on or hanging under apparatus using different body parts (see **Figure 27.2**)

Sample Movement Variety for More Experienced Children

- Flight onto apparatus, landing balanced
- Flight off of apparatus, landing with a stick, safety roll, or resilient jump
- Flight (vaulting) over apparatus

SAFETY AND LIABILITY 27.1

Increasing Safety and Decreasing Risk of Liability: Guidelines Relevant to Content in this Chapter

In this box, we discuss specific guidelines built on information discussed throughout this text on professional standards of practice, negligence, and liability. The goals of these guidelines are to increase children's safety and decrease teachers' risk of negligence and liability.

- To increase safety and decrease liability risk, teachers should plan and follow a written curriculum with a progression or sequence of tasks to develop children's skills safely. The curriculum is based on district, state, and national standards and guidelines. All tasks are developmentally appropriate and modified to accommodate individual differences. Safety issues within tasks are taught, and students are warned about potential dangers.
- In educational gymnastics, students select the skills to practice within a theme. Teach children they must select only those skills they can do safely, confidently, and with control. Teachers must monitor students' selections and modify selections when children select skills that are too difficult for them. The same principle applies when designing partner and group sequences. Select only those skills all children in the group can do safely, confidently, and with control.
- Performing with movement quality and appropriate performance techniques are two of the most important ways to increase safe participation. A reasonably prudent teacher focuses on movement quality throughout every lesson, teaches students the performance techniques that contribute to movement quality, and explicitly and repeatedly teaches students about movement quality.
- Teach children how to set up, arrange, and put away the gymnastics mats and apparatus.
- Before getting on an apparatus in a particular body position, know how you will get off safely.

Figure 27.2 Children supporting their weight by hanging from an apparatus

Courtesy of John Dolly.

- Rolling, balancing, steplike actions, and jumping onto apparatus
- Swinging actions

Shapes: Symmetrical and Asymmetrical

Chapter 26 includes considerable work on having children balance, roll, rock, and jump while making different shapes and discusses the general categories of round/curled, wide, straight, angular, and twisted shapes. In this chapter, we discuss symmetrical and asymmetrical shapes. In symmetrical shapes (see **Figure 27.3**), both sides of the body are the same in relation to a line of symmetry drawn vertically. In asymmetrical shapes, the two sides of the body differ (see **Figure 27.4**). We also focus on traveling in symmetrical and asymmetrical ways.

One important reason why we recommend that physical education teachers teach the movement concepts of symmetry and asymmetry is because of the importance of these concepts in mathematics from grade 1 onward. In terms of gymnastics, understanding asymmetry is the most important consideration because it helps children develop original and creative sequences.

Figure 27.3 Symmetrical shapes in gymnastics and mathematics

© Jones & Bartlett Learning. Photographed by Christine Myaskovsky.

Figure 27.4 Asymmetrical shape

Courtesy of John Dolly

In addition, in level 3, children can work on more difficult wide and curved shapes, such as arched, straddled, and split shapes while jumping, balancing, and transferring weight.

Movement Variety

When designing lessons on symmetry and asymmetry, you can focus on either the shape or the action of the body while traveling. You can design lessons to extend children's movement variety using different apparatus and partner work. For example, if you use low beams, you will elicit very different movements than if you use stacked mats and two-layer trapezoid sections.

Immature Movement Patterns

The first and most common immature pattern is for children to use only symmetrical shapes, especially when rolling and jumping. A second commonly encountered immature pattern is lack of clarity in asymmetrical shapes. In such a case, when children make a shape, it isn't precise, and they can't repeat the exact same shape. They have a general idea of the position of their body parts, but it isn't a clear, precise shape.

Levels

In gymnastics, children explore moving at three levels: high, medium, and low. When children are at developmental level 1, they experience jumping at high levels, rolling at low levels, and steplike actions at low and medium levels. When the movement concept of level is the theme of the lesson, the children's focus shifts from the foundational skill to the movement concept of levels—in particular, changing levels and the contrast between a high and low level. Thus, the theme of levels is an excellent theme for helping children learn about contrast as an element of quality sequence choreography.

Movement Variety

You can design several lessons that extend children's use of different levels simply by changing the apparatus and adding partners. For example, a two-layer trapezoid under a balance beam, a single stacked mat on an angle to the trapezoid, and a floor mat create a center with four levels to explore. Partner work, with each partner working simultaneously at a different level on apparatus, also creates many options to explore. In addition, pairing levels with other movement concepts, such as pushing or springing, will contribute increased movement variety.

Sample Movement Variety Experiences

Traveling and supporting weight at different levels

- Travel and jump at high levels about the gym, transition to moving at a low level across a mat.
- Perform skills with your hands first at high levels and then at low levels.
- Create a sequence emphasizing traveling and supporting weight at different levels.

Performing foundational skills onto and off of an apparatus set at different levels

- At an apparatus center, explore balancing on different body parts or in different shapes at each level.
- At an apparatus center, explore steplike actions on different levels.
- At an apparatus center, explore steplike actions to change levels (see **Figure 27.5**).
- At an apparatus center, explore balancing on one level and transitioning to a roll at a different level.
- At an apparatus center, explore jumping onto and off of an apparatus at all three levels.
- At an apparatus center, find different ways to link balances at different levels (e.g., rolling, stepping, over-balancing, sliding).
- At an apparatus center, find different ways to link rolling and steplike action (see **Figure 27.6**).

Changing levels to add interesting contrasts as an element of choreography

- Create a sequence on a floor mat, changing levels to add interesting contrasts.
- Create a sequence on apparatus, changing levels to add interesting contrasts.

Figure 27.5 Exploring steplike actions at different levels and to change levels

Courtesy of John Dolly

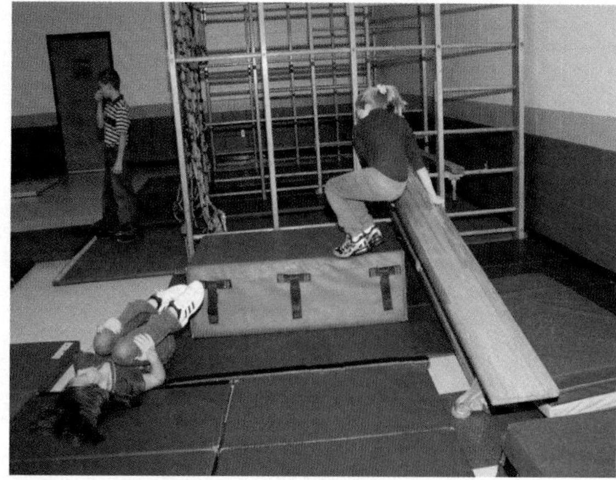

Figure 27.6 Exploring steplike actions connected to rolls at different levels

Speed

Varying the Speed of Foundational Skills from Slow to Moderately Fast

In gymnastics, speed constitutes a continuum from very slow to moderately fast. For safety, children perform few, if any, skills on apparatus or mats at a very fast speed. Children at ability levels 2 and 3 can explore rolling, rocking, and steplike actions at different speeds. Not all movements work equally well at both slow and fast speeds, however. Some movements have a natural speed that is most appropriate, such as moving into balances at slow speeds and galloping, skipping, and jumping at fast speeds. Avoid combining movements and speeds that are inappropriate for the movement, such as running at a slow speed or jumping at a slow speed. Make the speed of the movement appropriate.

Accelerating and Decelerating

In addition, children can work on accelerating and decelerating, in which the change of speed is continuous rather than abrupt. For example, they can start a sequence of three rolls in slow motion and then accelerate to a moderately fast motion.

Changing Speeds for Contrast

Similar to the theme of levels, speed is an excellent theme for lessons aimed at helping children understand contrast as an element of quality sequence choreography. They can work on sequences with a clear change of speed, sequences starting at a slow speed and steadily accelerating to a moderately fast speed, and sequences starting fast and decelerating to a slow speed. In addition, having children concentrate on the speed of their movement can help them acquire better control over the flow of their movement.

Stretching and Curling

In level 1, children perform foundational skills, such as rolling where the body is in a curled or straight shape. When children explore the theme of stretching and curling, however, they focus their attention on the feelings and actions of stretching and curling, rather than simply the shape.

Figure 27.7 Stretching and curling to change levels

Sample Movement Variety Experiences

Stretching and Curling

- Stretching and curling to travel (e.g., from a curled balance to a stretched steplike action)
- Stretching and curling to change levels (e.g., from a stretched steplike action to a curled roll) (see **Figure 27.7**)
- Stretching and curling to change the base of support (e.g., from a stretched balance on one hand and one foot to a curled balance on the shoulders) (see **Figure 27.8**)
- Combining stretching, curling, and twisting to change levels, locations, and positions

In designing lessons, you typically teach stretching and curling first on the floor. However, these are especially rich themes that can be extended across several lessons by using different apparatus and apparatus centers with several pieces of equipment.

Twisting and Turning

When you twist, one part of your body stays where it is, and other parts rotate to face a new direction. When you turn, the entire body rotates to face a new direction. Jumping is an excellent foundational skill with which to explore the themes of twisting and turning. Children also can explore twisting using weight transfer to different body parts to travel across a mat or twisting to change levels using stacked mats and trapezoids. In addition, twisting is an excellent theme to explore as a transition between balances; for example, children might be asked to hold a balance and then twist and tip into a new balance, roll, or steplike action. The primary focus with turning in gymnastics is turning jumps, including half-turns and full turns, turns on the floor on one foot or two feet, and spins on different body parts.

Figure 27.8 Stretching to change the base of support

Summary of Movement Variety

- Twisting and turning jumps
- Twisting to transfer weight
- Twisting to change the base of support and balance
- Twisting to change levels on apparatus
- Turns and spins on feet and different body parts on the floor

Swinging

In gymnastics, swinging is a theme applied to apparatus such as bars, ladders, ropes, and playground equipment. It is an excellent choice for building upper body strength. Children can explore swinging with half-turns, jumping to catch the bar and swinging, swinging and releasing at the top of the swing, and landing on the feet with a safety roll or stick.

Summary

In addition to using foundational skills and combinations of skills as themes, as demonstrated in Chapter 26, you can use movement concepts from the body, space, effort, and relationship aspects of the Laban framework as themes. During lessons that feature a movement concept as the theme, children perform a variety of foundational skills as they explore the movement concept, and their attention shifts to it.

Movement concepts, such as symmetrical and asymmetrical shapes; levels; speeds; stretching and curling; twisting and turning; and on, off, over, under, and through, are particularly strong themes that will greatly extend children's movement variety. Lessons on changing levels and speeds are helpful for improving the quality of contrast in children's choreography, whereas lessons on asymmetry help improve originality.

Review Questions

1. Which criteria let you judge whether children are ready to participate in lessons using movement concepts as the major theme? (Hint: Why is there no level 1 in this chapter?)
2. Describe and give an example of how movement concepts as lesson themes shift children's attention.
3. Why is teaching asymmetrical shapes important?
4. What are two immature patterns for children working on symmetrical and asymmetrical shapes, and how can you help the children improve them?
5. Describe how stretching, curling, and twisting are used as actions (as opposed to shapes). Give examples to illustrate your answer.

References

Rink, J. E. (2014). *Teaching physical education for learning* (7th ed.). New York: McGraw-Hill.

FYI

Summary of Task Label Abbreviations

I	Informing tasks
E	Extending/exploring tasks
R	Refinements
A	Application/assessment tasks
Org	Organizing task
Cog K	Cognitive knowledge: Explains or defines a concept
Social	Social skill or concept
Th	Thinking skill
Mot	Motivation concept
Safety	Safety information or reminder
MD	Modification to make the task more difficult
ME	Modification to make the task easier

Source: Adapted and Modified from Rink, J. E. (2014). *Teaching physical education for learning* (7th ed.).New York: McGraw-Hill.

Level 2 Sample Plans

SAMPLE PLAN 27.1

Theme: On, Off, Over, Under, and Through

Notes: These tasks are appropriate for children at ability level 2. This sample plan provides an example of how to design challenge courses and how to improve the clarity of children's movements using "the human videotape." It also includes an example of moderate scaffolding to help children and beginning teachers understand how to apply the foundational skills to the movement concepts.

Standards

This plan addresses National Standards 1 and 2 and CCSS for vocabulary acquisition.

Objectives

Children will learn to

Motor

1. Travel on, off, over, under, and through apparatus, landing gently and controlling the flow of the movement.
2. Perform and be able to repeat each movement with clear, precise shapes.

Cognitive

3. Understand the meaning of and accurately apply the concepts of on, off, over, under, and through.

CCSS

4. Acquire and use accurately domain-specific words and phrases, including those that signal spatial relationships.

Potential Refinements

- Land gently on your feet or absorb the force when you move on other body parts.
- Control the flow of your movement; don't let gravity take over.

Content Development

Org Scatter flat mats about general space. Set stacked mats on approximately half the flat mats. Set hoops in braces at the end of some other mats. Set low cones with paper canes on the floor, and set high cones with paper canes at the end of other mats.

Cog K/CCSS Today we are going to work on your relationship to apparatus, which means how you are positioned in relation to equipment, apparatus, or another person. We use words such as *on*, *off*, *over*, *under*, and *through* to describe these relationships. You can be on or off an apparatus. You can be under or over equipment and sometimes even go through equipment.

Exploring Over, Under, On, Off, and Through Using Equipment and Stacked Mats

I *Low canes:* Travel about the space, and, when you come to a low cane, find different ways to go over the cane. Which actions do you think you can use to go over a low cane? [Jump, hop, leap, 2-1, 1-2, steplike actions, rolls if the low cane is in front of a mat.] *Hoops in braces:* When you come to a free hoop, find different ways to go through the hoop without crawling. Which actions do you think you can use? [Roll, reach through, steplike actions.]

High canes: When you come to a high cane, find different ways to go either over or under the cane.

Stacked mats: When you come to a stacked mat, find different ways to get onto, travel on, and then off the stacked mat.

Focused Exploring Using Stacked Mats

E Go with your assigned partner to a stacked mat. I want you to explore movements on, off, and over the stacked mat only—we will use the small equipment again later.

Moderate Scaffolding If Needed

E Find different ways to jump on, off, and over the stacked mat. When jumping on the mat, use resilient landings. When jumping off, either stick or land and safety roll.

E Explore rolling on and off the stacked mat. By this, I mean to find different ways to mount onto the stacked mat using rolls. Find different ways to roll on the stacked mat, and find different ways to roll from the stacked mat.

MD If you feel safe and confident, find different ways to roll over the stacked mat.

SAMPLE PLAN 27.1

Theme: On, Off, Over, Under, and Through (*continued*)

E Now combine jumping and rolling. Find different ways to jump, land, and roll. Try the reverse order to roll, and immediately jump, going over, on, and off the stacked mat.

E Explore steplike actions on, over, and off the stacked mat. By this I mean, find different ways to mount onto the stacked mat using steplike actions, find different ways to do steplike actions on and over the stacked mat, and find different ways to use steplike actions to dismount from the stacked mat.

E Now combine steplike actions and rolling over, on, and off the stacked mat. Be sure you link your rolls and steplike actions so they become one continuous movement.

E Find different ways to arrive on the stacked mat in a balance and different ways to dismount from the mat from a balance. Be sure to vary the body part on which you are balancing and the shape of the balances.

E Now using all the actions—jumps, rolls, steplike actions, and balances—and moving continuously, find different ways to get onto, travel on, go over, and dismount from the stacked mat.

Culminating Activity: Designing Challenge Course Sequences

A With your assigned partner, pick up one cane on low cones, one cane on high cones, and one hoop near you. Then arrange your small equipment, a stacked mat, and floor mats in any order you want in a straight line. We call this a challenge course because it is an obstacle course that challenges you to improve your skills. Design a way to travel down your challenge course by going over, under, through, on, and off the equipment and apparatus. Design your sequence in three stages:

1. Experiment with different actions at each piece of equipment and apparatus.
2. Select the actions you think are most interesting and challenging and are actions you can perform well.
3. Figure out the transitions between the actions so one action leads immediately to another action. For example, you might jump over the cone and then roll but find you still have space to fill before you do a steplike action through your hoop. You need to add a transition movement after your roll that fills up this space. This action should start in the ending position from your roll and end in a position from which you are ready to do your steplike action.

Improving the Clarity of Sequences

R Now practice your sequence until you can repeat the exact same movements each time, and the shapes you make are very clear. You must be doing something definite at each piece of equipment, and you must know the exact shape and position of every body part. We call this quality *clarity*—it is an important part of gymnastics and dance sequences.

A Teach your sequence to your partner. You partner will become a "human videotape" and try to do your sequence exactly the same way you did. His or her performance will help you see if you had clarity. If your shapes or movements were not clear, your partner will have problems replaying them exactly in the same way a videotape would replay your sequence.

SAMPLE PLAN 27.2

Theme: Asymmetrical and Symmetrical Shapes

Notes: These tasks are appropriate for children at developmental ability level 2. This sample plan also explains how to introduce two key elements of choreography: (1) sequences have a beginning, a middle, and an end; and (2) in sequences, the parts fit together logically. It also includes an example of peer coaching.

Standards

This plan addresses National Standards 1 and 2 and CCSS for vocabulary acquisition.

Objectives

Children will learn to

Motor

1. Balance, jump, rock, and roll applying the movement concepts of symmetrical and asymmetrical shapes.

Cognitive and CCSS

2. Identify real-life connections between the words *symmetrical* and *asymmetrical* and their use.

(*continues*)

SAMPLE PLAN 27.2

Theme: Asymmetrical and Symmetrical Shapes (*continued*)

Potential Refinements

- Keep tight.
- Keep your legs straight when they are supposed to be straight and tucked tight when they are supposed to be bent.

Content Development

Cog K There are two kinds of shapes: symmetrical shapes and asymmetrical shapes. In *symmetrical shapes*, both sides of the body match. [Draw a line of symmetry through the middle of the shape to provide orientation.] You will be learning this in mathematics, too. Here is a picture of a person holding a symmetrical shape. Notice the line of symmetry; both sides are the same. In *asymmetrical shapes*, the sides of the body differ. Here are some pictures of asymmetrical body shapes.

CCSS What other symmetrical shapes do you know? [Circle, square, rectangle, equilateral triangle, cars viewed from the front, some trees, and so on.] What are some asymmetrical shapes? [Car viewed from the side.] Think about where you live. Is your house or apartment building symmetrical or asymmetrical?

Symmetrical and Asymmetrical Shapes of the Legs

I Balance on your back or shoulders, look at your legs, and make different symmetrical shapes with your legs. Now try different asymmetrical shapes.

E Explore jumping, first making symmetrical shapes and then making asymmetrical shapes.

E Combine the two movements: jump, and make a symmetrical shape. Then rock onto your back or shoulders, and make the exact same symmetrical shape. Hold this shape for three seconds, roll to your feet, and jump again, this time making a different symmetrical shape. Repeat the combination four times using four different shapes.

E Try the same combination, but this time make four different asymmetrical shapes. Jump, and make an asymmetrical shape. Then rock onto your back or shoulders, and make the exact same asymmetrical shape. Hold this shape for three seconds, roll to your feet, and jump again, this time making a different asymmetrical shape. Repeat the combination four times using four different shapes.

Symmetrical and Asymmetrical Shapes of the Body

E Now explore rocking and rolling while making symmetrical and asymmetrical shapes.

Cog K/CCSS *Peer coaching:* Select two rocks and two rolls showing asymmetrical and symmetrical shapes, and show them to a partner. See if your partner can label which you did. If you disagree, discuss why you think one way and your partner thinks another. Give reasons for your opinions.

E Now explore balancing while making symmetrical and asymmetrical shapes.

E Put three balances together in a sequence.

Cog K/CCSS *Peer coaching:* Show your sequence to your partner, and see if your partner can label which you did. If you disagree, discuss why you think one way and your partner thinks another. Give reasons for your opinions.

Culminating Activity: Designing Short Sequences

Structure of Sequences

Cog K Today you will be designing short sequences. You need to know two characteristics of sequences. First, all the parts fit together, the same way that all the words in a sentence fit together. If I said, "I want you to pick up your books, walk down to the library, return the books you read, and check out some new books you would like to read," you would understand me because I said a sentence. But, if I said, "Read speed like said your walk would new books some library," you wouldn't understand me because those were just a bunch of words. A sequence is like a sentence—all the movements fit together.

Second, a sequence has a beginning, a middle, and an end. In gymnastics, you begin in a shape, do your sequence, and end in a shape. Right now, start at one end of your mat and make a symmetrical shape. Walk to the other end of your mat and make an asymmetrical shape. That was the possible beginning and ending of a sequence.

A Today you will design a sequence with a beginning shape, three skills (rock, roll, jump, or balance), and an ending shape. You must have at least three different asymmetrical shapes.

Teaching Choreography

Cog K The criteria for deciding which shapes and skills work best for your sequence are originality and good transitions. Ask yourself the following questions [write abbreviated versions of these questions on a whiteboard]:

1. Are the starting and ending positions original or unusual?

SAMPLE PLAN 27.2

Theme: Asymmetrical and Symmetrical Shapes (*continued*)

2. Does the starting position allow you to move directly to your first skill with only one movement and no extra steps? If so, this is a good transition.
3. Does the ending position directly follow the third skill, with only one movement and no extra steps? If so, this is a good transition. If you are having problems with the transition between the starting and ending positions and the skills, but you really like the starting and ending positions, you might want to modify the skills.
4. Are all three skills different and interesting? Do you have at least one that is unusual?
5. Do the transitions between skills allow you to move directly from one to the next with only one movement and no extra steps? If so, you have good transitions.

A Begin to design your sequence. You can use the three most interesting or creative skills that you practiced before, or you can select new ones. Be sure to show a different leg shape on each skill.

R Practice your sequence until you can perform it exactly the same way each time.

A *Peer coaching:* Show your sequence to your assigned partner. Partners, watch for originality first. See if your partner has three different asymmetrical shapes and interesting beginning and ending shapes. Tell your partner which shape you thought was most interesting. Help your partner make his or her shapes more interesting.

A *Peer coaching:* This time, watch your partner's transitions. Tell him or her about any extra steps. Help your partner revise the transitions until all transitions are good.

A *Class show:* For those who want to show their sequences, we will do this in three groups. This third of the gym [gesture which children] will go first. The middle third will go second [gesture]. The last third will be this group near the stage [gesture]. Be prepared to offer compliments at the end.

SAMPLE PLAN 27.3

Major Theme: Different Levels; Minor Theme: Contrast as an Element of Choreography

Notes: These tasks are appropriate for children at developmental ability level 2. Teaching the content can take from two to three lessons. We provide two options for culminating activities, which you could do on different days. The first option for day 1 is a sequence without apparatus. The second option for days 2 and 3 includes exploring levels on an apparatus and then designing a sequence on that apparatus. This lesson provides an example of how to teach contrast as an element of sequence choreography.

Standards

This plan addresses National Standards 1 and 2 and CCSS for vocabulary acquisition.

Objectives

Children will learn to

Motor

1. Transfer weight and balance at different levels on mats and apparatus while maintaining body tension and landing lightly.

Critical Thinking

2. Understand and apply the concept of contrast in designing a sequence.

CCSS

3. Acquire and use accurately domain-specific words and phrases, including those that signal spatial relationships.

Potential Refinements

- Stay tight.
- Land lightly.

Content Development

Body at Different Levels

I Travel about space and jump, moving your body at a high level. Then approach a mat and travel by rolling, keeping your body at a low level.

(continues)

SAMPLE PLAN 27.3

Major Theme: Different Levels; Minor Theme: Contrast as an Element of Choreography (*continued*)

E Travel about space, moving your body at and to a high level. When you see a free mat, travel across it using steplike actions and moving the body at a medium level, and then reverse your direction and travel across the mat again while rolling, keeping the body at a low level.

Body Parts at Different Levels

E Travel about general space doing actions with your hands at a high level. Then, when you see a free mat, travel across it by taking your weight onto your hands at a low level.

E Travel about general space while you jump, hop, or leap, making your knee or knees the highest part of your leg. When you see a free mat, use a transition movement (roll, steplike action) to a balance in which your knee or knees are the highest part. Use a transition movement (roll, steplike action) out of the balance, and travel again. Repeat this process several times, finding different balances with your knee high and using different transitions into and out of balances.

E On a floor mat, find different ways to balance at all three levels while using different skills as transitions.

Culminating Activity Option 1: Creating Sequences with a Contrast in Levels

Cog K If you want to make a sequence interesting to watch, you need to include contrasts. *Contrast* means very different or opposite. A good way to add contrasts to gymnastics sequences is to vary the level from low to high as frequently as you can. A sequence will be boring if you stay at one level for a long time.

A Using a mat and the space around the mat, create a sequence showing movements at high, medium, and low levels. In your sequence, emphasize contrasts in levels by changing the level several times, going from high to low to high to low.

Culminating Activity Option 2: Apparatus at Low, Medium, and High Levels

Org Set up an apparatus section that two to three children can share. Have at least three pieces of apparatus that form three levels. For example, set a two-layer trapezoid under a balance beam and a single stacked mat on an angle to the trapezoid. Alternatively, use a ladder or bar, two stacked mats, and a trapezoid section.

Explore Balancing on Apparatus at Different Levels

E Explore different ways to balance at each level. Vary the body part on which you balance and your shapes.

E Find different ways to link your balances at different levels. For example, start with a balance on the apparatus at a medium level; then transition, with as few movements as possible, to a balance on the high apparatus; and finally transition to a balance at a low level.

E Vary the transitions. Try rolling, sliding, steplike actions, over-balancing into another balance, or jumping.

Explore Steplike and Rolling on Apparatus at Different Levels

E Explore steplike and rolling actions on the apparatus at different levels.

Explore Mounting and Dismounting an Apparatus at Different Levels

E Find different ways to approach and mount the apparatus at different levels and dismount from different levels.

Moderate Scaffolding If Needed

E Using an easy-approach jog, explore different ways to jump onto the apparatus, change levels, and find different ways to jump off. If you jump from a high level, land on your feet, and then safety roll. If you jump from a medium or low level, you can use resilient landings, land and stick, or land and safety roll.

E Find different ways to mount and dismount the apparatus using steplike actions at different levels.

E Find different ways to mount and dismount the apparatus at different levels using rolls.

E Mount the apparatus at one level, do two actions on the apparatus or to change levels, and then dismount from a different level.

Creating Apparatus Sequences with a Contrast in Levels

Cog K If you want to make a sequence interesting to watch, you need to include contrasts. *Contrast* means very different or the opposite. A good way to add contrasts to gymnastics sequences is to vary the level from low to high as frequently as you can. A sequence will be boring if you stay at one level for a long time.

A On the apparatus and the floor mats around it, create a sequence showing movements at high, medium, and low levels. In your sequence, emphasize contrasts in levels by changing the level several times, going from high to low to high to low.

SAMPLE PLAN 27.4

Theme: Different Speeds

Notes: These tasks are appropriate for children at developmental ability level 2.

Standards

This plan addresses National Standards 1 and 2 and CCSS for vocabulary acquisition.

Objectives

Children will learn to

Motor

1. Transfer weight at slow and moderately fast speeds, making the quick movements quick and the slow movements slow.

Thinking Skill

2. Compare and contrast skills based on how each skills works at slow and fast speeds.

CCSS

3. Acquire and use accurately domain-specific words and phrases, including those that signal temporal relationships, specifically, understand the movement concepts of slow and fast speeds, identify skills, and work better at slow and fast speeds.

Potential Refinements

- Make the quick movements quick and the slow movements slow.
- When you change speeds, make the change abruptly.
- When you accelerate or decelerate, spread the change in speed across the entire movement.

Introductory and Warm-up Activity

I Jog easily about general space, jumping over the corners of mats. Land on two feet or one foot with a resilient landing, spring away, and keep jogging.

E This time skip, gallop, or slide about the space using quick, light feet. Jump over the corner of the mat, taking off and landing sometimes on two feet and sometimes on one foot.

Content Development

Cog K Today we will be working at different speeds: fast and slow. Which animals move at slow speeds? [Tortoises, sloths, inchworms, worms moving through soil.] Which animals move fast? [Cheetahs, racehorses, greyhounds, roadrunners.] Which things move at fast speeds? [Racecars, jets, bullet trains.] Which things move in slow motion? [Bulldozers, drawbridges, glaciers, tectonic plates of the earth, locks on a river.] As you work today, think about something that moves slowly and something that moves quickly.

Safety You may move as quickly as you can as long as you are safe, are completely in control, and can stop instantly.

Traveling Quickly About General Space, Moving Slowly on a Mat

E Travel with quick, light feet. When you get to a free mat, roll across it in slow motion.

E Travel in different ways with quick, light feet. When you get to a free mat, slowly go into a balance, and slowly come down.

E Now we will travel quickly, jump, and land in a balance. Run with light, quick steps. At the edge of a mat, do a 1-2 jump, and perch balanced on the balls of your feet while stretching tall toward the ceiling. Hold this perch for three seconds, and then, in slow motion, travel across the mat in different ways each time.

E Now, travel about space using the five different kinds of flight from feet (jump, hop, leap, 2-1, and 1-2). Jump and land at the edge of a mat in a balance on one foot, then slowly lower yourself into a roll in slow motion. At the end of the roll, spring away.

Accelerating and Decelerating

E Starting at a mat, do three rolls in a row that you can perform confidently.

E Do the same three rolls, but start the first in slow motion, and then accelerate during the second roll, so the third roll is done quickly at a moderately fast speed.

E Try the reverse. Do the first roll fast, decelerate during the second roll, and do the third roll in slow motion.

(*continues*)

SAMPLE PLAN 27.4

Theme: Different Speeds (*continued*)

E Now select a different movement (steplike action, rock, or roll) and repeat it three times, starting fast and decelerating to slow motion.

E Reverse that process: Start in slow motion and end at a fast speed.

E Find a third movement, and try both accelerating and decelerating again. [Repeat several times.]

Slow and Fast Across a Mat

Th Let's work on comparing and contrasting skills. Did you find a movement that worked better at a fast speed than at a slow speed? Tell us which one, and explain why. Did you find a movement that worked better at a slow speed than at a fast speed? Tell us which one, and explain why.

E Find different ways to travel quickly across the mat, and then come back in slow motion. You may combine different ways of traveling in each pass.

Culminating Activity: Sequences

E Design a sequence showing movements at fast and slow speeds. Using any of the mats and general space, create a sequence that includes actions done at fast speeds and actions done at slow speeds.

SAMPLE PLAN 27.5

Major Theme: Twisting; Minor Theme: Turning

Notes: These tasks are appropriate for children at developmental ability level 3.

Standards

This plan addresses National Standards 1 and 2 and CCSS for vocabulary acquisition.

Objectives

Children will learn to

Motor and Cognitive

1. Apply the movement concepts of twisting and turning to different ways to jump, transfer weight, balance, and change levels on an apparatus while maintaining appropriate tension and controlling the flow of movement from flight and while traveling.

CCSS

2. Acquire and use accurately domain-specific words and phrases, including those that signal precise actions.

Potential Refinements

- Twisting in a jump is quick with lots of tension in the torso.
- When jumping, try to make your turns quick and sharp.
- In a turning jump, turn your head and look for where you will land; turn your shoulders to help initiate the turn.
- Land softly when you are traveling along the mat.

SAMPLE PLAN 27.5

Major Theme: Twisting; Minor Theme: Turning (*continued*)

Content Development

Cog K When you twist, one part of your body stays where it is, and other parts rotate to face a new direction. "Glue" one hand to the ground and walk around that arm. That's twisting your arm. Now, stand and twist at your waist and then twist back. A turn is when your whole body ends up facing a new direction. Turn so your back is to me. Turn and face me. Those were half-turns. Now do a full turn.

You are studying the planets in science. Does twisting or turning relate to the movement of planets? [Turning.] What term is used in science to describe how the planets turn? [Rotation.]

Twisting and Turning Jumps

I Travel about general space using an easy-approach jog. Jump from two feet to two feet, twisting one way and back in the air.

E Try twisting jumps in which you make different shapes with your legs and arms. Remember to twist one way and back before landing.

E Now try turning jumps in which you take off from either two feet or one foot.

E Try making different shapes with your legs and arms during the turning jump.

E Try jumping making a wide shape. As you bring your legs together to land, do a half-turn; land and spring away.

E Try the reverse: Jump, do a half-turn, and then, while you are still in the air, make a shape with your legs.

Twisting to Transfer Weight

I Find a mat, and start in a squat. Staying low, take your weight onto your hands, spring your legs up a few inches, twist, and bring your feet down in a different place.

MD If you are safe and confident, you can lift your legs higher. If you can do a handstand, you may choose to do that.

E Travel down your mat while taking your weight onto your hands, twisting, and bringing your feet down in a different place.

E Travel down the mat supporting your weight on different body parts and twisting to bring another body part down to support your weight.

Twisting and Balancing

E Now explore balancing on different body parts with one foot or two feet high. Twist to come down, and then twist again to go up into a different balance.

E Balance in a shoulder stand, twist your hips, and bring your legs down in a different place.

E Balance in a shoulder stand while varying the shape of your legs, twist, and let the twist take you into a different position or action (slide, steplike, roll, and balance).

E Start by kneeling with one hand on the floor. Twist by bringing one arm under your chest and through the space, letting the twist take you into a different position with your weight on your shoulders or back.

E Start by standing in either a straddle or lunge, and find a way to get down into a balance by twisting. Twist the balance, land on another body part, and do another action (roll, steplike action, slide, rock, balance).

Culminating Activity

The following tasks can be done with the whole class, or you can set up centers, and rotate the children to each center if you don't have enough apparatus.

E Stacked mat, floor mat: Run; land (two feet or one foot) on a stacked mat or aerobic box; jump and twist and untwist in the air; land and roll. Explore making different shapes in the air and using different rolls.

E Five hoops in a row: Transfer your weight while twisting to get into and out of each hoop.

E Mat, trapezoid section, mat: Balance on the first mat, twist to balance on the trapezoid, and twist down into a roll, steplike action, slide, or balance on the second mat.

E Stacked mat, floor mat: Run, jump on or over the stacked mat, make a half-turn before you land on floor mat, and safety roll sideways, backward, or backward diagonally over one shoulder.

SAMPLE PLAN 27.6

Theme: Stretching, Curling, and Twisting to Change Levels, Locations, and Positions

Notes: These learning experiences are appropriate for children at developmental ability level 3 and can be the basis for lessons for three to four days depending on the amount of lesson time and ability of the children. These experiences are excellent for extending children's movement variety. You can divide the tasks into one lesson on stretching and curling on flat mats, one lesson on stretching and curling using apparatus, one lesson on twisting using flat mats, and one lesson on twisting using apparatus. In addition, you can end by having children design sequences to show to the rest of the class, which will take an entire lesson.

Standards

This plan addresses National Standards 1 and 2 and CCSS for comprehension.

Objectives

Children will learn to

Motor and Cognitive

1. Apply the movement concepts of stretching, curling, and twisting to change levels, locations, and positions to extend the variety of gymnastics skills and actions they perform.
2. Move while stretching through the torso and maintaining continuity of flow.

CCSS

3. Describe details from information presented bodily through movement.

Potential Refinements

- When you stretch, feel the stretch throughout your whole body.
- Time your stretching and curling to be the action that takes you someplace, rather than just a body position.
- Stretching and curling to take you to a higher level often need to be forceful and fast.
- Maintain continuity of flow.

Content Development

Stretching and Curling to Change Levels, Locations, and Positions

I On a flat mat, explore different ways to start in a stretched position, and curl to take you to a new position.

E Now explore starting in a stretched position and curling to take you to a new level.

E Finally, explore curling to take you to a new location traveling across your mat.

E Try the reverse: Explore starting in a curled position, and stretch to take you to a new position while supporting your weight on different body parts.

E Explore starting curled, then stretch to take you to a new level while supporting your weight on different body parts.

E Explore starting curled, and then stretch to take you to a new location across your mat while supporting your weight on different body parts.

E Put all these skills together: Explore traveling on your mat by stretching and curling to take you to a new level, position, and location while supporting your weight on different body parts.

Twisting, Stretching, and Curling to Change Levels, Locations, and Positions

E Explore traveling on your mat by twisting to take you to a new level and position while supporting your weight on different body parts.

E Explore traveling on your mat by twisting to take you to a new level and location.

E Put all these skills together: Explore traveling on your mat by twisting, stretching, and curling to take you to a new level, position, and location while supporting your weight on different body parts.

Culminating Activity: Apparatus

Org Use whatever apparatus you have to set up centers. Each center should include at least three pieces of apparatus set at three different heights.

SAMPLE PLAN 27.6

Theme: Stretching, Curling, and Twisting to Change Levels, Locations, and Positions (*continued*)

Possible Apparatus Sections

- Playground equipment
- Boxes, stacked mats, trapezoids, vaulting horses, low beams arranged in a variety of ways
- High beams: sets of boxes, stacked mats, trapezoids arranged in a variety of ways under high beams
- Bars: sets of boxes, stacked mats, trapezoids arranged in a variety of ways under bars
- Climbing apparatus, Whittle equipment with mats

Stretching and Curling to Change Levels, Locations, and Positions

A We are going to take your floor work and apply it to the apparatus. First, support your weight on different body parts in curled positions, and see if you can stretch to take you to a new position, location, or level, ending on the same or different body parts.

E Now, support your weight on different body parts in stretched positions, and find ways to curl to take you to a new position, location, or level, ending on the same or different body parts.

E Moving as continuously as you can, stretch and curl to take you to a new position, location, or level. Try to vary the body parts on which you support your weight.

E Shift your focus, and explore stretching and curling to travel on, over, and off the apparatus.

Twisting, Stretching, and Curling to Change Levels, Locations, and Positions

E Support your weight on different body parts, and see if you can twist to take you to a new position, location, or level.

E Moving as continuously as you can, support your weight on different body parts, and twist to take you to a new position, location, or level; then twist again to travel again. Try to vary the body parts on which you support your weight.

E Now traveling on your hands and feet, find different ways to twist to travel on, over, and off the apparatus.

E Put everything together: Explore twisting, stretching, and curling to travel on, over, and off the apparatus.

Culminating Activity: Sequence on Apparatus

A Design a sequence showing stretching, curling, and twisting to take you to a different location on the apparatus. Avoid repetition of ordinary body shapes and actions; for example, don't rely on curling throughout the sequence. Work on having a variety of body shapes that are interesting and original. Have one unusual shape or movement.

CCSS After you have designed, refined, and practiced your sequence, I will put you with a partner who will assess your sequence on the following and then help you improve.

Repetition	A lot	Some	Very little	None
Originality	Ordinary	Some variety	A lot of interesting variety	Variety and at least one unusual shape or movement

If there was a lot or some repetition, the peer assessor should identify the shape or action that was repeated. The following are movements that beginners typically repeat too many times, so look for these:

- Repetition of curled shapes
- A lot of symmetrical shapes and movements
- Many movements at the same level; too few changes of level

If there were interesting and unusual shapes or movements, describe these shapes and movements clearly, and provide details about when and where they were performed.

CHAPTER

28

Partner and Group Work

OBJECTIVES

Students will learn:

1. Partner and group work is enjoyable for children and helps extend their movement vocabularies.
2. Children's ability to work cooperatively in groups determines whether they are ready for partner and group work.
3. Partner and group work requires only the foundational skills of rolling, balancing, steplike actions, and jumping but takes far more sophisticated social skills.

KEY TERMS

Canon
Complementing
Contrasting
Counterbalance
Countertension
Matching
Mirroring
Unison

CONNECTION TO STANDARDS

This chapter focuses on partner and group work while learning gymnastics skills; thus, it addresses National Standards 1, 2, and 4. The chapter also addresses Common Core and other State Standards (CCSS) for speaking, listening, and collaborating.

PROGRESSION OF CONTENT

Level 1 Foundational Skills

- Balancing
- Rolling and rocking
- Steplike actions
- Flight from feet
- Dynamic balancing

Level 2

Partner Work

Copying and following a leader

- Locomotor steps
- Pathway
- Foundational skills
- One off, over, under

Matching, mirroring contrasting, and complementing

- Matching and mirroring foundational skills and shapes
- Contrasting foundational skills and shapes
- Complementing a partner's shape and movement by matching the shape of the legs with partners performing two different skills
- Complementing shapes with partners performing the same skill in two different ways

Level 3

Partner Work

Countertension

- Combined with rolling
- Using like and unlike body parts
- Rising and lowering to different levels
- Rotating
- On an apparatus at different levels
- With matching, complementary, and contrasting shapes

Counterbalance

- Combined with rolling
- Using like and unlike body parts
- Rising and lowering to different levels
- Rotating
- On an apparatus at different levels
- With matching, complementary, and contrasting shapes

Countertension and Counterbalance Sequences

- Fluid transitions
- Parts that fit together logically
- Variety and originality
- Line

Partner and Group Sequences Based on Movement Concepts and Choreography Principles

- Different levels; contrast and aesthetic highlights
- Different speeds; contrast and aesthetic highlights
- Traveling over, under, and through partner shapes and balances; originality
- Partner and group shapes; originality and line

Group Work

Canon and unison

- Fitting all parts together logically with fluid transitions
- Varying skills and creating interesting shapes and body positions that bring out the aesthetic potential of canon and unison
- Determining interesting and appropriate rhythm of canon and unison movements
- Clarity of body positions and shapes

Pair and group balances

- Line
- Clarity of shapes
- Fluid transitions into and out of balances in sequences
- Fitting the balances into sequences logically

Group timing

- Timing approaches to an apparatus

Figure 28.1 Progression of Content

Introduction

This chapter focuses on partner and group work themes with lessons for children at ability levels 2 and 3. **Figure 28.1** summarizes the content discussed in this chapter, and the **FYI** box lists the sample plans found at the end of the chapter.

Partner work is one of the most enjoyable gymnastics activities for children. Partners capture children's interest, provide exciting challenges, and extend each other's movement vocabulary. In addition, the relatedness of working with a partner is motivating. Partner work is particularly useful in schools with few pieces of apparatus because partners can become obstacles to navigate as well as a means of support.

Older children especially enjoy working with others. Thus, teachers new to a school with children in the upper elementary grades who have not yet had gymnastics might find partner and group work motivating and some of the best ways to introduce skill and movement concept themes. Many lessons on foundational gymnastic skills and movement concepts can be modified easily to include partner work.

Partner work also gives teachers an opportunity to work on social responsibility objectives—which are the focus of National Standard 4 and CCSS for speaking, listening, and collaborating. In partner work, students learn and practice valuable communication and cooperation skills. They also learn how to contribute to a group project and to ensure their classmates have the opportunity to contribute. Finally, they learn to attend to the needs of other children by including only skills and shapes that all children in the group can do safely, and they learn to say no when group members suggest a skill they are not confident performing.

When Are Children Ready for Partner Work?

Whether children are ready for partner work depends more on their social and cognitive developmental level than on their movement ability. Partner and group work requires a level of social development that will support children in

- Working cooperatively and effectively with others
- Using thinking skills and choreographic processes, such as exploration, critical and creative thinking, problem solving, and decision making *with a partner or in groups*

To capitalize on children's usual pattern of social development, teachers typically use partner and group work with the upper elementary grades. Nevertheless, you can introduce some simple partner tasks, such as copying or following a leader, in the lower elementary grades.

Partner and group work, however, do not require children to perform advanced skills. Level 2 partner and group work themes require no more than side rolls, steplike actions with the feet at low and medium levels, balances on a variety of body parts, the five kinds of flight from feet (jump, hop, leap, 2-1, 1-2), and the ability to stay tight and control the flow of their movements. We have observed impressive group choreography on themes such as canon and unison from groups with only beginning-level skills.

FYI

Sample Plans in this Chapter

Level 2

1. Copying and Following a Leader (including a discussion about being a socially responsible leader)
2. Matching, Contrasting, and Complementary Shapes
3. Canon and Unison (including elements of sequence choreography for formations and transitions)

Level 3

4. Countertension Combined with Rolling (including an example of how you can integrate these skills with science/biomechanical principles)
5. Countertension Using Like and Unlike Body Parts (including teaching elements of choreography for transitions and variety)
6. Counterbalance (including teaching elements of choreography for transitions and variety)
7. Pair Balancing (including teaching elements of choreography for line and transitions)
8. Countertension and Counterbalance (including teaching elements of choreography for contrasts in speed and level)
9. Timing Approaches to Apparatus and Group Awareness (including a sample way to discuss increasing the social awareness of group members) (see text website)

SAFETY AND LIABILITY 28.1

Increasing Safety and Decreasing Risk of Liability: Guidelines Relevant to Content in this Chapter

In this box, we discuss specific guidelines built on information discussed throughout this text on professional standards of practice, negligence, and liability. The goals of these guidelines are to increase children's safety and decrease teachers' risk of negligence and liability.

- To increase safety and decrease liability risk, teachers should plan and follow a written curriculum with a progression or sequence of tasks to develop children's skills safely. The curriculum is based on district, state, and national standards and guidelines. All tasks are developmentally appropriate and modified to accommodate individual differences. Safety issues within tasks are taught, and students are warned about potential dangers.
- In educational gymnastics, students select the skills to practice within a theme. Teach children they must select only those skills they can do safely, confidently, and with control. When designing partner and group sequences, select only those skills all children in the group can do safely, confidently, and with control. Teachers must monitor students' selections and modify selections when children select skills that are too difficult for them.
- Performing with movement quality and appropriate performance techniques are two of the most important ways to increase safe participation. A reasonably prudent teacher focuses on movement quality throughout every lesson, teaches students the performance techniques that contribute to movement quality, and explicitly and repeatedly teaches students about movement quality.
- Teach children how to set up, arrange, and put away the gymnastics mats and apparatus.
- When assigning partners and groups, match size, weight, skill ability, and any other developmental characteristics relevant to safety within the tasks assigned.

Partner Work

Copying and Following the Leader

Copying a partner or following a leader is the simplest partner work. Even children in the youngest grades can work on these themes. You can design lessons using a wide range of foundational gymnastics and locomotor skills.

Potential Movement Variety Experiences

- Travel about the gym copying the locomotor steps of a partner.
- Follow a leader on straight, curved, and zigzag pathways, with the follower selecting his or her own locomotor steps.
- Follow a leader, copying both the locomotor steps and the pathway of the leader.
- Copy a partner's sequence of foundational skills (sequences can use any combination of rocking, rolling, steplike actions, jumping, and balancing).
- Follow a leader on, off, over, under, and through apparatus (copying just the pathway or copying both the pathways and movement of the leader).

Matching, Mirroring, Contrasting, and Complementary Shapes

Matching means doing the same shape or the same foundational skill in the same way (see **Figure 28.2**). **Mirroring** means doing the same shape but facing each other as if you were looking at a mirror (see **Figure 28.3**). **Contrasting** means doing the opposite. For example, if one child makes a big, wide shape, the other child makes a small, curled shape. If one child is twisted, the other is straight. **Complementing** means harmonizing or going together. In other words, one child's shape is similar to the other child's but with a slight variation, such as being at a different level or using slightly different body parts.

There is a wealth of material for designing lessons on matching, mirroring, contrasting, and complementing. Moreover, children enjoy repeating these themes and using them as a basis for partner sequences.

Figure 28.2 Matching

Courtesy of John Dolly

Figure 28.3 Mirroring

Courtesy of John Dolly

Possible Movement Variety Experiences

- Matching and mirroring foundational skills and shapes
- Contrasting foundational skills and shapes; for example, contrasting the shape with partners performing two different skills, such as a tucked jump contrasting a wide cartwheel, or performing the same skill in two different ways, such as two balances with contrasting leg shapes
- Complementing a partner's shape and movement by matching the shape of the legs with partners performing two different skills (e.g., the leg shape in a straddle side roll matching the leg shape in a cartwheel)
- Complementing shapes with partners performing the same skill in two different ways, such as two different jumps with complementing shapes

Designing sequences based on matching, mirroring, contrasting, and complementing shapes are opportunities to also focus on elements of choreography. The clarity of the shape and the lines formed by body parts are clearly necessary elements for making shapes match, contrast, or complement. Designing interesting and original shapes and movements as well as including an aesthetic highlight are additional elements of choreography that students can learn as they design sequences based on these themes. As always with gymnastic, designing fluid transitions and fitting the parts of a sequence together in a logical order that enhances the cohesiveness of the sequence are important elements of choreography students must learn.

Countertension and Counterbalance

In **countertension**, two children balance together by leaning away from each other, usually using a pulling action (see **Figure 28.4** and **Figure 28.5**). The base of support is typically narrow in such a skill. In **counterbalance**, two children balance together by leaning toward each other using a wide base of support (see **Figure 28.6** and **Figure 28.7**). In both

Figure 28.4 Countertension into a roll

countertension and counterbalance, each partner depends on the other to maintain balance.

To work on countertension and counterbalance, children not only need to be socially responsible, but also must be able to partly support their partner's weight. Moreover, they must be able to maintain body tension so their partner can partly support their weight.

We typically introduce countertension in combination with rolls, which are used as a transition from the countertension position. As children gain skill and increase their movement variety, there are many rich possibilities for developing lessons—in particular, with the use of stacked mats, trapezoid sections, or other apparatus. Countertension and counterbalance can also become part of other partner and group work lessons with movement concepts as themes, such as levels, contrasts, pushing and pulling, and matching and complementing shapes and movements.

Potential Movement Variety Experiences

- Countertension using hands and lowering the partner into different rolls
- Countertension and counterbalance using like and unlike body parts and lowering into rolls
- Rising and lowering countertensions and counterbalances at different levels
- Rotating or spinning while holding a countertension or counterbalance
- Countertension and counterbalance on an apparatus at different levels

Figure 28.5 Countertension into a roll

Figure 28.6 Counterbalance

Courtesy of John Dolly

Figure 28.7 Counterbalance into a roll

- Countertension and counterbalance with matching, contrasting, and complementing shapes

Sequences that include countertension and counterbalance require students to increase their knowledge of several elements of choreography. Foremost among the elements students need to learn are designing fluid transitions and fitting the parts of the sequence together in a logical order. In addition, students need to learn the importance of including a variety of and some original and unusual countertensions and counterbalances. The lines made by the position of partners' body parts when they hold a countertension or counterbalance are also clearly evident to observers and thus appropriate and worthy choreography content to teach when students design sequences.

Partner and Group Sequences Based on Movement Concepts and Choreography Principles

Partner and group work in gymnastics often focuses on designing sequences based on movement concept themes and elements of choreography. Children can work on these themes in partners, trios, or quads (groups of four). The following movement concepts and principles of choreography work well as lesson themes:

- Different levels; working on choreography principles of contrast and aesthetic highlights
- Different speeds; working on choreography principles of contrast and aesthetic highlights
- Traveling over, under, and through partner shapes and balances; working on the choreography principle of originality
- Partner and group shapes; working on choreography principles of originality and line

Group Work

Canon and Unison

Canon and unison are two different ways that individuals in a group can time their movements. **Unison** means that everyone moves at exactly the same time. **Canon** means that everyone moves in succession, starting one at a time. Canon is like the "wave" we see in sport stadiums, when the crowd stands and lifts their arms in a succession going all around the stadium.

For canon and unison sequences to be effective, children need to be in groups of three to five members. Consequently, we typically reserve this theme for fifth grade when children have developed the ability to work well in groups. We also start the children in groups of three and then put two groups together after they have generated several ideas. In groups of six, children have a difficult time completing the task because some children dominate the discussion, and others do not have the opportunity to contribute very much. When they start in groups of three, their classmates will listen to their ideas, and they enjoy creating their sequence and then combining it with another

Figure 28.8 Pairs balance

(A) © Jones & Bartlett Learning. Photographed by Christine Myaskovsky. (B) Courtesy of John Dolly.

group's sequence. Canon and unison are excellent themes for less-skilled children because they can create outstanding choreography without having to use difficult skills.

Canon and unison sequences are well matched to teaching students about the following elements of choreography:

- Fitting all parts together logically with fluid transitions
- Varying skills and creating interesting shapes and body positions that bring out the aesthetic potential of canon and unison
- Creating an aesthetic highlight
- Determining and practicing the rhythm of the canon and unison movements so that the rhythms are interesting and appropriate for the movements
- Understanding clarity and practicing until movements and shapes can be repeated accurately

Pair and Group Balances

Pair and group balances are good themes for older children who are socially responsible (see **Figure 28.8**). Such balances can be the focus of sequences if the children use other foundational skills as transitions. In addition, pair and group balances can be part of sequences based on other themes, such as level, speed, canon and unison, or countertension and counterbalance.

Pairs and multiple-person balances are excellent themes for teaching children about line as a choreographic principle. In designing their partner or group balance, they attend to the lines created by different body parts in relation to other body parts and how these lines complement each other. They also learn to attend to both the shape of their body and the shape created by the group and the clarity of those shapes. In addition, to move into and out of pair and group balances means students must learn how to design fluid transitions and figure out logical ways to fit the parts of a sequence together.

In terms of skill ability, pair and group balances require children to be able to support the body weight of a classmate either partly or totally. Children supported by another child must be able to maintain body tension.

Group Timing

Group timing is an advanced theme that refers to timing traveling actions so individuals cross paths but do not collide. *Timing* means knowing when to start the approach in relation to other members of the group. Children learn to be aware of where each group member is at all times and to anticipate where and when classmates will move.

In designing lessons, the apparatus and layout of the work space can elicit many different variations in timing. If mats are placed in an X-shaped formation, children are likely to design sequences with diagonal crossing patterns. If mats are parallel, timing patterns will be canon and unison with movements that are parallel or perpendicular. Because this is an advanced theme, we include sample plans on the text website, not in the text.

Summary

Partner and group work is enjoyable for children and helps extend their movement vocabularies. It requires that children be competent in only the level 1 foundational skills of rolling, balancing, steplike actions, and jumping. Partner and group work themes include copying and following a leader; matching, contrasting, and complementary shapes; canon and unison; countertension and counterbalance; and pair and group balances.

Partner and group work also require children to be able to work cooperatively and productively with others. These lessons enable teachers to teach social responsibility, communication, and collaboration skills, thus meeting National Standard 4 and CCSS for speaking, listening, and collaborating.

Review Questions

1. When are children ready for partner work?
2. Define and write a learning experience in gymnastics for each of the following movement elements: matching, contrasting, and complementing.
3. Describe the difference between countertension and counterbalance, and discuss how you could explain this distinction to children.
4. Which skill abilities do pair and group balances require?

Reference

Rink, J. E. (2014). *Teaching physical education for learning* (7th ed.). New York: McGraw-Hill.

FYI

Summary of Task Label Abbreviations

I	Informing tasks
E	Extending/exploring tasks
R	Refinements
A	Application/assessment tasks
Org	Organizing task
Cog K	Cognitive knowledge: Explains or defines a concept
Social	Social skill or concept
Th	Thinking skill
Mot	Motivation concept
Safety	Safety information or reminder
MD	Modification to make the task more difficult
ME	Modification to make the task easier

Source: Adapted and Modified from Rink, J. E. (2014). *Teaching physical education for learning* (7th ed.).New York: McGraw-Hill.

Level 2 Sample Plans

SAMPLE PLAN 28.1

Theme: Copying and Following a Leader

Notes: These tasks are designed for ability level 2. These learning experiences can take from two to three lessons. This sample plan also illustrates how to include a discussion about being a socially responsible leader.

Standards

This plan addresses National Standards 1, 2, and 4 and CCSS for collaboration.

Objectives

Children will learn to

Motor and Cognitive

1. Apply movement concepts to body actions and shapes with a partner copying and following a leader, making actions and shapes clear.

Social

2. Work responsibly as a leader making sure her or his shapes and body actions are safe for and match the ability level of her or his partner.

CCSS

3. Participate in collaborative discussions with a partner, listening carefully and both contributing ideas.

Potential Refinements

- Make your actions and shapes clear so you partner can copy you.

(*continues*)

SAMPLE PLAN 28.1

Theme: Copying and Following a Leader (*continued*)

Content Development

Following a Leader's Pathway and Actions About the Gym

I With your assigned partner, one of you lead while the other follows all about general space doing different locomotor steps and traveling on different pathways. Sometimes stop and jump in place or touch different body parts to the floor, and then stand and travel again. The follower must copy the leader's actions. Switch leads frequently.

Social Have a discussion with your partner about how to work responsibly as a leader. What does the leader need to think about to be responsible for the follower's safety? Be sure to listen carefully to your partner, and both of you contribute ideas. [Don't do anything that is too difficult for your partner. Be sure your pathway won't put the follower into any unsafe position. Make sure you don't cut in between another leader and follower or allow another leader to cut in between you and your follower.] [Call on several pairs to share their ideas with the class.]

What can you do if your partner does something you do not feel safe doing? [Tell them, and don't copy what they did.]

E Now, let's do the same task, but this time the follower must follow the pathway but not the actions of the leader. Switch leads frequently.

Sequence on Mats: Observe and Copy a Partner

E Find a space on a floor mat, and design a short sequence with a starting shape, one to three foundational skills [select a number appropriate for the age of the children], and an ending shape. Practice your sequence.

E Go with your assigned partner. Partner A teaches his or her sequence to partner B, who copies and follows the leader. Then switch roles.

R Work hard on making your movements exactly the same as your partner's movements.

Culminating Activity Options

The following are five options for a culminating activity for a lesson on copying a leader.

Option 1: Card Sequences: Read and Follow a Partner's Instructions

E [Give each child two black cards (squares) and one to three blank white cards. The black cards (on which children can't write) represent the starting and ending shape. The children write one foundational skill or one movement concept on each of the three white cards (e.g., roll, low level, slow, balance, round, jump, high level, rock), and give the five cards to their partners. Each partner does the sequence his or her partner wrote using whatever starting and ending shape they choose.

Alternatively, give the children three white cards on which you have written a foundational skill or movement concept. The leader can either use what you have written or turn the card over and write another foundational skill or movement concept. Then the partner does what the leader wrote.]

Option 2: Follow a Leader's Pathway On, Over, and Through Equipment and Small Apparatus

Org [Set up the following equipment scattered all around the gym: flat mats, stacked mats on flat mats, hoops flat on the floor, hoops braced vertically on a mat, trapezoids, low and medium cones with canes across, 2×4 beams, steppingstones (poly spots, beanbags), and whatever else is available.]

E There is lots of great equipment scattered about the space. Partner A leads, and partner B follows the leader's actions and pathways. Switch leads frequently. Repeat using the same equipment, but this time the follower follows the leader's pathway but not actions. Switch leads frequently.

Option 3: Follow a Leader's Pathway on Playground Equipment

E One partner leads, and the other follows the leader's actions and pathways. The leader travels all about the playground equipment, trying to get to each section. Then switch leads. Repeat, but this time the follower follows the leader's pathway but not actions. Switch leads.

Option 4: Reading a Map

E [Before class, draw a map of the playground equipment or the equipment and apparatus that will be set up in the gym.] I am going to hand each of you a map. Draw a pathway all around the equipment, and then give the map to your partner. The partner follows the pathway around the equipment doing any gymnastics action he or she chooses. [A second option is that the child who draws the pathway can also write which actions to do. Children can switch maps with another pair.]

SAMPLE PLAN 28.1

Theme: Copying and Following a Leader (*continued*)

Option 5: Whole-class Adventure Trail

E [You can do this activity using playground equipment supplemented with other small equipment or with indoor apparatus and equipment. Take out as many mats and apparatus as you have, along with carpet squares, tunnels, ropes, old hoses, hoops, 2×4 beams, poly spots, and beanbags. Arrange the equipment so children can travel from one piece to another without having to touch the floor (or ground). Design multiple pathways around the equipment.] As you can see, we have built an adventure trail. Partner A is the leader first and travels all around the adventure trail using different body actions and trying to get to all parts of the trail; partner B copies the leader's actions and pathway. Neither the leader nor the follower can touch the ground or another person. Switch leads.

SAMPLE PLAN 28.2

Theme: Matching, Contrasting, and Complementary Shapes

Notes: These learning experiences are for ability level 2 and will take from two to three lessons to complete.

Standards

This plan addresses National Standards 1, 2, and 4 and CCSS for vocabulary acquisition.

Objectives

Children will learn to

Motor and Cognitive

1. Apply the concepts of matching, contrasting, and complementing shapes to foundational skills with a partner, maintaining appropriate body alignment and having clear shapes.

Social

2. View the task from their partner's perspective, and make shapes that are easy to match or contrast.

CCSS

3. Acquire domain-specific vocabulary, including those that signal contrast and spatial relationships, specifically, matching, contrasting, and complementing.

Potential Refinements

- Ensure appropriate body alignment, pointing toes and keeping legs straight.
- Clear shapes match, contrast, or complement.

Content Development

Cog K There are three types of shapes you can make in relation to a partner: matching, contrasting, and complementary. What do you think matching means? Right: Matching shapes are the same. What might contrasting mean? Right: Contrasting shapes are the opposite of each other. If one person makes a big, wide shape, the other makes a small, curled shape. If one person is twisted, the other is straight. What do you think complementary shapes means? Complementary shapes harmonize or go together. That means one person's shape is similar to the other person's but with a slight variation, such as being at a different level or using slightly different body parts.

Explore Matching Shapes

I On your own, put together a sequence of a jump making a leg shape, land, roll on your back (or into a shoulder stand if you can do one confidently and competently), and end in a simple balance making the same leg shape. Roll to your feet, and repeat two more times. Practice this sequence until you can repeat it exactly the same way every time. Be sure your leg shapes are very clear, so your partner will be able to match them.

E Teach your partner your sequence, and work on matching exactly.

(*continues*)

SAMPLE PLAN 28.2

Theme: Matching, Contrasting, and Complementary Shapes (*continued*)

E Now, one of you balance or hold a shape at a low level, making a clear shape with your legs. The other partner jumps, matching that shape, and then safety rolls.

Safety The jumping partner has two choices. You can jump next to your partner's balance, or you can jump over one of your partner's body parts that is touching the ground. [If you do not know the class well, limit this task to jumping next to the partner.] The criterion you use for making this decision is safety. Only do what you are 100% sure you can do safely. If you are not sure you can jump over your partner, then jump next to her or him.

E Then the partner on the mat makes a new shape that is clear and easy to match, and the other partner jumps, lands, and rolls one more time. Then switch roles.

Explore Contrasting Shapes

E Explore shapes again, but this time the partner jumping contrasts the partner balancing low on the mat. Land the jump with a safety roll.

E Now explore different ways of traveling next to your partner's balance while making contrasting shapes. You can do steplike actions, rolls, or jumps.

Social Partners who are balancing, make your shape a good shape for your partner to contrast. Some shapes are difficult to contrast; try to be sure your shape is easy to contrast. Think about your partner's needs and ability.

Exploring Complementing Shapes

E Now explore the third kind of shape—complementary shapes. One partner balances or holds a shape at a low level, making a clear shape with her or his legs. The other partner jumps nearby, making a complementing shape and then finishing with a safety roll. An observer should be able to tell that you and your partner meant for your shapes to go together.

Culminating Activity: Sequences

E Now experiment with matching, contrasting, and complementing, jumping nearby your partner, alternating who is the obstacle on every jump. One partner makes a low-level balance or shape, and the other jumps nearby, matching, contrasting, or complementing shapes, and immediately transitions by rolling and ending in a balance at a low level. The other partner finds a way to smoothly transition from a low-level balance to her or his feet (by rolling, over-balancing, twisting, or steplike actions), does an easy-approach jog, and jumps nearby the partner, who by now should be holding a low-level balance. Keep alternating as you and your partner travel about general space.

Social You must be very aware of other pairs who also will be traveling about general space. When you make a balance, make sure your partner will have room to jump near you without landing on another child. You are responsible for your own and your partner's safety.

A Design a sequence with your partner showing matching, contrasting, and complementary shapes. Have at least two times when one of you jumps nearby the other. You also may add other ways of traveling nearby or over your partner, and you may have segments when you both are performing the same skill with matching, contrasting, or complementing shapes. For example, both partners might jump and roll at the same time, with one of you doing a wide jump and a tight, curled roll, while the other contrasts that movement with a curled jump and a straight log roll.

R Practice your sequence focusing on three related refinements:

- Body alignment: pointing toes, keeping legs straight when they are supposed to be straight and tucked tight when they are supposed to be tucked.
- Clarity: making a shape that is clearly a match, contrast, or complement to your partner's shape.
- You and your partner can accurately repeat the sequence to the last detail.

Then you can show your sequence to another pair. [Alternatively, you can have children show their sequences to the class, with one-third of the class showing at a time.]

CCSS Closure

I will assign two pairs to work together. Discuss the definitions of matching, contrasting, and complementing. Give examples that would help someone new to this school understand what you learned today.

SAMPLE PLAN 28.3

Major Theme: Canon and Unison; Minor Theme: Elements of Choreography—Parts Fit Together Logically with Fluid Transitions

Notes: These learning experiences are appropriate for ability level 2. Children need to be able to work well in groups of three to four for these learning experiences. As we discussed earlier, you can have groups of three combine their sequences in a group of six at the end of the lessons. Typically, we save this theme for fifth grade, but it also is an excellent theme to use with fourth- and fifth-grade children with little previous gymnastics experiences. Group the children within a class by ability level. Children who can do only the most basic rolls, steplike actions, and balances can design excellent sequences with canon and unison. It will take two to four lessons before the children can complete their sequence, practice it, and share their work with others. This is an excellent theme for the end of a gymnastics unit, and the teacher can assess the sequences.

Standards

This plan addresses National Standards 1, 2, and 4 and CCSS for collaboration.

Objectives

Children will learn to

Motor and Cognitive

1. Design group sequences using a variety of formations and skills with shapes and body positions that bring out the aesthetic potential of canon and unison.
2. Fit all the parts together logically with fluid transitions.
3. Practice the sequence until the group can repeat the sequence accurately.

Social and CCSS

4. Work collaboratively in a group being sensitive to the ability levels of all group members, listening carefully during discussions, building on each other's ideas, and ensuring everyone contributes at least one idea for the sequence.

Content Development

Cog K For the next few days, we will be working on group sequences based on canon and unison. Canon and unison are two different ways in which individuals in a group can time their movements. What does unison mean? Right: Unison means that everyone moves at exactly the same time. Anyone know what canon means? Canon means everyone moves in succession, starting one at a time. How many of you have ever been to a sport event in a stadium and seen the wave? Canon is like the wave we see in sport stadiums, when people in the crowd stand and lift their arms in a succession going all around the stadium.

Introducing Canon and Unison

I In your group of three, let's try both unison and canon with egg rolls. Get into one straight line standing sideways to a mat so all of you have room to roll sideways in a curled shape without touching anyone else. Have one person in your group say "Go"; then all of you take your weight onto the mat, roll sideways, and stand at exactly the same time. This is unison.

E Now try egg rolls in canon. For canon, the first person in line starts his or her roll. When that person is almost on the mat, the next person starts. When that person is almost on the mat, the third person starts, and then right down the line following the same timing pattern. That is canon.

E One aspect of your group sequence will be to include some canon movements and some unison movements. In your group, discuss and select three simple movement combinations. Starting from a line, try each combination in unison and in canon.

Social When you work in a group, can you tell the group members to do any movement you like? [No.] Why not? [Other people might not like the movement.] Good start at an answer, but there is more to it. In your groups, discuss why someone might not like the movement. [Call on a group.] [If you were in a group, and everyone in that group except you took gymnastics lessons after school, they might want to do things that I can't do. They might want to do difficult skills.] That's it. What do you think you can do if group wants to do a skill that you don't feel safe doing? [Tell them I can't do it. Tell them I am afraid to do it because I might get hurt.] So our rule is that you can do only skills that everyone in your group feels safe and confident doing.

Introducing Formations and Transitions

Cog K What is a formation? [How we stand in relation to each other. The shape on the floor created by where we stand.] A second aspect of your group sequence is formation. What kinds of group formations can you make? [Lines facing one leader, lines with everyone shoulder to shoulder, double lines, circles, squares, V shapes.] In your sequence, you need to have a lot of different formations and transitions that take you from one formation to the next without having to

(*continues*)

SAMPLE PLAN 28.3

Major Theme: Canon and Unison; Minor Theme: Elements of Choreography—Parts Fit Together Logically with Fluid Transitions (*continued*)

walk. As an example, let's try one. Go back and stand in your line facing the front of the gym. When I say "Go," the two outside people do one egg roll toward the front of the gym and then stand. The one inside person does two egg rolls, all moving toward the front of the gym. Ready, go. You should end up in a V formation, and no one had to walk to get there. The number of rolls created a new formation.

We will do one more example. Stand in a line following one leader. Using canon, the leader does an egg roll to the right. The next person in line does an egg roll to the left. The third person rolls right. You are now in a triangle formation. In none of these formation changes did you need to take extra steps.

Culminating Activity: Designing Sequences

A Working as a group, design a sequence showing canon and unison, a variety of formations, and different skills. You do not have to all do the same skills all the time. [Give the children plenty of time to design their sequences. This may take more than one lesson.]

Social and CCSS Before you begin, let's review our rules that will make your group discussions more productive and fair for everyone. [Elicit rules from children, and have a poster ready to post as a reminder.]

1. Everyone talks; everyone listens. (Each person gives his or her opinion, and everyone must listen.)
2. Initially, brainstorm to generate many ideas, many varied ideas, and some unusual ideas. When you brainstorm, don't criticize ideas; try to build on other people's ideas. The goal is to generate as many ideas as possible; evaluating ideas too early will limit your productive thinking.
3. Think while you move, and move while you think. Try ideas out before you make the decision to use them or not use them in your sequence.
4. Everyone contributes: Encourage a quiet classmate to contribute by saying, "What do you think, Jesse?" Everyone must contribute at least one idea to the sequence.

Social and CCSS Why do you think these rules are important? [We will all get a chance to give our ideas. Everyone will be respectful. Someone who is quiet and does not say very much will get a chance to contribute and maybe his or her ideas will be the best ideas. The more of us who contribute, the more ideas we will have for our sequence.]

E [After the children have practiced several ideas, intervene to teach the three following elements of sequence choreography. Teach one element, and let them work on that. Then teach the next. If the children are already using the element of choreography, compliment them on it, making sure that they know the element and are consciously applying it to their work.]

Three Elements of Choreography

1. *Variety of formations and skills with frequent changes:* Not only should you plan a variety of skills and formations, but you should also change formation frequently. Don't stay in the same formation for more than one or two skills.
2. *Select shapes and body positions that are the most effective shape for a formation that harmonize with that formation and that bring out the aesthetic potential of canon or unison:* Use a variety of leg shapes, and try to use the most effective shape for the formation. For example, if the audience is looking at you in a straight line following a leader in canon and they can see only the leader, which jump would be more effective and bring out the aesthetic potential of canon—a straight jump or a wide, straddle jump? Right, the straddle would have more of a visual impact when viewed from the front. Which would harmonize better with a transition from a line to a circle following a leader—doing forward rolls on a circular pathway or doing steplike, wheeling movements with all of you pointing your hands toward the center and wheeling your legs to the outside in unison? Right, the wheeling movements harmonize better with the circle and would catch the eye of the observers if you did them in perfect unison.
3. *Order your skills so you don't have to take extra steps in the transitions from one formation to the next:* Sometimes you have great ideas but problems with the transitions, and you end up having to take extra steps to get from one formation to the next. If this happens, try reordering the skills to see if a different order will solve your problem.

E I will now combine two groups to be a group of six. Create one sequence by combining your ideas. Canon, in particular, has more of a visual impact in groups of six, so pay careful attention to your formations and body positions for the canon parts of the sequence to make them aesthetically effective.

R Practice your sequence until you have it perfected—that is, your group movements are in perfect rhythm, and you can accurately repeat the sequence to the last detail. Then you can show your sequence to another group. [Alternatively, you can have children show their sequences to the class with one-third of the class showing at a time.]

SAMPLE PLAN 28.4

Theme: Countertension Combined with Rolling

Notes: These learning experiences are appropriate for ability level 3. Countertension and counterbalance require children to be socially responsible. We have found that it is helpful to introduce countertension by combining it with a roll. In the long run, this teaching strategy helps children develop sequences that have continuity and smooth transitions. This plan includes an example of how you can integrate science/biomechanical principles.

Standards

This plan addresses National Standards 1, 2, and 4 and CCSS for vocabulary acquisition.

Objectives

Children will learn to

Motor and Cognitive

1. Apply the concept of countertension to a balanced position, gently lowering the body and transiting into a roll.
2. Perform a variety of countertensions with different rolls, maintaining appropriate tension.

Social

3. Be sensitive to controlling their partner's weight, moving only as fast as the partner can move safely.

CCSS

4. Acquire domain-specific vocabulary, specifically countertension, and apply the concept in a variety of situations.

Potential Refinements

- Stay tight when your partner is supporting your weight.
- Feel the tension and pull between you.
- Lower your weight gently and smoothly into rolls.

Introductory Activity

I [Pair children with partners of comparable size. Use a wave organization pattern in which children start in lines, and each wave begins as soon as there is room in front of them, rather than waiting for the pairs in front to get to the end of the gym.] Partners, hold each other's right wrist securely and lean away from each other a little bit. Using small steps, jog slowly in a circle around each other *at the same time* traveling down the physical education space. Notice how the leadership (control) changes from one person to the other.

Social Be sensitive to feeling and controlling your partner's weight so you go only as fast as your partner can safely and confidently move.

Content Development

One Partner Lowers the Other into a Side Roll

Cog K and CCSS That was an example of countertension. Countertension is when two people balance by leaning away from each other, sometimes using a pulling action.

E [Demonstrate with a child being partner B and you being partner A.] In this next countertension task, one partner is the base, and the other is the roller. Begin with the base: partner A holding a very stable base, feet apart, knees bent, with one leg in front toward partner B, and the other leg behind in a line away from partner B. [Demonstrate as partner A.] The base holds the roller's wrist and leans back to support his or her weight as the base slowly lowers the roller to the ground into a side roll. The roller starts with his or her feet close to the base. Staying tight, the roller slowly extends his or her arm until it is straight and the base is partly supporting the roller's weight. Then the roller bends her or his knees, and the base slowly, smoothly, and gently lowers the roller into a side roll, with both partners letting go of each other's wrists at the start of the roll. Switch roles.

R Both of you must be tight and feel the tension and pull between you.

(*continues*)

SAMPLE PLAN 28.4

Theme: Countertension Combined with Rolling (*continued*)

Using countertension: the base lowers the partner into a side roll

Courtesy of John Dolly

Social Countertension requires the roller to trust the base and the base to be responsible for the safety of the roller. Bases, look after the rollers. It is your job to be sure the roller has a clear pathway in which to roll. Check whether any other roller might inadvertently roll into the path of your partner. It also is your job to make sure your partner is safe and you are supporting his or her weight by leaning back and pulling.

R Practice this until each of you can lower the other in a slow, smooth, continuous movement from the start of the countertension to the roll.

R Be sure you time the release of your wrists so the roller goes smoothly from the countertension into the roll. Do not release the roller early.

Cog K How can you increase the stability of your base? Link your answer to biomechanical principles. [When you bend your knees, you lower your center of gravity, which is more stable. When you move your feet farther apart, you form a wider base of support, which is also more stable.] Why is it more stable to have your legs in line with the roll rather than perpendicular to the roll? [With your legs in line, your base of support is wide in relation to the direction of force, which is your partner's weight. You can lean back away from your partner and your back leg will support your weight. If you lean back and your legs are perpendicular, then you have nothing supporting your weight or your partner's weight because the base of support is narrow in relation to the force.]

One Partner Lowers, the Other Varies the Roll

E Now, you may vary the roll at the end of the countertension. You can vary the shape of your legs in the roll, or you can vary the direction (forward, back diagonal/shoulder, forward/backward). *Do not do any roll that you are not safe, confident, and competent doing.*

Both Partners Lower into Side Rolls

E This time, we will make the countertension more challenging. Start by standing close together, holding each other's wrists securely. Slowly and at the same time, lean away from your partner while maintaining countertension. Both of you lower yourselves into side rolls. Concentrate on timing the release of your wrists so both of you gently and smoothly go into your side rolls at the same time.

R Practice this until you can both hold the countertension the entire time you are lowering your weight and can both roll smoothly in a continuous movement from the countertension.

Social Let's have a discussion about how to be a responsible base. What can the base partner do to help the roller trust you? What should the base partner not do?

Both Partners Lower, Vary Rolls

E Once you have mastered countertension into side rolls, you can vary your rolls. Both of you can do the same roll, or you can do different rolls.

Safety Make the decision about which roll you will do based on the criterion of safety. Do only rolls that you can perform safely. It is perfectly appropriate if one of you does side rolls and the other does front or back rolls.

SAMPLE PLAN 28.4

Theme: Countertension Combined with Rolling (*continued*)

Lower and Rise While Maintaining Countertension

E Stand facing your partner, hold both wrists, lean back into a countertension, and see if you can lower yourself to your hips and then, without pausing, slowly stand back up, maintaining the countertension the entire time.

MD Put your feet together and close to your partner.

ME Put your feet farther apart and farther from your partner.

E Experiment with the placement of your feet when you are standing and when you are on your hips (close together, farther apart) until you find a placement that is challenging but allows you to succeed each time. Memorize the position of your hips so you know how far apart you need to be from your partner.

Culminating Activity: Sequences

A Now we are going to put everything together into a short sequence. Select one of your best and most interesting countertension–roll combinations. Each of you, end your roll in a balance with an interesting shape. Your shapes can match, contrast, or complement each other. Then, from that balance, roll in slow motion toward your partner so you end up on your hips with your feet in the perfect position so you can grasp each other's wrists and stand up using countertension. You might have to do more than one roll to get to your partner, or you might have to do only half of a roll.

R Work on this sequence, modifying your rolls and shapes if necessary, until you can start standing, countertension, roll away, end in a balance, roll back, and countertension to a stand again without taking extra steps or having to readjust your positions.

R Practice your timing so both partners roll back together at the same time.

A Now select two other countertension–roll combinations, and add them to your sequence.

R Practice your sequence until you have it perfected—that is, your movement quality is the best you can do, and you and your partner can accurately repeat the sequence to the last detail. Then you can show your sequence to another pair. Have them assess your transitions to see if you take any extra steps. [Alternatively, you can have children show their sequences to the class, with one-third of the class showing at a time.]

SAMPLE PLAN 28.5

Theme: Countertension Using Like and Unlike Body Parts

Notes: These learning experiences are appropriate for ability level 3. We provide two possible culminating activities: (1) using countertension with stacked mats or trapezoid sections; and (2) designing sequences on countertension without apparatus. Teachers also can extend the learning experiences over two days and do sequences on apparatus. The elements of choreography taught in these learning experiences are fluid transitions and having a variety of skills done in a variety of ways.

Standards

This plan addresses National Standards 1 and 2 and CCSS for comprehension.

Objectives

Children will learn to

Motor

1. Perform countertensions using like and unlike body parts, maintaining appropriate tension.

CCSS

2. Describe key ideas or details from information presented through other media, in this case through gymnastics performances.

Potential Refinements

- Stay tight when your partner is supporting your weight.
- Feel the tension and pull between you.

(*continues*)

SAMPLE PLAN 28.5

Theme: Countertension Using Like and Unlike Body Parts (*continued*)

Content Development

Review

I Let's review what you learned about countertension. Start by holding your partner's wrist, and lean away from each other slowly into countertension; then slowly lower each other into a side roll.

E Now, vary your rolls.

Unlike Body Parts

E So far, we have been doing countertension by holding each other's wrists. These are like body parts. Instead of wrists, we will now explore countertension lowering into a roll but using different body parts. We will start with one partner being the base and the other partner being the roller. Bases, use both of your hands; rollers, give the base a different body part (such as a knee, foot, or elbow) each time you roll. Some body parts will work better than others. For example, the knee, foot, and elbow work very well, but many parts of the trunk don't work at all because the base can't hold the trunk with his or her hands. Shift roles and practice.

E Now both of you roll. Hold a countertension using any body parts you want. You can use like body parts—for example, hooking elbows—or unlike body parts. Whichever body parts you choose, make sure you lean away from each other, lower yourselves gently, and smoothly go into a roll.

E Another way you can vary countertension is by changing the initial relationship to each other. You can start face to face, back to back, face to back, or side to side. Explore these variations.

Pulling Past Each Other

E Now face your partner, and hold each other's right wrist. Lean back, and hold a countertension balance for three seconds. Then pull together, passing shoulders in the standing position and continuing into a roll in the other direction.

E Continue exploring different countertension–roll combinations while varying your body parts and rolls. Sometimes pull together and past each other to change direction, and sometimes lower yourselves in the original direction into a roll.

Culminating Activity Option 1: Apparatus: Trapezoids and Stacked Mats

A Each pair gets a stacked mat or trapezoid section and flat mats. Explore different ways of doing countertension combined with rolls. Start exploring with one person serving as base and lowering the other person into a roll. The base can start on the floor or on the trapezoid. The roller also can start on the floor or on the trapezoid. To ensure safety, begin by doing countertensions holding wrists and doing side rolls.

R Practice until you can consistently move from countertension to a roll smoothly, safely, and with control.

E After you have practiced, you may extend your countertensions to using different like and unlike body parts and varying your rolls.

Culminating Activity Option 2: Sequence (Can Be Done with Stacked Mats)

A Select your three best countertension–roll combinations, and put them into a sequence.

Elements of Choreography

Variety: Be sure the countertension–roll combinations are all different. Use a variety of body parts and rolls in different shapes. See if you can find one unusual combination.

Transitions: Add an ending shape to your rolls that can be the starting position for a roll, steplike action, or jump back to your partner. Plan ways to travel back together so you end in the starting position for the next countertension without having to take extra steps or shift positions. This can be very difficult, and you might need to do two skills to get into position for the next countertension.

R Practice your sequence until you have it perfected—that is, you are tight and maintaining appropriate tension between you, and you take no extra steps in your transitions.

A/CCSS Show your sequence to another pair. As you watch their sequence, select one countertension–roll combination you liked that was unusual or original. Describe the details of the movement that you liked.

SAMPLE PLAN 28.6

Theme: Counterbalance

Notes: These learning experiences are appropriate for ability level 3. Elements of choreography discussed in this plan are transitions and variety. Teaching this content will take several lessons.

Standards

This plan addresses National Standards 1, 2, 4, and 5 and CCSS for collaboration and presentation of ideas.

Objectives

Children will learn to

Motor

1. Counterbalance using like and unlike body parts, staying tight and maintaining appropriate tension.
2. Rise, lower, and rotate counterbalances and connect counterbalances.

Creative and Critical Thinking

3. Design a sequence with a variety of interesting counterbalances and transitions without taking extra steps.

Social

4. With a partner, critique the transitions in their sequences in a supportive way.

Affective

5. Enjoy the feelings of a variety of counterbalances and the challenge of designing an interesting sequence with a partner.

CCSS

6. Engage effectively in collaborative discussions with a partner, expressing their own ideas clearly and listening carefully to their partner's ideas.

Potential Refinements

- Stay tight.
- Use the appropriate amount of tension and force to counter your partner's tension and force.

Introductory Activity

Cog K Counterbalance is like countertension, but instead of leaning away from your partner, you lean toward your partner, balance together with a wide base of support, and depend on each other to maintain balance. For example, get back to back with your partner. Staying tight, walk your feet away from your partner so you are leaning against each other. This is a counterbalance.

E As a fun warm-up, we will try "addition stand-up." Get back to back with your partner, hook elbows, lean against each other, and lower yourselves to a sitting position. Briefly pick up your feet, put them down, and then, by counterbalancing, lean against your partner, and stand up again. Practice until you can do this confidently.

E If you are ready, form a group of four with another ready pair. All four get back to back, lean, sit, pick up your feet, place your feet back on the floor, lean in a counterbalance, and stand up again.

E [This task can be repeated with groups of eight to more than 30 students. With large groups, students end up in two long lines back to back. With large groups, remind student to check to be sure they are counterbalancing with only one person even though all students hook elbows with the people on either side of them.]

Content Development

Counterbalance into a Roll with Like and Unlike Body Parts

E Go back with your partner, start back to back in a counterbalance, and lower your weight. As you are just about to sit, each of you roll sideways to your right.

R Repeat until you can do this with tight tension and control.

E Starting on your feet, find different ways to counterbalance using like body parts. Lower your weight and roll out.

E Now find different counterbalances using unlike body parts, lowering your weight, and rolling out of the balance in different ways. You can do different rolls or the same rolls.

(*continues*)

SAMPLE PLAN 28.6

Theme: Counterbalance (*continued*)

Rising and Lowering, Counterbalancing at Different Levels

E Now explore counterbalances at different levels [high, medium, low]. You can use like or unlike body parts, but be sure both of you are at the same level.

E Try counterbalancing with each of you at a different level using like or unlike body parts.

E Remaining in your counterbalance, change levels by either rising or lowering. You can reverse, and rise or lower to your original position, or roll out.

Rotating the Counterbalance

E Another way to work in a counterbalance is to rotate as a pair while maintaining the counterbalance. For example, everyone face your partner. Put your hands on each other's shoulders, and lean toward each other forming a counterbalance. Then try moving your feet on a circular pathway and rotating together.

E Experiment with rotating different counterbalances.

E Sometimes you can rotate a counterbalance and also lower your weight onto the floor, letting the rotation lead each of you into a roll or spin. Experiment with different ways of releasing the counterbalance, leading smoothly into a different movement.

Connecting Counterbalances

E Start in a counterbalance, and see if you can transition into another counterbalance without any connecting skills. Try to go from one counterbalance to the next with a minimum of body part movements.

Culminating Activity: Trapezoids and Stacked Mats, Sequences

E Each pair, get a stacked mat or trapezoid section. Explore different ways of counterbalancing using the trapezoid. You can both be at the same level, or you can vary levels. You can both be on the trapezoid section, or you can be partly on the mat and partly on the trapezoid.

Social/CCSS Discuss with your partner different counterbalances you might use, trying to identify many, varied, and some unusual ideas.

A Select your three best counterbalances, and put them into a sequence.

Elements of Choreography

Variety: Be sure you use a variety of body parts and levels.

Transitions: Try different transitions between counterbalances. Work on making the counterbalance lead you smoothly into a different skill using as few movements as possible.

R Practice your sequence until you have it perfected—that is, you are tight, you maintain appropriate tension between you, and your transitions have no extra steps.

A Perform your sequence for another pair. Then share what you enjoyed most about the sequence or performing the sequence. Express your opinion clearly, and describe relevant details so your partner and the other pair understand why you enjoyed the part of the sequence or performance you enjoyed.

SAMPLE PLAN 28.7

Theme: Pair Balancing

Notes: These learning experiences are appropriate for ability level 3. We show you how to teach the elements of sequence choreography of line and transitions.

Standards

This plan addresses National Standards 1, 2, 4, and 5 and CCSS for presenting ideas.

Objectives

Children will learn to

Motor

1. Perform a variety of pair balances staying tight.

SAMPLE PLAN 28.7

Theme: Pair Balancing (*continued*)

Cognitive

2. Apply the choreography principle of line to their pair balances.

Social

3. Appreciate their partner's situation and try hard to maintain tension and support their partner's weight.

Affective

4. Appreciate the enjoyment and challenge of supporting a partner's weight in a pair balance.

CCSS

5. Present their ideas clearly and give reasons to support their opinions.

Potential Refinements

- Stay tight, stay tight, and stay tight! It is very difficult to support the weight of a partner who is loose.

Content Development

Cog K In pair balancing, one person supports part of or all of his or her partner's weight in a balance. A pair balance can be part countertension, part counterbalance, or it can simply be a balance with one person supporting the weight of the other.

I Start with one person making a stable base on hands and shins and the other experimenting with different ways the base can partially support the weight of the other. Rotate frequently.

E If you are confident, tight, and in control and have been able to maintain your balances for at least three seconds, you may try having the base completely support the weight of the other partner. If not, keep working on the movement quality of tightness. Rotate frequently.

E Now experiment with different bases and different ways to support part of the weight of your partner.

E If you are confident, tight, and in control and have been able to maintain your balances for at least three seconds, you may try having the base completely support the weight of the other partner. Rotate frequently.

E When you find several balances you think are interesting, and you can hold these balances for three seconds with tight, stretched bodies, you may explore different transitions by lowering your partner out of the balance into

- Rolls
- Steplike actions
- Other balances

Culminating Activity: Trapezoids and Stacked Mats, Sequences

E Now explore a variety of pair balances using a stacked mat or trapezoid section as part of the balance. You can both be at the same level, or you can vary levels. You can both be on the trapezoid section, or you can be partly on the mat and partly on the trapezoid.

Elements of Choreography

Cog K *Line:* To make a pair balance look good, you need to pay attention to the lines of your bodies that an observer will see. For example, you will have a good line if one of you is standing in a lunge on the trapezoid with your arm pointing toward the corner of the ceiling on the same diagonal as your straight leg and you are holding your partner's hand and partly supporting your partner's weight, with the partner being at a lower level and also forming a diagonal line. If your partner has one arm pointing toward the floor on the same diagonal, an observer will clearly see one diagonal line that goes from one person's arm pointing diagonally toward the ceiling to the other person's arm pointing diagonally toward the floor.

R Pick three of your favorite pair balances, and pretend you are observing these balances from the outside. Which lines would an observer see? How might you improve those lines? How might you modify the position of your body parts so you and your partner make lines that complement each other?

Transitions

A Now design a sequence that highlights your three best balances. You need to add transitions between the balances. For each transition skill, start from your balance, and end in a position ready to perform the next balance. Make your movements continuous, and time your movements with those of your partner so you both leave one balance at the same time and arrive at the next balance at the same time.

(*continues*)

SAMPLE PLAN 28.7

Theme: Pair Balancing (*continued*)

R Practice your sequence until you have it perfected—that is, you are both tight, tight, tight, and your transitions have no extra steps.

A Then you can show your sequence to another pair. [Alternatively, you can have children show their sequences to the class, with one-third of the class showing at a time.]

Closure

Discuss with your partner which balance you liked the best and why. Give reasons to support your opinions.

As a class, let's make a list on the whiteboard about all the positive feeling you have about working with a partner and pair balances.

SAMPLE PLAN 28.8

Theme: Countertension and Counterbalance

Notes: These learning experiences are appropriate for ability level 3. Elements of sequence choreography illustrated in this plan are contrasts in speed and level.

Standards

This plan addresses National Standards 1, 2, and 4 and CCSS for vocabulary acquisition.

Objectives

Children will learn to

Motor

1. Travel and rotate countertensions and counterbalances using appropriate tension and force.

Cognitive

2. Apply the principle of sequence choreography for contrast using the movement concepts of speed and levels.

Social

3. Be responsible for their safety and the safety of their partner.

CCSS

4. Acquire domain-specific knowledge about the principle of choreography for contrast.

Potential Refinements

- Focus on the tension in your body and between you and your partner.
- Pay attention to the amount of force you and your partner generate and need to perform countertensions and counterbalances. Make sure you are using the right amount of force.

Content Development

Traveling and Rotating Countertension and Counterbalance

I Holding your partner's right hand, run in a circle, leaning away from each other at the same time as you travel as a pair down the gym.

E Staying in one location, hold both hands and travel in a circle, leaning away from each other. Slowly lower yourselves. Just before you reach the ground, release your countertension and each of you roll or spin.

E Explore different ways to rotate a countertension position by lowering your weight and releasing into rolls or spins. One person can remain on one spot and turn, while the other runs around, or both partners can travel in space.

E Explore different ways to rotate counterbalances by lowering your weight and releasing into rolls or spins.

SAMPLE PLAN 28.8

Theme: Countertension and Counterbalance (*continued*)

Countertension and Counterbalance from a Height

I On the floor mat, one person does a balance on one leg; her or his partner holds the free leg and slowly lowers the other down into a roll. Switch roles. Explore going forward, backward, and sideways, ending in rolls that are safe for you to do.

E Try the same task from a single trapezoid section or stacked mat. The person lowering the other partner needs to be in a very stable position to support the partner's weight safely into a roll on the floor from the height of a trapezoid section.

E Now explore different ways to balance using countertension or counterbalance and one or more trapezoid sections, lowering your partner into rolls, other balances, or steplike actions.

Social/Safety You decide how much height you and your partner can manage safely, and select the appropriate number of stacked mats or trapezoid sections. You are responsible for your own and your partner's safety. If you don't feel confident about a movement your partner suggests, what do you do? [Say no. Tell my partner I don't feel confident about that move.]

Culminating Activity: Sequence with Apparatus

A Design a sequence of moving and stationary countertensions and counterbalances combined with rolls and steplike actions. Have at least one time when you rotate a countertension or counterbalance, and use at least one trapezoid section.

Elements of Choreography

Contrast: In your sequence, include very clear changes in speed. Sometimes you and your partner should move quickly and sometimes very slowly. Try to make the changes in speed obvious so an observer would be able to notice these moments. In addition, include variations in levels. Sometimes both of you work at a high level, sometimes both work at a low level, and sometimes partners can be at different levels. Make the changes in level frequent and obvious.

R Practice your sequence until you have it perfected.

Closure

Discuss with your partner and another pair what contrast means when applied as a principle of choreography. Discuss how a contrast in level and speed added to the quality of your sequence choreography. Be specific, and describe the details of the movements you used to support your ideas about contrast.

CHAPTER

29

Technical Reference Information for Teachers About Gymnastics Skills

OBJECTIVES

Students will learn:

1. Teachers need to know technical information about specific gymnastics skills to inform their observations and refinements of the movement quality of both specific skills and foundational skills performed in a variety of ways.
2. Knowing likely immature patterns informs teachers' observations and planning of lesson tasks.
3. Sometimes some children will be ready and interested in learning specific skills.
4. When teaching specific skills, an intraskill mastery progression is helpful.
5. Sometimes it is appropriate to integrate a progression for a specific skill into a theme.

KEY TERMS

Back handspring
Back roll
Back walk-over
Egg roll
Forward roll
Front handspring
Front shoulder roll
Handstand
Handstand forward roll
Headstand
Hollowing out
Hurdle
Interskill progression

Intraskill progression
Mule kick
Springboard hurdle
Track-start hands
Tripod
Tucked flank vault
Tucked front vault

CONNECTION TO STANDARDS

This chapter discusses the performance techniques for refining specific gymnastics skills and thus addresses National Standard 1.

Teaching Specific Skills

In this chapter, we provide technical reference information about specific named gymnastics skills, including descriptions of the performance techniques of the mature pattern, typical immature patterns, and progressions for teaching these skills. There is much information that teachers need to know that they do not necessarily teach to children. For example, information about the mature patterns of named skills, such as handstands and forward rolls, applies to many, if not most, of the variety of movements that children will perform when exploring the themes of balancing and rolling. Immature patterns of, for example, a back roll also generalize across rolling actions. When you know the mature and immature patterns of the named skills, you will be better able to observe and respond to children's actions during work on a theme.

Teaching Specific Skills Within Themes

All specific named skills are part of one theme or another. For example, a forward roll is part of the theme of rolling. A handstand is a balance. A cartwheel is a steplike action. When you teach using themes, children can choose to practice and learn specific skills related to the lesson theme.

What is critical to remember is that you are teaching the theme, not simply the specific skills categorized within that theme. For example, when you are teaching the theme of rolling, your lesson should not consist of tasks for teaching a side roll, forward roll, and backward roll. Rather, your tasks should have children work on rolling in a variety of ways. Children may work on forward and backward rolls if they choose, but the teacher focuses on rolling. Children not only need to understand the concept of rolling in all its variety, but also need to be able to work on those rolling skills that are safe for them. If you teach only the specific skills, you will put some children unnecessarily at risk for injury while under-challenging others.

In addition, when you observe a child attempting to perform a named skill, you can teach safety information about that skill in addition to critical performance techniques that will help the child perform the skill competently and safely. For example, if you see children attempting a backward roll and you judge they are ready to learn it, you can teach them the performance technique for hand placement. We find most children can safely learn the beginning-level named skills summarized in **Table 29.1**.

Table 29.1 Beginning-Level Named Skills

Theme	Related Named Beginning-level Skills
Rolling	Side rolls, forward shoulder rolls, backward shoulder rolls
Balancing	Shoulder stands, mule kicks/handstands
Steplike actions	Mini-cartwheels, mini-round-offs, cartwheels, round-offs

When and How to Teach Specific Skills Within a Theme

When should you teach specific skills as part of a theme? This is a good question. Any time you teach a theme, some children (even in kindergarten) will undoubtedly have mastered skills within that theme. Other children will be ready and want to learn specific skills. We deal with specific skills within a theme in two ways:

1. *If specific skills emerge when children are working on a theme and the children are practicing the skill safely, give performance feedback.* If you scan the class and see some children performing specific skills safely, then you can give them performance feedback to help them improve the quality of their skill. You might say, for example, "For those of you who are choosing to do handstands, remember to lock your elbows, and stay straight and tight."
2. *Teach a mastery progression to a small group or the entire class.* In this chapter, we present mastery intraskill progressions for teaching several specific skills. In brief, an **intraskill progression** is a series of subskills that progressively become more like the terminal skill the children are learning. The teacher teaches each subskill, and the child progresses to the next subskill *only* if he or she has mastered the previous subskill. Children do not *ever* have to move on to the next subskill in a progression and can continue practicing the subskill that best matches their ability level. No skill is sacred, and no child should feel pressured to learn the terminal skill. Thus, teachers can use a skill mastery progression to accommodate individual differences while teaching specific skills to a whole class.

Teachers need to use their professional judgment in deciding when to teach specific skills, if they do so at all. We typically use progressions for teaching skills with individual children

SAFETY AND LIABILITY 29.1

Increasing Safety and Decreasing Risk of Liability: Guidelines Relevant to Content in this Chapter

In this box, we discuss specific guidelines built on information discussed throughout this text on professional standards of practice, negligence, and liability. The goals of these guidelines are to increase children's safety and decrease teachers' risk of negligence and liability.

- Teaching using themes, such as rolling and balancing, allows children to work at their individual developmental levels. If you teach only specific skills within a theme, such as a side roll, forward roll, or backward roll from the theme of rolling, you will put some children unnecessarily at risk of injury and increase your risk of liability.
- Progressions for learning specific gymnastics skills are critical for safety and decrease the risks of injury and liability.
- If it is developmentally appropriate to teach a basic skill to a small group or the entire class, teachers must use a progression of subskills that builds step by step to the terminal skill. A child practices each subskill until he or she has mastered the subskill and is confident and interested in moving on to the next step in the progression. Children are never pressured to move on to the next subskill.
- If taught using a progression, most basic skills do not require spotting. The following advanced beginner and intermediate level skills do need a spotter, however: handstand forward roll, back walkover, front walkover, front handspring, and back handspring. We recommend teaching these skills only after school with a qualified spotter.
- A backwards roll is a difficult skill for children who are obese, overweight, or lack the arm strength to support their weight and can lead to serious neck injuries. We recommend you don't allow children to attempt backward rolls if they have inadequate strength to support their weight on their bent arms and hands.

before or after school. In addition, the progressions for mule kicks/handstands, cartwheels, and round-offs are easily integrated into whole-class lessons when the children are learning balancing and steplike actions.

Before using a progression with an entire class, it is important to answer two questions:

1. Do *all* children have the necessary skills and abilities to successfully and safely work on at least the first few subskills of the progression, and is it a skill that they all will find meaningful?
2. Have many children already mastered the skill and, therefore, will be bored doing the progression?

If the answer is yes to the first question and no to the second question, then the progression is a developmentally appropriate progression for that class or group of children.

In addition to intraskill progressions, we provide interskill progressions. An **interskill progression** is a suggested progression of different skills to master before working on a new skill.

The first progression presented in this chapter is written in a scripted format that includes refinements for a hypothetical group of children to illustrate how to refine performance techniques while teaching. The other progressions describe performance techniques before or within the progressions. You will need to provide refinements based on your children when using these progressions.

Progressions for Teaching Specific Skills

Mule Kicks and Handstands

A **mule kick** is a partial handstand. The weight is taken on the hands and straight arms; the legs are kicked one at a time, switching places in the air, and the legs reach waist to chest height. Technically, a mule kick is not a balance because it is not a held position. Nevertheless, because it is part of the progression for learning a handstand, we tell children they can substitute a mule kick for a handstand any time they choose.

A **handstand**, on the other hand, is a balance on the hands with the body perfectly straight, stretched, and tight. Many years ago, the style was to have an arched back, which we call a "banana back." Now the style is for handstands to be so straight that even the natural arch in the lower back is decreased by **hollowing out**—that is, tilting the top of the pelvis back and hollowing out the abdominal area.

Interskill Progression

- Travel on your hands and feet, keeping your arms straight.

Typical Immature Patterns

- Bent elbows
- **Track-start hands**—that is, putting the weight on the fingerprints and fingers, with the palms off the mat (resembling the hand position for starting a sprint in track, rather than putting their palms flat on the mat)
- Landing on the shins rather than the feet
- Landing with the feet too far from the hands so the child can't stand up
- Banana back: loose, sagging body, rather than stretched through the spine; the child arches the back rather than stretching with a "hollowed" hip position

Mule Kick/Handstand Intraskill Progression

Subskill 1: Weight on Hands, Tuck Position

Stand at the edge of the side of your mat. Squat down, transfer your weight from your feet to your hands [demonstrate as you talk], spring your feet one inch off the floor, stand, and stretch your arms toward the ceiling. [Repeat until mastered.]

R Keep your elbows locked. That means to keep them straight like this. [Demonstrate as you speak.]

R Be sure your palms are flat on the mat, and you are not in the track-start position. [Demonstrate both the palms-flat and immature track-start hand placements.]

Subskill 2: Weight on Hands, Switch Feet

If you feel safe and confident, and you have mastered the first subskill, you can now work on subskill 2. Stand on the edge of your mat with one foot slightly in front of the other, transfer your weight to your hands, spring your feet off the ground a few inches, switch legs in the air, and land one foot at a time with the other foot in front.

R Keep your elbows locked. [Repeat as needed throughout the remainder of the progression.]

R Be sure your palms are flat. [Repeat as needed throughout the remainder of the progression.]

R Look at the mat between your fingers. [Repeat as needed throughout the remainder of the progression.]

Subskill 3: Lift Your Feet a Little Higher

If you are safe, confident, and have mastered the previous task, you may move on to this next task. Do the same subskill, but lift your feet a little higher each time. [Demonstrate as you talk.] Do not go any higher than about 24 inches.

R Be sure to look at the mat between your fingers.

R Keep your elbows locked.

Subskill 4: Mini-Mule Kick

If you are ready to move on, stand in a lunge like this, with your front knee bent and your back leg straight (see **Figure 29.1A**). [Demonstrate as you speak.] Reach your arms toward the ceiling. Put your palms down, and kick the back leg up, pushing off the front foot. Switch legs in the air, and land in a lunge with your other foot in front and your hands pointing to the ceiling. You do not need to work on subskill 4; you can continue to work on the last task if you like.

R Be sure to land on your front foot, and stand up in a lunge; don't land on your knees.

R Land one foot at a time.

R When you land, reach for the ceiling.

Subskill 5: Full Mule Kick

If you are safe and confident, kick higher and higher until you are kicking waist high and then chest high.

R [Repeat previous refinements as needed.]

Subskill 6: Cartwheeling Out

If you have mastered the previous task, practice how to "cartwheel out," or turn out, of a handstand if you kick too high and are going over (see **Figure 29.2**). This is for safety. Kick up at least chest high, pick up one hand and move it into a cartwheel, and twist your feet down. *Do not, under any circumstance, go over into a backbend* or go over onto your back. Land on your feet and don't fall.

R Land on your feet.

Terminal Skill: Full Handstand

Once you can cartwheel out perfectly every time, you can practice full handstands (see **Figure 29.1B**).

R Shoulders over knuckles (Masser, 1993).

R Stretch through your back, and hollow out. *Hollow out* means to tilt the top of your pelvis back so you have less arch in your back, and your spinal column is as stretched and as straight as you can make it.

(A)

(B)

Figure 29.1 (A) Lunge (B) Handstand

Cartwheels

A mature cartwheel (see **Figure 29.3**) starts in a lunge. The hands are then placed one at a time sideways on a straight line, as the front leg pushes off and the back leg kicks and circles over in a wheeling motion. The legs are straddled in the air, and the child lands one foot at a time in a lunge with the feet on the same straight line. The body is stretched as it travels (and looks like the wheel of an old-fashioned cart). The rhythm is even: hand, hand, foot, foot.

Interskill Progression

- Taking your weight onto your hands in a curled position, spring your feet off the floor at a low level.

Typical Immature Patterns

- Track-start hands: Beginners put their weight on their fingerprints rather than their palms flat on the mat.
- They land on the same foot they used to push off—that is, the foot in front in the starting lunge position is the same foot in front on the landing, and the legs switch in the air (so they don't look like a "cart" wheel). For a mature pattern, the leg that started in back in the starting lunge position needs to end in front in the landing lunge position.
- Beginners put their hands down pointing to the left but have their right leg in front in the starting lunge position (or they put hands down pointing to the right with their

Figure 29.2 Cartwheeling out
Courtesy of John Dolly

Figure 29.3 Mature cartwheel
Courtesy of John Dolly

left leg in front in the starting lunge position). To deal with this immature pattern, it helps to remind children, "Left leg in front—hands to the left," or "Right leg in front—hands to the right."
- Beginners may bend their arms or pike their hips during the cartwheel.

Cartwheel Intraskill Progression

We find it is easier to learn a cartwheel if you use a stacked mat. Adding the height of the stacked mat means the child does not have to reach down to the floor, which is more difficult.

Potential Refinements

- Elbows straight
- Palms flat
- Land facing back where you started
- Legs straight and straddled in the air

Subskill 1: Weight on Hands

Put your hands on the stacked mat, and spring your hips up, sometimes landing on one foot and sometimes landing on two feet. Repeat subskill 1, but travel around the mat. Repeat subskill 1, but travel on and over the stacked mat.

Subskill 2: Weight on Hands, Spring Feet Over

Stand to the side of a stacked mat or single trapezoid section. Put your hands on the trapezoid to one side, put your weight on your hands, and, while keeping your feet at a low level, spring your feet to the other side.

Subskill 3: Stand, Spring Over, Stand

Start standing to the side of a stacked mat. In one motion, put your hands on the trapezoid to one side, spring your feet over at a low level, and stand with hands stretched toward the ceiling, looking back at the stacked mat.

Subskill 4: Lunge, Spring Over, Lunge

Start in a lunge (front leg bent, back leg straight) with one foot in front of the other. If your left leg is in front, put your hands to the left; if your right leg is in front, put your hands to the right. Lift your back leg, push off your front foot, and spring your legs (back leg first) one at a time over the trapezoid at a low level. End standing one foot in front of the other in a lunge, reaching your hands toward the ceiling and looking back at the stacked mat. If your left leg was in front at the start, your right leg will be in front at the end, and vice versa.

Subskill 5: Mini-Cartwheel

This is the same as subskill 4, but now you keep your legs straight and lift the legs higher each time. Be sure to end in a lunge.

Subskill 6: Progression on Floor Mat

Do subskills 3 through 5, but perform them on a floor mat rather than on a trapezoid section.

Terminal Skill: Full Cartwheel

Really stretch your legs toward the ceiling. Keep your legs straddled wide apart, so you look like an old-fashioned "cart" wheel! The rhythm is hand, hand, foot, foot. The hands and feet land on a straight line, and you end up looking back at your starting position. (You can draw a chalk line on the mat to help children cartwheel straight.)

Round-off

The interskill and intraskill progressions are the same as for the cartwheel, but for each subskill you land on two feet each time (see **Figure 29.4**).

More Mature Round-off Techniques

Once children can perform cartwheels and round-offs, they need to learn these skills from a hurdle and with increased speed. The round-off, in particular, is an important skill in that gymnasts use it to change from a forward to backward direction to be able to complete such skills as back handsprings and somersaults.

Potential Refinements

- After the hurdle, take a long lunge, and reach forward with the hands.
- Travel a far distance in the round-off to generate force.
- The first hand points to the side; the second hand points back toward the first hand.
- Shrug or push through the shoulders to help push off on the hands.
- Forcefully snap your legs down, and pop up.
- Do a resilient landing, and pop off the mat into high flight.

Rock and Roll Bar

Once children learn to pop up from a round-off, it helps to teach them the safety skill of the "roll bar." Have them rock on their back to their shoulders with their biceps by their ears and their forearms over their heads, palms facing the mat. Their arms and hands form a "roll bar cage" over their heads to prevent them from hurting their heads or necks. If they pop and fly backward off balance, they can land on their feet (they will still be off balance) and rock back using a roll bar.

Hurdle for Cartwheels and Round-offs

A **hurdle** before a cartwheel and round-off is technically a step-hop done in an uneven rhythm (i.e., a skip) and a long step (see **Figure 29.5**). During the hop, the arms stretch toward the ceiling, and the free knee lifts forward (as it does in a skip). A more difficult form of hurdle is to extend the free leg back and keep the body slightly arched during the hop.

Interskill Progression

1. Cartwheel
2. Round-off

Typical Immature Patterns

Beginners may get confused about which foot to hop on and which knee to lift. They often leave out the long step before the cartwheel, which is critical. They also hurdle on the wrong foot for the hand they want to put down first, which is why they end up leaving out the long step.

Figure 29.4 Round-off

Figure 29.5 Hurdle cartwheel
Courtesy of John Dolly

In the mature pattern for right-sided cartwheels, children lift the right knee during the hop (thus hopping on the left foot), step (long) on the right foot, and put their hands to the right, touching the right hand down first. In left-sided cartwheels, children lift the left knee during the hop, step on the left foot, and put the hands to the left.

Hurdle Cartwheel Intraskill Progression

The progression is the same for the cartwheel and round-off. Some children find the progression using the round-off easier.

Subskill 1: Skipping and Stepping

1. Skip about general space.
2. Travel about general space but moving more slowly. Do one skip on your right leg, then step on your left. Repeat the sequence over and over—skip, step, skip, step.
3. Reverse the sequence. Do one skip on your left leg, then step on your right.

O Arrange stacked mats and single-layer trapezoid sections at the side of flat mats scattered about general space. Put one plastic spot on the floor about three inches out on a diagonal from one corner of the trapezoid; put a second plastic spot about three inches out on a diagonal from the corner at the other end.

Subskill 2: Slow Hurdle with Mini-Cartwheel (or Round-off)

Most people have a favorite side for doing a hurdle cartwheel or round-off. Decide which direction you like best. Right-sided cartwheelers, stand facing a spot on the left side of the trapezoid, skip on your left leg by lifting your right knee, and step on the spot with your right foot. Then put your hands sideways, and do a mini-cartwheel (or round-off), with your right hand touching down first and fingers pointing right toward the middle of the trapezoid. Take your weight on your arms (straight arms), kick your left leg, and push off your right leg to travel over or around the end of the trapezoid, and land in a lunge facing the trapezoid. Left-sided cartwheelers, face a spot on the right side of the trapezoid, and do a mini-cartwheel (or round-off). Skip on your right leg by lifting your left knee, step on the spot with your left foot, put your hands sideways on the trapezoid with your fingers pointing left toward the middle, take your weight on your arms (straight arms), kick your right leg, and push off your left leg to travel over the end of the trapezoid, and land in a lunge facing the trapezoid.

R Stretch with arms overhead during the skip.

Subskill 3: Practice Until Hurdle Is Automatic

Practice the hurdle and mini-cartwheel (or round-off) over the end of the trapezoid until you feel confident and can hurdle without having to think about which leg goes where.

Terminal Skill: Full Hurdle and Cartwheel on the Floor

Try the hurdle cartwheel on the floor mat. Start slowly, and gradually increase your speed.

Shoulder Stand

The shoulder stand (see **Figure 29.6**) can be a dangerous skill for overweight and obese children and for children lacking core and arm strength, as it requires them to control their weight over their necks. Without control, their legs can flop over to

Figure 29.6 Shoulder stand

the mat, hyperextending their necks. We always offer children the option of doing a back stand (lying on the back with legs pointing toward the ceiling) rather than a shoulder stand, and we insist that all children master subskill 3 with perfect control, including being able to lift their head at least one inch off the mat, before attempting the terminal skill.

Interskill Progression

- Rock on your back while maintaining a tight tuck.

Typical Immature Patterns

- Loose body
- Rocking too far back without being in perfect control
- Piking at the hips rather than stretching the body straight toward the ceiling

Shoulder Stand Intraskill Progression

Potential Refinements

- Stay tight.
- Legs and hips straight.
- Stretch to the ceiling.

Subskill 1: Back Stand

Balance on your back in a pike position, with your legs pointing toward the ceiling. Stay tight, and try to pick your head up off the floor.

Subskill 2: Rocking

Staying in a tuck position, rock back onto your shoulders and then down again. Stay tight, and be sure you can control the flow of your movement so you can stop whenever you need to stop and you don't rock back on your head. Your weight should remain on your shoulders without straining or hyperflexing your neck. Repeat until you have this subskill mastered.

Subskill 3: Rocking and Stopping on the Shoulders

In a tuck position, rock back onto your shoulders and stop, put your elbows behind you, and put your hands on your hips to hold your hips off the mat. Stay tight, and be sure you control the flow of your movement so you can stop whenever you need to stop. Try to lift your head off the mat at least one inch. If you can't do this, practice subskill 2 until you can remain tight and in control of your movement.

Terminal Skill: Shoulder Stand

Rock back onto your shoulders, support your hips with your hands, and stretch your legs to the ceiling, keeping your body as straight as you can.

Front Shoulder Roll

A **front shoulder roll** is like a forward roll, except that the head stays to the side and the child rolls over her or his shoulder.

Interskill Progression

1. Do a variety of side rolls with control.
2. Rock on your back while maintaining a tight tuck.

Typical Immature Patterns

Many of these immature patterns are the same as those for the forward roll:

- Bodies open at the hips once the shoulders touch the mat
- Stop on the hips rather than rolling to the feet

Three Possible Front Shoulder Roll Intraskill Progressions

Potential Refinements

- Stay tucked (or piked) tightly in the hips.
- Roll to the feet.
- Use strong arms.
- Keep chin tucked.

Egg Roll Progression

Do a side roll in a tuck position—an **egg roll**—being sure to put your palms flat on the floor and push with strong arms (bent arms) as you go over. If you feel safe and confident, try to roll more and more on a diagonal over one shoulder each time you roll.

Kneeling Progression

Starting on your shins, put one shoulder on the floor next to your knees, with your head to the other side. Lift your hips, and push off your shins until you tip over onto your back. Stay tucked tight.

Another kneeling progression is to kneel on one leg with the other leg extended straight to the side. Reach between the legs with the same arm as the kneeling leg. Continue reaching until the shoulder touches and you tip onto your back.

Stacked Mat Progression

Starting on a stacked mat on your shins, and then reach down and put your palms on the floor with strong arms. Slowly lift your hips, and go into an egg roll on the floor. If you feel safe and confident, try to roll on a diagonal over your shoulder.

Back Shoulder Roll

A back shoulder roll is a backward roll that goes over the shoulder, with the head shifting to the side. The child lands either on two shins or on one shin with the other leg held up in a knee scale. A back shoulder roll is far easier than a back roll because it does not require that the child lift the body weight up off the mat to allow the head to fit through.

Interskill Progression

1. Do a variety of side rolls with control.
2. Shoulder stand in a tuck or pike position with a tight body and control over the flow of your movement.
3. Rock on your back while maintaining a tight tuck.

Typical Immature Patterns

- Loose bodies
- Landing on the knees rather than the shins
- Flopping onto the side rather than going over the shoulder

Back Shoulder Roll Intraskill Progression

Potential Refinements

- Land on the top of the foot (where your laces are on your sneakers) and then the shins, with the knees near your shoulder.
- Sit on your heels.
- Keep your arms to the side for balance.
- Once the shins are on the ground, put your palms on the mat to help push your head up.

Subskill 1

Rock back into a shoulder stand with legs tucked. Then master rocking back into a shoulder stand with your legs in a pike. (Children who are not flexible in their hamstrings might need to slightly bend their legs in the pike.)

Subskill 2

Rock back into a shoulder stand with your legs in a pike; twist and move the feet to one side or the other.

Terminal Skill

Rock back into a shoulder stand with legs in a pike, twist and move the feet to one side or the other, lower the top of the feet (laces) and shins onto the mat, and tip over, taking the body's weight on the shins. Then bring the hips down to the heels. Once you master this skill, try to land on the shin closest to your head with the other leg held high, put both hands on the mat, and push up into a knee scale (see **Figure 29.7**).

Headstand

In a **headstand**, the child balances on the front part of her or his head and two hands with the legs extended straight up. To do so safely, the child must have enough strength in the neck and core muscles to be able to support her or his weight. Consequently, a headstand will not be an appropriate skill for some children to learn, in particular obese children.

Interskill Progression

1. Ability to support the body's weight on the hands in a tucked body position
2. Side and forward shoulder rolls with control
3. Shoulder stand

Typical Immature Patterns

- Loose bodies
- Wobbly head and neck
- Hands and head in a line rather than a triangle
- Chin tucked too much or head back too much
- Back saggy, not stretched straight
- Crashing over onto the back due to stretching the toes toward the ceiling too quickly

Headstand Intraskill Progression

Potential Refinements

- Stay tight, especially through the torso and neck.
- Stretch through the torso.
- Keep the triangle.

Subskill 1

Kneel on both shins, put both palms flat on the mat shoulder-width apart, and put your head in front of your hands, forming a triangle. Repeat until you make a perfect triangle each time and you feel safe and comfortable.

Subskill 2

Kneel again, and form the triangle. Lift your hips up, keeping your feet on the floor so you have some weight on your head and hands and some weight on your feet. Stay tight, and stretch through your spinal column. Keep your neck and head tight and in line. Your weight is on the front part of your head, starting at your hairline. Keep your elbows bent and your forearms perpendicular to the

Figure 29.7 Back shoulder roll into a knee scale

Courtesy of John Dolly

floor. Repeat this subskill until you can maintain a stretched, tight position, holding your weight with control at all times.

Subskill 3

Repeat subskill 2, but lift your hips over your head more, and lift one foot off the floor (see **Figure 29.8**). Again, repeat this subskill until you can maintain a stretched, tight position holding your weight with control at all times.

Subskill 4: Tripod

Repeat subskill 2, but lift your hips in line over your head with both feet still on the floor. Then lower your knees or the upper part of your shins onto your elbow or humerus (see **Figure 29.9**). This is called a **tripod**. Do not, under any circumstance, allow yourself to tip over onto your back. If you feel like you might lose your balance, put your feet back down on the floor, and come down onto your shins. Repeat this subskill until you can maintain a stretched, tight position holding your weight with control at all times.

Terminal Skill

If you feel safe and confident in your tripod, slowly extend your legs to the ceiling. Stay tight and stretched. Do not, under any circumstance, allow yourself to tip over onto your back. If you feel like you might lose your balance, put your feet back down on the floor, and come down onto your shins. Headstands also can be performed with different leg shapes (see **Figure 29.10**).

Figure 29.9 Tripod
Courtesy of John Dolly

Forward Roll

Due to a lack of hamstring flexibility, most children start a **forward roll** from a squat position. (Starting from a pike or straddle position is an excellent progression if flexibility allows.) In such a case, the palms are flat on the mat and the arms bent. Using strong (bent) arms to support the weight, the child lifts the hips, pushes off both feet, and extends the legs completely, tucks the chin, slides the back of the head through the arms, and lands on the back of the shoulders in a pike position with the forehead near the knees. Without stopping, the child rolls on her or his back, tucks the legs (knees to chest, heels to bottom), and, without using the hands, rolls up to the feet, and stands.

Interskill Progression

1. A variety of side rolls with control
2. Forward shoulder roll while being tight and staying tucked

Immature Patterns

- Children land on their heads, or put a considerable amount of weight on their heads.
- Their hands and arms do not support their weight, and sometimes one elbow collapses to the side.

Figure 29.8 Subskill 3
Courtesy of John Dolly

Figure 29.10 Headstand with stag leg position
Courtesy of John Dolly

- They crash onto their backs because they are not round.
- Their push-off is incomplete, and their legs never straighten while piked at the hips before tucking again to stand.
- On their backs, they open the tuck; sometimes they remain lying down.
- They use their hands to roll to a stand.
- At the end of the roll, they don't tuck their heels close enough to their hips to allow them to roll to their feet.

Three Possible Forward Roll Intraskill Progressions

Inclined Mat Progression (Wedge Mat or "Cheese" Mat)

Start in a tuck on a stacked mat in front of a wedge mat. With palms flat and strong arms, lift your hips up, supporting your weight on bent, strong arms (like a weight lifter). Tuck your head, push off both feet by extending your legs straight, and lower the back of your neck and shoulders onto the mat. Put your forehead on your knees (Masser, 1993). Legs should be straight. Tuck your knees, and roll down the mat onto your feet.

Stacked Mat Progression

Starting on a stacked mat on your shins, reach down, and put your palms on the floor with strong arms. Slowly lift your hips, push off your shins by extending your legs straight, and then go into a forward roll to your feet on the floor.

Straddle Start onto Crash (Soft, Thick) Mat

This progression can help children who have problems lifting their hips as they push off for the forward roll. Have them start by standing in a straddle position (on or immediately in front of a crash mat), reach back between their legs, and roll onto a crash mat. After they are comfortable with this movement, they can add supporting their weight on their flat palms with strong, bent arms before rolling onto the crash mat.

Back Roll

Back rolls can be very dangerous for children who are overweight or obese or who have poor arm strength. We recommend teachers do not allow such children to attempt a back roll because of the possibility of injury to the neck.

To do the **back roll**, start standing, squat in a tucked position, and roll backward until the palms are flat on the mat and the body is curled over the shoulders. Push the palms strongly on the mat at the same time as you extend the arms in a reverse press (strong arms), lifting the body high enough for the head to pass through without putting any weight on the head. Land on your feet.

Interskill Progression

1. Shoulder stand with perfect control
2. Back shoulder roll (with complete mastery)
3. Forward roll (with complete mastery)

Typical Immature Patterns

- Landing on the shins or knees, rather than the feet
- Not placing both palms down on the mat
- One elbow collapsing so one hand does not support any weight
- Inadequate amount of force in the push with bent arms to allow the head to slip through
- Pushing too early or too late
- Opening up at the hips, rather than staying tucked tight

Back Roll Intraskill Progression

Potential Refinements

- Push with strong arms.
- Land on the feet.
- Stay tucked tight.

Subskill 1: Rock to Bunny Ears Position

To make bunny ears, put your hands near to your ears with your fingers pointing back and palms flat. Make sure you are not pushing your hands against your head. Rock back, remaining tucked into a shoulder stand with your hands by your ears, fingers pointing back, and palms flat on the mat (bunny ears). Rock back to your feet.

Back Roll on Inclined Mat

If your school has an inclined mat, this can be used as a very helpful scaffold for learning a back roll. It is not a necessary subskill. Squat on a stacked mat with your back to the wedge mat. Roll back onto the inclined wedge mat onto the shoulders. With palms flat, push hard, with strong arms lifting the body high enough for the head to pass through without putting any weight on the head. Land on your feet.

Terminal Skill on Floor Mat

Squat, and roll back onto the shoulders. With palms flat, push hard with strong arms, stay tucked, and land on your feet.

Handstand Forward Roll

A **handstand forward roll** is a forward roll done from the handstand position. We describe this skill in the intraskill progression in this section. We teach this skill only in before- or after-school clubs because it requires spotting to learn safely.

Interskill Progression

1. Straight, tight handstand with excellent control
2. Mature forward roll to the feet without using hands to assist standing up

Typical Immature Patterns

- Not over-balancing
- Quickly tucking the entire body in the handstand and picking up the arms so the body crashes to the mat
- Tucking and trying to put the feet back down in front
- Not making a smooth transition to the mat

Handstand Forward Roll Intraskill Progression

Subskill 1: Handstand Forward Roll with Teacher Spotter

The child kicks a straight, tight handstand and then over-balances so the center of gravity goes beyond the base of support and the child starts to fall in the direction of the back (see the second position in **Figure 29.11**). This over-balancing is critical because it generates force forward so the child can safely roll. If the child does not over-balance and starts to roll, injury can occur easily, as the neck is hyperflexed when the hips come

Figure 29.11 Handstand forward roll

down. Next, the child bends both arms and, using strong arms, lowers the back of the neck and shoulders to the mat, tucking the chin. A teacher spotter holds the child's ankles (or calves if the child is tall and the teacher short) and slowly and gently lowers the child to the mat. Once the child's shoulders are on the mat, the child tucks and rolls to the feet.

Terminal Skill: Handstand Forward Roll with Minimal Spotting

As the child improves in controlling the weight of his or her body and smoothly going from the handstand to the roll (consistently over-balancing to start the momentum of the roll forward), the spotter can assist less and less.

Back Walk-overs

For children who have flexible backs and can do backbends with ease, a **back walk-over** is a viable skill to learn. We describe this skill in subskill 2. It is critical that children not rely on lower back flexibility to do this skill; rather, they need to use their muscles and timing to kick over, staying stretched throughout the entire back. If you do not have large barrel or mailbox mats (see **Figure 29.12**), limit this skill to before- or after-school clubs, as it requires some spotting in the initial attempts.

Interskill Progression

1. Straight, tight handstand with excellent control
2. Backbend starting from a standing position

Typical Immature Patterns

- Kicking too early or too late
- Not rocking the weight backward toward the hands in the backbend
- Sagging through the spine
- Relying only on lower back flexibility, rather than stretching and arching the upper back as well
- Not kicking hard enough
- Letting the shoulders or head move forward out of line with the hands

Back Walk-over Intraskill Progression

Subskill 1: Backbend, Kick Off Stacked Mat

Lie down on a flat mat, knees bent, bottom touching a stacked mat, with feet on the stacked mat. Putting the hands back on the floor by the ears, push up to a backbend. With a spotter supporting the lower back and kick-off leg, kick one leg over while pushing off with the other leg to a handstand (the legs will be in a split position), and walk out of the handstand. The

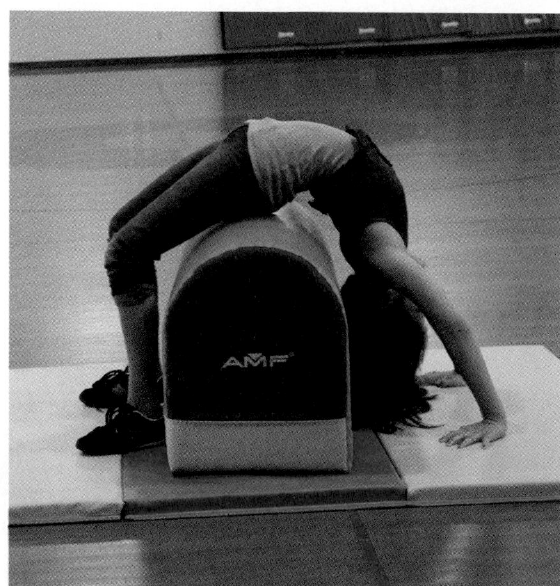

Figure 29.12 Mailbox mat used as a spotter for a backbend
Courtesy of John Dolly

child should practice this skill until he or she can perform it with confidence, doing a stretched handstand without assistance from the spotter.

Subskill 2: Back Walk-over Over a Barrel Mat or with a Spotter

Starting from a stand with the kick-off leg in front and stretching tall through the spine, arch back until the hands touch the floor. In a continuous, simultaneous movement, rock over the hands, kick up with the front leg, and push off with the back leg to the handstand position with legs split. Then step down from the handstand. If you have a barrel mat, the child starts behind the barrel and does the walk-over with the barrel there in case the child does not successfully kick over. If you don't have this kind of mat, spot the child by putting one hand under the front leg to assist with the push-off and the second hand under the lower back to support the child's weight up to the handstand. As the child acquires the control and timing of the kick, the spotter can assist less and less.

More advanced techniques for the back walk-over include the following:

- Starting with the front leg held as high as possible (the child will be balanced on one leg)
- Ending in a scale landing on the front leg while holding the back leg up and lifting the chest to the scale

Handsprings

There are many ways to teach front and back handsprings; some ways work better with some children, and other ways work better with other children. Both these skills require a lot of practice before children can perform them well. In schools, these skills need to be taught and practiced in before- or after-school clubs with a teacher who is a skilled spotter. In club settings, numerous kinds of mats (e.g., pits filled with foam, large barrel mats, inclined mats) are available that children can use for practice without a spotter.

Front Handspring

A **front handspring** (see **Figure 29.13**) begins with three running steps, a hurdle, and a long lunge. The child reaches forward with the hands and then kicks the back leg up and around, pushing off the front leg and swinging it around to join back leg in the air. Then, the child achieves flight from the hands by extending or shrugging the shoulders to push off the floor. During the flight from the hands to the landing on the feet, the child maintains a stretched back (very slight curve), with the head back between the arms (rather than tucking the chin to look for the mat) and the arms straight over the head (rather than reaching forward) to land with the body straight (rather than in a sitting or squatting position).

Interskill Progression

1. Straight, tight handstand with excellent control
2. Round-off from a hurdle

Typical Immature Patterns

- "Sitting" the landing (landing in a tucked position with head looking forward and arms forward)
- Not blocking out the shoulders (letting the shoulders come forward when the hands make contact with the mat and not having a straight line from the arms through the torso)
- Tucking and flexing the knees, hips, and torso throughout the skill (not keeping the legs straight and the body stretched)

Front Handspring Intraskill Progression

Subskill 1: Slow Front Handspring from Stacked Mat to Soft Landing Mat with Teacher Spotter

This subskill consists of performing the front handspring in slow motion with spotting. The child steps into a lunge and kicks up to and through a handstand on the edge of a stacked mat, staying very straight and tight. Looking at his or her hands, the child continues over, arching slightly to land standing on the landing mat. The spotter holds the shoulder and lower back and does not let go until the child is standing and in control.

Subskill 2: Increase Speed

The child gradually increases the speed of the skill, focusing on kicking and swinging the back leg forcefully around while pushing off and swinging the front leg forcefully around to the landing. It is critical for the child to maintain a straight, stretched body during flight and landing and not to reach forward, squat, or tuck the chin on landing.

Figure 29.13 Front handspring

Terminal Skill: Front Handspring on the Floor with Spotter

Once the child perfects the skill from the height of the stacked mat, he or she can move it to the floor. We suggest physical education teachers do not allow children to perform front handsprings without a spotter.

Additional Subskill

Another excellent subskill if you have the appropriate equipment is to practice a front handspring or a back handspring over a barrel (a large circular mat three to four feet in diameter). This mat must be large enough that the child can lie on top in a backbend position with either the hands or the feet touching the ground (but not both). The barrel rolls with the child and serves as a spotter if the child does not spring with sufficient force; the child lands on the barrel (Stork, 2006).

Back Handspring

A **back handspring** is a jump backward done from an off-balance position, landing on the hands, with the head back and the hands, shoulders, and hips in a line (with a very slight arch), then snapping the feet down (see **Figure 29.14** and **Figure 29.15**). The back handspring is long and low and generates horizontal force that can be converted on the snap down into vertical force to do somersaults.

Interskill Progression

1. Straight, tight handstand with excellent control
2. Backbend
3. Round-off from hurdle
4. Front handspring

Typical Immature Patterns

- Leaning the shoulders forward on the sit
- Sitting in a balanced position, rather than sitting back off balance
- Jumping up rather than back
- Lack of horizontal distance traveled
- Piking the legs too soon, sometimes before the hands land on the floor
- Landing with the shoulders forward, rather than blocked with the arms and torso aligned

Back Handspring Intraskill Progression

Subskill 1: Tilt or Sit Back

The key to traveling backward is to start the jump in an off-balance position. Some people teach a sit and jump. From a straight, tight stand, with the arms over the head or at shoulder height, the child sits back, falling off balance to the "sit" position in which the toes are in front of the knees and the knees are in front of the hips, while swinging the arms down. The body looks like it is sitting in a chair with a 90-degree angle at the knees and hips. From this "sit" position, the child then immediately swings the arms overhead and jumps back with a slightly curved body and the head looking at the hands. Children can practice the sit against a well-padded wall or on an appropriate height stack of mats. The sit and jump can be practiced with the teacher spotting or onto a three- to four-foot-high soft mat, like the mat used in pole vaulting.

Some teachers have the child stand absolutely straight and tight with arms pointing toward the ceiling, then have the child lean back, falling off-balance as he or she bends the knees and hips, swings the arms down and then back, and jumps back. This subskill is spotted by standing behind the child with the teacher's arms on the child's upper back and having the child first practice falling while keeping the body absolutely straight and tight (then push the child back up to a stand). Second, have the child fall and jump, with the spotter either catching the child or supporting the child's back and guiding the child back to a stand. This subskill can also be practiced without a spotter onto a three- to four-foot-high soft mat. Regardless of the technique, it is critical that the child's center of gravity be behind the feet so the jump travels backward.

Subskill 2: Spotted Back Handspring to the Hand Landing Position

From the jump, the body travels backward to land on the hands with the head looking at the mat, the shoulders extended (very slightly arched), the hips straight, and the body stretched and tight. The spotter stops the child in this orienting position, and then lets the child snap down. Stopping the child in this position helps her or him learn the feeling of flight through the air and landing stretched and straight on the hands. A typical beginner pattern is to try to pike the legs down as quickly as possible and

Figure 29.14 Standing back handspring

Courtesy of John Dolly

Figure 29.15 Round-off back handspring
Courtesy of John Dolly

land with the shoulders, hips, and knees flexed—an understandable response as the child is typically afraid of not completing the rotation and tries to get the feet back on the floor as quickly as possible. The teacher needs to start spotting behind the child and travel with the child during the jump and flight phases.

Terminal Skill: Back Handspring with Spotter

Once the child is consistently and confidently jumping backward from an off-balance position and landing stretched and straight on the hands, he or she can work on the terminal skill with a spotter. We suggest physical education teachers do not allow children to perform back handsprings without spotting.

Tucked Vaults Over a Trapezoid, Swedish Box, or Horse

We initially teach the approach and hurdle off the springboard separately from the vault. We put these together only after the children can do both well.

Springboard Hurdle

We start by teaching the hurdle onto the springboard, jumping in the air, and landing with a stick on a landing mat. A **springboard hurdle** is an *assemblé* (1-2 jump) done at a low level and traveling for a long distance—about the same distance as one running step.

The child runs toward the springboard while leaning forward in a normal running pattern but then must change the forward lean into a backward-leaning position in the hurdle and on the springboard to block. *To block* means to convert forward force into upward force, thereby enabling the child to take flight. To block, the child leans back and lands on the board with the toes in front of the knees, which are in front of the hips. Then, technically, he or she pops (jumps) off the board in a backward direction; however, the forward motion of the run interacts with the jump backward, so the child goes straight up in the air while still traveling forward.

The arms circle up around and back, ending up by the hips when the child jumps on the board. Then the arms continue circling up until they are reaching for the ceiling. The child lands on the board just in front of the peak of the hill (see **Figure 29.16**), which is about 10 inches from the end of the board. It helps to mark a landing area on the board.

The hurdle is long and low with a resilient pop to get flight. We have the children land on the mat within three feet of the board to help them learn to convert their forward running force into upward force using the blocking position and action on the board.

Typical Immature Patterns

- Landing at the end of the springboard, rather than just before the peak
- Leaning forward with hips in front of knees, knees in front of toes
- Doing the *assemblé* (hurdle) too high
- Pounding on the board (as if it is a trampoline) rather than making a quick, resilient pop off the board
- Running onto the board rather than the mature patterns of taking off from one foot well before the board
- Running and taking off from one foot rather than two feet
- Doing two two-foot jumps on the board rather than an *assemblé* (a 1-2 jump) (see **Figure 29.17**)

Figure 29.16 Landing appropriately before the end of the springboard

Courtesy of John Dolly

Figure 29.17 (A) Immature pattern of running and taking off from one foot (B) Got it!

Courtesy of John Dolly

Intraskill Progression for Hurdle Off a Springboard

Subskill 1: Spring Off Carpet Squares Using an Assemblé

Place carpet squares in front of flat mats. Place one very small foam ball about 12 inches in front of each carpet square, and two spots next to each other across each carpet square representing where the two feet should land. If carpet squares slip on your floor or ground surface, use plastic spots taped to floor. Pretend the carpet squares are springboards. Use an easy-approach jog to the carpet square, spring into the air off one foot (*assemblé*) over the small foam ball, and land on two feet on the two spots on the carpet square. Use a resilient landing, jump high, and land on the flat mat, and stick.

Subskill 2: Hurdle Off Springboard onto Landing Mat

Use an easy-approach jog to the springboard. Spring into the air off one foot (*assemblé*) over the small foam ball, and land on two feet on the springboard just before the peak, which is the area marked with tape. Use a resilient landing, jump high, land on the landing mat, and stick.

Terminal Skill: Hurdle Off Springboard to Vault Over Trapezoid

This skill may be attempted once children have mastered the vault progressions described in the next subsection.

Tucked Front Vault Over a Trapezoid

We build up to a tucked front vault through lessons on steplike actions traveling over a two- to three-layer trapezoid. The child springs off from two feet, puts her or his hands to the left or right parallel to the trapezoid, supports the body's weight on the arms, travels in a curled position over the trapezoid, and lands facing the trapezoid.

Once children have considerable experience supporting their weight on their hands while traveling over a trapezoid, you can add the springboard. Initially, you can use a carpet square as a pretend springboard if it does not slip on your floor or ground surface. If it slides, you can use two poly spots (one for each foot) taped to the floor or mat.

A **tucked front vault** is like a mini-round-off with a two-foot take-off (see **Figure 29.18**). The child runs, does an *assemblé* (hurdle) onto the springboard (or poly spots), puts the hands to the left or right in a mini-round-off position (using the child's preferred side), and springs the legs over the trapezoid to land facing the trapezoid.

Interskill Progression

1. Round-off (mastered)
2. Handstand (mastered)
3. Take off from two feet; lands on two feet; steplike actions over two-layer trapezoid or stacked mat with locked elbows and stable landings (mastered)

Tucked Front Vault Intraskill Progression

Subskill 1: Stand, 2-2 Over Two-Layer Trapezoid

Starting from a stand with your hands stretched toward ceiling, put your hands on the trapezoid, and spring your legs over the two-layer trapezoid or two stacked mats with your body in a tucked position. Land on two feet in a stable, stuck position

Figure 29.18 Tucked front vault

© Jones & Bartlett Learning. Photographed by Sarah Cebulski.

with hands up, stretching toward the ceiling. Keep your legs tucked and together.

Subskill 2: Mini Tucked Front Vault Over Two-Layer Trapezoid with Carpet Square

Put a carpet square six inches in front of a trapezoid and a small foam ball in front of the carpet square. Place a flat mat on the far side of the trapezoid. Take a short easy-approach jog, take off from one foot over the ball, land on the carpet square with two feet, put your hands to your favorite side, take your weight on your hands (arms straight), and spring your feet over the trapezoid with your body in a tucked position. Land facing the trapezoid on two feet. Bend your knees and stick the landing.

R Be sure to land backward directly facing the trapezoid with knees bent. Don't land sideways. If you land sideways, you can hurt your knees because your knees bend only forwards (not sideways).

R Keep your arms straight and elbows locked.

R Practice your mini-vault until you can vault over the trapezoid without any confusion about which foot goes where.

Subskill 3: Tucked Front Vault On and then Over Three-Layer Trapezoid with Carpet Square

Take an easy-approach jog, *assemblé* onto the carpet square (or two poly spots), put two hands toward your favorite side, spring from two feet onto the trapezoid, and then spring your feet off, and land on the other side facing the trapezoid.

Subskill 4: Tucked Front Vault Over Three-Layer Trapezoid with Carpet Square

This is the same as subskill 2 but with a three-layer trapezoid.

Terminal Skill: Tucked Front Vault with Springboard

This is the same as subskill 4 but uses a springboard.

Tucked Flank Vault

After the children can perform a tucked front vault, we teach a **tucked flank vault**. This is the same as the tucked front vault except that the child puts the hands on the trapezoid facing forward and springs the legs over the trapezoid with the side of the legs facing the trapezoid. The child lands with his or her back to the trapezoid.

Intraskill Progression for Tucked Flank Vault

The progression is the same as for the tucked front vault except that the child passes over the trapezoid with the side facing the trapezoid and lands with his or her back facing the trapezoid. Once they learn a tucked front vault, children can often start the tucked flank vault progression with subskill 3 of the tucked front vault progression.

Summary

Technical information about specific gymnastics skills informs your observations and refinements of the movement quality of foundational skills performed in a variety of ways. Some specific skills can be easily learned by most children, including side rolls (egg and log), front shoulder rolls, back shoulder rolls, mule kicks/handstands, mini-cartwheels, and mini-round-offs. When teaching these specific skills, an intraskill progression is helpful. In an intraskill progression, you teach a series of subskills leading up to the terminal skill. Children progress to each new subskill only when they are confident and have mastered the previous subskill. They are never required to learn the terminal skill, as it might not be a skill they can do safely. For any skill requiring spotting, it is wise to teach the skill in before- or after-school programs where the teacher can give one-on-one attention to students.

Review Questions

1. What is the difference between teaching the theme of rolling and teaching a side, forward, and back roll?
2. How does an intraskill mastery progression accommodate individual differences?
3. Under which two circumstances are skill progressions developmentally appropriate for an entire class?
4. What is the difference between an intraskill progression and an interskill progression?
5. True or false: In a lesson including a skill progression, all children will progress step by step through each subskill of the progression during the lesson.
6. What are three typical beginner or immature patterns for a mule kick? What can you say or do to help a child improve these patterns?
7. What are three typical beginner or immature patterns for a cartwheel? What can you say or do to help the child improve these patterns?
8. Why can a shoulder stand be dangerous for overweight children or children with weak core and arm strength?
9. Why is the hands–head triangle critical in a headstand?
10. Why are back rolls dangerous for overweight children or children with weak arm strength?

References

Masser, L. S. (1993). Critical cues to help first-grade students' achievement in handstands and forward rolls. *Journal of Teaching in Physical Education*, *12*, 291–312.

Stork, S. (2006). Teaching front handsprings from a developmental approach. *Teaching Elementary Physical Education*, *17*(3), 23–29.

SECTION V

Educational Dance Content

In this section, we describe the content of educational dance. This area of physical education includes creative dance and folk, line, and square dance.

Chapter 30 explains the importance of dance education to children's lives. As noted in this chapter, even physical education teachers with little prior experience with dance can still be effective dance teachers.

Chapters 31 and 32 describe in detail the content of creative dance, dividing the content into two levels—one for younger children and one for older children. At each level, we describe movement concepts from the body, effort, space, and relationship aspects of the Laban framework. These movement concepts can be used as the basis for learning experiences in dance, and we provide many examples to illustrate this process. We end each chapter with detailed sample lesson and unit segments to illustrate how dance content might be taught in school settings. Most of these examples integrate dance with a classroom topic or children's literature or poetry.

Chapter 33 focuses on multicultural folk dance. We include descriptions of modified dances from different cultures and show you how to teach children to design folk dances based on themes or modified dances from different cultures. We also discuss ways to teach children about different cultures in a respectful manner. We then discuss basic line and square dance steps and show you how to teach children to design their own line and square dances.

CHAPTER

30

Introduction to Educational Dance

PRE-READING REFLECTION

Before you begin reading this chapter, reflect on the following questions:

1. What are your feelings about dancing?
2. Have you ever watched friends dance at a social event and wished you could dance well?
3. Have you ever observed dance on television? What did you like or dislike about the dance?
4. What are your concerns about learning how to teach dance to elementary school children?

OBJECTIVES

Students will learn:

1. Dance is a culturally significant, health-related lifetime activity and, therefore, an important part of children's education.
2. Dance focuses on expressing and representing ideas and feelings.
3. Dance enhances critical and creative thinking.
4. Educational dance is designed for all children in school settings to meet educational goals.
5. Dance lessons have movement and topic themes that provide a context for inspiring dance movement.
6. Topic themes allow you to integrate dance and classroom content if desired.

KEY TERMS

Aesthetic experience
Aesthetic perception
Educational dance

CONNECTION TO STANDARDS

The National Standards for Physical Education for grades K to 5 (Society of Health and Physical Educators [SHAPE], 2014) consider games, educational gymnastics, and dance as the three areas of physical education. Competence in dance, dance techniques, and self-expression are required outcomes in National Standards 1, 2, and 5. In addition, we discuss how to teach vocabulary acquisition and integrate and design literature and informational texts based on the Common Core and other State Standards (CCSS).

Why Teach Dance?

We think the answer to this question is simple. Teaching is not about us; it's about the children.

Regardless of the physical activities teachers enjoy and feel confident teaching, we need to teach content based on the educational needs of children and the National Standards for Physical Education. Knowledge of and a basic competence in dance is not only critical to being well educated but recognizes that children find dance meaningful and joyful.

Most of us who chose to become physical education teachers followed this career pathway because of the positive experiences we had in sports, our deep love of sports, and our desire to make a difference in children's lives. It is the rare physical education major who has had experience on a dance team or in studio dance classes, however. The result is that too few physical education teachers include dance as a significant part of the physical education curriculum. We would like to convince you to add this content to your classes.

We think it is natural to want to share with our students those experiences we cherished when we were students. Early in our careers, the authors of this book most enjoyed teaching those activities we most enjoyed doing ourselves. However, as we grew as teachers, things changed. We found a great deal of pleasure in teaching activities that we never thought we would enjoy. Our focus and professional satisfaction shifted to what children found joyous and meaningful, what was important for their education, and what helped them understand and participate fully in the social and cultural world. Physical education must be bigger than sports and include all of the socially significant physical activities that children and adults find meaningful and worthwhile (see **Figure 30.1**).

Beginning Teachers Talk

First Experiences Teaching Dance

The following are comments from undergraduate students after their first experiences teaching dance as part of a methods course:

"I never thought that the students at Central Elementary would respond in the way that they did. I mean, I saw kids learning and enjoying what they learned."

"It basically was a shock to me that the kids really enjoyed the dances. I thought that they would brush it off when we got out there and taught."

"I had no idea of how the kids would react when teaching the dances. I thought they would think that they were boring and not want to do them. After we went to the school one time and taught dance, I knew they loved it. I watched as all of the kids were involved all over the room doing different dances."

"I saw the excitement in the students' eyes when we taught at Martin Luther King, Jr., Elementary. The children seemed to absolutely love what we were doing with them. They completely paid attention and didn't want to stop. I also saw some of the more timid students gain confidence in what they were doing and really begin to get involved in the dance."

"I think the biggest problem about dance is the actual teaching, not the children being interested in dance. If the teacher can get over the initial fear of teaching dance, then everything will go smoothly. The interest level of the children is there as soon as dance is mentioned."

I Can't Dance Myself, So How Can I Possibly Teach Dance?

This is an important question and one that has stopped many physical educators from teaching dance. We offer two points to consider.

First, we ask you to consider the assumption underlying this question. Many people assume that you must be able to perform a skill or activity to teach it. We do not accept this assumption. The fact is that few elite gymnastics coaches can do the skills they teach their athletes. Try to imagine Bela Karolyi (a long-time coach of both the U.S. and Romanian Olympic gymnastics teams) doing a back handspring on the balance beam! In fact, few Olympic and college coaches in any sport have the skills and talents of the elite athletes they coach. Being able to perform a skill is not a prerequisite for being able to teach it. One of us can't move to the beat of the music and can demonstrate only the simplest locomotor dance steps—but she has taught and enjoyed teaching dance for more than 25 years, and the students in her school get a strong dance education. You can learn to teach new activities successfully and in a way that is professionally satisfying and beneficial to the students under your care.

Second, teachers have a professional obligation to continue to expand their knowledge of the subject matter of their field in alignment with the National Standards. No one should expect that what they know when they graduate college at age 21 is all they will need to know for the rest of their lives. Being a good teacher means being a continual learner. It means "doing your homework," attending conferences, reading the professional literature and visiting Internet sites, taking risks, and trying new ideas. You need to be knowledgeable about all the subject

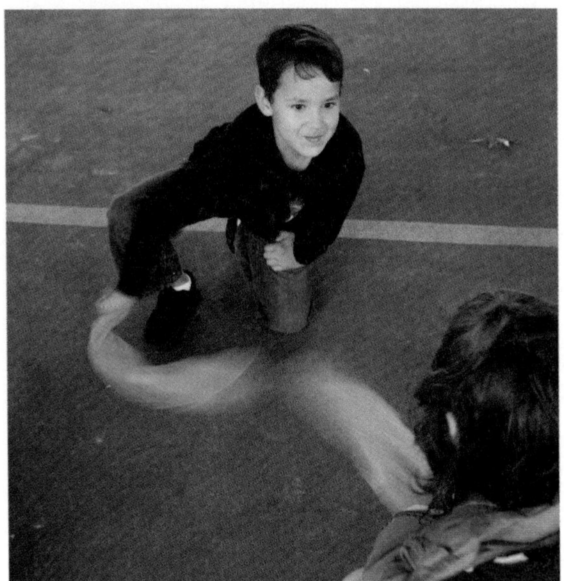

Figure 30.1 Enjoying dance using a scarf to explore movement at different levels

matter you are responsible for teaching, and there are many ways to acquire knowledge of physical activities in addition to performance.

Why Dance Is Important

The National Standards for Dance Education begin with the following explanation of the importance of the arts in society:

> The arts have been part of us from the very beginning. Since nomadic peoples first sang and danced for their ancestors, since hunters first painted their quarry on the walls of caves, since parents first acted out the stories of heroes for their children, the arts have described, defined, and deepened human experience. All peoples, everywhere, have an abiding need for meaning—to connect time and space, experience and event, body and spirit, intellect and emotion. People create art to make these connections, to express the otherwise inexpressible. A society and a people without the arts are unimaginable, as breathing would be without air. Such a society and people could not long survive (National Dance Association [NDA], 1994, p. 8).

Dance is essential for the school curriculum for at least seven major reasons.

1. Dance Is a Way of Knowing

The most important reason dance is essential for a school curriculum is that it is a way for children to know and understand their world. For example, in a dance lesson on the theme of prey and predator, children learn about moving with bound flow, curling, stillness, and traveling leading with different body parts. The theme is representing the idea of prey and predator, a topic they also encounter in their science classes. In dance, however, the children focus on the bodily feelings of prey and predator from the inside. The affective domain—that is, the kinesthetic and emotional feelings—along with the motor and cognitive domains contribute to what and how children learn about the concept of prey and predator. They "know" the concept of prey and predator in a different kinesthetic way because they have moved and felt bound flow as they stalked prey (see **Figure 30.2**) and curled into a position of stillness while being vigilant of their environment and anticipating the possibility of a predator. Having danced the roles of prey and predator, they have a deeper understanding of the concepts than they would have if they had learned about prey and predators only in science class.

2. Dance Is a Way of Expressing and Representing Ideas and Feelings

A goal of dance is for children to express, represent, and communicate ideas, concepts, and feelings (Cone & Purcell-Cone, 2003). Continuing the example from the preceding paragraph, in a dance about prey and predator, children are expressing, representing, and communicating to their peers their

Figure 30.2 Traveling with bound flow as prey

Experienced Teachers Talk

Teachers' Tales

When I was first learning to teach educational dance, a workshop leader told me this story. He said:

> Learning to teach this can be scary. It's like you are in a canoe traveling down this winding river, and all you can see is the dark forest closing in on you. You can't see what is around the next bend. You don't know if there are rapids ahead or water moccasins lurking in the swampy undergrowth. However, I am flying above you, and I can see that just around the bend is a beautiful wildflower meadow, deer drinking from the river, eagles soaring on wind currents, and staggering views of mountains in the distance.

And he was right. I just had to get in the canoe and paddle.

Misconception Alert

Physical education majors have told us they initially resisted learning dance because dance was an art, and the arts are only for those who have artistic talent. As one undergraduate said, "Previously, I thought of dance as something done to music by people who were very talented in the area." Research has shown this is a belief shared by many physical education majors (Allison, Pissanos, Turner, & Law, 2000). Certainly, not everyone has the talent or desire to be a professional dancer; however, all children, regardless of ability or financial wherewithal, deserve and have the right to dance education. We don't limit tennis lessons only to those individuals talented enough to make the professional circuit, nor do we limit math instruction only to those who will become mathematicians.

understanding and interpretation of the concept of prey and predator (see **Figure 30.3**). Children enjoy communicating their ideas to their classmates.

Recognizing the value of physical activity for self-expression is explicitly part of National Standard 5. Developing communication, idea representation, and self-expression skills are also general goals of education, part of the CCSS, and a focus of literacy, social studies, music, and art lessons. Dance can make a significant contribution toward these goals and standards.

3. Dance Enhances Critical and Creative Thinking and Develops Abilities to Create Artistic Products

Dance includes many opportunities for children to create movement responses and design dance sequences. Creating and designing dances requires the use of creative and critical thinking and problem solving. The development of critical-thinking, creative-thinking, and problem-solving skills are important general goals of education. Dance is an excellent content area for facilitating the development of such higher-order thinking skills.

Figure 30.3 Second-graders representing cats stalking and pouncing on a mouse

Experienced Teachers Talk

Why Experienced Teachers Enjoy Teaching Dance

"Dance puts students on an even playing field. It allows for tremendous amounts of creative thinking. I love watching them working within their groups to come up with a finished product. They love showing their creation to their classmates and receiving compliments from their classmates who watched them perform."

"What I love about teaching dance is watching the student experience joy: joy of moving, joy of learning to work in a group, joy of sharing ideas, and the joy of thinking. Oftentimes, the timid students or the ones with behavior problems excel in the dance area."

"I never knew how fun it would be to teach young children to dance. I was surprised to see how enthusiastic the children were and how involved they got in the lessons. Most of all, I was surprised to see how much the boys got into it."

4. Dance Can Enhance Aesthetic Perception and Provide Opportunities for Aesthetic Experiences

Aesthetic perception in dance is the capability to recognize and appreciate the expressive, symbolic, and artistic properties of dances. The development of aesthetic perception is most often associated with the arts, but its use is far broader and includes recognizing the aesthetic attributes of, for example, architecture, a new automobile model, a web page, a spectacular dunk shot in basketball, or an improbable diving catch to make the last out in a softball game. Thus, the development of aesthetic perception can be important for the workplace and in adult life in general.

An aesthetic experience is like watching a beautiful sunset over a mountain lake, looking over the Grand Canyon, or seeing the Northern Lights for the first time. It touches you in a memorable way. Stinson (1982) describes an **aesthetic experience** in children's dance as "an active response of the whole self. Just going through the motions, no matter how beautiful or interesting the motions are, is not enough. One must be stirred, touched, fully engaged" (p. 72). Thus, dance provides opportunities for children to develop and experience the aesthetic domain—which is a central goal of National Standard 5.

5. Dance Is a Culturally Significant Art Form

Dance is one of the arts. Because dance and the other arts are significant to our society, as are sports, they deserve to be taught for their intrinsic value. A well-educated person is knowledgeable about significant aspects of society, including the arts. For us to provide a good education for students, we must do more than simply focus on job training for adulthood. We must prepare students to live good, healthy, flourishing lives, appreciating all the world has to offer and contributing to society in meaningful ways. Curriculum scholars sometimes call this the goal of "living the good life." It is what many of us want for ourselves, and it is what we owe to children as well. Because of its importance as an art in society, dance has been part of a sound elementary school physical education curriculum for at least 100 years (Umstead, 1985).

6. Dance Contributes to a Multicultural Education

"Dance has existed in all societies throughout geographic space and historical time" (Vissicaro, 2004, p. 3). The universality of dance (it is practiced worldwide) and the diversity of dance forms offer teachers wonderful opportunities to provide a multicultural curriculum. Thus, dance is an excellent content area for helping children understand and appreciate not only aspects of their own culture, but also diverse cultures, ethnicities, and historical periods different from their own.

7. Dance Is a Lifelong, Health-Related Physical Activity

There are many ways people can enjoy dance as a lifelong, health-related physical activity (see **Figure 30.4**). Across the entirety of North America, from small towns to large cities, adolescents and adults participate in recreational dance groups, including folk dance, square dance, ballroom, hip-hop, swing, clogging, country, and Native American pow-wows. Weddings and other social gatherings and celebrations often include dancing. Private studios, town recreation departments, YMCAs, and other organizations offer lessons and support recreational dance groups. National and international organizations offer ability and age-group competitions for adults in a range of dance styles, including hip-hop, ballroom, country, and folk dancing. Fitness centers have long offered aerobic dance classes, and wide ranges of dance styles now serve as a basis for these aerobic classes. A growing number of television shows feature dance competitions ranging from hip-hop to high school and college dance teams to ballroom.

Thus, dance as a recreational and health-related fitness activity is a significant part of North American society and an

Beginning Teachers Talk

Learning to Value Dance for Children

Through our field experiences at Bryant Elementary and Central Elementary, I also learned that the children enjoyed dance as well. The kids at these schools seemed as if they looked forward to learning dance. You could tell by the smiles on their faces and the excitement they exerted that they thoroughly enjoyed dancing.

As I mentioned earlier, I had no background in dance and didn't really know that dance could play such a successful role in physical education. After seeing that I enjoyed dance, and after seeing how much fun the elementary children had with dance, I strongly agree that dance should be a part of every physical education curriculum in the country. Not only can dance be fun, but it also is a valuable learning experience for kids of all ages. Dance allows children to be creative, as well as letting children explore new ideas and movements.

I also learned that teaching dance can be rewarding to the teacher as well as the student. By this, I mean that as a teacher you can see your work paying off. You, as a teacher, can see the children working hard and enjoying themselves as well.

Figure 30.4 Dance is a lifetime physical activity

(left) © Hill Street Studios/Blend Images/age fotostock; (middle) ©AISPIX/Shutterstock; (right) ©Hemera/Thinkstock

activity enjoyed by many individuals. Preparing students to pursue participation in whatever form of dance they enjoy is a goal of the elementary dance curriculum.

Educational Dance

In this text, we present **educational dance**—that is, dance appropriate to, and designed for, all children in school settings to meet educational objectives. We recommend, for the elementary level, that the educational dance curriculum consist primarily of creative dance and multicultural folk dance (including square and line dancing).

The creative dance we advocate for physical education is not the same as studio dance instruction aimed at developing professional dancers for the stage or competitive hip-hop dance teams. The folk dance we propose does not encompass religious or classical forms of folk dance that take many years of study under dance masters. Instead, we aim to present a developmentally appropriate program that a competent, caring physical education teacher without extensive dance training can deliver successfully in public school settings. Of course, teachers with training in any of the wide range of dance forms can offer a broader curriculum for children.

There are three important forms of dance to teach:

- Creative dance
- Child-designed folk, line, and square dance
- Modified folk, line, and square dance

All three forms are worthwhile, but we do not recommend that you spend an equal amount of time on each form.

In our opinion, creative dance deserves the most time in the curriculum, followed by child-designed folk dance, with modified folk, line, and square dance being third in priority. Creative dance focuses most on the artistic, creative, and expressive aspects of dance, which are essential to a child's education. Modified folk dance allows children to learn forms and styles of dance from different cultures. Child-designed folk, line, and square dance allows teachers to deal with multicultural content in a richer way than modified folk dance, while also providing opportunities for developing the creative, expressive, and artistic elements of dance, albeit using a narrower range of movements than creative dance.

What Makes a Movement a Dance Movement?

Dance movement has four distinguishing characteristics.

First, dance movement is expressive, as opposed to functional movement, done simply to accomplish a task such as throwing a ball or brushing your teeth (see **Figure 30.5**).

Second, dance includes a heightened awareness of the kinesthetic and emotional feelings of the movement—that is, children need to be attentive to how the movement feels from the inside (Stinson, 1982). Stinson writes, "This awareness is the difference between an action like pointing to the door; compared to the process of extending the arm, feeling from the inside the energy travel to lengthen the arm and the hand, and then flow out the fingertip" (p. 72).

Third, dance includes a heightened awareness of the shape of the movement (Stinson, 1982). As a consequence, children focus on and are very aware of the shape of their bodies as they

SAFETY AND LIABILITY 30.1

Increasing Safety and Decreasing Risk of Liability: Guidelines Relevant to Content in this Chapter

In this box, we discuss specific guidelines built on information discussed throughout this text on professional standards of practice, negligence, and liability. The goals of these guidelines are to increase children's safety and decrease teachers' risk of negligence and liability.

- To increase safety and decrease liability risk, teachers plan and follow a written curriculum with a progression or sequence of tasks to develop children's skills safely. The curriculum is based on district, state, and national standards and guidelines. All tasks are developmentally appropriate and modified to accommodate individual differences. Safety issues within tasks are taught, and students are warned about potential dangers.
- All students are always supervised while they are in the physical education space and during transit to this space. Teachers cannot leave the children alone to step into the hallway for any reason, even to deal with an emergency situation, without another qualified supervisor in the physical education space. Classroom and physical education teachers must communicate when they transfer supervisory duties from one to the other.
- During all dance, but especially when teaching leaping, jumping, and other flight from feet skills, insist children perform with movement quality (e.g., light landings, controlling flow, absorbing force, maintaining tension in the body, and maintaining appropriate body alignment).
- Provide adequate space in front and overflow space when children are learning locomotor skills, such as galloping, sliding, and skipping. When children are traveling fast, provide even more space by using multiple lines (with no more than three children per line), starting each wave of children when there is adequate space in front or traveling on a large circular pathway around the space.
- Teach children the stop routine and how to travel in a scattered formation safely without falling down or colliding.
- When children practice movements with strong force and fast speed, such as thrusting, jabbing, and slashing, teach them that they must be very aware of the size of their personal space and not invade the personal space of other children.
- When children use implements, such as canes, wands, and ribbons on sticks, teach them that the size of their personal space increases considerably and they must be farther away from peers.

Figure 30.5 Feeling and expressing the difference between heavy tension (representing tiredness) and strong tension (representing anger)
Courtesy of John Dolly

are dancing. In attending to shape, children recognize that dance movement is special and understand that when they dance, it feels different from when they are not dancing.

Fourth, dance is an aesthetic experience that ought to "touch the spirit" (Stinson, 1982, p. 74). In essence, when children dance, teachers need to help them feel a connection to their inner selves, have a heightened awareness of their state of being, and appreciate the meaning of the movement (see **Figure 30.5**).

Representation, Expression, and Communication

Dance is an art form in which choreographers and dancers represent ideas, feelings, and events and communicate them to an audience. In dance, movement is the mode of communication, in the same way that words are the mode of communication in poetry and literature. A dance can tell a story, represent an idea, convey a message about an issue, or offer an interpretation of some element of the human condition.

> **Beginning Teachers Talk**
>
> Changing Beliefs About Dance
>
> "Never in my wildest dreams before this semester would I have thought that I had the ability to dance and teach dance."
>
> "I came into this class telling myself that I would never probably teach dance in a class, but going to the schools and seeing how well the students responded to the movement and their excitement toward the dances really has changed my mind."

Dance Lessons Have Movement Themes and Topic Themes

Because dance is expressive and communicates ideas about a topic, the dance lessons in this text include both a movement theme, which delineates the movement content, and a topic theme, which is the topic about which children will express ideas. Topic themes

- Help children create expressive shapes and movement patterns representing events, ideas, stories, emotions, and concepts
- Provide images that help children improve movement quality
- Help children make connections between movement and real-world experiences

For example, one dance lesson for the younger grades focuses on the movement theme of shape (round, straight, pointy, and twisted shapes) and the topic theme of autumn leaves. This lesson begins with children observing and discussing the differences in the shapes of autumn leaves. They then create round, straight, pointy, and twisted shapes related to the shapes of the leaves. Next, they explore swinging and swaying, falling gently, swirling, traveling on circular pathways, and turning jumps. The shapes of the leaves and the idea of leaves falling gently from a tree and then swirling around when a strong wind arises provide concrete images that help children create different shapes, move using different qualities of movement, and understand how movements can represent real-world events.

The Difference Between Representing and Imitating/Pantomiming

An important distinction must be drawn between using movement to represent an idea in dance and imitating or pantomiming. Imitating or pantomiming means to try to replicate the shape or movement of something exactly. Children imitating a cat might crawl on the floor meowing, stop and pretend to drink milk, and then crawl fast and bite a pretend mouse with their teeth. When children imitate or pantomime in dance, they often make stereotypical movements.

Representation, by comparison, is more abstract and emphasizes those aspects of what you are trying to represent that are most important or most telling or that capture its essence. Imitation is analogous to a photograph, whereas representation is like a painting. Children representing a cat might travel upright slowly while stepping on the balls of their feet quietly, then pause in a crouched position while staying perfectly still and looking straight ahead, concentrating on a point in space. Suddenly, they might leap in the air, making a slashing movement with their arms and legs (as the mouse scurries to safety), only to land gracefully and stare haughtily off to the side, pretending nothing had happened (see **Figure 30.3**)

Representations may range from literal to abstract. (Imitation is an extreme form of literal representation.) Purcell-Cone (2000) explains that in a literal representation, the portrayal is

(A)

(B)

(C)

Figure 30.6 (A) Imitating a buffalo in a stereotypical way (B and C) Making an abstract representation of a buffalo with powerful, stately movements and a large head

close to the original, whereas an abstract representation elaborates on the original or emphasizes only one portion—thereby capturing the main feeling or idea. Although the goal is for dance movement to represent ideas in abstract ways, this goal does not mean more literal representations are never appropriate. We support Purcell-Cone's (2000) stance:

> I believe that the creative process encompasses a full range of interpretative possibilities from literal to abstract.... Whether the interpretation is closer to the literal or abstract is dependent on the intent of the children in creating a dance....The role of the teacher is to help children explore the possibilities for their expression, not to make all the movement decisions about how to respond to the literature. The dance belongs to the children, and it is their meaning that should be expressed (p. 15).

Dance is about representation, so children need to understand the difference between representing and imitating (see **Figure 30.6**). Imitation, however, is not always negative. Often children begin to explore by imitating; then, as their feelings for and understanding of the movement become clearer, they start to explore different ways to represent the topic. For example, in the autumn leaves dance, children might begin by trying to imitate the shape of a particular round leaf by standing up and making a circle with their arms. As the lesson progresses, they will expand their explorations to creating different round shapes at different levels using their body parts in different ways. It is possible that imitation is an early developmental level in children who are learning to create their own movements. Research in other subject areas suggests this sequence of development is a strong possibility.

A fine line separates a literal representation and an imitation (which is rarely appropriate). When children imitate, the key is to encourage them to work on their ideas, rather than simply being satisfied with the first idea they have, and to help them move from imitating thoughtlessly to developing representations that are powerful and meaningful to them.

Integrating Dance, Classroom Content, and CCSS

Because dance includes both movement and topic themes, it provides a multitude of opportunities for integrating physical education and classroom subjects and meeting CCSS.

Integrating physical education with the content taught by classroom teachers can be beneficial for the following reasons:

- Children can acquire a deeper understanding of a topic when they learn through multiple modes, such as movement, reading, music, and art.
- When children create a dance about a topic they have studied, it can inspire their creativity and help them capture the feeling of the movement and topic—for example, how it might feel to be prey or a predator and which kinds of movement they can create to express that feeling. Integration helps children understand the world more holistically. Although we compartmentalize the world into separate subjects in school, outside of school and in the workplace, people deal with tasks, problems, issues, and events by integrating skills and information from a wide range of sources. Perceiving the big picture, seeing a problem or task from multiple perspectives, and being able to use information from different domains are valuable skills to have.
- Integrating their lessons with the work of classroom teachers can also help physical education teachers politically within their schools. It gives us a way to showcase what we do, lets other teachers know we care about what happens in their classrooms, and makes us more integral to the central function of educating children.

Integrating dance with other subject areas has a long, fruitful history in children's dance. Teachers have long used children's literature and poetry as a stimulus for dance. They have taught folk dance to help children appreciate cultures other than their own. In addition, teachers have had children create dance dramas or stories about historical and current cultural topics.

Is Integration of PE and Classroom Content the Latest Fad?

We don't think so. The current emphasis on state standards for literacy to which all subject areas are expected to contribute is likely to continue in one form or another or under one label or another. Moreover, integration of classroom content has stood the test of time and if teachers avoid the pitfall of trivialization, integration is beneficial for children's learning. As a teacher, you will undoubtedly encounter many ideas for teaching that sound good and appear promising for solving one problem or another. Some of these ideas will stand the test of time, and others won't—they will simply pass by as one of a long line of fads. How can you know which is which—that is, which are dross and which are pure gold? Sometimes you can't. However, you can critique what you read and hear and evaluate whether the new idea is in keeping with your philosophy. In the Air Force, aviators are taught that if they crash in the water, the environment can be very disorienting. If you watch which way the bubbles are moving, however, you will know which way is up. Your own teaching philosophy should be like those bubbles, leading you in the direction you need to go.

The Pitfall of Trivialization

Although integrating physical education and classroom subjects sounds wonderful, it has some pitfalls. The most common problem is trivializing either subject area or both of them. We have seen national and state workshop presentations and read about supposedly worthwhile ways to integrate physical education with classroom subjects that, in our opinion, are a waste of time. For example, scattering words or letters on cards about a gym and having children search for letters to make a word or words to make a sentence does not teach the children any physical education content and has dubious value in improving literacy. The children are physically active and having fun, but they are not learning anything. This kind of exercise would be an activity more appropriate for a birthday party.

Before you use an integration activity, ask these questions:

1. Which physical skill or movement are children performing, and will they improve their ability to perform it as a result of the activity?
2. Are they learning anything about that skill or movement that is a legitimate part of the game, gymnastics, or dance curriculum?

Dance and Meeting the Common Core and other State Standards

What we teach in dance contributes to children meeting three sections of the CCSS. We discuss these next.

Speaking and Listening

First, the speaking and listening section, with the subsections of comprehension, collaboration, and presentation of knowledge and ideas, focuses on teaching children how to ask and answer questions and collaborate with partners and within small groups. In dance, we frequently ask questions and present tasks applying movement concepts. We also have children alone, with partners, and in small groups design dance sequences, perform sequences for a small-group or whole-class audience, and require the audience to discuss positive details, the main ideas, and the reasons the dance sequence was successful, which are all part of the CCSS.

Vocabulary Acquisition

Second, dance also offers particularly rich content and context for vocabulary acquisition through the teaching of movement concepts and related movement vocabulary. Children learn vocabulary words most effectively within a relevant context as opposed to looking up words in a dictionary and memorizing definitions (Ruddell, 2009). In dance, children learn movement concepts within the context of physically experiencing movements related to the movement concept. Moreover, the movement concept is itself a broader concept that is comprised of categories of movements connected to events, objects, ideas, and feelings. When children learn a new vocabulary word within the context of a broader movement concept, they can connect that vocabulary word to related words and movements they experience bodily. These connections help children understand the meaning of the new vocabulary word. In addition, "Research has shown that active processing and substantial and varied practice with words promote solid recall of meaning vocabulary and that, in turn, results in improved comprehension" (Ruddell, 2009, p. 168). When we teach children a movement concept, such as floating, which is moving slowly with light force, they are physically, cognitively, and emotionally engaged. We help the children understand the vocabulary word *float* in a concrete and personal way. When children experience bodily a vocabulary word, they understand it at a deeper level and get considerable practice applying the word in different situations. The following brief outline of lesson content illustrates how several vocabulary words can be taught within the context of a lesson focused on the movement concept of *twisted.*

Brief Outline of Lesson Integrating Vocabulary Acquisition

Movement Theme: Twisted

Topic Theme: Exploring the haunted ring of stones by the gnarled old tree

Potential Vocabulary Words to Teach: gnarled, anguish, cauldron, wring (defined briefly within the lesson *when children need to know the meaning*)

1. Explore making different twisted shapes, twisting to the fullest extent you can.
2. Explore making different twisted shapes at low, medium, and high levels, using the image of a gnarled, old tree to stimulate explorations. Does anyone know what *gnarled* means? [Twisted into a state of deformity, full of knots.] As you move into your twisted shape, keep twisting through your full range of motion until you end in a twisted knot.
3. Now we are going to combine twisting with wringing. In dance, *wringing* means to move slowly, twisting while you maintain strong tension in all your muscles as if you were twisting a washcloth tightly to wring out all the water.

Start in a twisted shape, use wringing movements, keeping so tight that you squeeze your body into another twisted shape at a different level. Keep exploring wringing with strong tension and twisting to change levels to end in twisted shapes

4. Travel at a low level by twisting and pausing in different twisted shapes, scanning the environment like an anguished, human-like creature, such as Gollum from *The Hobbit* and *The Lord of the Rings*. Does anyone know what *anguished* means? [Extremely distressed, tormented, anxious.] Make your movements express how anxious and tormented you are. Look like you are extremely distressed.
5. Travel and jump, making different twisted shapes and slashing movements in the air like an evil bird (using the image of a bird such as the Nazgul when they flew like vultures in *The Lord of the Rings*).
6. Travel at a medium level in a circle by twisting and pausing in a twisted shape, wringing your hands and twisting with worry. You are a creature circling around a cauldron brewing a spell within a haunted ring of stones. Does anyone know what a cauldron is? [A large kettle for boiling liquids.]
7. Design a dance sequence:
   a. Starting in a twisted shape
   b. Using wringing and twisting movements to change levels to end in twisted shapes, representing a gnarled, old tree
   c. Traveling at a low level by twisting, pausing, and scanning, representing an anguished, human-like creature
   d. Traveling and jumping with slashing movements and twisted shapes, representing an evil bird.
   e. Traveling at a medium level in a circle, twisting and wringing hands, representing a creature brewing a spell in a cauldron within a haunted ring of stones
   f. Ending any way you want
8. Closure: Discuss vocabulary words: gnarled, anguish, cauldron, and wring.

The following subsections of vocabulary acquisition within the CCSS are relevant to dance. Children need to

- Acquire and use accurately domain-specific words and phrases, including those that signal spatial and temporal relationships, precise actions, emotions, or states of being and that are basic to a particular topic
- Identify real-life connections between words and their use
- Demonstrate understanding of words by relating them to their opposite (antonyms) and to words with similar but not identical meanings (synonyms)
- Explain the meaning of metaphors and similes in context
- Demonstrate understanding of word relationships and nuances in word meanings

[Adapted by the authors from the Common Core State Standards Initiative (2010), retrieved from www.corestandards.org].

We discuss each bulleted standard next.

Domain-Specific Vocabulary

In dance, acquiring domain-specific words and phrases relates primarily to the dance movement concepts that are part of the Laban framework. These movement concepts comprise the basic movement vocabulary of dance, including actions, such as rising, falling, opening, closing, gathering, scattering, and quivering; shapes, such as round, wide, straight, symmetrical, and asymmetrical; spatial concepts, such as pathways and directions; temporal concepts, such as duration and rhythm; and the many relationship concepts, such as in front of, behind, over, under, matching, contrasting, and complementing. The CCSS specify actions, emotions, spatial, temporal, and relational words and phrases. Consequently, as you teach the movement vocabulary of physical education, you are also addressing the CCSS for vocabulary acquisition.

Connections to Real-Life Situations

Critical to teaching dance is making connections to real-life situations. These connections help children not only understand the movement concept you are teaching, but also perform the movements more precisely and expressively. In addition, these connections help stimulate children's creative thinking about the movement concept. The teacher can provide examples of objects, events, and emotions related to the movement concept, but the children can also generate examples, thus developing a more elaborate understanding of the potential use of the term. We list real-life connections to the movement concept of *floating*, which means moving slowly with gentle, soft force, using space in an indirect, meandering way.

Examples of Real-Life Connections to Floating

- Balloons, hot air balloons, bubbles rising and floating in the air
- Leaves falling gently from a tree
- Feathers falling
- Flying, birds flying, eagles soaring
- Floating in water, floating down a river in a canoe or inner tube, feeling buoyant
- Cumulus clouds
- Floating weightless in space like an astronaut
- Whales swimming, manatees swimming
- Feeling airy, weightless, dreamy, tranquil, light

Antonyms and Synonyms

To help children understand movement concepts and also dance more competently, we also teach them about contrasting movements. The movements on the opposite end of the continuum from floating (slow, light, indirect movements) are the fast, strong, direct movements called thrusting and jabbing. Teaching the opposites to floating not only helps children understand floating, but also introduces a new set of connections between movement concepts and real life.

Examples of Antonyms to Floating and Real-Life Connections to Thrusting and Jabbing

- Punching, jabbing, thrusting
- Jumping
- Spearing fish
- Pounding or hammering something
- Bursting or exploding like popcorn, dynamite, or a star gone nova
- Lightning
- Fireworks exploding
- Waves crashing onto rocks
- Fighting (pretending to fight)
- Conflict between people

- Feeling angry, outraged, strong, powerful
- Moving impatiently, brusquely, or abruptly
- Moving as if you are energetic, vigorous, or spirited

Metaphors and Similes

In addition, in teaching dance we often use metaphors and similes to help children develop their ability to express their ideas and feeling through dance. To improve their ability to show strong tension in stillness, you might say, "Be as hard as a rock." Or, to express minimal tension in which the body feels heavy and relaxed, you might say, "Make your arms move slowly like cooked, limp spaghetti."

Nuances in Word Meanings

Dance is also a context in which teachers can work on the standards aimed at helping children understand nuances in the meanings of similar words. The following list of words illustrates many similar words with different nuances all connected to the movement concept of floating.

Examples of Nuances in Word Meanings Related to the Movements and Feelings of Floating

- Move leisurely, drift, hover, dawdle, linger, loiter, dillydally
- Don't let anything hurry you, waste time, procrastinate
- Feel calm, tranquil, placid, quiet, peaceful
- Feel gentle, kind, tender
- Feel weak, flimsy, fragile, frail

In working with the children, you can select similar words to *float*, and have the children show you through dance movement the often subtle differences and then discuss these differences in the closure section of the lesson.

Reading Standards

The third set of CCSS that can be met in dance lessons are selected sections of the reading standards for both literature and informational texts. These sections include asking and answering questions about key details in a text and explaining how specific aspects of a text's illustrations contribute to what is conveyed by the words.

We use children's literature, informational texts, or poetry in almost all dance lesson plans. Teachers have long used these forms of text as a stimulus for dance.

Guidelines for Integrating Literature and Informational Texts

The most important guideline to remember is that your first responsibility is to teach well the physical education content that addresses the National Standards for Physical Education. In addition, you need to keep the children physically active, learning skills and movements for at least 50% of class time. Despite the time constraints, you can effectively integrate literature and informational texts relevant to the physical education lessons.

A second guideline is that it is a far better learning experience for the children if the classroom teacher has taught the text or topic in reading, science or social studies before you integrate it into a physical education lesson. We suggest two ways to deal with this. First, at the start of the year, ask the classroom teachers what units and/or topics they plan to teach in social studies and science. Then you can design dance lessons on one of those topics. A second solution is to approach teachers and ask if they are willing to teach a book before you teach your dance lesson using the same book. We have found classroom teachers to be consistently willing to do this and appreciative that we are trying to support their work.

Teaching Strategies for Using Children's Literature, Informational Texts, and Poetry

In grades K to 2, texts are much shorter than the literature and informational texts read by children in grades 3 to 5. For the younger grades, you can read the entire story or poem at the start of class. Ask the children questions about the details they remember from the story, characters, images, and major events, and then explain that the dance lesson will be based on the story or poem. Your dance lesson can follow the events of the story or images in the poem in order. However, most often you will select those events and images that are most closely related to actions and movement concepts relevant for physical education. Our lesson titled "When Autumn Leaves Fall," using the children's book *Fall Leaves Fall!* (Hall & Halpern, 2000), illustrates this strategy, as does the lesson titled "The Sea and the Shore," based on a poem.

A second way to use the story or poem is to read a page or several pages that focus on one main idea. Then, have the children explore the movement concepts related to that idea using the text to stimulate their explorations. The children then gather around you, and you or the children all together read aloud the next page or section and then return to exploring dance movements. This read–dance–read sequence continues throughout the lesson. The lessons based on *In the Small, Small, Pond* (Fleming, 1993), *The Snowy Day* (Keats, 1962), and *If Not for the Cat* (Prelutsky & Rand, 2004) show you how to do this. When you examine these lesson plans, you will see that we selected portions of the text that were valuable for meeting our dance objectives. There is no rule that you must read the entire book to the children.

A third way to use texts, in particular informational texts in grades 3 to 5, is to select very small portions of text that teach important or interesting information related to your topic and movement themes. You can project these short portions on the wall and have the children read aloud all at the same time. Before you read, you can ask the following questions to facilitate comprehension of what you are about to read (from the lesson titled *In the Small, Small Pond*):

- Not only are there animals at a pond, but there are insects as well. Let's see what is at the pond. What's happening in this picture?
- What are the dragonflies doing? What do dragonflies look like when they fly?
- What else hovers? Yes, helicopters and some boats called hovercrafts.
- What do you think the frog is doing? How do frogs catch bugs?

Then you can ask them questions about the details or main ideas about what they read. We offer the following facts about predators as two options for helping children activate or elaborate their knowledge of predators as part of our lesson titled "Prey and Predator." The first introduces the idea that predators are also prey for animals further up the food chain and is an excellent introduction for the middle of the lesson, when children explore representing the feelings and movements of prey and predators.

> A group of penguins sun themselves on an ice floe. Splash! Hunger drives them into the cold water to hunt for fish. Soon the hunter becomes the hunted as a penguin finds itself in the jaws of a leopard seal, who kills it with a quick crunch. Its stomach full of penguin, the seal now climbs onto the empty ice to rest.
>
> Suddenly the hunter again becomes the hunted as the ice floe is surrounded by a pack of orcas, or killer whales. The doomed seal clings to the ice. It's only a matter of time until the intelligent orcas figure out a way to move the seal off the ice and into their waiting jaws (Baskin-Salzberg & Salzberg, 1991, p. 9).

The second set of excerpts is from the same book and describe three hunting strategies. These excerpts can be used to enhance the children's ideas about how to design their prey-and-predator dance sequence for the culminating activity.

"The Ambush"

> Some predators *ambush* their meals by waiting patiently out of sight behind a rock or under a leaf until their prey passes by. Then they rush out and grab their surprised victims. A high-speed attack may occur so quickly that a flock of birds may not even notice that one of their number is missing" (Baskin-Salzberg & Salzberg, 1991, p. 43).

"The Stalk"

> Many predators stalk, or sneak up on, prey by hiding behind plants, rocks, or trees until they're close enough to pounce. Big cats are expert stalkers. So are alligators, snakes, and polar bears.
>
> A stalking lion tries to make itself smaller by crouching low and keeping its head down. That way, it's less likely to be seen by a gazelle or a wildebeest. The big cat moves close only when its victim is looking the other way. Should the gazelle look up, the lion freezes in its tracks. When it's near enough, the lion will dash toward its quarry at full speed and jump on its back or knock it down with a huge swipe of its paw" (Baskin-Salzberg & Salzberg, 1991, p. 45).

"The Chase"

> When your food can run, fly, or swim away from you, you'd better be pretty fast yourself. And predators who chase their prey are fast, though they may lie in wait or stalk prey until they are within chasing range" (Baskin-Salzberg & Salzberg, 1991, p. 46–47).

After reading, ask the children to summarize the key idea of the text or to compare and contrast the three ways predators attack their prey and how each way might be represented in dance.

A final example of a way to use a children's book is via a text that is both a story and provides information. The book titled *Flash, Crash, Rumble, and Roll* (Branley & Kelley, 1999) describes and illustrates cumulus clouds developing into thunderheads, rain falling, and then lightning and thunder. The story matches the structure of the dance lesson "The Thunderstorm," and the illustrations show the curved clouds and zigzag pathways of lightning that are the lesson's movement themes. It is very short, and you can read it quickly at the start of the lesson. In the middle of the story, the authors describe how clouds, thunderheads, and lightning form. You could choose to teach this information during the lesson; however, we selected the information presented at the end of the book about what to do to be safe from lightning. Because this is an energetic lesson, teaching the children about safety and lightning during closure helps calm the children down and prepare to return to their classroom.

Designing Your Own Dance Lessons Based on Children's Literature

Designing dance lessons based on children's literature requires a somewhat different process than designing typical lessons in games, gymnastics, and dance. With typical lessons, you begin with the movement skill content. A children's book or poem, however, will often tell a story and provide images that require you to include multiple movement themes. Following is the five-step process that we use to design dance lessons based on children's literature (Rovegno, 2003).

1. Select the Book

We look for children's books with movements (e.g., the cat stalked the mouse; the tadpoles wiggled), movement images (e.g., the wind swirled the snow; the rain lashed the windowpanes; the house shook), or images related to movement terms (e.g., the blowfish grew bigger and bigger; people walked quickly with their heads down, looking only at the sidewalks). Books with animals often work well because animals have distinct movement patterns (e.g., hummingbirds flit; ponies prance; mice scurry). In addition, we look at the illustrations for movement images.

2. Read the Story, Examine the Illustrations, and List Possible Movements

Next, we read each page and list any possible movement content in the text and illustrations. We note the emotions of the characters and the shapes of objects illustrated. We also list events and movements that were implied but not directly described in the text. For example, one page of *In the Small, Small Pond* (Fleming, 1993) shows a heron wading and plunging its beak into the water and a frog, looking scared, jumping out of the water just seconds ahead of the heron's beak. The text reads, "lash, lunge, herons plunge." From this page, we generated the following list of movements:

Movements Illustrated and Described

- Lash: slashing movements (one of Laban's eight basic effort actions)
- Lunge and plunge: thrusting movements (one of Laban's eight basic effort actions) (see **Figure 30.7**)

Movements of Herons Not Illustrated

- Wading, stalking, and searching for prey: stepping slowly and gently, lifting knees high, and touching the water (i.e., floor) first with a toe, then with a heel, trying not to splash the water or disturb the soft bottom of the pond

3. Decide on the Structure of the Lesson and Final Dance Sequence

Similar to what happens with all lesson plans, in dance lessons, you typically decide your culminating dance sequence before

Figure 30.7 Herons plunge
Courtesy of John Dolly

you design the lesson tasks. The following are three possible lesson structures for dance lessons using children's literature:

- Read one to two pages, explore ideas in movement, read the next one to two pages, explore those ideas in movement, and so on; continue in this manner until you reach the end of the book. Final sequence: Read the book as the children perform short sequences of movement for each page.
- Divide the book into about three sections, read each section, and select one or two ideas from each section to explore in movement. Final sequence: Design a three-part sequence, and perform the sequence without reading the book.
- Read the entire book (quickly), and then explore selected ideas. Final sequence: Design individual or group sequences. Have groups show or teach their sequence to the class.

4. List Possible Movement Themes and Ways to Expand, Explore, and Refine the Performance of These Themes

Next, we list as many possible movement tasks as we can for helping children explore the movement themes for each page or section of the book. Using the Laban framework as a reference, we list exploration tasks beginning with single movement concepts, such as slashing. Then we expand concepts by combining them with other concepts from the Laban framework. For example, for herons lashing, you could include

- Slashing with different body parts
- Slashing at different levels
- Slashing while turning
- Slashing to end in pointy shapes at high, medium, and low levels

Finally, we list possible refinements to help children dance more skillfully, be aware of the feeling of the movement, or better represent their ideas about the text. **Table 30.1** illustrates

Table 30.1 Potential Movement Themes and Ways to Expand, Explore, and Refine Performance of Themes from the Lesson and Book *In the Small, Small Pond*

Book Segment	More Literal Movements Themes	More Abstract Movements: Extending and Exploring the Themes	Movement Quality to Refine
"Wiggle, jiggle, tadpoles wriggle"	Wiggle, jiggle, wriggle	Wiggling different body parts Spreading wiggle that starts with fingers and spreads through the whole body Spreading wiggle in groups of three: the wiggle starts with one person's fingers, spreads through his or her body, and then spreads to person 2 and then to person 3 Traveling while wiggling Traveling on a wiggly pathway Freezing in a wiggled shape Jiggling like Jell-O	Be sure every part of your body is wiggling. Make your wiggles fast and loose. Think about how wiggling feels in your muscles.
"Lash, lunge, herons plunge"	Lashing: slashing movements Lunging and plunging: thrusting movements Wading, stalking, and searching for prey: Stepping slowly and touching the water (i.e., floor) with a toe, then with a heel, trying not to splash or disturb the soft bottom of the pond	Slashing with different body parts Slashing at different levels Slashing while turning Slashing to end in pointy shapes at high, medium, and low levels Jumping in the air in a whirling action and landing with a stamping movement Do a slashing movement, then reach up and do a thrusting plunge, aiming directly down with your arms. End in a lunge or shape at a low level.	Step very slowly, and lift your knees high. Gently touch and then sink into the floor. Make your slashing and thrusting movements very fast and very strong. When slashing, try to use as much space as you can. When thrusting, try to move directly. Think how it feels to stalk a fish. Think how it feels inside your muscles when you move fast and strong.

Source: Fleming, D. (1993). *In the small, small pond.* New York: Henry Holt.

some of the lists used for the lesson plan correlated with *In the Small, Small Pond* (Fleming, 2003).

5. Evaluate the Ideas and Distribute Them into Lessons

Finally, we evaluate the quantity and quality of the ideas on our list and decide whether the book is worth one, two, three, or more lessons. We write the lesson plans, and ask the classroom teacher to teach the book before the dance lesson takes place. If he or she is unwilling to do so, we don't worry—we just do it ourselves.v

Summary

Dance is a culturally significant, health-related lifelong activity and, therefore, an important part of children's education. In dance, children learn to express and represent ideas and feelings. They develop their skills and understanding in the aesthetic domain and enhance their critical- and creative-thinking skills.

Dance lessons include both movement and topic themes. Topic themes inspire movement creativity and can easily be integrated with topics and books children are learning in their classroom. Thus, dance helps children learn about the world in a more holistic way.

This text was guided by the National Dance Standards and the philosophy of educational dance. Educational dance is designed for all children in school settings to meet educational goals.

Review Questions

1. How is dance a way of knowing? How can dance enhance children's understandings of concepts and vocabulary words?
2. What is aesthetic perception, and why might it be valuable as an adult in the work world?
3. Unfortunately, some school principals claim that the most important thing for children is to score well on standardized tests in math and literacy. Thus, they do not regard the arts as important. Outline an argument to support dance as an art form in school physical education.
4. What is educational dance?
5. Discuss four characteristics of dance movement that differentiate it from everyday movement.
6. What is the difference between representing and imitating or pantomiming?
7. List three benefits of integrating dance and classroom content.
8. What is the most commonly encountered pitfall in integrating dance with classroom subjects, and what questions can you ask yourself to ensure you avoid this pitfall?
9. How can you teach vocabulary during a dance lesson?
10. Find a children's book or poem that you think would be appropriate for a dance lesson. Create a list of movement themes you could use from the book and several extending and exploring tasks for each theme (see **Table 30.1** for help).

References

Allison, P. C., Pissanos, B. W., Turner, A. P., & Law, D. R. (2000). Preservice physical educators' epistemologies of skillfulness. *Journal of Teaching in Physical Education, 19*, 141–161.

Baskin-Salzberg & Salzberg, (1991). *Predators.* New York: Franklin Watts.

Branley, F. M., & Kelley, T. (1999). *Flash, Crash, Rumble, and Roll.* New York: HarperCollins.

Common Core State Standards Initiative. (2010). *Common core state standards for English language arts and literacy in history/social studies, science, and technical subjects.* Retrieved from www.corestandards.org.

Cone, S. L., & Purcell-Cone, T. (2003). Dancing, learning, creating, knowing. *Teaching Elementary Physical Education, 14*(5), 7–11.

Fleming, D. (1993). *In the small, small pond.* New York: Henry Holt.

Hall, Z., & Halpern, S. (2000). *Fall Leaves Fall.* New York: Scholastic.

Keats, E. J. (1962). *The snowy day.* New York: Puffin Books.

National Dance Association (NDA). (1994). *National standards for dance education: What every young American should know and be able to do in dance.* Reston, VA: Author.

Prelutsky, J., & Rand, T. (2004). *If not for the cat.* New York: Greenwillow Books.

Purcell-Cone, T. (2000). Off the page: Responding to children's literature through dance. *Teaching Elementary Physical Education, 11*(5), 11–34.

Rovegno, I. (2003). Children's literature and dance. *Teaching Elementary Physical Education 14*(4), 24–29.

Ruddell, R. B. (2009). *How to teach reading to elementary and middle school students: Practical ideas from highly effective teachers.* Boston: Pearson Education.

Stinson, S. (1982). Aesthetic experience in children's dance. *Journal of Physical Education, Recreation, and Dance, 53*(4), 72–74.

Umstead, E. C. (1985). History of elementary school physical education 1885–1920. In National Association for Sport and Physical Education, *The history of elementary school physical education 1885–1985* (pp. 6–17). Reston, VA: Author.

Vissicaro, P. (2004). *Studying dance cultures around the world: An introduction to multicultural dance education.* Dubuque, IO: Kendall/Hunt.

CHAPTER

31

Creative Dance Level 1

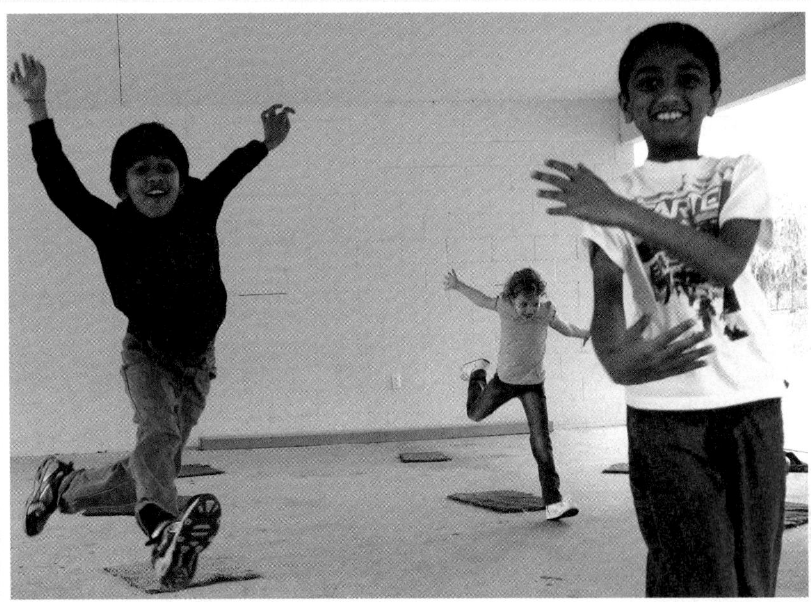

PRE-READING REFLECTION

Before reading this chapter, rate yourself on the following items. Then, after reading the chapter and after you have taught creative dance lessons in field experiences, rate yourself again.

1. How much experience have you had teaching creative dance?
   1 2 3 4 5
   None — A lot
2. How confident are you about teaching creative dance lessons to children?
   1 2 3 4 5
   Not confident at all — I am confident and ready to go!
3. How willing are you to learn to teach creative dance lessons to children?
   1 2 3 4 5
   Only if my professor forces me — Very willing
4. Do you think you could write a lesson plan for a creative dance lesson?
   1 2 3 4 5
   Not a chance — Absolutely
5. How do you think children will respond to creative dance lessons?
   1 2 3 4 5
   They will hate it. — They will love it.

OBJECTIVES

Students will learn:

1. The themes for dance lessons are derived from movement concepts from the body, effort, space, and relationship aspects of the Laban framework.
2. A strong progression for level 1 is to begin with movement concepts from body, then to address effort, then space, and finally relationships.

3. In level 2, you use a spiral progression and revisit the body, effort, space, and relationship aspects of the Laban framework but select content that is more complex.
4. Dance lessons focus on movement themes (movement concepts from the Laban framework) and topic themes.
5. Topic themes include ideas, feelings, and topics from children's literature, poetry, stories, the natural world, art, music, history, geography, and other classroom subjects.
6. Topic themes allow you to integrate dance with content children are learning in their classrooms.

KEY TERMS

Accent
Anti-gravity exertion
Complementing
Contrasting
Duration
Gallop
Heavy weight
Kinetic force
Line of symmetry
Matching
Meter
Mirroring
Rhythm
Skip
Slide
Speed
Static force
Sudden
Sustained
Swaying
Swinging
Turn
Twist

CONNECTION TO STANDARDS

This chapter focuses on content related to National Standards 1, 2, and 5. All dance content also has strong links to the Common Core and other State Standards (CCSS), and we illustrate how to meet these standards in all Sample Plans and throughout the chapter.

PROGRESSION OF CONTENT

Level 1: Introduction to Body Aspects

Motion and Stillness

- Motion, stillness, and part 1 of the stop routine
- Traveling and stopping still on a spot, focusing on feelings
- Traveling using different locomotor skills in general space and stopping
- Traveling slowly in a crowd and stopping in personal space

Sample Learning Experiences

- It's My Spot
- Travel and Freeze
- Hide and Seek in the Dark

Shapes

- Round, straight, wide, angular, twisted
- Related body actions of curling, stretching, and twisting
- Symmetrical and asymmetrical shapes
- Beginning and ending shapes and the structure of dance sequences

Sample Learning Experiences

- Make a Shape
- Moving into Shapes Quickly and Slowly
- Integrating Math Patterning and Shapes

Locomotor Skills: Skipping, Galloping, and Sliding

Sample Learning Experiences

- Teaching Sliding
- A Sliding Dance (can also be used for galloping and skipping)
- Teaching Galloping
- A Galloping Dance (can also be used for sliding and skipping)
- Teaching Skipping

Body Parts

- Exploring different ways to move and emphasize different body parts
- Exploring traveling leading with different body parts

Sample Learning Experiences

- Body Part Warm-up

Body Actions

- Twisting, turning, and spinning
  - At different levels
  - On different body parts
- Swinging and swaying
  - Individual body parts
  - Whole body
- Other body actions (e.g., wiggling, prancing, slithering, scurrying, pounding, shaking)

Figure 31.1 Progression of Content

Level 1: Introduction to Effort, Force (Kinetic, Static, Anti-gravity, Heavy), and Time (Speed, Duration, Rhythm, Accent, and Meter)

Sustained, Strong

- Strong static tension, feeling the firmness in muscles as you move slowly, exploring different actions, similes, events, and emotions

Sample Learning Experiences

- Hard as a Rock
- The Circus Clown Lifts Weights
- The Star Wars Trash Compactor
- The Tug-of-War

Sustained, Light

- Moving slowly with light kinetic and static force and light anti-gravity exertion exploring different actions, similes, events, and emotions

Sample Learning Experiences

- The Floating Hand
- The Floating Scarf

Sudden, Strong

- Moving quickly, generating and feeling strong kinetic force and firm static force

Sample Learning Experiences

- Freeze! Something Is Coming!
- The Mad, Mad Child
- Popcorn

Sudden, Light

- Moving quickly with light kinetic force and instantly stopping, holding positions with light static force and light, anti-gravity exertions
- Traveling with locomotor skills, such as skipping, while gesturing, making light, sudden gestures with the hands

Sample Learning Experiences

- The Fly on the Countertop
- The Campfire

Sustained, Heavy

- Moving slowly with minimal kinetic force and static tension in the muscles

Sample Learning Experiences

- The Tired, Bored Child

Sudden, Heavy

- Exploring fast sudden movement with minimal tension in the muscles, which feel heavy and limp

Sample Learning Experiences

- Cooked Spaghetti Arms
- The Ice Cream Cone

Level 1: Introduction to Space

Personal and General Space

- Exploring all areas of personal space
- Learning the limits of their and others' personal space while traveling in general space

Sample Learning Experiences

- Introducing Personal and General Space Using Spots for Younger Children
- Introducing Personal and General Space to Older Children

Levels

- Exploring shapes at high, medium, and low levels
- Exploring moving to different levels
- Changing levels during sequences to add contrast and interest

Pathways

- Exploring traveling on straight, curved, zigzag, and twisted pathways on the floor
- Exploring moving different body parts or equipment on straight, curved, zigzag, and twisted pathways in the air

Sample Learning Experiences

- Mud on the Kitchen Floor: Introducing Pathways
- The Name Dance

Directions

- Traveling using different locomotor skills in different directions (forward, backwards, sideways, and diagonally)
- Exploring gesturing and moving different body parts in different directions

Sample Learning Experiences

- The Haunted House

Level 1: Introduction to Relationships

Copying

- Copying a partner's shape
- Copying a partner's motor skill, pathway, direction, speed, or level

Sample Learning Experiences

- Cat and Copy Cat

Matching, Mirroring, Contrasting, and Complementing

- Matching, mirroring, contrasting, and complementing a partner's shape
- Matching a partner's motor skill, pathway, direction, speed, or level
- Contrasting a partner's motor skill, level, speed, or direction
- Complementing a partners motor skill, level, or pathway

Sample Learning Experiences

- Introducing Matching, Mirroring, Contrasting, and Complementing Shapes

Figure 31.1 Progression of Content (*continued*)

Progression in Dance

In this chapter, we describe creative dance content. We organize the content themes in a spiral progression, which is a simplified version of Preston-Dunlop's (1980) adaptation of Laban's (1948) original theme progression for dance.

In level 1, we begin with body themes, followed by effort, space, and relationship themes. When we move into level 2, we spiral around to body, effort, space, and relationship themes again, but this time addressing them at a more complex and difficult level. **Figure 31.2** illustrates this spiral progression.

In general, level 1 themes are appropriate for the lower elementary grades, and level 2 themes are geared toward the upper grades. Progression of dance content differs from that seen in gymnastics or games, however. In games and gymnastics, a particular progression is often essential for children's successful learning and safety. In dance, more leeway is permitted because you can modify many creative dance lessons to accommodate students with a wide range of abilities and experiences. We use the following guidelines to modify dance lessons for younger and older children.

Guidelines for Modifying Dance Lessons for Younger and Older Children

Younger Children

- Focus first on movement concepts from the body aspect of the Laban framework (e.g., locomotor skills, shape) before children work on combining body movement concepts with movement concepts from the effort, space, and relationship aspects.
- Limit the number of movement concepts you teach in one lesson.
- Keep the topic of the dance or the ideas the children are representing concrete and familiar to them.
- Keep formations and organizational patterns simple.
- Scaffold exploration.
- Call out the sequence of movements when children perform their dances.
- Focus on individual exploration of ideas. Limit partner work to copying and making simple decisions together.
- Talk more often, but give only small chunks of information each time you talk.

Older Children

- Extend the amount of time allocated to children for exploring movements and ideas.
- Include partner and small-group work in which children design their own dances.
- Include several parts and multiple movement concepts in dance sequences.
- Work on several movement concepts at the same time (e.g., stretching and curling to move to different levels, sometimes using strong force and sometimes using light force).
- Include more abstract and complex topic themes.

To help you understand how to modify dance lessons for different age groups, we have written two lessons that develop similar movement and topic themes. The lesson titled "The Thunderstorm" (**Sample Plan 31.6**) is for younger children. It focuses on traveling slowly and lightly on curved pathways while making round shapes, representing cumulus and then thunderhead clouds, traveling quickly on zigzag pathways, and then making strong, sharp, angular shapes representing lightning. By comparison, there is a lesson titled "Shelter in a Storm" that is appropriate for older children. Like "The Thunderstorm" lesson, it focuses on curved and zigzag pathways, round and angular shapes, and soft and strong effort qualities. However, it also includes meeting and parting with a partner, relating to a partner's shape, and exploring ways to represent the emotions of seeking and finding shelter in a storm, which are far more complex.

Should I Do Different Dance Lessons for Each Grade?

Yes, if it is possible within the constraints of your schedule. This kind of plan leads to the development of the children's skills and knowledge in a spiral progression. An additional benefit is that teachers can plan something special for each grade level. For example, fourth grade might be the year when children study

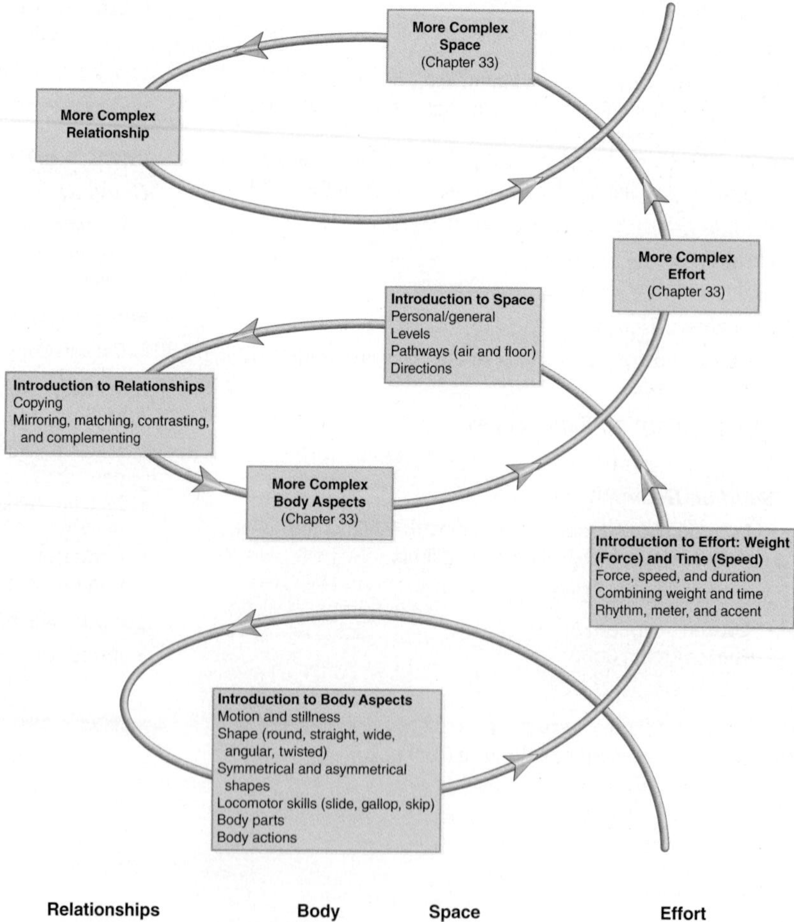

Figure 31.2 The Spiral Progression in Dance

FYI

Sample Plans in this Chapter

1. Movement Theme: Locomotor Skills and Body Actions

   Topic Theme: Animals Dancing

   Text: Mitton & Parker-Rees (2001). *Down by the Cool of the Pool*
2. Movement Theme: Shape (Symmetrical, Asymmetrical, Thin, Wide, Round, Twisted, Pointy), Swinging and Swaying

   Topic Theme: When Autumn Leaves Fall

   Text: Hall & Halpern (2000). *Fall Leaves Fall!*
3. Movement Theme: Shapes, Body Actions, and Pathways

   Topic Theme: The Snowy Dan

   Text: Keats (1962). *The Snowy Day*
4. Movement Theme: Effort: Light/Sudden, Light/Sustained, Heavy/Sudden, Heavy/Sustained, Strong/Sustained

   Topic Theme: The Summer Vacation
5. Movement Theme: Force and Speed

   Topic Theme: Animal Haiku

   Text: Prelutsky & Rand (2004.) *If Not for the Cat*
6. Movement Theme: Curved and Angular Pathways, Strong and Soft Force

   Topic Theme: The Thunderstorm

   Text: Branley & Kelley (1999). *Flash, Crash, Rumble, and Roll*
7. Movement Theme: Introducing Levels

   Topic Theme: Streamers

   Text: Thorpe & Roper (2000). *Follow the Lemming*
8. Movement Theme: Body Actions and Pathways

   Topic Theme: In the Small, Small Pond

   Text: Fleming (1993). *In the Small, Small Pond*

Native American cultures in social studies; the corresponding "special" unit in physical education might be to learn Native American dances and have an end-of-the-year pow-wow that the children perform for their peers or parents. Children enjoy looking forward to "things they get to do when they get bigger."

In some schools, teachers teach two or more classes from mixed grade levels at the same time. Consequently, these teachers will not be able to reserve separate lessons for separate grade levels. In addition, beginning teachers might be overwhelmed with planning and not have time to design different dance lessons for each grade. In these situations, teachers can set up a rotation of lessons and modify the lesson for each grade level using the guidelines given previously. **Table 31.1** compares a grade-level schedule and a rotating schedule using lessons (from this text) based on children's books.

Do Level 1 Lessons Work for Older Beginners?

When a teacher is new to a school and the previous teacher did not teach dance, children in the upper elementary grades are likely to be beginners in dance and consequently need to learn content in themes from level 1 body, effort, space, and relationship aspects. However, they are also more mature socially and cognitively. Thus, lessons from level 1 that will delight younger children might not be as effective with older children.

Table 31.1 Comparing a Grade-Level Schedule and a Rotating Schedule

Lesson Based on Book	Grade-Level Schedule	Rotating Schedule
In the Small, Small Pond	Kindergarten	Year A, grades K–2
The Snowy Day	First grade	Year B, grades K–2
If Not for the Cat	Second grade	Year C, grades K–2

We suggest two approaches. First, you can modify lessons from level 1 themes to include more sophisticated ways of approaching the topic theme, much in the way that we modified the level 1 "The Thunderstorm" lesson (clouds, thunder, lightning, and rain) to become a far more sophisticated lesson called "Shelter in the Storm" in level 2.

Second, you can do the reverse and simplify the movement themes of lessons from level 2. For example, there is a level 2 "Sport Tableaux" lesson that works very well with beginning fifth-grade students because it uses a comfortable topic—that is, sport—and the children design a dance in small groups. In general, fifth-grade children enjoy working in groups. The teacher can simplify the level 2 lesson on the theme of shape and teach the content across several lessons. Thus, the fifth-grade students can learn about shapes, which teachers typically introduce in the younger grades, in a lesson designed for their more mature social and cognitive levels of development.

Introduction to the Subject Matter of Level 1 Children's Dance

In this next section, we describe the subject matter of children's dance, beginning with body aspects and progressing through relationship aspects. Knowing your subject matter will help you be a better teacher. Research on expert teachers suggests that because they have strong subject matter knowledge, experts are better able to respond on their feet to children's ideas during creative dance, thus enriching the children's creativity and their understanding of the dance movements and topics of their dances (Chen & Cone, 2003).

To help you understand dance content, we describe sample learning experiences to help you imagine what this content might look like if taught in the school setting. At the end of the chapter, we provide detailed, annotated lesson and unit segments, which will help you understand how to combine these learning experiences into lessons and units. Although lesson and unit segments have been "child-tested" across many different settings, we have not taught them in *your* setting. Based on your knowledge of the content, you will be able to modify the lessons to best meet the needs of your children.

We also suggest ideas that you can use for designing your own lesson plans. Although designing dance lessons can be challenging, it can also be fun. Likewise, it is necessary when working with classroom teachers to integrate what children are learning in the classroom with what they are learning in physical education.

Level 1: Introduction to Body Aspects

Motion and Stillness

Have you ever wondered what to teach on the first day of school to kindergarteners? The two most basic and important themes for teaching young children are motion and stillness (from the body aspect of the Laban framework) and general and personal space (from the space aspect). One reason these themes are essential is safety. Children need to learn to travel about the gym safely, without bumping into other children, and to stop safely, without falling down.

The Stop Routine

The first content we teach children is how to stop. We have the children walk in a scattered formation about the gym and then stop on command from the teacher. We then have them focus on the feeling of motion and stillness. The stop routine is a necessary management routine for teaching physical education that you need to teach at the start of the school year.

You can introduce motion, stillness, and the stop routine in a games or gymnastics lesson. However, a dance lesson is an excellent opportunity for introducing this content and

SAMPLE LEARNING EXPERIENCES 31.1

Motion and Stillness

Potential Refinements

- Try to feel the stillness inside your whole body.
- Feel the stillness in your arms, hands, neck, tummy, legs, spine, and so on.
- Feel frozen, immobile, restricted.
- Even if you are still, feel alert, alive, ready to move.

It's My Spot

Set plastic spots in a scattered pattern about the gym with spots equidistant to each other ensuring that if a child stands on a spot, he or she can't touch another child. When the children enter the gym, assign them a spot. Have at least five more spots than children.

Kindergarteners standing on poly spots arranged in a scattered formation

Traveling Around the Spot and Stillness

I When I shake my tambourine, walk around your spot staying close to it like this [Demonstrate]. When the tambourine stops and I say, "Stop," stop and stand on your spot, remaining perfectly still. [Repeat several times.]

R Try to feel the stillness inside your whole body. [Repeat refinements throughout.]

E Now we will so the same thing, but this time I won't say "Stop." You have to listen carefully to the tambourine and stop the instant you don't hear it shaking. [Repeat several times.]

E Now do the same thing, but this time I will beat the tambourine. Listen for when the beat stops. [Repeat several times.]

E This time you can move in different ways around your spot. You can jump or hop to travel on your feet in different ways. When you stop, be very still. [Repeat several times.]

Traveling in a scattered formation

SAMPLE LEARNING EXPERIENCES 31.1

Motion and Stillness (*continued*)

R Tell me how you feel when you move and how you feel when you are standing still on the spot. How do movement and stillness feel different? [Various answers.] Let's try it again and this time, really concentrating on how movement and stillness feel.

Touching the Spot with Different Body Parts

Notes: This section illustrates scaffolding exploration for young children.

E This time when you stop, touch one part of your body to the spot. Watch me. I am jumping around my spot, the tambourines stops, and I put my hand on the spot. Everyone try that.

Traveling and stopping, touching different body parts to spots

R Feel the stillness in your arms, hands, neck, tummy, legs, spine, and so on. [Repeat refinements.]

E This time, let's pick a different body part—try your elbow.

E Now, try one foot. Feel the stillness.

E Now try your bottom. Now try your knee.

E This time, you select which body part you touch to the spot. You can choose any part you want, but you must be able to hold your position perfectly still. [Repeat several times; call out which body parts you see children touching to the spot.]

[If you are using these learning experiences to teach the stop routine, you can now teach **Sample Learning Experiences 31.11** on general and personal space. Children need to understand how to move within the limits of their personal space and how to move in general space before you teach the following lesson segments.]

Travel and Freeze

R Hold a still position, and concentrate on how your body feels from the inside. How do your legs feel? Your arms? How does it feel inside your chest and belly? Your head and neck?

E Walk about the gym, and stop the instant I say, "Stop." Go. [Wait no more than two seconds.] Freeze. [Repeat several times.]

R Feel frozen like an ice cube. [Repeat throughout.]

E Now I am going to let you walk a little bit longer. When you walk, you are not to touch or bump into any other child. You may walk anywhere in general space as long as you do not walk in someone else's personal space. Go. [Watch carefully for any bumping, and stop the children instantly if any is about to occur.] Freeze. [Repeat several times.]

R This time, think about how it feels to be moving and how it feels to be frozen still. Go. Stop. [Repeat.] Let's talk about the differences. How does it feel to be frozen still? Moving?

E Now travel about general space anyway you want. You can skip, hop, gallop, jump, or walk. Keep concentrating on how it feels inside to move and freeze. Go. Freeze. [Repeat several times.]

Hide and Seek in the Dark

I When I say, "Go," walk about the space in a scattered organization, making sure you don't touch or get close to anyone else. Stop still, and pay attention to how the stillness feels. [Repeat several times.]

R Even if you are still, feel alert, alive, and ready to move. [Repeat throughout.]

E Now we will try something more difficult. Come in closer, hold your arms at your sides, and walk about one another without touching. Walk slowly so you can avoid touching anyone else.

R Stop still. Feel the stillness in your arms, tummy, legs, and fingers. [Repeat several times.]

(*continues*)

SAMPLE LEARNING EXPERIENCES 31.1

Motion and Stillness (*continued*)

E Instead of me telling you when to move and when to stop, you decide. You can stop and hold a still position as long as you want and start moving again when you want. Go.

E Have you ever played hide and seek in the dark, and while you were hiding and staying still, the seeker walked right by you and didn't know you were there? That's the feeling I want you to get. As you are still, notice how it feels to be still and have someone walk by you and not see you. [Repeat several times.]

teaching the stop routine for several reasons. First, dance does not require equipment. In the beginning of the school year when teachers teach their rules and routines, it is easier for children to focus on moving and stopping their bodies without also having to think about moving and stopping equipment, such as a ball.

Second, dance focuses on the feeling of movement from the inside. Having children concentrate on moving and stopping and how these sensations feel inside their muscles, therefore, can help them not only learn how to control their movements, but also learn the difference between ordinary movement and dance. As Stinson (1982) explained, one simple way to teach children what makes movement become dance movement is to teach them to recognize when they are dancing and when they are not. Dancing feels different because children are highly aware of how the movement feels and of the shape of their bodies. Focusing on how the body feels in motion and stillness can be an aesthetic experience for children—one of our goals in dance, meeting National Standard 5.

You can combine the sample learning experiences below into one lesson. In addition, you can repeat each part as an introductory activity for other lessons throughout the year to reinforce the routine of stopping on the teacher's command.

Shape and the Related Body Actions of Curling, Stretching, and Twisting

Shape is also one of the most basic movement concepts of dance. As discussed, having a heightened awareness of the shape of the body is part of what turns movement into full-fledged dance (Stinson, 1982). The shape of the body is one way the dancer expresses feelings and ideas.

There are five basic shapes: round, straight, wide, twisted, and angular. Helping children explore many variations of each basic shape is important because these variations then become part of the children's movement vocabulary. Children use their movement vocabulary to express and communicate their ideas in dance in the same way that they use words to express and communicate their ideas when they speak and write.

Teachers typically include the related body actions in lessons focused on shape. For example, when you have children make a sharp, angular shape, you include a sharp, angular body action to create that shape. Similarly, twisted shapes require a twisting movement. A curling movement results in a round shape. Stretching wide results in a wide shape, and stretching tall results in a straight shape.

Round Shapes, Curling Movements

Other labels for round shapes include ball-like, curved, curled, circular, and curling movements (see **Figure 31.3**). Children create curled shapes by rounding the spine forward or sideways or arching the back. They bend their elbows slightly, giving the impression of a curved arm. They bend their knees—sometimes even keeping the knees tucked tight against the tummy. Round shapes work well with gentle, flowing, sustained movements. Curling movements can lower the body because the knees and back bend to produce a round shape.

Straight Shapes, Stretching Tall

Other labels for straight shapes include pin-like, pencil-like, narrow, and stretching tall (see **Figure 31.4**). Straight shapes have fewer variations than the other four shapes because they are not only straight but also narrow. Children can vary straight shapes most easily by changing the shape of the arms or one leg while keeping the sense of narrowness. Stretching tall and reaching for the sky creates a straight shape. Straight shapes work well with walking and other locomotor skills and are particularly effective when combined with traveling on straight pathways.

Wide Shapes, Stretching Wide

Other labels for wide shapes include wall-like, extended, big, and stretching movements (see **Figure 31.5**). Wide shapes are associated with wide, stretching movements. To explore the idea of wide shapes, children can explore the contrast between stretching to a big, wide shape with moving to narrow, straight shapes or curling into small, round shapes. Jumping and leaping, making stretched, wide shapes in the air, is another excellent task to explore.

Angular Shapes, Angular Movements

Other labels for angular shapes include pointy, sharp, jutting, jagged, and angular movements (see **Figure 31.6**). Children can create angular shapes with tightly bent elbows and knees or

Figure 31.3 Exploring a variety of curled shapes

Figure 31.4 Exploring moving into different straight shapes

(left) © Jones & Bartlett Learning. Photographed by Christine Myaskovsky. (right) © Jones & Bartlett Learning. Photographed by Sarah Cebulski.

Figure 31.5 Exploring stretching into a variety of wide shapes

© Jones & Bartlett Learning. Photographed by Christine Myaskovsky.

by pointing their arms and legs in different directions in space. Angular shapes come from angular movements done quickly with strong force or slowly with strong tension. Lessons on angular shapes work well with angular pathways on the floor and jumping in the air.

Figure 31.6 Exploring moving into a variety of angular shapes

(left) Courtesy of John Dolly; (right) © Jones & Bartlett Learning. Photographed by Christine Myaskovsky.

Twisted Shapes, Twisting Movement

Twisted shapes occur when one part of the body or a body segment faces one direction while another part or segment faces another direction (see **Figure 31.7**). For example, twisting at the waist causes the hips to face one way and the shoulders to face in the other direction. The legs can twist and twine around each other, arms and wrists can twist, and the head can twist at the neck. Twisted shapes come from twisting movements—the two go together, and you can easily teach them at the same time.

Symmetrical and Asymmetrical Shapes

In addition to the five basic shapes, there are two kinds of shapes: symmetrical and asymmetrical. Symmetrical means that the shapes (i.e., the positions of body parts) of the left and right sides of the body are the same. With asymmetrical shapes, the two halves of the body are different, thus offering a wider variety of options.

Symmetry and asymmetry in dance also can refer to actions, pathways, and formations. Symmetrical actions are movements that are the same on both sides of the body or actions that are repeated on one side and then the other—for example, a punch and a kick to the left, followed by a punch and a kick to the right. Asymmetry offers far more options, as the body can twist, turn, travel to one side, lead with different body parts, and move in several directions without repetition. Symmetrical pathways and formations include circles, horizontal lines, Vs, Xs, and figure 8s. There is a host of asymmetrical pathways and formations, most of which do not have names.

Choreographer Doris Humphrey (1959), who was one of the first authors to describe a theory of composition, wrote that symmetry suggests stability, balance, security, serenity, comfort, calmness, and rest. Rituals often rely on symmetry. Humphrey suggested that symmetry be used infrequently and judiciously, as it can be boring, predictable, and lifeless. By comparison, asymmetry suggests excitement, stimulation, unpredictability, freedom,

Figure 31.7 Exploring twisting into a variety of twisted shapes

passion, energy, and vitality. It leads to movement that can flow gently along unending curved lines or can zigzag on tormented, anxious pathways. Because it is unpredictable, asymmetry keeps the viewer's interest.

Combining Locomotor Skills and Other Movement Concepts with Shapes

Once children understand shapes and moving into shapes with their related actions, you can extend the content to combining shapes with other movement concepts and locomotor skills. The following are suggestions to get you started in designing your own combinations.

Combining Shapes and Locomotor Skills

- Explore different starting shapes, moving using different locomotor skills, and then ending in different shapes. (For example, start in a twisted shape, travel by jumping, and end in a curled shape.)

Combining Shapes and Traveling on Different Pathways

- Explore matching the starting shape, the pathway, and the ending shape. (For example, find a starting curled shape, travel on a curved pathway, and end in a curled shape.)
- Explore contrasting the shape with the pathway.

Combining Shapes and Levels

- Explore making different shapes at different levels. (For example, explore making curled shapes at a low level, then high level, and then medium level.) [The teacher calls out the level.]

Beginning and Ending Shapes and the Structure of Dance Sequences

The final important concept to teach children about shape is that dance sequences begin and end with a still shape. For young children, the structure of dance sequences is as follows:

- Beginning: Hold a starting still shape that tells the audience, "My dance is about to begin."
- Middle: Perform locomotor steps (e.g., skip, gallop, slide, hop, jump) and/or movements (e.g., stretch, curl, twist).
- End: Hold a still shape that tells the audience, "My dance has ended."

Ideas for Extending Movement Variety and Vocabulary

The following list of actions, events, objects, and emotions can be used as a basis for designing lessons on shape movement concepts that will not only extend children's movement vocabulary, but also help them meet CCSS for vocabulary acquisition. For example, you could design a dance lesson based on things associated with winter in the north after a snowstorm and teach the following vocabulary words: drift, drifting, icicles, bounding, fort, and stockpile. You could start by having the children explore the straight shapes of icicles, the angular shapes of snowflakes, the curved shapes of snow drifts, and the curved pathways and gentle movements of snowflakes drifting down. The children could then explore the movements and dance the story of a husky dog who loves staying outside in the cold, curled up sleeping peacefully as if she were in a den. She wakes up covered with snow, shakes herself free, and bounds across the yard with joy, making pathways in the snow. The children in her family come out to play, and they build a fort and stockpile snowballs for their planned battle. The battle begins, and the husky jumps and twists, trying to catch the snowballs in her teeth. The day ends with tired, happy children and their dog curling up in their beds.

Round Shapes, Curling Movements

- Curved letters
- Balls, clouds, balloons, bubbles, rocks
- Animals curled up in protective dens
- Animals with round shapes
- Curved shapes expressing softness, caring, and soothing emotions, like a mother cradling a baby in her arms
- Curling up into a tight ball with fright
- Sinking and curling up with sadness
- Curled up on the floor with loneliness, closed off from others
- Curled up sleeping peacefully

Straight Shapes, Stretching Movements

- Straight letters
- Marching toy soldiers
- Skyscrapers, monuments (e.g., Seattle Space Needle, Washington Monument)
- Forests
- Straight shapes representing balance and calmness
- Straight tall shapes expressing feeling stately, upright, or proud
- Straight shapes representing stiff, starched people or objects

Wide Shapes, Stretching Movements

- Leaves
- Gingerbread people
- Stars
- Walls
- Stretching wide to express freedom, joy, openness, and welcome

Angular Shapes, Angular Movements

- Angular letters
- Snowflakes
- Leaves
- Machines and machine-like movements
- Angular shapes and movements expressing anger, power, strength, and fighting

Twisted Shapes, Twisting Movements

- Gnarled, old tree
- Knots
- Washing machine actions
- Halloween witches and goblins
- Monsters
- Twisting and twisted shapes expressing anguish, tension, and worry
- Twisting and twisted shapes representing something that is coiled (like a snake), haunted, or contorted

Integrating Shapes with Classroom Content

Shapes provide an excellent opportunity for integrating physical education content with classroom content in the lower elementary grades. Teachers can ask children to identify letters and parts of letters that are curved, straight, and angular. Dance learning experiences can include having children travel on pathways writing letters and words. You can integrate lessons on symmetry and asymmetry with mathematics. In basic geometry, children study whether shapes such as squares, circles, different triangles, rectangles, and hexagons are symmetrical or asymmetrical. In mathematics, they learn about the **line of symmetry**, usually shown as a dotted line. Children use the line of symmetry to make a judgment about whether a shape is symmetrical or asymmetrical. In a human, if the line of symmetry is vertical, the body is symmetrical. In contrast, if the line of symmetry is placed at the belt, splitting the body horizontally, there is no symmetry.

Children also learn about congruent shapes in mathematics. When shapes are congruent, they are the same shape and the same size. In dance, we can translate congruent shapes to mean you can make congruent shapes only with someone who is approximately the same size as you.

SAMPLE LEARNING EXPERIENCES 31.2

Shape

Potential Refinements

We based these cues on the tendency of beginners to make shapes with only part of their bodies:

- Make your whole body round.
- Make your head and neck extend the curved line of your back in curled shapes.
- Really stretch through your spine.
- Make sure your legs and torso are part of your angular shape; don't use just your arms.
- Really twist all your body parts; feel the tension as part of you faces one direction, and another part faces another direction.
- Feel the wide stretch throughout your whole body in your wide shapes.

Make a Shape

In these experiences, we illustrate how to teach CCSS for vocabulary acquisition by briefly defining key words before and during the lesson and closing the lesson with discussion questions to reinforce an understanding of the vocabulary.

Teacher Calls Out a Shape, and Children Respond

Cog K There are different kinds of shapes you can make with your body. [Teach all five shapes (including angular shapes) if you are working with older beginners and three shapes if the class consists of kindergarteners.]

I Where you are sitting, curl up like a ball. [Demonstrate as you talk. If you teach outside, make these shapes while standing on your feet.] This is a round shape. When you make a round shape, all the parts of your body should be in curved positions. The overall appearance of your body is curved. The second shape is a straight shape. Stand up, and make your body look like a pencil. In straight shapes, most of your body parts are straight, but some can be bent if that bend contributes to the overall appearance of being straight and narrow. For example, reach one arm over your head, bend the

(continues)

SAMPLE LEARNING EXPERIENCES 31.2

Shape (*continued*)

other so your palm touches your cheek and your bent arm and elbow are touching your body. Your overall appearance is straight and narrow. Now, make your body look like a star by stretching your arms and legs out. This is a wide shape in which the overall appearance is stretched and big from one side to the other. Let's practice these shapes. Make a round ball shape; now make a straight pencil shape; now make a wide star shape. [Repeat, but mix up the order.]

E The last shape we will work on today is a twisted shape. Plant your feet firmly on the ground with your arms stretched out like a T. Now, twist at the waist, as I am doing. Now, twist your arms into an interesting shape.

Cog K This is a twisted shape. Twisted means that part of your body faces one way, and another part faces the other way.

E Try to make a different twisted shape. Now make another twisted shape.

R Twist all of your body parts, feel the tension as part of you faces one direction, and another part faces another. [Repeat throughout.]

E This time, try to twist your arms around each other and your legs around each other. Make your fingers twisted, too, and twist your head around. Your whole body is twisted, and your shapes are very interesting.

E Let's try to make interesting curled shapes. Make a round shape. Now another one. Now a different one.

Cog K How did you make your curled shapes interesting? Yes, you changed the positions of your arms and legs and you curved your back in different ways.

E Now try to make a different, interesting wide shape. Feel the wide stretch throughout your whole body.

E Now make a different interesting straight shape. Now a wide shape. Now a straight shape. Try to make a different wide shape and a different straight shape each time.

Sequence of Shapes

E Let's put together a sequence. Pick your favorite curled shape as your starting shape. Now move to your favorite wide shape. Now do your favorite straight shape, and end with your favorite twisted shape. [Repeat several times until the children can do the same four shapes each time. With younger children, select only three shapes.]

Transitions

E Now we will work on the transition between your shapes. Start in your curled shape. As I count to 3, slowly move to your wide shape. Pause, and then as I count to 3, slowly move to your straight shape and then your twisted shape. Let's practice your dances again. Really try to move slowly for the full three counts. If you move quickly, you will get to your new shape before I finish counting.

Three Options for Closure to Meet CCSS

With your assigned partner,

- Select one shape and define that shape.
- Contrast a wide and curled shape.
- Decide and give reasons for which of the following shapes can be combined:
  - Curled and twisted [yes]
  - Wide and twisted [yes]
  - Straight and curled [no]
  - Straight and wide [no]

Moving into Shapes Quickly and Slowly and at a Medium Speed

For younger children, choose three shapes. These learning experiences can also be adapted to symmetrical and asymmetrical shapes.

Fast Speed

Cog K Today, we are going to be moving into different shapes at different speeds. This means that sometimes you will move quickly into a shape, sometimes slowly, and sometimes at a medium speed.

I We will start with a fast speed. Each time I beat the tambourine, make a different twisted shape. Then hold the shape until I beat the tambourine again. [Repeat at least five times.]

Alternating Shapes, Fast Speed

E Now explore different round and wide shapes. Start in a round shape, and when I beat the tambourine, quickly move to a wide shape. Then alternate round, wide, round, wide. Try to do a different shape every time. [Repeat several times.]

E Now alternate twisted and straight shapes each time I beat the tambourine.

SAMPLE LEARNING EXPERIENCES 31.2

Shape (*continued*)

Alternating Shapes, Medium Speed

E We are going to change the speed to medium. Start in a round shape. As I beat the tambourine two counts, stretch to a straight shape. Take the full two counts to move from curled to straight. Then reverse, and take two counts to move back to a different curled shape. Alternate making round and straight shapes to a two-count beat, trying to come up with different and interesting shapes each time.

E Still moving at a two-count medium speed, alternate wide and twisted shapes. Try very hard to move the entire two counts and not get to your final shape until the last beat.

Sequence of Shapes, Slow Speed

E Select your four favorite shapes. This time I want you to move slowly from shape 1 to shape 2 to shape 3 to shape 4. I will beat a four-count phrase. It should take you the full four counts to move from one shape to the next. [Repeat several times until the children have their sequence memorized. With younger children, you might need to establish the order and call out the shapes—for example, Start twisted. Slowly move to a wide shape—1, 2, 3, 4. Now slowly move to a curled shape—1, 2, 3, 4. Now move to a straight shape—1, 2, 3, 4.]

E Now try your sequence, but don't even pause in your shape; just continue moving to the next shape.

Changing the Speed

E Now let's explore having a change of speed. Explore different ways to slowly move into a round shape, and then quickly stretch to a wide shape. Ready. Slowly curl—1, 2, 3, 4. [Beat the tambourine.] Now quickly stretch wide. [Strongly beat the tambourine once.] [Repeat several times.]

E [Repeat the task using different combinations and different orders of round, wide, twisted, angular, and straight shapes.]

Design a Sequence

A Now, design your own dance sequence with four different shapes and at least one fast movement and one very slow movement.

Integrating Math Patterning and Shapes

Symmetry, asymmetry, and patterning (i.e., different ways to sequence items) are important math concepts. These learning experiences combine all these ideas. After teaching children about symmetrical and asymmetrical shapes, give each pair four cones—two small and two medium-sized. (This lesson idea can also be adapted to focus on other shapes and other movement concepts.)

I Working with your partner, put your cones in a straight line in any pattern. You can do small, large, small, large, for example, or maybe small, large, large, small, or any pattern you want. [Demonstrate placing cones in a line, approximately five feet apart.]

CCSS You have studied symmetry and asymmetry in mathematics. Describe how you know if a shape is symmetrical. How do you know if a shape is asymmetrical?

E Now, working on your own, on either side of your cones, make a symmetrical shape next to the small cones, travel any way you want, and make an asymmetrical shape next to the large cones.

E Repeat your pattern, trying to make a smooth transition between the traveling movements and the shapes.

E Now, change the pattern of your cones, and try a new dance pattern. Keep making the symmetrical shape next to the small cone and the asymmetrical shape next to the large cone. Try to explore as many different symmetrical and asymmetrical shapes as you can.

E Discuss with your partner which pattern of cones you want for your final dance sequence. Then, make up your own dance sequence.

Social Share this decision, and be sure to listen to your partner's opinions.

This can be an opportunity to have a class discussion and demonstration of how partners can share decision making and listen to their partner's opinions.

CCSS Closure

With your assigned partner, draw three symmetrical shapes you have studied in mathematics, and give reasons why you know your shapes are symmetrical.

Locomotor Skills

The major locomotor skills used in creative dance include walking, running, galloping, skipping, sliding, and the five types of ways to get flight from feet: jumping, hopping, leaping, *assemblé* (1-2), and *sissone* (2-1).

We describe teaching jumping, hopping, leaping, *assemblé*, and *sissone* in the gymnastics chapters. In this chapter, we discuss teaching galloping, sliding, and skipping. When covering folk dance content, we discuss specific folk dance locomotor steps including the *schottische*, *chasse*, two-step, polka, grapevine, and waltz.

Skipping, sliding, and galloping all have uneven rhythms, as opposed to the even rhythm of walking and jogging. An uneven rhythm has an accent on the first step, which is longer in length and duration. The second beat is shorter and is either a step (gallop and slide) or a hop (skip).

- **Skip**: Skipping is a step-hop on one leg, followed by a step-hop on the other leg. The rhythm is uneven. The accent is on the step, which is long, followed by a short hop.
- **Gallop**: A gallop also has an uneven rhythm with an accent on the lead step. The same leg leads the entire time, and the child travels in a forward direction. The pattern is step–together–step–together. A gallop is a step on the lead foot and then a spring off that leg, bringing the back leg forward and together behind the lead leg and landing on the back leg. When a gallop is high and the legs come together in the air, dancers call it a *chassé*.
- **Slide**: The slide is the same as the gallop but travels sideways. The accent is on the lead step. The same leg leads the entire time. The rhythm is uneven. The pattern is step–together–step–together. Technically, the child steps sideways on the lead foot, closes the trailing leg to the lead leg while springing in the air and landing on the trailing foot, and then steps on the lead foot again.

Immature Movement Patterns

Our descriptions of immature movement patterns for skipping and galloping are based on research by Roberton and Halverson (1984). Children learning to skip often substitute a gallop for a skip; alternatively, they may skip on only one leg, their dominant leg, and step on their nondominant leg. In galloping, skipping, and sliding, a typical beginner pattern is to land flat-footed. Immature arm patterns are to hold the arms in the high guard position to assist in balancing or if the child falls.

As children mature, the arm action in the skip is opposition, in which the arm opposite to the lead leg swings forward. Once children can perform these locomotor skills to the stage of automaticity, they can use their arms to gesture for expressive purposes or perform actions, including catching, tossing, or manipulating equipment, such as scarves, ribbons, and wands.

Performance Techniques

The movement quality of skipping, galloping, sliding, and the five types of flight from feet in dance is most often *light, high, and resilient*, with attention being paid to aesthetically pleasing body alignment. In contrast, in track and field events, hopping, leaping, jumping, and 1–2 movements are intended to achieve distance or height. Children need many experiences to practice their locomotor skills, focusing on the movement of their feet to generate lightness and resilience.

General Potential Performance Refinements Appropriate for Skipping, Galloping, and Sliding in Dance

- Be light.
- Your legs are springs.
- Stretch tall.
- Extend through the ankles; point your feet.
- Land with resilience.

SAMPLE LEARNING EXPERIENCES 31.3
Sliding, Galloping, and Skipping

Teaching Sliding

Kindergarteners learning to slide around a hoop

(We thank Donna Stewart of Lecanto Primary School, Lecanto, Florida, for her ideas about teaching sliding.)

I [Each child with a hoop in scattered locations.] Each of you stands with your toes on your hula hoop, facing the center of the hoop. Take a step to the side with one foot.

SAMPLE LEARNING EXPERIENCES 31.3

Sliding, Galloping, and Skipping (*continued*)

Cog K We call this your lead leg. Then bring your other leg next to your lead leg. We call this leg your trail leg because it trails behind your lead leg.

E Keep stepping around your hoop, leading with your lead leg and then bringing your trail leg close together to your lead leg. The pattern is step, together, step, together. [Demonstrate.]

E Try the same thing around your hoop but not standing on your hoop. [Demonstrate.]

E Now, do it faster. [Demonstrate.] We call this locomotor pattern *sliding.* [Beat an uneven rhythm on a hand drum, with the strong accent on the lead step.]

E If you feel confident sliding, try sliding to another hoop, and slide around that hoop. If someone is using a hoop, go to a free hoop.

E This time when you slide, you may go faster, but you must remain in control.

Social If you bump into someone, you were going too fast. Only go as fast as you can go safely.

Changing the Lead Leg

Org [Class at one end of the physical education space.]

E When you slide, you can lead with either foot. We are going to slide to the other side of the space, leading with your right leg. Don't slide into the wall; stop on the red line that is about five feet away from the wall [or set up cones so children have an overflow area in case they miscalculate when to stop]. [Demonstrate.] Go.

E Now let's slide back, this time leading with the left leg.

E This time, when I make a big beat of the drum, change directions by changing lead legs. [Demonstrate.]

Th This is even harder. I know you like a challenge. When you challenge yourself, you will learn more.

E This time, slide across the space, and when I make a big beat of the drum, turn and change lead legs, continuing over to the other side of the gym. [Demonstrate.]

Kindergartners practicing sliding on a line

A Sliding Dance

[You also can use the following tasks with galloping and skipping.]

Adding Rhythm Sticks

[You can also add music your children enjoy.]

E Tap your sticks four times and then slide for four counts. [Repeat several times.]

E Explore different ways to tap your sticks:

- Changing levels
- Moving in different areas of personal space
- Tapping in the air without touching the sticks

E [For second- and third-grades] Make up a tapping and sliding dance with a starting shape, four taps, four slides, four taps, four slides, and an ending shape.

(*continues*)

SAMPLE LEARNING EXPERIENCES 31.3

Sliding, Galloping, and Skipping (*continued*)

Teaching Galloping

To teach galloping, start by teaching sliding (see the preceding Learning Experiences), and then extend the task to galloping.

Cog K Now that you can slide, you can do another skill we call *galloping*. Galloping is the same as sliding, but you travel facing forward. You still lead with one foot the entire time. It is like a horse race where your lead leg is in front and the back leg catches up, but the lead horse spurts ahead again to remain the lead horse.

I Slide, and then turn to move forward and do a gallop.

E Now try galloping leading with the other leg.

Kindergarteners learning to gallop

The Story of Fred and Sally

Here is another way to teach galloping we learned from Robin Litaker of Hoover, Alabama. This story helps children learn to gallop and remember that in a gallop, the same foot leads.

When You Gallop, the Same Foot Leads

There was a kindergarten boy named Fred. Everyone liked Fred because he was kind to everyone and always cheerful and happy. But Sally liked Fred so much she had a crush on him. One day during recess, Sally tried to give Fred a big old kiss. Fred knew he was way too young to be kissing a girl, and any way he didn't want Sally to kiss him. So he said no and ran away from her. Sally tried very hard to catch him, but Fred was faster. Every time Sally got close, Fred stayed ahead of her and got away.

When I tell you to gallop, I want you to think about the story of Fred and Sally. Your front leg is Fred and your back leg is Sally. Fred always stays in front, and when Sally catches up, Fred moves ahead.

A Galloping Dance

Org Get with your assigned partner, pick up a spot, and spread out, putting your spot on the floor. I am going to put on some music for galloping. ["The William Tell Overture" works well here—it also was used as the *Lone Ranger* theme song and is still used by many sports teams today.]

I One of you stands on the spot, and the other does eight gallops away and eight gallops back. Then switch.

E Now both of you do eight gallops away and eight gallops back, staying next to each other the whole time.

E Now both of you do eight gallops away and eight gallops back, but go on different pathways.

Teaching Skipping

Org Give every child a tambourine or hand drum. If you don't have children's musical instruments, give every child a ball. Play music that you can skip to easily.

I When I say, "Go," march about the space with your tambourine held below your waist. As you march, try to hit the tambourine with your knee.

E Keep marching, and try to lift your knee higher and higher. Soon you will be lifting it so high that you will be skipping.

E [The sliding dance and the galloping dance tasks in the previous lessons can be adapted and used here for developing skipping.]

SAMPLE LEARNING EXPERIENCES 31.3

Sliding, Galloping, and Skipping (*continued*)

Kindergartners learning to skip

Hot, Hot, Hot: Skipping on Hot Stones

This is another way to teach skipping that we learned from Robin Litaker. You can change the lead characters in the story to be characters important to children in your school.

> You are on a secret mission to rescue a baby mouse who is lost and about to be caught by a fox. As you are sneaking through the forest, you see the baby mouse on the other side of a hot lava river. You step across the lava river. Each time you step, you bring your other foot up in front of you and say "Hot," and brush the lava off your foot while hopping on the other foot. But that foot is hot, too, so you pick it up and brush the lava off that one. Continue across the river, lifting up and touching first one foot, then the other, saying "Hot, Hot, Hot" until you get across the river and save the baby mouse. What you are doing is called skipping. As you get more confident, try it without touching your foot. Don't forget to alternate legs.

Body Parts

In level 1, body part lessons can focus on the following content:

- Exploring different ways to move and emphasize different body parts
- Exploring traveling while leading with different body parts

Hands

Children can explore a lot of dance material focused on their hands. Hands can shake, vibrate, quiver, grip, and stretch. The shapes of their hands can be wide, narrow, pointy, round, or twisted and gnarled. The hands can draw designs in space—for example, hands can draw soft, gentle curves; angry, sharp zigzags; straight, piercing lines; and meandering, twisted lines. Different parts of the hands can lead the movement, evoking different feelings. Rising while leading with a fist can suggest strength, power, and confidence. Fingertips can pierce the space. Leading with the palm can suggest pushing away, pressing down, or pushing up. Leading with the side of the hand can suggest slicing, while leading with the back of the hand can suggest gentle flow.

Feet

Children can explore different ways to move their feet, both when they travel on their feet and when they support their body on another body part. Feet can tap, wiggle, flex, and point. The feet can draw patterns in the air, tap, jab, circle, stretch, flex, and wiggle.

Elbows and Knees, Arms and Legs, Shoulders, Hips, and Wrists

These body parts provide rich opportunities for children to explore different ways to move different body parts. Each part can move in isolation or move in relation to other body parts. For example, a lesson exploring ways for the elbows and knees to move in relation to each other can result in a variety of light, bouncy, angular movements resembling dancing puppets. The wrists can be the central body part in a lesson focusing on gathering and scattering, with children bringing their wrists together and then separating them in different ways. The arms and legs can shake, jab, wiggle, stretch, curl, swing, and circle.

Spine and Head

Having children explore how their spine can move is both an enjoyable learning experience and an excellent opportunity for acquiring a movement vocabulary. Spines can curl and stretch backward, forward, and sideways and make interesting shapes. Spines also twist and can twist and stretch or twist and curl at the same time, giving children a wide range of movements to explore. Having the movement of the spine initiate a movement is particularly important movement content, as it encourages children to use their whole body, rather than just their arms and legs, which is a typical developmental pattern exhibited by beginners.

SAMPLE LEARNING EXPERIENCES 31.4

Body Parts

Body Part Warm-up (Also an Activity Break)

The following activity is an excellent way to warm up the class. Select lively music that the children enjoy. For example, we have used the Pointer Sisters' song "I'm So Excited." Do all movements to a 16-count phrase that matches the music. If a phrase extends longer, you can extend the movement until the end of the phrase. Demonstrate and call out the body parts and actions.

To the beat of the music, do each movement 16 times each (or until the end of the music phrase).

Teacher Leads

1. Fingers: To the beat, alternate making a fist and stretching fingers wide.
2. Shake hands.
3. Shake hands in all areas of personal space.
4. Pointy hands: Pierce the air, leading with fingertips in all areas of personal space.
5. Pushing hands: Raise the roof. Push up with hands while jumping.
6. Push hands while jumping in a circle.
7. Punch: Punch fists down and up while jumping.
8. Slicing: Taking two beats for each slice, slice hands and arms to the left while stomping the left foot to the left, then slice hands and arms to the right while stomping the right foot.
9. Knees: Jog in place with a high knee lift.
10. Knees in and out: Jump and land with bent knees and feet apart pointed sideways. Jump and land with toes pointed in, feet apart, and knees together.
11. Add elbows. Repeat number 10, and point elbows out when knees are out and elbows in when knees are in.
12. Elbows and knees: Jog with a high knee lift, either pumping elbows or trying to touch elbows to knees.
13. Feet: Tap one foot all around while hopping on the other for eight counts. Then switch legs.
14. Legs: Alternate kicking legs, springing into the air each time you change legs.
15. Kick one leg eight times and then the other eight times while hopping.
16. Head nods: With feet apart and knees bent, put hands on knees and bounce the nodding head eight times looking left and eight times looking right.
17. Hips: Sway hips from side to side.
18. Wrists: Stick arms out straight in front, make fists, and bend one wrist up and the other down. Bend knees, and jump as you alternate wrists moving up and down.

Repeat the song, but this time the teacher calls out a body part, and the children invent their own movements. After the children have done the dance once, you can use the child-invented dance as a warm-up for other lessons.

Body Actions

Twisting, Turning, and Spinning

There is a difference between turning and twisting. When the body **turns**, the entire body rotates on an axis. When the body **twists**, one part of the body remains facing one direction while another part rotates to face in a different direction (see **Figure 31.8**). Spinning is turning, but the term *spinning* typically means the body rotates several times, as if it is spinning like a top. Children can turn and spin at different levels and on different body parts.

Figure 31.8 Exploring twisting

Courtesy of John Dolly

Swinging and Swaying

Swinging in creative dance means that the actions resemble the movements of a swing or pendulum. Individual body parts can swing one way and then reverse around a fixed point. For

Figure 31.9 Exploring swaying

example, the arms can swing forward and back at the shoulders, and one leg can swing from the hips. The whole body can also move in a swinging action, starting up to the left and moving down on a circular pathway and up again to the right; it can then reverse direction. The body can swing from side to side or forward and back. **Swaying** is similar but typically implies a smaller action in which the weight of the body shifts from one side to the other or in one direction and then the reverse (see **Figure 31.9**).

Critical to swinging and swaying is the repetitive rhythm—back and forth, back and forth (or side to side), over and over. A key aspect of swinging is the feeling of a pause at the height or apex of the swing, letting go and accelerating down and then up again, decelerating to a pause at the height of the swing on the other side. The feeling in the body is like the feeling of swinging on a swing. Children enjoy exploring swinging and swaying movements in much the same way they enjoy hanging from a bar and swinging forward and back.

Other Body Actions

Many other actions can be included in dance lessons. For example, these lessons may include bouncing, wiggling, prancing (like ponies), slithering (like snakes), scurrying (like mice), and pouncing (like a cat). Children can shake or vibrate different body parts or the whole body. Shaking typically incorporates a greater range of motion than vibrating. Children can use both types of movements to represent feelings, such as fear or being cold, and animals, such as hummingbirds or dragonflies.

Making Real-life Connection to Body Actions (CCSS)

Body actions provide many ways to connect dance vocabulary to real life, in particular to animals and other living creatures that capture children's interest and imaginations. We include three sample plans in which the characteristics of animals and insects serve as the stimulus for children to explore a range of body actions and movement concepts (see **Sample Plan 31.1**, "In the Cool of the Pool"; **Sample Plan 31.5**, "Animal Haiku"; and **Sample Plan 31.8**, "In the Small, Small Pond, at the end of this chapter.")

Level 1: Introduction to Effort: Force and Time

Theory Underlying Effort

The Laban framework identifies four movement concepts of effort: force (also called weight), time, use of space, and flow. These concepts are described as existing along a continuum. In creative dance level 1, we focus on force and time.

Force

Preston-Dunlop (1980) identified four strands of content in relation to force. At the elementary level, we suggest focusing on the following aspects of these four strands:

1. *Kinetic force (isotonic contractions): Light–strong continuum.* **Kinetic force** is generated by contracting the muscles, resulting in movement (the length of the muscle changes). Force is described as existing on a continuum from light to strong. Kinetic force can be strong, such as the actions of the legs while sprinting, or light, such as the action of the hands and arms when trying to catch a soap bubble without letting it burst.
2. *Static force or tension (isometric contractions): Fine–firm continuum.* **Static force** is generated by contracting or tightening the muscles but not moving (the length of the muscle remains the same). Strong static force results in tight, firm muscles. Light static force involves slight tension and feels like a soft touch. The continuum is from fine to firm. Static and kinetic forces often are combined into one movement, and combining them in different ways can elicit different feelings. For example, a vigorous gallop and a high hop (kinetic force) can be done with light static tension and give the suggestion of happiness or excitement, whereas a vigorous gallop and hop (kinetic force) done with strong static tension can represent anger or power.
3. *Light, anti-gravity exertion.* Although there are only two kinds of muscle contractions (isotonic and isometric), in dance, a third critical form of tension and force can be differentiated: anti-gravity exertion (Preston-Dunlop, 1980). **Anti-gravity exertion** is the light muscle tension used to hold the body stretched tall and upright (against the pull of gravity). Dancers almost always maintain anti-gravity exertion. For children, learning to maintain anti-gravity exertion is important because it helps children feel the movement from the inside and be aware of the positions of their body parts (Stinson, 1982).
4. *Heavy weight.* In contrast to anti-gravity exertion and strong static tension are a lack of tension and the feeling of **heavy weight**, or heaviness. The body feels heavy and the muscles loose.

Time

There are five movement concepts of time: speed, duration, rhythm, accent, and meter.

1. *Speed.* **Speed** is described as existing along a continuum from slow to fast.
2. *Duration.* **Duration** is the length of time a movement takes and is described as existing on a continuum from short to long.

Speed and duration are often combined in learning experiences for children to help them acquire a feeling for the speed of a movement. The most important combinations are sudden and sustained. **Sudden** is a fast speed of a short duration that helps children feel the urgency and quickness of fast speed. **Sustained** is a slow speed of a long duration that helps children feel how slow movement is endless, ongoing, lingering, and enduring. The terms *sudden* and *sustained* are often used in dance to replace *fast* and *slow* because the former terms better capture the feeling of the movements.

3. *Rhythm.* **Rhythm** is how the durations of movements are organized into patterns.
4. *Accent.* **Accent** is when one beat is emphasized.

   What is most important for dance movement is whether the rhythm is even or uneven. Typically, walking, jogging, running, and a step-hop are all performed at an even rhythm because the amount of time between each step is the same, and there is no accent. Skipping, galloping, and sliding use an uneven rhythm—the amount of time between each step is uneven, and there is an accent on the lead step. For example, when skipping (which is a step-hop), the lead step is longer, takes a longer period of time, and is the accent. By comparison, the hop takes a shorter period of time. You can say, "Long, short, long, short," in time with a skip.
5. *Meter.* **Meter** is a measurement of the ways duration is divided into phrases or measures.

The first beat of a measure is always the strong beat. Music used for children's dance most often uses a 4/4 meter, which means there are four beats in a measure and a quarter note has one beat. If you count 1, 2, 3, 4 to the beat of 4/4 music, you will hear how measures and phrases fit to the count with the accent on the count of 1. For example, the song "Row, Row, Row Your Boat," which is used in one lesson in this book, is in a 4/4 meter. The major beats of the song with the accent in **bold** are shown in the box 'The Meter of "Row, Row, Row Your Boat.'

The Meter of "Row, Row, Row Your Boat"

1	2	3	4
Row,	row,	row your	boat
1	2	3	4
Gently	down the	stream	(rest)
1	2	3	4
Merrily,	merrily,	merrily,	merrily,
1	2	3	4
Life is	but a	dream	(rest)

Combining Force and Time

We like to introduce the concept of effort by focusing on force and speed and combining these concepts with body actions and shapes. The body action or shape is the basic movement, and the effort element is how the action is performed or the quality of the movement. As Preston-Dunlop (1980) wrote, "After all, dynamics* [effort] is best seen as an adverb qualifying a 'doing' verb" (p. 13). Thus, lesson material might include the following items (the effort quality is italicized):

- Rising and falling *gently*
- Jumping *forcefully* and landing in a *tight*, angular shape
- Holding an *alert* shape to begin your dance phrase and then traveling *lightly* using a locomotor step
- Stretching *forcefully* to a wide, *powerful* shape, then *softy* curling into a *frail*, round shape

In level 1 lessons on effort, we combine the two movement concepts of force and speed to form the following combinations:

- Sustained, strong
- Sustained, light
- Sustained, heavy
- Sudden, strong
- Sudden, light
- Sudden, heavy

Combining two movement concepts of effort is a progression for later work in level 2, when three movement concepts are combined to form eight basic effort actions.

In lesson plans, we typically include three or more movement concepts and combinations. This approach allows the physical education teacher to show children the contrast between the different combinations, which will help them refine the quality of their movements and work on CCSS vocabulary standards for comparing and contrasting. In addition, children's muscles can become overly fatigued if they spend an entire lesson using strong force. Teaching several effort-based combinations will help keep them engaged.

Theme: Sustained, Strong

To teach children how to move with strong, sustained effort, focus on static force (isometric contractions) and the feeling of continuous tension and firmness in the muscles while moving slowly (see **Figure 31.10**). Children enjoy learning to move with strong, sustained effort because they get to tighten up all their muscles and look strong and powerful.

Immature Movement Patterns

Beginners tend to tighten only their arms and legs, so teachers need to remind them to tighten their tummies, bottoms, and torsos. For fun, have them tighten their faces and even teeth!

*Dancers often use the term *dynamics* instead of *effort*. We use the term *effort* throughout this text to be consistent with games and gymnastics content.

Figure 31.10 Exploring sustained, strong movement

Extending Movement Variety and Vocabulary

The following actions, feelings, and events from the theme of strong, sustained effort can be used to extend children's movement vocabulary and work on meeting CCSS for vocabulary acquisition:

- Gripping actions
- Pulling and pushing
- Lifting something heavy
- Bracing yourself against a strong wind
- Resisting pressure
- A tug-of-war
- A boa constrictor squeezing a victim
- Slow-motion fight scenes
- The pressure of the earth forming diamonds
- Demonstrating the feelings of power, strength, resistance, and firmness
- Demonstrating the feeling of tension, fear, and anger

SAMPLE LEARNING EXPERIENCES 31.5

Sustained, Strong Effort

Potential Refinements

- Be firm, be tight, be tense.
- Feel like you are braced, feel solid like a rock, feel like hardened steel.
- Show you are strong.
- Make yourself look mighty or brawny.
- Tighten up into an angry, icy stare.

Hard as a Rock

This activity is appropriate for introducing strong movement quality for the first time.

I Today, we are going to work on moving slowly with strong force. Standing straight with your arms at your sides, tighten up your entire body. Make every muscle as hard as a rock. Make your arms so tight and strong that I can't pull your arms away from your body. [Select several children and try (pretending to be trying very hard) to pull their arms away from their bodies.]

The Circus Clown Lifts Weights

This activity uses rising and falling actions.

I Today, we are going to work on moving slowly with strong force. With your feet apart and knees bent, reach down and pick up a heavy weight like a clown in a circus picking up a dumbbell. Showing tension in all your muscles, slowly lift the heavy weight to your chest and then over your head.

E This is a magic dumbbell. Once you get it over your head, you need to use just as much strength to lower it to the floor. Slowly press the dumbbell from over your head down to the floor.

E Lift the weight again. When you get the weight over your head, it is so heavy that you start to totter first to one side and then to the other side. Move your feet quickly, catching yourself just before you drop the weight.

E Explore lifting and lowering with different body parts (e.g., one hand, shoulders, head, elbows).

E Explore lifting and pressing down in different areas of personal space.

The Star Wars Trash Compactor

This activity uses pushing actions.

Org [Organize the class into a scattered formation, divided into four sections crosswise.]

(*continues*)

SAMPLE LEARNING EXPERIENCES 31.5

Sustained, Strong Effort (*continued*)

I Today we are going to work on moving slowly with strong force. The two outside sections are the trash compactor walls from the movie *Star Wars*. The two inside sections are Luke Skywalker, Princess Leia, Han Solo, and Chewbacca. Outside groups, slowly start to push the walls toward the middle of the gym. The walls are very heavy, so be tight in all your muscles and push slowly with great strength. The inside groups push back, trying to keep the walls from crushing you. [The groups do not touch each other.]

E Repeat, reversing roles.

The Tug-of-War

This activity uses pulling and gripping actions.

I Today we are going to work on moving slowly with strong force. Pretend you are in a tug-of war. Grip the rope with power and strength. Now, pull slowly. Oh no, the opposition is too strong! You are slowly losing ground. Now you feel yourself getting stronger and stronger. You brace yourself against the strength of your opponent. Now you are slowly winning.

E Turn and pull forward, now sideways, now backward, now forward, trudging one step at a time. Feel the power and strength.

Theme: Sustained, Light

Combining light and sustained movement concepts is an excellent way to introduce children to any of the following movement concepts: (1) moving slowly; (2) moving with light kinetic force; (3) moving with light static force; or (4) light, anti-gravity exertion. To help children learn to move with light and sustained movement, try to focus on having them move very slowly, feeling very light (see **Figure 31.11**).

Immature Movement Patterns

Some children find it difficult to move with light, sustained movements because their natural and preferred speed is fast! Most young children tend to move at medium, rather than slow, speeds. You will need to give lots of feedback on moving slowly and feeling light. It helps if you give the children images to think about as they move, such as a feather falling, a bubble floating on a breeze, clouds, or balloons rising into a clear, blue sky.

Figure 31.11 Exploring light, sustained movement

Extending Movement Variety and Vocabulary

The following actions, feelings, and events work well with the theme of light, sustained effort:

- Balloons, hot air balloons, bubbles rising and floating
- Leaves falling gently from a tree
- Feathers falling
- Flying, gliders, birds flying
- Floating in water, floating down a river in a canoe or inner tube, feeling buoyant
- Clouds
- Floating weightless in space like an astronaut
- Skaters gliding
- Herons stalking, eagles soaring, whales swimming, manatees swimming
- Showing the feelings of gentleness, kindness, and caring
- Feeling airy, dreamy, tranquil, calm

Sample Lesson Segment

Topic Theme: Riding Down a River in a Canoe

Movement Theme: Sustained, Light Movements

CCSS: Vocabulary Acquisition

Vocabulary words to briefly define during the lesson and discuss during closure: *soaring, buoyant, spiral pathways*

1. You are riding down a river in a canoe. The water is calm, and you feel calm and relaxed. Travel slowly with light tension and light force about the gymnasium. Let the calm of the water help you feel calm and relaxed.
2. Because you are calm, you take time to notice the beauty of the environment. Wander about the space slowly on random, curved pathways paying attention to the beauty around you.

3. You see an eagle soaring above. *Soaring* means flying at a great height, gliding on a spiral pathway, not using any energy to remain in flight. Soaring also means to rise majestically to a more exalted level. A *spiral pathway* is a circular pathway that rises (or falls) with each circle matching the shape of a spring, like the springs in our spring boards.
4. Fish are swimming lazily in the river. Travel on a twisted pathway leading with your hand. Explore leading with different body parts.
5. Bubbles from creatures under the water float gently to the surface. Sink and rise slowly and gently, then travel on a small circular pathway floating like a bubble.
6. You notice the clouds in the sky, which look like soft marshmallows. Travel on curved pathways, sometimes on small and sometimes on larger pathways.
7. Your canoe emerges onto a clear, calm lake. You and your family decide to tie up the canoes, sink into the cool water, and float on your backs, buoyant as the water supports your weight. *Buoyant* means capable of floating and also means cheerful. Continue floating and traveling on small circular pathways but look up, stretch your arms to the side, and lean back, lifting your chest toward the ceiling.
8. Meet your assigned partner and discuss, one at a time, the meaning of *soaring*, *spiral pathway*, and *buoyant*. Try to use each word in a sentence, and try to make a connection between each word and another real-life situation. [Write the words on the whiteboard.]

Theme: Sudden, Strong

When teaching the theme of strong, sudden movements, help children work on generating and feeling sharp, powerful,

SAMPLE LEARNING EXPERIENCES 31.6

Sustained, Light Effort

Potential Refinements

- Move gently.
- Feel calm, tranquil, placid.
- Make soothing, tender movements.
- Use a fine touch; touch softly.
- Feel quiet and peaceful.
- Move slowly, leisurely.
- Dawdle, linger.
- Don't let anything hurry you.
- Feel airy, weightless.
- Feel weak, flimsy, fragile, frail.

The Floating Hand

This activity is appropriate for introducing light, sustained movement quality for the first time.

Using Gestures in Personal Space

I Today we are going to work on moving slowly with light force. While sitting, move your hand very slowly around personal space, as if your hand was a bubble floating all around your body. Keep your movement soft and gentle. Try this with the other hand, then both hands at the same time.

Moving in General Space

E Stand and take a deep breath. Lift up your arms, and feel as if your body has become a bubble and you are lighter than air. Now travel slowly and gently. Imagine you are light and can float in the air above the ground looking down. Move very slowly so your bubble does not pop.

The Floating Scarf

This activity uses rising and sinking actions.

Org [Each child has a light scarf.]

I Today we are going to work on moving slowly with light force. While sitting, hold your scarf high in front of you, and spread it out. Drop the scarf, and watch it slowly fall to the floor. Gently toss your scarf up, and watch it fall again. Holding your scarf in one hand, slowly rise up until you are standing on tiptoes. Lift the scarf high, then slowly sink back to the floor, making the scarf float gently to the ground with you.

E Travel about the gym slowly, first reaching high with your scarf and then reaching low. Walk slowly, and move the scarf so it appears to be floating on a gentle breeze.

Figure 31.12 Exploring strong, sudden movement

instantaneous movements (see **Figure 31.12**). Children find these movements quite enjoyable because they are energetic and vigorous.

Immature Movement Patterns

Beginners have difficulty producing these movements with their entire body. They tend to use only their arms or legs, rather than having the movement originate from their core. To help them, suggest they tighten their tummies and bottoms and try to make their whole body move.

Extending Movement Variety and Vocabulary

The following actions, feelings, and events work well for designing tasks to teach the theme of strong, sudden effort and related vocabulary:

- Jumping
- Punching the air, jabbing, thrusting
- Spearing fish
- Pounding or hammering something
- Bursting or exploding like popcorn, dynamite, or a star gone nova
- Lightning
- Fireworks exploding
- Fighting (pretend)
- Waves crashing onto rocks
- Conflict between people
- Feeling angry, powerful

Theme: Sudden, Light

Light, sudden movements can be quick and end instantly, like a light tap, or can be repeated over a longer period, like a campfire flame. Children can learn these movement qualities as whole-body actions, such as skipping lightly, or in actions of individual body parts, such as tapping the hands all about personal space. You can help improve the quality and skillfulness of children's locomotor steps by working on light, sudden movement qualities. In addition, teaching light, sudden movements can help children learn to generate and recognize a quick, crisp feeling in movement (see **Figure 31.13**).

Extending Movement Variety and Vocabulary

The following actions, feelings, and events work well to help you design tasks to teach the theme of light, sudden effort:

- Skipping and galloping lightly
- Prancing; prancing ponies
- Tapping, dabbing, a delicate touch, a light tap

SAMPLE LEARNING EXPERIENCES 31.7

Sudden, Strong

Potential Refinements

- Feel powerful, strong.
- Move faster, instantly.
- Move as if you were angry, mad, or outraged.
- Move impatiently, brusquely, abruptly, or briskly.
- Be energetic, vigorous, spirited, or dynamic.

Freeze! Something Is Coming!

This activity uses stillness and walking actions.

I We are going to work on moving suddenly with force and strength. Walk about the space, and on the [loud] beat of the drum, do a small jump, stomp, and freeze in a wide, angular shape as if you were scared of the drumbeat. This time, land showing that the drum startled you, but you are ready to defend yourself. [Repeat.]

The Mad, Mad Child

This activity uses walking and stomping actions.

I Today we are going to work on moving suddenly with strong force. You are mad. Grit your teeth, tighten up, stamp your feet, and shake your head, "No, no, no!" Now walk as if you are mad. Walk fast, bend your elbows, make fists, and pump your arms back and forth. Be tight and walk fast, clicking your heels on the ground. Now stomp your feet—you are very mad. In fact, you are so mad, you go mad. Jump up and down. Stomp your feet. Travel quickly about the space. Thrust your arms every which way. Freeze with strong tension. You are the mad, mad child.

SAMPLE LEARNING EXPERIENCES 31.7
Sudden, Strong (*continued*)

The mad, mad child

(top left) Courtesy of John Dolly; (top right, bottom) © Jones & Bartlett Learning. Photographed by Sarah Cebulski.

Popcorn

This activity uses jumping.

I Today we are going to be moving suddenly with strong force. Start in a squatting position. When I say, "Jump," explode from the ground, reaching to the sky and jumping high in the air. Jump!

E This time, make a big shape in the air when you jump, and land in an angular shape. Jump!

E Let's be a class of popcorn. Pick your favorite number from 1 to 10. Everyone start low and bounce. I will count to 10. When I say your number, jump like a kernel of popcorn, and land in an angular popcorn shape with tight muscles.

Figure 31.13 Second-graders skipping making light, sudden gestures with their hands

© Jones & Bartlett Learning. Photographed by Sarah Cebulski.

- Darting; darting minnows, fish
- Scurrying; scurrying squirrels, chipmunks, mice
- Hummingbirds, dragonflies, bats, and birds flying
- Flames, fire, sparklers, twinkling stars
- Frisky dogs
- Babbling streams
- A quick smile, surprise
- Being excited, happy, jittery

For examples of tasks and lesson plans, at the end of this chapter see **Sample Plans 31.1**, "Down by the Cool of the Pool"; **31.5**, "Animal Haiku"; and **31.8**, "In the Small, Small Pond."

Theme: Sustained, Heavy

When children move with a heavy, sustained movement quality, they experience a sense of heaviness and lethargy—a feeling many of them are familiar with when they are tired and don't want to do chores or homework (see **Figure 31.14**). To help them recreate this feeling in dance, teach them to attend

SAMPLE LEARNING EXPERIENCES 31.8

Sudden, Light Effort

Potential Refinements

- Be light and quick.
- Look happy, be playful.
- Be excited, show excitement.

The Fly on the Countertop

This activity uses scurrying actions.

I Today we are going to be moving lightly and quickly. Hold yourself in a ready position. When I beat the drum, instantly move about one foot. Go. Move so abruptly and suddenly that an observer won't even see you move but just notice you are in a new location.

R Have light tension in your muscles.

E Now, pick a spot a short distance away from you. When you hear the drum, dart quickly to that spot. Go. Now select another spot. Move lightly and quickly, then pause and hold a ready position with light tension, anticipating your next move. Dart so lightly that the floor can't even feel your feet. [Repeat several times.] You are light like a fly on your kitchen counter.

E Oh no, your mom sees you! Quickly dart away, light as a fly. Your mom is trying to catch you! Dart again, and again. Pause and see if she can see you. Oh no, she has a fly swatter! What happens next?

The Campfire

This activity involves using gestures in personal space.

I Today we are going to work on moving quickly with light force. While sitting, quickly reach your hand up and then down. Now reach up and down with the other hand. This time when you reach, shake your hand and wiggle your fingers lightly like the flame of a fire. The fire starts small. Flicker with one hand quickly and lightly. Pause. Now flicker with the other hand. Pause. [Repeat several times.] Now flicker with both hands. The fire is getting bigger. Reach higher. Don't pause very long. Now you decide when to reach with one hand, the other hand, or both hands. Go. Look around—the whole gym is one big campfire. Now the fire starts to die down. Reach out only a little, and pause longer. The flames are flickering only now and then.

E Repeat the whole sequence while standing. Start at a low level, reach high to flicker the whole arm, and then sink back to a low level.

carefully to the feelings inside their muscles. They have to focus on maintaining loose, relaxed tension using only the minimal amount of kinetic force to move. When they lift a body part, it feels like it weighs a ton.

Figure 31.14 Exploring walking with heavy tension representing the tired, bored child

Extending Movement Variety and Vocabulary

The following actions, feelings, and events work well to help you design tasks to teach the theme of sustained, heavy movements. Children enjoy these tasks.

- Walking slowly. feeling tired and weary
- Creeping or sliding slowly along the floor on the torso
- Swaying with fatigue
- Moving like turtles, sloths, or slugs
- A sad clown wearing worn-out clothes in the circus
- Being slow as molasses
- Slowly flowing lava
- Being exhausted and crawling into bed
- Looking lethargic
- Dragging their feet
- Being totally bored

Sample Lesson Segment

Topic Theme: The Lethargic Child

Movement Theme: Sustained, Heavy Tension

CCSS: Vocabulary Acquisition

Vocabulary word to briefly define during the lesson and discuss during closure: *lethargic*

1. You were tired all day in school, and your mom has to go shopping and you must go with her, but you want to stay home and play a quiet game on your bed. Mom said, "Let's go," but you drag your feet. Travel about the classroom slowly with just enough tension in your body to remain standing. Drag your feet to show your mom you are too tired to go.
2. You get to the supermarket, and now you are totally lethargic. Your mom says, "Move along," but you move even more slowly, showing her how drowsy you are and how much you do not care about shopping—you are lethargic. *Lethargic* means being sluggish and feeling indifferent. Then your mom says, "After we get home and put away the groceries, we can go to the park, and you can play on the playground equipment. Suddenly, your mood changes, you start to feel excited and energetic, and you skip happily about the space making light gestures with your hands.
3. Repeat traveling slowly with heavy tension and then quickly with light tension on the teacher's command.
4. With a partner, define *lethargic*, and describe feelings and movements that reflect feeling lethargic. Then describe other feelings and movements that contrast lethargy.

Theme: Sudden, Heavy

Have you ever gone totally limp and sunken into a deep, soft mattress? That is a heavy, sudden movement. In dance, heavy, sudden movements are fast with a heavy feeling, loose muscles, floppy limbs, and just enough tension to prevent injury and loss of control. In a perfect world, you would introduce heavy, sudden movements in a space completely covered with large foam mattresses so children could simply eliminate all tension and control over their muscles and drop down on the mattress without fear of injury. In the real world, you need to teach children how to generate a heavy, sudden movement while maintaining enough control over the flow of their movement so they remain safe at all times.

To introduce heavy, sudden movements, you can use one or both arms. You can also use a swinging movement, starting with both hands high and to the side, then swinging down with a moment of heaviness before controlling the movement and swinging up to the other side.

Extending Movement Variety and Vocabulary

The following actions, feelings, and events work well to help you design tasks to teach the theme of heavy, sudden effort:

- Falling into something soft
- Collapsing, dropping
- Swinging with heavy tension on the middle part of the down swing
- Ice cream falling off a cone
- Dropping pudding on the floor
- Limp, cooked spaghetti
- A limp rag doll
- Snow dropping off a limb and plopping on the ground

■ Level 1: Introduction to Space

Level 1 space content focuses on four movement concepts:

- Personal and general space
- Levels
- Pathways (air and floor)
- Directions

It also combines these movement concepts with body actions.

SAMPLE LEARNING EXPERIENCES 31.9

Sustained, Heavy Effort

Potential Refinements

- Feel heavy.
- Feel loose in every muscle.
- Look bored.
- Look like you are weary, tired, or fatigued.
- Act sluggish and lethargic.
- Look like you are dejected and sad.

The Tired, Bored Child

This activity uses walking and sinking actions.

I We are going to move slowly and steadily with what is called *heavy effort*. As you stand there, try to relax every muscle in your body, maintaining just enough tension to remain standing. Let your head tip. Relax your shoulders. Sag through your spine. Just to feel the difference, tighten up every muscle, and be rigid as a board. Now relax. Alternate: tight, loose, tight, loose. Try to walk staying as relaxed as you can. Heavy, sustained movement is totally loose but never stops.

E Let's all look bored. How do you feel when you are bored? Can you show me bored? Make your muscles relaxed, loose. Relax your shoulders, tummy, legs, arms, face, jaw, and eyes. Strike a bored pose.

E Now let's walk slowly, looking bored. Keep all of your muscles as loose as you can. Walk slowly about the space, drag your feet, hang your head, and look bored. Move very slowly. Stop and hold a bored pose. Change to another bored pose.

SAMPLE LEARNING EXPERIENCES 31.10

Sudden, Heavy Effort

Potential Refinements

- Go limp.
- Lose all tension.
- Plop down.
- Show total relaxation.
- Collapse

Cooked Spaghetti Arms

This activity uses collapsing and sinking actions.

I We are going to move suddenly but with heavy effort. This means you will be totally loose and relaxed but move quickly. As you are standing there, lift your arms away from your sides. Make them stiff and straight like dried spaghetti before it is cooked. Now, by magic, the spaghetti has cooked. Suddenly relax your arm muscles, and let your arms collapse to your sides and then hang there limply. Keep your arms very loose and relaxed. Twist and let your arms flop around. Sway from side to side, and let your arms swing as if they were limp, cooked spaghetti.

E Now extend the movement to your whole body. Reach up, stretch up on your toes (balls of your feet), and tighten. Then suddenly relax, and flop back to a standing position, with every muscle in your body so loose that you have just enough tension to remain standing. Try again, being sure to have enough tension in your arms so you don't slap yourself when you relax.

The Ice Cream Cone

This activity combines light, sudden; heavy, sudden; and heavy, sustained effort using collapsing and sinking actions.

I This is the sad, sad story of my brother Bob's ice cream cone. We went to the store last summer, and it was so hot—over 100 degrees—and we were so hungry that we felt as if we hadn't eaten anything for the past year. We saw an ice cream shop, and we were so happy. We spent all our money and bought ice cream cones. Bliss! We thought we had it made. We started eating our ice cream, and we were really happy—in fact, we were so happy, we did not watch our ice cream. My brother's hand and arm started to relax, the ice cream cone started to tip, and it tipped farther and farther until plop, the ice cream fell out and landed on the hot, dirty sidewalk. Worse, it started to melt. Before our very eyes, it melted into a sorry, sticky puddle of goop. Bob looked as if he was going to cry. He was so sad and blue that a blue cloud settled over his head. The owner of the ice cream shop saw how blue he was and gave him a new scoop. And that's the end of the story.

E Let's do a dance about the ice cream cone. First, skip lightly and briskly about the gym, gesturing quickly and lightly with your hands to show how happy you are to buy ice cream [light, sudden arm actions]. Reach tall, making your muscles tight. Then, *with control*, collapse with loose muscles to a low level [heavy, sudden movement]. Next, slowly melt into the floor until you spread out in a sorry, sticky puddle of melted ice cream [heavy, sustained movement].

Theme: Personal and General Space

Helping children develop an awareness of all areas of their personal space is critical at all times, but especially so in dance. Typically, beginners explore movements in front of them at a medium level. Learning to explore all areas of their personal space helps children elicit a greater range of possible movement responses and makes their dances more interesting.

In addition, to ensure their own and other children's safety, children need always be aware of their personal space when moving in general space. If they are aware of the amount of space they occupy, they can avoid collisions and inadvertent body contact. Although we typically recommend that space movement concepts be introduced after children have explored body and dynamic movement concepts, personal and general space are the exceptions to this guideline. We suggest teachers introduce personal and general space during the first few days of school and revisit these concepts throughout the year.

Immature Movement Patterns

Children typically enjoy traveling in general space and then freezing when the teacher says, "Freeze." Some freeze in unstable positions and fall or wave their arms to keep balance. Some, of course, are just having fun and are off task. Nevertheless, this is a legitimate immature pattern for some children. Children have slower reaction times than adults, and children can *generate more speed than they can control.*

Once you extend the task to have children travel in general space by jogging or running, you will need to teach them how to stop skillfully by bending their knees, lowering their centers of gravity, and using stride positions for a wide base of support.

Another typical response of children traveling in general space is to travel in a circle as if they were jogging around a running track. You will need to emphasize that traveling in general space means traveling all about the space on different pathways and to different locations.

SAMPLE LEARNING EXPERIENCES 31.11

Personal and General Space to Be Taught in the First Days of School

Introducing Personal and General Space Using Spots for Younger Children

Set poly spots in a scattered pattern about the gym, with spots equidistant from each other. Ensure that if a child stands on a spot, he or she can't touch another child. When the children enter the gym, assign them a spot. Teach the lesson segment "It's My Spot" (from earlier in this chapter), directly followed by the lesson segment presented here. This content may take two lessons to cover. Have at least five more spots than children.

I Let's review what we did in the last class with the lesson "It's My Spot." When I beat my tambourine, move in different ways around your spot. When I stop beating the tambourine, stop still and touch one body part on the spot. You can pick any part you want, but you must be able to hold your position perfectly still. [Repeat several times.]

Cog K Now we are going to work on doing something the big kids are very good at doing. The first thing you have to learn is, "What is my personal space?" Stand over your spot with your feet apart as I am doing. [Demonstrate.] Do this with me. Without moving your feet, reach high with your hands; now reach to the sides; now reach low; now in front; now in back. The area around your body that you can reach we call your *personal space*. It is your space.

E Let's explore your personal space. Stay over your spot, and reach out with your hands (you can even reach out with your feet), and try to explore or reach to all areas of your personal space. [Demonstrate as you talk.]

Cog K Now that you know about your personal space, the second thing you need to understand is general space. General space is all the space in the gymnasium that has spots. When I say, "Go," all of you are going to walk all around the spots, *without moving into anyone else's personal space*—that is, *without bumping into or touching anyone else*. That is what the first-graders are great at doing. They can walk all around general space without touching anyone else.

I Do you think you can do this? Are you ready to try? Okay. Go. [Wait about two seconds.] Stop. Great job so far. Let's try longer. Go. [Wait about four seconds.] Stop. [Repeat several times, letting the children walk for a longer period of time each time.]

R Go back and sit on your spot. Let's talk about how to move in general space without touching anyone else. Some of you were great at doing this. Raise your hand if you want to share your secrets for doing a great job traveling in general space. [Responses to elicit: You look around, sometimes you have to stop and let someone go past you, and sometimes you have to turn or change where you are going.] You gave some great ideas. Let's try them out. Ready, go. [Repeat several times.]

E Let's make this even more challenging. When I say, "Personal space," you can travel around your own spot; when the tambourine stops, touch your spot with any body part you want. When I say, "General space," walk all about general space; when the tambourine stops, freeze right where you are, not standing on any spot. Ready, go. [Repeat several times.]

Introducing Personal and General Space to Older Children

Scattered Formation

Cog K Spread out throughout the gym so you can't touch any other person. Try to space yourselves as a class so you are all at an equal distance from each other. We call this a *scattered formation*. A scattered formation is one in which you can't touch another person, and no one is in your personal space.

Personal Space

Cog K Your personal space is the space around you that you can reach.

I Stand and reach to all areas of your personal space. Really explore this space. Reach behind you, to the side, down low and to the side, and up high.

General Space

Cog K The general space is the entire space in the gym. You need to learn to move about the general space of the gym without invading anyone's personal space.

Traveling in General Space and Stopping

E Now I want all of you to walk about the general space at the same time without bumping into anyone else. Go. I want you to go all about the space, to all areas, traveling on different pathways [demonstrate] without going in a circle like you were on a racetrack. Go. [Repeat several times.]

E Now jog. Try to be very aware of your classmates. Have eyes in the back of your head.

R Stop still. Check your spacing, and adjust it so you spread out evenly about the space as a class. What do you do with your body to freeze without falling? [Bend my knees, feet apart, feet in a stride position.] Those are good answers. When you freeze in a stable position, you lower your center of gravity and widen your base of support. This body position contributes to stability. Let's practice walking and freezing, and then jogging and freezing, until you can do this perfectly.

E Now jog faster. Stop. [Repeat several times, checking to make sure that the group is evenly spaced.] Now I am going to challenge you. You may run as long as you can run with control and without bumping into anyone else. Go only as fast as you can control your movement. Go. Stop. [Repeat several times.]

(*continues*)

SAMPLE LEARNING EXPERIENCES 31.11

Personal and General Space to Be Taught in the First Days of School (*continued*)

Through the Middle

E This next task is even more challenging. When I say, "Through the middle," I want everyone to jog through the middle of the space to the other side without bumping into anyone else and then continue jogging. Go. Through the middle.

R Share the secrets of what you did to go through the middle without bumping. [I had to slow down, wait for someone in front to pass, and watch very carefully.] Great answers. Let's do it again. [Repeat several times.]

Theme: Levels

Teaching children to be cognizant of working at all three levels (high, medium, and low) is critical in dance. Beginners tend to explore movements at a medium level. Having them explore moving at all three levels adds considerably to their movement vocabulary (see **Figure 31.15**).

More critical is helping children to explore changing levels while they dance. Changing levels is one way children can add interest and contrast to their dance sequences. A dance sequence at only one level can be monotonous, whereas a dance sequence with peaks and valleys is more interesting.

The ultimate goal is for children to be conscious of the level of their movements and to explore movements at a variety of levels without prompting from the teacher. In the beginning, however, children will need scaffolding (in this case, reminders) from the teacher. For an example of how to teach levels using streamers or ribbons, see **Sample Plan 31.7**, "Introducing Levels," at the end of this chapter.

Figure 31.15 Moving scarves at different levels

Theme: Pathways

In dance, pathways include straight, curved, twisted, and angular routes both on the floor and in the air. Children travel on

SAMPLE LEARNING EXPERIENCES 31.12

Pathways

Potential Refinements

- Make the zigzag pathway sharp and angular; don't round the points.
- Make the curves round.

Mud on the Kitchen Floor: Introducing Pathways

Cog K Something magical happens today—someone gives you your very own house, and you can make as much of a mess in it as you want. You decide you want to track mud all over the kitchen floor. You will get in big trouble if you do this at home, you know. But today is a magical day, and this is your house. Step into a big mud puddle.

I Walk around your kitchen on curved pathways like this [demonstrate], leaving a track of muddy footprints that make curved lines. Go.

E Make some curved pathways that are big and some that are small.

E Which letters of the alphabet have curved lines? Good answers. Let's write those letters with muddy footprints.

E Now, make zigzag pathways like the letter Z [demonstrate]. Make some small zigzags and some large zigzags. Look behind you and look at the mess we are making.

E The last muddy pathway I want you to make is a straight pathway. Walk on a straight pathway until you reach the boundary of our workspace, and then turn and walk on another straight pathway. Go.

E What a mess! But this is a magical house, so we can clap our hands and all the mud will disappear. Ready? Clap.

SAMPLE LEARNING EXPERIENCES 31.12

Pathways (*continued*)

The Name Dance

I Walk about the space on straight pathways. If you are about to travel into another student's personal space, pause until he or she walks by you. When you get to a barrier (e.g., a wall, desk, boundary), turn and continue.

E Now walk on zigzag pathways by walking straight, then turning sharply, and continuing on a straight pathway.

E Now try walking on curved pathways.

E Walk changing from curved to straight to zigzag pathways. You decide when to change pathways.

E Choose a letter and write that letter on the floor by walking on the appropriate pathways.

[Repeat with several letters.]

E Now write an imaginary letter using any pathway you want.

E We are going to work on representing different letters by using our imagination to add feelings and emotions to that letter. We will start with Z. Z is angular and sharp, forceful, and full of tension. When I hit the drum, move your arms fast with force on a zigzag pathway, and end in an angular shape. Be very tight. [Repeat several times.]

E Now let's imagine movements we can use with the letter M. An M (written in cursive) is curved and soft, with a hummmmmmming sound. Travel making soft, curved pathways in the air with your arms making a soft hum.

E Now let's make the letter E. E is frantic. Travel on straight pathways, changing directions and suddenly walking on a square as if you can't figure out where to go. Frantically say (*without screaming or screeching*), "Eeeeeeeeeee."

E Let's make up a name dance. Take two to four of the letters in your name and make up a short dance using those letters. Use your imagination to add any feeling you want to the letters you selected. Use both floor pathways and gesture with your arms on air pathways.

floor pathways. They gesture on air pathways with their hands, arms, feet, and other body parts. Air pathways also can result from bodily flight or children moving props in the air, such as ribbons, scarves, balls, or streamers.

The movement qualities of curved pathways feel flowing and smooth. Children can use curved air and floor pathways to represent ideas such as clouds, round letters, and bubbles. Moving in a circle can represent community and togetherness. Zigzag pathways feel sharp and abrupt. They can represent lightning, being lost, or running away from something scary. Straight pathways, if children move slowly and gently, can appear ongoing as if you are moving toward the horizon. If children march on straight pathways with firm tension, their movements can represent machines or soldiers. Twisted pathways can appear and feel convoluted, random, or flexible. Travelling slowly and gently on twisted pathways can represent wandering or meandering.

Immature Movement Patterns

Young children often make curved pathways that are not round, as they do when they learn to write letters. They also tend to make zigzag pathways without a sharp, angular change in pathway; in other words, they round out the points.

Theme: Directions

Directions include forward, backward, sideways, up, down, and diagonal. Initially, children learn they can travel forward, sideways, backward, and on diagonals using different locomotor steps. These directions are particularly important in folk dancing. Next, they learn to gesture and move their bodies or body parts forward, backward, sideways, up, down, and on a diagonal.

SAMPLE LEARNING EXPERIENCES 31.13

Directions

The Haunted House

This activity is done to the song "Monster Mash."

Org Today we are going to a haunted house. Put two red spots and two yellow spots in a square like this. [Place four spots in an eight-foot square, with the red and yellow spots on the diagonals.] Stand in the middle of your haunted house.

Cog K This dance is about traveling in different directions—up, down, sideways, forward, and backward. When the music starts, you will hear a bubbling noise. I want you move up and down, wiggling as if you were in a witch's brew.

E Now march sideways to one side of your house and then sideways to the other side of your house. Try to march on the beat of the music.

(*continues*)

SAMPLE LEARNING EXPERIENCES 31.13

Directions (*continued*)

E March sideways again, but this time lift your elbows up, let your hands hang down, and rattle your hands as if you were a skeleton.

MD You can also add a knee bend. Step to the side with your left foot, then bring your right foot next to your left and bend your knees. To the music, it is step, bend, step, bend, making your body wiggle and rattle like a skeleton.

E Now let's go forward and backward. Stand with your feet apart, arms up and out to the side. Try to walk without bending your knees so you look like Frankenstein. Just tip to one side, and then tip to the other, moving forward a little with each step. When you reach the front of your house, do the Frankenstein walk backward.

E Stand on one red spot, and travel like a ghost on the diagonal to the other red spot.

E Now turn into goblins. Travel on your hands and feet around the perimeter of your house looking like a goblin. [If the children have not learned about perimeter in mathematics, either explain the term or simply tell them to travel around all four walls.]

E End the dance in the middle, bubbling and wiggling as you move up and down in a witch's brew.

Walking like Frankenstein

Level 1: Introduction to Relationships

Most learning experience about relationships require working with a partner and consequently are appropriate only for children who are socially mature enough to work well with partners. If you keep tasks short and simple, even children in the youngest grades can copy a partner. Level 1 content from the relationship aspect includes four themes:

- Copying
- Matching
- Mirroring
- Contrasting and complementing

Theme: Copying

Copying means doing what a partner is doing—that is, one partner moves first, and the other copies that movement. Teachers can design learning experiences in which children copy movement concepts, such as shapes, locomotor skills, pathways, levels, directions, speed, and force. Children can copy the actions exactly or copy only part of the movement. For example, they

SAMPLE LEARNING EXPERIENCES 31.14

Copying

Cat and Copy Cat

Cog K Today we are going to work on trying to copy another person's movements. What does the word *copy* mean to you? *Copy* means to do exactly what your partner is doing. Go with your assigned partner.

I One of you, we will call "Cat." Cat will make a shape. The second person, we will call "Copy Cat." Copy Cat will make a shape that is an exact copy of Cat's shape. For example, I am standing with my legs together and arms out to the side. I am Cat.

SAMPLE LEARNING EXPERIENCES 31.14

Copying (*continued*)

All of you are Copy Cat and copy me. Great job. Now it's your turn. Cat will make three different shapes, and Copy Cat will copy the shapes. Then switch roles. [Switch several times.]

E Cat will walk on a pathway about the gym; Copy Cat will walk, too, copying the leader's pathway. Switch leaders. What will I see if you and your partner are good at copying?

E Now I am going to challenge you. Remember, if you want to learn and get better, you have to challenge yourself. Switch again. This time, Cat can choose any locomotor step, such as galloping, skipping, jogging, sliding, or walking. Copy Cat copies both the locomotor step and the pathway. [Switch several times.]

E This time, the leader will select any locomotor step and any pathway. You have some choices here. You can copy Cat's pathway, or you can challenge yourself and copy both the locomotor pattern and the pathway.

Social What does a good leader do so his or her partner is able to copy the movements? [Don't go too fast or get too far away.] You may begin. [Switch several times.]

E Now add traveling. Cat makes a starting shape, travels for four counts using one locomotor skill, and makes another shape. Copy Cat copies the starting shape, locomotor skill, and ending shape. Repeat the same sequence until Copy Cat is the exact copy of Cat.

Social Help each other. Discuss each other's shapes, and work hard to make them the same. If the shape is too difficult to copy, then discuss changing to an easier shape.

E After you have perfected this sequence, switch roles, and practice until you can do this second sequence as perfect duplicates of each other.

E If you want, you can add a prop to your dance. I have ribbons, scarves, and pompoms you can use.

Th/CCSS This is a potential opportunity to have a discussion requiring children to compare and contrast. You can ask the following questions:

- Which locomotor pattern did you use?
- Were these the same or different from the locomotor patterns of your partner?
- Which kind of shape did you choose (wide, straight, angular, twisted, round)?
- Did your first shape match your second shape, or were they different?
- Think about your shapes, and compare them to your partner's shapes. What did you notice?

Culminating Activity

A Put the two sequences together in a dance. Decide which sequence to do first. In addition, decide whether you will perform each of the sequences at the same time or have Cat perform first and Copy Cat perform second. Practice until you have your sequence perfect.

A Let's show your dances to your classmates. I will divide the class into three areas.

Social/CCSS Showing a sequence is strictly voluntary. Both of you must want to show your dance. If your partner does not want to show and you do, you may show with an invisible partner. Any pairs in area 1 can show now. Watch carefully because after the show, I will ask for compliments. Decide what you think is the best part of the pair's sequence, and then I will call on several of you to give them compliments. [Repeat with areas 2 and 3.]

can copy the pathway but not the locomotor skill of a leader, or they can copy the level but not the body actions. Lessons on copying are very enjoyable for children.

Themes: Matching, Mirroring, Contrasting, and Complementing

Matching means doing exactly the same actions (left side matches left side, and right side matches right side), with the same shapes and movement qualities as a partner (see **Figure 31.16**).

Mirroring means doing the same actions with the same shapes, with partners facing each other as if they were looking in a mirror (see **Figure 31.17**). The left side of one partner does the same thing as the right side of the other partner.

Contrasting means partners make shapes or perform actions that are different or opposite (see **Figure 31.18**). In dance, we typically first teach children about contrasting using shapes. Big, wide shapes are contrasts to small, curled shapes. Children also can contrast each other using different levels, directions, pathways, or effort movement concepts.

Complementing means the shapes and actions of the partners relate in some way so the pair looks as if they are dancing together. *Complement* means to harmonize or accompany. For example, one child might make an angular shape, and his or

Figure 31.16 Matching

Figure 31.17 Mirroring

her partner might make a slightly higher angular shape above the first child (see **Figure 31.19**). Alternatively, both children might make a shape pointing in the same direction, but one child is at a medium level and the other at a low level. With complementing shapes, the shapes are similar and highlight one common idea or body position.

Figure 31.18 Contrasting levels

Extending Movement Variety and Vocabulary

Typically, copying, matching, mirroring, and complementing represent doing something with someone else. Thus, children and teachers can use these movement concepts to represent abstract concepts such as friendship, camaraderie, caring, togetherness, harmony, and closeness. When you want to design a dance using children's literature or poetry or a story about friendship and related themes, then relationship movement themes work well.

Contrasting shapes, when combined with forceful effort actions, can represent fighting, anger, discord, tension, power, antagonism, and opposition. When combined with gentle effort actions, contrasting shapes and actions can represent conversations in which the partners have different, even antagonistic messages. Thus, the area of relationships has opportunities to teach rich vocabulary words and have children experience representing those words in movement.

Figure 31.19 Creating a sequence of mirroring, matching, and complementing

SAMPLE LEARNING EXPERIENCES 31.15

Matching, Mirroring, Contrasting, and Complementing Shapes

We designed the following learning experiences for teachers who must teach in classrooms during inclement weather. You also can teach the tasks in a physical education space and, if you choose, add traveling movements between each shape.

Mirroring

Cog K Today, we will start by having you mirror your partner's movements and shapes. Mirroring means doing the same actions with the same shapes, facing your partner as if you were looking in a mirror. If your partner moves his or her right arm, you will move your left arm. It is weird; you have to do the opposite to look the same.

I Go with your assigned partner. Face each other. Select who will lead first. Lead partner, move your arms only. Partner, mirror the leader's arm movements.

E Switch leads. Lead partner, move only your legs. Partner, mirror the leader's leg action.

Social What are important things you need to do to help your partner mirror you? [Go slow; sometimes repeat a movement several times. Do movements the partner can do.]

E Switch leads again. Lead partner, move slowly into a shape, and then pause. Partner, mirror the leader's movement and shape. Lead partner, you can then move to a second and third shape, pausing in each shape while the partner mirrors it. Switch leads.

E Repeat the task, but this time as you change shapes, add a change in level. Try to use different shapes. Switch leads.

E Repeat the task, but this time add a change in direction. Try to use different shapes.

Matching

Cog K Now, we will work on matching shapes. Matching means doing exactly the same shapes, with your left side matching the left side of your partner and your right side matching your partner's right side. You must move at the same time to be matching. If one moves first and then the other moves, it is copying. What do you think you will need to do to both move at the same time? [Move slowly. Plan your movements.]

E Stand side by side or one behind the other. Lead partner, move slowly, and make three shapes, pausing in each shape. Partner matches the lead. Try to vary your level and the direction you face. Switch leads. [Repeat several times.]

Contrasting

Cog K Contrasting means partners make shapes or perform actions that are different or opposite. For example, big, wide shapes are contrasts to small, curled shapes. A high shape contrasts a low shape.

E Do the same task as before, but this time contrast your partner's shape. Remember to move slowly from one shape to the next and pause so your partner has time to create a contrasting shape. [Repeat several times.]

Complementing

Cog K The last partner relationship is complementing shapes. Complementing means the shape and actions of the partners relate in some way, so you look like you are harmonizing and dancing together. I will demonstrate with LaKeisha. LaKeisha is sitting in a curled shape, and I am making a curled shape over her. Our curled shapes complement each other. The shapes are not matching, but they are similar, and you can tell we planned the shape.

E You and your partner create three complementing shapes. [Check to be sure that the children understand what *complementing shapes* means.]

E Now, add rising and falling. One partner starts high and falls, while the other starts low and rises. Use complementing starting and ending shapes. [Repeat several times.]

Designing Sequences

E Combine your favorite ideas into a short sequence. You can use matching, mirroring, contrasting, and complementing shapes. Select three or four of your best shapes, and put them together so both of you move at the same time from starting shape 1 to shape 2 to shape 3 to ending shape 4.

Summary

The themes for dance lessons are derived from movement concepts from the body, effort, space, and relationship aspects of the Laban framework. A time-tested progression is to begin with body aspects, then progress to the effort, space, and relationship aspects. Dance lessons focus on movement themes (i.e., movement concepts) and topic themes. Topic themes include ideas, feelings, and topics from children's literature, poetry, stories, the natural world, art, music, history, geography, and other classroom subjects. Topic themes stimulate ideas for dancing and allow you to integrate dance with content children are learning in their classrooms.

Review Questions

1. Identify guidelines for modifying a dance lesson for younger children.
2. Describe the five basic shapes and explain how they relate to body actions.
3. Describe a way to teach symmetrical and asymmetrical shapes to children.
4. What is different and what is the same about sliding, galloping, and skipping?
5. What are two performance techniques that you can teach that cross sliding, galloping, and skipping?
6. Describe a way to teach children about the difference between twisting and turning.
7. Define and describe kinetic force in relation to dance content.
8. Define and describe static force in relation to dance content.
9. Define and describe light, anti-gravity exertion in relation to dance content.
10. Define and describe heavy weight in relation to dance content.
11. Define *sudden and sustained* in relation to the movement concept of time.
12. Write a task different from those found in the text for teaching sustained, strong movements.
13. Write a task different from those found in the text for teaching sustained, light movements.
14. Write a task different from those found in the text for teaching sudden, strong movements.
15. Write a task different from those found in the text for teaching sudden, light movements.
16. How do personal and general space relate to safety?
17. Write a task different from those found in the text for teaching directions. Your task must include an image, story, or topic.
18. Define mirroring, matching, contrasting, and complementing.

References

Branley, F. M., & Kelley, T. (1999). *Flash, crash, rumble, and roll.* New York: HarperCollins.

Chen, W., & Cone, T. P. (2003). Links between children's use of critical thinking and expert teacher's teaching in creative dance. *Journal of Teaching in Physical Education, 22,* 169–185.

Ehlert, L. (1991). *Red leaf, yellow leaf.* Orlando, FL: Harcourt.

Fleming, D. (1993). *In the small, small pond.* New York: Henry Holt and Company.

Hall, Z., & Halpern, S. (2000). *Fall leaves fall.* New York: Scholastic.

Humphrey, D. (1959). *The art of making dances.* New York: Rinehart.

Keats, E. J. (1962). *The snowy day.* New York: Puffin Books.

Laban, R. (1948). *Modern educational dance.* London: MacDonald & Evans.

Mitton, T., & Parker-Rees, G. (2001). *Down by the cool of the pool.* New York: Scholastic

Prelutsky, J., & Rand, T. (2004). *If not for the cat.* New York: Greenwillow Books.

Preston-Dunlop, V. (1980). *A handbook for modern educational dance* (rev. ed.). Boston: Plays.

Purcell Cone, T. (2000). Off the page: Responding to children's literature through dance. *Teaching Elementary Physical Education, 11*(5), 11–34.

Rink, J. E. (2014). *Teaching physical education for learning* (7th ed.). New York: McGraw-Hill.

Robbins, K. (1998). *Autumn leaves.* New York: Scholastic.

Roberton, M. A., & Halverson, L. E. (1984). *Developing children: Their changing movement.* Philadelphia: Lea & Febiger.

Rovegno, I. (2003). Children's literature and dance. *Teaching Elementary Physical Education, 14* (4), 24–29.

Stinson, S. (1982). Aesthetic experience in children's dance. *Journal of Physical Education, Recreation, and Dance, 53*(4), 72–74.

Thorpe, K. & Roper, R. (2000). *Follow the lemming.* New York: Simon Spotlight/Nickelodeon.

FYI

Summary of Task Label Abbreviations

I	Informing tasks
E	Extending/exploring tasks
R	Refinements
A	Application/assessment tasks
Org	Organizing task
Cog K	Cognitive knowledge: Explains or defines a concept
Social	Social skill or concept
Th	Thinking skill
Mot	Motivation concept
Safety	Safety information or reminder
MD	Modification to make the task more difficult
ME	Modification to make the task easier

Source: Adapted and Modified from Rink, J. E. (2014). *Teaching physical education for learning* (7th ed.). New York: McGraw-Hill.

Sample Plans for Level 1

In this section, we annotate sample plans written to bring alive the content discussed in this chapter so you can imagine how it might look in actual learning environments. As you read these plans, imagine you are the teacher, and think about what is happening and how you might react. You can develop some of these plans into lesson plans and others into a series of lessons for a unit.

In the first four plans, we include tips for teaching, an observation plan, and potential interactive decisions, such as refinements and tasks for teaching social responsibility and thinking skills. We include these tasks to give you examples of how you might respond on your feet if the need for adjustment arises. In the last four lesson and unit segments, we list the major tasks. At the beginning of each segment, we list potential performance techniques to use for refinements.

SAMPLE PLAN 31.1

Down by the Cool of the Pool

Movement Theme: Locomotor Skills and Body Actions Topic Theme: Animals Dancing Text: Mitton & Parker-Rees (2001). *Down by the Cool of the Pool*	Notes and Potential Interactive Teaching Decisions
Standards This plan addresses National Standards 1, 2, 4, and 5 and CCSS for comprehension **Objectives** The children will learn to **Motor** 1. Move using the following skills and body actions in a variety of ways: jump, spin, bounce, wiggle, stomp, stamp, leap, gallop, skip, hop, and prance, while adding different arm gestures. 2. Move lightly while bouncing, leaping, galloping, skipping, hopping, and prancing. 3. Move forcefully while stomping and stamping. 4. Move with loose, floppy tension while wiggling. **Social** 5. Understand that people can be different and have fun dancing together. **Affective** 6. Appreciate and value the enjoyment of dancing. **CCSS** 7. Summarize a written text read aloud. Use information gained from the illustrations and words in a text to demonstrate an understanding of its characters, setting, or events.	**Observation Plan**  1. Watch for children moving and stopping safely in general space without bumping into other children or falling when they stop. 2. Watch the arm action in the jumps. 3. Watch for light, quick force in bouncing. 4. Watch for heavy force (loose, floppy) in wiggling. 5. Watch for soft, light actions in leaping, galloping, and prancing.
Introduction	
I Today we are going to be reading *Down by the Cool of the Pool*, written by Tony Mitton and illustrated by Guy Parker-Rees. [Show the cover.] What do you think is going to happen in this book? Yes, it does look like they are going to have a good time in the water. Let's see.	

(*continues*)

SAMPLE PLAN 31.1

Down by the Cool of the Pool (continued)

Content Development

Frog **Cog K** [Read the page with the frog.] "Down by the pool in the cool of the day, Frog cried, 'Wheeeee! Can you dance like me?'" What is the frog doing? [Flying in the air. Dancing, jumping, and leaping.] Yes, jumping. **I** Let's dance like the frog. Travel about the space jumping and leaping.	**R** Did the frog use his hands to help him jump? Yes. The frog is reaching straight over his head. Which performance technique did you learn for jumping? Right. Reach for the sky. Try to do that when you jump.
E Make different shapes in the air when you jump.	**R** Make big jumps. Really reach with your hands high over your head like the frog.
Cog K Now, let's have fun spinning. Spinning means to turn around as many times as you can without losing your balance. **I** Try spinning on your feet.	
E You can spin on one foot or both feet.	**R** Try to keep your back straight and stretched when you spin.
E You can spin to your right or your left, whichever you want.	**MD** Spin on one foot.
E Now try spinning on different body parts. Which parts can you use? [Bottom, belly, back, side.]	
Frog Dance: Shape, Spin, Two Jumps, Shape **E** We are going to do a frog dance by putting jumping and spinning together into a sequence. You will need to remember this sequence because we will do it again. Start in any shape you want. **CCSS** If you need an idea for a shape, you can look at Frog in this picture to see whether any part of his body gives you an idea. **E** Hold your shape. Spin on your feet, jump two times, and make another shape.	[Repeat several times.] *Notes:* You can accompany the dance by shaking a tambourine during the spin, hitting the tambourine loudly on the jumps and softly on the shapes.
Duck **Cog K** What's happening in this picture? [Read the next page of the book.] **Social** The duck doesn't dance the same way as Frog, but she can have fun and dance with the frog. **I** For the duck dance, we are going to bounce and flap. Bounce up and down to the beat of the tambourine.	
E Now travel as you bounce.	**R** Be light and quick.
E Bounce and turn.	
E Freeze in a shape like the duck.	**CCSS** Which shapes can you see in this picture of the duck? [Round, curved.] **R** Make your shape like the duck.
E Flap your arms up and down to the beat of the tambourine.	**R** Be loose.
E Now flap your arms all around your body, to the side, forward, behind you, and to the other side.	**R** Make your arms loose and floppy.
E Now combine bouncing on your feet and flapping your arms.	

SAMPLE PLAN 31.1

Down by the Cool of the Pool (continued)

Duck Dance: Shape, Bounce and Flap, Shape, Bounce and Flap, Shape **E** Now let's do the duck dance. Start in a round, still shape like Duck. Then bounce and flap your arms. Next, on the loud beat of the tambourine, freeze in a second shape. Then bounce and flap again; add a turn if you want. Then freeze again in a third shape. [Repeat several times.]	[You will need to cue the children on the dance actions and order. There are too many different dances (one for each animal), and the sequence of actions is too long for the children to remember.]
A Now let's put the dances together like in the book. First do the duck dance, then the frog. I will talk you through it.	*Duck dance:* shape, bounce and flap, shape, bounce and flap, shape *Frog dance:* shape, spin, two jumps, shape
Pig **I** [Holding up the book.] What other animal might come dance with Duck and Frog? [Children guess.] Let's see. [Turn page.] A pig. And the pig wiggles. Kids are great wigglers. Wiggle all over.	**R** Be really loose and floppy when you wiggle.
E Now, wiggle your arms, legs, shoulders, hands, belly, back, all over again. Freeze in a wiggly shape.	**R** Be really loose when you wiggle, and let your limbs flop all over the space.
E Now do a wiggling walk, traveling on a wiggly pathway, and freeze in a wiggly shape.	Repeat several times, shaking the tambourine to help the children feel wiggly.
Pig Dance: Wiggly Shape, Wiggling Walk, Shape, Walk Shape **E** Let's do the pig dance. The pattern will be shape, walk, shape, walk, shape. When I say, "Go," you will do a wiggly shape, then walk wiggling on a wiggly pathway, freeze in a wiggly shape, wiggle walk again, and then freeze in a different wiggly shape.	Beat and shake tambourine to movements. Repeat several times.
A Now put it together with the duck and frog dances.	*Pig dance:* wiggly shape, wiggling walk, shape, walk, shape *Duck dance:* shape, bounce and flap, shape, bounce and flap, shape *Frog dance:* shape, spin, two jumps, shape
Sheep **I** [Holding up the book.] Who is next? Yes, the sheep. The sheep can dance, too, but not in the same way as the other animals. The sheep stomps. Let's stomp to a beat.	**Social** Do you think the sheep will have fun dancing with the other animals even though the sheep dances differently?
E March about the space stomping your feet.	Stomp with strong force.
E Now add a step. Stomp your left foot, then step on that foot; stomp your right foot, and then step on your right foot.	[Continue cuing, "Stomp, step, stomp, step," until all children are comfortable with the pattern.]
E Now let's add a clap. Stomp and clap, then step; stomp and clap, then step.	[Continue cuing until all children are comfortable with the pattern.]
E Now let's add an arm gesture. Clap and stomp. As you step, move your arms any way you want. Then clap and stomp. Practice the arm pattern first. Clap, gesture, clap, gesture.	**R** Make all your movements sharp and strong.
E Put all the arm and leg patterns together. This is the sheep stomp dance. **E** Let's repeat all the animals' dances.	*Sheep dance:* stomp/clap, step/arm gesture *Pig dance:* wiggly shape, wiggling walk, shape, walk, shape *Duck dance:* shape, bounce and flap, shape, bounce and flap, shape *Frog dance:* shape, spin, two jumps, shape

(*continues*)

SAMPLE PLAN 31.1

Down by the Cool of the Pool (continued)

Cat **I** [Holding up the book, read about the cat, dog, and goat.] The cat suddenly bounds in to join the group. **E** Start in a shape, then leap about the space, and freeze in a new shape. **E** Let's do the cat dance. Make a shape, leap two times, and make a different shape.	**R** Land lightly when you leap. Be quiet like a cat.
Dog **I** The dog joins the party, frisking round and round. Start in a shape, and then gallop in a circle. Make light, frisky gestures with your hands. **E** Reverse direction, and gallop in another circle. Freeze in a shape.	**R** Gallop lightly by extending your ankles so you point your toes in the air.
Goat **I** The goat dances by skipping and hopping. Start in a shape, and then skip about the space. **E** Add hand gestures showing how much fun you have dancing with the other animals. Freeze in a shape.	[Repeat several times.] **R** Skip and hop lightly by extending your ankles so you point your toes in the air.
A Let's do the dances of the cat, dog, and goat. I will talk you through the dances.	*Cat bounds:* shape, leap two times, shape *Dog frisking:* shape, gallop in circle, shape, gallop in circle, shape *Goat dance:* shape, skip, shape, hop, shape
Pony and Donkey: Pony Prances, Donkey Stamps **I** [Read about the pony and the donkey.] The pony prances in, and the donkey drums a dance. Let's prance like the pony. **E** Now, drum a dance using your feet. Jog by stamping your feet each time you land.	**R** Point your toes, lift your knees high, and jog lightly, prancing about the space like a pony. **R** While the pony is light, the donkey is strong and pounding on the earth.
E Now alternate your light, high prance and your low, strong stamps. Pony, donkey, pony, donkey.	
All Animals Dance and then Fall into the Pool **E** [Finish the book.] Now the cow joins in, and all the animals dance. You join in and dance, too. Select any of the animal dances you want, and dance all about the space. Look, Robert is dancing like the cat. Shelia is dancing like the dog.	
E Oh, no. The animals fall into the pool. Everybody drop to the floor, making sure you land safely. Look at the picture. Did the animals stop dancing when they landed in the water? No. So you also keep dancing while staying on the floor. Make your hands and feet dance in the air.	**R** Keep your movements light, and quickly flick your hands and feet all about your personal space.
E Now one by one the animals drift away from the pool, and the sun goes down. Start to dance slower and slower, and then, one body part at a time, put your hands, feet, and legs down gently. Then roll over, and fall asleep. [Read the end of the story.]	

SAMPLE PLAN 31.1

Down by the Cool of the Pool (continued)

Culminating Activity

E Let's do the dance again. I will talk you through it to help you remember.

Frog dance: shape, spin, two jumps, shape

Duck dance: shape, bounce and flap, shape, bounce and flap, shape

Pig dance: wiggly shape, wiggling walk, shape, walk, shape

Sheep dance: stomp/clap, step/arm gesture

Cat bounds: shape, leap two times, shape

Dog frisking: shape, gallop in circle, shape, gallop in circle, shape

Goat dance: shape, skip, shape, hop, shape

Pony prances

Donkey stamps

All of the animals dance (select any animal).

The animals fall into the pool and dance in the pool.

The sun goes down, and they fall asleep.

CCSS Closure

With your assigned partner, retell the story, including key details.

Social Closure

All the animals were different and they did different dances, yet they had fun. Discuss how this idea can apply to children.

SAMPLE PLAN 31.2

When Autumn Leaves Fall

Movement Theme: Shape (Symmetrical, Asymmetrical, Thin, Wide, Round, Twisted, Pointy), Swinging, and Swaying

Topic Theme: When Autumn Leaves Fall

Text: Hall & Halpern (2000). *Fall Leaves Fall!*

Standards

This plan addresses National Standards 1, 2, 4, and 5 and CCSS for vocabulary acquisition.

Objectives

Children will learn to

Motor, Cognitive, and Affective

1. Understand, feel, and perform different body shapes (symmetrical, asymmetrical, thin, wide, round, twisted, pointy).
2. Increase their awareness of the kinesthetic feeling of movement (i.e., the tension in their muscles when they make shapes) and increase their awareness of the shape of the movement.
3. Perform turning jumps and travel fast and lightly on circular pathways, expressing swirling and whirling.
4. Swing and sway, expressing soft, slow, indirect movement, being aware of the feeling of floating.
5. Appreciate the different feelings dance provides.

Notes and Potential Interactive Teaching Decisions

Observation Plan

1. Scan to be sure when children travel fast, they are only traveling as fast as they can safely and in control of the flow of their movement.
2. Watch for a variety of shapes, not only across the class but also from individual students.
3. Identify whether children maintain anti-gravity tension in their shapes.

(continues)

SAMPLE PLAN 31.2

When Autumn Leaves Fall (*continued*)

Creative Thinking 6. Explore freely using images of autumn leaves to enhance their performance. **CCSS** 7. Sort common objects into categories and gain a sense of the concept of shape that the categories represent.	
Introductory Activity	
CCSS/Cog K Bring in some leaves that have a variety of shapes and, if possible, have started to change colors. Spread them on the floor. Have the children discuss the shapes of the leaves. Have them categorize the leaves and identify the characteristics that distinguish different categories (e.g., thin, wide, round, twisted, and angular shapes; smooth and rough edges). Quickly read *Fall Leaves Fall!* (Hall & Halpern, 2000) (or another book on leaves), assign partners, and have the children describe the major events of the story. Explain that the dance today will use some of these same events.	You can integrate this lesson with a science lesson on leaves. Ask the classroom teacher about key facts he or she has taught about leaves changing colors or the key ideas from an informational text the children have read about leaves, such as *Autumn Leaves* (Robbins, 1998) or *Red Leaf, Yellow Leaf* (Ehlert, 1991). Bring the book to physical education class, and ask the children questions about the key ideas. Project on the wall pages with the key ideas, and have the children read these aloud.
Content Development	
Awareness of the Feeling of Stillness and Body Shape **Cog K/CCSS** Today we will be dancing focusing on different shapes the body can make, using what you discovered about the shape of the leaves we just examined to help you. What were the categories of shapes you identified in the leaves? [Thin, round, wide, angular, pointy, twisted]. **I** Start by walking about the space, stop, and feel the shape of your body, where every body part is. [Repeat several times.]	
E Walk all about the space again, and stop. This time, focus on feeling the stillness in your body. [Repeat several times.]	**R** Feel how your body is still but also alert, as if you are ready to move but perfectly still.
E This time, you decide when to walk and when to stop and be still. Some of you will be moving, and some of you will be still. Go.	**R** Concentrate on how it feels to be still when others are traveling by you—like in hide and seek, when you are hiding and are very still and other people walk by you. Feel the stillness and alertness in your muscles.
R This time, concentrate on feeling the shape of your body and the location of each body part when you are still.	**R** Attend to your shape, the shape of your arms, how much tension you have in your legs, and so on.
Adding Different Locomotor Skills **E** Now you may travel faster. You can jog, skip, gallop, slide, or use any locomotor skill you want. Travel only as fast as you can do so safely and with control. Stop when you want, and travel when you want.	**R** Focus on the feeling of moving faster and being still while others travel fast by you.
E Travel any way you want, and stop in a thin shape.	[Repeat several times, cuing children to vary the shape each time.]
E Travel and stop in a wide shape. [Repeat several times, varying the shape each time.]	**R** Be sure to travel lightly, stretching through your spine.
E Travel and stop in a round shape.	[Repeat several times, cuing children to vary the shape each time.]
E Travel and stop in a twisted shape.	[Repeat several times, cuing children to vary the shape each time.]

SAMPLE PLAN 31.2

When Autumn Leaves Fall (*continued*)

E Travel and stop in a pointy shape.	[Repeat several times, cuing children to vary the shape each time.]
E Now remaining in your personal space, change to a different shape each time I beat the drum. Be sure to try all five kinds of shapes.	**R** Feel the shape of your body and the location of each body part.
E This time, take three counts to move to your new shape. I will beat the drum 1, 2, 3. Start changing to your new shape on the count of 1, and complete your new shape on the count of 3. Then move to another new shape as I count 1, 2, 3.	[Repeat several times.]
Symmetrical and Asymmetrical Shapes **E** This time, explore both symmetrical and asymmetrical shapes. Using three beats, start in a thin symmetrical shape, and then make a thin asymmetrical shape. Try a round symmetrical shape, and now try a round asymmetrical shape. **E** [Repeat with pointy and wide shapes.]	
Adding the Metaphor of Autumn Leaves **E** Now that you have been practicing your shapes, let's go back to the leaves we studied at the start of the lesson. I want you to imagine leaves swirling in the wind. Travel on curved pathways by taking long steps. Sometimes spin in place doing a full turn, and sometimes jump and turn in the air. Try to move like leaves swirling in the wind.	*CCSS Notes:* The point here is not to have the children pretend to be leaves but to use falling and blowing leaves as a metaphor to elicit movement. We want them to make the connection between the aesthetics of autumn leaves and their shapes (thin and pointed, wide and flat, curled, or ragged and decaying with holes) and the feelings of swirling, drifting, whirling, floating, and gently falling.
E Try spinning at different levels—sometimes low, medium, and high.	**R** Travel lightly.
E What kinds of shapes do autumn leaves have? [Round and pointed, pointy and angular, long and thin, curled, and so on.] Make the shape of an old dried-up leaf that is curled and full of holes.	Repeat until children are showing a variety of shapes and you see each child do a different shape each time. Cue: Change to another shape, and another shape. Vary your shapes.
E Make different holes in your shape.	
E Now change to a different leaf shape.	
E Choose a leaf shape as your starting shape. The wind starts and picks you up. All the leaves swirl around the room, the wind dies down, and the leaves slow down and fall gently to the ground.	[Repeat several times, starting in a different leaf shape each time.] **R** Travel lightly as the wind picks you up. **R** When the wind dies down, sink slowly and gently to the floor.
Leaves Falling from a Tree **E** Explore movements associated with leaves falling from trees. Make a leaf shape that is hanging by one point to a branch. Let one arm hang and sway gently back and forth; start with a very small movement brought about by a breeze so gentle that you can hardly see the movement of the leaf. Now swing your arm bigger, now bigger, and bigger.	
E Extend the swinging movement to your whole body. Swing down and up, down and up, down and up.	**R** Feel the acceleration as you swing down and the deceleration as you swing up.
E Now try it with the other arm. [Repeat the previous two tasks, starting with a small swing with one arm and building to a larger swing with the whole body.]	**R** Pause at the top of each swing, anticipating the start of the next swing.

(*continues*)

SAMPLE PLAN 31.2

When Autumn Leaves Fall (*continued*)

E Now repeat with both arms. Make a different shape, and explore other body parts swaying and swinging gently back and forth. Make your whole body sway.	
E Make another leaf shape at a high level. Swing or sway using one or more body parts. Suddenly the leaf comes free from the branch and gently falls to the ground. Sway as you slowly fall to the ground. Now swaying, rise again.	[Repeat several times, exploring falling and rising and starting and ending in different shapes.] **R** Sink slowly and gently.
Culminating Activity	
A We will begin our dance making a leaf shape. The leaf is hanging by one point from the tree. Gently sway, first one body part, then more body parts, then your whole body. Suddenly the leaf breaks away and falls gently to the ground. End in a different leaf shape. The wind picks up all the leaves and swirls them around the room, turning in the air, spinning at different levels, until the wind dies and the leaves come to rest in a different leaf shape. The wind picks up again and blows the leaves around the room, blowing them closer and closer to the center of the room until the wind has blown all the leaves into a pile. Form a large group shape, staying close together but not touching one another, with each of you making different leaf shapes. Obviously, a magic wind has blown the leaves into a pile so you don't have to rake them!	[Talk the children through the dance several times.] **Affective Closure** With your assigned partner, discuss the feelings you had when you were swirling and whirling like leaves blowing in a wind. Contrast the feeling you have now sitting still with the feelings you had when you were still holding the different shapes of leaves.

SAMPLE PLAN 31.3

The Snowy Day

Movement Theme: Shapes, Body Actions, and Pathways Topic Theme: The Snowy Day Text: Keats (1962). *The Snowy Day*	Notes and Potential Interactive Teaching Decisions
Standards This plan addresses National Standard 1, 2, and 4 and CCSS for comprehension. **Objectives** The children will learn to **Motor** 1. Make a variety of curled, straight, wide, pointy, and twisted shapes. 2. Perform a variety of rising, falling, slashing, and heavy (plopping) movements, falling slowly and gently, and being tight when they slash and relaxed when they plop. 3. Travel on straight, curved, and zigzag pathways in different ways.	**Observation Plan**  1. Scan to see if children are bumping into each other because they are not adjusting their pathways. 2. Watch for a variety of shapes, not only across the class but also from individual students. 3. Watch for gentle falling, forceful slashing, and heavy plopping.

SAMPLE PLAN 31.3

The Snowy Day (continued)

Creative Thinking Skills 4. Explore and represent movement ideas generated from children's literature about playing in the snow. **5.** Improve the clarity of their shapes. **CCSS** 6. Use information gained from the illustrations and words in a text to demonstrate an understanding of its characters, setting, or events.	
Introduction	
Read the first section of the text: **Cog K/CCSS** [Cover shows a boy in a city looking back at his footprints in the snow.] The title of this book is *The Snowy Day* by Ezra Jack Keats. Put your thumbs up if you have seen snow [Question for children living in warm climates]. Tell us when. Raise your hand, and tell me what is happening here. What is the boy doing? Where does he live? [Read the first section with Peter waking up, seeing the snow, going outside, and walking on pathways making different footprints in the snow. Stop on the page before he sees the tree.]	This is a Caldecott Award–winning book, which you can probably find in most school and public libraries. It was one of the first major children's books with an African American child as the main character. The story focuses on a little boy who wakes up, sees that it has snowed, and goes out to play in the snow. For dance, we divide the book into three sections. Read each section to the children, and then explore dance movements representing that section. If possible, have the classroom teacher teach the book first so the dance lesson can entail a quick review of the story and drawings to which children respond in their own ways.
Content Development	
Stretching and Curling (Waking Up), Falling and Rising Gently (Like Snow) **I** Start curled up in a round shape, as if you were sleeping. Slowly open your eyes, yawn, and stretch your arms. Now curl up again, and go to sleep. This time, stretch your legs, and then curl again. Now stretch your whole body and curl again, remaining at a low level.	**R** Make your whole body round. **R** Stretch throughout your whole body.
E This time, change levels. Try different ways to stretch and curl, each time curling, stretching, and twisting your spine in a different way and at a different level.	[Repeat several times.] **R** Really feel the stretch through your spine each time to wake your body up.
E Peter sees that it has snowed. Let's explore moving gently like falling snow. Stretch very tall, and then gently sink down to the floor. Now reverse these actions: Slowly rise again until you are stretched tall. As I beat the drum, slowly fall for four counts and then rise for four counts.	**R** Feel as light as snow falling.
E Each time you fall, try to end in a different curled shape, just like the mounds of snow Peter saw from his window.	**R** Feel lightness in your arms and whole body, as if you were as light as snow.
E This time, sway as you slowly fall, and then rise, keeping your arm movements light and gentle, and ending in a different round-mound-of-snow shape each time.	**R** Fall slowly, and gently drift down into a soft mound of snow. Let your arms just drift about the space as you fall.
Pathways in the Snow **E** Now explore making pathways in the snow. Start by walking on straight pathways, just like Peter, sometimes pointing your toes out and sometimes pointing your toes in.	

(*continues*)

SAMPLE PLAN 31.3

The Snowy Day (continued)

E	Make your own pathways in the snow. Explore walking on curved, zigzag, and twisted pathways. Sometimes point your toes in and out.	**R**	Make your pathways clear. Make your curved pathways perfectly round, your zigzag pathways very sharp and angular, and your twisted pathways very wavy and convoluted.
E	Write your name in the snow by leaving footprints on pathways with your feet.		
E	Explore making different footprint patterns by jumping and hopping in different ways. Sometimes slide your feet without lifting them off the ground to create a different pattern.		
Read the Next Section of the Text			
I	Let's see what happens next to Peter. [Read the page, "And he found something sticking out of the snow that makes a new track."] What do you think Peter found? What would make a pathway like that? [Call on several children.] Let's see what it was. [Turn page.] A stick. [Read the next section, stopping after Peter slides down the hill.] Let's review some of the fun things Peter did in the snow. Tell me what he did. [Call on children until they mention all of Peter's activities.] Notice the sky on this page when he is climbing up the hill and sliding down. What do these swirling lines represent? [Wind, swirling snow.]		
Slash and Plop			
I	Let's start by exploring the movements Peter made when he smacked the snow-covered tree. Staying in your personal space, do a slicing action with your arms, and stamp on one foot. Do another slicing action in a different direction, and stomp with the other foot. Continue to explore different ways to slash with your arms as you stomp with your feet.	**R**	Stay tight when you slash your arms. Be tight in your tummy, legs, chest, and arms. Your whole body should be tight.
E	Do three different slashing movements in a row as I beat the drum.		
E	Try again, adding a change of level.		
E	Try again, adding a turn and a change of level.		
E	Peter smacked the tree. Then what happened? Right. The snow plopped on his head. Let's explore the feeling of plop. Hold your arms out to the side and, without hurting yourself, totally relax your arms and let them drop to your hips with a plop. Try it again. [Repeat several times.]	**R**	When you plop, your arms feel heavy without any tension.
E	This time, extend the plopping feeling to your whole body. When you relax and plop your arms, also let your torso relax, and bend your knees so your whole body plops down a few inches. Don't plop onto the floor because you could hurt yourself. Just get the feeling of your whole body plopping down a little and then stopping yourself before you land on the floor.		[Repeat several times, cuing the children to try to end in a different shape each time.] **R** Feel the looseness in your muscles when you plop. **R** Relax and show you have very little tension after you plop.

SAMPLE PLAN 31.3

The Snowy Day (continued)

E Let's put the movements together into a short sequence: slash, slash, slash, plop.	[Repeat several times.]
Round, Wide, Straight and Twisted Shapes; Swirling Wind **E** What else did Peter do? Yes, he made snow angels. What kind of shape is that? Yes, wide. He also made a snowman. What shape was the snowman? Yes, round. When Peter slid down the hill, what shape did he make? Yes, straight. When the wind blew the snow, it swirled and twisted all around.	
Let's explore making these different shapes. Start at a low level in a round shape. Moving in slow motion, travel while keeping in a round shape, like a big, huge snowball for making a snowman. Now pause, and stretch into a wide shape. Then travel again, making different round shapes. Now pause, and stretch into a straight shape, and travel again in a round shape. Keep going, making different wide and straight shapes each time you pause.	**R** Really stretch when you make your straight and wide shapes. Travel slowly, and keep your body parts rounded when you make curled shapes.
E Travel about the room on a circular pathway like a swirling wind. Jump and make a twisted shape in the air, like snow being swirled and twisted by the wind.	**R** You can travel as fast as you want as long as you maintain control and don't bump into anyone else.
E Let's put the movements together into a short sequence. Start in a round shape, stretch slowly into a wide shape, and travel on a circular pathway by swirling, turning, and doing twisting jumps like a snow blizzard. Do a slashing jump, reach tall, and plop down to a medium level, holding your ending shape.	[Repeat several times.]
Read the Rest of the Book **I** Let's read the rest of the book. [Stop at one of the pages with snowflakes.] What are the shapes of snowflakes? Yes, they are pointy, most are symmetrical, and they all have six sides or points. **E** Let's dance to the rest of the story. Start by exploring different pointy shapes. Make some symmetrical and some asymmetrical. Make a new shape each time I beat the drum.	**R** Make as many body parts as you can be pointy in your pointy shapes. [Repeat this last dance sequence several times.] **CCSS Closure** With your assigned partner, discuss all the activities Peter did in the snow. Explain how Peter felt when he learned that his snowball melted. Do you think his snowball melting contributed to his dream that all the snow melted? Give reasons for your opinion.
E Now make a round shape like a snowball, and slowly melt into a puddle on the floor. Go to sleep sad, like Peter when his snowball melted.	
E Wake up, stretch, go outside with your friends, and skip about the space happy because it snowed again.	

SAMPLE PLAN 31.4

The Summer Vacation

<table>
<tr><th>Movement Themes: Light/Sudden, Light/Sustained, Heavy/Sudden, Heavy/Sustained, and Strong/Sustained Effort
Topic Theme: Summer Vacation</th><th>Notes and Potential Interactive Teaching Decisions</th></tr>
<tr><td>

Standards

This plan addresses National Standards 1, 2, 4, and 5 and CCSS for vocabulary acquisition.

Objectives

The children will learn to

Motor

1. Perform a variety of movements using different effort movement concepts, using light tension in light movements, using strong tension in strong movements, moving very slowly in sustained movements, and having loose muscles during heavy movements.

Thinking Skill, Cognitive Knowledge, CCSS

2. Compare and contrast movements with different effort movement concepts.
3. Demonstrate an understanding of verbs and adjectives by relating them to their opposites.

Affective

4. Appreciate how dance expresses emotions and enjoy expressing emotions through movement.

</td><td>

Notes: This lesson illustrates how to put sample learning experiences together into lesson segments. We started by thinking of a simple story that could incorporate several of the themes discussed in level 1 effort combining force and speed. We then planned exploration tasks for each theme and designed an introduction.

Observation Plan

1. Throughout the lesson, scan for children maintaining safe distances from each other.
2. Watch for the appropriate amount of tension for each task.

</td></tr>
<tr><th colspan="2">Introductory Activity</th></tr>
<tr><td>

I To warm up today, I want you to start by walking or, if you have a wheelchair, by rolling, all about general space. Travel on curved pathways, sometimes curving to the right and sometimes curving to the left.

Social Be sure to watch out for your classmates. Show you care about them by letting them pass in front of you or changing direction so you don't bump into each other.

</td><td></td></tr>
<tr><td>

E Skip all about the gym on different curved pathways. Make these happy skips. Pretend you are on summer vacation. Show how happy you are by making light gestures with your hands.

</td><td>

R Skip lightly.

R Keep your gestures light.

R Swing your arms.

R Make your arms gestures be quick, light, and happy.

</td></tr>
<tr><th colspan="2">Content Development</th></tr>
<tr><td>

Cog K Today we are going to work on moving with strong force, light force, and heavy force. In addition, we will be moving fast and slow. Let's start with strong force.

</td><td></td></tr>
<tr><td>

Hard as a Rock

I Standing straight with your arms at your sides, tighten up your entire body. Make every muscle as hard as a rock. Make your arms so tight and strong that I can't pull your arms away from your body.

E Rest a second, and try again.

</td><td>

[Select several children and try (pretending to be trying very hard) to pull their arms away from their bodies.]

R Try hard to be tight all over. You are using strong force.

[Repeat, "Rest, tight, rest, tight," several times.]

</td></tr>
</table>

SAMPLE PLAN 31.4
The Summer Vacation (*continued*)

E Let's try making different shapes while staying tight. Ready? Go. Try another shape. Now, another shape.	
E Make your shape angular and pointy. How do you make a shape angular? [You stick out your elbows, knees, legs, arms, and fingers and bend at the hips and knees.]	**R** Make as many parts of your body as you can be pointy.
The Tug-of-War **E** Now we are going to add moving slowly while maintaining strong force. Pretend you are in a tug-of-war. Grip the rope with power and strength and get into a ready position—that is, a strong position to resist the pull of the rope by the other team.	**R** What should your ready position look like? [Knees bent, hips bent, hands holding the rope, ready to lean back.] Right. Let's see excellent ready positions.
E Now pull slowly, pretending there is a team of very strong people pulling against you. Slowly move backward, pretending you are pulling the other team forward toward you.	**R** Really keep tight; be tight in your tummy, legs, torso, hips, and arms.
E Oh, no, the opposition is too strong! You are slowly losing ground and being pulled forward. Now you feel yourself getting stronger and stronger. You brace yourself against the strength of your opponent. Now you are slowly winning.	
E Let's try pulling facing different directions. Turn and pull forward, now sideways, now backward, now forward, trudging one step at a time.	**R** Feel and show power and strength.
Cog K We have just been working on strong, sustained force. That means you use strong force and move slowly. Next, we will move slowly but this time with light force.	
Floating Like a Bubble **I** Move your hand very slowly around your personal space as if your hand was a bubble floating all around your body. Try this with the other hand, then with both hands at the same time.	**R** Keep your movement soft and gentle. **R** Feel your arms become as light as can be. They feel as light as a bubble. **R** Move very slowly.
E Take a deep breath. Lift up your arms, and feel as if your body has become a bubble. You become lighter and lighter and finally lighter than air. Now travel slowly and gently floating in the air, feeling calm and peaceful as you look down at the ground.	**R** Move very slowly so your bubble does not pop.
Cog K With your assigned partner, compare and contrast the last two movements we practiced. [The force was different, but the speed was the same.] [Select one or two pairs to share their answers.]	
Alternating Strong/Sustained with Light/Sustained **E** Now let's alternate strong, sustained effort with light, sustained movements. See if you can feel the contrast in your body between strong and light movements. Everyone move slowly with strong force.	**R** Be really, really tight. Don't forget to tighten your torso.
E Without pausing, relax your muscles, and continue to move slowly but with light force. Reach your arms out in your personal space, and travel slowly on curved pathways about the gym.	**R** Feel really light and airy—like you are floating. **R** Don't speed up your movements; keep moving slowly.
E Now switch to strong force, now light.	[Continue alternating about every 10 seconds.]

(*continues*)

SAMPLE PLAN 31.4

The Summer Vacation (*continued*)

Freeze! Something Is Coming! **Cog K** Rest. Now we are going to change the speed of your movement, and move very quickly with strong force and strength. Walk about the space, and on the [loud] beat of the drum, quickly jump, stomp, and freeze, feeling tension in your body in a wide, angular shape as if you were scared the drum was a dangerous creature.	
E This time, walk faster, and when you hear the drum, suddenly jump, turning in the air, and land with tension in your body, showing that the drum startled you, but you are ready to defend yourself.	
E This time walk even faster, and when the drum beats turn faster, grit your teeth, glare at the drum, and look angry as if you were mad at the drum for bothering you.	**R** Feel the tightness and tension in your muscles.
The Mad, Mad Child **E** Now you are really mad at the annoying drum. Walk and stop. Make fists, stamp your feet, and shake your head, "No, no, no."	**R** Grit your teeth, and tighten up.
E Now walk mad. Walk fast, bend your elbows, make fists, and pump your arms back and forth. Now stomp your feet—you are very mad. **E** In fact, you are so mad that you go mad. Jump up and down. Stomp your feet. Thrust your arms in many directions. Travel quickly about the space jumping and stomping and thrusting your arms. You are the mad, mad child. (See **Figures** in Sample Learning Experiences 31.7)	**R** Be tight and walk fast, clicking your heels on the ground. **R** Be as tight as you can be. **R** Stomp hard.
The Tired, Bored Child **Cog K** Now we will contrast that movement. What is the opposite of moving fast? Right, moving slowly. One opposite of strong movements is light movement, which we practiced earlier. Another contrasting movement to tight and strong is heavy movement.	
E Let's work on heavy movement. As you are standing there, try to relax every muscle in your body, maintaining just enough tension to remain standing. Let your head tip. Relax in your shoulders. Sag through your spine. **E** Just to feel the difference, tighten up every muscle, and be rigid as a board. Now relax. Alternate tight, loose, tight, loose.	**R** Feel loose and relaxed during heavy movements.
E Now try to walk with heavy movements, staying as relaxed as you can.	**R** Heavy, sustained movement is totally loose but never stops.
E Let's all look bored. How do you feel when you are bored? Can you show me bored? Make your muscles relaxed, loose. Relax your shoulders, tummy, legs, arms, face, jaw, and eyes. Strike a bored pose.	
E Now walk slowly, looking bored. Keep all your muscles as loose as you can. Walk slowly about the space, drag your feet, hang your head, look bored. Stop and hold a bored pose. Change to another bored pose.	**R** Move slooooooowly.

SAMPLE PLAN 31.4
The Summer Vacation (*continued*)

Alternating the Mad Child and the Bored Child	
E Now let's alternate the two contrasting movements. First, stomp about the gym, being mad. When I hit the drum, suddenly get into a tight mad, shape.	**R** Be tight.
E Now relax, and let the tension leave your body. Walk about the space slowly with heavy tension. You are so tired that it is hard to even move. **E** Now you are mad again. Stomp about the space. Jump up and down, and thrust your arms out—you have gone mad from being mad. **E** Now move bored and slow. Relax all your muscles, and just drag your feet as you slowly walk about the gym. [Alternate the mad child and the bored child until the children move confidently.]	**R** Feel tired with no tension in your muscles.
Cooked Spaghetti Arms	
Cog K We have one more way to move—that is, moving suddenly but with heavy effort. This means you will be totally loose and relaxed but will move quickly.	
E As you are standing there, lift your arms away from your sides. Make them stiff and straight, like dried spaghetti before it is cooked. By magic, the spaghetti cooks. Now suddenly relax your arm muscles, and let your arms drop to your sides and then hang there limply. Twist and let your arms flop around. Sway from side to side, letting your arms swing as if they were limp, cooked spaghetti.	**R** Keep your arms very loose and relaxed.
E Now, extend the movement to your whole body. Reach up, stretch up on your toes (balls of your feet), and tighten your body. Then suddenly relax, and flop back to a standing position, with every muscle in your body so loose that you have just enough tension to remain standing. Try again, being sure to have enough tension in your arms so you don't slap yourself when you relax.	
Culminating Activity	
A Let's put everything together into a dance about a summer vacation. Here is the story: You have been waiting all summer to go away on a trip. You finally arrive at this cool vacation cabin, look out the window, and see that it's raining. It rains for an entire week. What do you do? You walk around bored.	
Bored Dance with Heavy, Slow Movements	
E Now let's walk slowly, looking bored. Keep all your muscles as loose as you can. Walk slowly about the space, drag your feet, hang your head, and look bored. Move very slowly. Stop and hold a bored pose. Change to another bored pose. **A** Let's make up a bored dance. Start in a bored shape. Now walk slowly, dragging your feet. Stop in another bored pose. Walk slowly. Now slowly sink down onto the floor, sit, and hold a bored pose. [Repeat the dance several times.]	

(*continues*)

SAMPLE PLAN 31.4

The Summer Vacation (*continued*)

Angry Dance with Strong, Sudden Movements

A Just when you think things can't get worse, they do! It rains another whole week, and you must stay inside. And you are mad. Let's do the mad dance. Walk about the space, and on the beat of the drum, stomp and land in an angry shape. You are mad. Grit your teeth, and tighten up. Walk again, and stop, stamp your feet, and shake your head, "No, no, no." Now walk mad. Walk fast, bend your elbows, make fists, and pump your arms back and forth. Be tight, and walk fast, clicking your heels on the ground. Now stomp your feet—you are very mad. In fact, you are so mad from staying inside another week that you go mad. Jump up and down. Stomp your feet. Thrust your arms every which way. Freeze and shake, making a funny face. You are the mad, mad child.

Skipping with Light, Sudden Movements

A Rest. The next week, you wake up, look out the window, and see that it is bright and sunny. It is a perfect day. You are so happy that you go outside and skip. Skip about the space, and make light happy gestures with your hands. You are so excited about being outside that you just skip and skip, showing you are happy by doing light, quick movements with your hands.

Tug-of-War with Strong, Slow Movements

A You see a friend and decide to have a tug-of-war. Go with your assigned partner, face each other, but don't touch each other. One of you faces the stage, and the other faces the exit door. Have a pretend tug-of-war. Start with the partner facing the stage winning, then the one facing the door. Move backward while pulling your partner with a pretend rope when you are winning, and be pulled in the other direction when your partner is winning. [Teacher calls out who is winning and finally ends the tug-of-war in a tie.]

Bubbles with Light, Slow Movements

A Now you decide to blow bubbles and watch them float on the breeze in the bright, sunny sky. Stand and take a deep breath. Lift up your arms, and feel as if your body has become a bubble and you are lighter than air. Imagine you are light and you can float in the air above the ground, looking down. Now you and your friend travel slowly and gently all around town. You look down at all the exciting things to see and do in the town, and you come to rest right in front of an ice cream store.

The Ice Cream Cone

[Combines light, sudden; heavy, sudden; and heavy, sustained effort.] This is the sad, sad story of my brother Bob's ice cream cone. We went to the store last summer and it was so hot—more than 100 degrees—and we were so hungry that we felt as if we hadn't eaten anything for the past year. We saw an ice cream shop and we were so happy. We spent all of our money and bought ice cream cones. Bliss! We thought we had it made. We started eating our ice cream and we were so happy. In fact, we were so happy that we did not watch our ice cream. My brother's hand and arm started to relax, the ice cream cone started to tip, and it tipped farther and farther until plop, the ice cream fell out and landed on the hot, dirty sidewalk. Worse, the ice cream started to melt. Before our very eyes, it melted into a sorry, sticky puddle of goop. Bob looked as if he was going to cry. He was so sad and blue that a blue cloud settled over his head. The owner of the ice cream shop saw how blue he was and gave him a new scoop. That's the end of the story.

A Let's do a dance about the ice cream cone. First, skip lightly and briskly about the gym, gesturing quickly and lightly with your hands to show how happy you are to buy ice cream [light, sudden arm actions]. Reach tall, making your muscles tight. Then, *with control*, collapse with loose muscles to a low level [heavy, sudden movement]. Slowly melt into the floor until you spread out in a sorry, sticky puddle of melted ice cream [heavy, sustained movement]. Here comes the storeowner. He gives you another ice cream cone. You get up and skip about the space again. That's the end of the vacation story. End in a happy shape.

CCSS Closure

With your assigned partner discuss the difference between (a) movements showing you were the bored child; (b) movements showing you were the angry child; and (c) movements like you were a bubble floating in the air. Then, discuss which of the three movements you enjoyed performing the most, and explain why.

SAMPLE PLAN 31.5

Animal Haiku

These lesson segments are based on children's poetry—in this case haiku, in a book written by Jack Prelutsky, a well-known author of children's poetry, and illustrated by Ted Rand. We highly recommend buying or borrowing this book because the illustrations are helpful in eliciting the movements you are trying to teach the children. The ideas in these learning experiences can also be adapted to other books about animals and to stories with similar emotions.

Movement Theme: Force and Speed
Topic Theme: Animal Haiku
Text: Prelutsky & Rand (2004). *If Not for the Cat*

Standards

This plan addresses National Standard 1, 2, 4, and 5 and CCSS for vocabulary acquisition and comprehension.

Objectives

Children will learn to

Motor

1. Perform a variety of light/sustained, strong/sudden, strong/sustained, light/sudden, and heavy/sustained movements, maintaining tight muscles when moving with strong force, light tension when moving with light force, and loose tension when moving with heavy force.
2. Move very slowly and continuously during sustained movements.
3. Move quickly during sudden and fast movements.

Affective

4. Appreciate that they can use different movement qualities to express their ideas and represent animals from haiku poetry.
5. Enjoy representing animals.

CCSS

6. Use sentence-level context and illustrations as clues to the meaning of a word of phrase.
7. Expand their vocabulary of verbs that specify nuanced meanings of movement concepts and enhance the situations and characteristics of animals.

Potential Refinements

Light, sustained effort:

- Light like a feather, gentle, soft, tender

Strong, sudden effort:

- Tight muscles
- Strong, powerful movements
- Energetic, spirited skips and jumps

Strong, sustained effort:

- Feel the tension
- Tight muscles

Light, sudden effort:

- Dart lightly, scurry quickly, tap lightly

Heavy, sustained effort:

- Molasses
- Heavy, loose
- Weary, tired, fatigued, sluggish, lethargic

Content Development

Cog K Today we are going to work on moving at different speeds and using different amounts of force. Let's start with light, slow movements.

(continues)

SAMPLE PLAN 31.5

Animal Haiku (*continued*)

Introducing Light, Sustained Effort

I Move your hand very slowly around personal space, as if you were drawing a never-ending line. Write lightly. Keep your movement soft and gentle. Move slowly.

E Try this with the other hand.

E Try both hands at the same time.

E Take a deep breath. Lift up your arms, and feel as if your body has become lighter than air.

E Now travel slowly and gently. Imagine you are light, like a feather (or balloon), and you can float and fly in the air above the ground looking down.

Introducing Light, Sudden Effort

I Now we are going to move lightly but instead of going slowly, we will move very quickly. Move your hands very quickly and lightly, tapping the air. Tap all around your personal space with your fingers.

E Another way to move your hands lightly and quickly is to make them quiver. Now make your arms quiver.

Cog K/CCSS A quiver is like a shiver when you are cold. See if you can make your entire body quiver.

E You can also move fast and light when you travel. Hold yourself in a ready position. When I beat the drum, instantly move about one foot. Go. Move so abruptly and suddenly that an observer won't even see you move, but just notice you are in a new location. Go.

E Now pick a spot a short distance away from you. When you hear the drum, dart quickly to that spot. Go. Now select another spot. Move lightly and quickly, then pause and hold a ready position anticipating your next move. Dart so lightly that the floor can't even feel your feet. [Repeat several times.]

Haiku

Cog K Let's take these two ways of moving with light/fast and light/sustained effort, and use them to create dances about animals. This is a book of haiku. Haiku is a form of poetry from Japan with a three-line structure. The first and third lines have five syllables, and the second line has seven syllables. Haiku typically describe, compare, contrast, or relate one or two images. The images are often from nature. The haiku poems written by Prelutsky are like riddles in that each one describes an animal, but the author does not use the name of the animal in the haiku. Here is the first one.

Jellyfish Dance

[Show the book, read the haiku, and discuss Ted Rand's illustration of a jellyfish (Prelutsky & Rand, 2004, pp. 10–11).]

Haiku by Jack Prelutsky

Boneless, translucent,
We undulate, undulate,
Gelatinously.

Cog K What animal is the haiku about? Put your thumbs up if you have seen a jellyfish in an aquarium. How do they move?

CCSS Listen to the word *gelatinously.* Can you hear another similar word you know based on the root word, which in *gelatinously* is the root word *gelatin*? Can anyone guess? Jell-O. Jell-O is the brand name for flavored, colored gelatin. Think about the texture of Jell-O or jelly as we do the jellyfish dance.

E Now we will move in the slow, gentle, flowing way under the sea of a jellyfish undulating. While standing, breathe in and out, lifting your arms up and down as if they were inflating and deflating like your lungs. Bend your knees as you exhale, and straighten them as you inhale. Twist and vary the positions of your arms each time you undulate up and down as if you were made of Jell-O.

E Keep bending your knees and moving your arms gently and slowly up and down, undulating and traveling very slowly first forward and then backward.

E Now, let's do a jellyfish dance. Undulate as you slowly walk forward, pause, turn, and extend your arms and fingers, pointing back toward your starting position. Wiggle your fingers like poisonous tendrils floating behind the jellyfish. [Repeat.]

Hummingbird Dance

Cog K Having the opposite quality of movement from the jellyfish is this animal. Does anyone know what it is? Yes, a hummingbird. [Read the haiku and discuss the illustrations.] Put your thumbs up if you have seen a hummingbird fly. How does it move?

E Start by extending your hands to the sides, and quiver by rotating them quickly. Now dart to another position and quiver again. Repeat three times.

SAMPLE PLAN 31.5

Animal Haiku (*continued*)

E Now alternate: Slowly walk and undulate like a jellyfish, and then quiver and dart like a hummingbird.

Cat and Mouse Dance: Introducing Strong, Sudden Effort

I We are still going to move suddenly, like the hummingbird, but this time with force and strength. On the [loud] beat of the drum, suddenly do a jump, and land in a wide, angular shape. Be tight in all your muscles in your shape.

Cog K Let's see if there is a haiku that we can dance to using strong, fast movements. [Show the book, read the haiku, and discuss the illustration—a mouse behind a hole in the wall with the face of the cat filling the hole (pp. 6–7).]

Haiku by Jack Prelutsky

If not for the cat,
And the scarcity of cheese,
I could be content.

CCSS Discuss with your assigned partner how the mouse feels. What problems does the mouse face that affect whether he or she is content?

E Let's do a dance representing the ideas in the haiku. Start by traveling about the gym moving slowly and silently like a cat. Pause. Look around to see if the mouse is visible.

E Walk again, stepping so gently that the mouse can't hear you moving. Freeze—you see the mouse! There he is, looking for cheese.

E Suddenly pounce on the mouse. Jump high, and come down with a strong stomp (see the chapter-opening photo.)

E Pounce again, making a shape in the air. Make your gestures powerful. Oh, no, you missed the mouse!

E Now, scurry about the space quickly and lightly like a mouse avoiding the claws of the cat. You see a hiding space, dart in it, and curl up safe from the cat. [Repeat the whole dance several times.]

Kangaroo and Baby Dance

Cog K Here is another haiku. [Read the haiku of the kangaroo (pp. 30–31) and discuss the illustration of the kangaroo and the baby in her pouch.]

Haiku by Jack Prelutsky

Safe inside my pouch
Sleeps the future of my kind—
Delicate and frail.

CCSS Discuss with your assigned partner how you think the mama kangaroo feels. Imagine how you might represent this in movement.

E Let's do a dance representing the ideas in this haiku. Start by traveling about the space using hopping, jumping, leaping, 2-1, and 1-2. Make big, strong jumps, springing high like a kangaroo bounding energetically all about the space.

E Stop in a big, wide, open shape. Now gently and slowly close up into a rounded, curled shape like a mama kangaroo protecting her baby. Your muscles feel light and soft. Show tenderness to your baby. [Repeat.]

Sloth Dance: Introducing Heavy, Sustained Effort

Affective We have been moving with strong and light force. How does it feel when you move with strong force? With light force? There is another kind of force that feels different. It is called heavy force. We will start with heavy, slow force. When you move with heavy force, you feel heavy, tired, sluggish, and very loose. [Call on several children.]

I As you are standing there, try to relax every muscle in your body, maintaining just enough tension to remain standing. Let your head tip. Relax your shoulders. Sag through your spine.

E Just to feel the difference, tighten up every muscle; be rigid as a board. Now relax. Alternate: tight, loose, tight, loose.

E Try to walk staying as relaxed as you can. Heavy, sustained movement is totally loose but never stops.

Sloth Dance

Cog K Let's read another haiku. This is about an animal called a sloth. [Show the book, read the children the haiku, and discuss the illustration by Ted Rand of the sloth (pp. 12–13).] Sloths live in the trees in the rainforest. They spend most of the time hanging upside down and holding onto branches with their claws. Sloths are the slowest-moving mammals on earth. Because they move slowly, it is very hard for predators to see them.

(*continues*)

SAMPLE PLAN 31.5

Animal Haiku (*continued*)

E Let's do a dance representing the very, very, very slow-moving sloth. At a low level, travel along the ground so slowly I wonder if you are moving or if it is just my imagination.

R Be very loose and heavy.

E Keep changing the body part supporting your weight.

Rattlesnake Dance

Cog K What is this animal (pp. 22–23)? Yes, a rattlesnake. Are rattlesnakes dangerous? Do you know why? [Read and discuss the haiku and illustration.]

E We are going to move in three different ways in the rattlesnake dance. First, we will slowly glide, then we will rattle, and finally we will strike. Start by gliding, traveling on your feet slowly and quietly all about the space. Which kind of pathway does the snake use? Yes, curved like an S.

E Now pause and rattle your hands and shake all over. Make a hissing noise.

E Suddenly jump and kick your legs, punch with your hands, and land with a sharp, striking movement. Repeat your dance.

Butterfly Metamorphosis Dance: Introducing Strong, Sustained Effort

Notes: This next set of learning experiences can be expanded to a lesson connecting dance to science. Metamorphosis is often a topic in fourth and fifth grade science.

Cog K For the next animal, we will use a new way to move—strong, slow movements.

I Standing straight with your arms at your sides, tighten up your entire body. Make every muscle as hard as a rock. Make your arms so tight and strong that I can't pull your arms away from your body.

E Reach up, and, showing tension in all your muscles, slowly push your hands down to the floor as if you were crushing something flat on the floor. Keep lowering down until your whole body is at a low level.

E Now, reverse, and press up as if you were in a box and to escape you had to lift the heavy box top up and then over your head. [Reverse and repeat several times.]

Cog K [Read the butterfly haiku, pp. 38–39.] What is this haiku about? Yes, the life cycle of a butterfly. What did you learn in science class about how butterflies grow? A butterfly isn't born with wings. It starts life as an egg. The egg hatches, and a caterpillar emerges. This is called the larva stage. The caterpillar eats leaves almost constantly. Next comes the pupa stage, in which the caterpillar is enclosed in a chrysalis and turns into an adult butterfly. In stage 4, the butterfly emerges from the chrysalis with beautiful wings and can fly.

Butterfly Metamorphosis Dance

E *Egg stage:* Start curled in a tight, little egg. Then, with strong, slow force, press your way out of the egg. It is hard to get out, and you have to push hard with lots of tension. Even then, you can only move slowly.

E *Larva stage:* Stay low to the ground, and move with a feeling of heaviness. Transfer your weight from one body part to the next, moving slowly and ponderously on the ground like a caterpillar.

E *Pupa stage:* Slowly rise to a medium level, and close up in a straight shape. Again, slowly and with strong tension, push your way out of the chrysalis.

E *Adult stage:* Oh joy! You are free and colorful. You can fly rather than crawl. Travel about the gym skipping, galloping, and jumping lightly. Show how happy you are to be flying about and what wonderful colors you have by moving lightly and making light, happy gestures with your arms.

E End in a wide shape showing your beautiful, colorful wings.

Culminating Activity

Let's review and put all the dances together.

Jellyfish dance: Undulate as you slowly walk forward, pause, turn, point back, and wiggle fingers like poisonous tendrils. Repeat.

Hummingbird dance: Hands to the sides and quiver; dart to another position and quiver again. Repeat three times.

Cat and mouse dance: Travel slowly and silently like a cat. Pause while searching for the mouse. Travel and search again for the mouse. Freeze. Jump high and pounce. Scurry quickly and lightly like a mouse. Dart into a hiding space. Curl up safe from the cat.

Kangaroo and baby dance: Travel using the five basic jumps, making big, strong jumps. Stop in a big, wide, open shape. Gently close up into a rounded curled shape like a mama kangaroo protecting her baby. Repeat.

Sloth dance: At a low level, travel along the ground very slowly, being loose and heavy.

SAMPLE PLAN 31.5

Animal Haiku (*continued*)

Rattlesnake dance: Slowly glide on curved pathways. Pause. Rattle and hiss. Jump and land with a striking movement. Repeat.

Butterfly metamorphosis dance:

1. Egg: Start curled in a tight, little egg. Press your way out slowly and with strong tension.
2. Larva: Move at a low level with heavy tension.
3. Pupa: Slowly rise, and close up in a straight shape. Slowly and with strong tension, push your way out.
4. Adult: Travel about the gym skipping, galloping, and jumping lightly. End in a wide shape.

Affective Closure

In the final dance, could you move at the same speed and with the same force to represent each animal? [No.] Name an animal, and explain how you had to move to represent that animal. What animal did you like dancing as the most, and why? Were there any you did not like representing? If so, why? Let's discuss with partners first and then share with the whole class.

CCSS Closure

With your partner, discuss the meaning of *quiver*, *undulate*, and *scurry*. Try to use the words in a sentence. Try to think of connections between the words and other real-life situations, things, animals, events, emotions, or objects.

SAMPLE PLAN 31.6

The Thunderstorm

We designed "The Thunderstorm" dance for first grade, but you can also teach it to children in kindergarten and second grade. The book *Flash, Crash, Rumble, and Roll* tells the story with interesting, rich illustrations that match the structure of this lesson. If you can't find this book, there are many others you can use on the same topic in both school and local libraries.

Movement Theme: Curved and Angular Pathways, Strong and Soft Force
Topic Theme: Thunderstorms
Text: Branley & Kelley (1999). *Flash, Crash, Rumble, and Roll*

Standards

This plan addresses National Standards 1, 2, and 5 and CCSS for comprehension.

Objectives

Children will learn to

Motor

1. Travel on curved pathways, moving slowly and gently.
2. Travel on zigzag pathways, moving fast with firm tension.
3. Create different curved and angular shapes with light and strong tension.

Creative Thinking Skills

4. Apply movement concepts to represent real-life natural phenomena.

Affective

5. Enjoy expressing their interpretations of thunderstorms.

CCSS

6. Use information gained from the illustrations and words in a text to demonstrate an understanding of its characters, setting, or events.
7. Make connections between the movement concepts used to represent clouds and lightning to other real-life natural phenomena.

(continues)

SAMPLE PLAN 31.6

The Thunderstorm (*continued*)

Immature Movement Patterns You Are Likely to See

Beginners have problems making their curved pathways round. They tend to flatten the curves. In addition, they have problems making angular pathways have sharp, angular changes in direction. They tend to round their points. Finally, beginners tend to perform slow movements at medium speeds.

Potential Refinements

- Feel tight.
- Feel soft.
- Make your slow movements very slow.
- Make your curved pathways round.
- Make your angular pathways have sharp changes of direction.

Introduction

I Today, we will be working on curved and angular shapes. Can you name some things that have curved shapes? Can you identify some things that have pointy, angular shapes?

Content Development

Explore Drawing Curved Lines with the Hands (Curved Pathways in the Air)

I Draw curved lines in space with one hand and arm. Make small curves and large curves. Draw curves all about your personal space—to your side, back, high, low.

E Try to make curves with your other hand.

E Try to make curves with both hands stretching way out in front of you, to the sides, and to the back.

E Make small curves and large curves.

Explore Walking on Curved Pathways

I Instead of drawing curved pathways in the air, we will now draw them on the ground by walking on a curved pathway. Pretend to paint the bottom of your feet. [Demonstrate as you explain.] When I say, "Go," walk and make a curved pathway so if we looked at the floor we would see the curved line you painted with your feet. Go.

E Make small curves and large curves.

E Sometimes go to the left, and sometimes go to the right.

Cog K Where in the classroom do you see curved pathways? Yes, the letters C, S, and so on.

Today we will be reading a story about a thunderstorm. [Either read aloud or project the pages on a wall, and have the children read it aloud together. Read just the story, not the informational text on lightning safety.]

Combining Traveling on Curved Pathways and Drawing Curved Pathways in the Air

E Now combine traveling on curved pathways and drawing curved pathways with your hands. Think about and feel the shapes of the cumulus clouds in this illustration [show the book].

E As you are traveling, draw a cloud in space. Be sure to draw the curves inside and outside of the clouds. Draw big, curved clouds.

E Come to a stop, and make your body a curved shape. Let's try that again: Travel, stop, and make all your body parts curved.

E Do it again, making a different curved shape each time you stop. Explore how your body can make different curved shapes.

Cloud Dance

E Let's put everything together and make a cloud dance. Start in a curved shape. As I beat the drum, travel on curved pathways, making curved shapes with your hands. When I stop beating the drum, end in a curved shape. [Repeat several times.]

Running on Zigzag Pathways

I Imagine the clouds getting bigger and darker—a storm is brewing. What happened next in the book? [The cumulus clouds turned into thunderheads. Then lightning, thunder, and rain started.] Let's work with lightning first. When I say, "Go," I want you to run as fast as you can on a sharp, angular, zigzag pathways. [Demonstrate as you explain.] Go. Stop. Try again, and again. [Beat the drum fast and loud.]

SAMPLE PLAN 31.6

The Thunderstorm (*continued*)

Making Strong, Angular Shapes

E This time when you stop, stop in an angular, sharp, pointy shape with firm, tight muscles. Go. When I beat the drum, make another angular shape, another, and another.

E Make three angular shapes in a row. Go. Go. Go.

E Which body parts can you make pointy? Yes, your elbows, knees, hips, fingertips, feet, and so on. [Repeat making three angular shapes in a row until you see a variety of shapes across the class and by individuals.]

E This time, change levels each time.

E Add a turn.

E This time I want you to think about lightning. What does lightning look like? How does it move? Which kinds of movements would you do to show lightning with your body? When I say, "Go," travel on an angular pathway, jump and make an angular shape in the air, and land in an angular shape.[Beat the drum fast and loud.] [Repeat several times.]

Lightning Dance

E Let's do a lightning dance. Start in an angular shape, and make three different angular shapes as I beat the drum. Then travel fast on sharp, angular pathways, and jump making an angular shape. Land in an angular shape. [Repeat several times.]

Thunder: Large, Forceful Jumps

Notes: For the thunder and rain, the sound made by children hitting and tapping a wood floor is effective. In other settings, give each child two rhythm sticks, hand drums, or other equipment they can beat to make thunder and then the quieter tapping of rain falling.

E Have a seat. What else happens in storms? What happens as a result of lightning? Yes, thunder. Let's make the sound of thunder by hitting the floor quickly, now. Without hurting yourself, try making thunder on different parts of your body. Try your thigh, chest, and arms. Open your mouth, and try your cheeks.

E Stand up, and then run on a straight pathway, building up to a huge jump when you thrust your legs and arms in the air. Go. Try it again.

Rain Dance

E What else happens in a storm? Yes, rain. How did we move as thunder? [Strong, fast, hard.] Rain is soft and fast. Tap your fingers softly and quickly on the floor and on different parts of your body—your thighs, arms, and chest. Be very soft and fast. Now the rain is slowing down. [Demonstrate, and have children tap as you talk.] The storm is passing; the rain is slowly stopping. Tap slower and slower, softer and softer. Now the rain has ended, and all that is left is a puddle. Sink down into the floor into a puddle shape.

Culminating Activity: Thunderstorm Dance

A Let's put everything together into a thunderstorm dance. We will start with clouds. Begin in a round shape, travel on curved pathways, and end in a round shape. [Use the drum the whole time to accompany the dance, and cue children to which movement is next.] Make three sharp lightning shapes, travel rapidly on a zigzag pathway, and end in a sharp, pointy shape. Beat the floor with your hands, your feet, and other body parts, run on a straight pathway, and do a thrusting jump in the air. Sit and tap gently on different body parts. Make your tapping very soft and fast. Now the rain is slowing down. [Demonstrate, and have children tap as you talk.] The storm is passing, and the rain is slowly stopping—tap slower and slower, softer and softer. Now the rain has ended, and all that is left is a puddle—sink down onto the floor into a puddle shape. [Repeat this dance several times, working on improving the children's ability to make curved and angular shapes, travel on curved and zigzag pathways, travel slow and fast, and maintain strong and soft muscles.]

Closure

Which part of the dance did you enjoy the most?

CCSS Today we represented clouds making curved shapes and traveling on curved pathways slowly and gently. Let's make a list of other things or events we could represent with slow, gentle movements and a second list for curved pathways and round shapes. [Repeat for strong, fast movements, zigzag pathways, and angular shapes.]

SAMPLE PLAN 31.7

Introducing Levels Using Streamers or Ribbons

Movement Theme: Introducing Levels
Topic Theme: Streamers
Text: Thorpe & Roper (2000). *Follow the Lemming*

Notes: The social content of this lesson can be connected to the children's book *Follow the Lemming* (Thorpe & Roper, 2000). This book describes how problems can arise when you follow a leader headed for trouble. It describes lemmings, which are rodents that live in cold places. The main characters are children who meet a pack of lemmings and play follow the leader. When Louie the lemming becomes the leader, the book portrays the legend that lemmings will follow each other right over a cliff no matter what. Ask the classroom teacher to teach the book, or read it yourself during closure.

Standards

This plan addresses National Standards 1, 2, and 4 and CCSS for listening.

Objectives

Children will learn to

Motor

1. Perform a variety of streamer movements at different levels.
2. Follow a leader, observing carefully and accurately copying the leader's movements.
3. Make the streamer circles round.

Creative Thinking Skills/Choreography

4. Select and arrange movements into a pattern, changing levels.

Social Responsibility and CCSS

5. Share decisions with a partner, following the rules for discussions, including listening and caring about your partner's opinions, asking for your partner's opinions, and asking questions to clarify what your partner said.
6. Understand what it means to be a good leader and a good follower and make connections between being a responsible leader and real-life situations in which you follow a leader headed for trouble.

Potential Refinements

- Follow the leader accurately.
- Make the streamer circles round.

Introductory Activity

I Today, we will be dancing with streamers, moving them at different levels. First, let's go over the different ways you can move streamers. Show me one way that you know how to move a streamer. Everyone copy that movement. Now show me another. [Repeat until the children have no more ideas. If any movements mentioned here are not shown, demonstrate these movements yourself, and have the children copy you.]

Basic Actions for Streamers or Scarves

Circles: Circle the streamer in front, to each side.

Helicopters: Circle the streamer overhead (with the streamer circling parallel to the ground).

Figure 8s: Make one circle on the right side, then one circle on the left side.

Rainbows: Starting with the streamer in one hand with that arm stretched to the side, reach up, over the head, and then down on the other side, drawing a half-circle, like a rainbow, with the streamer. Then reverse the action.

Spirals/tornados: Moving quickly, draw small circles with the end of the wand, which will cause the streamer to form a spiral in the air.

Zigzags: Draw a Z with the wand repeatedly, causing the streamer to make zigzags.

Snakes: Draw an S with the wand.

Hurricanes: Spin while holding the streamer out in front or to the side.

Write your name in big letters.

Write your name in tiny letters.

Whip the ribbon.

SAMPLE PLAN 31.7

Introducing Levels Using Streamers or Ribbons (*continued*)

Content Development

Cog K There are three levels: high, above your shoulders; medium, between your shoulders and your knees; and low, below your knees.

On Your Own, Explore Different Levels

[You can add music here. Tell the children that if they feel the beat, they can move to the music, but they must stay in their personal space.]

E Take your streamer, and try to find different ways to move it at a high level.

E Now explore a low level.

E Now explore a medium level.

E [Repeat with the teacher calling out different levels.] Try to make your streamer circles as round as you can make them.

E Try it traveling. Travel and move your streamer in different ways at a high level, now at a medium level, and now at a low level. [Repeat with the teacher calling out different levels.]

E Travel in a different way while moving your streamer at different levels. You can gallop, slide, walk, jog, or use any other locomotor pattern.

Follow a Leader

E Let's play follow the leader. First, everyone follows me. [Call out the level as you do a variety of movements.] Try to follow my movements exactly.

E With your assigned partner, decide which one of you will be the leader first; the other partner will try to copy what the leader is doing. Leaders, do something with your streamer at different levels. Followers, try to copy what the leader is doing exactly. Rotate leaders frequently. You have to decide when you will change the leader.

[This task offers an opportunity to have a class discussion about how to be a good leader and a good follower.]

Social What do you need to do to be a good follower? [Pay attention. Watch carefully.] What do you need to do to be a good leader? [Make sure you are leading your partner on a safe path. Don't do anything too hard for your partner. Volunteer to change leadership after a fair amount of time.]

E Leaders, travel and move your streamer at different levels. Partners, follow the leader, and try to copy where the leader is moving the streamer.

Make a Pattern and Design a Sequence

E With your partner, make a pattern consisting of streamer movements at different levels. Do you remember what a pattern in art is? Right, it is a design that you repeat. One pattern with a streamer might be "high, low, high, medium," repeated over and over. You and your partner can do this pattern either facing each other or traveling.

Social You can choose any of the streamer actions you both like. You need to discuss your ideas with your partner, and share in the decision making. What are the rules for a good discussion? [Listening and caring about your partner's opinions, asking for your partner's opinions, and asking questions to clarify what your partner said.]

Show and Identify Patterns

E If you want to show your sequence to the class, raise your hands. This half of the class will show first and then the other half. [Select one to three pairs to show a second time, after asking them if they are willing to have the class discuss their sequence.]

E Let's watch Katie and Jessie's sequence, and see if we can identify the pattern. Which pattern did you see? [Repeat with several groups.]

Closure

Does anyone want to share an experience when they or someone they know followed a leader and got into trouble? Do not say the person's name, just say, "someone I know" (which could even be you).

Does anyone want to share an experience when someone they know stood up to a leader who was not being responsible and refused to follow that person or stopped what the irresponsible leader was doing? Do not reveal anyone's name or give any clues about who they are.

SAMPLE PLAN 31.8

*In the Small, Small Pond**

* An earlier version of this lesson was originally published by Rovegno (2003) in *Teaching Elementary Physical Education.*

The ideas presented here can take up to three lessons, depending on the length of time you have for teaching. You can easily shorten the length by limiting the number of pages you explore through movement. Simply read the other pages to the children. We thank Theresa Purcell Cone for the suggestion to use this book (Purcell-Cone, 2000).

Movement Themes: Body Actions and Pathways
Topic Theme: In the Small, Small Pond
Text: Fleming (1993). *In the Small, Small Pond*

Standards

This plan addresses National Standards 1, 2, and 5 and CCSS for vocabulary acquisition.

Objectives

Children will learn to

Motor

1. Perform the following movements and apply the relevant movement concepts using a variety of body parts while traveling on different pathways: wiggling, marching, hovering, shivering, traveling very slowly, slashing, plunging, scattering, swirling, twirling, swooping, making rhythmic sounds with body parts, running, and freezing.

Creative Thinking

2. Explore and represent images and ideas about pond animals from children's literature through dance movement.

Affective

3. Increase their awareness of their feelings during different dance movements.
4. Appreciate the opportunity for self-expression in dance.

CCSS

5. Improve their understanding of vocabulary words from *In the Small, Small Pond* by making connections to additional real-life events, objects, animals, emotions, or things and by expressing the vocabulary words bodily in dance.
6. Use information gained from the illustrations and words in a text to demonstrate an understanding of its characters, setting, or events.

Introduction

The cover and first page of the book show a boy with his hands in a pond watching with surprise as a frog jumps out of and back into the water. Start the lesson by holding the book up and having the children read along with you. Ask several of the following questions. After a brief discussion, proceed to segment 1.

Facilitating Comprehension and Making Connections

- The title of this book is *In the Small, Small Pond.*
- Put your thumbs up if you have seen a pond. Tell us when. [Call on several children.]
- Denise Fleming wrote this book. Do you think she has written any other books? Yes. She has.
- Raise your hand, and tell me what is happening here. What is the frog doing? What is the boy doing? What is he feeling?
- What do you think will happen next? Could be—let's read and see.

Content Development

Segment 1: Tadpoles

Text: "Wiggle, jiggle, tadpoles wriggle." [Book illustrates tadpoles swimming around the frog.]

Facilitating Comprehension and Making Connections

- Have you ever seen tadpoles? What do they look like? Which other animals wiggle?
- Have you ever wiggled when you should not have and your mom or dad said, "Stop wiggling?" Tell us when.
- Can you try to hold a wiggle inside and not let it get out?
- Now, we are going to do a wiggling dance.

SAMPLE PLAN 31.8

In the Small, Small Pond (continued)

Movement Tasks

1. What does a wiggle look like? Everyone wiggle.
2. Wiggle different body parts: Wiggle your fingers, now your hands, shoulders, toes, feet, legs, whole body.
3. Spreading wiggle: As you are standing, a wiggle starts in one finger, then it spreads to that hand, then it spreads up your arm so your fingers, hand, and arm are wiggling. Now it spreads to the shoulders, now the torso, now your whole body. Repeat. Let's do it again, but this time start the wiggle in your toes and have it spread up through your whole body.
4. [Assign groups of three] Hold hands. One person at one end start a wiggle in one hand, and have it spread to your arm, your shoulder, your other arm, and the person next to you. The wiggle then spreads across the second person to the third person. Now all of you are wiggling. [Repeat several times.]
5. On your own, travel on a wiggly pathway, pause, wiggle, and freeze in a wiggled shape. [Repeat several times.]
6. Wiggle sequence: In your group of three, travel on a wiggly pathway around each other, pause, person 1 wiggles and pauses, person 2 wiggles and pauses, person 3 wiggles and pauses, and then all wiggle and freeze in a group wiggle shape.
7. Jiggle like Jell-O: Instead of wiggling, let's jiggle like Jell-O. Jiggle up and down, and now jiggle so much that you move about the space jiggling.
8. Jiggle different body parts: fingers, hands, arms, shoulders, feet, legs, and your whole body.
9. Rest. Can you try to hold a jiggle inside and not let it get out?

Refinements and Questions to Help Children Increase Awareness of Feelings

- Be loose and very wiggly.
- Think about how wiggling feels in your muscles.
- What does a wiggle feel like? Wiggle again, and concentrate on how the wiggle feels.
- What does a jiggle feel like? Jiggle again, and concentrate on how the jiggle feels.

Segment 2: Geese

Text: "Waddle, wade, geese parade." [Book shows a mother goose leading her babies into the pond.]

Facilitating Comprehension and Making Connections

- We read that the frog saw wiggling tadpoles in the pond. What other animals might you see in a pond? Let's see what the frog in this book sees.
- What's happening in this picture?
- What are the colors of the mother? What are the colors of the babies?
- Have you ever seen geese marching? Where? Have you ever marched behind someone? When? Have you ever seen people marching? Tell us when.

Movement Tasks

1. Let's march! Stand up. When I beat the drum, march all about the space. Really lift your knees high like this, and swing your arms.
2. As you march, try different arm movements.
3. Now march on different pathways. Try marching on straight pathways. Now try curved pathways. Now try angular pathways.
4. Now march while adding different arm movements.
5. Let's try marching in a line. Everyone get in line behind me. Let's march to the beat of the drum.
6. Get into your group of three and form a follow-the-leader line. Each of you will have a turn to be the leader and lead your line about the gym. The first person in line is leader number one. Leader adds an arm movement, and the other group members follow the leader's movement. Repeat the same arm movement with each step. Make the movement simple to copy.
7. Leader one walks to the end of the line, and the second person in line is now the leader who marches and adds arm movements. [Change one more time to a new leader, and repeat marching, adding arm movements.]

Refinements and Questions to Help Children Increase Awareness of Feelings

- Really stand tall and proud when you march.
- Keep your head up, lift your knees high, and swing your arms.
- Listen to the beat of the drum, and try to march to the beat.

(*continues*)

SAMPLE PLAN 31.8

In the Small, Small Pond (continued)

- When you march on an angular pathway, really make each change in direction sharp and precise.
- What do you like about marching? What do you like about being the leader? What do you like about following the leader?

Segment 3: Dragonflies

(See opening photograph for Section V.)

Text: "Hover, shiver, wings quiver." [Book shows dragonflies hovering over lily pads. The frog is in the water looking up at a dragonfly.]

Facilitating Comprehension and Making Connections

- Not only are there animals at a pond, but there are insects as well. Let's see what is at the pond. What's happening in this picture?
- What are the dragonflies doing? What do dragonflies look like when they fly?
- What else hovers? Yes, helicopters and some boats called hovercrafts.
- What do you think the frog is doing? How do frogs catch bugs?

Movement Tasks

1. *Shiver and quiver:* Imagine you are getting into bed on a cold night, and the sheets are cold. Grab yourself and shiver. Now just have your fingers shiver. Now just shiver with your arms, now one leg, now the other leg, and now your whole body. Try extending your arms and shivering like dragonfly wings.
2. *Darting and hovering:* What do dragonflies look like when they fly? Sometimes they stay in place; we call this hovering. Sometimes they dart about quickly. Run lightly, darting about the gym, and stop on your toes when you hear the sound of the tambourine. Breathe in, lift your chest and arms, balance on your toes, hover, and make your arms quiver.
3. Can you think of any other time when you might shiver or quiver? Yes, when you are afraid. Now quiver by shaking and trembling very quickly.
4. Dart lightly about the gym; stop and quiver when you hear the sound of the tambourine.
5. How does a frog catch a bug? Sit; reach out one hand slowly, stretching as far as you can into space. Then quickly retract your hand, bringing your hand back in. Slowly reach out again to a different spot in your personal space, and then quickly retract your hand. Try reaching out to all areas of your personal space.
6. *Sequence for older children:* Divide the class in half. Half the class sits scattered on the ground as if on lily pads, while the other half runs lightly about the space. Children on the ground reach out, stretch, and then quickly retract their arms. Runners hover, quiver, and dart.

Refinements and Questions to Help Children Increase Awareness of Feelings

Darting: Run as lightly as you can; feel as if you are skimming over water.

Hovering: Stretch your body tall. Breathe in, and feel the lightness. Stretch the top of your head right to the ceiling.

Feel how the quiver is quick and light.

Dart quickly around the lily pads and frogs.

How does it feel to hover over the pond? How does it feel to skim by the frogs?

Segment 4: Turtles

Text: "Drowse, doze, eyes close." [Book shows three turtles moving along the bank of the pond and one turtle partially in the water. The frog is behind the turtle with its eye almost closed. Lily pads are in the background.]

Facilitating Comprehension and Making Connections

- What do you think is happening in this picture?
- What do you think will happen next?
- How do turtles move?
- What do turtles look like when they sleep?
- What shape are the turtles?

Movement Tasks

1. Explore traveling in different ways very slowly at a low level. Transfer your weight slowly onto different body parts, travel on different body parts, and move one body part at a time. Sometimes have your back on the ground, sometimes your belly; sometimes travel on hands and feet only.

SAMPLE PLAN 31.8

In the Small, Small Pond (continued)

2. Create a short sequence. Start in a curled body shape at a low level, just like a turtle in its shell. Travel slowly on different body parts, pause, look around for your favorite rock in the sun, travel to the rock, and sink down in a different curled shape as if you were taking a nap in the sun.

Refinements and Questions to Help Children Increase Awareness of Feelings

- Be sure to move very slowly.
- What does it feel like to move very slowly?
- How does it feel to curl up in a round shape?

Segment 5: Herons

(See **Figure 31.8**.)

Text: "Lash, lunge, herons plunge." [Book shows a heron wading near the shore and plunging its beak into the water and the frog, looking scared, jumping out of the water just seconds ahead of the heron's beak.]

Facilitating Comprehension and Making Connections

- What is happening in this picture?
- Have you ever seen a heron fishing for dinner? Where did you see this?
- How do herons try to catch fish? How do they move? Why do they move slowly?
- Have you ever played a tag game when you tried to run and jump to avoid the tagger tagging you? How does it feel when you just barely escape the tag?
- Have you ever played hide and seek? How does it feel when someone walks by you, you keep very still, and he or she does not see you?

Movement Tasks

1. *Slashing:* Imagine you are very mad. When I beat the drum, lash out with your arms and legs, and show in your body fast, indirect, strong movements—slashing movements. Twist and turn your body, jump in the air in a whirling action, and land with a stamping movement. [Slashing is one of Laban's eight basic effort actions. Slashing movements have strong force and fast speed, and they travel indirectly through space—that is, they involve traveling in a roundabout way using a large amount of space.]
2. Now combine slashing and thrusting in a short sequence. Do a slashing movement, then reach up, and do a thrusting plunge down, aiming directly down with your arms as you take a large step and bend your knee, ending in a lunge position. Pierce into the water. [Thrusting is one of Laban's eight basic effort actions. Thrusting movements have strong force and fast speed, and they travel directly through space—that is, they involve traveling efficiently in a straight, direct way using a small, precise amount of space.]
3. Now alternate slashing and thrusting movements when I beat the drum. Try ending at a different level each time. Sometimes slash and lunge down, pointing your arms down; then slash and lunge, pointing at a medium or high level. Sometimes lunge in different directions or end in different shapes.
4. Walk about the space slowly, stepping first on your toes, then on your heel. Feel your toes and feet sink into the floor. Next, reverse the action, and peel your feet off the floor by lifting your heel first, then your sole, then your toes. Then slowly step toe–heel again. Try to show how a heron would stalk and search for prey in the water without scaring fish by making a splash or disturbing the soft bottom of the pond.
5. Put the two together in a sequence. Walk, slash, walk, and thrust-plunge down. Walk on the soft beat of the drum, and lash or lunge on the strong double beat of the drum. Be very precise, slow, and deliberate as you stalk the fish, then attack suddenly with a lunge and plunge into space to represent catching a fish. Try to slash and plunge in a different way each time.

Refinements and Questions to Help Children Increase Awareness of Feelings

- Step very slowly and gently. Lift your knees high. Gently touch the floor first with your toes, then with your heel. Sink gently, taking your weight onto your foot.
- Make your slashing movements very fast and very strong. Try to use as much space as you can.
- Make your thrusting movements very fast and very strong. Try to move directly to your ending position.
- Think how it feels to stalk a fish.
- How does it feel when you stalk slowly and then suddenly plunge down on the fish?

(*continues*)

SAMPLE PLAN 31.8

In the Small, Small Pond (continued)

Segment 6: Whirligigs

Text: "Circle, swirl, whirligigs twirl." [Looking down from above the pond, the illustrations show whirligigs on top of the water, with expanding circles around each representing water ripples. The frog is under the water.]

Facilitating Comprehension and Making Connections

- Let's see what else lives in a pond. Does anyone know what these are? Yes, insects. A whirligig is a beetle that lives on the surface of the water and swims in circles.
- There are many circles in this picture. What else has a round, circular shape?
- Put your thumbs up if you have ever tossed a rock into a pond. What happens to the surface? Which shapes do you see?

Movement Tasks

1. Let's do circular movements. Try spinning on one foot. Now try spinning on different body parts.
2. Travel about the gym on circular pathways. Sometimes travel in large circles and sometimes in small circles.
3. Now sometimes travel on circular pathways and sometimes spin on different body parts.

Refinements and Questions to Help Children Increase Awareness of Feelings

- How do you feel when you spin and spin?
- Where in this room do you see circles? What has a circular shape?
- When outside of physical education do you travel on circular pathways?

Segment 7: Swallows

Text: "Sweep, swoop, swallows scoop." [Book shows swallows swooping down, one skimming along the surface of the pond with its beak in the water scooping.]

Facilitating Comprehension and Making Connections

- What do you think the birds are doing in this picture?
- Has anyone seen how birds swoop down to the water to catch fish?
- How many of you have seen swallows fly in the evening? What do they look like? What do their pathways in the air look like?

Movement Tasks

1. Reach up with one hand as high as you can, and then swoop down with that hand on a circular pathway down and back up. Bend your knees as you swoop down. Make your whole body swoop down and up with your hand. Now try the other hand. Now try both hands.
2. Now swoop by leading with the tips of your fingers, now the side of your hands, now with your palms up and then down.
3. Now add traveling: Run a few steps, reach high, swoop down by sweeping your hand gently along the floor, reach up, and pause.
4. Try again. Sometimes travel using many steps; sometimes take only one step.
5. Now try swooping to one side, now to the other side.
6. Now add legs. Start by standing tall and reaching with one hand. Lift one knee, and swoop down and up with your whole body.

Refinements and Questions to Help Children Increase Awareness of Feelings

- Really stretch through your whole body just before you swoop. Take a deep breath in, and feel the lightness just before you swoop down.
- When you swoop down, feel your body fall. Collapse, let the air out, let go of the tension, and when you get near the ground, tighten up and swing up again—just like a swing.

Segment 8: Crawfish

Text: "Click, clack, claws clack." [Illustrations show crawfish on the bottom of the pond with their claws open and held up.]

Facilitating Comprehension and Making Connections

- What is happening in this picture?
- Have you ever seen a crawfish? They look like lobsters but live in fresh water. When you see lobsters in the supermarket, they have big rubber bands on their claws. Why do you think the rubber bands are placed there?

SAMPLE PLAN 31.8

In the Small, Small Pond (continued)

Movement Tasks

1. Explore making clicking and clacking noises with your body. Click your fingers, clap your hands, clap your hands on different body parts, and make clicking noises with your tongue.
2. Create a short rhythm sequence consisting of different clicks and claps. This will be your own personal rhythm. Select three different sounds, and put them together in a rhythm. For example, click your fingers twice, clap once, and slap your thighs three times fast.
3. Now add movements to your click-clack rhythm sequence.
4. Now teach your rhythm to a partner.
5. Let's have a conversation with clicking and clacking movements. One partner make a rhythm, and the other respond with a different rhythm.

Refinements and Questions to Help Children Increase Awareness of Feelings

- Listen carefully to your rhythm, and try to repeat it in exactly the same way and at the same tempo.
- Try to follow your partner's rhythm exactly.

Segment 9: Ducks

Text: "Dabble, dip, tails flip." [Illustrations show ducks with their tails in the air and their heads underwater trying to catch minnows.]

Facilitating Comprehension and Making Connections

- What is happening in this picture? What are the ducks doing? The minnows? The frog?
- How many of you have ever seen ducks diving for food?
- What is happening with the water?

Movement Tasks

1. Let's work on dabbing movements. (Dabbing is one of Laban's eight basic effort actions; it includes movements that are fast, light, and direct.) Gently and quickly move your hands by making dabbing movements, as if you were touching something with a cotton ball. Now, skip about the space making light gestures with your hands. Do a light turning jump, and continue skipping. Keep your hands light. This is a happy movement.
2. Let's do a dabbing dance: Skip and do a turning jump. Skip again, making light gestures with your hands. Jump and end with your head down, looking between your legs, with your arms up and fingers pointing to the ceiling, representing the ducks in the illustration.

Refinements and Questions to Help Children Increase Awareness of Feelings

- Skip lightly. Make it a happy skip, an excited skip.
- How does it feel to skip lightly?
- Concentrate on the feeling of quick, gentle, and soft movements.
- Make your turning jumps carefree, fun, and light.

Segment 10: Raccoon

Text: "Splish, splash, paws flash." [Book shows a raccoon on the bank catching a fish in its paws with a splash. The frog is jumping away. There are cattails on the bank.]

Facilitating Comprehension and Making Connections

- What kind of animal is this? What tells you that it is a raccoon?
- How is the raccoon catching fish?
- What kind of plant is growing on the bank? Does anyone know what is inside a cattail pod?
- Have you ever tried to catch a fish with your hands? What happened? Is it hard?

Movement Tasks

1. Let's work on flicking—like flicking a fly off your arm. [Flicking is one of Laban's eight basic effort actions. A flick is a soft, fast, indirect movement.] Move your hands quickly and lightly all about your personal space as if they were twinkling lights.

(*continues*)

SAMPLE PLAN 31.8

In the Small, Small Pond (continued)

2. Now do three flicking movements followed by a thrusting movement. Flick your hands in three different places in your personal space, and then do a thrusting action by jumping and stamping while you extend your hands and fingers out. Hold that shape. Try it to the rhythm of the text—splish (flick), splash (flick), paws (flick) flash (thrust)—and hold that shape.
3. Now add traveling by skipping and hopping. Make happy, twisting, excited movements with your hands, arms, and head. Then do the rhythm to the text—splish, splash, paws flash—and hold that shape.

Refinements and Questions to Help Children Increase Awareness of Feelings

- Keep your flicking movements light and quick. Your fingers should feel alive, dancing all about your personal space.
- The thrusting action should be sudden and end in an unexpected shape.
- Make your skips light and happy. Spring high when you skip, letting your arms swing all about your personal space.

Segment 11: End of Story

Text: "Chill breeze, winter freeze…cold night, sleep tight, small, small pond." [The first illustration is of a goose, cattails, leaves, and snow blowing across the pond. The last page shows snow falling on the pond at night and the frog curled up inside a den under the bank.]

Facilitating Comprehension and Making Connections

- Let's see how the story ends. What is happening in these pictures? What shows you that the wind is blowing? Is the wind blowing gently or strongly? Do you think it is cold or hot?
- What do you think the goose is feeling? What do you think the frog is feeling?
- Has it been a long day for the frog? How do you feel at the end of a long day? What do you like to do when you feel that way?
- How do you feel when you are outside and the wind is blowing?
- What are some fun things to do when you are playing outside and it is very windy?

Movement Tasks

1. Imagine that there is a strong wind blowing. Travel quickly by running, leaping, turning, and spinning about the gym; then stop and freeze.
2. Let's do a sequence to end the story. Travel quickly and freeze three times, then slowly turn and sink down into a cozy den by making a round shape on the floor.

Refinements and Questions to Help Children Increase Awareness of Feelings

- Really swing your arms as you leap and turn; swirl your arms around your body.
- Lift your knees as you do a turning jump.
- How did you feel when there was a strong wind blowing?
- How did you feel in the cozy den?

Culminating Dance

Children enjoy hearing stories repeatedly, and they enjoy repeating their dances several times. At the end of each lesson, the teacher can read the book, pause after each segment, and cue the children through a short, individual dance sequence for each segment of the book. The dance ends with all individuals sinking into a cozy den.

Another option is a whole-class dance representing what the frog sees, feels, and experiences. Have three children be a frog group and design a way to travel from group to group. Divide the rest of the class into 10 groups. Each group performs a sequence for one segment. The frogs travel to each group in order around the room and stop to watch each group's sequence. The dance ends with all children performing an individual sequence for the last segment of the book, ending by sinking into a cozy den.

Closure

Did you enjoy moving like different animals and insects? What animal or insect did you enjoy the most, and why?

CHAPTER 32

Creative Dance Level 2

OBJECTIVES

Students will learn:

1. Level 2 content revisits the body, effort, space, and relationship aspects of the Laban framework in a spiral progression from level 1.
2. Level 2 content does not require a higher level of skill ability.
3. The cognitive and social aspects of level 2 content are more complex than level 1 and, therefore, are appropriate for the upper elementary grades.

KEY TERMS

Dimensional cross
Eight basic effort actions

CONNECTION TO STANDARDS

This chapter addresses developing dance skills and body actions, applying movement concepts, principles of choreography, and principles of movement quality, social responsibility during group work, and the value of self-expression in dance. Thus, it addresses National Standards 1, 2, 4, and 5 and also the Common Core and other State Standards (CCSS) for reading literature and information texts, speaking, listening, collaboration, and vocabulary acquisition.

PROGRESSION OF CONTENT

Level 2: More Complex Body Aspects

Expanding Range and Combining Body Actions into Sequences

- Leaping and Jumping
- Turning
- Body Action Sequences

Using Body Actions and Gestures to Represent Objects, Events, Abstract Ideas, and Stories

- Moving from Imitation to Representation

Sample Learning Experiences

- Body Action Sequences

Level 2: More Complex Effort

Flow

Eight Basic Effort Actions

- Theory Underlying the Eight Basic Effort Actions

Sample Learning Experiences

- Eight Basic Effort Actions

Level 2: More Complex Space

Directions

- Theory Underlying Directions: The Dimensional Cross
- Linking Directions in Space to Meaningful Body Actions
- Using the Dimensional Cross to Design Learning Experiences

Levels and Pathways

Sample Learning Experiences and Representations

Level 2: More Complex Relationships

Group Formations

Sample Learning Experiences

- Formations and Streamers

Group Shapes

- Angular, Flat, Round, and Straight Group Shapes
- Internal and External Focus and Line

Group Actions

- Cannon and Unison
- Action and Reaction
- Meeting and Parting

Sample Learning Experiences

- Cannon and Unison
- Action and Reaction (Fight Scene)
- Meeting and Parting (Magnetism)

Figure 32.1 Progression of Content

Introduction

In this chapter, we discuss level 2 dance content. We spiral around and revisit the body, effort, space, and relationship aspects of the Laban framework at a more complex level. The dance content in level 2 does not require a higher level of skill ability, but the cognitive and social aspects are more complex than level 1. Thus, level 2 is appropriate for children in the upper elementary grades.

Level 2: More Complex Body Aspects

Level 2 lessons working on body aspects have two major goals. The first goal is to expand the range of body actions in children's movement vocabulary and to develop their abilities to combine these body actions into sequences. The second goal is to develop children's use of body actions to represent objects, events, ideas, and stories.

Expanding Range and Combining Body Actions into Sequences

In level 2, children are ready to work on expanding their variety of body actions and designing longer sequences. The following are the body actions most commonly performed in such sequences:

- Turning, spinning
- Stretching, curling, twisting
- Rising, falling
- Opening, closing
- Gathering, scattering
- Shaking, wiggling
- Pushing, pulling
- Swinging, swaying

This is just a small sample of the many body actions that children can use in dance. Table 32.1 lists other body actions

FYI

Sample Plans in this Chapter

1. Movement Theme: Body Actions
   Topic Theme: Ashanti to Zulu
   Text: Musgrove (1976). *African Traditions*
2. Movement Theme: Bound Flow, Stretching, and Curling
   Topic Theme: Prey and Predators
   Text: Baskin-Salzberg & Salzberg (1991). *Predators*
3. Movement Theme: Wringing, Slashing, and Twisted Shapes
   Topic Theme: Invasive Species
   Text: Drake, Love, & Thurman (2008). *Alien Invaders: Species that Threaten Our World*
4. Movement Theme: Glide, Float, Thrust, and Press
   Topic Theme: The Sea and the Shore
   Text: Stokes (1970). *The Sea and the Shore*
5. Movement Theme: Eight Basic Effort Actions
   Topic Theme: Planets
   Text: Aguilar (2008). *Eleven Planets: A New View of the Solar System*
6. Movement Theme: Directions, Rising, Falling, Closing, Opening, Advancing, and Retreating
   Topic Theme: The Dimensional Cross
7. Movement Theme: Pathways, Levels, Meeting and Parting
   Topic Theme: Shelter in a Storm
   Text: Branley & Kelley (1999). *Flash, Crash, Rumble, and Roll*
8. Movement Theme: Canon
   Topic Theme: "Row, Row, Row Your Boat"
9. Movement Theme: Group Shapes and Transitions
   Topic Theme: Sports and Sport Tableaux (Living Statues)

you can use as the basis for learning experiences in dance. You will find other body actions on the text website.

Leaping and Jumping

Two important body actions children can develop in level 2 work are leaps and jumps. Children work on combining leaping and jumping with different locomotor skills, such as galloping, skipping, and running. More complex leaping and jumping includes adding half- and full turns with the legs straight or bent. It also includes leaps and jumps making different shapes in the air.

Children enjoy learning leaps and jumps with names, such as split, stag, double stag, straddle, arched, and the wolf jump and leap. Finally, more complex leaping and jumping includes combining several leaps and jumps in a row.

Turning

You also can teach different ways to turn in level 2. More complex turning includes teaching children to turn on one foot. Four variations are possible: Turning to the left on the left leg and turning to the right on the right leg are easier turns; turning to the left on the right leg and turning to the right on the left leg are more difficult. All four variations require children to initiate the turn with their shoulders while remaining stretched tall through the backbone.

Children also can explore different ways to turn on one foot by holding the free leg in different positions. The easiest position is to bend the free leg at the knee held in front with the foot either touching the inside of the supporting leg or being held in an interesting position. A more difficult turn is to hold the free leg straight either forward or backward at waist height or to kick the leg forward, backward, or sideways while turning. Other interesting positions include turning on one foot with the back arched and the free leg back or to the side and turning with both knees bent and the body curled.

Body Action Sequences

Lists

You can design level 2 dance lessons on body actions in several ways. One way is to give children a list of body actions that form

Table 32.1 Action Words: Select One Movement from Each Column for Your Dance

First Movement	Second Movement	Third Movement	Fourth Movement	Last Movement
Twist	March	Leap	Pounce	Hover, perch
Turn	Hustle/bustle	Jump, explode	Prance	Statue
Spiral, twirl	Scurry	Pound, stomp	Bounce	Freeze, grip
Quiver, vibrate	Dart	Squash	Sway	Collapse, fall
Shake	Slither	Lunge, plunge	Swing	Droop, drip, melt
Wiggle			Swoop, scoop	
			Scatter, gather	
			Close, open	
			Throb	

Figure 32.3 The machine dance

Moving from Imitation to Representation

Although children represented ideas and events in level 1 lessons, in level 2, they assume more responsibility for designing dance movements individually, in pairs, and in small groups. To do so, they need to learn how to move from imitation to representations that are more abstract. You can help children make this transition in the following ways.

Changing a Movement from Imitation to Representation

Start by imitating a movement (such as signing your name on a whiteboard, swinging a softball bat, or digging a hole in the dirt with a shovel). Then do the following:

- Exaggerate it; highlight one part of it.
- Extend it from one body part to the whole body. or condense it from a whole-body action to a hand gesture.
- Repeat the actions using different body parts.
- Change the level, direction, or pathway.
- Change the force or speed.
- Change the shape.
- Enlarge the emotional content by emphasizing the relevant effort qualities of the movement—for example, make an angry movement very tight, forceful, and angular.

Here, we present an example of how to take the concrete actions from a children's book and turn them into abstract dance movements. The full lesson plan appears at the end of this chapter.

The children's book is *Ashanti to Zulu: African Traditions*, written by Musgrove (1976). This book describes a different African tribe for each letter of the alphabet. You can find this book in most school and public libraries. Following is the text from the book describing the *Ga* tribe:

> Ga (gah) women make *foufou* by pounding boiled white yams with long thick sticks. This makes the hot yams smooth and pasty. Before eating it the family members roll the steamy *foufou* between their fingers and dip it into a stew. The whole family eats the *foufou* from the same bowl. It is Ga tradition to use only the right hand to touch food (Musgrove, 1976).

The illustration with the text depicts a family. Two women are working together to pound yams. A man is going off to work with a farming tool; his hand touches one of the women on her shoulder. A boy is in a hut looking out the window. The feelings represented are positive—a sense of family, community, togetherness, and pride in work.

Table 32.3 lists the actions described in the text in the first column, ways to imitate these actions in the second column, and then the more abstract movements you can derive from the imitations in the third column. The dance lesson based on the information about the Ga tribe takes the ideas of pounding yams, the smooth texture of the yams, and eating the yams as a family and represents these ideas with pounding, smoothing, and dabbing movements performed in a range of ways and group shapes representing family, sharing, and togetherness.

Table 32.3 Transforming Work Actions and Family Life into Literal and then Abstract Movements

Book Text	Imitation	More Abstract Movement
Pounding yams	Pretend to hold a stick in hands; pretend to pound yams imitating the illustration in the book.	Pounding and thrusting actions (strong, direct, fast) using different body parts (hands, feet, elbows, knees) at high, medium, and low levels; adding turns; varying the size of the movements; and adding a rhythm, such as small, small, big, small, small, big.
Yams smooth and pasty; rolling foufou between fingers	Smoothing movement with hands at a medium level	Smoothing movements with the arms at different levels in all areas of personal space, smoothing and gliding movements with the whole body
Dip foufou into stew	Pretend to dip foufou into stew at a medium level.	Dabbing movements (light, fast, direct) at different levels, in all areas of personal space, dabbing with different body parts, dabbing to create a conversation with a partner
Whole family eats from the same bowl, using only the right hand	Sit in a circle; pretend to eat.	Group shape symbolizing family, togetherness, sharing; end with gesture with right hands

Movement concepts from the Laban framework expand the movement patterns of the body actions.

Level 2: More Complex Effort

Level 2 effort content builds on level 1 by focusing on all four movement concepts of effort, either alone or in combinations. We discuss flow first, then cover the eight basic effort actions.

Flow

Laban defined flow on a continuum from bound to free (Laban, 1948; Preston-Dunlop, 1980). *Free flow* means the movement is difficult to stop and feels continuously ongoing. At its most extreme, free flow is unstoppable and flowing so freely that it is out of control, like a loose ski falling down a snow-covered ski slope. Clearly, we do not want children to experience "extreme" free flow in a gymnasium, as it is difficult—if not impossible—to create a safe environment in which they can do so. Children can experience brief moments of free flow when there is adequate space by running, skipping fast, galloping fast, or spinning.

For safety, children need to experience free flow at a more moderate speed without attempting to work at the extreme end of the continuum. Because dance focuses on the feeling of movement, you can work on feeling unrestricted, carefree, wild, and almost uncontrolled while children travel at fast but controllable speeds.

Bound flow means being able to stop the flow of the movement instantly (see **Figure 32.4**). The feelings associated with bound flow are safe and easy for children to experience. They include feeling restricted, careful, hesitant, constrained, and cautious. They must be ready to stop at any time and be completely in control of their motion. Bound flow can also be meticulous.

To introduce bound flow, we use a task similar to the game "Red Light, Green Light" and continue with a lesson or unit on prey and predators, helping children feel bound flow and representing the actions of prey and predators. A sample plan for teaching prey and predator is written in detail at the end of this chapter.

Figure 32.4 Bound flow

Ideas for Designing Learning Experiences About Flow

One possible learning experience for introducing bound flow is to have children pretend they are in *Jurassic Park* and the Tyrannosaurus rex is near. They try to walk to safety but must be able to stop instantly because the dinosaur can't see them unless they move. You can extend this idea to become a lesson on the topic theme of *Jurassic Park*. Have small groups of children design brief sequences representing different dinosaurs. Select dinosaurs with different movements and shapes, and suggest a few action words for each dinosaur. Then have the class travel with bound flow to each group to watch their dance sequence.

Eight Basic Effort Actions

Theory Underlying the Eight Basic Effort Actions

Laban combined the six components at the ends of the continua of speed, force, and use of space to form the **eight basic effort actions** (Laban, 1948; Preston-Dunlop, 1980).

The Six Components

Speed:	Slow ____	Fast
Force:	Light ____	Strong
Use of Space:	Indirect ____	Direct

Each effort action combines three components: one each from speed, force, and use of space. There are eight effort actions because there are eight possible combinations, listed in **Table 32.4**. Laban labeled each effort action with a term that describes the resulting quality of the movement. Because it is difficult to describe movement with words, these labels are inadequate to capture the full range of feelings and images each effort action can represent.

Next, we provide learning experiences and images for each effort action that teachers can use to introduce and help children perform each effort action. At the end of this chapter, we present three sample plans illustrating how to teach the effort actions.

Table 32.4 The Eight Basic Effort Actions

	Speed	Force	Use of Space
Float	Slow	Light	Indirect
Glide	Slow	Light	Direct
Wring	Slow	Strong	Indirect
Press	Slow	Strong	Direct
Flick	Fast	Light	Indirect
Dab	Fast	Light	Direct
Slash	Fast	Strong	Indirect
Thrust	Fast	Strong	Direct

SAMPLE LEARNING EXPERIENCES 32.2

The Eight Basic Effort Actions

Float

Travel slowly and gently, using space in an indirect, flexible, meandering way:

- Float like a bubble or balloon.
- Move gently and slowly, meandering about the gym.
- Drift in space as if you were a feather carried on a light breeze.
- Take a deep breath, lift up your chest, rise up on the balls of your feet, lift your arms, and then travel slowly, feeling the air supporting your body as if you were floating off the ground.
- Pretend you are weightless in space. Suspend yourself in a weightless void, then tip and drift about space.
- Rise like vapor or steam, and then meander about the room.
- Rise up as if you are in a dream, then drift about in a dreamy state.
- Travel about the gym lingering here and there.

Exploring floating, traveling at different levels

Glide

Travel slowly and gently using space in a smooth, direct way:

- Fly like a glider riding the air currents.
- Soar like a bird riding the air currents over the sea.
- Glide like a skater balancing on one leg.
- Travel serenely straight across the gym like a majestic king or queen approaching the throne.
- Travel straight and gently as if you were a beam of moonlight coming down to touch the glistening snow.

Gliding

- Look toward the horizon, and travel calmly on your journey to the end of the gym.
- Travel smoothly and directly toward a goal seeking something.
- Glide like a crew row boat skimming the water.

Wring

Move slowly with great tension in your muscles, twisting and moving indirectly:

- Wring yourself out like a wet towel.
- Twist all of your body parts until you contort the body as if you were in agony.
- Pretend your body is a powerful machine that grinds and pulverizes rocks into sand.
- Grow to become a gnarled, twisted monster.
- Moving in slow motion, fight the pain that is growing inside you; twist away from its torturous talons.

Wringing

Press

Move slowly with tension, showing strength and moving directly:

- Pretend you are pulling a heavy load, gripping it with your hands.

Pressing

SAMPLE LEARNING EXPERIENCES 32.2

The Eight Basic Effort Actions(*continued*)

- Lift a heavy weight over your head. You are powerful and strong.
- Push straight ahead slowly and strongly. Do not be deterred from your steady progress.
- Squeeze your body so tight you become a thin line.
- Travel low to the ground, filled with tension; you are a poisonous, unstoppable ooze.

Flick

Move quickly and lightly, indulging in space and using space flexibly:

- Flick a mosquito off your arm.
- Flick your hands and fingers in the air.
- Make your hands and fingers move like a sparkler or glitter falling.
- Make your arms, hands, and fingers move like a fire, flame, or sparkling star.
- Skip while making gestures that show you are happy, playful, flippant, or excited.
- Gallop lightly like a frisky pony.
- Quiver or shiver.
- Wiggle and jiggle.
- Bounce up and down, with your arms loose and floppy.
- Make your body move as if it was giggling.
- Travel as if you were a babbling stream.
- Flit like a bird from spot to spot.

Skipping and flicking

Dab

- Move quickly, lightly, and directly, using space efficiently.
- Tap the air gently with the tips of your fingers, your elbows, or your nose.
- Pretend you are gently patting your pet dog, who is scared.
- Lightly touch the air or ground with your feet.
- Sit and tap the air with your feet and toes.
- Prance lightly like a proud pony.
- Dart quickly and lightly to a different space in the room.
- Bounce lightly up and down.

Skipping and dabbing

Slash

Move fast with strong force, using a lot of space in an indirect way:

- Slash your arms strongly in the air, like Zorro's sword.
- Make a vigorous jump, and whip your arms and legs in the air.
- Make an energetic leap, and fling, lash, or flail your arms and legs in the air.
- Jump as if you were popcorn bursting.
- Jump as if you were an explosion.
- Run on angular pathways like lightning.
- Walk urgently about the space, changing directions frequently.
- Thrash out against a net that has captured you.

Slashing

Thrust

Move fast with strength in a direct way, using space efficiently:

- Stab the air with a sudden explosion of force.
- Punch, pierce, or jab the air with your arms and legs powerfully.

(*continues*)

SAMPLE LEARNING EXPERIENCES 32.2

The Eight Basic Effort Actions(*continued*)

- Vigorously punch your way out of a sac of air that has captured you.
- React forcefully as if someone punched you.
- Hammer or pound the air strongly with your fists, elbows, knees, and feet.
- Stomp off angrily.
- Jump and land in a defensive position as if you were frightened of being attacked.
- Plunge or stab as if you were spearing fish.

Thrusting jumps

Courtesy of John Dolly

Integrating with Literacy: Teaching Vocabulary

Learning new vocabulary words is critical for developing children's literacy and a major section of the CCSS. The eight basic effort actions provide many rich and powerful ways to help children learn new vocabulary words. Because the children dance the vocabulary word, they can experience the feelings associated with the word. This experience enriches their understanding and can help them remember the meanings of vocabulary words. Physical education teachers can work with classroom teachers in selecting movement words that teachers use in lessons, or the physical education teacher can teach the terms on his or her own.

Level 2: More Complex Space

Level 2 space focuses on using movement concepts (directions, levels, and pathways) of space in ways that are expressive, linking space movement concepts to body actions. We begin with the movement element of directions and describe Laban's dimensional cross and scale. We then explain how Laban linked directions to six meaningful body actions.

Directions

Theory Underlying Directions: The Dimensional Cross

To help students understand directions in space, Laban developed the dimensional cross (see **Figure 32.5**). The **dimensional cross** connects six directions in space (up, down, left, right, backward, and forward) to six body actions (rising, falling, closing, opening, retreating, and advancing). This connection helps children understand how to use space for expressing and representing ideas and feelings.

Three axes or imaginary lines cross at the center of the body: an up-and-down axis, a side-to-side axis, and a forward-and-back axis. Laban defined this set of axes as the dimensional cross because the three lines relate to three-dimensional space and the three dimensions of the body—that is, height, width, and depth. These dimensions, in turn, relate to the three planes—frontal (door), horizontal (table), and sagittal (wheel) (see **Figure 32.6**).

Laban developed a movement scale, called the dimensional scale, for practicing movements that follow the lines of the dimensional cross. A movement scale is similar to musical scales in which the student practices basic movements in a set order. The dimensional scale (performed with the right hand) is up, down, left, right, back, and forward. (Performed with the left hand, it would be up, down, right, left, back, and forward.) In performing the dimensional scale, the dancer traces the lines of the dimensional cross. The actions that result

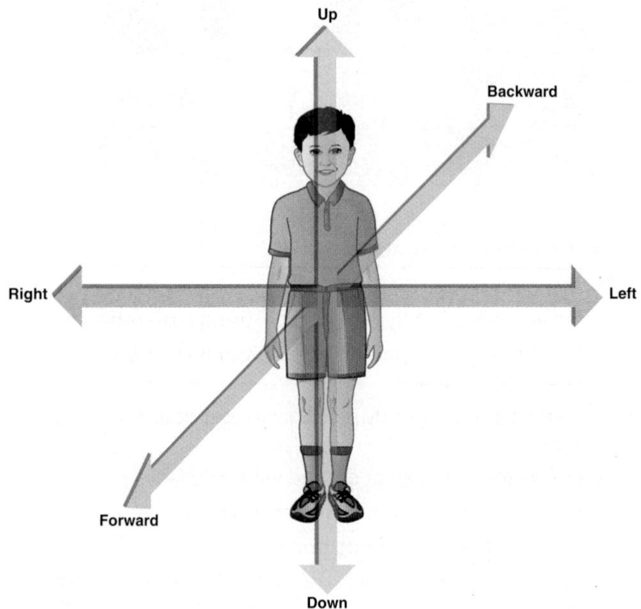

Figure 32.5 The dimensional cross

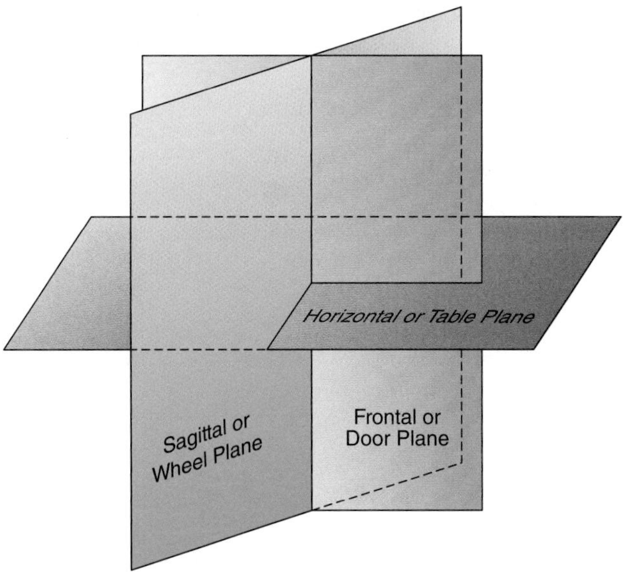

Figure 32.6 The three planes

from performing the scale are rising, falling, closing, opening, retreating, and advancing. Table 32.5 shows the scale and the related actions.

Linking Directions in Space to Meaningful Body Actions

The dimensional scale links the three body axes to six meaningful actions. When children move on the up-and-down axis, they are rising and falling. When they move on the side-to-side axis, they are closing and opening. Moving on the backward-and-forward axis, they are retreating and advancing.

The six actions can be used in different ways to express or represent many different meanings. For example, you can rise with triumph; rise with defiance; fall showing sadness; fall into a comforting, safe, restful place; close showing shyness; open with a welcoming gesture; retreat in fear; or advance seeking adventure. The list of possible representations can go on and on.

Using the Dimensional Cross to Design Learning Experiences

The dimensional scale and cross are simply theoretical tools. As a teacher, you need to take the theory and use it to design learning experiences about space. We suggest you begin by having children explore the six body actions. Body actions give the spatial dimensions their meanings: I am rising, I am falling, I am closing, and so on. After children have experienced many ways to perform these actions, it can be fun for them to learn about the dimensional scale. This scale can then serve as a framework for dance sequences. If you start with the scale, however, it can easily become a rote experience of moving up, down, left, right, backward, and forward and can lose the expressive quality of dance.

Table 32.5 Dimensional Cross Scale and the Related Six Body Actions (for the Right Hand)

Movement of the Scale	Direction in Space	Body Action
Reach straight up over the head	Up	Rising
Reach down to the feet	Down	Falling
Cross the right hand over to the left side	Left	Closing
Reach the right hand to the right side	Right	Opening
Reach the right hand back	Backward	Retreating
Reach the right hand forward	Forward	Advancing

Levels and Pathways

In level 2 work, children can also explore using levels and pathways to represent feelings and ideas.

Sample Learning Experiences and Representations

Levels with a Partner or in Groups

- Being with a partner or group at a high level can represent triumph, success, or reaching for something.
- Being at a high level above someone else can represent protection, oppression, or power.
- Being below someone can represent oppression, lack of power, or helplessness.
- Being with a partner or group at a low level can represent community, home, or togetherness.

Angular and Twisted Pathways

Traveling quickly on angular pathways can represent

- Feeling frantic, scared, or nervous
- Escaping from something
- Being pushed and pulled by an outside force

With light tension, traveling quickly on angular and twisted pathways can represent

- Being playful
- Having fun

Traveling slowly on angular or twisted pathways can represent

- Wandering
- Being lost

Circular Pathways

Traveling in a group on a circular pathway can represent

- Community, togetherness, closeness, or comfort
- Endlessness or enclosure
- Going around in circles
- Getting nowhere
- Being locked in, being unable to break away, or captured

Level 2: More Complex Relationships

The goal of level 2 relationships is to further develop children's understanding of group work. This includes group formations, group shapes, and group actions. Work in this theme depends on children's abilities to work productively and responsibly in small groups. They need to generate many, varied, and some unusual ideas; critique their ideas; solve problems as a group; and stay focused on the task even when there are ample opportunities to socialize with their friends. Designing dances in groups can be very meaningful and satisfying for children.

Group Formations

Since their first days of school, children have been sitting in circles and walking in lines. They have also learned about shapes, such as triangles, circles, and squares, in mathematics. Consequently, children have experience with group formations before they are ready for group work in dance. **Figure 32.7** shows common dance formations.

Formations are central to and often taught first in folk dance lessons. They can also be interesting content in creative dance. Circles can represent community, family, togetherness, and inclusion. Lines can represent militaristic themes and following a leader.

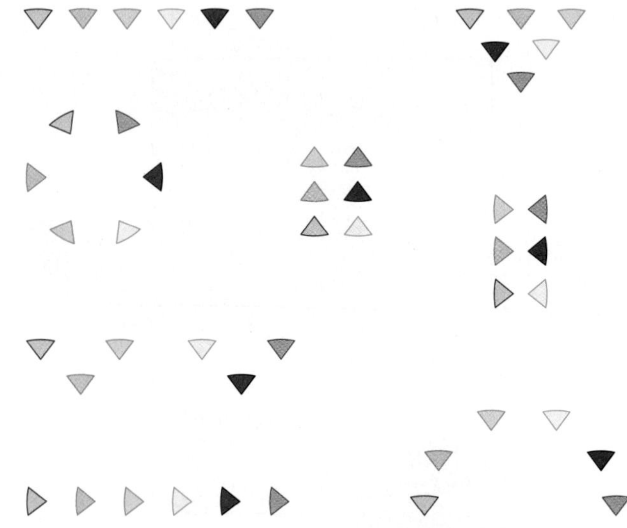

Figure 32.7 Dance formations

SAMPLE LEARNING EXPERIENCES 32.3

Group Formations

Theme: Formations and Streamers

Notes: One way to teach children formations is by using props, such as streamers, canes, and scarves. Begin the unit by teaching the children a set of basic actions with the prop you select. Then have them design a group dance moving in different formations. Music is particularly helpful for these lessons. Select a song that has a steady, obvious beat with a melody (or singing) that goes as much as possible to the underlying beat.

Introductory Activity

I Today, we will be designing a dance using streamers (or ribbons, wands, canes, scarves) and different formations. Let's review the basic actions you can do with streamers. I will show you one. [Select one from the list below.] Follow my lead. Can you think of any others? [Have children demonstrate different ideas. If they don't come up with any of the ideas in the list, then show these to your students.]

Circling ribbons, traveling in a circle

Basic Actions for Streamers (Attached to a Small Wand), Ribbons, and Scarves

- *Circles:* Circle the streamer in front, to each side.
- *Helicopters:* Circle the streamer overhead (with the streamer circling parallel to the ground).
- *Figure 8s:* Make one circle on the right side and then one circle on the left side.
- *Rainbows:* Starting with the streamer in the right hand and the arm stretched to the right, reach up, over the head, and then down on the left side, drawing a half-circle, like a rainbow, with the streamer. Then reverse the action.

SAMPLE LEARNING EXPERIENCES 32.3

Group Formations (*continued*)

- *Spirals/tornados:* Moving quickly, draw small circles with the end of the wand, which will cause the streamer to form a spiral in the air.
- *Zigzags:* Draw a Z with the wand over and over, causing the streamer to make zigzags.
- *Snakes:* Draw an S with the wand.
- *Hurricanes:* Spin while holding the streamer out in front or to the side.
- Write your name in big letters.
- Write your name in tiny letters.
- Whip the streamer.

Rainbows
Courtesy of John Dolly

Basic Actions for Canes (Light, Plastic Tubes or Dance Canes)

- Make circles and rainbows (same as above).
- Tap on the ground and in the air.
- Holding the cane on both ends, reach (and tap) forward, sideways, up, and down.

Content Development

E [Optional.] I have designed a short sequence to the music using different actions. Follow my lead.

1. Do eight figure 8s.
2. Make a big circle in front of you while sliding to the left. Reverse and make a circle with the streamer while you slide to the right. Repeat again to the left and to the right.
3. Make four rainbows.
4. Gallop in a circle around your streamer, making a spiral with your ribbon.
5. Stretch and swing the streamer high, then sink and let the streamer sink into a shape on the floor.

E On your own, explore different ways to move the streamer to the music. Try to change the actions of the streamer when the music changes to a different phrase.

E Experiment with the streamer at different levels.

E Now I will assign you to groups of three or four. [For older children, if you start with groups of three and have children design a sequence, then you can combine two groups to have groups of six and put their sequences together into a longer sequence. Six children and streamers have a more dramatic visual impact than groups of three or four.] Experiment by using different streamer actions in the following formations:

- *Circle formation:* all facing in, move in to the center and back out
- *Circle formation:* all facing out, move away from the center and back in
- *Alternating:* every other child moving in while the others move out
- *Circle formation:* all facing in (or out), sliding sideways
- *Single-line formation:* all facing the child at the head of the line
- *Single-line formation:* children standing shoulder to shoulder and traveling forward, backward, or sideways
- *Double-line formation*

(*continues*)

SAMPLE LEARNING EXPERIENCES 32.3

Group Formations (*continued*)

Culminating Activity

A Now, as a group, design a dance to the music. Try to change formations and streamer actions frequently. Listen carefully to the music, and try to make changes in formations or in streamer actions when there is a change in the music, such as when the singers start a new phrase. For example, when the singer is singing a verse, make one movement. When the singer is singing the chorus, change to a different formation. If you count, you will notice that the phrases of the music are eight counts long. [Most simple pop and children's songs have phrases of four, eight, or 16 counts. Help children listen to the counts and hear when the music changes. Then help them change formations or streamer actions when there is a new phrase.]

R Work on the transitions between formations. Make sure you have a planned way to change formations that does not make you stop and walk or shift positions. For example, if you are in a circle and the next formation is a line, figure out a way to get from the circle to the line that looks like it is part of the dance. For example, you can have one child lead and the rest follow in a line from the circle to a line. Select a locomotor skill and streamer movement for the transition. Your transitions should be coordinated locomotor skills and streamer actions so the transitions look like the other parts of your sequence.

A [Put two groups of three together.] Show the other group your sequence. Then put the sequences together to be a longer sequence. You may need to eliminate formations you did that were the same. You can also add new formations that neither group originally used.

R Practice your sequence until you have it perfected and can repeat it every time doing the same movements. Work on your group timing so you all move in time with one another and with the music. Then we will show your sequences to your classmates.

Group Shapes

There are many different ways that individuals can work together to form interesting group shapes in dance. Although everyone in the group can make the same shape, the dance is usually more effective if everyone makes different shapes that complement one another.

In the same way that individuals can make ball-like, pin-like, wall-like, angular, pointy, and twisted shapes, so can groups. Group can also form one united shape, creating a line of sight that directs an observer's eye on a line to a particular point in space. Finally, group shapes can have an internal focus, an external focus, or several foci.

In making a group shape, children need to attend to different levels and directions. Some children will need to be at low and high levels; some will be in front, in back, and to the sides. Children also need to consider how their group shape will look to an observer.

SAMPLE LEARNING EXPERIENCES 32.4

Group Shapes

Theme: Angular, Flat, Round, and Straight Group Shapes
Content Development

I Today, we will experiment with ball-like, pin-like, wall-like, angular, and pointy group shapes. I will assign you to a group of four. Start by standing still close together but not touching. One person breaks away, travels to a new spot, and forms an angular shape. A second child travels to this new spot and forms an angular shape slotting in and complementing or relating to the first angular shape. A third child and a fourth child then follow suit.

E We will do this again but making flat shapes. Try to decide who breaks away to form the new shape without talking. One child breaks away and makes a flat shape against the wall. The others follow one at a time.

E All at the same time, in slow motion, slide down the wall, and slowly roll away from the wall (using side rolls or transferring weight onto your hips, shins, or hands). Meet together, and form a ball-like shape as a group.

E Instantly, with all children moving at the same time, change the ball to a pointy shape with everyone facing out, and arms, legs, fingers, and feet pointing in all directions.

SAMPLE LEARNING EXPERIENCES 32.4

Group Shapes (*continued*)

E At a medium speed, move all at the same time to end in a big, wall-like shape.

E Moving slowly and at the same time, gather close together, and end with all of you looking up in a pinnacle of arms, hands, and fingers reaching to the sky.

Culminating Activity

A As a group, design a short sequence showing different group shapes. Vary your transitions. Sometimes move at the same time, and sometimes move one at a time. Also, try to vary the speed of your transitions.

R Practice until you have perfected your movement quality and can repeat the sequence precisely the same way every time. Then you will show your sequences to your classmates.

Ball-like group shape

Wall-like group shape learned by using a wall

Theme: Internal and External Focus and Line

Cog K When you make group shapes, sometimes you have an internal focus. This means an observer will notice that everyone in the group focuses on some point in space that is inside or internal to the group. Other group shapes have an external focus. In this kind of group shape, a line of sight created by the group draws an observer's attention to a particular point in space outside of the group. Today we will experiment with making different group shapes that have a particular focus of attention.

I I will put you into groups of four. Start by standing close together in a scattered formation. One child travels a few steps and forms a shape, focusing at a low level internal to the group. Next, a second child travels and joins the first, making a complementary shape that also points to the same internal focus. Then, the other two members of the group, one at a time, travel and join the group shape, pointing to an internal focus.

E Repeat the task, but, this time create a group shape with an external focus in which the group forms a shape with a line of sight pointing to a spot on the wall. One child travels a few steps and forms a shape focusing on a spot on one wall. Next, a second child travels and joins the first, making a complementary shape that also points to the same spot on the wall external to the group. Then, the other two members of the group, one at a time, travel and join the group shape. Be sure group members are present at different levels. Remember, a complementary shape is a shape that is similar to, but not the same as, the shapes made by the other group members. Some of you might point to the spot using your arms. Others might point using your legs, torso, or head.

E Repeat again, but this time travel to a new place, and make a group with many external foci. Your group shape should have many points aiming out into space.

E Moving all at the same time, slowly turn inward and surround a point in space internal to the group.

E As a group, bounce up and down, starting slowly and going faster and faster until you suddenly freeze in a group shape with a focus that is high and external to the group.

(*continues*)

SAMPLE LEARNING EXPERIENCES 32.4

Group Shapes (*continued*)

A In your groups, design a dance sequence showing internal and external focus and line. Practice until you have perfected your movement quality and can repeat the sequence precisely the same way every time.

Cone-like group shape

External focus, pointy shape

Group shape with low diagonal line

Courtesy of John Dolly

Group Actions

There are three group action themes that are important for children to explore: canon and unison, action and reaction, and meeting and parting.

Canon and Unison

Unison means that all dancers move at the same time. Canon means that the dancers move in succession, like the "wave" in a sports stadium. With canon, each child can finish the movement before the next child begins or their movements can overlap. Canon can be done in groups so group 1 moves, then group 2, then group 3. In addition, you can do canon movements starting at one side and moving to the other side, or from front to back. Canon and unison are standard choreographic tools for dance and drill teams and are enjoyable for children to perform.

Action and Reaction

In action and reaction, one child or group acts and others react. You can use action–reaction movements to represent different events and ideas. For example, action–reaction can represent fighting, discord, or making friends. In the lesson titled "The Sea and the Shore," action and reaction are used to represent first the aggressive, antagonistic feelings of huge ocean waves crashing against a rocky cliff and then the peaceful conversation between gentle waves rushing onto a sandy beach.

Meeting and Parting

Meeting and parting refers to individuals meeting together, typically doing some movements together, and then parting, going on about their lives. Meeting and parting can also refer to nonhuman forces, such as magnetism. Gathering and scattering is a form of meeting and parting but has a different nuance, implying a crowd of individuals that forms and then disperses. Gathering and scattering can also refer to harvesting and planting grain. We use meeting and parting as themes in two lessons: "Shelter in a Storm," in which the emotions represented are comfort and safety, and "The Sea and the Shore," which portrays gentle waves on a beach and human relationships that linger but don't last.

SAMPLE LEARNING EXPERIENCES 32.5

Group Actions

Theme: Cannon and Unison

Cog K Today we will be working on canon and unison. I am going to start by having you demonstrate canon. In your group (of three or four children), get in a line by kneeling shoulder to shoulder. Put your hands on the floor. Starting at one end, do the wave. The first person stretches her or his hands to the ceiling and then back to the floor. After the first person is halfway up, the second person starts. Continue down the line.

Cog K/I Now I will have you demonstrate unison. Stand, turn, and all face one line leader. In unison, make a big circle with your arms and body reaching far to the side and to the floor as you circle. Carefully watch the line leader. Repeat.

SAMPLE LEARNING EXPERIENCES 32.5

Group Actions (*continued*)

E Repeat the circle action but this time in canon.

E Repeat the circle action again in canon but now alternating first person to the right, second person to the left, third person to the right, and so on, and without stopping, start a second circle. When your hands get near the floor, break away, traveling at a low level to end in a round shape on the floor with the group in a scattered formation.

E A new leader stands up and travels while making a simple rhythm by clapping, stamping, and making arm gestures that repeat. One at a time, each group member joins in matching and moving in unison with the leader's movements. Continue adding children to the line until the whole group is moving in unison. The leader says, "Freeze," and everyone freezes, making her or his own shape.

E A new leader starts traveling while making a simple rhythm by clapping, stamping, and making arm gestures. One at a time, each group member joins the line behind the leader. The leader says, "Freeze," and all group members stand straight. The leader makes one big, slow movement, and all group members follow in unison.

E Repeat the movement in canon.

E Repeat the movement in canon again but without pausing, transition to a low level, and end in a curled position on the floor.

A In your groups, design a dance sequence showing canon and unison. Practice until you have perfected your movement quality and can repeat the sequence precisely the same way every time.

Theme: Action and Reaction

Fight Scene

I With your assigned partner, one person does a punching action *without touching your partner*, and the other person reacts. Then the second partner does a punching action, and the first person reacts.

Safety Safety is critical in this task. Before you start, move far enough apart so you won't be able to actually touch each other—even by mistake. Be certain that you control and stop your punching action without getting close to your partner.

E Now, do punching actions using different body parts. Make your actions interesting. [Repeat several times, changing which partner acts and which partner reacts.]

E What are some actions that cause a reaction? [Someone calls me a name and I do not like it. Put your hand in a fire and you get burned.] Are all reactions quick? Can you think of some that might be slow?

A Now, with your partner, plan three different action–reaction segments, and put them together into a sequence. Select a theme to help you plan your movements. Your theme can be fighting, or you can think of a different theme. Have at least one change in level and one turn in your sequence. Practice until you have perfected your movement quality and can repeat the sequence precisely the same way every time.

Theme: Meeting and Parting

Magnetism

I Pretend your wrists are electromagnets. When the current is on, they pull together; when the current is off, they drift apart. Take four beats to bring your wrists together and four beats to pull them apart. Current is on—1, 2, 3, 4. Current is off—1, 2, 3, 4. Each time the current turns on, bring your wrists together in a different position around your body. [Repeat current on and off several times.]

E Now your elbows are electromagnets. Try to vary the ways you bring your elbows together and pull them apart. [Repeat current on and off several times.]

E In groups of three, explore making your wrists and elbows electromagnets. Find different ways you can gather and become stuck together at your wrists and elbows and then drift apart.

A Now you select which body parts are electromagnets. Design a sequence in which the three of you meet and gather together and then part or scatter. Practice until you have perfected your movement quality and can repeat the sequence precisely the same way every time.

Summary

In level 2, you revisit the body, effort, space, and relationship aspects of the Laban framework in a spiral progression from level 1. You select movement concepts that are more complex and combine several elements, such as the eight basic effort actions. The dance sequences you ask children to design require that they can (or learn to) cooperate with partners and small groups in making decisions and solving choreographic problems. The ideas children represent in their dances are more abstract and complex than in level 1.

Review Questions

1. In what ways is level 2 a progression from level 1?
2. What implications does a spiral progression have for teaching?
3. Design a task for a body action dance sequence for children.
4. From **Table 32.2**, select one topic (or come up with your own topic), and list at least five different ideas within that topic that you could use for a dance lesson.
5. Carefully study **Table 32.4**, and figure out the logic of the order of the eight basic effort actions. Then, without looking, reproduce the table.
6. Select one effort action, and design a lesson segment ending in a very short sequence to teach that effort action. In your tasks, overlay a story that will help children understand the effort action and become the basis for a short sequence.
7. Describe the dimensional cross, and explain how it links to the axes of the body.
8. Describe how the dimensional cross is transformed into six meaningful actions.
9. Design an outline of tasks for a short lesson segment that uses levels or pathways to represent an idea, topic, or feeling.
10. Write a story or topic not discussed in the text that you could use to teach action and reaction.

References

Aguilar, D. A. (2008). *Eleven planets: A new view of the solar system.* Washington DC: National Geographic Society.

Baskin-Salzberg & Salzberg, (1991). *Predators.* New York: Franklin Watts.

Branley, F. M., & Kelley, T. (1999). *Flash, Crash, Rumble, and Roll.* New York: HarperCollins.

Drake, J., Love, A., & Thurman, M. (2008). *Alien invaders: Species that threaten our world.* Plattsburgh, NY: Tundra.

Galiano, D. (Rev. Ed. 2003). *Thunderstorms and lightning.* New York: Rosen.

Laban, R. (1948). *Modern educational dance.* London: MacDonald & Evans.

Musgrove, M. (1976). *Ashanti to Zulu: African traditions.* New York: Dial.

Preston-Dunlop, V. (1980). *A handbook for modern educational dance* (rev. ed.). Boston: Plays.

Rovegno, I., & Bandhauer, D. (2000). Teaching elements of choreography. *Teaching Elementary Physical Education, 11*(5), 6–10, 34.

Stokes, E. M. (1970). *Word pictures as a stimulus for creative dance.* London: MacDonald & Evans.

FYI

Summary of Task Label Abbreviations

I	Informing tasks	Th	Thinking skill
E	Extending/exploring tasks	Mot	Motivation concept
R	Refinements	Safety	Safety information or reminder
A	Application/assessment tasks	MD	Modification to make the task more difficult
Org	Organizing task	ME	Modification to make the task easier
Cog K	Cognitive knowledge: Explains or defines a concept		
Social	Social skill or concept		

Source: Adapted and Modified from Rink, J. E. (2014). *Teaching physical education for learning* (7th ed.). New York: McGraw-Hill.

Sample Plans for Level 2 Creative Dance

SAMPLE PLAN 32.1

Ashanti to Zulu

Movement Theme: Body Actions
Topic Theme: *Ashanti to Zulu*
Text: Musgrove (1976). *Ashanti to Zulu: African Traditions*

Notes: This lesson is based on the children's book *Ashanti to Zulu: African Traditions*. Because the book is a Caldecott winner (a yearly award for the "most distinguished American picture book for children"), you can find it in most school and public libraries and bookstores. We designed the lesson for older children who can work in groups.

This is an excellent unit to integrate with social studies. Ask the classroom teacher to teach the book and have it available in the classroom as a reference. Ask if it is possible to have the children research their tribes as part of a social studies lesson. If not, the lesson works fine on its own. Once the children have selected their tribes, try to provide copies of the book for each group or photocopy the relevant page.

Standards

This plan addresses National Standards 1, 2, 4, and 5 and CCSS for reading key ideas and details and integration of knowledge and ideas.

Objectives

The children will learn to

Motor

1. Perform a variety of body actions, varying body positions, pathways, and effort actions.
2. Make light movements light, strong movements forceful, fast movements fast, and slow movements slow.
3. Work from their center by using their whole body to perform a shape or effort action, not just the arms and legs.

Creative Thinking and Choreography Concepts

4. Apply the concept of contrast and good transitions to their dance compositions.

Social

5. Work cooperatively in a small group during the choreographic process.

CCSS

6. Use information gained from illustrations and the words in a text to demonstrate an understanding of the text orally and then through representation of the ideas in a dance.
7. Refer to details and examples in a text when drawing inferences from the text.

Introductory and Warm-up Activity

I The title of this book is *Ashanti to Zulu: African Traditions*, by Margaret Musgrove. It is an alphabet book about 26 African tribes. Today we are going to create a dance based on one of the tribes in this book. Then in the next two to three lessons, you will select your own tribe and create your own dance. You will be able to use props and, if you want, make costumes for the dance.

Reading and Facilitating Understanding of the Text

Cog K Let's start by reading the story about the Ga tribe. [Project the text and illustration on a wall.] What do you see in the illustration? What do you think they are doing? [Call on several children.] Let's read and see. [Have the children read aloud.] Let's review:

- What did the text say about the Ga tribe?
- What surprised you?
- What might be the advantages of that style of eating?
- What do you think the dad is feeling?
- What do you think the mom is feeling?
- What do you think the little boy is thinking?
- What do you think the family is thinking?

(*continues*)

SAMPLE PLAN 32.1

Ashanti to Zulu (*continued*)

Content Development

Pounding (Thrusting)

Potential Refinements

- Keep tight when you pound.
- Show the force in your body.
- Feel the strong pounding force inside you.

Cog K Which kind of movements do you think they are doing to squash the yams? Which kind of force do you need?

I In your own space, make some pounding movements. I see some of you look like you are using a stick. Let's begin by pounding yams like the Ga. Start by holding two hands on a pretend stick and pound.

E I am going to add a drum beat. [Teacher beats a drum while the children pound.] Try to stay with the rhythm I am beating.

E Most of you have been pounding by using your arms. Which other parts can you use for pounding? Now let's take the pounding movement and explore pounding with other body parts. [Call out the parts that you see children using. If necessary, scaffold the following parts.] Can you pound with your hands? Feet? One elbow? Other elbow? Now try pounding with your head, now your knee. Now do whole-body actions representing pounding with your whole body.

E Try pounding with your hands at different levels—low, now medium, now high. [Repeat several times.] Now do five pounding movements in a row to the beat of the drum: high, medium, low, medium, high. Now try pounding in all areas of your personal space.

E Now try pounding at different levels with different body parts. Let's explore feet first. Pound with your feet low, then at a medium level. Now try elbows. Now travel each time you pound. Travel forward, back, sideways. Now add a turn as you travel.

E Let's vary the size of the movement. We will do three pounding movements (at different levels and with different body parts)—small, small, big. [Beat the drum quiet, quiet, loud.] Move with the beat: small movement, small movement, big pounding movement. [Continue repeating and cuing the children, if necessary, to vary the levels and body parts.] Now try a different rhythm—small, big, small, big. [Repeat several times.] Now try one more—small, small, small, big, big, big. [Repeat several times.]

Smoothing Yams

Potential Refinements

- Keep your movements smooth and gentle.

E Another part of the story was smoothing yams. Let's explore smoothing yams. Start by imitating smoothing yams with your hands. Do this at a medium level as if you were smoothing the yams on a table.

E Now try smoothing movements with your hands in other areas of your personal space.

E Try smoothing movements at other levels.

E Put together a sequence of two smoothing movements—for example, medium level, high level, medium level, high level or low level, very low level, low level, very low level.

Dabbing

Potential Refinements

- Dab gently and quickly.

E While you are sitting, let's explore a dabbing action to represent dipping the foufou into the stew. Gently, dab with your hands as if you are patting a scraped knee with a cotton ball.

E Now, explore dabbing in all areas of your personal space. Dab to the side, behind you, up high, behind your head, reaching out to all areas around your body.

E Now face a partner, and we will have a movement conversation. Without talking, one person dab a message by moving your hands to different positions in a rhythm. [Demonstrate two or three dabbing movements to a partner.] Then the other person responds by dabbing a message back. Continue the movement conversation. [Repeat with several different partners, cuing the children to dab in all areas of their personal space.]

SAMPLE PLAN 32.1

Ashanti to Zulu (*continued*)

Culminating Activity

A Take the main movement ideas, and in your assigned groups of four, create a dance interpreting the story of the Ga. There are three main movement ideas: pounding movements, smoothing movements, and dabbing movements. Use them as the basis for your dance, but expand on the ideas so you are representing the story and not imitating the movements of pounding yams, smoothing yams, and dipping the foufou into the stew. For example, although the book illustrates pounding yams with a stick, take the idea of pounding and pound in many different ways, with different body parts, and at different levels. End the dance by representing the feeling of a family being together eating from the same bowl using their right hands. Don't be constrained by the story line—represent the main ideas.

Social It is important when you work in a group that everyone gets to contribute ideas. Today we will have the rule, "Everyone speaks and everyone listens." Select one member of your group to be the monitor of group discussions. If not everyone is listening, the monitor should say, "Let's all listen to John now." If someone has not contributed to the discussion, the monitor can say, "George, what is your opinion?"

Refine Your Dance

R After you design the rough draft of your dance, call the group in and discuss how to refine the choreography.

- *Transitions:* First, check that you have good transitions. Try to have each section of the dance lead seamlessly to the next. You should not be able to tell when one section ends and the next section begins because the transition is part of the dance.
- *Contrasts:* Now add contrasts and aesthetic highlights. Dances are monotonous without contrasts. To add contrasts, try adding a change in levels, speeds, or directions. Two of the most important contrasts are changing formations and relationships frequently. Sometimes move in unison, and sometimes have each person doing different movements. Sometimes face in as a group, and sometimes face out.

A Now that you have finished your dances, do any groups volunteer to show their dance to their classmates? Everyone watch, and be ready to identify what you like about their dance and what the strengths of their choreography are. Then we will give the group compliments.

Extending the Content in Future Lessons

If you want to extend this lesson into a unit, you can assign different tribes to groups of three or four children.

A I will assign you to groups of four. Each group will select a different letter and design a group dance. You may use drums or other musical instruments to accompany your dance. In addition, you can use props such as sticks, poles, ribbons, and scarves. You may add costumes if you like.

Suggested Tribes Identified by Letters

Following are some suggestions you can give the children for other letters:

E Design a dance in which you have movement conversations and create different dances to different rhythmical beats on drums. Each dancer can use a drum, or you can use one drum for the entire group.

F Themes could be chopping trees, sipping, pouring wine on the ground as an invitation, and gathering.

P Themes could be slashing, jabbing, and thrusting movements, pair dances, and a group dance.

T You could use different instruments and have each person create a dance to an instrument. In this case, the dance is like a story, and the rest of group watches.

W Themes could be anglers moving carefully, rapids, building traps, fish swimming and the anglers catching them in traps, and repairing traps.

Z You could create a group dance sequence to drums.

More Difficult Letters

A Weaving kente, personal identity, making your own dance with a cloth as a prop.

B Dance drama: a story of war, escape, sacrifice, and related emotions.

I Humans and animals working together: a story of a bird leading humans to honey.

Q Different family identities.

V Group movement in unison with heads level, then each person does a sequence showing movements while changing levels. Children also could use ABACADA rondo form, in which A is a group sequence repeated in between each individual sequence, represented by the letters B, C, and D.

SAMPLE PLAN 32.2

Prey and Predators

Movement Theme: Bound Flow, Stretching, and Curling
Topic Theme: Prey and Predators
Text: Baskin-Salzberg & Salzberg (1991). *Predators*

Notes: For teachers who have no large space, you can teach this lesson on rainy days in a classroom with desks. We designed the lesson especially for fourth- and fifth-graders to connect with classroom study of prey and predators, which is part of the elementary science curriculum in many schools. For dance, the lesson goal is to interpret the theme of prey and predator in an artistic mode—that is, dance. In addition, this lesson connects with drama and literature. The theme of prey and predator is a major theme represented in literature, film, and television (for example, most police dramas). You can begin the lesson by asking children to discuss different stories they have heard or seen about prey and predators.

Standards

This plan addresses National Standards 1, 2, 4, and 5 and CCSS for reading key ideas and details and vocabulary acquisition.

Objectives

The children will learn to

Motor

1. Feel and show bound flow (especially those aspects of bound flow movement that are cautious, wary, frightened, calculating, and alert).
2. Stretch and curl in different ways, feeling the contrast between stretching and curling, stretching through all parts of the body, and keeping all parts of the body in a curled shape.
3. Travel with bound flow, leading with different body parts while moving hesitantly, maintaining an alert tension in their muscles.

Creative Thinking Skills/Choreography Concepts

4. Design a dance representing the feelings and idea of prey and predators.
5. Select an interesting ending to their dance, and explain their reasons for their choices.

CCSS

6. Determine the main idea of a text, and explain how it is supported by key details.
7. Identify real-life connections between words and their use.

Potential Refinements

- Be able to stop your movement at any time.
- Move hesitantly.
- Feel the movement from the inside.
- Feel constrained and cautious.
- Feel the anticipation of having to stop at any time.
- Stretch through all parts of your body.

Introduction

Cog K We will work on several movement concepts today. The first is bound flow. Spread out at the end of the physical education space and face me. Slowly and cautiously, walk toward me. Stop. [Repeat several times.] Be ready to stop the instant I say, "Stop." Pay attention to the feeling inside you of knowing that you must travel slowly and stop instantly. We call this bound flow. *Bound flow* means you can stop your movement at any time. You are so in control of your movement that your movements are constrained and cautious.

Content Development

Traveling with Bound Flow

E This time, watch me, and stop the instant you see me start to move. If you think I have stopped moving, start walking again. [As the children walk toward you, suddenly move your arm. Repeat until some children have reached the front of the room.]

SAMPLE PLAN 32.2

Prey and Predators (*continued*)

E You are such a trustworthy class that we are going to repeat the task, but this time I am going to turn my back. When my back is turned, you can move, but you must move in such a way that I can't hear you. I won't even know you are in the room. Then, I will suddenly turn around, and all I will see is an entire class of frozen children. I will not see one body or even one eyebrow moving. It will look like no one has moved at all. [Randomly (and often), turn around. Turn around within one second the first time. Then vary the timing.]

E We are going to do the same thing, but this time travel on different pathways about the space (throughout the desks if you are in a classroom) with bound flow. Don't move into anyone else's personal space. Stop when you see me move (or hear me say, "Stop").

E This time, you decide when to stop, how long to hold your still position, and when to move again. [If you are in a big gym, have the children get relatively close together in the middle of the space.] Concentrate on the feeling of being still and being aware of another child moving close to you. This is like the feeling of playing hide and seek in the dark, when you hide and someone walks right by you without seeing you.

Traveling as Prey

Cog K In science, you have been talking about predators and prey, and that topic is the theme for your dance today. [Project the text on the wall and have the children read aloud together.]

A group of penguins sun themselves on an ice floe. Splash! Hunger drives them into the cold water to hunt for fish. Soon the hunter becomes the hunted as a penguin finds itself in the jaws of a leopard seal, who kills it with a quick crunch. Its stomach full of penguin, the seal now climbs onto the empty ice to rest.

Suddenly the hunter again becomes the hunted as the ice floe is surrounded by a pack of orcas, or killer whales. The doomed seal clings to the ice. It's only a matter of time until the intelligent orcas figure out a way to move the seal off the ice and into their waiting jaws (Baskin-Salzberg & Salzberg, 1991, p. 9).

Cog K With your assigned partner, discuss the main idea of these paragraphs. Give details to support your answer.

E We will start as prey. Select what you think is a safe spot in the room. Plan a pathway to this spot that will get you there without anyone detecting where you are trying to go. Move with bound flow. Stop when you feel the need to be cautious, when you want to disguise your pathway, or when you think someone dangerous to you can see you move. When you get there, stop, and slowly, warily scan the terrain as if you are prey for some unseen predator.

E Repeat the task, but this time travel at three different levels. Sometimes travel at a low level, sometimes at a high level, and sometimes at a medium level. Concentrate on how it feels to move with bound flow while scanning for predators.

E Repeat the task, but this time when you get to your safe spot, scan and then change your level by curling and ending in a shape that represents hiding and fear.

E [Repeat the preceding task several times.] Be sure to curl into a different curled shape each time. Think about the feeling of being prey. Try to represent this feeling in your movements and shapes. Try to have original, creative shapes, rather than plain shapes.

E Now, each time you travel, lead with a different body part, while maintaining the sense of being prey. Sometimes lead with your back, sometimes with your side, and sometimes with your front. Each time you stop, slowly curl into a shape that shows you are prey. Try to make a different shape each time. Be aware of the feeling inside your muscles when you travel with bound flow.

Stretching and Curling

E Now beginning in your safe space, explore stretching slowly out of your den to see if it is safe, look around, and curl back into your den. [Repeat several times.]

E Now travel again, pause, and curl into a different den. Be sure to travel at different levels. Attend to the feeling of bound flow.

Moving as a Predator

Cog K Let's read together some facts about predator hunting strategies [project text on the wall, and have children read aloud together].

"The Ambush"

Some predators *ambush* their meals by waiting patiently out of sight behind a rock or under a leaf until their prey passes by. Then they rush out and grab their surprised victims. A high-speed attack may occur so quickly that a flock of birds may not even notice that one of their number is missing (Baskin-Salzberg & Salzberg, 1991, p. 43).

"The Stalk"

Many predators *stalk*, or sneak up on, prey by hiding behind plants, rocks, or trees until they're close enough to pounce. Big cats are expert stalkers. So are alligators, snakes, and polar bears.

(*continues*)

SAMPLE PLAN 32.2

Prey and Predators (*continued*)

A stalking lion tries to make itself smaller by crouching low and keeping its head down. That way, it's less likely to be seen by a gazelle or a wildebeest. The big cat moves close only when its victim is looking the other way. Should the gazelle look up, the lion freezes in its tracks. When it's near enough, the lion will dash toward its *quarry* at full speed and jump on its back or knock it down with a huge swipe of its paw (Baskin-Salzberg & Salzberg, 1991, p. 45).

"The Chase"

When you food can run, fly, or swim away from you, you'd better be pretty fast yourself. And predators who chase their prey are fast, though they may lie in wait or stalk prey until they are within chasing range (Baskin-Salzberg & Salzberg, 1991, pp. 46–47).

E We will start with the stalking strategy. Still moving with bound flow and being cautious not to let anyone catch you moving, change your attitude to that of a predator. Imagine your prey is somewhere in this room. Decide on a pathway that will get you very close to the prey but on which you can move undetected. Be calculating and patient. When you reach the spot, hold a position at a different level that will enable you to pounce on the prey when the time comes. [Repeat several times.] Be sure to travel at different levels.

E This time as you travel, try leading with different body parts. Think about the feeling of being a predator. Try to represent this feeling in your movements and shapes.

E Now explore stretching but as a predator. Slowly stretch out of your hiding place to see if you can see your prey. Look around; if your prey is looking your way, freeze. When you can move undetected, curl back into your hiding place. [Repeat several times.]

E Now, stretch out of your hiding place, and travel while searching for prey. Move so the prey won't see you. Every so often, curl into a different hiding place that allows you to look for prey but in which your prey won't see you. Be aware of the feeling inside your muscles. How does the feeling differ when you are prey and predator?

E Now you are close enough to pounce on your prey. Move a few steps quickly, jump with firm tension, making an angular shape in the air, and land in an angular shape representing your attack on your prey.

E Explore different ways to jump with strong force and firm tension, and do a jabbing action. Land in a different shape each time.

E Add a turn, and make a large, circular gesture with your arms.

E Put stalking and attacking together. Stalk about the space, and attack when you get close to your prey. Repeat several times. You decide when to stalk and when to attack.

Culminating Activity

A With your assigned partner, create a sequence that represents the theme of predator and prey and captures in movement the feelings of prey and predator and information from the text. Show a variety of relationships (e.g., apart, together, back to back, facing, side by side) and different levels. Express the feeling of prey and predator. One of you will be the prey, and the other will be the predator. Here is the dance structure, but you can modify it if you think your modifications will tell a better story [It helps to write this sequence on a whiteboard]:

1. The prey moves and freezes, feels safe, and then curls into a den.
2. The predator then moves and freezes. The prey senses but cannot see the predator.
3. The prey moves, freezes, moves to a new spot, and curls into hiding.
4. The predator sees the prey and begins to stalk it. The prey continues to move, sensing the predator.
5. The predator closes in.
6. Make up your own ending. (Children will come up with a variety of endings, including having the prey successfully defend itself against the predator.)

R Refine your sequence. Check whether you both have starting complementary shapes. In other words, your shapes should relate to each other so an observer will know that you are partners even though you are not near each other. Next, be sure you have complementary shapes or movements during your dance. You might travel around each other in a similar way but at different levels, or you might travel in opposite directions but in similar ways. You might also pause near each other in complementary shapes.

A If you want, you may show your sequence. [For teachers with multiple classes, have one-third of the pairs show at the same time. For teachers with single classes, let two or three pairs show at the same time.] Audience members, watch carefully, and be prepared to give compliments. Performers, after your sequence, be prepared to discuss why you selected your ending. Before you show your dance, is there anything you would like to tell us about your sequence?

SAMPLE PLAN 32.3

Invasive Species

Movement Themes: Wringing, Slashing, Scurrying, and Twisted Shapes
Topic Theme: Invasive Species
Text: Drake, Love, & Thurman (2008). *Alien Invaders: Species that Threaten Our World*

Notes: Invasive species are typically part of fourth or fifth grade science; thus, it is likely you can integrate the lesson with the unit taught by the classroom teacher. We have included enough information in this plan for you to teach concepts from the topic and successfully teach this dance unit. The unit will take several lessons to complete, in particular if you want students to refine their group dances.

Asian Long-horned Beetles

These beetles attack many varieties of tree, in particular maple, and can kill a tree in three years. The larvae eat vital cells within the trunk, leaving tunnels and disrupting sap flow. In essence they strangle the tree. Controlling the beetles can be done only by cutting down and burning infected trees. From Asia, they are now in North America, England, and Austria.

Hydrilla

Once popular plants for fish tanks, hydrilla live in lakes and rivers and can grow to be nine meters tall. The plants form mats that smother other plants, block streams, create stagnant water and mosquito infestations, and clog boat engines. Once established, it is difficult to eradicate. Originally from India, Korea, and Australia, hydrilla has invaded every continent except Antarctica.

Yellow Crazy Ants

Crazy ants kill by spraying acid in the eyes of, and then eating, their prey. They damage the food chain by killing other small animals, such as spiders, crabs, clams, and snails. In turn, vegetation typically eaten by small animals, grows out of control, which, in turn, has an impact on larger mammals, birds, and reptiles. They are now found in Australia and on Pacific, Caribbean, and Indian Ocean islands.

Cane Toads

Cane toads live in sugar cane farms in Australia. Their skin is covered with lumpy, poisonous glands that ooze venom, and their eggs and tadpoles are poisonous, too. Their poison can kill small animals, such as dogs, cats, frogs, lizards, and other small mammals. They kill their predators and take over their habitat. From South and Central America, they have spread to Hawaii and other South Pacific and Caribbean islands.

Standards

These learning experiences meet National Standards 1, 2, 4, and 5 and CCSS for reading informational texts.

Objectives

By the end of these unit tasks, children will learn to

Motor and Cognitive Knowledge

1. Maintain firm tension throughout the body, especially the torso, while wringing and traveling at low levels.
2. Rise and fall using floating effort actions, maintaining light force and fine tension.
3. Travel using quick, scurrying movements.
4. Jump and leap, using slashing effort actions and a lot of space indirectly.

Creative Thinking Skills/Choreography Concepts

5. Design a group dance with originality, line, and clarity.

Social Responsibility and CCSS

6. Listen attentively to other group members' ideas, build on others' ideas, and encourage everyone in the group to contribute.

CCSS

7. Determine the main idea of a text, explain how it is supported by key details, and summarize the text. Refer to details and examples in a text when explaining what the text says explicitly and when drawing inference from the text.

Potential Refinements

- Have a lot of tension in your muscles while wringing.
- Have light force and fine tension while floating
- Use a lot of space indirectly during slashing jumps and leaps.

(continues)

SAMPLE PLAN 32.3

Invasive Species (*continued*)

Introduction

[Project the text on the wall and have children read aloud together:]

Millions cross oceans, clinging to ships' hulls or as stowaways in cargo holds. Thousands hitchhike on truck trailers or in packing crates. Untold numbers curl up in airplane landing gear at night, or sneak into the folds of luggage. Some even swagger across borders in broad daylight, their passage provided by unknowing, careless humans.

Once they arrive, their numbers grow, slowly at first—and silently. Then the killing begins. They strangle, suffocate, drown, sting, trample, starve, suck out the lifeblood, and even eat their victims. Only then do we notice our homeland has been invaded and we could be overwhelmed by alien invaders (Drake, et al., 2008, p. 5).

Questions for Comprehension

- What is the main idea the authors are trying to capture in the starting paragraphs of the text? What feelings are they trying to elicit in the reader? What was the tone? What did you think about and feel as you listened?
- These ideas and feeling will be the theme of our dance. Keep the meaning and tone of these introductory paragraphs in mind, and later we will discuss how you might represent the theme of invasive species in a dance.

Content Development

Wringing and Traveling at a Low Level, Twisting

CCSS We will start working on movements representing the Asian long-horned beetle. What did you learn about these beetles? [They eat tunnels in the wood strangling and killing a tree in just three years (Drake, et al., 2008)].

I Start sitting. Using firm tension, slowly curl your fingers one at a time, keeping a lot of tension in your finger muscles, as if your fingers were pinchers at the end of an insect's segmented leg. Then uncurl your fingers one at a time. Now try it with the other hand. Now, both hands.

E Curl and uncurl your fingers and stretch one arm in personal space, twisting your arm with firm tension. Slowly, tortuously, twist that arm all the way until the twist moves into your shoulder, and then slowly untwist it. Repeat with the other arm. Repeat with both arms at the same time.

E Using the same wringing action, take your pinchers and reach out to the edge of your personal space; move as if you are clawing wood and digging a tunnel within the tree, and slowly travel, staying at a low level.

E Now, explore reaching to different areas of your personal space and traveling on different body parts at a low level. Twist as you travel maintaining strong tension. [Repeat several times.]

E Try to use original movements and body positions that are grotesque and threatening.

Rising and Sinking Using Floating Effort Actions

E Now we are working on representing hydrilla. What did you learn about hydrilla? [It is a plant that invades lakes and rivers with dense, tall leaves that choke streams and smother the habitat of animals and waterfowl.]

I Starting low, slowly rise, floating as if you were a tall leaf drifting in a river, sway side to side gently, and then sink to a low level.

E Explore rising, swaying, and sinking with floating effort, that is, moving slowly and gently, letting your arms, shoulders, head, and body drift about in space. [Repeat many times.]

E Try to find original shapes and movements that capture the feeling of tall hydrilla weeds floating in a river.

E The hydrilla has won. Use strong tension, press down with your hands and arms, and slowly sink showing strong tension throughout your body. You are pressing your victim onto the riverbed suffocating it. Then reverse, and press while you rise.

E Explore different ways to rise and sink using pressing effort actions (slow, forceful, with firm tension). Vary the position of your hands and arms each time. Try to find original and unusual positions.

E Crash into a slimy heap on the floor, defeated.

Scurrying

E Suddenly and without warning, you become the crazy ants. The ants scurry, running on zigzag pathways and moving quickly. Stop. [Repeat several times.]

E Now try scurrying on all fours (traveling on your hands and feet). Travel on zigzag pathways quickly like crazy ants. Stop. Scan, looking for prey to attack. Scurry again. [Repeat several times.]

SAMPLE PLAN 32.3

Invasive Species (*continued*)

Slashing Leap and Landing at a Low Level

Cog K What did you learn about how yellow crazy ants kill prey? [They spray acid in their eyes.]

E This time, rise, run, and leap, slashing at the air and trying to use as much space as possible. [Repeat several times.]

E This time, leap or jump, land, and immediately move to a low level with a jabbing movement. Practice a slashing leap and landing with a jab at a low level several times.

E Now expand the phrase. Run, leap, land at a low level, and quickly rise tall and jab low again as if attacking prey.

E Explore making different shapes and gestures in the jump and the jab.

Exploring in Trios Wringing and Traveling at a Low Level

E I will assign you to groups of three. First, explore and find three different group shapes that are twisted and grotesque. Then connect the shapes by twisting to move from one to the next.

E Two of you make twisted shapes, number one at a medium level and number two at a low level. The third person will travel twisting using strong tension going under some body part of the first person and going over the second person. Be sure to have some space where your partner can travel under you. Then rotate roles. Person two is now the traveler, person three moves with strong tension to a medium level, and the previous traveler twists into a shape at a low level. Continue to switch roles as the three of you travel as a group. Maintain tension in your whole body as you move or hold the still, twisted shape. Think of being one creature, with all of you moving and relating to each other continually.

E Now, focus on the shape of your body trying to complement the shape of your group members' bodies.

E Now, focus on making precise shapes that your group members can complement or even match.

Exploring Rising, Swaying, and Sinking with Floating Effort

E Now, as a group, explore different ways to rise and fall as a group, matching and or complementing shapes.

E Try to vary the levels, sometimes rising only to a medium level and sinking only to a medium level, and your relationships, such as back to back, side by side, front to back.

Exploring Pressing While Rising and Sinking

E Now, explore pressing while rising and sinking as a group, relating your body shapes to each other. Match and/or complement shapes. Vary the levels and your relationships, such as back to back, side by side, and front to back.

E Explore sinking with strong force, pause, and find different ways to collapse as a group into a huddled, curved mass on the floor.

Exploring Scurrying, Slashing Jumps, and Jabs

E Now explore ways to scurry at a low level, run and do slashing jumps, and then as a group jab, moving from a high to a low level. Work on finding many, varied, and some unusual jabbing movements as a group, matching and complementing your shapes.

E One person scurries away at a low level to a new spot and, with a slow, tense wringing motion, ends in a twisted shape. The second person scurries and joins in, wringing and making a twisted shape that relates to the first person's shape. Then the third person scurries over and joins the group shape. Repeat several times.

E Repeat, but scurry and then do a slashing leap before forming the group shape. Repeat several times. Use a lot of space in your leap by flinging your arms and legs out.

Pulsing and Jabbing

E Travel as a group at a medium level while rising and sinking, expanding and contracting, pulsating together as if you were one heart beating. Think about how the cane toads you studied ooze venom. As you pulsate, you are oozing venom.

E Pause. Quickly jump two times moving sideways. Pause. Repeat the sequence of traveling while pulsating, jump, jump, and then pause.

E This time after you pause, make a quick, jabbing movement, ending in pointy shapes, sending your venom into a predator, who has now become a prey. Repeat several times exploring different shapes.

Culminating Activity

CCSS Now that you have explored many movement possibilities, it is time to design your dance representing four invasive species you studied: Asian long-horned beetles, hydrilla, yellow crazy ants, and cane toads from Australia. First, as a group, discuss the details you learned about each species. Next discuss the main theme and feeling you want to represent in your dance.

(*continues*)

SAMPLE PLAN 32.3

Invasive Species (*continued*)

Soc Remember our class rule: Everyone talks, everyone listens. Build on your group members' ideas. Ask your group members for their opinions and ideas. Discuss why you like particular ideas.

Cog K Let's have a class discussion and list all the movements you explored that could be used for each species. I will write your ideas on the while board. [List the four species, and call on many students to identify possible movements for each species.]

A Now, create your group dance. Work on one section at a time. Work hard to make your beginning and ending shapes for each section original. Try to make all of your movements and shapes related to each other in matching or complementing ways.

R Practice until you have perfected your movement quality and can repeat the sequence precisely the same way every time. Then we will show the sequences.

SAMPLE PLAN 32.4

The Sea and the Shore

Movement Theme: Glide, Float, Thrust, and Press
Topic Theme: The Sea and the Shore
Text: Stokes (1970). *The Sea and the Shore*

Notes: These learning experiences integrate dance with poetry written for children's dance. The learning experiences can take several class periods. Children will need time to design, practice, and then show their sequences. These learning experiences are designed for older children.

Standards

This plan addressed National Standards 1, 2, 4, and 5 and CCSS for reading craft and structure.

Objectives

The children will learn to

Motor

1. Show and feel the following effort actions: gliding, floating, thrusting, and pressing; gliding and floating with gentle, slow movement; thrusting with fast, strong, direct movements; and pressing with strong, slow, direct movements.

Affective

2. Appreciate aesthetic aspects of the sea and the shore—in particular, two contrasting relations: the gentle sea and sandy beaches and the powerful waves and rock cliffs.

Creative Thinking/Choreography Concepts

3. Create a sea-and-shore partner dance sequence to represent the poem "The Sea and the Shore" about the characteristics of the sea and the shore, and interpret these characteristics through different effort actions.

CCSS

4. Compare and contrast the treatment of similar topics about the sea and the shore and patterns of events in the two verses of a poem.

Potential Refinements

- Make the slow movements slow.
- Make gentle movements soft; feel light.
- Make fast movements fast.
- Make strong movements forceful; feel strong, powerful, and in control.

SAMPLE PLAN 32.4

The Sea and the Shore (continued)

Introduction

In today's lesson, we will interpret a poem about the sea and the shore. Does anyone want to read the first verse of the poem? [Have the poem written on a whiteboard so all children can read it.] What was this verse about? Who would like to read the second verse? What was this verse about? Let's contrast the movement images of the two verses. Which kinds of movements do you visualize with the first verse? Which kinds of movements and feelings do you visualize with the second verse?

The Sea and the Shore **by Edith M. Stokes**

Golden smooth sands
Lie spread open, inviting
The gentle approaching sea.
They meet and linger
But an unseen hand
Once again separates them.
Their conversation never ends,
For it never has time to begin,
Yet it does not matter.

Dark angry rocks
Jagged and threatening
Ready for armed combat
Stand their ground
Against repeated attacks
Of hateful resentment
The barrage is maintained
Until the unseen hand,
Sensing destruction, separates them.

Content Development

Cog K We will use different dance movements to interpret this poem. Specifically, we will work on moving with strong and light force and fast and slow movements. Who can tell me a fast movement we have worked on in an earlier lesson? How about a slow movement? A strong movement? A light movement? What does it feel like when you do a strong movement? A light movement?

Darting and Leaping

I Spread out in a scattered formation. Pick a spot in the room and when I say, "Go," run quickly, dart to that spot, and freeze. Be aware of everyone else in the room. Go.

E Pick another spot, dart quickly, then freeze. Go. What do you need to do to "dart"? [Move quickly, suddenly.] [Repeat several times.]

R When you freeze, be alert. Feel the tension in your muscles.

R Dart again, and feel like you are moving on a hot surface; start suddenly, and stop suddenly.

E Dart, and when I beat the drum, do a punching jump or leap. This effort action is called a punch or thrust. [Repeat several times.]

Three Angular Shapes

E Dart, leap or jump, and land in an angular shape. Make sharp points with your elbows and knees.

E On the drumbeat, make three sharp, angular shapes. Go. Go. Go. Make thrusting actions fast and firm.

E Dart, leap, land, and make three angular shapes. Make a different shape each time. [If the children have problems varying their shapes, suggest wide, twisted, and narrow angular shapes.]

E Repeat three sharp movements, and change levels with each shape.

R Be very firm in your arms, legs, back, and belly.

E Repeat again, and change the direction you are facing at least once. Make bold, aggressive gestures that say, "I'm ready to fight."

Action–Reaction

E Now, travel and do a punching jump; land facing your assigned partner. One partner does a thrusting or punching action, and the other reacts.

(continues)

SAMPLE PLAN 32.4

The Sea and the Shore (continued)

Safety *Be very sure you do not touch your partner; be far enough apart so you don't actually punch each other.* Go.

E Repeat several times, changing who acts and who reacts. Try to do a variety of thrusting movements when acting and reacting. Thrusting movements originate from your torso or the center of your body.

R You need to be tight in your whole torso and use your torso when you thrust with your arms or legs.

E Add a change in level.

E Change the direction you are facing when you act and when you react.

E Thrust with different body parts.

E With your partner, put together three action–reaction movements.

R Be sure you thrust from the core with your tummy tight.

Pressing

I Alone, start in a shape on the floor, then slowly press with your hands as you rise to a stand. Now, press back down into the floor. This effort action is called a press.

E Rise again, and imagine you are pressing your way out of a box and pressing a very heavy weight up.

R Show tension and force in your muscles and body shape.

E Repeat several times, varying your shape each time you rise and sink.

Cog K What is the difference between a press effort action and a thrust? [Speed.]

E Go back with your partner. One person starts low and presses to rise, while the other partner presses down, trying to press you into a box. Don't touch hands. Once the person rising is stretched tall, reverse, and press your partner down into the box. [Repeat several times, reversing each time.]

E Vary your shape, starting position, and ending position each time.

E Vary the body parts you use to press and vary the way you relate your body parts to each other.

Floating and Gliding

I Now, we are going to change to very different effort actions. We will work on floating and gliding. Slowly and gently, travel about the space by wandering on curved pathways, feeling very soft and light and showing this feeling in your body.

R Feel as if the clouds are just lifting you up and holding you up—feel the gentleness in floating.

E Now glide by, moving more directly on straight pathways.

R Make your movements very smooth. Don't stop.

E Alternate floating and gliding. Move so gently that no one can hear your feet. [Repeat several times.]

E Now travel by, floating or gliding, pause, sway several times, and travel again. [Repeat several times.]

E Travel by floating or gliding, gently sink, and then rise.

Culminating Activity

Cog K For your dance today, we will be interpreting the poem we read at the beginning of class. [Read the poem again.]

Potential Questions to Ask

- Which effort actions and movements does the first verse suggest to you?
- Which sort of partner relationships does it suggest?
- What is the relationship between a gentle sea and a sandy beach?
- How does the water move?
- What does the sand look like?
- What does a wave look like after it breaks on the sand?
- What does it look like when the foam fingers reach up on the sand?
- What happens after the wave reaches up onto the sand?
- Which movements and effort actions does the second verse suggest to you?
- Which partner relationships might this verse suggest?
- What happens when waves crash against rocks?
- Which shapes do you see on a jagged rock cliff?
- What happens to the wave after it hits the rock? What happens to the rock?

SAMPLE PLAN 32.4

The Sea and the Shore (continued)

A Go with your assigned partner. Your partner dance will have two verses like the poem. The structure of each verse will be as follows [It helps to write this information on a whiteboard]:

1. Start apart in a shape.
2. Come together.
3. Dance together.
4. Move apart.
5. Create an ending shape.

You can come together and move apart several times if you want. Within each of the two parts, work on the relationships among your body parts and your partner's body parts so your shapes are clear and complement each other.

R After you have your sequence designed, work on refining the quality of your movements. Feel the difference between the tension when you move softly and when you move quickly and firmly. Tense up your muscles when you are being firm. Keep your muscles soft when you are moving gently and slowly. Practice your dance until you can repeat the movements exactly the same way each time you perform the dance. Then we will show sequences.

SAMPLE PLAN 32.5

Journey Through the Solar System

Movement Theme: Eight Basic Effort Actions
Topic Theme: Planets (or Colors)
Text: Aguilar (2008). *Eleven Planets: A New View of the Solar System*

Notes: This lesson is based on an informational text published by the National Geographic Society. If possible, ask the classroom teacher to teach it before you do the dance lesson. If not, you can read the paragraphs about each planet in physical education and show children the illustrations.

You can easily modify these learning experiences to be about the colors yellow, gray, red, brown, green, and blue by eliminating all references to the planets. The learning experiences begin with a review of the eight basic effort actions. If the children have no experience with the effort actions, you will need to modify the review tasks to include an introduction to each effort action.

Standards

This plan addresses National Standards 1, 2, 4, and 5 and CCSS for reading and vocabulary acquisition.

Objectives

The children will learn to

Motor

1. Perform a variety movements, clearly demonstrating the movement qualities of the eight basic effort actions: light, sparkling flicking movements; holding their head high; remaining stretched through the backbone moving gently and slowly while turning; gliding and floating; and using strong force, maintaining tight tension while thrusting, slashing, pressing, and wringing.

Creative Thinking/Choreography

2. Design a dance representing abstract images, feelings, and colors.

Social Responsibility

3. Work cooperatively in a small group.
4. Demonstrate appropriate audience behavior in watching dance performances; discuss their opinions about the dances with their peers in a supportive and constructive way.

(continues)

SAMPLE PLAN 32.5

Journey Through the Solar System (*continued*)

CCSS

5. Compare and contrast the treatment of similar topics in myths. Use information gained from illustrations and the words in a text to demonstrate an understanding of the text.
6. Determine the main ideas and supporting details of information presented visually in classmates' dances.
7. Use domain-specific words, especially those that signal precise actions and emotions associated with the eight effort actions that are basic to a particular topic.

Potential Refinements

- Light, sparkling flicking movements.
- Head high, stretched through backbone, moving slowly and gently while turning, gliding, and floating.
- Strong force and tight torsos while thrusting, slashing, pressing, and wringing.

Introductory Activity

We are going to be doing a dance about an imaginary journey through the solar system (or about colors) using the eight basic effort actions to represent each of the planets we visit. Let's begin by reviewing the eight effort actions.

Content Development

Flick and Dab

I Let's start with flicking and dabbing. While sitting, dab your hands in all areas of your personal space. Now flick.

Cog K Remember that the difference is that a dab is a more direct movement, while a flick is more flexible. [Repeat several times.]

E Stand and travel about the gym, skipping lightly. Flick or dab your hands, making light, quick gestures. Your movements should be crisp and sparkle like glitter or a twinkling star.

E Skip and leap lightly. Land in a spiky shape with your arms, fingers, elbows, knees, and feet sticking out in a mass of points.

E Do three spiky shapes in a row, and then skip again.

E This time, do three pointy, spiky shapes, and add a turn.

E Add a jump.

E Add a change of level.

A Put together a sequence. Start in a pointy shape, skip while dabbing or flicking, leap lightly, and land in a spiky shape. Make three different spiky shapes in a row with at least one turn and one jump.

Glide and Float

Cog K Gliding and floating are slow, sustained movements. Gliding uses space directly, while floating indulges in space.

E Travel about the space, sometimes gliding and sometimes floating, with your head high and stretched through your entire backbone to the top of your head.

E Pause when reaching to a high level, and then turn or spin on one leg.

E Turn again, changing the position of your free leg and arms.

E Travel about the space gliding and floating. Add turns. Each time you turn, have your free leg and arms in different positions.

E Do a spin, varying the level and shape of your arms and legs.

A Put together a short sequence. Start in a closed position. Open and step into a swirling spin. Glide and float, adding turns as you travel. Pause when reaching to a high level. Turn in a different shape, and end opened or closed.

Thrust and Slash

Cog K Now, we are going to change from light to strong force and fast speed. Thrusting is a direct use of space, while slashing is flexible.

E Start by marching boldly and proudly about the space to the beat of the drum.

E When I hit the drum hard, do three fast thrusting or slashing actions.

E Try three thrusting or slashing actions again, but add a turn.

E Add a jump.

E Let's do a dance sequence in rhythm. Start with eight counts, marching boldly. Then do four thrusting or slashing actions with a one-count pause in between. Ready: March, 2, 3, 4, 5, 6, 7, 8, action (slash or thrust), pause, action, pause, action, pause, action, pause. Repeat several times.

SAMPLE PLAN 32.5

Journey Through the Solar System (*continued*)

Wring and Press

Cog K The last effort actions are wringing and pressing. Both are slow and firm. Pressing is direct; wringing is indirect.

E Start by wringing and slowly falling, then press and rise. Repeat several times, ending low.

E Now travel along the ground pressing or wringing. Keep transferring your weight slowly from one body part to another. Sometimes twist to move; sometimes press and travel using space more directly.

E Now try traveling along the ground with heaviness—that is, with loose tension.

E Now alternate heavy, wring/press, heavy, wring/press, changing the part of your body supporting your weight.

R When you are heavy, keep your muscles very, very loose. When you are wringing or pressing, be very firm and tight. Don't forget to be tight in your torso, too.

A Design a brief sequence. Select a starting position; travel using three wringing, pressing, or heavy actions; and select an ending position.

Culminating Activity

Cog K Here is the story that will form the basis for the dance:

Once upon a time, there were some space voyagers. They took off from their planet and after many years, they found themselves in a distant solar system, our solar system. They landed on the first planet from the sun. What is the name of this planet? [Mercury]

What do you know about Mercury? Who is Mercury named after? [The winged Roman god of travel, who served as a messenger for the other gods.] The Roman god Mercury was known to be a speedy traveler. Likewise, the planet Mercury travels fast in its orbit around the sun. Its year is only 88 earth days long. Daytime is very hot, reaching 800 degrees Fahrenheit and the nights very cold at –300 degrees.

In our imaginary journey, the sky of Mercury is bright yellow. The people who lived there were all bright and sparkly, and their bodies were spiky and pointed. They looked like they were made of flames. The ground of the planet Mercury was hot, so the people darted quickly from crater to crater.

Next, the space voyagers came to the second planet from the sun. What planet is this? What do you know about Venus? Who is Venus named after? [The Roman goddess of love and beauty.] Because Venus is so bright in our sky, it often is considered to be the most beautiful planet. It is covered by dense clouds of carbon dioxide.

In our imaginary journey, Venus is covered with misty clouds of gray that swirled around the planet. The people were ghostly gray and did not even appear to be solid. They floated around Venus gently like the fog in which they lived.

The space voyagers then traveled to the fourth planet. What is this planet? What do you know about Mars? Mars has a 17-mile-high volcano, polar ice caps, and huge canyons. Who is Mars named after? [The Roman god of war, so named because of the planet's red color.]

In our imaginary journey, Mars is bold, red, and mighty. Powerful, forthright people marched about the planet in columns. The planet had tree-lined streets, and the trees were tall with bright red leaves. The air was vibrant, and everything felt red.

The travelers then went many miles near the edge of the solar system and visited Pluto, one of three dwarf planets. What do you know about Pluto? Pluto travels on an egg-shaped orbit. Who is Pluto named after? [The Roman god of the underworld, who could become invisible.]

In our imaginary journey, Pluto was dark, cold, and murky brown. The creatures crawled along the ground writhing with tension—sometimes wringing and pressing, sometimes moving with a heaviness that looked like dismay, and sometimes suddenly slithering with fast, unexpected speed.

Finally, the travelers settled on the third planet from the sun, called Earth. From high above Earth, the planet looked like a shimmering blue-and-white marble. The space voyagers landed on a clearing next to a clear, blue lake, surrounded by lush green forests and, in the distance, majestic purple mountains.

Organization

Choose which planet dance you want to create (Mercury, Venus, Mars, or Pluto). Then I will organize groups of three or four within each planet selected. Multiple groups can be working on sequences representing the same planet. Each group should design a sequence representing life on the planet selected. [Sequences can be short or long, depending on how many lessons you want to devote to this unit. Children can also design these sequences individually.]

CCSS With your group, compare and contrast the themes and images of the imaginary journeys to the four planets. On the white board and on one sheet of paper per group, list the eight effort actions and the four planets. See if you can connect the eight basic effort actions to the images and themes related to the four planets. Draw lines from each effort action to one planet. [You can stop the discussion here and instead of children brainstorming to come up with possible movements, you can list the movements enclosed in [brackets] on the whiteboard.] Then brainstorm shapes and movements you can use in your dance to represent your planet and the Roman god or goddess for which it was named.

(*continues*)

SAMPLE PLAN 32.5

Journey Through the Solar System (*continued*)

Mercury

- Feeling of bright yellow; fiery, hot ground; pointy fire people with 10 fingers on each hand.

[Movements students need to identify: flick and dab; spiky shapes; fast footwork; quick jumps from stone to stone; skipping and darting on angular pathways.]

Venus

- Feeling of soft gray; swirling mists and fog.

[Movements students need to identify: float and glide; gentle movements; swirling, turning, and traveling on curved pathways; leading a partner through the mists, traveling at medium and high levels.]

Mars

- Feeling of bright vibrant red; boldness, power, might.

[Movements students need to identify: thrust and slash; marching; big, bold jumps; thrusting jabs; energetic jumps.]

Pluto

- Feeling of murky brown; cold; creatures who crawl underground.

[Movements students need to identify: wring and press, alternating with heavy movements; crawling; slithering; traveling at low levels.]

A Now that you have ideas about the movements, design your dance. Work hard as a group to include originality and an aesthetic highlight in your dance.

Single Lesson or Short Unit Ending with a Whole-Class Culminating Dance

If you want a shorter unit, have each group design short sequences quickly. Then have each group teach its sequence to the rest of the class. End the lesson with the whole class "traveling" to each of the four planets—i.e., performing each of the sequences from the four planets.

Longer Sequences with the Unit Ending with a Whole-Class Culminating Dance

If you want the children to work on sequences that are more complex, then the final dance can be structured as follows:

Whole-Class Sequence

1. The class begins the journey in a variety of curled, sitting positions.
2. Everyone slowly rises to a stretched position.
3. On the teacher's signal, all children travel on a large circular pathway around the gym doing turns and turning leaps, representing a journey and circular pathways of planets in a solar system.
4. On the teacher's signal, everyone stretches tall, then sinks into another sitting position.
5. The groups from each of the four planets step into the middle, one at a time, and perform their sequences. Observers change to a different sitting position with each new group performance.
6. The entire class performs the Earth dance as individuals.

Whole-Class Earth Dance

1. From a sitting position, rise slowly.
2. Travel by walking majestically about the space in scattered formations, taking a tour of the beautiful planet Earth.
3. Glide smoothly with long gestures, showing a serene feeling, like the blue color of a clear mountain lake.
4. On the teacher's signal, everyone does a big, opening gesture and then closes to a low level. Next they travel briefly along the ground, transferring weight to different body parts and enjoying the lush, green Earth.
5. Everyone rises again with an opening gesture and continues walking serenely.
6. Repeat the pattern of closing, traveling along the ground, and rising and opening.
7. End by gathering together in the center of the space, rising to a high position with everyone gesturing to the sky.

Possible Discussion Topics Related to the Dance Sequences

Identify the following aesthetic criteria in one of the dance sequences you observed, and explain why it was effective. Include their use of the effort actions they chose in your description:

- Originality
- Aesthetic highlight

SAMPLE PLAN 32.6

The Dimensional Cross

Notes: This set of learning experiences will take several days to teach. Following the introduction of the content, we give you several suggestions for dance sequences that children can design.

Learning experiences on rising and falling, closing and opening, and retreating and advancing offer excellent opportunities to help children learn nuances in word meaning and distinguish shades of meaning. Discussing the meanings of these words will not only help children understand the words, but also improve their ability to represent the words in movement. For example, you would slowly *withdraw* (a retreating movement) when you see a raccoon (who might have rabies) ahead on a woodland path, but you might *recoil* (another retreating movement) if you saw that raccoon frothing at the mouth eating another animal alive. These two retreating actions would look very different and have different nuances and shades of meaning. Withdrawing would include showing an alert, cautious, maybe fearful retreat, whereas recoiling would include movements showing disgust, revulsion, or horror.

Standards

This plan addresses National Standards 1, 2, 4, and 5 and CCSS for vocabulary acquisition.

Objectives

The children will learn to

Motor, Cognitive Knowledge, and Affective

1. Rise, fall, open, close, retreat, and advance, understanding the relationships of these actions to the dimensional cross.
2. Match, contrast, and complement a partner's movements, and understand how these patterns can represent different feelings.
3. Understand and use effort actions to represent feelings.

Creative Thinking/Choreography Concepts

4. Design a sequence combining directional aspects of space and body actions to represent feelings or ideas.

CCSS

5. Distinguish shades of meaning among related words and phrases, including those that signal spatial relationships.

Potential Refinements

- Make fast movements fast.
- Make slow movements slow.
- Make forceful movements strong and firm.
- Make gentle movements soft.

Content Development

Introducing Rising and Falling

The teacher beats a hand drum—four counts for rising, four counts for falling.

I Start in a shape at a low level. As I beat the drum four counts, rise to a high level. Then, sink to a low level for four counts.

E Repeat rising and falling to the drum beats, but vary your starting and ending positions each time. [Repeat several times.]

E *Varying levels:* Now vary your level. Sometimes rise only to a medium level; sometimes rise, but remain at a low level the entire time. Sometimes fall from a high to a medium level. [Repeat several times.]

E *Symmetry and asymmetry:* Find three ways to rise and fall with symmetry. Then find three ways to rise and fall with asymmetry.

E *Varying duration:* Now let's vary the duration. Take two beats to rise and six beats to fall. [Repeat.] Now take six beats to rise and two beats to fall. [Repeat several times, varying the starting and ending positions.] Now rise in one beat and fall in one beat. [Repeat several times.]

E *Varying force:* Start in a high position, and press (slow, firm tension) down to the floor, pushing with your palms straight down until you are curled. Now reverse your direction, pressing up as if you are lifting a heavy weight. [Repeat several times.]

E *Using force to represent different feelings:* Now fall with weakness, let the tension out of your muscles, droop, and wilt by melting down into the floor. Then rise with strength.

E Experiment with different ways to rise showing strength, power, triumph, or success, and to sink showing sadness, despair, or defeat.

(*continues*)

SAMPLE PLAN 32.6

The Dimensional Cross (*continued*)

E Now explore leading with different parts of your hands. Rise and fall while leading with your fist. Now rise and fall while piercing with your fingertips to a two-count beat. Explore using a slicing movement leading with the side of one hand, and finally lead with the back of your hand in a flowing movement.

E Combine speed and force. Rise strong and fast; fall slow and gentle. Rise strong and slow; fall fast and gentle. Continue exploring different combinations of force and speed.

E Experiment with ways to rise while representing an uplifting image, lightness, or inspiration and falling into a restful place like a comforting home or a cozy den.

E Now try rising to meet the start of the day and falling representing the end of the day in a peaceful place.

Introducing Closing and Opening

I *Hiding and sliding:* Try to hide yourself away on the wall and close yourself off from other people. Then suddenly open up, and slide across the room. Stop suddenly, look around, and try to hide on the other wall, closed up against the wall.

E Now open slowly, look about the room, and see all your friends. Slide while opening wider still among your friends, independent and loving the world. Pause. You are not sure of yourself, so you close and hide against an imaginary wall. Then awaken again, and travel about the world.

E *Wrists and elbows:* Explore closing and opening in place. On four beats of the drum, bring both wrists together; then on the next four beats of the drum, push them apart, opening up. Close and open the wrists again, each time in a different area of your personal space. Repeat with elbows.

E *Different shapes:* Now explore closing and opening ending in different shapes. On four beats of the drum, close to the left; then on the next four beats, open to the right, using a different gesture and ending in a different position each time (and the reverse). [Repeat several times.]

E *Adding twists and turns:* Close with a twist, then untwist and end in an open position. [Repeat several times, varying your positions.]

E Turn and end in a closed position; open with a turn and end in an open position.

E *Varying speed and force:* Explore closing and opening, sometimes varying the speed and sometimes varying the force.

E *Representing feelings:* Now you are ready to work on expressing feelings. Let's start with opening showing happiness and closing showing fear or wariness. [Repeat several times.]

E Open and travel appearing approachable, friendly, sympathetic, and interested in everyone around you. Next travel closed, showing isolation and introversion. Now travel with a closed position showing shyness or loneliness. Then open up with a greeting of welcome. Now close yourself from everyone in the world. Now open and travel with a sense of adventure, opening a door and yourself to the world.

Introducing Retreating and Advancing

Gather the children at one end of the physical education space.

I *Walk and freeze:* Start walking slowly toward me. When I beat the drum, you are caught; jump back and freeze. Walk forward again, pause, look straight ahead to the horizon, and feel as if the movement could go on and on; advance forward again. This time when you hear the drum, freeze and jump back as if someone punched you.

E [If the children are safe and responsible, increase the speed.] Dart forward with an urgency, a driving force of expectancy. On my drumbeat [after the children take three to five steps], you suddenly meet an unexpected force; in response, you retreat or hesitate. Then on my signal, move forward again.

E Walk forward. On the beat, quickly retreat to a position representing cautious hiding. Walk forward more bravely this time. Be daring. Oh, no! You see something scary. On the beat, back off and retreat in fear.

E Now advance with stealth, periodically withdrawing but maintaining an alert caution. You are sneaky, and sometimes you have to hide and wait until it is safe to move on.

E Now at a low level on the floor, advance as if you have been traveling forever and you are so tired, but you must press forward or you won't get home. Pause and gather your strength. Still at a low level, search by looking to the horizon to see if you can see your destination. Back off and rest.

E At a medium level, advance as if you were going on an adventure or you were on a quest. The quest will take a long time. Sometimes you move to the brink of danger and then withdraw. But the quest is important, so you move on again, conquering your fear. You stand up for what you believe.

SAMPLE PLAN 32.6
The Dimensional Cross (*continued*)

Combining the Six Actions of the Dimensional Scale

I Explain the three axes, the dimensional cross, and the way that the six actions can be combined to create the dimensional scale. In this discussion, it helps to show them an image of the dimensional cross and the three planes (see **Figures 32.6** and **32.7**). Have the children learn the order by trying the scale with their right hand and then the left hand several times by tracing the three axes. If you have ribbons or scarves, these props will help children see the lines in space. Have them practice on a four-count beat, counting "up, 2, 3, 4, down, 2, 3, 4, left, 2, 3, 4, back, 2, 3, 4, forward, 2, 3, 4." Once the children are familiar with the order, change the vocabulary to "rise, 2, 3, 4, fall, 2, 3, 4, close, 2, 3, 4, open, 2, 3, 4, retreat, 2, 3, 4, advance, 2, 3, 4."

Culminating Activity Option 1: Designing an Individual Dance Sequence

A Now that you know the dimensional scale, design a dance using the six actions. Have at least one contrast in speed or force.

Culminating Activity Option 2: Designing a Partner Dance Sequence

The Dimensional Scale with a Partner: Matching, Complementing, and Contrasting

One of the most interesting ways for children to explore the dimensional scale is with a partner. Children can match, complement, and contrast their partner's movements and body positions. In particular, finding ways to complement each other's positions can offer a wide range of choreographic possibilities. The following are suggested culminating sequences.

A *Matching:* Design a dimensional scale sequence matching your partner's movements.

A *Contrasting:* Design a dimensional scale sequence contrasting your partner's movements. One partner starts high, while the other starts low. One falls and the other rises, and then both reverse. One closes and the other opens, and then both reverse. One retreats and the other advances, and then both reverse.

R To improve your choreography, make the positions of your arms, legs, and torsos relate to each other. Add a turn at some point in the sequence. Sometimes face in different directions, and sometimes face in the same direction.

E *Complementing:* Find different ways to rise and fall while complementing each other. You can do this in any of the following ways:

- End at different levels with similar shapes.
- Relate the positions and lines of your arms, legs, and torsos.
- Face in different directions but do similar movements.

E Find different ways to close and open, complementing each other. You can do this in any of the following ways:

- Move at different levels.
- Switch levels.
- End at different levels.
- Relate the positions and lines of your arms, legs, and torsos.
- Face in different directions but do similar movements.

E Find different ways to retreat and advance complementing each other. You can do this in any of the following ways:

- Relate the positions and lines of your arms, legs, and torsos.
- Add turns at the same time.
- Face in different directions.
- Move at different levels.

A Design a dimensional scale sequence complementing your partner's movements.

The Dimensional Scale: Long Sequence

Using the dimensional scale as the framework, children can easily design a longer dance with several phrases. For example,

- Phrase 1: Perform your own dimensional scale sequence as an individual. Travel to a partner.
- Phrase 2: With a partner, perform a dimensional scale while matching each other.
- Phrase 3: With a partner, perform a dimensional scale while contrasting each other.
- Phrase 4: With a partner, perform a dimensional scale while complementing each other; then separate.
- Phrase 5: Perform your own dimensional scale as an individual.

You can easily set this dance sequence to music. If the phrasing of the music is in counts of eight, then simply repeat an action—for example, rise, fall, close, open, retreat, advance, advance, advance or rise, fall, rise, fall, close, open, retreat, advance.

SAMPLE PLAN 32.7

Shelter in a Storm

Movement Theme: Pathways, Levels, Meeting and Parting
Topic Theme: Shelter in a Storm
Text: Branley & Kelley (1999). *Flash, Crash, Rumble, and Roll*

Notes: The learning experience in this lesson plan shows how the material in **Sample Plan 31.6**, "The Thunderstorm," which is designed for kindergartners and first-graders, can be expanded and made appropriate for an older class. To do so, we add a more sophisticated idea for the children to represent in their dances, that is, seeking shelter in a storm, partner work, and a focus on multiple movement concepts. It will probably take two lessons for the children to design and refine their dances.

We connect this lesson to a combined literature and informational text on safety in thunderstorms: *Flash, Crash, Rumble, and Roll* (Branley & Kelley, 1999). You can have the children read the story aloud and briefly discuss the safety information provided at the end of the lesson. Alternatively, you can link this lesson to more complex knowledge of lightning and its dangers by having students read portions of *Thunderstorms and Lightning* (Galiano, 2003).

Standards

This plan addresses National Standards 1, 2, 4, and 5 and CCSS for listening and comprehension.

Objectives

Children will learn to

Motor

1. Move on curved and angular pathways using gentle and strong force.
2. Create curved and angular shapes, while relating their shapes to a partner's shapes.

Creative Thinking/Choreography Concepts

3. Design complementary shapes and actions that are clear, with the position of every body part planned in relation to their partner's shapes and actions.

CCSS

4. Summarize the points the speakers make about their dance and explain how each claim is supported by reasons and evidence in their dance. Review the key ideas expressed and draw conclusions in light of information and knowledge gained by listening to performers and watching their dances.

Potential Refinements

- Maintain light, anti-gravity tension in your whole body.
- Curve and stretch through your entire spine.

Content Development

Explore Drawing Curved Lines with the Hands (Curved Pathways in the Air)

I In this unit, the topic theme is the representation of a thunderstorm and then seeking shelter, feeling safe within the shelter while the storm rages on. This book is the inspiration for the lesson. Let's read it together. [Project the book on the wall, and have the children read aloud together.] Let's start exploring movements connected to cumulus clouds before they develop into thunderheads.

I As you are sitting on the ground, draw curved lines in space with one hand and arm. Make small curves and large curves, and draw curves all about your personal space—to your side, back, high, and low.

E Try making curves with your other hand.

E Try making curves with both hands.

E Make small curves and large curves, and vary the level.

E Stand. [Repeat previous tasks while standing.]

Combining Traveling on Curved Pathways and Drawing Curved Pathways in the Air

I Travel on curved pathways while drawing curves in the air with your hands.

E Travel on both small and large curved pathways. You can make your curves so small you turn in place. Sometimes turn to the left, and sometimes turn to the right. Try to capture the image of clouds moving gently and slowly.

E Vary the level, reaching high and low as you travel on small and large curved pathways.

E Try turning at different levels, making a curved shape as you turn.

SAMPLE PLAN 32.7

Shelter in a Storm (*continued*)

E Come to a stop, and make your body a curved shape.

E Travel again. This time, meet one or two other children, and together, make a curved shape. Make complementing shapes by relating your body parts to each other.

E Part and travel again. This time, meet one or two different children, and make a group curved shape. Try to make the shape interesting by being at different levels. [Repeat several times.]

Cloud Dance

E Design a short sequence with your assigned partner. Start by making a curved shape complementing your partner. As I beat the drum, travel together on curved pathways, relating to each other in some way and drawing curved shapes with your hands. When I stop beating the drum, end in a curved shape. Try to make every body part relate to the overall shape in some way.

Meeting and Parting

Affective Now we are shifting to images and feelings you can connect to feeling safe and having shelter in a storm.

E Now explore meeting and parting with your partner. Start together in a curved shape, separate and travel in different directions, and pause in another curved shape. Then travel to meet again. Each time you meet, create a different shape, varying your levels. When you part, try to find ways to make your movements and shapes relate to each other.

E This time when you meet, instead of pausing, walk in a circle around each other, and then part again. Repeat several times, exploring different arm positions as you circle around each other. Vary your levels. Have one of you at a low level and the other at a medium or high level, still relating your body shapes and arm positions.

Running on Zigzag Pathways

I Imagine the clouds getting bigger and darker and becoming thunderheads—a storm is brewing. What happens in a storm? Let us work with lightning first. When I say, "Go," I want you to run as fast as you can on a sharp, angular, zigzag pathway. [Demonstrate as you explain.] Go. Stop. [Repeat several times.] [Beat the drum fast and loud.]

Making Strong, Angular Shapes

E This time when you stop, stop in an angular, sharp, pointy shape. Go. When I beat the drum, make another angular shape. Another. Another.

E Make three shapes in a row. Go. Go. Go. Which body parts can you make pointy? [Elbows, knees, hips, and so on.]

E Make three shapes again, changing levels each time.

E Add a turn.

E This time, I want you to think about lightning. What does lightning look like? How does it move? What kinds of movements would you do to show lightning with your body? When I say "Go," make three angular shapes, travel on an angular pathway, jump and make an angular shape in the air, and land in an angular shape. [Repeat several times.]

E Get with your partner, and explore making angular shapes using an action–reaction relationship. With action—reaction, one person makes an angular shape, and the other person reacts to that shape. Repeat three times, and then switch roles.

E Add changes in level so each partner moves at all three levels. You can be at the same level or at different levels. Work on making your angular shapes relate to each other. You can do this by matching, contrasting, or complementing each other's shapes. Try to make every body part relate to your partner's shape.

Lightning Dance

E Let's do a lightning dance. Start alone in an angular shape, and do three different angular shapes as I beat the drum. Then, travel fast on sharp, angular pathways, and jump while making an angular shape. Land facing your partner in an angular shape. Do three action–reaction movements. End by running, jumping, making an angular shape in the air, and ending in an angular shape together. [Repeat several times.]

Affective Compare the feelings of the lightning and cloud dances. How do the movements differ?

Culminating Activity

A Today we are going to design a dance we will call "Shelter in a Storm." [Children can work in groups of two to four, depending on their developmental levels and choreographic capabilities. The smaller the group, the easier the choreographic process.] Let's talk about your experiences during powerful thunderstorms. [Call on many children.]

(*continues*)

SAMPLE PLAN 32.7

Shelter in a Storm (*continued*)

Potential Questions to Ask

- How do you feel during a thunderstorm? [Call on many children.]
- Let's brainstorm some images about storms. What are some positive images? [Being inside and dry from the rain, sitting on your grandmother's lap on her porch as you watch a storm approaching, parched soil during a drought finally getting some needed rain.]
- What are some movements you can use to represent storms?
- What are some movements you can use to represent feeling safe within a shelter in a storm?
- How can you use different levels and pathways in your dance?

A With your partner (or group), design a dance representing the idea of shelter in a storm. Work hard on making all shapes and movements relate to and complement each other in some way. Here is a rubric to help you understand what I mean by saying all shapes and movements relate to and complement each other.

Level 1: Partners' body lines, shapes, and movement do not relate to or complement each other. There are no similar shapes and no lines formed by body parts that relate to the overall shape or to the partner's shape. You don't feel like the partners are dancing the same dance.

Level 2: The positions of some body parts are planned and show a relationship between both partners' shapes. Some shapes are similar and at different levels; thus, the partners complement each other. Some body parts form intended lines, and some lines of one partner relate to the lines of the other.

Level 3: The positions of body parts are well planned and show a clear relationship to the position of the partner's body parts. One partner's shapes complement the other partner's shapes throughout the entire sequence. You can tell the pair is dancing together and are intentionally matching shapes but varying the level or the direction they are facing, thus complementing each other.

R Practice until you perfect your movement quality and can repeat the sequence precisely the same every time.

Peer Coaching

R Once you have designed and practiced your dance, show it to another pair. Before you show your dance, explain to the observers your goals and reasons for selecting the movements you selected—that is, why you thought they were interesting, and what you were trying to represent. Observers, summarize what you see, and connect what the pair said they were trying to represent with specific shapes and movements in their sequence. Your job is to give your peers positive and constructive comments to help improve the dance in relation to the goals of the choreographers.

R Refine your dance based on your peers' comments. At the end of class, we will show the final dances to the class.

SAMPLE PLAN 32.8

"Row, Row, Row Your Boat"

Movement Theme: Canon
Topic Theme: "Row, Row, Row Your Boat"

Standards

This sample plan addresses National Standard 1, 2, 4, and 5 and CCSS for acquiring domain-specific vocabulary.

Objectives

The children will learn to

Motor

1. Perform a basic dance demonstrating the structure of canon.
2. Move in rhythm and timing to a simple round moving in canon.

Thinking/Choreography Concepts

3. Think creatively to design movements to interpret a song.
4. Think critically to analyze and improve the visual impact of moving in canon.

SAMPLE PLAN 32.8

"Row, Row, Row Your Boat" (*continued*)

CCSS

5. Acquire and use domain-specific words and phrases, especially those that signal temporal relationships that are basic to group dances.

Potential Refinements

- Move to the beat of the song.

Introductory Activity

Cog K Today we will be doing a dance in canon. Canon means you perform the same movements, but you begin at different times in a sequence. You may have done a canon before while singing and didn't know there was a name for it. In music, we also call canons *rounds.* Many people sing "Row, Row, Row Your Boat" in rounds. We will try that now. First, let's sing it in unison. [Sing it together.]

E I am going to divide you into three groups, and we will sing this song in rounds. The first group starts and sings, "Row, row, row your boat" alone. Then the second group starts. After the second group sings "Row, row, row your boat," the third group starts. Does the first group stop and wait for the other groups to catch up? Which group finishes first? Which group finishes last? What are some of the ways you can keep your group from getting mixed up with the other groups? Great. Let's sing the round.

Content Development

E Before we make up a dance to "Row, Row, Row Your Boat," let's try a simple dance in canon. We will do this dance in unison first. Get in one line (shoulder to shoulder) across the gym. Walk forward for eight beats. Now, press upward as if you were raising the roof for eight beats. Then, walk backward for eight beats. [Repeat several times until the children have the sequence memorized.]

E I am going to divide you into three groups. The right end of the line to here [indicate a child] is group 1, the middle is group 2, and the left end of the line is group 3. I will count eight beats. Group 1 starts and walks eight steps forward. While group 1 moves on to raising the roof, group 2 walks eight steps forward. Then group 3 starts the dance. What do groups 2 and 3 do while group 1 is walking forward? [Stand still.] Does group 1 wait for the other groups to catch up? [No.] Which group will finish first, second, and last? Ready? Go.

Culminating Activity

A Now I will put you with a partner to make up a dance to "Row, Row, Row Your Boat."

Phrase 1: *Row, row, row, your boat, gently down the stream*

First, design a push-and-pull action (two counts) that you repeat four times to the first phrase of the song. Either match each other, or work in opposition. Move to the beat of the song, practicing until you can move and sing at the same time.

Phrase 2: *Merrily, merrily, merrily, merrily, life is but a dream*

Next, design an eight-count unison, matching sequence to the words "Merrily, merrily, merrily, merrily, life is but a dream." Use a locomotor pattern (e.g., skipping, galloping) with arm gestures on a planned, repeatable pathway, and end in a happy shape on the word *dream.* Practice until you can do the unison, matching sequence perfectly.

E Put the two phrases together and practice your dance as you sing along until you can do it perfectly.

Canon in Groups of Four

A I will put you with another pair. Show them your sequence. Then put together a canon dance. One pair starts and does four counts of pushing and pulling ("Row, row, row your boat"). Then the second pair starts. Try it again with singing.

E Reverse and let the other pair start. Discuss the differences when one pair starts as opposed to the other. Decide which you like best.

Think Critically About and Refine Phrase 1

E Now decide on starting shapes and a formation so the four of you relate to each other and the audience will know that you are dancing together. You might want to face each other or stand side by side. Maybe one pair looks good behind the other. Think about what the audience will see, and then decide on an effective formation and group starting shape. For example, the pair closest to the audience might be at a lower level. You might need to modify the starting shape of your dances.

(*continues*)

SAMPLE PLAN 32.8

"Row, Row, Row Your Boat" (*continued*)

Think Critically About and Refine Phrase 2

E Then examine the second phrase. If necessary, modify the pathways so at some point in the dance, you are relating to the other pair. You might move through or around them, you might move on parallel pathways, or you might move in opposition. Choose pathways that you find interesting and relate to each other.

E Finally, create an ending shape in which all four of you relate in some way. You may need to change the ending shape of one or both pairs' original dance.

E Practice your dance while adding singing.

Culminating Activity for a Second Lesson

A In the last class, you designed dances in canon based on the song "Row, Row, Row Your Boat." Today I will assign you to groups of three, four, or five. Each group will make up a canon dance using at least four different movements. You have to include both locomotor and nonlocomotor movements in your dance. Each person must contribute one part to the group's dance. Design and practice your dance in unison first, until all of you have it memorized and can perform it confidently.

E Now discuss how to divide the dance and how many beats the first child performs before the second, third, and fourth children start. Practice the dance in canon.

R Practice until you perfect your movement quality and can repeat the sequence precisely the same way every time. Then we will show the sequences.

CCSS Closure

With your partner, define the word *canon*. Explain how *canon* connects to timing the start of the movement.

Affective Closure

What part of your dance did you enjoy most? What part of your dance did you think was your best work?

SAMPLE PLAN 32.9

Sport Tableaux (Living Statues)

Movement Theme: Group Shape and Transitions
Topic Theme: Sports

Notes: This lesson was designed to be taught, if necessary, in a small space or a classroom. It is intended to enable teachers who do not have gymnasiums to work on important content on rainy days when they must teach indoors. You will need to be able to move the desks. Because the lesson relies on group work, it is appropriate only for children in grade 3 and above. These learning experiences were originally published by Rovegno and Bandhauer (2000).

Integrating Dance with Classroom Content

We used sport as a topic theme to make this dance comfortable for older students with little dance experiences because sport is a topic familiar to them. This lesson can be modified to deal with other cultural content and to integrate physical education with classroom subjects. Classes studying Greek mythology have developed a series of tableaux about Hercules, Icarus, Narcissus and Echo, and Persephone and Demeter. You can also design tableaux lessons around more abstract themes, such as power, community, isolation, togetherness, support, caring, confusion, unity, curiosity, individuality, justice, or freedom.

Standards

This plan addressed National Standards 1, 2, 4, and 5 and CCSS for vocabulary acquisition.

Objectives

The children will learn to

SAMPLE PLAN 32.9

Sport Tableaux (Living Statues) (*continued*)

Motor

1. Create group shapes that represent, rather than imitate, an idea.
2. Relate their individual shapes to the shapes of other individuals at different levels.
3. Make each part of the body contribute to both their own shape and the group's shape.

Creative Thinking/Choreography

4. Design different transitions between group shapes that are well planned, smooth, and fluent, without hesitations or extra steps.
5. Express and represent an idea, story, or event by selecting a critical movement that captures the idea, story, or event.

CCSS

6. Acquire and use domain-specific words and phrases that signal spatial relationships.
7. Report on their topic using relevant descriptive details to support their ideas.

Potential Refinements

- Make each part of your body contribute to the line and shape intended.
- Make your body lines contribute to the group shape.

Introduction

Cog K A tableau is a living statue or group scene that depicts a moment in time. It is not the same as a photograph because in a photograph you see everything in the scene. In a tableau, you see only some of what is in a photograph—that is, you see just the most significant parts. A sport tableau is more like an expressionist painting of a moment in sports rather than a photograph. When you design a sport tableau, you try to represent an important moment in a sport by capturing what was significant about the event and the feelings associated with the event.

Content Development

I We will begin by creating individual statues. Get in a shape that is exactly like me. [Demonstrate the starting position for a standing broad jump]. Be very relaxed. Now slowly start to tighten your muscles until you can feel tension but you are not completely rigid. Feel the tension in your legs, tummy, and arms. Still doing what I do, change your shape. [Demonstrate a free-throw position.] Think about the feeling in your muscles. Keep light tension in your muscles. Continue to follow me. [Demonstrate a follow-through for a basketball shot, a preparation for a discus throw, a single-leg take-off for a high jump, a gymnastics landing, and a preparation for baseball hit.] Can you tell me which sports we are representing?

E Now, explore making your own individual sport statues.

E Go with your assigned partner, and show your partner your best four sport statues. Ask your partner to guess which sport you are representing.

E Working on your own again, select one of your sport movements. Make three shapes—one that represents the beginning phase of the movement, one for the middle phase, and one for the ending phase. Do that with all three of your sport statues.

R Now we are going to work on the quality of your representations with your partner. Show your partner three different ways to represent one sport action. Discuss which of the three is the best representation of that action and why. Which shape is the most powerful representation? Which is most aesthetic? Which is the most exciting? There will not always be one best representation, and you and your partner can have different opinions. For example, one of you might like the representation of the beginning phase of a running race because it shows the excitement you feel when you anticipate the start of action. The other person might prefer a representation of the end of the race as one runner breaks the tape to win because it represents triumph, relief, or joy.

R Work with your partner. Discuss with your partner which shape you think depicts the "best" shape for that sport movement and why. You will end up with your four best shapes.

R When you have selected your four best statues, watch the other person and help him or her select the best of his or her statues. In your discussion, try to give reasons for your opinions.

(*continues*)

SAMPLE PLAN 32.9

Sport Tableaux (Living Statues) (*continued*)

Culminating Activity: Sport Tableaux Dance

A I will assign you to groups of three to five. Create five (or four or three, depending on your time) sport tableaux. I will demonstrate a tableau with this group.

The students who designed this tableau called it "The Hit." [Set up "The Hit" sport tableaux with children from your class matching the photo in this text.] Notice we left out the pitcher, umpire, and other players, and we included four fans. The fans illustrate the emotional reaction to hitting a home run. In addition, all group members are focused on one location in space, that is, the place where the ball was hit. You can also see the group shape is a diagonal line that points to the place where the ball was hit. Thus, the group shape and each individual's shape relate to each other and to the idea the students were trying to represent.

The hit

Courtesy of John Dolly

After selecting a moment in a sport for your tableau, try to figure out the best way to represent and express the main idea or main feeling. Do not imitate—do not try to make the group statue include everything that you would see in a photograph.

R Now, as a group, critique each of your tableaux based on the following elements:

1. Are there any people you can eliminate from the scene who distract the audience's attention or distract from the focus? If so, how can you modify their shape to support your main idea?
2. Does the shape of each individual relate to the other participants' shapes to create a line or focus?
3. Does every person contribute to the group shape, line, or focus in an important way to express the idea you are trying to represent in your tableau?

R Now, consider the feeling you are trying to represent:

4. Is there some message or shape that is so important that you need to have more people making the same or similar shape to make the statement stronger?
5. Is your tableau an imitation (i.e., a photograph), or is it a representation of a moment in sport?
6. Will the audience's attention be drawn to too many places?
7. Is what you are trying to express *clear*? Is it *powerful*?

E Now we will combine the five tableaux into one dance. First, you need to practice all five in order. Then we will add transitions. All groups, when I say "One," make your first tableau: One. Now make your second tableau: Two. Now three. Now four. Now five. [Repeat the entire sequence until all groups quickly and confidently perform all five tableaux in a row without talking.]

Adding Transitions

E We will take your five tableaux and turn them into a dance by adding transitions. First, we will experiment with a variety of ways to move from one tableau to the next. Get into your first tableau.

1. In the first kind of transition, all the dancers move at the same time. Go. [Repeat for all five tableaux.]
2. In the second type of transition, one person moves at a time. Do your first tableau. Now the first person move; now the second, the third, the fourth, and the fifth. [Repeat for all five tableaux.]
3. In the third type of transition, all of you move to a neutral position (like standing in a group) and then make the new tableau in one group motion.
4. The fourth type of transition is sending a signal movement through your group. For example, each individual successively and quickly turns her or his head; after the last head turns, the entire group moves. Try this for all five tableaux.

E Put the whole dance together. Select a neutral beginning shape so you must move to your first tableau. Select a different type of transition to move to each of the next four tableaux. Try to vary your transitions. Practice your dance until it is perfected and you can perform the whole dance without talking or cuing each other.

CCSS Closure

Within your group, describe the difference between imitation and representation.

Select your best tableaux that is clearly a representation and not an imitation to show to the class. First within your group and then to your classmates, describe the main idea for your tableaux and how you selected the group shape and individual shapes to represent the main idea you are trying to express.

A I will divide the class in half, and you can show your entire dance to the class. Observers, be prepared to say what you liked about each dance.

CHAPTER

33

Folk, Square, and Line Dance

PRE-READING REFLECTION

1. Have you ever been at (or known about) a social or cultural event in which folk or cultural dancing (e.g., performing the "Chicken Dance" at sporting events, attending an African American step show, attending an ethnic wedding) occurred? If so, describe what happened.
2. Are there any folk or cultural dance clubs or groups at your university? If so, list them.
3. Go to a video Internet site and view current folk dances by searching for the following: Serbian folk dance, Korean folk dance, Korean sword dance, martial arts dance, African American stepping or step shows, Chinese ribbon dance, and Greek folk dance.

OBJECTIVES

Students will learn:

1. Folk dance is a universal part of human culture.
2. Many folk dances represent aspects of daily life.
3. Folk dances include locomotor steps, formations, and pathways, usually performed in a repeatable pattern.
4. In many countries and communities, traditional folk dance has evolved to become a popular form of performance art.
5. Folk dance lessons integrate easily with social studies.
6. Folk dance lessons are excellent opportunities for teaching children how to be respectful of other cultures.

skills and learn to move to the beat of the music, facilitating, if they desire, their participation in school and community dance activities as adolescents and throughout adulthood.

Second, you can easily design folk dance lessons to meet or exceed the guidelines for providing moderate to vigorous physical activity. For example, Native American pow-wow steps are highly vigorous.

Finally, folk dance provides important opportunities to include multicultural content in the curriculum and teach children to appreciate and value cultural diversity. These units can be truly powerful, especially if you collaborate with classroom teachers to design a unit integrating folk dance and social studies.

Integrating Folk Dance with Social Studies

When classroom teachers teach *any* unit about a culture, cultural event, or historical period, you can integrate physical education lessons with the unit. It is especially easy to integrate physical education with social studies lessons if you use child-designed folk dances, as you will not need to become an expert on the dances of the culture. Rather, you can build on the content taught by the classroom teacher and have children design dances representing what they have learned about the topic. Topics can come from the following categories:

- Nations
- Ethnicities
- Geographical regions
- States
- Historical periods
- Historical people and cultures
- Cities, communities, and cultural events (e.g., New Orleans and Mardi Gras)

The benefit for children of learning through integrated units is that they acquire broader, well-connected knowledge of a topic. For example, if students learn some basic dance steps and modified folk dances from a different country, they will understand that country in a more holistic way. Moreover, if children design their own folk dances incorporating basic steps and representing information they learned in their classroom, they will extend and elaborate their knowledge of the culture they have studied, while also being able to express their knowledge in their own way.

We suggest that physical education teachers ask the classroom teachers at the beginning of the year about the topics they plan to teach in social studies and science and offer to collaborate on an integrated unit at that time. You also can request classroom teachers to teach a unit. For example, if you are interested in teaching a unit on Native American dance culminating in a pow-wow, many classroom teachers might be willing to work with you in designing this unit.

If the classroom teachers are not willing or able to work with you, then you can briefly teach information about the culture that is relevant to your folk dance lessons. For each unit in this chapter, we provide brief descriptions of information you can teach about the culture from which the dance unit was developed.

Respectfully Teaching About Cultures

Researchers in multicultural education suggest the following guidelines to teach respectfully about different cultures (Banks, 2004; Cornelius, 1999; Gay, 2004).

Teach Children that They Must Respect Cultural Differences

Different cultures choose to do things in different ways. For example, they might have a different religion, political system, customs, language, music, art, and/or beliefs about family life. Children might not understand why a culture does things the way it does, but they need to know that the members of that culture do understand their culture and deserve the right to practice their customs without criticism from outsiders (Cornelius, 1999).

Teach Children Not to View Other Cultures as Exotic with Strange Tastes in Food, Clothing, and Housing

A culture's food, clothing, and housing evolve because people solve the problems of living in their geographic region and climate using the available natural resources. For example, traditionally Hawaiian people living on a Pacific island in a tropical climate built houses with thatched roofs because that building material was readily available, whereas people who lived in alpine regions were known for constructing homes with steep-pitched roofs to enable the winter snows to slide off rather than build up, causing the roof to collapse under the weight of the snow. Szechwan Chinese people developed a cuisine in which food is chopped into small pieces and cooked quickly in woks because of a shortage of fuel, whereas people from cold, northern countries with plentiful forests were known for stews that were cooked all day over the fire used to warm the house. As these examples suggest, the teacher's goal is to enable children to see connections between their own and other cultures and to appreciate differences as reasonable choices people make, rather than viewing these choices as weird or inferior.

Teach Children About the Harm and Inaccuracies of Stereotypes

It is important not to allow children to remain ignorant and believe that stereotypes accurately represent cultures. For example, one inaccurate stereotype of Native Americans is that they all live in tipis and wear feather headdresses. In the past, some Native American tribes lived in tipis if they lived on the plains and followed the buffalo herds for food. In contrast, other tribes in the Southeast were farmers who lived in permanent houses. Native Americans today live in the same types of houses and apartments as other Americans in their particular region of the country. Today, Native Americans might wear feather headdresses when they attend a pow-wow to celebrate their heritage, but they dress like other North Americans in everyday life. Assuming that people from other cultures always dress in traditional regalia would be the same as thinking that all American children dress in their Halloween costumes throughout the entire year!

Anticipate Teachable Moments

We find folk dance lessons to be excellent opportunities to address stereotyping. You can anticipate which stereotypes children will have and counteract these misperceptions in your introduction. For example, when we do child-designed folk dance on a Native American theme, we anticipate children will do the "tomahawk chop" (imitating fans at Atlanta Braves games). Consequently, we begin with a discussion of why this is an inappropriate stereotype of all Native Americans as warlike peoples and how the "tomahawk chop" is disrespectful.

The Benefits of Child-Designed and Modified Folk Dances

In this chapter, we present both modified and child-designed folk dances. Although we favor child-designed folk dances (see **Figure 33.2**), there are benefits to both teaching approaches.

Figure 33.2 Children designing a folk dance
Courtesy of John Dolly

Benefits of Child-Designed Folk Dance

- Allows children to express their interpretations of information they have learned about another culture and to choose themes meaningful to them. For example, in a child-designed Israeli dance lesson one of the authors taught, one group of boys represented the Arab–Israeli wars, while a group of girls represented the Dead Sea and fish swimming in the Jordan River.
- Helps develop children's creative- and critical-thinking skills and ability to engage in collaborative group work, thus meeting National Standard 4 and CCSS for speaking, listening, collaboration, and comprehension.
- Teaches children how to combine locomotor steps on different pathways and in different formations and design smooth transitions from one formation to the next.
- Teaches children how to listen to the phrasing of music and appropriately select locomotor skills for each phrase.
- Accommodates individual difference by allowing children (and teachers) who feel embarrassed or incompetent because they have difficulty performing the steps of authentic folk dances to the beat of the music to design dances that they can successfully perform.

Benefits of Modified and Authentic Folk Dance

- Teaches children new dance steps and dance styles from other cultures and historical periods.
- Helps children learn to appreciate cultural and ethnic diversity.
- Teaches children dances they might do in other settings.
- Gives teachers who are inexperienced with child-designed dances and cooperative learning techniques a way to include dance that is within their comfort zone.

Music

Try to select simple music that has a clear, steady beat and comes from the country you have selected for the lesson. You do not have to use authentic music if you can't find it—just select music that sounds like your theme. You can download and purchase folk dance CDs produced for elementary school physical education (they are advertised in equipment companies' catalogs). We have typically used the songs on these CDs for child-designed folk dances based on the country in which the folk dance originated. However, we have used these same tunes for child-designed folk dances for other countries as well. These CDs may have the steps of the folk dance written for you, but we feel free to modify these dances or create our own.

For square and line dances, we suggest you use music that the children in your school enjoy. Rap and salsa music work just as well as contemporary country music does. You need to be able to walk and skip to the music at a moderately brisk pace.

Try to find music that is not complicated. Complicated music has a melody, different harmonies, and multiple underlying beats that change or do not match the beat of the melody. A developmental pattern exhibited by children learning to move to the beat of the music is moving with the melody or the singers, rather than moving to the underlying beat. Children (and adult beginners) can have problems hearing and moving to the underlying beat of complicated music.

You also can have students bring in music they like. We require all music be free from vulgar, sexist, racist, and derogatory language and not be overtly sexual or religious. Some stores and Internet sources sell popular music recorded or modified for children.

We find it very helpful to record the song for the dance about 15 times in a row on a CD or to put the CD player on repeat play so you can continue teaching without having to run over to stop the music and find the song again. A remote control can be invaluable when you are working on folk dance lessons.

Internet Resources

The Internet can be an excellent resource when teaching folk dance. You can quickly access information about different countries and folk dances, or you can have children do so as homework assignments or during computer labs. In addition, many people have posted videos of folk dance performances on Internet sites. You can use these videos to show children some of the dances and the style of movement of the country you are studying; such performances can serve as excellent stimuli for child-designed folk dance lessons. Once children view, for example, a Chinese ribbon dance or a Korean sword dance, they can generate ideas for their own ribbon or sword dances.

Modifications

Although we have written modified versions of the folk dances in this chapter, we might not have modified the dances enough for your children. You can make all dances less complex, if necessary, by using the following suggestions:

- *Allow children to step on either foot.* In general, we do not worry about whether children are on the "correct" foot. Unless it is essential for safety or for the dance to work, we do not insist that all children be on the same foot.
- *Use longer repetitions.* One thing that makes a dance complex is when the dance steps change frequently. To make a dance less complex, add more repetitions. For example, if the dance has four step-hops in a row, you can change this to eight.
- *Eliminate steps, eliminate crossover steps, and substitute easier steps.* If children are having problems performing a certain step, then you can eliminate it from the dance and substitute an easier step. For example, a walk is easier than a step-hop, and a step-together-step is easier than a grapevine (which requires one leg to cross over and then behind the other leg).

- *Simplify formations.* Most dance formations can be simplified. One of the easiest ways to organize students is by having children in a scattered formation all facing the same directions. Single circles also are relatively easy formations to implement. Dances that require partners, sets of four, or changing partners as the dance progresses can usually be simplified to having children dance alone or in a circle.

Modifying Folk Dance for Children in Wheelchairs

Children in wheelchairs can participate in folk dance lessons with simple modifications. Instead of stepping, they push their wheel rims. A small step is equivalent to a light push; a running step or a series of running steps matches a medium push. For hops and jumps, children in wheelchairs can tap their rims with their hands or, for those who can do wheelies (raise their chair onto their two main wheels), lift their front wheels up and back to the ground. For partner turns, some children will be able to use elbow and hand holds, whereas other children can do the turn without touching their partners. Children in wheelchairs can use arm gestures as leg gestures and can design arm gestures to match the spirit of the music and dance or interpret the dance in their own way.

We provide an example of how to modify a folk dance for children in wheelchairs in the lesson segment on teaching the modified *Tarantella*. Child-designed folk dance works especially well for this population, as the children can find many creative ways to use their wheelchairs.

Holding Hands

In some schools, children resist holding hands in folk and square dances. This attitude seems to go in and out of fashion. In many schools, we simply have the children hold hands and, once they begin the lessons, their resistance fades. In other schools, you may need to have children hold scarves between them or substitute hooking elbows or holding shoulders. If need be, most folk and square dances can be done without holding hands.

With square dancing, we do not require girl–boy partners, even if that results in all-girl and all-boy groups. Instead of having dance steps designated for boys and girls, we simply have children wear pinnies or vests and call out the color of the pinnie, rather than calling, "ladies and gents," as is traditional in square dancing. Only a rare group of boys will resist holding hands; we tell that group to dance without touching one another. As the teacher, you should not let a few children who complain dictate the educational opportunities of all children.

Teaching Folk Dances

Breaking Down a Dance into Sections

When teaching a modified folk dance, try to break the dance down into short sections. Teach the first section, and practice it to the music until the children are confident in their performance. Then teach another brief section, and practice both sections 1 and 2 to the music. Continue and teach section 3, and then practice all three sections. Keep adding a section and practicing the new section with previously learned sections until the children have learned the entire dance.

Demonstrating Dance Steps

Four formations are commonly used for demonstrating folk dance steps. Each has its own benefits and limitations:

1. *Children facing the teacher and matching the teacher's movements; teacher in the front with back to children.* Some dance steps are easier for children to learn if you and they face the same direction and you demonstrate with your back toward the class. This way, the children can match your steps and directions exactly: When you move forward, they move forward; when you move right, they move right; and so on. The grapevine and rock steps are two steps that are more easily learned when you face the same direction as the children. The obvious problem with this formation is that you need to twist your head to watch the children, both for management and to see how they are learning the steps.
2. *Children facing the teacher and mirroring the teacher's movements; teacher in front facing the children.* Some steps are just as easily learned with the teacher facing the children. Step–together–step moving sideways is one such step. When you teach facing the children, you must reverse your left and right actions so the children can mirror you. In other words, when you say "Step sideways to your right," you as the teacher will have to point and move to your left (which will be the children's right).
3. *Children in scattered formation.* Some steps are so simple that you can demonstrate from the edge and cue the children while they travel in a scattered formation. A step-hop and a *schottische* are two such steps.
4. *Children in a circle.* There are a few dances that you can teach while the class is in a circle as long as the steps are very simple or require children to move into the center and back. Such a formation is very difficult for beginners, however, because the children on the opposite side of the circle will appear to be moving in the opposite direction and on the opposite foot.

Organization of this Chapter

We have organized the rest of this chapter by countries and dance forms. First, however, we list the fundamental locomotor skills used as folk dance steps and their definitions. We then introduce a sample plan for a child-designed New Orleans Mardi Gras folk dance. You can easily modify this generic child-designed folk dance plan for use with any country, historical period, or cultural topic the children have studied in their classroom. In this plan, we provide examples of how to teach basic locomotor skills, formations, and pathways. We also show you how to scaffold children's brainstorming for topic themes and how to help them design and refine their dance.

For most countries, we include child-designed sample learning experiences based on steps, formations, and stories from that country. Having children design, practice, and then show their dances to classmates may take three or four lessons. For some countries, we include descriptions of modified and authentic folk dances. By comparing these versions, you will be able to see how you can modify those folk dances you want to teach. In a few countries, we include sample learning experiences to show you how to teach and demonstrate modified folk dances. Finally, we provide background information on the dance or country that you can teach children if you are not integrating the lesson with content taught by the classroom teacher.

Fundamental Locomotor Folk Dance Steps, Formations, and Pathways

Fundamental Locomotor Skills

Walk, run.

Hop: Take off from one foot, land on the same foot.

Jump: Take off from two feet, land on two feet.

Leap: Take off from one foot, land on the opposite foot.

Assemblé (1 to 2): Take off from one foot, land on two feet; also called a *hurdle* in diving and gymnastics vaulting.

Sissone (2 to 1): Take off from two feet, land on one foot.

Skip: Step on left foot, hop on left foot; step on right foot, hop on right foot. Alternate the lead leg, and use an uneven rhythm: long (step), short (hop), long (step), short (hop). The accent is on the step.

Gallop: Uneven rhythm, forward direction, same leg leads, step–together–step–together. Technically, a gallop is performed as "step on the lead foot, close the back leg to the front while leaping onto the back foot, step on the lead foot again, and continue." A gallop is the same as a slide but moves forward.

Slide: Uneven rhythm, sideways, same leg leads, step–together–step–together. Technically, a slide is performed as "step on the lead foot, close the trailing leg to the lead leg while leaping onto the trailing foot, step on the lead foot again, and continue." A slide is the same as a gallop but moves sideways.

Step-hop: Step on the left foot, hop on the left foot; step on the right foot, hop on the right foot; even rhythm. A step-hop is the same as a skip but done with an even rhythm.

Schottische: A **schottische** consists of three steps and a hop in an even rhythm: Left, right, left, hop on left, right, left, right, hop on right.

Step–together–step (step–close–step): This folk dance step is used in many countries and is called by different names. It is derived from the *Gallopade*, which was popular in the early 1800s, and is the same basic pattern of a gallop.

Named Variations of Step–Together–Step

Two-step: A **two-step** is a step–together–step moving forward, alternating the lead leg: Left step–together–step, pause; right step–together–step, pause. Performed slowly, it is done with an even rhythm.

Chassé: A **chassé** is a step–together–step–together moving forward, backward, or sideways in an uneven rhythm. The body springs in the air with toes pointed. It is the same basic movement as a gallop. *Chassé* and *sashay* are pronounced the same way.

Sashay: A **sashay** is a square dance term for a step–together–step moving sideways in an uneven rhythm. It is the same as a slide.

Polka: The **polka** is the same as a two-step but faster and with a hop added, alternating the lead leg: Left step–together step–hop; right step–together–step–hop. It has an uneven rhythm.

Waltz: A **waltz** is danced in a 3/4 meter (three beats to a measure). Step forward on the left foot; step to side on the right foot; close the left foot next to the right foot. Repeat starting on the right foot. It is performed "down, up, up."

Mazurka: A **Mazurka** is danced in a 3/4 meter. Step with the left foot; close right to left foot while leaping onto right foot (called a "cut"); hop on the right foot; the same leg leads.

Pas de basque (pas de bas): In a **pas de basque (pas de bas)**, the dancer leaps to the right side, steps lightly on the ball of the left foot placed next to the right foot, steps on the right foot in place, and repeats to the left. It is sometimes called a "three."

Rock (or balance): In a **rock (or balance)**, the dancer steps forward on the left foot, transfers weight forward, and then transfers weight back on the right foot; it can be done on either leg.

Grapevine: A **grapevine** involves moving continuously to the right or left—step right foot to side; cross left foot behind right; step right foot to side; cross left foot in front of right (repeat).

Large Group Floor Pathways and Actions

Serpentine: Dancers in a line, usually holding hands, travel on a curved, snake-like pathway.

Spirals: Dancers are in a long line holding hands (not letting go) while the leader walks on a spiral pathway into the center; when the group is in a spiral, the leader turns, reverses, and spirals out.

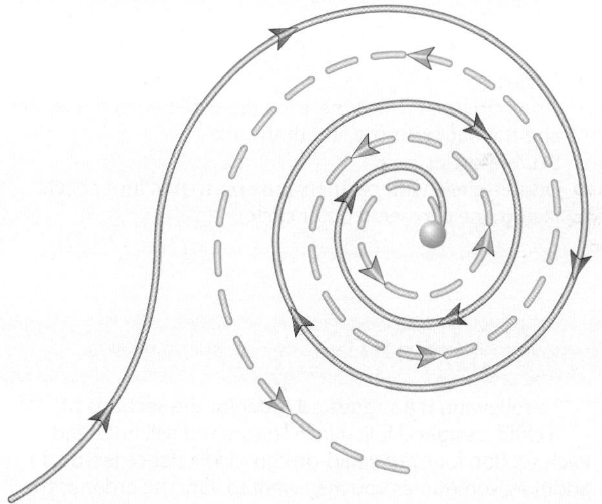

How to lead the spiral in and out

Maze: Dancers are in a long line holding hands with arms raised; the leader leads the line in weaving in and out.

Bridges/arches: Couples form an arch like "London bridges" with both arms; other couples walk under the arch.

(*continues*)

Fundamental Locomotor Folk Dance Steps, Formations, and Pathways (*continued*)

The maze

Waves: Partners are in longways sets (two parallel lines). Couples 1, 3, 5, 7, 9, and so on, turn to face the rear of the set; couples 2, 4, 6, 8, and so on, face the head of the set. All pairs hold the partner's inside hand. Even-numbered pairs hold hands up, and odd-numbered pairs walk under one couple; then odd-numbered pairs hold hands up, and even-numbered pairs walk under one couple. They continue walking under one couple's arms and then moving arms over another couple. When a couple reaches the end, they turn and come back, following the same over–under pattern (see **Figure 33.3**).

Basic Formations

- Circles
- Open circles in which there is a break between the leader and the dancer at the end of the line
- Double circles
- Double circle with partners (one partner in inner circle facing one partner in outer circle)
- Partners in a circle facing in
- Partners in a circle facing around the circle
- Line (standing shoulder to shoulder)
- Line (school line with each child facing the child in front)
- Double lines with partners facing each other
- Double lines with partners facing the pair in front
- Partner square/square dance set (four sets of partners facing in; each pair parallel to one wall of the gym)

Other Folk Dance Terms for Turns, Partner Positions, and Formations

Elbow swings: **Elbow swings** involve hooking elbows and walking around the partner.

Star turns: In **star turns**, partners or groups of four touch palms and hold hands high above head height; dancers walk around each other, completing one full circle back to their original place.

Promenade: In a **promenade**, dancers hold left hands with left hands and right hands with right hands, with arms crossed in front, typically walking forward in a circle formation.

Varsovienne: In a **varsovienne**, the man puts his right hand behind the woman's shoulder and holds the woman's right hand at shoulder height. The woman puts her left hand palm down across the man's chest and holds the man's left hand.

Longways set: In a **longways set**, six to eight couples are arranged in two parallel lines. Partners either face each other or hold inside hands and face the head of the set.

Do-sa-do (sometimes spelled do-si-do): A **do-sa-do** involves walking forward toward one's partner; passing by right shoulders; walking sideways around the partner (without turning), and then walking backward to one's starting location.

Outline of Generic Child-Designed Folk Dance Lesson (As Written in Sample Plan 33.1) Using New Orleans and Mardi Gras as an Example

The following is a suggested order for the sections of a child-designed folk dance lesson. You will not need each section for every child-designed folk dance lesson. In addition, sometimes you may want to vary the order of the sections. For example, you might introduce the topic for the dance as the first section of the culminating activity just before the children brainstorm ideas.

Warm-up Activity: Introduction of Topic or Story

Content Development

1. Teach selected locomotor steps if necessary.
2. Move to the beat of the music using selected locomotor steps.
3. Hear the phrasing of the music.
4. Design a repeatable pattern of locomotor steps to the phrasing of the music.
5. Learn the potential formation, pathways, and/or partner relationships.

Culminating Activity: Designing the Folk Dance

1. Brainstorm ideas based on the topic or story to represent in the dance.
2. Explore different gestures and actions to represent ideas in the dance.
3. Select ideas for each part of the dance, and add formations, pathways, and/or partner relationships.
4. Arrange the parts of the dance, and plan transitions from one formation to the next.
5. Match the parts of the dance to the phrases of the music, deciding how many times to repeat a locomotor step or gesture.
6. Refine and practice (stretching tall, light landings, moving to the beat and phrasing of the music, movements synchronized, movements precisely repeatable, good transitions).

Assessment and Showing Dances

Figure 33.3 The wave

SAMPLE PLAN 33.1

Generic Child-Designed Folk Dance Lesson Using New Orleans and Mardi Gras as an Example

Movement Theme: Basic Locomotor Steps, Formations, and Pathways

Topic Theme: New Orleans and Mardi Gras

Standards

This plan addresses National Standards 1, 2, and 4 and CCSS for speaking, listening, and collaborating.

Objectives

Children will learn to:

Motor

1. Walk, hop, jump, slide, and skip, traveling in different directions, moving lightly to the beat of the music, and stretching tall through the spine.

Creative Thinking and Knowledge of Choreography

2. Design gestures that represent topics based on New Orleans and Mardi Gras.
3. Design smooth transitions between different formations that do not require extra steps or jumps to shift positions.

Teaching Notes and Potential Interactive Decisions

Integrating with Social Studies

You can use this generic lesson plan for any cultural or historical topic the children are studying in their classroom by substituting the country and possible themes and topics for the dance.

Observation Plan

1. Watch for children moving to the beat of the music.
2. Watch for children stretching tall and landing lightly.
3. Watch whether group work is productive and children are generating and exploring ideas.
4. Watch whether all children are contributing to their group's dance.

(continues)

SAMPLE PLAN 33.1

Generic Child-Designed Folk Dance Lesson Using New Orleans and Mardi Gras as an Example (*continued*)

Social

4. Work cooperatively by listening to everyone and encouraging everyone to contribute ideas to the dance.

CCSS

5. Engage effectively in a range of collaborative discussions with diverse partners on topics, listening carefully, building on partners' ideas, and expressing their own ideas clearly.

Warm-up Activity

I To warm up your body, travel about the gym using different locomotor steps to the music. [Select upbeat music that has a clear beat.]

Scaffold Exploration if Necessary

E Have you tried hopping? Jumping? Walking? Skipping? Sliding?

Introduction of Topic or Story

I In your classroom, you have been studying New Orleans. What are some of the things New Orleans is famous for? [Jazz, Mardi Gras, Hurricane Katrina, floodwalls, some sections below sea level, beignets, po boy sandwiches, good food, the French Quarter, ironwork balconies, above-ground cemeteries.] Tell me more about what you have learned about Mardi Gras. [Masks; parades; floats representing organizations; beads; the colors purple, green, and gold; parties; jazz bands.] Today we are going to be designing folk dances representing topics from New Orleans and Mardi Gras.

Content Development

Moving to the Beat of the Music Using Selected Locomotor Steps

I Let's start by working on moving to the beat of the music. Follow me, and let's clap to the underlying beat. [Put on music, and clap to beat.]

E Now, walk about general space as you clap to the beat.

E Continue walking, but stop clapping, and see if you can keep walking to the beat of the music.

E Explore doing other locomotor steps to the beat of the music, or continue walking.

Scaffold Exploration if Necessary

E Try jumping, hopping, 2-1, 1-2, jogging, skipping, sliding, or galloping.

Hearing the Phrasing of the Music

Cog K This music is in phrases of eight counts. [Eight-count phrases are commonly heard in music, as are 16-count phrases.] I will count out the major beats of each phrase as you listen. [Count aloud 1–8 on the major beats for each major phrase or verse of the song, starting at 1 with each new verse or major phrase. You will need to practice this before class time. Some music has phrases of different durations during the song. For example, the first three phrases might be 16 counts, and then the next phrase might be 12 counts.] Can you hear when the major phrases or new verses begin?

E Let's do a short task to help you hear and move to the phrasing of the music. Start by walking to the beat of the music. When you hear a new verse or phrase, jog. When the phrase changes again, go back to walking. See if you can change from jogging to walking with each phrase of the song.

SAMPLE PLAN 33.1

Generic Child-Designed Folk Dance Lesson Using New Orleans and Mardi Gras as an Example (*continued*)

Designing a Repeatable Pattern of Locomotor Steps to the Phrasing of the Music **E** All folk dances have locomotor steps done in a repeatable pattern. Select an easy pattern such as eight walks, eight skips, eight walks, eight skips or eight walks, eight jumps, eight walks, and eight jumps, and try that to the beat of the music. **E** That's great. Try a different pattern.	**R** Stretch tall. People are proud of their folk dancing. **R** Land lightly from jumps, hops, and leaps.
Learning Potential Formations, Pathways, and Partner Relationships *Formations* **E** All folk dances have different formations. Let's try some as a group. Get in a circle, and follow me as we walk around to the beat of the music. Stop. Reverse direction. Stop and face in. • Walk four steps into the center and back. [Repeat several times.] • Walk four steps into the center, and clap high on step 4; then walk four steps back. [Repeat several times.] • Walk three steps into the center, and then clap and jump, landing with a stomp on beat 4; walk four steps back. [Repeat several times.]	*Notes:* To help you understand how to teach formations, pathways, and partner relationships, we describe far more than you need for a lesson. When designing your lesson, select only some of these formations, and then do others on a different day.
E Let's try some other formations. [Let go of the hand of the child in front of you.] Follow my lead. [Lead the class in a line.] We just transitioned from a circle to a line. Now starting with me, every other person takes a giant step to the left. Now we are in a double line. Now each line faces the other.	
Partner Relationships **Org** Starting at the front of the line, partner up with the person in front of you. [If there is an odd number of children, the teacher can be a partner.] **E** Sometimes folk dances have partner work. Let's try some: • Walk four steps backward, moving away from your partner. Walk four steps in and four steps back. • Walk four steps in and "high five" (clap) both your partner's hands. • Can anyone think of a partner action we can try? A turn is a great idea. • Let's try an elbow turn first. Walk toward your partner, hook right elbows, walk around your partner, and go back to your original place. Now link left elbows. [Repeat several times.]	**E** If you want to try more variations, you can try star turns and do-sa-do.
Pathways **E** Sometimes folk dances move on different pathways. Get back into one line, and follow me, and we will do a serpentine pattern [big S curves]. Does anyone know where the word *serpentine* comes from? Yes. That's right, a serpent or a snake. We are moving in a snake-like pattern. **E** Now we will do a spiral—this is fun. Don't let go of each other's hands no matter what. [See the earlier figure for a diagram of the spiral pattern.]	

(*continues*)

SAMPLE PLAN 33.1

Generic Child-Designed Folk Dance Lesson Using New Orleans and Mardi Gras as an Example (*continued*)

Culminating Activity: Designing the Folk Dance	
Brainstorm Ideas Based on the Topic or Story to Represent in the Dance **E** I will put you into groups of three or four. Using your best brainstorming skills, discuss all of the possible ideas about New Orleans and Mardi Gras that you can use for your folk dance.	Play the music over and over the entire time the children are working. **Social/CCSS** Remember when we work in groups, everyone talks (one at a time), and everyone listens. Build on each other's ideas.
Exploring Different Gestures and Actions to Represent Ideas in the Dance **E** Now, select one of your ideas, and explore different ways to do a locomotor step and make arm and body gestures that represent that idea. **E** Select three to five other ideas, and do the same. **Social/CCSS** It is important that everyone contributes to the dance. If someone in your group has not made a suggestion, encourage her or him to add an idea. Listen carefully.	*Scaffold Exploration if Necessary* **E** Someone tell me one of your ideas. Jazz is a great idea. Everyone stand up, and I will start the music. Travel about the space doing any locomotor step you choose, and explore different arm and body gestures that represent a jazz musician playing a trombone. **E** Someone tell me another idea. Masks are another great idea. Everyone use your hands to represent a mask. Now show a different mask; now a third mask. Now, select a locomotor step, add a mask, and represent someone in a Mardi Gras parade wearing a mask. You had some wonderful ideas. Now, go back to your group, and see if you can come up with ways to represent the ideas for your group dance. **R** Try to find interesting ways to represent your ideas.
Selecting Ideas for Each Part of the Dance and Adding Formations, Pathways, and/or Partner Relationships **E** Now, select a formation for each idea. The formations you select can help highlight your ideas. For example, if you want to represent marching in a parade, which formation might you use? Yes, a line or double line. If you want to highlight a high gesture, which formation might you use? Yes, good idea—you could use a circle walking into the center and gesturing high, then walking back.	**R** Remember that in creative dance we discussed the difference between representing and imitating? What is the difference? That's right. *Imitating* means doing something exactly the way it is done or doing a stereotyped movement that is not very interesting. *Representing* means taking the idea and making the movement bigger, or doing it with different body parts, or taking only part of the idea and exaggerating that part.
Arranging the Parts of the Dance and Planning Transitions from One Formation to the Next **E** Start to put your folk dance together. Decide on an order for your formations, and then figure out how to transition from one formation to the next. For example, if you are in a circle, how could you transition to a line? Right, one person could be the leader and lead the group from a circle into a line, or two people could lead the group into a double line.	**R** If you have a problem with a transition, try changing the order of your ideas to make the transitions easier.
Matching the Parts of the Dance to the Phrases of the Music, and Deciding How Many Times to Repeat a Locomotor Step or Gesture **E** Work on putting your dance to the music. Listen to the phrases of the music. Change to a new formation or a new locomotor step only when you hear a new major phrase or new verse. Decide how many times to repeat each locomotor step and gesture to match the phrases.	*Notes:* This task is designed for older children or children who are experienced in designing their own folk dances.
Refine and Practice **R** Now refine and practice your dance to improve your performance. Work on all moving at the same time to the beat of the music. If you are all doing the same gesture, try to match one another perfectly.	**Other Potential Refinements** **R** If you are doing the same locomotor step, try to all start on the same foot. **R** Work on making your formations precise (e.g., circles are round, lines are straight, spacing between children is the same). **R** Stretch tall. Use light landings.

SAMPLE PLAN 33.1

Generic Child-Designed Folk Dance Lesson Using New Orleans and Mardi Gras as an Example (*continued*)

Showing Dances

E Now let's show your dances to your classmates. If you do not want to show your dance, come up by me, and I will tell you your "watching" assignment.

Social Let's review how to be a good audience. What should you do? Yes, you remembered the class rules perfectly. Be silent. Don't laugh at anyone. Applaud at the end of the performance. Watch carefully, and be prepared to offer a compliment to the group, telling them specifically what you liked about their dance.

Balkan Countries: Teaching Basic Folk Dance Steps

The Balkan countries are on the peninsula between the Mediterranean Sea to the west and south and the Black Sea to the east. These countries include Slovenia, Croatia, Bosnia and Herzegovina, the Republic of Montenegro, Macedonia, Serbia, Albania, Greece, Bulgaria, Romania, Moldova, and the European part of Turkey.

In this unit, we include modified folk dances for the *Poskok*, an energetic folk dance from Serbia, and the *Kalamatianos*, which is a national folk dance of Greece. We focus on these dances because they include four important but simple folk dance steps: the step-hop, *schottische*, grapevine, and rock. In addition, dances from the Balkan region consist of simple, repeatable patterns performed in circles and serpentine lines with a leader who often improvises variations on the movements. Children can easily design their own Balkan-style sequence of dance steps in groups of two to four.

Serbia: Teaching the Step Hop and *Schottische* Steps

We begin by describing the dance called the *Poskok*. We selected this dance because it includes two common and simple folk dance steps: a step-hop and a *schottische* step. You can also find dances from other countries to teach these two steps.

Next, we present a sample lesson segment that demonstrates how to teach folk dance steps, how to cue children while they are dancing, and how to put the steps together into a dance. Using the outline for a generic folk dance lesson presented earlier in this chapter, we then explain how you can teach a simple child-designed folk dance. This dance consists of a repeatable pattern of locomotor steps.

Potential Information to Use for an Introduction to Serbian Dance

Show a Video Clip of Serbian Folk Dancers

We found an excellent example of a performance of folk dances from Serbia titled *Folk Dances from Central Serbia* on a popular Internet video site. This demonstration shows the energetic, smooth dance style and the steps in the folk dance. It also shows a dance with the dancers using the alternating cross-V handhold (see **Figure 33.4**) and doing interesting sequences of steps forward, backward, and sideways. Showing the children this video is one way to introduce either a modified *Poskok* or a child-designed folk dance lesson using the Serbian style.

Figure 33.4 Alternating cross-V handhold

Courtesy of John Dolly

Discuss Information About Serbia

Serbia is a Balkan country that was once part of Yugoslavia. For hundreds of years, the Slavic peoples living in the Balkan Peninsula were conquered and subjugated by invaders from the south and north. In 1945, at the end of World War II, the Federal People's Republic of Yugoslavia was formed from six republics: Serbia, Montenegro, Slovenia, Bosnia–Herzegovina, Croatia, and Macedonia. In the early 1990s, a civil war in Yugoslavia resulted in the separation of the republics.

Discuss Baltic Dances

A circle formation, called a *kolo*, predominates in Baltic dances, but some interesting dances are performed in lines of about six people, with the line moving sideways, forward, and backward. Circle dances are the most ancient of the dance formations. Dance historians have documented circle dances back to early Stone Age peoples.

Discuss and Demonstrate Interesting Handholds

Several interesting handholds are used in Baltic dances. In a "W" handhold, the elbows are bent and the hands or pinkies joined at shoulder height. In an alternating cross-V handhold, count off 1, 2, 1, 2, and so on. The 1s hold hands by reaching in front of the 2s, making a V. The 2s hold hands by reaching in front of the 1s, also making a V. Everyone's right arm is in front of the left arm of the person next to him or her (see **Figure 33.4**).

Description of the *Poskok*

Poskok: Modified Version

This dance is performed to lively music with a beat that matches a comfortable jog.

Formation: Circle with children holding hands (or holding scarves between hands or hand on shoulder of child in front), facing center.

Part A

Summary: Move to center of circle with step-hops and back out with *schottische* step four times.

Counts	*Step-Hop and Schottische*
1–4	Step, hop, step, hop moving toward the center, raising arms high.
5–8	*Schottische* (step, step, step, hop) back to place, lowering arms.

Repeat for a total of four times.

Part B

Summary: Eight *schottische* steps traveling around the circle to the right.

Counts	*Schottische Steps*
1–32	Turn to right and perform eight *schottische* steps (step, step step, hop) traveling around the circle.

***Poskok:* Authentic Version**

The authentic version is the same as the modified version, except in part A: Now when the dancers move into the center of the circle, they move forward on a diagonal to the right and then back on a diagonal to the right. They then retrace the diagonal pathway, moving forward on a diagonal to the left and back to their original place on a diagonal to the left (see the accompanying figure).

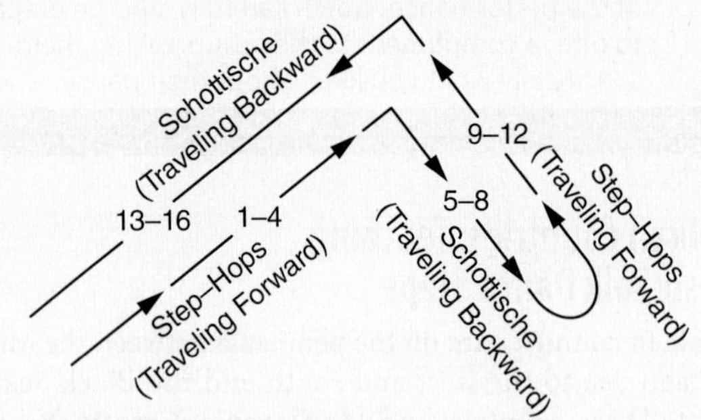

Floor pattern of the authentic *Poskok*

SAMPLE LEARNING EXPERIENCES 33.1

Teaching the Modified *Poskok*

Organization

In teaching the step-hop and *schottische* for the *Poskok*, you can have the children travel about the gym rather than face in one direction: In this dance, it does not matter if beginners step and hop on the same leg. Once the children have the dance mastered, you can add having them step and hop on the same foot, but, for beginners, this is an unnecessary criterion.

Potential Refinements

- Body stretched tall
- Small light hops and running steps
- Energetic feeling
- Free foot stays near the floor

Content Development

Teaching the Step-Hop

I Today I am going to teach you a modified version of an energetic dance from Serbia. The dance is called the *Poskok*. There are two steps to this dance: a step-hop and a *schottische*. Let's start with the step-hop. It is like a skip, but the rhythm is even. Watch me, and listen: step, hop, step, hop. Join in with me: Step on one foot, hop on that foot, step on the other foot, hop on that foot. That's it—step, hop, step, hop. [Repeat over and over until the children are comfortable and performing competently.]

E Now I will cue you faster. [Increase the speed of your cues until the children are moving at about the speed of the music.]

E Let's try it to the music. When you hear the music, travel about the gym doing a step-hop.

Teaching the *Schottische*

E The second step is called a *schottische*. It consists of three steps and one hop. Let's try that together. Step, step, step, hop on the same leg; step, step, step, hop. [Continue giving cues until the children can perform the *schottische* competently.]

E Now try the *schottische* to the music. [Continue cuing: step, step, step, hop.]

Putting the Dance Together

Org Everyone get in a circle facing in. [Holding hands is helpful to learning this dance but not necessary.]

SAMPLE LEARNING EXPERIENCES 33.1

Teaching the Modified *Poskok* (*continued*)

E Do two step-hops toward the center and then a *schottische* back to place. Let me cue you on moving forward. Ready? Step, hop, step, hop. Now reverse, and move backward back to place: step, step, step, hop. Great. Let's do that again. [Repeat until the children are comfortable and competent.]

E In part 1 of the dance, we go into the center and back out four times. As you go in, reach your arms up high; as you go back, bring your arms back to your sides. Let's try that four times to the music. I will cue you. Ready? [Cue part 1.]

E In part 2, we travel around the circle doing eight *schottische* steps. Everyone hold hands and turn right [or hold the shoulder of the person in front of you], and move to your right. Ready. [Cue part 2: step, step, step, hop eight times.]

E Now let's do the whole dance to the music. We will repeat it several times. [Cue parts 1 and 2 until the children can perform the steps. Then simply cue the number of steps: into the center 1 and back, into the center 2 and back, 3, 4, traveling around the circle 1, 2, 3, 4, 5, 6, 7, 8. Back to the beginning, into the center 1, 2, 3, 4, and so on.]

SAMPLE LEARNING EXPERIENCES 33.2

Child-Designed Sequence of Locomotor Steps, Balkan-Style

See the generic child-designed folk dance lesson for suggestions in designing a complete lesson plan.

Content Development

Moving to the Beat of the Music Using Selected Locomotor Steps

I Travel about the space doing different locomotor steps to the music. Which kinds of steps might you do? Great suggestions: jog, skip, hop, jump, slide, gallop, step–together–step.

Hearing the Phrasing of the Music

E Now try to listen to the music, and count phrases of eight. Let's do this together first. [Count aloud with the children—1, 2, 3, 4, 5, 6, 7, 8 to the beat of the music.]

Designing a Repeatable Pattern of Locomotor Steps to the Phrasing of the Music

E Now travel about the gym, and I will count out the phrases of eight. Change locomotor steps each time I start at number 1. Ready? 5, 6, 7, and go: 1, 2, 3, 4, 5, 6, 7, 8, and so on. [Repeat several times until the children can perform a step for eight counts and change to another step.]

E Great! You are moving to the beat of the music and changing to a different step every eight counts. Now, I want you to select two steps and put them into a sequence that you can repeat over and over. For example, you might do step-hop, step-hop, step-hop, step-hop moving forward and then jump eight times. [Demonstrate.] Or you might walk forward eight times, and then turn and jog eight times back to your original place. [Repeat until children can do the sequence confidently.]

Culminating Activity

A In our last class, we did a folk dance from Serbia called the *Poskok*. Today you will be designing your own folk dance in the same style. I am going to assign partners. With your partner, design a sequence of two different locomotor steps. The music is in counts of four, so you can do one locomotor step eight times and then the second locomotor step eight times. Or you can do each step four times and repeat.

Potential Partner Relationships, Pathways, and Directions

E Now, decide on your partner relationships, pathway, and directions. For partner relationships, you can stand side by side or one person in front and one person behind. You can move on straight, curved, or zigzag pathways. You can move forward, backward, or sideways. You have many choices and many decisions to make.

MD For those of you who want a more difficult challenge, after you have designed and practiced your dance, join with another group. Each group teaches the other group their dance, and then the two groups combine their dances.

Potential Formations

E With groups of four, you have different formations you can use. If you want, you can add different formations to your dance.

Refine and Practice

E Once your dance is designed, practice the dance until your group can perform the dance accurately over and over.

Assess and Show

Description of the *Kalamatianos*

Kalamatianos: Modified Version

Music: You can use the tune "Zorba the Greek" for this dance. The music increases in speed each time the verse is played, which makes the dance enjoyable for children. A version of this song can be found on the CD *Folk Dance Fun* by Georgiana Stewart from Kimbo Educational.

Formation: Line

Part A

Summary: Four grapevine steps moving sideways to the right.

Counts	*Grapevine Step*
1	Step to side on right
2	Cross and step on left behind right
3	Step to side on right
4	Cross and step on left in front of right (this completes one grapevine step)

Repeat, completing a total of four grapevine steps.

Cues: Side, behind, side, front.

Part B

Summary: Two rocks

Counts	*Rocks*
1, 2	Step right to side (slow)
3	Rock forward on left (quick)
4	Rock back on right (quick)
1, 2	Step to side left (slow)
3	Rock forward on right (quick)
4	Rock back on left (quick)

Cues: Side, rock, rock, side, rock, rock.

Kalamatianos: Authentic Version

The authentic *Kalamatianos* is performed to a 7/8 meter called *epitritos.* The rhythm of the steps is slow, quick, quick, slow, quick, quick, and the rhythm is uneven. We provide counts for more simple music with four-count phrases at a walking speed.

The difference in Part A from the modified version is that the dancers only do one and a half grapevine steps, adding a quick, small hop after the first grapevine then move immediately into Part B, which is exactly the same as the modified version.

Cues for Part A

Side (slow)
Behind (quick)
Side and small hop (quick)
Front (slow)
Side (quick)
Behind (quick)

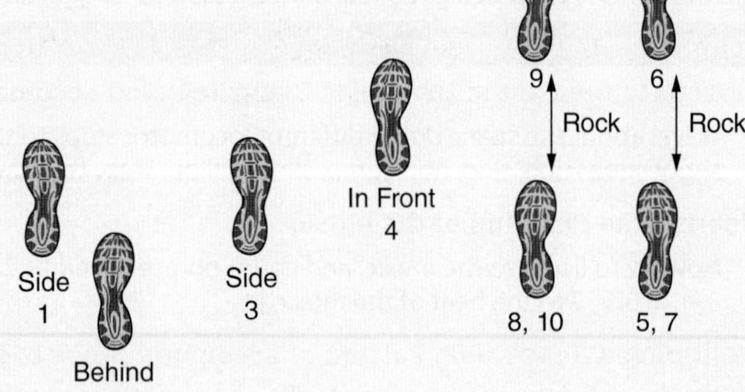

Footprint pattern of one grapevine step and two rocks

Greece: Teaching the Grapevine Step and Rocks

Potential Information to Use for an Introduction to Greek Dance

Show Photos of Greek Pottery

Writers in ancient Greece described Greek dancing for festivities, religious ceremonies, and fitness (Freeman, 2012). Depictions of these dances can be seen on Greek pottery that has survived to the present day. You can find photos of Greek folk dances on ancient pottery on the Internet and show these photos to children to introduce the lesson, or you can use these images to inspire ideas for child-designed Greek folk dances.

Discuss How Traditional Greek Folk Dances Are Still Performed Today

Do you believe a dance can be handed down from ancient times to today? When the Romans conquered the Greeks, they did not eliminate the Greek culture or traditions, but rather assimilated these traditions into the Roman culture. Thus, the Greeks continued to perform their folk dances. The Ottoman Empire was another major invader of the Greek islands. The Greeks who lived in rural, mountainous regions resisted the Turkish overlords and continued performing Greek folk dances. Scholars, in fact, believe that the ancient Greek dances represented on ancient Greek art have survived into modern times (Lawson, 1970).

In ancient times, men and women were segregated when they danced. Today, however, they dance together.

Tell a Folk Tale

One interesting story connected with the *Kalamatianos* is that invaders entered a Greek village. Rather than be taken by the invaders, the women of the village danced the *Kalamatianos* to the edge of a cliff and then, one by one, jumped off the cliff, preferring death to capture.

Use Scarves as Props

Traditionally, a handkerchief is held between the leader and the second person in the *Kalamatianos*, while the rest of the people in the line hold hands. In physical education, you can have all children hold scarves between their hands. This is especially helpful if the children are designing their own variations, as scarves allow them to turn and make arches easily without having to twist their hands. In addition, children can add gestures using the scarves.

SAMPLE LEARNING EXPERIENCES 33.3

Teaching the Modified *Kalamatianos*

Potential Refinements

- In the grapevine step, the body twists and turns while maintaining a smooth style of movement (without bouncing up and down). When the dancers rock forward, the entire body shifts forward over the foot. The line of dancers moves as if all were one and looks like a painting on an ancient Greek vase.
- Dancers hold their heads high and stretch tall.

Content Development

Cog K Now that you have heard the story of the *Kalamatianos*, let's try a modified version. It starts with the grapevine step. The grapevine step represents a grapevine twisting around an arbor.

Org Everyone face me, and move a few steps to the left. [Initially turn your back toward the class so children can match your leg actions exactly without getting confused by having to reverse the direction in which their legs move. Twist your head so you can see the children as you teach this step.]

Teaching the Grapevine Step

1. Follow me, and step sideways to your right on your right foot. [Point to the right with your right hand.]
2. Cross your left leg behind your right, and step on your left foot. [Continue to point right.]
3. Step sideways again on your right foot.
4. Cross your left leg in front of your right, and step on your left foot. This is one grapevine step. Let's repeat it several times. I will do it with you and say the cues.
5. Side, behind, side, in front. [Repeat several times until the class is close to the edge of the physical education space.]
6. Slide back to the other side of the gym, be in personal space, and let's grapevine across the gym while I cue you. Side, behind, side, in front. [Repeat cues the entire time, and repeat until the children are moving confidently.]

E That's great. You are ready to practice to the music. Move to the other side of the gym again. [Repeat cues to the music.]

E In the dance, we do four grapevine steps followed by two rocks. Let's do the four grapevine steps and then stop. Ready? Side, behind, side, in front, 2 behind, side in front, 3, and 4.

Teaching the Rock

E Here is the rock step. Do this with me. [Again, initially teach with your back to the class because children will get confused trying to reverse the directions in which you move as you demonstrate. Try to twist your head to see them.]

1. Standing on your left leg, step sideways to the right on your right foot, and pause. [Point your hand to the right.]
2. Step forward on your left foot, rocking your weight forward.
3. Step back on your right foot, rocking your weight backward.
4. Now repeat to the other side. [Point your hand to the left.] Step sideways to your left on your left foot, and pause.
5. Step forward on your right foot, rocking your weight forward.
6. Step back on your left foot, rocking your weight backward.

E Let's repeat this over and over while I cue you. The rhythm is slow (side), quick (rock forward), quick (rock backward). [Demonstrate the rhythm.] Do the rock with me. [Cue in rhythm; midway, switch from cuing the steps to cuing the rhythm.] Side, rock, rock; side, rock, rock; slow, quick, quick; slow, quick, quick. [Repeat until the children are comfortable performing the rocking step.]

E Now let's try it to the music [continue cuing].

Putting the Dance Together

E Now put the two parts together: four grapevines, two rocks, four grapevines, two rocks. Do this with me while I cue you. [Repeat cues for grapevine and rocks.]

E [If the children are comfortable and competent performing the dance facing the front of the gym, then put them in lines of four to six. If they master dancing in a line, they can dance in a circle.] Let's try it to the music in lines of four to six. Everyone pick up a scarf and hold it in your right hand. Hold onto the scarf of the child next to you with your left hand. [You can also have the children simply hold hands.] I will cue you to the music. [Stop while the music is still at a slow pace.]

E What is fun about this folk dance is that the music called "Zorba the Greek" keeps getting faster (or changes from fast to slow to fast to slow, depending on the version of the song). Let's try dancing to the entire song. Listen to me as I cue you on your steps and your speed. Ready? Grapevine right. [Continue cuing until the children no longer need the cues.]

Italy: The *Tarantella*

The *Tarantella* is a popular Italian folk dance still performed in social and recreational settings today. There is an interesting story about why people invented and danced the *Tarantella*. In Sicily, an island off the tip of the "boot" of Italy, people believed that if a tarantula spider bit them, they could dance vigorously to get the poison out of their systems. They would dance the *Tarantella* with such frenzy and for so long that they would drop from exhaustion (Tillman-Hall, 1969). This very energetic dance is one of the most well-known dances of Italy. You can purchase the music from the Internet.

Description of the *Tarantella*

Tarantella: Modified Version

Formation: Entire class in one circle; do not hold hands.

Repeat Part A and Part B of the authentic version for the entire dance.

Tarantella: Authentic Version

Formation: Double circle with partners facing each other; two couples next to each other, making a set of four. A more simple variation is to simply do the dance in partners or leave out parts E and F.

Part A

Counts	*Two Step-Kicks, Four Runs in Place*
1	Step left
2	Kick right (swing and lift right leg across) and clap
3	Step right
4	Kick left (swing and lift left leg across) and clap
5, 6, 7, 8	Run in place left, right, left, right, and click fingers four times

Repeat counts 1–8 for a total of four times.

Part B

Counts	*Run into Center and Back Four Times*
1, 2, 3, 4	Four runs into center, bending low and clicking fingers
5, 6, 7, 8	Four runs back to place, raise arms up and click fingers

Repeat counts 1–8 for a total of four times into the center and back.

Repeat part A: two step-kicks, four runs in place, four times.

Part C

Counts	*Two Elbow Swings*
1–8	Hook right elbows, walk eight steps around partner, and end back in place
1–8	Hook left elbows, walk eight steps around partner, and end back in place

Part D

Counts	*Two Do-Sa-Do*
1–4	Walk toward partner, pass right shoulders, pass back to back
5–8	Continue circling around partner, pass left shoulders, walk backward to place
1–8	Repeat do-sa-do, but pass left shoulders, pass back to back, pass right shoulders, and walk backward to place

Part E

Counts	*Four-Elbow Turn*
1–8	Set of four walks to the center with hands on hips, put left elbows in (nearly touching), and skip eight times (counterclockwise) in a circle and back to place
1–8	Repeat four-elbow turn with right elbows (circling clockwise)

Part F

Counts	*Star Turn*
1–8	Set of four walks to the center touching palms high, skip eight times (counterclockwise) in a circle and back to place
1–8	Repeat star turn with right palms (circling clockwise)

SAMPLE LEARNING EXPERIENCES 33.4

Teaching a Modified *Tarantella* with Modifications for Children Using Wheelchairs

In this lesson segment, we illustrate how to modify a folk dance for children using wheelchairs. These same modifications can be applied in other dances. We also include sample objectives. Dancers can shake tambourines throughout the dance if you have enough equipment.

Objectives

Children will learn to

Motor

1. Jog, hop, and swing/kick a leg, push the wheelchair, do-sa-do, elbow-swing partner, and clap and finger click while moving to the beat of the music and stretching the head tall.
2. Perform a modified version of the *Tarantella* with competence and confidence.

SAMPLE LEARNING EXPERIENCES 33.4

Teaching a Modified *Tarantella* with Modifications for Children Using Wheelchairs (*continued*)

Cognitive

3. Understand that dances can represent stories, ideas, and events, such as how a bite from a tarantula spider is represented in the *Tarantella* folk dance.

Social

4. Elbow-swing their partners without pulling their partner off balance.

Affective

5. Appreciate that dance can be fun for all children.

Potential Refinements

- Bouncy, light movements
- Heads high
- Be energetic.

Introductory Warm-up Activity

Play the music for the *Tarantella.*

I Travel about the gym doing different locomotor patterns to the music. You can jog, skip, step-hop, jump, hop, 2 -1 (*sissone*), and 1-2 (*assemblé*). For students who use wheelchairs, work on wheelies or hops if you can (tilting the chair back onto its main wheel), turns, and fast and slow movements.

Introduction of the Story

I Today we are going to learn a folk dance called the *Tarantella.* There is an interesting story about why people invented and danced the *Tarantella.* In Sicily, an island off the tip of the "boot" of Italy, people believed that if a tarantula spider bit them, they could dance vigorously to get the poison out of their systems. They would dance the *Tarantella* with such frenzy and for so long that they would drop from exhaustion. This is a very energetic dance and one of the most well-known dances of Italy.

Content Development

Hearing and Moving to the Beat of the Music

I [Use tambourines (which are authentic for this dance), shakers, wrist bells, or any instruments if there are enough for each child to have an instrument.] Listen to the music, and see if you can play your instrument or clap to the beat of the music.

E Now, walk about general space while clapping or playing to the music. For students who use wheelchairs, move to the beat of the music, and push and use wrist bells to tap the beat on your wheel rims.

E We have been clapping or playing on every beat. Now, clap on every other beat while doing a step-hop. Step-hop, clapping on the hop, like this. [Demonstrate as you call out the steps.] Step-hop [clap at the same time], step-hop [clap at the same time]. Students who use wheelchairs, push, clap, push, clap; or push and then tap hand rims—push, tap, push, tap. Ready. Go.

Cue: Step-hop, step-hop, step-clap, step-clap. [Say "hop" or "clap" depending on what helps the children put the two together.]

E Now try jogging about the space to the beat while clicking your fingers. Students who use wheelchairs, move about the space using strong pushes; while gliding, click fingers to the beat.

E Now, using any locomotor step you want and clapping or clicking (or using your instrument), travel about the space to the music. Explore different locomotor steps and different combinations of clapping and clicking. Students who use wheelchairs, work on moving in different ways and clicking and clapping—push, glide, clap, click; wheelie, push, clap, click; and so on.

Modified Version of the *Tarantella*

Part A

E Everyone face the front of the gym, and join with me. I will show you a modified version of the *Tarantella.* [Demonstrate while facing the group but reversing the left and right legs.] Start by stepping sideways to your left and kick your right leg. Then step right and kick with your left leg. Again and again. [Keep repeating until all children are doing this accurately.] Let's put on the music, and do it to the music.

E Now add a hop when you kick. [Keep repeating until all children are doing this accurately.]

E In the dance, you do two step-kicks, then four runs in place. Do this with me as I cue you through it four times. *Cue four times:* Step-kick, step-kick, run, run, run, run.

E Now add a clap on the kick, and click your fingers when you run. *Cue four times:* Step-clap, step-clap, click, click, click, click.

(*continues*)

SAMPLE LEARNING EXPERIENCES 33.4

Teaching a Modified *Tarantella* with Modifications for Children Using Wheelchairs (*continued*)

Modifications for Students Who Use Wheelchairs

E If you use a wheelchair, for the step-kick, step-kick, run, run, run, run:

Option A: Face front, turn left 45 degrees, face front, turn right 45 degrees, return forward, and click, click, click, click for the run. *Cue four times:* Turn, turn, click, click, click, click.

Option B: Students who can do wheelies can add a wheelie when they turn. Face front, turn left 45 degrees and do a wheelie, turn to the front (either staying in the wheelie or returning the front wheels to the floor), turn right 45 degrees and do a wheelie, turn to the front, and click, click, click, click. *Cue four times:* Turn, turn, click, click, click, click.

Part B

E The next section of the dance is to run forward four steps, then back four steps, clicking and reaching down as you go forward and then up as you go back. We do that four times.

Modifications for Students Who Use Wheelchairs

If you use a wheelchair, you have two options:

Option A: Push forward using small pushes for each count, then pull back using small pushes for each count—2, 3, 4.

Option B: One medium push forward, arms reaching up on 2, 3, 4, then one medium pull back, arms down 2, 3, 4.

Cue four times: Forward, 2, 3,4; back, 2, 3, 4.

Putting the Dance Together

E Let's put it all together. Ready, to the music. *Cue four times (alternating wheelchair cues)*:

- Step-kick, step-kick, run, run, run, run.
- Turn, turn, click, click, click, click.

Cue four times:

- Forward, 2, 3, 4; back, 2, 3, 4.
- Reach down, 2, 3, 4; reach up, 2, 3, 4.

Double Circle with Partners

E Now that you have parts A and B learned, we are going to change formations to a double circle. Starting here (pair up two children) and moving around the circle, partner up. One of you moves into the center about four steps, then turns and faces your partner. We will end up in a double circle. [The teacher should partner up with a child if there is an odd number of children and teach from the outside circle.]

E Let's repeat parts A and B but facing your partner.

MD Because both of you will start stepping on your left foot and kicking your right leg, will you be mirroring or matching your partner? Right, matching. That means it will look like you are moving in opposite directions.

E Ready. Go. [Repeat if necessary.]

Part C: Elbow Swings

Social You did such a great job with parts A and B, let's add part C elbow swings. You must be very careful not to pull your partner off balance.

E Move together, hook right elbows, walk in a circle around each other for eight steps, let go, and go back to your place. Now do the same thing again, but hook left elbows and count eight steps. For students who use wheelchairs, you can circle your partner without hooking elbows or you can hook elbows. If you hook elbows, the person using the wheelchair should hook with the right elbow and push with the left hand and then hook with the left elbow and push with the right hand. Let's try the entire dance to music. *Cue:* Elbow-swing right elbows. Elbow-swing left elbows.

Part D: Do-sa-do

E Part D is called a do-sa-do. Walk or roll toward your partner passing right shoulders, pass back to back, then move back to your original place passing left shoulders. Then we do the do-sa-do in reverse, starting by passing left shoulders. For students who use wheelchairs, the do-sa-do is the same.

Cue: Do-sa-do.

E Let's try the whole dance to music. [Cue the entire dance.]

SAMPLE LEARNING EXPERIENCES 33.5

Child-Designed Folk Dance Based on the *Tarantella*

You can teach these learning experiences either before or after teaching a modified *Tarantella.* Alternatively, it can stand alone.

Movement Theme

Meeting, parting, passing, and accompanying, using energetic locomotor steps.

Topic Theme

Folk dance based on the historical folk belief that if you are bitten by a tarantula spider, you can dance energetically to help rid the body of poison.

Potential Refinements

- Bouncy, light movements
- Heads high
- Be energetic

Introductory Warm-up Activity

I Listen to the music, and travel about general space doing different energetic steps. If you use a wheelchair, push and do energetic arm movements.

E Try some bouncy movements.

Content Development

Exploring Locomotor Steps in a Pattern

E Which movements have you done? Great, I heard tapping your wheel rims, tapping in the air, skipping, jumping, hopping, sliding, galloping, and jogging. Select two movements, and make a short sequence to a count of eight. If you want, add some kicks. For example, you might have a pattern of four kicks (hopping while you kick), four slides, four kicks, and four slides back to place. Once you have a pattern you like, repeat it over and over.

Adding a Musical Instrument

Use tambourines if possible, but have at least one instrument for every child. If some instruments are more interesting than others, set up a system of rotation.

E Around the room you will see bins with tambourines (or any instruments you have available, such as shakers, bells, rattles, small drums, or rain sticks). Pick up one, and then spread out into a scattered formation. To the beat of the music, explore different ways to make different sounds and to move your tambourine.

E Now, add traveling in different ways while making different sounds.

E Experiment with making different rhythmic patterns. Maybe you will tap the tambourine every other beat, or every fourth beat, or maybe you will tap the tambourine four times and then shake it for two beats. Once you find a pattern you like, repeat it over and over.

Meeting and Parting

E I will assign you a partner. Stand at least six feet away from your partner. Find different ways to meet and then part. Start by one of you teaching the other a pattern of locomotor steps you designed. Try meeting and parting using that pattern. Then the second partner teaches her or his pattern. Then experiment together and come up with several patterns for meeting and parting that are energetic and that both of you like.

E [If the children are having problems coming up with ideas, you can scaffold the exploration process.] If you are having problems thinking of ideas, you can try meeting and parting with your tambourines

- At different levels
- Using different body parts
- Using different rhythms
- Using different locomotor steps

E Now experiment with different ways to circle around each other.

E [If the children are having problems coming up with ideas, you can scaffold the exploration process.] You and your partner can turn in different ways; for example, you can do an elbow turn. Walk toward each other, hook left elbows, and walk around each other, being very careful not to pull your partner or swing him or her off balance. You can also circle around each other without touching. When I say, "Go," explore different ways you and your partner can circle and turn around each other, connecting with different body parts in different ways. Go.

(*continues*)

SAMPLE LEARNING EXPERIENCES 33.5

Child-Designed Folk Dance Based on the *Tarantella* (*continued*)

E Now explore different ways to travel in relationship to each other. What are the different kinds of relationships? Great answers: traveling side by side, one leading and the other following, facing each other and traveling first toward each other and then away, turning your backs to each other and traveling sideways. [You can have the children demonstrate, and then have the class try each suggestion or simply demonstrate each one, and then let the children explore on their own.]

Culminating Activity

Story

A Today, you are going to start designing your own dance in the spirit of the Italian *Tarantella*. Let me tell you the story about this dance. In Sicily, an island off the tip of the "boot" of Italy, people believed that if a tarantula spider bit them, they could dance vigorously to get the poison out of their systems. They would dance the *Tarantella* with such frenzy and for so long that they would drop from exhaustion. This is a very energetic dance and one of the most well-known dances of Italy. The *Tarantella* is a dance done by partners in sets of four. It involves meeting and parting in different ways with the dancers using tambourines.

E I am going to put two pairs together to form groups of four. Now in groups of four, design your own *Tarantella* dance using the ideas you have explored in the lesson so far. What are some of the different formations you can use?

- Circles (facing in and out, traveling in and out)
- Lines
- Double lines
- One pair leading and the other pair following
- Crossing through the middle and changing partners

What are some of the partner relationships and turns you can use?

- Side-by side
- Follow the leader
- Do-sa-do
- Star turns
- Hand turns

What are some locomotor and movement patterns you can use?

- Jumps
- Slides
- Skips
- Hops
- Leg kicks
- Turns
- Taps

Try to design a very energetic dance to represent the idea of the original dancers dancing so vigorously they would eliminate the poison from a tarantula bite.

R Once you have decided on your dance, practice it over and over until you can do it accurately. Make your dance very energetic. Keep your movements light and bouncy.

Ireland: Teaching Reel Dances, Step–Together–Step, and Polka

In this section, we describe the reel as a dance form and basic step–together–step and polka dance steps, which are common to many cultural dances. On the text website, we also include learning experiences for a child-designed folk dance lesson based on the effect of geography—in this case, islands—on culture.

Potential Information to Use for an Introduction to Irish Dance

An important part of the history of Ireland is the Potato Famine of 1845 to 1849. At that time, Ireland was crowded with approximately 8 million, mostly poor, landless people who worked for landlords in return for a small plot of land on which to grow food for their families. Most of the land had been confiscated by the English during previous invasions and wars; the English ruling class also attempted to suppress the Irish culture, language, and religion. The Irish people kept their language and culture alive through storytelling, songs, and dance.

A field of potatoes could feed a family while taking up less space and using poorer-quality soil than other crops. In the mid-1800s, however, a potato blight (a plant disease) struck across the island. Millions of Irish people died of starvation while millions of others emigrated, many to the United States.

The population continued to decline, due to poverty and political repression for about 70 years, to approximately 4 million people—half of what it was before the famine. During the famine, the English landowners exported food and raised cattle on farmable land to export meat back to England.

Reels and the Waves of Tory Folk Dance

The Waves of Tory is a folk dance from the island of Tory, located off the coast of Ireland. It is a Celtic reel. The Celts were ancient people who lived across what is now continental Europe and Ireland, Scotland, England, and Wales. **Reels** are folk dances done in longways sets—that is, six to eight couples arranged in parallel lines. Many different Celtic reels evolved, and, when Celtic people came to America, they brought these reels with them. The Virginia Reel is very similar to the Waves of Tory. In the Waves of Tory, however, the dancers do an enjoyable pattern called "the wave" that represents the rough seas and strong waves that crash onto the coast of the island (see **Figure 33.3**).

You can teach the Waves of Tory using any lively, Irish jig-type music. Irish music offers a wonderful opportunity for children to practice the step-together-step pattern that is the basis for many other patterns, such as the two-step, polka, *chassé*, and sashay.

Description of the Waves of Tory

Waves of Tory: Modified Version

Formation: Double line of partners. Partners number off 1, 2, 3, 4, 5, 6, 7, 8, and so on. Start with facing partners about six feet apart.

Part A

Summary: Travel to the partner and back out twice.

Counts	*Step–Together–Step*
1–4	Step–together–step, pause; [change leg] step–together–step, pause, moving forward to partner
5–8	Repeat (two step–together–step/pause sequences), moving backward to place
9–16	Repeat counts 1–8, moving toward and away from partner

Part B

Summary: Star turns

Counts	*Star Turns*
1–8	Walk four steps to partner, touch palms high, walk around partner, and take four steps back to place

Part C

Summary: The wave

Counts	*The Wave*
As many as needed	Odd-numbered partners (1, 3, 5, 7, and so on) turn to face the rear of the lines. Even-numbered partners (2, 4, 6, 8, and so on) face the front of the lines. All hold their partners' inside hand (or hold scarves). Even numbers hold hands up, and odd numbers walk under one couple; then odd numbers hold hands up, and even numbers walk under one couple. Partners continue walking under one pair's arms and then moving their arms over another pair. When a pair reaches the end, they turn and come back, following the same over-under pattern.

Part D

Counts	*Cast Off and Form an Arch*
As many as needed	Pair 1 casts off—let go of hands, both turn to outside, and walk or two-step down the outside of their lines, with the other dancers in each line following the leader. At the end of the set, pair 1 forms an arch with both hands held high; the rest of the couples join hands as they pass under the arch and walk back to place. Pair 2 is now the new head pair. The dance is repeated until all pairs have been head pair.

Description of the Virginia Reel

The Virginia Reel was derived from similar Celtic reels.

Formation: Longways set of six to eight pairs (traditionally done in male–female couples, but this is not necessary). Start facing partners.

Part A

Counts	*Five Times In and Back*
1–8	Four steps in, bow, four steps back to place
1–8	Right-hand star turn with partner, back to place
1–8	Left-hand star turn with partner, back to place
1–8	Hold both hands, turn with partner, back to place
1–8	Do-sa-do with partner

Part B

Counts	*Head Pair Sashays, Reels the Set*
1–16	Head pair sashays (slides) down the set and back to place
As many as needed	Head pair reels the set—hook right elbows and elbow-turn one and a half turns to end facing the opposite line; hook left elbows with the second person in the opposite line, and elbow-swing one turn. End facing the partner. Hook right

(*continues*)

Description of the Waves of Tory (*continued*)

	elbows, and elbow-swing partner one turn to the end, facing the third person. Continue swinging each person in the line, alternating with a swing of the partner. At the end of the set, sashay back to place.	
Part C		
Counts	*Cast Off and Form an Arch*	
As many as needed	Pair 1 casts off—split, both turn to outside, and walk or two-step down the outside of their lines, with the other dancers in each line following the leader. At the end of the set, pair 1 forms an arch with both hands held high, and the rest of the couples join hands as they pass under the arch and walk back to place. Pair 2 is now the new head pair. The dance is repeated until all pairs have had the chance to be head pair.	

SAMPLE LEARNING EXPERIENCES 33.6

Teaching Step–Together–Step and the Polka Step

Teaching Step–Together–Step and Polka

Music: Select Irish music to which you can gallop at a reasonable speed. Many Irish jigs work well.

Prerequisites: Galloping and sliding are prerequisite skills for learning the step–together–step and polka, which are simply variations of the gallop. Review dance lessons on teaching sliding and galloping.

Introductory Warm-up Activities

I Explore locomotor patterns to Irish music by traveling in general space, galloping and sliding to the music.

Content Development

Teaching Step–Together–Step and Polka

Org Today we are going to learn two dance steps based on galloping and sliding. Everyone stand on the side of the gym behind the cones (placed approximately 10 feet from the wall). Get in lines of three. We will use the wave pattern so you have room but get lots of practice.

E When I say wave 1, the first person in line slides across to the cones, then walks closer to the wall to make space for wave 2. I will call wave 2 when wave 1 has gone about three yards. I will call wave 3 when wave 2 has gone about three yards. Ultimately, all of you will be sliding at the same time, but your starts will be staggered. [Practice sliding across the gym in waves several times until the children work well with the formation. You also can have the children decide when to start by telling them they can begin when the person ahead of them is far enough away that they will not bump into them. The ultimate goal is for children to become self-responsible and make appropriate decisions about when to start on their own.]

E This time, slide across the space four times facing me. [Stand at the front of the gym.] You will be leading with your right leg. Then turn so you are facing the back of the gym and continue sliding across the space, leading with your left leg and sliding four times. Keep changing your lead leg after every four slides. [Repeat until the children have this skill mastered.]

E Now slide and change lead legs every two slides. [Repeat until children have this skill mastered.]

E Now slide and change lead legs every slide. [Repeat until children have this skill mastered.]

Cog K You have successfully learned what we call a step–together–step. Notice how you are naturally adding a little hop when you change lead legs. This is good because the hop is part of the polka step.

E Now, change to a gallop. This step–together–step–hop (changing lead legs) is the basic two-step and polka step.

E Now, try to polka (step–together–step, hop) traveling in general space.

Philippines: *Tinikling*

Potential Information to Use for an Introduction to *Tinikling*

Honored as a popular, traditional Philippine dance, *tinikling* began in the Visayan region islands and the Leyte province of the Philippines. This dance represents the movements of the *tikling*, graceful birds that run quickly over tree branches and tall grass stems. The birds also leap over bamboo traps set by rice farmers, who capture the birds for food and feathers (Tillman-Hall, 1969).

In *tinikling*, dancers jump and leap over two poles (traditionally bamboo). The poles are held at each end by pole beaters, who tap the poles together and apart in a rhythm. Dancers leap and jump over the poles using different locomotor steps and patterns. Jumping and leaping in and out of the poles without getting trapped makes *tinikling* a challenging, captivating dance, but one that children can learn in a few lessons. For this reason, *tinikling* has been a favorite folk dance in American physical education programs for many years.

Equipment

Traditionally, the poles used in *tinikling* are made from bamboo. However, we use 10- to 12-feet lengths of PVC pipe (one and half or two inches in diameter) because such pipe is cheap and readily available at home improvement stores. Elastic jump bands (long elastic bands worn around the ankles so the students at the ends jump the bands in a closed, closed, open, open pattern) can also be used and add an aerobic component for the beaters. We suggest purchasing two poles for each group of four dancers.

For beginners, it is also helpful to have two 24-inch-long 2×4 boards on which the pole beaters strike the poles. This setup prevents them from hitting their fingers on the ground. Although the beaters are supposed to hold the poles on the top, this positioning is difficult for beginners, and they tend to forget the instructions once the dancers start dancing. We color the outside (with markers or paint) for five inches on each side, designating where the pole beaters need to tap the poles when apart. We find this step is essential for beginners, who get excited and tend to separate the poles only about eight inches, making it difficult for the dancers to jump inside.

Music

Music is not necessary. If you use music, select music your children like (anything from rap, to rock, to pop, to country), or use ethnic music with a clear, steady beat that is comfortable for walking briskly, jogging, and hopping. If you search "tinikling" on the Internet, you can easily find videos of both Filipino dancers and collegiate international folk dancers who have designed *tinikling* dances for performances at their universities, often adding their own creative interpretations to *tinikling* using current popular music.

The *Tinikling* Rhythm

Traditionally, *tinikling* is done to a 3/4 rhythm, which means there are three beats to each measure and the dance pattern is repeated in sets of three. For example,

Beat 1: jump feet apart

Beat 2: jump feet together

Beat 3: jump feet together

In teaching children, we use music with a 4/4 rhythm, which makes the dance much easier to learn. To a 4/4 rhythm, you can teach either a four-beat action (two jumps with feet apart, two jumps with feet together) or a slower two-beat action (jump apart, jump together). **Table 33.1** outlines the pole actions for 3/4 and 4/4 rhythms with a simple jump step.

Table 33.1 Tinikling Pole Actions

Most Difficult: Traditional 3/4 Rhythm						
Counts	**1**	**2**	**3**	**1**	**2**	**3**
Poles	Closed	Open	Open	Closed	Open	Open
Jump feet	Apart	Together	Together	Apart	Together	Together
Feet	Outside poles	Inside poles	Inside poles	Outside poles	Inside poles	Inside poles
Easier: 4/4 Rhythm						
Counts		**1**	**2**	**3**	**4**	
Poles		Closed	Closed	Open	Open	
Jump feet		Apart	Apart	Together	Together	
Feet		Outside poles	Outside poles	Inside poles	Inside poles	
Easiest: 4/4 Rhythm						
Counts		**1**	**and**	**2**	**And**	
Poles		Closed	Pause	Open	Pause	
Jump feet		Apart		Together		
Feet		Outside poles		Inside poles		

SAMPLE LEARNING EXPERIENCES 33.7

Teaching *Tinikling*

Introductory Warm-up Activity and Topic Introduction

Org Face your assigned partner. One of you do a simple hopping, jogging, or jumping pattern with two locomotor steps. For example, jump feet apart, jump feet together, apart, together; or, two hops on left foot, two hops on right foot; or four jogs, four jumps. [Demonstrate as you explain.] Keep it simple. Your partner will mirror your movements. Repeat your pattern until I say, "New leader"; then the other partner will be the leader. I will keep the music on, so quickly start your pattern. Each time I say, "Newleader," try to design a new pattern.

I [Discuss the background information on *tinikling*—specifically its representation of the movement of the *tikling* bird.]

Outline of Major Tasks for Content Development

Exploring Using the Equipment

I I will put you in groups of four. Walk over to the sides of the gym and two of you pick up two poles, holding the poles at the ends. The other two pick up one 2×4 each. The four of you set up the poles 15 inches apart flat on the ground; place a 2×4 at each end, touching the poles. We will not use the 2×4 boards yet. [Demonstrate the setup with one group. Alternatively, you can tape lines on the floor 15 inches apart, or have each child set up two spots (to represent being outside the poles) on either side of a carpet square (representing being inside the poles).] Explore different combinations of hopping, jumping, and jogging to the music on your own over and in and out of the stationary poles (or spots and carpet squares), traveling inside and outside the stationary poles.

E Design a pattern of hops, jumps, and jogs that takes you inside and outside the stationary poles.

Learning the Three Basic Step Patterns

E Now we will be learning the three basic steps of a dance called the *tinikling.*

E The first step is jumping. We will practice each step with the stationary poles first. Then after learning the three steps, we will try it with moving poles.

Jumping feet apart

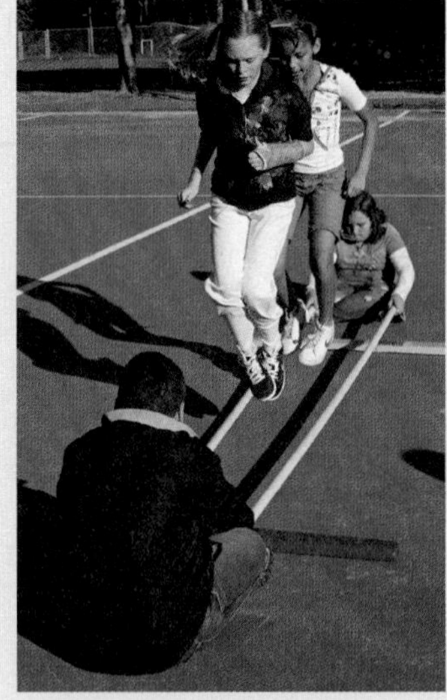

Jumping feet together

Jump	*Apart, Apart, Together, Together*
1	Jump both feet outside poles [poles closed]
2	Jump both feet outside poles [poles closed]
3	Jump both feet inside poles [poles open]
4	Jump both feet inside poles [poles open]

Cue: Apart, apart, together, together.

SAMPLE LEARNING EXPERIENCES 33.7

Teaching *Tinikling* (continued)

Hop outside of poles

Hop inside of poles

Hop	*Start Standing to the Right of the Poles*
1	Hop on right foot outside poles [poles closed]
2	Hop on right foot outside poles [poles closed]
3	Leap on left foot inside poles [poles open]
4	Hop on left foot inside poles [poles open]

Turn and face the other end, and try it again, starting by hopping on the left foot.

Cue: Outside, outside, inside, inside.

Leap	*Start Standing to the Right of the Poles*
1	Hop on right foot outside poles [poles closed]
2	Hop on right foot outside poles [poles closed]
3	Leap on left foot inside poles [poles open]
4	Leap on right foot inside poles [poles open]
5	Leap on left foot to the left of poles [poles closed]
6.	Hop on left foot outside poles [poles closed]
7	Leap on right foot inside poles [poles open]
8	Leap on left foot inside poles [poles closed]

Cue: Hop, hop, leap, leap, hop, hop, leap, leap.

R As you become more confident, try to make smaller jumps, hops, and leaps. If you take really big jumps, you will have a harder time changing direction and moving into the next pattern.

Typical Beginner Patterns: Beating *Tinikling* Poles

When beginners first learn to beat the poles, they tend to do the following:

- Lift the poles much too high. This makes it difficult for the dancers to jump and leap over the poles. Telling the children to keep the poles low and slide the poles out and in helps.
- Separate the poles only about 10 inches. This makes it difficult for the dancers to dance inside of the poles. Painting the ends of each 2×4 and telling the children that they must reach the painted areas at the ends of the 2×4 helps.
- Grab the poles too tight and hold their hands under the poles. This can cause an injury if the dancers step on the poles. The pole beaters need to hold the poles from the top; then, if the dancer steps on the pole, it will slide out of their hands.

Learning to Beat the Poles

E Now that you have learned the steps, you need to learn how to beat the poles to the beat of the music in the appropriate pattern. First, hold the poles from the top. If your fingers get caught underneath the poles, you can smash your fingers. Second, tap the poles twice together in the middle of the 2×4 and then slide the poles out, keeping the poles low so the dancers can easily jump over the poles; tap the poles twice on the painted part of the 2×4. You must keep a steady beat to the music.

(*continues*)

SAMPLE LEARNING EXPERIENCES 33.7

Teaching *Tinikling* (*continued*)

E Let's start by all practicing on the floor (without poles) to the beat of the music. Just tap the floor lightly. Listen carefully to the music, and be exactly on the beat. *Cue:* Closed, closed, open, open.

E Now two of you try it with the poles while your partners coach you.

R Keep poles low.

R Hit the paint.

Putting the Poles and Steps Together

E Now you are ready for a new challenge. Two of you beat the poles, and the other two practice the three basic steps. Partners, coach each other. Cue each other on the actions, and help your partners. [This phase of the unit will take a considerable amount of time—often more than one lesson.]

Designing Your Own Patterns

E You are doing the basic patterns perfectly. Now I want you and your partner to design a sequence, adding half-turns. Sometimes mirror each other, sometimes match each other. Sometimes move in the same sideways direction, sometimes move in opposite directions. You also can trade places and add low kicks. Start designing the sequence over stationary poles or on the ground so all four of you can work at the same time. Then practice your sequence using the poles. Rotate being dancers and pole beaters fairly. [This phase of the unit may take several lessons.]

More Advanced Choreography Possibilities for Experienced Learners

E You have been doing *tinikling* for several years. This year I want you to choreograph a four-person sequence with two sets of poles. Two groups of four will work near each other and will be pole beaters for each other. We will divide the time equally so each group of four has the same time to practice its dance. Here are some possible variations.

Pole Formations

- Four poles in a row
- Two poles crossed over the other two in a tic-tac-toe formation so dancers can travel in a circle around the poles
- Have the pole beaters move to a new formation while the dance continues

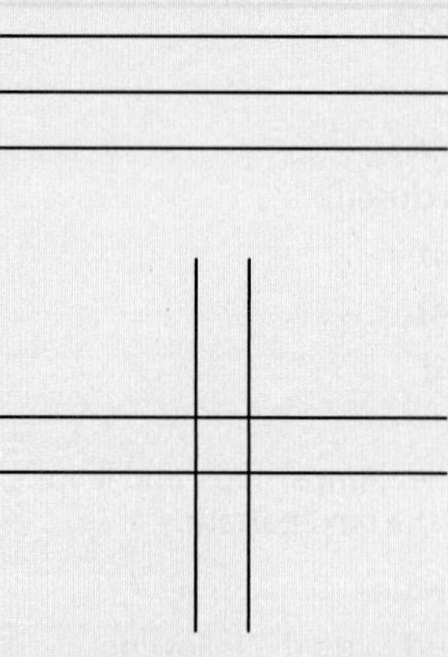

Pole formations for *tinikling*

E You can also vary the relationships within your dance—for example, using canon and unison, follow the leader, mirroring and matching, and changing places. You also can add kicks, claps, turns, and gestures.

Native American Traditional Intertribal Dance

The Importance of Native American Dance

Folk dance has traditionally included only Western European folk dances, square dance, and, more recently, line dancing. We think it is critical for children also to learn about the indigenous dances of North America.

The study of Native American culture is required in most North American elementary schools. Consequently, Native American dance is the dance form most easily integrated with classroom lessons. Working with classroom teachers, you can provide a rich learning experience for the children. You also can use this opportunity to counteract stereotypes of Native Americans.

Figure 33.5 The aerobic value of Native American dance
Courtesy of John Dolly

Potential Information to Teach About Pow-wows

As in the past, pow-wows are part of Native American culture today. "A pow-wow is an event where American Indians of all nations come together to celebrate their culture through the medium of music and dance" (Browner, 2002, p. 1). In Canada and the United States, people can attend a pow-wow within a three-hour drive of all populated areas (Browner, 2002).

Native American tribes also hold tribal and intertribal dances that are closed to the public and may include dances that are spiritual and religious in nature (L. Taylor, personal communication, January 23, 2006). In addition, Native Americans hold many traditional tribal and traditional intertribal pow-wows that are open to the public.

Pow-wow dance competitions are plentiful, and some dancers make a living from competitive dancing (Browner, 2002). In these competitions, Fancy Dancers dance free form (designing their own dance sequence) in full regalia and are judged on originality, skill, and regalia. Women's competitions may include jingle dancing, shawl dancing, and traditional dancing, while men's competition may include grass dancing. You can see video clips of national competitions at http://www.powwows.com (and other Internet sites). This website also describes pow-wows, explains the pow-wow structure and drum and dance competitions, and describes the regalia. You can download video clips of dances as well.

In this text, we focus on traditional intertribal dance steps, free-style dancing, child-designed dances using the traditional steps, and a few traditional intertribal and tribal dances. These are recreational and historical but not religious dances.

The Aerobic Exercise Value of Native American Dance

Native American intertribal dance steps can provide an excellent aerobic workout for children (see **Figure 33.5**). We organize the dance steps into three difficulty levels. Steps in levels 2 and 3 are often highly energetic (continual hopping and jumping) and easily learned in grades 3 through 5. When children design or practice free-style dancing, in which they perform the steps they select in any order they choose, this can contribute to a fine aerobic workout.

For interval training, we have half the children sitting in a circle keeping the beat with shakers and the other half performing free style in the center, with roles rotating every 30 seconds. As children's fitness improves, the shakers can remain standing doing a simple, level 1 step as they keep the beat for their classmates. Alternatively, teachers may divide the class into three groups, with one group keeping the beat while the other two dance.

Music

In traditional (i.e., open to the public) intertribal pow-wows, Native American dancers perform with "drums." "Drums" in this sense means a group of singers and drummers. Teachers can purchase Native American drum music off the Internet. Alternatively, you can have children simply keep a beat with hand drums, homemade shakers, and bells. Teachers can purchase ankle bells, which are like sleigh bells (about one and one-quarter inches diameter) attached to a leather strap tied to the ankle with leather ties. We made low-cost ankle bells by stringing jingle bells on elastic that children can pull over their shoes and wear on their ankles. The bells helped children move to the beat of the drum and shakers.

How to Make Low-Cost Shakers and Ankle Bells

Shakers

1. Collect water bottles with caps (pure water only; no soft drinks or any drink that requires you to wash the bottle). We collected more than 100 in three days by emailing teachers and posting a sign over garbage bags in the hall.
2. Take off the caps, and let the bottles air dry (this can take several days).
3. Put one inch of pea gravel in each bottle. Tighten the cap.
4. Optional: Duct-tape the cap closed.

Ankle Bells

1. Purchase low-cost, small jingle bells (about four per child) and quarter-inch elastic.
2. Measure a length of elastic that, when tied, can be slipped over your shoe.
3. Cut one length of elastic for each child.
4. Pinch the end of an elastic in half lengthwise so it is about one-eighth of an inch wide; push this end through the top of the bell. String three more bells on, and then tie the elastic in a double knot.

Descriptions of Traditional Intertribal Dance Steps

The basic dance steps described in this section are used today—and were used historically—by many Native American tribes. As a consequence, these steps are called traditional intertribal dance steps. We thank Leon Taylor of the Choctaw Tribe for his help with several of these steps and dances. The other steps we learned in childhood, found in historical books, learned by studying dancing on the website http://www.powwows.com, and learned by attending local pow-wows.

Style

- *Soft knees:* Bend the knees slightly as the heel or foot lands or stomps.
- *Body bounces:* The whole body bounces up and down with soft knees. The movement is fluid and relaxed.
- *Short steps/up-and-down movements:* Steps are typically short, with the feet remaining under the body. Many steps are done in place. The movement is predominantly up and down.

Definition of Terms

- *Toe:* Step on the ball of the foot.
- *Stomp:* A sharp (light to moderately forceful) drop of the heel or a sharp step on a flat foot, done by bending the knees and dropping the entire body. This downward body action is part of the up-and-down bounce done throughout many steps.
- *Trot:* Jog with an up-and-down bouncing action.

Level 1 Basic Steps

Step–Together–Step–Together Moving Sideways

- Use small steps that cover very little distance (less than 12 inches).
- Step to the right on the right foot.
- Close left (left foot lands next to right foot) with a stomp on a flat left foot, bending the knee and letting the body drop. Pick up the right leg at the same time. The force of the stomp is moderate, not strong.

Variation: When stomping on the left (bending the knee), pick up the bent right knee high in front to about thigh level. Can also move forward.

Toe–Heel

- Step on the right toe (ball of foot).
- Stomp the right heel.
- Step on the left toe.
- Stomp the left heel.

Performance Cues

- Toe, heel, toe, heel
- Bounce, bounce, bounce, bounce
- Short steps, soft knees

Teaching Progression

1. Teach the toe–heel step without bounces.
2. Add one bounce (drop down) when the heel stomps.
3. Add one bounce when the toe steps and one bounce when the heel stomps.

Canoe Step

- Beat 1: Tap right toe.
- Beat 2: Slide right foot forward, and stomp right heel.
- Beat 3: Tap left toe.
- Beat 4: Slide left foot forward, and stomp left heel.

Cue: Tap, step, tap, step.

Teaching Progression

Teach the tap-step, leaving out the slide.

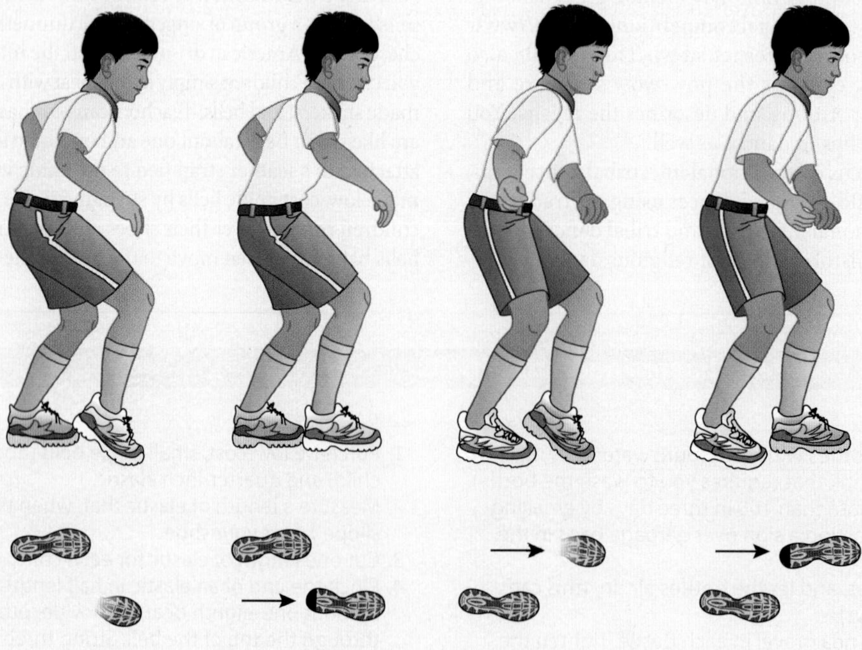

Canoe step

Descriptions of Traditional Intertribal Dance Steps (*continued*)

Level 2: Flat-Foot Steps

The following steps are all done with a flat-footed landing, in which the entire foot lands at the same time. The ankles are continuously flexed.

Trot

Jog landing on a *flat foot*:

- Very short steps (the front toe is no farther than five inches ahead of the back toe)
- Soft knees
- Bounce whole body up and down
- Movement is relaxed and fluid

This is a difficult step for children because their natural energy and enthusiasm quickly leads to jogging with normal-length steps without a flat-footed landing. That is why we categorize the trot as level 2.

2-1-2-1 (Double Flat-Foot)

From two feet, spring forward and land on one foot (left). Spring forward and land on two feet. Spring forward and land on one foot (right). Continue 2-1-2-1.

Style

The height of the spring forward is very low; landings are flat-footed with soft knees. The distance traveled is short. The movement is bouncing and relaxed.

Step–Hop (Even Rhythm)

Step right, hop on right foot, step left, hop on left foot.

Pawing Step

This step resembles the pawing foot movement of horses and buffalos. It is done on either the right or left leg, and the same foot does the pawing each time.

- Beat 1: Hop on the left foot (with the right knee up).
- Beat 2: Make a pawing movement with the right leg by stretching the right leg forward, circling the foot to the floor, brushing the right foot back along the floor to the left foot, and then lifting the right knee again.

Level 3 (Most Energetic)

Level 3 steps can give children a great aerobic workout. You can see these steps and more advanced variations in modern-day pow-wows. Pow-wow competitive dancing is free form—that is, there are neither choreographed dances nor particular steps that must be done in a prescribed order. Once children have learned the steps described in this section, they can add their own variations and practice free-form dancing.

Three Hops and Stomp (Four Beats)

- Hop three times on the left foot (traveling forward), and stomp on the right foot, shuffling the right foot back to land on the same location as the last hop.
- Hop three times on the right foot (traveling forward), and stomp on the left foot, shuffling the left foot back to land on the same location as the last hop.
- During the hops, the free-leg knee is bent and circles from back, high to the side, then to the front, and then slides in to replace the supporting leg.

Three Hops with Pivot and Stomp (Pivot in Either Direction)

- To add the pivot, turn left while hopping on the right foot, or turn right while hopping on the left foot.
- Alternatively, do the reverse: Turn right while hopping on the right foot, or turn left while hopping on the left foot.
- While hopping, circle the free leg with knee bent from front to side to back, or do the reverse, from back to side to front.

Three Hops with Taps (Four Beats)

- Beats 1, 2, 3: Hop three times on the left foot while at the same time tapping the right foot three times (back, side, forward).
- Beat 4: Stomp on the right foot, sliding it onto the same location as and replacing the left foot.
- Repeat on the right side.

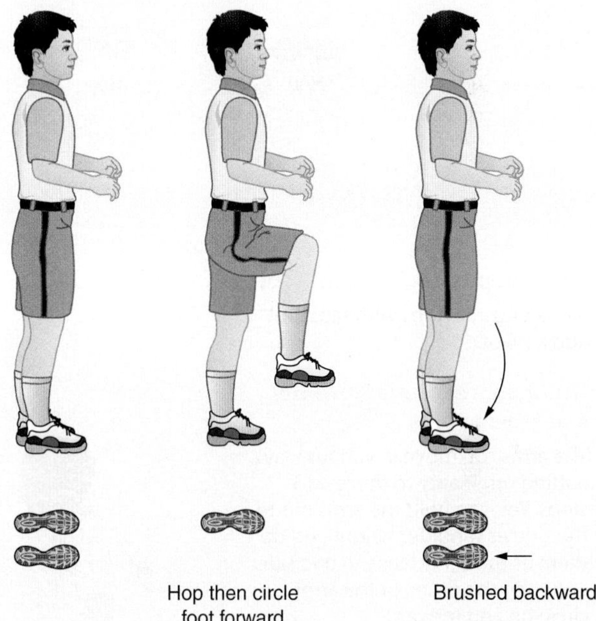

Pawing step

Children practicing level 3 steps

Courtesy of John Dolly

(*continues*)

Descriptions of Traditional Intertribal Dance Steps (*continued*)

Three hops and stomp

Three Hops with Tap and Pivot

Same as three hops with taps, but add a pivot.

Arm Actions for All Three Hop and Stomp Steps

The arms can move in various ways, adding originality to the level 3 steps. You can hold the arms out to the side at shoulder height and tip them as the body leans to one side and then the other, or the arms can circle up and forward.

Shuffle Steps

The heel shuffle and toe shuffle are more challenging for children to learn than the three hop steps. We encourage you to persevere in teaching the shuffle steps because they form the basis for the other "fancy dance" steps and are fun to do.

With these steps, the last step on the three hop steps is a shuffle step. Children typically perform the three hop steps without the shuffle (which makes the steps easier) until they have mastered the heel and toe shuffle.

Heel shuffle

Descriptions of Traditional Intertribal Dance Steps (*continued*)

Heel Shuffle

- Hop on the left foot, while at the same time tapping the right heel on the ground in front.
- Spring up and slide the right foot back to replace the left foot, landing on the right foot (this is the "shuffle").
- Hop on the right foot and tap the left heel in front.
- Spring up and slide the left foot back to replace the right foot.

Children learning the progression for the heel shuffle

Courtesy of John Dolly

Progressions

Two different progressions can help children learn this step. The first progression is described under "Heel Shuffle" and the second progression is described under "Toe Shuffle."

Progression: Hops and Heel Taps in Eights, Fours, and Twos (Leaving Out the Slide)

- Eights: Hop eight times on the left foot, tapping the right heel on the floor (bringing the right heel back near the left leg between each tap), and then change legs. Remain in place. Eight hops on the right foot while tapping the left heel; change. Eight hops on the left foot while tapping the right heel; change. *Cue:* 1, 2, 3, 4, 5, 6, 7, change. Repeat until children can perform eights smoothly.
- Fours: Four hops on the left foot while tapping the right heel; change. Four hops on the right foot while tapping the left heel; change. *Cue:* 1, 2, 3, change. Repeat until children can perform fours smoothly.
- Twos: Two hops on the left foot while tapping the right heel; change. Two hops on the right foot while tapping the left heel; change.
- Ones: Change after every heel tap. This is the heel shuffle step.

Toe Shuffle

This is the same as the heel shuffle, but the toe taps in front rather than the heel. It is an important step to learn, as it forms the basis for the more advanced steps discussed later.

Progression: Leaving Out the Hop

- Stand on the left foot and tap the right toe in front.
- Slide the right toe back and then spring up so the right foot replaces the left foot.
- Tap the left toe in front.
- Slide the left toe back and then spring up so the left foot replaces the right foot.
- Slowly increase the speed and amount of height on the spring from one foot to the other.

Crossover

(*continues*)

Descriptions of Traditional Intertribal Dance Steps (*continued*)

Crossover

This is like the three hops with tap and stomp patterns but with a crossover on tap 2.

- Beat 1: Hop on the left foot; tap the right toe to the right side of the body.
- Beat 2: Hop on the left foot; cross over and tap the right toe on the left side of the body.
- Beat 3: Hop on the left foot; tap the right toe extended far forward in front of the body.
- Beat 4: Spring forward, sliding the right foot slightly back; land on the flat right foot, bending forward at the hips.
- Repeat hopping on the right foot.

Children learning the crossover

Courtesy of John Dolly

SAMPLE LEARNING EXPERIENCES 33.8

Overview of Unit for Teaching Native American Free-Style Dancing

In free-style dancing, children select their own dance steps and continue dancing for the length of the song, changing steps frequently whenever they choose. The goal is to demonstrate their skills and endurance in dancing. To teach free-style dancing, we do the following.

Content Development

I [Each day, teach several dance steps, breaking them down using the progressions given previously.]

Culminating Activity

Org [Write the dance steps the children have learned on a whiteboard. Each day, add new steps.]

E As I beat a drum, practice the dance steps you learned. [If you do not observe children practicing a variety of steps, you can call out the steps they have learned until the children remember the steps.]

A Select which steps you want to include in your free-style dance. You decide which steps to do and when to change steps. You can plan the order of a sequence of steps if you want, but that is not necessary.

R Practice your free-style dancing, adding new steps you have learned.

A Now that you have mastered some of the more energetic (level 3) steps, we are going to rotate dancing inside the circle and standing in the circle while keeping the beat by shaking your shakers. Because these dance steps are energetic, they get your heart beating faster, and you are building cardiorespiratory endurance. When you work very hard for 30 seconds and then rest for 30 seconds, we call this interval training. Group A will be dancers first, and group B will be shakers. Then we will switch. Practice the three-hop steps, shuffle steps, 2-1s, step-hops, and pawing steps.

R Take short, low steps and hops.

Children rotating, showing their free-style dances and shaking their shakers

Courtesy of John Dolly

Planning a Pow-wow

Because Native American dance is an excellent unit to integrate with content taught by classroom teachers, you can plan a celebratory pow-wow at the end of this unit. **Table 33.2** provides an overview of the physical education portion of the unit, which ends with the "Song Within My Heart" pow-wow. During the pow-wow, the children perform their free-style dance, an individual child-designed dance representing an animal, and a group child-designed dance. Sample lesson segments for the child-designed dances are outlined here or on the text website.

Before the pow-wow, each group selects an animal to represent its tribe and then makes a tribal flag, which is placed at the entry to the arena.

Ask the classroom teacher to teach the following book or teach it yourself: "The Song Within My Heart" (Bouchard & Sapp, 2002). In this book, a Native American boy learns about pow-wows as times to celebrate the song within one's heart that expresses what one wants to contribute to the world (Rovegno & Gregg, 2007). Potential poetry selections include, "Dry and Parched," "I go forth to move about the earth," and "Celebration" (Lopez, 1972).

Following is the pow-wow program.

"The Song Within My Heart" Pow-wow

1. Grand entry into the arena from the east (class marches in using the toe–heel step, ankle bells, and shakers).
2. Cherokee snake dance (using shakers and ankle bells; the teacher accompanies the dance on the drum). In the snake dance, the class is in one line with their hand on the shoulder of the child in front of her or him. Using a canoe step or step–together–step, the leader leads the line on a spiral pathway until the group is in a tight spiral. Then the leader reverses and spirals out. See the illustration of the spiral pathway in and then out located in this chapter in the box "Fundamental Locomotor Folk Steps, Formations, and Pathways."
3. Free-style dance demonstration: Group A dances; group B beats the rhythm with shakers.
4. Free-style dance demonstration: Group B dances; group A beats the rhythm with shakers.
5. Demonstration of individual child-designed dances representing a Southeast forest or river animal.
6. Demonstration of group child-designed dances representing a Native American food source and housing linked to the geography of where the tribe lived.
7. Friendship dance: All parents, guests, and students do a round dance in a single circle moving sideways using a step–together–step footwork pattern. If desired, they can hold hands.
8. Hope Ceremony: Write the title or main idea from your reflection paper based on the book *The Song Within My Heart* (Bouchard & Sapp, 2002) on a small piece of paper. Tear the paper and bury it in a school garden to become part of the soil. Celebrate with a feast of cornbread and blackberry jam.

Child-Designed Folk Dances on Native American Themes

Here we describe one child-designed folk dance unit representing aspects of Native American culture, focusing on food and clothing sources for one tribe living in historical times to match tribes representative of those children typically study in their classroom. You can easily modify this unit to represent other tribes. Other child-designed folk dance units can be found on the text website.

Table 33.2 Suggested Native American Dance Unit Leading to a Pow-wow

For all lessons, use homemade shakers or rattles for each child and ankle bells.

Day 1	Steps: step–together–step, toe heel, canoe step. Dances: Snake dance (on text website), round dance in a circle moving sideways using a step–together–step footwork pattern, first with teacher beating a drum and, if time permits, with children beating the rhythm using their shakers.
Days 2–3	Steps: Review steps. Teach trot, 2-1-2-1, step-hop, three hops and stomp, three hops and tap, and add pivots. Dance: Have children design their own free-style dance sequences.
Day 3	Steps: Review steps. Teach pawing step. Dance: Practice free-style dancing. Child-Designed Folk Dance: Begin the lesson on the individual child-designed folk dances representing Southeast forest and river animals.
Days 4–6	Steps: Review steps. Teach heel shuffle. Dance: Practice free-style dancing, increasing the time for this activity each day. Child-Designed Folk Dance: Continue the Southeast forest and river animal dances.
Days 7–10	Dance: Practice free-style dancing. Child-Designed Folk Dance: Teach one of the lessons on group child-designed folk dance representing housing or food sources for one or two tribes (see text website).
Days 11–13	Plan and Practice Pow-wow: Either integrating the physical education with the classroom teacher's content or on your own, read *The Song Within My Heart* by Bouchard and Sapp (2002) with the children, and assign them to write a reflection paper on the song within their heart, describing what they would like to do when they grow up.
Day 14	Pow-wow: Parents, teachers, and principals invited.

SAMPLE LEARNING EXPERIENCES 33.10

Child-Designed Folk Dance Lesson Based on Hawai`i (*continued*)

The Hog Dance

(Barrère et al., 1980, p. 83)
The hairless pig up on Haupu
Announces the calm, hu! hu! hu!
The bristling pig on Kalanipu
Announces a storm, u! u! u!
They drink the water of Kemamo
Kipu is but a small hill, uhu! uhu! uhu!
At Mahaulepu are my conch shells,
I shake my hips!

Introduction of Topic or Story

Cog K Begin the lesson by asking children what they know about Hawai`i and about the hula. Then present relevant information from the background information section about Hawai`i and the hula. You also can show the children authentic hula dances on the Internet. The ancient hula-style dancing with chanting and rattles/drums is both informative and shows both men and women dancing the hula, rather than the more overtly sexual hula sometimes portrayed in the media.

Content Development

Teaching Selected Locomotor Steps

I [Teach the children a few hula steps using a rattle/drum or Hawaiian music as an accompaniment.]

I [Teach the children a few authentic hula gestures.]

E Now that you have seen the video and learned a few hula steps and gestures, go with your assigned partner, and invent two different gestures with two different hula steps.

Culminating Activity: Designing the Folk Dance

Brainstorm Ideas Based on the Topic or Story to Represent in the Dance

A Now design a folk dance representing aspects of Hawaiian culture. Start by brainstorming ideas. You can select stories, events, customs, recreational activities such as surfing and swimming, food and food production, land forms such as volcanoes and waterfalls, or any aspect of Hawaiian culture that you like. [Alternatively, you can give each group a Hawaiian chant and a rattle/drum and have the children represent the chant in their dance.]

Explore Different Gestures and Actions to Represent Ideas in the Dance

E Select several ideas, and explore different gestures and locomotor steps for each idea. Try to come up with several movements for each idea. Include at least one turn.

Select Ideas for Each Part of the Dance, and Add Formations, Pathways, and Partner Relationships

E Now, select your best ideas, and put them together in a sequence. Decide how many times you will repeat each locomotor step and gesture. Decide on your formations. Decide when you will travel and when you will dance in place. Decide on the number of turns and the direction in which you will turn. Plan your transitions from one formation or dance step to the next.

R Refine and practice your dance. Work on moving at the same time and matching your partner precisely. Practice until you can repeat the dance doing the exact same movements each time.

Assessment and Showing Dances

Korea, Japan, and China: Child-Designed Folk Dances with Props

In this section, we outline learning experiences for child-designed folk dances based on current artistic Asian folk dances, focusing primarily on Korean dancing. Starting in the early 1900s, folk dancers began to take traditional folk dance movements, modify them, and choreograph new artistic dances for stage productions (Malborg, 2005). Today, traditional folk dances are performed recreationally across Asian countries and also form the basis for artistic folk dance performances by dancers ranging from school children and university students to professional dance troupes. Although many of these dances had religious origins, the artistic and recreational goals predominate now.

We divide dance forms into two groups. Group 1 includes dances that use props—that is, the Korean sword dance, tambour dance, scarf dance, and Chinese ribbon dance. Group 2 consists of a martial arts dance. You can see performances of all these dances on Internet video sites.

Dances with Props

Swords

Traditionally, only women performed Korean sword dances; today, however, both men and women may perform these dances. Some sword dancers use long swords, whereas others use short swords. You can use short, cardboard swords painted silver, foam wands, or plastic wands. Dancers swing the swords in many patterns, such as circles and figures 8s, while turning, traveling, and making different formations.

Tambours

In the tambour dance, dancers hold a tambour with a wooden handle in one hand and a drumstick in the other. You can use any kind of hand drum. A drumstick is not necessary. Similar to sword dance movements, the dancers swing the tambour while hopping, traveling, and creating different formations, beating the tambour for accents.

Scarves

Scarf dancers use one or two long, light, flowing scarves about two yards long and half a yard wide. The epitome of Korean folk dance is the monk dance, in which the dancers wear a tunic with very long, light, flowing sleeves (about three yards long) (Malborg, 2005). Chinese and Japanese scarf dancers use light scarves about the size of a large handkerchief. Chinese ribbon dancers hold a very long, light ribbon about five inches wide and two to three yards long. You can substitute any scarf or long ribbon equipment for these dances. In these dances, the flowing movement of the scarves accentuates the traveling and turning movements and formations of the dancers, creating interesting patterns in the air.

Arm Actions with Props

Figures 33.6 through **33.13** depict the arm actions that are basic to all dances with props. There are two ways you can teach these actions. If your children have some experience with creative dance, you can readily elicit ideas for how they might move the prop. With less experienced beginners, you can show them the movements or make up and teach the children a simple sequence of movements to the first verse of the music. Then have the children design their own dance for the remainder of the song. We provide one example of a simple dance you can teach in **Sample Learning Experiences 33.11**.

Basic Steps and Style

Korean folk dances use the following basic steps:

- Step–together–step (or slides)
- Skips
- Light jogging steps
- Hops
- Multiple turns on two feet

The style incorporates continuous, flowing movements.

The beauty and excitement of Korean group folk dance derive from the many changes in formations done by the dancers as they use the props. For children, these formations can include the following options:

- Circles facing in and out
- Traveling around a circle
- Traveling in lines and double lines
- Lines passing and merging

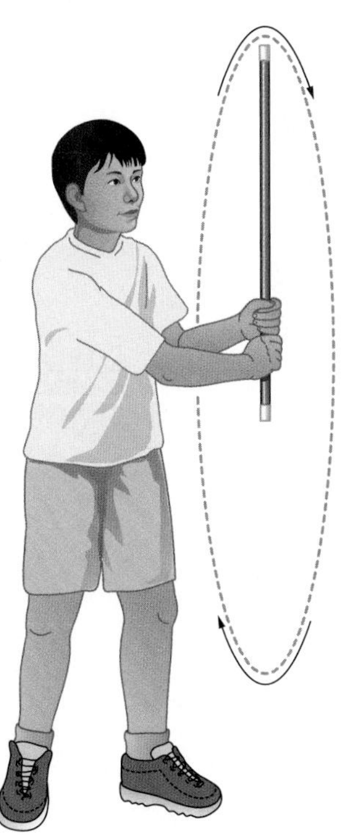

Figure 33.6 Side circles with sword held in two hands

Figure 33.7 Front circles with two scarves

Figure 33.8 Helicopters with a long ribbon

Figure 33.10 Front and back circles with long ribbon

Figure 33.9 Figure 8s with sword held in two hands

Figure 33.11 Hurricanes with large scarf

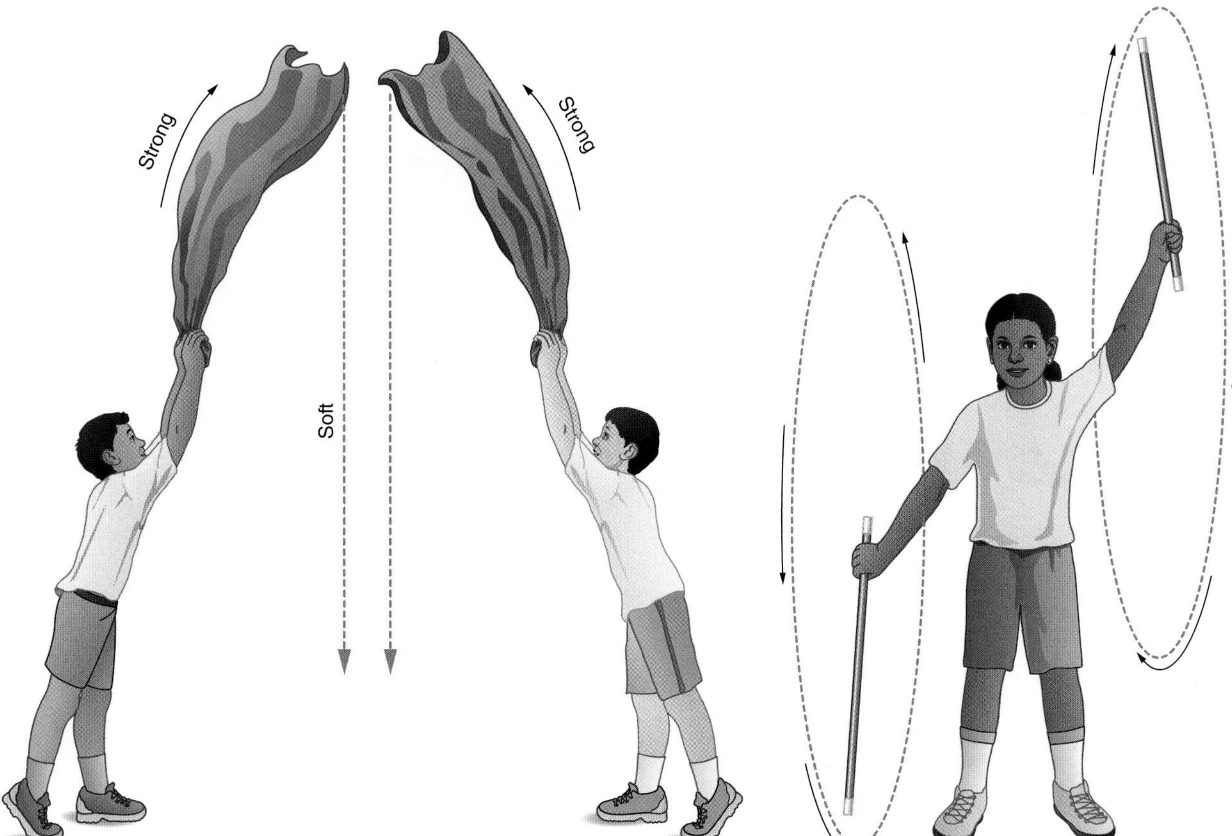

Figure 33.12 Slash up, float down with 2 dancers and large scarves

Figure 33.13 Swimming with two swords

SAMPLE LEARNING EXPERIENCES 33.11

Child-Designed Korean Scarf Dance

Movement Theme

Dancing with scarves, making different patterns in different formations.

Topic Theme

Korean scarf dancing

Introductory Activity

I Today we will be designing a Korean scarf dance or monk dance. [Show a video clip of one of these dances downloaded from the Internet.] If you decide to design a scarf dance, you will use one scarf. If you design a monk dance, you will use two scarves, representing the very long sleeves of the tunics worn by monks for dancing. Your aim is to move continuously while producing interesting patterns with your scarves. I will put on the music. Travel in general space using step–together–step, slides, skips, hops, and jogging, exploring different ways to move your scarf.

Content Development

Short Teacher-Designed Sequence to Illustrate Combining Scarf and Locomotor Movements

E Face me, and I will show you a short sequence of movements you can do.

1. Step–together–step-hop to your left; then repeat moving to your right: step–together–step-hop. [Repeat until the children have this sequence mastered.]
2. Now let's add the scarf action. Hold your scarf out to your right. As you step–together–step moving left, circle your scarf in front of your body down, all the way around, and then end up on the left as you hop. [Repeat until the children have this mastered.] (See **Figure 33.14**.)
3. The next movement is a turn while holding the scarf out at waist height. This is called a hurricane. Let's turn four times, with each turn taking four beats. Reverse direction each time (see **Figure 33.11**).

(*continues*)

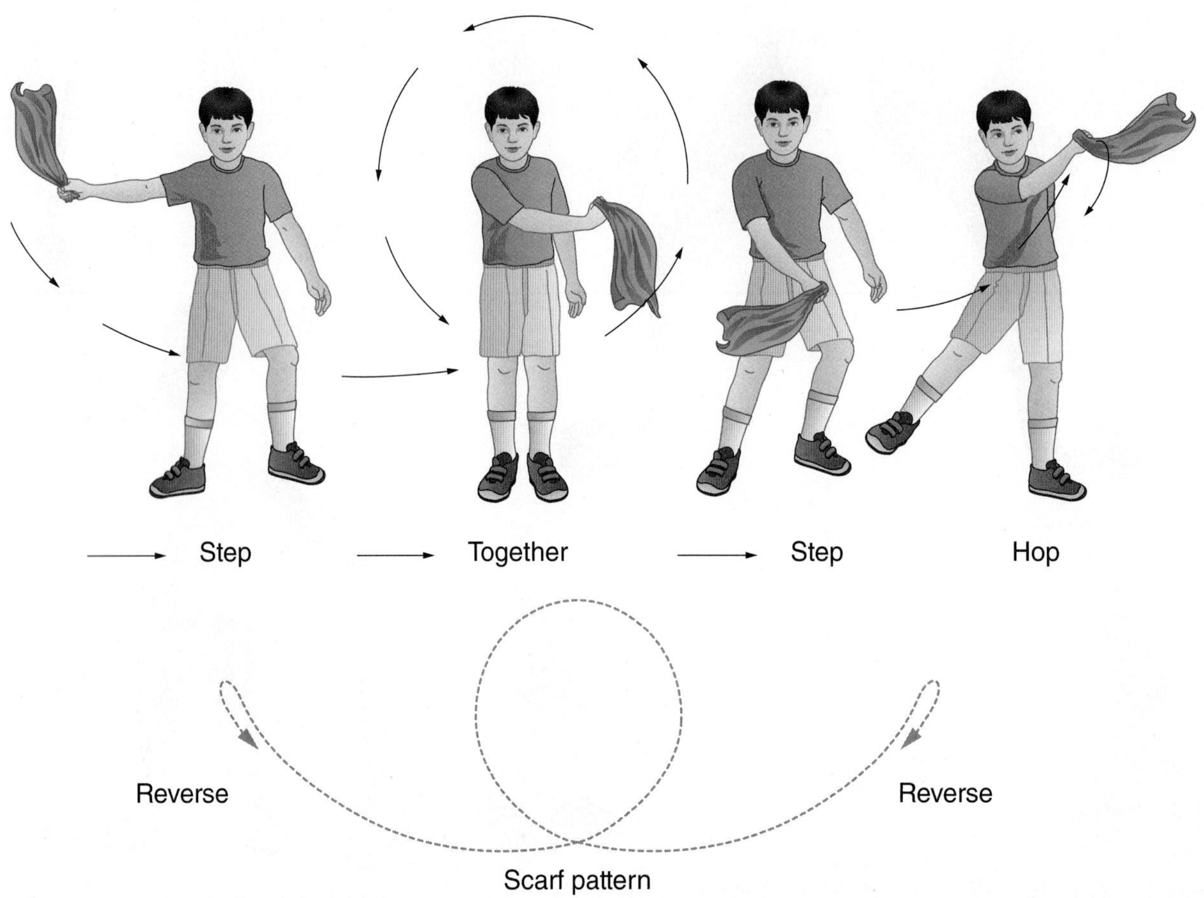

Figure 33.14 Step-together-step-hop with circling scarf

SAMPLE LEARNING EXPERIENCES 33.11

Child-Designed Korean Scarf Dance (*continued*)

4. Next try figure 8s, circling the scarf first on your right and then on your left (see **Figure 33.9**). Do a total of four figure 8s.
5. We will end by strongly whipping up the scarf high using a slashing movement, then letting it gently lower to the ground for three beats. Do this four times in total (see **Figure 33.12**).
6. Let's put the dance together, doing each movement four times.

Cues: Step–together–step (four times).

Turn, 2, 3, 4; reverse, 2, 3, 4 (four times).

Figure 8 (four times).

Slash up, float down, 2, 3, 4 (four times).

E On your own, explore other kinds of movements you can make with the scarf.

E Who wants to share one idea? [Call on different children, and have the whole class try their ideas until you and the children have elicited all the basic arm actions and the children have many ideas from which to choose to design their dances.]

Culminating Activity

A I will put you into groups of three. Design a scarf dance inspired by the Korean scarf folk dance movements you saw on the video. You have three criteria.

1. The dance must flow continuously. You can use step–together–step, slides, hops, lots of turns, and any other locomotor steps you want.
2. You must have many changes in formation.
3. The scarves should enhance your movements and formations.

SAMPLE LEARNING EXPERIENCES 33.11

Child-Designed Korean Scarf Dance (*continued*)

Exploring Different Scarf Actions in Different Formations

E Start by exploring different scarf actions and locomotor steps in different formations. Try to come up with as many ideas as you can, while using as many different formations as you can.

Selecting and Arranging the Parts of the Dance, and Planning Transitions from One Formation to the Next

E Once you have many ideas, select your best ideas, and put them into a sequence. Plan the transitions from one formation to the next so you don't have to take extra steps. Remember, sometimes you can solve a transition problem by reordering your formations.

R Refine and practice your dance until your movements are synchronized and you can repeat it precisely the same way each time.

Peer Assessment and Coaching

A I will pair you up with another group. Here is a checklist with the three criteria for your dance. Watch the group, and then fill out the checklist. Then coach the group to help them improve on the criteria.

Checklist

Dance flows continuously:	Perfect	Looks Good	Not Yet
Many different formations:	Perfect	Looks Good	Not Yet
Scarves enhance movement and formations:	Perfect	Looks Good	Not Yet

Class Show/Teacher Assessment

Martial Arts Dances

Martial arts dancers take the stances, positions, poses, and movements used in the martial arts (ranging from Tae Kwon Do to Tai Chi), add music, and choreograph a dance using simple dance steps, including hops, jumps, turns, turning jumps, and slides. Sometimes these dances represent animals, such as a tiger or lion; sometimes they tell a story; and often they show the virtuosity of the dancer in performing high turning leaps and moves that resemble break-dancing. Both men and women perform these dances.

One of the oldest forms of martial arts dance is *Capoeira*, which was developed by African slaves in Brazil approximately 400 years ago. They wanted to practice and preserve their fighting abilities but were forbidden to do so. In response, they invented *Capoeira*, which is part dance, part martial arts, and part game. In this dance, two dancers imitate a sparring match and perform gymnastics-like movements in an effort to show who has the most skill. We have seen different versions of martial arts dancing from Korea, Japan, and China. Some include gymnastics-like movements, such as cartwheels.

Basic Styles and Steps

The basic style includes the following actions:

- Held martial arts–like positions
- Slow, strong martial arts–like movements
- Fast, strong, thrusting and slashing movements and jumps
- Effort actions, predominately pressing, wringing, slashing, and thrusting

All the arm actions described in **Figures 33.6** through **33.14**, with or without a sword, also appear in martial arts dances. The following basic steps also are included:

- Kicks to the front, side, and back
- Leaps with bent front leg and second leg kicked high, switching legs in the air
- Lunges at a medium level, thrusting or circling a sword
- Lunges at a very low level
- Wide, balanced stances with knees bent
- Stork stands (see **Figure 33.15**)
- Full turning jumps with straight and bent legs
- Turning jumps with kicks

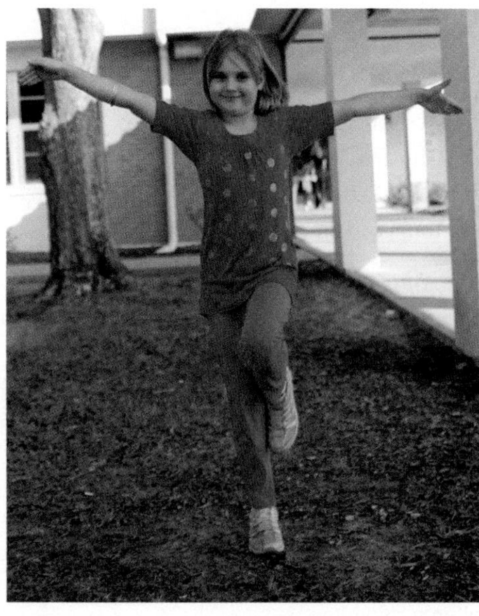

Figure 33.15 Stork stand

SAMPLE LEARNING EXPERIENCES 33.12

Child-Designed Martial Arts Dance Lesson with Swords

These learning experiences can take several lessons, especially if you decide to progress from individual sequences to partner sequences.

Movement Themes

Pressing, wringing, slashing, thrusting actions and jumps

Topic Theme

Martial arts dance with swords

Potential Refinements

- Maintain strong tension in the body.
- Use strong force when jumping and kicking.

Introduction of Topic or Story

I How many of you have taken martial arts lessons? How many of you have seen martial arts? Which kinds of movements did you see? [Kicks, chopping arm actions, turns, jumps with kicks.] Martial arts are used for self-defense, but, in countries like China, Korea, Japan, and Brazil, people also turn martial arts movements into dances. That's what we are going to do today. [Show video clips from the Internet of one or two different martial arts dances.]

Content Development

Moving to the Beat of the Music While Exploring Different Gestures and Actions to Represent Ideas in the Dance

Exploring movements for a child-designed martial arts dance

Courtesy of John Dolly

Slow Martial Arts Steps and Lunges

E Let's start by traveling slowly in general space to the music (or to the beat of a drum—music is not necessary to this dance), using lunges and wide-stance plies or knee bends and moving your arms in slow-motion slicing actions. Explore different slicing actions with each step.

E Lunge and end at different levels.

E Sometimes slice your arms in the same direction and sometimes in different directions.

E Add a turn each time you step or lunge.

Jumping and Landing in Angular Shapes, Three Fast Kicking Movements

E Now jog in general space, jump, and land in a martial arts position. Each time you jump and land, make a different angular shape. [Repeat several times.]

E This time when you land, do three sharp, fast kicking movements. Make each kicking movement different. [Repeat several times.]

E Jump and explore kicking in different directions—to the side, front, and back.

E Explore kicking at different levels.

E At least one time in your kicking movements, add a turn. One time, try a full turn. [Repeat several times.]

E Now try high jumps with a kick or switching legs in the air. Be sure to land in control of your body and still holding a martial arts fighting position.

E Explore turning jumps.

SAMPLE LEARNING EXPERIENCES 33.12

Child-Designed Martial Arts Dance Lesson with Swords (*continued*)

Adding the Swords

Org Walk over to the wall and pick up a foam pole (plastic pole or a swimming pool noodle cut into two-foot lengths). We will use these poles to represent swords.

Social When you swing a sword, the size of your personal space is much larger. What does this mean you must remember? [To stay farther away from others.]

E Explore different ways to circle your sword (overhead, figure 8s, in front, to the sides).

E Explore lunges while circling and thrusting your sword in different ways.

E Explore lunging and thrusting your sword at different levels.

E Explore doing different circular actions with your sword before you lunge and thrust.

E Explore jumping and landing in different martial arts positions, using the sword to enhance the movement.

E Explore jumping, landing, and doing three kicking movements, using the sword in different ways to enhance your movements.

Culminating Activity

Selecting Different Gestures and Actions to Represent Ideas in the Dance

A Design a short sequence that starts with three martial arts positions performed in slow motion. Then, design a fast section. What might you include in the fast section? [Jumps, kicks, turns.] Then create an ending in which you move slowly. What are some of the different movements you can do with swords? [Thrusts, circles, figures 8s, helicopters, and so on.] You can use any of those movements, too.

Refining and Practicing

R Once you have the sequence designed, practice it until you can repeat it. Work on maintaining tension during your slow movements and showing strong force and tension in your fast movements.

A I will put you with a partner. First, show your sequences to each other. Then design a matching-and-mirroring partner sequence to the music (or without music). Be sure you use some part of each of your individual sequences in the partner sequence. What are some possible partner relationships and formations? [Facing each other, side by side, one in front and one behind, traveling meeting and parting, traveling and going by each other.] You have many choices and decisions to make about your dance.

R Practice your sequence until you have synchronized your actions and can match or mirror each other perfectly.

Assessment and Showing Sequences to Classmates

Other Potential Martial Arts Dances

We first saw an interpretive Japanese lion dance performed by Mary Ohno, in Tacoma, Washington. She used two fans representing the jaws of the lion, with scarves added to create a mane and tail. She performed a slow dance with poses emphasizing the graceful, yet deadly movements of the lion hunting.

We also have seen a Chinese group of physical education majors performing a series of strong, fast martial arts dances interpreting the movements of a tiger, monkey, and wild boar, sometimes using a long pole or a sword. These dance ideas can be adapted for elementary schools by modifying the lesson in **Sample Learning Experiences 33.12**.

African American Stepping

Stepping was developed by African American university and college fraternities and sororities, who designed routines and competed in step shows (Fine, 2003; Malone, 1996). It has been highlighted in films such as *School Daze* (1988), *Drum Line* (2002), and *Stomp the Yard* (2007). This type of performance has now spread to church, school, cheerleading, and community groups as well.

African American stepping is not typically called dance. It involves creating rhythmic movements using foot patterns, stomps, clapping, slapping different body parts, chanting, and verbal call-and-response, in which a leader speaks a phrase and the other group members respond (Hastie, Martin, & Buchanan, 2006). In essence, the body becomes a drum, and the dancers create complex rhythmic routines with their body and voices.

Stepping can include the use of props, such as canes, sticks, and swords, for visual effects and for creating rhythmic beats. Over the years, it has expanded to include elements from military drills, hip hop, gymnastics, and martial arts.

Step routines are performed in groups. Unison is emphasized, although step routines may also effectively use canon. Formations often include single, double, and multiple lines, rotating lines, and triangles. Routines are two to five minutes long.

Overview of Stepping Unit

As there are no "step" dances and the tradition is to design your own routines, stepping units focus on student-designed group routines (Hastie et al., 2006). If possible, show the children video clips of step routines. Such performance videos are readily found on Internet sites. It will take several lessons for children to design their own routine. You can integrate this unit with the content taught by classroom teachers by having the children write chants for their step routines in the classroom.

A typical lesson begins with children reviewing their step routines from the previous lesson, learning a few new steps, and then designing new sections of their step routine. Following are some steps and clapping actions. Claps and steps are typically performed at the same time—for example, double stomp while clapping and then slapping thighs.

Descriptions of Potential Hand Actions and Steps

Claps and Body Slaps

- Clap in front
- Clap over head
- Clap under leg while bending forward at waist
- *Slicing clap:* one hand starts high and the other low; make a slicing action and clap the hands as they pass each other in front of the body
- Clap behind back
- Slap side of thigh, slap front of thigh
- Slap shoe inside, slap shoe outside
- Slap opposite foot behind back by bending knee and twisting leg
- Slap floor
- *Digging:* imitate digging by leaning forward on a diagonal while stomping one foot, then throwing the dirt over the shoulder while leaning back on the diagonal and stomping the back foot
- Clap high, then bend and clap low under leg
- *Diagonals:* clap high to one side, then move hands on a diagonal down to the other side and clap under leg

Steps

- *Single stomp:* step with a stomp
- *Double stomp:* stomp and then step with a stomp on the same foot
- *Leap and knee lift:* spring into the air, land on one foot with a stomp and the other knee lifted
- *Leap and kick:* spring into the air, land on one foot while kicking the other
- Knee lift and hop
- Stomping, turn a full circle by running in place
- Tap foot behind, then kick forward
- *Stomp jump:* low jump almost sliding the feet forward with bent knees, landing with a stomp
- Stomp walk in circle, clapping low
- Stomp jump in circle with knees bent the whole time
- *Tuck jump:* jump, tuck knees up, land with bent knees and a stomp
- *Rock:* rock forward, hop with a stomp, rock back, hop, and lift front knee

Example Combination

- Clap two times while stomping two times
- Slap top of thighs, swinging arms back while stomping foot to side with bent knee; slap side of thighs, swinging arms forward while stomping other foot to side with bent knee
- Clap two times while stomping two times
- Slap top of thighs, swinging arms back while stomping foot to side with bent knee; slap side of thighs, swinging arms forward while stomping other foot to side with bent knee
- Jump four times, knees bent, feet apart, turning one full turn and pointing with one arm
- Clap under leg while hopping; change to other leg; repeat four times
- Stomp jump forward four times while reaching hands up to raise the roof

SAMPLE LEARNING EXPERIENCES 33.13

Child-Designed African American Step Routines

Introduction of Topic or Story

I Show a video clip of a step routine from the Internet. Discuss the history of stepping.

Content Development

Teaching Selected Claps and Steps

I Let's begin by learning a few steps and then putting them together into a short routine. Follow me, and try to clap and stomp following my rhythm.

- Clap while stomping. *Cue:* Clap, clap. [Repeat until children are moving in unison.]
- Slap top of thighs, swinging arms back while stomping foot to side with bent knee; slap side of thighs, swinging arms forward while stomping other foot to side with bent knee. *Cue:* Slap, slap. [Repeat until children are moving in unison.]
- Jump four times, knees bent, feet apart, turning one full turn while pointing with one arm. *Cue:* Jump, jump, jump, jump. [Repeat turning in the other direction. Keep repeating until children are moving in unison.]

SAMPLE LEARNING EXPERIENCES 33.13

Child-Designed African American Step Routines (*continued*)

- Clap under leg while hopping; change to other leg. *Cue:* Clap, change, clap, change. [In the change from hopping on one leg to the other, there is a small jump on two feet to allow the change to hop on the other leg. Repeat until children are moving in unison.]
- Stomp jump forward four times while reaching palms up and down to raise the roof.

Cue: Raise the roof. [Repeat until children are moving in unison.]

Combining Movements into a Routine

E We will put these together to be a routine. Let's start with the first two moves.

- Clap two times while stomping two times (counts 1, 2).
- Slap top of thighs, swinging arms back while stomping foot to side with bent knee (count 3).
- Slap side of thighs, swinging arms forward while stomping other foot to side with bent knee (count 4).

Cue: Clap, clap, slap, slap. [Repeat counts 1, 2, 3, 4 until the children can perform confidently in unison.]

E Now we will add the next step. Do clap, clap, slap, slap (counts 1, 2, 3, 4) twice. Ready? *Cue:* Clap, clap, slap, slap; clap, clap, slap, slap (1, 2, 3, 4; 1, 2, 3, 4).

E Now, jump four times with knees bent and feet apart, turning one full turn while pointing with one arm. *Cue:* Jump, jump, jump, jump.

E Let's practice the dance so far.

- *Cue:* Clap, clap, slap, slap; clap, clap, slap, slap.
- *Cue:* Jump, jump, jump, jump.

[Repeat until children can do the sequence confidently.]

E Now for the end. Stomp jump forward four times while reaching hands up to raise the roof. *Cue:* Raise the roof.

E Let's do the entire sequence. [Cue the entire dance until children can do it without cueing.]

Culminating Activity: Designing Routines

These learning experiences can take several, if not many, lessons depending on the length of the routines. In addition, if the children want to add chants, it will take even more time. Finally, although we begin with groups of three to ensure all children contribute ideas, we then progress to combining two groups of three, which also takes time.

Brainstorming and Exploring Different Gestures and Actions for the Routine

E I will put you in groups of three. Now you will begin to design your own sequence. Start by exploring different actions using slaps, claps, and stomps. You also can add different arm gestures and dance steps. Brainstorm and explore until you have many, varied, and some unusual ideas.

Selecting Ideas for Each Part of the Routine, Deciding How Many Times to Repeat Each Action

E Now select your best ideas, and design a routine. Be sure everyone contributes at least one idea. You need to decide how many times to repeat each action. In addition, you can add words. Sometimes you can all chant the same words, and sometimes you can use a call-and-response like you saw in the video clips.

Adding Formations

E Once you have a sequence, add formations, and add new actions if needed for transitions between formations.

Combining into Groups of Six

E I have combined two groups of three, so you are now in groups of six. Show your routine to the other group, and then combine routines. You may have to design new formations because you have many more options with six people.

R Refine and practice moving together, matching movements precisely, synchronizing movement, and repeating the routine the exact same way each time.

Assessment and Showing Dances

Square Dancing

Square dance developed from the French *quadrille* of the 1600s. When immigrants brought these dances to North America, the dances were modified and evolved, with different forms developing in different parts of the country (Pittman, Waller, & Dark, 2005). Square dance is now a distinctly American form of dance. Today, national organizations have standardized the steps and calls.

Square dancing is wonderful fun because of the feeling of community when a group works together and changes positions and patterns in interesting ways (Adams, 2006). Traditionally, people square dance with a caller who calls out the patterns a beat ahead of the dancers so the dancers do not know ahead of time the order of patterns in the dance. This is one reason square dance is exciting. In physical education, we do both dances that the teacher calls and dances in which each group of students designs their own pattern.

Music

We recommend using music your children enjoy. Square dance has always been a recreational form of dance done to music popular at the time. Rap works just as well as country. You can even design rap calls (Adams, 2006). Salsa music also works well—salsa can be performed using positions and patterns like square dance. Find music with a brisk walking beat.

Varying the Size of Sets and Using Pinnies Rather than Gender

Traditionally, square dance is done in sets of eight people (four couples) in a square formation.

The man is on the left and the woman on the right. **Figure 33.16** illustrates the traditional set formation. This arrangement can be difficult for physical education classes, however, as you rarely have a class that can be divided into groups of eight with no children left out. You can easily modify square dance steps for sets of six (three pairs) and four (no partners; each person has a number), and many steps can be done as a whole class in single or double circles.

Because it also is unusual for a class to include an equal number of boys and girls and because children in the upper elementary grades sometimes prefer same-gender partners, we have children wear pinnies or vests of two different colors. We call the dance using the colors rather than genders—for example, saying, "Greens to the center and back; now reds to the center and back." If we are using groups of four with no partners, we number the pinnies 1 through 4 and call either the number or "Odd" and "Even."

Some children resist holding hands with partners. In these situations, we use groups of four with no partners (see **Figure 33.17**) or have children form their own groups, which can be all girls, all boys, or mixed boys and girls. If some children still resist holding hands, we tell them to design their dance without touching each other. This is more difficult but works just as well. Basic square dance steps can be seen at http://www.squaredancecd.com.

Figure 33.17 Square dance in set of four

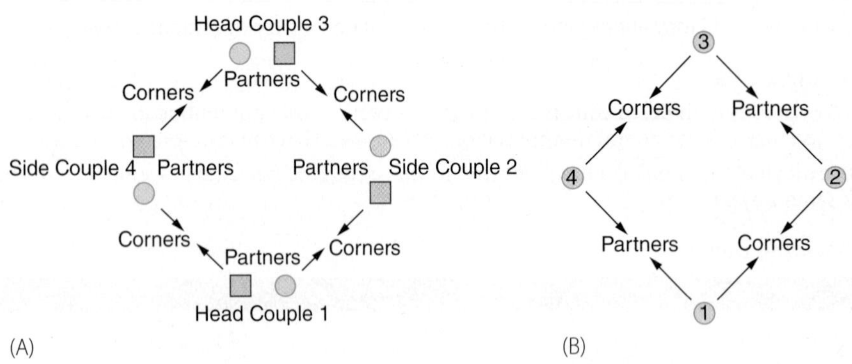

Figure 33.16 (A) Traditional square dance set with head and side couples marked (B) Individual square dance set individuals numbered 1 through 4

Descriptions of Sample Square Dance Steps

Here we describe the basic square dance steps.

Square Your Sets

This means to stand in your original position next to your partner facing the center of the square (or circle if using sets of six or whole-group formations). Pairs are numbered 1 through 4, also called head couples (1 and 3) and side couples (2 and 4). Individuals are numbered 1 through 4.

Honor Your Partner and Corner

Traditionally men bow to their partner and women curtsey. We have children all bow or nod or design their own form of greeting, such as fist bumps or high fives. Your partner stands next to you. Your corner is the person standing on the other side of you. If groups of four, individuals 1 and 2 are corners, as are 3 and 4. Individuals 1 and 4 are partners, as are 2 and 3.

Swing Partner and Corner

In traditional square dance, partners use the social dance position to swing. We teach children an elbow swing using the right elbows, emphasizing the importance of caring for your partner and not swinging your partner or corner too hard or fast, causing the partner or corner to go off balance.

Join Hands, Circle Left, Circle Right

Holding hands or not, walk in a circle to the left or right, ending up back in place. The caller will often say, "Reverse." You can vary this by having only reds or greens step into the middle and circle left or right, or partners 1 and 3 or partners 2 and 4 step into the middle and circle left or right.

Into the Middle and Back

Dancers walk into the center of the square and back. You can vary this to be greens and reds into the middle and back, or partners 1 and 3, then partners 2 and 4. You can have children add gestures in the center, such as raising arms, waving, or clapping.

Do-Sa-Do

Face your partner (or corner), walk forward toward your partner, pass by right shoulders, walk sideways one step around your partner (without turning), and then walk backward back to place.

Star Left, Star Right

Partners or groups of four touch palms, and hands are held high above head height; dancers walk around each other, completing one full circle and going back to place. Star left means hold your left hands together and travel counterclockwise. Star right means hold your right hands together and travel clockwise.

Promenade

Standing next to your partner with one inside and the other outside, walk around the circle back to place. Partners can hold inside hands, or hold both hands with left hand holding left hand, right hand holding right hand, and the arms crossed in front of the dancers' bodies. With groups of four, walk single file around the circle.

Allemande Left

Face your corner and extend left hands; walk and circle around your corner back to place.

Grand Right and Left

This call typically follows the allemande left call. Extend the right hand to the partner and walk past the partner, still holding right hands. Extend the left hand to the person facing you. Drop the right hand, and while holding left hands, walk past that person while extending the right hand to the next dancer. Reds will all be traveling in one direction and greens in the other direction. Continue alternating left and right hands as you travel around the circle until you meet your partner. Then promenade home.

Weave the Ring

This is the same as the grand right and left without touching. A modification can be to have greens stand still and reds walk around traveling first on the left side and then on the right side of the greens.

Head Couples Make an Arch, Side Couples Circle Under

Head couples 1 and 3 make an arch with their inside hands and turn and face side couples 2 and 4. Side couples duck under the arch and circle back to place. Then you can reverse roles.

Chains (Traditionally Called Ladies Chains)

Green partners 1 and 3 (ladies or the partner on the right) walk to the middle and extend the right hand to the green on the opposite side, pass by, and extend the left hand to the red opposite the partner's left hand. In our modified version, circle around each other until facing the center again. In the authentic version, the man does a courtesy turn, as described next.

Chain with Courtesy Turn

Green partners 1 and 3 (ladies or the partner on the right) walk to the middle and extend the right hand to the green on the opposite side, pass by, and extend the left hand to the red opposite the partner's left hand. Red puts the right arm behind the back of green, who holds red's right arm at the waist with the right arm. Circle around until facing the center again.

Promenade

(*continues*)

Descriptions of Sample Square Dance Steps (*continued*)

Chain Combinations

You can have greens 1 and 3 chain across and then immediately chain back to their original partners, or you can alternate and have greens 2 and 4 chain across, then 1 and 3 chain back, and 2 and 4 chain back. You also can have all four greens chain across at the same time, touching their hands together as if they were doing a star turn.

Basic Dances Called by the Teacher

We suggest teaching a few steps, then having the children do the steps with you calling the dance to the music and telling them what to do. Next, teach a few more steps and have them dance again, adding the new calls to the mix. Continue this way until you have taught all the basic steps. Following are some sample combination calls you can use to practice the basic steps.

Simple Combination Calls for Sets of Four, Six, and Eight Children, or an Entire Class in Single Circle with Partners

Combination 1

- Honor your partner, honor your corner
- Do-sa-do your corner
- Swing your partner
- Allemande left your corner
- Swing your partner
- Promenade

Combination 2

- Allemande left your corner
- Do-sa-do your partner
- Allemande left your corner
- Grand right and left
- When you meet your partner, promenade home

Combination 3

- Allemande left your corner
- Swing your partner
- Allemande left your corner
- Grand right and left
- When you meet your partner, promenade home
- Honor your partner, honor your corner, turn to the teacher and wave

Simple Combination Calls for No-Partner Sets of Four

Before beginning, assign each child a number. Individuals 1 and 4 will be partners to each other. Individuals 2 and 3 will be partners to each other. Individuals 1 and 2 will be corners to each other, and 3 and 4 will be corners (see **Figure 33.16B**).

Combination 4

- All to the middle, greet your set, and back (let children design their own greeting)
- 1 and 3, do-sa-do
- 2 and 4, do-sa-do
- All four do a left-hand star, then back to place
- Allemande left your corner
- Swing your partner
- Square your set and promenade (single file)

Simple Combination Calls for Sets of Four, Six, or Eight

Combination 5

- Greens to the middle with a right-hand star
- When you see your partner, do-sa-do and square your set
- Reds to the middle with a left-hand star
- When you see your partner, swing
- Square your set

Combination 6

- Honor your corner, swing your corner
- Allemande left your partner
- Do-sa-do your corner
- Swing your partner
- Greens 1 and 3, chain across and courtesy turn
- Greens 2 and 4, chain across and courtesy turn
- Greens 1 and 3, chain back and courtesy turn
- Greens 2 and 4, chain back and courtesy turn
- Reds to the middle with a right-hand star
- When you see your corner, allemande left
- Grand right and left; when you meet your partner, promenade

SAMPLE LEARNING EXPERIENCES 33.14

Child-Designed Square Dance

We outline two versions of these learning experiences. The first uses rock or rap music, with the students adding clapping and stomping gestures similar to African American stepping (see the previous section on teaching stepping for more information and ideas, as well as the article by Adams [2006]). The second version uses country music and the theme of living on a farm. You can modify these lessons using any kind of music and different themes.

Introductory Activity

I On a whiteboard, write the different square dance steps the students have learned. Review the steps by putting on the music the students will use for their dance and doing several practice calls.

SAMPLE LEARNING EXPERIENCES 33.14

Child-Designed Square Dance (*continued*)

Content Development: Rap or Rock

E I have put you in groups of four. You are going to make up your own square dance by taking the basic steps, modifying them, and adding gestures that go with the music. For example, get with a partner, and face the other pair in your group. Start by honoring your partner. Which ways might you greet someone? [Bumping fists, handshake routines.] Make up a short handshake routine or other greeting that your group will use to honor your partner and honor your corner.

E Now design a way to walk into the center and back, adding a gesture when you meet in the center. What might you do? Yes, you can slap palms, tap fists, tap forearms, and so on. Great ideas. You decide what your group will use.

E On the whiteboard, I have listed the steps you have learned. Your task is to take these steps and modify them. For example, how might you modify the promenade? Great idea—you can move back to back using a dip and a two-step. Figure out how your group will promenade.

Culminating Activity

A Now that you have the idea of how to modify steps, design a square dance to the song. You must include the following elements (write on a whiteboard):

1. Gestures, stomps, and claps
2. Three different formations and ways to move into and out of the formations
3. At least one step, one hand position, and one turn you invented

In square dance, there are many different ways to change positions and to change formations from squares to lines, so find some interesting and original ways to do this.

Content Development: Country Music and Living on a Farm

E Today we will make up a square dance to Tim McGraw's song "Down on the Farm," based on the theme of living on a farm. What are some of the things you do when you live on a farm? [Ride tractors, grow food, dig holes for fence posts, ride horses, cross over streams, and travel on winding country roads.] I have put you in groups of four. Let's start by designing a way to honor your partner by greeting someone. You select what your group will do to start your dance by honoring your partner.

E Now take the idea of traveling on winding country roads and crossing over streams. What can you use to represent that? [Arches, grand right and left, and chains.] Design a pattern that includes an arch in some way and travels on a winding pathway.

Culminating Activity

A On the whiteboard, I have listed the steps you have learned. Your task is to take these steps and modify them by adding gestures to create a square dance representing the idea of living on a farm. You can also use ideas from the song. What are some ideas Tim McGraw sings about in the song? [Don't mess with the bull, close the gate, and stay out of the beans.] You must include the following elements (write on the whiteboard):

1. Gestures and actions representing ideas in the song
2. Three different formations and ways to move into and out of the formations
3. At least one step, one hand position, and one turn you invented

In square dance, there are many different ways to change positions and to change formations from squares to lines, so find some interesting and original ways to do this.

Line Dancing

Line dancing is one form of Country-and-Western dancing that originated with Country-and-Western music. Both men and women dancers wear cowboy boots and tight jeans (Pittman et al., 2005).

Line dancing is popular in many parts of the United States. It requires no partners and no formations, and consists of footwork with arms held behind the back or thumbs hooked on the belt (Pittman et al., 2005). Dancers typically stand in several lines filling the general space and perform the footwork in unison. Often the dance includes a quarter-turn at the end and is repeated facing a different wall. These are called four-wall line dances.

Use any music your children like, including hip hop, country, rap, R&B, or rock. You can find many line dances set to current music on the Internet, but children also may enjoy designing their own. Next, we outline a child-designed line dance lesson.

SAMPLE LEARNING EXPERIENCES 33.15

Child-Designed Line Dance

Introductory Activity

I Toady you will be making up your own line dance to this music. To warm up, as the music plays, travel about general space exploring a variety of locomotor patterns to find ones you like to do to the music.

Content Development

E One fun part of line dancing is moving in unison. Let's try some locomotor steps together to the music. Stay in personal space. Does anyone have any suggestions? Grapevines. Great idea. Let's do grapevines in unison.

E [Play the music in a continuous loop.] Do a grapevine to the left and tap your right heel, then do a grapevine to the right and tap your left heel. Repeat eight times to practice.

Cue: Step left, right behind, step left, right heel tap.

Step right, left behind, step right, left heel tap.

Step, behind, step, heel.

Step, behind, step, heel.

E Does anyone have another suggestion? Rock. Good idea. Rock (and step) forward on your left foot and bounce, rock your weight back on your right foot and bounce. Repeat eight times to practice.

E How about a scuff heel step and leg swings? Step left, scuff the right heel forward; keeping your weight on your left foot, cross and swing the right foot over the left; kick the right foot forward, step on the right foot, and repeat using the left foot. Repeat eight times to practice.

Cue: Step, scuff, cross, kick.

E Let's end by walking eight steps in a circle in personal space turning 450 degrees (circle one and a quarter times) so you end up facing the side wall of the gym.

E Let's put the dance together by doing each step four times.

- Grapevine left
- Grapevine right
- Grapevine left
- Grapevine right
- Rock forward
- Rock back
- Rock forward
- Rock back
- Step left, scuff right, cross, kick
- Step right, scuff left, cross, kick
- Step left, scuff right, cross, kick
- Step right, scuff left, cross, kick

Circle 1, 2, 3, 4, 5, 6, 7, 8; face the new wall, and start again.

Culminating Activity

E Now that you have the idea of line dancing, I will assign you to groups of four, and you can create your own dance. Use any dance steps all of you can do competently and like doing. Practice your sequence until you have it perfected. Then I will have you teach another group your dance, and they will teach you theirs.

Acknowledgment

We thank Dr. Margaret Stran for her suggestions for wheelchair modifications.

Summary

Folk dance has been a universal part of human culture since prehistory. Folk dances include locomotor steps, formations, and pathways that are usually performed in a repeatable pattern and often represent aspects of daily life. Folk dance continues to evolve, and it remains a popular social and recreational activity in countries and communities around the world. In many countries, current folk dancers take elements of traditional folk dance and design their own dances. Teaching children to design folk dances reflects this tradition. Folk dance lessons can be easily integrated with social studies units and are excellent opportunities for teaching children how to be respectful of other cultures.

Review Questions

1. What are the three basic elements of folk dances you need to teach?
2. Think of a song you believe would be appropriate at the elementary school level. List at least four actions or ideas from the song that children can represent in a folk dance they design.
3. List three reasons to teach folk dance.
4. How can you teach children to be respectful of diverse cultures?
5. Discuss at least four benefits of child-designed folk dance.
6. Discuss the benefits and limitations of four ways to demonstrate folk dance steps.
7. Discuss three ways to modify a folk dance to make it easier for children.
8. What is the difference between a gallop and a slide? A step-hop and a skip?
9. What is a *schottische*?
10. Describe an overview of a child-designed folk dance lesson. Include typical activities in the introduction, content development, and culminating activity sections.
11. Describe an overview of a modified folk dance lesson. Include typical activities in the introduction, content development, and culminating activity sections.
12. What is the story behind the *Tarantella*?
13. Describe *tinikling*.
14. What props can you use to represent Korean, Japanese, and Chinese artistic folk dances?
15. What is stepping, and who invented it?
16. How can you modify the traditional "four men and four women" square dance sets?

References

Adams, D. (2006). Squaring to the rap! Using rap music to teach square dancing to today's students. *Teaching Elementary Physical Education, 17*(2), 14–16.

Banks, J. A. (2004). Multicultural education: Historical development, dimensions, and practice. In J. A. Banks & C. A. McGee Banks (Eds.), *Handbook of research on multicultural education* (2nd ed.) (pp. 3–29). San Francisco: Jossey-Bass.

Barrère, D. B., Kawena Pukui, M., & Kelly, M. (1980). *Hula: Historical perspectives, Pacific anthropological records No. 30.* Honolulu, HI: Department of Anthropology, Bernice Pauahi Bishop Museum.

Bouchard, D., & Sapp, A. (2002). *The song within my heart.* Vancouver: Raincoast Books.

Browner, T. (2002). *Heartbeat of the people: Music and dance of the northern powwow.* Urbana, IL: University of Illinois Press.

Cone, S. L., & Purcell Cone, T. (2003). Dancing, learning, creating, knowing. *Teaching Elementary Physical Education, 14*(5), 7–11.

Cornelius, C. (1999). *Iroquois corn in a culture-based curriculum: A framework for respectfully teaching about cultures.* Albany, NY: State University of New York Press.

Fine, E. (2003). *Soulstepping: African American step shows.* Chicago, IL: University of Illinois Press

Freeman, W. H. (2012). *Physical education, exercise, and sport science in a changing society* (7th ed.). Burlington, MA: Jones & Bartlett Learning.

Gay, G. (2004). The importance of multicultural education. *Educational Leadership, 61*(4), 30–35.

Hastie, P. A., Martin, E., & Buchanan, A. M. (2006). Stepping out of the norm: As examination of praxis for a culturally-relevant pedagogy for African-American children. *Journal of Curriculum Studies, 38*, 293–306.

Johnston, R., Hixon, K., & Anton, V. (2009). The Native American dance legacy: The never-ending circle of life: Native American hoop dancing from its origin to the present day. *Journal of Physical Education, Recreation and Dance, 80*(6), 21–25, 30.

LaPointe-Crump, J. (2006). Dance movement and spirit: Issues in the dance education curriculum. *Journal of Physical Education, Recreation and Dance, 77*(5), 3–4, 12.

Lawson, J. (1970). *European folk dance: Its national and musical characteristics.* London: Pitman.

Lopez, A. (1972). Celebration. In T. Allen (Ed.), *The whispering wind: Poetry by young American Indians* (p. 3). Garden City, NY: Doubleday.

Lopez, A. (1972). Dry and parched. In T. Allen (Ed.), *The whispering wind: Poetry by young American Indians* (p. 9). Garden City, NY: Doubleday.

Lopez, A. (1972). I go forth to move about the earth. In T. Allen (Ed.), *The whispering wind: Poetry by young American Indians* (p. 8). Garden City, NY: Doubleday.

Malborg, K. (2005). *Korean dance* (L. J. Young, Trans.). Seoul, Korea: Ewha Womans [sic] University Press.

Malone, J. (1996). *Steppin' on the blues: The visible rhythms of African American dance.* Urbana, IL: University of Illinois Press.

Menton, L., & Tamura, E. (1989). *A history of Hawai`i.* Honolulu: University of Hawai`i.

National Dance Association (NDA). (1994). *National standards for dance education.* Reston, VA: Author.

Pittman, A. M., Waller, M. S., & Dark, C. L. (2005). *Dance a while.* San Francisco: Pearson/Benjamin Cummings.

Porter-Hearn, C. (2009). The Native American dance legacy: Transcending rhythms: A celebration of Native and African American culture. *Journal of Physical Education, Recreation and Dance, 80*(6), 26–30.

Public Broadcasting System. (2007). *Hula steps and gestures.* Retrieved December 21, 2007, from http://www.pbs.org/wnet/gperf/shows/holomaipele/multimedia/mant1.html

Rovegno, I., & Gregg, M. (2007). Using folk dance and geography to teach interdisciplinary, multicultural subject matter: A school-based study. *Physical Education and Sport Pedagogy, 12*, 205–223.

Tillman-Hall, J. (1969). *Folk dance.* Pacific Palisades, CA: Goodyear.

SECTION VI

Working in Schools

The final section of this text discusses working in schools. We begin with a chapter on the importance of continued professional development. We discuss research-proven ways to facilitate teacher development. In addition, we describe resources within schools and professional organizations that support teachers.

In the last chapter, we discuss the politics of schools and tactics that can help physical education teachers manage school politics. We also discuss ways to promote the physical education program.

In both chapters, we include stories and advice from teachers who have successfully managed the politics of elementary schools and continued their professional development throughout their careers.

CHAPTER

34

Continued Professional Development

PRE-READING REFLECTION

1. What do you know about continued professional development?
2. Which questions and concerns do you have about continued professional development?

OBJECTIVES

Students will learn:

1. Continued professional development is required for teachers.
2. Reflecting on your teaching is an important way to improve your effectiveness as a physical education teacher.
3. Research shows that a disposition to be a continual learner, to recognize that it takes time and effort to improve your program, to want to do the job right, to experiment with new ideas, to take responsibility for what happens, and to have a sound philosophy and make your program match your philosophy will contribute to successful, positive professional development.
4. Having support in the workplace is important for teachers.

KEY TERMS

National Board of Professional Teaching Standards
Stages of teacher development

CONNECTION TO STANDARDS

To meet current and future National Standards of Physical Education and Common Core and other State Standards (CCSS), you must continue to develop your knowledge of curriculum and instruction. We seem to be getting more and more standards, and the standards we have change over time. It is our job to remain current and continue to develop as teachers and to ensure that our students can meet current National Standards.

Introduction

It is common in commencement ceremonies for speakers to note that *commencement* means beginning. When you graduate, you will commence your career as a teacher. Although you have been well prepared in your teacher education program, the process of developing as a teacher will just be starting.

We hope that you have learned in your teacher education program about the importance of continuing professional development throughout your career. Being a professional in any field—including medicine, law, dentistry, engineering, and education—carries the responsibility to keep up with the latest developments. To do so, you need to attend workshops and conferences, read the professional literature, and further your formal education. In many states, teachers are required to earn a master's degree or complete a certain number of university credit-bearing courses every three years.

Reflecting on Your Teaching for Professional Development

Probably the most important source for your continued development as a teacher is your reflections on how and what your students are learning and feeling and how their learning is linked to your teaching. Engaging in reflection means taking time to think back on lessons, units, and your program and to reflect on questions such as the following:

1. How are the students progressing and meeting the CCSS and National Standards of Physical Education?
2. What learning outcomes did I want to accomplish in this lesson, this week, and this month?
3. Why are these outcomes important and justified, and how are they linked to the National Standards?
4. Did the children achieve the learning outcomes?
5. What contributed to children's successful learning? What could I do to increase successful learning?
6. If there were problems, what factors contributed to them? What could I have done differently to prevent the problems?
7. What have I learned about teaching and children's learning? Am I growing as a teacher?
8. Did this lesson and my objectives reflect my philosophy and beliefs? Do I have any moral or ethical concerns about what happened? Am I the teacher I want to be?

Research shows that teachers who observe children's learning outcomes carefully and reflect on their teaching improve and can set themselves on the road to true teaching expertise (Behets & Vergauwen, 2006; Jung, 2012; Rovegno, 2003).

Stages of Teacher Development

Teachers can progress through different **stages of teacher development** as they develop from beginner to veteran. You may or may not experience these changes, but, if you do, you should know that you are not alone. Initially, many beginning teachers are concerned about survival, management, and discipline (Behets & Vergauwen, 2006; Stroot & Ko, 2006). Consequently, they focus on establishing management routines that work in their settings.

Unfortunately, some beginning teachers feel pressure from veteran teachers to fit in with the status quo and not teach in ways they learned during their teacher education. They shift from the way they want and know how to teach to teaching within a "zone of curricular safety" that does not challenge students to work hard and learn or threaten the veterans who do not want to change (Rovegno, 1994). Other beginning teachers are determined to be the best teachers they can be and do not succumb to peer pressure; these individuals refuse to let the system set limits on what they can be and do (Stroot & Ko, 2006).

After they pass through the survival stage, teachers stop focusing on themselves and start focusing on students' learning. By this phase in their evolution as teachers, they have developed classroom routines, they know more about how students learn, and they are able to solve the problems that arise in the typical school day (Behets & Vergauwen, 2006).

If teachers continue to work on their professional development, they can move to the expert stage. It is important to remember that expertise is not the same as experience. Teachers who have taught for many years might simply be experienced, without having learned enough during their years of experience to become experts.

Some research suggests that it could take a minimum of five to seven years before teachers truly can be labeled expert teachers (Berliner, 2000). This does not mean you cannot be a good teacher in your first year—you can. Rather, it simply means that developing true expertise is a long-term process.

Dispositions that Facilitate Teacher Development

Becoming an expert at anything is never easy. It requires time and effort. Research shows that certain dispositions—that is, attitudes, beliefs, and actions—can help you develop as a teacher.

Experienced Teachers Talk

Continued Professional Development

"Your teacher education does not end with your college diploma."

Being a Teacher Means Being a Learner

One of the most important dispositions good teachers have is the drive to be a continual learner. Good teachers are always trying to learn more. First, they try to learn more about the content they teach. Typically, physical education teachers know a few skills and sports well. No one can possibly graduate from college and know everything possible about all the skills, sports, dance, and lifelong activities we teach. Even with activities we know well, there are always teachers and coaches developing new techniques, new skills, and new tactics for these activities to evolve in new directions. Research shows that teachers who study content in workshops can improve their knowledge of content, which, in turn, has a significant, positive impact on student learning (Ward, Kim, Ko, & Li, 2015).

Good teachers also continuously seek information on instructional and assessment techniques, different ways to create a learning environment, new ideas about motivation, and new visions for what they want schools to be. They know that being a teacher means being a continual learner.

Figure 34.1 Reflecting on and assessing your teaching

Good Teachers (and Programs) Develop Over Time Due to Effort and Hard Work

A second disposition that can help you develop into an excellent teacher is an acceptance that the process will take time and effort. Do not think that there is something wrong with you if you have to work hard to master teaching. Learning to teach well and to have an impact on children's lives is a difficult skill to develop fully; that is simply a fact. Be prepared to have days when things do not go well, but don't let those aberrations overwhelm you. One study highlighted the power of resiliency, with the researchers noting that resilient teachers could face and solve problems while remaining optimistic with a sense of personal power (Woods & Lynn, 2001). Just because learning to teach is difficult does not mean you cannot be resilient and feel positive about your efforts.

In addition, it takes time to develop a program in a new school. Not only do you need to learn about your new environment, but the children must also adjust to a new physical education environment. Children tend to like physical education whether it is poorly or well taught, whether they learn anything or not. When you begin work in a school in which the children were used to physical education being recess-like, you can expect some initial complaints. (Children enjoy free play in the same way we enjoy our vacations.) Such demurrals do not mean that they won't value learning skills more; they will. Accept that it will take time to develop your program.

The Disposition to Do the Job Right: It's About the Kids

The following quote, attributed to Walt Disney, sums up the disposition of good teachers: "Whatever you do, do it well. Do it so well that when people see you do it they will want to come back and see you do it again and they will want to bring others and show them how well you do what you do."

Good teachers are not born; they work hard to become good teachers. They want to do the job right. They have a conscientious work ethic. Moreover, they want to do a good job because they know teaching is ultimately about the children, not about the teacher. The following quotes are from research studies on successful teachers.

> *Lori:* You know when I started to see them increase in their skillfulness in games, dance, and gymnastics…it changed my opinion of what I was doing….What I could see was the end product, not just that they were skillful, but I could see their pleasure in being able to do it [the skill]….That fostered a lot of my pleasure in being a physical educator and my feelings that my content was important, that it did have an impact on the lives of the children (Pissanos & Allison, 1996, p. 6).

To do the job right, you must be willing to critique yourself and your program (see **Figure 34.1**). Research shows that teachers who continue to grow professionally often change their programs because they have looked critically at what they were doing and been dissatisfied with the results of that analysis. As one said,

> *Karen:* It was kind of like the saying, "If it ain't broke, don't fix it." Well, it was broke. We were having kids who were not

Experienced Teachers Talk

Teacher Learning

"The best teachers are the best students."

Experienced Teachers Talk

Rome Wasn't Built in a Day

The following quote is from a research study by Cothran (2001, p. 76) focusing on teachers who successfully learned new curriculum approaches and improved their program:

> *Vicki:* At first you'll make a lot of mistakes and it won't be easy. It will be rough and crude the first unit you try it on. Then you refine it and go ahead and then put it in another unit.

taking responsibility for their own discipline. I was really open to finding something that would really affect them in their heart, not just in their head. I was having trouble reaching what I considered a connected level with the kids on the issue of their social responsibilities in class. I was ready to try something and the something that I was fortunate to find was the Hellison Model (Cothran, 2001, p. 72).

Believe in Your Philosophy and Develop a Practice that Matches It

Another disposition that can help your professional development is the willingness to build a sound educational philosophy that can guide you. A sound philosophy is rooted in theory and research. It provides justifications for your decisions. For example, a belief that every child has the right to equitable physical education regardless of gender, race, ethnicity, and ability gives you a moral stance upon which you can base decisions about how to divide children into groups, how to design tasks, and how to modify equipment. If you believe physical education should be developmentally appropriate for all children, you will differentiate instruction.

The goal, then, is to make your practice match your philosophy. This is not an easy task. If it were, we would have solved the problems of inequitable schooling, alienated students, and lack of student success and achievement years ago. You will need to reflect on and evaluate your own teaching. Videorecord your lessons to assess whether you are meeting goals, such as to facilitate learning, giving children maximum practice opportunities, having children be active for more than 50% of class time, ensuring low-skilled children are successful, and ensuring all children have positive experiences.

A sound philosophy will not only guide you, but also sustain you as you work to improve your program and your skills as a teacher. The "Experienced Teachers Talk" feature titled "Having a Sound Philosophy" describes how this process worked for one teacher.

Finally, a sound philosophy can help you evaluate ideas you glean from equipment companies, the Internet, and conferences (Langton, 2007). Not every new idea is a good idea, of course. Sometimes you can feel overwhelmed. Your philosophy, however, can be like the bubbles of air that guide surfers and boaters underwater. When boaters capsize and their boat overturns or when surfers are tossed in the whitewater of a wave, they can become disoriented underwater. They blow out some air and watch which way the bubbles go. The bubbles' path points out which way is up, and they can swim to the surface.

Similarly, let your philosophy guide you when you feel overwhelmed with choices.

Experienced Teachers Talk

Having a Sound Philosophy

The following quote is from a teacher in a research study who believed in the philosophy of an approach named "Every Child a Winner," which promoted a learning environment in which all children would learn and be successful (Rovegno & Bandhauer, 1997, p. 144). She believed in the philosophy so strongly that she could not go back to her old way of teaching even though the new approach was difficult.

> I believed so strongly in that that I couldn't give up on the idea no matter what...I couldn't go back. I was totally convinced they were right, so I couldn't go back—totally committed to the notion that everybody had the right to participate, and everybody had the right to be a winner.

Take Risks and Suspend Judgment

Another disposition that helps teachers continue to develop professionally is a willingness to take risks and try new ideas. At a conference, on an Internet site, or in a journal, you may encounter a new instructional strategy or a new curricular approach. Good teachers are willing to evaluate new ideas in relation to their own sound philosophy and then take risks and to experiment with these ideas. They don't say, "That's a good idea, but it won't work with my kids"; they give it a try.

More importantly, good teachers know that they may have to struggle with new ideas for a while before they learn how to make the ideas work in their own setting. They suspend judgment until they have worked with the new idea or approach extensively.

If you expect instant success, any attempt to change and improve your program is doomed to fail. You can get trapped in the status quo, however, if you assume there is nothing new you can learn that will work in your school. In contrast, recognizing that teaching is difficult and that it will take time to learn how to make new ideas work in your school will give you freedom to grow as a teacher.

It also will help to remember that in learning any new idea, we all have preconceptions about the idea—and some of these ideas may be misconceptions. Separating out the truth in this way is simply part of learning. It takes time to understand any complex idea, and you need to invest the time to get beyond your initial conceptions.

The field of physical education continues to grow and develop better ways to teach. To grow with the field, you just need to be willing to take risks and experiment with new ideas.

Take Responsibility Rather than Blame the Children

Another disposition of good teachers is their belief that it is their responsibility to ensure that children learn. Several studies have found that beginning teachers may initially blame the children for what happens in the lesson. Beginning teachers sometimes think that because they have worked hard at writing their lessons and planning activities, the students will automatically have the same enthusiasm. In turn, they may become angry with the students when they don't respond the way the teacher wanted or predicted. With experience, beginners grow to realize that the problem does not lie with the children, but rather with their teaching and their interpretations of the children's responses.

Finding Support in the Workplace

There is no doubt that having support from other teachers and administrators will help you develop as a teacher. Many school systems set up formal mentoring systems for new teachers.

Beginning Teachers Talk

Learning to Take Responsibility for Students' Learning

This feature presents quotes from research studies on beginning teachers when they shifted from blaming the students to taking responsibility for students' learning.

> *Brenda:* It was tough at the beginning because we did not plan well. They got a bad first impression because then we didn't make the drills at their level. But the biggest problem was that we didn't see it; we thought it was all them and not us (McCaughtry & Rovegno, 2003, p. 360).
>
> *Amber:* It was bad the first couple of weeks because they were bored. I don't blame them for hating our drills. They were not the problem, we were.... Not only were they hating what they were doing, but they hated us because we did not solve problems. We just blamed them (McCaughtry & Rovegno, 2003, p. 364).
>
> *Tyler:* They're eager, very eager. I never saw that before....I worked with school-aged kids in a day camp situation and the only thing that I perceived out of that was they are very lazy as a group and they don't want to do anything. And I had to be the cheerleader all the time and get them to do things. And I'm not sure now; maybe that had something to do with my activities and how I was getting them across (Rovegno, 1991, p. 209).

These systems can provide you with guidance on improving your teaching and emotional support.

If your school does not have a support system, or if the one it has isn't helping you, then you can create your own. First, find a mentor. Talk to other teachers, and ask for advice. Most veteran teachers are very willing to help newcomers. In addition, talk to administrators. Part of their job is to support teachers. Keep talking to different teachers and administrators until you find someone who seems able and willing to be an informal mentor. You might need to find a mentor from a different school.

Second, socialize with other beginning teachers at your school or in your community. Informal time spent together after work can be an excellent opportunity to talk about the problems you are facing and ways to solve them. You will soon learn that you are all having similar problems and that you can help one another discover solutions.

Try to find like-minded people, and spend time discussing your ideas (see **Figure 34.2**). Avoid people who leave you feeling negative or discouraged. Unfortunately, some staff rooms can be places where teachers simply complain, rather than places that are supportive environments for teacher development.

Maintain contact with your peers from your teacher education program. You can also maintain contact with faculty and cooperating teachers who can give you the support and guidance you want.

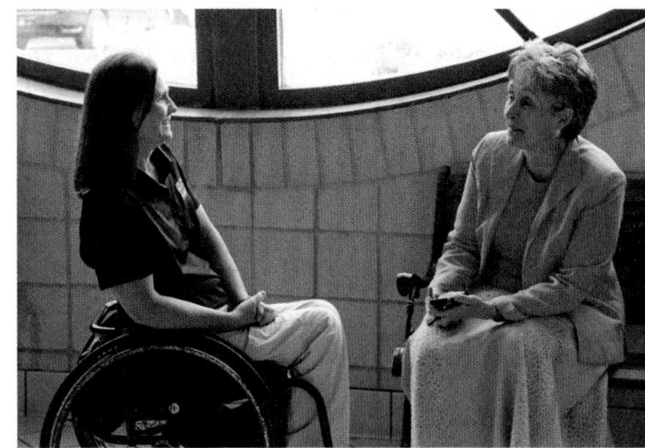

Figure 34.2 Seeking support from colleagues

Courtesy of John Dolly

Teachers need to be part of productive learning communities. Beginners, in particular, need support and guidance when they enter a new school (Stroot & Ko, 2006).

Teacher Evaluations

In almost all schools, principals evaluate teachers. They evaluate beginning teachers formally for at least their first three years. Most states or school districts have an evaluation tool they use for formal evaluations. Teacher evaluations can be an excellent way for you to improve your teaching.

Teacher evaluation tools typically are based on research on effective teachers. In general, they assess instructional strategies that have been shown to increase student learning. We cannot generalize about all state and district assessment tools, but the ones that we have examined include basic teaching techniques that all teachers want to develop.

We suggest you think politically about evaluations and study the evaluation tool well before the time of your evaluation. Because most tools were designed for classroom teachers, you will need to translate any item that doesn't appear to apply to you. You can ask your principal about these items and can negotiate what they mean in terms of your subject area. Then

SAFETY AND LIABILITY 34.1

Increasing Safety and Decreasing Risk of Liability: Guidelines Relevant to Content in this Chapter

In this box, we discuss specific guidelines built on information discussed throughout this text on professional standards of practice, negligence, and liability. The goals of these guidelines are to increase children's safety and decrease teachers' risk of negligence and liability.

- Administrators must provide teachers opportunities for training in current professional practice and safety procedures, such as CPR and first aid.

be prepared to teach for the test. Know how you can demonstrate all the evaluation items in your lessons. This will show the principal that you have a quality program equivalent to those offered by the classroom teachers.

Professional Organizations and Internet Support

There are many professional organizations you can join to help you continue your professional development. Physical educators' national organization is the Society of Health and Physical Educators, called SHAPE America. Each regional district has a branch, and all states have a state-level organization. Each of these organizations holds a conference at least once a year that you can attend; conference information is available on their websites.

Your state organization associated with SHAPE is often the first choice for teachers because the conferences are within driving distance and the dues and conference fees are less expensive than national organizations' fees. State SHAPE organizations offer excellent opportunities to meet and share ideas with other professionals within your state. You can also become involved with the many committees, task forces, advocacy initiatives, leadership positions, and activities run by the state organizations. Your involvement gives you a voice in our profession and provides the much-needed service on which all professional organizations depend.

When you join our national organization, SHAPE America, you select journals to receive each month. The *Journal of Physical Education, Recreation, and Dance* (JOPERD) and *Strategies* are written for teachers. SHAPE maintains an Internet forum in which members discuss common problems and issues. SHAPE emails monthly newsletters informing teachers about the latest research proving the benefits of physical education. These articles can help you promote and justify your program. They also alert teachers about issues, political initiatives, and new research on injuries and safety issues. SHAPE also maintains a Facebook page that provides information about research, political actions, new initiatives, resources, issues, and new ideas for your program.

SHAPE's website includes teaching tools, advocacy toolkits, teacher toolboxes, and position statements on topics ranging from dodgeball, recess, and use of physical activity as punishment, to appropriate class length for elementary physical education and appropriate practices. In addition, SHAPE provides links to other organizations and national promotional efforts, such as U.S. First Lady Michelle Obama's "Let's Move!" and SHAPE's "Let's Move in School" campaigns.

Other organizations that offer online newsletters and websites of interest are the American Heart Association and the National Coalition for Promoting Physical Activity.

Several other websites have provided useful information for physical educators for many years. PE Central has lesson plans, examples of special events, assessments, bulletin boards, summaries of research, and job listings. PE Universe also offers lesson ideas, discussions, and blogs. Teacher Tube has videos of lessons, and Sportplan has information about teaching and coaching many different sports.

Twitter can also be an excellent professional development tool, linking you to teacher blogs, chat rooms, and other educational sites that offer conference-type sessions. For example, search the hashtags #pechat, #pegeeks, #PhysEdSummit, and #Edcamphome.

Finally, many universities offer evening and summer courses and institutes for teachers. In addition, a variety of online courses for teachers are available. (You can find listings of online courses on the PE Central website.)

The Teaching Profession and the National Board of Professional Teaching Standards

One excellent professional development opportunity for teachers is to work to become a board-certified teacher. The **National Board of Professional Teaching Standards**, for example, has designed a set of tools for assessing accomplished teaching. In doing so, it has established standards for each subject area, including physical education, based on the five core propositions described in this section (National Board of Professional Teaching Standards, 2002). These propositions, which were developed by teachers and are supported by research, provide excellent goals for beginning teachers to aspire to meet. You can read detailed descriptions of the propositions and the standards for physical education at the website for the National Board (http://www.nbpts.org).

Teachers Are Committed to Students and Their Learning

The first proposition is that accomplished teachers are committed to all students and hold high expectations for all learners, regardless of their ability. They not only recognize and accept individual differences, but also differentiate instruction and establish a learning environment so that all children are challenged and successful. Moreover, they respect and value diversity and ensure students treat one another respectfully.

Teachers Know the Subjects They Teach and How to Teach Those Subjects to Students

Accomplished teachers know their subject matter in depth. They know how to translate their knowledge into developmentally appropriate teaching. They know how students learn particular content, which immature patterns they are likely to see, and which difficulties they are likely to encounter, and they plan lessons based on that knowledge. Accomplished teachers understand and promote the benefits of physical activity for children's health across their lifespan.

Teachers Are Responsible for Managing and Monitoring Student Learning

Accomplished teachers effectively use a range of teaching techniques to motivate and inspire students to engage in learning. They use multiple assessment tools appropriate for different learners and use their assessments to provide feedback for students and to improve instruction.

Teachers Think Systematically About Their Practice and Learn from Experience

Accomplished teachers reflect on their teaching to improve their knowledge and teaching. They are aware of current theories, instructional strategies, and issues within physical education.

Teachers Are Members of Learning Communities

Accomplished teachers avoid isolation, instead striving to collaborate with others in learning communities. They work with parents and members of the community to advocate physical education. They seek ways to involve parents in the physical education program.

Summary

One of your responsibilities as a teacher will be to continue your professional development. Building your program and developing your skills so you become an excellent teacher takes time and effort. A sound philosophy can guide you in this process.

Having support in the workplace from other teachers and administrators will help you adjust to the school environment and develop your expertise as a teacher. You can also find support from professional organizations. The bottom line, however, is that you will need to take responsibility for keeping up with new developments in your field by reading, attending conferences, and finding colleagues with whom you can work to support one another's professional development.

Review Questions

1. Why is reflecting on teaching important? In your opinion, what is the most important question to ask to guide your reflection on a lesson?
2. During field experiences in your undergraduate coursework, did you ever experience the survival stage of teaching? If so, why, and what happened? If not, what helped you avoid or move beyond this stage?
3. Think back on all the teachers and coaches you have known. Which ones do you think were experts, and what is the basis for your opinion? Which teachers were experienced but not experts, and what is the basis for your opinion?
4. When have you experienced the idea that being a teacher means being a learner? What contributed to your learning?
5. When have you been frustrated because your teaching was not as effective as you wanted it to be? How did you respond to your frustration?
6. Have you ever taken risks in teaching? If so, how did you feel, and how did it work? If not, why not, and when might you find opportunities to take risks?
7. Have you ever blamed the students for problems in a lesson (as most beginning teachers do at some point)? What could you have done differently in that situation?
8. What are three of the most important beliefs you hold as part of your philosophy of teaching?
9. What is your opinion of the five propositions for accomplished teachers from the National Board of Professional Teaching Standards?

References

Behets, D., & Vergauwen, L. (2006). Learning to teach in the field. In D. Kirk, D. MacDonald, & M. O'Sullivan (Eds.). *The handbook of physical education* (pp. 407–424). London: Sage.

Berliner, D. C. (2000). A personal response to those who bash teacher education. *Journal of Teacher Education, 51*, 358–371.

Cothran, D. J. (2001). Curricular change in physical education: Success stories from the front line. *Sport, Education and Society, 6*, 67–79.

Jung, J. (2012). The focus, role, and meaning of experienced teachers' reflection in physical education. *Physical Education and Sport Pedagogy, 17*, 157–175.

Langton, T. (2007). Applying Laban's movement framework in elementary physical education. *Journal of Physical Education, Recreation and Dance, 78*(1), 17–24, 39, 53.

McCaughtry, N., & Rovegno, I. (2003). The development of pedagogical content knowledge: Moving from blaming students to predicting skillfulness, recognizing motor development, and understanding emotion. *Journal of Teaching in Physical Education, 22*, 355–368.

National Board for Professional Teaching Standards. (2002). *What Teachers Should Know and Be Able to Do.* Arlington, VA: NBPTS.

Pissanos, B. W., & Allison, P. C. (1996). Continued professional learning: A topical life history. *Journal of Teaching in Physical Education, 16*, 2–19.

Rovegno, I. (1991). A participant-observation study of knowledge restructuring in a field-based elementary physical education methods course. *Research Quarterly for Exercise and Sport, 62*, 205–212.

Rovegno, I. (1994). Teaching within a curricular zone of safety: School culture and the situated nature of student teachers' pedagogical content knowledge. *Research Quarterly for Exercise and Sport, 65*, 269–279.

Rovegno, I. (2003). Teachers' knowledge construction. In S. J. Silverman & C. D. Ennis (Eds.), *Student learning in physical education: Applying research to enhance instruction* (2nd ed.) (pp. 295–310). Champaign, IL: Human Kinetics.

Rovegno, I., & Bandhauer, D. (1997). Psychological dispositions that facilitated and sustained the development of knowledge of a constructivist approach to physical education. *Journal of Teaching in Physical Education, 16*, 136–154.

Stroot, S., & Ko, B. (2006). Induction of beginning physical educators into the school setting. In D. Kirk, D. MacDonald, & M. O'Sullivan (Eds.), *The handbook of physical education* (pp. 425–448). London: Sage.

Ward, P., Kim, I., Ko, B., & Li, W. (2015). Effects of improving teachers' content knowledge on teaching and student learning in physical education. *Research Quarterly for Exercise and Sport, 86*, 130–139.

Woods, A. M., & Lynn, S. K. (2001). Through the years: A longitudinal study of physical education teachers from a research-based preparation program. *Research Quarterly for Exercise and Sport, 72*, 219–231.

CHAPTER

35

Managing the Politics of Schools

PRE-READING REFLECTION

1. What do you want to know about the politics of the school where you student teach or have your first job?
2. How do you think you can acquire this information?

OBJECTIVES

Students will learn:

1. School politics can influence your job satisfaction either positively or negatively.
2. You can learn the politics of your school and have a positive impact on the workplace environment.

KEY TERM

School politics

CONNECTION TO STANDARDS

Providing a quality program based on the National Standards and promoting your program as such is important for improving the status of physical education in your school. The Common Core and other State Standards (CCSS) also offer physical education teachers opportunities to increase and promote their centrality in their school because we are working toward the same standards as classroom teachers. When physical education meets standards in the ways that classroom teachers do, we increase our visibility and our contribution to the mission of schools as educational institutions.

Schools Are Political Places

In every school we have ever worked in, school "politics" have been part of the environment. **School politics** comprises the relationships among teachers, staff, and administrators that lead to power in the school. *Power* in this context includes the power to influence or control funds, schedules, workload, policies, procedures, curricula, instruction, and status.

Sometimes the politics of a school create a positive atmosphere that promotes a good work environment and enhances teachers' satisfaction with the school and their jobs. At other times, the politics create a negative, discouraging environment that limits teachers' efforts to focus on student learning. Research suggests that the latter scenario is especially likely to be realized by beginning teachers who start their first job eager to apply what they have learned in their teacher training and then are surprised when confronted with teachers and administrators who are not supportive (Stroot & Ko, 2006).

It can be easy to assume as a beginning teacher or a student teacher that you can do little about school politics. In some schools, that perception is accurate. Nevertheless, research also shows there is much you can do politically to improve your work environment, to contribute to a positive atmosphere, and to increase your impact on the school. What follows are suggestions from the research (Rovegno & Bandhauer, 1997) and advice from experienced teachers who have successfully managed the politics of elementary schools.

Know Your Rights and Responsibilities

All states and schools have policies that spell out teachers' rights and responsibilities, and you need to know what these policies say. Often, they are stated in your contract and in teachers' handbooks or school policy and mission statements. These are important documents for you to have and understand. In particular, pay attention to safety regulations and procedures to follow if a child is injured. In addition, you need to know the disciplinary procedures and any policies related to interacting with parents.

Sometimes, the written policies and procedures do not match what administrators and teachers actually do in practice. Be aware of this possibility. Typically, experienced teachers are willing to help you understand the policies and procedures that actually function in your school.

Figure Out Who Has Power

Your first task is simply to pay attention to the politics and identify how things work and who has power. For example, the principal probably has the most power in the school. In some cases, however, the assistant principals will have a more direct impact on your day-to-day life. In many schools, principals formally share power with teachers through committees, such as budget and curriculum committees. They also may share power informally with teachers who have gained the principal's trust and who provide valuable advice and guidance. As you might imagine, it is in your best interest to become one of these teachers.

Although this might surprise you, for physical education teachers, another important person with power is the custodian.

Custodians maintain the school's fields and keep the facilities clean and safe. Having a good relationship with the custodian will make your job easier. Once you know who has power and understand power structures, such as committees, your goal should be to become a positive part of the political structure of the school and to position yourself as central to the school. Research shows that many physical education teachers are marginalized—that is, administrators and classroom teachers do not consider them and their programs to be central to the school (Stroot & Ko, 2006). This perspective can result in smaller budgets, less time in the curriculum, and a heavier workload. More significantly, if you are marginalized, it means less respect for you and your work.

SAFETY AND LIABILITY 35.1

Increasing Safety and Decreasing Risk of Liability: Guidelines Relevant to Content in this Chapter

In this box, we discuss specific guidelines built on information discussed throughout this text on professional standards of practice, negligence, and liability. The goals of these guidelines are to increase children's safety and decrease teachers' risk of negligence and liability.

In relation to safety and decreasing risk of liability, your school should have and provide you with the following (Eckhoff-Shemek, 2009; Nohr, 2009):

- Written plans for medical emergencies and written emergency procedures in the event of a serious injury to a student.
- Accident report forms and a place to maintain written records of accidents and injuries.
- A first aid kit.
- Written emergency procedures in the event of serious threats to the safety and health of children and school personnel.
- Written procedures for fire and other reasons for evacuations and lockdowns.

It is your responsibility to know these procedures and be prepared to respond appropriately and to offer aid if needed.

Experienced Teachers Talk

School Atmosphere

The following quotes describe the atmospheres of two schools. The first speaker is a substitute teacher and the second an experienced teacher:

> [School X] puts too much emphasis on the negative....It goes down to the cafeteria workers—I feel it is contagious. I don't even go into the teachers' room [there]. It's like a competition who has the worst kids and who had the worst experience that day. Here [school Y], I hear the teachers talking about doing things together. In general, the whole atmosphere is better, and that carries through to the kids, and they have a better opportunity to learn... [Here] they are more open to changes and to trying new things, whereas [there] most teachers fight change: "This is the way we have done it, and we're not going to change."

> I think we have a really good, a very good situation here where we learn from each other. There's a lot of sharing and ideas coming back and forth as open as we are. You know I've been at places where you were in your own room... and the door was closed,...and there were people who were guarding, "Don't-look-at-my-bulletin-boards kind of thing."...And [here] there's a lot of, "Would you like a copy of the worksheet that we did?" Or, "We've used these materials and I've finished with them. Would you like to try it?" There's a lot of sharing going on as far as sharing activities, sharing information.

In part, some people may perceive physical education as a marginal subject because they assume the mind is separate from—and more important than—the body. Even so, physical education teachers can and do eliminate marginalization in their school.

Be a Positive Influence and Play a Central Role in the Life of the School

One of the best ways to overcome marginality is to become a positive influence and play a central role in the life of your school. You can do this several ways.

Participate in School Functions

First, try to participate in school events. If the classroom teachers have planned a special academic program, such as a Renaissance Faire or a parents' night to showcase children's social studies projects on different countries, volunteer to help or, better yet, find a way to include physical education in the event. For example, you can have children design a dance to represent the country or historical period they studied and perform it during the parents' night.

Volunteer to be on school committees, and try to contribute to their work (see **Figure 35.1**). As an assistant principal said about her physical education teacher, "You can't help but have respect for her and what she has done. I love it when she is on committees. On committees, she is full of ideas. If you want something done, you have her involved." If the school has social functions, attend and speak positively about your classes and your program.

Figure 35.1 Physical education teachers participating in school committees

At the very least, you want those in power to view you as a professional with a positive influence. Try to avoid engaging in conversations with teachers who constantly complain about the school, children, other teachers, and administrators. In addition, try to avoid listening to gossip, and don't spread gossip yourself.

Understand the Needs of Classroom Teachers

As one politically astute physical education teacher said, "I pay attention to the complaints of the classroom teachers because they outnumber the specials [art, music, and physical education teachers] 41 to 5." To understand the needs and concerns of others, learn the history of the problem, and listen carefully to what people say. One teacher explained,

> I go to all the meetings, and I know what they say....That's why I'm so powerful in Little League: because I know what went on before, and I know what went on after. They keep bringing up the same issues. You know, they all think I'm this great person that has these great ideas. Well, I'm just one of the few people that know past history and peoples' wishes because I pay attention to that.

Once you understand the concerns and issues, help solve the problem. For example, in one school, the classroom teachers complained for several years that there was no recess. The physical education teacher tracked down the state requirements for instructional time during each day, called other districts to learn about different recess procedures, figured out how much time was legally available for recess, and developed a schedule and set of recess procedures that were accepted by principals and teachers.

Taking a leadership role in solving the problems of classroom teachers and administrators will increase your power in the school. When you care about other teachers' needs, they will care about yours. Moreover, it is very difficult for classroom teachers to suggest cuts to physical education if you have helped them solve their problems.

Finally, when problems arise in which two sides hold competing interests, scout out the opposition. Anticipate how your opponents will perceive the issue and their needs. Often, you can broker a compromise if you can address the needs of the teachers on both sides of the debate.

Be Conversant with the Latest Educational Theories and Instructional Techniques

Physical education is a school subject focused on children's learning outcomes. In that sense, it is the same as any other subject area. We base the physical education curriculum and instruction on national standards and on the same learning, motivation, and cultural theories and research as classroom subjects. Being aware of the current educational research and recommendations for curricula and instruction gives you common ground with classroom teachers, and discussing these issues with your classroom peers can help them recognize you as a teacher just like them. As one classroom teacher said about the physical education teacher with whom she recognized common ground, "She believes in what I believe in." When you are working toward the same goals as the classroom teachers, you are at the center of the school mission, not the margins.

The CCSS, which apply to all subject areas, give you an opportunity to connect what you do to the same standards that apply to classroom subjects. Classroom teachers are under pressure to improve children's test scores in reading and mathematics and, in our experience, are grateful for the contributions physical education can make in meeting the CCSS.

Many of the professional development workshops on the latest research and theory about curricula and instruction that take place at your elementary school will be geared—unfairly—toward the classroom teachers. Nevertheless, we can find ways to translate educational theories for classroom curricula and instruction into the physical education realm. For example, critical thinking in social studies; a hands-on, experiment-based approach in science; cooperative learning; and the thinking curriculum that is prominent in current classroom subject areas are also important to physical education.

The problem, of course, is that you end up having to translate the classroom research recommendations to the physical education sphere. Sometimes, this will be easy for you; at other times, it will be more difficult. Try to listen to the big message and don't worry about irrelevant details. For example, if the workshop is on problem solving in mathematics, focus on what the presenters are saying about how to teach the process of problem solving and try to apply it to problem solving in physical education, such as the problem-solving process children use to design a dance, gymnastics sequence, or game.

What the Research Says

School Politics

In a study of the influence of school politics on three beginning teachers (Schempp, Sparkes, & Templin, 1993, p. 460), one teacher said, "The social–political dynamics within a building are important in how you are viewed. The things that you do, that you get involved with, the staff functions, the committees you get on to do different things, really come into play in how you are viewed in the school."

Dress for Success

We understand that how you dress is a personal decision and makes a statement about how you want others to perceive you. Try to be aware that the attire your generation considers fashionable and appropriate might be considered inappropriate attire by administrators and members of older generations. Whether these judgments are fair or not, it is in your best interest to remember schools are multigenerational—and to recognize that the older generation often holds the most power.

Some schools have explicit dress codes. All schools, however, have implicit dress codes. Until you understand the politics of your school, we suggest you try to dress conservatively. We have seen too many young teachers draw lines in the sand about their dress and win the battle but lose the war; we know of too many student teachers sent home because their shorts were too short or too tight or their tops too revealing. Obviously, appropriate physical education attire differs from classroom attire. You will always be safe if you follow the lead of the best-dressed college football coaches you see on television.

In addition, Rubinstein (2012) points out that when beginning teachers dress too casually, attempting not to look like a traditional older teacher, they are taking a big risk with students' perceptions and, in turn, behaviors. He says, "If you look like a teacher, they will treat you like a teacher" (p. 52).

When you interview for a job, dress in conservative business attire, not physical education attire. Your goal is to get the job and show the people you meet that you are competent and understand what it means to dress like a professional.

Provide a Quality Program

Probably nothing is more important for gaining respect and centrality for your program than providing a quality program. Classroom teachers respect physical education teachers who share the same commitment to teaching and work hard to provide quality learning experiences for children. In addition, many classroom teachers suffered through poor-quality physical education programs when they were children and expect physical education to be the same as the programs they experienced. They need to know how your program is different.

Promoting Your Program Within the School

Classroom teachers and principals will not automatically watch your program and see that it is a quality program. You will have to tell them. As a principal said, "[The physical education teacher] is another reason the program is successful, and she communicates that well. . . . She calls our attention to it, as it should be."

One way to promote your program is to talk with the classroom teachers when they pick up their classes from physical education (see **Figure 35.2**). Tell them what the children learned, or comment on positive achievements. For example, if you were working on transitions between gymnastic moves, you can tell the teacher how you related that to transitions in writing. If you were working on asymmetrical and symmetrical shapes, you can tell the teacher you talked about the line of symmetry and congruent shapes. If the students designed games in groups, you can tell the teacher you discussed what children needed to do to be good group members and how to work productively in groups.

Figure 35.2 Promoting your program with classroom teachers

In addition, find out what the children are learning in their classrooms, and try to make connections. You will be surprised at the many ways physical education and classroom subjects connect. In describing the centrality of physical education, one assistant principal said,

> It's so much a part of what we do, I don't see it any more as separate....so much of what they do in PE ties directly into the classroom....The concepts tie in....the content itself is powerful—like the kids doing sequences with beginning and ending shapes and cooperating. That is powerful...and ties right in with math and reading. You teach sequencing to kids when they are reading. Sequencing in a story would be what happened first in the story—did he get out of bed before he brushed his teeth? And being able to repeat a story back. Kindergarten teachers work on the concepts under, over, behind, in front of, and PE teachers work on it constantly.

In addition, teaching interdisciplinary units in which you work with a classroom teacher to combine two (or more) subject areas can enhance children's learning in both subject areas (Purcell Cone, Werner, & Cone, 2008). These units highlight your work and show classroom teachers you share their concern for children's learning in all subject areas.

We do not recommend interdisciplinary units that trivialize physical education content, such as laying out hundreds of cards with words and having children run around collecting words to form sentences. Interdisciplinary units should not try to teach reading or math with a physical activity component. Rather, they should begin with important and worthwhile physical education content and find links to what children are learning in other subject areas.

In addition to talking with classroom teachers, promote your program with the principal(s). It is possible, if not likely, that you will be hired in a school to replace a physical education teacher who ran a recreational, rather than educational, program. In these instances, you should start promoting your program when you interview for the job and continue to do so every chance you get. When you talk about the program, use the language of elementary education. Explain how you will focus on learning outcomes and differentiate instruction. Inform administrators about research showing the benefits of physical activity for academic learning and cognitive functioning. Believe in your program and in the positive contribution of physical education, and share this belief and your enthusiasm with others in your school and community.

Experienced Teachers Talk

Classroom Teachers' Perspectives

The following comments are from classroom teachers about why they liked the physical education program at their school:

> It's a real dynamic as opposed to static program. Every child is moving. I really like it a lot—a lot. I think it's an incredible program....I was a fat little girl, and I hated PE. I learned how to not stand up straight. I learned not to play....And so I think it's a wonderful program....They're doing their homework. They are doing the education part of it and doing the political arena—getting the money.

> I remember comparing their PE to mine, and it was so much higher quality and humane, and it was really individualized. And what we were subjected to was inhumane. As a classroom teacher, I had a hard time teaching PE and that too made my respect for them increase because they made it look easy and kids came back pumped.

Experienced Teachers Talk

Connecting to Classroom Subjects

Both teachers and children can identify ways to connect classroom subjects and physical education. It will help children to recognize the connections if you use the same vocabulary as the classroom teachers. The following is a classroom teacher's comments on how physical education can connect with classroom content:

> I'll say to the kids, "We're going to do some sequencing today. Who knows what sequencing is?"...I always have a hand up that says, "Oh yeah, we do sequences in PE."...a lot of times that there is some tie-in as far as what's happening there with what happens here. I see that as a real positive thing because it helps the kids to see that things are not done in isolation.... In science, we talk about forces. I'll get started on a force as a push or a pull, and they'll say, "Yeah we push with our bodies and do light force." They relate that....I've watched PE classes, and I've heard them talk about using high-level movements and low-level and forces...but the kids bring it.

Promoting Your Program in the Community

Promoting your program in the community also is important, but more difficult. School boards and state departments of education have considerable power over what happens in schools. Dolly Lambdin, a leader in our field who is an elementary physical educator and a past president of SHAPE America, was interviewed by Steve Stork, editor of *Teaching Elementary Physical Education* (TEPE). Here is an excerpt from that interview:

TEPE: What do you see as the major challenges facing physical education teachers today?

DL: I think the major challenge has been the same for a long time. That is, learning how to be part of the political process, instead of just doing good work. I think it's very difficult. People now appreciate physical education more than they have in the past for lots of reasons: because we've improved quality of programs, and because of obvious health needs that have been documented over and over. But, on a local basis, we are still not part of the political process in the way we need to be. It's difficult. How do you do that on top of everything else you do every day? I mean, teach kids all day long, and still have the energy to write your school board member or talk to legislators. I think the answer comes in people being able to articulate better and better what it is they do on an individual basis. We've decided in our district that if each teacher had one supportive parent they talked to on regular basis that would be enough. They don't have to have dozens. If each [teacher] just identified one [parent] who would be their advocate in talking to the school board, or principal, or sharing with other parents in the community that would be incredibly powerful. But we're not even there yet. It's very difficult to begin to nurture that support system for yourself (Stork, 2004, pp. 7–8).

One way to begin to promote your program in the community is to learn about your community. Learn about what parents want for their children, and discover their concerns. Get to know the families in your school. Talk to parents when they pick up their children. Learn about the recreational and after-school opportunities that you can recommend for children. Attend parent–teacher organization (PTO) and school board meetings. Become involved in community events that you enjoy. Become visible in your community. Attend Little League games, soccer games, gymnastics competitions, and dance competitions.

As Dolly Lambdin suggested, parents can be a strong advocate for your program. Typically, this relationship starts with their children talking positively about what they learn in their physical education classes. However, you can also initiate these conversations and communicate directly with parents. The box titled "Promoting Your Program with Parents and Guardians" highlights some suggestions.

Promoting Your Program with Parents and Guardians

- Send an email newsletter describing what you have been teaching.
- Send home notes titled "Ask your child what he or she learned in physical education today," followed by suggested questions and correct answers.
- Create a newsletter using MyPlate materials from MyPlate for Kids and MyPlate for My Family (http://www.choosemyplate.gov/kids) (U.S. Department of Agriculture Food and Nutrition Service, 2011).
- Put short articles in the school newsletter describing research on safety issues, such as children wearing backpacks and high-heeled shoes.
- Send home information from the U.S. government's *Let's Move!* website (http://www.letsmove.gov) about simple things families can do to promote healthy eating and physical activity habits.
- Send home information about the NFL Play 60 campaign (http://www.NFL.com/play60) to get children to play actively 60 minutes a day.

You can use special events, such as field days, to get parents involved in your program. You can also organize events such as Family Fitness Nights, during which the children teach their parents what they have learned about health-related physical activity and have the parents join in with the physical activities. Having children perform dance and gymnastics sequences at PTO meetings is another well-established way to showcase your program. Finally, you can plan special events during National Physical Education and Sport week, such as inviting parents to participate in physical education classes or doing a student program at the local mall.

Promoting your program in the community can be difficult, but it is worth the effort. One parent explained, "I just love our PE teacher. There was a 5K run that included kids and there she was at the finish line cheering on and hugging *every* kid who came across. One of those kids was mine, and she made his day. Mine, too."

Summary

All schools have their own school politics, which can have a positive or negative effect on your work experiences. As a teacher, you need to be aware of your school's politics and understand how they work. Over time, you can find ways to work within the political structures to improve your work environment.

In many schools, physical education is marginalized. Ways to overcome marginality include playing a central role in the life of the school, understanding and responding to the needs of the classroom teachers, being conversant with the latest educational theories, providing a quality program, and promoting your program in the school and community.

Review Questions

1. What are school politics, and why are they important?
2. (a) What is marginality? (b) Think about a time you experienced marginality because of your major and you were taken by surprise and did not respond. Describe how you might respond if you were to be faced with a similar situation in the future.
3. Discuss how to play a central role in the life of the school.
4. What is your opinion about the implicit dress codes of schools?
5. In relation to school politics, why is it important to provide a quality program?
6. Discuss two ways to promote your physical education program within the school. Figure out and describe one way that was not presented in the chapter.
7. Discuss how you can promote your program with parents.

References

Purcell Cone, T., Werner, P., & Cone, S. (2008). *Interdisciplinary elementary physical education: Connecting, sharing, partnering* (2nd ed.). Champaign, IL: Human Kinetics.

Rovegno, I., & Bandhauer, D. (1997). Norms of the school culture that facilitated teacher adoption and learning of a constructivist approach to physical education. *Journal of Teaching in Physical Education, 16*, 401–425.

Rubinstein, G. (2012). The don'ts and don's of teaching. *Educational Leadership, 69*(8), 50–52.

Schempp, P. G., Sparkes, A. C., & Templin, T. J. (1993). The micropolitics of teacher induction. *American Educational Research Journal, 30*, 447–472.

Stork, S. (2004). Interview with Dolly Lambdin. *Teaching Elementary Physical Education, 15*(3), 6–8.

Stroot, S., & Ko, B. (2006). Induction of beginning physical educators into the school setting. In D. Kirk, D. MacDonald, & M. O'Sullivan (Eds.), *The handbook of physical education* (pp. 425–448). London: Sage.

U.S. Department of Agriculture Food and Nutrition Service. (2011). *MyPlate for kids*. Washington, DC: Author. Retrieved from http://www.MyPlate.gov

Glossary

Accent: An accent occurs when one beat is emphasized.

ActivityGram: The ActivityGram assesses the amount of children's physical activity across a three-day period in a variety of activities.

Adult error detection model: In contrast to a developmental perspective, the teacher compares what he or she sees against the adult or expert model and views any derivation from an adult performance as an error.

Aesthetic experience: An aesthetic experience in children's dance is "an active response of the whole self. Just going through the motions, no matter how beautiful or interesting the motions are, is not enough. One must be stirred, touched, fully engaged" (Stinson, 1982, p. 72). An aesthetic experience is like watching a beautiful sunset over a mountain lake, looking over the Grand Canyon, or seeing the Northern Lights for the first time. It touches you in a memorable way.

Aesthetic highlight: An aesthetic highlight is part of a sequence that stands out as distinctive, exceptional, or particularly interesting.

Aesthetic perception: In dance, an aesthetic perception is the ability to recognize and appreciate the expressive, symbolic, and artistic properties of a dance.

Affordances: Affordances are possible actions that the environment allows (i.e., affords) in relation to an individual's capabilities and goals.

Aligned developmental feedback: In aligned developmental feedback, the intended learning outcome and, in turn, the assessment and feedback, focus on performance techniques matched to the child's current developmental levels on different body components that the child can learn and develop within a lesson or unit. Research has shown that such feedback increases student learning more than specific feedback that is not aligned developmentally (Cohen, Goodway, & Lidor, 2012).

Alternative strategies: Creating alternative strategies involves planning ways to modify tasks if what you are doing isn't working.

Anti-gravity exertion: Although there are only two kinds of muscle contractions (isotonic and isometric), in dance a third critical form of tension and force can be differentiated: anti-gravity exertion (Preston-Dunlop, 1980). Anti-gravity exertion is the light muscle tension used to hold the body stretched tall and upright (against the pull of gravity). Dancers almost always maintain anti-gravity exertion.

Apex: The apex is highest point of the parabolic pathway of a tossed or thrown ball.

Application tasks (A): Application, or assessment, tasks are tasks that apply lesson content to a culminating activity, such as a dance, gymnastics sequence, game, or game-like task. With such tasks, the children's focus of attention shifts from how to perform a skill to using the skill in different situations and broader contexts. Application tasks also include self-challenges, such as "Try to improve the number of times you hit the target," and self-competition tasks, such as "Each time you dribble, try to dribble the ball more times in a row without losing control." Again, the children's focus of attention shifts to applying the skill in a broader, more complex context. Assessment tasks give children the opportunity to assess their progress.

Asymmetrical shapes: Asymmetrical shapes are shapes in which the positions of body parts on each side of the body are different.

Autonomy: Autonomy is the extent to which one has choices and control over his or her behaviors. Student autonomy leads to increased engagement, self-sufficiency, and enjoyment.

Back handspring: A back handspring is a jump backward done from an off-balance position, landing on the hands with the head back and the hands, shoulders, and hips in a line (with a very slight arch), then snapping the feet down.

Back roll: In a back roll, the child starts standing, squats in a tucked position, and rolls backward until the palms are flat on the mat and the body is curled over the shoulders. The palms are pushed strongly on the mat at the same time as the child extends his or her arms in a reverse press (using strong arms), lifting the body high enough for the head to pass through without putting any weight on the head. The roll ends landing on the feet.

Back walk-over: In a back walk-over, the child involves staring from a standing position with the kick-off leg in front, stretching tall through the spine, and arching back until the hands touch the floor in a back bend. In a continuous, simultaneous movement, the child rocks over the hands, kicks up with the front leg, and pushes off with the back leg to the handstand position with legs split. The move is completed with a step down from the handstand.

Balance: When children balance, they support their weight on one or several body parts and hold that position still. Balancing implies positions that are hard to hold. By "hard to hold," we don't mean the child attempts a difficult or advanced skill, but rather that the child needs to concentrate and maintain tension in the body to remain balanced.

"Ball, me, defender" position: In the "ball, me, defender" position, a dribbler puts his or her body between the ball and the defender to shield the ball.

Ballistic stretches: Ballistic stretches stretch the muscles by bouncing. This form of stretching is no longer recommended for any age group due to its potential for injury.

Basal metabolism: Basal metabolism consists of the minimum amount of energy required for the body's basic physiological functions, such as repairing cell damage, building new cells, and growth, while the body is at complete rest.

Beehive soccer: In beehive soccer, crowds of children chase after one ball like a mass of bees swarming about a hive. There is no passing, no attempts to get into an open space, and no defense other than intimidation and trying to run and kick the ball somewhere.

Block plan: A block plan is a form of unit plan that lists the major tasks and the culminating activity for the set of lessons within the unit.

Block tackling: Block tackling is a form of defense used in invasion games in which the defender blocks the ball with the stick or foot, positioning the body to the side of the offense so the foot of the defender aligns with the foot and ball of the offense.

Bloom's taxonomy: Bloom's taxonomy describes six levels of cognitive processing for educational objective knowledge, comprehension, application, analysis, synthesis, and evaluation.

Body aspect of the Laban framework: The body aspect of the Laban framework describes what the body is doing and the shape of the body.

Body composition: Body composition is the percentage of fat in the body in relation to the percentage of lean body tissue.

Breach of duty: Breach of duty means that a teacher failed to meet the standard of professional care of a child that a reasonably prudent teacher would have met in the same or similar situation. A breach of duty can be an action or a failure to act.

Canon: In a canon group action, everyone moves in succession, starting one at a time.

Cardiorespiratory endurance: "Cardiorespiratory endurance is the ability to perform large-muscle, whole-body exercise at moderate to high intensity for an extended period of time" (Institute of Medicine, 2012, pp. 7–8).

Central ready position: To deny the offense the most space, position yourself in the center, and be in a ready position. In tennis-type and one-wall handball-type games, this is just behind the baseline and is called the *base position.* In badminton-type games, the central ready position is in the middle of the court because the shuttlecock does not bounce. In racquetball-type wall games with four walls, it is the center of the court, with both players trying to control the same spot. In volleyball-type games, the players' positions vary depending on the number of players and the size of the court. In all net/wall games, stand in a ready position with weight on the balls of the feet, knees bent, and feet shoulder-width apart, ready to move quickly. Quickly recover and/or return to the central ready position after you hit.

***Chassé*:** A *chassé* is a step–together–step–together moving forward, backward, or sideways in an uneven rhythm. The body springs in the air with toes pointed. It is the same basic movement as the gallop.

Checking for understanding: After you teach a concept or give instructions about a task, ask questions and assess the children's responses as to whether the children have understood what you have just said.

Checklists: Similar to rubrics, checklists describe learning outcomes. Most often in physical education, a checklist is a list of performance techniques for skills that teachers have taught that are performance techniques critical to developing the mature movement pattern of the skill. Typically, checklists require a yes/no answer and assess whether the student is doing the performance technique or has yet to master the technique and needs more practice. Checklists can also be used with tally marks to count the number of times an action is observed, such as the number of times an offensive player appropriately cuts into an open space in a game-like situation. This approach to checklists is particularly valuable in assessing game play. Like rubrics, checklists provide detailed, specific information about intended learning outcomes and are used to provide feedback on performance and improvement. Thus, they can be a learning tool for students.

Child-centered teaching: In child-centered teaching, the teacher focuses on what children are learning and experiencing, how they are thinking and feeling, and what they can do. Teachers base teaching decisions on what children, need not on a predetermined curriculum script.

Clarity: Clarity refers to being precise and making a definite, repeatable movement or shape. Clarity requires that children know the exact shape they want to make and the position of every body part necessary to create that shape.

Classroom ecology: The classroom ecology is the work environment resulting from the teacher's tasks, the students' responses to those tasks, the social interactions among students, and the teachers' response to students' responses.

Closed skills: Closed skills are skills performed in stable, unchanging environments.

Closure: Closure occurs at the end of the culminating activity, once the children have put away the equipment. This phase of the class is typically used to make informal assessments of what each child has learned during the lesson, review the content, and/or discuss how the content connects to other content in children's lives.

Cold call: In a cold call, the teacher does not have children raise their hands indicating they want to answer a question; instead the teacher always selects who will answer the question. Students soon learn that they can't avoid participating in class because they know that the teacher will call on them at some point in time.

Collectivistic cultural values: Collectivistic cultural values are values focused on groups, such as interdependence within the family, concern for group well-being and success, group responsibility, cooperation, modesty, and respect for elders.

Complementing: Complementing means that the shapes and actions of each partner relate in some way so that the pair looks as if they are performing together. Complementing means to harmonize or accompany. For example, one child might make an angular shape and his or her partner might make an angular shape at a slightly higher level, above the first child. Alternatively, both children might make a shape pointing in the same direction but with one child at a medium level and the other at a low level. With complementing shapes, the shapes are similar and highlight one common idea or body position.

Components of fitness: The components of fitness are cardiorespiratory endurance, muscle fitness (muscle strength, muscle endurance, and muscle power), flexibility, and body composition.

Comprehensive School Physical Activity Program (CSPAPs): CSPAPs have multiple components that jointly aim to increase students' physical activity levels and develop the knowledge, skills, and dispositions to engage lifelong in physical activity (Centers for Disease Control and Prevention, 2013). These components include quality physical education, before- and after-school programs, physical activity breaks, and recess.

Congruent feedback: Congruent feedback is feedback that matches the performance technique the teacher gave as the focus of the task.

Constructivism: Constructivism is a cognitive learning theory describing how individuals learn. Constructivism has many implications for teaching. Even so, it is not a theory of instruction, nor does it tell teachers how to teach. In the constructivist approach, teaching and learning are considered to be two sides of the same coin: they are connected, but one side does not dictate what the other side must look like.

Content development: Content development consists of content that will enable children to meet your lesson objectives. The content development tasks break that content down into smaller parts and are arranged into a progression that leads to learning.

Contrasting: In contrasting, partners make shapes or perform opposite actions. For example, if one child makes a big, wide shape, the other child makes a small, curled shape. If one child is twisted, the other is straight.

Cooperative learning: Cooperative learning is group work in which students work together cooperatively to complete a project.

Counterbalance: In counterbalance, two children balance together by leaning toward each other using a wide base of support.

Countertension: In countertension, two children balance together by leaning away from each other, usually using a pulling action. The base of support is typically narrow in such a skill.

Criterion-referenced tests: Criterion-referenced tests indicate whether the student's score on a test meets the level of fitness recommended for health.

Critical performance techniques: Critical performance techniques focus on a few critical performance techniques based on children's developmental levels.

Critical thinking: Critical thinking in physical education can be defined as reflective thinking that is used to make reasonable and defensible decisions about movement tasks or challenges. *Reflective* refers to the ability to draw upon information from one's general and domain-specific knowledge areas; *reasonable* implies a logical thought process; and *defensible* refers to being held accountable for the decisions made from the critical-thinking process (McBride, 1991, p. 115).

Culminating activity: A culminating activity occurs after content development and has the children use the skills and movements they have practiced in more complex settings, application tasks, assessments, or centers.

Cultural sensitivity: Cultural sensitivity is an awareness of cultural differences and responding in ways that are affirming and equitable.

Curriculum script: A curriculum script is a familiar progression taught year after year in the same way, regardless of the students' prior knowledge and experiences.

Cutting to receive a pass: To receive a pass, cut into an open space called a passing lane. If a defender is covering you, fake, feint, dodge, and then accelerate (explode) on a straight pathway to get free. Cut on an angle toward the passer so the passer can send a short pass.

Damage: In an allegation of damage, the child's lawyer must prove that the child suffered actual damage or that an actual injury occurred.

Dance forms of movement: Dance forms of movement consist of movements that are expressive and rhythmic and occur within creative, folk, square, line, and social dances.

Developmental perspective: With a developmental perspective, the teacher recognizes individual differences and what each child can do along the developmental continuum and designs developmentally appropriate lessons differentiating instruction by matching tasks and feedback to the capabilities of individual children to help them progress.

Developmental sequence (or continuum): A developmental sequence (or continuum) consists of the qualitative changes that occur in children's movement patterns of skills as they develop from less mature to more mature levels of performance.

Developmentally appropriate: A developmentally appropriate curriculum and instructional approach (1) take into account children's developmental capabilities in the motor, cognitive, social, and affective domains; and (2) differentiate instructional tasks to accommodate individual differences among children.

Differentiated instruction: In differentiated instruction, the teacher modifies and adapts content and feedback, designs tasks, selects equipment, changes group sizes, and makes other adjustments to match the developmental levels of different children within one class.

Dimensional cross: The dimensional cross connects six directions in space (up, down, left, right, backward, and forward) to six body actions (rising, falling, closing, opening, retreating, and advancing).Three axes or imaginary lines cross at the center of the body: an up-and-down axis, a side-to-side axis, and a forward-and-back axis. Laban defined this set of axes as the dimensional cross because the three lines relate to three-dimensional space and the three dimensions of the body—that is, height, width, and depth. These dimensions, in turn, relate to the three planes: frontal (door), horizontal (table), and sagittal (wheel).

Disciplinary mastery value orientation: With a disciplinary mastery value orientation, teachers focus on subject-matter mastery as the primary goal.

Discovery learning: In discovery learning, the learner actively seeks information from the environment and discovers which movement to produce by exploring the relations among individual capabilities and the current task and environmental constraints.

Do-sa-do: In a do-sa-do (sometimes spelled "do-si-do"), partners walk forward toward each other, pass by right shoulders, walk sideways around each other (without turning), and then walk backward back to their original places.

Double dribble: A double dribble, in which the individual dribbles with two hands simultaneously is a violation according to the regulation rules of basketball. For children learning to dribble when changing pathways, however, it is a temporary scaffold that children will not use once they have mastered the skill of hand dribbling. This scaffold allows them to work at a more advanced level while learning the movement pattern with a temporary assist.

Duct tape and Velcro approach: The duct tape and Velcro approach involves believing you can modify any equipment or activity to make activities accessible. The duct tape and Velcro approach encourages you to never give up on finding ways to make games and activities inclusive. It is an approach that shouts, "We can figure out a way to make this work, and we won't let traditional ways of doing things get in our way or block our thinking!"

Duration: Duration is the length of time a movement takes and is described as existing on a continuum from short to long.

Duty: Duty means that there is some relationship between individuals, such as employer and employee, teacher and student, or coach and player. The dominant party in the relationship (e.g., employer, teacher, coach) has a duty to protect the other party (e.g., employee, student, player) from harm. The potential for harm by an action or lack of action is considered to be foreseeable.

Dynamic balancing: Dynamic balancing involves traveling on a narrow surface without falling. This skill is most often associated with traveling on balance beams.

Dynamic stretches: Dynamic stretches slowly move the joints through their full range of motion to loosen the joint and eliminate any tension in the muscles.

Ecological integration value orientation: With an ecological integration value orientation, teachers emphasize the integration of the individual within the total physical, social, and cultural environment. Neither individual nor social needs predominate.

Educational dance: Educational dance is dance appropriate to, and designed for, all children in school settings to meet educational objectives.

Educational gymnastics: Educational gymnastics is designed for school settings with the goal for *all* children to develop competency in a variety of gymnastics skills performed in a variety of ways (such as rolling in different directions and in different shapes and balancing on different body parts), to learn and apply movement concepts from the Laban framework to develop movement variety (such as jumping while making different shapes in the air and balancing at different levels), to learn and apply elements of quality sequence choreography, and to learn and apply principles of movement quality to improve performance. Educational gymnastics takes a broader view of the kinds of apparatus that can be used. Educational gymnastics uses inexpensive, even homemade, apparatus and equipment readily available in many schools and through catalogs. This includes equipment such as cones, jump ropes, hoops, crates, and canes, as well as larger apparatus such as playground equipment, sturdy gymnastics benches, aerobic boxes, inexpensive 2×4 beams, foam trapezoids, stacked mats, and swinging ropes.

Educational gymnastics themes: Educational gymnastics themes are groups of skills organized around a common action, movement concept, or both.

Effort aspect of the Laban framework: The effort aspect of the Laban framework escribes how the body moves.

Effort movement concepts: Effort movement concepts describe how the body moves, including the speed and duration of movement, the force (from light to strong), the use of space (from indirect to direct), and the flow of movement (from bound to free).

Egg roll: An egg roll is a side roll in a tuck position.

Ego orientation: Students with an ego orientation focus most on how their performance compares to that of others. They are very concerned with looking good and having others perceive that they are smart and highly skilled. They don't like challenging tasks because they are afraid they will fail and appear inept. This attitude, in turn, has a negative impact on learning, because such individuals will be reluctant to attempt skills they have not yet mastered.

Egocentrism: With an egocentric perspective, children believe their perspective is the only perspective.

Eight basic effort actions: Laban combined the six components at the ends of the continua of speed, force, and use of space to form the eight basic effort actions: floating (slow, light, indirect), gliding (slow, light, direct), wringing (slow, strong, indirect), pressing (slow, strong, direct), flicking (fast, light, indirect), dabbing (fast, light, direct), slashing (fast, strong, indirect), and jabbing or thrusting (fast, strong, direct).

Elbow swings: When doing elbow swings, partners hook elbows and walk around each other.

Eliciting tasks: Eliciting tasks are tasks that elicit a particular movement pattern or performance technique through task and/or environmental constraints designed by the teacher.

Elimination games: Elimination games have a rule that when a child makes a poor play or a mistake, he or she is eliminated from the game.

Elongate the spine: Elongating the spine involves stretching through the spine to create as much space as possible between each vertebra.

Engaging the core: Core engagement means that the muscles in the torso (the rectangular area from shoulders to hips) are part of the action. *Moving from the core* means that any action of the arms, head, and/or legs originates from the core muscles.

Environmental constraints: Environmental constraints include gravity, the weather, and the type of surface; the amount of space, light, and noise; and social and cultural constraints, such as classmates, teachers, peer groups, parents, siblings, societal expectations, and cultural expectations and support.

Exit slip: An exit slip is a simple, quick form of assessment in which the students respond to a question or prompt from the teacher on an index card, slip of paper, or though their smartphones or tablets (Marzano, 2012).

Exploration tasks (E): Exploration tasks ask children to discover, invent, find different solutions to a problem, and/or generate multiple responses.

Extending tasks (E): Extending tasks are tasks that are part of a progression that builds from simple to more complex or from easier to more difficult. Extending tasks break content down into a series of tasks that lead to students learning the skill or movement pattern that is your objective.

External feedback: Children often get external feedback about the results of their movement. We call this "knowledge of results," and it includes things like seeing whether the ball hit the target and seeing whether a kicked ball went into the air or traveled along the ground.

Feedback: Feedback is information that a teacher (or a peer) gives to a child about his or her responses in relation to the learning goal of the task. Feedback gives students specific information about their responses that tells them if, how, and the extent to which they are learning the objective of the lesson or task.

Field games: Field games include major sports, such as softball, baseball, and cricket. In field games, the offense hits a ball, usually with a bat, into a field space covered by defenders. The offense scores by running to bases ahead of a throw by the defenders.

Fitness model: The fitness model predates the current health-related physical activity model and was an adult exercise prescription model focused on improving physical fitness with continuous, vigorous aerobic activities lasting for 30 minutes, performed three to four days per week.

FitnessGram: The FitnessGram is a criterion-referenced battery of tests from which teachers can select those that best meet their needs. Designed by the Cooper Institute, the tests report whether children's scores are in the healthy fitness zone or need improvements in the following areas: aerobic capacity, body composition, abdominal strength and endurance, trunk extensor strength and flexibility, upper body strength and endurance, hamstring flexibility, and shoulder flexibility. The FitnessGram includes three questions about the number of days in the past week in which the child engaged in aerobic activity, strength activity, and flexibility activity.

FITT: FITT is an acronym for four key principles of health-related physical fitness: frequency, intensity, time, and type.

Fixed mindset: Students with a fixed mindset believe that abilities are innate and there is nothing they can do to change their abilities because they are fixed traits. Students with fixed mindsets attribute success to ability, rather than to effort and hard work. When they make mistakes or fail at a task, they believe this result shows that they lack ability and are not smart and that working harder will not make any difference.

Flexibility: Flexibility is the range of motion of the joints and connected muscles. The term *stretching* is often used synonymously with *flexibility.*

Focus: Focus in gymnastics and dance means that the body shapes and body parts focus the observer's attention on a particular point in space.

Focused observations: When a teacher is engaged in focused observation, he or she pauses his or her scanning of the class to observe one child or group of children long enough to see how they are learning. The teacher looks up frequently to scan the entire class because at the elementary level, children can get off task and into unsafe situations very quickly.

Folk dances: In general, folk dances originated with everyday people who were not part of the courts or circles of power (National Dance Association, 1994). They often represent the lives, geography, values, and heritage of the people who perform them (Cone & Purcell Cone, 2003). Folk dances most often consist of simple locomotor steps, such as walking and hopping, done in different formations, such as circles and lines, while traveling on floor pathways. The locomotor steps are typically performed in a repeatable pattern to lively cultural music and are easily learned.

Formal assessments: Formal assessments are planned, rely on criteria for making judgments, and yield results for every child and are recorded in writing or electronically.

Formative assessments: Formative assessments occur before and during a unit to assess what students currently know, can do, and feel; their improvement on those fronts; and the extent to which they have learned the objective for the teacher's lesson or unit.

Forward roll: In a forward roll, the child starts from a squat position using strong (bent) arms to support the weight, lifts the hips, pushes off both feet, extends the legs completely, tucks the chin, slides the back of the head through the arms, and lands on the back of the shoulders in a pike position with the forehead near the knees. Without stopping, the child rolls onto her or his back, tucks the legs (knees to chest, heels to bottom), and, without using the hands, rolls up to the feet and stands.

Frequency: Frequency refers to the number of recommended days of physical activity per week, whereas time refers to the recommended number of minutes devoted to such activity. For children, the current guidelines call for a minimum of 60 minutes or more physical activity daily (U.S. Department of Health and Human Services, 2008).

Friedrich Ludwig Jahn: Born in Prussia, Friedrich Ludwig Jahn (1778–1852) is considered the father of physical education and modern gymnastics. Influenced by the ideas of Guts Muths, he was a leader in developing "German gymnastics" and *Turnverein* (gymnastics societies).

Front handspring: A front handspring begins with three running steps, a hurdle, and a long lunge. The child reaches forward with the hands and then kicks the back leg up and around, pushing off the front leg and swinging it around to join back leg in the air. Then, the child achieves flight from the hands by extending or shrugging the shoulders to push off the floor. During the flight from the hands to the landing on the feet, the child maintains a stretched back (with a very slight curve), with the head back between the arms (rather than tucking the chin to look for the mat) and the arms straight over the head (rather than reaching forward) to land with the body straight (rather than in a sitting or squatting position).

Front shoulder roll: A front shoulder roll is like a forward roll, except that the head stays to the side and the child rolls over her or his shoulder.

Fundamental game skills: Fundamental game skills are basic ball handling skills that are foundational to one or more game or sport, such as catching, throwing, dribbling, and kicking.

Future orientation: A future orientation is an orientation in which children can envision a different future for themselves—a future in which they are self-directed and can have careers that are meaningful to them and productive: a future filled with possibilities, and not dead ends (Husman & Lens, 1999; Kauffman & Husman, 2004).

Gallop: A gallop is a step on the lead foot, close the back foot to the front, and leap onto the back foot, step on the lead foot again. It has an uneven rhythm with an accent on the lead step. The same leg leads the entire time, and the child travels in a forward direction.

Game forms of movement: Game forms of movement are functional movements, skills, and tactics related to games and sports.

Game structures: Game structures include boundaries, rules, consequences for breaking rules, scoring goals, scoring systems, a competitive/cooperative structure, the number of players, and the equipment and skills used.

"Goldilocks Principle": The "Goldilocks Principle" states that the level of defense cannot be too intense or too slack, but needs to be just right—that is, challenging yet also allowing for success.

Good life: According to curriculum scholars, a good life is a life that is satisfying, meaningful, and productive.

Grapevine: The grapevine movement involves moving continuously to the right or left—step right foot to side; cross left foot behind right; step right foot to side; cross left foot in front of right (repeat).

Growth mindset: Students with a growth mindset believe that they can develop their abilities. They attribute success to effort and hard work, rather than to innate abilities. They believe that if they work hard, they will become more skilled and more intelligent and consequently will perform better. If they make mistakes or fail at a task, they view the setback as simply a sign that they need to work harder or find a different way to tackle the task.

Gymnastics forms of movement: Gymnastics forms of movement are functional (i.e., not expressive) movements used to demonstrate bodily skill, strength, flexibility, power, precision, and prowess.

Gymnastics wars: Much as in the "reading wars" and the "math wars" of recent times, educators in the late 1800s debated whether the German or Swedish system was best. Educators sometimes called these debates the "gymnastics wars" or the "battle of the systems" (Freeman, 2012).

Hall of Shame practices: Hall of Shame practices are inappropriate teaching behaviors that do not meet professional standards of practice because they alienate students and harm the learning environment. Neil Williams (1992, 1994, 1996) nominated a number of common teaching practices and games for the "The Physical Education Hall of Shame," including putting children on display and having captains publicly pick their teams.

Handstand: A handstand is a balance on the hands with the body perfectly straight, stretched, and tight.

Handstand forward roll: A handstand forward roll is a forward roll done from the handstand position.

Headstand: In a headstand, the child balances on the front part of her or his head and two hands with the legs extended straight up.

Health-related physical activity model: The health-related physical activity model suggests 30 minutes of moderate to vigorous physical activity most days of the week for adults and 60 minutes every day for children.

Heavy weight: In contrast to anti-gravity exertion and strong static tension are a lack of tension and the feeling of heaviness, or heavy weight. The body feels heavy and the muscles loose.

Hollowing out: Hollowing out involves tilting the top of the pelvis back and hollowing out the abdominal area during gymnastics skills such as handstands.

Hula: Hula is a traditional dance of native Hawaiians that uses gestures to represent words, ideas, and emotions. In prehistoric times, ancient hula was part of the oral tradition for passing down stories, history, rituals, and prayers from one generation to the next (Menton & Tamura, 1989). Ancient hula consisted of dance accompanied by drums, chants, recitations, or song. Sometimes the dancers moved in unison; at other times, someone would lead while other participants gestured with their hands and kept the beat with drums. Both men and women danced the hula.

Hurdle: A hurdle before a cartwheel or round-off is technically a step-hop done in an uneven rhythm (i.e., a skip) followed by a long step. During the hop, the arms stretch toward the ceiling and the free knee lifts forward (as it does in a skip). A more difficult form of hurdle is to extend the free leg back and keep the body slightly arched during the hop.

Imitation: In comparison to representation, imitation is a surface-level characterization of an idea or theme. For example, standing straight with the arms circled overhead is a static, surface-level characterization of a tree.

Inclusion tasks: Inclusion tasks are asks that have built-in choices for the level of difficulty, such as by modifying speed, force, height, or distance, and in which each child selects his or her own level of difficulty.

Individual accountability: Individual accountability during group work means that everyone is responsible and held accountable through assessments for learning and developing skills.

Individual constraints: Individual constraints include factors such as the child's height, strength, and fitness level; physical, cognitive, and social development; current ability level; anxiety; motivation; attention; knowledge; and memory.

Individualistic cultural values: Individualistic cultural values are values focused on individuals, such as independence (e.g., working alone on assignments), individual achievement (taking tests individually, being graded on work individually, competition, succeeding as an individual), self-expression, and individual responsibility.

Inert knowledge: Inert knowledge is knowledge that is not well connected, not used, often forgotten, and not very meaningful to children.

Informal assessments: Informal assessments include criteria for making judgments, but the results are typically not recorded. Teachers rely on informal assessments in every lesson. These ongoing assessments include observing children's responses to assess the extent to which the children are improving and checking for understanding by asking questions to individuals and partners.

Informing tasks (I): Informing tasks (introductory tasks) introduce new content and are the first tasks in the progression of tasks for your lesson. Typically, informing tasks are used at the beginning of your lesson and at the beginning of each new section that works on a different skill. These tasks give children just enough information to begin practicing. With informing tasks, the key is to not lecture or review excessive amounts of information beyond the children's attention and memory capabilities.

Inquiry-oriented teaching: Inquiry-oriented teaching involves setting exploration, creative and critical-thinking, problem-solving, and decision-making tasks and asking questions. Inquiry-oriented teaching strategies require children to think and engage actively in constructing knowledge.

Instructional task system: The instructional task system comprises the set of tasks for learning the lesson content, including teachers' methods of holding students accountable for learning the content (Hastie & Siedentop, 2006).

Intensity: Intensity is how hard you work. Intensity recommendations for cardiorespiratory endurance for children are to engage in moderate levels of physical activity daily and in vigorous intensity at least three days a week (U.S. Department of Health and Human Services, 2008).

Interactive teaching: Interactive teaching is as a cycle of observing children, interpreting those observations, and then making a decision about what to do (Barrett, 2009).

Interskill progression: An interskill progression is a suggested progression of different skills to master before working on a new skill.

Intertask developmental sequence: An intertask developmental sequence is a sequence of different skills that develop or emerge across time. For example, walking emerges before running, which emerges before hopping, which emerges before skipping.

Intraskill progression: An intraskill progression is a series of subskills that progressively become more like the terminal skill the children are learning. The teacher teaches each subskill, and the child progresses to the next subskill *only* if he or she has mastered the previous subskill. Children do not *ever* have to move on to the next subskill in a progression and can continue practicing the subskill that best matches their ability level. No skill is sacred, and no child should feel pressured to learn the terminal skill. Thus, teachers can use a skill mastery progression to accommodate individual differences while teaching specific skills to a whole class.

Intratask developmental sequence (or continuum): An intratask developmental sequence (or continuum) describes the most common changes that occur in the movement patterns of one skill over time as children learn the skill. For example, when very young children first throw, they do not step with either foot as they throw; this is labeled an immature pattern. As they develop, an intermediate pattern is to take a step as they throw, but they will step with the foot on the same side of their body as their throwing arm. A second intermediate pattern is to take a short step with the opposite foot. With practice (and instruction), they will learn the mature pattern to take a long step with the opposite foot (Roberton & Halverson, 1984).

Intrinsic feedback: Intrinsic feedback is feedback children get through their own senses, such as the feeling of hitting a ball.

Introductory and warm-up activities: Introductory and warm-up activities prepare students for the lesson. When you introduce the lesson, you inform children about what they will be learning and why it is important. You also try to capture children's interest and build enthusiasm. Warm-up activities warm up the children's bodies and get them physically active quickly.

Invasion games: Invasion games include games in which the offense and defense play in the same space—that is, they invade the space of the other team to score. Examples include basketball, soccer, field hockey, ice hockey, team handball, lacrosse, football, and water polo. Although tactics vary when these sports are played at the elite level, for elementary-age children, the invasion game tactics we teach, such as cutting into open spaces to receive passes, are the same or similar whether you are using kicking skills or throwing and catching skills.

Johann Christoph Friedrich Guts Muths: The modern era of physical education began in Germany in the late 1700s, as part of a movement led by Johann Christoph Friedrich Guts Muths (1759–1839) (Gerber, 1971). Guts Muths was a physical education teacher who taught and wrote about his work for more than 50 years (Freeman, 2012). Historians call him the grandfather of physical education. Guts Muths provided individualized gymnastics programs for students, focusing on wrestling, running, leaping, throwing, balancing, climbing, lifting, skipping rope, swimming, dancing, hiking, and military exercises. He also included games that contributed to building strength, speed, and flexibility.

Kinetic force: Kinetic force (isotonic contractions) is generated by contracting the muscles, resulting in movement (the length of the muscle changes). Force is described as existing on a continuum from light to strong. Kinetic force can be strong, such as the actions of the legs while sprinting, or light, such as the action of the hands and arms when trying to catch a soap bubble without letting it burst.

Laban's framework: Laban's framework is a conceptual framework to analyze movement and describe its content. It is based on the work of Hungarian dance artist and theorist Rudolf Laban (1879–1958).

Large-group, one-ball games: These games limit practice time because only a few children are active at a time. Such games should be eliminated from your curriculum.

Lead pass: A lead pass is a pass sent into the space ahead of the receiver so the receiver does not have to change stride or speed to catch the ball.

Learning process value orientation: With a learning process value orientation, teachers help children learn how to learn.

Lesson objectives: Lesson objectives are the intended learning outcomes for a lesson. Lesson objectives are written as sentences that state exactly what the children will learn in the lesson. They are specific and detailed. Objectives are not what the teacher will do, but rather describe the content that the children will learn and the specific ways in which they will improve a movement, thinking, or social skill.

Line: In gymnastics and dance, line refers to the lines formed by intentionally positioning several body parts.

Line of symmetry: To determine if a shapes is symmetrical, use a line of symmetry. In a human, if the line of symmetry is vertical, the body is symmetrical. In contrast, if the line of symmetry is placed at the belt, horizontally splitting the body, there is no symmetry.

Locomotor skills: Locomotor skills are skills used to travel on one's feet, such as skipping, walking, running, hopping, galloping, sliding, jumping, and leaping.

Longways set: A longways set is used in dance and consists of six to eight couples arranged in two parallel lines. Partners either face each other or hold inside hands and face the head of the set.

Major learning outcome: A major learning outcome is a superordinate objective for the unit—it is your main goal for what you want the children to learn. It typically comprises the most important content within the culminating activity of the unit, such as the theme and concepts of the final dance or gymnastics sequence, the tactical skills of the game or game-like experience for older children, or the skill movement variety and quality for younger children.

Management task system: The management task system encompasses the set of tasks and accountability measures designed to create a smoothly running, nondisruptive work environment (Hastie & Siedentop, 2006).

Manipulative skills: Manipulative skills are skills such as throwing and striking, in which the body manipulates equipment, such as balls and bats.

Mastery orientation: Students who have a mastery orientation are most concerned about learning the content, mastering the task or skill, and accomplishing their own self-improvement. They embrace challenging tasks, don't give up when the going gets tough, and persist in working hard even when they encounter difficulties in learning the content.

Mastery progressions: Mastery progressions involve breaking a skill down into a series of subskills that increase in difficulty. In such a progression, the teacher teaches the series of subskills and tells the children to work on the subskill that is developmentally appropriate for them. Children should move on to the next subskill only if they are confident, competent, and sure they can safely progress.

Matching: Matching means doing the same shape or the same foundational skill in the same way.

***Mazurka*:** A *Mazurka* is danced in a 3/4 meter. Step with the left foot; close right to left foot while leaping onto right foot (called a "cut"); hop on the right foot; the same leg leads.

***Mens sana en corpore sano*:** This phrase means "a strong mind in a healthy body" and was promoted in ancient Greek and Roman society.

Metacognition: Metacognition means "reflecting on and evaluating one's own thoughts and learning" (Alexander, 2006, p. 157).

Meter: Meter is a measurement of the ways duration is divided into phrases or measures.

Middle childhood: The elementary school years, called middle childhood, constitute a phase of life that is qualitatively different from adolescence and adulthood. During this phase, children are full of energy, curiosity, and playfulness. They are inventive and creative and like to build things, try new activities, play with friends, and develop competency (Berk, 2010). The kinds of physical activities meaningful to children are the antithesis of the regimented exercise workouts that adolescents and adults enjoy in health clubs across America.

Mirroring: Mirroring means doing the same actions with the same shapes, with partners facing each other as if they were looking in a mirror. The left side of one partner does the same thing as the right side of the other partner.

Motor development: Motor development consists of changes in motor behavior over time that reflect the interaction of the human organism with its environment.

Movement approach: In a movement approach, teachers use the Laban framework to analyze movement and teach the skills, movement concepts, tactics, health-related physical activity concepts, and choreographic concepts within games, dance, and gymnastics tasks. The focus is clearly on developing skill and movement variety. Teachers select skills and tactics related to invasion, net/wall, field, and target games as learning objectives. Teachers provide appropriate situations for practicing the skill or tactic and modify all games to be small-sided.

Movement concepts: Movement concepts are elements of the four aspects of the Laban framework and describe the shape, where and how a skill or body action is performed, and the relationships among body parts, equipment, and other individuals.

Mule kick: A mule kick is a partial handstand. The weight is taken on the hands and straight arms; the legs are kicked one at a time, switching places in the air; and the legs reach waist to chest height.

Muscle endurance: Muscle endurance is "the ability of skeletal muscle to perform repeated contractions against a load" (Institute of Medicine, 2012b, p.8).

Muscle fitness: Muscle fitness consists of muscle strength, muscle endurance, and muscle power.

Muscle power: Muscle power is "the peak force of a skeletal muscle multiplied by the velocity of the muscle contraction" (Institute of Medicine, 2012b, p. 8). A jump for height and a jump for distance use muscle power in the legs, torso, and arms.

Muscle strength: Muscle strength is "the ability of skeletal muscle to produce force under controlled conditions" (Institute of Medicine, 2012b, p. 8). Lifting a heavy weight is an example of muscle strength.

MyPlate: MyPlate illustrates the five food groups and the recommended proportions to eat daily. It was developed by the U.S. Department of Agriculture Food and Nutrition Service (2011).

National Board of Professional Teaching Standards: The National Board of Professional Teaching Standards is a professional organization that has designed a set of tools for assessing accomplished teaching. Teachers who pass the assessments become board-certified teachers.

Negligence: Negligence is the failure to do what a reasonably prudent person would do in the same or similar circumstances. Negligence can also be considered a failure to exercise the reasonable care that a reasonably prudent person would have exercised in the same or similar circumstances.

Net/wall games: In net/wall games, a net separates the teams, an arrangement found in games such as volleyball, tennis, badminton, pickleball, table tennis, and deck tennis. Tactics such as hitting into open space where no defender can reach the ball and covering space to prevent the ball or shuttlecock from hitting the ground or bouncing twice are the same or similar across all net games. Wall games, such a racquetball, handball, and squash, are grouped with net games because the tactics are the same or similar. Net/wall games usually use striking skills with the hands, forearms, or rackets.

Newell's constraints theory: Newell's constraints theory states that the movement patterns of skills exhibited by an individual result from interactions among (1) individual constraints; (2) environmental constraints; and (3) task constraints.

Nonlocomotor skills: Nonlocomotor skills are skills in which the body remains in one place, such as balancing, turning, twisting, stretching, and curling.

Norm-referenced tests: Norm-referenced tests compare student's scores to each other and identify the percentile rank of one student compared to other students. Experts agree that fitness tests, if used, must be criterion referenced, not norm referenced (Pangrazi, 2000).

Observation plan: In an observation plan, first plan to observe for safety. Think about which safety problems might potentially arise in your tasks and what you need to look for to be sure the children are safe. Second, plan to observe for learning. Think about your lesson objectives and what you need to observe and assess to determine whether the children are meeting these objectives.

Olympic gymnastics: Olympic gymnastics is the sport of gymnastics as performed in the Olympics. The content taught in Olympic gymnastics consists of specific skills from the four Olympic events for women (floor, vault, balance beam, and uneven parallel bars) and the six events for men (floor, vault, rings, parallel bars, high bar, and pommel horse). Olympic gymnastics uses only one piece of apparatus for routines.

Open skills: Open skills are skills performed in variable environments and therefore must be repeatedly adapted to the changing demands of the environment.

Open space: An open space is the space between the defender and the boundary or between defenders. Open spaces change based on defenders' positions. When defenders cover the center space, open spaces are typically near the sidelines, corners, very close to the net (or wall), or at the far back end of the court.

Originality: Originality means that movements are varied, different, and interesting, with some being unusual.

Overload principle: The overload principle states that you must do more physical activity or work harder than you do at rest in order to improve your physical fitness. Your body adapts to an overload of work by becoming stronger or more flexible.

***Pas de basque* (*pas de bas*):** In a *pas de basque (pas de bas)*, the dancer leaps to the right side, steps lightly on the ball of the left foot placed next to the right foot, steps on the right foot in place, and repeats to the left. It is sometimes called a "three."

Passing lane: A passing lane is a lane, or area of space, in which there are no defenders between the passer and receiver.

***PE Metrics*:** *PE Metrics* are a set of standardized tests for assessing learning outcomes based on the National Standards for Physical Education (National Association of Sport and Physical Education, 2010.)

Peer assessment: A checklist or other assessment tool that peers use to assess their partners. Research has shown that when teachers prepare a checklist or other assessment tool that describes specifically what peer assessors need to look for and assess in their partners, students learn and retain more than students doing the same lesson without the assessment tool (Iserbyt, Elen, & Behets, 2010; Vande Broek, Boen, Claessens, Feys, & Ceux, 2011).

Per Henrik Ling: Per Henrik Ling was an educator who developed the Swedish system of gymnastics. The Swedish system emphasized exercises and body positions performed in highly precise ways, much like many aerobic and fitness classes today. Swedish exercising concentrated on posture development rather than the stunts employed in German gymnastics. Ling invented a variety of apparatus for his system, including the stall bars and the Swedish box used for vaulting. We still use these and similar apparatus today.

Perceived competence: When children enter a classroom believing that they can be successful and competent in the content being taught, they have perceived competence.

Personal interest: Personal interest is interest that students already possess based on their own experiences or opinions of activities.

Physical activity breaks: Physical activity breaks are short, five-minute breaks in which children engage in physical activity in their classroom while being directed by the classroom teacher. They are often also called *brain breaks.*

Play–discuss–play cycle: In this cycle, children make decisions about their game structures or tactics and then play the game for several minutes. At that point, they stop to discuss the game structures or tactics briefly, make any needed modifications, and then play again. This play–discuss–play cycle continues throughout the lesson.

Polka: The polka is the same as a two-step but faster and with a hop added, alternating the lead leg: Left step–together step–hop; right step–together–step–hop. It has an uneven rhythm.

Pop culture: Pop culture consists of how sports, fitness, dance, and the body are represented by television, magazines, Internet sites, advertisements, radio, peers, and adults in children's daily lives. Pop culture contributes a significant part of the knowledge and experiences children bring to physical education classes.

Positive interdependence: Positive interdependence during group work involves group members working together to complete the project, helping each other, depending on each other, and caring about the success of the group, and everyone contributing to the project and the learning of other group members (Dean et al., 2012; Slavin, 2014).

Praise (general, positive feedback): Praise, or general, positive feedback, is general, nonspecific feedback that makes a positive statement about student performance.

Proficiency barrier: A proficiency barrier is a minimal level of proficiency in fundamental motor skills that children must acquire to allow for enjoyable participation in physical activity and active recreation throughout their lifespan.

Progression principle: To continue to improve in any area of fitness, you must follow the progression principle by working harder or longer than you have before.

Promenade: In a promenade, dancers hold left hands with left hands and right hands with right hands, with arms crossed in front, typically walking forward in a circle formation.

Proximate cause: Proximate cause means the teacher's actions or failure to act caused the injury or harm to the child. For example, if the child asked to try a back handspring (a difficult gymnastics skill) and the teacher said yes but failed to spot the child and the child was injured, the failure to provide spotting is a proximate cause of the injury. To help you understand proximate cause, you can apply the "but for" test. *But for* the teacher's negligence in not providing spotting, the child would not have been injured.

Rating scale: A rating scale is an elaboration of a checklist. Like checklists, rating scales describe performance techniques that are linked directly to student learning outcomes. Unlike checklists, rating scales also include a way to assess the extent to which a performance technique has been mastered or the developmental level of the performance. Rating scales often include assessing the frequency with which an important movement pattern or action is observed. Whereas a checklist with tally marks counts the number of times an assessor observes a movement, a rating scale uses scales that require a judgment, such as always, often, sometimes, or rarely (Brookhart, 2013).

Reels: Reels are folk dances done in longways sets—that is, six to eight couples arranged in parallel lines.

Refinements (R): Refinements work on improving the movement quality or performance techniques.

Reflective teaching: Reflective teaching occurs when teachers reflect on long-term goals, such as the goal of physical education defined in our national standards, and the extent to which their teaching, curriculum, and the responses of children in the motor, cognitive, affective, and social domains indicate children are likely to meet these goals.

Relationship aspect of the Laban framework: The relationship aspect of the Laban framework consists of the relationships between the body or body parts and the equipment or apparatus, between individuals, and among individuals in groups.

Relationship movement concepts: Relationship movement concepts describe the relationship between the body and the equipment, between one individual and other individuals, or between body parts and other body parts—for example.

Reporting: A critical way to decrease bullying, harassment, and children being mean is to teach children the importance of reporting incidents of negative behavior. Reporting means trying to keep someone or something (e.g., equipment) safe from harm, as opposed to tattling, in which a child tries to get someone in trouble who is breaking a rule but not harming anyone (Cooper & Snell, 2003).

Representation: Representation means taking the main idea, abstracting it, and transforming it into movement. By abstracting, we mean taking an idea (about, for example, a feeling, object, animal, person, or event) and focusing on one portion that captures the essence of the idea—what is most essential. Representing an idea is thus not trying to portray an exact duplicate of the idea, nor is it pantomiming the movements associated with the idea. Representing an idea means expressing what that idea means to you.

Rhythm: Rhythm is how the durations of sounds in a piece of music are organized into patterns.

Rock (or balance): In a rock (or balance), the dancer steps forward on the left foot, transfers weight forward, and then transfers weight back on the right foot; it can be done on either leg.

Routines: Routines are standard procedures you use frequently in class to organize and manage students, such as routines for lining up for a fire drill or getting out equipment.

Rubric: A rubric is an assessment tool that describes specifically and in detail levels of performance from beginner to competent performer for each component of the skill or physical activity students are expected to learn.

Sashay: A sashay is a square dance term for a step–together–step moving sideways in an uneven rhythm. It is the same as a slide.

Scaffolding: Scaffolding in physical education includes temporary sets of procedures, prompts, assistance, and/or equipment modifications to help children learn a motor, cognitive, or social skill.

Scanning: Scanning involves observing the class, starting at one side and systematically sweeping your eyes across the class back and forth, without stopping to watch a particular child.

School politics: School politics comprise the relationships among teachers, staff, and administrators that lead to power in the school. *Power* in this context includes the power to influence or control funds, schedules, workload, policies, procedures, curriculum, instruction, and status.

Schottische: A *schottische* consists of three steps and a hop in an even rhythm: Left, right, left, hop on left, right, left, right, hop on right.

Self-actualization value orientation: With a self-actualization value orientation, teachers focus on individual development and help children develop autonomy, self-confidence, self-management skills, self-understanding, and the ability to identify and work toward their own goals.

Self-regulation: Self-regulation involves reflecting on and evaluating your motor, cognitive, and emotional responses and the environment during learning (Alexander, 2006).

Shape movement concepts: Shape movement concepts describe different shapes of the body, including straight round, angular, twisted, wide, symmetrical, and asymmetrical.

Situated cognition: In situated cognition, the individual, the activity in which he or she is engaged, and the social–cultural environment are inseparable parts of what is learned and how learning occurs. Situated cognition argues against teaching decontextualized skills and in favor of authentic activities that are meaningful to learners.

Situational interest: Situational interest is interest in an activity created by a teacher in a school situation.

Skip: A skip is a step-hop on one leg, followed by a step-hop on the other leg. The rhythm is uneven. The accent is on the step, which is long, followed by the hop, which is short.

Slide: A slide is the same as a gallop but travels sideways.

Social constructivism: Social constructivism is a theory of learning and development which focuses on the role of social interactions with parents, peers, teachers, and other individuals in children's learning.

Social responsibility value orientation: With a social responsibility value orientation, teachers focus on developing responsible citizenship.

Social task system: The social task system consists of students' attempts to interact with their peers during the physical education lesson. Talking with peers is often part of group work in physical education, such as when groups or partners are designing dance, gymnastics, jump rope, and fitness routines, and when groups are designing games or planning game tactics. Moreover, there are times during physical education when students can talk with their friends without being off task, such as when they are carrying equipment out to the field.

Space aspect of the Laban framework: The space aspect of the Laban framework describes where in space the body moves.

Space movement concepts: Space movement concepts describe where the body moves, including general and personal space, at different levels, on different pathways, and in different directions.

Specificity principle: The specificity principle states that physiological changes in the body relate closely to the type of physical activity being done. For example, stretching exercises will not improve strength, and upper body strength exercises will not improve lower body strength.

Speed: Speed is described as existing along a continuum from slow to fast.

Springboard hurdle: A springboard hurdle is an *assemblé* (1-2 jump) done at a low level and traveling for a long distance—about the same distance as one running step. The child runs toward the springboard, takes off from one foot, and lands on the board on two feet just in front of the peak of the hill of the springboard and springs into the air, landing on a landing mat.

Stages of motor learning: Learning is considered to occur in three broad stages. In stage one, children focus on the basic movement patterns of skills. In stage two, children develop versatility and adapt movements to different environmental conditions. In stage three, children become proficient, do not need to think consciously about their movements, and can attend to complex game situations.

Stages of teacher development: Teachers can progress through different stages as they develop from beginner to veteran. The first stage is survival, in which beginning teachers are concerned about survival, management, and discipline. After they pass through the survival stage, teachers stop focusing on themselves and start focusing on students' learning. By this phase in their evolution as teachers, they have developed classroom routines, they know more about how students learn, and they are able to solve the problems that arise in the typical school day (Behets & Vergauwen, 2006). If teachers continue to work on their professional development, they can move to the expert stage.

Star turns: In star turns, partners or groups of four touch palms and hold hands high above head height; dancers walk around each other, completing one full circle back to their original place.

Static force: Static force is generated by contracting or tightening the muscles but not moving (the length of the muscle remains the same). Strong static force results in tight, firm muscles. Light static force involves slight tension and feels like a soft touch. The continuum is from fine to firm.

Static stretches: Static stretches are stretches in which the muscle, ligaments, and tendons are stretched and lengthened in a held position. Although in the past static stretches were used during warm-up activities, current recommendations are to work on static stretches only after the body is warmed up or at the end of an exercise session. Because static stretching can be boring for children (Sanders & Graham, 1995) and is typically unnecessary for children's health, it is probably not a good investment of limited lesson time to work on static stretching other than for educating children about different types of flexibility exercises (Mally, 2006).

Stem: Learning objectives are written as complete sentences and begin with what we call a stem—that is, a starting phrase that is the same for all objectives. Teachers, principals, and professors sometimes disagree with what is an appropriate stem. At the elementary level, teachers often use stems focused on improvement because the performance techniques for skills such as throwing, catching, and dribbling develop over years of practice.

Stereotyping: Stereotyping occurs when a characteristic that may be an appropriate descriptor of one individual is assumed to be a characteristic of all people of that ethnicity or race.

Stick handling (ball control): Stick handling and ball control are other terms for field hockey dribbling.

Student journal: A student journal is an assessment tool in which students respond to prompts from the teacher and write about what they have learned or how they felt about the physical education lesson or unit (Mohnsen, 1998).

Sudden: The term *sudden* describes a fast speed of a short duration.

Summative assessments: Summative assessments occur at the end of a unit or grade level and assess what students have learned in that unit or across the school year.

Sustained: The term *sustained* describes a slow speed of a long duration.

Swaying: Swaying is similar to swinging, but typically implies a smaller action in which the weight of the body shifts from one side to the other or in one direction and then the reverse.

Swinging: Swinging in creative dance means that the actions resemble the movements of a swing or pendulum. Individual body parts can swing one way and then reverse around a fixed point. For example, the arms can swing forward and back at the shoulders, and one leg can swing from the hips. The whole body can also move in a swinging action, starting up to the left and moving down on a circular pathway and up again to the right; it can then reverse direction. The body can swing from side to side or forward and back.

Symmetrical shapes: Symmetrical shapes are shapes in which the positions of body parts on each side of the body are the same.

Tactical game skills: Tactical game skills are fundamental skills in which the child adapts a movement pattern in a variety of game-like ways derived from the tactical situations of games.

***Tarantella*:** The *Tarantella* is a popular Italian folk dance originating in Sicily and still performed in social and recreational settings today. It is believed to have originated from a belief that if a tarantula spider were to bite a person, he or she could dance vigorously to get the poison out of his or her system. The *Tarantella* would be danced with such frenzy and for so long that the person would drop from exhaustion (Tillman-Hall, 1969).

Target games: Target games are typically individual sports focused on hitting a target, often using an implement. Target sports include golf, bowling, and archery.

Target hands: When a receiver cuts into an open space to receive a pass, he or she stretches his or her arms and hands out to create "target hands." This gives the passer a target and tells the passer that the receiver is free to receive a pass.

Task constraints: Task constraints include the goals of the activity, movements specified, rules, equipment, and number of players.

Tattling: Tattling occurs when a child tries to get someone in trouble who is breaking a rule but not harming anyone (Cooper & Snell, 2003). This is opposed to reporting, which involves trying to keep someone or something (e.g., equipment) safe from harm.

Teaching for transfer: Teachers want children to be able to use and apply the skills, movement concepts, and tactics learned in one context within other contexts. Transfer does not happen automatically. Teachers can teach for transfer by helping children make connections between previously learned content and new content and by helping them understand similarities and differences in performance when the context changes.

Think–pair–share: With this technique, the teacher asks the class a question and has the children think on their own for approximately 30 seconds about the answer. The teacher then has the children discuss their answers with a partner, and finally, has pairs share their answers with the entire class.

***Tinikling*:** In the well-known dance from the Philippines called *tinikling*, two people hit bamboo poles on the ground twice apart and then once together while a dancer jumps and performs intricate steps in and out of the middle. The dancer represents the movement of the *tikling* birds (which have long legs like flamingos) as they walk over tree branches or dodge bamboo traps set by farmers.

Top-down and bottom-up planning: Top-down and bottom-up planning is a process in which the teacher builds a progression by simultaneously considering the desired learning outcome, unit objectives, and culminating activity she or he wants for the end of the unit, and ensuring a progression of content from simple to complex that begins with students' prior knowledge and experience. In other words, the teacher thinks both top down from her or his objectives and bottom up from where students begin.

Track-start hands: Track-start hands are an immature pattern in which the performer supports her or his weight on the fingerprints and fingers, with the palm off the mat (resembling the hand position for starting a sprint in track, rather than putting the palms flat on the mat).

Trading off: Trading off is when "teachers negotiate with students to produce the necessary cooperation in the managerial system by reducing the demands of the instructional system" (Hastie & Siedentop, 2006, p. 216).

Traditional sport approach: With a traditional sport approach, teachers teach adult versions of traditional sports, often with regulation-sided games. Teachers teach traditional skills related to a specific sport, such as a chest pass, bounce pass, and overhand pass in basketball.

Transitions: Transitions are the movements between skills, shapes, and formations that make the movements in a sequence flow one after the other as if they were one continuous movement.

Tripod: A tripod is part of the progression of a headstand in which the weight is placed on the head and hands in a triangle, with the hips over the shoulders and the knees or upper part of the shins resting on the elbows or humerus.

Tucked flank vault: A tucked flank vault is the same as a tucked front vault, except that the child puts the hands on the trapezoid facing forward and springs the legs over the trapezoid with the side of the legs facing the trapezoid. The child lands with his or her back to the trapezoid.

Tucked front vault: In a tucked front vault, the child springs off from two feet, puts her or his hands to the left or right parallel to the trapezoid, supports the body's weight on the arms, travels in a curled position over the trapezoid, and lands facing the trapezoid.

Turn: When the body turns, the entire body rotates on an axis.

Twist: When the body twists, one part of the body remains facing one direction while another part rotates to face in a different direction.

Two-step: A two-step is a step–together–step moving forward, alternating the lead leg: Left step–together–step, pause; right step–together–step, pause. Performed slowly, it is done with an even rhythm.

Type of activity: For children, the Centers for Disease Control and Prevention (U.S. Department of Health and Human Services, 2008) recommend four types of activities: vigorous physical activities, moderate physical activities, muscle strength and endurance activities, and muscle power activities for bone strengthening. Type of activity is important because it relates to the specificity principle.

Unison: In unison, everyone moves at exactly the same time.

Unit objectives: Unit objectives are similar to lesson objectives except that unit objectives are broader and encompass more content. Unit objectives break down the major learning outcome into the motor, cognitive knowledge, thinking skill/motivation, social skill, and affective content on which the teacher plans to focus.

Variable practice: Variable practice involves practicing a skill under a variety of task and environmental constraints.

***Varsovienne*:** In a *varsovienne*, the man puts his right hand behind the woman's shoulder and holds the woman's right hand at shoulder height. The woman puts her left hand palm down across the man's chest and holds the man's left hand.

Waltz: A waltz is danced in a 3/4 meter (three beats to a measure). Step forward on the left foot; step to side on the right foot; close the left foot next to the right foot. Repeat starting on the right foot. It is performed "down, up, up."

Wave organization: When children must practice a skill, such as dribbling or galloping, at a fast speed and you teach in a small space, the wave organization is designed to accommodate these constraints. With this approach, you have as many short lines as you can while still ensuring enough room between the lines. Assign a maximum of two to four children to each line. The first children in line are wave 1, the second are wave 2, and so on. Tell the first wave to start. When they are roughly one-third of the way down the gym, tell wave 2 to start. When wave 2 is one-third of the way down the gym, start wave 3. In the meantime, wave 1 stops at cones set up approximately eight feet from the wall and forms a line facing the direction from which they started. As each wave finishes, its members get in line and you repeat the task moving in the other direction. With this strategy, most children are active most of the time, and each child has enough space to travel safely at a fast speed without worrying about another child crossing his or her path.

Web form graphic organizers: Graphic organizers in the form of a web are assessment tools in which students write the main topic in a center circle; the concepts related to the topic are then written in circles surrounding this topic, with lines connecting the circles showing the relations among concepts. Webs give children a visual picture of the most important concepts they need to learn about a topic.

Weight bearing: A precursor to balancing is weight bearing. Weight bearing involves children supporting their weight on one or several body parts in a position of momentary, rather than sustained, stillness. All balances are weight-bearing skills, but not all weight bearing is balancing because *weight bearing* does not imply *hard to hold.*

Weight transfer skills: Weight transfer skills are skills such as rolling and step-like actions (e.g., cartwheels) in which the body travels and is supported by a sequence of different body parts.

Index

A

B

D

E

H

I

N

O

P

R

S

T

U

V

W

Y